WW Spelmer

THE WISDOM OF CHINA AND INDIA

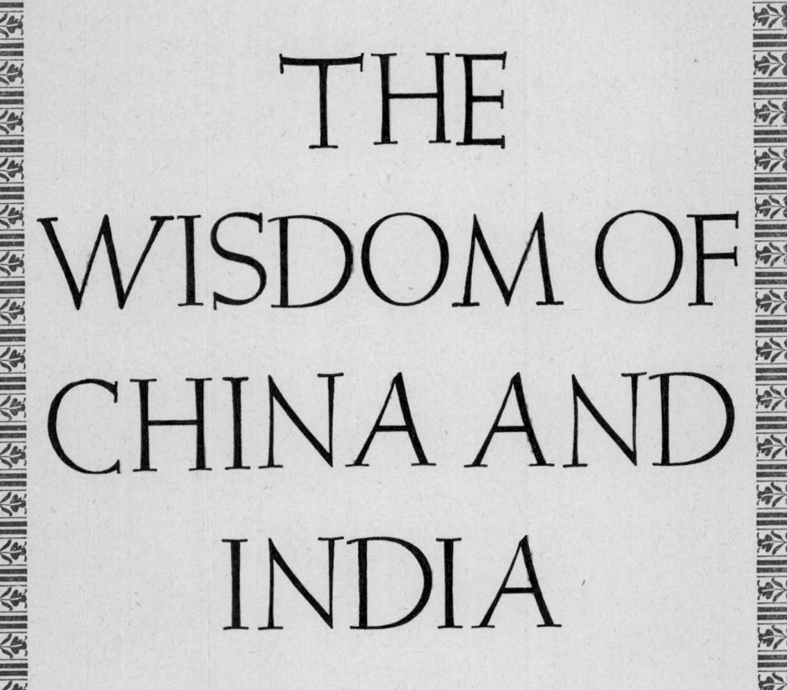

THE WISDOM OF CHINA AND INDIA

EDITED BY LIN YUTANG

RANDOM HOUSE · NEW YORK

FIRST PRINTING

Manufactured in the U.S.A. by H. Wolff, New York

ACKNOWLEDGMENTS

We wish to acknowledge our indebtedness to the following publishers for their courtesy in granting permission to reprint sections of books issued and copyrighted by them:

"The Tale of Ch'ienniang," from *My Country and My People* by Lin Yutang; Letter VIII and a postscript to Letter XIII in "Letters of a Chinese Poet," and sections from the "Six Chapters of a Floating Life," from *The Importance of Living* by Lin Yutang, copyrighted and published by The John Day Company, Inc.

"The Sermon at Benares," the "Sermon on Abuse" and the legends, "The Marriage Feast in Jambunada," "Kisa Gotami," and "Following the Master over the Stream," copyrighted and published by The Open Court Publishing Company, La Salle, Illinois.

Selections from *The Panchatantra,* translated by Arthur W. Ryder, and copyrighted and published by The University of Chicago Press.

"The Tale of Meng Chiang," from *The Lady of the Long Wall,* translated by Genevieve Wimsatt and Geoffrey Chen, and published by Columbia University Press.

Selections from *The Jade Mountain,* translated by Witter Bynner, copyrighted, 1920, 1929, by Alfred A. Knopf, Inc.

"Aphorisms of Confucius" and "The Golden Mean," from *The Wisdom of Confucius,* translated and edited by Lin Yutang, copyrighted, 1938, by Random House, Inc.

Selections from *The Surangama* and "What is Nirvana?" from *The Lankavatara,* translated by Dwight Goddard and Wei-Tao, published by Dwight Goddard.

Other acknowledgments have been made in the individual introductions.

Contents

PART ONE: THE WISDOM OF INDIA

PART TWO: THE WISDOM OF CHINA

THE
WISDOM
OF
INDIA

Introduction

I AM NOT a Sanskrit or Pali scholar, but, better than that, a lover of books that are eternal in their wisdom. The purpose of including the wisdom of India with the wisdom of China is to communicate a joyful experience of the beauty and wisdom of that country's literature and share it with my readers. In the process of compilation, I could not have enjoyed it more if I had taken a trip to India. How could it be otherwise? The contact with poets, forest saints and the best wits of the land, the glimpse into the first awakening of Ancient India's mind as it searched, at times childishly and naïvely, at times with a deep intuition, but at all times earnestly and passionately, for the spiritual truths and the meaning of existence—this experience must be highly stimulating to anyone, particularly because the Hindu culture is so different and therefore has so much to offer. One sees the ideas and the ethos of a nation as revealed in its literature, which have activated and moulded that people for three thousand years. Not until we see the richness of the Hindu mind and its essential spirituality can we understand India or hope to share with it the freedom and equality of peoples which we in some lame and halting fashion are trying to create out of this morally and politically chaotic world.

In accordance with Chinese courtesy, I have put the section on the wisdom of India first, reversing the order suggested by the title. If I have put China first in the title, it is because I strongly suspect that the average reader does not suspect India has as rich a culture, as creative an imagination and wit and humor as any China has to offer, and that India was China's teacher in religion and imaginative literature, and the world's teacher in trigonometry, quadratic equations, grammar, phonetics, Arabian Nights, animal fables, chess, as well as in philosophy, and that she inspired Boccaccio, Goethe, Herder, Schopenhauer, Emerson, and probably also old Aesop.

But the great age of Western appreciation of Indian literature and philosophy, the age of Sir William Jones, Franz Bopp and Sir Edwin Arnold, has passed. The enthusiasm that came with the discovery of Sanskrit and the founding of the science of Indo-Germanic philology, directly inspired by it, soon evaporated. 1860 marked the turning point. G. T. Garratt writes in his extremely informative article "Indo-British Civilization" in *The Legacy of India* (Oxford): "This phase was not fated to last. His [Sir William Jones's] successors soon began to adopt that slightly hostile and superior attitude which characterizes the work of Englishmen writing on Indian subjects. . . . From about 1836, this tradition had become firmly established. India was the 'Land of Regrets' in which Englishmen spent years of exile amongst a people half savage, half decadent." "After the Mutiny . . . new types of Englishmen went out East, including journalists and schoolmasters; they brought their wives, and were visited by tourists; within India a domiciled English and Eurasian population was growing in numbers and developing a life of its own. . . . The British were rapidly developing into a separate caste, strongly reinforced by the new officials, planters, and business men who came crowding out East after 1860. There was a natural tendency for writers to concentrate more upon this colony of their expatriated countrymen," producing a mass of cheap novels, "nearly all of which are grossly offensive to (the Hindu) race." "They are interesting for the light they throw upon the bureaucracy during the most static, self-satisfied, and sterile era of British rule, from about 1870, till the end of the century. The greater part of Rudyard Kipling's Indian works is directly in this tradition, though it is illumined by his own genius. . . . Apart from the 'Jungle' books, the greater part of his Indian fiction and verse is concerned with these two [European and Eurasian] tiny communities, the officials and military officers, and the subordinate Europeans and Eurasians. Round them surges the immense sea of Indians, but nearly all of this subjected race who appear as individuals are minor characters, mostly domestic servants or women kept by Englishmen. The few educated Indians who come into his pages seem to have been introduced to satisfy the deep-seated prejudices of the English in India. . . . Kipling allowed himself the most astounding generalizations about Indian duplicity and mendacity, or the physical cowardice of certain races." When Sir Edwin Arnold wrote about 1860 in his Preface to his translation of the *Hitopadesa,* "No one listens now to the precipitate ignorance which would set aside as 'heathenish' the high civilization of this great race," he did not know what he was talking about. India today has become an untouchable topic, and the most untouchable topic is about the untouchable caste of the Englishmen in India—I must forbear to touch the topic now.

The average Western attitude toward India may be summed up in a sentence which contains a fourfold untruth: "All I know about India is that the Hindus are Buddhists, and as the Nirvana of Buddha's teachings means extinction, obviously India has nothing to contribute to the world civilization." The first untruth is that the Hindus are Buddhists, which they as a nation are not. Characteristically, the Hindus have rejected Buddhism as the Jews have rejected Christianity. The second untruth is the assumption that the meaning of Nirvana is ever understood by the conditioned, finite, logical intelligence of man. The third untruth rises from the fact that India has actually produced a vast, rich imaginative literature and philosophy, besides Buddhism, and that the Indian culture is highly creative and in fact has enriched the world literature with the droll humor that we associate with the *Arabian Nights*. And the fourth untruth is the denial that the essential spiritual concept of man in both Hinduism and Buddhism, their essential denial of materialism, and their stand on non-violence arising from those religions, have anything to teach to the modern world. Buddha taught that the greatest sin is ignorance or thoughtlessness, and that the holy life begins with, and is founded upon, moral earnestness and the spirit of inquiry and self-examination. This sin of thoughtlessness about India has to cease. Nobody is going to profit by making the problem of India or British rule in India an untouchable topic. It is my firm belief that this generation of elderly statesmen is hopeless, and that we must begin by educating a new generation toward a more correct view of the Indian nation.

The basic material concerning the beliefs of Hinduism, the national religion of present-day Hindus and their leaders like Gandhi and Nehru, is to be found in the first section on Hindu piety. It is characteristic of Indian thought that, in India, religion and philosophy are inseparable. In India, no "link" between philosophy and religion is necessary and the problem of finding that fatal missing link in the modern world does not exist. Hindu philosophy and the knowledge of

God are inseparable as Chinese philosophy and the questions of human conduct are inseparable. We do not know whether we are coming to the close of an epoch; we do not know whether our highly specialized and departmentalized thinkers are capable of reuniting science, philosophy and religion. But it is evident that India is a land overflowing with religion and with the religious spirit. India produced too much religion, and China, too little. A trickle of Indian religious spirit overflowed to China and inundated the whole of Eastern Asia. Not too little, but too much is India's trouble. It would seem logical and appropriate that any one suffering from a deficiency of the religious spirit should turn to India rather than to any other country in the world. It is apparent that only in India is religion still a living emotion today, and that the Christian doctrine of turning the other cheek could be turned into a national movement, practiced by the masses, only in India and in no other country in the world. India's paradox is the pacifist's paradox the world over. But peace can come only from non-violence and disbelief in force, and non-violence can come only from India, because the Indians seem really to believe in it.

In the realm of imaginative literature, the great Indian epics will speak for themselves. The comparison with the *Iliad* and the *Odyssey* is inevitable. I have preferred to give the whole story of the *Ramayana,* rather than give incomplete selections from both; those interested may read the *Mahabharata* in the Everyman's Library edition. I have, for reasons of space, also found it necessary to exclude the great dramatic poetry of *Shakuntala,* by Kalidasa, "the Indian Shakespeare" (Everyman's) and the popular classical drama, *Little Clay Cart* (tr. by Arthur William Ryder, Harvard Oriental Series).

It may also be a complete revelation to find that the fabulous Hindu mind is responsible for the genre of animal fables and many stories of the *Arabian Nights* type, in which Buddhist and non-Buddhist literature abounds. "Numerous European fairy stories, to be found in Grimm or Hans Andersen, including the magic mirror, the seven-leagued boots, Jack and the beanstalk, and the purse of Fortunatus, have been traced to Indian sources," writes H. G. Rawlinson, in his article "India in European Literature and Thought" in *The Legacy of India.* "Many of them are to be found in the *Gesta Romanorum,* the *Decameron,* and Chaucer's *Canterbury Tales.*" The story of the Three Caskets, used in the *Merchant of Venice,* is found in the romance of *Barlaam and Josaphat,* which is too clearly the story of Buddha, who was changed into a Christian garb, and later canonized as a Christian saint as St. Josaphat! And everyone of course knows the story of the Milkmaid who dreamt of her wedding and overthrew the milk pail, now to be recognized in its original form as the story of the Brahman's Dream, included in the selections from the *Panchatantra.*

Lastly, I have included important selections from Buddhist canons and non-canonical works, chiefly from the Mahayana, or the "Greater Vehicle School," or the school of "Northern Buddhism." I confess to a personal bias, and have largely used Mahayana texts based on Chinese translations from the Sanskrit. The study of Pali, which rose to importance about 1880, has shifted the emphasis to the Hinayana texts of the school of "Southern Buddhism." And I believe that, apart from scholarly convenience in the study of Pali, any satisfactory interpretation of Buddhism as a religion for the common man must come from the Mahayana texts. This I have tried to make plain in my introduction to the selection from the *Surangama Sutra.* In spite of the wealth of the Pali *Tripitaka,* I rather think the final gleanings as a living belief for the student of larger human truths must be somewhat barren.

I think it is possible to take the three selections, the *Hymns from the Rigveda,* the *Bhagavad-Gita* and the *Dhammapada,* the latter two being reproduced here complete, as milestones in the development of Hindu thought and find therein the best fruit of the Hindu speculation about the meaning of man's existence on earth.

India's achievements in the field of the positive sciences have naturally not been included. It is interesting to note that when Houston Chamberlain, the English apostle of Aryanism, wanted to prove Aryan superiority, he had to point out Panini as the world's first grammarian. Readers who are interested should read the relevant chapters in *The Legacy of India* or the less obtainable *"Positive Sciences of the Ancient Hindus"* by Sarkar.

In a book for the general reader such as this, it is advisable to use a simple system of transcription of Indian words. I have, therefore, eliminated all accent marks except those for long vowels in the selections. For variations in spellings of the same word, see the short note preceding the "Glossary of Hindu Words."

Finally I have to thank Dr. Taraknath Das of the College of the City of New York who has been helpful in guiding me to certain interesting references, as well as explaining certain obscure Indian terms, and in going over the proofs of the Indian section of this book.

INDIAN PIETY

Hymns from the Rigveda

INTRODUCTION

INDIA IS A LAND and a people intoxicated with God. This is the impression of anyone who reads through the Hymns from the *Rigveda,* and follows through the *Upanishads* to the arrival of Buddha in 563 B.C. The Hindu preoccupation with questions of the world soul and the individual soul is so intense that at times it must seem oppressive to a less spiritual people. I doubt there is a nation on earth that equals the Hindus in religious emotional intensity except the Jews. It is therefore entirely natural that we find the earliest creation of the Hindu spirit assumed a form and passion very similar to the Psalms of the Old Testament.

Max Müller has called the *Rigveda* (*rig* means "verse" and *veda* means "knowledge," the title meaning "songs of spiritual knowledge") "the first word spoken by the Aryan man." The *Vedas* cover ten books and 1,028 hymns. In point of antiquity, the earliest of the *Vedas* probably went as far back as 1,500 or 1,200 B.C., covering eight centuries of development, during which they grew to their present form. Throughout this development and down to present-day Hinduism, we see this preoccupation with God and the mystic conception of the universe. Hindus are natural mystics, mysticism meaning a form of religion aiming at achieving direct union with God. To achieve the union of the individual soul (*atman*) with the world soul (*brahma*) behind all things may be said to be the whole effort of the Vedic philosophy.

In these Hymns one sees, at the very birth of this religious spirit, such utterances expressing an awakening of man's soul and sense of wonder and doubt and intellectual inquiry, in such characteristic fashion like something that hits one in the eye. It may sound frivolous, yet profoundly true, to say that Hindu intoxication with God began with the drink of the soma-juice, a fermented drink from the soma-plant, used in Vedic rituals. For, says the early Hindu poet:

Not as a mote within the eye count the five tribes of men with me:
Have I not drunk of soma-juice?

The heavens and earth themselves have not grown equal to half of me:
Have I not drunk of soma-juice?

I in my grandeur have surpassed the heavens and all this spacious earth:
Have I not drunk of soma-juice?

Aha! this spacious earth will I deposit either here or there:
Have I not drunk of soma-juice?

One of my flanks is in the sky: I let the other trail below:
Have I not drunk of soma-juice?

The case for intoxication with God is therefore established. And readers may well regard these Hymns as the first cocktail sips of the Hindu religious philosophy.

The suggestion of similarity with the Psalms is inevitable, when one reads lines like the following, in the able version by Ralph T. H. Griffith:

Far from me, Varuna, remove all danger: accept me graciously, thou holy sovran.
Cast off, like cords that hold a calf, my troubles: I am not even mine eyelid's lord without thee.

O mighty Varuna, now and hereafter, even as of old, will we speak forth thy worship.
For in thyself, invincible god, thy statutes ne'er to be moved as fixed as on a mountain. (To Varuna)

Or listen to the first fervent cry of joy at the glories of the sunrise at dawn:

Bright leader of glad sounds, our eyes behold her: splendid in hue she hath unclosed the portals.
She, stirring up the world, hath shown us riches; Dawn hath awakened every living creature.

Dawns giving sons all heroes, kine and horses, shining upon the man who brings oblations—
These let the soma-presser gain when ending his glad songs louder than the voices of Vayu. (To Dawn)

Equally reminiscent of the Psalms are the Hymns to Indra, the "fierce god":

He who hath smitten, ere they knew their danger, with his hurled weapon many grievous sinners;
Who pardons not his boldness who provokes him, who slays the Dasyu, he, O men, is Indra.
Even the heaven and earth bow down before him, before his very breath the mountains tremble.
Known as the soma-drinker, armed with thunder, who wields the bolt, he, O men, is Indra. (To Indra)

And the sense of intellectual inquiry and doubt naturally followed the sense of wonder and worship:

What was the tree, what wood in sooth produced it, from which they fashioned out the earth and heaven?
Ye thoughtful men inquire within your spirit whereon he stood when he established all things. (To Visvakarman)

Skepticism arose at the end of the "Song of Creation":

He, the first origin of this creation, whether he formed it all or did not form it,
Whose eye controls this world in highest heaven, he verily knows it, or perhaps he knows not.

And so on, until in the Hymn to Prajapati (the Creator), which Max Müller has entitled "To the Unknown god," the Vedic poet in ten successive verses asks the question, "What god shall we adore with our oblation?"

I notice among certain European students of Hinduism the constant insinuation of polytheism with a tone of reproach. That Hindu monotheism developed in the *Upanishads* with the Vedanta belief in the One behind all things is a minor point. It is my belief that it is entirely unimportant what god one worships, monotheistic or polytheistic; what is important is that belief should produce the true spirit of devotion in the life of the worshipper. In modern terms, what is important is that religion be "efficient," that is, that it produce results, and I may say that modern monotheism is less efficient than when men believed in the spirituality of trees and rocks, and mountains and rivers.

Hymns from the Rigveda

Translated by Ralph J. H. Griffith

TO INDRA[1]

This, even this was my resolve, to win a cow, to win a steed:
Have I not drunk of soma-juice?

Like violent gusts of wind the draughts that I have drunk have lifted me:
Have I not drunk of soma-juice?

The draughts I drank have borne me up, as fleet-foot horses draw a car:
Have I not drunk of soma-juice?

The hymn hath reached me, like a cow who lows to meet her darling calf:
Have I not drunk of soma-juice?

As a wright bends a chariot-seat, so round my heart I bend the hymn:
Have I not drunk of soma-juice?

Not as a mote within the eye count the five tribes of men with me:
Have I not drunk of soma-juice?

The heavens and earth themselves have not grown equal to one half of me:
Have I not drunk of soma-juice?

[1] The favorite national deity of the Vedic age. He hurls thunderbolts.

in my grandeur have surpassed the heavens and all this spacious earth:
ɪave I not drunk of soma-juice?

\ha! this spacious earth will I deposit either here or there:
ɪave I not drunk of soma-juice?

n one short moment will I smite the earth in fury here or there
ɪave I not drunk of soma-juice?

)ne of my flanks is in the sky; I let the other trail below:
ɪave I not drunk of soma-juice?

, greatest of the mighty ones, am lifted to the firmament:
ɪave I not drunk of soma-juice?

seek the worshipper's abode; oblation-bearer to the gods:
ɪave I not drunk of soma-juice? (*Book X, 119*)

THE SONG OF CREATION

ᴛHEN was not non-existent nor existent: there was no realm of air, no sky beyond it.
Vhat covered in, and where? and what gave shelter? Was water there, unfathomed depth of water?

)eath was not then, nor was there aught immortal: no sign was there, the day's and night's divider.
ᴛhat one thing, breathless, breathed by its own nature: apart from it was nothing whatsoever.

)arkness there was: at first concealed in darkness, this All was indiscriminated chaos.
\ll that existed then was void and formless: by the great power of warmth was born that unit.

ᴛhereafter rose desire in the beginning, Desire, the primal seed and germ of spirit.
ˢages who searched with their heart's thought discovered the existent's kinship in the non-existent.

Transversely was their severing line extended: what was above it then and what below it?
There were begetters, there were mighty forces, free action here and energy up yonder.

Who verily knows and who can here declare it, whence it was born and whence comes this creation?
The gods are later than this world's production. Who knows, then whence it first came into being?

He, the first origin of this creation, whether he formed it all or did not form it,
Whose eye controls this world in highest heaven, he verily knows it or perhaps he knows not. (*Book X, 129*)

TO PRAJĀPATI[1]

In the beginning rose Hiranyagarbha,[2] born only lord of all created beings.
He fixed and holdeth up this earth and heaven. What god shall we adore with our oblation?

Giver of vital breath, of power and vigour, he whose commandments all the gods acknowledge:
The lord of death, whose shade is life immortal. What god shall we adore with our oblation?

Who by his grandeur hath become sole ruler of all the moving world that breathes and slumbers:
He who is lord of men and lord of cattle. What god shall we adore with our oblation?

His, through his might, are these snow-covered mountains, and men call sea and Rasā[3] his possession:
His arms are these, his are these heavenly regions. What god shall we adore with our oblation?

[1] The Creator, ruler of the universe.
[2] *Hiranyagarbha:* the sun-god.
[3] *Rasā,* the mythical river of the firmament.

By him the heavens are strong and earth is stedfast, by him light's realm and sky-vault are supported:
By him the regions in mid-air were measured. What god shall we adore with our oblation?

To him, supported by his help, two armies embattled look with trembling in their spirit,
When over them the risen sun is shining. What god shall we adore with our oblation?

What time the mighty waters came, containing the universal germ, producing Agni,[1]
Thence sprang the god's one spirit into being. What god shall we adore with our oblation?

He in his might surveyed the floods containing productive force and generating worship.
He is the god of gods, and none beside him. What god shall we adore with our oblation?

Ne'er may he harm us who is earth's begetter, nor he whose laws are sure, the heavens' creator,
He who brought forth the great and lucid waters. What god shall we adore with our oblation?

Prajāpati! thou only comprehendest all these created things, and none beside thee.
Grant us our hearts' desire when we invoke thee: may we have store of riches in possession. (*Book X, 121*)

TO VARUNA[2]

This laud of the self-radiant wise Aditya[3] shall be supreme o'er all that is in greatness.
I beg renown of Varuna the mighty, the god exceeding kind to him who worships.

[1] The god of fire and light.
[2] King of air and sea.
[3] Son of Aditi. Both Varuna and the Sun are Adityas.

Having extolled thee, Varuna, with thoughtful care may we have high fortune in thy service.
Singing thy praises like the fires at coming, day after day, of mornings rich in cattle.

May we be in thy keeping, O thou leader, wide ruling Varuna, Lord of many heroes.
O sons of Aditi, for ever faithful, pardon us, gods, admit us to your friendship.

He made them flow, the Aditya, the sustainer: the rivers run by Varuna's commandment.
These feel no weariness, nor cease from flowing: swift have they flown like birds in air around us.

Loose me from sin as from a band that binds me: may we swell, Varuna, thy spring of order.
Let not my thread, while I weave song, be severed, nor my work's sum, before the time, be shattered.

Far from me, Varuna, remove all danger: accept me graciously, thou holy sovran.
Cast off, like cords that hold a calf, my troubles: I am not even mine eyelid's lord without thee.

Strike us not, Varuna, with those dread weapons which, Asura, at thy bidding wound the sinner.
Let us not pass away from light to exile. Scatter, that we may live, the men who hate us.

O mighty Varuna, now and hereafter, even as of old, will we speak forth our worship.
For in thyself, invincible god, thy statutes ne'er to be moved are fixed as on a mountain.

Move far from me what sins I have committed: let me not suffer, King, for guilt of others.
Full many a morn remains to dawn upon us: in these, O Varuna, while we live direct us.

O King, whoever, be he friend or kinsman, hath threatened me affrighted in my slumber—
If any wolf or robber fain would harm us, therefrom, O Varuna, give thou us protection.

May I not live, O Varuna, to witness my wealthy, liberal, dear friend's destitution.
King, may I never lack well-ordered riches. Loud may we speak with heroes in assembly. (*Book II, 28*)

TO VARUNA

SING forth a hymn sublime and solemn, grateful to glorious Varuna, imperial ruler,
Who hath struck out, like one who slays the victim, earth as a skin to spread in front of Sūrya.[1]

In the tree-tops the air he hath extended, put milk in kine and vigorous speed in horses,
Set intellect in hearts, fire in the waters, Sūrya in heaven and Soma on the mountain.

Varuna lets the big cask, opening downward, flow through the heaven and earth and air's mid-region.
Therewith the universe's sovran waters earth as the shower of rain bedews the barley.

When Varuna is fain for milk, he moistens the sky, the land, and earth to her foundation.
Then straight the mountains clothe them in the raincloud: the heroes, putting forth their vigour, loose them.

I will declare this mighty deed of magic, of glorious Varuna, the lord immortal,
Who, standing in the firmament, hath meted the earth out with the sun as with a measure.

[1] The Sun God.

None, verily, hath ever let or hindered this the most wise god's mighty deed of magic,
Whereby with all their flood, the lucid rivers fill not one sea wherein they pour their waters.

If we have sinned against the man who loves us, have ever wronged a brother, friend, or comrade,
The neighbour ever with us, or a stranger, O Varuna, remove from us the trespass.

If we, as gamesters cheat at play, have cheated, done wrong unwittingly or sinned of purpose,
Cast all these sins away like loosened fetters, and, Varuna, let us be thine own beloved. (*Book V, 85*)

TO VISVAKARMAN[1]

He who sate down as Hotar-priest,[2] the Rishi,[3] our father, offering up all things existing—
He, seeking through his wish a great possession, came among men on earth as archetypal.

What was the place whereon he took his station? What was it that supported him? How was it?
Whence Visvakarman, seeing all, producing the earth, with mighty power disclosed the heavens.

He who hath eyes on all sides round about him, a mouth on all sides, arms and feet on all sides,
He, the sole god, producing earth and heaven, weldeth them, with his arms as wings, together.

What was the tree, what wood in sooth produced it, from which they fashioned out the earth and heaven?
Ye thoughtful men inquire within your spirit whereon he stood when he established all things.

[1] Visvakarman is represented in this hymn as the creator of all things and architect of the worlds.
[2] The priest who invokes the gods to receive the offerings.
[3] A saint, anchorite, a term commonly used.

Thine highest, lowest, sacrificial natures and these thy midmost here, O Visvakarman,
Teach thou thy friends at sacrifice, O Blessed, and come thyself, exalted, to our worship.

Bring thou thyself, exalted with oblation, O Visvakarman, earth and heaven to worship.
Let other men around us live in folly: here let us have a rich and liberal patron.

Let us invoke to-day, to aid our labour, the lord of speech, the thought-swift Visvakarman.
May he hear kindly all our invocations who gives all bliss for aid, whose works are righteous. (*Book X, 81*)

TO INDRA

He who, just born, chief god of lofty spirit by power and might became the gods' protector,
Before whose breath through greatness of his valour the two worlds trembled, he, O men, is Indra.

He who fixed fast and firm the earth that staggered, and set at rest the agitated mountains,
Who measured out the air's wide middle region and gave the heaven support, he, men, is Indra.

Who slew the dragon, freed the seven rivers, and drove the kine forth from the cave of Vala,
Begat the fire between two stones, the spoiler in warrior's battle, he, O men, is Indra.

By whom this universe was made to tremble, who chased away the humbled brood of demons,
Who, like a gambler gathering his winnings, seized the foe's riches, he, O men, is Indra.

Of whom, the terrible, they ask, Where is he? or verily they say of him, He is not.
He sweeps away, like birds, the foe's possessions. Have faith in him, for he, O men, is Indra.

Stirrer to action of the poor and lowly, of priest, of suppliant who sings his praises;
Who, fair-faced, favours him who presses soma with stones made ready, he, O men, is Indra.

He under whose supreme control are horses, all chariots, and the villages, and cattle;
He who gave being to the sun and morning, who leads the waters, he, O men, is Indra.

To whom two armies cry in close encounter, both enemies the stronger and the weaker;
Whom two invoke upon one chariot mounted, each for himself, he, O ye men, is Indra.

Without whose help our people never conquer; whom, battling, they invoke to give them succour;
He of whom all this world is but the copy, who shakes things moveless, he, O men, is Indra.

He who hath smitten, ere they knew their danger, with his hurled weapon many grievous sinners;
Who pardons not his boldness who provokes him, who slays the Dasyu, he, O men, is Indra.

He who discovered in the fortieth autumn Sambara as he dwelt among the mountains;
Who slew the dragon putting forth his vigour, the demon lying there, he, men, is Indra.

Who with seven guiding reins, the bull, the mighty, set free the seven great floods to flow at pleasure;
Who, thunder-armed, rent Rauhina [1] in pieces when scaling heaven, he, O ye men, is Indra.

[1] A demon of drought.

Even the heaven and earth bow down before him, before his very breath the mountains tremble.
Known as the soma-drinker, armed with thunder, who wields the bolt, he, O ye men, is Indra.

Who aids with favour him who pours the soma and him who brews it, sacrificer, singer,
Whom prayer exalts, and pouring forth of soma, and this our gift, he, O ye men, is Indra.

Thou verily art fierce and true who sendest strength to the man who brews and pours libation.
So may we evermore, thy friends, O Indra, speak loudly to the synod with our heroes. *(Book II, 12)*

HYMN OF MAN

A THOUSAND heads hath Purusha,[1] a thousand eyes, a thousand feet.
On every side pervading earth he fills a space ten fingers wide.

This Purusha is all that yet hath been and all that is to be,
The lord of immortality which waxes greater still by food.

So mighty is his greatness; yea, greater than this is Purusha.
All creatures are one-fourth of him, three-fourths eternal life in heaven.

With three-fourths Purusha went up: one-fourth of him again was here.
Thence he strode out to every side over what eats not and what eats.

From him Virāj[2] was born; again Purusha from Virāj was born.
As soon as he was born he spread eastward and westward o'er the earth.

[1] *Purusha,* embodied spirit, or man personified and regarded as the soul and original source of the universe, the personal and life-giving principle in all animated beings, is said to have a *thousand,* that is innumerable, *heads, eyes, and feet,* as being one with all created life. *A space ten fingers wide:* the region of the heart of man, wherein the soul was supposed to reside. Although as the universal soul he pervades the universe, as the individual soul he is enclosed in a space of narrow dimensions.
[2] One of the sources of existence.

When gods prepared the sacrifice with Purusha as their offering,
Its oil was spring; the holy gift was autumn; summer was the wood.

They balmed as victim on the grass Purusha born in earliest time.
With him the deities and all Sādhyas [1] and Rishis sacrificed.

From that great general sacrifice the dripping fat was gathered up.
He formed the creatures of the air, and animals both wild and tame.

From that great general sacrifice Richas and Sāma-hymns were born:
Therefrom were spells and charms produced; the Yajus had its birth from it.

From it were horses born, from it all cattle with two rows of teeth:
From it were generated kine, from it the goats and sheep were born.

When they divided Purusha, how many portions did they make?
What do they call his mouth, his arms? What do they call his thighs and feet?

The Brāhman [2] was his mouth, of both his arms was the Rājanya [3] made.
His thighs became the Vaisya,[4] from his feet the Sudra [5] was produced.

The moon was gendered from his mind, and from his eye the sun had birth;
Indra and Agni from his mouth were born, and Vāyu [6] from his breath.

Forth from his navel came mid-air; the sky was fashioned from his head;
Earth from his feet, and from his ear the regions. Thus they formed the worlds.

Seven fencing-sticks had he, thrice seven layers of fuel were prepared,
When the gods, offering sacrifice, bound, as their victim, Purusha.

[1] Celestial beings.
[2] The first caste of Brahman priests.
[3] The second caste of kings.
[4] The third caste of traders.
[5] The fourth caste of laborers.
[6] God of Wind.

Gods, sacrificing, sacrificed the victim: these were the earliest holy ordinances.
The mighty ones attained the height of heaven, there where the Sādhyas, gods of old, are dwelling. (*Book X, 90*)

TO LIBERALITY

The gods have not ordained hunger to be our death: even to the well-fed man comes death in varied shape.
The riches of the liberal never waste away, while he who will not give finds none to comfort him.

The man with food in store who, when the needy comes in miserable case begging for bread to eat,
Hardens his heart against him—even when of old he did him service—finds not one to comfort him.

Bounteous is he who gives unto the beggar who comes to him in want of food and feeble.
Success attends him in the shout of battle. He makes a friend of him in future troubles.

No friend is he who to his friend and comrade who comes imploring food, will offer nothing.
Let him depart—no home is that to rest in—and rather seek a stranger to support him.

Let the rich satisfy the poor implorer, and bend his eye upon a longer pathway.
Riches come now to one, now to another, and like the wheels of cars are ever rolling.

The foolish man wins food with fruitless labour: that food—I speak the truth—shall be his ruin.
He feeds no trusty friend, no man to love him. All guilt is he who eats with no partaker.

The ploughshares ploughing makes the food that feeds us, and with its feet cuts through the path it follows.
Better the speaking than the silent Brāhman: the liberal friend outvalues him who gives not.

He with one foot hath far outrun the biped, and the two-footed catches the three-footed.
Four-footed creatures come when bipeds call them, and stand and look where five are met together.

The hands are both alike: their labour differs. The yield of sister milch-kine is unequal.
Twins even differ in their strength and vigour: two, even kinsmen, differ in their bounty. *(Book X, 117)*

TO FAITH

By faith is Agni kindled, through faith is oblation offered up.
We celebrate with praises faith upon the height of happiness.

Bless thou the man who gives, O Faith; Faith, bless the man who fain would give.
Bless thou the liberal worshippers; bless thou the word that I have said.

Even as the deities maintained faith in the mighty Asuras,[1]
So make this uttered wish of mine true for the liberal worshippers.

Guarded by Vāyu, gods and men who sacrifice draw near to faith.
Man winneth faith by yearnings of the heart, and opulence by faith.

Faith in the early morning, Faith at noonday will we invocate,
Faith at the setting of the sun. O Faith, endow us with belief.

(Book X, 151)

[1] Primeval Aryan gods, later believed as demons working against God.

TO NIGHT

WITH all her eyes the goddess Night looks forth approaching many a spot:
She hath put all her glories on.

Immortal, she hath filled the waste, the goddess hath filled height and depth:
She conquers darkness with her light.

The goddess as she comes hath set the Dawn her sister in her place:
And then the darkness vanishes.

So favour us this night, O thou whose pathways we have visited
As birds their nest upon the tree.

The villagers have sought their homes, and all that walks and all that flies,
Even the falcons fain for prey.

Keep off the she-wolf and the wolf; O Ūrmya,[1] keep the thief away:
Easy be thou for us to pass.

Clearly hath she come nigh to me who decks the dark with richest hues:
O morning, cancel it like debts.

These have I brought to thee like kine. O Night, thou child of heaven, accept
This laud as for a conqueror. (*Book X. 127*)

TO DAWN

THIS light is come, amid all lights the fairest; born is the brilliant, far-extending brightness.
Night, sent away for Savitar's[2] uprising, hath yielded up a birthplace for the morning.

[1] Epithet for "night" personified.
[2] *Savitar:* the sun, the life-giver.

The fair, the bright is come with her white offspring; to her the dark one hath resigned her dwelling.
Akin, immortal, following each other, changing their colours, both the heavens move onward.

Common, unending is the sisters' pathway: taught by the gods, alternately they travel.
Fair-formed, of different hues and yet one-minded, Night and Dawn clash not, neither do they tarry.

Bright leader of glad sounds, our eyes behold her: splendid in hue she hath unclosed the portals.
She, stirring up the world, hath shown us riches: Dawn hath awakened every living creature.

Rich Dawn, she sets afoot the coiled-up sleeper, one for enjoyment, one for wealth or worship,
Those who saw little for extended vision: all living creatures hath the Dawn awakened.

One to high sway, one to exalted glory, one to pursue his gain and one his labour;
All to regard their different vocations, all moving creatures hath the Dawn awakened.

We see her there, the child of heaven, apparent, the young maid, flushing in her shining raiment.
Thou sovran lady of all earthly treasure, flush on us here, auspicious Dawn, this morning.

She, first of endless morns to come hereafter, follows the path of morns that have departed.
Dawn, at her rising, urges forth the living: him who is dead she wakes not from his slumber.

As thou, Dawn, hast caused Agni to be kindled, and with the sun's eye hast revealed creation,
And hast awakened men to offer worship, thou hast performed, for gods, a noble service.

How long a time, and they shall be together.—Dawns that have shone and dawns to shine hereafter?
She yearns for former dawns with eager longing, and goes forth gladly shining with the others.

Gone are the men who in the days before us looked on the rising of the earlier morning.
We, we the living, now behold her brightness, and they come nigh who shall hereafter see her.

Foe-chaser, born of Law, the law's protectress, joy-giver, waker of all pleasant voices,
Auspicious, bringing food for gods' enjoyment, shine on us here, most bright, O Dawn, this morning.

From days eternal hath Dawn shone, the goddess, and shows this light to-day, endowed with riches.
So will she shine on days to come; immortal she moves on in her own strength, undecaying.

In the sky's borders hath she shone in splendour: the goddess hath thrown off the veil of darkness.
Awakening the world with purple horses, on her well-harnessed chariot Dawn approaches.

Bringing all life-sustaining blessings with her, showing herself, she sends forth brilliant lustre.
Last of the countless mornings that have vanished, first of bright morns to come hath Dawn arisen.

Arise! the breath, the life, again hath reached us: darkness hath passed away, and light approacheth.
She for the sun hath left a path to travel: we have arrived where men prolong existence.

Singing the praises of refulgent mornings with his hymn's web, the priest, the poet, rises.
Shine then to-day, rich maid, on him who lauds thee, shine down on us the gift of life and offspring.

Dawns giving sons all heroes, kine and horses, shining upon the man who brings oblations—
These let the soma-presser gain when ending his glad songs louder than the voice of Vāyu.

Mother of gods, Āditi's form of glory, ensign of sacrifice, shine forth exalted.
Rise up, bestowing praise on our devotion: all-bounteous, make us chief among the people.

Whatever splendid wealth the dawns bring with them to bless the man who offers praise and worship,
Even that may Mitra, Varuna vouchsafe us, and Āditi[1] and Sindhu,[2] earth and heaven. (*Book I, 113*)

[1] The Infinite.
[2] The Indus, or any great river.

The Upanishads

INTRODUCTION

Schopenhauer is credited to have read a Latin translation of a Persian translation of the *Upanishads,* which influenced his philosophic speculations about the world as will and as idea, and I trust many English readers hear of the *Upanishads* in connection with Schopenhauer, if not with Emerson. The age of "Brahmin" transcendentalism has passed, yet W. B. Yeats, George Russell and a number of contemporary poets seem to entertain a curiosity about what is contained in the mystic-metaphysical view of man and God and the universe in the *Upanishads.*[1] When one comes to read the *Upanishads* themselves, many may have been repelled by what Yeats calls the "polyglot, hyphenated, latinised, muddied muddle of distortion that froze belief" in some of the scholarly translations. Furthermore, the *Upanishads,* being the earliest speculations about the universe and encasing some very naïve dogmatizations as well as later and more mature developments, are often not easy to follow or enjoy, made worse by commentaries by scholars, who help to split the hair, not yet split fine enough by the forest sages of ancient India. A discriminating selection is therefore necessary. Personally I have been kept away from many of the world's masterpieces because in my young days I happened to stumble upon some bad edition or translation of a certain work.

The *Upanishads* are believed to have been mostly written before the time of Buddha, although some (the last five in the present selection) might be as late as 400 B.C. They represented the development of

[1] See Yeats' Preface to *The Ten Principal Upanishads* which he helped to translate in collaboration with a Hindu scholar Shree Purohit Swami (Macmillan, 1937).

probably three or four centuries, and this fact explains why the different *Upanishads* are of uneven value to the modern reader. Compare, for instance, the first selection with the last in the present volume, and one can readily see the difference in language and thought. It may be surprising that the *Upanishads* as a whole are regarded by the Hindus today as holy scriptures, which are still sung daily as a form of devotion by the learned Brahmans. Yet an analogy with the Old Testament should make the matter clear. The fact that the books of the Old Testament present different views of Jahveh, now a tribal god, now a supreme ruler, now jealous and fierce with vengeance, and now benevolent, does not make any difference to the average believer in Christianity. The modern Christian who believes God is the Father of all mankind still finds it possible to enjoy the story of Joshua who prayed to God to stay the sun in order to allow him time to annihilate the enemy.

The *Upanishads* are strictly speaking the speculations of the Indian forest sages about the world system, and therefore quite different from the Hymns of the *Rigveda*. "It is this brooding on the meaning of existence which distinguishes the spirit of the Hymns from the *Upanishads*," says Tagore. The entire collection breathes the spirit of a troubled inquiry into the problems of the reality, the individual soul and the world soul behind the phenomena. What is the Ultimate Self, the Atman? What is the spirit of the universe, the Brahman? What is mind and what is matter, and what is that personality behind our consciousness, the Purusha? Finally, what is God? Is he transcendent or immanent? The Sankhya philosophers believed that the world consists of two principles, souls and the material world, the *Prakriti,* or Nature, while the Vedanta philosophers believed in one all-comprising unity. Out of such debates in the forest grew these books. These questions are vexing in their very nature, whether to the ancient or to the better-equipped modern man. Two important conclusions are: first, that the ultimate reality, or Brahman, is incomprehensible and surpasses all understanding. "And he (the Atman) can only be described as no, no!" The second result, the most important discovery, is that the individual soul, or Self, within is identical with the soul without, and that by discovering this real Self, man achieves freedom and emancipation from Mara, or the illusions. Still, as Tagore rightly points out, the whole approach is too intellectual, and the final consummation of Vedic philosophy is to be found in *Bhagavad-Gita,* written perhaps two centuries later, when an ardent devotion to a personal God took the place of these barren speculations. According to Buddhist records, there were as many as sixty-three confusing schools of philosophy at the time of Buddha (563–483 B.C.), which explained Buddha's revolt at their futile reasonings and ritualism. Buddha came as a giant, and attacked the same problem from a human approach, and preached the fourfold truth: that there is human suffering, that there is a cause for this suffering, that there is an escape, and that his teachings of emancipation from illusions and senses and desires constitute that escape. Against that Brahmanic background, Buddhism had an austere clarity of method and goal, but as will be seen from the *Upanishads,* it was from this soil that Buddha's teachings naturally grew.

It is the "troubled intensity" of man's search after the soul and its moral earnestness that seems to constitute the value and significance of the *Upanishads*. Nor can it be said that the final message of the *Upanishads* can be ignored even today:

> "Only when men shall roll up the sky like a hide, will there be an end to misery, unless God has first been known."
>
> —*The Svetāsvatara Upanishad*

The Upanishads

Translated by F. Max Müller

THE STORY OF THE CREATION[1]

In the beginning this was Self alone, in the shape of a person (*Purusha*). He looking round saw nothing but his Self. He first said, 'This is I'; therefore he became I by name. Therefore even now, if a man is asked, he first says, 'This is I,' and then pronounces the other name which he may have. And because before all this, he burnt down all evils, therefore he was a person. Verily he who knows this, burns down everyone who tries to be before him.

He feared, and therefore anyone who is lonely fears. He thought, 'As there is nothing but myself, why should I fear?' Thence his fear passed away. For what should he have feared? Verily fear arises from a second only.

But he felt no delight. Therefore a man who is lonely feels no delight. He wished for a second. He was so large as man and wife together. He then made this his Self to fall in two and thence arose husband and wife. Therefore Yājñavalkya said: 'We two are thus (each of us) like half a shell.' Therefore the void which was there, is filled by the wife. He embraced her, and men were born.

She thought, 'How can he embrace me, after having produced me from himself? I shall hide myself.'

She then became a cow, the other became a bull and embraced her, and hence cows were born. The one became a mare, the other a stallion;

[1] This curious and rather crude story of the creation contains nevertheless many germinal ideas of Hinduism.

the one a male ass, the other a female ass. He embraced her, and hence one-hoofed animals were born. The one became a she-goat, the other a he-goat; the one became a ewe, the other a ram. He embraced her, and hence goats and sheep were born. And thus he created everything that exists in pairs, down to the ants.

He knew, 'I indeed am this creation, for I created all this.' Hence he became the creation, and he who knows this lives in this his creation.

Next he thus produced fire by rubbing. From the mouth, as from the fire-hole, and from the hands he created fire. Therefore both the mouth and the hands are inside without hair, for the fire-hole is inside without hair.

And when they say, 'Sacrifice to this or sacrifice to that god,' each god is but his manifestation, for he is all gods.

Now, whatever there is moist, that he created from seed; this is Soma. So far verily is this universe either food or eater. Soma indeed is food, Agni eater. This is the highest creation of Brahman, when he created the gods from his better part, and when he, who was (then) mortal, created the immortals. Therefore it was the highest creation. And he who knows this, lives in this his highest creation.

Now all this was then undeveloped. It became developed by form and name, so that one could say, 'He, called so and so, is such a one.' Therefore at present also all this is developed by name and form, so that one can say, 'He, called so and so, is such a one.'

He (Brahman or the Self) entered thither, to the very tips of the finger-nails, as a razor might be fitted in a razor-case, or as fire in a fire-place.

He cannot be seen, for, in part only, when breathing, he is breath by name; when speaking, speech by name; when seeing, eye by name; when hearing, ear by name; when thinking, mind by name. All these are but the names of his acts. And he who worships (regards) him as the one or the other, does not know him, for he is apart from this (when qualified) by the one or the other (predicate). Let men worship him as Self, for in the self all these are old.[1] This Self is the footstep of everything, for through it one knows everything. And as one can find again by footsteps what was lost, thus he who knows this finds glory and praise.

This, which is nearer to us than anything, this Self, is dearer than a son, dearer than wealth, dearer than all else.

[1] The Brahman "Self" is almost what we mean by the divine nature immanent in ourselves as well as in the external world.

And if one were to say to one who declares another than the Self dear, that he will lose what is dear to him, very likely it would be so. Let him worship the Self alone as dear. He who worships the Self alone as dear, the object of his love will never perish.

Here they say: 'If men think that by knowledge of Brahman they will become everything, what then did that Brahman know, from whence all this sprang?'

Verily in the beginning this was Brahman, that Brahman knew (its) Self only, saying, 'I am Brahman.' From it all this sprang. Thus, whatever Deva was awakened (so as to know Brahman), he indeed became that (Brahman); and the same with Rishis and men. The Rishi Vāmadeva saw and understood it, singing, 'I was Manu (moon), I was the sun.' Therefore now also he who thus knows that he is Brahman, becomes all this, and even the Devas cannot prevent it, for he himself is their Self.

Now if a man worships another deity, thinking the deity is one and he another, he does not know. He is like a beast for the Devas. For verily, as many beasts nourish a man, thus does every man nourish the Devas. If only one beast is taken away, it is not pleasant; how much more when many are taken! Therefore it is not pleasant to the Devas that men should know this.

Verily in the beginning this was Brahman, one only. That being one, was not strong enough. It created still further the most excellent Kshatra (power), viz. those Kshatras (powers) among the Devas—Indra, Varuna, Soma, Rudra, Parjanya, Yama, Mrityu, Isāna. Therefore there is nothing beyond the Kshatra, and therefore at the Rājasūya sacrifice the Brāhmana sits down below the Kshatriya. He confers that glory on the Kshatra alone. But Brahman is (nevertheless) the birthplace of the Kshatra. Therefore though a king is exalted, he sits down at the end (of the sacrifice) below the Brahman, as his birthplace. He who injures him, injures his own birthplace. He becomes worse, because he has injured one better than himself.

He was not strong enough. He created the people, the classes of Devas which in their different orders are called Vasus, Rudras, Ādityas, Visve Devas, Maruts.

He was not strong enough. He created the Sūdra caste, as nourisher. This earth verily is Pūshan (the nourisher); for the earth nourishes all this whatsoever.

He was not strong enough. He created still further the most excellent

Law. Law is the Kshatra (power) of the Kshatra, therefore there is nothing higher than the Law. Thenceforth even a weak man rules a stronger with the help of the Law, as with the help of a king. Thus the Law is what is called the true. And if a man declares what is true, they say he declares the Law; and if he declares the Law, they say he declares what is true. Thus both are the same.

There are then this Brahman, Kshatra, Vis, and Sūdra. Among the Devas that Brahman existed as fire only, among men as Brāhmana, as Kshatriya through the (divine) Kshatriya, as Vaisya through the (divine) Vaisya, as Sūdra through the (divine) Sūdra. Therefore people wish for their future state among the Devas through the sacrificial fire only; and among men through the Brāhmana, for in these two forms did Brahman exist.

Now if a man departs this life without having seen his true future life (in the Self), then that Self, not being known, does not receive and bless him, as if the Veda had not been read, or as if a good work had not been done. Nay, even if one who does not know that (Self), should perform here on earth some great holy work, it will perish for him in the end. Let a man worship the Self only as his true state. If a man worships the Self only as his true state, his work does not perish, for whatever he desires that he gets from that Self.

Now verily this Self (of the ignorant man) is the world of all creatures. In so far as man sacrifices and pours out libations, he is the world of the Devas; in so far as he repeats the hymns, etc., he is the world of the Rishis; in so far as he offers cakes to the fathers and tries to obtain offspring, he is the world of the fathers; in so far as he gives shelter and food to men, he is the world of men; in so far as he finds fodder and water for the animals, he is the world of the animals; in so far as quadrupeds, birds, and even ants live in his houses, he is their world. And as everyone wishes his own world not to be injured, thus all beings wish that he who knows this should not be injured. Verily this is known and has been well reasoned.

In the beginning this was Self alone, one only. He desired, 'Let there be a wife for me that I may have offspring, and let there be wealth for me that I may offer sacrifices.' Verily this is the whole desire, and, even if wishing for more, he would not find it. Therefore now also a lonely person desires, 'Let there be a wife for me that I may have offspring, and let there be wealth for me that I may offer sacrifices.' And so long as he does not obtain either of these things, he thinks he is incomplete.

Now his completeness (is made up as follows): mind is his Self (husband); speech the wife; breath the child; the eye all worldly wealth, for he finds it with the eye; the ear his divine wealth, for he hears it with the ear. The body (ātman) is his work, for with the body he works. This is the fivefold sacrifice, for fivefold is the animal, fivefold man, fivefold all this whatsoever. He who knows this, obtains all this.

(*From the Brihadāranyaka Upanishad*)

THE SUBTLE ESSENCE[1]

'As the bees, my son, make honey by collecting the juices of distant trees, and reduce the juice into one form.

'And as these juices have no discrimination, so that they might say, I am the juice of this tree or that, in the same manner, my son, all these creatures, when they have become merged in the True (either in deep sleep or in death), know not that they are merged in the True.

'Whatever these creatures are here, whether a lion, or a wolf, or a boar, or a worm, or a midge, or a gnat, or a mosquito, that they become again and again.

'Now that which is that subtle essence, in it all that exists has its self. It is the True. It is the Self, and thou, O Svetaketu, art it.'

'Please, Sir, inform me still more,' said the son.

'Be it so, my child,' the father replied.

'These rivers, my son, run, the eastern (like the Gangā) toward the east, the western (like the Sindhu) toward the west. They go from sea to sea. They become indeed sea. And as those rivers, when they are in the sea, do not know, I am this or that river.

'In the same manner, my son, all these creatures, when they have come back from the True, know not that they have come back from the True. Whatever these creatures are here, whether a lion, or a wolf, or a boar, or a worm, or a midge, or a gnat, or a mosquito, that they become again and again.

'That which is that subtle essence, in it all that exists has its self. It is the True. It is the Self, and thou, O Svetaketu, art it.'

'Please, Sir, inform me still more,' said the son.

'Be it so, my child,' the father replied.

[1] This is the teaching of Uddālaka Aruni to his son Svetaketu.

'If someone were to strike at the root of this large tree here, it would bleed, but live. If he were to strike at its stem, it would bleed, but live. If he were to strike at its top, it would bleed, but live. Pervaded by the living Self that tree stands firm, drinking in its nourishment and rejoicing;

'But if the living Self leaves one of its branches, that branch withers; if it leaves a second, that branch withers; if it leaves a third, that branch withers. If it leaves the whole tree, the whole tree withers. In exactly the same manner, my son, know this.' Thus he spoke:

'This body indeed withers and dies when the living Self has left it; the living Self dies not.

'That which is that subtle essence, in it all that exists has its self. It is the Self, and thou, Svetaketu, art it.'

'Please, Sir, inform me still more,' said the son.

'Be it so, my child,' the father replied.

'Fetch me from thence a fruit of the nyagrodha tree.'

'Here is one, Sir.'

'Break it.'

'It is broken, Sir.'

'What do you see there?'

'These seeds, almost infinitesimal.'

'Break one of them.'

'It is broken, Sir.'

'What do you see there?'

'Not anything, Sir.'

The father said: 'My son, that subtle essence which you do not perceive there, of that very essence this great nyagrodha tree exists.

'Believe it, my son. That which is the subtle essence, in it all that exists has its self. It is the True. It is the Self, and thou, O Svetaketu, art it.'

'Please, Sir, inform me still more,' said the son.

'Be it so, my child,' the father replied.

'Place this salt in water, and then wait on me in the morning.'

The son did as he was commanded.

The father said to him: 'Bring me the salt, which you placed in the water last night.'

The son having looked for it, found it not, for, of course, it was melted.

The father said: 'Taste it from the surface of the water. How is it?'
The son replied: 'It is salt.'
'Taste it from the middle. How is it?'
The son replied: 'It is salt.'
'Taste it from the bottom. How is it?'
The son replied: 'It is salt.'
The father said: 'Throw it away and then wait on me.'
He did so; but salt exists for ever.

Then the father said: 'Here also, in this body, forsooth, you do not perceive the True, my son; but there indeed it is.

'That which is subtle essence, in it all that exists has its self. It is the True. It is the Self, and thou, Svetaketu, art it.'

'Please, Sir, inform me still more,' said the son.

'Be it so, my child,' the father replied.

(*From the Chhāndogya Upanishad*)

THE TRUE BRAHMAN

All this is Brahman. Let a man meditate on that visible world as beginning, ending, and breathing in it.

Now man is a creature of will. According to what his will is in this world, so will he be when he has departed this life. Let him therefore have this will and belief:

The intelligent, whose body is spirit, whose form is light, whose thoughts are true, whose nature is like ether, from whom all works, all desires, all sweet odours and tastes proceed; he who embraces all this, who never speaks, and is never surprised,

He is my self within the heart, smaller than a corn of rice, smaller than a corn of barley, smaller than a mustard seed, smaller than a canary seed or the kernel of a canary seed. He also is my self within the heart, greater than the earth, greater than the sky, greater than heaven, greater than all these worlds.

He from whom all works, all desires, all sweet odours and tastes proceed, who embraces all this, who never speaks and who is never surprised, he, my self within the heart, is that Brahman. When I shall have departed from hence, I shall obtain that Self. He who has this faith has no doubt; thus said Sāndilya,[1] yea, thus he said.

(*From the Chhāndogya Upanishad*)

[1] This chapter is frequently quoted as the Sāndilya-vidyā.

EMANCIPATION

Hari, Om. There is this city of Brahman (the body), and in it the palace, the small lotus of the heart, and in it that small ether. Now what exists within that small ether, that is to be sought for, that is to be understood.

And if they should say to him: 'Now with regard to that city of Brahman, and the palace in it, i.e. the small lotus of the heart, and the small ether within the heart, what is there within it that deserves to be sought for, or that is to be understood?'

Then he should say: 'As large as this ether is, so large is that ether within the heart. Both heaven and earth are contained within it, both fire and air, both sun and moon, both lightning and stars; and whatever there is of him here in the world, and whatever is not, all that is contained within it.'

And if they should say to him: 'If everything that exists is contained in that city of Brahman, all beings and all desires, then what is left of it, when old age reaches it and scatters it, or when it falls to pieces?'

Then he should say: 'By the old age of the body, the ether does not age; by the death of the body, the ether is not killed. That is the true Brahma-city. In it all desires are contained. It is the Self, free from sin, free from old age, from death and grief, from hunger and thirst, which desires nothing but what it ought to desire, and imagines nothing but what it ought to imagine. Now as here on earth people follow as they are commanded, and depend on the object which they are attached to, be it a country or a piece of land,

'And as here on earth, whatever has been acquired by exertion perishes, so perishes whatever is acquired for the next world by sacrifices and other good actions performed on earth. Those who depart from hence without having discovered the Self and those true desires, for them there is no freedom in all the worlds. But those who depart from hence, after having discovered the Self and those true desires, for them there is freedom in all the worlds.

(*From the Chhāndogya Upanishad*)

THE CONQUEST OF DEATH

I

VĀJASRAVASA, desirous of heavenly rewards, surrendered at a sacrifice all that he possessed. He had a son of the name of Nachiketas.

When the promised presents were being given (to the priests), faith entered into the heart of Nachiketas, who was still a boy, and he thought:

'Unblessed, surely, are the worlds to which a man goes by giving cows which have drunk water, eaten hay, given their milk, and are barren.'

He (knowing that his father had promised to give up all that he possessed, and therefore his son also) said to his father: 'Dear father, to whom wilt thou give me?'

He said it a second and a third time. Then the father replied:

'I shall give thee unto Death.'

(The father, having once said so, though in haste, had to be true to his word and to sacrifice his son.)

The son said: 'I go as the first, at the head of many (who have still to die); I go in the midst of many (who are now dying). What will be the work of Yama[1] which to-day he has to do unto me?

'Look back how it was with those who came before, look forward how it will be with those who come hereafter. A mortal ripens like corn, like corn he springs up again.'

(Nachiketas enters into the abode of Yama Vaivasvata, and there is no one to receive him. Thereupon one of the attendants of Yama is supposed to say:)

'Fire enters into the houses, when a Brāhmana enters as a guest. That fire is quenched by this peace-offering—bring water, O Vaivasvata!

'A Brāhmana that dwells in the house of a foolish man without receiving food to eat, destroys his hopes and expectations, his possessions, his righteousness, his sacred and his good deeds, and all his sons and cattle.'

(Yama, returning to his house after an absence of three nights, during which time Nachiketas had received no hospitality from him, says:)

'O Brāhmana, as thou, a venerable guest, hast dwelt in my house three nights without eating, therefore choose now three boons. Hail to thee! and welfare to me!'

[1] The King of Death.

II

Nachiketas said: 'O Death, as the first of the three boons I choose that Gautama, my father, be pacified, kind, and free from anger towards me; and that he may know me and greet me, when I shall have been dismissed by thee."

Yama said: 'Through my favour Auddālaki Āruni, thy father, will know thee, and be again towards thee as he was before. He shall sleep peacefully through the night, and free from anger, after having seen thee freed from the mouth of death.'

Nachiketas said: 'In the heaven-world there is no fear; thou art not there, O Death, and no one is afraid on account of old age. Leaving behind both hunger and thirst, and out of the reach of sorrow, all rejoice in the world of heaven.

'Thou knowest, O Death, the fire-sacrifice which leads us to heaven; tell it to me, for I am full of faith. Those who live in the heaven-world reach immortality—this I ask as my second boon.'

Yama said: 'I tell it thee, learn it from me, and when thou understandest that fire-sacrifice which leads to heaven, know, O Nachiketas, that it is the attainment of the endless worlds, and their firm support, hidden in darkness.'

Yama then told him that fire-sacrifice, the beginning of all the worlds, and what bricks are required for the altar, and how many, and how they are to be placed. And Nachiketas repeated all as it had been told to him. Then Mrityu, being pleased with him, said again:

The generous, being satisfied, said to him: 'I give thee now another boon; that fire-sacrifice shall be named after thee, take also this many-coloured chain.

'He who has three times performed this Nāchiketa rite, and has been united with the three (father, mother, and teacher), and has performed the three duties (study, sacrifice, almsgiving) overcomes birth and death. When he has learnt and understood this fire, which knows (or makes us know) all that is born of Brahman, which is venerable and divine, then he obtains everlasting peace.

'He who knows the three Nāchiketa fires, and knowing the three, piles up the Nāchiketa sacrifice, he, having first thrown off the chains of death, rejoices in the world of heaven, beyond the reach of grief.

'This, O Nachiketas, is thy fire which leads to heaven, and which thou hast chosen as thy second boon. That fire all men will proclaim. Choose now, O Nachiketas, thy third boon.'

Nachiketas said: 'There is that doubt, when a man is dead—some saying, he is; others, he is not. This I should like to know, taught by thee; this is the third of my boons.'

Death said: 'On this point even the gods have doubted formerly; it is not easy to understand. That subject is subtle. Choose another boon, O Nachiketas, do not press me, and let me off that boon.'

Nachiketas said: 'On this point even the gods have doubted indeed, and thou, Death, hast declared it to be not easy to understand, and another teacher like thee is not to be found—surely no other boon is like unto this.'

Death said: 'Choose sons and grandsons who shall live a hundred years, herds of cattle, elephants, gold, and horses. Choose the wide abode of the earth, and live thyself as many harvests as thou desirest.

'If you can think of any boon equal to that, choose wealth, and long life. Be king, Nachiketas, on the wide earth. I make thee the enjoyer of all desires.

'Whatever desires are difficult to attain among mortals, ask for them according to thy wish; these fair maidens with their chariots and musical instruments—such are indeed not to be obtained by men—be waited on by them whom I give to thee, but do not ask me about dying.'

Nachiketas said: 'These things last till to-morrow, O Death, for they wear out this vigour of all the senses. Even the whole of life is short. Keep thou thy horses, keep dance and song for thyself.

'No man can be made happy by wealth. Shall we possess wealth, when we see thee? Shall we live, as long as thou rulest? Only that boon which I have chosen is to be chosen by me.

'What mortal, slowly decaying here below, and knowing, after having approached them, the freedom from decay enjoyed by the immortals, would delight in a long life, after he has pondered on the pleasures which arise from beauty and love?

'No, that on which there is this doubt, O Death, tell us what there is in that great hereafter. Nachiketas does not choose another boon but that which enters into the hidden world.'

III

Death said: 'The good is one thing, the pleasant another; these two, having different objects, chain a man. It is well with him who clings to the good; he who chooses the pleasant, misses his end.

'The good and pleasant approach man: the wise goes round about them and distinguishes them. Yea, the wise prefers the good to the pleasant, but the fool chooses the pleasant through greed and avarice.

'Thou, O Nachiketas, after pondering all pleasures that are or seem delightful, hast dismissed them all. Thou hast not gone into the road that leadeth to wealth, in which many men perish.

'Wide apart and leading to different points are these two, ignorance, and what is known as wisdom. I believe Nachiketas to be one who desires knowledge, for even many pleasures did not tear thee away.

'Fools dwelling in darkness, wise in their own conceit, and puffed up with vain knowledge, go round and round, staggering to and fro, like blind men led by the blind.

'The hereafter never rises before the eyes of the careless child, deluded by the delusion of wealth. "This is the world," he thinks, "there is no other"—thus he falls again and again under my sway.

'He (the Self) of whom many are not even able to hear, whom many, even when they hear of him, do not comprehend; wonderful is a man, when found, who is able to teach him (the Self); wonderful is he who comprehends him, when taught by an able teacher.

'That Self, when taught by an inferior man, is not easy to be known, even though often thought upon; unless it be taught by another, there is no way to it, for it is inconceivably smaller than what is small.

'That doctrine is not to be obtained by argument, but when it is declared by another, then, O dearest, it is easy to understand. Thou hast obtained it now; thou art truly a man of true resolve. May we have always an inquirer like thee!'

Nachiketas said: 'I know that what is called a treasure is transient, for that eternal is not obtained by things which are not eternal. Hence the Nāchiketa fire-sacrifice has been laid by me first; then, by means of transient things, I have obtained what is not transient.'

Yama said: 'Though thou hadst seen the fulfilment of all desires, the foundation of the world, the endless rewards of good deeds, the shore where there is no fear, that which is magnified by praise, the wide abode, the rest, yet being wise thou hast with firm resolve dismissed it all. . . .

'The knowing Self is not born, it dies not; it sprang from nothing, nothing sprang from it. The Ancient is unborn, eternal, everlasting; he is not killed, though the body is killed.

'If the killer thinks that he kills, if the killed thinks that he is killed, they do not understand; for this one does not kill, nor is that one killed.

'The Self, smaller than small, greater than great, is hidden in the heart of that creature. A man who is free from desires and free from grief, sees the majesty of the Self by the grace of the Creator.

'Though sitting still, he walks far; though lying down, he goes everywhere. Who, save myself, is able to know that God who rejoices and rejoices not?

'The wise who knows the Self as bodiless within the bodies, as unchanging among changing things, as great and omnipresent, does never grieve.

'That Self cannot be gained by the Veda, nor by understanding, nor by much learning. He whom the Self chooses, by him the Self can be gained. The Self chooses his body as his own.

'But he who has not first turned away from his wickedness, who is not tranquil, and subdued, or whose mind is not at rest, he can never obtain the Self even by knowledge.

'Who then knows where He is, He to whom the Brahmans and Kshatriyas are (as it were) but food, and death itself a condiment?

(*From the Katha Upanishad*)

THE ONE GOD

The snarer who rules alone by his powers, who rules all the worlds by his powers, who is one and the same, while things arise and exist—they who know this are immortal.

For there is one Rudra only, they do not allow a second, who rules all the worlds by his powers. He stands behind all persons, and after having created all worlds he, the protector, rolls it up at the end of time.

That one god, having his eyes, his face, his arms, and his feet in every place, when producing heaven and earth, forges them together with his arms and his wings.

He, the creator and supporter of the gods, Rudra, the great seer, the ord of all, he who formerly gave birth to Hiranyagarbha, may he endow us with good thoughts.

O Rudra, thou dweller in the mountains, look upon us with that most blessed form of thine which is auspicious, not terrible, and reveals no evil!

O lord of the mountains, make lucky that arrow which thou, a dweller in the mountains, holdest in thy hand to shoot. Do not hurt man or beast!

Those who know beyond this the High Brahman, the vast, hidden in the bodies of all creatures, and alone enveloping everything, as the Lord, they become immortal.

I know that great person (purusha) of sunlike lustre beyond the darkness. A man who knows him truly, passes over death; there is no other path to go.

This whole universe is filled by this person (purusha), to whom there is nothing superior, from whom there is nothing different, than whom there is nothing smaller or larger, who stands alone, fixed like a tree in the sky.

That which is beyond this world is without form and without suffering. They who know it, become immortal, but others suffer pain indeed.

That Bhagavat exists in the faces, the heads, the necks of all, he dwells in the cave (of the heart) of all beings, he is all-pervading, therefore he is the omnipresent Siva.

That person is the great lord; he is the mover of existence, he possesses that purest power of reaching everything; he is light, he is undecaying.

The person, not larger than a thumb, dwelling within, always dwelling in the heart of man, is perceived by the heart, the thought, the mind; they who know it become immortal.

The person with a thousand heads, a thousand eyes, a thousand feet, having compassed the earth on every side, extends beyond it by ten fingers' breadth.

That person alone (purusha) is all this, what has been and what will be; he is also the lord of immortality; he is whatever grows by food.

Its hands and feet are everywhere, its eyes and head are everywhere, its ears are everywhere, it stands encompassing all in the world.

Separate from all the senses, yet reflecting the qualities of all the senses, it is the lord and ruler of all, it is the great refuge of all.

The embodied spirit within the town with nine gates, the bird, flutters outwards, the ruler of the whole world, of all that rests and of al that moves.

Grasping without hands, hasting without feet, he sees without eyes he hears without ears. He knows what can be known, but no one know him; they call him the first, the great person.

The Self, smaller than small, greater than great, is hidden in the hear of the creature. A man who has left all grief behind, sees the majesty, th Lord, the passionless, by the grace of the creator.

I know this undecaying, ancient one, the self of all things, being infinite and omnipresent. They declare that in him all birth is stopped for the Brahma-students proclaim him to be eternal.

(*From the Svetāsvatara Upanishad*)

THE IMMANENCE OF GOD

He, the sun, without any colour, who with set purpose by means of his power produces endless colours, in whom all this comes together in the beginning, and comes asunder in the end—may he, the god, endow us with good thoughts.

That Self indeed is fire, it is the sun, it is wind, it is moon; the same also is the starry firmament, it is Brahman, it is water, it is Prajāpati.

Thou art woman, thou art man; thou are youth, thou art maiden; thou, as an old man, totterest along on thy staff; thou art born with thy face turned everywhere.

Thou art the dark-blue bee, thou art the green parrot with red eyes, thou art the thunder-cloud, the seasons, the seas. Thou art without beginning, because thou art infinite, thou from whom all worlds are born.

There is one unborn being (female), red, white, and black, uniform, but producing manifold offspring. There is one unborn being (male) who loves her and lies by her; there is another who leaves her, while she is eating what has to be eaten.

Two birds, inseparable friends, cling to the same tree. One of them eats the sweet fruit, the other looks on without eating.

On the same tree man sits grieving, immersed, bewildered, by his own impotence. But when he sees the other lord contented, and knows his glory, then his grief passes away.

He who does not know that indestructible being of the Rigveda, that highest ether-like Self wherein all the gods reside, of what use is the Rigveda to him? Those only who know it, rest contented.

That from which the maker (māyin) sends forth all this—the sacred verses, the offerings, the sacrifices, the panaceas, the past, the future, and all that the Vedas declare—in that the other is bound up through that art (māyā).

Know then nature is art, and the great Lord the maker; the whole world is filled with what are his members.

If a man has discerned him, who being one only, rules over every cause, in whom all this comes together and comes asunder again, who is the lord, the bestower of blessing, the adorable god, then he passes for ever into that peace.

He, the creator and supporter of the gods, Rudra, the great seer, the lord of all, who saw Hiranyagarbha being born, may he endow us with good thoughts.

He who is the sovereign of the gods, he in whom all the worlds rest, he who rules over all two-footed and four-footed beings, to that god let us sacrifice an oblation.

He who has known him who is more subtle than subtle, in the midst of chaos, creating all things, having many forms, alone enveloping everything, the happy one (Siva) passes into peace for ever.

He also was in time the guardian of this world, the lord of all, hidden in all beings. In him the Brahmarshis and the deities are united, and he who knows him cuts the fetters of death asunder.

He who knows the blessed (Siva) hidden in all beings, like the subtle film that rises from out the clarified butter, alone enveloping everything —he who knows the god, is freed from all fetters.

That god, the maker of all things, the great Self, always dwelling in the heart of man, is perceived by the heart, the soul, the mind;—they who know it become immortal.

When the light has risen, there is no day, no night, neither existence nor non-existence; the blessed (Siva) alone is there. That is the eternal, the adorable light of Savitri—and the ancient wisdom proceeded thence.

No one has grasped him above, or across, or in the middle. There is no image of him whose name is Great Glory.

His form cannot be seen, no one perceives him with the eye. Those who through heart and mind know him thus abiding in the heart, become immortal.

'Thou art unborn,' with these words some one comes near to thee, trembling. O Rudra, let thy gracious face protect me for ever!

O Rudra! hurt us not in our offspring and descendants, hurt us not in our own lives, nor in our cows, nor in our horses! Do not slay our men in thy wrath, for, holding oblations, we call on thee always.

(*From the Svetāsvatara Upanishad*)

GOD IS WITHIN YOU

In the imperishable and infinite Highest Brahman, wherein the two, knowledge and ignorance, are hidden, the one, ignorance, perishes, the other, knowledge, is immortal; but he who controls both, knowledge and ignorance, is another.

It is he who, being one only, rules over every cause, over all forms, and over all germs; it is he who, in the beginning, bears in his thoughts the wise son, the fiery, whom he wishes to look on while he is born.

In that field in which the god, after spreading out one net after another in various ways, draws it together again, the Lord, the great Self, having further created the lords, thus carries on his lordship over all.

As the car of the sun shines, lighting up all quarters, above, below, and across, thus does that god, the holy, the adorable, being one, rule over all that has the nature of a germ.

He, being one, rules over all and everything, so that the universal germ ripens its nature, diversifies all natures that can be ripened, and determines all qualities.

Brahma knows this, which is hidden in the upanishads, which are hidden in the Vedas, as the Brahma-germ. The ancient gods and poets who knew it, they became it and were immortal.

But he who is endowed with qualities, and performs works that are to bear fruit, and enjoys the reward of whatever he has done, migrates through his own works, the lord of life, assuming all forms, led by the three Gunas,[1] and following the three paths.

That lower one also, not larger than a thumb, but brilliant like the sun, who is endowed with personality and thoughts, with the quality of mind and the quality of body, is seen small even like the point of a goad.

That living soul is to be known as part of the hundredth part of the point of a hair, divided a hundred times, and yet it is to be infinite.

[1] Three primeval elements, light, passion and dullness which compose the world. See the Glossary under *Gunas*.

It is not woman, it is not man, nor is it neuter; whatever body it takes, with that it is joined only.

By means of thoughts, touching, seeing, and passions the incarnate Self assumes successively in various places various forms, in accordance with his deeds, just as the body grows when food and drink are poured into it.

That incarnate Self, according to his own qualities, assumes many shapes, coarse or subtile, and having himself caused his union with them, he is seen as another and another, through the qualities of his acts, and through the qualities of his body.

He who knows him who has no beginning and no end, in the midst of chaos, creating all things, having many forms, alone enveloping everything, is freed from all fetters.

Those who know him who is to be grasped by the mind, who is not to be called the body, who makes existence and non-existence, the happy one (Siva) who also creates the elements, they have left the body.

(*From the Svetāsvatara Upanishad*)

KNOW GOD

Some wise men, deluded, speak of Nature, and others of Time as the cause of everything; but it is the greatness of God by which this Brahma-wheel is made to turn.

It is at the command of him who always covers this world, the knower, the time of time, who assumes qualities and all knowledge, it is at his command that this creation unfolds itself, which is called earth, water, fire, air, and ether;

He who, after he has done that work and rested again, and after he has brought together the self with matter, with one, two, three, or eight, with time also and with the subtle qualities of the mind,

Who after starting the works endowed with the three qualities,[1] can order all things, yet when, in the absence of all these, he has caused the destruction of the work, goes on, being in truth different from all he has produced;

He is the beginning, producing the causes which unite the soul with the body, and, being above the three kinds of time, past, present, future, he is seen as without parts, after we have first worshipped that adorable

[1] The Gunas referred to in the preceding section.

god, who has many forms, and who is the true source of all things, as dwelling in our own mind.

He is beyond all the forms of the world and of time, he is the other, from whom this world moves round, when one has known him who brings good and removes evil, the lord of bliss, as dwelling within the self, the immortal, the support of all.

Let us know that highest great lord of lords, the highest deity of deities, the master of masters, the highest above, as God, the lord of the world, the adorable.

There is no effect and no cause known of him, no one is seen like unto him or better; his high power is revealed as manifold, as inherent, acting as force and knowledge.

There is no master of his in the world, no ruler of his, not even a sign of him. He is the cause, the lord of the lords of the organs, and there is of him neither parent nor lord.

That only God who spontaneously covered himself, like a spider, with threads drawn from the first cause, grant us entrance into Brahman.

He is the one God, hidden in all beings, all-pervading, the self within all beings, watching over all works, dwelling in all beings, the witness, the perceiver, the only one, free from qualities.

He is the one ruler of many who do not act; he makes the one seed manifold. The wise who perceive him within their self, to them belongs eternal happiness, not to others.

He is the eternal among eternals, the thinker among thinkers, who, though one, fulfils the desires of many. He who has known that cause which is to be apprehended by Sāmkhya (philosophy) and Yoga (religious discipline), he is freed from all fetters.

The sun does not shine there, nor the moon and the stars, nor these lightnings, and much less this fire. When he shines, everything shines after him; by his light all this is lightened.

He is the one bird in the midst of the world; he is also like the sun that has set in the ocean. A man knows him truly, passes over death; there is no other path to go.

He makes all, he knows all, the self-caused, the knower, the destroyer of time, who assumes qualities and knows everything, the master of nature and of man, the lord of the three qualities, the cause of the bondage, the existence, and the liberation of the world.

He who has become that, he is the immortal, remaining the lord, the knower, the ever-present guardian of this world, who rules this world for ever, for no one else is able to rule it.

Seeking for freedom I go for refuge to that God who is the light of his own thoughts, he who first creates Brahman and delivers the Vedas to him;

Who is without parts, without actions, tranquil, without fault, without taint, the highest bridge to immortality—like a fire that has consumed its fuel.

Only when men shall roll up the sky like a hide, will there be an end of misery, unless God has first been known.[1]

Through the power of his penance and through the grace of God has the wise Svetāsvatara truly proclaimed Brahman, the highest and holiest, to the best of ascetics, as approved by the company of Rishis.

This highest mystery in the Vedānta, delivered in a former age, should not be given to one whose passions have not been subdued, nor to one who is not a son, or who is not a pupil.

If these truths have been told to a high-minded man, who feels the highest devotion for God, and for his Guru[2] as for God, then they will shine forth—then they will shine forth indeed.

[1] This may be considered the final message of the Upanishads.
[2] Preceptor.

The Lord's Song

(THE BHAGAVAD-GITA)

INTRODUCTION

THE BHAGAVAD-GITA stands in relation to Hinduism as the Sermon on the Mount stands in relation to the Christian teachings. It has been described as the "Essence of the Vedas." An Indian saint has said: "All the Upanishads are the cows, the Lord Himself is the Milker, Arjuna, the calf, and those of purified understanding are the drinkers of the milk, the supreme nectar of the Gita."

Originally it formed a section of Book Six of the great Hindu epic, the *Mahabharata*. It is in the form of a conversation between the warrior Arjuna and his charioteer, who really was the "Blessed Lord," the god Krishna. War had become inevitable between the sons of Pandu (of which Arjuna was one) and their cousin Duryodhana and his brothers, the sons of the blind King Dhritarashtra, or briefly between the Pandavas and the Kurus. Just before the beginning of the battle, Arjuna refused to fight, when he saw he was going to kill his own kinsmen. The god Krishna explained to him that no one could be killed, since men's souls live for ever, and thereon the conversation began, extending to eighteen chapters, covering every phase of ethical and religious questions, concerning the yoga of action, the justification for rituals and sacrifices, the manifestations of god in this physical world, and ending with the important injunction on accepting Krishna as a refuge to whom all people of all classes could come and find peace and salvation. The old blind King, unable to watch the battle was offered sight by a great sage, but declined it, for he had no wish to see the slaughter among his own kinsmen. The great sage then granted Sanjaya the power of perceiving at a distance all that happened on the battlefield. Therefore, principally in the beginning and in the end, we see the remarks of Sanjaya, concerning the battle, while the questions and answers between Arjuna and the Lord Krishna, as reported by Sanjaya, form the substance of the main body of the work.

The whole book breathes the Hindu mental and religious atmosphere, although some of the teachings, such as the emphasis on action and doing it without regard to selfish benefit but for devotion to God, and particularly the denial of materialism and emphatic Vedic assertion of the spirit behind all things, offer viewpoints that are either present or are greatly needed in the modern world. Anyway, the contrasts are as important as the similarities, and it is because the work is characteristically the most important product of the Hindu religious spirit that its influence and position in India have been so great. Dr. E. J. Thomas calls it "one of the greatest of the religious phenomena of the world" and "the earliest and still the greatest monument of Hindu religion."

The *Bhagavad-Gita* has not the same appeal for me as the Buddhist *Dhammapada,* but that is no reason why it should be less important to the Hindu nation. What is important is to note the progress of the Hindu mind from the *Upanishads* to the *Gita* and its increasing clarity of thought and ways of thinking closer to our own. The work was probably written in the second century before the Christian era, although no approximate date can be assigned. So important did it become in the Hindu religious thought that every system had to square itself with the teachings of the Lord's Song. There are strands of pantheism, monotheism, theism and deism in it. Whether it was added to by successive writers is less important than the fact that these teachings were, and still are, accepted by the Hindu people as the ultimate embodiment of religious wisdom. Any attempt by Western higher critics to separate the several strands of belief from one another in the Song and "restore" the "original text" is bound to be both foolish and ridiculous. Certain scholars, presupposing that one man could hold only one consistent system of belief and that that system must be the one they hold to be the original one, and ignoring the fact that such a document was necessarily a synthesis of many streams of influence, satisfactory to its believers, have attempted the foolish task of determining its original composition. It never occurs to them that the world could be God and at the same time a personal God could exist—rather fine distinctions that exist in academic minds only. The great power of the Gita lies in the fact that it teaches a "loving faith" or devotion (*bhakti*) to a personal God, Krishna. The final message of Krishna is: "Giving up all Dharmas, come unto me alone for refuge. I shall free thee from all sins; grieve not." (XVIII, 66)

It is extremely important that such a testimony of the Hindu religious spirit should not be translated by a scholar of Sanskrit, but by a Hindu follower who is at home with its language and at one with the spirit of its teachings, and who knows what the different verses mean, directly and simply, to the Indian people.

The Bhagavad-Gita has engaged the loving labors of many translators, and many excellent translations exist, such as Lionel D. Barnett's "Lord's Song" (Temple Classics) with a long introduction and copious notes, E. J. Thomas's "The Song of the Lord" (Wisdom of the East Series), the well-known version by Annie Besant (Theosophical Press), Sir Edwin Arnold's "The Song Celestial" (Trübner), M. M. Chatterji's "The Lord's Lay" (Houghton), with commentary and notes and references to the Christian Scriptures, and the scholarly translation by Telang in the Sacred Books of the East. I have, however, chosen the translation by Swami Paramananda (The Vedanta Center) because I believe, more than the others, it shows that mastery of the languages and that profound understanding of the thought content, so that the result is, as it should be, an easy, effective and mature version, without either the cumbersomeness of the scholarly or the surreptitious paraphrasing of the over-interpretative. As the editor of the book remarks, "The letter must be illumined by the spirit; and none can read the translation without feeling convinced that the head, heart, and life have co-operated in the making of it." That is no mean compliment. I have kept the footnotes by Swami Paramananda.

The Blessed Lord's Song

SRIMAD-BHAGAVAD-GITA

Translated by Swami Paramananda

CHAPTER I

Dhritarāshtra asked:

1. O Sanjaya, assembled together on the sacred plain of Kurukshetra, being desirous to fight, what did my people and the Pāndavas do?

Sanjaya replied:

2. The Prince Duryodhana, having seen the Pāndava forces arrayed, approached his teacher (Drona) and spoke these words:

3. Behold this mighty host of the sons of Pāndava arrayed by the son of Drupada, thy gifted pupil.

4-6. Here are heroes, mighty bowmen, equals in battle to Bhima and Arjuna—the great warriors, Yuyudhāna, Virāta, Drupada; valiant Drishtaketu, Chekitāna and the King of Kāshi; Purujit, Kunti-Bhoja and Shaibya, the greatest of men; the powerful Yudhamanyu and the brave Uttamaujas; the son of Subhadrā and the sons of Draupadi; all of them mighty car-warriors.

7. O best of twice-born,[1] hear also of those who are distinguished among ourselves, the leaders of my army; I relate their names for thy information.

[1] A Brāhmin is called a twice-born because he is born for the second time when he receives his holy thread or badge for spiritual life.

8. Thyself and Bhishma and Karna, and Kripa, the victorious in battle, Aswatthamā, Vikarna, Jayadratha, the son of Somadatta.

9. Also there are many heroes skillful in battle armed with many kinds of weapons, determined to lay down their lives for my sake.

10. Yet this army of ours, though commanded by Bhishma, seems insufficient; but their army, commanded by Bhima, seems sufficient.

11. Therefore ye all, being stationed in your proper places in the divisions of the army, support Bhishma alone.

12. The powerful, the eldest of the Kurus (Bhishma), the grandsire, in order to cheer him (Duryodhana), sounded aloud a lion's roar and blew his conch.

13. Then (following Bhishma), conchs, kettledrums, tabors, trumpets and cowhorns suddenly sounded. The noise was tremendous.

14. Then Mādhava (Krishna) and Pāndava (Arjuna) stationed in their great war chariot, yoked to white horses, also blew their divine conchs.

15. Hrishikesha[1] (Krishna) blew the Pānchajanya; and Dhananjaya[2] (Arjuna), Devadatta[3] (God-given); and Vrikodara[4] (Bhima), doer of terrible deeds, blew his large conch Paundra.

16. King Yudhishthira, son of Kunti, blew the conch named Anantavijaya (endless victory). Nakula and Sahadeva their Sughosha and Manipushpaka.

17. The King of Kāshi, the great bowman, and the mighty warrior Shikhandi, Dhrishtadyúmna, Virāta and the unconquered hero, Sātyaki;

18. (King) Drupada and the sons of Draupadi and the mighty-armed son of Subhadrā, each blew respectively his own conch, O Lord of the Earth!

19. That tremendous uproar, filling earth and sky with sound, rent the hearts of Dhritarāshtra's party.

20. Then, O Lord of the Earth! the son of Pāndu (Arjuna), whose ensign was the monkey, seeing Dhritarāshtra's army arrayed and the throwing of weapons about to begin, raised his bow and spoke the following words to Krishna:

[1] The Lord of the senses.
[2] Conqueror of wealth.
[3] Name of the conch.
[4] Having the belly of a tiger, indicating the physical formation of a hero.

Arjuna said:

21-23. O Achyuta (changeless, Krishna), place my chariot between the two armies desirous of battle, so that I may see with whom I have to fight in this outbreak of war, for I desire to observe those who are assembled here for battle wishing to please the evil-minded son of Dhritarāshtra by taking his side.

Sanjaya said:

24-25. O King! Requested thus by Gudākesha[1] (Arjuna), Krishna, having placed the war chariot between the two armies in front of Bhishma, Drona and all the rulers of the earth, spoke thus: O son of Prithā (Arjuna), behold all the Kuru forces gathered together.

26. Then Pārtha (Arjuna) saw there in both armies arrayed grandfathers, fathers-in-law, uncles, brothers and cousins, his own sons and their sons and grandsons, comrades, teachers and friends.

27. Then he, the son of Kunti (Arjuna), seeing all his kinsmen stationed in their ranks, spoke thus sorrowfully, overwhelmed with deep compassion:

Arjuna said:

28. O Krishna, seeing these my kinsmen, gathered here desirous to fight, my limbs fail me, my mouth is parched;

29. My body shivers, my hair stands on end, my Gandiva (bow) slips from my hand, my skin is burning.

30. O Keshava (Krishna, the slayer of Keshi), I am not able to stand upright, my mind is in a whirl and I see adverse omens.

31. O Krishna, neither do I see any good in slaying my own people in this strife. I desire neither victory, nor kingdom, nor pleasures.

32-34. Teachers, uncles, sons and grandsons, grandfathers, fathers-in-law, brothers-in-law, besides other kinsmen, for whose sake empire, enjoyment and pleasures are desired, they themselves stand here in battle, forsaking life and wealth. What avail, then, is kingdom, enjoyment, or even life, O Govinda (Krishna)?

35. These warriors I do not wish to kill, even though I am killed by them, not even for the dominion over the three worlds, how much less for the sake of this earth, O slayer of Madhu.

[1] The conqueror of sleep.

36. O Janārdana (giver of prosperity and salvation, Krishna), what pleasure could there be for us by killing the sons of Dhritarāshtra? Sin alone would take possession of us by slaying these evil-doers.

37. Therefore we ought not to kill these sons of Dhritarāshtra who are our relations; for how can we, O Mādhava (Krishna), obtain happiness by destroying our own kinsmen?

38. Although these (my enemies), their understanding being overpowered by greed, see no evil from extinction of families and no sin in hostility to friends.

39. But, O Janārdana, why should not we turn away from this sin, seeing clearly the evil in destruction of family?

40. From the destruction of a family the immemorial religious rites of that family perish. Spirituality being destroyed, that whole family is overpowered by unrighteousness.

41. O Krishna, from the predominance of unrighteousness, the women of that family become corrupt; and women being corrupted, there arises intermingling of castes.

42. This intermingling of castes leads the destroyers of the family to hell, as also the family itself; for their ancestors fall, being deprived of the offerings of rice ball and water.[1]

43. By these misdeeds of the slayers of the family, bringing about confusion of caste, the immemorial religious rites of family and caste are destroyed.

44. O Janārdana, we have heard that for such men, whose household religious rites have been destroyed, the dwelling in hell is inevitable.

45. Alas! what a great sin we are resolved to incur, being prepared to slay our kinsmen, actuated by greed of kingdom and pleasure.

46. Verily, it would be better for me if the sons of Dhritarāshtra, weapons in hand, should slay me in the battle, unresisting and unarmed.

Sanjaya said:

47. Speaking thus in the midst of the battlefield, Arjuna sank down on the seat of his war chariot, casting aside his bow and arrows, his mind overwhelmed with sorrow.

Here ends the First Chapter called
"The Grief of Arjuna"

[1] Certain funeral rites performed for the welfare of the departed ones.

CHAPTER II

Sanjaya said:

1. To him (Arjuna) whose mind was thus overpowered by pity and grief and eyes dimmed with tears, Madhusudana (Krishna) spoke these words:

The Blessed Lord said:

2. O Arjuna, whence comes upon thee in this critical moment this depression unworthy of an Aryan, disgraceful, and contrary to the attainment of heaven?

3. O son of Prithā, yield not to unmanliness; it does not befit thee. Casting off this mean faint-heartedness, arise, O terror of thy foes!

Arjuna said:

4. O destroyer of enemies and slayer of Madhu (Krishna), how can I fight with arrows in battle against Bhishma and Drona, who are worthy to be worshipped (by me).

5. Instead of slaying these great-souled masters, it would be better even to live in this life by begging; but killing them, all our enjoyments of wealth and desires, even in this world, will be stained with blood.

6. Indeed I know not which of the two is better for us, whether we should conquer them or they should conquer us. For those very sons of Dhritarāshtra stand before us, after slaying whom we should not care to live.

7. With my nature overpowered by pity and depression and mind confused about duty, I implore Thee (O Krishna) tell me with certainty what is good for me. I am Thy disciple, instruct me, who have taken refuge in Thee.

8. For I see not what can remove this grief which withers my senses, even if I should obtain unrivalled and flourishing dominion over the earth and rulership over the gods.

Sanjaya said:

9. Gudākesha (Arjuna), the conqueror of his foes, having thus spoken to the Lord of the senses (Krishna), said: "I shall not fight, O Govinda!" and became silent.

10. O descendant of King Bharata, Hrishikesha (Krishna), as if

smilingly, spoke these words to him (Arjuna), who was thus grief-stricken in the midst of the two armies.

The Blessed Lord said:

11. Thou hast been mourning for those who should not be mourned for and yet thou speakest (apparent) words of wisdom; but the truly wise mourn not either for the dead or for the living.

12. It is not that I have never existed before, nor thou, nor all these kings. Nor is it that all of us shall cease to exist hereafter.

13. As in this body the embodied soul passes through childhood, youth and old age, in the same manner it goes from one body to another; therefore the wise are never deluded regarding it (the soul).

14. O son of Kunti, the feelings of heat, cold, pleasure, pain, are produced from the contact of the senses with sense-objects; they are with beginning and end, transitory. Therefore, O Bhārata, endure them (bravely).

15. O mighty among men, he is fit to attain immortality who is serene and not afflicted by these sensations, but is the same in pleasure and pain.

16. There is no existence for the unreal and the real can never be non-existent. The Seers of Truth know the nature and final ends of both.

17. Know That to be indestructible by which all this is pervaded. No one is ever able to destroy that Immutable.

18. These bodies are perishable; but the dwellers in these bodies are eternal, indestructible and impenetrable. Therefore fight, O descendant of Bharata!

19. He who considers this (Self) as a slayer or he who thinks that this (Self) is slain, neither of these knows the Truth. For It does not slay, nor is It slain.

20. This (Self) is never born, nor does It die, nor after once having been, does It go into non-being. This (Self) is unborn, eternal, changeless, ancient. It is never destroyed even when the body is destroyed.

21. O son of Prithā, how can he slay or cause the slaying of another who knows this (Self) to be indestructible, eternal, unborn and immutable?

22. As man casts off worn-out garments and puts on others which are new, similarly the embodied soul, casting off worn-out bodies, enters into others which are new.

23. Sword cannot pierce It (Self), fire cannot burn It, water cannot wet It, and air cannot dry It.

24. It cannot be pierced, nor burned, nor wet, nor dried. It is eternal, all-pervading, unchangeable, immovable, everlasting.

25. This (Self) is said to be unmanifested, unthinkable, unchangeable; therefore knowing this to be so, thou shouldst not grieve.

26. But even if thou thinkest that this (Self) is subject to constant birth and death, even then, O mighty-armed, thou shouldst not grieve.

27. For that which is born death is certain, and for the dead birth is certain. Therefore grieve not over that which is unavoidable.

28. O Bhārata, all creatures are unmanifested in the beginning, manifested in their middle state, unmanifested again in the end. What is there to grieve about?

29. Some look upon It (Self) with wonder, some speak about It with wonder, some hear about It with wonder and yet others, even after hearing about It, know It not.

30. The dweller in the body of everyone is ever indestructible; therefore, O Bhārata, thou shouldst not grieve over any creature.

31. Looking upon it even from the standpoint of thine own Dharma,[1] thou shouldst not waver, for nothing is higher for a Kshatriya (warrior) than a righteous war.

32. O son of Prithā, fortunate indeed are Kshatriyas to whom comes unsought, as an open gate to heaven, such a war.

33. But if thou shouldst not take part in this righteous war, then forfeiting thine own duty and honor, thou shalt incur sin.

34. People will ever speak ill of thee; for the esteemed, dishonor is even worse than death.

35. These great car-warriors will think that thou hast withdrawn from the battle through fear. And thou shalt be thought of lightly by those who once honored thee highly.

36. Thine enemies will speak unutterable disgraceful things against thee and blame thy valor. What can be more painful than this?

37. If thou fallest in battle, thou shalt obtain heaven; if thou conquerest, thou shalt enjoy the earth. Therefore, O son of Kunti, arise and be resolved to fight.

38. Regarding alike pleasure and pain, gain and loss, victory and defeat, fight thou the battle. Thus sin will not stain thee.

39. Thus I have declared unto thee the wisdom of Self-realization.

[1] Moral and religious duty.

Listen now, O son of Prithā, regarding Yoga, by knowing which thou shalt be freed from the bonds of Karma (cause and effect).

40. In this (Yoga) there is neither waste of effort nor possibility of evil results. Even a little practice of this (Yoga) delivers one from great fear.

41. O son of Kuru, in this (Yoga), the well-resolved mind is single and one-pointed; but the purposes of the irresolute mind are many-branched and endless.

42. O son of Prithā, those who delight in the flowery speech of the unwise and are satisfied with the mere letter of the Vedas (Scriptures) saying: "There is naught else";

43. And those who are full of desires for self-gratification, regarding heaven[1] as their highest goal, and are engaged in many intricate Scriptural rites just to secure pleasure and power as the result of their deeds for their future incarnations;

44. Whose discrimination is stolen away by the love of power and pleasure and who are thus deeply attached therein, (for such people) it is impossible to obtain either firm conviction (in purpose) or God-consciousness.

45. The Vedas deal with the three *Gunas*.[2] O Arjuna, be thou free from these three Gunas; free from the pairs of opposites (cold and heat, pleasure and pain); ever steadfast, be thou free from (thoughts of) acquiring or keeping and self-possessed.

46. To the Brāhmana, the knower of Truth, all the Vedas are of as little use as a small water-tank is during the time of a flood, when water is everywhere.[3]

47. To work alone thou hast the right, but never to the fruits thereof. Be thou neither actuated by the fruits of action, nor be thou attached to inaction.

48. O Dhananjaya, abandoning attachment and regarding success and failure alike, be steadfast in Yoga and perform thy duties. Even-mindedness is called Yoga.

49. O Dhananjaya, work (with desire for results) is far inferior to work with understanding. Therefore seek refuge in the Yoga of understanding. Wretched indeed are those who work for results.

50. Being possessed with this understanding, one frees one's self even

[1] Heaven is the temporary abode of highest pleasure.

[2] Sattwa, quality of goodness; Rajas, quality of activity and passion; Tamas, quality of darkness and inertia.

[3] This verse shows the difference between mere book knowledge and direct vision of Truth.

in this life from good and evil. Therefore engage thyself in this Yoga. Skillfulness in action is called Yoga.

51. The wise, possessed with knowledge, abandoning the fruits of their actions, become freed from the fetters of birth and reach that state which is beyond all evil.

52. When thine intellect will cross beyond the mire of delusion, then alone shalt thou attain to indifference regarding things heard and yet to be heard.

53. When thine intellect, tossed by the various conflicting opinions of the Scriptures, will become firmly established in the Self, then thou shalt attain Yoga (Self-realization or union with God).

Arjuna said:

54. O Keshava, what are the signs of the man of steady wisdom, one who has attained God-consciousness? How does the man of steady wisdom speak? How does he sit? How does he walk?

The Blessed Lord said:

55. O Pārtha, when a man is satisfied in the Self by Self alone and has completely cast out all desires from the mind, then he is said to be of steady wisdom.

56. He whose mind is not agitated in calamities and who has no longing for pleasure, free from attachment, fear and anger, he indeed is said to be a saint of steady wisdom.

57. He who is free from all attachment and neither rejoices on receiving good nor is vexed on receiving evil, his wisdom is well-established.

58. When he completely withdraws his senses from sense-objects as the tortoise withdraws its limbs, then his wisdom becomes well-established.

59. The embodied, through the practice of abstinence (i.e. not giving food to the senses), can deaden the feelings of the senses, but longing still lingers in the heart; all longings drop off when he has seen the Supreme.

60. O son of Kunti, dangerous are the senses, they even carry away forcibly the mind of a discriminative man who is striving for perfection.

61. The man of steady wisdom, having subdued them all (senses), becomes fixed in Me, the Supreme. His wisdom is well-established whose senses are under control.

Thinking of sense-objects, man becomes attached thereto. From attachment arises longing and from longing anger is born.

63. From anger arises delusion; from delusion, loss of memory is caused. From loss of memory, the discriminative faculty is ruined and from the ruin of discrimination, he perishes.[1]

64. But the self-subjugated attains peace and moves among objects with the senses under control, free from any longing or aversion.

65. In peace there is an end to all misery and the peaceful mind soon becomes well-established in wisdom.

66. There is no wisdom for the unsteady and there is no meditation for the unsteady and for the unmeditative there is no peace. How can there be any happiness for the peaceless?

67. For the mind that yields to the uncontrolled and wandering senses, carries away his wisdom just as a boat on water is carried away by wind.

68. Therefore, O mighty-armed, his wisdom is established whose senses are well-restrained from all objects of sense.

69. That which is night to all beings, therein the self-subjugated remains awake; and in that where all beings are awake, that is night for the knower of Self.[2]

70. As the ocean remains calm and unaltered though the waters flow into it, similarly a self-controlled saint remains unmoved when desires enter into him; such a saint alone attains peace, but not he who craves the objects of desire.

71. That man attains peace who, abandoning all desires, moves about without attachment and longing, without the sense of "I" and "mine."

72. O son of Prithā, this is the state of dwelling in Brahman (absolute Truth); having attained this, no one is ever deluded. Being established in this knowledge even at the end of life, one attains oneness with Brahman (the Supreme).

Here ends the Second Chapter called
"Sānkhya-Yoga, or The Path of Wisdom"

[1] When a greedy man sees a bag of gold and begins to think of its value, attachment for the thing grows in his heart; from attachment he feels intense longing to get possession of it and when anything or anybody interferes with the gratification of his desire, it results in anger. From anger delusion rises, i.e., confusion of understanding; then his memory fails him, i.e., he forgets his position and duty in life; and when he is in this state, without discrimination of right and wrong, he does things to cause his own ruin.

[2] The spiritual plane, which to ordinary mortals is like night, full of darkness, is like day, full of clearness and light, to the wise ones; and the sense plane, where the ordinary minds are wide awake and active, there the wise men are as if asleep, knowing the futility of sense desire. These are the two poles of human existence represented by night and day.

CHAPTER III

Arjuna said:

1. O Janārdana, O Keshava (Krishna), if to thy mind (the path of) wisdom is superior to (the path of) action, then why art thou engaging me in this terrible action?

2. By these seemingly conflicting words[1] thou art bewildering my understanding; therefore tell me with certainty that one of these, by following which I can attain the highest.

The Blessed Lord said:

3. O sinless one, in this world twofold is the path already described by me. The path of wisdom is for the meditative and the path of work is for the active.

4. A man does not attain to freedom from action by non-performance of action, nor does he attain to perfection merely by giving up action.

5. No one can ever rest even for an instant without performing action, for all are impelled by the Gunas (qualities), born of Prakriti (Nature), to act incessantly.

He who, restraining the organs of action, sits holding thoughts of sense-objects in his mind, that self-deluded one is called a hypocrite.

7. But, O Arjuna, he who, controlling the senses by the mind, follows without attachment the path of action with his organs of action, he is esteemed.

8. Do thou therefore perform right and obligatory actions, for action is superior to inaction. Without work, even the bare maintenance of thy body would not be possible.

9. This world is bound by actions, except when they are performed for the sake of *Yajna*.[2] Therefore, O son of Kunti, do thou perform action without attachment.

10. In the beginning the Lord of creatures, having created mankind, together with Yajna, said: "By this (Yajna) ye shall prosper and obtain all desired results, like Kāmadhuk.[3]

11. "By this (Yajna) ye shall please the Devas (bright ones) and the

[1] Sometimes praising work, sometimes praising wisdom.

[2] Religious ceremonies, sacrifices, worship, etc.

[3] The symbolic cow who possesses the extraordinary quality of giving to the milker whatever he desires.

Devas, in their turn, will cherish you. Thus by cherishing one another, ye shall obtain the highest good.

12. "The Devas, pleased by the Yajna, will bestow upon you all the objects of your desire." He who enjoys the objects given by the Devas without offering to them, he is indeed a thief.

13. The righteous, eating the remnants of Yajna (sacrifice), become free from all sins; but the unrighteous, who cook for themselves, eat sin.

14. Creatures come forth from food; food is produced from rain; rain comes as the result of Yajna; and Yajna is born of Karma (action).

15. Know that Karma rises from the Vedas and Vedas from the Imperishable. Therefore the all-pervading Truth (Brahman) is ever established in Yajna (sacrifice).

16. He who here (on earth) does not follow the wheel thus set revolving, lives in sin and sensuality; O Pārtha, he lives in vain.

17. That man, who is devoted to the Self, is satisfied with Self and is content in the Self alone, for him there is nothing to do.

18. For him there is nothing in this world to gain by action or to lose by inaction; nor does he need to depend on any being for any object.

19. Therefore, being unattached, perform thy duties (the work that ought to be done) unceasingly; for through the performance of action, unattached, man attains the highest.

20. Verily, by work alone, Janaka[1] and other (great souls) attained perfection. Also just from the point of view of benefiting mankind, thou shouldst perform action.

21. Whatsoever a superior (man) does, that alone inferior men do. Whatever example he sets by his actions, that the people (masses) follow.

22. O Pārtha, there is nothing for Me to accomplish; nothing there is in the three worlds unattained or to be attained by Me, and yet I continue in action.

23. For if I do not work unceasingly, O Pārtha, men would follow my path (example) in every way.

24. If I did not work, these worlds would perish.[2] I should cause the confusion of castes,[3] and also the destruction of all beings.

25. O descendant of Bharata, as the ignorant (who are attached to

[1] The great king who was noted for his wisdom and non-attachment.

[2] From the lack of social, moral and spiritual examples.

[3] Order or division of qualities among men.

esults) work, so also (with the same fervor) the wise should act, devoid of attachment, being desirous to help mankind.

26. One should not unsettle the understanding of the ignorant who are attached to action; the man of wisdom, by steadily performing actions, should engage (the ignorant) in all right action.

27. All actions are performed by the Gunas, born of Prakriti (Nature). One whose understanding is deluded by egoism alone thinks: "I am the doer."

28. But, O mighty-armed, the Seer of Truth, understanding the divisions of Guna and Karma (qualities, senses and actions), and knowing that it is only the senses which run after sense-objects, does not become deluded therein.

29. A man of perfect wisdom should not unsettle the people of small and imperfect understanding, who are deluded by the qualities born of Nature and are attached to the function of the Gunas (senses).

30. Surrendering all action to Me and fixing the mind on the Self, devoid of hope[1] and egoism,[2] and free from the fever (of grief), fight, O Arjuna.

31. Those who constantly practise this teaching of Mine with true faith and devotion and unflinching heart, they too are freed from (the fetters of) action.

32. But those who find fault with my teaching and do not follow it, such self-deluded ones, devoid of all knowledge and discrimination, know them to be ruined.

33. Even a wise man acts according to his nature; beings follow nature: What can restraint do?

34. Attachment and aversion of the senses are based on sense-objects; let none come under the sway of these two. They are his enemies.

35. Better one's own duty, though devoid of merit, than the duty of another, well performed. Better is death, in following one's own duty; the duty of another is full of danger.

Arjuna said:

36. But, O Descendant of Vrishni (Krishna), impelled by what power does a man commit sin even against his wish, constrained, as it were, by force?

[1] Longing for results.
[2] Sense of "I" and "Mine."

The Blessed Lord said:

37. It is desire, it is anger, born of Rajo-Guna (quality of passion) of unappeasable craving and of great sin; know this as the foe in thi world.[1]

38. As fire is enveloped by smoke, as a mirror by dust, as an embry by the womb, so is this (Self) covered by that.

39. O son of Kunti, wisdom is covered by this insatiable fire of desire the constant enemy of the wise.

40. The senses, mind and intellect are said to be its seats; through thes it deludes the embodied one by covering his wisdom.

41. Therefore, O mightiest of the Bharata race, first subduing th senses, kill this (desire), the sinful, destroyer of wisdom and Self-knowl edge.

42. The senses are said to be superior (to the body), the mind is super ior to the senses and intellect is superior to the mind; and that which i superior to the intellect is He (Atman, Self).

43. O mighty-armed, thus knowing Him who is superior to the intel lect, and subduing self by the Self, destroy this enemy in the form o desire, difficult to overcome.

Here ends the Third Chapter called
"Karma-Yoga, or The Path of Work"

CHAPTER IV

The Blessed Lord said:

1. I declared this imperishable Yoga to Vivasvān, and Vivasvān tol it to Manu, Manu taught it to Ikshvāku.

2. Thus, handed down in regular succession, the royal sages knew it This Yoga through long lapse of time has been lost in this world, O Parantapa (Arjuna).

3. That same ancient Yoga has been (again) today declared to thee by Me, for thou art my devotee and my friend. This is the supreme secret.

Arjuna said:

4. Later was thy birth and the birth of Vivasvān was prior to thine How, then, am I to know that thou didst declare this in the beginning?

[1] Desire and anger are inseparable, as anger is caused by obstructed desire.

The Blessed Lord said:

5. O Arjuna, both you and I have gone through many births. I know hem all, but thou knowest them not, O Parantapa.

6. Though I am unborn and of unchangeable nature, and though I m Lord of all beings, yet by ruling over my Prakriti (Nature) I come nto being by my own Māyā (mysterious power).

7. O Bhārata, whenever there is decline of virtue and predominance f vice, then I embody Myself.

8. For the protection of the good and for the destruction of evil-doers nd for the re-establishment of Dharma (virtue and religion) I am born rom age to age.

9. He who thus understands truly My Divine birth and action is not orn again on leaving his body, O Arjuna, but he attains unto Me.

10. Freed from attachment, fear and anger, being absorbed in Me and aking refuge in Me, purified by the fire of wisdom, many have attained My Being.

11. In whatever way men worship Me, in the same way I fulfil their lesires. O Pārtha, in every way men follow My path.

12. Those who long for success in this world worship the gods, for n the human world success is quickly attained by actions.

13. The fourfold caste[1] was created by Me according to Guna and Karma (qualities and actions). Although I am the author (of that), yet now me to be the non-doer and changeless.

14. Actions pollute Me not, nor have I any desire for the fruits of ction. He who knows Me thus, is not bound by action.

15. Knowing this, the ancient seekers after liberation performed action. Do thou, therefore, also perform action as did the ancients in olden ime.

16. Even wise men are bewildered regarding what is action and what s inaction. Therefore I shall teach thee that action, by knowing which hou shalt be freed from all evil.

17. For verily the nature of right action should be understood, also hat of unlawful action and of inaction. The nature of Karma (action) s indeed very difficult to understand.

Brāhmana represents spiritual qualities,—goodness, serenity, etc. Kshatrya stands for he combination of Sattwa (goodness) and Rajas (passion, ambition). Vaisya, merchant lass, is represented by Rajas (passion) and Tamas (dullness). Sudra, or the servant class, s typified by Tamas (dullness, ignorance and inertia). In short, this fourfold caste gives an rganized form of division of labor, placing each one in a position according to his quality nd capacity.

18. He who sees inaction in action and action in inaction, he is intelli
gent among men; he is a man of established wisdom and a true per
former of all actions.[1]

19. Him the sages call wise whose undertakings are devoid of desir
for results and of plans, whose actions are burned by the fire of wisdom

20. Having abandoned attachment for the fruits of action, ever con
tent and dependent on none, though engaged in action, yet he doe
nothing.

21. Being freed from longing, with self under control, and giving u
all sense of possession (ownership), he is not tainted by sin merely b
performing bodily action.

22. Content with whatever comes without effort, undisturbed by th
pairs of opposites (pleasure and pain, heat and cold), free from envy
even-minded in success and failure, though acting (he) is not bound

23. One whose attachment is gone, who is liberated, whose mind i
well-established in wisdom, who works for sacrifice alone, his whol
Karma melts away.

24. Brahman (absolute Truth) is the offering, Brahman is the obla
tion, the sacrificial fire is (another form of) Brahman and by Brahman
is the sacrifice performed. Thus, by performing actions with the con
sciousness of Brahman, he reaches Brahman alone.

25. Some Yogis offer sacrifices to the Devas, while others perform
sacrifice in the fire of Brahman by offering self by the self alone.

26. Some offer the sense of hearing and other senses as oblation in the
fire of control; still others offer sound and other sense-objects as oblation
in the fire of the senses.

27. Others offer all the actions of the senses and the functions of the
vital forces as oblation in the fire of self-control, lighted by wisdom.

28. Some offer wealth as sacrifice; some, austerity and Yoga as sacrifice;
still others, of rigid vow and self-control, offer study of the Scriptures
and wisdom as sacrifice.

29. Yet others offer as sacrifice the outgoing breath in the incoming
and the incoming breath in the outgoing, stopping the courses of the
outgoing and incoming breaths; thus they constantly practise Prānāyāma.[2] Whereas others, regulating their food, offer the functions of the
vital forces in the Prāna itself as sacrifice.

[1] This verse means that a truly wise man knows how to differentiate body, mind and senses from the Self. Even when activity is going on, on the physical plane, he knows that the true Self is not acting.

[2] Certain breathing exercises for the control of Prāna; vital force.

30-31. All the knowers of sacrifice, burning off their sins (impurities) by the performance of sacrifice and drinking the nectar of the remnant of sacrifice, go to the eternal Brahman (absolute Truth). O best of the Kurus (Arjuna), not even this world is for the non-performer of sacrifice, how much less is the other (world).

32. All these various sacrifices are given in the Vedas (the revelation of Brahman or absolute Truth). Know them all to be born of action; knowing thus thou shalt be freed.

33. O Parantapa (Arjuna), wisdom-sacrifice is far superior to the sacrifice performed with material objects. The entire realm of action, O Pārtha, ends in wisdom.

34. Learn this by reverence, by enquiry and by humble service. Those men of wisdom, who have realized the Truth, will teach thee supreme wisdom.

35. Knowing which, O Pāndava, thou shalt not again thus fall into error (delusion) and by which thou shalt see all beings in (thy) Self and also in Me.

36. Even if thou art the most sinful of the sinful, thou shalt cross over (the ocean of) sin by the bark of wisdom.

37. As kindled fire reduces fuel to ashes, O Arjuna, so does the wisdom fire reduce all actions (Karma) to ashes.

38. Nothing indeed in this world purifies like wisdom. He who is perfected by Yoga, finds it in time within himself by himself.

39. The man of (unflinching) faith, who has mastered his senses, attains wisdom. Having gained wisdom, immediately he attains to supreme peace.

40. The ignorant, the faithless and one of doubting mind perishes. There is neither this world nor the next nor any happiness for the doubting self.

41. O Dhananjaya, one who has renounced actions by Yoga and has cut asunder doubt by wisdom and who is self-possessed, actions bind him not.

42. Therefore, cutting asunder with the sword of wisdom this doubt of Self, born of ignorance, lying in the heart, take refuge in Yoga and arise, O Bhārata!

Here ends the Fourth Chapter called
"Jnāna-Yoga, or The Path of Wisdom"

CHAPTER V

Arjuna said:

1. O Krishna, renunciation of action thou praisest and then again Yoga (performance of action); tell me with certainty which of the two is better?

The Blessed Lord said:

2. Renunciation (of action) and performance of action both lead to liberation. But of the two, performance of action is superior to renunciation of action.

3. Know him to be a perpetual renouncer (Sannyāsi) who has neither longing nor aversion, O mighty-armed; being free from the pairs of opposites (cold and heat, pleasure and pain, etc.), he is easily liberated from all bondage.

4. Children (the ignorant) alone say, not wise men, that wisdom and Yoga are different. He who is truly established in one obtains the fruits of both.

5. That place which is attained by the Jnānis (wise men), is also reached by the Karma Yogins (men of action). He who looks upon wisdom and the performance of action as one, is a true Seer.

6. O mighty-armed, renunciation of action is difficult to attain without performance of action. The wise man, being devoted to Yoga (action), ere long attains to Brahman (absolute Truth).

7. One who is devoted to Yoga, of purified mind, self-subjugated and a master of the senses, realizes his Self as the Self of all beings; though acting he is not tainted.

8-9. The self-possessed knower of Truth should think: "I do nothing at all," though seeing, hearing, touching, smelling, eating, walking, sleeping, breathing, speaking, letting go and holding, opening and closing the eyes, firmly convinced that senses alone move among sense-objects.

10. He who performs actions, surrendering them to Brahman and abandoning all attachment, is not polluted by sin, as a lotus-leaf[1] by water.

11. Karma Yogins, for self-purification alone, perform actions with

[1] The lotus-leaf, though it grows in water, is not moistened by it.

ody, with mind, with intellect, even with the senses, abandoning all ttachment.

12. The steady-minded, by giving up all (attachment for) the fruits f action, obtains peace, born of steadfastness. The unsteady (fickle), eing attached to fruits through desire, is ever bound (by action).

13. The self-subjugated embodied one, by renouncing all actions hrough mental discrimination, rests happily in the city of nine gates (body), neither acting (himself) nor causing (others) to act.

14. The Lord creates neither the agency (sense of "I"), nor actions for he world, nor union with the fruit of action. It is nature that leads to ction.

15. The omnipresent Lord partakes neither of the good nor of the vil deed of any. Wisdom is covered by ignorance, thus mortals are leluded.

16. But those, whose ignorance is destroyed by Self-knowledge, their nowledge of the Self, like the sun, illumines the Supreme.

17. Those whose heart and soul are absorbed in That (Supreme), vho are steadily devoted to That and regard That as their highest goal, hey go never to return, their sins (impurities) being washed off by visdom.

18. The wise look upon a Brāhmana endowed with learning and umility, a cow, an elephant, a dog, and a Pariah (dog-eater) with equal egard.[1]

19. Even here (in this world), existence (earthly life) is conquered y them whose mind rests in equality, for Brahman is without imper-ection and equal. Therefore they abide in Brahman.

20. The steady-minded, undeluded knower of Brahman, being well-stablished in Brahman, neither rejoices on receiving the pleasant nor rieves on receiving the unpleasant.

21. He, whose heart is unattached to external contacts (of the senses), ealizes the happiness that is in the Self; being united with Brahman by neditation, he attains to eternal bliss.

22. The enjoyments which are born through contact (with sense-ob-ects) are ever generators of misery; (they are) with beginning and end.) son of Kunti, the wise do not seek pleasure in them.

23. He who can withstand the impulse of lust and anger even here (in is life), before he is separated from the body, is steadfast and truly a appy man.

[1] They see the same underlying Self everywhere.

24. He whose joy is within, whose pleasure is within, and whose ligh
is within, that Yogi, being well-established in Brahman, attains to abs
lute freedom.

25. The self-subjugated Rishis (Truth-Seers), whose impurities a
washed off, whose doubts are destroyed, and who are engaged in doin
good to all beings, attain supreme liberation.

26. The Sannyāsins, who are freed from lust and anger, with hear
well-subdued and Self realized, for them absolute freedom exists he
and hereafter.

27-28. Shutting out the external contact with sense-objects, the ey
fixed between the eyebrows,[1] and equalizing the currents of Prāna (i
coming breath) and Apāna (the outgoing breath) inside the nostrils, th
meditative man, having mastered the senses, mind and intellect, bein
freed from desire, fear and anger, and regarding freedom as his suprem
goal, is liberated forever.

29. Knowing Me to be the receiver and dispenser of Yajna (sacrifice
and austerity, the Supreme Lord of the Universe and the Friend of a
beings, he attains to peace.

Here ends the Fifth Chapter called
"Sannyāsa-Yoga, or The Path of Renunciation"

CHAPTER VI

The Blessed Lord said:

1. He who performs his duty without depending on the fruits o
action, he is a Sannyāsi (a true renouncer), and a Yogi (a true worker
not he who is without sacrificial fire or without action.

2. O Pāndava, that which is called Sannyāsa (renunciation) know th
to be also Yoga (true performance of action), for none can become a Yo
without giving up fancies for the fruits of action.

3. For the meditative who is striving to attain Yoga, action is said t
be the means; for the same man, when he has attained to Yoga, inactio
is said to be the means.

4. He who is unattached to sense-objects and to actions, and has give
up all fancies for the fruits of action, he is said to have attained Yoga.

5. Let a man raise himself by his Self, let him never lower himself; fo
he alone is the friend of himself and he alone is the enemy of himself.

[1] A form of concentration.

6. He who has conquered himself by the Self, he is the friend of him-
·lf; but he whose self is unconquered, his self acts as his own enemy like
ı external foe.

7. The Supreme Self of the self-subjugated and serene-minded, is ever
ndisturbed in heat and cold, pleasure and pain, as well as in honor and
ishonor.

8. He who is satisfied with wisdom and direct vision of Truth, who
as conquered the senses and is ever undisturbed, to whom a lump of
ırth, a stone and gold are the same, that Yogi is said to be a Yukta (a
ıint of established wisdom).

9. He is esteemed who looks with equal regard upon well-wishers,
iends, enemies, neutrals, a mediator, the hateful, relatives, upon the
ghteous and the unrighteous.

10. A Yogi[1] should constantly practise concentration of the heart, re-
ıaining in seclusion alone, subduing his body and mind and being free
om longing and possession (sense of ownership).

11. In a cleanly spot having established his seat firmly, neither too
igh nor too low, with a cloth, skin and Kusha grass, placed one on the
her;

12. Being seated there, making the mind one-pointed and subduing
ıe activities of mind and senses, let him practise Yoga for self-purifica-
on.

13. Let him hold his body, head and neck erect and motionless, fixing
ıe gaze on the tip of his nose, not looking around.[2]

14. Being serene-hearted and fearless, ever steadfast in the vow of
rahmacharya[3] and controlling the mind, let him sit steadfastly ab-
rbed in thoughts of Me, regarding Me as his supreme goal.

15. Thus ever keeping himself steadfast, the Yogi of subdued mind
tains eternal peace and freedom, which abide in Me.

16. But, O Arjuna, (the practice of) Yoga is not for him who eats too
ıuch or who does not eat at all, nor for him who sleeps too much or
eeps awake (in excess).

17. He who is moderate in eating and recreation, moderate in his ef-
rts in work, moderate in sleep and wakefulness (his practice of) Yoga
ecomes the destroyer of all misery.

)ne who is striving for union with God through the practice of concentration and
editation.

\ form of concentration.

/ow of godly life and continence.

18. When the mind, completely subdued, rests in Self alone, free fro longing for all objects of desire, then he is said to be a Yukta (steadfa in Self-knowledge).

19. As a lamp placed in a windless spot does not flicker, the sam simile is used to define a Yogi of subdued mind, practising union wit the Self.

20. In that state, when the mind is completely subdued by the practic of Yoga and has attained serenity, in that state, seeing Self by the self, h is satisfied in the Self alone.

21. In that state, transcending the senses, he (the Yogi) feels that i finite bliss which is perceived by the purified understanding; knowin that and being established therein, he never falls back from his real sta (of Self-knowledge);

22. After having attained which, no other gain seems greater; bein established wherein, he is not overwhelmed even by great sorrow.

23. Know that (state) of separation from the contact with pain Yoga. This Yoga should be practised with perseverance and undepresse heart.

24. Abandoning without reserve all the desires born of mental fancie and restraining completely by the mind the entire group of the sens from all directions,

25. With understanding held by firmness, and mind established i the Self, let him (thus) by degrees attain tranquility; let him not thin of anything else.

26. Wheresoever the restless and unsteady mind may wander awa let him withdraw it from there and bring it under the control of the Se alone.

27. He whose passions are quieted and mind perfectly tranquil, wh has become one with Brahman, being freed from all impurities, to suc a Yogi comes supreme bliss.

28. Thus constantly holding the mind steadfast, the Yogi, whose si are shaken off, easily attains the infinite bliss, born of contact wi Brahman.

29. He whose heart is steadfastly engaged in Yoga, looks everywhe with the eyes of equality, seeing the Self in all beings and all beings the Self.

30. He who sees Me in all and all in Me, from him I vanish not, n does he vanish from Me.

31. He who, being established in unity, worships Me dwelling in all ings, that Yogi, howsoever living, abides in Me.
32. O Arjuna, he who looks upon pleasure and pain everywhere with e same regard as when it is applied to himself, that Yogi is highly teemed.

rjuna said:

33. O Destroyer of Madhu (Krishna), this Yoga, which has been de- ared by Thee as even-mindedness, I do not see (the possibility) of its sting existence, owing to the restlessness of the mind.
34. O Krishna, the mind is restless, turbulent, strong and unyielding; consider it as difficult to subdue as the wind.

he Blessed Lord said:

35. Doubtless, O mighty-armed, the mind is restless and difficult to ntrol; but O son of Kunti, through practice and dispassion (renuncia- on) it can be conquered.
36. Yoga is difficult to attain by him who is of uncontrolled self: such my conviction; but the self-subjugated can attain it by following the ght means.

rjuna said:

37. O Krishna, he who, though possessed with faith, yet lacks in con- ol and whose mind wanders away from Yoga, what end does he meet, iling to reach perfection in Yoga?
38. O Mighty-armed (Krishna), does he not perish like a rent cloud, pportless, fallen from both (here and hereafter), deluded in the path Brahman (Truth)?
39. O Krishna, this doubt of mine Thou oughtest to dispel, for there none but Thee who is able to destroy this doubt.

he Blessed Lord said:

40. O Pārtha, there is no destruction for him either here or hereafter, r the well-doer (devotee), O Beloved, never comes to an evil end.
41. One who is fallen from Yoga, after having attained the regions of e righteous and dwelling there for unlimited time, reincarnates in the ouse of the pure and prosperous.
42. Or else he is born in the family of wise Yogis; but such a birth is ery rare to obtain in this world.

43. O descendant of Kuru, there (in that incarnation) he gains th
knowledge acquired in his previous incarnation, and he strives agai
more (fervently) than before for perfection.

44. He is irresistibly led by the previous practice (of Yoga). Even th
enquirer of Yoga goes beyond the letter-Brahman.[1]

45. But the Yogi, striving with perseverance, purified from all sir
perfected through many births, reaches the supreme goal.

46. The Yogi is superior to ascetics, and superior to those who hav
attained wisdom through books; he is also superior to performers c
action (according to the Scriptures). Therefore, O Arjuna! be thou
Yogi.

47. And among all the Yogis, to Me he is the highest, who, with h
inner self absorbed in Me, worships Me with (unflinching) faith.

Here ends the Sixth Chapter called
"Dhyāna-Yoga, or The Path of Meditation"

CHAPTER VII

The Blessed Lord said:

1. O Pārtha, practising Yoga, with thy mind fixed on Me and takin
refuge in Me, do thou hear how without doubt thou shalt know M
fully.

2. I shall declare unto thee without reserve this knowledge (spec
uiative) and wisdom (practical), having known which nothing mor
here (in this world) remains to be known.

3. Among thousands of human beings, scarcely one strives for perfe
tion; and among (the thousands of) faithful strivers after perfectio
scarcely one knows Me in truth.

4. Earth, water, fire, air, ether, mind, intellect, egotism, thus m
Prakriti (Nature) is divided eightfold.

5. This Prakriti is inferior; but different from this, know tho
mighty-armed, my higher Prakriti in the form of life-consciousness, b
which this universe is supported.

6. Know that all beings are generated from these two (Prakritis).
am the origin and also the dissolution of the entire universe.

7. O Dhananjaya (Arjuna), there is naught else (existing) highe
than I. Like pearls on a thread, all this (universe) is strung in Me.

[1] The performance of rites and rituals given in the Scriptures.

8. O son of Kunti, I am the sapidity in waters and the radiance in sun nd moon, I am Om[1] in all the Vedas, sound in Akāsha (ether), self-nsciousness in mankind.

9. I am the sacred fragrance in earth and brilliance in fire; I am the fe in all beings and austerity in ascetics.

10. Know Me, O Pārtha, as the eternal seed of all beings. I am the in-llect of the intelligent and the prowess of the powerful.

11. O mighty of the Bharata race, of the strong I am the strength, evoid of desire and attachment; I am (also) desire in all beings, unop-osed to Dharma (spiritual duty).

12. Whatever conditions there are pertaining to the states of Sattwa quality of goodness), Rajas (passion), Tamas (ignorance, inertia), now them all to proceed from Me. I am not in them, but they are in Me.

13. Being deluded by these states, composed of the three Gunas qualities), all this world does not know Me, who am beyond these and nmutable.

14. Verily this divine Māyā of mine (elusive mystery), composed of Gunas, is difficult to surmount; those who take refuge in Me alone, they ross over this Māyā.

15. The deluded, evil-doers, the lowest of men, robbed of understand-ig by Māyā and following demonic tendencies, do not attain unto Me.

16. O Prince of the Bharata race, O Arjuna, four kinds of virtuous ien worship Me: the distressed, the seeker of knowledge, the seeker of aterial prosperity and the wise.

17. Among them the wise, ever steadfast, devoted to the One (to Me), xcels; for I am supremely dear to the wise and he is dear to Me.

18. Noble are all these, but I regard the wise as my very Self; for with oul ever steadfast, he is established in Me alone as his supreme goal.

19. At the end of many births the man of wisdom comes unto Me, eeing that all this is (pervaded by) one Self. Such a great-souled one is ery difficult to find.

20. Those whose discrimination is stolen away by diverse desires, wor-hip other deities by observing various external rites (with the hope of aining pleasure, power, etc.), being impelled by their own nature.

21. Whatever devotee seeks to worship whatever (Divine) form with ith, I make his faith unwavering.

22. Possessed with that faith, he engages himself in worship of (that

[1] The Pranava or Word-God. The same as the *Logos* of Christian theology.

deity); and from that he gains the desired results, those being grante by Me alone.

23. But the fruit (acquired) by these men of small understanding i limited and perishable. The worshippers of the Devas (bright ones) g to the Devas; but my devotees come unto Me.

24. The ignorant, not knowing my Eternal, Immutable and Suprem state, consider Me as the unmanifested coming into manifestation.

25. I am not manifest to all, being veiled by Yoga-Māyā.[1] This delude world knows Me not, the Unborn and Immutable.

26. O Arjuna, I know the past, present and future of all beings, but n one knows Me.

27. O Bhārata, terror of thy foes, all beings at birth fall into delusior caused by the pairs of opposites, arising from desire and aversion.

28. But those men of virtuous deeds, whose sin has come to an enc freed from the delusion of the pairs of opposites, worship Me with firn resolve.

29. Those who, having taken refuge in Me, strive to attain freedon from old age and death, they know Brahman, the whole of the individua Self and the entire realm of Karma (action).

30. Those who know Me in the physical realm, in the Divine realn and in the realm of sacrifice, being steadfast in heart, they know M even at the time of death.

Here ends the Seventh Chapter called "Jnāna-Vijnāna-Yoga, or The Path of Wisdom and Realization"

CHAPTER VIII

Arjuna said:

1. O Best of Beings (Krishna), what is Brahman, what is Adhyātm (embodied soul), and what is Karma? What is the physical realn (Adhibhuta), and what is called the Divine realm (Adhidaiva)?

2. O Destroyer of Madhu, how and who dwells in this body as Ad hiyajna (deity of sacrifice); and how art Thou known at the time o death by the self-subjugated ones?

[1] Delusion composed of the three Gunas.

The Blessed Lord said:

3. The Imperishable Supreme Being is Brahman, its manifestation as the embodied soul is called Adhyātman. The prescribed sacrifice, which causes the creation and support of beings, is called Karma.

4. O best of the embodied (Arjuna), perishable existence is called Adhibhuta (the physical); the Supreme Self is the Adhidaivata (Universal Spirit). I am the Adhiyajna (the presiding deity of sacrifice) in the body.

5. He who, at the time of death, thinking of Me alone, goes forth, leaving the body, he attains unto my Being. There is no doubt in this.

6. O son of Kunti, whatever state (or being) one dwells upon in the end, at the time of leaving the body, that alone he attains, because of his constant thought of that state or being.

7. Therefore, at all times, think of Me and fight (perform actions). Having offered thy mind and intellect to Me, thou shalt without doubt come unto Me.

8. O son of Prithā, by the steadfast practice of meditation with unwavering mind (not moving elsewhere) and constant thought of the Supreme Divine Being, one goes to Him.

9. He who thinks upon the Omniscient, the Ancient, the Ruler, the minutest of the minute, the Sustainer of all, whose form is inconceivable, Self-effulgent like the sun, and beyond the darkness (of ignorance);

10. (He who thus meditates on Him) at the time of death, with unflinching mind, possessed with devotion, fully fixing the Prāna (life-breath) between the eyebrows by the power of Yoga, he attains to the Supreme Divine Being.

11. That which the knowers of Veda (Truth, Wisdom) speak of as imperishable, that which the unattached Sannyāsins [1] enter into, by desiring which they practise Brahmacharya,[2] that state I shall declare unto thee in brief.

12. Closing all the gates of the senses, confining the mind in the heart, and fixing the Prāna in the head (between the eyebrows), thus engaged in the practice of concentration (Yoga);

13. Uttering the monosyllable "Om," (the sound) Brahman, and meditating on Me, he who departs, leaving his body, he attains the supreme goal.

[1] Self-controlled renouncers.

[2] Life of continence and purity.

14. He who is without any other thought (but Me), who remembers Me daily and constantly, O Pārtha, I am easily attained by that ever-devoted Yogi.

15. The great-souled ones, having reached Me, do not come to re-birth, the ever-changing abode of misery, for they have attained the highest perfection.

16. O Arjuna, all worlds, from the abode of Brahmā to this world, are subject to return; but, O son of Kunti, after having attained Me, there is no re-birth.

17. Those who know that Brahmā's day ends in a thousand Yugas (ages) and his night in a thousand Yugas, they are the true knowers of the night and day.

18. At the approach of (Brahmā's) day, all manifestations proceed from the Unmanifested, and at the approach of the night, they merge into that which is called the Unmanifested.[1]

19. O Pārtha, the multitude of beings, coming into birth again and again, helplessly merge into (the Unmanifested) at the approach of night and again remanifest at the approach of day.

20. But beyond this Unmanifested, there is another Unmanifested, which is eternally existent and is not destroyed even when all beings are destroyed.

21. That which has been described as Unmanifested and Imperishable is called the Highest Goal, having attained which there is no return (re-births). That is my Supreme Abode.

22. O son of Prithā, that Supreme Self, in whom all beings abide and by whom all this is pervaded, can be attained by whole-hearted and exclusive devotion to Him.

23. O Prince of the Bharata race, now I shall declare to thee that time, at which in departing (leaving the body) the Yogis return (to re-birth), and also that time at which in departing they do not return.

24. Fire, light, day-time, the bright fortnight (ascending moon), the six months of the sun's northern course, departing at such time, the knowers of Brahman go to Brahman.

25. Smoke, night-time, the dark fortnight (waning moon), the six months of the sun's southern course, the Yogi departing at such time and receiving the lunar light, returns.

[1] These two verses signify the evolution and involution of the sum-total of Cosmic energy, represented by Brahmā's day and night.

26. These two are considered as eternal paths of the world, the bright and the dark (path of wisdom and path of ignorance). By one, (man) attains to non-return (freedom); by the other, he returns again.

27. O son of Prithā, by knowing these (two) paths, the Yogis are never deluded. Therefore, O Arjuna, in all times be thou steadfastly engaged in Yoga.

28. Whatever fruits of good deeds are promised in the study of the Vedas, in sacrifices, in the practice of austerities, in charitable gifts, the Yogi, having known these and rising above all, attains to the primeval Supreme Abode.

Here ends the Eighth Chapter called "Akshara-Brahma-Yoga, or The Path of the Imperishable Brahman"

CHAPTER IX

The Blessed Lord said:

1. (Now) I shall declare to thee, who art without evil thought, this great secret, wisdom together with realization, knowing which thou shalt be freed from evil.

2. This is the king of sciences, king of secrets, the supreme purifier; it is realized by direct perception and is endowed with righteousness, easily performed and imperishable.

3. O Parantapa (Arjuna), the men who have no faith in this Dharma (science of Self-knowledge), without attaining Me, return to the path of death and re-birth.

4. By My unmanifested Form all this world is pervaded; all beings dwell in Me, but I do not dwell in them.

5. Behold My Divine Yoga! Beings do not dwell in Me; (although) the Creator and Supporter of all beings, (yet) My Self dwells not in them.

6. As the air, vast and always moving everywhere, exists in Akāsha (space and ether), even so, know thou, all beings exist in Me.

7. O son of Kunti, all beings, at the end of a cycle, go back to my Prakriti (Nature); again, at the beginning of a cycle, I send them forth.

8. Ruling over My Prakriti, I send forth again and again this vast multitude of beings, who are helplessly impelled by Nature.

9. O conqueror of wealth (Arjuna), these acts (of creation and dissolution) do not bind Me, sitting as one unconcerned and unattached to these acts.

10. O son of Kunti, with Me as the presiding Deity, Prakriti (Nature) sends forth the moving and the unmoving. For this reason the world wheels round and round.

11. Fools, unaware of My Supreme state, as the great Lord of beings, disregard Me dwelling in human form.

12. They are of vain hopes, of vain deeds, of vain knowledge, and senseless, possessed with the deluding nature of Rākshasas (unclean, passionate and godless creatures) and Asuras (creatures of darkness and of ignorance).

13. But, O son of Kunti, the great-souled ones, possessing the Divine Nature, knowing Me as Immutable and as the Source of beings, worship Me with single-minded devotion.

14. Ever singing My glory and striving with steadfast vows, bowing down to Me in devotion, (they) perpetually worship Me.

15. Others again by performing the wisdom-sacrifice worship Me, the All-facing, as One, as separate, or in manifold forms.

16. I am Kratu,[1] I am Yajna,[2] I am Svadhā,[3] I am medicinal herbs, I am the Mantra,[4] I am the oblation, I am the fire and I am the act of sacrifice.

17. I am the Father of the universe, the Mother, the Sustainer, the Grandsire, the One to be known, the Purifier, Om (Sound-Brahman), the Rik, Saman and Yajur.[5]

18. (I am) the Way, the Supporter, the Lord, the Witness, the Abode, the Refuge, the Friend, the Origin, the Dissolution, the Resting-Place, the Storehouse and the Eternal Seed.

19. O Arjuna, I give heat, I send forth rain and withhold it; I am Immortality and also Death. I am being and non-being (the manifested and the unmanifested).

20. The knowers of the three Vedas,[6] having worshipped Me with sacrifice, drinking the Soma [7] and thus being purified from sin, pray for

[1] Certain Vedic rite.
[2] Sacrifice.
[3] Offering for the benefit of the departed ancestors.
[4] The sacred text, by repeating and meditating on which one is purified.
[5] Different branches of the Vedas.
[6] Mentioned in verse 17.
[7] Nectar, remnant of the sacrifice.

the goal of heaven; they, having reached the region of the ruler of the Devas, enjoy in heaven the celestial pleasures of the Devas.

21. Having enjoyed that vast celestial world, they, at the exhaustion of the merit (of their good deeds), again enter into the mortal world; thus following the religion of the three Vedas, with the craving for objects of desire, they attain coming and going (birth and re-birth).

22. Those who worship Me and meditate on Me without any other thought, to these ever steadfast devotees I secure safety and supply all their needs (I carry their burden).

23. O son of Kunti, even those devotees who worship other gods with faith, they too worship Me, but contrary to the law.

24. For I am alone the Enjoyer and Lord of all sacrifice; but they do not know Me in truth, hence they return (fall into re-birth).

25. The worshippers of the gods go to the gods; to the ancestors go the ancestor-worshippers; the spirit-worshippers go to the spirits; but My worshippers come unto Me.

26. He who, with devotion offereth to Me a leaf, a flower, a fruit and water, that love-offering I accept, made by the pure-hearted.

27. Whatever thou doest, whatever thou eatest, whatever thou offerest as oblation, whatever thou givest and the austerities thou performest, O son of Kunti, do that as an offering to Me.

28. Thus thou shalt be freed from the bonds of action that bears good and evil fruit; and thy soul, being steadfastly engaged in this devotion of renunciation, liberated thou shalt come unto me.

29. Alike am I to all beings; hated or beloved there is none to Me. But those who worship Me with devotion, they are in Me and I am in them.

30. Even if the most wicked worships Me with undivided devotion, he should be regarded as good, for he is rightly resolved.

31. Very soon he becomes a righteous soul and attains to eternal peace. Know thou, O son of Kunti, that my devotee never perishes.

32. O Pārtha, even those who are of inferior birth,—women, Vaishyas (merchant class) and Sudras (servant class),—even they, by taking refuge in Me, attain to the Supreme Goal.

33. What need is there, then, to speak of the holy Brāhmanas and the royal Sages![1] Having come into this transitory and joyless world, do thou worship Me.

[1] How much more easily is the goal attained by them.

34. Fill thy mind with Me, be thou My devotee, worship Me and bow down to Me; thus, steadfastly uniting thy heart with Me alone and regarding Me as thy Supreme Goal, thou shalt come unto Me.

Here ends the Ninth Chapter called
"The Path of Royal Science
and Royal Secret"

CHAPTER X

The Blessed Lord said:

1. O mighty-armed, again do thou listen to My Supreme Word, which I, wishing thy welfare, declare unto thee who art rejoiced (to hear Me).

2. All the Devas know not My origin, nor do the great Rishis (Seers); for I am the Source of all the Devas and the great Rishis.

3. He who knows Me as birthless and beginningless, the Supreme Lord of the universe, he among mortals is undeluded and is freed from all sins.

4. Intelligence, wisdom, non-delusion, forgiveness, truth, control of the senses, serenity of the heart, pleasure and pain, birth and death, fear and fearlessness.

5. Non-injury, equanimity, contentment, austerity, benevolence, fame and infamy; these different states of beings arise from Me alone.

6. The seven great Rishis, the elder four [1] as well as the Manus, were born of My mind and endowed with My nature, from whom (are generated) all these creatures in the world.

7. He who comprehends in reality these My various manifestations and My Yoga power, he becomes well-established in unshakable Yoga. There is no doubt in this.

8. I am the Origin of all, everything evolves from Me. Knowing this, the wise worship Me with loving ecstasy.

9. With their heart fixed on Me, with their life absorbed in Me, mutually enlightening (one another), and perpetually singing My glory, they are contented and rejoiced.

10. To these ever steadfast and loving worshippers, I give that Yoga of wisdom by which they come unto Me.

11. Out of pure compassion for them, I, dwelling in their hearts, destroy the darkness born of ignorance, by the effulgent light of wisdom.

[1] Elder than the seven.

Arjuna said:

12–13. Thou art the Supreme Brahman, the Supreme Abode and Supreme Purity. All the Rishis (Sages), the divine sage Nārada, as well as Asita, Devala and Vyāsa, have declared Thee as the Eternal and Self-effulgent Being, the primeval Deity, unborn and all-pervading; and Thou Thyself declarest to me the same.

14. O Keshava (Krishna), I regard all that Thou sayest to me as true. O Blessed Lord, neither the Devas nor the Dānavas (demi-gods) know Thy manifestations.

15. O Supreme Being, O Source of beings, O Lord of beings, O God of gods, O Ruler of the universe, Thou Thyself alone knowest Thyself by Thyself.

16. (O Lord), Thou oughtest to tell me, without reserve, of Thy Divine manifestations, by which Divine attributes Thou abidest, pervading all the worlds.

17. O Yogin (Krishna), how by constantly meditating on Thee shall I know Thee? O Blessed Lord, in what aspects art Thou to be meditated upon by me?

18. O Janārdana (Krishna), tell me again in detail of Thy Yoga power and Divine attributes, for I am never satiated in listening to Thy words of nectar.

The Blessed Lord said:

19. O best of the Kurus, I shall declare to thee My principal Divine attributes, for there is no end to the vastness of My manifestations.

20. O Gudākesha (Arjuna), I am the Self existing in the heart of all beings. I am the beginning, the middle and also the end of beings.

21. I am Vishnu of the Adityas, of the luminaries I am the radiant Sun, among the winds I am Marichi, among the constellations I am the Moon.

22. Of the Vedas I am the Sāma-Veda, and of the Devas I am Vāsava (Indra). Of the senses I am the mind and I am the consciousness of all living beings.

23. Of the Rudras I am Sankara; I am the Lord of wealth of the Yakshas and Rākshasas; of the Vasus I am the Fire-god; I am Meru among the mountains.

24. O Pārtha, know Me to be Brihaspati, the high priest; of generals, I am Skanda; among waters, I am the ocean.

25. I am Bhrigu among the great Rishis; of words, I am the monosyllable "Om." Of Yajnas (sacrifices), I am Japa;[1] of the immovable, I am the Himālaya.

26. I am Aswattha among all the trees; among the divine Rishis, I am Nārada. I am Chitraratha of the Gandharvas;[2] I am the sage Kapila[3] among the perfected ones.

27. Among horses, know Me as Uchchaisrava, born of nectar; and of the lordly elephants as Airāvata, and among men as Monarch.

28. I am the Thunderbolt among weapons; among cows, I am Kāmadhuk. I am Kandarpa, the cause of offspring; and of serpents, I am Vāsuki.

29. I am Ananta among the snakes; I am Varuna among water-beings; of ancestors, I am Aryamā; I am Yama among rulers.

30. I am Prahlāda among the Daityas; of measures, I am Time; among wild beasts, I am the lord of beasts (the lion); and among birds, I am Vainateya.

31. Among purifiers, I am the wind; among warriors, I am Rāma; among fishes, I am Makara (shark); and among rivers, I am the Ganges.

32. O Arjuna, of all creations I am the beginning, the middle and also the end; of all the sciences, I am the science of Self-knowledge; among the disputants, I am Vāda.[4]

33. Of syllables, I am "A," and Dvandva[5] of all compound words. I am inexhaustible Time; I am the Dispenser (of fruits of actions), facing everywhere.

34. I am all-seizing Death; I am the origin of all that is to be; of the female I am fame, prosperity, speech, memory, intelligence, constancy and forgiveness.

35. I am the Brihat-sāman of the Vedic hymns; I am Gāyatri[6] of metres. Of months I am Mārgashirsha and of seasons I am the flowering season.

36. I am gambling among the fraudulent; I am the prowess of the powerful. I am Victory, I am Perseverance, I am the Goodness of the good.

37. Of the Vrishnis I am Vāsudeva; among the Pāndavas I am

[1] Silent repetition of the sacred text.
[2] Celestial musicians.
[3] Founder of the Sankya system of philosophy.
[4] Truth-seeking arguments.
[5] Copulative.
[6] A verse of twenty-four syllables.

Dhananjaya; among the saints I am Vyāsa and among the sages I am Ushanā.

38. I am the Rod of disciplinarians; I am the Polity of the seekers of conquest. I am the Silence of secrets; I am the Wisdom of the wise.

39. O Arjuna, whatever is the seed of all beings, that also am I. Without Me there is no being existent, whether moving or unmoving.

40. O Parantapa, there is no end to the manifestations of My Divine Power; what I have declared is only a partial statement of the vastness of my Divine manifestation.

41. Whatever being there is, glorious, prosperous or powerful, know thou that to have sprung from a portion of My splendor.

42. O Arjuna, what need is there for thee to know these details? I alone exist, sustaining this whole universe by a portion of Myself.

Here ends the Tenth Chapter called "Vibhuti-Yoga, or The Path of Divine Manifestation"

CHAPTER XI

Arjuna said:

1. The supremely profound word regarding Self-knowledge, spoken by Thee out of compassion for me, has dispelled this my delusion.

2. O Lotus-Eyed (Krishna), I have heard at length from Thee of the creation and dissolution of beings, as well as of Thine inexhaustible glory.

3. O Great Lord, as Thou hast declared Thyself, so it is. O Supreme Being, I desire to see Thy Godly Form.

4. O Lord, if Thou thinkest me able (worthy) to see that (Form), then, O Lord of Yogis, show me Thine Infinite Self.

The Blessed Lord said:

5. Behold, O Pārtha, My various celestial Forms, of different colors and shapes, by hundreds and by thousands.

6. O descendant of Bharata, behold the Adityas, the Rudras, the Vasus, the twin Asvins and the Maruts.[1] Behold many wonders that were not seen before.

[1] Names for celestial beings.

7. O Gudākesha (Arjuna), behold in this body of Mine the entire universe together, with all that is moving and unmoving and whatever else thou desirest to perceive.

8. But with these eyes of thine thou canst not see Me; therefore I give thee Divine sight. Behold my Supreme Yoga power!

Sanjaya said:

9. O King, having spoken thus, the great Lord of Yoga, Hari (Krishna), then showed to Pārtha His Supreme Godly Form.

10. With many faces and eyes, with many wondrous sights, with many celestial ornaments and with many celestial weapons uplifted,

11. Wearing celestial garlands and garments, anointed with celestial fragrant perfumes; the all-wonderful Deity, infinite, facing the universe everywhere.

12. If the effulgence of a thousand suns were to shine at once in the sky, that might resemble the splendor of that great Being.

13. Then the son of Pāndu (Arjuna) saw the entire universe resting together, with its manifold divisions, in the body of the God of gods.

14. Then Dhananjaya, overpowered with wonder, and his hair standing on end, bending down his head in awe to the Deity, spoke with folded hands:

Arjuna said:

15. O God! in Thy body I see all the gods, as well as multitudes of all kinds of beings; the Lord Brahmā, seated on the lotus throne, all the Rishis and all the celestial serpents.

16. O Lord of the universe, O Universal Form, I see Thee with manifold arms, bellies, mouths and eyes, boundless on every side; neither do I see Thy beginning, nor middle nor end.

17. I see Thee with diadems, maces, discus, shiningly effulgent everywhere, blazing all around like the burning fire and the sun, dazzling to the sight and immeasurable.

18. Thou art the Imperishable, the Supreme, the One to be known. Thou art the Supreme Refuge of this universe; Thou art the ever unchanging Guardian of the Eternal Dharma (religion); Thou art, I know, the Ancient Being.

19. I see Thee without beginning, middle or end, with infinite power, with numberless arms, the sun and moon as Thine eyes, Thy mouth as the blazing fire, heating this universe with Thine own radiance.

20. By Thee alone the space between heaven and earth and all the quarters is pervaded. O Great Soul, seeing this, Thy wonderful and terrifying Form, the three worlds are stricken with fear.

21. Verily, these hosts of Devas are entering into Thee; some in fear, praising Thee with folded hands. The host of great Rishis and Siddhas, saying "Svasti" (peace, may it be well), are singing Thy glory in beautiful hymns.

22. The Rudras, Adityas, Vasus, Sadhyas, the Visvas, the Asvins, the Maruts, the Ushmapās, the host of Gandharvas, Yakshas, Asuras, Siddhas, they are all looking at Thee wonderstruck.

23. O Mighty-armed, seeing Thine immeasurable form, with many mouths and eyes, with many arms, thighs and feet, with many loins, and fearful with many large teeth, the worlds and I, as well, are agitated with terror.

24. O Vishnu, seeing Thee touching the sky, shining in many colors, with mouths wide open, and with large blazing eyes, my heart is terrified and I find neither peace nor tranquillity.

25. O Lord of gods! seeing Thy mouths, terrible with long teeth, blazing like the fires of destruction, I know not the four quarters, nor do I find any peace. Have mercy, O Abode of the universe!

26. All these sons of Dhritarāshtra, with the multitude of monarchs, Bhishma, Drona and Sutaputra (Karna), as well as our own principal warriors,

27. Enter rushingly into Thy mouths, terrible with long teeth and fearful to look at. Some are seen hanging between Thy teeth, with their heads crushed to powder.

28. As the many torrents of rivers rush towards the ocean, similarly do these heroes amongst men enter into Thy mouths, blazing fiercely on all sides.

29. As the moths rush into the burning fire with headlong speed for destruction, in the same manner do these creatures rush into Thy mouths with headlong speed, only to perish.

30. O Vishnu! swallowing all the worlds with Thy blazing flames, Thou art licking all around. Thy fierce, radiant rays, filling the whole universe, are burning.

31. Tell me, who art Thou, in this terrible Form? Salutation to Thee! O Supreme Deity, have mercy! O Primeval One, I desire to know Thee, for indeed I know not Thy purpose.

The Blessed Lord said:

32. I am eternal, world-destroying Time, manifested here for the destruction of these people. Even without Thee, none of these warriors, arrayed here in the hostile armies, shall live.

33. Therefore, do thou arise and acquire glory. Conquering the enemies, enjoy the unrivalled kingdom. By Me alone have they already been slain; be thou merely an instrumental cause, O Savyasāchin[1] (Arjuna).

34. Drona, Bhishma, Jayadratha, Karna, as well as the other brave warriors, are already slain by Me. Do thou kill and be not distressed by fear. Fight! and thou shalt conquer thine enemies in battle.

Sanjaya said:

35. Having heard these words of Keshava (Krishna), (Arjuna) the diadem-wearer, with folded hands, trembling, prostrating himself, again spoke to Krishna in a choked voice, bowing down, overwhelmed with fear.

Arjuna said:

36. O Lord of the senses (Krishna), it is right that the world delights and rejoices in Thy glory. The Rākshasas (demonic creatures) fly with fear in all directions and the host of Siddhas bow down to Thee in adoration.

37. Why should they not bow down to Thee, O Mighty Being, O Infinite One, O Lord of the gods, O Abode of the universe, greater than Brahmā and even the primeval cause of Brahmā; for Thou art the Imperishable; (Thou art) Existence and Non-existence and all that is beyond.

38. O boundless Form, Thou art the Primeval Deity, the Ancient Being, Thou art the Supreme Refuge of this universe; Thou art the Knower, the One to be known and the Supreme Abode. By Thee alone is this universe pervaded.

39. Thou art Vāyu, Yama, Agni, Varuna, the Moon; Thou art the Lord of creatures and the great Grandsire. Salutations to Thee, my salutations a thousand times, again and again my salutations to Thee!

40. Salutations to Thee before, salutations to Thee behind, salutations

[1] Who could shoot arrows even with his left hand.

to Thee on all sides! O All, infinite in power, and immeasurable in valor, Thou pervadest all, therefore Thou art All.

41. Not knowing this Thy glory and regarding Thee merely as a friend, whatever I may have said presumptuously, out of either carelessness or fondness, addressing Thee as "O Krishna," "O Yādava," "O Friend";

42. O Changeless One, in whatever manner I may have been disrespectful to Thee, in jesting, in walking, in reposing, sitting, or at meals, alone, or in the presence of others; O Unfathomable One, I implore Thee to forgive all that.

43. Thou art the Father of the moving and unmoving world, and its object of worship; greater than the great, O Incomparable Power, no one in the three worlds exists equal to Thee. How can, then, anyone excell Thee?

44. O Adorable Lord! prostrating my body in adoration, I beg Thy forgiveness. O God, as a father forgives his son, a friend his dear friend, a beloved one his love, even so do Thou forgive me!

45. O God, joyous am I to have seen (Thy form) which I never saw before; yet my heart is agitated with terror, therefore show me that Form of Thine. O God of gods! O Abode of the universe, have mercy.

46. I desire to see Thee as before, with diadem, mace and discus. O Universal Form of thousand arms, do Thou manifest Thyself in that same Four-armed Form (form of Vishnu).

The Blessed Lord said:

47. O Arjuna, mercifully have I shown thee this Supreme Form by My own Yoga power. This effulgent, infinite, primeval, great universal Form of Mine, which has not been seen by anyone else before thee.

48. O great hero of the Kurus, not by the study of the sacred Vedas or by sacrifice, not by charity or rituals, not by severe austerities, am I visible in such Form in this world of men to any other than thee.

49. Be not frightened, nor bewildered, having seen this terrific Form of Mine, getting rid of thy fear and with gladdened heart, behold thou again this My former Form.

Sanjaya said:

50. Vāsudeva (Krishna), having thus spoken to Arjuna, showed again His own Form. The Great-souled One, having assumed again His gentle Form, pacified him (Arjuna) who was terrified.

Arjuna said:

51. O Janārdana, seeing this, Thy gentle human Form, now my thoughts are collected and I have recovered myself.

The Blessed Lord said:

52. This Form of Mine which thou hast seen is very difficult to perceive; even gods ever long to behold this Form.
53. Neither by the Vedas, nor by austerities, nor by charitable gifts, nor by sacrifice, can I be seen as thou hast seen Me,
54. But by single-hearted devotion alone I can be known in this manner, O Arjuna, and perceived in reality and also entered into, O Parantapa.
55. O Pāndava, he who works for Me, has Me for his highest goal, is devoted to Me, is free from attachment and bears enmity towards no creature, he enters into Me.

Here ends the Eleventh Chapter called "Vishya-Rupa-Darsanam, or The Vision of the Universal Form"

CHAPTER XII

Arjuna said:

1. Those devotees who, ever steadfast, thus worship Thee and those who worship the Unmanifested Imperishable, which of them are better knowers of Yoga?

The Blessed Lord said:

2. Those who, fixing their minds on Me, worship Me with perpetual devotion, endowed with supreme faith, to My mind they are the best knowers of Yoga.
3. But those who contemplate the Imperishable, the Undefinable, Unmanifested, Omnipresent, Unthinkable, Unchangeable, Immovable and Eternal,
4. Having subdued all the senses, even-minded everywhere, and engaged in doing good to all beings, verily they attain unto Me.
5. Greater is their difficulty whose minds are set on the Unmanifested,

for the goal of the Unmanifested is very arduous for the embodied to attain.

6. But those who, surrendering all actions to Me and regarding Me as the Supreme Goal, worship Me with single-hearted devotion,

7. For them whose hearts are thus fixed on Me, O son of Prithā, I become ere long the Saviour from the ocean of mortal Samsāra (world of birth and death).

8. Fix thy mind on Me alone and rest thine understanding in Me, thus thou shalt doubtlessly live in Me hereafter.

9. O Dhananjaya, if thou art unable to fix thy mind steadfastly on Me, then, by faithful practice of devotion, do thou seek to reach Me.

10. If thou art also unable to practise devotion, then be thou intent on working for Me. Even by performing actions for My sake, thou shalt attain perfection.

11. If thou art not able to do even this, then, taking refuge in Me alone, and self-controlled, do thou surrender the fruits of all actions.

12. Knowledge is indeed better than blind practice; meditation excels knowledge; surrender of the fruits of action is more esteemed than meditation. Peace immediately follows surrender.

13. He who hates no creature and is friendly and compassionate to all, who is free from attachment and egotism, equal-minded in pleasure and pain, and forgiving,

14. Who is ever content and meditative, self-subjugated and possessed with firm conviction, with mind and intellect dedicated to Me, he who is thus devoted to Me is dear to Me.

15. He by whom the world is not afflicted and who is not afflicted by the world, who is free from elation, envy, fear and anxiety, he is dear to Me.

16. He who is free from all external dependence, pure, efficient, unattached, undisturbed, and has given up all (selfish) undertakings, he who is thus devoted to Me is dear to Me.

17. He who neither rejoices, nor hates, nor sorrows, nor desires and who has renounced good and evil, he who is thus full of devotion is dear to Me.

18. He who is the same to friend and foe and also in honor and dishonor, the same in heat and cold, pleasure and pain, free from all attachment,

19. He who is alike in praise and blame, is silent, content with everything, homeless, steady-minded, such a devoted soul is dear to Me.

20. Those who follow this immortal Dharma (teaching) as declared (by Me) and who are possessed with faith, regarding Me as the Supreme Goal, such devotees are exceedingly dear to Me.

Here ends the Twelfth Chapter called "Bhakti-Yoga, or The Path of Devotion"

CHAPTER XIII

[*Arjuna said:* O Keshava, Prakriti (Nature) and Purusha (Self), Kshetra and the knower of Kshetra, knowledge and that which ought to be known, these I desire to learn.]

The Blessed Lord said:

1. O son of Kunti, this body is called Kshetra (field), the wise call the knower of it as Kshetrajna (knower of the field).

2. O descendant of Bharata, know Me to be the Kshetrajna (conscious Soul) in all Kshetras (bodies). To My mind, the knowledge of Kshetra (body) and Kshetrajna (Soul) is the true knowledge.

3. What the Kshetra (field) is, of what nature, what are its modifications, whence it arises; also who is he (knower, Soul) and what are his powers, do thou hear that from me in brief.

4. This truth has been sung by the Rishis (Seers) in various ways, in many different hymns, in Brahma-Sutra-Aphorisms, full of sound reasoning and conviction.

5. The great elements (earth, water, fire, air, ether), egoism, intellect, the Unmanifested (Nature), the ten organs (of sense and action) and the one (mind), the five sense-objects;

6. Desire, aversion, pleasure, pain, combination (of these), consciousness, fortitude, thus the Kshetra (body) has been briefly described with its modifications.

7. Humility, unostentatiousness, non-injuring, forgiveness, simplicity, service to the Guru (spiritual teacher), purity, steadfastness, self-control;

8. Renunciation of sense-objects as well as absence of egoism, realization of the evils of birth, death, old age, disease, pain;

9. Non-attachment, non-identification of self with son, wife, home and the rest; equal-mindedness in beneficial and non-beneficial happenings;

10. One-pointed and unwavering devotion to Me, resort to secluded places, distaste for assemblies;

11. Constant devotion to spiritual knowledge, realization of the essence of Truth, this is declared to be wisdom; what is opposed to this is ignorance.

12. I shall declare now that which is to be known, by knowing which one attains immortality. The Supreme Brahman is beginningless; It is said to be neither Sat (existence) nor Asat (non-existence).

13. With hands and feet everywhere, with eyes, heads and mouths everywhere and with ears everywhere in the universe, That alone exists enveloping all.

14. It shines through the functions of all the senses, and yet It is without senses; unattached, yet It sustains all; devoid of Gunas (qualities), yet It is the experiencer of Gunas.

15. It exists within and without all beings; It is unmoving as well as moving, incomprehensible because of Its subtlety; It is far and also near.

16. Indivisible, yet It exists as if divided in beings; It is to be known as the Sustainer of beings; It destroys and also generates.

17. It is the Light of lights and is said to be beyond darkness. It is knowledge, the One to be known, and the Goal of knowledge, dwelling in the hearts of all.

18. Thus Kshetra (field), knowledge and that which is to be known, have been told briefly. My devotee, knowing this, becomes fitted to enter into My Being (oneness with Me).

19. Know thou both Prakriti (Nature) and Purusha (Soul) to be without beginning. Know thou also that all the modifications and Gunas (qualities) are born of Prakriti.

20. Prakriti is said to be the productive source of cause and effect; while the embodied soul is the cause of experiences of pleasure and pain.

21. For the Purusha (Soul) experiences the Gunas, born of Prakriti; attachment to the Gunas is the cause of its birth in good and evil wombs.

22. The great Soul (that dwells) in this body is called the Witness or Looker-on, the Sanctioner, the Sustainer, the Experiencer, the mighty Lord and also the Supreme Self.

23. He who thus knows Purusha (Soul) and Prakriti (Nature) with the Gunas (qualities), howsoever he may be living, is not born again.

24. Some, by meditation, behold the Self by the self within themselves; others by the path of wisdom; still others by the path of action.

25. Others again, not possessing such knowledge themselves, worship as they have heard from others (illumined Souls); even they surmount death, by following with faith what they have heard.

26. O mighty of the Bharata race, whatever is born, whether moving or unmoving, know it to be (produced) from the union of Kshetra and Kshetrajna (Nature and Soul).

27. The Supreme Lord abides in all beings equally; (He is) undying in the dying: He who sees (thus) sees truly.

28. Seeing the same Lord existing everywhere equally, he does not hurt Self by the self and thus attains the highest goal.

29. And he who sees that all actions are being performed by Prakriti (Nature) alone and that the Self is not acting, he sees truly.

30. When he sees the separate existence of all beings established in One, and their expansion from that One alone, then he becomes Brahman (one with Brahman).

31. O son of Kunti, being without beginning and devoid of Gunas, the Supreme Self is immutable; though dwelling in the body, It neither acts nor is affected (by the fruits of action).

32. As the all-pervading ether (Akāsha) is not tainted, because of its subtlety, similarly this Self, (though) existing everywhere in the body, is not tainted.

33. O descendant of Bharata, as one sun illumines all this world, similarly He who dwells in the body illumines all bodies.

34. They who thus, by the eyes of wisdom, perceive the distinction between body and Soul, and the liberation of beings from Nature (Prakriti), they attain to the Supreme.

Here ends the Thirteenth Chapter called
"Yoga of Kshetra and Kshetrajna, or
The Path of Discrimination
between Body and Soul"

CHAPTER XIV

The Blessed Lord said:

1. Now I shall again declare unto thee that supreme wisdom, which is above all wisdom, by knowing which all the Sages after this life attain to the highest perfection.

2. Abiding by this wisdom, and having attained to My Being, neither do they come forth in evolution[1] nor are they affected in involution.[2]

3. O descendant of Bharata, the great Prakriti is My womb; in that I place the seed, from thence is the birth of all beings.

4. O son of Kunti, whatever forms are produced in all the wombs, the great Prakriti is the womb and I am the seed-giving Father.

5. O mighty-armed, Sattwa, Rajas, Tamas,[3] these Gunas (qualities), born of Prakriti, bind the immutable, embodied soul in the body.

6. O sinless one, of these (Gunas) Sattwa, being transparent, luminous and free from evil, binds (the embodied) by attachment to happiness and attachment to knowledge.

7. O son of Kunti, know thou Rajas to be of the nature of passion, giving rise to thirst (for pleasure) and attachment. It binds the embodied by attachment to action.

8. O Bhārata (Arjuna), know thou Tamas to be born of ignorance; it deludes all embodied beings and binds by false perception, indolence and sleep.

9. O Bhārata, Sattwa attaches one to happines; Rajas to action; while Tamas, covering wisdom, attaches one to false perception.

10. O Bhārata (sometimes) Sattwa predominates over Rajas and Tamas; (sometimes) Rajas predominates over Sattwa and Tamas; and (sometimes) Tamas over Sattwa and Rajas.

11. When through all the senses of this body the light of understanding shines forth, then it is to be known that Sattwa is predominant.

12. O Prince of the Bharata race, greed, (excessive) activity, enterprise, restlessness, longing, these prevail when Rajas is predominant.

13. O descendant of Kuru, darkness, inertia, false perception, and also delusion prevail when Tamas is predominant.

14. If the embodied meets with death when Sattwa is predominant, then he attains the spotless regions of the knowers of the Highest.

15. Meeting with death in Rajas, one is born among those attached to action; and dying in Tamas, one is born in the wombs of senseless beings.

16. The fruit of good deeds is declared to be Sāttwika and pure; the fruit of Rajas (passionate deeds) is pain; and ignorance is the fruit of Tamas.

[1] Creation.
[2] Dissolution.
[3] Goodness, passion, darkness.

17. Wisdom is born of Sattwa; greed, of Rajas; false perception, delusion and ignorance arise from Tamas.

18. The dwellers of Sattwa go upward; the Rājasic (of passionate natures) stay in the middle; and the Tāmasic, abiding in the functions of the lowest Guna, go downward.

19. When the Seer beholds no other agent than the Gunas, and knows also That which is higher than the Gunas, then he attains to My Being.

20. The embodied, having gone beyond these three Gunas, out of which the body is evolved, is liberated from birth, death, decay and pain, and attains to immortality.

Arjuna said:

21. O Lord, what are the signs of him who has gone beyond the three Gunas? What are his characteristics and how does he go beyond these three Gunas?

The Blessed Lord said:

22. O Pāndava, he who neither hates the presence of illumination (Sattwa), activity (Rajas) or delusion (Tamas), nor craves for them when they are absent;

23. He who is seated unconcerned (like a witness) and is not moved by the Gunas, who is established and unshaken, knowing that the Gunas alone operate;

24. He who is alike in pleasure and pain; self-possessed; regarding alike a lump of earth, a stone and gold; who is the same in pleasant and unpleasant, in praise and blame, and steady;

25. He who is alike in honor and dishonor, the same to friend and foe, giving up all (selfish) undertakings, he is said to have crossed beyond the Gunas.

26. And he who, crossing over these Gunas, serves me with unwavering devotion, becomes fit to attain oneness with Brahman.

27. For I am the Abode of Brahman, the Immutable, the Immortal, the eternal Dharma and Absolute Bliss.

Here ends the Fourteenth Chapter called
"Distinction of the Three Gunas"

CHAPTER XV

The Blessed Lord said:

1. They speak of an eternal Ashwattha (tree), rooted above and branching below, whose leaves are the Vedas. He who knows it knows the Vedas.

2. Its branches are spread below and above, nourished by the Gunas; the sense-objects are its buds; its roots stretch down below in the world of men, creating actions.

3. Its form is not visible here, neither its end nor its origin, nor its basis. Having cut down this firm-rooted Ashwattha tree by the mighty sword of non-attachment,

4. Then that Goal is to be sought after, attaining which they (the wise) do not return again. I take refuge in that Primeval Being from which streams forth the Eternal (creative) Energy.

5. Free from pride and false conceit, the evil of attachment conquered, ever devoted to spiritual knowledge, desires completely pacified, liberated from the pairs of opposites known as pleasure and pain, the undeluded reach that eternal Goal.

6. That (Goal) the sun does not illumine, nor the moon, nor fire; going there, they (the wise) do not return. That is My Supreme Abode.

7. A portion of Myself has become the living Soul in the world of life from time without beginning. It draws the (five) senses and mind, the sixth (sense), which are in Prakriti.

8. When the Lord (Soul) obtains a body and when He leaves it, He takes these (senses and mind) and goes forth as the wind (goes forth), carrying away the scents from their seats (the flowers).

9. The embodied soul, presiding over the ear, eye, the sense of touch, of taste and smell, as well as over the mind, experiences sense-objects.

10. Either going forth from the body, or residing in it, or experiencing, or united with the Gunas, the deluded do not see It (the Soul); but those who have the eye of wisdom perceive It.

11. The self-subjugated perceive It, dwelling in themselves; but the impure-hearted and the unintelligent, even though striving, behold It not.

12. The light which resides in the sun, in the moon, in fire, and which illumines the whole world, know that light to be Mine.

13. Entering the earth with My energy, I support all beings and I nourish all the herbs, becoming the watery moon.

14. Dwelling in the body of living beings as Fire, I, being united with Prāna (ingoing breath) and Apāna (outgoing breath), digest four kinds of food.[1]

15. I am seated in the hearts of all, from Me alone comes memory, wisdom, and also their loss. I am that which is known in all the Vedas. Verily I am the Author of Vedanta and the knower of the Vedas am I.

16. There are two kinds of beings in the world: the perishable and the imperishable; all beings are perishable, but the Purusha (Self) is imperishable.

17. But there is another, the Highest Being, called the Supreme Self, who is the Immutable Lord, pervading the three worlds and supporting them.

18. As I am beyond the perishable and am above even the imperishable, therefore in the world and in the Veda I am known as the Supreme Being.

19. O descendant of Bharata, he who, free from delusion, thus knows Me as the Supreme Being, he, knowing all, worships Me with his whole heart.

20. Thus, O sinless Bhārata, has been declared by Me the most profound teaching, knowing this one attains enlightenment and the fulfillment of all duties.

Here ends the Fifteenth Chapter called "The Path of the Supreme Being"

CHAPTER XVI

The Blessed Lord said:

1. Fearlessness, purity of heart, steadfastness in Yoga of Self-knowledge, charitable gifts, control of the senses, sacrifice, study of the Sacred Scriptures, austerity and simplicity,

2. Non-injury, truthfulness, absence of anger, renunciation, peace, absence of calumny, compassion to beings, non-covetousness, gentleness, modesty and absence of fickleness,

3. Vigor, forgiveness, fortitude, purity, absence of hatred and pride,

[1] Fourfold foods which require masticating, sucking, licking and swallowing or drinking.

these, O descendant of Bharata, belong to one born with the divine property.

4. O Pārtha, ostentatiousness, arrogance and self-conceit, anger as well as cruelty and ignorance, belong to one born with the demonic property.

5. The divine property is for liberation and the demonic for bondage. Grieve not, O Pāndava, thou art born with the divine property.

6. O Pārtha, in this world there are twofold manifestations of beings; the divine and the demonic. The divine has been described at length. Hear from Me now of the demonic state.

7. The demonic people know not how to follow right or how to refrain from wrong; there is neither purity, nor good conduct, nor truth in them.

8. They say that "this universe is without truth, without a basis, without God, born of mutual union caused by lust. What else is there?"

9. Holding this view, these ruined souls, of small understanding and of fierce deeds, rise as the enemies of the world for its destruction.

10. Filled with insatiable desires, possessed with hypocrisy, pride and arrogance, holding evil fancies through delusion, they work with unholy resolve;

11. Beset with immense cares, ending only in death; regarding sensual enjoyment as the highest and feeling sure that that is all there is;

12. Bound by a hundred ties of hope, given over to lust and anger, they strive to secure hoards of wealth by unjust means, for sensual gratification.

13. "This has been gained by me today and this desire I shall obtain, this is mine and this wealth also shall be mine."

14. "That enemy has been slain by me, others also shall I slay. I am the lord, I am the enjoyer, I am successful, powerful and happy."

15. "I am rich and well-born; who is equal to me? I shall sacrifice, I shall give, I shall rejoice": thus deluded by ignorance,

16. Bewildered by many fancies, enwrapped in the net of delusion, addicted to the gratification of the senses, they fall into a foul hell.

17. Self-glorifying, haughty, filled with the vanity and intoxication of wealth, they perform sacrifices (merely) in name out of hypocrisy, disregarding the Scriptural injunctions.

18. Possessed by egoism, power, insolence, lust and anger, these malignant people hate Me (dwelling) in their own bodies and in those of others.

19. I hurl these malignant and cruel evil doers, most degraded of mer into the wombs of Asuras[1] in the world (of birth and death).

20. O son of Kunti, entering into the Asuric (unclean) wombs an deluded birth after birth, without attaining Me they fall into a stil lower state.

21. Lust, anger and greed, these three are the soul-destroying gate of hell. Therefore one should forsake these three.

22. O son of Kunti, he who is free from these three gates of darknes practises what is good for his soul and thus attains the Supreme Goa

23. He who, setting aside the injunctions of the Scriptures, follow the impulse of desire, attains neither perfection, nor happiness, nor th highest goal.

24. Therefore let the Scriptures be thy authority in ascertaining wha ought to be done and what ought not to be done. Having learned th injunctions declared in the Scriptures, thou shouldst act here (in thi world).

Here ends the Sixteenth Chapter called
"Distinction between the Divine and
the Demonic Property"

CHAPTER XVII

Arjuna said:

1. O Krishna, those who, disregarding the injunctions of the Scrip tures, perform sacrifice with faith, what is their state? Is it Sattwa (good ness), Rajas (passion) or Tamas (darkness)?

The Blessed Lord said:

2. Threefold is the faith of the embodied, born of their inherent nature Sāttwica (good), Rājasica (passionate), Tāmasica (ignorant). Do tho hear of that.

3. O descendant of Bharata, the faith of each is according to his in herent nature. The man consists of his faith; he is verily what his faith is

4. The men of purity worship the gods; the men of passionate natur worship Yakshas and Rākshasas; while the others, men of Tāmasic (ignorant) nature, worship ghosts (departed spirits) and goblins.

[1] Unclean, cruel and godless creatures.

5. The men who practise severe austerities, not enjoined by the Scriptures, being possessed with hypocrisy and egoism, impelled by lust and attachment.

6. Torturing, senseless as they are, all the organs of the senses and Me, dwelling in the body, know them to be of demonic resolve.

7. The foods also are of threefold nature which are liked respectively by each of these; and so also sacrifice, austerity and charitable gifts. Do thou hear the distinction of these.

8. The foods which increase life-force, energy, strength, health, joy and cheerfulness, and which are savory, soothing, substantial and agreeable, are liked by the Sāttwica nature.

9. The Rājasica nature likes foods which are bitter, sour, saline, overhot, pungent, dry, burning, and which produce pain, grief and disease.

10. That which is stale, insipid, putrid, cooked over night, even leavings or unclean food is liked by the Tāmasica nature.

11. That sacrifice is Sāttwica which is performed by men desiring no fruit, as it is enjoined by the Scriptural laws, with the mind fixed on the sacrifice alone, just for its own sake.

12. But, O best of the Bharatas, that which is performed with the desire for fruits and for ostentation, know that to be Rājasica sacrifice.

13. The sacrifice which is performed, without regard to Scriptural injunctions, in which no food is distributed, and which is without sacred texts, charitable gifts and faith, is said to be Tāmasica.

14. Worship of the gods, of the twice-born,[1] of Gurus[2] and wise men; purity, simplicity, continence, non-injury; these are called the austerity of the body.

15. Speech, which causes no pain (to others) and is true as well as pleasant and beneficial; regular study of the Scriptures: these are called the austerity of speech.

16. Cheerfulness of mind, kindliness, silence, self-control, purity of heart: these are called austerity of the mind.

17. When this threefold austerity is practised, by men of steadfast devotion, with great faith, without desiring fruits, it is said to be Sāttwica.

18. When this austerity is performed with the object of gaining welcome, honor and worship, or from ostentation, it is said to be Rājasica, unstable and fleeting.

19. The austerity which is performed with deluded understanding, by

[1] Brāhmanas.
[2] Spiritual teachers.

self-torture or for the purpose of injuring another, that is said to be Tāmasica.

20. "To give is right": with this thought, giving to one who does nothing in return, in a fit place, time and to a worthy person, is regarded as a Sāttwica gift.

21. That gift which is made with the thought of receiving in return or of looking for the fruits, or given reluctantly, is known as a Rājasica gift.

22. The gift which is made in the wrong place or time, to unworthy persons, with disrespect and contempt, that is said to be a Tāmasica gift.

23. "Om, Tat, Sat" (Yes, That, the Real), this is declared to be the triple name of Brahman, by which were made of old the Brāhmanas, the Vedas and sacrifices.

24. Therefore the followers of the Vedas always begin their acts of sacrifice, gift and austerity by uttering "Om" as enjoined in the Scriptures.

25. By uttering "Tat," without looking for fruits, the seekers after liberation perform various acts of sacrifice, austerity and gift.

26. O Pārtha, the word "Sat" is used in the sense of reality and of goodness; and the word "Sat" is also used in the sense of auspicious act.

27. Steadfastness in sacrifice, austerity and gift is called "Sat," and action performed for the sake of That (Supreme) is also called "Sat."

28. O Pārtha, whatever is sacrificed, or given, or performed, or whatever austerities are practised without faith, that is called "Asat" (Unreal). It is neither good for here nor for hereafter.

Here ends the Seventeenth Chapter called
"Division of the Threefold Faith"

CHAPTER XVIII

Arjuna said:

1. O Lord of the senses, O Mighty-armed, O Destroyer of Keshi, I desire to know respectively the truth regarding Sannyāsa (renunciation) as well as of Tyāga (relinquishment).

The Blessed Lord said:

2. The Sages declare that the renunciation of actions with desire (for fruits) is Sannyāsa, and the learned declare that the relinquishment of the fruits of all actions is Tyāga.

3. Some philosophers declare that all actions should be given up as an evil; while others say that the work of sacrifice, gift and austerity should never be given up.

4. O best of the Bharatas, O tiger among men, hear from Me the final truth regarding relinquishment; for relinquishment has been declared to be of three kinds.

5. The acts of sacrifice, gift and austerity are not to be relinquished, but should indeed be performed; for sacrifice, gift and austerity are purifying to the discriminative.

6. But, O Pārtha, even these acts are to be performed, giving up attachment and the fruits. This is My best and sure conviction.

7. Relinquishment of the prescribed actions is not proper. Abandonment of the same, through delusion, is declared to be Tāmasica.

8. He who relinquishes action out of fear of bodily trouble, thinking "it is painful," thus performing Rājasica relinquishment, does not obtain the fruit thereof.

9. O Arjuna, giving up attachment and fruit, when prescribed action is performed because it should be done, such relinquishment is regarded as Sāttwica.

10. The relinquisher, imbued with Sattwa and steady understanding, with his doubts destroyed, does not hate a disagreeable work, nor is he attached to an agreeable one.

11. It is not possible for the embodied to relinquish actions entirely; but he who relinquishes the fruits of action is called a (true) relinquisher.

12. Good, evil and mixed, threefold is the fruit of action obtained by non-relinquishers after death; but never by relinquishers.

13. O mighty-armed, learn from Me the five causes for the accomplishment of all action, as it is declared in the Sānkhya philosophy.

14. The body, the agent, the various senses, the different and manifold functions and the presiding deity as the fifth.

15. Whatever action man performs with his body, speech and mind, whether right or the reverse, these five are its causes.

16. This being the case, he who, through impure understanding, looks upon his Self, the One, as the agent, he of perverted mind, sees not (the Truth).

17. He who has no egotistical notion (such as "I am the doer"), whose understanding is not affected (by good and evil), even though slaying these people, he neither slays nor is bound (by action).

18. The knowledge, the knowable, and the knower are the threefold cause of action; the instrument (senses), the object and the agent, are the threefold basis of action.

19. Knowledge, action and agent are declared in the Sānkhya philosophy to be threefold, according to the distinction of the Gunas. Hear them also duly.

20. Know that knowledge to be Sāttwica, by which is seen in all beings the One Immutable, inseparate in the separate.

21. But the knowledge which sees in all beings the distinct entities of diverse kinds as different from one another, know that knowledge to be Rājasica (passionate).

22. While that knowledge which is confined to one single effect, as if it were the whole, without reason, not founded on truth, and trivial, that is declared to be Tāmasica.

23. The action which is ordained, performed by one not desirous of fruits, free from attachment and without love or aversion, is declared to be Sāttwica.

24. But the action which is performed with longing for objects of desire or with egoism, or with much effort, is declared to be Rājasica.

25. The action which is undertaken from delusion, without heed to ability and consequence, loss and injury (to others) is said to be Tāmasica.

26. Free from attachment, non-egotistic, endued with perseverance and enthusiasm, unaffected in success or failure, such an agent is called Sāttwica.

27. He who is passionate and desirous of the fruits of action, greedy, malignant, impure, easily moved by joy or sorrow, such an agent is called Rājasica.

28. Unsteady, vulgar, arrogant, dishonest, malicious, indolent, despondent, procrastinating, such an agent is called Tāmasica.

29. O Dhananjaya, hear thou the distinction of understanding and fortitude according to the threefold Gunas, as I declare them exhaustively and distinctively.

30. O Pārtha, know that understanding to be Sāttwica which knows when to act and when to abstain from action; also right and wrong action, fear and fearlessness, bondage and liberation.

31. O Pārtha, that by which the understanding is distorted regarding right and wrong, proper and improper action, that is called Rājasic understanding.

32. That understanding which is covered with darkness and regards unrighteousness as righteousness, and looks upon all things in a perverted light, that, O Pārtha, is Tāmasica understanding.

33. That firmness, O Pārtha, by which one can control the activity of the mind, Prāna and senses, through the unwavering practice of Yoga, that firmness is Sāttwica.

34. But that firmness by which one clings to duty, desire and wealth, being attached therein and desirous of fruits, that firmness is Rājasica.

35. O Pārtha, that by which a stupid man does not give up sleep, fear, grief, despondency and vanity, that firmness is Tāmasica.

36. O Prince of the Bharata race, now hear from Me regarding the threefold happiness, that happiness which one enjoys by habit and by which one comes to the end of pain.

37. That which is like poison in the beginning and like nectar in the end, that happiness is said to be Sāttwica (pure), born of the blissful knowledge of the Self.

38. That happiness which arises from the contract of the senses with sense-objects and is like nectar in the beginning but like poison in the end, is declared to be Rājasica.

39. That happiness which begins and ends in self-delusion, arising from sleep, indolence and false perception, is declared to be Tāmasica.

40. There is no being on earth or in heaven among the gods, who is free from these three Gunas, born of Prakriti (Nature).

41. O Parantapa (Arjuna), the duties of Brāhmanas, Kshatriyas, Vaisyas and also of Sudras, are distributed according to their Gunas, born of their nature.

42. Control of mind and senses, austerity, purity, forgiveness and also simplicity, knowledge, realization and faith in God, these are the duties of Brāhmanas, born of their nature.

43. Bravery, energy, firmness, skill and also not flying from the battle, generosity, lordliness, are the duties of Kshatriyas, born of their nature.

44. Agriculture, rearing of cattle and trade are the duties of the Vaisyas, born of their nature. Service is the duty of Sudras, born of their nature.

45. Man attains perfection, being engaged in his own duty. Hear now how one engaged in his own duty attains perfection.

46. Him from Whom is the evolution of all beings, by Whom all this is pervaded, by worshipping Him with his own duty man attains perfection.

47. Better is one's own duty, although imperfect, than that of another

well performed. He who does the duty born of his own nature incurs no sin.

48. O son of Kunti, one should not relinquish the duty to which he is born, though it is defective, for all undertakings are surrounded by evil as fire by smoke.

49. He, whose understanding is unattached everywhere, who is self-subjugated, devoid of desires, he, by renunciation, attains the supreme perfection, consisting in freedom from action.

50. O son of Kunti, after reaching such perfection, how he attains to Brahman, the highest Goal of Wisdom, do thou hear that from Me in brief.

51. Endued with pure understanding; subduing self by firmness; relinquishing sound and other sense-objects; abandoning longing and aversion;

52. Resorting to a secluded spot; eating little; controlling body, speech and mind; ever steadfastly engaged in meditation and concentration; endued with dispassion;

53. Forsaking egoism, power, pride, lust, anger and possession; freed from the notion of "mine" and tranquil: one is thus fit to become one with Brahman.

54. Becoming one with Brahman, serene-minded, he neither grieves nor desires; alike to all beings, he attains supreme devotion unto Me.

55. By devotion he knows Me in truth, what and who I am; having thus known Me in truth, he forthwith enters into Me.

56. Even though constantly performing all actions, taking refuge in Me, through My grace he attains to the Eternal, Immutable Abode.

57. Surrendering mentally all actions to Me, regarding Me as the highest goal, resorting to Self-knowledge, do thou ever fix thy heart on Me.

58. Fixing thy heart on Me, thou shalt, by My grace, overcome all obstacles; but if, through egoism, thou wilt not hear Me, thou shalt perish.

59. If, actuated by egoism, thou thinkest: "I will not fight," in vain is this thy resolve. Thine own nature will impel thee.

60. O son of Kunti, being bound by thine own Karma, born of thine own nature, thou shalt be helplessly led to do that which from delusion thou desirest not to do.

61. O Arjuna, the Lord dwells in the heart of all beings, causing all beings to revolve, as if mounted on a wheel.

62. O Bhārata, take refuge in Him with all thy heart; through His grace thou shalt attain Supreme Peace and the Eternal Abode.

63. Thus wisdom, most profound of all secrets, has been declared unto thee by Me; pondering over it fully, do as thou likest.

64. Hear again My Supreme Word, most profound of all; for thou art My dearly beloved, therefore I shall speak for thy good.

65. Fill thy heart with Me, be thou devoted to Me, do thou worship Me and bow down to Me. Thus thou shalt attain unto Me. Truly I promise thee, for thou art dear to Me.

66. Giving up all Dharmas (righteous and unrighteous actions), come unto Me alone for refuge. I shall free thee from all sins; grieve not.

67. This should never be spoken by thee to one who is devoid of austerity or without devotion, nor to one who does not render service, nor to one who speaks ill of Me.

68. He who, with supreme devotion to Me, will declare this deeply profound secret to My devotees, doubtless he shall come unto Me.

69. There is none among men who does dearer service to Me than he, nor shall there be any other on earth dearer to Me than he.

70. And he who shall study this Sacred Dialogue between us, by him I shall be worshipped with sacrifice of wisdom. Such is My conviction.

71. And even that man who shall hear this, full of faith and without malice, he too, being freed from evil, shall attain to the sacred region of those of righteous deeds.

72. O son of Prithā, has this been heard by thee with an attentive mind? O Dhananjaya, has the delusion of thine ignorance been destroyed?

Arjuna said:

73. My delusion is destroyed and I have regained my memory through Thy grace, O Changeless One. I stand firm with doubts dispelled; I will do Thy Word.

Sanjaya said:

74. Thus have I heard this wonderful Dialogue between Vāsudeva (Krishna) and great-souled Pārtha, causing my hair to stand on end.

75. Through the grace of Vyāsa have I heard this supreme and most profound Yoga, declared directly by Krishna Himself, the Lord of Yoga.

76. O King, as I remember, over and over, this wonderful and holy Dialogue between Keshava and Arjuna, I rejoice again and again.

77. And as I remember, over and over, that most wonderful Form of Hari (the Lord), great is my wonder, O King, and I rejoice again and again.

78. Wherever is Krishna, the Lord of Yoga, wherever is Pārtha, the bowman, there are prosperity, victory, glory, sound polity. Such is my firm conviction.

Here ends the Eighteenth Chapter called "The Path of Liberation through Renunciation" in the Srimad-Bhagavad-Gita, the Essence of the Upanishads, the Science of Brahman, the Scripture of Yoga, the Dialogue between Sri Krishna and Arjuna

Peace! Peace! Peace be unto all.

The Yoga Aphorisms of Patanjali

INTRODUCTION

THE MOST CURIOUS, most distinctive and at the same time probably the most widely known aspect of Hindu mysticism is the philosophy and practice of *yoga*. If the sum of Brahmanism may be defined as teaching the mystic union of man's true self with the world-soul (*brahman,* God, etc.), *yoga* represents the most direct and well-formulated method for achieving that goal, and as such constitutes a form of religious experience and a religious technique. The reason for the popularity of *yoga* philosophy and its particular appeal to the modern world is twofold; it arises from the combination of a system of physical regimen that has something to do with physical and mental health with a mystic search for inner stability and the psychic depths of man's soul, which seems to underly a broad and deep undercurrent of modern life. "To me," says C. G. Jung, "the crux of the spiritual problem of today is to be found in the fascination which psychic life exerts upon the modern man." It is needless to point out that it is modern psychoanalysis itself, which has awakened our interest in, and opened our way to the exploration of, the subconscious, and by changing our whole conception of the human "mind," has exhibited to us the tyrannous demoniac power of our primordial instincts, impulses and "urges" which govern our lives in that vast psychological underworld. Lastly, it must be pointed out that popularity of *yoga* is due to its claims of supernatural powers and to the general interest in the hocus-pocus of all forms of occultism.

Yoga (meaning "yoke") represents a form of personal discipline, with the object of "yoking" the body to the soul, and the individual soul to the universal soul. From a practical aspect, its aim is to help cultivate emotional stability. It begins with a unique and unparalleled exploration in the region of the involuntary muscles and bringing them under the control of the mind, and proceeds to the liberation of the mind from its sense impressions and the deeper residuents and impedimenta that not only clog but form the very fabric of our subconscious life which Freud has summed up as *Eros,* or the life-principle, comprising the sex instinct and the ego-instinct. Finally, it aims at the destruction of the "mind" for the liberation of the "soul" (which is variously interpreted), at which point it has a religious character and goes beyond the fields and aims of psychoanalytic research.

Before the coming of Freud and Jung, we might have easily laughed off *yoga* philosophy and put it on the same level with the much debated Hindu rope trick and levitation. *Yoga* does claim powers of levitation. In the first week of July, 1942, I read in the *New York Herald Tribune* a factual account by a responsible Hindu professor of a *yogi* buried under publicly tested conditions and coming to life again after six months in the presence of thousands of Hindu peasants. It is these sensational reports that appeal to the popular fancy. After the modern experiments of freezing of patients under ice, these feats seem less incredible and are not any more inexplicable than the hibernation of animals. Still, they are bound to detract our attention from the more normal and earnest problems of achieving emotional stability and psychological health.

Luckily, modern psychology offers the key to our understanding of *yoga.* Breathing exercises and the mastery of ordinarily involuntary muscles by practice require no explanation; the deeper problems of the psyche do. Jung has written a full and highly illuminating introduction to a Chinese *yoga* book (*The Secret of the Golden Flower,* Harcourt, Brace, 1938, not to be confused with the Buddhistic *Lotus Gospel;* see especially the sections, "Difficulties encountered by a European in trying to understand the East," and "Modern psychology offers a possibility of understanding"). Kovoor T. Behanan, in his *"Yoga: a Scientific Evaluation"* (Macmillan, 1937) has also drawn interesting parallels in the chapter, "Yoga and Psychoanalysis." The curious thing about this book is that in Behanan, a Hindu by birth, his scientific training in Toronto and Yale seems to have got the upper hand of his native Hindu blood and his early training at Calcutta; I rather think his approach to *yoga* is more "university trained" and therefore more trivial than that of a continental mind like Jung.

Readers of the *yoga* section of the *Bhagavad-Gita* must have been impressed by its concern with what lies in the subconscious life. The overwhelming emphasis on the subconscious and the dependence of the *yoga* disciple upon the *guru,* or spiritual teacher, are points of similarity with the practice of psychoanalysis. "*Yoga* can only be safely learned by direct contact with a teacher," warns Swami Vivekananda. When we come to the analysis of the mind itself, only modern psychology makes the doctrine intelligible to us. The process of destruction of the mind (*chitta*) in order to save the soul (*purusha*) can be understood only in psychological terms. The mind with its incrusted layers of sense-attachments, which *yoga* teaches as the hindrances to our seeing of the ultimate soul, is no more than the sepulchre of primordial life-urges that psychology has shown us; the doctrine of the rebirth is no more than that survival in individual of a superpersonal or collective race inheritance phylogenetically acquired; the impersonal, collective nature of these primordial forces is apparently the same as that of the "collective unconscious" of Jung. Finally, the urge for release and liberation is what Freud has negatively called the "death-instinct," the opposite of the "life-instinct," very inadequately illustrated, I am afraid, in sadism and masochism. Freud says very correctly, in the subconscious, "instinctive impulses . . . exist independently side by side, and are exempt from mental contradiction. . . . There is in this system no negation, no dubiety, no varying degrees of certainty. . . . Its processes are timeless, they are not ordered temporarily, are not altered by the passage of time, in fact bear no relation to time at all." It is these forces, as well as the body that must be brought under control by *yoga* practice.

It is also important to point out that the theories of psychoanalysis, like the theories of *yoga,* are speculative, and only a portion of these subjective interpretations are amenable to proof by experimentation. We have not even the vocabulary for these inner phenomena, and when psychoanalysis begins to tackle the depths of the psyche, it is compelled to invent terms that are in their nature quasi-scientific make-shifts—terms like *life-urge,* the *Id, animus, anima, libido* (a form of discharge of energy which unfortunately cannot be measured in volts), and that elusive spiritual entity called *Eros.* Hindu psychology, Buddhist and non-Buddhist, abounds in such terms. It is said that there is a greater psychological vocabulary in Sanskrit and Pali than in the "modern languages" combined. (For example, see the "Table of the Eighty-Nine Consciousnesses" in Henry Clarke Warren's *Buddhism in Translations.*)

Jung says, "We have not yet clearly grasped the fact that Western Theosophy is an amateurish imitation of the East. We are just taking up astrology again, and that to the Oriental is his daily bread. Our studies of sexual life, originating in Vienna and England, are matched or surpassed by Hindu teachings on the subject. Oriental texts ten centuries old introduce us to philosophical relativism,[1] while the idea of indetermination, newly broached in the West, furnishes the very basis of Chinese science.[2] Richard Wilhelm has even shown me that certain complicated processes discovered by analytical psychology are recognizably described in ancient Chinese texts.[3] Psycholanalysis itself and the lines of thought to which it gives rise—surely a distinctly Western development—are only a beginner's attempt compared to what is an immemorial art in the East."[4]

I can do no better than quote Swami Vivekananda on the nature and character of the *yoga* discipline. "For thousands of years such phenomena have been studied, investigated, and generalised, the whole ground of the religious faculties of man has been analysed, and the practical result is the science of *Rāja-Yoga*. . . . It declares that each man is only a conduit for the infinite ocean of knowledge and power that lies beyond mankind. It teaches that desires and wants are in man, that the power of supply is also in man; and that wherever and whenever a desire, a want, a prayer has been fulfilled, it was out of this infinite magazine that the supply came, and not from any supernatural being. The idea of supernatural beings may arouse to a certain extent the power of action in man, but it also brings spiritual decay. It brings dependence; it brings fear; it brings superstition. It degenerates into a horrible belief in the natural weakness of man. There is no supernatural, says the *Yogi,* but there are in nature gross manifestations and subtle manifestations. The subtle are the causes, the gross the effects. The gross can be easily perceived by the senses; not so the subtle. The practice of *Rāja-Yoga* will lead to the acquisition of the more subtle perceptions."

The *Yoga Aphorisms of Patanjali* is the classic and textbook of *yoga,* acknowledged by all schools to be the highest authority on the subject.

[1] Relativism is really as old as Taoism in China.
[2] Jung is referring to *Yi-ching,* one of the Chinese *Five Classics.*
[3] For instance, the case of narcissism in Miss Feng Hsiao-ch'ing.
[4] C. G. Jung: *Modern Man in Search of a Soul,* p. 249.

It was written, according to Professor J. H. Woods, in the fourth or fifth centuries of our era. In this complete text, without the commentaries, a brief glimpse may be had of the contents of *yoga* teachings. I have used the free and easily understandable translation of Swami Vivekananda, and those who are interested should read his commentaries (*Rāja-Yoga,* Ramakrishna-Vivekananda Center, New York, 1939). The classic Comment, and Explanations of the Comment, together with Professor James Haughton Woods' scholarly translation of the text *Yoga-System of Patanjali,* Harvard Oriental Series, Vol. 17, may be consulted only by the academically-minded. Professor Woods seems to err on the scholarly side: his "sources-of-valid-ideas" are translated by Vivekananda as "right knowledge," his "predicate-relation" (*vikalpa*) is simply the latter's "verbal delusion," and "Memory is not-adding-surreptitiously to a once experienced object" simply means, according to the Hindu *yoga* teacher, "Memory is when perceived objects do not slip away." In the same way, I believe "non-attachment" is better English than "passionlessness" and "egoism" better than "feeling-of-personality." "Undifferentiated-consciousness" may be etymologically more exact than "ignorance" for the rendering of *avidyā,* but the important thing is what a Hindu word means to a Hindu, for etymological meaning is always altered by a current meaning which usage has acquired. A brief, but clear exposition of the *yoga* mysticism may be found in *Hindu Mysticism,* by S. N. Dasgupta (Open Court), a lucid introduction to Hindu thought, in general, as against the same author's heavy and scholarly *History of Indian Philosophy.* I have supplied the sectional headings for the convenience of the reader.

The Yoga Aphorisms of Patanjali

Translated by Swami Vivekananda

CHAPTER I: CONCENTRATION: ITS SPIRITUAL USES

Goal of Concentration

1. Now concentration is explained.
2. Yoga is restraining the mind-stuff *(Chitta)* from taking various forms *(Vrittis)*.
3. At that time (the time of concentration) the seer *(Purusha)* rests in his own (unmodified) state.

Forms of Mind-Stuff

4. At other times (other than that of concentration) the seer is identified with the modifications.
5. There are five classes of modifications, (some) painful and (others) not painful.
6. (These are) right knowledge, indiscrimination, verbal delusion, sleep and memory.
7. Direct perception, inference, and competent evidence, are proofs.
8. Indiscrimination is false knowledge not established in real nature.
9. Verbal delusion follows from words having no (corresponding) reality.
10. Sleep is a *Vritti* which embraces the feeling of voidness.

11. Memory is when (*Vrittis* of) perceived subjects do not slip away (and through impressions come back to consciousness).

Methods of Control

12. Their control is by practice and non-attachment.

13. Continuous struggle to keep them (the *Vrittis*) perfectly restrained is practice.

14. It becomes firmly grounded by long constant efforts with great love (for the end to be attained).

15. That effect which comes to those who have given up their thirst after objects either seen or heard, and which wills to control the objects, is non-attachment.

16. That is extreme non-attachment which gives up even the qualities, and comes from the knowledge of (the real nature of) the *Purusha*.[1]

Kinds of Concentration

17. The concentration called right knowledge is that which is followed by reasoning, discrimination, bliss, unqualified egoism.

18. There is another *Samādhi*[2] which is attained by the constant practice of cessation of all mental activity, in which the *Chitta* retains only the unmanifested impressions.

Different Ways of Attaining Samādhi

19. (This *Samādhi* when not followed by extreme non-attachment) becomes the cause of the re-manifestation of the gods and of those that become merged in nature.

[1] *Note by Vivekananda.* "We have first to understand what the *Purusha,* the Self, is, and what are the qualities. According to *Yoga* philosophy the whole of nature consists of three qualities or forces; one is called *Tamas,* another *Rajas* and the third *Sattva.* These three qualities manifest themselves in the physical world as darkness or inactivity; attraction or repulsion; and equilibrium of the two. Everything that is in nature, all manifestations, are combinations and recombinations of these three forces. Nature has been divided into various categories by the *Sānkhyas;* the Self of man is beyond all these, beyond nature. It is effulgent, pure and perfect. Whatever of intelligence we see in nature is but the reflection of this Self upon nature."

[2] Superconscious state, trance.

20. To others (this *Samādhi*) comes through faith, energy, memory, concentration, and discrimination of the real.

21. Success is speedy for the extremely energetic.

22. The success of *Yogis* differs according as the means they adopt are mild, medium or intense.

23. Or by devotion to *Isvara*.

The "Om"

24. *Isvara* (the Supreme Ruler) is a special *Purusha,* untouched by misery, actions, their results and desires.

25. In Him becomes infinite that all-knowingness which in others is (only) a germ.

26. He is the Teacher of even the ancient teachers, being not limited by time.

27. His manifesting word is *Om*.

28. The repetition of this (*Om*) and meditating on its meaning (is the way).

29. From that is gained (the knowledge of) introspection, and the destruction of obstacles.

Forms of Meditation and Samādhi

30. Disease, mental laziness, doubt, lack of enthusiasm, lethargy, clinging to sense-enjoyments, false perception, non-attaining concentration, and falling away from the state when obtained, are the obstructing distractions.

31. Grief, mental distress, tremor of the body, irregular breathing, accompany non-retention of concentration.

32. To remedy this, the practice of one subject (should be made).

33. Friendship, mercy, gladness and indifference, being thought of in regard to subjects, happy, unhappy, good and evil respectively, pacify the *Chitta*.

34. By throwing out and restraining the Breath.

35. Those forms of concentration that bring extraordinary sense perceptions cause perseverance of the mind.

36. Or (by the meditation on) the Effulgent Light, which is beyond all sorrow.

37. Or (by meditation on) the heart that has given up all attachment to sense-objects.

38. Or by meditating on the knowledge that comes in sleep.

39. Or by the meditation on anything that appeals to one as good.

40. The *Yogi's* mind thus meditating, becomes unobstructed from the atomic to the infinite.

41. The *Yogi* whose *Vrittis* have thus become powerless (controlled) obtains in the receiver, (the instrument of) receiving, and the received (the Self, the mind, and external objects), concentratedness and sameness, like the crystal (before different coloured objects).

42. Sound, meaning, and resulting knowledge, being mixed up, is (called) *Samādhi* with-question.

43. *Samādhi* called 'without-question' (comes) when the memory is purified, or devoid of qualities, expressing only the meaning (of the meditated object).

44. By this process (the concentrations) with discrimination and without discrimination, whose objects are finer, are (also) explained.

45. The finer objects end with the *Pradhāna.*

46. These concentrations are with seed.

47. The concentration "without discrimination" being purified, the *Chitta* becomes firmly fixed.

48. The knowledge in that is called "filled with Truth."

49. The knowledge that is gained from testimony and inference is about common objects. That from the *Samādhi* just mentioned is of a much higher order, being able to penetrate where inference and testimony cannot go.

50. The resulting impression from this *Samādhi* obstructs all other impressions.

51. By the restraint of even this (impression, which obstructs all other impressions), all being restrained, comes the "seedless" *Samādhi.*

CHAPTER II: CONCENTRATION: ITS PRACTICE

The Pain-Bearing Obstructions

1. Mortification, study, and surrendering fruits of work to God are called *Kriyā-yoga.*

2. (It is for) the practice of *Samādhi* and minimising the pain-bearing obstructions.

3. The pain-bearing obstructions are—ignorance, egoism, attachment, aversion, and clinging to life.

4. Ignorance is the productive field of all these that follow, whether they are dormant, attenuated, overpowered, or expanded.

5. Ignorance is taking the non-eternal, the impure, the painful, and the non-Self, as the eternal, the pure, the happy, and the Atman or Self (respectively).

6. Egoism is the identification of the seer with the instrument of seeing.

7. Attachment is that which dwells on pleasure.

8. Aversion is that which dwells on pain.

9. Flowing through its own nature, and established even in the learned, is the clinging to life.

10. The fine *Samskāras*[1] are to be conquered by resolving them into their causal state.

11. By meditation, their (gross) modifications are to be rejected.

12. The 'receptacle of works'[2] has its root in these pain-bearing obstructions, and their experience is in this visible life, or in the unseen life.

13. The root being there, the fruition comes (in the form of) species, life, and experience of pleasure and pain.

14. They bear fruit as pleasure or pain, caused by virtue or vice.

15. To the discriminating, all is, as it were, painful on account of everything bringing pain, either as consequence, or as anticipation of loss of happiness or as fresh craving arising from impressions of happiness, and also as counter-action of qualities.

16. The misery which is not yet come is to be avoided.

The Independence of the Soul as Seer

17. The cause of that which is to be avoided is the junction of the seer and the seen.

18. The experienced is composed of elements and organs, is of the nature of illumination, action, and inertia, and is for the purpose of experience and release (of the experiencer).

19. The states of the qualities are the defined, the undefined, the indicated only, and the signless.

[1] *Samskāras* are the subtle impressions that manifest themselves into gross forms later on—original note.

[2] By the 'receptacle of works' is meant the sum total of *Samskāras*—original note.

20. The seer is intelligence only, and though pure, sees through the colouring of the intellect.

21. The nature of the experienced is for him.

22. Though destroyed for him whose goal has been gained, yet it is not destroyed, being common to others.

23. Junction is the cause of the realisation of the nature of both the powers, the experienced and its Lord.

24. Ignorance is its cause.

25. There being absence of that (ignorance) there is absence of junction, which is the thing-to-be-avoided; that is the independence of the seer.

26. The means of destruction of ignorance is unbroken practice of discrimination.

27. His knowledge is of the sevenfold highest ground.

The Eight Stages

28. By the practice of the different parts of *Yoga* the impurities being destroyed, knowledge becomes effulgent up to discrimination.

29. *Yama, Niyama, Asana, Prānāyāma, Pratyāhāra, Dhāranā, Dhyāna,* and *Samādhi,* are the eight limbs of *Yoga.*

1. FIVE VOWS (*Yama*)

30. Non-killing, truthfulness, non-stealing, continence, and non-receiving, are called *Yama.*

31. These, unbroken by time, place, purpose and caste-rules, are (universal) great vows.

2. FIVE OBSERVANCES (*Niyama*)

32. Internal and external purification, contentment, mortification, study, and worship of God, are the *Niyamas.*

33. To obstruct thoughts which are inimical to *Yoga,* contrary thoughts should be brought.

34. The obstructions to *Yoga* are killing, falsehood, etc., whether committed, caused, or approved; either through avarice, or anger or ignorance; whether slight, middling, or great; and result in infinite ignorance and misery. This is (the method of) thinking the contrary.

35. Non-killing being established, in his presence all enmities cease (in others).

36. By the establishment of truthfulness the *Yogi* gets the power of attaining for himself and others the fruits of work without the works.

37. By the establishment of non-stealing all wealth comes to the *Yogi*.

38. By the establishment of continence energy is gained.

39. When he is fixed in non-receiving he gets the memory of past life.

40. Internal and external cleanliness being established, arises disgust for one's own body, and non-intercourse with others.

41. There also arises purification of the *Sattva*,[1] cheerfulness of the mind, concentration, conquest of the organs, and fitness for the realisation of the Self.

42. From contentment comes superlative happiness.

43. The result of mortification is bringing powers to the organs and the body, by destroying the impurity.

44. By repetition of the *Mantra*[2] comes the realisation of the intended deity.

45. By sacrificing all to *Iswara*[3] comes *Samādhi*.

3. POSTURE: (*Asana*)

46. Posture is that which is firm and pleasant.

47. By lessening the natural tendency (for restlessness) and meditating on the unlimited (posture becomes firm and pleasant).

48. Seat being conquered, the dualities do not obstruct.

4. RESPIRATION (*Prānāyāma*)

49. Controlling the motion of the exhalation and the inhalation follows after this.

50. Its modifications are either external or internal, or motionless, regulated by place, time, and number, either long or short.

51. The fourth is restraining the *Prāna* by reflecting on external or internal objects.

52. From that, the covering to the light of the *Chitta* is attenuated.

53. The mind becomes fit for *Dhāranā*.

5. WITHDRAWING OF THE ORGANS (*Pratyāhāra*)

54. The drawing in of the organs is by their giving up their own objects and taking the form of the mind-stuff, as it were.

55. Thence arises supreme control of the organs.

[1] The good element; see note to I, 16.
[2] Prayer formula.
[3] The Lord (also *Isvara*).

CHAPTER III: POWERS

We have now come to the chapter in which the *Yoga* powers are described.

6. CONCENTRATION ON ONE OBJECT (*Dhāranā*)

1. *Dhāranā* is holding the mind on to some particular object.

7. MEDITATION (*Dhyāna*)

2. An unbroken flow of knowledge in that object is *Dhyāna*.

8. SUPERCONSCIOUSNESS (*Samādhi*)

3. When that, giving up all forms, reflects only the meaning, it is *Samādhi*.

Description of the Last Three Stages

4. (These) three (when practised) in regard to one object is *Samyama*.
5. By the conquest of that comes light of knowledge.
6. That should be employed in stages.
7. These three are more internal than those that precede.
8. But even they are external to the seedless *(Samādhi)*.
9. By the suppression of the disturbed impressions of the mind, and by the rise of impressions of control, the mind, which persists in that moment of control, is said to attain the controlling modifications.
10. Its flow becomes steady by habit.
11. Taking in all sorts of objects, and concentrating upon one object, these two powers being destroyed and manifested respectively, the *Chitta* gets the modification called *Samādhi*.
12. The one-pointedness of the *Chitta* is when the impression that is past and that which is present are similar.
13. By this is explained the threefold transformation of form, time and state, in fine or gross matter, and in the organs.
14. That which is acted upon by transformations, either past, present or yet to be manifested, is the qualified.
15. The succession of changes is the cause of manifold evolution.

The Transformation of Mental Powers

16. By making *Samyama* on the three sorts of changes comes the knowledge of past and future.

17. By making *Samyama* on word, meaning, and knowledge, which are ordinarily confused, comes the knowledge of all animal sounds.

18. By perceiving the impressions, (comes) the knowledge of past life.

19. By making *Samyama* on the signs in another's body, knowledge of his mind comes.

20. But not its contents, that not being the object of the *Samyama*.

21. By making *Samyama* on the form of the body, the perceptibility of the form being obstructed, and the power of manifestation in the eye being separated, the *Yogi's* body becomes unseen.

22. By this the disappearance or concealment of words which are being spoken and such other things, are also explained.

23. *Karma* is of two kinds, soon to be fructified, and late to be fructified. By making *Samyama* on these, or by the signs called *Arishta,* portents, the *Yogis* know the exact time of separation from their bodies.

24. By making *Samyama* on friendship, mercy, etc. (I:33), the *Yogi* excels in respective qualities.

25. By making *Samyama* on the strength of the elephant, and others, their respective strength comes to the *Yogi*.

26. By making *Samyama* on the effulgent light (I:36) comes the knowledge of the fine, the obstructed and the remote.

27. By making *Samyama* on the sun, (comes) the knowledge of the world.

28. On the moon, (comes) the knowledge of the cluster of stars.

29. On the pole-star, (comes) the knowledge of the motion of the stars.

30. On the navel circle, (comes) the knowledge of the constitution of the body.

31. On the hollow of the throat, (comes) cessation of hunger.

32. On the nerve called *Kurma* (comes) fixity of the body.

33. On the light emanating from the top of the head, sight of the *Siddhas*.[1]

34. Or by the power of *Prātibha*[2] all knowledge.

35. In the heart, knowledge of minds.

[1] The *Siddhas* are beings who are a little above ghosts. When the *Yogi* concentrates his mind on the top of his head he will see these *Siddhas*—original note.

[2] Spontaneous enlightenment from purity.

36. Enjoyment comes by the non-discrimination of the Soul and *Sattva* which are totally different. The latter whose actions are for another is separate from the self-centred one. *Samyama* on the self-centred one gives knowledge of the *Purusha*.

37. From that arises the knowledge belonging to *Prātibha* and (supernatural) hearing, touching, seeing, tasting, and smelling.

38. These are obstacles to *Samādhi:* but they are powers in the worldly state.

Supernatural Powers

39. When the cause of bondage of the *Chitta* has become loosened, the *Yogi,* by his knowledge of its channels of activity (the nerves), enters another's body.

40. By conquering the current called *Udāna*[1] the Yogi does not sink in water, or in swamps, he can walk on thorns, etc., and can die at will.

41. By the conquest of the current *Samāna* he is surrounded by a blaze of light.

42. By making *Samyama* on the relation between the ear and the *Akāsa*[2] comes divine hearing.

43. By making *Samyama* on the relation between the *Akāsa* and the body and becoming light as cotton wool, etc., through meditation on them, the *Yogi* goes through the skies.

44. By making *Samyama* on the 'real modifications' of the mind, outside of the body, called great disembodiedness, comes disappearance of the covering to light.

45. By making *Samyama* on the gross and fine forms of the elements, their essential traits, the inherence of the *Gunas*[3] in them and on their contributing to the experience of the soul, comes mastery of the elements.

46. From that comes minuteness, and the rest of the powers, 'glorification of the body,' and indestructibleness of the bodily qualities.

47. The 'glorification of the body' is beauty, complexion, strength, adamantine hardness.

48. By making *Samyama* on the objectivity and power of illumination of the organs, on egoism, the inherence of the *Gunas* in them and on their contributing to the experience of the soul, comes the conquest of the organs.

[1] The name of the nerve current that governs the lungs, and all the upper parts of the body.
[2] The ether.
[3] The three elements.

49. From that comes to the body the power of rapid movement like the mind, power of the organs independently of the body, and conquest of nature.

50. By making *Samyama* on the discrimination between *Sattva* and the *Purusha* come omnipotence and omniscience.

Isolation or Complete Freedom

51. By giving up even these powers comes the destruction of the very seed of evil, which leads to *Kaivalya.*[1]

52. The *Yogi* should not feel allured or flattered by the overtures of celestial beings, for fear of evil again.

53. By making *Samyama* on a particle of time and its precession and succession comes discrimination.

54. Those things which cannot be differentiated by species, sign and place, even they will be discriminated by the above *Samyama.*

55. The saving knowledge is that knowledge of discrimination which simultaneously covers all objects, in all their variations.

56. By the similarity of purity between the *Sattva* and the *Purusha* comes *Kaivalya.*

CHAPTER IV: INDEPENDENCE

Desires and Objects of the Mind

1. The *Siddhis* (powers) are attained by birth, chemical means, power of words, mortification or concentration.

2. The change into another species is by the filling in of nature.

3. Good and bad deeds are not the direct causes in the transformations of nature, but they act as breakers of obstacles to the evolutions of nature: as a farmer breaks the obstacles to the course of water, which then runs down by its own nature.

4. From egoism alone proceed the created minds.

5. Though the activities of the different created minds are various, the one original mind is the controller of them all.

6. Among the various *Chittas* that which is attained by *Samādhi* is desireless.

[1] Complete isolation or independence.

7. Works are neither black nor white for the *Yogis;* for others they are three-fold—black, white, and mixed.

8. From these threefold works are manifested in each state only those desires (which are) fitting to that state alone. (The others are held in abeyance for the time being.)

9. There is consecutiveness in desires, even though separated by species, space and time, there being identification of memory and impressions.

10. Thirst for happiness being eternal desires are without beginning.

11. Being held together by cause, effect, support, and objects, in the absence of these is its absence.

12. The past and future exist in their own nature, qualities having different ways.

13. They are manifested or fine, being of the nature of the *Gunas.*[1]

14. The unity in things is from the unity in changes.

15. Since perception and desire vary with regard to the same object, mind and object are of different nature.

16. Things are known or unknown to the mind, being dependent on the colouring which they give to the mind.

17. The states of the mind are always known because the lord of the mind, the *Purusha,* is unchangeable.

18. The mind is not self-luminous, being an object.

19. From its being unable to cognise both at the same time.

20. Another cognising mind being assumed there will be no end to such assumptions and confusion of memory will be the result.

21. The essence of knowledge (the *Purusha*) being unchangeable, when the mind takes its form, it becomes conscious.

22. Coloured by the seer and the seen the mind is able to understand everything.

23. The mind though variegated by innumerable desires acts for another (the *Purusha*), because it acts in combination.

Complete Isolation

24. For the discriminating the perception of the mind as Atman ceases.

[1] The *Gunas* are the three substances, *Sattva, Rajas,* and *Tamas,* whose gross state is the sensible universe. Past and future arise from the different modes of manifestation of these *Gunas*—original note.

25. Then bent on discriminating, the mind attains the previous state of *Kaivalya* (isolation).

26. The thoughts that arise as obstructions to that are from impressions.

27. Their destruction is in the same manner as of ignorance, egoism, etc., as said before (II:10).

28. Even when arriving at the right discriminating knowledge of the essences, he who gives up the fruits, unto him comes as the result of perfect discrimination, the *Samādhi* called the cloud of virtue.

29. From that comes cessation of pains and works.

30. Then knowledge, bereft of covering and impurities, becoming infinite, the knowable becomes small.

31. Then are finished the successive transformations of the qualities, they having attained the end.

32. The changes that exist in relation to moments, and which are perceived at the other end (at the end of a series) are succession.

33. The resolution in the inverse order of the qualities, bereft of any motive of action for the *Purusha,* is *Kaivalya,* or it is the establishment of the power of knowledge in its own nature.

INDIAN IMAGINATION

The Ramayana

INTRODUCTION

MY LOVE AND TRUE RESPECT for India were born when I first read the Indian epics, the *Ramayana* and the *Mahabharata* in the present translation in my college days. In these two masterpieces we are brought closer to the atmosphere, ideals and customs of ancient Hindu life than by a hundred volumes of commentary on the *Upanishads,* and through them Hindu ideals, as well as Hindu men and women, become real to us. And the fact that Hindu imagination produced such masterpieces of literature, closely rivalling Homer in antiquity and in beauty and power of portraying human passions, is a definite pledge of the worth and richness of the Hindu civilization.

It is more than a figure of speech to say that the *Mahabharata* must be compared, if compared at all, with Homer's *Iliad,* and the *Ramayana,* with the *Odyssey*. To take the *Mahabharata,* the subject of the epic was the same, dealing with a long-drawn-out war between the Kurus and the Panchalas, as Homer dealt with the Trojan War. The treatment was the same: the delineation of the character of the warriors, the "tiger-waisted" Bhima, the "helmet-wearing" Arjuna (the Achilles of the epic), the royal and dignified Yudhishthir (suggesting Agamemnon), the vengeance of Arjuna for the death of his boy, the fierce contests and rounds of combats between heroes of the opposing camps, the Homeric speeches before the combats, the Councils of War, and the presence of gods and celestial spirits all reproduce the epic impression. The Hindu epic abounds more in episodic developments and discourses (such as the long discourse between Yudhishthir and Bhishma on the art of government) and has a wider canvas, with descriptions of forest life and later interpolations of discussions on questions of spiritual truth (such as the *Bhagavad-Gita,* which is merely a reported conversa tion between the god Krishna and Arjuna before the battle, nov accepted as a separate book). In magnitude, the *Mahabharata* comprise 100,000 couplets, which is the result of successive accretions in the eas *sloka* verse-form, while the *Ramayana* comprises 24,000 couplets, anc is more the unified work of one writer. In so far as the *Ramayana* deal with the story of wanderings of Rama and his wife Sita, it may be saic to resemble the *Odyssey*. Beyond that, the resemblance ceases, for whil the story of Sita is that of the test of a woman's loyalty, like that o Penelope, the main theme is not that of Ulyssean adventures, but o domestic human passions, comprising such tragic material as is founc in *King Lear, Macbeth* and *Othello*. It is also extremely important tc note the tragic ending of Sita, where a happy ending would have been easy.

In modern terms, the *Mahabharata* may be said to be realistic, and the *Ramayana,* idealistic, in their respective handling of human characters. Sita in *Ramayana* is all that a woman could or should be, and is impressive by her sweetness and devotion. Draupadi in *Mahabharata,* on the other hand, may be any of the high-spirited modern women who live off one of New York's avenues, with her anger and her brooding for revenge—and for that reason more human. There is greater "realistic" truth in the full-blooded characters of the *Mahabharata,* higher passion and nobler resolve, fiercer jealousy and more biting scorn, and greater grandeur in many of its scenes. Yet it is undeniable there is greater spiritual beauty, greater softness and tenderness of emotion in *Ramayana*. The subject of *Mahbharata* is men and war; the subject of *Ramayana* is women and the home. If I judge human nature correctly, by the preference of fathers for daughters and mothers for sons, then it is inevitable that *Mahabharata* is the women's epic, while *Ramayana* is the men's. As it is impossible to include both epics, and highly desirable to reproduce one of them complete, therefore, as a man, I have chosen the *Ramayana*.

Truly, as the translator says, "The two together comprise the whole of the epic literature of the ancient Hindus; and the two together present us with the most graphic and lifelike picture that exists of the civilization and culture, the political and social life, the religion and thought of ancient India." And "to know the Indian epics is to understand the Indian people better." For it must be remembered, also, that these are not dead literature of long ago; they have influenced and molded

Indian life for thousands of years and are still a living factor today in the innermost depths of Indian consciousness.

Eventually, I am convinced India must win her freedom, not by fighting, because they will not resort to violence, and not by politics, for the English are superb at politics, but by Englishmen falling in love with Sita. Whether English stockholders will ever read Indian literature and poetry is doubtful, and it is not implied that the prospect is bright, for the great age of English appreciation of Hindu thought has declined. But anyone can see that one who loves Phidias would not like to bomb the Acropolis, and no one in his senses could believe that a people that could produce such epics ought to be ruled by others. It does not make sense.

Having said so much, I believe I am not in a position to improve upon an introduction to the *Ramayana,* which Romesh Dutt has so ably written in his "Epilogue." The following abstracts from the "Epilogue" will make the contents of this epic and its significance to the Indian people clear. The translation, reproduced here complete, is a condensation of the original. I have therefore kept the separate introductions to the different Books, which supply the outline of the epic story.

"It would appear that the original work ended with the sixth Book, which describes the return of the hero to his country and to his loving subjects. The seventh Book is called *Uttara* or Supplemental, and in it we are told something of the dimensions of the poem, apparently after the fatal process of additions and interpolations had gone on for centuries. We are informed that the poem consists of six Books and a Supplemental Book; and that it comprises 500 cantos and 24,000 couplets. And we are also told in this Supplemental Book that the descendants of Rama and his brothers founded some of the great towns and states which, we know from other sources, flourished in the fifth and fourth centuries before Christ. It is probable therefore that the Epic, commenced after 1000 B.C., had assumed something like its present shape a few centuries before the Christian Era.

"The *Mahabharata* grew out of the legends and traditions of a great historical war between the Kurus and the Panchalas; the *Ramayana* grew out of the recollections of the golden age of the Kosalas and the Videhas. The characters of the *Mahabharata* are characters of flesh and blood, with the virtues and crimes of great actors in the historic world; the characters of the *Ramayana* are more often the ideals of manly devotion to truth, and of womanly faithfulness and love in domestic life. . . . As an heroic poem the *Mahabharata* stands on a higher level; as a poem delineating the softer emotions of our everyday life the *Ramayana* sends its roots deeper into the hearts and minds of the millions in India. . . . Without rivalling the heroic grandeur of the *Mahabharata,* the *Ramayana* is immeasurably superior in its delineation of those softer and perhaps deeper emotions which enter into our everyday life and hold the world together. And these descriptions, essentially of Hindu life, are yet so true to nature that they apply to all races and nations.

"There is something indescribably touching and tender in the description of the love of Rama for his subjects and the loyalty of his people towards Rama,—that loyalty which has ever been a part of the Hindu character in every age—

'As a father to his children to his loving men he came,
Blessed our homes and maids and matrons till our infants lisped his name,

For our humble woes and troubles Rama hath the ready tear,
To our humble tales of suffering Rama lends his willing ear!'

"Deeper than this was Rama's duty towards his father and his father's fondness for Rama; and the portion of the Epic which narrates the dark scheme by which the prince was at last torn from the heart and home of his dying father is one of the most powerful and pathetic passages in Indian literature. The stepmother of Rama, won by the virtues and the kindliness of the prince, regards his proposed coronation with pride and pleasure, but her old nurse creeps into her confidence like a creeping serpent, and envenoms her heart with the poison of her own wickedness. She arouses the slumbering jealousy of a woman and awakens the alarms of a mother, till—

'Like a slow but deadly poison worked the ancient nurse's tears,
And a wife's undying impulse mingled with a mother's fears!'

"The nurse's dark insinuations work on the mind of the queen till she becomes a desperate woman, resolved to maintain her own influence on her husband, and to see her own son on the throne. The determination of the young queen tells with terrible effect on the weakness and vacillation of the feeble old monarch, and Rama is banished at last. And the scene closes with a pathetic story in which the monarch recounts his misdeed of past years, accepts his present suffering as the fruit of that misdeed, and dies in agony for his banished son. The inner workings of the human heart and of human motives, the dark intrigue of a scheming dependant, the awakening jealousy and alarm of a wife and a mother, the determination of a woman and an imperious queen, and the feebleness and despair and death of a fond old father and husband, have never been more vividly described. . . .

"It is truth and power in the depicting of such scenes, and not in the delineation of warriors and warlike incidents, that the *Ramayana* excels. It is in the delineation of domestic incidents, domestic affections, and domestic jealousies, which are appreciated by the prince and the peasant alike, that the *Ramayana* bases its appeal to the hearts of the millions in India. And beyond all this, the righteous devotion of Rama, and the faithfulness and womanly love of Sita, run like two threads of gold through the whole fabric of the Epic, and ennoble and sanctify the work in the eyes of Hindus.

"Sita holds a place in the hearts of women in India which no other creation of a poet's imagination holds among any other nation on earth. There is not a Hindu woman whose earliest and tenderest recollections do not cling round the story of Sita's sufferings and Sita's faithfulness, told in the nursery, taught in the family circle, remembered and cherished through life. Sita's adventures in a desolate forest and in a hostile prison only represent in an exaggerated form the humbler trials of a woman's life; and Sita's endurance and faithfulness teach her devotion to duty in all trials and troubles of life. 'For,' said Sita:

'For my mother often taught me and my father often spake,
That her home the wedded woman doth beside her husband make,
As the shadow to the substance, to her lord is faithful wife,
And she parts not from her consort till she parts with fleeting life!
Therefore bid me seek the jungle and in pathless forests roam,
Where the wild deer freely ranges and the tiger makes his home,
Happier than in father's mansions in the woods will Sita rove,
Waste no thought on home or kindred, nestling in her husband's love!'

"The ideal of life was joy and beauty and gladness in ancient Greece; the ideal of life was piety and endurance and devotion in ancient India. The tale of Helen was a tale of womanly beauty and loveliness which charmed the western world. The tale of Sita was a tale of womanly faith and self-abnegation which charmed and fascinated the Hindu world. Repeated trials bring out in brighter relief the unfaltering truth of Sita's character; she goes to a second banishment in the woods with the same trust and devotion to her lord as before, and she returns once more, and sinks into the bosom of her Mother Earth, true in death as she had been true in life. The creative imagination of the Hindus has conceived no loftier and holier character than Sita; the literature of the world has not produced a higher ideal of womanly love, womanly truth, and womanly devotion."

The Epic of Rama

Translated by Romesh Dutt

BOOK I SITA-SWAYAMVARA
(*The Bridal of Sita*)

THE EPIC relates to the ancient traditions of two powerful races, the Kosalas and the Videhas, who lived in Northern India between the twelfth and tenth centuries before Christ. The names Kosala and Videha in the singular number indicate the kingdoms—Oudh and North Behar—and in the plural number they mean the ancient races which inhabited those two countries.

According to the Epic, Dasa-ratha king of the Kosalas had four sons, the eldest of whom was Rama the hero of the poem. And Janak king of the Videhas had a daughter named Sita, who was miraculously born of a field furrow, and who is the heroine of the Epic.

Janak ordained a severe test for the hand of his daughter, and many a prince and warrior came and went away disappointed. Rama succeeded, and won Sita. The story of Rama's winning his bride, and of the marriage of his three brothers with the sister and cousins of Sita, forms the subject of this Book.

The portions translated in this Book form Section vi., Sections lxvii. to lxix., Section lxxiii., and Section lxxvii. of Book i. of the original text.

I *Ayodhya, the Righteous City*

Rich in royal worth and valour, rich in holy Vedic lore,
Dasa-ratha ruled his empire in the happy days of yore,

Loved of men in fair Ayodhya, sprung of ancient Solar Race,
Royal *rishi* in his duty, saintly *rishi*[1] in his grace,
Great as INDRA in his prowess, bounteous as KUVERA kind,
Dauntless deeds subdued his foemen, lofty faith subdued his mind!
Like the ancient monarch Manu, father of the human race,
Dasa-ratha ruled his people with a father's loving grace,
Truth and Justice swayed each action and each baser motive quelled
People's Love and Monarch's Duty every thought and deed impelled,
And his town like INDRA's city,—tower and dome and turret brave—
Rose in proud and peerless beauty on Sarayu's limpid wave!
Peaceful lived the righteous people, rich in wealth in merit high,
Envy dwelt not in their bosoms and their accents shaped no lie,
Fathers with their happy households owned their cattle, corn, and gold,
Galling penury and famine in Ayodhya had no hold,
Neighbours lived in mutual kindness helpful with their ample wealth,
None who begged the wasted refuse, none who lived by fraud and stealth!
And they wore the gem and earring, wreath and fragrant sandal paste,
And their arms were decked with bracelets, and their necks with *nishkas*[2] graced,
Cheat and braggart and deceiver lived not in the ancient town,
Proud despiser of the lowly wore not insults in their frown,
Poorer fed not on the richer, hireling friend upon the great,
None with low and lying accents did upon the proud man wait!
Men to plighted vows were faithful, faithful was each loving wife,
Impure thought and wandering fancy stained not holy wedded life,
Robed in gold and graceful garments, fair in form and fair in face,
Winsome were Ayodhya's daughters, rich in wit and woman's grace!
Twice-born men were free from passion, lust of gold and impure greed,
Faithful to their Rites and Scriptures, truthful in their word and deed,
Altar blazed in every mansion, from each home was bounty given,
Stooped no man to fulsome falsehood, questioned none the will of Heaven.
Kshatras bowed to holy Brahmans, Vaisyas to the Kshatras bowed
Toiling Sudras lived by labour, of their honest duty proud,
To the Gods and to the Fathers, to each guest in virtue trained,
Rites were done with true devotion as by holy writ ordained.

[1] Saint or anchorite.
[2] Coins often used for ornament.

Pure each caste in due observance, stainless was each ancient rite,
And the nation thrived and prospered by its old and matchless might,
And each man in truth abiding lived a long and peaceful life,
With his sons and with his grandsons, with his loved and honoured wife.
Thus was ruled the ancient city by her monarch true and bold,
As the earth was ruled by Manu in the misty days of old,
Troops who never turned in battle, fierce as fire and strong and brave,
Guarded well her lofty ramparts as the lions guard the cave.
Steeds like INDRA's in their swiftness came from far Kamboja's land,
From Vanaya and Vahlika and from Sindhu's rock-bound strand,
Elephants of mighty stature from the Vindhya mountains came,
Or from deep and darksome forests round Himalay's peaks of fame,
Matchless in their mighty prowess, peerless in their wondrous speed,
Nobler than the noble tuskers sprung from high celestial breed.
Thus Ayodhya, "virgin city,"—faithful to her haughty name,—
Ruled by righteous Dasa-ratha won a world-embracing fame,
Strong-barred gates and lofty arches, tower and dome and turret high
Decked the vast and peopled city fair as mansions of the sky.
Queens of proud and peerless beauty born of houses rich in fame,
Loved of royal Dasa-ratha to his happy mansion came,
Queen Kausalya blessed with virtue true and righteous Rama bore
Queen Kaikeyi young and beauteous bore him Bharat rich in lore,
Queen Simitra bore the bright twins, Lakshman and Satrughna bold,
Four brave princes served their father in the happy days of old!

II Mithila, and the Breaking of the Bow

Janak monarch of Videha spake his message near and far,—
He shall win my peerless Sita who shall bend my bow of war,—
Suitors came from farthest regions, warlike princes known to fame,
Vainly strove to wield the weapon, left Videha in their shame.
Viswa-mitra royal *rishi,* Rama true and Lakshman bold,
Came to fair Mithila's city from Ayodhya famed of old,
Spake in pride the royal *rishi:* "Monarch of Videha's throne,
Grant, the wondrous bow of RUDRA be to princely Rama shown."
Janak spake his royal mandate to his lords and warriors bold:
'Bring ye forth the bow of RUDRA decked in garlands and in gold,"
And his peers and proud retainers waiting on the monarch's call,
Brought the great and goodly weapon from the city's inner hall.

Stalwart men of ample stature pulled the mighty iron car
In which rested all-inviolate Janak's dreaded bow of war,
And where midst assembled monarchs sat Videha's godlike king,
With a mighty toil and effort did the eight-wheeled chariot bring.
"This the weapon of Videha," proudly thus the peers begun,
"Be it shewn to royal Rama, Dasa-ratha's righteous son."
"This the bow," then spake the monarch to the *risha* famed of old,
To the true and righteous Rama and to Lakshman young and bold,
"This the weapon of my fathers prized by kings from age to age,
Mighty chiefs and sturdy warriors could not bend it, noble sage!
Gods before the bow of RUDRA have in righteous terror quailed,
Rakshas[1] fierce and stout *Asuras*[2] have in futile effort failed,
Mortal man will struggle vainly RUDRA's wondrous bow to bend,
Vainly strive to string the weapon and the shining dart to send,
Holy saint and royal *rishi,* here is Janak's ancient bow,
Shew it to Ayodhya's princes, speak to them my kingly vow!"
Viswa-mitra humbly listened to the words the monarch said,
To the brave and righteous Rama, Janak's mighty bow displayed,
Rama lifted high the cover of the pond'rous iron car,
Gazed with conscious pride and prowess on the mighty bow of war.
"Let me," humbly spake the hero, "on this bow my fingers place,
Let me lift and bend the weapon, help me with your loving grace."
"Be it so," the *rishi* answered, "be it so," the monarch said,
Rama lifted high the weapon on his stalwart arms displayed,
Wond'ring gazed the kings assembled as the son of Raghu's race
Proudly raised the bow of RUDRA with a warrior's stately grace,
Proudly strung the bow of RUDRA which the kings had tried in vain,
Drew the cord with force resistless till the weapon snapped in twain!
Like the thunder's pealing accent rose the loud terrific clang,
And the firm earth shook and trembled and the hills in echoes rang,
And the chiefs and gathered monarchs fell and fainted in their fear,
And the men of many nations shook the dreadful sound to hear!
Pale and white the startled monarchs slowly from their terror woke,
And with royal grace and greetings Janak to the *rishi* spoke:
"Now my ancient eyes have witnessed wond'rous deed by Rama done,
Deed surpassing thought or fancy wrought by Dasa-ratha's son,
And the proud and peerless princess, Sita glory of my house,
Sheds on me an added lustre as she weds a godlike spouse,

[1] Night demons. [2] Evil spirits.

True shall be my plighted promise, Sita dearer than my life,
Won by worth and wond'rous valour shall be Rama's faithful wife!
Grant us leave, O royal *rishi,* grant us blessings kind and fair,
Envoys mounted on my chariot to Ayodhya shall repair,
They shall speak to Rama's father glorious feat by Rama done,
They shall speak to Dasa-ratha, Sita is by valour won,
They shall say the noble princes safely live within our walls,
They shall ask him by his presence to adorn our palace halls!"
Pleased at heart the sage assented, envoys by the monarch sent,
To Ayodhya's distant city with the royal message went.

III The Embassy to Ayodhya

Three nights halting in their journey with their steeds fatigued and spent,
Envoys from Mithila's monarch to Ayodhya's city went,
And by royal mandate bidden stepped within the palace hall,
Where the ancient Dasa-ratha sat with peers and courtiers all,
And with greetings and obeisance spake their message calm and bold,
Softly fell their gentle accents as their happy tale they told.
"Greetings to thee, mighty monarch, greetings to each priest and peer,
Wishes for thy health and safety from Videha's king we bear,
Janak monarch of Videha for thy happy life hath prayed,
And by Viswa-mitra's bidding words of gladsome message said:
'Know on earth my plighted promise, spoke by heralds near and far,—
He shall win my peerless Sita who shall bend my bow of war,—
Monarchs came and princely suitors, chiefs and warriors known to fame,
Baffled in their fruitless effort left Mithila in their shame,
Rama came with gallant Lakshman by their proud preceptor led,
Bent and broke the mighty weapon, he the beauteous bride shall wed!
Rama strained the weapon stoutly till it snapped and broke in twain,
In the concourse of the monarchs, in the throng of armèd men,
Rama wins the peerless princess by the righteous will of Heaven,
I redeem my plighted promise—be thy kind permission given!
Monarch of Kosala's country! with each lord and peer and priest,
Welcome to Mithila's city, welcome to Videha's feast,
Joy thee in thy Rama's triumph, joy thee with a father's pride,
Let each prince of proud Kosala win a fair Videha-bride!'

These by Viswa-mitra's bidding are the words our monarch said,
This by Sata-nanda's counsel is the quest that he hath made."
Joyful was Kosala's monarch, spake to chieftains in the hall,
Vama-deva and Vasishtha and to priests and Brahmans all:
"Priests and peers! in far Mithila, so these friendly envoys tell,
Righteous Rama, gallant Lakshman, in the royal palace dwell,
And our brother of Videha prizes Rama's warlike pride,
To each prince of proud Kosala yields a fair Videha-bride,
If it please ye, priests and chieftains, speed we to Mithila fair,
World-renowned is Janak's virtue, Heaven-inspired his learning rare!
Spake each peer and holy Brahman: "Dasa-ratha's will be done!"
Spake the king unto the envoys: "Part we with the rising sun!"
Honoured with a regal honour, welcomed to a rich repast,
Gifted envoys from Mithila day and night in gladness passed!

IV Meeting of Janak and Dasa-ratha

On Ayodhya's tower and turret now the golden morning woke,
Dasa-ratha girt by courtiers thus to wise Sumantra spoke:
"Bid the keepers of my treasure with their waggons lead the way,
Ride in front with royal riches, gold and gems in bright array,
Bid my warriors skilled in duty lead the four-fold ranks of war,
Elephants and noble chargers, serried foot and battle-car,
Bid my faithful chariot-driver harness quick each car of state,
With the fleetest of my coursers, and upon my orders wait.
Vama-deva and Vasishtha versed in *Veda's* ancient lore,
Kasyapa and good Jabali sprung from holy saints of yore,
Markandeya in his glory, Katyayana in his pride,
Let each priest and proud preceptor with Kosala's monarch ride,
Harness to my royal chariot strong and stately steeds of war,
For the envoys speed my journey and the way is long and far."
With each priest and proud retainer Dasa-ratha led the way,
Glittering ranks of forces followed in their four-fold dread array,
Four days on the way they journeyed till they reached Videha's land,
Janak with a courteous welcome came to greet the royal band.
Joyously Videha's monarch greeted every priest and peer,
Greeted ancient Dasa-ratha in his accents soft and clear:
"Hast thou come, my royal brother, on my house to yield thy grace,
Hast thou made a peaceful journey, pride of Raghu's royal race?

Welcome! for Mithila's people seek my royal guest to greet,
Welcome! for thy sons of valour long their loving sire to meet,
Welcome to the priest Vasishtha versed in *Veda's* ancient lore,
Welcome every righteous *rishi* sprung from holy saints of yore!
And my evil fates are vanquished and my race is sanctified,
With the warlike race of Raghu thus in loving bonds allied,
Sacrifice and rites auspicious we ordain with rising sun,
Ere the evening's darkness closes, happy nuptials shall be done!"
Thus in kind and courteous accents Janak spake his purpose high,
And his royal love responding, Dasa-ratha made reply:
"Gift betokens giver's bounty,—so our ancient sages sing,—
And thy righteous fame and virtue grace thy gift, Videha's king!
World-renowned is Janak's bounty, Heaven-inspired his holy grace,
And we take his boon and blessing as an honour to our race!"
Royal grace and kingly greeting marked the ancient monarch's word
Janak with a grateful pleasure Dasa-ratha's answer heard,
And the Brahmans and preceptors joyously the midnight spent,
And in converse pure and pleasant and in sacred sweet content.
Righteous Rama, gallant Lakshman piously their father greet,
Duly make their deep obeisance, humbly touch his royal feet,
And the night is filled with gladness for the king revered and old,
Honoured by the saintly Janak, greeted by his children bold,
On Mithila's tower and turret stars their silent vigils keep,
When each sacred rite completed, Janak seeks his nightly sleep.

V *The Preparation*

All his four heroic princes now with Dasa-ratha stayed
In Mithila's ancient city, and their father's will obeyed,
Thither came the bold Yudhajit prince of proud Kaikeya's line,
On the day that Dasa-ratha made his gifts of gold and kine,
And he met the ancient monarch, for his health and safety prayed,
Made his bow and due obeisance and in gentle accents said:
"List, O king! my royal father, monarch of Kaikeya's race,
Sends his kindly love and greetings with his blessings and his grace,
And he asks if Dasa-ratha prospers in his wonted health,
If his friends and fond relations live in happiness and wealth.
Queen Kaikeyi is my sister, and to see her son I came,
Bharat prince of peerless virtue, worthy of his father's fame,

Aye, to see that youth of valour, by my royal father sent,
To Ayodhya's ancient city with an anxious heart I went,
In the city of Mithila,—thus did all thy subjects say,—
With his sons and with his kinsmen Dasa-ratha makes his stay,
Hence in haste I journeyed hither, travelling late and early dawn,
For to do thee due obeisance and to greet my sister's son!"
Spake the young and proud Kaikeya, dear and duly-greeted guest,
Dasa-ratha on his brother choicest gifts and honours pressed.
Brightly dawned the happy morning, and Kosala's king of fame
With his sons and wise Vasishtha to the sacred *yajna* [1] came,
Rama and his gallant brothers decked in gem and jewel bright,
In th' auspicious hour of morning did the blest *Kautuka* [2] rite,
And beside their royal father piously the princes stood,
And to fair Videha's monarch spake Vasishtha wise and good:
"Dasa-ratha waits expectant with each proud and princely son,
Waits upon the bounteous giver, for each holy rite is done,
'Twixt the giver and the taker sacred word is sacred deed,
Seal with gift thy plighted promise, let the nuptial rites proceed!"
Thus the righteous-souled Vasishtha to Videha's monarch prayed,
Janak versed in holy *Vedas* thus in courteous accents said:
"Wherefore waits the king expectant? Free to him this royal dome,
Since my kingdom is his empire and my palace is his home,
And the maidens, flame-resplendent, done each fond *Kautuka* rite,
Beaming in their bridal beauty tread the sacrificial site!
I beside the lighted altar wait upon thy sacred hest,
And auspicious is the moment, sage Vasishtha knows the rest,
Let the peerless Dasa-ratha, proud Kosala's king of might,
With his sons and honoured sages enter on the holy site,
Let the righteous sage Vasishtha, sprung from Vedic saints of old,
Celebrate the happy wedding; be the sacred *mantras* [3] told!"

VI The Wedding

Sage Vasishtha skilled in duty placed Videha's honoured king,
Viswa-mitra, Sata-nanda, all within the sacred ring,

[1] Sacrifice.
[2] Wedding investiture with the nuptial chord.
[3] Hymns or incantations.

And he raised the holy altar as the ancient writs ordain,
Decked and graced with scented garlands grateful unto gods and men,
And he set the golden ladles, vases pierced by artists skilled,
Holy censers fresh and fragrant, cups with sacred honey filled,
Sanka bowls and shining salvers, *arghya*[1] plates for honoured guest,
Parchéd rice arranged in dishes, corn unhusked that filled the rest,
And with careful hand Vasishtha grass around the altar flung,
Offered gift to lighted AGNI and the sacred *mantra* sung!
Softly came the sweet-eyed Sita,—bridal blush upon her brow,—
Rama in his manly beauty came to take the sacred vow,
Janak placed his beauteous daughter facing Dasa-ratha's son,
Spake with father's fond emotion and the holy rite was done:
"This is Sita child of Janak, dearer unto him than life,
Henceforth sharer of thy virtue, be she, prince, thy faithful wife,
Of thy weal and woe partaker, be she thine in every land,
Cherish her in joy and sorrow, clasp her hand within thy hand,
As the shadow to the substance, to her lord is faithful wife,
And my Sita best of women follows thee in death or life!"
Tears bedew his ancient bosom, gods and men his wishes share,
And he sprinkles holy water on the blest and wedded pair.
Next he turned to Sita's sister, Urmila of beauty rare,
And to Lakshman young and valiant spake in accents soft and fair:
"Lakshman, dauntless in thy duty, loved of men and Gods above,
Take my dear devoted daughter, Urmila of stainless love,
Lakshman, fearless in thy virtue, take thy true and faithful wife,
Clasp her hand within thy fingers, be she thine in death or life!"
To his brother's child Mandavi, Janak turned with father's love,
Yielded her to righteous Bharat, prayed for blessings from above:
"Bharat, take the fair Mandavi, be she thine in death or life,
Clasp her hand within thy fingers as thy true and faithful wife!"
Last of all was Sruta-kriti, fair in form and fair in face,
And her gentle name was honoured for her acts of righteous grace,
"Take her by the hand, Satrughna, be she thine in death or life,
As the shadow to the substance, to her lord is faithful wife!"
Then the princes held the maidens, hand embraced in loving hand,
And Vasishtha spake the *mantra,* holiest priest in all the land,
And as ancient rite ordaineth, and as sacred laws require,
Stepped each bride and princely bridegroom round the altar's lighted fire,

[1] Offering to an honored guest.

Round Videha's ancient monarch, round the holy *rishis* all,
Lightly stepped the gentle maidens, proudly stepped the princes tall!
And a rain of flowers descended from the sky serene and fair,
And a soft celestial music filled the fresh and fragrant air,
Bright *Gandharvas* skilled in music waked the sweet celestial song,
Fair *Apsaras*[1] in their beauty on the greensward tripped along!
As the flowery rain descended and the music rose in pride,
Thrice around the lighted altar every bridegroom led his bride,
And the nuptial rites were ended, princes took their brides away,
Janak followed with his courtiers, and the town was proud and gay!

VII Return to Ayodhya

With his wedded sons and daughters and his guard in bright array,
To the famed and fair Ayodhya, Dasa-ratha held his way,
And they reached the ancient city decked with banners bright and brave,
And the voice of drum and trumpet hailed the home-returning brave.
Fragrant blossoms strewed the pathway, song of welcome filled the air,
Joyous men and merry women issued forth in garments fair,
And they lifted up their faces and they waved their hands on high,
And they raised the voice of welcome as their righteous king drew nigh.
Greeted by his loving subjects, welcomed by his priests of fame,
Dasa-ratha with the princes to his happy city came,
With the brides and stately princes in the town he held his way,
Entered slow his lofty palace bright as peak of Himalay.
Queen Kausalya blessed with virtue, Queen Kaikeyi in her pride,
Queen Sumitra sweetly loving, greeted every happy bride,
Soft-eyed Sita noble-destined, Urmila of spotless fame,
Mandavi and Sruta-kirti to their loving mothers came.
Decked in silk and queenly garments they performed each pious rite,
Brought their blessings on the household, bowed to Gods of holy might,
Bowed to all the honoured elders, blest the children with their love,
And with soft and sweet endearment by their loving consorts moved.
Happy were the wedded princes peerless in their warlike might,
And they dwelt in stately mansions like KUVERA's mansions bright.
Loving wife and troops of kinsmen, wealth and glory on them wait,
Filial love and fond affection sanctify their happy fate.

[1] Celestial nymphs.

Once when on the palace chambers bright the golden morning woke,
To his son the gentle Bharat, thus the ancient monarch spoke:
"Know, my son, the prince Kaikeya, Yudajit of warlike fame,
Queen Kaikeyi's honoured brother, from his distant regions came,
He hath come to take thee, Bharat, to Kaikeya's monarch bold,
Go and stay with them a season, greet thy grandsire loved of old."
Bharat heard with filial duty and he hastened to obey,
Took with him the young Satrughna in his grandsire's home to stay,
And from Rama and from Lakshman parted they with many a tear,
From their young and gentle consorts, from their parents ever dear,
And Kaikeya with the princes, with his guards and troopers gay,
To his father's western regions gladsome held his onward way.
Rama with a pious duty,—favoured by the Gods above,—
Tended still his ancient father with a never-faltering love,
In his father's sacred mandate still his noblest Duty saw,
In the weal of subject nations recognised his foremost Law!
And he pleased his happy mother with a fond and filial care,
And his elders and his kinsmen with devotion soft and fair,
Brahmans blessed the righteous Rama for his faith in gods above,
People in the town and hamlet blessed him with their loyal love!
With a woman's whole affection fond and trusting Sita loved,
And within her faithful bosom loving Rama lived and moved,
And he loved her, for their parents chose her as his faithful wife,
Loved her for her peerless beauty, for her true and trustful life,
Loved and dwelt within her bosom though he wore a form apart,
Rama in a sweet communion lived in Sita's loving heart!
Days of joy and months of gladness o'er the gentle Sita flew,
As she like the QUEEN OF BEAUTY brighter in her graces grew,
And as VISHNU with his consort dwells in skies, alone, apart,
Rama in a sweet communion lived in Sita's loving heart!

BOOK II VANA-GAMANA-ADESA
(*The Banishment*)

THE EVENTS NARRATED in this Book occupy scarcely two days. The description of Rama's princely virtues and the rejoicings at his proposed coronation, with which the Book begins, contrast with much dramatic force and effect with the dark intrigues which follow, and which end in his cruel banishment for fourteen years.

The portions translated in this Book form Sections i., ii., vi., and vii., portions of Sections x. to xiii., and the whole of Section xviii. of Book ii. of the original text.

I The Council Convened

Thus the young and brave Satrughna, Bharat ever true and bold,
Went to warlike western regions where Kaikeyas lived of old,
Where the ancient Aswa-pati ruled his kingdom broad and fair,
Hailed the sons of Dasa-ratha with a grandsire's loving care.
Tended with a fond affection, guarded with a gentle sway,
Still the princes of their father dreamt and thought by night and day,
And their father in Ayodhya, great of heart and stout of hand,
Thought of Bharat and Satrughna living in Kaikeya's land.
For his great and gallant princes were to him his life and light,
Were a part of Dasa-ratha like his hands and arms of might,
But of all his righteous children righteous Rama won his heart,
As SWAYAMBHU of all creatures, was his dearest, holiest part,
For his Rama strong and stately was his eldest and his best,
Void of every baser passion and with every virtue blest!
Soft in speech, sedate and peaceful, seeking still the holy path,
Calm in conscious worth and valour, taunt nor cavil waked his wrath,
In the field of war excelling, boldest warrior midst the bold,
In the palace chambers musing on the tales by elders told,
Faithful to the wise and learned, truthful in his deed and word,
Rama dearly loved his people and his people loved their lord!
To the Brahmans pure and holy Rama due obeisance made,
To the poor and to the helpless deeper love and honour paid,
Spirit of his race and nation was to high-souled Rama given,
Thoughts that widen human glory, deeds that ope the gates of heaven.
Not intent on idle cavil Rama spake with purpose high,
And the God of speech might envy when he spake or made reply,
In the learning of the *Vedas* highest meed and glory won,
In the skill of arms the father scarcely matched the gallant son!
Taught by sages and by elders in the manners of his race,
Rama grew in social virtues and each soft endearing grace,
Taught by inborn pride and wisdom patient purpose to conceal,
Deep determined was his effort, dauntless was his silent will!

Peerless in his skill and valour steed and elephant to tame,
Dauntless leader of his forces, matchless in his warlike fame,
Higher thought and nobler duty did the righteous Rama move,
By his toil and by his virtues still he sought his people's love!
Dasa-ratha marked his Rama with each kingly virtue blest,
And from lifelong royal duties now he sought repose and rest:
"Shall I see my son anointed, seated on Kosala's throne,
In the evening of my lifetime ere my days on earth be done,
Shall I place my ancient empire in the youthful Rama's care,
Seek for me a higher duty and prepare for life more fair?"
Pondering thus within his bosom counsel from his courtiers sought,
And to crown his Rama, Regent, was his purpose and his thought,
For strange signs and diverse tokens now appeared on earth and sky,
And his failing strength and vigour spoke his end approaching nigh,
And he witnessed Rama's virtues filling all the world with love,
As the full-moon's radiant lustre fills the earth from skies above!
Dear to him appeared his purpose, Rama to his people dear,
Private wish and public duty made his path serene and clear,
Dasa-ratha called his Council, summoned chiefs from town and plain,
Welcomed too from distant regions monarchs and the kings of men,
Mansions meet for prince and chieftain to his guests the monarch gave.
Gracious as the Lord of Creatures held the gathering rich and brave!
Nathless to Kosala's Council nor Videha's monarch came,
Nor the warlike chief Kaikeya, Aswa-pati king of fame,
To those kings and near relations, ancient Dasa-ratha meant,
Message of the proud anointment with his greetings would be sent.
Brightly dawned the day of gathering; in the lofty Council Hall
Stately chiefs and ancient burghers came and mustered one and all,
And each prince and peer was seated on his cushion rich and high,
And on monarch Dasa-ratha eager turned his anxious eye,
Girt by crownéd kings and chieftains, burghers from the town and plain,
Dasa-ratha shone like INDRA girt by heaven's immortal train!

II The People Consulted

With the voice of pealing thunder Dasa-ratha spake to all,
To the princes and the burghers gathered in Ayodhya's hall:
"Known to all, the race of Raghu rules this empire broad and fair,
And hath ever loved and cherished subjects with a father's care,

In my fathers' footstops treading I have sought the ancient path,
Nursed my people as my children, free from passion, pride and wrath,
Underneath this white umbrella, seated on this royal throne,
I have toiled to win their welfare and my task is almost done!
Years have passed of fruitful labour, years of work by fortune blest,
And the evening of my lifetime needs, my friends, the evening's rest,
Years have passed in watchful effort, Law and Duty to uphold,
Effort needing strength and prowess—and my feeble limbs are old!
Peers and burghers, let your monarch, now his lifelong labour done,
For the weal of loving subjects on his empire seat his son,
INDRA-like in peerless valour, *rishi*-like in holy lore,
Rama follows Dasa-ratha, but in virtues stands before!
Throned in Pushya's constellation shines the moon with fuller light,
Throned to rule his father's empire Rama wins a loftier might,
He will be your gracious monarch favoured well by FORTUNE'S QUEEN,
By his virtue and his valour lord of earth he might have been!
Speak your thoughts and from this bosom lift a load of toil and care,
On the proud throne of my fathers let me place a peerless heir,
Speak your thought, my chiefs and people, if this purpose please you well,
Or if wiser, better counsel in your wisdom ye can tell,
Speak your thoughts without compulsion, though this plan to me be dear,
If some middle course were wiser, if some other way were clear!"
Gathered chieftains hailed the mandate with applauses long and loud,
As the peafowls hail the thunder of the dark and laden cloud,
And the gathered subjects echoed loud and long the welcome sound,
Till the voices of the people shook the sky and solid ground!
Brahmans versed in laws of duty, chieftains in their warlike pride,
Countless men from town and hamlet heard the mandate far and wide,
And they met in consultation, joyously with one accord,
Freely and in measured accents, gave their answer to their lord:
"Years of toil and watchful labour weigh upon thee, king of men,
Young in years is righteous Rama, Heir and Regent let him reign,
We would see the princely Rama, Heir and Regent duly made,
Riding on the royal tusker in the white umbrella's shade!"
Searching still their secret purpose, seeking still their thought to know,
Spake again the ancient monarch in his measured words and slow:
"I would know your inner feelings, loyal thoughts and whispers kind,
For a doubt within me lingers and a shadow clouds my mind,

True to Law and true to Duty while I rule this kingdom fair,
Wherefore would you see my Rama seated as the Regent Heir?"
"We would see him Heir and Regent, Dasa-ratha, ancient lord,
For his heart is blessed with valour, virtue marks his deed and word,
Lives not man in all the wide earth who excels the stainless youth,
In his loyalty to Duty, in his love of righteous Truth,
Truth impels his thought and action, Truth inspires his soul with grace,
And his virtue fills the wide earth and exalts his ancient race!
Bright Immortals know his valour; with his brother Lakshman bold
He hath never failed to conquer hostile town or castled hold,
And returning from his battles, from the duties of the war,
Riding on his royal tusker or his all-resistless car,
As a father to his children to his loving men he came,
Blessed our homes and maids and matrons till our infants lisped his name,
For our humble woes and troubles Rama hath the ready tear,
To our humble tales of suffering Rama lends his willing ear!
Happy is the royal father who hath such a righteous son,
For in town and mart and hamlet every heart hath Rama won,
Burghers and the toiling tillers tales of Rama's kindness say,
Man and infant, maid and matron, morn and eve for Rama pray,
To the Gods and bright Immortals we our inmost wishes send,
May the good and godlike Rama on his father's throne ascend,
Great in gifts and great in glory, Rama doth our homage own,
We would see the princely Rama seated on his father's throne!"

III The City Decorated

With his consort pious Rama, pure in deed and pure in thought,
After evening's due ablutions NARAYANA's chamber sought,
Prayed unto the Lord of Creatures, NARAYANA Ancient Sire,
Placed his offering on his forehead, poured it on the lighted fire,
Piously partook the remnant, sought for NARAYANA's aid,
As he kept his fast and vigils on the grass of *kusa*[1] spread.
With her lord the saintly Sita silent passed the sacred night,
Contemplating World's Preserver, Lord of Heaven's ethereal height,
And within the sacred chamber on the grass of *kusa* lay,
Till the crimson streaks of morning ushered in the festive day,

[1] Grass strewn round the altar at sacrifice.

Till the royal bards and minstrels chanted forth the morning call,
Pealing through the holy chamber, echoing through the royal hall.
Past the night of sacred vigils, in his silken robes arrayed,
Message of the proud anointment Rama to the Brahmans said,
And the Brahmans spake to burghers that the festive day was come,
Till the mart and crowded pathway rang with note of pipe and drum,
And the townsmen heard rejoicing of the vigils of the night,
Kept by Rama and by Sita for the day's auspicious rite.
Rama shall be Heir and Regent, Rama shall be crowned to-day,—
Rapid flew the gladdening message with the morning's gladsome ray,
And the people of the city, maid and matron, man and boy,
Decorated fair Ayodhya in their wild tumultuous joy!
On the temple's lofty steeple high as cloud above the air,
On the crossing of the pathways, in the garden green and fair,
On the merchant's ample warehouse, on the shop with stores displayed,
On the mansion of the noble by the cunning artist made,
On the gay and bright pavilion, on the high and shady trees,
Banners rose and glittering streamers, flags that fluttered in the breeze!
Actors gay and nimble dancers, singers skilled in lightsome song,
With their antics and their music pleased the gay and gathered throng,
And the people met in conclaves, spake of Rama, Regent Heir,
And the children by the roadside lisped of Rama brave and fair!
Women wove the scented garland, merry maids the censer lit,
Men with broom and sprinkled water swept the spacious mart and street,
Rows of trees and posts they planted hung with lamps for coming night,
That the midnight dark might rival splendour of the noonday light!
Troops of men and merry children laboured with a loving care,
Woman's skill and woman's fancy made the city passing fair,
So that good and kindly Rama might his people's toil approve,
So that sweet and soft-eyed Sita might accept her people's love!
Groups of joyous townsmen gathered in the square or lofty hall,
Praised the monarch Dasa-ratha, regent Rama young and tall:
"Great and good is Dasa-ratha born of Raghu's royal race,
In the fulness of his lifetime on his son he grants his grace,
And we hail the rite auspicious for our prince of peerless might,
He will guard us by his valour, he will save our cherished right,
Dear unto his loving brothers in his father's palace hall,
As is Rama to his brothers dear is Rama to us all,

Long live ancient Dasa-ratha king of Raghu's royal race,
We shall see his son anointed by his father's righteous grace!"
Thus of Rama's consecration spake the burghers one and all,
And the men from distant hamlets poured within the city wall,
From the confines of the empire, north and south and west and east,
Came to see the consecration and to share the royal feast!
And the rolling tide of nations raised their voices loud and high,
Like the tide of sounding ocean when the full moon lights the sky,
And Ayodhya thronged by people from the hamlet, mart and lea,
Was tumultuous like the ocean thronged by creatures of the sea!

IV Intrigue

In the inner palace chamber stood the proud and peerless queen,
With a mother's joy Kaikeyi gaily watched the festive scene,
But with deep and deadly hatred Manthara, her nurse and maid,
Marked the city bright with banners, and in scornful accents said:
"Take thy presents back, Kaikeyi, for they ill befit the day,
And when clouds of sorrow darken, ill beseems thee to be gay,
And thy folly moves my laughter though an anguish wakes my sigh,
For a gladness stirs thy bosom when thy greatest woe is nigh!
Who that hath a woman's wisdom, who that is a prudent wife,
Smiles in joy when prouder rival triumphs in the race of life,
How can hapless Queen Kaikeyi greet this deed of darkness done,
When the favoured Queen Kausalya wins the empire for her son?
Know the truth, O witless woman! Bharat is unmatched in fame,
Rama, deep and darkly jealous, dreads thy Bharat's rival claim,
Younger Lakshman with devotion doth on eldest Rama wait,
Young Satrughna with affection follows Bharat's lofty fate,
Rama dreads no rising danger from the twins, the youngest-born,
But thy Bharat's claims and virtues fill his jealous heart with scorn!
Trust me, queen, thy Bharat's merits are too well and widely known,
And he stands too near and closely by a rival brother's throne,
Rama hath a wolf-like wisdom and a fang to reach the foe,
And I tremble for thy Bharat, Heaven avert untimely woe!
Happy is the Queen Kausalya, they will soon anoint her son,
When on Pushya's constellation gaily rides to-morrow's moon,
Happy is the Queen Kausalya in her regal pomp and state,
And Kaikeyi like a bond-slave must upon her rival wait!

Wilt thou do her due obeisance as we humble women do,
Will thy proud and princely Bharat as his brother's henchman go,
Will thy Bharat's gentle consort, fairest princess in this land,
In her tears and in her anguish wait on Sita's proud command?"
With a woman's scornful anger Manthara proclaimed her grief,
With a mother's love for Rama thus Kaikeyi answered brief:
"What inspires thee, wicked woman, thus to rail in bitter tone,
Shall not Rama, best and eldest, fill his father's royal throne,
What alarms thee, crooked woman, in the happy rites begun,
Shall not Rama guard his brothers as a father guards his son?
And when Rama's reign is over, shall not Gods my Bharat speed,
And by law and ancient custom shall not younger son succeed,
In the present bliss of Rama and in Bharat's future hope,
What offends thee, senseless woman, wherefore dost thou idly mope?
Dear is Rama as my Bharat, ever duteous in his ways,
Rama honours Queen Kausalya, loftier honour to me pays,
Rama's realm is Bharat's kingdom, ruling partners they shall prove,
For himself than for his brothers Rama owns no deeper love!"
Scorn and anger shook her person and her bosom heaved a sigh,
As in wilder, fiercer accents Manthara thus made reply:
"What insensate rage or madness clouds thy heart and blinds thine eye,
Courting thus thy own disaster, courting danger dread and high,
What dark folly clouds thy vision to the workings of thy foe,
Heedless thus to seek destruction and to sink in gulf of woe?
Know, fair queen, by law and custom, son ascends the throne of pride,
Rama's son succeedeth Rama, luckless Bharat steps aside,
Brothers do not share a kingdom, nor can one by one succeed,
Mighty were the civil discord if such custom were decreed!
For to stop all war and tumult, thus the ancient laws ordain,
Eldest son succeeds his father, younger children may not reign,
Bharat barred from Rama's empire, vainly decked with royal grace,
Friendless, joyless, long shall wander, alien from his land and race!
Thou hast borne the princely Bharat, nursed him from thy gentle breast,
To a queen and to a mother need a prince's claims be pressed,
To a thoughtless heedless mother must I Bharat's virtues plead,
Must the Queen Kaikeyi witness Queen Kausalya's son succeed?
Trust thy old and faithful woman who hath nursed thee, youthful queen,
And in great and princely houses many darksome deeds hath seen,

Trust my word, the wily Rama for his spacious empire's good,
Soon will banish friendless Bharat and secure his peace with blood!
Thou hast sent the righteous Bharat to thy ancient father's land,
And Satrughna young and valiant doth beside his brother stand,
Young in years and generous-hearted, they will grow in mutual love,
As the love of elder Rama doth in Lakshman's bosom move.
Young companions grow in friendship, and our ancient legends tell,
Weeds protect a forest monarch which the woodman's axe would fell,
Crownéd Rama unto Lakshman will a loving brother prove,
But for Bharat and Satrughna, Rama's bosom owns no love,
And a danger thus ariseth if the elder wins the throne,
Haste thee, heedless Queen Kaikeyi, save the younger and thy son!
Speak thy mandate to thy husband, let thy Bharat rule at home,
In the deep and pathless jungle let the banished Rama roam,
This will please thy ancient father and thy father's kith and kin,
This will please the righteous people, Bharat knows no guile or sin!
Speak thy mandate to thy husband, win thy son a happy fate,
Doom him not to Rama's service or his unrelenting hate,
Let not Rama in his rancour shed a younger brother's blood,
As the lion slays the tiger in the deep and echoing wood!
With the magic of thy beauty thou hast won thy monarch's heart,
Queen Kausalya's bosom rankles with a woman's secret smart,
Let her not with woman's vengeance turn upon her prouder foe,
And as crownéd Rama's mother venge her in Kaikeyi's woe,
Mark my word, my child Kaikeyi, much these ancient eyes have seen,
Rama's rule is death to Bharat, insult to my honoured queen!"
Like a slow but deadly poison worked the ancient nurse's tears,
And a wife's undying impulse mingled with a mother's fears,
Deep within Kaikeyi's bosom worked a woman's jealous thought,
Speechless in her scorn and anger mourner's dark retreat she sought.

V The Queen's Demand

Rama shall be crowned at sunrise, so did royal bards proclaim,
Every rite arranged and ordered, Dasa-ratha homeward came,
To the fairest of his consorts, dearest to his ancient heart,
Came the king with eager gladness joyful message to impart,
Radiant as the Lord of Midnight, ere the eclipse casts its gloom,
Came the old and ardent monarch heedless of his darksome doom!

Through the shady palace garden where the peacock wandered free,
Lute and lyre poured forth their music, parrot flew from tree to tree,
Through the corridor of creepers, painted rooms by artists done,
And the halls where scented *Champak*[1] and the flaming *Asok*[2] shone,
Through the portico of splendour graced by silver, tusk and gold,
Radiant with his thought of gladness walked the monarch proud and bold.
Through the lines of scented blossoms which by limpid waters shone,
And the rooms with seats of silver, ivory bench and golden throne,
Through the chamber of confection, where each viand wooed the taste,
Every object in profusion as in regions of the blest,
Through Kaikeyi's inner closet lighted with a softened sheen,
Walked the king with eager longing,—but Kaikeyi was not seen!
Thoughts of love and gentle dalliance woke within his ancient heart,
And the magic of her beauty and the glamour of her art,
With a soft desire the monarch vainly searched the vanished fair,
Found her not in royal chamber, found her not in gay parterre!
Filled with love and longing languor loitered not the radiant queen,
In her soft voluptuous chamber, in the garden, grove or green.
And he asked the faithful warder of Kaikeyi loved and lost,
She who served him with devotion and his wishes never crost,
Spake the warder in his terror that the queen with rage distraught,
Weeping silent tears of anguish had the mourner's chamber sought!
Thither flew the stricken monarch; on the bare and unswept ground,
Trembling with tumultuous passion was the Queen Kaikeyi found,
On the cold uncovered pavement sorrowing lay the weeping wife,
Young wife of an ancient husband, dearer than his heart and life!
Like a bright and blossoming creeper rudely severed from the earth,
Like a fallen fair *Apsara,*[3] beauteous nymph of heavenly birth,
Like a female forest-ranger bleeding from the hunter's dart,
Whom her mate the forest-monarch soothes with soft endearing art,
Lay the queen in tears of anguish! And with sweet and gentle word
To the lotus-eyéd lady softly spake her loving lord:
"Wherefore thus, my Queen and Empress, sorrow-laden is thy heart,
Who with daring slight or insult seeks to cause thy bosom smart?

[1] A tree with yellow blossoms; its blossom.
[2] Name of a bright flower.
[3] Celestial nymph.

If some unknown ailment pains thee, evil spirit of the air,
Skilled physicians wait upon thee, priests with incantations fair,
If from human foe some insult, wipe thy tears and doom his fate,
Rich reward or royal vengeance shall upon thy mandate wait!
Wilt thou doom to death the guiltless, free whom direst sins debase,
Wilt thou lift the poor and lowly or the proud and great disgrace,
Speak, and I and all my courtiers Queen Kaikeyi's hest obey,
For thy might is boundless, Empress, limitless thy regal sway!
Rolls my chariot-wheel revolving from the sea to farthest sea,
And the wide earth is my empire, monarchs list my proud decree,
Nations of the eastern regions and of Sindhu's western wave,
Brave Saurashtras and the races who the ocean's dangers brave,
Vangas, Angas and Magadhas, warlike Matsyas of the west,
Kasis and the southern races, brave Kosalas first and best,
Nations of my world-wide empire, rich in corn and sheep and kine,
All shall serve my Queen Kaikeyi and their treasures all are thine,
Speak, command thy king's obedience, and thy wrath will melt away,
Like the melting snow of winter 'neath the sun's reviving ray!"
Blinded was the ancient husband as he lifted up her head,
Heedless oath and word he plighted that her wish should be obeyed,
Scheming for a fatal purpose, inly then Kaikeyi smiled,
And by sacred oath and promise bound the monarch love-beguiled:
"Thou hast given, Dasa-ratha, troth and word and royal oath,
Three and thirty Gods be witness, watchers of the righteous truth,
Sun and Moon and Stars be witness, Sky and Day and sable Night,
Rolling Worlds and this our wide Earth, and each dark and unseen wight,
Witness Rangers of the forest, Household Gods that guard us both,
Mortal beings and Immortal,—witness ye the monarch's oath,
Ever faithful to his promise, ever truthful in his word,
Dasa-ratha grants my prayer, Spirits and the Gods have heard!
Call to mind, O righteous monarch, days when in a bygone strife,
Warring with thy foes immortal thou hadst almost lost thy life,
With a woman's loving tendance poor Kaikeyi cured thy wound,
Till from death and danger rescued, thou wert by a promise bound,
Two rewards my husband offered, what my loving heart might seek,
Long delayed their wished fulfilment,—now let poor Kaikeyi speak,
And if royal deeds redeem not what thy royal lips did say,
Victim to thy broken promise Queen Kaikeyi dies to-day!

By these rites ordained for Rama,—such the news my menials bring,—
Let my Bharat, and not Rama, be anointed Regent King,
Wearing skins and matted tresses, in the cave or hermit's cell,
Fourteen years in Dandak's forests let the elder Rama dwell,
These are Queen Kaikeyi's wishes, these are boons for which I pray,
I would see my son anointed, Rama banished on this day!"

VI The King's Lament

"Is this torturing dream or madness, do my feeble senses fail,
O'er my darkened mind and bosom doth a fainting fit prevail?"
So the stricken monarch pondered and in hushed and silent fear,
Looked on her as on a tigress looks the dazed and stricken deer,
Lying on the unswept pavement still he heaved the choking sigh,
Like a wild and hissing serpent quelled by incantations high!
Sobs convulsive shook his bosom and his speech and accent failed,
And a dark and deathlike faintness o'er his feeble soul prevailed,
Stunned awhile remained the monarch, then in furious passion woke,
And his eyeballs flamed with redfire, to the queen as thus he spoke:
"Traitress to thy king and husband, fell destroyer of thy race,
Wherefore seeks thy ruthless rancour Rama rich in righteous grace,
Traitress to thy kith and kindred, Rama loves thee as thy own,
Wherefore then with causeless vengeance as a mother hate thy son?
Have I courted thee, Kaikeyi, throned thee in my heart of truth,
Nursed thee in my home and bosom like a snake of poisoned tooth,
Have I courted thee, Kaikeyi, placed thee on Ayodhya's throne,
That my Rama, loved of people, thou shouldst banish from his own?
Banish far my Queen Kausalya, Queen Sumitra saintly wife,
Wrench from me my ancient empire, from my bosom wrench my life,
But with brave and princely Rama never can his father part,
Till his ancient life is ended, cold and still his beating heart!
Sunless roll the world in darkness, rainless may the harvests thrive,
But from righteous Rama severed, never can his sire survive,
Feeble is thy aged husband, few and brief on earth his day,
Lend me, wife, a woman's kindness, as a consort be my stay!
Ask for other boon, Kaikeyi, aught my sea-girt empire yields,
Wealth or treasure, gem or jewel, castled town or smiling fields,
Ask for other gift, Kaikeyi, and thy wishes shall be given,
Stain me not with crime unholy in the eye of righteous Heaven!"

Coldly spake the Queen Kaikeyi: "If thy royal heart repent,
Break thy word and plighted promise, let thy royal faith be rent,
Ever known for truth and virtue, speak to peers and monarchs all,
When from near and distant regions they shall gather in thy hall,
Speak if so it please thee, monarch, of thy evil-destined wife,
How she loved with wife's devotion, how she served and saved thy life,
How on plighted promise trusting for a humble boon she sighed,
How a monarch broke his promise, how a cheated woman died!"
"Fair thy form," resumed the monarch, "beauty dwells upon thy face,
Woman's winsome charms bedeck thee, and a woman's peerless grace,
Wherefore then within thy bosom wakes this thought of cruel wile,
And what dark and loathsome spirit stains thy heart with blackest guile?
Ever since the day, Kaikeyi, when a gentle bride you came,
By a wife's unfailing duty you have won a woman's fame,
Wherefore now this cruel purpose hath a stainless heart defiled,
Ruthless wish to send my Rama to the dark and pathless wild?
Wherefore, darkly-scheming woman, on unrighteous purpose bent,
Doth thy cruel causeless vengeance on my Rama seek a vent,
Wherefore seek by deeds unholy for thy son the throne to win,
Throne which Bharat doth not covet,—blackened by his mother's sin?
Shall I see my banished Rama mantled in the garb of woe,
Reft of home and kin and empire to the pathless jungle go,
Shall I see disasters sweeping o'er my empire dark and deep,
As the forces of a foeman o'er a scattered army sweep?
Shall I hear assembled monarchs in their whispered voices say,
Weak and foolish in his dotage, Dasa-ratha holds his sway,
Shall I say to righteous elders when they blame my action done,
That by woman's mandate driven I have banished thus my son?
Queen Kausalya, dear-loved woman! she who serves me as a slave,
Soothes me like a tender sister, helps me like a consort brave,
As a fond and loving mother tends me with a watchful care,
As a daughter ever duteous doth obeisance sweet and fair,
When my fond and fair Kausalya asks me of her banished son,
How shall Dasa-ratha answer for the impious action done,
How can husband, cold and cruel, break a wife's confiding heart,
How can father, false and faithless, from his best and eldest part?"
Coldly spake the Queen Kaikeyi: "If thy royal heart repent,
Break thy word and plighted promise, let thy royal faith be rent,

Truth-abiding is our monarch, so I heard the people say,
And his word is all inviolate, stainless virtue marks his sway,
Let it now be known to nations,—righteous Dasa-ratha lied,
And a trusting, cheated woman broke her loving heart and died!"
Darker grew the shades of midnight, coldly shone each distant star,
Wilder in the monarch's bosom raged the struggle and the war:
"Starry midnight, robed in shadows! give my wearied heart relief,
Spread thy sable covering mantle o'er an impious monarch's grief,
Spread thy vast and inky darkness o'er a deed of nameless crime,
Reign perennial o'er my sorrows heedless of the lapse of time,
May a sinful monarch perish ere the dawning of the day,
O'er a dark life sin-polluted, beam not morning's righteous ray!"

VII The Sentence

Morning came and duteous Rama to the palace bent his way,
For to make his salutation and his due obeisance pay,
And he saw his aged father shorn of kingly pomp and pride,
And he saw the Queen Kaikeyi sitting by her consort's side.
Duteously the righteous Rama touched the ancient monarch's feet,
Touched the feet of Queen Kaikeyi with a son's obeisance meet,
"Rama!" cried the feeble monarch, but the tear bedimmed his eye,
Sorrow choked his failing utterance and his bosom heaved a sigh,
Rama started in his terror at his father's grief or wrath,
Like a traveller in the jungle crossed by serpent in his path!
Reft of sense appeared the monarch, crushed beneath a load of pain,
Heaving oft a sigh of sorrow as his heart would break in twain,
Like the ocean tempest-shaken, like the sun in eclipse pale,
Like a crushed repenting *rishi* when his truth and virtue fail!
Breathless mused the anxious Rama,—what foul action hath he done,
What strange anger fills his father, wherefore greets he not his son?
"Speak, my mother," uttered Rama, "what strange error on my part,
Unremembered sin or folly fills with grief my father's heart,
Gracious unto me is father with a father's boundless grace,
Wherefore clouds his altered visage, wherefore tears bedew his face?
Doth a piercing painful ailment rack his limbs with cruel smart,
Doth some secret silent anguish wring his torn and tortured heart,
Bharat lives with brave Satrughna in thy father's realms afar,
Hath some cloud of dark disaster crossed their bright auspicious star?

Duteously the royal consorts on the loving monarch wait,
Hath some woe or dire misfortune dimmed the lustre of their fate,
I would yield my life and fortune ere I wound my father's heart,
Hath my unknown crime or folly caused his ancient bosom smart?
Ever dear is Queen Kaikeyi to her consort and her king,
Hath some angry accent escaped thee thus his royal heart to wring,
Speak, my ever-loving mother, speak the truth, for thou must know,
What distress or deep disaster pains his heart and clouds his brow?"
Mother's love nor woman's pity moved the deep-determined queen,
As in cold and cruel accents thus she spake her purpose keen:
'Grief nor woe nor sudden ailment pains thy father loved of old,
But he fears to speak his purpose to his Rama true and bold,
And his loving accents falter some unloving wish to tell,
Till you give your princely promise, you will serve his mandate well!
Listen more, in bygone seasons,—Rama thou wert then unborn,—
I had saved thy royal father, he a gracious boon had sworn,
But his feeble heart repenting is by pride and passion stirred,
He would break his royal promise as a caitiff breaks his word,
Years have passed and now the monarch would his ancient word forego,
He would build a needless causeway when the waters ceased to flow!
Truth inspires each deed attempted and each word by monarchs spoke,
Not for thee, though loved and honoured, should a royal vow be broke,
If the true and righteous Rama binds him by his father's vow,
I will tell thee of the anguish which obscures his royal brow,
If thy feeble bosom falter and thy halting purpose fail,
Unredeemed is royal promise and unspoken is my tale!"
"Speak thy word," exclaimed the hero, "and my purpose shall not fail,
Rama serves his father's mandate and his bosom shall not quail,
Poisoned cup or death untimely,—what the cruel fates decree,—
To his king and to his father Rama yields obedience free,
Speak my father's royal promise, hold me by his promise tied,
Rama speaks and shall not falter, for his lips have never lied."
Cold and clear Kaikeyi's accents fell as falls the hunter's knife,
"Listen then to word of promise and redeem it with thy life,
Wounded erst by foes immortal, saved by Queen Kaikeyi's care,
Two great boons your father plighted and his royal words were fair,
I have sought their due fulfilment,—brightly shines my Bharat's star,
Bharat shall be Heir and Regent, Rama shall be banished far!

If thy father's royal mandate thou wouldst list and honour still,
Fourteen years in Dandak's forest live and wander at thy will,
Seven long years and seven, my Rama, thou shalt in the jungle dwell,
Bark of trees shall be thy raiment and thy home the hermit's cell,
Over fair Kosala's empire let my princely Bharat reign,
With his cars and steeds and tuskers, wealth and gold and armèd men!
Tender-hearted is the monarch, age and sorrow dim his eye,
And the anguish of a father checks his speech and purpose high,
For the love he bears thee, Rama, cruel vow he may not speak,
I have spoke his will and mandate, and thy true obedience seek."
Calmly Rama heard the mandate, grief nor anger touched his heart,
Calmly from his father's empire and his home prepared to part.

BOOK III DASA-RATHA-VIYOGA

(*The Death of the King*)

THE FIRST SIX DAYS of Rama's wanderings are narrated in this Book. Sita and the faithful Lakshman accompanied Rama in his exile, and the loyal people of Ayodhya followed their exiled prince as far as the banks of the Tamasa river, where they halted on the first night. Rama had to steal away at night to escape the citizens, and his wanderings during the following days give us beautiful glimpses of forest life in holy hermitages. Thirty centuries have passed since the age of the Kosalas and Videhas, but every step of the supposed journey of Rama is well known in India to this day, and is annually traversed by thousands of devoted pilgrims. The past is not dead and buried in India, it lives in the hearts of millions of faithful men and faithful women, and shall live for ever.

On the third day of their exile, Rama and his wife and brother crossed the Ganges; on the fourth day they came to the hermitage of Bharad-vaja, which stood where Allahabad now stands, on the confluence of the Ganges and the Jumna; on the fifth day they crossed the Jumna, the southern shores of which were then covered with woods; and on the sixth day they came to the hill of Chitrakuta, where they met the saint Valmiki, the reputed author of this Epic. "We have often looked," says a writer in *Calcutta Review,* vol. xxii, "on that green hill: it is the holiest spot of that sect of the Hindu faith who devote themselves to this incarnation of Vishnu. The whole neighbourhood is Rama's country. Every headland has some legend, every cavern is connected with his name, ome of the wild fruits are still called Sita-phal, being the reputed food of the exile. Thousands and thousands annually visit the spot, and round he hill is raised a footpath on which the devotee, with naked feet, treads ull of pious awe."

Grief for the banished Rama pressed on the ancient heart of Dasa-ratha. The feeble old king pined away and died, remembering and re-counting on his death-bed how in his youth he had caused sorrow and death to an old hermit by killing his son. Scarcely any passage in the Epic is more touching than this old sad story told by the dying monarch.

The portions translated in this Book form the whole or the main portions of Sections xxvi., xxvii., xxxi., xxxix., xl., xlvi., lii., liv., lv., lvi., lxiii., and lxiv. of Book ii. of the original text.

I *Woman's Love*

'Dearly loved, devoted Sita! daughter of a royal line,
Part we now, for years of wand'ring in the pathless woods is mine,
For my father, promise-fettered, to Kaikeyi yields the sway,
And she wills her son anointed,—fourteen years doth Rama stray,
But before I leave thee, Sita, in the wilderness to rove,
Yield me one more tender token of thy true and trustful love!
Serve my crownéd brother, Sita, as a faithful, duteous dame,
Tell him not of Rama's virtues, tell him not of Rama's claim,
Since my royal father willeth,—Bharat shall be regent-heir,
Serve him with a loyal duty, serve him with obeisance fair,
Since my royal father willeth,—years of banishment be mine,
Brave in sorrow and in suffering, woman's brightest fame be thine!
Keep thy fasts and vigils, Sita, while thy Rama is away,
Faith in Gods and faith in virtue on thy bosom hold their sway,
In the early watch of morning to the Gods for blessings pray,
To my father Dasa-ratha honour and obeisance pay,
To my mother, Queen Kausalya, is thy dearest tendance due,
Offer her thy consolation, be a daughter fond and true!
Queen Kaikeyi and Sumitra equal love and honour claim,
With a soothing soft endearment sweetly serve each royal dame,
Cherish Bharat and Satrughna with a sister's watchful love,
And a mother's true affection and a mother's kindness prove!
Listen, Sita, unto Bharat speak no heedless angry word,
He is monarch of Kosala and of Raghu's race is lord,

Crownéd kings our willing service and our faithful duty own,
Dearest sons they disinherit, cherish strangers near the throne!
Bharat's will with deep devotion and with faultless faith obey,
Truth and virtue on thy bosom ever hold their gentle sway,
And to please each dear relation, gentle Sita, be it thine,
Part we love! for years of wand'ring in the pathless woods is mine!"
Rama spake, and soft-eyed Sita, ever sweet in speech and word,
Stirred by loving woman's passion boldly answered thus her lord:
"Do I hear my husband rightly, are these words my Rama spake,
And her banished lord and husband will the wedded wife forsake?
Lightly I dismiss the counsel which my lord hath lightly said,
For it ill beseems a warrior and my husband's princely grade!
For the faithful woman follows where her wedded lord may lead,
In the banishment of Rama, Sita's exile is decreed,
Sire nor son nor loving brother rules the wedded woman's state,
With her lord she falls or rises, with her consort courts her fate,
If the righteous son of Raghu wends to forests dark and drear,
Sita steps before her husband wild and thorny paths to clear!
Like the tasted refuse water cast thy timid thoughts aside,
Take me to the pathless jungle, bid me by my lord abide,
Car and steed and gilded palace, vain are these to woman's life,
Dearer is her husband's shadow to the loved and loving wife!
For my mother often taught me and my father often spake,
That her home the wedded woman doth beside her husband make,
As the shadow to the substance, to her lord is faithful wife,
And she parts not from her consort till she parts with fleeting life!
Therefore bid me seek the jungle and in pathless forests roam,
Where the wild deer freely ranges and the tiger makes his home,
Happier than in father's mansions in the woods will Sita rove,
Waste no thought on home or kindred, nestling in her husband's love!
World-renowned is Rama's valour, fearless by her Rama's side,
Sita will still live and wander with a faithful woman's pride,
And the wild fruit she will gather from the fresh and fragrant wood,
And the food by Rama tasted shall be Sita's cherished food!
Bid me seek the sylvan greenwoods, wooded hills and plateaus high,
Limpid rills and crystal *nullas*[1] as they softly ripple by,
And where in the lake of lotus tuneful ducks their plumage lave,
Let me with my loving Rama skim the cool translucent wave!

[1] Rivulets.

Years will pass in happy union,—happiest lot to woman given,—
Sita seeks not throne or empire, nor the brighter joys of heaven,
Heaven conceals not brighter mansions in its sunny fields of pride,
Where without her lord and husband faithful Sita would reside!
Therefore let me seek the jungle where the jungle-rangers rove,
Dearer than the royal palace, where I share my husband's love,
And my heart in sweet communion shall my Rama's wishes share,
And my wifely toil shall lighten Rama's load of woe and care!"
Vainly gentle Rama pleaded dangers of the jungle life,
Vainly spake of toil and trial to a true and tender wife!

II Brother's Faithfulness

Tears bedewed the face of Lakshman as he heard what Sita said,
And he touched the feet of Rama and in gentle accents prayed:
"If my elder and his lady to the pathless forests wend,
Armed with bow and ample quiver Lakshman will on them attend,
Where the wild deer range the forest and the lordly tuskers roam,
And the bird of gorgeous plumage nestles in its jungle home,
Dearer far to me those woodlands where my elder Rama dwells,
Than the homes of bright Immortals where perennial bliss prevails!
Grant me then thy sweet permission,—faithful to thy glorious star,
Lakshman shall not wait and tarry when his Rama wanders far,
Grant me then thy loving mandate,—Lakshman hath no wish to stay,
None shall bar the faithful younger when the elder leads the way!"
"Ever true to deeds of virtue, duteous brother, faithful friend,
Dearer than his life to Rama, thou shall not to forests wend,
Who shall stay by Queen Kausalya, Lakshman, if we both depart,
Who shall stay by Queen Sumitra, she who nursed thee on her heart?
For the king our aged father, he who ruled the earth and main,
Is a captive to Kaikeyi, fettered by her silken chain,
Little help Kaikeyi renders to our mothers in her pride,
Little help can Bharat offer, standing by his mother's side.
Thou alone can'st serve Kausalya when for distant woods I part,
When the memory of my exile rankles in her sorrowing heart,
Thou alone can'st serve Sumitra, soothe her sorrows with thy love,
Stay by them, my faithful Lakshman, and thy filial virtues prove,
Be this then they sacred duty, tend our mothers in their woe,
Little joy or consolation have they left on earth below!"

Spake the hero: "Fear no evil, well is Rama's prowess known,
And to mighty Rama's mother Bharat will obeisance own,
Nathless if the pride of empire sways him from the righteous path,
Blood will venge the offered insult and will quench our filial wrath!
But a thousand peopled hamlets Queen Kausalya's hests obey,
And a thousand armèd champions own her high and queenly sway,
Aye, a thousand village-centres Queen Sumitra's state maintain,
And a thousand swords like Lakshman's guard her proud and prosperous reign!
All alone with gentle Sita thou shalt track thy darksome way,
Grant it, that thy faithful Lakshman shall protect her night and day,
Grant it, with his bow and quiver Lakshman shall the forests roam,
And his axe shall fell the jungle, and his hands shall rear the home!
Grant it, in the deepest woodlands he shall seek the forest fruit,
Berries dear to holy hermits and the sweet and luscious root,
And when with thy meek-eyed Sita thou shalt seek the mountain crest,
Grant it, Lakshman ever duteous watch and guard thy nightly rest!"
Words of brother's deep devotion Rama heard with grateful heart,
And with Sita and with Lakshman for the woods prepared to part:
"Part we then from loving kinsmen, arms and mighty weapons bring,
Bows of war which Lord Varuna rendered to Videha's king,
Coats of mail to sword impervious, quivers which can never fail,
And the rapiers bright as sunshine, golden-hilted, tempered well,
Safely rest these goodly weapons in our great preceptor's hall,
Seek and bring them, faithful brother, for me thinks we need them all!"
Rama spake; his valiant brother then the wondrous weapons brought,
Wreathed with fresh and fragrant garlands and with gold and jewels wrought,
"Welcome, brother," uttered Rama, "stronger thus to woods we go,
Wealth and gold and useless treasure to the holy priests bestow,
To the son of saint Vasishtha, to each sage is honour due,
Then we leave our father's mansions, to our father's mandate true!"

III Mother's Blessings

Tears of sorrow and of suffering flowed from Queen Kausalya's eye,
As she saw departing Sita for her blessings drawing nigh,
And she clasped the gentle Sita and she kissed her moistened head,
And her tears like summer tempest choked the loving words she said:

"Part we, dear devoted daughter, to thy husband ever true,
With a woman's whole affection render love to husband's due!
False are women loved and cherished, gentle in their speech and word,
When misfortune's shadows gather, who are faithless to their lord,
Who through years of sunny splendour smile and pass the livelong day,
When misfortune's darkness thickens, from their husband turn away,
Who with changeful fortune changing oft ignore the plighted word,
And forget a woman's duty, woman's faith to wedded lord,
Who to holy love inconstant from their wedded consort part,
Manly deed nor manly virtue wins the changeful woman's heart!
But the true and righteous woman, loving spouse and changeless wife,
Faithful to her lord and consort holds him dearer than her life,
Ever true and righteous Sita, follow still my godlike son,
Like a God to thee is Rama in the woods or on the throne!"
"I shall do my duty, mother," said the wife with wifely pride,
"Like a God to me is Rama, Sita shall not leave his side,
From the Moon will part his lustre ere I part from wedded lord,
Ere from faithful wife's devotion falter in my deed or word,
For the stringless lute is silent, idle is the wheel-less car,
And no wife the loveless consort, inauspicious is her star!
Small the measure of affection which the sire and brother prove,
Measureless to wedded woman is her lord and husband's love,
True to Law and true to Scriptures, true to woman's plighted word,
Can I ever be, my mother, faithless, loveless to my lord?"
Tears of joy and mingled sorrow filled the Queen Kausalya's eye,
As she marked the faithful Sita true in heart, in virtue high,
And she wept the tears of sadness when with sweet obeisance due,
Spake with hands in meekness folded Rama ever good and true:
"Sorrow not, my loving mother, trust in virtue's changeless beam,
Swift will fly the years of exile like a brief and transient dream,
Girt by faithful friends and forces, blest by righteous Gods above,
Thou shalt see thy son returning to thy bosom and thy love!"
Unto all the royal ladies Rama his obeisance paid,
For his failings unremembered, blessings and forgiveness prayed,
And his words were soft and gentle, and they wept to see him go,
Like the piercing cry of curlew rose the piercing voice of woe,
And in halls where drum and tabor rose in joy and regal pride,
Voice of grief and lamentation sounded far and sounded wide!

Then the true and faithful Lakshman parted from each weeping dame,
And to sorrowing Queen Sumitra with his due obeisance came,
And he bowed to Queen Sumitra and his mother kissed his head,
Stilled her anguish-laden bosom and in trembling accents said:
"Dear devoted duteous Lakshman, ever to thy elder true,
When thy elder wends to forest, forest-life to thee is due,
Thou hast served him true and faithful in his glory and his fame,
This is Law for true and righteous,—serve him in his woe and shame,
This is Law for race of Raghu known on earth for holy might,
Bounteous in their sacred duty, brave and warlike in the fight!
Therefore tend him as thy father, as thy mother tend his wife,
And to thee, like fair Ayodhya be thy humble forest life,
Go, my son, the voice of Duty bids my gallant Lakshman go,
Serve thy elder with devotion and with valour meet thy foe!

IV Citizens' Lament

Spake Sumantra chariot-driver waiting by the royal car,
"Haste thee, mighty-destined Rama, for we wander long and far,
Fourteen years in Dandak's forest shall the righteous Rama stray,
Such is Dasa-ratha's mandate, haste thee Rama and obey."
Queenly Sita bright-apparelled, with a strong and trusting heart,
Mounted on the car of splendour for the pathless woods to part,
And the king for needs providing gave her robes and precious store,
For the many years of exile in a far and unknown shore,
And a wealth of warlike weapons to the exiled princes gave,
Bow and dart and linkéd armour, sword and shield and lances brave.
Then the gallant brothers mounted on the gold-emblazoned car,
For unending was the journey and the wilderness was far,
Skilled Sumantra saw them seated, urged the swiftly-flying steed,
Faster than the speed of tempest was the noble coursers' speed.
And they parted for the forest; like a long unending night,
Gloomy shades of grief and sadness deepened on the city's might,
Mute and dumb but conscious creatures felt the woe the city bore,
Horses neighed and shook their bright bells, elephants returned a roar!
Man and boy and maid and matron followed Rama with their eye,
As the thirsty seek the water when the parchéd fields are dry,
Clinging to the rapid chariot, by its side, before, behind,
Thronging men and wailing women wept for Rama good and kind:

"Draw the reins, benign Sumantra, slowly drive the royal car,
We would once more see our Rama, banished long and banished far,
Iron-hearted is Kausalya from her Rama thus to part,
Rends it not her mother's bosom thus to see her son depart?
True is righteous-hearted Sita cleaving to her husband still,
As the ever present sunlight cleaves to Meru's golden hill,
Faithful and heroic Lakshman! thou hast by thy brother stood,
And in duty still unchanging thou hast sought the pathless wood,
Fixed in purpose, true in valour, mighty boon to thee is given,
And the narrow path thou choosest is the righteous path to heaven!"
Thus they spake in tears and anguish as they followed him apace,
And their eyes were fixed on Rama, pride of Raghu's royal race,
Meanwhile ancient Dasa-ratha from his palace chamber came,
With each weeping queen and consort, with each woe-distracted dame!
And around the aged monarch rose the piercing voice of pain,
Like the wail of forest creatures when the forest-king is slain,
And the faint and feeble monarch was with age and anguish pale,
Like the darkened moon at eclipse when his light and radiance fail!
Rama saw his ancient father with a faltering footstep go,
Used to royal pomp and splendour, stricken now by age and woe,
Saw his mother faint and feeble to the speeding chariot hie,
As the mother-cow returneth to her young that loiters by,
Still she hastened to the chariot, "Rama! Rama!" was her cry,
And a throb was in her bosom and a tear was in her eye!
"Speed, Sumantra," uttered Rama, "from this torture let me part,
Speed, my friend, this sight of sadness breaks a much-enduring heart,
Heed not Dasa-ratha's mandate, stop not for the royal train,
Parting slow is lengthened sorrow like the sinner's lengthened pain!"
Sad Sumantra urged the coursers and the rapid chariot flew,
And the royal chiefs and courtiers round their fainting monarch drew,
And they spake to Dasa-ratha: "Follow not thy banished son,
He whom thou wouldst keep beside thee comes not till his task is done!"
Dasa-ratha, faint and feeble, listened to these words of pain,
Stood and saw his son departing,—saw him not on earth again!

V *Crossing the Tamasa: The Citizens' Return*

Evening's thickening shades descended on Tamasa's distant shore,
Rama rested by the river, day of toilsome journey o'er,

And Ayodhya's loving people by the limpid river lay,
Sad and sorrowing they had followed Rama's chariot through the day!
"Soft-eyed Sita, faithful Lakshman," thus the gentle Rama said,
"Hail the first night of our exile mantling us in welcome shade,
Weeps the lone and voiceless forest, and in darksome lair and nest,
Feathered bird and forest creature seek their midnight's wonted rest,
Weeps methinks our fair Ayodhya to her Rama ever dear,
And perchance her men and women shed for us a silent tear,
Loyal men and faithful women, they have loved their ancient king,
And his anguish and our exile will their gentle bosoms wring!
Most I sorrow for my father and my mother loved and lost,
Stricken by untimely anguish, by a cruel fortune crost,
But the good and righteous Bharat gently will my parents tend,
And with fond and filial duty tender consolation lend,
Well I know his stainless bosom and his virtues rare and high,
He will soothe our parents' sorrow and their trickling tear will dry!
Faithful Lakshman, thou hast nobly stood by us when sorrows fell,
Guard my Sita by thy valour, by thy virtues tend her well,
Wait on her while from this river Rama seeks his thirst to slake,
On this first night of his exile food nor fruit shall Rama take,
Thou Sumantra, tend the horses, darkness comes with close of day,
Weary was the endless journey, weary is our onward way!"
Store of grass and welcome fodder to the steeds the driver gave,
Gave them rest and gave them water from Tamasa's limpid wave,
And performing night's devotions, for the princes made their bed,
By the softly rippling river 'neath the tree's umbrageous shade.
On a bed of leaf and verdure Rama and his Sita slept,
Faithful Lakshman with Sumantra nightly watch and vigils kept,
And the stars their silent lustre on the weary exiles shed,
And on wood and rolling river night her darksome mantle spread.
Early woke the righteous Rama and to watchful Lakshman spake:
"Mark the slumb'ring city people, still their nightly rest they take,
They have left their homes and children, followed us with loyal heart,
They would take us to Ayodhya, from their princes loth to part!
Speed, my brother, for the people wake not till the morning's star,
Speed by night the silent chariot, we may travel fast and far,
So my true and loving people see us not by dawn of day,
Follow not through wood and jungle Rama in his onward way,

For a monarch meek in suffering should his burden bravely bear,
And his true and faithful people may not ask his woe to share!"
Lakshman heard the gentle mandate, and Sumantra yoked the steed,
Fresh with rest and grateful fodder, matchless in their wondrous speed,
Rama with his gentle consort and with Lakshman true and brave,
Crossed beneath the silent starlight dark Tamasa's limpid wave.
On the farther bank a pathway, fair to view and far and wide,
Stretching onwards to the forests spanned the spacious country-side,
"Leave the broad and open pathway," so the gentle Rama said,
"Follow yet a track diverging, so the people be misled.
Then returning to the pathway we shall march ere break of day,
So our true and faithful people shall not know our southward way."
Wise Sumantra hastened northward, then returning to the road,
By his master and his consort and the valiant Lakshman stood,
Raghu's sons and gentle Sita mounted on the stately car,
And Sumantra drove the coursers travelling fast and travelling far.
Morning dawned, the waking people by Tamasa's limpid wave,
Saw not Rama and his consort, saw not Lakshman young and brave,
And the tear suffused their faces and their hearts with anguish burned,
Sorrow-laden and lamenting to their cheerless homes returned.

VI Crossing the Ganges. Bharad-Vaja's Hermitage

Morning dawned, and far they wandered, by their people loved and lost,
Drove through grove and flowering woodland, rippling rill and river crost,
Crossed the sacred Vedasruti on their still unending way,
Crossed the deep and rapid Gumti where the herds of cattle stray,
All the toilsome day they travelled, evening fell o'er wood and lea,
And they came where sea-like Ganga rolls in regal majesty,
'Neath a tall Ingudi's shadow by the river's zephyrs blest,
Second night of Rama's exile passed in sleep and gentle rest.
Morning dawned, the royal chariot Rama would no further own,
Sent Sumantra and the coursers back to fair Ayodhya's town,
Doffing then their royal garments Rama and his brother bold
Coats of bark and matted tresses wore like anchorites of old.
Guha, chief of wild Nishadas, boat and needed succour gave,
And the princes and fair Sita ventured on the sacred wave.

And by royal Rama bidden strong Nishadas plied the oar,
And the strong boat quickly bounding left fair Ganga's northern shore.
"Goddess of the mighty Ganga!" so the pious Sita prayed,
"Exiled by his father's mandate, Rama seeks the forest shade,
Ganga! o'er the three worlds rolling, bride and empress of the sea,
And from BRAHMA's sphere descended! banished Sita bows to thee.
May my lord return in safety, and a thousand fattened kine,
Gold and gifts and gorgeous garments, pure libations shall be thine,
And with flesh and corn I worship unseen dwellers on thy shore,
May my lord return in safety, fourteen years of exile o'er!"
On the southern shore they journeyed through the long and weary day,
Still through grove and flowering woodland held their long and weary way,
And they slayed the deer of jungle and they spread their rich repast,
Third night of the princes' exile underneath a tree was past.
Morning dawned, the soft-eyed Sita wandered with the princes brave,
To the spot where ruddy Ganga mingles with dark Jumna's wave,
And they crost the shady woodland, verdant lawn and grassy mead,
Till the sun was in its zenith, Rama then to Lakshman said:
"Yonder mark the famed Prayaga, spot revered from age to age,
And the line of smoke ascending speaks some *rishi's* hermitage,
There the waves of ruddy Ganga with the dark blue Jumna meet,
And my ear the sea-like voices of the mingling waters greet.
Mark the monarchs of the forest severed by the hermit's might,
And the logs of wood and fuel for the sacrificial rite,
Mark the tall trees in their blossom and the peaceful shady grove,
There the sages make their dwelling, thither, Lakshman, let us rove."
Slowly came the exile-wand'rers, when the sun withdrew his rays,
Where the vast and sea-like rivers met in sisters' sweet embrace,
And the *asram's*[1] peaceful dwellers, bird of song and spotted deer,
Quaked to see the princely strangers in their warlike garb appear!
Rama stepped with valiant Lakshman, gentle Sita followed close,
Till behind the screening foliage hermits' peaceful dwellings rose,
And they came to Bharad-vaja, anchorite and holy saint,
Girt by true and faithful pupils on his sacred duty bent.
Famed for rites and lofty penance was the anchorite of yore,
Blest with more than mortal vision, deep in more than mortal lore,

[1] Hermitage.

And he sat beside the altar for the *agni-hotra*[1] rite,
Rama spake in humble accents to the man of holy might:
"We are sons of Dasa-ratha and to thee our homage bring,
With my wife, the saintly Sita, daughter of Videha's king,
Exiled by my royal father in the wilderness I roam,
And my wife and faithful brother make the pathless woods their home,
We would through these years of exile in some holy *asram* dwell,
And our food shall be the wild fruit and our drink from crystal well,
We would practise pious penance still on sacred rites intent,
Till our souls be filled with wisdom and our years of exile spent!"
Pleased the ancient Bharad-vaja heard the prince's humble tale,
And with kind and courteous welcome royal strangers greeted well,
And he brought the milk and *arghya* where the guests observant stood,
Crystal water from the fountain, berries from the darksome wood,
And a low and leafy cottage for their dwelling-place assigned,
As a host receives a stranger, welcomed them with offerings kind.
In the *asram's* peaceful courtyard fearless browsed the jungle deer,
All unharmed the bird of forest pecked the grain collected near,
And by holy men surrounded 'neath the trees' unbrageous shade,
In his pure and peaceful accents *rishi* Bharad-vaja said:
"Not unknown or unexpected, princely strangers, have ye come,
I have heard of sinless Rama's causeless banishment from home,
Welcome to a hermit's forest, be this spot your place of rest,
Where the meeting of the rivers makes our sacred *asram* blest,
Live amidst these peaceful woodlands, still on sacred rites intent
Till your souls be filled with wisdom and your years of exile spent!"
"Gracious are thy accents, *rishi*," Rama answered thus the sage,
"But fair towns and peopled hamlets border on this hermitage,
And to see the banished Sita and to see us, much I fear,
Crowds of rustics oft will trespass on thy calm devotions here,
Far from towns and peopled hamlets, grant us, *rishi*, in thy grace,
Some wild spot where hid in jungle we may pass these years in peace."
"Twenty miles from this Prayaga," spake the *rishi* pond'ring well,
"Is a lonely hill and jungle where some ancient hermits dwell,
Chitra-kuta, Peak of Beauty, where the forest creatures stray,
And in every bush and thicket herds of lightsome monkeys play,
Men who view its towering summit are on lofty thoughts inclined,
Earthly pride nor earthly passions cloud their pure and peaceful mind,

[1] Sacrifice to the fire with offering of milk.

Hoary-headed ancient hermits, hundred autumns who have done,
By their faith and lofty penance heaven's eternal bliss have won,
Holy is the fair seclusion for thy purpose suited well,
Or if still thy heart inclineth, here in peace and comfort dwell!"
Spake the *rishi* Bharad-vaja, and with every courteous rite,
Cheered his guests with varied converse till the silent hours of night,
Fourth night of the princes' exile in Prayaga's hermitage,
Passed the brothers and fair Sita honoured by Prayaga's Sage.

VII Crossing the Jumna—Valmiki's Hermitage

Morning dawned, and faithful Sita with the brothers held her way,
Where the dark and eddying waters of the sacred Jumna stray,
Pondering by the rapid river long the thoughtful brothers stood,
Then with stalwart arms and axes felled the sturdy jungle wood,
Usira[1] of strongest fibre, slender bamboo smooth and plain,
Jambu[2] branches intertwining with the bent and twisting cane,
And a mighty raft constructed, and with creepers scented sweet,
Lakshman for the gentle Sita made a soft and pleasant seat.
Then the rustic bark was floated, framed with skill of woodman's craft,
By her loving lord supported Sita stepped upon the raft,
And her raiments and apparel Rama by his consort laid,
And the axes and the deerskins, bow and dart and shining blade,
Then with stalwart arms the brothers plied the bending bamboo oar,
And the strong raft gaily bounding left for Jumna's southern shore.
"Goddess of the glorious Jumna!" so the pious Sita prayed,
"Peaceful be my husband's exile in the forest's darksome shade,
May he safely reach Ayodhya, and a thousand fattened kine,
Hundred jars of sweet libation, mighty Jumna, shall be thine,
Grant that from the woods returning he may see his home again,
Grant that honoured by his kinsmen he may rule his loving men!"
On her breast her arms she folded while the princes plied the oar,
And the bright bark bravely bounding reached the wooded southern shore.
And the wanderers from Ayodhya on the river's margin stood,
Where the unknown realm extended mantled by unending wood,
Gallant Lakshman with his weapons went before the path to clear,
Soft-eyed Sita followed gently, Rama followed in the rear.

[1] A kind of hard wood. [2] Name of a tree.

Oft from tree and darksome jungle, Lakshman ever true and brave,
Plucked the fruit or smiling blossom and to gentle Sita gave,
Oft to Rama turned his consort, pleased and curious evermore,
Asked the name of tree or creeper, fruit or flower unseen before.
Still with brotherly affection Lakshman brought each dewy spray,
Bud or blossom of wild beauty from the woodland bright and gay,
Still with eager joy and pleasure Sita turned her eye once more,
Where the tuneful swans and *saras*[1] flocked on Jumna's sandy shore.
Two miles thus they walked and wandered and the belt of forest passed,
Slew the wild deer of the jungle, spread on leaves their rich repast,
Peacocks flew around them gaily, monkeys leaped on branches bent,
Fifth night of their endless wanderings in the forest thus they spent.
"Wake, my love, and list the warblings and the voices of the wood,"
Thus spake Rama when the morning on the eastern mountains stood,
Sita woke and gallant Lakshman, and they sipped the sacred wave,
To the hill of Chitra-kuta held their way serene and brave.
"Mark, my love," so Ramu uttered, "every bush and tree and flower,
Tinged by radiant light of morning sparkles in a golden shower,
Mark the flaming flower of *Kinsuk* and the *Vilwa* in its pride,
Luscious fruits in wild profusion ample store of food provide,
Mark the honeycombs suspended from each tall and stately tree,
How from every virgin blossom steals her store the faithless bee!
Oft the lone and startled wild cock sounds its clarion full and clear,
And from flowering fragrant forests peacocks send the answering cheer,
Oft the elephant of jungle ranges in this darksome wood,
For yon peak is Chitra-kuta loved by saints and hermits good,
Oft the chanted songs of hermits echo through its sacred grove,
Peaceful on its shady uplands, Sita, we shall live and rove!"
Gently thus the princes wandered through the fair and woodland scene,
Fruits and blossoms lit the branches, feathered songsters filled the green,
Anchorites and ancient hermits lived in every sylvan grove,
And a sweet and sacred stillness filled the woods with peace and love!
Gently thus the princes wandered to the holy hermitage,
Where in lofty contemplation lived the mighty Saint and Sage,
Heaven inspired thy song, Valmiki! Ancient Bard of ancient day,
Deeds of virtue and of valour live in thy undying lay!
And the Bard received the princes with a father's greetings kind,
Bade them live in Chitra-kuta with a pure and peaceful mind,

[1] *Sarasa* the Indian crane.

To the true and faithful Lakshman, Rama then his purpose said,
And of leaf and forest timber Lakshman soon a cottage made.
"So our sacred *Sastras*[1] sanction," thus the righteous Rama spake,
"Holy offering we should render when our dwelling-home we make,
Slay the black buck, gallant Lakshman, and a sacrifice prepare,
For the moment is auspicious and the day is bright and fair."
Lakshman slew a mighty black-buck, with the antlered trophy came,
Placed the carcass consecrated by the altar's blazing flame,
Radiant round the mighty offering tongues of red fire curling shone,
And the buck was duly roasted and the tender meat was done.
Pure from bath, with sacred *mantra* Rama did the holy rite,
And invoked the bright Immortals for to bless the dwelling site,
To the kindly VISWA-DEVAS, and to RUDRA fierce and strong,
And to VISHNU Lord of Creatures, Rama raised the sacred song.
Righteous rite was duly rendered for the forest-dwelling made,
And with true and deep devotion was the sacred *mantra* prayed,
And the worship of the Bright Ones purified each earthly stain,
Pure-souled Rama raised the altar and the *chaitya's*[2] sacred fane.
Evening spread its holy stillness, bush and tree its magic felt,
As the Gods in BRAHMA's mansions, exiles in their cottage dwelt,
In the woods of Chitra-kuta where the Malyavati flows,
Sixth day of their weary wand'rings ended in a sweet repose.

VIII Tale of the Hermit's Son

Wise Sumantra chariot-driver came from Ganga's sacred wave,
And unto Ayodhya's monarch, banished Rama's message gave,
Dasa-ratha's heart was shadowed by the deepening shade of night,
As the darkness of the eclipse glooms the sun's meridian light!
On the sixth night,—when his Rama slept in Chitra-kuta's bower,—
Memory of an ancient sorrow flung on him its fatal power,
Of an ancient crime and anguish, unforgotten, dark and dread,
Through the lapse of years and seasons casting back its death-like shade!
And the gloom of midnight deepened, Dasa-ratha sinking fast,
To Kausalya sad and sorrowing spake his memories of the past:
"Deeds we do in life, Kausalya, be they bitter, be they sweet,
Bring their fruit and retribution, rich reward or suffering meet.

[1] Scriptures. [2] A shrine or temple.

Heedless child is he, Kausalya, in his fate who doth not scan
Retribution of his *karma,*[1] sequence of a mighty plan!
Oft in madness and in folly we destroy the mango grove,
Plant the gorgeous gay *palasa*[2] for the red flower that we love,
Fruitless as the red *palasa* is the *karma* I have sown,
And my barren lifetime withers through the deed which is my own!
Listen to my tale, Kausalya, in my days of youth renowned,
I was called a *sabda-bedhi,*[3] archer prince who shot by sound,
I could hit the unseen target, by the sound my aim could tell,—
Blindly drinks a child the poison, blindly in my pride I fell!
I was then my father's Regent, thou a maid to me unknown,
Hunting by the fair Sarayu in my car I drove alone,
Buffalo or jungle tusker might frequent the river's brink,
Nimble deer or watchful tiger stealing for his nightly drink,
Stalking with a hunter's patience, loitering in the forests drear,
Sound of something in the water struck my keen and listening ear,
In the dark I stood and listened, some wild beast the water drunk,
'Tis some elephant, I pondered, lifting water with its trunk.
I was called a *sabda-bedhi,* archer prince who shot by sound,
On the unseen fancied tusker dealt a sure and deadly wound,
Ah! too deadly was my arrow and like hissing cobra fell,
On my startled ear and bosom smote a voice of human wail,
Dying voice of lamentation rose upon the midnight high,
Till my weapons fell in tremor and a darkness dimmed my eye!
Hastening with a nameless terror soon I reached Sarayu's shore,
Saw a boy with hermit's tresses, and his pitcher lay before,
Weltering in a pool of red blood, lying on a gory bed,
Feebly raised his voice the hermit, and in dying accents said:
'What offence, O mighty monarch, all-unknowing have I done,
That with quick and kingly justice slayest thus a hermit's son?
Old and feeble are my parents, sightless by the will of fate,
Thirsty in their humble cottage for their duteous boy they wait,
And thy shaft that kills me, monarch, bids my ancient parents die,
Helpless, friendless, they will perish, in their anguish deep and high!
Sacred lore and lifelong penance change not mortal's earthly state,
Wherefore else they sit unconscious when their son is doomed by fate,

[1] A man's deeds with their consequences in this or future life.
[2] A tree bearing large, red blossoms with no scent.
[3] An archer who shoots by sound, not by sight of his object.

Or if conscious of my danger, could they dying breath recall,
Can the tall tree save the sapling doomed by woodman's axe to fall?
Hasten to my parents, monarch, soothe their sorrow and their ire,
For the tears of good and righteous wither like the forest fire,
Short the pathway to the *asram,* soon the cottage thou shalt see
Soothe their anger by entreaty, ask their grace and pardon free!
But before thou goest, monarch, take, O take thy torturing dart,
For it rankles in my bosom with a cruel burning smart,
And it eats into my young life as the river's rolling tide
By the rains of summer swollen eats into its yielding side.'
Writhing in his pain and anguish thus the wounded hermit cried,
And I drew the fatal arrow, and the holy hermit died!
Darkly fell the thickening shadows, stars their feeble radiance lent,
As I filled the hermit's pitcher, to his sightless parents went,
Darkly fell the moonless midnight, deeper gloom my bosom rent,
As with faint and falt'ring footsteps to the hermits slow I went.
Like two birds bereft of plumage, void of strength, deprived of flight,
Were the stricken ancient hermits, friendless, helpless, void of sight,
Lisping in their feeble accents still they whispered of their child,
Of the stainless boy whose red blood Dasa-ratha's hands defiled!
And the father heard my footsteps, spake in accents soft and kind:
'Come, my son, to waiting parents, wherefore dost thou stay behind,
Sporting in the rippling water didst thou midnight's hour beguile,
But thy faint and thirsting mother anxious waits for thee the while,
Hath my heedless word or utterance caused thy boyish bosom smart,
But a feeble father's failings may not wound thy filial heart,
Help of helpless, sight of sightless, and thy parents' life and joy,
Wherefore art thou mute and voiceless, speak, my brave and beauteous boy!'
Thus the sightless father welcomed cruel slayer of his son,
And an anguish tore my bosom for the action I had done,
Scarce upon the sonless parents could I lift my aching eye,
Scarce in faint and faltering accents to the father make reply,
For a tremor shook my person and my spirit sank in dread,
Straining all my utmost prowess, thus in quavering voice I said:
'Not thy son, O holy hermit, but a Kshatra warrior born,
Dasa-ratha stands before thee by a cruel anguish torn,
For I came to slay the tusker by Sarayu's wooded brink,
Buffalo or deer of jungle stealing for his midnight drink,

And I heard a distant gurgle, some wild beast the water drunk,—
So I thought,—some jungle tusker lifting water with its trunk,
And I sent my fatal arrow on the unknown, unseen prey,
Speeding to the spot I witnessed,—there a dying hermit lay!
From his pierced and quivering bosom then the cruel dart I drew,
And he sorrowed for his parents as his spirit heavenward flew,
Thus unconscious, holy father, I have slayed thy stainless son,
Speak my penance, or in mercy pardon deed unknowing done!'
Slow and sadly by their bidding to the fatal spot I led,
Long and loud bewailed the parents by the cold unconscious dead,
And with hymns and holy water they performed the funeral rite,
Then with tears that burnt and withered, spake the hermit in his might:
'Sorrow for a son beloved is a father's direst woe,
Sorrow for a son beloved, Dasa-ratha, thou shalt know!
See the parents weep and perish, grieving for a slaughtered son,
Thou shalt weep and thou shalt perish for a loved and righteous son!
Distant is the expiation,—but in fulness of the time,
Dasa-ratha's death in anguish cleanses Dasa-ratha's crime!'
Spake the old and sightless prophet; then he made the funeral pyre,
And the father and the mother perished in the lighted fire,
Years have gone and many seasons, and in fulness of the time,
Comes the fruit of pride and folly and the harvest of my crime!
Rama eldest born and dearest, Lakshman true and faithful son,
Ah! forgive a dying father and a cruel action done,
Queen Kaikeyi, thou hast heedless brought on Raghu's race this stain,
Banished are the guiltless children and thy lord and king is slain!
Lay thy hands on mine, Kausalya, wipe thy unavailing tear,
Speak a wife's consoling accents to a dying husband's ear,
Lay thy hands on mine, Sumitra, vision falls my closing eyes,
And for brave and banished Rama wings my spirit to the skies!
Hushed and silent passed the midnight, feebly still the monarch sighed,
Blessed Kausalya and Sumitra, blest his banished sons, and died.

BOOK IV RAMA-BHARATA-SAMBADA

(*The Meeting of the Princes*)

THE SCENE OF THIS BOOK is laid at Chitra-kuta. Bharat returning from the kingdom of the Kaikeyas heard of his father's death and his brother's exile, and refused the throne which had been reserved for him. He wandered through the woods and jungle to Chitra-kuta, and implored Rama to return to Ayodhya and seat himself on the throne of his father. But Rama had given his word, and would not withdraw from it.

Few passages in the Epic are more impressive than Rama's wise and kindly advice to Bharat on the duties of a ruler, and his firm refusal to Bharat's passionate appeal to seat himself on the throne. Equally touching is the lament of Queen Kausalya when she meets Sita in the dress of an anchorite in the forest.

But one of the most curious passages in the whole Epic is the speech of Jabali the Sceptic, who denied heaven and a world hereafter. In ancient India as in ancient Greece there were different schools of philosophers, some of them orthodox and some of them extremely heterodox, and the greatest latitude of free thought was permitted. In Jabali, the poet depicts a free-thinker of the broadest type. He ridicules the ideas of Duty and of Future Life with a force of reasoning which a Greek sophist and philosopher could not have surpassed. But Rama answers with the fervour of a righteous, truth-loving, God-fearing man.

All persuasion was in vain, and Bharat returned to Ayodhya with Rama's sandals, and placed them on the throne, as an emblem of Rama's sovereignty during his voluntary exile. Rama himself then left Chitra-kuta and sought the deeper forests of Dandak, so that his friends and relations might not find him again during his exile. He visited the hermitage of the Saint Atri; and the ancient and venerable wife of Atri welcomed the young Sita, and robed her in rich raiments and jewels, on the eve of her departure for the unexplored wildernesses of the south.

The portions translated in this Book are the whole or the main portions of Sections xcix., c., ci., civ., cviii., cix., cxii., and cxix. of Book ii. of the original text.

I The Meeting of the Brothers

Sorrowing for his sire departed Bharat to Ayodhya came,
But the exile of his brother stung his noble heart to flame,
Scorning sin-polluted empire, travelling with each widowed queen,
Sought through wood and trackless jungle Chitra-kuta's peaceful scene.
Royal guards and Saint Vasishtha loitered with the dames behind,
Onward pressed the eager Bharat, Rama's hermit-home to find,

Nestled in a jungle thicket, Rama's cottage rose in sight,
Thatched with leaves and twining branches, reared by Lakshman's faithful might.
Faggots hewn of gnarléd branches, blossoms culled from bush and tree,
Coats of bark and russet garments, *kusa*[1] spread upon the lea,
Store of horns and branching antlers, fire-wood for the dewy night,—
Spake the dwelling of a hermit suited for a hermit's rite.
"May the scene," so Bharat uttered, "by the righteous *rishi* told,
Markalvati's rippling waters, Chitra-kuta's summit bold,
Mark the dark and trackless forest where the untamed tuskers roam,
And the deep and hollow caverns where the wild beasts make their home,
Mark the spacious wooded uplands, wreaths of smoke obscure the sky,
Hermits feed their flaming altars for their worship pure and high.
Done our weary work and wand'ring, righteous Rama here we meet,
Saint and king and honoured elder! Bharat bows unto his feet,
Born a king of many nations, he hath forest refuge sought,
Yielded throne and mighty kingdom for a hermit's humble cot,
Honour unto righteous Rama, unto Sita true and bold,
Theirs be fair Kosala's empire, crown and sceptre, wealth and gold!"
Stately *Sal*[2] and feathered palm-tree on the cottage lent their shade.
Strewn upon the sacred altar was the grass of *kusa* spread,
Gaily on the walls suspended hung two bows of ample height,
And their back with gold was pencilled, bright as INDRA's bow of might,
Cased in broad unfailing quivers arrows shone like light of day,
And like flame-tongued fiery serpents cast a dread and lurid ray,
Resting in their golden scabbards lay the sword of warriors bold,
And the targets broad and ample bossed with rings of yellow gold,
Glove and gauntlet decked the cottage safe from fear of hostile men,
As from creatures of the forest is the lion's lordly den!
Calm in silent contemplation by the altar's sacred fire,
Holy in his pious purpose though begirt by weapons dire,
Clad in deer-skin pure and peaceful, poring on the sacred flame,
In his bark and hermit's tresses like an anchorite of fame,
Lion-shouldered, mighty-arméd, but with gentle lotus eye,
Lord of wide earth ocean-girdled, but intent on penance high,
Godlike as the holy BRAHMA, on a skin of dappled deer
Rama sat with meek-eyed Sita, faithful Lakshman loitered near!

[1] Grass strewn around the altar at sacrifice. [2] *Sala,* a tall forest tree.

"Is this he whom joyous nations called to fair Ayodhya's throne,
Now the friend of forest-rangers wandering in the woods alone,
Is this he who robed in purple made Ayodhya's mansions bright,
Now in jungle bark and deer-skin clad as holy anchorite,
Is this he whose wreathéd ringlets fresh and holy fragrance shed,
Now a hermit's matted tresses cluster round his royal head,
Is this he whose royal *yajnas* filled the earth with righteous fame,
Now inured to hermit's labour by the altar's sacred flame,
Is this he whose brow and forehead royal gem and jewel graced,
Heir to proud Kosala's empire, eldest, noblest, and the best?"
Thus lamented pious Bharat, for his heart was anguish-rent,
As before the feet of Rama he in loving homage bent,
"Arya!"[1] in his choking accents this was all that Bharat said,
"Arya!" spake the young Satrughna and he bent his holy head!
Rama to his loving bosom raised his brothers from his feet,
Ah, too deep is love for utterance when divided brothers meet,
Faithful Guha, brave Sumantra, bowed to Rama's righteous feet,
And a joy and mingled sadness filled the hermit's calm retreat!

II *Bharat's Entreaty and Rama's Reply*

"Speak, my true, my faithful Bharat," so the righteous Rama cried,
"Wherefore to this jungle dwelling hast thou from Ayodhya hied,
Speak, my fond and loving brother, if our father bade thee come,
Leaving throne and spacious empire in this wilderness to roam?
Heir and Regent of Kosala! Dost thou tend our father well,
And obey the lofty mandate from his royal lips that fell,
And the ancient Dasa-ratha, glorious still in regal might,
Doth he pass his bright life's evening in each pure and holy rite?
Doth my mother, Queen Kausalya, still for Rama wet her eye,
And the gentle Queen Sumitra for her banished Lakshman sigh,
Doth the peerless Queen Kaikeyi pass her days in duties fair,
Guard her Bharat's mighty empire, tend him with a mother's care?
Is each holy rite and homage to the Gods and Fathers done,
Is the honour due to elders rendered by each duteous son,
Do thy warriors guard thy kingdom as of yore with matchless skill,
And with counsel deep and duteous do thy min'sters serve thy will?

[1] Honorable person, an Aryan.

Rich thy fields in corn and produce fed by rivers broad and deep,
Rich thy green unending pastures with the kine and fattened sheep,
Tend the herdsman and his cattle, tend the tiller of the soil,
Watch and help with all thy bounty workmen in their peaceful toil,
For the monarch's highest duty is to serve his people's weal
And the ruler's richest glory is to labour and to heal!
Guard thy forts with sleepless caution with the engines of the war,
With the men who shoot the arrow and who drive the flying car,
Guard Kosala's royal treasure, make thy gifts of wealth and food,
Not to lords and proud retainers, but to worthy and the good!
Render justice pure and spotless as befits thy royal line,
And to save the good and guiltless, Bharat, be it ever thine,
For the tears of suffering virtue wither like the thunder levin,
And they slay our men and cattle like the wrath of righteous heaven,
Fruitful be thy lore of Veda, fruitful be each pious rite,
Be thy queen a fruitful mother, be thy empire full of might!"
Weeping, weeping, Bharat answered Dasa-ratha's eldest son,
"Dasa-ratha walks the bright sky, for his earthly task is done!
For impelled by Queen Kaikeyi to the woods he bade thee go,
And his spotless fame was clouded and his bosom sank in woe,
And my mother, late repenting, weeps her deed of deepest shame,
Weeps her wedded lord departed, and a woman's tarnished fame!
Thou alone canst wipe this insult by a deed of kindness done,—
Rule o'er Dasa-ratha's empire, Dasa-ratha's eldest son,
Weeping queens and loyal subjects supplicate thy noble grace,—
Rule o'er Raghu's ancient empire, son of Raghu's royal race!
For our ancient Law ordaineth and thy Duty makes it plain,
Eldest-born succeeds his father as the king of earth and main,
By the fair Earth loved and welcomed, Rama, be her wedded lord,
As by planet-jewelled Midnight is the radiant Moon adored!
And thy father's ancient min'sters and thy courtiers faithful still,
Wait to do thy righteous mandate and to serve thy royal will,
As a pupil, as a brother, as a slave, I seek thy grace,—
Come and rule thy father's empire, king of Raghu's royal race!"
Weeping, on the feet of Rama, Bharat placed his lowly head,
Weeping for his sire departed, tears of sorrow Rama shed,
Then he raised his loving brother with an elder's deathless love,
Sorrow wakes our deepest kindness and our holiest feelings prove!

"But I may not," answered Rama, "seek Ayodhya's ancient throne,
For a righteous father's mandate duteous son may not disown,
And I may not, gentle brother, break the word of promise given,
To a king and to a father who is now a saint in heaven!
Not on thee, nor on thy mother, rests the censure or the blame,
Faithful to his father's wishes Rama to the forest came,
For the son and duteous consort serve the father and the lord,
Higher than an empire's glory is a father's spoken word!
All inviolate is his mandate,—on Ayodhya's jewelled throne,
Or in pathless woods and jungle Rama shall his duty own,
All inviolate is the blessing by a loving mother given,
For she blessed my life in exile like a pitying saint of heaven!
Thou shalt rule the kingdom, Bharat, guard our loving people well,
Clad in wild bark and in deer-skin I shall in the forests dwell,
So spake saintly Dasa-ratha in Ayodhya's palace hall,
And a righteous father's mandate duteous son may not recall!"

III *Kausalya's Lament and Rama's Reply*

Slow and sad with Saint Vasishtha, with each widowed royal dame,
Unto Rama's hermit-cottage ancient Queen Kausalya came,
And she saw him clad in wild bark like a hermit stern and high,
And an anguish smote her bosom and a tear bedewed her eye.
Rama bowed unto his mother and each elder's blessings sought,
Held their feet in salutation with a holy reverence fraught,
And the queens with loving fingers, with a mother's tender care,
Swept the dust of wood and jungle from his head and bosom fair,
Lakshman too in loving homage bent before each royal dame,
And they blessed the faithful hero spotless in his righteous fame.
Lastly came the soft-eyed Sita with obeisance soft and sweet,
And with hands in meekness folded bent her tresses to their feet,
Pain and anguish smote their bosoms, round their Sita as they prest,
As a mother clasps a daughter, clasped her in their loving breast!
Torn from royal hall and mansions, ranger of the darksome wood,
Reft of home and kith and kindred by her forest hut she stood!
"Hast thou, daughter of Videha," weeping thus Kausalya said,
"Dwelt in woods and leafy cottage and in pathless jungle strayed,
Hast thou, Rama's royal consort, lived a homeless anchorite,
Pale with rigid fast and penance, worn with toil of righteous rite?

But thy sweet face, gentle Sita, is like faded lotus dry,
And like lily parched by sunlight, lustreless thy beauteous eye,
Like the gold untimely tarnished is thy sorrow-shaded brow,
Like the moon by shadows darkened is thy form of beauty now!
And an anguish scathes my bosom like the withering forest fire,
Thus to see thee, duteous daughter, in misfortunes deep and dire,
Dark is wide Kosala's empire, dark is Raghu's royal house,
When in woods my Rama wanders and my Rama's royal spouse!"
Sweetly, gentle Sita answered, answered Rama fair and tall,
That a righteous father's mandate duteous son may not recall!

IV *Jabali's Reasoning and Rama's Reply*

Jabali a learned Brahman and a Sophist skilled in word,
Questioned Faith and Law and Duty, spake to young Ayodhya's lord:
"Wherefore, Rama, idle maxims cloud thy heart and warp thy mind,
Maxims which mislead the simple and the thoughtless human kind?
Love nor friendship doth a mortal to his kith or kindred own,
Entering on his wide earth friendless, and departing all alone,
Foolishly upon the father and the mother dotes the son,
Kinship is an idle fancy,—save thyself thy kith is none!
In the wayside inn he halteth who in distant lands doth roam,
Leaves it with the dawning daylight for another transient home,
Thus on earth are kin and kindred, home and country, wealth and store,
We but meet them on our journey, leave them as we pass before!
Wherefore for a father's mandate leave thy empire and thy throne,
Pass thy days in trackless jungle sacrificing all thy own,
Wherefore to Ayodhya's city, as to longing wife's embrace,
Speed'st thou not to rule thy empire, lord of Raghu's royal race?
Dasa-ratha claims no duty, and this will is empty word,
View him as a foreign monarch, of thy realm thou art the lord,
Dasa-ratha is departed, gone where all the mortals go,
For a dead man's idle mandate wherefore lead this life of woe?
Ah! I weep for erring mortals who on erring duty bent
Sacrifice their dear enjoyment till their barren life is spent,
Who to Gods and to the Fathers vainly still their offerings make,
Waste of food! for God nor Father doth our pious homage take!
And the food by one partaken, can it nourish other men,
Food bestowed upon a Brahman, can it serve our Fathers then?

Crafty priests have forged these maxims and with selfish objects say,
Make thy gifts and do thy penance, leave thy worldly wealth and pray!
There is no Hereafter, Rama, vain the hope and creed of men,
Seek the pleasures of the present, spurn illusions poor and vain,
Take the course of sense and wisdom, cast all idle faith aside,
Take the kingdom Bharat offers, rule Ayodhya in thy pride!"
"Fair thy purpose," answered Rama, "false thy reason leads astray,
Tortuous wisdom brings no profit, virtue shuns the crooked way,
For the deed proclaims the hero from the man of spacious lies,
Marks the true and upright *Arya* from the scheming worldly-wise!
If assuming virtue's mantle I should seek the sinful path,
Gods who judge our secret motives curse me with their deepest wrath,
And thy counsel helps not, *rishi,* mansions of the sky to win,
And a king his subjects follow adding deeper sin to sin!
Sweep aside thy crafty reasoning, Truth is still our ancient way,
Truth sustains the earth and nations and a monarch's righteous sway,
Mighty Gods and holy sages find in Truth their haven shore,
Scorning death and dark destruction, Truth survives for evermore!
Deadlier than the serpent's venom is the venom of a lie,
From the false, than from the cobra, men with deeper terror fly,
Dearer than the food to mortals, Truth as nourishment is given,
Truth sustains the wide creation, Truth upholds the highest heaven,
Vain were gifts and sacrifices, rigid penances were vain,
Profitless the holy *Vedas* but for Truth which they sustain,
Gifts and rites and rigid penance have no aim or purpose high,
Save in Truth which rules the wide earth and the regions of the sky!
I have plighted truth and promise and my word may not unsay,
Fourteen years in pathless forests father's mandate I obey,
And I seek no spacious reasons my relinquished throne to win,
Gods nor Fathers nor the *Vedas* counsel tortuous paths of sin!
Pardon, *rishi,* still unchanging shall remain my promise given
To my mother Queen Kaikeyi, to my father now in heaven,
Pardon, *rishi,* still in jungle we shall seek the forest fare,
Worship Gods who watch our actions, and pervade the earth and air!
Unto AGNI, unto VAYU, shall my constant prayers run,
I shall live like happy INDRA, hundred sacrifices done,
And the deep and darksome jungle shall be Rama's royal hall,
For a righteous father's mandate duteous son may not recall!"

V The Sandals

Tears nor sighs nor sad entreaty Rama's changeless purpose shook,
Till once more with hands conjoinéd Bharat to his elder spoke:
"Rama, true to royal mercy, true to duties of thy race,
Grant this favour to thy mother, to thy brother grant this grace,
Vain were my unaided efforts to protect our father's throne,
Town and hamlet, lord and tiller, turn to thee and thee alone!
Unto Rama, friends and kinsmen, chiefs and warriors, turn in pain,
And each city chief and elder, and each humble village swain,
Base thy empire strong, unshaken, on a loyal nation's will,
With thy worth and with thy valour serve thy faithful people still!"
Rama raised the prostrate Bharat to his ever-loving breast,
And in voice of tuneful *hansa*[1] thus his gentle speech addrest:
"Trust me, Bharat, lofty virtue, strength and will to thee belong,
Thou could'st rule a worldwide empire in thy faith and purpose strong,
And our father's ancient min'sters, ever faithful, wise and deep,
They shall help thee with their counsel and thy ancient frontiers keep.
List! the Moon may lose his lustre, Himalaya lose his snow,
Heaving Ocean pass his confines surging from the caves below,
But the truth-abiding Rama will not move from promise given,
He hath spoke and will not palter, help him righteous Gods in heaven!"
Blazing like the Sun in splendour, beauteous like the Lord of Night,
Rama vowed his Vow of Duty, changeless in his holy might!
"Humble token," answered Bharat, "still I seek from Rama's hand,
Token of his love and kindness, token of his high command,
From thy feet cast forth those sandals, they shall decorate the throne,
They shall nerve my heart to duty and shall safely guard thy own,
They shall to a loyal nation absent monarch's will proclaim,
Watch the frontiers of the empire and the people's homage claim!"
Rama gave the loosened sandals as his younger humbly prayed,
Bharat bowed to them in homage and his parting purpose said:
"Not alone will banished Rama barks and matted tresses wear,
Fourteen years the crowned Bharat will in hermit's dress appear,
Henceforth Bharat dwells in palace guised as hermit of the wood,
In the sumptuous hall of feasting wild fruit is his only food,
Fourteen years shall pass in waiting, weary toil and penance dire
Then, if Rama comes not living, Bharat dies upon the pyre!"

[1] Swan or goose.

VI The Hermitage of Atri

With the sandals of his elder Bharat to Ayodhya went,
Rama sought for deeper forests on his arduous duty bent,
Wandering with his wife and Lakshman slowly sought the hermitage,
Where resided saintly Atri, Vedic Bard and ancient sage.
Anasuya, wife of Atri, votaress of Gods above,
Welcomed Sita in her cottage, tended her with mother's love,
Gave her robe and holy garland, jewelled ring and chain of gold,
Heard the tale of love and sadness which the soft-eyed Sita told:
How the monarch of Videha held the plough and tilled the earth,
From the furrow made by ploughshare infant Sita sprang to birth,
How the monarch of Videha welcomed kings of worth and pride,
Rama 'midst the gathered monarchs broke the bow and won the bride,
How by Queen Kaikeyi's mandate Rama lost his father's throne,
Sita followed him in exile in the forest dark and lone!
Softly from the lips of Sita words of joy and sorrow fell,
And the pure-souled pious priestess wept to hear the tender tale,
And she kissed her on the forehead, held her on her ancient breast,
And in mother's tender accents thus her gentle thoughts exprest:
"Sweet the tale you tell me, Sita, of thy wedding and thy love,
Of the true and tender Rama, righteous as the Gods above,
And thy wifely deep devotion fills my heart with purpose high,
Stay with us my gentle daughter for the night shades gather nigh.
Hastening from each distant region feathered songsters seek their nest,
Twitter in the leafy thickets ere they seek their nightly rest,
Hastening from their pure ablutions with their pitcher smooth and fair,
In their dripping barks the hermits to their evening rites repair,
And in sacred *agni-hotra*[1] holy anchorites engage,
And a wreath of smoke ascending marks the altar of each sage.
Now a deeper shadow mantles bush and brake and trees around,
And a thick and inky darkness falls upon the distant ground,
Midnight prowlers of the jungle steal beneath the sable shade,
But the tame deer by the altar seeks his wonted nightly bed.
Mark! how by the stars encircled sails the radiant Lord of Night,
With his train of silver glory streaming o'er the azure height,
And thy consort waits thee, Sita, but before thou leavest, fair,
Let me deck thy brow and bosom with these jewels rich and rare,

[1] A sacrifice to the fire with daily offering of milk morning and evening.

Old these eyes and grey these tresses, but a thrill of joy is mine,
Thus to see thy youth and beauty in this gorgeous garment shine!"
Pleased at heart the ancient priestess clad her in apparel meet,
And the young wife glad and grateful bowed to Anasuya's feet,
Robed and jewelled, bright and beauteous, sweet-eyed Sita softly came,
Where with anxious heart awaited Rama prince of righteous fame.
With a wifely love and longing Sita met her hero bold,
Anasuya's love and kindness in her grateful accents told,
Rama and his brother listened of the grace by Sita gained,
Favours of the ancient priestess, pious blessings she had rained.
In the *rishi's* peaceful *asram* Rama passed the sacred night,
In the hushed and silent forest silvered by the moon's pale light,
Daylight dawned, to deeper forests Rama went serene and proud,
As the sun in midday splendour sinks within a bank of cloud!

BOOK V PANCHAVATI

(On the Banks of the Godavari)

THE wanderings of Rama in the Deccan, his meeting with Saint Agastya, and his residence on the banks of the Godavari river, are narrated in this Book. The reader has now left Northern India and crossed the Vindhya mountains; and the scene of the present and succeeding five Books is laid in the Deccan and Southern India. The name of Agastya is connected with the Deccan, and many are the legends told of this great Saint, before whom the Vindhya mountains bent in awe, and by whose might the Southern ocean was drained. It is likely that some religious teacher of that name first penetrated beyond the Vindhyas, and founded the first Aryan settlement in the Deccan, three thousand years ago. He was pioneer, discoverer and settler,—the Indian Columbus who opened out Southern India to Aryan colonization and Aryan religion.

Two *yojanas*[1] from Agastya's hermitage, Rama built his forest dwelling in the woods of Panchavati, near the sources of the Godavari river, and within a hundred miles from the modern city of Bombay. There he lived with his wife and brother in peace and piety, and the Book closes with the description of an Indian winter morning, when the brothers and Sita went for their ablutions to the Godavari, and thought of their

[1] A *yōjana* is about nine English miles.

distant home in Oudh. The description of the peaceful forest-life of the exiles comes in most appropriately on the eve of stirring events which immediately succeed, and which give a new turn to the story of the Epic. We now stand therefore at the turning point of the poet's narrative; he has sung of domestic incidents and of peaceful hermitages so far; he sings of dissensions and wars hereafter.

The portions translated in this Book form Sections i., xii., xiii., xv., and xvi. of Book iii. of the original text.

I The Hermitage of Agastya

Righteous Rama, soft-eyed Sita, and the gallant Lakshman stood
In the wilderness of Dandak,—trackless, pathless, boundless wood,
But within its gloomy gorges, dark and deep and known to few,
Humble homes of hermit sages rose before the princes' view.
Coats of bark and scattered *kusa* spake their peaceful pure abode,
Seat of pious rite and penance which with holy splendour glowed,
Forest songsters knew the *asram* and the wild deer cropt its blade,
And the sweet-voiced sylvan wood-nymph haunted oft its holy shade,
Brightly blazed the sacred altar, vase and ladle stood around,
Fruit and blossom, skin and faggot, sanctified the holy ground.
From the broad and bending branches ripening fruits in clusters hung,
And with gifts and rich libations hermits raised the ancient song,
Lotus and the virgin lily danced upon the rippling rill,
And the golden sunlight glittered on the greenwoods calm and still,
And the consecrated woodland by the holy hermits trod,
Shone like BRAHMA's sky in lustre, hallowed by the grace of God!
Rama loosened there his bow-string and the peaceful scene surveyed,
And the holy sages welcomed wanderers in the forest shade,
Rama bright as Lord of Midnight, Sita with her saintly face,
Lakshman young and true and valiant, decked with warrior's peerless grace!
Leafy hut the holy sages to the royal guests assigned,
Brought them fruit and forest blossoms, blessed them with their blessings kind,
"Raghu's son," thus spake the sages, "helper of each holy rite,
Portion of the royal INDRA, fount of justice and of might,
On thy throne or in the forest, king of nations, lord of men,
Grant us to thy kind protection in this hermit's lonely den!"

Homely fare and jungle produce were before the princes laid,
And the toil-worn, tender Sita slumbered in the *asram's* shade.
Thus from grove to grove they wandered, to each haunt of holy sage,
Sarabhanga's sacred dwelling and Sutikshna's hermitage,
Till they met the Saint Agastya, mightiest Saint of olden time,
Harbinger of holy culture in the wilds of Southern clime!
"Eldest born of Dasa-ratha, long and far hath Rama strayed,"—
Thus to pupil of Agastya young and gallant Lakshman said,—
'With his faithful consort Sita in these wilds he wanders still,
I am righteous Rama's younger, duteous to his royal will,
And we pass these years of exile to our father's mandate true,
Fain to mighty Saint Agastya we would render homage due!"
Listening to his words the hermit sought the shrine of Sacred Fire,
Spake the message of the princes to the Saint and ancient Sire:
"Righteous Rama, valiant Lakshman, saintly Sita seeks this shade,
And to see thee, radiant *rishi,* have in humble accents prayed."
"Hath he come," so spake Agastya, "Rama prince of Raghu's race,
Youth for whom this heart hath thirsted, youth endued with righteous grace,
Hath he come with wife and brother to accept our greetings kind,
Wherefore came ye for permission, wherefore linger they behind?"
Rama and the soft-eyed Sita were with gallant Lakshman led,
Where the dun deer free and fearless roamed within the holy shade,
Where the shrines of great Immortals stood in order thick and close,
And by bright and blazing altars chanted songs and hymns arose.
BRAHMA and the flaming AGNI, VISHNU lord of heavenly light,
INDRA and benign VIVASAT ruler of the azure height,
SOMA and the radiant BHAGA, and KUVERA lord of gold,
And VIDHATRI great Creator worshipped by the saints of old,
VAYU breath of living creatures, YAMA monarch of the dead,
And VARUNA with his fetters which the trembling sinners dread,
Holy Spirit of GAYATRI goddess of the morning prayer,
VASUS and the hooded NAGAS, golden-winged GARUDA fair,
KARITKEYA heavenly leader strong to conquer and to bless,
DHARMA god of human duty and of human righteousness,
Shrines of all these bright Immortals ruling in the skies above,
Filled the pure and peaceful forest with a calm and holy love!
Girt by hermits righteous-hearted then the Saint Agastya came,
Rich in wealth of pious penance, rich in learning and in fame,

Mighty-arméd Rama marked him radiant like the midday sun,
Bowed and rendered due obeisance with each act of homage done,
Valiant Lakshman tall and stately to the great Agastya bent,
With a woman's soft devotion Sita bowed unto the saint.
Saint Agastya raised the princes, greeted them in accents sweet,
Gave them fruit and herb and water, offered them the honoured seat,
With libations unto Agni offered welcome to each guest,
Food and drink beseeming hermits on the wearied princes pressed.
"False the hermits," spake Agastya, "who to guests their dues deny,
Hunger they in life hereafter—like the speaker of a lie.
And a royal guest and wanderer doth our foremost honour claim,
Car-borne kings protect the wide earth by their prowess and their fame,
By these fruits and forest blossoms be our humble homage shewn,
By some gift, of Rama worthy, be Agastya's blessings known!
Take this bow, heroic Rama,—need for warlike arms is thine,—
Gems of more than earthly radiance on the goodly weapon shine,
Worshipper of righteous Vishnu! Vishnu's wondrous weapon take,
Heavenly artist Viswa-karman shaped this bow of heavenly make!
Take this shining dart of Brahma radiant like a tongue of flame,
Sped by good and worthy archer never shall it miss its aim,
And this Indra's sample quiver filled with arrows true and keen,
Filled with arrows still unfailing in the battle's dreadful scene!
Take this sabre golden-hilted in its case of burnished gold,
Not unworthy of a monarch and a warrior true and bold,
Impious foes of bright Immortals know these weapons dread and dire,
Mowing down the ranks of foemen, scathing like the forest fire!
Be these weapons thy companions,—Rama thou shall need them oft,—
Meet and conquer still thy foemen like the Thunder-God aloft!"

II The Counsel of Agastya

"Pleased am I," so spake Agastya, "in these forests dark and wild,
Thou hast come to seek me, Rama, with the saintly Janak's child,
But like pale and drooping blossoms severed from the parent tree,
Far from home in toil and trouble, faithful Sita follows thee,
True to wedded lord and husband she hath followed Raghu's son,
With a woman's deep devotion woman's duty she hath done!
How unlike the fickle woman, true while Fame and Fortune smile,
Faithless when misfortunes gather, loveless in her wicked wile,

How unlike the changeful woman, false as light the lightnings fling,
Keen as sabre, quick as tempest, swift as bird upon its wing!
Dead to Fortune's frown or favour, Sita still in truth abides,
As the star of Arundhati in her mansion still resides,
Rest thee with thy gentle consort, farther still she may not roam,
Holier were this hermit's forest as the saintly Sita's home!"
"Great Agastya!" answered Rama, "blessèd is my banished life,
For thy kindness to an exile and his friendless homeless wife,
But in wilder, gloomier forests lonesome we must wander still,
Where a deeper, darker shadow settles on the rock and rill."
"Be it so," Agastya answered, "two short *yojans* from this place,
Wild is Panchavati's forest where unseen the wild deer race,
Godavari's limped waters through its gloomy gorges flow,
Fruit and root and luscious berries on its silent margin grow,
Seek that spot and with thy brother build a lonesome leafy home,
Tend thy true and toil-worn Sita, farther still she may not roam!
Not unknown to me the mandate by thy royal father given,
Not unseen thy endless wanderings destined by the will of Heaven,
Therefore Panchavati's forest marked I for thy woodland stay,
Where the ripening wild fruit clusters and the wild bird trills his lay,
Tend thy dear devoted Sita and protect each pious rite,
Matchless in thy warlike weapons peerless in thy princely might!
Mark yon gloomy *Mahua* forest stretching o'er the boundless lea,
Pass that wood and turning northward seek an old *Nyagrodha* tree,
Then ascend a sloping upland by a steep and lofty hill,
Thou shalt enter Panchavati, blossom-covered, calm and still!"
Bowing to the great Agastya, Rama left the mighty sage,
Bowing to each saint and hermit, Lakshman left the hermitage,
And the princes tall and stately marched where Panchavati lay,
Soft-eyed Sita followed meekly where her Rama led the way!

III The Forest of Panchavati

Godavari's limpid waters in her gloomy gorges strayed,
Unseen rangers of the jungle nestled in the darksome shade!
"Mark the woodlands," uttered Rama, "by the Saint Agastya told,
Panchavati's lonesome forest with its blossoms red and gold,
Skilled to scan the wood and jungle, Lakshman, cast thy eye around,
For our humble home and dwelling seek a low and level ground,

Where the river laves its margin with a soft and gentle kiss,
Where my sweet and soft-eyed Sita may repose in sylvan bliss,
Where the lawn is fresh and verdant and the *kusa* young and bright,
And the creeper yields her blossoms for our sacrificial rite."
"Little can I help thee, brother," did the duteous Lakshman say,
"Thou art prompt to judge and fathom, Lakshman listens to obey!"
"Mark this spot," so answered Rama, leading Lakshman by the hand
"Soft the lawn of verdant *kusa,* beauteous blossoms light the land,
Mark the smiling lake of lotus gleaming with a radiance fair,
Wafting fresh and gentle fragrance o'er the rich and laden air,
Mark each scented shrub and creeper bending o'er the lucid wave,
Where the bank with soft caresses Godavari's waters lave!
Tuneful ducks frequent this margin, *Chakravakas*[1] breathe of love,
And the timid deer of jungle browse within the shady grove,
And the valleys are resonant with the peacock's clarion cry,
And the trees with budding blossoms glitter on the mountains high,
And the rocks in well-marked strata in their glittering lines appear,
Like the streaks of white and crimson painted on our tuskers fair!
Stately *Sal* and feathered palm-tree guard this darksome forest-land,
Golden date and flowering mango stretch afar on either hand,
Asok thrives and blazing *Kinsuk, Chandan* wafts a fragrance rare,
Aswa-karna and *Khadira* by the *Sami* dark and fair,
Beauteous spot for hermit-dwelling joyous with the voice of song,
Haunted by the timid wild deer and by black buck fleet and strong!"
Foe-compelling faithful Lakshman heard the words his elder said,
And by sturdy toil and labour stately home and dwelling made,
Spacious was the leafy cottage walled with moistened earth and soft,
Pillared with the stately bamboo holding high the roof aloft,
Interlacing twigs and branches, corded from the ridge to eaves,
Held the thatch of reed and branches and of jungle grass and leaves,
And the floor was pressed and levelled and the toilsome task was done,
And the structure rose in beauty for the righteous Raghu's son!
To the river for ablutions Lakshman went of warlike fame,
With a store of fragrant lotus and of luscious berries came,
Sacrificing to the Bright Gods sacred hymns and *mantras* said,
Proudly then unto his elder shewed the home his hand had made.
In her soft and grateful accents gentle Sita praised his skill,
Praised a brother's loving labour, praised a hero's dauntless will,

[1] The male and female geese, as symbols of conjugal love.

.ama clasped his faithful Lakshman in a brother's fond embrace,
pake in sweet and kindly accents with an elder's loving grace:
How can Rama, homeless wand'rer, priceless love like thine requite,
.et him hold thee in his bosom, soul of love and arm of might,
.nd our father good and gracious, in a righteous son like thee,
.ives again and treads the bright earth, from the bonds of YAMA free!"
'hus spake Rama, and with Lakshman and with Sita child of love,
)welt in Panchavati's cottage as the Bright Gods dwell above!

IV Winter in Panchavati

;ame and passed the golden autumn in the forest's gloomy shade,
.nd the northern blasts of winter swept along the silent glade,
Vhen the chilly night was over, once at morn the prince of fame,
'or his morning's pure ablutions to the Godavari came.
/leek-eyed Sita softly followed with the pitcher in her arms,
;allant Lakshman spake to Rama of the Indian winter's charms:
Comes the bright and bracing winter to the royal Rama dear,
.ike a bride the beauteous season doth in richest robes appear,
'rosty air and freshening zephyrs wake to life each mart and plain,
\nd the corn in dewdrop sparkling makes a sea of waving green,
3ut the village maid and matron shun the freezing river's shore,
3y the fire the village elder tells the stirring tale of yore!
Vith the winter's ample harvest men perform each pious rite,
To the Fathers long departed, to the Gods of holy might,
Vith the rite of *agrayana*[1] pious men their sins dispel,
\nd with gay and sweet observance songs of love the women tell,
\nd the monarchs bent on conquest mark the winter's cloudless glow,
.ead their bannered cars and forces 'gainst the rival and the foe!
Southward rolls the solar chariot, and the cold and widowed North
Reft of 'bridal mark' and joyance coldly sighs her sorrows forth,
Southward rolls the solar chariot, Himalaya, 'home of snow,'
True to name and appellation doth in whiter garments glow,
Southward rolls the solar chariot, cold and crisp the frosty air,
And the wood of flower dismantled doth in russet robes appear!
Star of Pushya rules December and the night with rime is hoar,
And beneath the starry welkin in the woods we sleep no more,

[1] The autumn harvest festival, with offerings of new grain.

And the pale moon mist-enshrouded sheds a faint and feeble beam,
As the breath obscures the mirror, winter mist obscures her gleam,
Hidden by the rising vapour faint she glistens on the dale,
Like our sun-embrownéd Sita with her toil and penance pale!
Sweeping blasts from western mountains through the gorges whistle by
And the *saras* and the curlew raise their shrill and piercing cry,
Boundless fields of wheat and barley are with dewdrops moist and wet
And the golden rice of winter ripens like the clustering date,
Peopled marts and rural hamlets wake to life and cheerful toil,
And the peaceful happy nations prosper on their fertile soil!
Mark the sun in morning vapours—like the moon subdued and pale—
Brightening as the day advances piercing through the darksome veil
Mark his gay and golden lustre sparkling o'er the dewy lea,
Mantling hill and field and forest, painting bush and leaf and tree,
Mark it glisten on the green grass, on each bright and bending blade,
Lighten up the long-drawn vista, shooting through the gloomy glade!
Thirst-impelled the lordly tusker still avoids the freezing drink,
Wild duck and the tuneful *hansa* doubtful watch the river's brink,
From the rivers wrapped in vapour unseen cries the wild curlew,
Unseen rolls the misty streamlet o'er its sandbank soaked in dew,
And the drooping water-lily bends her head beneath the frost,
Lost her fresh and fragrant beauty and her tender petals lost!
Now my errant fancy wanders to Ayodhya's distant town,
Where in hermit's barks and tresses Bharat wears the royal crown,
Scorning regal state and splendour, spurning pleasures loved of yore,
Spends his winter day in penance, sleeps at night upon the floor,
Aye! perchance Sarayu's waters seeks he now, serene and brave,
As we seek, when dawns the daylight, Godavari's limpid wave!
Rich of hue, with eye of lotus, truthful, faithful, strong of mind,
For the love he bears thee, Rama, spurns each joy of baser kind,
'False he proves unto his father who is led by mother's wile,'—
Vain this ancient impious adage—Bharat spurns his mother's guile,
Bharat's mother Queen Kaikeyi, Dasa-ratha's royal spouse,
Deep in craft, hath brought disaster on Ayodhya's royal house!"
"Speak not thus," so Rama answered, "on Kaikeyi cast no blame,
Honour still the righteous Bharat, honour still the royal dame,
Fixed in purpose and unchanging still in jungle wilds I roam,
But thy accents, gentle Lakshman, wake a longing for my home!

And my loving mem'ry lingers on each word from Bharat fell,
Sweeter than the draught of nectar, purer than the crystal well,
And my righteous purpose falters, shaken by a brother's love,
May we meet again our brother, if it please the Gods above!"
Waked by love, a silent tear-drop fell on Godavari's wave,
True once more to righteous purpose Rama's heart was calm and brave,
Rama plunged into the river 'neath the morning's crimson beam,
Sita softly sought the waters as the lily seeks the stream,
And they prayed to Gods and Fathers with each rite and duty done,
And they sang the ancient *mantra* to the red and rising Sun,
With her lord, in loosened tresses Sita to her cottage came,
As with RUDRA wanders UMA in Kailasa's hill of fame!

BOOK VI SITA-HARANA

(Sita Lost)

WE EXCHANGE the quiet life of Rama in holy hermitages for the more stirring incidents of the Epic in this Book. The love of a Raksha princess for Rama and for Lakshman is rejected with scorn, and smarting under insult and punishment she fires her brother Ravan, the king of Ceylon, with a thirst for vengeance. The dwellers of Ceylon are described in the Epic as monsters of various forms, and able to assume different shapes at will. Ravan sends Maricha in the shape of a beautiful deer to tempt away Rama and Lakshman from the cottage, and then finds his chance for stealing away the unprotected Sita.

The misfortunes of our lives, according to Indian thinkers, are but the results of our misdeeds; calamities are brought about by our sins. And thus we find in the Indian Epic, that a dark and foul suspicion against Lakshman crossed the stainless mind of Sita, and words of unmerited insult fell from her gentle lips, on the eve of the great calamity which clouded her life ever after. It was the only occasion on which the ideal woman of the Epic harboured an unjust thought or spoke an angry word; and it was followed by a tragic fate which few women on earth have suffered. To the millions of men and women in India, Sita remains to this day the ideal of female love and female devotion; her dark suspicions against Lakshman sprang out of an excess of her affection for her husband; and her tragic fate and long trial proved that undying love.

The portions translated in this Book form the whole or the main portions of Sections xvii., xviii., xliii., xlv., xlvi., xlvii., and xlix. of Book iii of the original text.

I Surpa-nakha in Love

As the Moon with starry Chitra dwells in azure skies above,
In his lonesome leafy cottage Rama dwelt in Sita's love,
And with Lakshman strong and valiant, quick to labour and obey,
Tales of bygone times recounting Rama passed the livelong day.
And it so befell, a maiden, dweller of the darksome wood,
Led by wand'ring thought or fancy once before the cottage stood,
Surpa-nakha, Raksha maiden, sister of the Raksha lord,
Came and looked with eager longing till her soul was passion-stirred!
Looked on Rama lion-chested, mighty-arméd, lotus-eyed,
Stately as the jungle tusker, with his crown of tresses tied,
Looked on Rama lofty-fronted, with a royal visage graced,
Like KANDARPA young and lustrous, lotus-hued and lotus-faced!
What though she a Raksha maiden, poor in beauty plain in face,
Fell her glances passion-laden on the prince of peerless grace,
What though wild her eyes and tresses, and her accents counselled fear,
Soft-eyed Rama fired her bosom, and his sweet voice thrilled her ear,
What though bent on deeds unholy, holy Rama won her heart,
And, for love makes bold a female, thus did she her thoughts impart:
"Who be thou in hermit's vestments, in thy native beauty bright,
Friended by a youthtful woman, arméd with thy bow of might,
Who be thou in these lone regions where the Rakshas hold their sway,
Wherefore in a lonely cottage in this darksome jungle stay?"
With his wonted truth and candour Rama spake sedate and bold,
And the story of his exile to the Raksha maiden told:
"Dasa-ratha of Ayodhya ruled with INDRA's godlike fame,
And his eldest, first-born Rama, by his mandate here I came,
Younger Lakshman strong and valiant doth with me these forests roam,
And my wife, Videha's daughter, Sita makes with me her home.
Duteous to my father's bidding, duteous to my mother's will,
Striving in the cause of virtue in the woods we wander still.
Tell me, female of the forest, who thou be and whence thy birth,
Much I fear thou art a Raksha wearing various forms on earth!"

"Listen," so spake Surpa-nakha, "if my purpose thou wouldst know,
I am Raksha, Surpa-nakha, wearing various shapes below,
Know my brothers, royal Ravan, Lanka's lord from days of old,
Kumbha-karna dread and dauntless, and Bibhishan true and bold,
Khara and the doughty Dushan with me in these forests stray,
But by Rama's love emboldened I have left them on the way!
Broad and boundless is my empire and I wander in my pride,
Thee I choose as lord and husband,—cast thy human wife aside,
Pale is Sita and misshapen, scarce a warrior's worthy wife,
To a nobler, lordlier female consecrate thy gallant life!
Human flesh is food of Rakshas! weakling Sita I will slay,
Slay that boy the stripling brother,—thee as husband I obey,
On the peaks of lofty mountains, in the forests dark and lone,
We shall range the boundless woodlands and the joys of dalliance prove!"

II *Surpa-nakha Punished*

Rama heard her impious purpose and a gentle smile repressed,
To the foul and forward female thus his mocking words addressed:
"List, O passion-smitten maiden! Sita is my honoured wife,
With a rival loved and cherished cruel were thy wedded life!
But no consort follows Lakshman, peerless is his comely face,
Dauntless is his warlike valour, matchless is his courtly grace,
And he leads no wife or consort to this darksome woodland grove,
With no rival to thy passion seek his ample-hearted love!"
Surpa-nakha passion-laden then on Lakshman turned her eye,
But in merry mocking accents smiling Lakshman made reply:
"Ruddy in thy youthful beauty like the lotus in her pride,
I am slave of royal Rama, wouldst thou be a vassal's bride?
Rather be his younger consort, banish Sita from his arms,
Spurning Sita's faded beauty let him seek thy fresher charms,
Spurning Sita's faded graces let him brighter pleasures prove,
Wearied with a woman's dalliance let him court a Raksha's love!"
Wrath of unrequited passion raged like madness in her breast,
Torn by anger strong as tempest thus her answer she addrest:
"Are these mocking accents uttered, Rama, to insult my flame,
Feasting on her faded beauty dost thou still revere thy dame?
But beware a Raksha's fury and an injured female's wrath,
Surpa-nakha slays thy consort, bears no rival in her path!"

Fawn-eyed Sita fell in terror as the Raksha rose to slay,
So beneath the flaming meteor sinks Rohini's softer ray,
And like Demon of Destruction furious Surpa-nakha came,
Rama rose to stop the slaughter and protect his helpless dame.
"Brother, we have acted wrongly, for with those of savage breed,
Word in jest is courting danger,—this the penance of our deed,
Death perchance or death-like stupor hovers o'er my lovéd dame,
Let me wake to life my Sita, chase this female void of shame!"
Lakshman's anger leaped like lightning as the female hovered near,
With his sword the wrathful warrior cleft her nose and either ear,
Surpa-nakha in her anguish raised her accents shrill and high,
And the rocks and wooded valleys answered back the dismal cry,
Khara and the doughty Dushan heard the far-resounding wail,
Saw her red disfigured visage, heard her sad and woeful tale!

III Rama's Departure

Vainly fought the vengeful Khara, doughty Dushan vainly bled,
Rama and the valiant Lakshman strewed the forest with the dead,
Till the humbled Surpa-nakha to her royal brother hied,
Spake her sorrows unto Ravan and Maricha true and tried.
Shape of deer unmatched in beauty now the deep Maricha wore,
Golden tints upon his haunches, sapphire on his antlers bore,
Till the woodland-wand'ring Sita marked the creature in his pride,
Golden was his neck of beauty, silver-white his flank and side!
"Come, my lord and gallant Lakshman," thus the raptur'd Sita spake,
"Mark the deer of wondrous radiance browsing by the forest brake!"
"Much my heart misgives me, sister," Lakshman hesitated still,
" 'Tis some deep deceitful Raksha wearing every shape at will,
Monarchs wand'ring in this forest, hunting in this lonely glen,
Oft waylaid by artful Rakshas are by deep devices slain,
Bright as day-god or *Gandharva,*[1] woodland scenes they love to stray,
Till they fall upon the heedless, quick to slaughter and to slay,
Trust me, not in jewelled lustre forest creatures haunt the green,
'Tis some *maya*[2] and illusion, trust not what thy eyes have seen!"
Vainly spake the watchful Lakshman in the arts of Rakshas skilled,
For with forceful fascination Sita's inmost heart was thrilled,

[1] A celestial musician.

[2] *Maya* is illusion.

"Husband, good and ever gracious," sweetly thus implored the wife,
"I would tend this thing of beauty,—sharer of my forest life!
I have witnessed in this jungle graceful creatures passing fair,
Chowri[1] and the gentle roebuck, antelope of beauty rare,
I have seen the lithesome monkey sporting in the branches' shade,
Grizzly bear that feeds on *Mahua*,[2] and the deer that crops the blade,
I have marked the stately wild bull dash into the deepest wood,
And the *Kinnar*[3] strange and wondrous as in sylvan wilds he stood,
But these eyes have never rested on a form so wondrous fair,
On a shape so full of beauty, decked with tints so rich and rare!
Bright his bosom gem-bespangled, soft the lustre of his eye,
Lighting up the gloomy jungle as the Moon lights up the sky,
And his gentle voice and glances and his graceful steps and light,
Fill my heart with eager longing and my soul with soft delight!
If alive that beauteous object thou canst capture in thy way,
As thy Sita's sweet companion in these woodlands he will stay,
And when done our days of exile, to Ayodhya will repair,
Dwell in Sita's palace chamber nursed by Sita's tender care,
And our royal brother Bharat oft will praise his strength and speed,
And the queens and royal mothers pause the gentle thing to feed!
If alive this wary creature be it, husband, hard to take,
Slay him and his skin of lustre cherish for thy Sita's sake,
I will as a golden carpet spread the skin upon the grass,
Sweet memento of this forest when our forest days will pass!
Pardon if an eager longing which befits a woman ill,
And an unknown fascination doth my inmost bosom fill,
As I mark his skin bespangled and his antlers' sapphire ray,
And his coat of starry radiance glowing in the light of day!"
Rama bade the faithful Lakshman with the gentle Sita stay,
Long through woods and gloomy gorges vainly held his cautious way,
Vainly set the snare in silence by the lake and in the dale,
'Scaping every trap, Maricha, pierced by Rama's arrows fell,
Imitating Rama's accents uttered forth his dying cry:
"Speed, my faithful brother Lakshman, helpless in the woods I die!"

[1] Properly *chamari*, the yak.
[2] Properly *madhuka*, a tree.
[3] A being with the body of a man, and face of a horse.

IV Lakshman's Departure

"Heardst that distant cry of danger?" questioned Sita in distress,
"Woe, to me! who in my frenzy sent my lord to wilderness,
Speed, brave Lakshman, help my Rama, doleful was his distant cry,
And my fainting bosom falters and a dimness clouds my eye!
To the dread and darksome forest with thy keenest arrows speed,
Help thy elder and thy monarch, sore his danger and his need,
For perchance the cruel Rakshas gather round his lonesome path,
As the mighty bull is slaughtered by the lions in their wrath!"
Spake the hero: "Fear not, Sita! Dwellers of the azure height,
Rakshas nor the jungle-rangers match the peerless Rama's might,
Rama knows no dread or danger, and his mandate still I own,
And I may not leave thee, Lady, in this cottage all alone!
Cast aside thy causeless terror; in the sky or earth below,
In the nether regions, Rama knows no peer or equal foe,
He shall slay the deer of jungle, he shall voice no dastard cry,
'Tis some trick of wily Rakshas in this forest dark and high!
Sita, thou hast heard my elder bid me in this cottage stay,
Lakshman may not leave thee, Lady, for this duty—to obey.
Ruthless Rakshas roam the forest to revenge their leader slain,
Various are their arts and accents; chase thy thought of causeless pain!"
Sparkled Sita's eye in anger, frenzy marked her speech and word,
For a woman's sense is clouded by the danger of her lord:
"Markest thou my Rama's danger with a cold and callous heart,
Courtest thou the death of elder in thy deep deceitful art,
In thy semblance of compassion dost thou hide a cruel craft,
As in friendly guise the foeman hides his death-compelling shaft,
Following like a faithful younger in this dread and lonesome land,
Seekest thou the death of elder to enforce his widow's hand?
False thy hope as foul thy purpose! Sita is a faithful wife,
Sita follows saintly Rama, true in death as true in life!"
Quivered Lakshman's frame in anguish and the tear stood in his eye,
Fixed in faith and pure in purpose, calm and bold he made reply:
"Unto me a Queen and Goddess,—as a mother to a son,—
Answer to thy heedless censure patient Lakshman speaketh none,
Daughter of Videha's monarch,—pardon if I do thee wrong,—
Fickle is the faith of woman, poison-dealing is her tongue!

And thy censure, trust me, Lady, scathes me like a burning dart,
Free from guile is Lakshman's purpose, free from sin is Lakshman's heart,
Witness ye my truth of purpose, unseen dwellers of the wood,
Witness, I for Sita's safety by my elder's mandate stood,
Duteous to my queen and elder, I have toiled and worked in vain,
Dark suspicion and dishonour cast on me a needless stain!
Lady! I obey thy mandate, to my elder now I go,
Guardian Spirits of the forest watch thee from each secret foe,
Omens dark and signs of danger meet my pained and aching sight,
May I see thee by thy Rama, guarded by his conquering might!"

V *Ravan's Coming*

Ravan watched the happy moment burning with a vengeful spite,
Came to sad and sorrowing Sita in the guise of anchorite,
Tufted hair and russet garment, sandals on his feet he wore,
And depending from his shoulders on a staff his vessel bore,
And he came to lonely Sita, for each warlike chief was gone,
As the darkness comes to evening lightless from the parted Sun,
And he cast his eyes on Sita, as a *graha*[1] casts its shade
On the beauteous star Rohini when the bright Moon's glories fade.
Quaking Nature knew the moment; silent stood the forest trees,
Conscious of a deed of darkness fell the fragrant forest breeze,
Godavari's troubled waters trembled 'neath his lurid glance,
And his red eye's fiery lustre sparkled in the wavelets' dance!
Mute and still were forest creatures when in guise of anchorite,
Unto Sita's lonely cottage pressed the Raksha in his might,
Mute and voiceless was the jungle as he cast on her his eye,
As across the star of Chitra, planet Sani walks the sky!
Ravan stood in hermit's vestments,—vengeful purpose unrevealed,—
As a deep and darksome cavern is by grass and leaf concealed,
Ravan stood sedate and silent, and he gazed on Rama's queen,
Ivory brow and lip of coral, sparkling teeth of pearly sheen!
Lighting up the lonely cottage, Sita sat in radiance high,
As the Moon with streaks of silver fills the lonely midnight sky,
Lighting up the gloomy woodlands with her eyes serenely fair,
With her bark-clad shape of beauty mantled by her raven hair!

[1] The power of darkness, supposed to seize the sun or the moon at eclipse.

Ravan fired by impure passion fixed on her in lustful eye,
And the light that lit his glances gave his holy texts the lie,
Ravan in his flattering accents, with a soft and soothing art,
Praised the woman's peerless beauty to subdue the woman's heart:
"Beaming in thy golden beauty, robed in sylvan russet dress,
Wearing wreath of fragrant lotus like a nymph of wilderness,
Art thou *Sri*[1] or radiant *Gauri,*[2] maid of Fortune or of Fame,
Nymph of Love or sweet Fruition, what may be thy sacred name?
On thy lips of ruddy coral teeth of tender jasmine shine,
In thy eyes of limpid lustre dwells a light of love divine,
Tall and slender, softly rounded, are thy limbs of beauty rare,
Like the swelling fruit of *tala*[3] heaves thy bosom sweetly fair!
Smiling lips that tempt and ravish, lustre that thy dark eyes beam,
Crush my heart, as rolling waters crush the margin of the stream.
And thy wealth of waving tresses mantles o'er thy budding charms,
And thy waist of slender beauty courts a lover's circling arms!
Goddess or Gandharva maiden wears no brighter form or face,
Woman seen by eyes of mortals owns not such transcendent grace,
Wherefore then, in lonesome forest, nymph or maiden, make thy stay,
Where the jungle creatures wander and the Rakshas hold their sway?
Royal halls and stately mansions were for thee a meeter home,
And thy steps should grace a palace, not in pathless forest roam,
Blossoms rich, not thorn of jungle, decorate a lady's bower,
Silken robes, not sylvan garments, heighten Beauty's potent power!
Lady of the sylvan forest! other destiny is thine,—
As a bride beloved and courted in thy bridal garments shine,
Choose a loved and lordly suitor who shall wait on thee in pride,
Choose a hero worth thy beauty, be a monarch's queenly bride!
Speak thy lineage, heaven-descended! who may be thy parents high,
Rudras or the radiant *Maruts, Vasus* leaders of the sky,
All unworthy is this forest for a nymph or heavenly maid,
Beasts of prey infest the jungle, Rakshas haunt its gloomy shade,
Lions dwell in lovely caverns, tuskers ford the silent lake,
Monkeys sport on pendant branches, tigers steal beneath the brake,
Wherefore then this dismal forest doth thy fairy face adorn,
Who are thou and whence descended, nymph or maid or goddess-born?"

[1] Goddess of beauty and wealth, wife of Vishnu.
[2] A goddess, wife of Siva.
[3] A species of palm-tree with round fruit.

VI Ravan's Wooing

"Listen, Brahman!" answered Sita,—unsuspecting in her mind
That she saw a base betrayer in a hermit seeming kind,—
"I am born of royal Janak, ruler of Videha's land,
Rama prince of proud Kosala by his valour won my hand.
Years we passed in peaceful pleasure in Ayodhya's happy clime,
Rich in every rare enjoyment gladsome passed our happy time,
Till the monarch Dasa-ratha,—for his days were almost done,—
Wished to crown the royal Rama as his Heir and Regent son.
But the scheming Queen Kaikeyi claimed a long-forgotten boon,
That my consort should be exiled and her son should fill the throne,
She would take no rest or slumber, nourishment of drink or food,
Till her Bharat ruled the empire, Rama banished to the wood!
Five and twenty righteous summers graced my good and gracious lord,
True to faith and true to duty, true in purpose, deed, and word,
Loved of all his loyal people, rich in valour and in fame,
For the rite of consecration Rama to his father came.
Spake Kaikeyi to my husband:—'List thy father's promise fair,
Bharat shall be ruling monarch, do thou to the woods repair,'—
Ever gentle, ever duteous, Rama listened to obey,
And through woods and pathless jungles we have held our lonely way.
This, O pious-hearted hermit, is his story of distress,
And his young and faithful brother follows him in wilderness,
Lion in his warlike valour, hermit in his saintly vow,
Lakshman with his honoured elder wanders through the forest now.
Rest thee here, O holy Brahman, rich in piety and fame,
Till the forest-ranging brothers greet thee with the forest game,
Speak, if so it please thee, father, what great *rishi* claims thy birth,
Wherefore in this pathless jungle wand'rest friendless on this earth."
"Brahman nor a righteous *rishi*," royal Ravan made reply,
"Leader of the wrathful Rakshas, Lanka's lord and king am I,
He whose valour quells the wide-world, Gods above and men below,
He whose proud and peerless prowess Rakshas and Asuras know!
But thy beauty's golden lustre, Sita, wins my royal heart,
Be a sharer of my empire, of my glory take a part,
Many queens of queenly beauty on the royal Ravan wait,
Thou shalt be their reigning empress, thou shalt own my regal state!

Lanka girt by boundless ocean is of royal towns the best,
Seated in her pride and glory on a mountain's towering crest,
And in mountain paths and woodlands thou shalt with thy Ravan stray
Not in Godavari's gorges through the dark and dreary day,
And five thousand gay-dressed damsels shall upon my Sita wait,
Queen of Ravan's true affection, proud partaker of his state!"
Sparkled Sita's eyes in anger and a tremor shook her frame,
As in proud and scornful accents answered thus the royal dame:
"Knowest thou Rama great and godlike, peerless hero in the strife,
Deep, uncompassed, like the ocean?—I am Rama's wedded-wife!
Knowest thou Rama proud and princely, sinless in his saintly life,
Stately as the tall *Nyagrodha?*[1]—I am Rama's wedded wife!
Mighty-armèd, mighty-chested, mighty with his bow and sword,
Lion midst the sons of mortals,—Rama is my wedded lord!
Stainless as the Moon in glory, stainless in his deed and word,
Rich in valour and in virtue,—Rama is my wedded lord!
Sure thy fitful life is shadowed by a dark and dreadful fate,
Since in frenzy of thy passion courtest thou a warrior's mate,
Tear the tooth of hungry lion while upon the calf he feeds,
Touch the fang of deadly cobra while his dying victim bleeds,
Aye, uproot the solid mountain from its base of rocky land,
Ere thou win the wife of Rama stout of heart and strong of hand!
Pierce thy eye with point of needle till it racks thy tortured head,
Press thy red tongue cleft and bleeding on the razor's shining blade,
Hurl thyself upon the ocean from a towering peak and high,
Snatch the orbs of day and midnight from their spheres in azure sky,
Tongues of flaming conflagration in thy flowing dress enfold,
Ere thou take the wife of Rama to thy distant dungeon hold,
Ere thou seek to insult Rama unrelenting in his wrath,
O'er a bed of pikes of iron tread a softer easier path!"

VII Ravan's Triumph

Vain her threat and soft entreaty, Ravan held her in his wrath,
As the planet Budha captures fair Rohini in his path,
By his left hand tremor-shaken, Ravan held her streaming hair,
By his right the ruthless Raksha lifted up the fainting fair!

[1] The banyan or Indian fig-tree.

Unseen dwellers of the woodlands watched the dismal deed of shame,
Marked the mighty-arméd Raksha lift the poor and helpless dame,
Seat her on his car celestial yoked with asses winged with speed,
Golden in its shape and radiance, fleet as INDRA's heavenly steed!
Angry threat and sweet entreaty Ravan to her ears addressed,
As the struggling fainting woman still he held upon his breast,
Vain his threat and vain entreaty, "Rama! Rama!" still she cried,
To the dark and distant forest where her noble lord had hied.
Then arose the car celestial o'er the hill and wooded vale,
Like a snake in eagle's talons Sita writhed with piteous wail,
Dim and dizzy, faint and faltering, still she sent her piercing cry,
Echoing through the boundless woodlands, pealing to the upper sky:
"Save me, mighty-arméd Lakshman, stainless in thy heart and deed,
Save a faithful wife and woman from a Raksha's lust and greed,
True and faithful was thy warning,—false and foul the charge I made,
Pardon, friend, an erring sister, pardon words a woman said!
Help me, ever righteous Rama, duty bade thee yield thy throne,
Duty bids thee smite the sinful, save the wife who is thy own,
Thou art king and stern chastiser of each deed of sin and shame,
Hurl thy vengeance on the Raksha who insults thy faithful dame!
Deed of sin, unrighteous Ravan, brings in time its dreadful meed,
As the young corn grows and ripens from the small and living seed,
For this deed of insult, Ravan, in thy heedless folly done,
Death of all thy race and kindred thou shalt reap from Raghu's son!
Darksome woods of Panchavati, Janasthana's smiling vale,
Flowering trees and winding creepers, murmur to my lord this tale,
Sweet companions of my exile, friends who cheered my woodland stay,
Speak to Rama, that his Sita ruthless Ravan bears away!
Towering peaks and lofty mountains, wooded hills sublime and high,
Far-extending gloomy ranges heaving to the azure sky,
In your voice of pealing thunder to my lord and consort say,
Speak of Rama, that his Sita ruthless Ravan bears away!
Unseen dwellers of the woodlands, spirits of the rock and fell,
Sita renders you obeisance as she speaks her sad farewell,
Whisper to my righteous Rama when he seeks his homeward way,
Speak to Rama, that his Sita ruthless Ravan bears away!
Ah, my Rama, true and tender! thou hast loved me as thy life,
From the foul and impious Raksha thou shalt still redeem thy wife,

Ah, my Rama, mighty-arméd! vengeance soon shall speed thy way,
When thou hearest helpless Sita is by Ravan torn away!
And thou royal bird, Jatayu, witness Ravan's deed of shame,
Witness how he courts destruction, stealing Rama's faithful dame,
Rama and the gallant Lakshman soon shall find their destined prey,
When they know that trusting Sita is by Ravan torn away!"
Vainly wept the anguished Sita; vain Jatayu in his wrath,
Fought with beak and bloody talons to impede the Raksha's path,
Pierced and bleeding fell the vulture; Raven fled with Rama's bride,
Where amidst the boundless ocean Lanka rose in towering pride!

BOOK VII KISHKINDHA

(In the Nilgiri Mountains)

RAMA'S WANDERINGS in the Nilgiri mountains, and his alliance with Sugriva the chief of these regions, form the subject of the Book. With that contempt for aboriginal races which has marked civilized conquerors in all ages, the poet describes the dwellers of these regions as monkeys and bears. But the modern reader sees through these strange epithets; and in the description of the social and domestic manners, the arts and industries, the sacred rites and ceremonies, and the civic and political life of the Vanars, the reader will find that the poet even imports Aryan customs into his account of the dwellers of Southern India. They formed an alliance with Rama, they fought for him and triumphed with him, and they helped him to recover his wife from the king of Ceylon.

The portions translated in this Book from Sections v., xv., xvi., xxvi., a portion of Section xxviii., and an abstract of Sections xl. to xliii. of Book iv. of the original text.

I *Friends in Misfortune*

Long and loud lamented Rama by his lonesome cottage door,
Janasthana's woodlands answered, Panchavati's echoing shore,
Long he searched in wood and jungle, mountain crest and pathless plain,
Till he reached the Malya mountains stretching to the southern main.
There Sugriva king of Vanars, Hanuman his henchman brave,
Banished from their home and empire lived within the forest cave,

To the exiled king Sugriva, Hanuman his purpose told,
As he marked the pensive Rama wand'ring with his brother bold:
"Mark the sons of Dasa-ratha banished from their royal home,
Duteous to their father's mandate in these pathless forests roam,
Great was monarch Dasa-ratha famed for sacrifice divine,
Raja-suya,[1] *Aswa-medha*,[2] and for gift of gold and kine,
By a monarch's stainless duty people's love the monarch won,
By a woman's false contrivance banished he his eldest son!
True to duty, true to virtue, Rama passed his forest life,
Till a false perfidious Raksha stole his fair and faithful wife,
And the anguish-stricken husband seeks thy friendship and thy aid,
Mutual sorrow blends your fortunes, be ye friends in mutual need!"
Bold Sugriva heard the counsel, and to righteous Rama hied,
And the princess of Ayodhya with his greetings gratified:
"Well I know thee, righteous Rama, soul of piety and love,
And thy duty to thy father and thy faith in God above,
Fortune favours poor Sugriva, Rama courts his humble aid,
In our deepest direst danger be our truest friendship made!
Equal is our fateful fortune,—I have lost a queenly wife,
Banished from Kishkindha's empire here I lead a forest life,
Pledge of love and true alliance, Rama, take this proffered hand,
Banded by a common sorrow we shall fall or stoutly stand!"
Rama grasped the hand he offered, and the tear was in his eye,
And they swore undying friendship o'er the altar blazing high,
Hanuman with fragrant blossoms sanctified the sacred rite,
And the comrades linked by sorrow walked around the altar's light,
And their word and troth they plighted: "In our happiness and woe
We are friends in thought and action, we will face our common foe!"
And they broke a leafy *Sal* tree, spread it underneath their feet,
Rama and his friend Sugriva sat upon the common seat,
And a branch of scented *Chandan*[3] with its tender blossoms graced,
Hanuman as seat of honour for the faithful Lakshman placed.
"Listen, Rama," spake Sugriva, "reft of kingdom, reft of wife,
Fleeing to these rugged mountains I endure a forest life,
For my tyrant brother Bali rules Kishkindha all alone,
Forced my wife from my embraces, drove me from my father's throne,
Trembling in my fear and anguish I endure a life of woe,
Render me my wife and empire from my brother and my foe!"

[1] An imperial sacrifice. [2] Horse sacrifice. [3] Sandal tree.

"Not in vain they seek my succour," so the gallant Rama said,
"Who with love and offered friendship seek my counsel and my aid,
Not in vain these glistening arrows in my ample quiver shine,
Bali dies the death of tyrants, wife and empire shall be thine!
Quick as INDRA's *forked lightning are these arrows feather-plumed,*
Deadly as the hissing serpent are these darts with points illumed,
And this day shall not be ended ere it sees thy brother fall,
As by lurid lightning severed sinks the crest of mountain tall!"

II The Counsel of Tara

Linked in bonds of faithful friendship Rama and Sugriva came,
Where in royal town Kishkindha, Bali ruled with warlike fame,
And a shout like troubled ocean's or like tempest's deafening roar
Spake Sugriva's mighty challenge to the victor king once more!
Bali knew that proud defiance shaking sky and solid ground,
And like sun by eclipse shaded, dark and pale he looked around,
And his teeth were set in anger and a passion lit his eye,
As a tempest stirs a torrent when its lilies scattered lie,
And he rose in wrath terrific with a thought of vengeance dread,
And the firm earth shook and trembled 'neath his proud and haughty tread!
But the true and tender Tara held her husband and her lord,
And a woman's deeper wisdom spake in woman's loving word:
"Wherewore like a rain-fed torrent swells thy passion in its sway,
Thoughts of wrath like withered blossoms from thy bosom cast away,
Wait till dawns another morning, wait till thou dost truly know,
With what strength and added forces comes again thy humbled foe.
Crushed in combat faint Sugriva fled in terror and in pain,
Trust me, not without a helper comes he to the fight again,
Trust me, lord, that loud defiance is no coward's falt'ring cry,
Conscious strength not hesitation speaks in voice so proud and high!
Much my woman's heart misgives me, not without a mighty aid,
Not without a daring comrade comes Sugriva to this raid,
Not with feeble friend Sugriva seeks alliance in his need,
Nor invokes a powerless chieftain in his lust and in his greed.
Mighty is his royal comrade,—listen, husband, to my word,
What my son in forest confines from his messengers hath heard,—

Princes from Ayodhya's country peerless in the art of war,
Rama and the valiant Lakshman in these forests wander far,
Much I fear, these matchless warriors have their aid and counsel lent
Conscious of his strength Sugriva hath this proud defiance sent!
To his foes resistless Rama is a lightning from above,
To his friends a tree of shelter, soul of tenderness and love,
Dearer than his love of glory is his love to heal and bless,
Dearer than the crown and empire is his hermit's holy dress,
Not with such, my lord and husband, seek a vain unrighteous strife,
For, like precious ores in mountains, virtues dwell in Rama's life.
Make Sugriva thy companion, make him Regent and thy Heir,
Discord with a younger brother rends an empire broad and fair,
Make thy peace with young Sugriva, nearest and thy dearest kin,
Brother's love is truest safety, brother's hate is deadliest sin!
Trust me, monarch of Kishkindha, trust thy true and faithful wife,
Thou shalt find no truer comrade than Sugriva in thy life,
Wage not then a war fraternal, smite him not in sinful pride,
As a brother and a warrior let him stand by Bali's side.
Listen to thy Tara's counsel if to thee is Tara dear,
If thy wife is true in duty scorn not Tara's wifely tear,
Not with Rama prince of virtue wage a combat dread and high,
Not with Rama prince of valour, peerless like the Lord of sky!"

III The Fall of Bali

Star-eyed Tara softly counselled pressing to her consort's side,
Mighty Bali proudly answered with a warrior's lofty pride:
"Challenge of a humbled foeman and a younger's haughty scorn
May not, shall not, tender Tara, by a king be meekly borne!
Bali turns not from encounter even with his dying breath,
Insult from a foe, unanswered, is a deeper stain than death,
And Sugriva's quest for combat Bali never shall deny,
Though sustained by Rama's forces and by Rama's prowess high!
Free me from thy sweet embraces and amidst thy maids retire,
Woman's love and soft devotion woman's timid thoughts inspire,
Fear not, Tara, blood of brother Bali's honour shall not stain,
I will quell his proud presumption, chase him from this realm again,
Free me from thy loving dalliance, midst thy damsels seek thy place,
Till I come a happy victor to my Tara's fond embrace!"

Slow and sad with sweet obeisance Tara stepped around her lord,
Welling tear-drops choked her accents as she prayed in stifled word,
Slow and sad with swelling bosom Tara with her maids retired,
Bali issued proud and stately with the thought of vengeance fired!
Hissing like an angry cobra, city's lofty gates he past,
And his proud and angry glances fiercely all around he cast,
Till he saw bold Sugriva, gold-complexioned, red with ire,
Girded for the dubious combat, flaming like the forest fire!
Bali braced his warlike garments and his hand he lifted high,
Bold Surgiva raised his right arm with a proud and answering cry,
Bali's eyes were red as copper and his chain was burnished gold,
To his brother bold Sugriva thus he spake in accents bold:
"Mark this iron fist, intruder, fatal is its vengeful blow,
Crushed and smitten thou shalt perish and to nether world shalt go,"
"Nay that fate awaits thee, Bali," spake Sugriva armed for strife,
"When this right arm smites thy forehead, from thy bosom rends thy life!"
Closed the chiefs in fatal combat, each resistless in his pride,
And like running rills from mountains poured their limbs the purple tide,
Till Sugriva quick uprooting *Sal* tree from the jungle wood,
As the dark cloud hurls the lightning, hurled it where his brother stood,
Staggering 'neath the blow terrific Bali reeled and almost fell,
As a proud ship overladen reels upon the ocean's swell!
But with fiercer rage and fury Bali in his anguish rose,
And with mutual blows they battled,—brothers and relentless foes,
Like the sun and moon in conflict or like eagles in their fight,
Still they fought with cherished hatred and an unforgotten spite,
Till with mightier force and fury Bali did his younger quell,
Faint Sugriva fiercely struggling 'neath his brother's prowess fell!
Still the wrathful rivals wrestled with their bleeding arms and knees,
With their nails like claws of tigers and with riven rocks and trees,
And as INDRA battles Vritra in the tempest's pealing roar,
Blood-stained Bali, red Sugriva, strove and struggled, fought and tore,
Till Sugriva faint and falt'ring fell like Vritra from the sky,
To his comrade and his helper turned his faint and pleading eye!
Ah! those soft and pleading glances smote the gentle Rama's heart,
On his bow of ample stature Rama raised the fatal dart,

Like the fatal disc of YAMA was his proudly circled bow,
Like a snake of deadly poison flew his arrow swift and low,
Wingéd dwellers of the forest heard the twang with trembling fear,
Echoing woods gave back the accent, lightly fled the startled deer,
And as INDRA's flag is lowered when the Aswin winds prevail,
Lofty Bali pierced and bleeding by that fatal arrow fell!

IV The Consecration of Sugriva

Tears of love the tender Tara on her slaughtered hero shed,
E'en Sugriva's bosom melted when he saw his brother dead,
And each Vanar chief and warrior, *maha-matra,*[1] lord and peer,
Gathered round the sad Sugriva wet with unavailing tear!
And they girt the victor Rama and they praised his wond'rous might,
As the heavenly *rishis* gather circling BRAHMA's throne of light,
Hanuman of sun-like radiance, lofty as a hill of gold,
Clasped his hands in due obeisance, spake in accents calm and bold:
"By thy prowess, peerless Rama, prince Sugriva is our lord,
To his father's throne and empire, to his father's town restored,
Cleansed by bath and fragrant unguents and in royal garments gay,
He shall with his gold and garlands homage to the victor pay,
To the rock-bound fair Kishkindha do thy friendly footsteps bend,
And as monarch of the Vanars consecrate thy grateful friend!"
"Fourteen years," so Rama answered, "by his father's stern command,
In a city's sacred confines banished Rama may not stand,
Friend and comrade, brave Sugriva, enter thou the city wall,
And assume the royal sceptre in thy father's royal hall.
Gallant Angad, son of Bali, is in regal duties trained,
Ruling partner of thy empire be the valiant prince ordained,
Eldest son of eldest brother,—such the maxim that we own,—
Worthy of his father's kingdom, doth ascend his father's throne.
Listen! 'tis the month of *Sravan,*[2] now begins the yearly rain,
In these months of wind and deluge thoughts of vengeful strife were vain,
Enter then thy royal city, fair Kishkindha be thy home,
With my ever faithful Lakshman let me in these mountains roam.
Spacious is yon rocky cavern fragrant with the mountain air,
Bright with lily and with lotus, watered by a streamlet fair,

[1] A royal officer.
[2] *Sravana,* July-August.

Here we dwell till month of *Kartik*[1] when the clouded sky will clear,
And the time of war and vengeance on our foeman shall be near."
Bowing to the victor's mandate brave Sugriva marched in state,
And the host of thronging Vanars entered by the city gate,
Prostrate chiefs with due obeisance rendered homage, one and all,
And Sugriva blessed his people, stepped within the palace hall.
And they sprinkled sacred water from the vases jewel-graced,
And they waved the fan of *chowri*,[2] raised the sun-shade silver-laced,
And they spread the gold and jewel, grain and herb and fragrant *ghee*,[3]
Sapling twigs and bending branches, blossoms from the flowering tree,
Milk-white garments gem-bespangled, and the *Chandan's* fragrant dye,
Wreaths and spices, snow-white lilies, lotus azure as the sky,
Jatarupa and *Priyangu*,[4] honey, curd and holy oil,
Costly sandals gilt and jewelled, tiger-skin the hunter's spoil!
Decked in gold and scented garlands, robed in radiance rich and rare,
Sweetly stepped around Sugriva sixteen maidens passing fair,
Priests received the royal bounty, gift and garment gold-belaced,
And they lit the holy altar with the sacred *mantra* graced,
And they poured the sweet libation on the altar's lighted flame,
And on throne of royal splendour placed the chief of royal fame!
On a high and open terrace with auspicious garlands graced,
Facing eastward, in his glory was the brave Sugriva placed,
Water from each holy river, from each *tirtha* famed of old,
From the broad and boundless ocean, was arranged in jars of gold,
And from vase and horn of wild bull, on their monarch and their lord,
Holy consecrating water chiefs and loyal courtiers poured.
Gaya and the great Gavaksha, Gandha-madan proud and brave,
Hanuman held up the vases, Jambman his succour gave,
And they laved the king Sugriva as Immortals in the sky
Consecrate the star-eyed INDRA in his mansions bright and high,
And a shout of joy and triumph, like the pealing voice of war,
Spake Sugriva's consecration to the creatures near and far!
Duteous still to Rama's mandate, as his first-born and his own,
King Sugriva named young Angad sharer of his royal throne,
Gay and bannered town Kishkindha hailed Sugriva's gracious word,
Tender Tara wiped her tear-drops bowing to a younger lord!

[1] *Kartika*, October-November.
[2] Fan made from the tail of the Indian yak.
[3] Or *ghrita*, clarified butter.
[4] Fragrant ointment.

V *The Rains in the Nilgiri Mountains*

"Mark the shadowing rain and tempest," Rama to his brother said,
As on Malya's cloud-capped ranges in their hermit-guise they strayed,
'Massive clouds like rolling mountains gather thick and gather high,
Lurid lightnings glint and sparkle, pealing thunders shake the sky,
Pregnant with the ocean moisture by the solar ray instilled,
Now the skies like fruitful mothers are with grateful waters filled!
Mark the folds of cloudy masses, ladder-like of smooth ascent,
One could almost reach the Sun-god, wreath him with a wreath of scent,
And when glow these heavy masses red and white with evening's glow,
One could almost deem them sword-cuts branded by some heavenly foe!
Mark the streaks of golden lustre lighting up the checkered sky,
Like a lover *chandan*-painted in each breeze it heaves a sigh,
And the earth is hot and feverish, moistened with the tears of rain,
Sighting like my anguished Sita when she wept in woe and pain!
Fresh and sweet like draught of necta is the rain-besprinkled breeze,
Fragrant with the *ketak*[1] blossom, scented by the camphor trees,
Fresh and bold each peak and mountain bathed in soft descending rain,
So they sprinkle holy water when they bless a monarch's reign!
Fair and tall as holy hermits, stand yon shadow-mantled hills,
Murmuring *mantras* with the zephyr, robed in threads of sparkling rills,
Fair and young as gallant coursers neighing forth their thunder cries,
Lashed by golden whips of lightning are the dappled sunlit skies!
Ah, my lost and loving Sita! writhing in a Raksha's power,
As the lightning shakes and quivers in this dark tempestuous shower,
Shadows thicken on the prospect, flower and leaf are wet with rain,
And each passing object, Lakshman, wakes in me a thought of pain!
Joyously from throne and empire with my Sita I could part,
As the stream erodes its margin, Sita's absence breaks my heart,
Rain and tempest cloud the prospect as they cloud my onward path,
Dubious is my darksome future, mighty is my foeman's wrath!
Ravan monarch of the Rakshas,—so Jatayu said and died,—
In some unknown forest fastness doth my sorrowing Sita hide,
But Sugriva true and faithful seeks the Raksha's secret hold,
Firm in faith and fixed in purpose we will face our foeman bold!"

[1] A strong-scented plant.

VI The Quest for Sita

Past the rains, the marshalled Vanars gathered round Sugriva bold,
And unto a gallant chieftain thus the king his purpose told:
"Brave in war and wise in counsel! take ten thousand of my best,
Seek the hiding-place of Ravan in the regions of the East.
Seek each ravine rock and forest and each shadowy hill and cave,
Far where bright Sarayu's waters mix with Ganga's ruddy wave,
And where Jumna's dark blue waters ceaseless roll in regal pride,
And the Sone through leagues of country spreads its torrents far and wide.
Seek where in Videha's empire castled towns and hamlets shine,
In Kosala and in Malwa and by Kasi's sacred shrine,
Magadh rich in peopled centres, Pundra region of the brave,
Anga rich in corn and cattle on the eastern ocean wave.
Seek where clans of skilful weavers dwell upon the eastern shore,
And from virgin mines of silver miners work the sparkling ore.
In the realms of uncouth nations, in the islets of the sea,
In the mountains of the ocean, wander far and wander free!"
Next to Nila son of AGNI, Jambaman VIDAHATA's son,
Hanuman the son of MARUT, famed for deeds of valour done,
Unto Gaya and Gavaksha, Gandha-madan true and tried,
Unto Angad prince and regent, thus the brave Sugriva cried:
"Noblest, bravest of our chieftains, greatest of our race are ye,
Seek and search the southern regions, rock and ravine, wood and tree,
Search the thousand peaks of Vindhya lifting high its misty head,
Through the gorges of Narmada rolling o'er its rocky bed,
By the gloomy Godovari and by Krishna's wooded stream,
Through Utkala's sea-girt forests tinged by morning's early gleam.
Search the towns of famed Dasarna and Avanti's rocky shore,
And the uplands of Vidarbha and the mountains of Mysore,
Land of Matsyas and Kalingas and Kausika's regions fair,
Trackless wilderness of Dandak seek with anxious toil and care.
Search the empire of the Andhras, of the sister-nations three,—
Cholas, Cheras and the Pandyas dwelling by the southern sea,
Pass Kaveri's spreading waters, Malya's mountains towering brave,
Seek the isle of Tamra-parni, gemmed upon the ocean wave!"
To Susena chief and elder,—Tara's noble sire was he,—
Spake Sugriva with obeisance and in accents bold and free:

"Take my lord, a countless army of the bravest and the best,
Search where beats the sleepless ocean on the regions of the West.
Search the country of Saurashtras, of Bahlikas strong and brave,
And each busy mart and seaport on the western ocean wave,
Castles girt by barren mountains, deserts by the sandy sea,
Forests of the fragrant *ketak*, regions of the *tamal* tree!
Search the ocean port of Pattan shaded by its fruitful trees,
Where the feathery groves of cocoa court the balmy western breeze,
Where on peaks of Soma-giri lordly lions wander free,
Where the waters of the Indus mingle with the mighty sea!"
Lastly to the valiant chieftain Satavala strong and brave,
For the quest of saintly Sita thus his mighty mandate gave:
"Hie thee, gallant Satavala, with thy forces wander forth,
To the peaks of Himalaya, to the regions of the North!
Mlechchas and the wild Pulindas in the rocky regions dwell,
Madra chiefs and mighty Kurus live within each fertile vale,
Wild Kambojas of the mountains, Yavanas of wondrous skill,
Sakas swooping from their gorges, Pattanas of iron will!
Search the woods of *devadaru*[1] mantling Himalaya's side,
And the forests of the *lodhra*[2] spreading in their darksome pride,
Search the land of Soma-srama where the gay *Gandharvas* dwell
In the tableland of Kala search each rock and ravine well!
Cross the snowy Himalaya, and Sudarsan's holy peak,
Deva-sakha's wooded ranges which the feathered songsters seek,
Cross the vast and dreary region void of stream or wooded hill,
Till you reach the white Kailasa, home of Gods, serene and still!
Pass Kuvera's pleasant regions, search the Krauncha mountain well,
And the land where warlike females and the horse-faced women dwell,
Halt not till you reach the country where the Northern Kurus rest,
Utmost confines of the wide earth, home of Gods and Spirits blest!"

BOOK VIII SITA-SANDESA

(*Sita Discovered*)

Among the many chiefs sent by Sugriva in different directions in search of Sita, Hanuman succeeded in the quest and discovered Sita in Ceylon. Ceylon is separated from India by a broad channel of the sea, and

[1] The Himalayan pine. [2] A tree.

Hanuman leaped, or rather flew through the air, across the channel, and lighted on the island. Sita, scorning the proposals of Ravan, was kept in confinement in a garden of *Asoka* trees, surrounded by a terrible guard of Raksha females; and in this hard confinement she remained true and faithful to her lord. Hanuman gave her a token from Rama, and carried back to Rama a token which she sent of her undying affection and truth.

The portions translated in this Book form the whole of the main portions of Sections xv., xxxi., xxxvi., and lxvi. of Book v. of the original text.

I Sita in the Asoka Garden

Crossed the ocean's boundless waters, Hanuman in duty brave,
Lighted on the emerald island girded by the sapphire wave,
And in tireless quest of Sita searched the margin of the sea,
In a dark *Asoka*[1] garden hid himself within a tree.
Creepers threw their clasping tendrils round the trees of ample height,
Stately palm and feathered cocoa, fruit and blossom pleased the sight,
Herds of tame and gentle creatures in the grassy meadow strayed,
Kokils[2] sang in leafy thicket, birds of plumage lit the shade,
Limpid lakes of scented lotus with their fragrance filled the air,
Homes and huts of rustic beauty peeped through bushes green and fair,
Blossoms rich in tint and fragrance in the checkered shadow gleamed,
Clustering fruits of golden beauty in the yellow sunlight beamed!
Brightly shone the red *Asoka* with the morning's golden ray,
Karnikara and *Kinsuka*[3] dazzling as the light of day,
Brightly grew the flower of *Champak* in the vale and on the reef,
Punnaga and *Saptaparna* with its seven-fold scented leaf,
Rich in blossoms many tinted, grateful to the ravished eye,
Gay and green and glorious Lanka was like garden of the sky,
Rich in fruit and laden creeper and in beauteous bush and tree,
Flower-bespangled golden Lanka was like gem-bespangled sea!
Rose a palace in the woodlands girt by pillars strong and high,
Snowy-white like fair Kailasa cleaving through the azure sky,
And its steps were ocean coral and its pavements yellow gold,
White and gay and heaven-aspiring rose the structure high and bold!

[1] Name of a flower, orange and scarlet.
[2] An Indian singing bird.
[3] All names of flowers.

By the rich and royal mansion Hanuman his eyes did rest,
On a woman sad and sorrowing in her sylvan garments drest,
Like the moon obscured and clouded, dim with shadows deep and dark,
Like the smoke-enshrouded red fire, dying with a feeble spark,
Like the tempest-pelted lotus by the wind and torrent shaken,
Like the beauteous star Rohini by a *graha*[1] overtaken!
Fasts and vigils paled her beauty, tears bedimmed her tender grace,
Anguish dwelt within her bosom, sorrow darkened on her face,
And she lived by Rakshas guarded, as a faint and timid deer,
Severed from her herd and kindred when the prowling wolves are near,
And her raven locks ungathered hung behind in single braid,
And her gentle eye was lightless, and her brow was hid in shade!
"This is she! the peerless princess, Rama's consort loved and lost,
This is she! the saintly Sita, by a cruel fortune crost,"
Hanuman thus thought and pondered: "On her graceful form I spy,
Gems and gold by sorrowing Rama oft depicted with a sigh,
On her ears the golden pendants and the tiger's sharpened tooth,
On her arms the jewelled bracelets, tokens of unchanging truth,
On her pallid brow and bosom still the radiant jewels shine,
Rama with a sweet affection did in early days entwine!
Hermit's garments clothe her person, braided in her raven hair,
Matted bark trees of forest drape her neck and bosom fair,
And a dower of dazzling beauty still bedecks her peerless face,
Though the shadowing tinge of sorrow darkens all her earlier grace!
This is she! the soft-eyed Sita, wept with unavailing tear,
This is she! the faithful consort, unto Rama ever dear,
Unforgetting and unchanging, truthful still in deed and word,
Sita in her silent suffering sorrows for her absent lord,
Still for Rama lost but cherished, Sita heaves the choking sigh,
Sita lives for righteous Rama, for her Rama she would die!"

II The Voice of Hope

Hanuman from leafy shelters lifts his voice in sacred song,
Till the tale of Rama's glory Lanka's woods and vales prolong:
"Listen, Lady, to my story;—Dasa-ratha famed in war,
Rich in steeds and royal tuskers, armèd men and battle car,

[1] The spirit of darkness, responsible for eclipse.

Ruled his realm in truth and virtue, in his bounty ever free,
Of the mighty race of Raghu mightiest king and monarch he,
Robed in every royal virtue, great in peace in battle brave,
Blest in bliss of grateful nations, blest in blessings which he gave!
And his eldest-born and dearest, Rama soul of righteous might,
Shone, as mid the stars resplendent shines the radiant Lord of Night,
True unto his sacred duty, true unto his kith and kin,
Friend of piety and virtue, punisher of crime and sin,
Loved in all his spacious empire, peopled mart and hermit's den,
With a truer deeper kindness Rama loved his subject men!
Dasa-ratha, promise-fettered, then his cruel mandate gave,
Rama with his wife and brother lived in woods and rocky cave,
And he slayed the deer of jungle and he slept in leafy shade,
Stern destroyer of the Rakshas in the pathless forests strayed,
Till the monarch of the Rakshas,—fraudful is his impious life,—
Cheated Rama in the jungle, from his cottage stole his wife!
Long lamenting lone and weary Rama wandered in the wood,
Searched for Sita in the jungle where his humble cottage stood,
Godavari's gloomy gorges, Krishna's dark and wooded shore,
And the ravine, rock and valley, and the cloud-capped mountain hoar!
Then he met the sad Sugriva in wild Malya's dark retreat,
Won for him his father's empire and his father's royal seat,
Now Sugriva's countless forces wander far and wander near,
In the search of stolen Sita still unto his Rama dear!
I am henchman of Sugriva and the mighty sea have crost,
In the quest of hidden Sita, Rama's consort loved and lost,
And methinks that form of beauty, peerless shape of woman's grace,
Is my Rama's dear-loved consort, Rama's dear-remembered face!"
Hushed the voice: the ravished Sita cast her wond'ring eyes around,
Whence that song of sudden gladness, whence that soul-entrancing sound?
Dawning hope and rising rapture overflowed her widowed heart,
Is it dream's deceitful whisper which the cruel Fates impart?

III Rama's Token

"'Tis no dream's deceitful whisper!" Hanuman spake to the dame,
As from darksome leafy shelter he to Rama's consort came,

"Rama's messenger and vassal, token from thy lord I bring,
Mark this bright ring, jewel-lettered with the dear name of thy king,
For the loved and cherished Sita is to Rama ever dear,
And he sends his loving message and his force is drawing near!"
Sita held that tender token from her loved and cherished lord,
And once more herself she fancied to his loving arms restored,
And her pallid face was lighted and her soft eye sent a spark,
As the Moon regains her lustre freed from *Rahu's*[1] shadows dark!
And with voice of deep emotion in each softly whispered word,
Spake her thoughts in gentle accents of her consort and her lord:
"Messenger of love of Rama! Dauntless is thy deed and bold,
Thou hast crossed the boundless ocean to the Raksha's castled hold,
Thou hast crossed the angry billows which confess no monarch's sway,
O'er the face of rolling waters found thy unresisted way,
Thou hast done what living mortal never sought to do before,
Dared the Raksha in his island, Ravan in his sea-girt shore!
Speak, if Rama lives in safety in the woods or by the hill,
And if young and gallant Lakshman faithful serves his brother still,
Speak, if Rama in his anger and his unforgiving ire,
Hurls destruction on my captor like the world-consuming fire,
Speak, if Rama in his sorrow wets his pale and drooping eye,
If the thought of absent Sita wakes within his heart a sigh!
Doth my husband seek alliance with each wild and warlike chief,
Striving for a speedy vengeance and for Sita's quick relief,
Doth he stir the warlike races to a fierce and vengeful strife,
Dealing death to ruthless Rakshas for this insult on his wife,
Doth he still in fond remembrance cherish Sita loved of yore,
Nursing in his hero-bosom tender sorrows evermore!
Didst thou hear from far Ayodhya, from Kausalya royal dame,
From the true and tender Bharat prince of proud and peerless fame,
Didst thou hear if royal Bharat leads his forces to the fight,
Conquering Ravan's scattered army in his all-resistless might,
Didst thou hear if brave Sugriva marshals Vanars in his wrath,
And the young and gallant Lakshman seeks to cross the ocean path?"
Hanuman with due obeisance placed his hand upon his head,
Bowed unto the queenly Sita and in gentle accents said:
"Trust me, Lady, valiant Rama soon will greet his saintly wife,
E'en as INDRA greets his goddess, SACHI dearer than his life,

[1] The spirit of darkness.

Trust me, Sita, conquering Rama comes with panoply of war,
Shaking Lanka's sea-girt mountains, slaying Rakshas near and far!
He shall cross the boundless ocean with the battle's dread array,
He shall smite the impious Ravan and the cruel Rakshas slay,
Mighty Gods and strong Asuras shall not hinder Rama's path,
When at Lanka's gates he thunders with his more than godlike wrath,
Deadly YAMA, all-destroying, pales before his peerless might,
When his red right arm of vengeance wrathful Rama lifts to smite!
By the lofty Mandar mountains, by the fruit and root I seek,
By the cloud-obstructing Vindhyas, and by Malya's towering peak,
I will swear, my gentle Lady, Rama's vengeance draweth nigh,
Thou shalt see his beaming visage like the Lord of Midnight Sky,
Firm in purpose Rama waiteth on the Prasra-vana hill,
As upon the huge Airavat, INDRA, motionless and still!
Flesh of deer nor forest honey tasteth Rama true and bold,
Till he rescues cherished Sita from the Raksha's castled hold,
Thoughts of Sita leave not Rama dreary day or darksome night,
Till his vengeance deep and dreadful crushes Ravan in his might,
Forest flower nor scented creeper pleases Rama's anguished heart,
Till he wins his wedded consort by his death-compelling dart!"

IV Sita's Token

Token from her raven tresses Sita to the Vanar gave,
Hanuman with dauntless valour crossed once more the ocean wave,
Where in Prasra-vana's mountain Rama with his brother stayed,
Jewel from the brow of Sita by her sorrowing consort laid,
Spake of Ravan's foul endearment and his loathsome loving word,
Spake of Sita's scorn and anger and her truth unto her lord,
Tears of sorrow and affection from the warrior's eyelids start,
As his consort's loving token Rama presses to his heart!
"As the mother-cow, Sugriva, yields her milk beside her young,
Welling tears upon this token yields my heart by anguish wrung,
Well I know this dear-loved jewel sparkling with the ray of heaven,
Born in sea, by mighty INDRA to my Sita's father given,
Well I know this tender token, Janak placed it on her hair,
When she came my bride and consort decked in beauty rich and rare,
Well I know this sweet memorial, Sita wore it on her head,
And her proud and peerless beauty on the gem a lustre shed!

Ah, methinks the gracious Janak stands again before my eye,
With a father's fond affection, with a monarch's stature high,
Ah, methinks my bride and consort, she who wore it on her brow,
Stands again before the altar, speaks again her loving vow,
Ah, the sad, the sweet remembrance! ah, the happy days gone by,
Once again, O loving vision, wilt thou gladden Rama's eye!
Speak again, my faithful vassal, how my Sita wept and prayed,
Like the water to the thirsty, dear to me what Sita said,
Did she send this sweet remembrance as a blessing from above,
As a true and tender token of a woman's changeless love,
Did she waft her heart's affection o'er the billows of the sea,
Wherefore came she not in person from her foes and fetters free?
Hanuman, my friend and comrade, lead me to the distant isle,
Where my soft-eyed Sita lingers midst the Rakshas dark and vile,
Where my true and tender consort like a lone and stricken deer,
Girt by Rakshas stern and ruthless sheds the unavailing tear,
Where she weeps in ceaseless anguish, sorrow-stricken, sad and pale,
Like the Moon by dark clouds shrouded then her light and lustre fail!
Speak again, my faithful henchman, loving message of my wife,
Like some potent drug her accents renovate my fainting life,
Arm thy forces, friend Sugriva, Rama shall not brook delay,
While in distant Lanka's confines Sita weeps the livelong day,
Marshal forth thy bannered forces, cross the ocean in thy might,
Rama speeds on wings of vengeance Lanka's impious lord to smite!"

BOOK IX RAVANA-SABHA

(*The Council of War*)

Ravan was thoroughly frightened by the deeds of Hanuman. For Hanuman had not only penetrated into his island and discovered Sita in her imprisonment, but had also managed to burn down a great portion of the city before he left the island. Ravan called a Council of War, and as might be expected, all the advisers heedlessly advised war.

All but Bibhishan. He was the youngest brother of Ravan, and condemned the folly and the crime by which Ravan was seeking a war with the righteous and unoffending Rama. He advised that Sita should be restored to her lord and peace made with Rama. His voice was drowned in the cries of more violent advisers.

It is noticeable that Ravan's second brother, Kumbha-karna, also had the courage to censure his elder's action. But unlike Bibhishan he was determined to fight for his king whether he was right or wrong. There is a touch of sublimity in this blind and devoted loyalty of Kumbha-karna to the cause of his king and his country.

Bibhishan was driven from the court with indignity, and joined the forces of Rama, to whom he gave much valuable information about Lanka and its warriors.

The passages translated in this Book form Sections vi., viii., ix., portions of Sections xii. and xv., and the whole of Section xvi. of Book vi. of the original text.

I Ravan Seeks Advice

Monarch of the mighty Rakshas, Ravan spake to warriors all,
Spake to gallant chiefs and princes gathered in his Council Hall:
"Listen, Princes, Chiefs, and Warriors! Hanuman our land hath seen,
Stealing through the woods of Lanka unto Rama's prisoned queen.
And audacious in his purpose and resistless in his ire,
Burnt our turret tower and temple, wasted Lanka's town with fire!
Speak your counsel, gallant leaders, Ravan is intent to hear,
Triumph waits on fearless wisdom, speak your thoughts without a fear,
Wisest monarchs act on counsel from his men for wisdom known,
Next are they who in their wisdom and their daring act alone,
Last, unwisest are the monarchs who nor death nor danger weigh,
Think not, ask not friendly counsel, by their passions borne away!
Wisest counsel comes from courtiers who in holy lore unite,
Next, when varying plans and reasons blending lead unto the right,
Last and worst, when stormy passions mark the hapless king's debate,
And his friends are disunited when his foe is at the gate!
Therefore freely speak your counsel and your monarch's task shall be
But to shape in deed and action what your wisest thoughts decree,
Speak with minds and hearts united, shape your willing monarch's deed,
Counsel peace, or Ravan's forces to a war of vengeance lead,
Ere Sugriva's countless forces cross the vast and boundless main,
Ere the wrathful Rama girdles Lanka with a living chain!"

II Prahasta's Speech

Dark and high as summer tempest mighty-armed Prahasta rose,
Spake in fierce and fiery accents hurling challenge on his foes:
"Wherefore, Ravan, quails thy bosom, gods against thee strive in vain,
Wherefore fear the feeble mortals, homeless hermits, helpless men?
Hanuman approached in secret, stealing like a craven spy,
Not from one in open combat would alive the Vanar fly,
Let him come with all his forces, to the confines of the sea
I will chase the scattered army and thy town from foeman free!
Not in fear and hesitation Ravan should repent his deed,
While his gallant Raksha forces stand beside him in his need,
Not in tears and vain repentance Sita to his consort yield,
While his chieftains guard his empire in the battle's gory field!"

III Durmukha's Speech

Durmukha of cruel visage and of fierce and angry word,
Rose within the Council Chamber, spake to Lanka's mighty lord:
"Never shall the wily foeman boast of insult on us flung,
Hanuman shall die a victim for the outrage and the wrong!
Stealing in unguarded Lanka through thy city's virgin gate,
He hath courted deep disaster and a dark untimely fate,
Stealing in the inner mansions where our dames and damsels dwell,
Hanuman shall die a victim,—tale of shame he shall not tell!
Need is none of Ravan's army, bid me seek the foe alone,
If he hides in sky or ocean or in nether regions thrown,
Need is none of gathered forces, Ravan's mandate I obey,
I will smite the bold intruder and his Vanar forces slay!"

IV Vajra-danshtra's Speech

Iron-toothéd Vajra-danshtra then arose in wrath and pride,
And his blood-stained mace of battle held in fury by his side,
"Wherefore, Ravan, waste thy forces on the foemen poor and vile,
Hermit Rama and his brother, Hanuman of impious wile,
Bid me,—with this mace of battle proud Sugriva I will slay,
Chase the helpless hermit brothers to the forests far away!

Or to deeper counsel listen! Varied shapes the Rakshas wear,
Let them wearing human visage, dressed as Bharat's troops appear,
Succour from his ruling brother Rama will in gladness greet,
Then with mace and blood-stained sabre we shall lay them at our feet,
Rock and javelin and arrow we shall on our foemen hail,
Till no poor surviving Vanar lives to tell the tragic tale!"

V *Speech of Nikumbha and Vajra-Hanu*

Then arose the brave Nikumbha,—Kumbha-karna's son was he,—
Spake his young heart's mighty passion in his accents bold and free:
"Need is none, O mighty monarch, for a battle or a war,
Bid me meet the homeless Rama and his brother wand'ring far,
Bid me face the proud Sugriva, Hanuman of deepest vile,
I will rid thee of thy foemen and of Vanars poor and vile!"
Rose the chief with jaw of iron, Vajra-hanu fierce and young,
Licked his lips like hungry tiger with his red and lolling tongue:
"Wherefore, monarch, dream of battle? Rakshas feed on human gore,
Let me feast upon thy foemen by the ocean's lonely shore,
Rama and his hermit brother, Hanuman who hides in wood,
Angad and the proud Sugriva soon shall be my welcome food!"

VI *Bibhishan's Warning*

Twenty warriors armed and girded in the Council Hall arose,
Thirsting for a war of vengeance, hurling challenge on the foes,
But Bibhishan deep in wisdom,—Ravan's youngest brother he,—
Spake the word of solemn warning, for his eye could farthest see:
"Pardon, king and honoured elder, if Bibhishan lifts his voice
'Gainst the wishes of the warriors and the monarch's fatal choice,
Firm in faith and strong in forces Rama comes with conqu'ring might,
Vain against a righteous warrior would unrighteous Ravan fight!
Think him not a common Vanar who transpassed the ocean wave,
Wrecked thy city tower and temple and a sign and warning gave,
Think him not a common hermit who Ayodhya ruled of yore,
Crossing India's streams and mountains, thunders now on Lanka's shore!
What dark deed of crime or folly hath the righteous Rama done,
That you stole his faithful consort unprotected and alone,

What offence or nameless insult hath the saintly Sita given,
She who chained in Lanka's prison pleads in piteous tear to Heaven?
Take my counsel, king and elder, Sita to her lord restore,
Wipe this deed of wrong and outrage, Rama's righteous grace implore,
Take my counsel, Raksha monarch, vain against him is thy might,
Doubly arméd is the hero,—he who battles for the right!
Render Sita to her Rama ere with vengeance swift and dire,
He despoils our peopled Lanka with his bow and brand and fire,
Render wife unto her husband ere in battle's dread array,
Rama swoops upon thy empire like a falcon on its prey,
Render to the lord his consort ere with blood of Rakshas slain,
Rama soaks the land of Lanka to the margin of the main!
Listen to my friendly counsel,—though it be I stand alone,—
Faithful friend by fiery foeman is this Dasa-ratha's son,
Listen to my voice of warning,—Rama's shafts are true and keen,
Flaming like the with'ring sunbeams on the summer's parchéd green,
Listen to my soft entreaty,—righteousness becomes the brave,
Cherish peace and cherish virtue and thy sons and daughters save!"

VII Kumbha-karna's Determination

Ravan's brother Kumbha-karna, from his wonted slumber woke:
Mightiest he of all the Rakshas, thus in solemn accents spoke:
"Truly speaks the wise Bibhishan; ere he stole a hermit's wife,
Ravan should have thought and pondered, courted not a causeless strife,
Ere he did this deed of folly, Ravan should have counsel sought,
Tardy is the vain repentance when the work of shame is wrought!
Word of wisdom timely spoken saves from death and dangers dire,
Vain is grief for crime committed,—offerings to unholy fire,
Vain is hero's worth or valour if by foolish counsel led,
Toil and labour fail and perish save when unto wisdom wed,
And the foeman speeds in triumph o'er a heedless monarch's might,
As through gaps of Krauncha mountains *hansas*[1] speed their southern flight!
Ravan, thou hast sought unwisely Sita in her calm retreat,
As the wild and heedless hunter feeds upon the poisoned meat,
Nathless, faithful Kumbha-karna will his loyal duty know,
He shall fight his monarch's battle, he shall face his brother's foe!

[1] Geese.

True to brother and to monarch, be he right or be he wrong,
Kumbha-karna fights for Lanka 'gainst her foemen fierce and strong,
Recks not if the mighty Indra and Vivasvat cross his path,
Or the wild and stormy Maruts, Agni in his fiery wrath!
For the Lord of Sky shall tremble when he sees my stature high,
And he hears his thunders echoed by my loud and answering cry,
Rama armed with ample quiver shall no second arrow send,
Ere I slay him in the battle and his limb from limb I rend!
Wiser heads than Kumbha-karna right and true from wrong may know,
Faithful to his race and monarch he shall face the haughty foe,
Joy thee in thy pleasure, Ravan, rule thy realm in regal pride,
When I slay the hermit Rama, widowed Sita be thy bride!"

VIII Indrajit's Assurance

Indrajit the son of Ravan then his lofty purpose told,
'Midst the best and boldest Rakshas none so gallant, none so bold:
"Wherefore, noble king and father, pale Bibhishan's counsel hear,
Scion of the race of Rakshas speaks not thus in dastard fear,
In this race of valiant Rakshas, known for deeds of glory done,
Feeble-hearted, faint in courage, save Bibhishan, there is none!
Matched with meanest of the Rakshas what are sons of mortal men,
What are homeless human brothers hiding in the hermit's den,
Shall we yield to weary wand'rers, driven from their distant home,
Chased from throne and father's kingdom in the desert woods to roam?
Lord of sky and nether region, Indra 'neath my weapon fell,
Pale Immortals know my valour and my warlike deeds can tell,
Indra's tusker, huge Airavat, by my prowess overthrown,
Trumpeted its anguished accents, shaking sky and earth with groan,
Mighty God and dauntless Daityas fame of Indrajit may know,
And he yields not, king and father, to a homeless human foe!"

IX Ravan's Decision

Anger swelled in Ravan's bosom as he cast his blood-red eye
On Bibhishan calm and fearless, and he spake in accents high:
"Rather dwell with open foemen or in homes where cobras haunt,
Than with faithless friends who falter and whom fears of danger daunt!

O, the love of near relations!—false and faithless, full of guile,—
How they sorrow at my glory, at my danger how they smile,
How they grieve with secret anguish when my loftier virtues shine,
How they harbour jealous envy when deserts and fame are mine,
How they scan with curious vision every fault that clouds my path,
How they wait with eager longing till I fall in Fortune's wrath!
Ask the elephants of jungle how their captors catch and bind,—
Not by fire and feeble weapons, but by treason of their kind,
Not by javelin or arrow,—little for these arms they care,—
But their false and fondling females lead them to the hunter's snare!
Long as nourishment and vigour shall impart the milk of cow,
Long as woman shall be changeful, hermits holy in their vow,
Aye, so long shall near relations hate us in their inner mind,
Mark us with a secret envy though their words be ne'er so kind!
Rain-drops fall upon the lotus but unmingling hang apart,
False relations round us gather but they blend not heart with heart,
Winter clouds are big with thunder but they shed no freshening rain,
False relations smile and greet us but their soothing words are vain,
Bees are tempted by the honey but from flower to flower they range,
False relations share our favour but in secret seek a change!
Lying is thy speech, Bibhishan, secret envy lurks within,
Thou wouldst rule thy elder's empire, thou wouldst wed thy elder's queen,
Take thy treason to the foemen,—brother's blood I may not shed,—
Other Raksha craven-hearted by my royal hands had bled!"

X *Bibhishan's Departure*

"This to me!" Bibhishan answered, as with fiery comrades four,
Rose in arms the wrathful Raksha and in fury rushed before,
"But I spare thee, royal Ravan, angry words thy lips have passed,
False and lying and unfounded is the censure thou hast cast!
True Bibhishan sought thy safety, strove to save his elder's reign,—
Speed thee now to thy destruction since all counsel is in vain,
Many are thy smiling courtiers who with honeyed speech beguile,—
Few are they with true and candour speak their purpose void of guile!
Blind to reason and to wisdom, Ravan, seek thy destined fate,
For thy impious lust of woman, for thy dark unrighteous hate,

Blind to danger and destruction, deaf to word of counsel given,
By the flaming shafts of Rama thou shalt die by will of Heaven!
Yet, O! yet, my king and elder, let me plead with latest breath,
'Gainst the death of race and kinsmen, 'gainst my lord and brother's death,
Ponder yet, O Raksha monarch, save thy race and save thy own,
Ravan, part we now for ever,—guard thy ancient sea-girt throne!"

BOOK X YUDDHA

(*The War in Ceylon*)

RAMA CROSSED over with his army from India to Ceylon. There is a chain of islands across the strait, and the Indian poet supposes them to be the remains of a vast causeway which Rama built to cross over with his army.

The town of Lanka, the capital of Ceylon, was invested, and the war which followed was a succession of sallies by the great leaders and princes of Lanka. But almost every sally was repulsed, every chief was killed, and at last Ravan himself who made the last sally was slain and the war ended.

Among the numberless fights described in the original work, those of Ravan himself, his brother Kumbha-karna, and his son Indrajit, are the most important, and oftenest recited and listened to in India; and these have been rendered into English in this Book. And the reader will mark a certain method in the poet's estimate of the warriors who took part in these battles.

First and greatest among the warriors was Rama; he was never beaten by an open foe, never conquered in fair fight. Next to him, and to him only, was Ravan the monarch of Lanka; he twice defeated Lakshman in battle, and never retreated except before Rama. Next to Rama and to Ravan stood their brothers, Lakshman and Kumbha-karna; it is difficult to say who was the best of these two, for they fought only once, and it was a drawn battle. Fifth in order of prowess was Indrajit the son of Ravana, but he was the first in his magic art. Concealed in mists by his magic, he twice defeated both Rama and Lakshman; but in his last battle he had to face combat with Lakshman, and was slain. After these five warriors, pre-eminent for their prowess, various Vanars and Rakshas took their rank.

The war ended with the fall of Ravan and his funerals. The portions translated in this Book form the whole or portions of Sections xliv., xlviii., lix., lxvi., lxvii., and lxxiii., an abstract of Sections lxxv. to xci., and portions of Sections xciii., xcvi., ci., cii., ciii., cix., cx., and cxiii. of Book vi. of the original text.

I Indrajit's First Battle—The Serpent-Noose

Darkly round the leaguered city Rama's countless forces lay,
Far as Ravan cast his glances in the dawning light of day,
Wrath and anguish shook his bosom and the gates he opened wide,
And with ranks of charging Rakshas sallied with a Raksha's pride!
All the day the battle lasted, endless were the tale to tell,
What unnumbered Vanars perished and what countless Rakshas fell,
Darkness came, the fiery foemen urged the still unceasing fight,
Struggling with a deathless hatred fiercer in the gloom of night!
Onward came resistless Rakshas, laid Sugriva's forces low,
Crushed the broken ranks of Vanars, drank the red blood of the foe,
Bravely fought the scattered Vanars facing still the tide of war,
Struggling with the charging tusker and the steed and battle car,
Till at last the gallant Lakshman and the godlike Rama came,
And they swept the hosts of Ravan like a sweeping forest flame,
And their shafts like hissing serpents on the falt'ring foemen fell,
Fiercer grew the sable midnight with the dying shriek and yell!
Dust arose like clouds of summer from each thunder-sounding car,
From the hoofs of charging coursers, from the elephants of war,
Streams of red blood warm and bubbling issued from the countless slain,
Flooded battle's dark arena like the floods of summer rain,
Sound of trumpet and of bugle, drum and horn and echoing shell,
And the neigh of charging coursers and the tuskers' dying wail,
And the yell of wounded Rakshas and the Vanars' fierce delight,
Shook the earth and sounding welkin, waked the echoes of the night!
Six bright arrows Rama thundered from his weapon dark and dread,
Iron-toothéd Vajra-dranshtra and his fainting comrades fled,
Dauntless still the serried Rakshas, wave on wave succeeding came,
Perished under Rama's arrows as the moths upon the flame!
Indrajit the son of Ravan, Lanka's glory and her pride,
Matchless in his majic weapons came and turned the battle's tide,
What though Angad in his fury had his steeds and driver slayed,
Indrajit hid in the midnight battled from its friendly shade,

Shrouded in a cloud of darkness still he poured his darts like rain,
On young Lakshman and on Rama and on countless Vanars slain,
Matchless in his magic weapons, then he hurled his *Naga*[1]-dart,
Serpent noose upon his foemen draining lifeblood from their heart!
Vainly then the royal brothers fought the cloud-enshrouded foe,
Vainly sought the unseen warrior dealing unresisted blow,
Fastened by a noose of *Naga*[1] forced by hidden foe to yield.
Rama and the powerless Lakshman fell and fainted on the field!

II Sita's Lament

Indrajit ere dawned the morning entered in his father's hall,
Spake of midnight's darksome contest, Rama's death and Lakshman's fall,
And the proud and peerless Ravan clasped his brave and gallant son,
Praised him for his skill and valour and his deed of glory done,
And with dark and cruel purpose bade his henchmen yoke his car,
Bade them take the sorrowing Sita to the gory field of war!
Soon they harnessed royal coursers and they took the weeping wife,
Where her Rama, pierced and bleeding, seemed bereft of sense and life,
Brother lay beside his brother with their shattered mail and bow,
Arrows thick and dark with red blood spake the conquest of the foe,
Anguish woke in Sita's bosom and a dimness filled her eye,
And a widow's nameless sorrow burst in widow's mournful cry:
"Rama, lord and king and husband! didst thou cross the billowy sea,
Didst thou challenge death and danger, court thy fate to rescue me,
Didst thou hurl a fitting vengeance on the cruel Raksha force,
Till the hand of hidden foeman checked thy all-resistless course?
Breathes upon the earth no warrior who could face thee in the fight,
Who could live to boast his triumph o'er thy world-subduing might,
But the will of Fate is changeless, Death is mighty in his sway,—
Peerless Rama, faithful Lakshman, sleep the sleep that knows no day!
But I weep not for my Rama nor for Lakshman young and brave,
They have done a warrior's duty and have found a warrior's grave,
And I weep not for my sorrows,—sorrow marked me from my birth,—
Child of Earth I seek in suffering bosom of my mother Earth!
But I grieve for dear Kausalya, sonless mother, widowed queen,
How she reckons day and seasons in her anguish ever green.

[1] A snake; name of a tribe.

How she waits with eager longing till her Rama's exile o'er,
He would soothe her lifelong sorrow, bless her agéd eyes once more,
Sita's love! Ayodhya's monarch! Queen Kausalya's dearest born!
Rama soul of truth and virtue sleeps the sleep that knows no morn!"
Sorely wept the sorrowing Sita in her accents soft and low,
And the silent stars of midnight wept to witness Sita's woe,
But Trijata her companion,—though a Raksha woman she,—
Felt her soul subdued by sadness, spake to Sita tenderly:
"Weep not, sad and saintly Sita, shed not widow's tears in vain,
For thy lord is sorely wounded, but shall live to fight again,
Rama and the gallant Lakshman, fainting, not bereft of life,
They shall live to fight and conquer,—thou shalt be a happy wife,
Mark the Vanars' marshalled forces, listen to their warlike cries,
'Tis not thus the soldiers gather when a chief and hero dies,
'Tis not thus round lifeless leader muster warriors true and brave,
For when falls the dying helmsman, sinks the vessel in the wave!
Mark the ring of hopeful Vanars, how they watch o'er Rama's face,
How they guard the younger Lakshman beaming yet with living grace,
Trust me, sad and sorrowing Sita, marks of death these eyes can trace,
Shade of death's decaying fingers sweeps not o'er thy Rama's face!
Listen more, my gentle Sita, though a captive in our keep,
For thy woes and for thy anguish see a Raksha woman weep,
Though thy Rama armed in battle is our unrelenting foe,
For a true and stainless warrior see a Raksha filled with woe!
Fainting on the field of battle, blood-ensanguined in their face,
They shall live to fight and conquer, worthy of their gallant race,
Cold nor rigid are their features, darkness dwells not on their brow,
Weep not thus, my gentle Sita,—hasten we to Lanka now."
And Trijata spake no falsehood, by the winged Garuda's skill,
Rama and the valiant Lakshman lived to fight their foemen still!

III Ravan's First Battle—The Javelin-Stroke

'Gainst the God-assisted Rama, Ravan's efforts all were vain,
Leaguered Lanka vainly struggled in her adamantine chain,
Wrathful Rakshas with their forces vainly issued through the gate,
Chiefs and serried ranks of warriors met the same resistless fate!
Dark-eyed chief Dhumraksha sallied with the fierce tornado's shock,
Hanuman of peerless prowess slayed him with a rolling rock,

Iron-toothéd Vajra-danshtra dashed through countless Vanars slain,
But the young and gallant Angad laid him lifeless on the plain,
Akampan unshaken warrior issued out of Lanka's wall,
Hanuman was true and watchful, speedy was the Raksha's fall,
Then the mighty-armed Prahasta strove to break the hostile line,
But the gallant Nila felled him as the woodman fells the pine!
Bravest chiefs and countless soldiers sallied forth to face the fight,
Broke not Rama's iron circle, 'scraped not Rama's wondrous might,
Ravan could no longer tarry, for his mightiest chiefs were slain,
Foremost leaders, dearest kinsmen, lying on the gory plain!
"Lofty scorn of foes unworthy spared them from my flaming ire,
But the blood of slaughtered kinsmen claims from me a vengeance dire,"
Speaking thus the wrathful Ravan mounted on his thundering car,
Flame-resplendent was the chariot drawn by matchless steeds of war!
Beat of drum and voice of *sankha*[1] and the Raksha's battle cry,
Song of triumph, chanted *mantra,* smote the echoing vault of sky,
And the troops like cloudy masses with their eyes of lightning fire
Girt their monarch, as his legions girdle RUDRA in his ire!
Rolled the car with peal of thunder through the city's lofty gate,
And each fierce and fiery Raksha charged with warrior's deathless hate,
And the vigour of the onset cleft the stunned and scattered foe,
As a strong bark cleaves the billows riding on the ocean's brow!
Brave Sugriva king of Vanars met the foeman fierce and strong,
And a rock with mighty effort on the startled Ravan flung,
Vain the toil, disdainful Ravan dashed aside the flying rock,
Brave Sugriva pierced by arrows fainted neath the furious shock.
Next Susena chief and elder, Nala and Gavaksha bold,
Hurled them on the path of Ravan speeding in his car of gold,
Vainly heaved the rock and missile, vainly did with trees assail,
Onward sped the conquering Ravan, pierced the fainting Vanars fell.
Hanuman the son of MARUT next against the Raksha came,
Fierce and strong as stormy MARUT, warrior of unrivalled fame,
But the Raksha's mighty onset gods nor mortals might sustain,
Hanuman in red blood welt'ring rolled upon the gory plain.
Onward rolled the car of Ravan, where the dauntless Nila stood,
Armed with rock and tree and missile, thirsting for the Raksha's blood,
Vainly fought the valiant Nila, pierced by Ravan's pointed dart,
On the gory field of battle poured the red blood of his heart.

[1] Conch-shell, used as bugle in war and festivities.

Onward through the scattered forces Ravan's conquering chariot came,
Where in pride and dauntless valour Lakshman stood of warlike fame,
Calm and proud the gallant Lakshman marked the all-resistless foe,
Boldly challenged Lanka's monarch as he held aloft his bow:
"Welcome, mighty Lord of Lanka! wage with me an equal strife,
Wherefore with thy royal prowess seek the humble Vanars' life!"
"Hath thy fate," so answered Ravan, "brought thee to thy deadly foe,
Welcome, valiant son of Raghu! Ravan longs to lay thee low!"
Then they closed in dubious battle, Lanka's Lord his weapon bent,
Seven bright arrows, keen and whistling, on the gallant Lakshman sent,
Vain the toil, for watchful Lakshman stout of heart and true of aim,
With his darts like shooting sunbeams cleft each arrow as it came.
Bleeding from the darts of Lakshman, pale with anger, wounded sore,
Ravan drew at last his *Sakti,*[1] gift of Gods in days of yore,
Javelin of flaming splendour, deadly like the shaft of Fate,
Ravan hurled on dauntless Lakshman in his fierce and furious hate.
Vain were Lakshman's human weapons aimed with skill directed well,
Pierced by *Sakti,* gallant Lakshman in his red blood fainting fell,
Wrathful Rama saw the combat and arose in godlike might,
Bleeding Ravan turned to Lanka, sought his safety in his flight.

IV Fall of Kumbha-Karna

Once more healed and strong and valiant, Lakshman in his arms arose,
Safe behind the gates of Lanka humbled Ravan shunned his foes,
Till the stalwart Kumbha-karna from his wonted slumbers woke,
Mightiest he of all the Rakshas;—Ravan thus unto him spoke:
"Thou alone, O Kumbha-karna, can the Raksha's honour save,
Strongest of the Raksha warriors, stoutest-hearted midst the brave,
Speed thee like the Dread Destroyer to the dark and dubious fray,
Cleave through Rama's girdling forces, chase the scattered foe away!"
Like a mountain's beetling turret Kumbha-karna stout and tall,
Passed the city's lofty portals and the city's girdling wall,
And he raised his voice in battle, sent his cry from shore to shore,
Solid mountains shook and trembled and the sea returned the roar!
INDRA nor the great VARUNA equalled Kumbha-karna's might,
Vanars trembled at the warrior, sought their safety in their flight,

[1] Javelin.

But the prince of fair Kishkindha, Angad chief of warlike fame,
Marked his panic-stricken forces with a princely warrior's shame.
"Wither fly, ye trembling Vanars?" thus the angry chieftain cried,
"All forgetful of your duty, of your worth and warlike pride,
Deem not stalwart Kumbha-karna is our match in open fight,
Forward let us meet in battle, let us crush his giant might!"
Rallied thus, the broken army stone and tree and massive rock,
Hurled upon the giant Raksha speeding with the lightning's shock,
Vain each flying rock and missile, vain each stout and sturdy stroke,
On the Raksha's limbs of iron stone and tree in splinters broke.
Dashing through the scattered forces Kumbha-karna fearless stood,
As a forest conflagration feasts upon the parchéd wood,
Far as confines of the ocean, to the causeway they had made,
To the woods or caves or billows, Vanars in their terror fled!
Hanuman of dauntless valour turned not in his fear nor fled,
Heaved a rock with mighty effort on the Raksha's towering head,
With his spear-head Kumbha-karna dashed the flying rock aside,
By the Raksha's weapon stricken Hanuman fell in his pride.
Next Rishabha and brave Nila and the bold Sarabha came,
Gavaksha and Gandha-madan, chieftains of a deathless fame,
But the spear of Kumbha-karna hurled to earth his feeble foes,
Dreadful was the field of carnage, loud the cry of battle rose!
Angad prince of fair Kishkindha, filled with anger and with shame,
Tore a rock with wrathful prowess, to the fatal combat came,
Short the combat, soon the Raksha caught and turned his foe around
Hurled him in his deadly fury, bleeding, senseless on the ground!
Last, Sugriva king of Vanars with a vengeful anger woke,
Tore a rock from bed of mountain and in proud defiance spoke,
Vain Sugriva's toil and struggle, Kumbha-karna hurled a rock,
Fell Sugriva crushed and senseless 'neath the missile's mighty shock!
Piercing through the Vanar forces, like a flame through forest wood,
Came the Raksha where in glory Lakshman calm and fearless stood,
Short their contest,—Kumbha-karna sought a greater, mightier foe,
To the young and dauntless Lakshman spake in accents soft and low:
"Dauntless prince and matchless warrior, fair Sumitra's gallant son,
Thou hast proved unrivalled prowess and unending glory won,
But I seek a mightier foeman, to thy elder let me go,
I would fight the royal Rama, or to die or slay my foe!"

"Victor proud!" said gallant Lakshman, "peerless in thy giant might,
Conquerer of great Immortals, Lakshman owns thy skill in fight,
Mightier foe than bright Immortals thou shalt meet in fatal war,
Death for thee in guise of Rama tarries yonder, not afar!"
Ill it fared with Kumbha-karna when he strove with Rama's might,
Men on earth nor Gods immortal conquered Rama in the fight,
Deadly arrows keen and flaming from the hero's weapon broke,
Kumbha-karna faint and bleeding felt his death at every stroke,
Last, an arrow pierced his armour, from his shoulders smote his head,
Kumbha-karna, lifeless, headless, rolled upon the gory bed,
Hurled unto the heaving ocean Kumbha-karna's body fell,
And as shaken by a tempest, mighty was the ocean's swell!

V *Indrajit's Sacrifice and Second Battle*

Still around beleaguered Lanka girdled Rama's living chain,
Raksha chieftain after chieftain strove to break the line in vain,
Sons of Ravan,—brave Narantak was by valiant Angad slain,
Trisiras and fierce Devantak, Hanuman slew on the plain,
Atikaya, tall of stature, was by gallant Lakshman killed,
Ravan wept for slaughtered princes, brave in war in weapons skilled.
"Shed no tears of sorrow, father!" Indrajit exclaimed in pride,
"While thy eldest son surviveth triumph dwells on Ravan's side,
Rama and that stripling Lakshman, I had left them in their gore,
Once again I seek their lifeblood,—they shall live to fight no more.
Hear my vow, O Lord of Rakshas! ere descends yon radiant sun,
Rama's days and gallant Lakshman's on this wide earth shall be done,
Witness INDRA and VIVASWAT, VISHNU great and RUDRA dire,
Witness Sun and Moon and Sadhyas, and the living God of Fire!"
Opened wide the gates of Lanka; in the spacious field of war,
Indrajit arranged his army, foot and horse and battle car,
Then with gifts and sacred *mantras* bent before the God of Fire,
And invoked celestial succour in the battle dread and dire.
With his offerings and his garlands, Indrajit with spices rare,
Worshipped holy VAISWA-NARA on the altar bright and fair,
Spear and mace were ranged in order, dart and bow and shining blade
Sacred fuel, blood-red garments, fragrant flowers were duly laid,
Head of goat as black as midnight offered then the warrior brave,
And the shooting tongue of red fire omens of a conquest gave,

Curling to the right and smokeless, red and bright as molten gold,
Tongue of flame received the offering of the hero true and bold!
Victory the sign betokens! Bow and dart and shining blade,
Sanctified by holy *mantras,* by the Fire the warrior laid,
Then with weapons consecrated, hid in mists as once before,
Indrajit on helpless foemen did his fatal arrows pour!
Fled the countless Vanar forces, panic-stricken, crushed and slain,
And the dead and dying warriors strewed the gory battle plain,
Then on Rama, and on Lakshman, from his dark and misty shroud,
Indrajit discharged his arrows bright as sunbeams through a cloud.
Scanning earth and bright sky vainly for his dark and hidden foe,
Rama to his brother Lakshman spake in grief and spake in woe:
"Once again that wily Raksha, slaying all our Vanar train,
From his dark and shadowy shelter doth on us his arrows rain,
By the grace of great SWAYAMBHU, Indrajit is lost to sight,
Useless is our human weapon 'gainst his gift of magic might,
If SWAYAMBHU wills it, Lakshman, we shall face these fatal darts,
We shall stand with dauntless patience, we shall die with dauntless hearts!"
Weaponless but calm and valiant, from the foeman's dart and spell
Patiently the princes suffered, fearlessly the heroes fell!

VI Indrajit's Third Battle and Fall

Healing herbs from distant mountains Hanuman in safety brought,
Rama rose and gallant Lakshman, once again their foemen sought.
And when night its sable mantle o'er the earth and ocean drew,
Forcing through the gates of Lanka to the frightened city flew!
Gallant sons of Kumbha-karna vainly fought to stem the tide,
Hanuman and brave Sugriva slew the brothers in their pride,
Makaraksha, shark-eyed warrior, vainly struggled with the foe,
Rama laid him pierced and lifeless by an arrow from his bow.
Indrajit arose in anger for his gallant kinsmen slayed,
In his arts and deep devices Sita's beauteous image made,
And he placed the form of beauty on his speeding battle car,
With his sword he smote the image in the gory field of war!
Rama heard the fatal message which his faithful Vanars gave,
And a deathlike trance and tremor fell upon the warrior brave,

But Bibhishan deep in wisdom to the anguished Rama came,
With his words of consolation spake of Rama's righteous dame:
"Trust me, Rama, trust thy comrade,—for I know our wily house,—
Indrajit slays not the woman whom his father seeks as spouse,
'Tis for Sita, impious Ravan meets thee on the battle-field,
Stakes his life and throne and empire, but thy Sita will not yield,
Deem not that the king of Rakshas will permit her blood be shed,
Indrajit slays not the woman whom his father seeks to wed!
'Twas an image of thy Sita, Indrajit hath cleft in twain,
While our army wails and sorrows,—he performs his rites again,
To the holy Nikumbhila, Indrajit in secret hies,
For the rights which yield him prowess, hide him in the cloudy skies.
Let young Lakshman seek the foeman ere his magic rites be done,—
Once the sacrifice completed, none can combat Ravan's son,—
Let young Lakshman speed through Lanka till his wily foe is found,
Slay the secret sacrificer on the sacrificial ground!"
Unto holy Nikumbhila, Lakshman with Bibhishan went
Bravest, choicest of the army, Rama with his brother sent,
Magic rites and sacrifices Indrajit had scarce begun,
When surprised by arméd foemen rose in anger Ravan's son!
"Art thou he," thus to Bibhishan, Indrajit in anger spake,
"Brother of my royal father, stealing thus my life to take,
Raksha born of Raksha parents, dost thou glory in this deed,
Traitor to thy king and kinsmen, false to us in direst need?
Scorn and pity fill my bosom thus to see thee leave thy kin,
Serving as a slave of foemen, stooping to a deed of sin.
For the slave who leaves his kindred, basely seeks the foeman's grace,
Meets destruction from the foeman after he destroys his race!"
"Untaught child of impure passions," thus Bibhishan answer made,
"Of my righteous worth unconscious bitter accents hast thou said,
Know, proud youth, that Truth and Virtue in my heart precedence take,
And we shun the impious kinsman as we shun the pois'nous snake!
Listen, youth! this earth no longer bears thy father's sin and strife,
Plunder of the righteous neighbour, passion for the neighbour's wife,
Earth and skies have doomed thy father for his sin-polluted reign,
Unto Gods his proud defiance and his wrongs to sons of men!
Listen more! this fated Lanka groans beneath her load of crime,
And shall perish in her folly by the ruthless hand of Time,

Thou shalt perish and thy father and this proud presumptuous state,
Lakshman meets thee, impious Raksha, by the stern decree of Fate!"
"Hast thou too forgot the lesson," Indrajit to Lakshman said,
"Twice in field of war unconscious thee with Rama have I laid,
Dost thou stealing like a serpent brave my yet unconquered might,
Perish, boy, in thy presumption, in this last and fatal fight!"
Spake the hero: "Like a coward hid beneath a mantling cloud,
Thou hast battled like a caitiff safe behind thy sheltering shroud,
Now I seek an open combat, time is none to prate or speak,
Boastful word is coward's weapon, weapons and thy arrows seek!"
Soon they mixed in dubious combat, fury fired each foeman's heart,
Either warrior felt his rival worthy of his bow and dart,
Lakshman with his hurtling arrows pierced the Raksha's golden mail,
Shattered by the Raksha's weapons Lakshman's useless armour fell,
Red with gore and dim in eyesight still the chiefs in fury fought,
Neither quailed before his foeman, pause nor grace nor mercy sought,
Till with more than human valour Lakshman drew his bow amain,
Slayed the Raksha's steeds and driver, severed too his bow in twain.
"If the great and godlike Rama is in faith and duty true,
Gods assist the cause of virtue!"—Lakshman uttered as he drew,
Fatal was the dart unerring,—Gods assist the true and bold,—
On the field of Nikumbhila, Lakshman's foeman headless rolled!

VII Ravan's Lament

"Quenched the light of Rakshas' valour!" so the message-bearer said,
"Lakshman with the deep Bibhishan hath thy son in battle slayed,
Fallen is our prince and hero and his day on earth is done,
In a brighter world, O monarch, lives thy brave, thy gallant son!"
Anguish filled the father's bosom and his fleeting senses failed,
Till to deeper sorrow wakened Lanka's monarch wept and wailed:
"Greatest of my gallant warriors, dearest to thy father's heart,
Victor over bright Immortals,—art thou slain by Lakshman's dart,
Noble prince whose peerless arrows could the peaks of Mandar stain,
And could daunt the Dread Destroyer,—art thou by a mortal slain?
But thy valour lends a radiance to elysium's sunny clime,
And thy bright name adds a lustre to the glorious rolls of time,
In the skies the bright Immortals lisp thy name with terror pale,
On the earth our maids and matrons mourn thy fall with piercing wail

Hark! the voice of lamentation waking in the palace halls,
Like the voice of woe in forests when the forest monarch falls,
Hark! the wailing widowed princess, mother weeping for her son,
Leaving them in tears and anguish, Indrajit, where are thou gone?
Full of years,—so oft I pondered,—when the monarch Ravan dies,
Indrajit shall watch his bedside, Indrajit shall close his eyes,
But the course of nature changes, and the father weeps the son,
Youth is fallen, and the aged lives to fight the foe alone!"
Tears of sorrow, slow and silent, fell upon the monarch's breast,
Then a swelling rage and passion woke within his heaving chest,
Like the sun of scorching summer glowed his face in wrathful shame,
From his brow and rolling eyeballs issued sparks of living flame!
"Perish she!" exclaimed the monarch, "she-wolf Sita dies to-day,
Indrajit but cleft her image, Ravan will the woman slay!"
Followed by his trembling courtiers, regal robes and garments rent,
Ravan shaking in his passion to *Asoka's* garden went,
Maddened by his wrath and anguish, with his drawn and flaming sword,
Sought the shades where soft-eyed Sita silent sorrowed for her lord.
Woman's blood the royal sabre on that fatal day had stained,
But his true and faithful courtiers Ravan's wrathful hand restrained.
And the watchful Raksha females girdled round the sorrowing dame,
Flung them on the path of Ravan to withstand a deed of shame.
"Not against a woman, Ravan, mighty warriors raise their hand,
In the battle," spake the courtiers, "duty bids thee use thy brand,
Versed in *Vedas* and in learning, court not thus a caitiff's fate,
Woman's blood pollutes our valour, closes heaven's eternal gate!
Leave the woman in her sorrow, mount upon thy battle car,
Faithful to our king and leader we will wake the voice of war,
'Tis the fourteenth day auspicious of the dark and waning moon,
Glory waiteth thee in battle and thy vengeance cometh soon,
All-resistless in the contest slay thy foeman in his pride,
Seek as victor of the combat widowed Sita as thy bride!"
Slow and sullen, dark and silent, Ravan then his wrath restrained,
Vengeance on his son's destroyer deep within his bosom reigned!

VIII Ravan's Second Battle and Vengeance

Voice of woe and lamentation and the cry of woman's wail,
Issuing from the homes of Lanka did the monarch's ears assail,

And a mighty thought of vengeance waked within the monarch's heart,
And he heaved a sigh of anguish as he grasped his bow and dart:
"Arm each chief and gallant Raksha! be our sacred duty done,
Ravan seeks a fitting vengeance for his brave and noble son,
Mahodar and Virupaksha, Mahaparshwa warrior tall,
Arm! this fated day will witness Lakshman's or your monarch's fall!
Call to mind each slaughtered hero,—Khara, Dushan, slain in fight,
Kumbha-karna giant warrior, Indrajit of magic might,
Earth nor sky shall hide my foemen nor the ocean's heaving swell,
Scattered ranks of Rama's forces shall my speedy vengeance tell,
Be the red-earth strewn and covered with our countless foemen slain,
Hungry wolves and blood-beaked vultures feed upon the ghastly plain,
For his great and gallant brother, for his brave and beauteous son,
Ravan seeks a fitting vengeance, Rakshas be your duty done!"
House to house, in Lanka's city, Ravan's royal hest was heard,
Street and lane poured forth their warriors by a mighty passion stirred,
With the javelin and sabre, mace and club and axe and pike,
Sataghni[1] and *bhindipala,*[2] quoit and discus quick to strike.
And they formed the line of tuskers and the line of battle car,
Mule and camel fit for burden and the fiery steed of war,
Serried ranks of armèd soldiers shook the earth beneath their tread,
Horsemen that on wings of lightning o'er the field of battle spread.
Drum and conch and sounding trumpet waked the echoes of the sky,
Pataha[3] and loud *mridanga*[4] and the people's maddening cry,
Thundering through the gates of Lanka, Ravan's lofty chariot passed
Destined by his fortune, Ravan ne'er again those portals crost!
And the sun was dim and clouded and a sudden darkness fell,
Birds gave forth their boding voices and the earth confessed a spell,
Gouts of blood in rain descended, startled coursers turned to fly,
Vultures swooped upon the banner, jackals yelled their doleful cry,
Omens of a dark disaster mantled o'er the vale and rock,
And the ocean heaved in billows, nations felt the earthquake shock!
Darkly closed the fatal battle, sturdy Vanars fell in fight,
Warlike leaders of the Rakshas perished neath the foeman's might,
Mahodhar and Virupaksha were by bold Sugriva slain,
Crushed by Angad, Mahaparshwa slumbered lifeless on the plain.

[1] A weapon of war, supposed to kill a hundred men at one discharge.
[2] A weapon of war. [3] A drum. [4] A drum.

But with more than mortal valour Ravan swept the ranks of war,
Warriors fell beneath his prowess, fled before his mighty car,
Cleaving through the Vanar forces, filled with vengeance deep and dire,
Ravan marked the gallant Lakshman flaming like a crimson fire!
Like the tempest cloud of summer Ravan's wingéd courses flew,
But Bibhishan in his prowess soon the gallant charges slew,
Dashing from his useless chariot Ravan leaped upon the ground,
And his false and traitor brother by his dearest foeman found!
Wrathful Ravan marked Bibhishan battling by the foeman's side,
And he hurled his pond'rous weapon for to slay him in his pride.
Lakshman marked the mighty jav'lin as it winged its whizzing flight,
Cleft it in its onward passage, saved Bibhishan by his might!
Grimly smiled the angry Ravan gloating in his vengeful wrath,
Spake to young and dauntless Lakshman daring thus to cross his path:
"Welcome, Lakshman! thee I battle for thy deed of darkness done,
Face the anger of a father, cruel slayer of the son,
By thy skill and by thy valour, false Bibhishan thou hast saved,
Save thyself! Deep in this bosom is a cruel grief engraved!"
Father's grief and sad remembrance urged the lightning-wingéd dart,
Ravan's *Sakti* fell resistless on the senseless Lakshman's heart,
Wrathful Rama saw the combat and arose in godlike might,
Carless, steedless, wounded Ravan sought his safety in his flight.

IX Rama's Lament

"Art thou fallen," sorrowed Rama, "weary of this endless strife,
Lakshman, if thy days are ended, Rama recks not for his life,
Gone is Rama's wonted valour, weapons leave his nerveless hand,
Drop his bow and shining arrows, useless hangs his sheathéd brand!
Art thou fallen, gallant Lakshman, death and faintness on me creep,
Weary of this fatal contest let me by my brother sleep,
Weary of the strife and triumph, since my faithful friend is gone,
Rama follows in his footsteps and his task on earth is done!
Thou hast from the far Ayodhya, followed me in deepest wood,
In the thickest of the battle thou hast by thy elder stood,
Love of woman, love of comrade, trite is love of kith and kind,
Love like thine, true-hearted brother, not on earth we often find!
When Sumitra seeks thee, Lakshman, ever weeping for thy sake,
When she asks me of her hero, what reply shall Rama make,

What reply, when Bharat questions,—Where is he who went to wood,
Where is true and faithful Lakshman who beside his elder stood?
What great crime or fatal shadow darkens o'er my hapless life,
Victim to the sins of Rama sinless Lakshman falls in strife,
Best of brothers, best of warriors, wherefore thus unconscious lie,
Mother, wife, and brother wait thee, ope once more thy sleeping eye!"
Tara's father, wise Susena, gentle consolation lent,
Hanuman from distant mountains herbs of healing virtue rent,
And by loving Rama tended, Lakshman in his strength arose,
Stirred by thoughts of fatal vengeance Rama sought the flying foes.

X *Celestial Arms and Chariot*

Not in dastard terror Ravan sought his safety in his flight,
But to seek fresh steeds of battle ere he faced his foeman's might,
Harnessing his gallant coursers to a new and glorious car,
Sunlike in its radiant splendour, Ravan came once more to war.
Gods in wonder watched the contest of the more than mortal foes,
Ravan mighty in his vengeance, Rama lofty in his woes,
Gods in wonder marked the heroes, lion-like in jungle wood,
INDRA sent his arms and chariot where the human warrior stood!
"Speed, Matali," thus spake INDRA, *"speed thee with my heavenly car,*
Where on foot the righteous Rama meets his mounted foe in war,
Speed, for Ravan's days are ended, and his moments brief and few,
Rama strives for right and virtue,—Gods assist the brave and true!"
Brave Matali drove the chariot drawn by steeds like solar ray,
Where the true and righteous Rama sought his foe in fatal fray,
Shining arms and heavenly weapons he to lofty Rama gave,—
When the righteous strive and struggle, God assist the true and brave!
"Take this car," so said Matali, "which the helping Gods provide,
Rama, take these steeds celestial, INDRA's golden chariot ride,
Take this royal bow and quiver, wear this falchion dread and dire,
VISWA-KARMAN forged this armour in the flames of heavenly fire,
I shall be thy chariot driver and shall speed the thund'ring car,
Slay the sin-polluted Ravan in this last and fatal war!"
Rama mounted on the chariot clad in arms of heavenly sheen,
And he mingled in a contest mortal eyes have never seen!

XI Ravan's Third Battle and Fall

Gods and mortals watched the contest and the heroes of the war,
Ravan speeding on his chariot, Rama on the heavenly car,
And a fiercer form the warriors in their fiery frenzy wore,
And a deeper weight of hatred on their anguished bosoms bore,
Clouds of dread and deathful arrows hid the radiant face of sky,
Darker grew the day of combat, fiercer grew the contest high!
Pierced by Ravan's pointed weapons bleeding Rama owned no pain,
Rama's arrows keen and piercing sought his foeman's life in vain,
Long and dubious battle lasted, and with fury wilder fraught,
Wounded, faint, and still unyielding, blind with wrath the rivals fought,
Pike and club and mace and trident scaped from Ravan's vengeful hand,
Spear and arrows Rama wielded, and his bright and flaming brand!
Long and dubious battle lasted, shook the ocean, hill and dale,
Winds were hushed in voiceless terror and the livid sun was pale,
Still the dubious battle lasted, until Rama in his ire
Wielded BRAHMA's deathful weapon flaming with celestial fire!
Weapon which the Saint Agastya had unto the hero given,
Winged as lightning dart of INDRA, fatal as the bolt of heaven,
Wrapped in smoke and flaming flashes, speeding from the circled bow,
Pierced the iron heart of Ravan, laid the lifeless hero low,
And a cry of pain and terror from the Raksha ranks arose,
And a shout from joyous Vanars as they smote their fleeing foes!
Heavenly flowers in rain descended on the red and gory plain,
And from unseen harps and timbrels rose a soft celestial strain,
And the ocean heaved in gladness, brighter shone the sunlit sky,
Soft and cool the gentle zephyrs through the forest murmured by,
Sweetest scent and fragrant odours wafted from celestial trees,
Fell upon the earth and ocean, rode upon the laden breeze!
Voice of blessing from the bright sky fell on Raghu's valiant son,—
"Champion of the true and righteous! now thy noble task is done!"

XII Mandodari's Lament and the Funerals

"Hast thou fallen," wept in anguish Ravan's first and eldest bride,
Mandodari, slender-waisted, Queen of Lanka's state and pride,
"Hast thou fallen, king and consort, more than Gods in warlike might,
Slain by man, whom bright Immortals feared to face in dubious fight?

Not a man!—the Dark Destroyer came to thee in mortal form,
Or the heaven-traversing VISHNU, INDRA ruler of the storm,
Gods of sky in shape of Vanars helped the dark and cruel deed,
Girdling round the Discus-Wielder in the battle's direst need!
Well I knew,—when Khara, Dushan, were by Rama's prowess slain,
Rama was no earthly mortal, he who crossed the mighty main,
Well I knew,—when with his army he invested Lanka's gate,
Rama was no earthly mortal but the messenger of Fate,
And I prayed,—the faithful Sita might unto her consort go,
For 'tis writ that nations perish for a righteous woman's woe,
But for impious lust of woman,—all forgetful of thy wife,
Thou hast lost thy crown and kingdom, thou hast lost thy fated life!
Woe to me! the sad remembrance haunts my tortured bosom still,
Of our days on famed Kailasa or on Meru's golden hill,
Gone the days of joy and gladness, Mandodari's days are done,
Since her lord and king and husband from her dear embrace is gone!"
Sorely wept the Queen of Lanka; Rama, tender, tearful, true,
Bade the funeral rites and honours to a fallen foeman due,
And they heaped the wood of *Chandan* and the fragrant garland laid,
On the pyre they lifted Ravan in the richest robes arrayed,
Weeping queens and sorrowing Rakshas round their fallen leader stood,
Brahmans with their chaunted *mantras* piled the dry and scented wood,
Oil and cords and sacred offerings were upon the altar laid,
And a goat of inky darkness as a sacrifice was slayed.
Piously the good Bibhishan lighted Ravan's funeral pyre,
And the zephyrs gently blowing fanned the bright and blazing fire,
Slow and sad with due ablutions mourners left the funeral site,
Rama then unstrung his weapon, laid aside his arms of might.

BOOK XI RAJYA-ABHISHEKA

(*Rama's Return and Consecration*)

THE REAL EPIC ends with the war, and with Rama's happy return to Ayodhya. Sita proves her stainless virtue by an Ordeal of Fire, and returns with her lord and with Lakshman in an aërial car, which Ravan had won from the Gods, and which Bibhishan made over to Rama. Indian poets are never tired of descriptions of nature, and the poet of the Ramayana takes advantage of Rama's journey from Ceylon to Oudh to give us a bird's-eye view of the whole continent of India, as well as to recapitulate the principal incidents of his great Epic.

The gathering of men at Arodhya, the greetings to Rama, and his consecration by the Vedic bard Vasishtha, are among the most pleasing passages in the whole poem. And the happiness enjoyed by men during the reign of Rama—described in the last few couplets of this Book—is an article of belief and a living tradition in India to this day.

The portions translated in this Book form the whole or portions of Sections cxviii., cxx., cxxv., cxxix., and cxxx., of Book vi. of the original text.

I Ordeal by Fire

For she dwelt in Ravan's dwelling,—rumour clouds a woman's fame—
Righteous Rama's brow was clouded, saintly Sita spake in shame:
"Wherefore spake ye not, my Rama, if your bosom doubts my faith,
Dearer than a dark suspicion to a woman were her death!
Wherefore, Rama, with your token came your vassal o'er the wave,
To assist a fallen woman and a tainted wife to save,
Wherefore with your mighty forces crossed the ocean in your pride,
Risked your life in endless combats for a sin-polluted bride?
Hast thou, Rama, all forgotten?—Saintly Janak saw my birth,
Child of harvest-bearing furrow, Sita sprang from Mother Earth,
As a maiden true and stainless unto thee I gave my hand,
As a consort fond and faithful roved with thee from land to land!
But a woman pleadeth vainly when suspicion clouds her name,
Lakshman, if thou lov'st thy sister, light for me the funeral flame,
When the shadow of dishonour darkens o'er a woman's life,
Death alone is friend and refuge of a true and trustful wife,
When a righteous lord and husband turns his cold averted eyes,
Funeral flame dispels suspicion, honour lives when woman dies!"
Dark was Rama's gloomy visage and his lips were firmly sealed,
And his eye betrayed no weakness, word disclosed no thought concealed,
Silent heaved his heart in anguish, silent drooped his tortured head,
Lakshman with a throbbing bosom funeral pyre for Sita made,
And Videha's sinless daughter prayed unto the Gods above,
On her lord and wedded consort cast her dying looks of love!
"If in act and thought," she uttered, "I am true unto my name,
Witness of our sins and virtues, may this Fire protect my fame!

If a false and lying scandal brings a faithful woman shame,
Witness of our sins and virtues, may this Fire protect my fame!
If in lifelong loving duty I am free from sin and blame,
Witness of our sins and virtues, may this Fire protect my fame!"
Fearless in her faith and valour Sita stepped upon the pyre,
And her form of beauty vanished circled by the clasping fire,
And an anguish shook the people like the ocean tempest-tost,
Old and young and maid and matron wept for Sita true and lost,
For bedecked in golden splendour and in gems and rich attire,
Sita vanished in the red fire of the newly lighted pyre!
Rishis and the great *Gandharvas,* Gods who know each secret deed,
Witnessed Sita's high devotion and a woman's lofty creed,
And the earth by ocean girdled with its wealth of teeming life,
Witnessed deed of dauntless duty of a true and stainless wife!

II Woman's Truth Vindicated

Slow the red flames rolled asunder, God of Fire incarnate came,
Holding in his radiant bosom fair Videha's sinless dame,
Not a curl upon her tresses, not a blossom on her brow,
Not a fibre of her mantle did with tarnished lustre glow!
Witness of our sins and virtues, God of Fire incarnate spake,
Bade the sorrow-stricken Rama back his sinless wife to take:
"Ravan in his impious folly forced from thee thy faithful dame,
Guarded by her changeless virtue, Sita still remains the same,
Tempted oft by female Rakshas in the dark and dismal wood,
In her woe and in her sadness true to thee hath Sita stood,
Courted oft by royal Ravan in the forest far and lone,
True to wedded troth and virtue Sita thought of thee alone,
Pure is she in thought and action, pure and stainless, true and meek,
I, the witness of all actions, thus my sacred mandate speak!"
Rama's forehead was unclouded and a radiance lit his eye,
And his bosom heaved in gladness as he spake in accents high:
"Never from the time I saw her in her maiden days of youth,
Have I doubted Sita's virtue, Sita's fixed and changeless truth,
I have known her ever sinless,—let the world her virtue know,
For the God of Fire is witness to her truth and changeless vow!
Ravan in his pride and passion conquered not a woman's love,
For the virtuous like the bright fire in their native radiance move,

Ravan in his rage and folly conquered not a faithful wife,
For like ray of sun unsullied is a righteous woman's life,
Be the wide world now a witness,—pure and stainless is my dame,
Rama shall not leave his consort till he leaves his righteous fame!"
In his tears the contrite Rama clasped her in a soft embrace,
And the fond forgiving Sita in his bosom hid her face!

III Return Home by the Aërial Car

"Mark my love," so Rama uttered, as on flying Pushpa car,
Borne by swans, the home-returning exiles left the field of war,
"Lanka's proud and castled city on Trikuta's triple crest,
As on peak of bold Kailasa mansions of Immortals rest!
Mark the gory fields surrounding where the Vanars in their might,
Faced and fought the charging Rakshas in the long and deathful fight,
Indrajit and Kumbha-karna, Ravan and his chieftains slain,
Fell upon the field of battle and their red blood soaks the plain.
Mark where dark-eyed Mandodari, Ravan's slender-waisted wife,
Wept her widow's tears of anguish when her monarch lost his life,
She hath dried her tears of sorrow and bestowed her heart and hand,
On Bibhishan good and faithful, crownéd king of Lanka's land.
See my love, round Ceylon's island how the ocean billows roar,
Hiding pearls in caves of corals, strewing shells upon the shore,
And the causeway far-extending,—monument of Rama's fame,—
'Rama's Bridge' to distant ages shall our deathless deeds proclaim!
See the rockbound fair Kishkindha and her mountain-girdled town,
Where I slayed the warrior Bali, placed Sugriva on the throne,
And the hill of Rishyamuka where Sugriva first I met,
Gave him word,—he would be monarch ere the evening's sun had set.
See the sacred lake of Pampa by whose wild and echoing shore,
Rama poured his lamentations when he saw his wife no more,
And the woods of Janasthana where Jatayu fought and bled,
When the deep deceitful Ravan with my trusting Sita fled.
Dost thou mark, my soft-eyed Sita, cottage on the river's shore,
Where in righteous peace and penance Sita lived in days of yore,
And by gloomy Godavari, Saint Agastya's home of love,
Holy men by holy duties sanctify the sacred grove!
Dost thou, o'er the Dandak forest, view the Chitrakuta hill,
Deathless bard the Saint Valmiki haunts its shade and crystal rill,

Thither came the righteous Bharat and my loving mother came,
Longing in their hearts to take us to Ayodhya's town of fame,
Dost thou, dear devoted Sita, see the Jumna in her might,
Where in Bharad-waja's *asram* passed we, love, a happy night,
And the broad and ruddy Ganga sweeping in her regal pride,
Forest-dweller faithful Guha crossed us to the southern side.
Joy! joy! my gentle Sita! Fair Ayodhya looms above,
Ancient seat of Raghu's empire, nest of Rama's hope and love,
Bow, bow, to bright Ayodhya! Darksome did the exiles roam,
Now their weary toil is ended in their father's ancient home!"

IV Greetings

Message from returning Rama, Vanars to Ayodhya brought,
Righteous Bharat gave his mandate with a holy joy distraught:
"Let our city shrines and *chaityas* [1] with a lofty music shake,
And our priests to bright Immortals grateful gifts and offerings make,
Bards, reciters of *Puranas,*[2] minstrels versed in ancient song,
Women with their tuneful voices lays of sacred love prolong,
Let our queens and stately courtiers step in splendour and in state,
Chieftains with their marshalled forces range along the city gate,
And our white-robed holy Brahmans hymns and sacred *mantras* sing,
Offer greetings to our brother, render homage to our king!"
Brave Satrughna heard his elder and his mandate duly kept:
"Be our great and sacred city levelled, cleansed, and duly swept,
And the grateful earth be sprinkled with the water from the well,
Strewn with parchéd rice and offering and with flower of sweetest smell,
On each turret, tower, and temple let our flags and colours wave,
On the gates of proud Ayodhya plant Ayodhya's banners brave,
Gay festoons of flowering creeper home and street and dwelling line,
And in gold and glittering garment let the gladdened city shine!"
Elephants in golden trappings thousand chiefs and nobles bore,
Chariots, cars, and gallant chargers speeding by Sarayu's shore,
And the serried troops of battle marched with colours rich and brave,
Proudly o'er the gay procession did Ayodhya's banners wave.
In their stately gilded litters royal dames and damsels came,
Queen Kausalya first and foremost, Queen Sumitra rich in fame,

[1] Shrines or temples. [2] Sacred chronicles.

Pious priest and learned Brahman, chief of guild from near and far,
Noble chief and stately courtier with the wreath and water jar.
Girt by minstrel, bard, and herald chanting glorious deeds of yore,
Bharat came,—his elder's sandals still the faithful younger bore,—
Silver-white his proud umbrella, silver-white his garland brave,
Silver-white the fan of *chowri* which his faithful henchmen wave.
Stately march of gallant chargers and the roll of battle car,
Heavy tread of royal tuskers and the beat of drum of war,
Dundubhi[1] and echoing *sankha,* voice of nations gathered nigh,
Shook the city's tower and temple and the pealing vault of sky!
Sailing o'er the cloudless ether Rama's Pushpa chariot came,
And ten thousand jocund voices shouted Rama's joyous name,
Women with their loving greetings, children with their joyous cry,
Tottering age and lisping infant hailed the righteous chief and high.
Bharat lifted up his glances unto Rama from afar,
Unto Sita, unto Lakshman, seated on the Pushpa car,
And he wafted high his greetings and he poured his pious lay,
As one wafts the chaunted *mantra* to the rising God of Day!
Silver swans by Rama's bidding soft descended from the air,
And on earth the chariot lighted,—car of flowers divinely fair,—
Bharat mounting on the chariot, sought his long-lost elder's grace,
Rama held his faithful younger in a brother's dear embrace.
With his greetings unto Lakshman, unto Rama's faithful dame,
To Bibhishan and Sugriva and each chief who hither came,
Bharat took the jewelled sandals with the rarest gems inlaid,
Placed them at the feet of Rama and in humble accents said:
"Tokens of thy rule and empire, *these* have filled thy royal throne,
Faithful to his trust and duty Bharat renders back thine own,
Bharat's life is joy and gladness, for returned from distant shore,
Thou shalt rule thy spacious kingdom and thy loyal men once more,
Thou shalt hold thy rightful empire and assume thy royal crown,
Faithful to his trust and duty,—Bharat renders back thine own!"

V The Consecration

Joy! joy! in bright Ayodhya gladness filled the hearts of all,
Joy! joy! a lofty music sounded in the royal hall,

[1] Drum.

Fourteen years of woe were ended, Rama now assumed his own,
And they placed the weary wand'rer on his father's ancient throne,
And they brought the sacred water from each distant stream and hill,
From the vast and boundless ocean, from each far and sacred rill.
Vasishtha the Bard of *Vedas* with auspicious rites and meet
Placed the monarch and his consort on the gemmed and jewelled seat,
Gautama and Katyayana, Vamadeva priest of yore,
Jabali and wise Vijaya versed in holy ancient lore,
Poured the fresh and fragrant water on the consecrated king,
As the Gods anointed INDRA from the pure ethereal spring!
Vedic priests with sacred *mantra,* dark-eyed virgins with their song,
Warriors girt in arms and weapons round the crownéd monarch throng,
Juices from each fragrant creeper on his royal brow they place,
And his father's crown and jewels Rama's ample forehead grace,
And as Manu, first of monarchs, was enthroned in days of yore,
So was Rama consecrated by the priests of Vedic lore!
Brave Satrughna on his brother cast the white umbrella's shade
Bold Sugriva and Bibhishan waved the *chowri* gem-inlaid,
VAYU, God of gentle zephyrs, gift of golden garland lent,
INDRA, God of rain and sunshine, wreath of pearls to Rama sent,
Gay *Gandharvas* raised the music, fair *Apsaras* [1] formed the ring,
Men in nations hailed their Rama as their lord and righteous king!
And 'tis told by ancient sages, during Rama's happy reign,
Death untimely, dire diseases, came not to his subject men,
Widows wept not in their sorrow for their lords untimely lost,
Mothers wailed not in their anguish for their babes by YAMA *crost,*
Robbers, cheats, and gay deceivers tempted not with lying word,
Neighbour loved his righteous neighbour and the people loved their lord!
Trees their ample produce yielded as returning seasons went,
And the earth in grateful gladness never failing harvest lent,
Rains descended in their season, never came the blighting gale,
Rich in crop and rich in pasture was each soft and smiling vale,
Loom and anvil gave their produce and the tilled and fertile soil,
And the nation lived rejoicing in their old ancestral toil.

[1] Celestial nymph.

BOOK XII ASWA-MEDHA
(*Sacrifice of the Horse*)

The real Epic ends with Rama's happy return to Ayodhya. An *Uttara-Kanda* or Supplement is added, describing the fate of Sita, and giving the poem a sad ending.

The dark cloud of suspicion still hung on the fame of Sita, and the people of Ayodhya made reflections on the conduct of their king, who had taken back into his house a woman who had lived in the palace of Ravan. Rama gave way to the opinion of his people, and he sent away his loving and faithful Sita to live in forests once more.

Sita found an asylum in the hermitage of Valmiki, and reputed author of this Epic, and there gave birth to twins, Lava and Kusa. Years passed on, and Lava and Kusa grew up as hermit boys, and as pupils of Valmiki.

After years had passed, Rama performed a great Horse-sacrifice. Kings and princes were invited from neighbouring countries, and a great feast was held. Valmiki came to the sacrifice, and his pupils, Lava and Kusa, chanted there the great Epic, the *Ramayana,* describing the deeds of Rama. In this interesting portion of the poem we find how songs and poetry were handed down in ancient India by memory. The boys had learnt the whole of the Epic by heart, and chanted portions of it, day after day, till the recital was completed. We are told that the poem consists of seven books, 500 cantos, and 24,000 couplets. Twenty cantos were recited each day, so that the recital of the whole poem must have taken twenty-five days. It was by such feats of memory and by such recitals that literature was preserved in ancient times in India.

Rama recognised his sons in the boy-minstrels, and his heart yearned once more for Sita, whom he had banished but never forgotten. He asked the Poet Valmiki to restore his wife to him, and he desired that Sita might once more prove her purity in the great assembly, so that he might take her back with the approval of his people.

Sita came. But her life had been darkened by an unjust suspicion, her heart was broken, and she invoked the Earth to take her back. And the Earth, which had given Sita birth, yawned and took back her suffering child into her bosom.

In the ancient hymns of the *Rig Veda,* Sita is simply the goddess of the field-furrow which bears crops for men. We find how that simple conception is concealed in the *Ramayana,* where Sita the heroine of the Epic is still born of the field-furrow, and after all her adventures returns to the Earth. To the millions of men and women in India, however, Sita is not an allegory; she lives in their hearts and affections as the model of womanly love, womanly devotion, and a wife's noble self-abnegation.

The portions translated in this Book form the whole or portions of Sections xcii., xciii., xciv., and xcvii. of Book vii. of the original text.

I The Sacrifice

Years have passed; the lonely Rama in his joyless palace reigned,
And for righteous duty yearning, *Aswa-medha*[1] rite ordained,
And a steed of darkest sable with the valiant Lakshman sent,
And with troops and faithful courtiers to Naimisha's forest went.
Fair was far Naimisha's forest by the limpid Gumti's shore,
Monarchs came and warlike chieftains, Brahmans versed in sacred lore,
Bharat with each friend and kinsman served them with the choicest food,
Proud retainers by each chieftain and each crownéd monarch stood.
Palaces and stately mansions were for royal guests assigned,
Peaceful homes for learnéd Brahmans were with trees umbrageous lined,
Gifts were made unto the needy, cloth by skilful weavers wrought,
Ere the suppliants spake their wishes, ere they shaped their inmost thought!
Rice unto the helpless widow, to the orphan wealth and gold,
Gifts they gave to holy Brahmans, shelter to the weak and old,
Garments to the grateful people crowding by their monarch's door,
Food and drink unto the hungry, home unto the orphan poor.
Ancient *rishis* had not witnessed feast like this in any land,
Bright Immortals in their bounty blest not with a kinder hand,
Through the year and circling seasons lasted Rama's sacred feast,
And the untold wealth of Rama by his kindly gifts increased!

II Valmiki and His Pupils

Foremost midst the gathered Sages to the holy *yajna*[2] came
Deathless Bard of Lay Immortal—Saint Valmiki rich in fame,
Midst the humble homes of *rishis,* on the confines of the wood,
Cottage of the Saint Valmiki in the shady garden stood.
Fruits and berries from the jungle, water from the crystal spring,
With a careful hand Valmiki did unto his cottage bring,

[1] Horse sacrifice.

[2] Sacrifice.

And he spake to gentle Lava, Kusa child of righteous fame,—
Sita's sons, as youthful hermits to the sacred feast they came:
"Lift your voices, righteous pupils, and your richest music lend,
Sing the Lay of *Ramayana* from the first unto the end,
Sing it to the holy Brahman, to the warrior fair and tall,
In the crowded street and pathway, in the monarch's palace hall,
Sing it by the door of Rama,—he ordains this mighty feast,
Sing it to the royal ladies,—they shall to the story list,
Sing from day to day unwearied, in this sacrificial site,
Chant to all the gathered nations Rama's deeds of matchless might,
And this store of fruits and berries will allay your thirst and toil,
Gentle children of the forest, unknown strangers in this soil!
Twenty cantos of the Epic, morn to night, recite each day,
Till from end to end is chanted *Ramayana's* deathless Lay,
Ask no alms, receive no riches, nor of your misfortunes tell,
Useless unto us is bounty who in darksome forests dwell,
Children of the wood and mountain, cruel fortune clouds your birth,
Stainless virtue be your shelter, virtue be your wealth on earth!
If the royal Rama questions and your lineage seeks to know,
Say,—Valmiki is our Teacher and our Sire on earth below,
Wake your harps to notes of rapture and your softest accents lend,
With the music of the poet music of your voices blend,
Bow unto the mighty monarch, bow to Rama fair and tall,
He is father of his subjects, he is lord of creatures all!"

III Recital of the Ramayana

When the silent night was ended, and their pure ablutions done,
Joyous went the minstrel brothers, and their lofty lay begun,
Rama to the hermit minstrels lent a monarch's willing ear,
Blended with the simple music dulcet was the lay to hear,
And so sweet the chanted accents, Rama's inmost soul was stirred,
With his royal guests and courtiers still the deathless lay he heard!
Heralds versed in old *Puranas,* Brahmans skilled in pious rite,
Minstrels deep in lore of music, poets fired by heavenly might,
Watchers of the constellations, min'sters of the festive day,
Men of science and of logic, bards who sang the ancient lay,
Painters skilled and merry dancers who the festive joy prolong,
Hushed and silent in their wonder listed to the wondrous song!

And as poured the flood of music through the bright and livelong day,
Eyes and ears and hearts insatiate drank the nectar of the lay,
And the eager people whispered: "See the boys, how like our king
As two drops of limpid water from the parent bubble spring!
Were the boys no hermit-children, in the hermit's garments clad,
We would deem them Rama's image,—Rama as a youthful lad!"
Twenty cantos of the Epic thus the youthful minstrels sung,
And the voice of stringéd music through the Epic rolled along,
Out spake Rama in his wonder: "Scarce I know who these may be,
Eighteen thousand golden pieces be the children-minstrels' fee!"
"Not so," answered thus the children, "we in darksome forests dwell,
Gold and silver, bounteous monarch, forest life beseem not well!"
"Noble children!" uttered Rama, "dear to me the words you say,
Tell me who composed this Epic,—Father of this deathless Lay?"
"Saint Valmiki," spake the minstrels, "framed the great immortal song
Four and twenty thousand verses to this noble Lay belong,
Untold tales of deathless virtue sanctify his sacred line,
And five hundred glorious cantos in this glorious Epic shine,
In six Books of mighty splendour was the poet's task begun,
With a seventh Book, supplemental is the poet's labour done,
All thy matchless deeds, O monarch, in this Lay will brighter shine,
List to us from first to ending if thy royal heart incline!"
"Be it so," thus Rama answered, but the hours of day were o'er,
And Valmiki's youthful pupils to their cottage came once more.
Rama with his guests and courtiers slowly left the royal hall,
Eager was his heart to listen, eager were the monarchs all,
And the voice of song and music thus was lifted day to day,
And from day to day they listened to Valmiki's deathless Lay!

IV Lava and Kusa Recognised

Flashed upon the contrite Rama glimpses of the dawning truth,
And with tears of love paternal Rama clasped each minstrel youth,
Yearned his sorrow-stricken bosom for his pure and peerless dame,
Sita banished to the forest, stainless in her righteous fame!
In his tears repentant Rama to Valmiki message sent,
That his heart with eager longing sought her from her banishment:
"Pure in soul! before these monarchs may she yet her virtue prove,
Grace once more my throne and kingdom, share my unforgotten love,

Pure in soul! before my subjects may her truth and virtue shine,
Queen of Rama's heart and empire may she once again be mine!"

V Sita Lost

Morning dawned; and with Valmiki, Sita to the gathering came,
Banished wife and weeping mother, sorrow-stricken, suffering dame,
Pure in thought and deed, Valmiki gave his troth and plighted word,—
Faithful still the banished Sita in her bosom held her lord!
"Mighty Saint," so Rama answered as he bowed his humble head,
"Listening world will hear thy mandate and the word that thou hast said,
Never in his bosom Rama questioned Sita's faithful love,
And the God of Fire incarnate did her stainless virtue prove!
Pardon, if the voice of rumour drove me to a deed of shame,
Bowing to my people's wishes I disowned my sinless dame,
Pardon, if to please my subjects I have bade my Sita roam,
Tore her from my throne and empire, tore her from my heart and home!
In the dark and dreary forest was my Sita left to mourn,
In the lone and gloomy jungle were my royal children born,
Help me, Gods, to wipe this error and this deed of sinful pride,
May my Sita prove her virtue, be again my loving bride!"
Gods and Spirits, bright Immortals to that royal *Yajna* came,
Men of every race and nation, kings and chiefs of righteous fame,
Softly through the halls of splendour cool and scented breezes blew,
Fragrance of celestial blossoms o'er the royal chambers flew.
Sita saw the bright Celestials, monarchs gathered from afar,
Saw her royal lord and husband bright as heaven-ascending star,
Saw her sons as hermit-minstrels beaming with a radiance high,
Milk of love suffused her bosom, tear of sorrow filled her eye!
Rama's queen and Janak's daughter, will she stoop her cause to plead,
Witness of her truth and virtue can a loving woman need?
Oh! her woman's heart is bursting, and her day on earth is done,
And she pressed her heaving bosom, slow and sadly thus begun:
"If unstained in thought and action I have lived from day of birth,
Spare a daughter's shame and anguish and receive her, Mother Earth!
If in duty and devotion I have laboured undefiled,
Mother Earth! who bore this woman, once again receive thy child!
If in truth unto my husband I have proved a faithful wife,
Mother Earth! relieve thy Sita from the burden of this life!"

Then the earth was rent and parted, and a golden throne arose,
Held aloft by jewelled *Nagas* as the leaves enfold the rose,
And the Mother in embraces held her spotless sinless Child,
Saintly Janak's saintly daughter, pure and true and undefiled,
Gods and men proclaim her virtue! But fair Sita is no more,
Lone is Rama's loveless bosom and his days of bliss are o'er!

CONCLUSION

In the concluding portion of the *Uttara* or Supplemental Book, the descendants of Rama and his brothers are described as the founders of the great cities and kingdoms which flourished in Western India in the fourth and fifth centuries before the Christian Era.

Bharat had two sons, Taksha and Pushkala. The former founded Taksha-sila, to the east of the Indus, and known to Alexander and the Greeks as Taxila. The latter founded Pushkala-vati, to the west of the Indus, and known to Alexander and the Greeks as Peukelaotis. Thus the sons of Bharat are said to have founded kingdoms which flourished on either side of the Indus river in the fourth century before Christ.

Lakshman had two sons, Angada and Chandraketu. The former founded the kingdom of Karupada, and the latter founded the city of Chandrakanti in the Malwa country.

Satrughna had two sons, Suvahu and Satrughati. The former became king of Mathura, and the latter ruled in Vidisha.

Rama had two sons, Lava and Kusa. The former ruled in Sravasti, which was the capital of Oudh at the time of the Buddha in the fifth and sixth centuries before Christ. The latter founded Kusavati at the foot of the Vindhya mountains.

The death of Rama and his brothers was in accordance with Hindu ideas of the death of the righteous. Lakshman died under somewhat peculiar circumstances. A messenger from heaven sought a secret conference with Rama, and Rama placed Lakshman at the gate, with strict injunctions that whoever intruded on the private conference should be slain. Lakshman himself had to disturb the conference by the solicitation of the celestial *rishi* Durvasa, who always appears on earth to create mischief. And true to the orders passed by Rama, he surrendered his life by penances, and went to heaven.

In the fulness of time, Rama and his other brothers left Ayodhya, crossed the Sarayu, surrendered their mortal life, and entered heaven.

INDIAN HUMOR

The Fables of Panchatantra

INTRODUCTION

India is the home of fables, which are usually associated in our minds with the Greek slave, mentioned by Herodotus, by the name of Aesop. Few users of allusions to Aesop's fables which have crept into our everyday language realize that these stories, their special form and technique, can be traced to very remote sources in India. Ernest Rhys, in his Introduction to *Fables, Aesop and Others* (Everyman's) justly remarks, "We have to admit that the beast-fable did not begin with him (Aesop), or in Greece at all. We have, in fact, to go East and to look to India and burrow in the 'tales within tales' of *Hitopadesa* to get an idea how old the antiquity of the fable actually is."

There are two outstanding collections of animal fables in Indian literature, the *Panchatantra* and the *Hitopadesa*. The first is the older and richer collection, consisting of 87 stories, the second, of 43, of which 25 are found in the *Panchatantra*. According to Dr. Hertel, the *Panchatantra* was probably written down in the second century B.C. in Kashmir, but the stories themselves are much older from evidences in Sanskrit works. It was the German Sanskrit scholar, Theodor Benfey, who translated the *Panchatantra* in 1859, and started the comparative study of beast fables, while the science of comparative philology had been started by the English pioneer of Sanskrit studies, Sir William Jones in 1789, and its foundation laid by Franz Bopp in 1816 through the comparison of Greek, Latin, Sanskrit, Celtic and Teutonic words. (Note that *Pancha* means "five," *Panchatantra* meaning "Five Sections"; cf. *Pentateuch*.) Curiously, a German version of these animal fables, made in 1481, was one of the earliest printed books in Europe, and an English version was among the books that came from Caxton's printing press. Also, the *Hito-*

padesa was one of the first printed Sanskrit books in the beginning of the nineteenth century. Sir Edwin Arnold translated the *Hitopadesa* (*Book of Good Counsels*) from the Sanskrit in 1861. On the other hand, the *Panchatantra* was not directly translated from the Sanskrit until 1924 by Stanley Rice,[1] and by Arthur W. Ryder in 1925.

While the indebtedness of Aesop to the Indian fables is open to question and can never be settled by conclusive evidence, the established route of migration of Indian fables into Europe has been interestingly described by Max Müller.[2] The stories from one of the collections of the *Panchatantra* (of which there are twenty-five recensions), were translated into Pahlawi (Pehlevi) in the sixth century. From the Persian, it was translated into Syriac in A.D. 570 (under the title *Kalilag and Damnag*, names of the jackals telling the stories, Tarataka and Damnaka), and into Arabic in the eighth century as the *Fables of Pilpay*. In this Arabic garb, it spread through the Islam world and reached Spain, Sicily, Provence and France, while through Constantinople, it reached Eastern Europe and was translated into Greek, Latin, German, Italian and English. In an English translation from the Italian it was probably known to Shakespeare. Such tales have inspired similar stories of *Boccaccio;* see *The Gullible Husband* and *The Butter-Blinded Brahman* in the present selection. La Fontaine, in the edition of his *Fables* published in 1678, says in the Preface, "It is not necessary that I should say whence I have taken the subjects of these new fables. I shall only say, from a sense of gratitude that I owe the largest portion of them to Pilpay the Indian Sage."[3]

The *Panchatantra* was therefore one of the most widely known and widely translated books of the world in the Middle Ages. As to the intriguing question of the origin of Aesop's fables, different views are possible and are held by different scholars. Max Müller believed that these fables found their way to Greece in or before Herodotus' time; others held the opposite; while still others believe in a common Aryan origin, or in independent origins. The question will probably never be settled. Rawlinson points out, however, "That the migration of fables was originally from East to West, and not vice versa, is shown by the

[1] Stanley Rice wrote in 1924 in his introduction to *Ancient Fables and Stories* (Wisdom of the East Series): "Indeed, a search in the British Museum and in the India Office libraries has failed to discover any English translation whatsoever."

[2] "On the Migration of Fables," in *Chips from a German Workshop*, vol. IV.

[3] Quoted by H. H. Gowen, *History of Indian Literature*.

fact that the animals and birds who play the leading parts, the lion, the jackal, the elephant, and the peacock, are mostly Indian ones. In the European versions the jackal becomes the fox: the relation between the lion and the jackal is a natural one, whereas that between the lion and the fox is not."[1] What seems to me common sense is that tigers, monkeys and crocodiles abound in Indian jungles and not in Greece. One cannot read Indian literature without being constantly impressed by the sense of the forest.

The important thing to point out is that the fables have had a too luxuriant growth in native Indian literature to permit of the theory of borrowed origins. With an apology for punning, one must say that the Hindu mind is fabulous. The genius for creating fables seems inexhaustible in Indian literature, while Aesop stood almost alone in Greece. Witness the *Buddhist Birth Stories* (the *Jatakas*),[2] and the *Dhammapada Commentary* by Buddhaghosha,[3] running each into four or five hundred stories, a great part of them animal fables, and the *Panchatantra* and the *Hitopadesa*. When one remembers also that many of the stories in the *Arabian Nights,* including that of the famous Sindbad the Sailor, are of Hindu origin, it is not easy to accept the view that such tales are not of native Indian growth.

Like the *Arabian Nights,* the *Panchatantra* uses a framework: that of a king despairing of teaching his two dull princes and finally engaging a wise Brahman who pledged to teach these two dull boys the complete *niti,* or wisdom of human intercourse, in six months, and who proceeded to teach these lessons on human nature through the fables, cleverly weaving one tale within another and very often making one character in the story start telling another story before one is completed.

The gift for moralizing that we see in *Aesop* exists in rather uncomfortable abundance. For it is quite clear that here the tale adorns the moral, rather than the moral adorns the tale. Many of these maxims are quotations from older books, like the *Vedas,* and some of them are extremely appropriate today. One might choose the following as the maxim for the present work and all folk literature:

> All things that are seen or heard
> In science or the Sacred Word,

[1] "India in European Thought and Literature" in *The Legacy of India,* Oxford.
[2] Translated by T. W. Rhys Davids, London, 1880.
[3] Translated by E. W. Burlingame, *Buddhist Legends,* in 3 vols. Harvard Oriental Series, Nos. 28, 29, 30.

All things in interstellar space
Are known among the populace.

And in an age when scholars build airplanes without knowing how to use them, one could agree in the tale of *Lion-Makers* that

Scholarship is less than sense,
Therefore seek intelligence.

The folly of appeasers was once wittily expressed by Heywood Broun in Aesop fashion when he said that "appeasers believe that if you keep on throwing steaks to a tiger, the tiger will become a vegetarian." The author of *Panchatantra* had some thing similar to say:

Caress a rascal as you will,
He was, and is, a rascal still:
All salve and sweating-treatments fail
To take the kink from doggy's tail.

Conciliation simply makes
A foeman's indignation splutter,
Like drops of water sprinkled on
A briskly burning pan of butter.

And we may derive some comfort in hearing that mankind eventually always overcomes its schemers:

Since scamp and sneak and snake
So often undertake
A plan that does not thrive,
The world wags on, alive.

The purpose of the book may be said to teach wisdom about human nature by libeling the animal world. Like Aesop, the author's morals are sharp and shrewd. But on the whole, it is a good procedure to make the animal kingdom bear all the sins of hypocrisy and cunning and avarice of mankind. When the wolf chides the lamb for fouling the water he is drinking, the people of the weak nations know who the wolf is if not the aggressor himself. And when a fox condemns "sour grapes," I feel that he is distinctly human: a fox is too honest for that, only humans indulge in the luxury of rationalizing errors. There is an advantage in making animals talk like men, rather than make gods do the same. When animals talk like men, we at least feel as if we were hearing children talk like grown-ups, which is pleasurable, but when we make the gods talk like human beings, we feel as if we were listening to old men talking like children. Rather than be anthropomorphic with the gods, let's be anthropomorphic with the animals.

The present selection is taken from the translation by Arthur W. Ryder,[1] who has also translated the beautiful *Sakuntala,* the classic Indian drama, for us. I have often found it necessary to omit some of the too many verse comments. In an age when men still fight like animals, it may be sometimes quite refreshing to re-enter the world of simple human truths and recognize ourselves or our fellowmen whose names may appear in the morning papers. I have included some fables at the end of this selection, which are recognizable as familiar to us. The best known is that containing the classical example of anti-climax, *The Brahman's Dream,* known to us as the story of the Milkmaid who dreamed of her wedding and overthrew her milk pail. The story of the *Loyal Mungoose,* so heroically pathetic and worthy of a Walt Disney cartoon, can be recognized as the Welsh story of Llewellyn and Gelert, where the mungoose has been transformed into a faithful dog.

But I do wish that the wise, learned and calculating appeasers of America and Europe had read *The Frogs that Rode Snakeback* in their childhood and taken that simple wisdom to heart, for I believe Waterfoot who gave away the plebeian frogs to the snake was the first of the race of appeasers. And the first of the isolationists were the little monkeys in the story of *The Unforgiving Monkey.*

[1] *The Panchatantra,* University of Chicago Press, 1925.

The Panchatantra

Translated by Arthur W. Ryder

INTRODUCTION TO THE STORIES

IN THE SOUTHERN COUNTRY is a city called Maidens' Delight. There lived a king named Immortal-Power. He was familiar with all the works treating of the wise conduct of life. His feet were made dazzling by the tangle of rays of light from jewels in the diadems of mighty kings who knelt before him. He had reached the far shore of all the arts that embellish life. This king had three sons. Their names were Rich-Power, Fierce-Power, Endless-Power, and they were supreme blockheads.

Now when the king perceived that they were hostile to education, he summoned his counselors and said: "Gentlemen, it is known to you that these sons of mine, being hostile to education, are lacking in discernment. So when I behold them, my kingdom brings me no happiness, though all external thorns are drawn. For there is wisdom in the proverb:

> Of sons unborn, or dead, or fools,
> Unborn or dead will do:
> They cause a little grief, no doubt;
> But fools, a long life through.

And again:

> To what good purpose can a cow
> That brings no calf nor milk, be bent?
> Or why beget a son who proves
> A dunce and disobedient?

Some means must therefore be devised to awaken their intelligence."

And they, one after another, replied: "O King, first one learns grammar, in twelve years. If this subject has somehow been mastered, then one masters the books on religion and practical life. Then the intelligence awakens."

But one of their number, a counselor named Keen, said: "O King, the duration of life is limited, and the verbal sciences require much time for mastery. Therefore let some kind of epitome be devised to wake their intelligence. There is a proverb that says:

> Since verbal science has no final end,
> Since life is short, and obstacles impend,
> Let central facts be picked and firmly fixed,
> As swans extract the milk with water mixed.

"Now there is a Brahman here named Vishnusharman,[1] with a reputation for competence in numerous sciences. Intrust the princes to him. He will certainly make them intelligent in a twinkling."

When the king had listened to this, he summoned Vishnusharman and said: "Holy sir, as a favor to me you must make these princes incomparable masters of the art of practical life. In return, I will bestow upon you a hundred land-grants."

And Vishnusharman made answer to the king: "O King, listen. Here is the plain truth. I am not the man to sell good learning for a hundred land-grants. But if I do not, in six months' time, make the boys acquainted with the art of intelligent living, I will give up my own name. Let us cut the matter short. Listen to my lion-roar. My boasting arises from no greed for cash. Besides, I have no use for money; I am eighty years old, and all the objects of sensual desire have lost their charm. But in order that your request may be granted, I will show a sporting spirit in reference to artistic matters. Make a note of the date. If I fail to render your sons, in six months' time, incomparable masters of the art of intelligent living, then His Majesty is at liberty to show me His Majestic bare bottom."

When the king, surrounded by his counselors, had listened to the Brahman's highly unconventional promise, he was penetrated with wonder, intrusted the princes to him, and experienced supreme content.

Meanwhile, Vishnusharman took the boys, went home, and made them learn by heart five books which he composed and called: (I) "The Loss of Friends," (II) "The Winning of Friends," (III) "Crows and Owls," (IV) "Loss of Gains," (V) "Ill-considered Action."

[1] It is possible that Vishnusharman was the real author of the book.

These the princes learned, and in six months' time they answered the prescription. Since that day this work on the art of intelligent living, called *Panchatantra,* or the "Five Books," has traveled the world, aiming at the awakening of intelligence in the young. To sum the matter up:

> Whoever learns the work by heart,
> Or through the story-teller's art
> Becomes acquainted,
> His life by sad defeat—although
> The king of heaven be his foe—
> Is never tainted.

THE FROGS THAT RODE SNAKEBACK

THERE WAS ONCE an elderly black snake in a certain spot, and his name was Slow-Poison. He considered the situation from this point of view: "How in the world can I get along without overtaxing my energies?" Then he went to a pond containing many frogs, and behaved as if very dejected.

As he waited thus, a frog came to the edge of the water and asked: "Uncle, why don't you bustle about today for food as usual?"

"My dear friend," said Slow-Poison, "I am afflicted. Why should I wish for food? For this evening, as I was bustling about for food, I saw a frog and made ready to catch him. But he saw me and, fearing death, he escaped among some Brahmans intent upon holy recitation, nor did I perceive which way he went. But in the water at the edge of the pond was the great toe of a Brahman boy, and stupidly deceived by its resemblance to a frog, I bit it, and the boy died immediately. Then the sorrowing father cursed me in these terms: 'Monster! Since you bit my harmless son, you shall for this sin become a vehicle for frogs, and shall subsist on whatever they choose to allow you.' Consequently, I have come here to serve as your vehicle."

Now the frog reported this to all the others. And every last one of them, in extreme delight, went and reported to the frog-king, whose name was Water-Foot. He in turn, accompanied by his counselors, rose hurriedly from the pond—for he thought it an extraordinary occurrence—and climbed upon Slow-Poison's hood. The others also, in order of age, climbed on his back. Yet others, finding no vacant spot, hopped along behind the snake. Now Slow-Poison, with an eye to making his living, showed them fancy turns in great variety. And Water-Foot, enjoying contact with his body, said to him:

> I'd rather ride Slow-Poison than
> The finest horse I've seen,
> Or elephant, or chariot,
> Or man-borne palanquin.

The next day, Slow-Poison was wily enough to move very slowly. So Water-Foot said: "My dear Slow-Poison, why don't you carry us nicely, as you did before?"

And Slow-Poison said: "O King, I have no carrying power today because of lack of food." My dear fellow," said the king, "eat the plebeian frogs."

When Slow-Poison heard this, he quivered with joy in every member and made haste to say: "Why, that is a part of the curse laid on me by the Brahman. For that reason I am greatly pleased at your command." So he ate frogs uninterruptedly, and in a very few days he grew strong. And with delight and inner laughter he said:

> The trick was good. All sorts of frogs
> Within my power have passed.
> The only question that remains,
> Is: How long will they last?

Water-Foot, for his part, was befooled by Slow-Poison's plausibilities, and did not notice a thing.

THE UNFORGIVING MONKEY

In a certain city was a king named Moon, who had a pack of monkeys for his son's amusement. They were kept in prime condition by daily provender and pabulum in great variety.

For the amusement of the same prince there was a herd of rams. One of them had an itching tongue, so he went into the kitchen at all hours of the day and night and swallowed everything in sight. And the cooks would beat him with any stick or other object within reach.

Now when the chief of the monkeys observed this, he reflected: "Dear me! This quarrel between ram and cooks will mean the destruction of the monkeys. For the ram is a regular guzzler, and when the cooks are infuriated, they hit him with anything handy. Suppose some time they find nothing else and beat him with a firebrand. Then that broad, woolly back will very easily catch fire. And if the ram, while burning, plunges into the stable near by, it will blaze—for it is mostly thatch—and the horses will be scorched. Now the standard work on veterinary science prescribes monkey-fat to relieve burns on horses. This being so, we are threatened with death."

Having reached this conclusion, he assembled the monkeys and said:

"A quarrel of the ram and cooks
Has lately come about;
It threatens every monkey life
Without a shade of doubt.

"Because, if senseless quarrels rend
A house from day to day,
The folk who wish to keep alive
Had better move away.

"Therefore let us leave the house and take to the woods before we are all dead."

But the conceited monkeys laughed at his warning and said: "Oho! You are old and your mind is slipping. Your words prove it. We have no intention of foregoing the heavenly dainties which the princes give us with their own hands, in order to eat fruits peppery, puckery, bitter, and sour from the trees out there in the forest."

Having listened to this, the monkey chief made a wry face and said: "Come, come! You are fools. You do not consider the outcome of this pleasant life. Just at present it is sweet, at the last it will turn to poison. At any rate, I will not behold the death of my household. I am off for that very forest."

With these words the chief left them all behind, and went to the forest.

One day after he had gone, the ram entered the kitchen. And the cook, finding nothing else, picked up a firebrand, half-consumed and still blazing, and struck him. Whereat, with half his body blazing, he plunged bleating into the stable near by. There he rolled until flames started up on all sides—for the stable was mostly thatch—and of the horses tethered there some died, their eyes popping, while some, half-burned to death and whinnying with pain, snapped their halters, so that nobody knew what to do.

In this state of affairs, the saddened king assembled the veterinary surgeons and said: "Prescribe some method of giving these horses relief from the pain of their burns." And they, recalling the teachings of their science, prescribed for this emergency the remedy of applying monkey-fat.

When the king heard this, he ordered the slaughter of the monkeys. And, not to waste words, every one was killed.

Now the monkey chief did not with his own eyes see this outrage perpetrated on his household. But he heard the story as it passed from one to another, and did not take it tamely. As the proverb says:

> If foes commit an outrage on
>   A house, and one forgives—
> Be it from fear or greed—he is
>   The meanest man that lives.

Now as the elderly monkey wandered about thirsty, he came to a lake made lovely by clusters of lotuses. And as he observed it narrowly, he noticed footprints leading into the lake, but none coming out. Thereupon he reflected: "There must be some vicious beast here in the water. So I will stay at a safe distance and drink through a hollow lotus-stalk."

When he had done so, there issued from the water a man-eating fiend with a pearl necklace adorning his neck, who spoke and said: "Sir, I eat everyone who enters the water. So there is none shrewder than you, who drink in this fashion. I have taken a liking to you. Name your heart's desire."

"Sir," said the monkey, "how many can you eat?" And the fiend replied: "I can eat hundreds, thousands, myriads, yes, hundreds of thousands, if they enter the water. Outside, a jackal can overpower me."

"And I," said the monkey, "I live in mortal enmity with a king. If you will give me that pearl necklace, I will awaken his greed with a plausible narrative, and will make that king enter the lake along with his retinue." So the fiend handed over the pearl necklace.

Then people saw the monkey roaming over trees and palace-roofs with a pearl necklace embellishing his throat, and they asked him: "Well, chief, where have you spent this long time? Where did you get a pearl necklace like that? Its dazzling beauty dims the very sun."

And the monkey answered: "In a spot in the forest is a shrewdly hidden lake, a creation of the god of wealth. Through his grace, if anyone bathes there at sunrise on Sunday, he comes out with a pearl necklace like this embellishing his throat."

Now the king heard this from somebody, summoned the monkey, and asked: "Is this true, chief?" "O King," said the monkey, "you have visible proof in the pearl necklace on my throat. If you, too, could find a use for one, send somebody with me, and I will show him."

On hearing this, the king said: "In view of the facts, I will come myself with my retinue, so that we may acquire numbers of pearl necklaces." "O King," said the monkey, "your idea is delicious."

So the king and his retinue started, greedy for pearl necklaces. And the king in his palanquin clasped the monkey to his bosom, showing him honor as they traveled. For there is wisdom in the saying:

> The hair grows old with aging years;
> The teeth grow old, the eyes and ears.
> But while the aging seasons speed,
> One thing is young forever—greed.

At dawn they reached the lake and the monkey said to the king: "O King, fulfilment comes to those who enter at sunrise. Let all your attendants be told, so that they may dash in with one fell swoop. You, however, must enter with me, for I will pick the place I found before and show you plenty of pearl necklaces." So all the attendants entered and were eaten by the fiend.

Then, as they lingered, the king said to monkey: "Well, chief, why do my attendants linger?" And the monkey hurriedly climbed a tree before saying to the king: "You villainous king, your attendants are eaten by a fiend that lives in the water. My enmity with you, arising from the death of my household, has been brought to a happy termination. Now go. I did not make you enter there, because I remembered that you were the king. Thus you plotted the death of my household, and I of yours."

When the king heard this, he hastened home, grief-stricken.

THE LION-MAKERS

In a certain town were four Brahmans who lived in friendship. Three of them had reached the far shore of all scholarship, but lacked sense. The other found scholarship distasteful; he had nothing but sense.

One day they met for consultation. "What is the use of attainments," said they, "if one does not travel, win the favor of kings, and acquire money? Whatever we do, let us all travel."

But when they had gone a little way, the eldest of them said: "One of us, the fourth, is a dullard, having nothing but sense. Now nobody gains the favorable attention of kings by simple sense without scholarship. Therefore we will not share our earnings with him. Let him turn back and go home."

Then the second said: "My intelligent friend, you lack scholarship. Please go home." But the third said: "No, no. This is no way to behave. For we have played together since we were little boys. Come along, my noble friend. You shall have a share of the money we earn."

With this agreement they continued their journey, and in a forest they found the bones of a dead lion. Thereupon one of them said: "A good opportunity to test the ripeness of our scholarship. Here lies some kind of creature, dead. Let us bring it to life by means of the scholarship we have honestly won."

Then the first said: "I know how to assemble the skeleton." The second said: "I can supply skin, flesh, and blood." The third said: "I can give it life."

So the first assembled the skeleton, the second provided skin, flesh, and blood. But while the third was intent on giving the breath of life, the man of sense advised against it, remarking: "This is a lion. If you bring him to life, he will kill every one of us."

"You simpleton!" said the other, "it is not I who will reduce scholarship to a nullity." "In that case," came the reply, "wait a moment, while I climb this convenient tree."

When this had been done, the lion was brought to life, rose up, and killed all three. But the man of sense, after the lion had gone elsewhere, climbed down and went home.

"And that is why I say:

> Scholarship is less than sense;
> Therefore seek intelligence:
> Senseless scholars in their pride
> Made a lion; then they died."

MOUSE-MAID MADE MOUSE

THE BILLOWS of the Ganges were dotted with pearly foam born of the leaping of fishes frightened at hearing the roar of the waters that broke on the rugged, rocky shore. On the bank was a hermitage crowded with holy men devoting their time to the performance of sacred rites—chanting, self-denial, self-torture, study, fasting, and sacrifice. They would take purified water only, and that in measured sips. Their bodies wasted under a diet of bulbs, roots, fruits, and moss. A loin-cloth made of bark formed their scanty raiment.

The father of the hermitage was named Yajnavalkya. After he had bathed in the sacred stream and had begun to rinse his mouth, a little female mouse dropped from a hawk's beak and fell into his hand. When he saw what she was, he laid her on a banyan leaf, repeated his bath and mouth-rinsing, and performed a ceremony of purification. Then through the magic power of his holiness, he changed her into a girl, and took her with him to his hermitage.

As his wife was childless, he said to her: "Take her, my dear wife. She has come into life as your daughter, and you must rear her carefully." So the wife reared her and spoiled her with petting. As soon as the girl reached the age of twelve, the mother saw that she was ready for marriage, and said to her husband: "My dear husband, how can you fail to see that the time is passing when your daughter should marry?"

And he replied: "You are quite right, my dear. The saying goes:

For if she bides a maiden still,
She gives herself to whom she will;
Then marry her in tender age:
So warns the heaven-begotten sage.

If she, unwed, unpurified,
Too long within the home abide,
She may no longer married be:
A miserable spinster, she.

A father then, avoiding sin,
Weds her, the appointed time within
(Where'er a husband may be had)
To good, indifferent, or bad.

Now I will try to give her to one of her own station. You know the saying:

Where wealth is very much the same,
And similar the family fame,
Marriage (or friendship) is secure;
But not between the rich and poor.

"But

> Get money, good looks,
> And knowledge of books,
> Good family, youth,
> Position, and truth.

"So, if she is willing, I will summon the blessèd sun, and give her to him." "I see no harm in that," said his wife. "Let it be done."

The holy man therefore summoned the sun, who appeared without delay, and said: "Holy sir, why am I summoned?" The father said: "Here is a daughter of mine. Be kind enough to marry her." Then, turning to his daughter, he said: "Little girl, how do you like him, this blessèd lamp of the three worlds?" "No, father," said the girl. "He is too burning hot. I could not like him. Please summon another one, more excellent than he is."

Upon hearing this, the holy man said to the sun: "Blessèd one, is there any superior to you?" And the sun replied: "Yes, the cloud is superior even to me. When he covers me, I disappear."

So the holy man summoned the cloud next, and said to the maiden: "Little girl, I will give you to him." "No," said she. "This one is black and frigid. Give me to someone finer than he."

Then the holy man asked: "O cloud, is there anyone superior to you?" And the cloud replied: "The wind is superior even to me."

So he summoned the wind, and said: "Little girl, I give you to him." "Father," said she, "this one is too fidgety. Please invite somebody superior even to him." So the holy man said: "O wind, is there anyone superior even to you?" "Yes," said the wind. "The mountain is superior to me."

So he summoned the mountain and said to the maiden: "Little girl, I give you to him." "Oh, father," said she. "He is rough all over, and stiff. Please give me to somebody else."

So the holy man asked: "O kingly mountain, is there anyone superior even to you?" "Yes," said the mountain. "Mice are superior to me." [1]

Then the holy man summoned a mouse, and presented him to the little girl, saying: "Little girl, do you like this mouse?"

The moment she saw him, she felt: "My own kind, my own kind," and her body thrilled and quivered, and she said: "Father dear, turn me into a mouse, and give me to him. Then I can keep house as my kind of people ought to do."

[1] Because mice bore holes in the mountain sides.

And her father, through the magic power of his holiness, turned her into a mouse, and gave her to him.

"And that is why I say:

Though mountain, sun, and cloud, and wind
  Were suitors at her feet,
The mouse-maid turned a mouse again—
  Nature is hard to beat."

THE DUEL BETWEEN ELEPHANT AND SPARROW

In a dense bit of jungle lived a sparrow and his wife, who had built their nest on the branch of a tamal tree, and in course of time a family appeared.

Now one day a jungle elephant with the spring fever was distressed by the heat, and came beneath that tamal tree in search of shade. Blinded by his fever, he pulled with the tip of his trunk at the branch where the sparrows had their nest, and broke it. In the process the sparrows' eggs were crushed, though the parent-birds—further life being predestined—barely escaped death.

Then the hen-sparrow lamented, desolate with grief at the death of her chicks. And presently, hearing her lamentation, a woodpecker bird, a great friend of hers, came grieved at her grief, and said: "My dear friend, why lament in vain? For the Scripture says:

For lost and dead and past
  The wise have no laments:
Between the wise and fools
  Is just this difference."

"That is good doctrine," said the hen-sparrow, "but what of it? This elephant—curse his spring fever!—killed my babies. So if you are my friend, think of some plan to kill this big elephant. If that were done, I should feel less grief at the death of my children."

"Madam," said the woodpecker, "your remark is very true. For the proverb says:

A friend in need is a friend indeed,
  Although of different caste;
The whole world is your eager friend
  So long as riches last.

"Now see what my wit can devise. But you must know that I, too, have a friend, a gnat called Lute-Buzz. I will return with her, so that this villainous beast of an elephant may be killed."

So he went with the hen-sparrow, found the gnat, and said: "Dear madam, this is my friend the hen-sparrow. She is mourning because a villainous elephant smashed her eggs. So you must lend your assistance while I work out a plan for killing him."

"My good friend," said the gnat, "there is only one possible answer. But I also have a very intimate friend, a frog named Cloud-Messenger. Let us do the right thing by calling him into consultation."

So all three went together and told Cloud-Messenger the entire story. And the frog said: "How feeble a thing is that wretched elephant when pitted against a great throng enraged! Gnat, you must go and buzz in his fevered ear, so that he may shut his eyes in delight at hearing your music. Then the woodpecker's bill will peck out his eyes. After that I will sit on the edge of a pit and croak. And he, being thirsty, will hear me, and will approach expecting to find a body of water. When he comes to the pit, he will fall in and perish."

When they carried out the plan, the fevered elephant shut his eyes in delight at the song of the gnat, was blinded by the woodpecker, wandered thirst-smitten at noonday, followed the croak of a frog, came to a great pit, fell in, and died.

"And that is why I say:

> Woodpecker and sparrow,
> With froggy and gnat,
> Attacking *en masse,* laid
> The elephant flat."

THE HERON THAT LIKED CRABMEAT

THERE WAS ONCE a heron in a certain place on the edge of a pond. Being old, he sought an easy way of catching fish on which to live. He began by lingering at the edge of his pond, pretending to be quite irresolute, not eating even the fish within his reach.

Now among the fish lived a crab. He drew near and said: "Uncle, why do you neglect today your usual meals and amusements?" And the heron replied: "So long as I kept fat and flourishing by eating fish, I spent my time pleasantly, enjoying the taste of you. But a great disaster will soon befall you. And as I am old, this will cut short the pleasant course of my life. For this reason I feel depressed."

"Uncle," said the crab, "of what nature is the disaster?" And the heron continued: "Today I overheard the talk of a number of fishermen as they passed near the pond. 'This is a big pond,' they were saying, 'full of fish. We will try a cast of the net tomorrow or the day after. But today we will go to the lake near the city.' This being so, you are lost, my food supply is cut off, I too am lost, and in grief at the thought, I am indifferent to food today."

Now when the water-dwellers heard the trickster's report, they all feared for their lives and implored the heron, saying: "Uncle! Father! Brother! Friend! Thinker! Since you are informed of the calamity, you also know the remedy. Pray save us from the jaws of this death."

Then the heron said: "I am a bird, not competent to contend with men. This, however, I can do. I can transfer you from this pond to another, a bottomless one." By this artful speech they were so led astray that they said: "Uncle! Friend! Unselfish kinsman! Take me first! Me first! Did you never hear this?

Stout hearts delight to pay the price
Of merciful self-sacrifice,
Count life as nothing, if it end
In gentle service to a friend."

Then the old rascal laughed in his heart, and took counsel with his mind, thus: "My shrewdness has brought these fishes into my power. They ought to be eaten very comfortably." Having thus thought it through, he promised what the thronging fish implored, lifted some in his bill, carried them a certain distance to a slab of stone, and ate them there. Day after day he made the trip with supreme delight and satisfaction, and meeting the fish, kept their confidence by ever new inventions.

One day the crab, disturbed by the fear of death, importuned him with the words: "Uncle, pray save me, too, from the jaws of death." And the heron reflected: "I am quite tired of this unvarying fish diet. I should like to taste him. He is different, and choice." So he picked up the crab and flew through the air.

But since he avoided all bodies of water and seemed planning to alight on the sun-scorched rock, the crab asked him: "Uncle, where is that pond without any bottom?" And the heron laughed and said:

"Do you see that broad, sun-scorched rock? All the water-dwellers have found repose there. Your turn has now come to find repose."

Then the crab looked down and saw a great rock of sacrifice, made horrible by heaps of fish-skeletons. And he thought: "Ah me!

> If you will, with serpents play;
> Dwell with foemen who betray:
> Shun your false and foolish friends,
> Fickle, seeking vicious ends.

Why, he has already eaten these fish whose skeletons are scattered in heaps. So what might be an opportune course of action for me? Yet why do I need to consider?

> Fear fearful things, while yet
> No fearful thing appears;
> When danger must be met,
> Strike, and forget your fears.

So, before he drops me there, I will catch his neck with all four claws."

When he did so, the heron tried to escape, but being a fool, he found no parry to the grip of the crab's nippers, and had his head cut off.

Then the crab painfully made his way back to the pond, dragging the heron's neck as if it had been a lotus-stalk. And when he came among the fish, they said: "Brother, why come back?" Thereupon he showed the head as his credentials and said: "He enticed the water-dwellers from every quarter, deceived them with his prevarications, dropped them on a slab of rock not far away, and ate them. But I—further life being predestined—perceived that he destroyed the trustful, and I have brought back his neck. Forget your worries. All the water-dwellers shall live in peace."

THE UNTEACHABLE MONKEY

In a part of a forest was a troop of monkeys who found a firefly one winter evening when they were dreadfully depressed. On examining the insect, they believed it to be fire, so lifted it with care, covered it with dry grass and leaves, thrust forward their arms, sides, stomachs, and chests, scratched themselves, and enjoyed imagining that they were warm. One of the arboreal creatures in particular, being especially chilly, blew repeatedly and with concentrated attention on the firefly.

Thereupon a bird named Needle-Face, driven by hostile fate to her own destruction, flew down from her tree and said to the monkey: "My dear sir, do not put yourself to unnecessary trouble. This is not fire. This is a firefly." He, however, did not heed her warning but blew again, nor did he stop when she tried more than once to check him. To cut a long story short, when she vexed him by coming close and shouting in his ear, he seized her and dashed her on a rock, crushing face, eyes, head, and neck so that she died.

"And that is why I say:

> No knife prevails against a stone;
> Nor bends the unbending tree;
> No good advice from Needle-Face
> Helped indocility."

THE BRAHMAN'S GOAT

In a certain town lived a Brahman named Friendly who had undertaken the labor of maintaining the sacred fire. One day in the month of February, when a gentle breeze was blowing, when the sky was veiled in clouds and a drizzling rain was falling, he went to another village to beg a victim for the sacrifice, and said to a certain man: "O sacrificer, I wish to make an offering on the approaching day of the new moon. Pray give me a victim." And the man gave him a plump goat, as prescribed in Scripture. This he put through its paces, found it sound, placed it on his shoulder, and started in haste for his own city.

Now on the road he was met by three rogues whose throats were pinched with hunger. These, spying the plump creature on his shoulder, whispered together: "Come now! If we could eat that creature, we should have the laugh on this sleety weather. Let us fool him, get the goat, and ward off the cold."

So the first of them changed his dress, issued from a by-path to meet the Brahman, and thus addressed that man of pious life: "O pious Brahman, why are you doing a thing so unconventional and so ridiculous? You are carrying an unclean animal, a dog, on your shoulder.

At that the Brahman was mastered by anger, and he said: "Are you blind, man, that you impute doghood to a goat?" "O Brahman," said the rogue, "do not be angry. Go whither you will."

But when he had traveled a little farther, the second rogue met him and said: "Alas, holy sir, alas! Even if this dead calf was a pet, still you should not put it on your shoulder."

Then the Brahman spoke in anger: "Are you blind, man? You call a goat a calf." And the rogue said: "Holy sir, do not be angry. I spoke in ignorance. Do as you will."

But when he had walked only a little farther through the forest, the third rogue, changing his dress, met him and said: "Sir, this is most improper. You are carrying a donkey on your shoulder. Pray drop this thing, before another sees you."

So the Brahman concluded that it was a goblin in quadruped form, threw it on the ground, and made for home, terrified. Meanwhile, the three rogues met, caught the goat, and carried out their plan.

"And that is why I say:

> The strong, deft, clever rascals note,
> Who robbed the Brahman of his goat."

"Moreover, there is sound sense in this:

> Is any man uncheated by
> New servants' diligence,
> The praise of guests, the maiden's tears,
> And roguish eloquence?

Furthermore, one should avoid a quarrel with a crowd, though the individuals be weak. As the verse puts it:

> Beware the populace enraged;
> A crowd's a fearsome thing:
> The ants devoured the giant snake
> For all his quivering."

THE SNAKE IN THE PRINCE'S BELLY

In a certain city dwelt a king whose name was Godlike. He had a son who wasted daily in every limb because of a snake that used his belly as a home instead of an ant-hill. So the prince became dejected and went to another country. In a city of that country he begged alms, spending his time in a great temple.

Now in that city was a king named Gift, who had two daughters in early womanhood. One of these bowed daily at her father's feet with the greeting: "Victory, O King," while the other said: "Your deserts, O King."

At this the king grew very angry, and said: "See, counselors. This young lady speaks malevolently. Give her to some foreigner. Let her have her own deserts." To this the counselors agreed, and gave the princess, with very few maid-servants, to the prince who made his home in the temple.

And she was delighted, accepted her husband like a god, and went with him to a far country. There by the edge of a tank in a distant city she left the prince to look after the house while she went with her maids to buy butter, oil, salt, rice, and other supplies. When her shopping was done, she returned and found the prince with his head resting on an ant-hill. And from his mouth issued the head of a hooded snake, taking the air. Likewise another snake crawled from the ant-hill, also to take the air.

When these two saw each other, their eyes grew red with anger, and the ant-hill snake said: "You villain! How can you torment in this way a prince who is so perfectly handsome?" And the snake in the prince's mouth said: "Villain yourself! How can you bemire those two pots full of gold?" In this fashion each laid bare the other's weakness.

Then the ant-hill snake continued: "You villain! Doesn't anybody know the simple remedy of drinking black mustard and so destroying you?" And the belly-snake retorted: "And doesn't anybody know the simple way to destroy you, by pouring in hot water?"

Now the princess, hiding behind a branch, overheard their conversation, and did just as they suggested. So she made her husband sound and well, and acquired vast wealth. When she returned to her own country, she was highly honored by father, mother, and relatives, and lived happily. For she had her deserts.

"And that is why I say:

Be quick with mutual defense
In honest give-and-take;
Or perish like the ant-hill beast
And like the belly-snake."

THE GULLIBLE HUSBAND

THERE WAS ONCE A CARPENTER in a certain village. His wife was a whore, and reputed to be such. So he, desiring to test her, thought: "How can I put her to the test? For the proverb says:

> Fire chills, rogues bless, and moonlight burns
> Before a wife to virtue turns.

"Now I know from popular gossip that she is unfaithfu.. For the saying goes:

> All things that are not seen or heard
> In science or the Sacred Word,
> All things in interstellar space
> Are known among the populace."

After these reflections, he said to his wife: "Tomorrow morning, my dear, I am going to another village, where I shall be detained several days. Please put me up a nice lunch." And her heart quivered when she heard this; she eagerly dropped everything to make delicious dishes, almost pure butter and sugar. In fact, the old saw was justified:

> When lowering clouds
> Shut in the day,
> When streets are mired
> With sticky clay,
> When husband lingers
> Far away,
> The flirt becomes
> Supremely gay.

Now at dawn the carpenter rose and left his house. When she had made sure that he was gone, with laughing countenance she spent the dragging day in trying on all her best things. Then she called on an old lover and said: "My husband has gone to another village—the rascal! Please come to our house when the people are asleep." And he did so.

Now the carpenter spent the day in the forest, stole into his own house at twilight by a side entrance, and hid under the bed. At this juncture the other fellow arrived and got into bed. And when the carpenter saw him, his heart was stabbed by wrath, and he thought: "Shall I rise and smite him? Or shall I wait until they are asleep and kill them both without effort? Or again, shall I wait to see how she behaves, listen to what she says to him?" At this moment she softly locked the door and went to bed.

But as she did so, she stubbed her toe on the carpenter's body. And she thought: "It must be that carpenter—the rascal!—who is testing me. Well, I will give him a taste of woman's tricks."

While she was thinking, the fellow became insistent. But she clasped her hands and said: "Dear and honored sir, you must not touch me." And he said: "Well, well! For what purpose did you invite me?"

"Listen," said she. "I went this morning to Gauri's shrine to see the goddess. There all at once I heard a voice in the sky, saying: 'What am I to do, my daughter? You are devoted to me, yet in six months' time, by the decree of fate, you will be a widow.' Then I said: 'O blessèd goddess, since you are aware of the calamity, you also know the remedy. Is there any means of making my husband live a hundred years?' And the goddess replied: 'Indeed there is—a remedy depending on you alone.' Of course I said: 'If it cost my life, pray tell me, and I will do it.' Then the goddess said: 'If you go to bed with another man, and embrace him, then the untimely death that threatens your husband will pass to him. And your husband will live another hundred years.' For this purpose I invited you. Now do what you had in mind. The words of a goddess must not be falsified—so much is certain." Then his face blossomed with noiseless laughter, and he did as she said.

Now the carpenter, fool that he was, felt his body thrill with joy on hearing her words, and he issued from under the bed, saying: "Bravo, faithful wife! Bravo, delight of the family! Because my heart was troubled by the gossip of evil creatures, I pretended a trip to another village in order to test you, and lay hidden under the bed. Come now, embrace me!"

With these words he embraced her and lifted her to his shoulder, then said to the fellow: "My dear and honored sir, you have come here because my good deeds earned this happiness. Through your favor I have won a full hundred years of life. You, too, must mount my shoulder."

So he forced the fellow, much against his will, to mount his shoulder, and then went dancing about to the doors of the houses of all his relatives.

"And that is why I say:

> It argues utter want of sense
> To pardon obvious offense;
> The carpenter upon his head
> Took wife and him who fouled his bed."

THE BUTTER-BLINDED BRAHMAN

THERE WAS ONCE A BRAHMAN named Theodore in a certain town. His wife, being unchaste and a pursuer of other men, was forever making cakes with sugar and butter for a lover, and so cheating her husband.

Now one day her husband saw her and said: "My dear wife, what are you cooking? And where are you forever carrying cakes? Tell the truth."

But her impudence was equal to the occasion, and she lied to her husband: "There is a shrine of the blessèd goddess not far from here. There I have undertaken a fasting ceremony, and I take an offering, including the most delicious dishes." Then she took the cakes before his very eyes and started for the shrine of the goddess, imagining that after her statement, her husband would believe it was for the goddess that his wife was daily providing delicious dishes. Having reached the shrine, she went down to the river to perform the ceremonial bath.

Meanwhile her husband arrived by another road and hid behind the statue of the goddess. And his wife entered the shrine after her bath, performed the various rites—laving, anointing, giving incense, making an offering, and so on—bowed before the goddess, and prayed: "O blessèd one, how may my husband be made blind?"

Then the Brahman behind the goddess' back spoke, disguising his natural tone: "If you never stop giving him such food as butter and butter-cakes, then he will presently go blind."

Now that loose female, deceived by the plausible revelation, gave the Brahman just that kind of food every day. One day the Brahman said: "My dear, I don't see very well." And she thought: "Thank the goddess."

Then the favored lover thought: "The Brahman has gone blind. What can he do to me?" Whereupon he came daily to the house without hesitation.

But at last the Brahman caught him as he entered, seized him by the hair, and clubbed and kicked him to such effect that he died. He also cut off his wicked wife's nose, and dismissed her.

THE BRAHMAN, THE THIEF, AND THE GHOST

There was once a poor Brahman in a certain place. He lived on presents, and always did without such luxuries as fine clothes and ointments and perfumes and garlands and gems and betel-gum. His beard and his nails were long, and so was the hair that covered his head and his body. Heat, cold, rain, and the like had dried him up.

Then someone pitied him and gave him two calves. And the Brahman began when they were little and fed them on butter and oil and fodder and other things that he begged. So he made them very plump.

Then a thief saw them and the idea came to him at once: "I will steal these two cows from this Brahman." So he took a rope and set out at night. But on the way he met a fellow with a row of sharp teeth set far apart, with a high-bridged nose and uneven eyes, with limbs covered with knotty muscles, with hollow cheeks, with beard and body as yellow as a fire with much butter in it.

And when the thief saw him, he started with acute fear and said: "Who are you, sir?"

The other said: "I am a ghost named Truthful. It is now your turn to explain yourself."

The thief said: "I am a thief, and my acts are cruel. I am on my way to steal two cows from a poor Brahman."

Then the ghost felt relieved and said: "My dear sir, I take one meal every three days. So I will just eat this Brahman today. It is delightful that you and I are on the same errand."

So together they went there and hid, waiting for the proper moment. And when the Brahman went to sleep, the ghost started forward to eat him. But the thief saw him and said: "My dear sir, this is not right. You are not to eat the Brahman until I have stolen his two cows."

The ghost said: "The racket would most likely wake the Brahman. In that case all my trouble would be vain."

"But, on the other hand," said the thief, "if any hindrance arises when you start to eat him, then I cannot steal the two cows either. First I will steal the two cows, then you may eat the Brahman."

So they disputed, each crying "Me first! Me first!" And when they became heated, the hubbub waked the Brahman. Then the thief said:

"Brahman, this is a ghost who wishes to eat you." And the ghost said: "Brahman, this is a thief who wishes to steal your two cows."

When the Brahman heard this, he stood up and took a good look. And by remembering a prayer to his favorite god, he saved his life from the ghost, then lifted a club and saved his two cows from the thief.

"And that is why I say:

From enemies expect relief,
If discord pierce their host;
Thus, life was given by the thief
And cattle by the ghost."

THE LOYAL MUNGOOSE

THERE WAS ONCE A BRAHMAN named Godly in a certain town. His wife mothered a single son and a mungoose. And as she loved little ones, she cared for the mungoose also like a son, giving him milk from her breast, and salves, and baths, and so on. But she did not trust him, for she thought: "A mungoose is a nasty kind of creature. He might hurt my boy."

One day she tucked her son in bed, took a water-jar, and said to her husband: "Now, Professor, I am going for water. You must protect the boy from the mungoose." But when she was gone, the Brahman went off somewhere himself to beg food, leaving the house empty.

While he was gone, a black snake issued from his hole and, as fate would have it, crawled toward the baby's cradle. But the mungoose, feeling him to be a natural enemy, and fearing for the life of his baby brother, fell upon the vicious serpent halfway, joined battle with him, tore him to bits, and tossed the pieces far and wide. Then, delighted with his own heroism, he ran, blood trickling from his mouth, to meet the mother; for he wished to show what he had done.

But when the mother saw him coming, saw his bloody mouth and his excitement, she feared that the villain must have eaten her baby boy, and without thinking twice, she angrily dropped the water-jar upon him, which killed him the moment that it struck. There she left him without a second thought, and hurried home, where she found the baby safe and sound, and near the cradle a great black snake, torn to bits. Then, overwhelmed with sorrow because she had thoughtlessly killed her benefactor, her son, she beat her head and breast.

At this moment the Brahman came home with a dish of rice gruel which he had got from someone in his begging tour, and saw his wife bitterly lamenting her son, the mungoose. "Greedy! Greedy!" she cried. "Because you did not do as I told you, you must now taste the bitterness of a son's death, the fruit of the tree of your own wickedness. Yes, this is what happens to those blinded by greed."

THE MICE THAT SET ELEPHANTS FREE

There was once a region where people, houses, and temples had fallen into decay. So the mice, who were old settlers there, occupied the chinks in the floors of stately dwellings with sons, grandsons (both in the male and female line), and further descendants as they were born, until their holes formed a dense tangle. They found uncommon happiness in a variety of festivals, dramatic performances (with plots of their own invention), wedding-feasts, eating-parties, drinking-bouts, and similar diversions. And so the time passed.

But into this scene burst an elephant-king, whose retinue numbered thousands. He, with his herd, had started for the lake upon information that there was water there. As he marched through the mouse community, he crushed faces, eyes, heads, and necks of such mice as he encountered.

Then the survivors held a convention. "We are being killed," they said, "by these lumbering elephants—curse them! If they come this way again, there will not be mice enough for seed. Therefore let us devise a remedy effective in this crisis."

When they had done so, a certain number went to the lake, bowed before the elephant-king, and said respectfully: "O King, not far from here is our community, inherited from a long line of ancestors. There we have prospered through a long succession of sons and grandsons. Now you gentlemen, while coming here to water, have destroyed us by the thousand. Furthermore, if you travel that way again, there will not be enough of us for seed. If then you feel compassion toward us, pray travel another path. Consider the fact that even creatures of our size will some day prove of some service."

And the elephant-king turned over in his mind what he had heard, decided that the statement of the mice was entirely logical, and granted their request.

Now in the course of time a certain king commanded his elephant-trappers to trap elephants. And they constructed a so-called water-trap, caught the king with his herd, three days later dragged him out with a great tackle made of ropes and things, and tied him to stout trees in that very bit of forest.

When the trappers had gone, the elephant-king reflected thus: "In what manner, or through whose assistance, shall I be delivered?" Then it occurred to him: "We have no means of deliverance except those mice."

So the king sent the mice an exact description of his disastrous position in the trap through one of his personal retinue, an elephant-cow who had not ventured into the trap, and who had previous information of the mouse community.

When the mice learned the matter, they gathered by the thousand, eager to return the favor shown them, and visited the elephant herd. And seeing king and herd fettered, they gnawed the guy-ropes where they stood, then swarmed up the branches, and by cutting the ropes aloft, set their friends free.

"And that is why I say:

Make friends, make friends, however strong
Or weak they be:
Recall the captive elephants
That mice set free."

THE ASS IN THE TIGER-SKIN

THERE WAS ONCE A LAUNDRYMAN named Clean-Cloth in a certain town. He had a single donkey who had grown very feeble from lack of fodder.

As the laundry man wandered in the forest, he saw a dead tiger, and he thought: "Ah, this is lucky. I will put this tiger-skin on the donkey and let him loose in the barley fields at night. For the farmers will think him a tiger and will not drive him out."

When this was done, the donkey ate barley to his heart's content. And at dawn the laundryman took him back to the barn. So as time passed, he grew plump. He could hardly squeeze into the stall.

But one day the donkey heard the bray of a she-donkey in the distance. At the mere sound he himself began to bray. Then the farmers perceived that he was a donkey in disguise, and killed him with blows from clubs and stones and arrows.

"And that is why I say:

However skilful in disguise,
However frightful to the eyes,
Although in tiger-skin arrayed,
The ass was killed—because he brayed."

THE FARMER'S WIFE

There was once a farmer who lived with his wife in a certain place. And because the husband was old, the wife was forever thinking of lovers, and could not possibly be contented at home. Her one idea was strange men.

Now a rogue who lived by pilfering, noticed her and said: "You lovely creature, my wife is dead, and I am smitten with love at the sight of you. Pray enrich me with love's perfect treasure."

And she said: "You beautiful man, if you feel that way, my husband has a great deal of money, and he is so old that he cannot stir. I will bring it, so that I may go somewhere with you and enjoy the delights of love."

"That is satisfactory to me," he replied. "Suppose you hasten to this spot at dawn, so that we may go together to some fascinating city where life may bear for me its perfect fruit." "Very well," she agreed, and went home with laughing countenance.

Then at night, while her husband slept, she took all the money, and reached the rendezvous at dawn. The rogue, for his part, put her in front, started south, and traveled two leagues, gaily enjoying the delights of conversation with her. But when he saw a river ahead, he reflected: "What am I to do with this middle-aged female? Besides, someone might perhaps pursue her. I will just take her money and be off."

So he said to her: "My dear, this is a great river, hard to cross. I will just take the money and put it safe on the far bank, then return to carry you alone on my back, and so transport you in comfort." "Do so, my belovèd," said she.

So he took the money to the last penny, and then he said: "Dearest, hand me your dress and your wrap, too, so that you may travel through the water unembarrassed." And when she did so, the rogue took the money and the two garments and went to the place he had in mind.

Then the farmer's wife sat down woebegone on the river-bank, digging her two hands into her throat. At that moment a she-jackal came to the spot, carrying a piece of meat. As she came up and peered about, a great fish leaped from the water and was stranded on the bank. On spying him, she dropped the meat and darted at the fish. Whereupon a vulture swooped from the sky and flew off with the meat. And the fish, perceiving the jackal, struggled into the river. So the she-jackal had her pains for nothing, and as she gazed after the vulture, the naked woman smiled and said:

"You poor she-jackal!

> The vulture has your meat;
> The water holds your fish:
> Of fish and flesh forlorn,
> What further do you wish?"

And the she-jackal, perceiving that the woman was equally forlorn, having lost her husband's money and her lover, said with a sneer:

"You naked thing!

> Your cleverness is twice
> As great as mine, 'twould seem;
> Lover and husband lost,
> You sit beside the stream."

THE BRAHMAN'S DREAM

In a certain town lived a Brahman named Seedy, who got some barley-meal by begging, ate a portion, and filled a jar with the remainder. This jar he hung on a peg one night, placed his cot beneath it, and fixing his gaze on the jar, fell into a hypnotic reverie.

"Well, here is a jar full of barley-meal," he thought. "Now if famine comes, a hundred rupees will come out of it. With that sum I will get two she-goats. Every six months they will bear two more she-goats. After goats, cows. When the cows calve, I will sell the calves. After cows, buffaloes; after buffaloes, mares. From the mares I shall get plenty of horses. The sale of these will mean plenty of gold. The gold will buy a great house with an inner court. Then someone will come to my house and offer his lovely daughter with a dowry. She will bear a son, whom I shall name Moon-Lord. When he is old enough to ride on my knee, I will take a book, sit on the stable roof, and think. Just then Moon-Lord will see me, will jump from his mother's lap in his eagerness to ride on my knee, and will go too near the horses. Then I shall get angry and tell my wife to take the boy. But she will be busy with her chores and will not pay attention to what I say. Then I will get up and kick her."

Being sunk in his hypnotic dream, he let fly such a kick that he smashed the jar. And the barley-meal which it contained turned him white all over.

SHELL-NECK, SLIM, AND GRIM

In a certain lake lived a turtle named Shell-Neck. He had as friends two ganders whose names were Slim and Grim. Now in the vicissitudes of time there came a twelve-year drought, which begot ideas of this nature in the two ganders: "This lake has gone dry. Let us seek another body of water. However, we must first say farewell to Shell-Neck, our dear and long-proved friend."

When they did so, the turtle said: "Why do you bid me farewell? I am a water-dweller, and here I should perish very quickly from the scant supply of water and from grief at loss of you. Therefore, if you feel any affection for me, please rescue me from the jaws of this death. Besides, as the water dries in this lake, you two suffer nothing beyond a restricted diet, while to me it means immediate death. Consider which is more serious, loss of food or loss of life."

But they replied: "We are unable to take you with us since you are a water-creature without wings." Yet the turtle continued: "There is a possible device. Bring a stick of wood." This they did, whereupon the turtle gripped the middle of the stick between his teeth, and said: "Now take firm hold with your bills, one on each side, fly up, and travel with even flight through the sky, until we discover another desirable body of water."

But they objected: "There is a hitch in this fine plan. If you happen to indulge in the smallest conversation, then you will lose your hold on the stick, will fall from a great height, and will be dashed to bits."

"Oh," said the turtle, "from this moment I take a vow of silence, to last as long as we are in heaven." So they carried out the plan, but while the two ganders were painfully carrying the turtle over a neighboring city, the people below noticed the spectacle, and there arose a confused buzz of talk as they asked: "What is this cartlike object that two birds are carrying through the atmosphere?"

Hearing this, the doomed turtle was heedless enough to ask: "What are these people chattering about?" The moment he spoke, the poor simpleton lost his grip and fell to the ground. And persons who wanted meat cut him to bits in a moment with sharp knives.

The Enchanted Parrot

INTRODUCTION

THE ENCHANTED PARROT, or the *Suka Saptati,* "Seventy Stories," told by a parrot to keep her mistress from going out with her lovers for sixty-nine successive nights when her husband was away, is a charming collection of tales of feminine, and also masculine, infidelity, with a predominant sense of the comic, happening in a world of easy make-believe such as suggested by the *Arabian Nights.* The tales are for the most part simple and naïve. Like the *Arabian Nights* and the *Panchatantra,* it employs a framing story; like the *Panchatantra* and the *Hitopadesa,* it employs, but to a less extent, the device of a tale within a tale and delights in insertions of moral maxims for the edification of the hearers; and like the *Ocean of Stories,*[1] it rather delights in comments at the expense of women, dull husbands and Brahman monks, and in stories of rogues. Again the author is unknown, but the book was widely circulated and was certainly known to have existed before the eleventh century. These stories suggest Boccaccio.

What lifts *The Enchanted Parrot* from the rest is that here the comments are no longer broad generalities of impersonal proverbs, but have the distinct individual charm of a modern cynic and woman-hater. Cynicism, like that of the *Ecclesiastes,* is always refreshing, and even modern women can stand a few jokes at their expense.

The arts of women are these: deceitful speech; craft; oaths; pretended emotions; pretended weeping; pretended laughter; meaningless pleasures and

[1] *Ocean of Stories,* a giant collection of Hindu short stories, (Somadeva's *Kathā Sarit Sagara*), translated by C. H. Tawny, 2 vols., Calcutta, 1880. A beautiful edition, in 10 volumes, was privately printed for subscribers only in London.

pain; asking questions with a deferential air; indifference; equanimity, in prosperity or in adversity; making no difference between good and evil; sidelong glances directed toward lovers—that is the list of the accomplishments practiced by the ladies of the town.

At any rate, no woman of the country need be offended.

But the author is usually defter and less explicit; besides, he classifies women with kings and serpents, all three of whom he hates heartily.

Kings, women and creepers generally lay hold of what is near to them.

Put not your trust in rivers, in savage beasts, in horned cattle, in armed men, in women, in princes. Kings are like soldiers clad in mail, savage, crooked in their ways as serpents creep on you for evil. A king slays with his smile; he may pay honor, but he is dangerous; the elephant kills with a touch, the serpent with a caress.

His comments are by no means confined to the subject of women:

How should one sleep who is overwhelmed with debt, who has a disagreeable wife, who is surrounded by enemies?

It is the speaker of unpleasant but wholesome truths who cannot find a listener.

Cleanliness in a crow, honesty in a gambler, mildness in a serpent, women satisfied with love, vigor in a eunuch, truth in a drunkard, friendship in a king—who ever heard of these things?

A stranger, if he is a rich man, is a relation; but a kinsman, if he be poor, is an outcast.

And there is something delightfully insinuating in the following:

Giving, receiving, imparting secrets, asking questions, eating in company—these are the five proofs of friendship.

The following selection is taken from the translation by the Rev. B. Hale Wortham (Luzac, London, 1911), with its rather unusual punctuation somewhat revised. In the words of the translator:

"The *Suka Saptati,* seventy tales of a parrot, are quite characteristic of Eastern story. The peg on which they hang is a certain Prabhāvatī. This lady's husband, whose name is Madana, has gone on a long journey. He has, however, left her his parrot, a bird which appears to be under a charm. Prabhāvatī, after her husband has been absent some little time, begins to feel rather dull, and her attendants, or friends, suggest that she had better look out for some admirer to console her during his absence. She accordingly is preparing to start on this errand, when the parrot suddenly finds his voice, and remarks very strongly on Prabhāvatī's disreputable intentions. Prabhāvatī makes up her mind to have the parrot's neck wrung, but before actually departing, and ordering the bloodthirsty deed to be carried out, she reflects that after all it is only a bird speaking, and tells him that she means to go in spite of his well-meant advice. This starts the parrot off, and he bids her go by all means, if she is as clever as someone whom he knows. Prabhāvatī asks him who this person may be, and wherein his cleverness consists. This leads to Story I, and just when the climax arrives, the parrot stops, and asks Prabhāvatī and her friends how they think the story ends. Of course they don't know, and the parrot keeps them on tenterhooks for a bit, and finally tells them. By this time the evening is tolerably far advanced, so that it is of no use for Prabhāvatī to set out on her love-making expeditions, and she goes to bed with her attendants. This process is repeated for sixty-nine evenings, and finally Prabhāvatī's husband returns. From what he gathers, he does not altogether approve of his wife's goings on in his absence, and seems as if he meant to proceed to extremities, when the eloquent parrot calms him down with the seventieth story, after which Madana's father observes a great festival in honor of his son and daughter-in-law, and the parrot, having worked out the charm (or the curse), ascends to heaven in a rain of flowers."

The Enchanted Parrot

Translated by the Rev. B. Hale Wortham

YASODEVĪ AND HER TRANSMIGRATIONS

THE NEXT EVENING Prabhāvatī began to think over her pursuit of a lover and asked the parrot for his advice. The parrot said: "Go, by all means if you desire to go! That is to say, if you are as clever in getting out of difficulties as Yasodevī was."

"And pray who was Yasodevī?" rejoinded Prabhāvatī.

"If I tell you," replied the parrot, "and keep you here, perhaps you will carry out your intention of wringing my neck."

"Never mind," answered Prabhāvatī, "be the result what it may, I must hear the story of Yasodevī."

So the parrot began:

"There is a town called Nandana, whose prince bore the same name. He had a son, Rājasekhara, and Rājasekhara's wife was called Sasiprabhā. Now a certain Dhanasena came across her, and fell violently in love with her. He was absolutely consumed with the flame of his passion, and at last his mother, Yasodevī, asked him what was the matter. With many sighs and tears he told her. He must have the prince's wife. She was very difficult to get hold of, but he could not live without her. On hearing this, Yasodevī bid him be of good cheer, and said she would see what could be done. So she abstained from all food, and putting on her best clothes went to Sasiprabhā, taking with her a bitch. She assumed an appearance of grief, and taking Sasiprabhā aside, said to her: 'You see this bitch; well, you and I and this bitch were sisters in a former existence. As for me, I had no compunction in accepting the advances of my lovers; you received their addresses, but with some hesitation. But this was not the case with our sister. She would not have anything to do with men at any price; she kept them at a distance, and now you see to what a condition she is reduced. She has to live as a bitch, all the time recollecting what she was. You, through your reluctance, may or may not remember your former state; but as far as I am concerned, I have no recollection of it whatever, for I thoroughly enjoyed myself. And so I am sorry for you, and I come to warn you by showing you this bitch, and telling you her story. If you have got a lover I advise you to give him all he wants, and save yourself from the disagreeables of a future state like this. For the person who gives liberally will himself be the recipient of endless favors. It is said: "Those who beg from house to house, merely let you know that they are there; they do not ask for anything, for the liberal always give alms freely according to their condition, to those in need of assistance."'

"Sasiprabhā was quite overcome by this address, and embracing Yasodevī wept over her and entreated her assistance in escaping from the fate which seemed to impend. So Yasodevī introduced Sasiprabhā to her own son and Rājasekhara, who had been bribed with magnificent presents of gold and jewels, was quite willing to let her go, and thought that a great piece of good luck had befallen him.

"So Yasodevī by her skill and cleverness cheated the prince of the princess, and gained her own ends. If you are as clever as she was, go; if not, stay at home—go to bed, and don't make a fool of yourself."

THE QUEEN AND THE LAUGHING FISH[1]

I

There is a city called Ujjayinī, and the king's name is Vikramāditya. His queen was Kāmalīnā. She was a lady of very noble family, and was the king's favorite wife. One day the king was dining with her and he gave her some roast fish. She looked at them (the men present) and said, "Sir! I cannot bear to look at these men, much less to touch them!" On these words the fish burst into a loud laugh, so loud that it was heard by all the people in the town. The king could not understand this, so he asked the astrologers, who were acquainted with the language of birds, what the fish meant by their laughter. None of them could tell him; so he sent for his private chaplain, who was the head of the Brahmans in the town, and said: "If you don't tell me what those fish

[1] This is another example of enclosing stories within a story, and of the abundance of wise-cracking comments in a Hindu story.

meant by laughing at what the queen said, I shall send you and all the Brahmans into exile." The chaplain, on hearing this, was a good deal upset, and was quite sure that he and the rest of the reverend gentlemen would have to go, for it seemed impossible to find any answer to the question. His daughter observed his depressed condition and said: "Father! What's the matter? Why do you look so dismal? Tell me the cause of the trouble. You know people possessed of wisdom should not lose their self-possession even if difficulties arise. For it has been said: 'The man who is not overjoyed in prosperity, who is not cast down in adversity, who is steadfast in difficulties, such a man as this has been born for an everlasting ornament and protection to the world.' "

So the Brahman told his daughter the whole story, and how the king had threatened to banish him; since—

"There is not a single person in this world on whose friendship or affection one can rely: how much less on that of a king who walks in the ways of treachery."

For it has been said—"Cleanliness in a crow; honesty in a gambler; mildness in a serpent; women satisfied with love; vigor in a eunuch; truth in a drunkard; friendship in a king—who ever heard of these things?"

Moreover—"Put not your trust in rivers, in savage beasts, in horned cattle, in armed men, in women, in princes. Kings are like soldiers clad in mail, savage, crooked in their ways as serpents creep on you for evil. A king slays with his smile; he may pay honor, but he is dangerous; the elephant kills with a touch, the serpent with a caress."

"I have served the king," continued the Brahman, "faithfully all these years, yet he has become my enemy, and will send me and my fellow Brahmans into exile. It has been said—

" 'A man may give up something for the sake of his village; he may give up his village for the sake of his country; but he will give up the whole world to save his life.' "

When the Brahman's daughter heard that, she said: "This, Father, is all very true, but no respect will be paid to a servant that has been sent adrift by his master.

"For it has been said—'A man may be of the highest character, or very commonplace. If he devotes himself to the service of the ruler, whichever he may be, he will get nothing out of it. The king will take the first man he comes across, be he ignorant, or learned, honorable or dishonorable, into his service; for kings, women, and creepers generally lay hold of what is nearest to them.'

"Besides this—'A man may be learned, energetic, skilful, ambitious, well versed in all his duties, but he is nothing without the prince's favor. A man may be nobly born, possessed of ability, but if he does not pay court to the prince he may just as well spend his life in begging or perpetual penance. One who falls into the power of diseases, crocodiles or kings, and the stupid man who does not know how to get out of a difficulty, will never keep his position in life.'

"For it has been said—'Kings are as nothing to those wise and skilful persons who by their power bring lions, tigers, serpents and elephants into subjection. But men who are wise rely on the king's favor, and so attain to eminence. The sandal grove only flourishes on Mount Malaya.'

"All the insignia of rank—parasols, elephants, horses—are given by the king to those whom he delights to honor. You are the object of the king's affection and honor, therefore, my dear father, do not be downcast. The chief minister's duty is to clear up, from time to time, all doubts which beset the king's mind. Therefore cheer up! I will find out for you what the fish meant by their laughter."

The Brahman at this advice felt somewhat comforted, and went and told the king what his daughter had said. The king was delighted, and immediately sent for the damsel. She came and made an elaborate obeisance to his majesty and said, "Sir! pray do not treat these Brahmans so ill; it is not their fault. Pray tell me what kind of a laugh was it that you heard from the fish? Still, I am only a woman, and I wonder you are not ashamed to ask me to clear the matter up. For—

" 'A king may be vile, yet he is even then not as another man, but bears a divine form.' You, Vikramāditya, as your name tells us, are the bearer of divine power. For it has been said—'From Indra comes might; from fire comes heat; from Yama wrath; from Kuvera riches; but a king is formed from Kā and Vishnu combined.'

"The person you ought to blame is yourself, for it is your business to remove doubts and difficulties.

"Hear, then, what I have to tell you:

"And if you can't find out the answer send for me. At any rate you cannot possibly doubt the queen's fidelity, seeing that she never goes out of doors."

Neither the king nor his wise men had the slightest idea what these

verses meant, and so the Brahman's clever daughter went away, and left
them in their bewilderment.

2

The king spent a sleepless night trying to puzzle out the meaning of
the verses. For, as it has been said—

"How should one sleep who is overwhelmed with debt, who has a dis
agreeable wife, who is surrounded by enemies?"

So after a miserable night the king sent again for the wise maiden and
said: "I cannot make out what the fish meant by their laughter."

"Your majesty had better not ask me," she replied, "or perhaps you
may repent of it as the merchant's wife did when she was determined
to find out where the cakes came from." The king said: "And wha
was that?" She told him the following story:—

"There is a town called Jayantī, and a merchant whose name wa
Sunmata lived in it. His wife was Padiminī. He was unlucky enough
to lose all his money; in consequence his family would have nothing
more to do with him, for it is well known that wealth and friendship
go together—

" 'He who has money has friends; he who has money has relations
He who has money has wisdom; in fact, he is a man of importance.

"It is said in the Mahābhārata—'There are five conditions in which
a man though living may be regarded as dead: Poverty, disease, stupidity
exile, hopeless slavery.' Also—'A stranger, if he is a rich man, is a rela
tion; but a kinsman, if he be poor, is an outcast.'

"So this merchant used to take straw and wood into the market fo
sale. One day he could not find either, but he came across an image o
Ganesa, made of wood. He thought to himself, 'This will suit my pur
pose very well.'

"For it has been said—'There is nothing that a hungry man will no
do for bread; and a man who is ruined has no conscience. Such will b
guilty of any crime; what a respectable man would not dream of doing
comes natural to them."

"So he made up his mind to break the image up for the sake of th
wood, when Ganesa said to him: 'If you will leave my image alone,
will give you every day five cakes made of sugar and butter; you ca
come here for them. Only you must not tell anyone how you come b
them. If you let the secret out, I shall be clear of my promise.'

"He gladly consented, and Ganesa gave him five cakes which he took home and gave to his wife. With some of them she supplied the wants of her own house, and gave what was left over to a friend. The friend asked her one day where the cakes came from; Padminī could not answer the question, and the friend said, 'If you don't tell me, then there is an end of our friendship.' For, as the saying is—

" 'Giving, receiving, imparting secrets, asking questions, eating in company: these are the five proofs of friendship.'

"Padminī replied: 'My husband knows, but he says it is a secret and will not tell me; even if I were to ask him a hundred times, I should get nothing out of him.' The friend replied: 'Then all I have to say is that you must make a very bad use of your youth and beauty, if you can't find this out.'

"So Padminī asked her husband again, 'Where do those cakes come from?' 'By the favor of destiny,' he replied, 'for it has been said, Fate, if it is on your side will accomplish your wishes. She will bring you what you want, even from a distant land, from the ends of the world, from the bottom of the sea. Once upon a time a mouse, making a hole for itself, fell into the jaws of a serpent. The serpent could not find anything to eat and was in the last stage of starvation, but refreshed by the lucky meal he went on his way rejoicing. So fate is the cause of a man's rise or fall.'

"Padminī, when she found her husband would not tell her, refused to eat. He was put in a difficulty and said: 'If I tell you what you want to know disaster will follow, and you will be sorry for it.' Padminī, however, took no heed of warnings, but continued to be obstinate, and at last her husband was obliged to tell her; for it is said, 'When the gods want to ruin a man, they first take away his senses, so that he does not know evil from good.'

"Then, your majesty," continued the Brahman's daughter, "Sumati was prevailed on by his foolish wife to tell her the secret. For—

" 'Even Rāma failed to recognize the golden deer; Nahusha harnessed the Brahmans to his chariot; Arjuna carried off both cow and calf; Yudhisthira gambled away his wife and four brothers. So often even a good man, in a crisis, becomes the victim of folly.'

"Well! Padminī got the secret out of her husband, and went and told her friend, and the result was the friend sent her own husband to Ganesa, who gave him the cakes. Next day Padminī went with Sumati to Ganesa for the daily present, and he told them plainly that it was no use their coming any more to him, for the bargain had been broken and the cakes had been given to someone else. So Padminī's husband gave her a good scolding, and they went home very sorry for what they had done. In the same way your majesty should not ask me to explain the meaning of the verses to you lest you repent of your knowledge. You had better make them out by yourself, without my help." So saying, she got up and went home.

3

After another sleepless night the king not being able to find out the meaning of the verses, sent for the Brahman's daughter again, and said, "Pray, tell me the meaning of the verses without any more delay."

She answered: "You must not importune the gods with entreaties, or repentance will follow, as was the case with the Brahman who fell in love with Sthagikā. There is a town somewhere or other—it matters not where—whose king is Vīrābhya, and in it lived a Brahman called Keshava. One day the thought occurred to him: 'Why should I not increase the wealth my father has left me?' For it has been said—

" 'The glory that you gain from your own virtues is the truest; next best is that which you gain from your father; but that which comes to you from a remoter source is worth nothing.'

"So he started with a view of getting more money, and in the course of his wandering passed through several towns, and places of sacred pilgrimage. At last he reached an out-of-the-way place where he saw an ascetic sitting cross-legged in meditation.

"The Brahman came up to him and made a respectful obeisance. The ascetic ceased meditating for a moment, and seeing the Brahman said: 'To whom in this world should liberality be shown? Who should be protected? To whom should be granted what seems almost impossible of acquirement?'

"The Brahman rose up from his humble posture and said, 'Sir, to *me*. I am the pursuit of wealth.'

"The ascetic knew that his visitor was a Brahman and was quite shocked to hear him utter such an unworthy sentiment, for it has been said—

" 'To see a distinguished person begging, in a state of poverty, asking for what he ought not to want, troubles the mind, though one is prepared to give. For a good man, though he may be himself in trouble, performs his duty to another. The sandal tree may be broken in a thousand pieces, but it still keeps its cooling power.'

"The ascetic therefore gave his visitor a magic cloak, and said: 'Whenever you shake this, 500 gold pieces will fall from it; but you must not give it to anyone, or say where the money comes from.'

"The Brahman thanked the ascetic and departed with his cloak. Next morning he shook it, and immediately became the possessor of 500 gold pieces. He then proceeded on his travels and reached a town called Ratuavatī, where he fell violently in love with a young lady called Sthagikā. She could not make out where all the money came from, and her mother to whom she confided her doubts said: 'Well, what is this Brahman's business, for he seems to have plenty of money. How does he come by it?' So she asked her admirer but he would not tell her. By dint of worrying, however, she got it out of him, and he let out all about the magic cloak. The consequence was that she waited till he was asleep and then stole the cloak, and as now he had lost all his money, the girl's mother showed him the door. It has been said—

" 'There is not much cleverness required to deceive one who has confidence in us, nor is much courage required to kill one who is asleep.'

"The Brahman, when he woke up, could not find his cloak, and went and laid a complaint before the magistrates, asserting with great vehemence that he had been robbed. The case was therefore tried, and the mother and daughter were charged with the theft. The mother said: 'This good-for-nothing fellow made love to my daughter. He has invented this story about his cloak—no sensible person could believe such nonsense. The whole thing is a fabrication from beginning to end. He came to my house, and my servants finding that he was a foreigner turned him out of doors, and we sent the cloak back to the holy man who gave it to him.' This decided the case against the Brahman, and he lost both Sthagikā and his cloak, all through letting out the secret, and this may be your majesty's fate too, if you persist in your curiosity."

With these words the damsel got up and went home.

4

The king was still unable to fathom the meaning of the verses, so the next day he sent for the Brahman's daughter. She said: "Your majesty! You should not be so importunate. A king should not be so pertinacious, whether the objects at which he aims be good or bad. Kings are as the body, and their subjects are only their limbs. Still if I obey your commands evil will befall you, as it befell the merchant who lost his home and all that he had." "How was that?" said the king. The Brahman's daughter answered: "There is a place called Tripura, and in it lived Prince Vikrama. A merchant inhabited that city whose wife's name was Sabhagā. She was a person of very light frivolous disposition, and do what he would he could not keep her within bounds. One day when she was wandering about town and getting into mischief, she came across a merchant who lived in the house of a Yaksha. She promptly fell in love with him, and as he very willingly responded to her advances she made up her mind to run away with him. Before going she called a confidential maid-servant and said: 'I am going away for a bit: directly after I have started do you set the house on fire, and my husband will be so taken up trying to put it out that he will not find out I am gone I shall be back again before long.' So no sooner had Sabhagā started than her confidante set the place on fire, and her husband who had had his suspicions of the merchant, left keeping guard over Yaksha's house and came home to try and put the fire out. Meanwhile her plan succeeded perfectly, while the house was burnt down.

"Thus the merchant lost house and everything, and that will be your majesty's fate if you are so determined. If, however, you permit, I will tell you what you want to know myself."

So saying, she departed.

5

Next morning the king, who was still quite unable to find the answer, sent for the Brahman's daughter and said: "You promised to tell me the meaning of those verses, for I cannot make out what they mean myself." The girl replied: "If you cannot find out the meaning, then listen to me. You have among your soothsayers and wise men, one called Pushpakāra. He is their head. I believe he is a very prudent discreet person. Tell me, why is he called Pushpakāra?" The king replied: "He is rightly called Pushpakāra, because when he smiles it seems as if a shower of blossoms fell from his countenance. This was reported to be his characteristic, and so messengers were sent to fetch him to prove the truth of this report about him. When he came he neither laughed nor was there any shower of blossoms that fell from him, and for that reason they called him 'The bond of secrecy.'" The Brahman's daughter said: "And why did not Pushpakāra laugh? Do you know the reason?" "I haven't the least idea," replied the king. "Then you should make him tell you," rejoined the Brahman's daughter. "You have asked me what the fish meant by laughing. You ask him the same question. Perhaps he will answer it and tell you at the same time why he did not laugh himself."

So the king sent for Pushpakāra, and as he was a wise man, and of some importance, he made him valuable presents and asked him why he did not laugh, and why the fish did. He replied: "Family scandals should not be talked about. Loss of money, sorrow of mind, difficulties at home, fraud, contempt—these are things which no wise man ever publishes. Still the command of the king, equal to that of Sudra, has surpassing power on the earth; the very name of a righteous, energetic king, surpasses the sun in magnificence. Therefore I will answer your majesty's question. I found out that my wife was in love with someone else, and therefore grief stopped my laughter."

Then the king put his own difficulty before the wise man, and the latter gave no answer but struck the queen full in the face. The queen pretended to faint, and Pushpakāra burst into a fit of laughter. The king was extremely angry and looking at the magician and the Brahman's daughter, said, "What is there to laugh at? What do you mean by this?" "Sir," replied the magician, making a profound bow, "the queen did not faint the other night because she was struck by the young men in whose company she was. Now when I strike her she faints, or pretends to faint." The king grew still more angry and said, "What is this? Do you know it of your own knowledge? The magician answered, "I saw it with my own eyes, and if your majesty is not convinced I will prove it to you." The king went into the matter and found out everything. The magician said, "I suppose your majesty sees now why the Brahman's daughter would not tell you the reason why the fish laughed (when they heard her say that she could not bear to look at the men)." The end of it was that Pushpakāra and the Brahman's daughter were sent home in a considerable state of trepidation, while the queen and her lovers were sewn up in a sack and thrown into the river.

THE SON OF PROMISE

Next day Prabhāvatī's friends addressed her and said: "Go where the sandalwood ointment is rubbed off by the sweat which falls. Go where the sounds of love are manifold; where the tinkle of the anklets is silent: where everything incites to love. Go where the universal law of love prevails. For—

" 'Health, pleasure, peace, power, lordship: these are nothing without love.' It has been said—'The woman with long half-closing eyes, looking at their own forms resplendent with beauty in the curving mirrors, wait with longing for the lover's approach. It is through their attractiveness that women gain the fruit of love.' "

The parrot answered: Men are easily won over; they always speak fair. It is the speaker of unpleasant though wholesome truths who cannot find a listener. But why say more? You and your friends are determined on evil deeds.

(The parrot continued:)

There is a town called Padmavatī, where the rays of the sun shine on streets paved with jewels, as though the glow of the gems on the hood of the serpent king had come down to earth. When the sun scorches, when the long days are unbearable, when the wind is the breath of a furnace, when everything is dried up or perishes through the heat, sandalwood ointment, light clothing, refreshing drink—these things bringing coolness and delight in conquering the heat. The heat is but a slave to those who at midday anoint themselves with the sandal, who bathe at evening, whose nights are tempered by the wind of the fans.

There was a merchant in the town called Chandana, and he and his wife Prabhāvatī passed the hot season on the roof of their house.

Even the sun supported in the heaven by his rays descends into the ocean when his day is done. For it has been said—"When fate is hostile it is useless to try and reach greatness!"

Even the thousand rays cannot support the sun when his time for setting is come. Then the sun, sunk low in the heaven, his brilliancy departed, shines like a piece of coral; and presently the wide-eyed moon comes forward and takes up his place, rising over the Eastern mountain, accompanied by the myriads of stars, to kill the darkness. The moon standing with her head above the Eastern mountain in the beginning of the night shines forth—a torch to the world overwhelmed by the gloom. The moon rising from behind the Eastern mountain shines resplendent as she lies in the lap of her beloved night, or as she stands gleaming on Krishna's head.

Such were the days and nights when Chandana and his wife passed their time together. They had a son whose name was Rāma, and to him his father taught the mysteries of the divine wisdom.

His mother prayed to Chandra and said: "I have but one only son: I am therefore exceedingly pained with anxiety." Chandra replied: "It is best for you that you should have but one son. For a son that is clever, gentle, self-denying, discreet, the abode of the arts, the dwelling-place of virtue; one only son such as this is all sufficient. Besides, what is the good of more sons? They may produce grief and care. It is better to be satisfied with one whose nature, whose disposition is noble."

But Prabhāvatī was not satisfied; so she took a woman called Dhūrtamāyā into her confidence, and said: "If you will train a son for me, able to resist all deceitful arts of women, I will give you 100 pieces of gold." "I will give you a son," replied Dhūrtamāyā, "and if he falls a victim to female seduction, I will forfeit to you twice as many pieces of money." So the bargain was concluded and signed and the son was placed in the merchant's house, where he became the object of all the wiles that women could devise.

The arts of women are these: deceitful speech; craft; oaths; pretended emotions; pretended weeping; pretended laughter; meaningless expressions of pleasure and pain; asking questions with a deferential air; indifference; equanimity, in prosperity or in adversity; making no difference between good and evil; sidelong glances directed toward lovers—that is the list of the accomplishments practiced by the ladies of the town.

So the son, handed over according to the agreement with Dhūrtamāyā, was sent by his father to the island of Suvarna to acquire wealth. In that island lived a lady called Kalāvatī, and with her he spent a whole year. One day he said to Kalāvatī: "Pray tell me! My youngest sister has often said that, although she was skilled in all the arts of attracting men, she never could succeed in getting anything out of her admirers. How is this to be accomplished?" Kalāvatī repeated this to her mother. "My dear," replied the old lady, "it is quite clear that this admirer of yours is well up in the ways of women: you can't catch him like this; perhaps flattery might succeed. When he is thinking of going back home, you say that you want to go with him, and that if he leaves you, you will drown yourself—and so on. I daresay he would give you anything you liked to ask for." Kalāvatī answered, "My dear mother, don't put it in that way: I care nothing for his money without him, and it has been said—

"'Do not set your heart on riches gained by wickedness, or from an enemy whom you have humiliated.'"

Her mother answered: "Not at all, my daughter; riches are the cause of death or life. It has been said—

" 'A man who acts with energy is sure to prosper; for energy in all matters is the road to fortune. Those who have not revealed secrets, who have done no evil, who have not slain without cause—they attain glory. Fate is the cause of justice and injustice: the cause of honor and of dishonor. Fate makes a man both a giver and an asker.'

"You do as I have told you," continued her mother. "I will manage all the rest." So she listened to the advice her mother had given, and the end of it was, that the merchant's son gave her all his money, and after she had got hold of several millions which had belonged to him, he was turned out of doors and sent adrift.

So Kalāvatī's admirer returned home, having lost both money and credit. His father, seeing him in this condition, was much distressed, and asked how it had all come about. He did not like to tell him, but told his spiritual father, who said: "My son, do not be cast down! Good luck and bad luck are equally the lot of man. Why should wise men think so much of money? If it goes, grieve not after it: if it comes back, care not for it."

When his father heard all that had happened, he went to Dhūrtamāyā and said: "I have come to tell you that a great misfortune has happened. My son has fallen a victim to the treachery of a woman." "Who has not been ruined by women?" replied Dhūrtamāyā, "for it has been said, 'A man who gains wealth becomes proud; he who falls into calamities loses his senses. Who can be the friend of a king? Who has not come into the power of death? Who does not respect a rich man? Who that falls into the net of the evil escapes without loss?' Therefore if you will take a passage for me in a ship, I will go back with your son. It has been said, 'Damage may be repaid with damage, injury with injury; if you pull out my feathers, I will pull out your hair.'

"I agreed that if your son were cheated by a woman I would be responsible. For, 'Though the earth, supported by the serpent king, the mighty mountain, the tortoise, the elephant, may move, that which has been determined by the wise and thoughtful is never moved, even in the course of ages.' "

So Dhūrtamāyā and Chandana's son went back to Survana. All the inhabitants including Kālavatī welcomed him, but he did not recover his money. The question was therefore, what could Dhūrtamāyā do? Well, as the money was not forthcoming, she put on the disguise of a Chandalā and went about trying to find an opportunity of getting it back. In the course of her wanderings she came across Chandana's son in the company of Kālavatī. He saw her at the same time, and rushed to meet her, a line of action which had been already agreed upon between them. Kālavatī followed him, and exclaimed, "Pray who is this?" He replied, "This is my mother; I have not seen her since I lost all my money!" Dhūrtamāyā seizing hold of his hand greeted him affectionately, and said: "My son! You went to this lady's house! You fell a victim to her wiles, but after a time you escaped. You know all the money you took away belonged to me."

This she kept on asserting with oaths and imprecations, until Kālavatī and her mother took the woman disguised as a Chandalā into the house and said: "Madam! tell us, where do you come from? What is your name? In short, who are you?" "I," she replied, "am one of Sundarasana's minstrels, the king of Padmavatī. This son of mine took away all my money, and you stole it from him." Kālavatī and her mother were thoroughly frightened and said, "Here is the money! Pray take it!" "No," answered Dhūrtamāyā, "not unless the king of this country gives me permission."

Then they fell down at her feet and said: "We pray you accept it and have mercy on us!" So she took it, and having been treated with the greatest respect by Kālavatī and her mother, went back with Rāma rejoicing to their own country.

DEVIKĀ AND HER FOOLISH HUSBAND

THERE IS A LARGE VILLAGE called Kukhādā; in it dwelt a certain Jarasa, who was a great fool. His wife's name was Devikā; she was a flighty, ill-conducted person, and had a lover—a Brahman—whom she used to meet under a Vibhītaka tree, some way from the village. These meetings were a great subject of gossip in the place, and in the course of time her husband heard of them. So he made up his mind to see into the matter himself and went and climbed into the tree. What he saw from his hiding place fully justified all the gossip and he called out to his wife: "You good-for-nothing hussy! You have been up to this game for some time past." She was put into somewhat of a difficulty and said: "I don't know what you mean!" "I will let you know what I mean," he answered, "if you will just wait till I come down." So she promised to wait till he came down from the tree, and meanwhile sent her lover away. At last her husband reached the ground. "It is of no use your making excuses," he said, "you have been caught in the act." "My dear husband!" she replied. "You must know that this tree has very peculiar properties: any one who climbs up into it can see at once whether his or her spouse has been faithful." Her husband replied, "Well, you climb up and see if it is so," which she did, and cried out, "You good-for-nothing wretch! You have been running after other women for days and days." As this was perfectly true, the fool had nothing to say, and so he made up with his wife and they went home together.

THE LADY AND THE TIGER

In a village called Devalākhya lived a prince whose name was Rājasinha. His wife was a person of irreproachable reputation, but very ill-tempered and quarrelsome. One day she had a violent altercation with her husband, and in consequence left home and started off with her two sons to her father's house. She traveled through several towns and villages, and at last reached a large wood near Malaya, where she saw a tiger. The tiger saw her too, and came toward her lashing his tail with rage. She felt somewhat alarmed, but put on a bold front, and administering a smart slap to her sons she said: "What do you mean by quarreling over who is to have a tiger to eat? Can't you see one here close by? Eat him first and then we will go and find another." The tiger heard all this, and thinking to himself, "Surely this lady must be indeed a formidable person," took to his heels and ran away in terror.

Presently a jackal met him. He burst into a fit of laughter and said: "Hullo! Here is a tiger running away from something in a fright." "Friend jackal," replied the tiger, "the sooner you go off to some far distant country the better, for there is a most terrible person hereabouts —a regular tiger-eater!—such as one only hears of in fables. She has almost been the death of me; as soon as I saw her, I ran away as fast as I could." "Well, I am surprised," said the jackal. "Do you mean that you are afraid of what after all is only a piece of human flesh?" "I was close to her," answered the tiger, "and what she did and said was enough to frighten any one." The jackal answered: "Well, I think I shall go by myself and see if I can find this tiger-eating lady. You had perhaps better not come, as she might recognize you again." "Whether you go with me or without me," replied the tiger, "it will make no difference; you are certain to be destroyed."

"Well, then," said the jackal, "let me mount on your back, and we will go together." So the jackal was tied on the tiger's back and off they started, and very soon found the tiger-eater with her two sons. She felt a little nervous at first, seeing the tiger had come back accompanied by a jackal, but reflecting a minute she cried out: "You rascally jackal! Once upon a time you used to bring me three tigers at once; what do you mean by coming here with only one?" The tiger heard this, and was so frightened that he turned and fled with the jackal on his back.

The tiger continued his headlong course, while the jackal, tied on the tiger's back, suffered the greatest discomfort and inconvenience. The question for him was how to get out of this unfortunate position, for the tiger in deadly fear, tore through rivers, over mountains, through forests. Suddenly he burst into a loud fit of laughter. The tiger exclaimed: "Well! I can't see what there is to laugh at!" "A great deal, I think," replied the jackal. "It just occurred to me how cleverly we have cheated that scoundrelly tiger-eater. Here I am safe and sound with your help, and she has been left behind, no one knows where. That was why I laughed. So, my dear tiger, do let me get down and see where we are." The tiger felt flattered and willingly loosed the jackal off his back. No sooner had he done so than he suddenly fell down dead, and the jackal went off rejoicing. For it has been said—

"Wisdom is better than pomp and display, for by it men gain place, riches, and honor; but he who is devoid of wisdom falls into dire misfortune. The strength of the ignorant is used to carry out the business of another, even as the surpassing might of an elephant is made subject to man."

THE CONCLUDING STORY

At the conclusion of these stories, Madana returned from his expedition, and was received by Prabhāvatī with every demonstration of affection.

The parrot said, very slowly and solemnly—

"Affection in woman means nothing; pride in woman means nothing. All the time that you have been absent, she has been my friend and devoted to me."

Madana heard what the parrot said, but he did not pay much attention to it. The parrot smiled and continued: "He who hears good advice and follows it is blessed both in this world and in the next." Madana therefore was induced to ask the parrot what he meant. Prabhāvatī at this felt a little bit anxious as to what might come out, for it has been said—"The good are always bold, sustained by consciousness of the good. The wicked are always afraid, for their evil conscience makes cowards of them."

So Prabhāvatī said to her husband, "Sir! your place has been well supplied, for in this house dwells a parrot, who seems to have come direct from the abode of the gods, and who speaks words of wisdom. He has been even as a husband and son to me."

The parrot at these words felt a little ashamed of himself, for it did not seem to him that he had merited such compliments. So Madana turned to Prabhāvatī and said: "Pray, what were the words of wisdom with which the parrot consoled you?"

She replied: "My lord, a speaker of truth may be found, but it is not so easy to find a listener, for it has been said—'Men who say what is pleasant are always welcome, but those who tell unpalatable truths, will not find an audience.'

"Now, my husband, hear me. After your departure, for a time I kept you in remembrance, though there was separation between us. Then evil friends came by, and tried to lead me astray. This bird prevented my following after them, and held me back seventy nights, by means of the stories which he told me. So I was prevented from following my desires, and my designs of evil were not fulfilled. From today—whether in life or in death—you, my husband, shall be my chief object."

At the conclusion of this harangue, Madana turned to the parrot and asked what in the world it all meant.

The parrot answered: "Speech must not be uttered hastily by the wise; those who know what is right and proper must act accordingly. Sir, I say nothing of the foolish, drunkards, women, persons afflicted with disease, those in love, the weak, the wrathful. The mad, the careless, the timid, the starving, such as these have but few virtues. There are ten who know not the way of righteousness—the mad, the careless, the drunkard, the feeble, the wrathful, the glutton, the hasty, the coward, the covetous, the lustful.

"Pray grant Prabhāvatī pardon for her shortcomings. Indeed they were not her fault, but the fault of her evil companions. For it is said—

" 'The virtuous fall into evil ways through contact with the depraved. Even Bhishma stole a cow under the influence of Duryodhana. The king's daughter was led astray by a Vidyādhara; but, though her fault was plain, she was forgiven by her father.' "

The parrot then told Madana the following story—

"There is a mountain called Malaya, and on the top of it is Manohara, a city of the Gandharvas. In it lived a certain Madana, a Gandharva, and he had a wife whose name was Ratnāvalī. Their daughter was Madanamanjarī. She was extremely beautiful and fascinating, and everyone who saw her absolutely lost his senses, whether god or hero. It was quite impossible to find a husband for her sufficiently good-looking. It so happened one day that a certain Nārada came by; when he saw her he was so fascinated by her charms that he went off his head. After a time, however, Nārada, who was a Rishi, came to himself. And he solemnly cursed her, in these words: 'Since the fire of passion has been kindled in me at the sight of your beauty, you shall be the victim of deceit.' Then her father, hearing the curse, bowed to the ground before the Rishi, and said: 'Sir, show compassion on my daughter, and grant her forgiveness!' Nārada replied: 'She shall indeed be deceived, but she shall not suffer loss, nor shall she fail in gaining a husband. On the top of Mount Meru is a city called Vipula, and in it dwells the Gandharva, Kanaprabha. He shall be your daughter's husband.' With these words Nārada departed, and according to his promise Madanamanjarī was given in marriage to the Gandharva.

Soon after this, her husband left her, and went on a journey to Kailasa. She was inconsolable at his departure, and lay full length on a stone slab in the courtyard of her home. Here she was seen by a Vidyādhara, who made advances of love to her. She declined them without hesitation, but eventually, putting on the form of her husband, he accomplished his object. Before long her husband returned, but it appeared to him that she was not particularly glad to see him. He thought that there must be some counter-attraction, and eventually he worked himself up to such a state of jealousy that he contemplated putting an end to his wife's existence. So Madanamanjarī, seeing her end in view, went to the shrine of the goddess Durgā, and made loud lamentation. The goddess heard her complaints and said to her husband, "Noble Gandharva! Your wife is guiltless; she was deceived by a Vidyādhara, who put on your form. Since she was ignorant of the real state of things, how could she be to blame? Besides, the cause of all this is the curse pronounced on her by the Rishi Nārada. Now the curse is worked out, and since she is free from guilt you must take her back.' Hearing the words of the goddess, Kanaprabha took his wife home, and they lived happily together.

"So, Madana," continued the parrot, "if you have any confidence in my words, receive your wife kindly, for there is no evil in her."

Then Madana, obedient to the parrot's wish, took Prabhāvatī home, and his father Haridatta, rejoicing at his son's return, made a great feast. While the festival was proceeding, a rain of flowers fell from heaven, and the parrot—the adviser and confidant of Prabhāvatī—freed from the curse which had compelled him to wear a parrot's form, ascended to the abode of the gods, and Madana and Prabhāvatī passed the remainder of their lives in peace and happiness.

BUDDHISM

The Dhammapada

INTRODUCTION

The Dhammapada, or "Words of the Doctrine," is a book of Buddhist aphorisms in 423 verses, but to say this is to mislead. It is not a collection of wise sayings in haphazard order, but a continuous, original, rare work of literature, unified in rhythm, style, themes and treatment, and infused with a high moral passion. The words are ascribed to Buddha himself; while scholars disagree on the subject, as scholars must, the layman stands on the sure ground that the thoughts represent correctly and truly Buddha's own teachings. The author of the verses is unknown. Whoever wrote this book must have caught the fire of a valiant call to the religious life and felt the spiritual joy that we associate with Thomas à Kempis. The obvious common-sense conclusion is that if Buddha himself had not spoken with this valiant voice, he could not have communicated it to his disciple, the unknown author. What we must be thankful for is that the voice of Buddha can still be distinctly heard through his work, which must be read continuously from the beginning to the end. That the sayings are often sharp and witty like aphorisms is the incidental literary quality of this work; behind them all, we hear the voice of someone who had something very important to say. It is a convincing voice; few works share this genuine moral passion.

It is, in short, a clear call to rouse oneself from the life of sloth, indolence and thoughtlessness of the common man, to achieve that greatest of all conquests, the conquest of self, to escape from the snares of evil passions, lust, hatred and anger, and to attain that highest human freedom, the moral freedom of one who has overcome himself. But this call for moral effort and struggle is coupled with a sense of urgency of escape and gives us the sensation of a race, as with St. Paul:

Earnest among the thoughtless, awake among the sleepers, the wise man advances like a racer, leaving behind the hack.

Again:

He whose conquests cannot be conquered again, into whose conquest no one in this world enters, by what track can you lead him, the Awakened, the Omniscient, the trackless?

He whom no desire with its snares and poisons can lead astray, by what track can you lead him, the Awakened, the Omniscient, the trackless?

And why? Because all of us know that the body is transient, and all of us are seeking salvation:

Long is the night to him who is awake; long is the mile to him who is tired; long is life to the foolish who do not know the true law.

Because:

As a cow-herd with his staff drives his cows into the stable, so do Age and Death drive the life of men.

But, because we are subject to the temptations of this illusory world, the foolish keep on living their futile, indolent, weak and licentious life, which is a life in vain, a life not worth having:

And he who lives a hundred years, ignorant and unrestrained, a life of one day is better if a man is wise and reflecting.

And he who lives a hundred years, idle and weak, a life of one day is better if a man has attained firm strength. . . .

And he who lives a hundred years, not seeing the highest law, a life of one day is better if a man sees the highest law.

It is entirely possible for one to grow "old in vain":

A man is not an elder because his head is gray; his age may be ripe, but he is called "Old-in-Vain."

For there is such a thing as moral growth:

A man who has learnt little, grows old like an ox; his flesh grows, but his knowledge does not grow.

Hence we hear the clarion call to rouse oneself from that life of moral sloth and indolence and futile mischief:

Rouse thyself! Do not be idle! Follow the law of virtue!
The virtuous rest in bliss in this life and in the next.
Come, look at this world, glittering like a royal chariot;
The foolish are immersed in it, but the wise do not touch it.

The first and last step is the conquest of self:

Rouse thyself by thyself, examine thyself by thyself; thus self-protected and attentive wilt thou live happily, O Bikkshu!

For self is the lord of self, self is the refuge of self; therefore curb thyself as the merchant curbs a noble horse.

Mules are good, if tamed, and the noble Sindhu horses, and elephants with large tusks; but he who tames himself is better still.

For with these animals does no man reach the untrodden country (Nirvāna), where a tamed man goes on a tamed animal!—on his well-tamed self.

This essential thought recurs again and again, like a theme in a symphony:

If one man conquer in battle a thousand times a thousand men, and if another conquer himself, he is the greatest of conquerors.

The process of salvation must come from within:

By one's self the evil is done, by one's self one suffers; by one's self evil is left undone, by one's self one is purified. The pure and the impure stand and fall by themselves, *no one can purify another.*

Hence Buddha's call for constant vigilance and individual effort:

You yourself must make an effort. The Tathāgatas (Buddhas) are only preachers. The thoughtful who enter the way are freed from the bondage of Māra . . .

And I like something which is so simple, so direct:

If anything is to be done, let a man do it, let him attack it vigorously! A careless pilgrim only scatters the dust of his passion more widely.

But one has first to rid oneself of the illusions of the false life and attain a moral height, from which he can see a different world:

When the learned man drives away vanity by earnestness, he, the wise, climbing the terraced heights of wisdom, looks down upon the fools: free from sorrow he looks upon the sorrowing crowd, as one that stands on a mountain looks down upon them that stand upon the plain.

Curiously, salvation comes from knowledge:

The channels run everywhere, the creeper of passion stands sprouting; if you see the creeper springing up, *cut its root by means of knowledge.*

Or again:

Knowing that this body is fragile like a jar, and making his thought firm like a fortress, one should attack Māra, the tempter, *with the weapon of knowledge,* one should watch him when conquered, and should never rest.

Because the greatest of all evils is the evil of ignorance:

But there is a taint worse than all taints—ignorance is the greatest taint. O mendicants, throw off that taint, and become taintless!

The evil life is really the *thoughtless* life:

Earnestness is the path of immortality (Nirvāna), thoughtlessness the path of death. Those who are in earnest do not die, those who are thoughtless are as if dead already.

For after all, evil and pain are identical; it is those unable to see pain as the natural result of doing evil that continue to do evil:

If a man commits a sin, let him not do it again; let him not delight in sin: *the accumulation of evil is painful.*

And good and happiness are identical:

If a man does what is good, let him do it again, let him delight in it: *the accumulation of good is delightful.*

For the virtuous man alone is happy, for he has that happiness which cannot be taken away from him:

The virtuous man is happy in this world, and he is happy in the next; he is happy in both. He is happy when he thinks of the good he has done; he is still more happy when going on the good path.

Again:

We live happily indeed, not hating those who hate us! among men who hate us we dwell free from hatred!

We live happily indeed, free from greed among the greedy! among men who are greedy let us dwell free from greed!

We live happily indeed, though we call nothing our own! We shall be like the bright gods, feeding on happiness!

For the power of good pervades:

The scent of flowers does not travel against the wind, nor that of sandalwood, or of Tagara and Mallikā flowers; but the odor of good people travels even against the wind; a good man pervades every place.

Again:

Good people are seen from afar, like the snowy mountains; bad people are not seen, like arrows shot by night.

The good man, who has achieved freedom from the senses, is even worthy of the envy of the gods:

The gods even envy him whose senses, like horses well broken in by the driver, have been subdued, who is free from pride, and free from appetites; such a one who does his duty is tolerant like the earth, like the threshold; he is like a lake without mud; no new births are in store for him.

And there we reach the spiritual joy of the calm, saintly life, strong above the trammels of passion and worldly cares:

The gift of the law exceeds all gifts; the sweetness of the law exceeds all sweetness; the delight in the law exceeds all delights; the extinction of thirst overcomes all pain.

Again, we hear the note of inner peace:

A Bikkshu who has entered his empty house, and whose mind is tranquil, feels more than a human delight when he sees the law clearly.

That is why one must allow no thoughts of hatred, anger and lust to enter the mind, and why one must not requite evil with evil, but must overcome evil with good:

He who holds back rising anger like a rolling chariot, him I call a real driver; other people are but holding the reins.

Let a man overcome anger by love, let him overcome evil by good; let him overcome the greedy by liberality, the liar by truth!

For the man who is tainted with hatred and anger, or who injures others but injures himself:

If a man offend a harmless, pure, and innocent person, the evil falls back upon that fool, like light dust thrown up against the wind.

What the world calls victory is not victory, because it breeds more hatred:

Victory breeds hatred, for the conquered is unhappy. He who has given up both victory and defeat, he, the contented, is happy.

For what the saint prizes and values is moral victory:

Silently I endured abuse as the elephant in battle endures the arrow sent from the bow: for the world is ill-natured.

They lead a tamed elephant to battle, the king mounts a tamed elephant; the tamed is the best among men, he who silently endures abuse.

Here we reach the moral heights of the Sermon on the Mount. And having disabused our minds of the common passions of men, we arrive at a new set of moral values, the values of the inner life:

A man is not learned because he talks much; he who is patient, free from hatred and fear, he is called learned.

A man is not an elect (Ariya) because he injures living creatures; because he has pity on all living creatures, therefore is a man called Ariya.

The ordinary conventional values of society do not hold any more:

A man does not become a Brahmana by his plaited hair, by his family, or by birth; in whom there is truth and righteousness, he is blessed, he is a Brahmana.

I do not call a man a Brahmana because of his origin or of his mother. He is indeed arrogant, and he is wealthy; but the poor who is free from attachments, him I call indeed a Brahmana.

The externals of the religious practice are no substitutes for the inner spiritual life, for priests also go to hell:

Many men whose shoulders are covered with the yellow gown are ill-conditioned and unrestrained; such evil-doers by their evil deeds go to hell.

Better it would be to swallow a heated iron ball, like flaring fire, than that a bad, unrestrained fellow should live on the charity of the land.

Such are the main themes that occur again and again in the *Dhammapada*. While such doctrines afford no more glimpse into Buddhist philosophy than the Sermon on the Mount affords any glimpse of Christian theology, they are the central ethical teachings of Buddhism. Here we do not run into abstruse metaphysics (see the section, *The Surangama Sutra*), but see on the other hand, the clarity, the simplicity and great humanity of Buddha's teachings, a humanity that is easy to appreciate:

If the occasion rises, friends are pleasant; enjoyment is pleasant, whatever be the cause; a good work is pleasant in the hour of death; the giving up of grief is pleasant.

Pleasant in the world is the state of a mother; pleasant the state of a father; pleasant the state of a Samana (ascetic); pleasant the state of a Brahmana.

Pleasant is virtue lasting to old age; pleasant is a faith firmly rooted; pleasant is attainment of intelligence; pleasant is avoiding of sin.

The following translation was made by Max Müller in 1870. There have been a number of succeeding efforts to re-translate the *Dhammapada*, by F. L. Woodward (1921), and by Wagiswara and Saunders (1920) in prose, and by A. L. Edmunds in verse (*Hymns of the Faith*, 1902), for this unique work has attracted many scholars. The late Irving Babbitt's translation is based on the version by Max Müller.[1] Some translators may have improved upon Max Müller in literalness, but I doubt very much in aptness of expression or in producing the smooth-flowing rhythm, for as must be evident to the reader, the great translator was concerned not only with the words, as scholars are, but had a pleasing acquaintance with the sense of words. The Chinese version of the *Dhammapada* has been rendered into English by Samuel Beal (*Texts from the Buddhist Canon known as Dhammapada*, London and Boston, 1878). Its closeness to Confucian and Taoist teachings (e.g., advice on good friends, distinction between the wise and the fools, emphasis on self-examination, freedom from fear, moral strength and inner repose) explains why Buddhism is so readily acceptable to the Chinese people.

The *Dhammapada* is a great spiritual testimony, one of the very few religious masterpieces in the world, combining genuineness of spiritual passion with a happy gift of literary expression. It is closer to the modern man than the *Bhagavad-Gita;* the latter, with all its lofty moral conceptions, is bound to strike deeper a Hindu than a non-Hindu mind, while the *Dhammapada* speaks directly on common ethical terms, such as many a self-made man would like to present to his licentious-living son, but usually has not the courage to because he is his own father. The *Dhammapada* therefore belongs to the world and to all time.

[1] Published posthumously, Oxford, 1936. It contains a valuable essay by Babbitt on *Buddha and the Occident*. What interests Babbitt in Buddhism is the emphasis on the principle of the "inner check" and self-mastery.

The Dhammapada

Translated by F. Max Müller

CHAPTER I: THE TWIN-VERSES

ALL THAT WE ARE is the result of what we have thought: it is founded on our thoughts, it is made up of our thoughts. If a man speaks or acts with an evil thought, pain follows him, as the wheel follows the foot of the ox that draws the carriage.

All that we are is the result of what we have thought: it is founded on our thoughts, it is made up of our thoughts. If a man speaks or acts with a pure thought, happiness follows him, like a shadow that never leaves him.

"He abused me, he beat me, he defeated me, he robbed me"—in those who harbor such thoughts hatred will never cease.

"He abused me, he beat me, he defeated me, he robbed me"—in those who do not harbor such thoughts hatred will cease.

For hatred does not cease by hatred at any time: hatred ceases by love—this is an old rule.

The world does not know that we must all come to an end here; but those who know it, their quarrels cease at once.

He who lives looking for pleasures only, his senses uncontrolled, immoderate in his food, idle, and weak, Māra (the tempter) will certainly overthrow him, as the wind throws down a weak tree.

He who lives without looking for pleasures, his senses well controlled, moderate in his food, faithful and strong, him Māra will certainly not overthrow, any more than the wind throws down a rocky mountain.

He who wishes to put on the yellow dress without having cleansed himself from sin, who disregards also temperance and truth, is unworthy of the yellow dress.

But he who has cleansed himself from sin, is well grounded in all virtues, and endowed also with temperance and truth: he is indeed worthy of the yellow dress.

They who imagine truth in untruth, and see untruth in truth, never arrive at truth, but follow vain desires.

They who know truth in truth, and untruth in untruth, arrive at truth, and follow true desires.

As rain breaks through an ill-thatched house, passion will break through an unreflecting mind.

As rain does not break through a well-thatched house, passion will not break through a well-reflecting mind.

The evil-doer mourns in this world, and he mourns in the next; he mourns in both. He mourns and suffers when he sees the evil result of his own work.

The virtuous man delights in this world, and he delights in the next; he delights in both. He delights and rejoices, when he sees the purity of his own work.

The evil-doer suffers in this world, and he suffers in the next; he suffers in both. He suffers when he thinks of the evil he has done; he suffers more when going on the evil path.

The virtuous man is happy in this world, and he is happy in the next; he is happy in both. He is happy when he thinks of the good he has done; he is still more happy when going on the good path.

The thoughtless man, even if he can recite a large portion of the law, but is not a doer of it, has no share in the priesthood, but is like a cowherd counting the cows of others.

The follower of the law, even if he can recite only a small portion of the law, but, having forsaken passion and hatred and foolishness, possesses true knowledge and serenity of mind, he, caring for nothing in this world or that to come, has indeed a share in the priesthood.

CHAPTER II: ON EARNESTNESS

Earnestness is the path of immortality (Nirvāna), thoughtlessness the path of death. Those who are in earnest do not die, those who are thoughtless are as if dead already.

Having understood this clearly, those who are advanced in earnestness delight in earnestness, and rejoice in the knowledge of the elect.

These wise people, meditative, steady, always possessed of strong powers, attain to Nirvāna, the highest happiness.

If an earnest person has roused himself, if he is not forgetful, if his deeds are pure, if he acts with consideration, if he restrains himself, and lives according to law—then his glory will increase.

By rousing himself, by earnestness, by restraint and control, the wise man may make for himself an island which no flood can overwhelm.

Fools follow after vanity. The wise man keeps earnestness as his best jewel.

Follow not after vanity, nor after the enjoyment of love and lust! He who is earnest and meditative, obtains ample joy.

When the learned man drives away vanity by earnestness, he, the wise, climbing the terraced heights of wisdom, looks down upon the fools: free from sorrow he looks upon the sorrowing crowd, as one that stands on a mountain looks down upon them that stand upon the plain.

Earnest among the thoughtless, awake among the sleepers, the wise man advances like a racer, leaving behind the hack.

By earnestness did Maghavan (Indra) rise to the lordship of the gods. People praise earnestness; thoughtlessness is always blamed.

A Bhikshu (mendicant) who delights in earnestness, who looks with fear on thoughtlessness, moves about like fire, burning all his fetters, small or large.

A Bhikshu (mendicant) who delights in reflection, who looks with fear on thoughtlessness, cannot fall away from his perfect state—he is close upon Nirvāna.

CHAPTER III: THOUGHT

As a fletcher makes straight his arrow, a wise man makes straight his trembling and unsteady thought, which is difficult to guard, difficult to hold back.

As a fish taken from his watery home and thrown on the dry ground, our thought trembles all over in order to escape the dominion of Māra, the tempter.

It is good to tame the mind, which is difficult to hold in and flighty, rushing wherever it listeth; a tamed mind brings happiness.

Let the wise man guard his thoughts, for they are difficult to perceive, very artful, and they rush wherever they list: thoughts well guarded bring happiness.

Those who bridle their mind which travels far, moves about alone, is without a body, and hides in the chamber of the heart, will be free from the bonds of Māra, the tempter.

If a man's faith is unsteady, if he does not know the true law, if his peace of mind is troubled, his knowledge will never be perfect.

If a man's thoughts are not dissipated, if his mind is not perplexed, if he has ceased to think of good or evil, then there is no fear for him while he is watchful.

Knowing that this body is fragile like a jar, and making his thought firm like a fortress, one should attack Māra, the tempter, with the weapon of knowledge, one should watch him when conquered, and should never rest.

Before long, alas! this body will lie on the earth, despised, without understanding, like a useless log.

Whatever a hater may do to a hater, or an enemy to an enemy, a wrongly-directed mind will do him greater mischief.

Not a mother, not a father, will do so much, nor any other relatives; a well-directed mind will do us greater service.

CHAPTER IV: FLOWERS

Who shall overcome this earth, and the world of Yama, the lord of the departed, and the world of the gods? Who shall find out the plainly shown path of virtue, as a clever man finds the right flower?

The disciple will overcome the earth, and the world of Yama, and the world of the gods. The disciple will find out the plainly shown path of virtue, as a clever man finds the right flower.

He who knows that this body is like froth, and has learnt that it is as unsubstantial as a mirage, will break the flower-pointed arrow of Māra, and never see the king of death.

Death carries off a man who is gathering flowers, and whose mind is distracted, as a flood carries off a sleeping village.

Death subdues a man who is gathering flowers, and whose mind is distracted, before he is satiated in his pleasures.

As the bee collects nectar and departs without injuring the flower, or its color or scent, so let a sage dwell in his village.

Not the perversities of others, not their sins of commission or omission, but his own misdeeds and negligences should a sage take notice of.

Like a beautiful flower, full of color, but without scent, are the fine but fruitless words of him who does not act accordingly.

But, like a beautiful flower, full of color and full of scent, are the fine and fruitful words of him who acts accordingly.

As many kinds of wreaths can be made from a heap of flowers, so many good things may be achieved by a mortal when once he is born.

The scent of flowers does not travel against the wind, nor that of sandal-wood, or of Tagara and Mallikā flowers; but the odor of good people travels even against the wind; a good man pervades every place.

Sandal-wood or Tagara, a lotus-flower, or a Vassikī, among these sorts of perfumes, the perfume of virtue is unsurpassed.

Mean is the scent that comes from Tagara and sandal-wood; the perfume of those who possess virtue rises up to the gods as the highest.

Of the people who possess these virtues, who live without thoughtlessness, and who are emancipated through true knowledge, Māra, the tempter, never finds the way.

As on a heap of rubbish cast upon the highway the lily will grow full of sweet perfume and delight, thus among those who are mere rubbish the disciple of the truly enlightened Buddha shines forth by his knowledge above the blinded worldling.

CHAPTER V: THE FOOL

LONG IS THE NIGHT to him who is awake; long is a mile to him who is tired; long is life to the foolish who do not know the true law.

If a traveller does not meet with one who is his better, or his equal, let him firmly keep to his solitary journey; there is no companionship with a fool.

"These sons belong to me, and this wealth belongs to me," with such thoughts a fool is tormented. He himself does not belong to himself; how much less sons and wealth?

The fool who knows his foolishness, is wise at least so far. But a fool who thinks himself wise, he is called a fool indeed.

If a fool be associated with a wise man even all his life, he will perceive the truth as little as a spoon perceives the taste of soup.

If an intelligent man be associated for one minute only with a wise man, he will soon perceive the truth, as the tongue perceives the taste of soup.

Fools of poor understanding have themselves for their greatest enemies, for they do evil deeds which bear bitter fruits.

That deed is not well done of which a man must repent, and the reward of which he receives crying and with a tearful face.

No, that deed is well done of which a man does not repent, and the reward of which he receives gladly and cheerfully.

As long as the evil deed done does not bear fruit, the fool thinks it is like honey; but when it ripens, then the fool suffers grief.

Let a fool month after month eat his food (like an ascetic) with the tip of a blade of Kusa-grass, yet is he not worth the sixteenth particle of those who have well weighed the law.

An evil deed, like newly-drawn milk, does not turn suddenly; smouldering, like fire covered by ashes, it follows the fool.

And when the evil deed, after it has become known, turns to sorrow for the fool, then it destroys his bright lot, nay, it cleaves his head.

Let the fool wish for a false reputation, for precedence among the Bhikshus, for lordship in the convents, for worship among other people!

"May both the layman and he who has left the world think that this is done by me; may they be subject to me in everything which is to be done or is not to be done," thus is the mind of the fool, and his desire and pride increase.

"One is the road that leads to wealth, another the road that leads to Nirvāna"—if the Bhikshu, the disciple of Buddha, has learnt this, he will not yearn for honor, he will strive after separation from the world.

CHAPTER VI: THE WISE MAN

If you see a man who shows you what is to be avoided, who administers reproofs, and is intelligent, follow that wise man as you would one who tells of hidden treasures; it will be better, not worse, for him who follows him.

Let him admonish, let him teach, let him forbid what is improper!—he will be beloved of the good, by the bad he will be hated.

Do not have evil-doers for friends, do not have low people for friends: have virtuous people for friends, have for friends the best of men.

He who drinks in the law lives happily with a serene mind: the sage rejoices always in the law, as preached by the elect.

Well-makers lead the water wherever they like; fletchers bend the arrow; carpenters bend a log of wood; wise people fashion themselves.

As a solid rock is not shaken by the wind, wise people falter not amidst blame and praise.

Wise people, after they have listened to the laws, become serene, like a deep, smooth, and still lake.

Good men indeed walk warily under all circumstances; good men speak not out of a desire for sensual gratification; whether touched by happiness or sorrow wise people never appear elated or depressed.

If, whether for his own sake, or for the sake of others, a man wishes neither for a son, nor for wealth, nor for lordship, and if he does not wish for his own success by unfair means, then he is good, wise, and virtuous.

Few are there among men who arrive at the other shore (become Arhats); the other people here run up and down the shore.

But those who, when the law has been well preached to them, follow the law, will pass over the dominion of death, however difficult to cross.

A wise man should leave the dark state of ordinary life, and follow the bright state of the Bhikshu. After going from his home to a homeless state, he should in his retirement look for enjoyment where enjoyment seemed difficult. Leaving all pleasures behind, and calling nothing his own, the wise man should purge himself from all the troubles of the mind.

Those whose mind is well grounded in the seven elements of knowledge, who without clinging to anything, rejoice in freedom from attachment, whose appetites have been conquered, and who are full of light, they are free even in this world.

CHAPTER VII: THE VENERABLE

There is no suffering for him who has finished his journey, and abandoned grief, who has freed himself on all sides, and thrown off all fetters.

They exert themselves with their thoughts well-collected, they do not tarry in their abode; like swans who have left their lake, they leave their house and home.

Men who have no riches, who live on recognized food, who have perceived void and unconditioned freedom (Nirvāna), their path is difficult to understand, like that of birds in the air.

He whose appetites are stilled, who is not absorbed in enjoyment, who has perceived void and unconditioned freedom (Nirvāna), his path is difficult to understand, like that of birds in the air.

The gods even envy him whose senses, like horses well broken in by the driver, have been subdued, who is free from pride, and free from appetites; such a one who does his duty is tolerant like the earth, or like a threshold; he is like a lake without mud; no new births are in store for him.

His thought is quiet, quiet are his word and deed, when he has obtained freedom by true knowledge, when he has thus become a quiet man.

The man who is free from credulity, but knows the uncreated, who has cut all ties, removed all temptations, renounced all desires, he is the greatest of men.

In a hamlet or in a forest, on sea or on dry land, wherever venerable persons (Arahanta) dwell, that place is delightful.

Forests are delightful; where the world finds no delight, there the passionless will find delight, for they look not for pleasures.

CHAPTER VIII: THE THOUSANDS

Even though a speech be a thousand (of words), but made up of senseless words, one word of sense is better, which if a man hears, he becomes quiet.

Even though a Gāthā (poem) be a thousand (of words), but made up of senseless words, one word of a Gāthā is better, which if a man hears, he becomes quiet.

Though a man recite a hundred Gāthās made up of senseless words, one word of the law is better, which if a man hears, he becomes quiet.

If one man conquer in battle a thousand times a thousand men, and if another conquer himself, he is the greatest of conquerors.

One's own self conquered is better than all other people; not even a god, a Gandharva, not Māra (with Brāhman), could change into defeat the victory of a man who has vanquished himself, and always lives under restraint.

If a man for a hundred years sacrifice month by month with a thousand, and if he but for one moment pay homage to a man whose soul is grounded in true knowledge, better is that homage than a sacrifice for a hundred years.

If a man for a hundred years worship Agni (fire) in the forest, and if he but for one moment pay homage to a man whose soul is grounded in true knowledge, better is that homage than sacrifice for a hundred years.

Whatever a man sacrifice in this world as an offering or as an oblation for a whole year in order to gain merit, the whole of it is not worth a quarter a farthing; reverence shown to the righteous is better.

He who always greets and constantly reveres the aged, four things will increase to him: life, beauty, happiness, power.

But he who lives a hundred years, vicious and unrestrained, a life of one day is better if a man is virtuous and reflecting.

And he who lives a hundred years, ignorant and unrestrained, a life of one day is better if a man is wise and reflecting.

And he who lives a hundred years, idle and weak, a life of one day is better if a man has attained firm strength.

And he who lives a hundred years, not seeing beginning and end, a life of one day is better if a man sees beginning and end.

And he who lives a hundred years, not seeing the immortal place, a life of one day is better if a man sees the immortal place.

And he who lives a hundred years, not seeing the highest law, a life of one day is better if a man sees the highest law.

CHAPTER IX: EVIL

A MAN should hasten towards towards the good, and should keep his thought away from evil; if a man does what is good slothfully, his mind delights in evil.

If a man commits a sin, let him not do it again; let him not delight in sin: the accumulation of evil is painful.

If a man does what is good, let him do it again; let him delight in it: the accumulation of good is delightful.

Even an evil-doer sees happiness so long as his evil deed does not ripen; but when his evil deed ripens, then does the evil-doer see evil.

Even a good man sees evil days so long as his good deed does not ripen; but when his good deed ripens, then does the good man see good things.

Let no man think lightly of evil, saying in his heart, It will not come nigh unto me. Even by the falling of water-drops a water-pot is filled; the fool becomes full of evil, even if he gather it little by little.

Let no man think lightly of good, saying in his heart, It will not come nigh unto me. Even by the falling of water-drops a water-pot is filled; the wise man becomes full of good, even if he gather it little by little.

Let a man avoid evil deeds, as a merchant, if he has few companions and carries much wealth, avoids a dangerous road; as a man who loves life avoids poison.

He who has no wound on his hand, may touch poison with his hand; poison does not affect one who has no wound; nor is there evil for one who does not commit evil.

If a man offend a harmless, pure, and innocent person, the evil falls back upon that fool, like light dust thrown up against the wind.

Some people are born again; evil-doers go to hell; righteous people go to heaven; those who are free from all worldly desires attain Nirvāna.

Not in the sky, not in the midst of the sea, not if we enter into the clefts of the mountains, is there known a spot in the whole world where a man might be freed from an evil deed.

Not in the sky, not in the midst of the sea, not if we enter into the clefts of the mountains, is there known a spot in the whole world where death could not overcome the mortal.

CHAPTER X: PUNISHMENT

All men tremble at punishment, all men fear death; remember that you are like unto them, and do not kill, nor cause slaughter.

All men tremble at punishment, all men love life; remember that thou art like unto them, and do not kill, nor cause slaughter.

He who, seeking his own happiness, punishes or kills beings who also long for happiness, will not find happiness after death.

He who, seeking his own happiness, does not punish or kill beings who also long for happiness, will find happiness after death.

Do not speak harshly to anyone; those who are spoken to will answer thee in the same way. Angry speech is painful: blows for blows will touch thee.

If, like a shattered metal plate (gong), thou utter nothing, then thou hast reached Nirvāna; anger is not known to thee.

As a cow-herd with his staff drives his cows into the stable, so do Age and Death drive the life of men.

A fool does not know when he commits his evil deeds: but the wicked man burns by his own deeds, as if burnt by fire.

He who inflicts pain on innocent and harmless persons, will soon come to one of these ten states:—

He will have cruel suffering, loss, injury of the body, heavy affliction, or loss of mind.

A misfortune coming from the king, or a fearful accusation, or loss of relations, or destruction of treasures.

Lightning-fire will burn his houses; and when his body is destroyed, the fool will go to hell.

Not nakedness, not platted hair, not dirt, not fasting, or lying on the earth, not rubbing with dust, not sitting motionless, can purify a mortal who has not overcome desires.

He who, though dressed in fine apparel, exercises tranquility, is quiet, subdued, restrained, chaste, and has ceased to find fault with all other beings, he indeed is a Brāhmana, an ascetic (sramana), a friar (bhikshu).

Is there in this world any man so restrained by shame that he does not provoke reproof, as a noble horse the whip?

Like a noble horse when touched by the whip, be ye strenuous and eager, and by faith, by virtue, by energy, by meditation, by discernment of the law, you will overcome this great pain, perfect in knowledge and in behavior, and never forgetful.

Well-makers lead the water wherever they like; fletchers bend the arrow; carpenters bend a log of wood; good people fashion themselves.

CHAPTER XI: OLD AGE

How is there laughter, how is there joy, as this world is always burning? Do you not seek a light, ye who are surrounded by darkness?

Look at this dressed-up lump, covered with wounds, joined together, sickly, full of many schemes, but which has no strength, no hold!

This body is wasted, full of sickness, and frail; this heap of corruption breaks to pieces, life indeed ends in death.

After one has looked at those gray bones, thrown away like gourds in the autumn, what pleasure is there left in life!

After a stronghold has been made of the bones, it is covered with flesh and blood, and there dwell in it old age and death, pride and deceit.

The brilliant chariots of kings are destroyed, the body also approaches destruction, but the virtue of good people never approaches destruction—thus do the good say to the good.

A man who has learnt little, grows old like an ox; his flesh grows, but his knowledge does not grow.

Looking for the maker of this tabernacle, I have run through a course of many births, not finding him; and painful is birth again and again. But now, maker of the tabernacle, thou hast been seen; thou shalt not make up this tabernacle again. All thy rafters are broken, thy ridge-pole is sundered; the mind, approaching the Eternal (visankhāra, nirvāna), has attained to the extinction of all desires.

Men who have not observed proper discipline, and have not gained wealth in their youth, perish like old herons in a lake without fish.

Men who have not observed proper discipline, and have not gained wealth in their youth, lie, like broken bows, sighing after the past.

CHAPTER XII: SELF

If a man hold himself dear, let him watch himself carefully; during one at least out of the three watches a wise man should be watchful.

Let each man direct himself first to what is proper, then let him teach others; thus a wise man will not suffer.

If a man make himself as he teaches others to be, then, being himself well subdued, he may subdue others; for one's own self is difficult to subdue.

Self is the lord of self, who else could be the lord? With self well subdued, a man finds a lord such as few can find.

The evil done by one's self, self-forgotten, self-bred, crushes the foolish, as a diamond breaks even a precious stone.

He whose wickedness is very great brings himself down to that state where his enemy wishes him to be, as a creeper does with the tree which it surrounds.

Bad deeds, and deeds hurtful to ourselves, are easy to do; what is beneficial and good, that is very difficult to do.

The foolish man who scorns the rule of the venerable (Arhat), of the elect (Ariya), of the virtuous, and follows a false doctrine, he bears fruit to his own destruction, like the fruits of the Katthaka reed.

By one's self the evil is done, by one's self one suffers; by one's self evil is left undone, by one's self one is purified. The pure and the impure stand and fall by themselves, no one can purify another.

Let no one forget his own duty for the sake of another's, however great; let a man, after he has discerned his own duty, be always attentive to his duty.

CHAPTER XII: THE WORLD

Do not follow the evil law! Do not live on in thoughtlessness! Do not follow false doctrine! Be not a friend of the world.

Rouse thyself! do not be idle! Follow the law of virtue! The virtuous rest in bliss in this world and in the next.

Fellow the law of virtue; do not follow that of sin. The virtuous rest in bliss in this world and in the next.

Look upon the world as you would on a bubble, look upon it as you would on a mirage: the king of death does not see him who thus looks down upon the world.

Come, look at this world, glittering like a royal chariot; the foolish are immersed in it, but the wise do not touch it.

He who formerly was reckless and afterwards became sober, brightens up this world, like the moon when freed from clouds.

He whose evil-deeds are covered by good deeds, brightens up this world, like the moon when freed from clouds.

This world is dark, few only can see here; a few only go to heaven, like birds escaped from the net.

The swans go on the path of the sun, they go miraculously through the ether; the wise are led out of this world, when they have conquered Māra and his train.

If a man has transgressed the one law, and speaks lies, and scoffs at another world, there is no evil he will not do.

The uncharitable do not go to the world of the gods; fools only do not praise liberality; a wise man rejoices in liberality, and through it becomes blessed in the other world.

Better than sovereignty over the earth, better than going to heaven, better than lordship over all worlds, is the reward of Sotāpatti, the first step in holiness.

CHAPTER XIV: THE BUDDHA—THE AWAKENED

He whose conquest cannot be conquered again, into whose conquest no one in this world enters, by what track can you lead him, the Awakened, the Omniscient, the trackless?

He whom no desire with its snares and poisons can lead astray, by what track can you lead him, the Awakened, the Omniscient, the trackless?

Even the gods envy those who are awakened and not forgetful, who are given to meditation, who are wise, and who delight in the repose of retirement from the world.

Difficult to obtain is the conception of men, difficult is the life of mortals, difficult is the hearing of the True Law, difficult is the birth of the Awakened (the attainment of Buddhahood).

Not to commit any sin, to do good, and to purify one's mind, that is the teaching of all the Awakened.

The Awakened call patience the highest penance, long-suffering the highest Nirvāna; for he is not an anchorite (pravragita) who strikes others, he is not an ascetic (sramana) who insults others.

Not to blame, not to strike, to live restrained under the law, to be moderate in eating, to sleep and sit alone, and to dwell on the highest thoughts—this is the teaching of the Awakened.

There is no satisfying lusts, even by a shower of gold pieces; he who knows that lusts have a short taste and cause pain, he is wise; even in heavenly pleasures he finds no satisfaction, the disciple who is fully awakened delights only in the destruction of all desires.

Men, driven by fear, go to many a refuge, to mountains and forests, to groves and sacred trees.

But that is not a safe refuge, that is not the best refuge; a man is not delivered from all pains after having gone to that refuge.

He who takes refuge with Buddha, the Law, and the Church; he who, with clear understanding, sees the four holy truths: pain, the origin of pain, the destruction of pain, and the eightfold holy way that leads to the quieting of pain;—that is the safe refuge, that is the best refuge; having gone to that refuge, a man is delivered from all pain.

A supernatural person (a Buddha) is not easily found: he is not born everywhere. Wherever such a sage is born, that race prospers.

Happy is the arising of the Awakened, happy is the teaching of the True Law, happy is peace in the church, happy is the devotion of those who are at peace.

He who pays homage to those who deserve homage, whether the awakened (Buddha) or their disciples, those who have overcome the host of evils, and crossed the flood of sorrow, he who pays homage to such as have found deliverance and know no fear, his merit can never be measured by anyone.

CHAPTER XV: HAPPINESS

We live happily indeed, not hating those who hate us! among men who hate us we dwell free from hatred! We live happily indeed, free from ailments among the ailing! among men who are ailing let us dwell free from ailments!

We live happily indeed, free from greed among the greedy! among men who are greedy let us dwell free from greed!

We live happily indeed, though we call nothing our own! We shall be like the bright gods, feeding on happiness!

Victory breeds hatred, for the conquered is unhappy. He who has given up both victory and defeat, he, the contented, is happy.

There is no fire like passion; there is no losing throw like hatred; there is no pain like this body; there is no happiness higher than rest.

Hunger is the worst of diseases, the elements of the body the greatest evil; if one knows this truly, that is Nirvāna, the highest happiness.

Health is the greatest of gifts, contentedness the best riches; trust is the best of relationships, Nirvāna the highest happiness.

He who has tasted the sweetness of solitude and tranquillity, is free from fear and free from sin, while he tastes the sweetness of drinking in the law.

The sight of the elect (Ariya) is good, to live with them is always happiness; if a man does not see fools, he will be truly happy.

He who walks in the company of fools suffers a long way; company with fools, as with an enemy, is always painful; company with the wise is pleasure, like meeting with kinsfolk.

Therefore, one ought to follow the wise, the intelligent, the learned, the much enduring, the dutiful, the elect; one ought to follow such a good and wise man, as the moon follows the path of the stars.

CHAPTER XVI: PLEASURE

He who gives himself to vanity, and does not give himself to meditation, forgetting the real aim of life and grasping at pleasure, will in time envy him who has exerted himself in meditation.

Let no man ever cling to what is pleasant, or to what is unpleasant. Not to see what is pleasant is pain, and it is pain to see what is unpleasant.

Let, therefore, no man love anything; loss of the beloved is evil. Those who love nothing, and hate nothing, have no fetters.

From pleasure comes grief, from pleasures comes fear; he who is free from pleasure knows neither grief nor fear.

From affection comes grief, from affection comes fear; he who is free from affection knows neither grief nor fear.

From lust comes grief, from lust comes fear; he who is free from lust knows neither grief nor fear.

From love comes grief, from love comes fear; he who is free from love knows neither grief nor fear.

From greed comes grief, from greed comes fear; he who is free from greed knows neither grief nor fear.

He who possesses virtue and intelligence, who is just, speaks the truth, and does what is his own business, him the world will hold dear.

He in whom a desire for the Ineffable (Nirvāna) has sprung up, who in his mind is satisfied, and whose thoughts are not bewildered by love, he is called ūrdhvamsrotas (carried upwards by the stream).

Kinsmen, friends, and lovers salute a man who has been long away, and returns safe from afar.

In like manner his good works receive him who has done good, and has gone from this world to the other;—as kinsmen receive a friend on his return.

CHAPTER XVII: ANGER

Let a man leave anger, let him forsake pride, let him overcome all bondage! No sufferings befall the man who is not attached to name and form, and who calls nothing his own.

He who holds back rising anger like a rolling chariot, him I call a real driver; other people are but holding the reins.

Let a man overcome anger by love, let him overcome evil by good; let him overcome the greedy by liberality, the liar by truth!

Speak the truth, do not yield to anger; give, if thou art asked for little; by these three steps thou wilt go near the gods.

The sages who injure nobody, and who always control their body, they will go to the unchangeable place (Nirvāna), where, if they have gone, they will suffer no more.

Those who are ever watchful, who study day and night, and who strive after Nirvāna, their passions will come to an end.

This is an old saying, O Atula, this is not as if of to-day: "They blame him who sits silent, they blame him who speaks much, they also blame him who says little; there is no one on earth who is not blamed."

There never was, there never will be, nor is there now, a man who is always blamed, or a man who is always praised.

But he whom those who discriminate praise continually day after day, as without blemish, wise, rich in knowledge and virtue, who would dare to blame him, like a coin made of gold from the Gambū river? Even the gods praise him, he is praised even by Brāhman.

Beware of bodily anger, and control thy body! Leave the sins of the body, and with thy body practise virtue!

Beware of the anger of the tongue, and control thy tongue! Leave the sins of the tongue, and practise virtue with thy tongue!

Beware of the anger of the mind, and control thy mind! Leave the sins of the mind, and practise virtue with thy mind!

The wise who control their body, who control their tongue, the wise who control their mind, are indeed well controlled.

CHAPTER XVIII: IMPURITY

THOU ART NOW like a sear leaf, the messengers of death (Yama) have come near to thee; thou standest at the door of thy departure, and thou hast no provision for thy journey.

Make thyself an island, work hard, be wise! When thy impurities are blown away, and thou art free from guilt, thou wilt enter into the heavenly world of the elect (Ariya).

Thy life has come to an end, thou art come near to death (Yama), there is no resting-place for thee on the road, and thou hast no provision for thy journey.

Make thyself an island, work hard, be wise! When thy impurities are blown away, and thou art free from guilt, thou wilt not enter again into birth and decay.

Let a wise man blow off the impurities of himself, as a smith blows off the impurities of silver, one by one, little by little, and from time to time.

As the impurity which springs from the iron, when it springs from it, destroys it; thus do a transgressor's own works lead him to the evil path.

The taint of prayers is non-repetition; the taint of houses, non-repair; the taint of complexion is sloth; the taint of a watchman, thoughtlessness.

Bad conduct is the taint of woman, niggardliness the taint of a benefactor; tainted are all evil ways, in this world and in the next.

But there is a taint worse than all taints—ignorance is the greatest taint. O mendicants! throw off that taint, and become taintless!

Life is easy to live for a man who is without shame: a crow hero, a mischief-maker, an insulting, bold, and wretched fellow.

But life is hard to live for a modest man, who always looks for what is pure, who is disinterested, quiet, spotless, and intelligent.

He who destroys life, who speaks untruth, who in the world takes what is not given him, who goes to another man's wife; and the man who gives himself to drinking intoxicating liquors, he, even in this world, digs up his own root.

O man, know this, that the unrestrained are in a bad state; take care that greediness and vice do not bring thee to grief for a long time!

The world gives according to their faith or according to their pleasure: if a man frets about the food and the drink given to others, he will find no rest either by day or by night.

He in whom that feeling is destroyed, and taken out with the very root, finds rest by day and by night.

There is no fire like passion, there is no shark like hatred, there is no snare like folly, there is no torrent like greed.

The fault of others is easily perceived, but that of one's self is difficult to perceive; a man winnows his neighbor's faults like chaff, but his own fault he hides, as a cheat hides the bad die from the player.

If a man looks after the faults of others, and is always inclined to be offended, his own passions will grow, and he is far from the destruction of passions.

There is no path through the air, a man is not a Samana outwardly. The world delights in vanity, the Tathāgatas (the Buddhas) are free from vanity.

There is no path through the air, a man is not a Samana outwardly. No creatures are eternal; but the awakened (Buddha) are never shaken.

CHAPTER XIX: THE JUST

A MAN IS NOT JUST if he carries a matter by violence; no, he who distinguishes both right and wrong, who is learned and guides others, not by violence, but by the same law, being a guardian of the law and intelligent, he is called just.

A man is not learned because he talks much; he who is patient, free from hatred and fear, he is called learned.

A man is not a supporter of the law because he talks much; even if a man has learnt little, but sees the law bodily, he is a supporter of the law, a man who never neglects the law.

A man is not an elder because his head is gray; his age may be ripe, but he is called "Old-in-vain."

He in whom there is truth, virtue, pity, restraint, moderation, he who is free from impurity and is wise, he is called an elder.

An envious, stingy, dishonest man does not become respectable by means of much talking only, or by the beauty of his complexion.

He in whom all this is destroyed, and taken out with the very root, he, when freed from hatred, is called respectable.

Not by tonsure does an undisciplined man who speaks falsehood become a Samana [1]; can a man be a Samana who is still held captive by desire and greediness?

He who always quiets the evil, whether small or large, he is called a Samana (a quiet man), because he has quieted all evil.

A man is not a mendicant (Bhikshu) simply because he asks others for alms; he who adopts the whole law is a Bhikshu, not he who only begs.

He who is above good and evil, who is chaste, who with care passes through the world, he indeed is called a Bhikshu.

A man is not a Muni [2] because he observes silence if he is foolish and ignorant; but the wise who, as with the balance, chooses the good and avoids evil, he is a Muni, and is a Muni thereby; he who in this world weighs both sides is called a Muni.

A man is not an elect (Ariya) because he injures living creatures; because he has pity on all living creatures, therefore is a man called Ariya.

Not only by discipline and vows, not only by much learning, not by entering into a trance, not by sleeping alone, do I earn the happiness of release which no worldling can know. O Bhikshu, he who has obtained the extinction of desires, has obtained confidence.

CHAPTER XX: THE WAY

THE BEST OF WAYS is the eightfold [3]; the best of truths the four words [4]; the best of virtues passionlessness; the best of men he who has eyes to see.

This is the way, there is no other that leads to the purifying of intelligence. Go on this path! This is the confusion of Māra, the tempter.

[1] Pali form of Sanskrit *Sramana*, an ascetic.

[2] A holy sage.

[3] Right Doctrine, Right Purpose, Right Discourse, Right Behavior, Right Purity, Right Thought, Right Solitude, Right Rapture.

[4] See Chap. XIV.

If you go on this way, you will make an end of pain! The way preached by me, when I had understood the removal of the thorns in the flesh.

You yourself must make an effort. The Tathāgatas (Buddhas) are only preachers. The thoughtful who enter the way are freed from the bondage of Māra.

"All created things perish," he who knows and sees this becomes passive in pain; this is the way to purity.

"All created things are grief and pain," he who knows and sees this becomes passive in pain; this is the way that leads to purity.

"All forms are unreal," he who knows and sees this becomes passive in pain; this is the way that leads to purity.

He who does not rouse himself when it is time to rise, who, though young and strong, is full of sloth, whose will and thought are weak, that lazy and idle man never finds the way to knowledge.

Watching his speech, well restrained in mind, let a man never commit any wrong with his body! Let a man but keep these three roads of action clear, and he will achieve the way which is taught by the wise.

Through zeal knowledge is gained, through lack of zeal knowledge is lost; let a man who knows this double path of gain and loss thus place himself that knowledge may grow.

Cut down the whole forest of desires, not a tree only! Danger comes out of the forest of desires. When you have cut down both the forest of desires and its undergrowth, then, Bhikshus, you will be rid of the forest and of desires!

So long as the desire of man towards women, even the smallest, is not destroyed, so long is his mind in bondage, as the calf that drinks milk is to its mother.

Cut out the love of self, like an autumn lotus, with thy hand! Cherish the road of peace. Nirvāna has been shown by Sugata (Buddha).

"Here I shall dwell in the rain, here in winter and summer," thus the fool meditates, and does not think of death.

Death comes and carries off that man, honored for his children and flocks, his mind distracted, as a flood carries off a sleeping village.

Sons are no help, nor a father, nor relations; there is no help from kinsfolk for one whom death has seized.

A wise and well-behaved man who knows the meaning of this, should quickly clear the way that leads to Nirvāna.

CHAPTER XXI: MISCELLANEOUS

IF BY LEAVING A SMALL PLEASURE one sees a great pleasure, let a wise man leave the small pleasure, and look to the great.

He who, by causing pain to others, wishes to obtain pleasure for himself, he, entangled in the bonds of hatred, will never be free from hatred.

What ought to be done is neglected, what ought not to be done is done; the desires of unruly, thoughtless people are always increasing.

But they whose whole watchfulness is always directed to their body, who do not follow what ought not to be done, and who steadfastly do what ought to be done, the desires of such watchful and wise people will come to an end.

A true Brāhmana goes scathless, though he have killed father and mother, and two valiant kings, though he has destroyed a kingdom with all its subjects.

A true Brāhmana goes scathless, though he have killed father and mother, and two holy kings, and an eminent man besides.

The disciples of Gotama (Buddha) are always well awake, and their thoughts day and night are always set on Buddha.

The disciples of Gotama are always well awake, and their thoughts day and night are always set on the law.

The disciples of Gotama are always well awake, and their thoughts day and night are always set on the church.

The disciples of Gotama are always well awake, and their thoughts day and night are always set on their body.

The disciples of Gotama are always well awake, and their mind day and night always delights in compassion.

The disciples of Gotama are always well awake, and their mind day and night always delights in meditation.

It is hard to leave the world to become a friar, it is hard to enjoy the world; hard is the monastery, painful are the houses; painful it is to dwell with equals to share everything in common, and the itinerant mendicant is beset with pain. Therefore let no man be an itinerant mendicant, and he will not be beset with pain.

A man full of faith, if endowed with virtue and glory, is respected, whatever place he may choose.

Good people shine from afar, like the snowy mountains; bad people are not seen, like arrows shot by night.

Sitting alone, lying down alone, walking alone without ceasing, and alone subduing himself, let a man be happy near the edge of a forest.

CHAPTER XXII: THE DOWNWARD COURSE

He who says what is not, goes to hell; he also who, having done a thing, says I have not done it. After death both are equal: they are men with evil deeds in the next world.

Many men whose shoulders are covered with the yellow gown[1] are ill-conditioned and unrestrained; such evil-doers by their evil deeds go to hell.

Better it would be to swallow a heated iron ball, like flaring fire, than that a bad unrestrained fellow should live on the charity of the land.

Four things does a reckless man gain who covets his neighbor's wife—demerit, an uncomfortable bed, thirdly, punishment, and lastly, hell.

There is demerit, and the evil way to hell: there is the short pleasure of the frightened in the arms of the frightened, and the king imposes heavy punishment; therefore let no man think of his neighbor's wife.

As a grass-blade, if badly grasped, cuts the arm, badly-practised asceticism leads to hell.

An act carelessly performed, a broken vow, and hesitating obedience to discipline (Brāhma-kariyam), all this brings no great reward.

If anything is to be done, let a man do it, let him attack it vigorously! A careless pilgrim only scatters the dust of his passions more widely.

An evil deed is better left undone, for a man repents of it afterwards; a good deed is better done, for having done it, one does not repent.

Like a well-guarded frontier fort, with defences within and without, so let a man guard himself. Not a moment should escape, for they who allow the right moment to pass, suffer pain when they are in hell.

They who are ashamed of what they ought not to be ashamed of, and are not ashamed of what they ought to be ashamed of, such men, embracing false doctrines, enter the evil path.

They who fear when they ought not to fear, and fear not when they ought to fear, such men, embracing false doctrines, enter the evil path.

They who see sin where there is no sin, and see no sin where there is sin, such men, embracing false doctrines, enter the evil path.

They who see sin where there is sin, and no sin where there is no sin, such men, embracing the true doctrine, enter the good path.

[1] Priests.

CHAPTER XXIII: THE ELEPHANT

SILENTLY I endured abuse as the elephant in battle endures the arrow sent from the bow: for the world is ill-natured.

They lead a tamed elephant to battle, the king mounts a tamed elephant; the tamed is the best among men, he who silently endures abuse.

Mules are good, if tamed, and noble Sindhu horses, and elephants with large tusks; but he who tames himself is better still.

For with these animals does no man reach the untrodden country (Nirvāna), where a tamed man goes on a tamed animal—on his own well-tamed self.

The elephant called Dhanapālaka, his temples running with pungent sap, and who is difficult to hold, does not eat a morsel when bound; the elephant longs for the elephant grove.

If a man becomes fat and a great eater, if he is sleepy and rolls himself about, that fool, like a hog fed on grains, is born again and again.

This mind of mine went formerly wandering about as it liked, as it listed, as it pleased; but I shall now hold it in thoroughly, as the rider who holds the hook holds in the furious elephant.

Be not thoughtless, watch your thoughts! Draw yourself out of the evil way, like an elephant sunk in mud.

If a man find a prudent companion who walks with him, is wise, and lives soberly, he may walk with him, overcoming all dangers, happy, but considerate.

If a man find no prudent companion who walks with him, is wise, and lives soberly, let him walk alone, like a king who has left his conquered country behind—like an elephant in the forest.

It is better to live alone: there is no companionship with a fool; let a man walk alone, let him commit no sin, with few wishes, like an elephant in the forest.

If the occasion arises, friends are pleasant; enjoyment is pleasant, whatever be the cause; a good work is pleasant in the hour of death; the giving up of all grief is pleasant.

Pleasant in the world is the state of a mother, pleasant the state of a father, pleasant the state of a Samana, pleasant the state of a Brāhmana.

Pleasant is virtue lasting to old age, pleasant is a faith firmly rooted; pleasant is attainment of intelligence, pleasant is avoiding of sins.

CHAPTER XXIV: THIRST

THE THIRST of a thoughtless man grows like a creeper; he runs from life to life, like a monkey seeking fruit in the forest.

Whomsoever this fierce poisonous thirst overcomes, in this world, his sufferings increase like the abounding Bīrana grass.

But from him who overcomes this fierce thirst, difficult to be conquered in this world, sufferings fall off, like water-drops from a lotus leaf.

This salutary word I tell you, "Do ye, as many as are here assembled, dig up the root of thirst, as he who wants the sweet-scented Usīra root must dig up the Bīrana grass, that Māra, the tempter, may not crush you again and again, as the stream crushes the reeds."

As a tree, even though it has been cut down, is firm so long as its root is safe, and grows again, thus, unless the feeders of thirst are destroyed, this pain of life will return again and again.

He whose thirty-six streams are strongly flowing in the channels of pleasure, the waves—his desires which are set on passion—will carry away that misguided man.

The channels run everywhere, the creeper of passion stands sprouting; if you see the creeper springing up, cut its root by means of knowledge.

A creature's pleasures are extravagant and luxurious; given up to pleasure and deriving happiness, men undergo again and again birth and decay.

Beset with lust, men run about like a snared hare; held in fetters and bonds, they undergo pain for a long time, again and again.

Beset with lust, men run about like a snared hare; let therefore the mendicant drive out thirst, by striving after passionlessness for himself.

He who, having got rid of the forest of lust (after having reached Nirvāna), gives himself over to forest-life (to lust), and who, when free from the forest (from lust), runs to the forest (to lust), look at that man! though free, he runs into bondage.

Wise people do not call that a strong fetter which is made of iron, wood, or hemp; passionately strong is the care for precious stones and rings, for sons and a wife.

That fetter wise people call strong which drags down, yields, but is difficult to undo; after having cut this at last, people leave the world, free from cares, and leaving the pleasures of love behind.

Those who are slaves to passions, run down the stream of desires, as a spider runs down the web which he has made himself; when they have cut this, at last, wise people go onwards, free from cares, leaving all pain behind.

Give up what is before, give up what is behind, give up what is between, when thou goest to the other shore of existence; if thy mind is altogether free, thou will not again enter into birth and decay.

If a man is tossed about by doubts, full of strong passions, and yearning only for what is delightful, his thirst will grow more and more, and he will indeed make his fetters strong.

If a man delights in quieting doubts, and, always reflecting, dwells on what is not delightful, he certainly will remove, nay, he will cut the fetter of Māra.

He who has reached the consummation, who does not tremble, who is without thirst and without sin, he has broken all the thorns of life: this will be his last body.

He who is without thirst and without affection, who understands the words and their interpretation, who knows the order of letters (those which are before and which are after), he has received his last body, he is called the great sage, the great man.

"I have conquered all, I know all, in all conditions of life I am free from taint; I have left all, and through the destruction of thirst I am free; having learnt myself, whom should I indicate as my teacher?"

The gift of the law exceeds all gifts; the sweetness of the law exceeds all sweetness; the delight in the law exceeds all delights; the extinction of thirst overcomes all pain.

Riches destroy the foolish, if they look not for the other shore; the foolish by his thirst for riches destroys himself, as if he were destroying others.

The fields are damaged by weeds, mankind is damaged by passion: therefore a gift bestowed on the passionless brings great reward.

The fields are damaged by weeds, mankind is damaged by hatred: therefore a gift bestowed on those who do not hate brings great reward.

The fields are damaged by weeds, mankind is damaged by vanity: therefore a gift bestowed on those who are free from vanity brings great reward.

The fields are damaged by weeds, mankind is damaged by lust: therefore a gift bestowed on those who are free from lust brings great reward.

CHAPTER XXV: THE BHIKSHU[1]

Restraint in the eye is good, good is restraint in the ear, in the nose restraint is good, good is restraint in the tongue.

In the body restraint is good, good is restraint in speech, in thought restraint is good, good is restraint in all things. A Bhikshu, restrained in all things, is freed from all pain.

He who controls his hand, he who controls his feet, he who controls his speech, he who is well controlled, he who delights inwardly, who is collected, who is solitary and content, him they call Bhikshu.

The Bhikshu who controls his mouth, who speaks wisely and calmly, who teaches the meaning and the law, his word is sweet.

He who dwells in the law, delights in the law, meditates on the law, recollects the law: that Bhikshu will never fall away from the true law.

Let him not despise what he has received, nor ever envy others: a mendicant who envies others does not obtain peace of mind.

A Bhikshu who, though he receives little, does not despise what he has received, even the gods will praise him, if his life is pure, and if he is not slothful.

He who never identifies himself with name and form, and does not grieve over what is no more, he indeed is called a Bhikshu.

The Bhikshu who behaves with kindness, who is happy in the doctrine of Buddha, will reach the quiet place (Nirvāna), happiness arising from the cessation of natural inclinations.

O Bhikshu, empty this boat! if emptied, it will go quickly; having cut off passion and hatred, thou wilt go to Nirvāna.

Cut off the five fetters, leave the five, rise above the five. A Bhikshu, who has escaped from the five fetters, he is called Oghatinna—"saved from the flood."

Meditate, O Bhikshu, and be not heedless! Do not direct thy thought to what gives pleasure, that thou mayest not for thy heedlessness have to swallow the iron ball in hell, and that thou mayest not cry out when burning, "This is pain."

Without knowledge there is no meditation, without meditation there is no knowledge: he who has knowledge and meditation is near unto Nirvāna.

A Bhikshu who has entered his empty house, and whose mind is tran-

[1] Monk, mendicant, a religious devotee.

quil, feels a more than human delight when he sees the law clearly.

As soon as he has considered the origin and destruction of the elements of the body, he finds happiness and joy which belong to those who know the immortal (Nirvāna).

And this is the beginning here for a wise Bhikshu: watchfulness over the senses, contentedness, restraint under the law; keep noble friends whose life is pure, and who are not slothful.

Let him live in charity, let him be perfect in his duties; then in the fulness of delight he will make an end of suffering.

As the Vassikā plant shed its withered flowers, men should shed passion and hatred, O ye Bhikshus!

The Bhikshu whose body and tongue and mind are quieted, who is collected, and has rejected the baits of the world, he is called quiet.

Rouse thyself by thyself, examine thyself by thyself, thus self-protected and attentive wilt thou live happily, O Bhikshu!

For self is the lord of self, self is the refuge of self; therefore curb thyself as the merchant curbs a noble horse.

The Bhikshu, full of delight, who is happy in the doctrine of Buddha will reach the quiet place (Nirvāna), happiness consisting in the cessation of natural inclinations.

He who, even as a young Bhikshu, applies himself to the doctrine of Buddha, brightens up this world, like the moon when free from clouds.

CHAPTER XXVI: THE BRĀHMANA[1]

STOP THE STREAM VALIANTLY, drive away the desires, O Brāhmana! When you have understood the destruction of all that was made, you will understand that which was not made.

If the Brāhmana has reached the other shore in both laws, in restraint and contemplation, all bonds vanish from him who has obtained knowledge.

He for whom there is neither the hither nor the further shore, nor both, him, the fearless and unshackled, I call indeed a Brāhmana.

He who is thoughtful, blameless, settled, dutiful, without passions, and who has attained the highest end, him I call indeed a Brāhmana.

The sun is bright by day, the moon shines by night, the warrior is bright in his armor, the Brāhmana is bright in his meditation; but Buddha, the Awakened, is bright with splendor day and night.

[1] Usually called "Brahmin" in English.

Because a man is rid of evil, therefore he is called Brāhmana; because he walks quietly, therefore he is called Samana; because he has sent away his own impurities, therefore he is called Pravragita (Pabbagita,[1] a pilgrim).

No one should attack a Brāhmana, but no Brāhmana, if attacked, should let himself fly at his aggressor! Woe to him who strikes a Brāhmana, more woe to him who flies at his aggressor!

It advantages a Brāhmana not a little if he holds his mind back from the pleasures of life; the more all wish to injure has vanished, the more all pain will cease.

Him I call indeed a Brāhmana who does not offend by body, word, or thought, and is controlled on these three points.

He from whom he may learn the law, as taught by the Well-awakened (Buddha), him let him worship assiduously, as the Brāhmana worships the sacrificial fire.

A man does not become a Brāhmana by his plaited hair, by his family, or by birth; in whom there is truth and righteousness, he is blessed, he is a Brāhmana.

What is the use of plaited hair, O fool! what of the raiment of goatskins? Within thee there is ravening, but the outside thou makest clean.

The man who wears dirty raiments, who is emaciated and covered with veins, who meditates alone in the forest, him I call indeed a Brāhmana.

I do not call a man a Brāhmana because of his origin or of his mother. He is indeed arrogant, and he is wealthy: but the poor, who is free from all attachments, him I call indeed a Brāhmana.

Him I call indeed a Brāhmana who, after cutting all fetters, never trembles, is free from bonds and unshackled.

Him I call indeed a Brāhmana who, after cutting the strap and the thong, the rope with all that pertains to it, has destroyed all obstacles, and is awakened.

Him I call indeed a Brāhmana who, though he has committed no offence, endures reproach, stripes, and bonds: who has endurance for his force, and strength for his army.

Him I call indeed a Brāhmana who is free from anger, dutiful, virtuous, without appetites, who is subdued, and has received his last body.

Him I call indeed a Brāhmana who, does not cling to sensual pleasures, like water on a lotus leaf, like a mustard seed on the point of a needle.

[1] Pali for Sanskrit *Pravragita.*

Him I call indeed a Brāhmana who, even here, knows the end of his own suffering, has put down his burden, and is unshackled.

Him I call indeed a Brāhmana whose knowledge is deep, who possesses wisdom, who knows the right way and the wrong, and has attained the highest end.

Him I call indeed a Brāhmana who keeps aloof both from laymen and from mendicants, who frequents no houses, and has but few desires.

Him I call indeed a Brāhmana who without hurting any creatures, whether feeble or strong, does not kill nor cause slaughter.

Him I call indeed a Brāhmana who is tolerant with the intolerant, mild with the violent, and free from greed among the greedy.

Him I call indeed a Brāhmana from whom anger and hatred, pride and hypocrisy have dropped like a mustard seed from the point of a needle.

Him I call indeed a Brāhmana who utters true speech, instructive and free from harshness, so that he offend no one.

Him I call indeed a Brāhmana who takes nothing in the world that is not given him, be it long or short, small or large, good or bad.

Him I call indeed a Brāhmana who fosters no desires for this world or for the next, has no inclinations, and is unshackled.

Him I call indeed a Brāhmana who has no interests, and when he has understood the truth, does not say How, how? and who has reached the depth of the Immortal.

Him I call indeed a Brāhmana who in this world has risen above both ties, good and evil, who is free from grief, from sin, and from impurity.

Him I call indeed a Brāhmana who is bright like the moon, pure, serene, undisturbed, and in whom all gayety is extinct.

Him I call indeed a Brāhmana who has traversed this miry road, the impassable world, difficult to pass, and its vanity, who has gone through, and reached the other shore, is thoughtful, steadfast, free from doubts, free from attachment, and content.

Him I call indeed a Brāhmana who in this world, having abandoned all desires, travels about without a home, and in whom all concupiscence is extinct.

Him I call indeed a Brāhmana who, having abandoned all longings, travels about without a home, and in whom all covetousness is extinct.

Him I call indeed a Brāhmana who, after leaving all bondage to men, his risen above all bondage to the gods, and is free from all and every bondage.

Him I call indeed a Brāhmana who has left what gives pleasure and what gives pain, who is cold, and free from all germs of renewed life: the hero who has conquered all the worlds.

Him I call indeed a Brāhmana who knows the destruction and the return of beings everywhere, who is free from bondage, welfaring (Sugata), and awakened (Buddha).

Him I call indeed a Brāhmana whose path the gods do not know, nor spirits (Gandharvas), nor men, whose passions are extinct, and who is an Arhat.

Him I call indeed a Brāhmana who calls nothing his own, whether it be before, behind, or between; who is poor, and free from the love of the world.

Him I call indeed a Brāhmana, the manly, the noble, the hero, the great sage, the conqueror, the indifferent, the accomplished, the awakened.

Him I call indeed a Brāhmana who knows his former abodes, who sees heaven and hell, has reached the end of births, is perfect in knowledge, a sage, and whose perfections are all perfect.

Three Sermons by Buddha

INTRODUCTION

SOME CHRISTIANS may feel humiliated to find that the Buddhist teachings of love and mercy and kindness to fellowmen and animals, and particularly of not requiting evil with evil, stand on the same ethical height with the best of the Christian teachings. It may be a shock to learn that there is real truth even in revealed truth, and that that truth can be arrived at by independent human minds, or that there is something in the nature of human relationships and of this universe which calls for righteousness and mercy, apart from any special revelation. Yet it is undeniable that the hold of Buddhism upon its millions of believers rests not upon the desire to enter Nirvana, but upon the preaching of such common truths as gentleness and kindness, and that the charm of Buddha's personality is exactly that charm of gentleness and kindness.

To this day I cannot find out the differences in teachings of the Mormon Church from the non-Mormon sects except the claim of a special Revelation to its founder. So many different priestcrafts are trying to sell their particular brands of religion to the populace that only the claim to some "special patented process" can help to make the sale convincing. And so we come upon the curious phenomenon in religion that narrow-minded sectarianism is always a prominent feature of any religion of universal love. There is never a devout saint or believer in universal love who is not a "heretic" to some other believer, whether Christian or Buddhist. Tolstoi says somewhere that those who believe their religion is greater than God will believe that their sect is greater than their religion, and end up by believing that they are greater than their sect.

Consonant with my bias for Chinese sources, I have selected here the famous "Sermon at Benares" from *The Fo-Sho-Hing-Tsan-King,* a Life of Buddha by Asvaghosha, translated from the Sanskrit into Chinese by Dharmaraksha in A.D. 420 and from Chinese into English by Samuel Beal. This emphasizes the Middle Way, between extreme indulgence and extreme asceticism, with some sane comment on the wholesome mind in a wholesome body. It also contains a summary in bare outline of the basic Buddhist teachings concerning the "eightfold path," the existence of suffering, the cause of suffering, and the escape from suffering. The "Sermon on Abuse," which teaches requiting not evil with evil,[1] is taken from the *Sutra of Forty-two Sections,* probably the earliest Buddhist scripture to be translated into Chinese, soon after A.D. 67. Both are reproduced as edited or revised by Dr. Paul Carus. Finally I include the "Fire Sermon," from the *Mahā-Vagga* (translated by Henry Clarke Warren), referred to in T. S. Eliot's *Wasteland,* because it breathes something of the direct, impetuous fire of a prophet. But, as we shall see in the "Fire Sermon," there is one thing in Buddhism which can never convince the truly modern man, and that is the doctrine of the aversion for the body, taught in this Sermon, as well as elsewhere. So long as any religion teaches other-worldliness, I do not care whether it teaches a Heaven of Pearly Gates or a Nirvana. The body is not bad, that is all there is to it. The body is transient, but it is not bad. It goes through old age and death, but it is not bad. Our passions must be brought under control, but they are not bad in themselves. Our sense impressions are mere illusions, but they are not bad. This is the feeling of the modern man about the truth of the body.

[1] See also the parable of the Patient Elephant, *Gospel of Buddha,* p. 215, and the *Dhammapada.*

Three Sermons by Buddha

THE SERMON AT BENARES

On seeing their old teacher approach, the five bhikkhus agreed among themselves not to salute him, nor to address him as a master, but by his name only. "For," so they said, "he has broken his vow and has abandoned holiness. He is no bhikkhu but Gotama, and Gotama has become a man who lives in abundance and indulges in the pleasures of worldliness."

But when the Blessed One approached in a dignified manner, they involuntarily rose from their seats and greeted him in spite of their resolution. Still they called him by his name and addressed him as "friend Gotama."

When they had thus received the Blessed One, he said: "Do not call the Tathāgata by his name nor address him as 'friend,' for he is the Buddha, the Holy One. The Buddha looks with a kind heart equally on all living beings, and they therefore call him 'Father.' To disrespect a father is wrong; to despise him, is wicked.

"The Tathāgata," the Buddha continued, "does not seek salvation in austerities, but neither does he for that reason indulge in worldly pleasures, nor live in abundance. The Tathāgata has found the middle path.

"There are two extremes, O bhikkhus, which the man who has given up the world ought not to follow—the habitual practice, on the one hand, of self-indulgence which is unworthy, vain and fit only for the worldly-minded—and the habitual practice, on the other hand, of self-mortification, which is painful, useless and unprofitable.

"Neither abstinence from fish or flesh, nor going naked, nor shaving the head, nor wearing matted hair, nor dressing in a rough garment, nor covering oneself with dirt, nor sacrificing to Agni, will cleanse a man who is not free from delusions.

"Reading the Vedas, making offerings to priests, or sacrifices to the gods, self-mortification by heat or cold, and many such penances performed for the sake of immortality, these do not cleanse the man who is not free from delusions.

"Anger, drunkenness, obstinacy, bigotry, deception, envy, self-praise, disparaging others, superciliousness and evil intentions constitute uncleanness; not verily the eating of flesh.

"A middle path, O bhikkhus, avoiding the two extremes, has been discovered by the Tathāgata—a path which opens the eyes, and bestows understanding, which leads to peace of mind, to the higher wisdom, to full enlightenment, to Nirvāna!

"What is that middle path, O bhikkhus, avoiding these two extremes, discovered by the Tathāgata—that path which opens the eyes, and bestows understanding, which leads to peace of mind, to the higher wisdom, to full enlightenment, to Nirvāna?

"Let me teach you, O bhikkhus, the middle path, which keeps aloof from both extremes. By suffering, the emaciated devotee produces confusion and sickly thoughts in his mind. Mortification is not conducive even to worldly knowledge; how much less to a triumph over the senses!

"He who fills his lamp with water will not dispel the darkness, and he who tries to light a fire with rotten wood will fail. And how can any one be free from self by leading a wretched life, if he does not succeed in quenching the fires of lust, if he still hankers after either worldly or heavenly pleasures. But he in whom self has become extinct is free from lust; he will desire neither worldly nor heavenly pleasures, and the satisfaction of his natural wants will not defile him. However, let him be moderate, let him eat and drink according to the needs of the body.

"Sensuality is enervating; the self-indulgent man is a slave to his passions, and pleasure-seeking is degrading and vulgar.

"But to satisfy the necessities of life is not evil. To keep the body in good health is a duty, for otherwise we shall not be able to trim the lamp of wisdom, and keep our mind strong and clear. Water surrounds the lotus-flower, but does not wet its petals.

"This is the middle path, O bhikkhus, that keeps aloof from both extremes."

And the Blessed One spoke kindly to his disciples, pitying them for their errors, and pointing out the uselessness of their endeavors, and the ice of ill-will that chilled their hearts melted away under the gentle warmth of the Master's persuasion.

Now the Blessed One set the wheel of the most excellent law rolling, and he began to preach to the five bhikkhus, opening to them the gate of immortality, and showing them the bliss of Nirvāna.

The Buddha said:

"The spokes of the wheel are the rules of pure conduct: justice is the uniformity of their length; wisdom is the tire; modesty and thoughtfulness are the hub in which the immovable axle of truth is fixed.

"He who recognizes the existence of suffering, its cause, its remedy, and its cessation has fathomed the four noble truths. He will walk in the right path.

"Right views will be the torch to light his way. Right aspirations will be his guide. Right speech will be his dwelling-place on the road. His gait will be straight, for it is right behavior. His refreshments will be the right way of earning his livelihood. Right efforts will be his steps: right thoughts his breath; and right contemplation will give him the peace that follows in his footprints.

"Now, this, O bhikkhus, is the noble truth concerning suffering:

"Birth is attended with pain, decay is painful, disease is painful, death is painful. Union with the unpleasant is painful, painful is separation from the pleasant; and any craving that is unsatisfied, that too is painful. In brief, bodily conditions which spring from attachment are painful.

"This, then, O bhikkhus, is the noble truth concerning suffering.

"Now this, O bhikkhus, is the noble truth concerning the origin of suffering:

"Verily, it is that craving which causes the renewal of existence, accompanied by sensual delight, seeking satisfaction now here, now there, the craving for the gratification of the passions, the craving for a future life, and the craving for happiness in this life.

"This, then, O bhikkhus, is the noble truth concerning the origin of suffering.

"Now this, O bhikkhus, is the noble truth concerning the destruction of suffering:

"Verily, it is the destruction, in which no passion remains, of this very thirst; it is the laying aside of, the being free from, the dwelling no longer upon this thirst.

"This, then, O bhikkhus, is the noble truth concerning the destruction of suffering.

"Now this, O bhikkhus, is the noble truth concerning the way which leads to the destruction of sorrow. Verily! it is this noble eightfold path; that is to say:

"Right views; right aspirations; right speech; right behavior; right livelihood; right effort; right thoughts; and right contemplation.

"This, then, O bhikkhus, is the noble truth concerning the destruction of sorrow.

"By the practice of lovingkindness I have attained liberation of heart, and thus I am assured that I shall never return in renewed births. I have even now attained Nirvāna."

And when the Blessed One had thus set the royal chariot wheel of truth rolling onward, a rapture thrilled through all the universes.

The devas left their heavenly abodes to listen to the sweetness of the truth; the saints that had parted from life crowded around the great teacher to receive the glad tidings; even the animals of the earth felt the bliss that rested upon the words of the Tathāgata: and all the creatures of the host of sentient beings, gods, men, and beasts, hearing the message of deliverance, received and understood it in their own language.

And when the doctrine was propounded, the venerable Kondanna, the oldest one among the five bhikkhus, discerned the truth with his mental eye, and he said: "Truly, O Buddha, our Lord, thou hast found the truth!" Then the other bhikkhus too, joined him and exclaimed: "Truly, thou art the Buddha, thou hast found the truth."

And the devas and saints and all the good spirits of the departed generations that had listened to the sermon of the Tathāgata, joyfully received the doctrine and shouted: "Truly, the Blessed One has founded the kingdom of righteousness. The Blessed One has moved the earth; he has set the wheel of Truth rolling, which by no one in the universe, be he god or man, can ever be turned back. The kingdom of Truth will be preached upon earth; it will spread; and righteousness, good-will, and peace will reign among mankind."

THE SERMON ON ABUSE

AND THE BLESSED ONE observed the ways of society and noticed how much misery came from malignity and foolish offences done only to gratify vanity and self-seeking pride.

And the Buddha said: "If a man foolishly does me wrong, I will return to him the protection of my ungrudging love; the more evil comes from him, the more good shall go from me; the fragrance of goodness always comes to me, and the harmful air of evil goes to him."

A foolish man learning that the Buddha observed the principle of great love which commends the return of good for evil, came and abused him. The Buddha was silent, pitying his folly.

When the man had finished his abuse, the Buddha asked him, saying: "Son, if a man declined to accept a present made to him, to whom would it belong?" And he answered: "In that case it would belong to the man who offered it."

"My son," said the Buddha, "thou hast railed at me, but I decline to accept thy abuse, and request thee to keep it thyself. Will it not be a source of misery to thee? As the echo belongs to the sound, and the shadow to the substance, so misery will overtake the evil-doer without fail."

The abuser made no reply, and Buddha continued:

"A wicked man who reproaches a virtuous one is like one who looks up and spits at heaven; the spittle soils not the heaven, but comes back and defiles his own person.

"The slanderer is like one who flings dust at another when the wind is contrary; the dust does but return on him who threw it. The virtuous man cannot be hurt and the misery that the other would inflict comes back on himself."

The abuser went away ashamed, but he came again and took refuge in the Buddha, the Dharma, and the Sangha.[1]

THE FIRE SERMON

Then the Blessed One, having dwelt in Uruvelā as long as he wished, proceeded on his wanderings in the direction of Gayā Head, accompanied by a great congregation of priests, a thousand in number, who had all of them aforetime been monks with matted hair. And there in Gayā Head, the Blessed One dwelt, together with the thousand priests.

And there the Blessed One addressed the priests:

"All things, O priests, are on fire. And what, O priests, are all these things which are on fire?

[1] *Dharma,* the Law of the Path of Buddhist teachings; *Sangha,* the Buddhist Church. These, with Buddha, constitute the "three refuges."

"The eye, O priests, is on fire; forms are on fire; eye-consciousness is on fire; impressions received by the eye are on fire; and whatever sensation, pleasant or unpleasant, or indifferent, originates in dependence on impressions received by the fire, that also is on fire.

"And with what are these on fire?

"With the fire of passion, say I, with the fire of hatred, with the fire of infatuation; with birth, old age, death, sorrow, lamentation, misery, grief, and despair are they on fire.

"The ear is on fire; sounds are on fire; . . . the nose is on fire; odors are on fire; . . . the tongue is on fire; tastes are on fire; . . . the body is on fire; things tangible are on fire; . . . the mind is on fire; ideas are on fire; . . . mind-consciousness is on fire; impressions received by the mind are on fire; and whatever sensation, pleasant or unpleasant, or indifferent, originates in dependence on impressions received by the mind, that also is on fire.

"And with what are these on fire?

"With the fire of passion, say I, with the fire of hatred, with the fire of infatuation; with birth, old age, death, sorrow, lamentation, misery, grief, and despair are they on fire.

"Perceiving this, O priests, the learned and noble disciple conceives an aversion for the eye, conceives an aversion for forms, conceives an aversion for eye-consciousness, conceives an aversion for impressions received by the eye; and whatever sensation, pleasant or unpleasant, or indifferent, originates in dependence on impressions received by the eye, for that also he conceives an aversion. Conceives an aversion for the ear, conceives an aversion for sounds . . . conceives an aversion for the nose, conceives an aversion for odors . . . conceives an aversion for the tongue, conceives an aversion for tastes . . . conceives an aversion for the body, conceives an aversion for things tangible . . . conceives an aversion for the mind, conceives an aversion for ideas, conceives an aversion for mind-consciousness, conceives an aversion for the impressions received by the mind; and whatever sensation, pleasant or unpleasant, or indifferent, originates in dependence on impressions received by the mind, for this also he conceives an aversion. And in conceiving this aversion, he becomes divested of passion, and by the absence of passion he becomes free, and when he is free, he becomes aware that he is free; and he knows that rebirth is exhausted, that he has lived the holy life, that he has done what behooved him to do, and that he is no more for this world."

Some Buddhist Parables and Legends

INTRODUCTION

THAT AESOP'S FABLES originated from India,[1] is proved by the whole character of Hindu literature, in which the instinct for the fable abounds. The *Panchatantra,* the *Hitopadesa,* the Buddhist *Jātaka* (fables and stories of Buddhist previous lives, technically called "birth-stories," in which Buddha was born as a snake, or an elephant, etc.), and Buddhaghosha's Commentary on the *Dhammapada*[2] all attest to this truth. In Buddhaghosha's Commentary, a story, or sometimes several stories, are told to illustrate each of the 423 ethical epigrams of the *Dhammapada,* with which the story always ends in Aesop fashion.

In the following selections may be found one of the best wedding sermons and one of the best funeral sermons I have ever come across. The story of *Kisā Gotamī,* which tells a great truth in a simple story, is one of the best in the whole Buddhist literature, and its introduction transports us to the magic world of the *Arabian Nights.* Its subject is none other than Death.

The *Marriage Feast in Jambūnada* illustrates many striking parallels between the Buddhist and Christian Gospels, as also does the following story of *Following the Master over the Stream.* The first is taken from the Chinese Life of Buddha, *Fo Pen Hsing Chi Ching,* tr. by Samuel Beal, while the second is taken from the Chinese Dhammapada, *Texts*

[1] See Introduction to *Panchatantra.*

[2] Translated by E. W. Burlingame, "*Buddhist Legends,*" Harvard Oriental Series, Vols. 28, 29 & 30. Also *Buddhaghosha's Parables,* translated by T. Rogers, London, 1870.

from the Buddhist Canon, tr. by Beal. The above three stories are reproduced as arranged by Dr. Paul Carus in *The Gospel of Buddha* (Open Court). For another striking parallel, see the story of the lost son who returned to his father's house as a common laborer, in *Gospel of Buddha,* by Paul Carus, p. 182.

The *Greedy Monk* from the *Dhammapada* Commentary illustrates the same technique of enclosing a tale within a tale, characteristic of the *Panchatantra.* The story of *Ocean-of-Beauty,* from the same collection, contains some remarks about womanhood which shows the New York lady in an apartment flat has nothing to teach the Hindu women in methods of attracting a man. The translation is by Eugene Watson Burlingame.

Some Buddhist Parables and Legends

KISĀ GOTAMĪ

THERE WAS A RICH MAN who found his gold suddenly transformed into ashes; and he took to his bed and refused all food. A friend, hearing of his sickness, visited the rich man and learned the cause of his grief. And the friend said: "Thou didst not make good use of thy wealth. When thou didst hoard it up it was not better than ashes. Now heed my advice. Spread mats in the bazaar; pile up these ashes, and pretend to trade with them."

The rich man did as his friend had told him, and when his neighbors asked him, "Why sellest thou ashes?" he said: "I offer my goods for sale."

After some time a young girl, named Kisā Gotamī, an orphan and very poor, passed by, and seeing the rich man in the bazaar, said: "My lord, why pilest thou thus up gold and silver for sale."

And the rich man said: "Wilt thou please hand me that gold and silver?" And Kisā Gotamī took up a handful of ashes, and lo! they changed back into gold.

Considering that Kisā Gotamī had the mental eye of spiritual knowledge and saw the real worth of things, the rich man gave her in marriage to his son, and he said: "With many, gold is no better than ashes, but with Kisā Gotamī ashes become pure gold."

And Kisā Gotamī had an only son, and he died. In her grief she carried the dead child to all her neighbors, asking them for medicine, and the people said: "She has lost her senses. The boy is dead."

At length Kisā Gotamī met a man who replied to her request: "I canno
give thee medicine for thy child, but I know a physician who can."

And the girl said: "Pray tell me, sir; who is it?" And the man replied
"Go to Sakyamuni, the Buddha."

Kisā Gotamī repaired to the Buddha and cried: "Lord and Master, give
me the medicine that will cure my boy."

The Buddha answered: "I want a handful of mustard-seed." And wher
the girl in her joy promised to procure it, the Buddha added: "The mus
tard-seed must be taken from a house where no one has lost a child, hus
band, parent, or friend."

Poor Kisā Gotamī now went from house to house, and the peopl
pitied her and said: "Here is mustard-seed; take it!" But when she asked
"Did a son or daughter, a father or mother, die in your family?" they
answered her: "Alas! the living are few, but the dead are many. Do no
remind us of our deepest grief." And there was no house but some be
loved one had died in it.

Kisā Gotamī became weary and hopeless, and sat down at the way
side, watching the lights of the city, as they flickered up and were ex
tinguished again. At last the darkness of the night reigned everywhere
And she considered the fate of men, that their lives flicker up and are ex
tinguished. And she thought to herself: "How selfish am I in my grief
Death is common to all; yet in this valley of desolation there is a path
that leads him to immortality who has surrendered all selfishness."

Putting away the selfishness of her affection for her child, Kisā Gotamī
had the dead body buried in the forest. Returning to the Buddha, she
took refuge in him and found comfort in the Dharma, which is a balm
that will soothe all the pains of our troubled hearts.

The Buddha said:

"The life of mortals in this world is troubled and brief and combined
with pain. For there is not any means by which those that have been
born can avoid dying; after reaching old age there is death; of such a
nature are living beings.

"As ripe fruits are early in danger of falling, so mortals when born are
always in danger of death.

"As all earthen vessels made by the potter end in being broken, so is
the life of mortals.

"Both young and adult, both those who are fools and those who are
wise, all fall into the power of death; all are subject to death.

"Of those who, overcome by death, depart from life, a father cannot save his son, nor kinsmen their relations.

"Mark! while relatives are looking on and lamenting deeply, one by one mortals are carried off, like an ox that is led to the slaughter.

"So the world is afflicted with death and decay, therefore the wise do not grieve, knowing the terms of the world.

"In whatever manner people think a thing will come to pass, it is often different when it happens, and great is the disappointment; see, such are the terms of the world.

"Not from weeping nor from grieving will any one obtain peace of mind; on the contrary, his pain will be the greater and his body will suffer. He will make himself sick and pale, yet the dead are not saved by his lamentation.

"People pass away, and their fate after death will be according to their deeds.

"If a man live a hundred years, or even more, he will at last be separated from the company of his relatives, and leave the life of this world.

"He who seeks peace should draw out the arrow of lamentation, and complaint, and grief.

"He who has drawn out the arrow and has become composed will obtain peace of mind; he who has overcome all sorrow will become free from sorrow, and be blessed."

THE MARRIAGE-FEAST IN JAMBŪNADA

There was a man in Jambūnada who was to be married the next day, and he thought, "Would that the Buddha, the Blessed One, might be present at the wedding."

And the Blessed One passed by his house and met him, and when he read the silent wish in the heart of the bridegroom, he consented to enter.

When the Holy One appeared with the retinue of his many bhikkhus, the host whose means were limited received them as best he could, saying: "Eat, my Lord, and all thy congregation, according to your desire."

While the holy men ate, the meats and drinks remained undiminished, and the host thought to himself: "How wondrous is this! I should have had plenty for all my relatives and friends. Would that I had invited them all."

When this thought was in the host's mind, all his relatives and friends entered the house; and although the hall in the house was small there was room in it for all of them. They sat down at the table and ate, and there was more than enough for all of them.

The Blessed One was pleased to see so many guests full of good cheer and he quickened them and gladdened them with words of truth, proclaiming the bliss of righteousness:

"The greatest happiness which a mortal man can imagine is the bond of marriage that ties together two loving hearts. But there is a greater happiness still: it is the embrace of truth. Death will separate husband and wife, but death will never affect him who has espoused the truth.

"Therefore be married unto the truth and live with the truth in holy wedlock. The husband who loves his wife and desires for a union that shall be everlasting must be faithful to her so as to be like truth itself, and she will rely upon him and revere him and minister unto him. And the wife who loves her husband and desires a union that shall be everlasting must be faithful to him so as to be like truth itself; and he will place his trust in her, he will provide for her. Verily, I say unto you, their children will become like unto their parents and will bear witness to their happiness.

"Let no man be single, let every one be wedded in holy love to the truth. And when Māra, the destroyer, comes to separate the visible forms of your being, you will continue to live in the truth, and you will partake of the life everlasting, for the truth is immortal."

There was no one among the guests but was strengthened in his spiritual life, and recognized the sweetness of a life of righteousness; and they took refuge in the Buddha, the Dharma, and the Sangha.

FOLLOWING THE MASTER OVER THE STREAM

South of Sāvatthi is a great river, on the banks of which lay a hamlet of five hundred houses. Thinking of the salvation of the people, the World-honored One resolved to go to the village and preach the doctrine. Having come to the riverside he sat down beneath a tree, and the villagers seeing the glory of his appearance approached him with reverence; but when he began to preach, they believed him not.

When the world-honored Buddha had left Sāvatthi, Sāriputta felt a desire to see the Lord and to hear him preach. Coming to the river where the water was deep and the current strong, he said to himself: "This stream shall not prevent me. I shall go and see the Blessed One," and he stepped upon the water which was as firm under his feet as a slab of granite.

When he arrived at a place in the middle of the stream where the waves were high, Sāriputta's heart gave way, and he began to sink. But rousing his faith and renewing his mental effort, he proceeded as before and reached the other bank.

The people of the village were astonished to see Sāriputta, and they asked how he could cross the stream where there was neither a bridge nor a ferry.

And Sāriputta replied: "I lived in ignorance until I heard the voice of the Buddha. As I was anxious to hear the doctrine of salvation, I crossed the river and I walked over its troubled waters because I had faith. Faith, nothing else, enabled me to do so, and now I am here in the bliss of the Master's presency."

The World-honored One added: "Sāriputta, thou hast spoken well. Faith like thine alone can save the world from the yawning gulf of migration and enable men to walk dryshod to the other shore."

And the Blessed One urged to the villagers the necessity of ever advancing in the conquest of sorrow and of casting off all shackles so as to cross the river of worldliness and attain deliverance from death.

Hearing the words of the Tathāgata, the villagers were filled with joy and believing in the doctrines of the Blessed One embraced the five rules and took refuge in his name.

THE GREEDY MONK

THE STORY GOES that the Elder, who was skilled to teach the Law, after listening to a discourse on the subject of being satisfied with but little, accepted a large number of robes with which several monks who had taken upon themselves the Pure Practices honored him, and besides took all the utensils which they had left and carried them off with him. As the season of the rains was near at hand, he went off into the country. He stopped at a certain monastery to preach the Law, and the novices and probationers liked the way he talked so well that they said to him, "Spend the rainy season here, Reverend Sir." "What allowance is made to a monk who spends the season of rains here?" asked the Elder. "A single cloak," was the reply. The Elder left his shoes there and went to the next monastery. When he reached the second monastery, he asked the same question, "What allowance is made here?" "Two cloaks," was the reply.

There he left his walking stick. Then he went to the third monastery and asked the same question, "What is the allowance made here?" "Three cloaks," was the reply. There he left his water-pot.

Then he went to the fourth monastery and asked the same question, "What is the allowance made here?" "Four cloaks," was the reply. "Very good," said the Elder, "I will take my residence here"; and there he went into residence. And he preached the Law to the laymen and the monks who resided there so well that they honored him with a great number of garments and robes. When he had completed residence, he sent a message to all the other monasteries, saying, "I left my requisites behind me, and must have whatever is required for residence; pray send them to me." When he gathered all of his possessions together, he put them in a cart and continued his journey.

Now at a certain monastery two young monks who had received two cloaks and a single blanket found it impossible to make a division satisfactory to both of them, and therefore settled themselves beside the road and began to quarrel, saying, "You may have two cloaks, but the blanket belongs to me." When they saw the Elder approaching, they said, "Reverend Sir, you make a fair decision and give us what you think fit." "Will you abide by my decision?" "Yes indeed; we will abide by your decision." "Very good, then." So the Elder divided the two cloaks between the two monks; then he said to them, "This blanket should be worn only by us who preach the law"; and when he had thus said, he shouldered the costly blanket and went off with it.

Disgusted and disappointed, the two young monks went to the Teacher and reported the whole occurrence to him. Said the Teacher, "This is not the first time he has taken what belongs to you and left you disgusted and disappointed; he did the same thing also in a previous state of existence." And he related the following:

The Otters and the Jackal

Once upon a time, long, long ago, two otters named Anutīracārī and Gambhīracārī, caught a big redfish and fell to quarreling over it, saying, "The head belongs to me; you may have the tail." Unable to effect a division satisfactory to both of them, catching sight of a certain jackal, they appealed to him for a decision, saying, "Uncle, you make such a division of this fish as you think proper and render an award." Said the jackal, "I have been appointed judge by the king, and am obliged to sit in court for hours at a time; I came out here merely to stretch my legs; I have no time now for such business." "Uncle, don't say that, make a division and render an award." "Will you abide by my decision?" "Yes indeed, uncle, we will abide by your decision." "Very good, then," said the jackal. The jackal cut the head and laid that aside, then cut off the tail and laid that aside. When he had done so, he said to them, "Friends, that one of you who runs along the bank (Anutīracārī) shall have the tail, and that one of you who runs in deep water (Gambhīracārī) shall have the head; as for this middle portion, however, this shall be mine, inasmuch as I am justice." And to make them see the matter in better light, he pronounced the following Stanza,

Anutīracārī shall have the tail, and Gambhīracārī shall have the head;
But as for this middle portion, it shall belong to the justice.

Having pronounced this Stanza, the jackal picked up the middle portion of the fish and went off with it. As for the otters, they were filled with disgust and disappointment, and stood and eyed the jackal as he went away.

When the Teacher finished this Story of the Past, he said, "And thus it was that in times long past this Elder filled you with disgust and disappointment." Then the Teacher consoled these monks and rebuked Upananda, saying, "Monks, a man who admonishes others should first direct himself in the way he should go." And when he had thus spoken, he pronounced the following Stanza,

A man should first direct himself in the way he should go.
Only then should he instruct others; a wise man will do so and not grow weary.[1]

A COURTESAN TEMPTS THE MONK OCEAN-OF-BEAUTY

At Sāvatthi, we are told, in a great household possessing forty crores[2] of treasure, was reborn a certain youth of station named Ocean-of-Beauty, Sundarasamudda Kumāra. One day after daybreak, seeing a great company of people carrying perfumes and garlands in their hands, going to Jetavana to hear the Law, he asked, "Where are you going?" "To the teacher to hear the Law," they replied. "I will go too," said he, and accompanying them, sat down on the outer circle of the congregation. The

[1] This verse is from the *Dhammapada,* of which the story is told as a "commentary."
[2] Ten millions.

Teacher, knowing the thoughts of his heart, preached the Law in orderly sequence. Thought Ocean-of-Beauty, "It is impossible to live the life of a householder and at the same time live the Life of Holiness, whereof a polished shell is the image and likeness."

The Teacher's discourse made him eager to retire from the world. Therefore, as the congregation departed, he asked the Teacher to admit him to the order. Said the Teacher, "The Tathāgatas admit no one to the Order who has not obtained permission of his mother and father." So Ocean-of-Beauty went home, and so like youth Ratthapāla and others, by dint of great effort, prevailed upon his mother and father to give him permission to enter the Order. Having obtained their permission, he retired from the world and was admitted to the Order by the Teacher. Subsequently he made his full profession as member of the Order. Then he thought to himself, "What is the use of my living here?" So departing from Jetavana, he went to Rājagaha and spent his time going his rounds for alms.

Now one day there was a festival at Sāvatthi, and on that day Ocean-of-Beauty's mother and father saw their son's playfellows diverting themselves amid great splendor and magnificence. Thereupon they began to weep and lament, saying, "This is past our son's getting now." At that moment a certain courtesan came to the house, and seeing his mother as she sat weeping, asked her, "Mother, why do you weep?" "I keep thinking of my son; that is why I weep." "But, Mother, where is he?" "Among the monks, retired from the world." "Would it not be proper to make him return to the world?" "Yes, indeed; but he doesn't wish to do that. He has left Sāvatthi and gone to Rājagaha." "Suppose I were to succeed in making him return to the world; what would you do for me?" "We would make you mistress of all the wealth of this household." "Very well, give me my expenses." And taking the amount of her expenses, she surrounded herself with a large retinue and went to Rājagaha.

Taking note of the street in which the Elder was accustomed to make his rounds for alms, she obtained a house in this street and took her abode therein. And early in the morning she prepared choice food, and when the Elder entered the street to make his round for alms, she gave him alms. After a few days had passed, she said to him, "Reverend Sir, sit down right here and eat your meal." So saying, she offered to take the bowl, and the Elder yielded his bowl willingly. Then she served him with choice food, and having so done, said to him, "Reverend Sir, right here is the most delightful spot to which you could come on your rounds for alms." For a few days she enticed him to sit on the veranda, and there provided him with choice food.

Next she won the favor of some small boys by treating them with cakes, and said to them, "See here, boys; when the Elder comes to the house, you come too. And when you come, kick up the dust. And even if I tell you to stop, pay no attention to what I say." So on the following day, while the Elder was eating his meal, the boys came to the house and kicked up the dust. And when the mistress of the house told them to stop, they paid no attention to what she said. On the next day she said to the Elder, "Reverend Sir, these boys keep coming here and kicking up the dust, and, even when I tell them to stop, pay no attention to what I say; sit inside of the house." For a few days she seated him inside of the house and there provided him with choice food. Then she treated the boys again and said to them, "Boys, while the Elder is eating his meal, make a loud noise. And even if I tell you to stop, pay no attention to what I say." The boys did as they were told.

On the following day she said to the Elder, "Reverend Sir, the noise in this place is unbearable. In spite of all I do to stop them, these boys pay no attention to what I say; sit on the upper floor of the mansion." The Elder gave his consent. She then climbed to the top of the mansion, making the Elder precede her, and closing the door after her. Now the Elder had taken upon himself the strict obligation to receive alms only by making an unbroken round from door to door. But in spite of this fact, so firmly bound was he by the bonds of the craving of taste that he complied with her suggestion and climbed to the topmost floor of the seven-storied mansion. The woman provided the Elder with a seat.

In forty ways, friend Punnamukha, does a woman accost a man: She yawns, she bows down, she makes amorous gestures, she pretends to be abashed, she rubs the nails of one hand or foot with the nails of the other hand or foot, she places one foot on another foot, she scratches on the ground with a stick. She causes her boy to leap up, she causes her boy to leap down, she dallies with her boy and makes him dally with her, she kisses him and makes him kiss her, she eats food and makes him eat food, she gives and begs for gifts, she imitates whatever he does. She talks in a loud tone, she talks in a low tone; she talks as in public, she talks as in private. While dancing, singing, playing musical instruments, weeping, making amorous gestures, adorning herself, she laughs and looks. She sways her hips, she jiggles her waist-gear, uncovers her thigh, covers her thigh, displays her breast, displays her armpit, and displays her navel.

She buries the pupils of her eyes, lifts her eyebrows, scratches her lips, and dangles her tongue. She takes off her loin-cloth, puts on her loin-cloth, takes off her turban, and puts on her turban.

Thus did that woman employ all the devices of a woman, all the graces of a woman. And standing before the Elder, she recited the following Stanza,

> Dyed in lac and clad in slippers are the feet of a harlot.
> You are young and you are mine; I am young and I am yours.
> We will both retire from the world later on, and lean on a staff.

Thought the Elder, "Alas! I have committed a grievous sin! I did not consider what I was doing." And he was deeply moved. At that moment the Teacher, although seated within Jetavana, forty-five leagues distant, saw the whole affair and smiled. Elder Ananda asked him, "Reverend Sir, what is the cause, what is the occasion of your smiling?" "Ananda, in the city of Rājagaha, on the topmost floor of a seven-storied palace, there is a battle on between the monk Ocean-of-Beauty and a harlot." "Who is going to win, Reverend Sir, and who is going to lose?" The Teacher replied, "Ananda, Ocean-of-Beauty is going to win, and the harlot is going to lose." Having thus proclaimed that the Elder would win the victory, the Teacher, remaining seated where he was, sent forth a luminous image of himself and said, "Monk, renounce both lusts and free yourself from desire." So saying, he pronounced the following Stanza,

> Whoever in this world renounces lusts, whoever abandons the house life and retires from the world,
> Whoever has extinguished the essence of lust, such a man I call a Brahman.[1]

[1] This verse is in the *Dhammapada,* of which the story is told as a "commentary."

The Light of Asia

(LIFE OF BUDDHA)

INTRODUCTION

INDIA PRODUCED too much religion, China too little. A dribble of this religious spirit overflowed from India and innudated the whole Eastern Asia. One cannot help being curious about the fact that the Hindus have rejected Buddhism as the Jews have rejected Christianity. One should have thought that a nation would have embraced teachings which seem to other nations their most important contribution to the world and the highest manifestation of their spirit. Yet this is not the case. The only clue I can find seems to lie in the fact that Jesus attacked the established priestcraft of His time, as Buddha rebelled against the teachings and the sacerdotalism of the Brahmans. That Buddhism represents a revolt against Brahmanism is especially clear in his conversation with the two Brahmans.[1] He was the agnostic and the doubter regarding the *Brahmā* and the *Atman* (universal and individual soul) of the *Upanishads*. It seems that the established priesthood was too strong for the revolutionary teachings, and the Brahmans felt an injured pride in the presence of Buddha, as the Pharisees and Sadducees felt an injured pride in the challenge of Jesus. Yet this cannot be the whole explanation. Why should not the Jews have felt the charm, beauty and the greatness of Jesus's teachings, and why should not the Hindus have felt the charm, beauty and the greatness of Buddha? Probably a better explanation is that Judaism in Judea and Brahmanism in India, in neither case to be despised as religious and ethical systems and both being still very vital to-

[1] *Sacred Books of the East,* XI, pp. 157-202. Buddha was opposed to the priestcraft and preached directly to the people in their spoken tongue instead of in the classical Sanskrit of the Brahman.

day,[1] had older, truer and deeper roots in their racial consciousness, and that Buddhism and Christianity had those universal, idealistic qualities which detracted from their national character. If this is so, we may learn a lesson about the power of history and the strength of national beliefs.

Whatever the explanation, the strength and power of Buddhism in Asia, excepting India, clearly lies in the Mahayana conception of Buddha as Savior of the world, his great compassion and gentleness and kindness, and his message of saving mankind and freeing it from the sorrows and sufferings of this world. These constitute the great driving power of world religions.

In the study of Buddhism, we may take the poetic approach or the philosophic approach, through moral surrender or through intellectual belief. Sir Edwin Arnold's famous life of Buddha, *Light of Asia,* gives the best poetic approach, while the selection from the *Surangama,* which follows, gives the best philosophic approach.

There is a reason for reprinting the *Light of Asia* complete in this volume, although it was written by an Englishman. This long poem ran to sixty editions in England and eighty editions in the United States in the course of a few years when it was published about a century ago, and sold hundreds of thousands of copies at a time when there were neither best-seller lists, nor the Book-of-the-Month Club. More curiously still, it was a greater success than the author's later volume, *Light of the World,* depicting the life of Jesus. Most Western readers of the elderly generation owe their impression of Buddha to this poem. This is easy to understand. While it raised Buddha to cosmic heights, it never lost the human interest of its story. This is essentially the story of St. Josaphat, borrowed from the Buddhist *Lalitavistara,* who in the romance of *Barlaam and Josaphat,* became a Christian prince who was touched by the sorrows of this world and renounced his palatial glories to become an ascetic. Thus Buddha became actually canonized as a Christian saint in the sixteenth century.[2] (For instances of Christian and Buddhist parallels see the section "Some Buddhist Fables and Legends.") The influence must have been mutual, for while the Christian story of St. Josaphat was written in the eighth century A.D., the story of King Solomon dividing the child between two

[1] Witness Gandhi, Tagore, Ramakrishna and Vivekenanda.

[2] See H. G Rawlinson's article *India in European Thought and Literature,* in *The Legacy of India,* p. 26.

mothers certainly antedated a similar story in the Buddhist Jātakas.[1]

While the poem does not present the metaphysical system on which Buddhism is based, and which fascinated the Chinese scholars, it gives a true popular picture of Buddha as it appears to the average believer. To put the reader into the state of moral surrender, with all its miracles, the author chose to put the story in the mouth of an Indian Buddhist, and elaborated a full tapestry of Indian jungles and cities with great artistic skill. The poem has one of the noblest themes of all poetry, the theme of human sorrows. The full title of the poem reads: "The Light of Asia, or the Great Renunciation, being the Life and Teaching of Gautama, Prince of India and Founder of Buddhism (as told by an Indian Buddhist), by Edwin Arnold, Companion of the Star of India, Officer of the Order of the Elephant of Siam, Third Class of the Imperial Order of the Medjideh, etc." Sir Edwin Arnold also translated one story *Nala and Damayantī* from the *Mahābhārata* and wrote the very charming *Indian Idylls* (Boston, 1883).

Sir Edwin Arnold's poem is based on the life of Buddha, the *Buddha-Charita*,[2] written by Asvaghosha, the great Mahayanist teacher, whom I regard as the St. Paul of Buddhism. He lived toward the end of the first century and was author of the famous *Mahāyāna Sraddhotpāda*, or "The Awakening of Faith," translated into Chinese in the beginning of the fifth century. Roughly Buddhism was introduced into China at the beginning of the Christian era, and Buddhist texts were first translated in or soon after A.D. 67, while contact with Buddhist practices through Chinese Turkestan must have taken place as early as the time of the great Chinese Emperor, Han Wuti (140-85 B.C.), when several references were made to the subject. Concerning the important division into Mahayana and Hinayana Buddhism, see the introduction to the selection, *Surangama Sutra*.

There is a good translation of the life of Buddha from the introduction to the *Jātaka* in Chapter One of *Buddhism in Translations*, by Henry Clarke Warren (in *Harvard Oriental Series*, vol. 3, and *Harvard Classics*).

[1] Rhys Davids, *Buddhist Birth-Stories*, I, 13, 44. See also the Chinese version of the "Judgment between Two Mothers" in the section "Chinese Tales."

[2] See English translation from the Sanskrit by E. B. Cowell, *Sacred Books of the East*, vol. 49. For the Chinese version, see *Fo Sho Hing Tsan King*, which was translated by Dharmaraksha, and retranslated into English by Samuel Beal, *Sacred Books of the East*, vol. 19.

The Light of Asia

by Sir Edwin Arnold

BOOK THE FIRST

The Scripture of the Saviour of the World,
Lord Buddha—Prince Siddārtha styled on earth—
In Earth and Heavens and Hells Incomparable,
All-honoured, Wisest, Best, most Pitiful;
The Teacher of Nirvāna and the Law.

Thus came he to be born again for men.

Below the highest sphere four Regents sit
Who rule our world; and under them are zones
Nearer, but high, where saintliest spirits dead
Wait thrice ten thousand years, then live again;
And on Lord Buddha, waiting in that sky,
Came for our sakes the five sure signs of birth,
So that the Devas [1] knew the signs, and said
"Buddha will go again to help the World."
"Yea!" spake He, "now I go to help the World
This last of many times; for birth and death
End hence for me and those who learn my Law.
I will go down among the Sākyas,[2]
Under the southward snows of Himalay,
Where pious people live and a just King."

[1] Celestial spirits.
[2] Name of a royal race in the northern frontiers of Magadha, hence Buddha's title "Sākya-muni," or the Sākya sage.

That night the wife of King Suddhōdana,
Maya the Queen, asleep beside her Lord,
Dreamed a strange dream; dreamed that a star from heaven—
Splendid, six-rayed, in colour rosy-pearl,
Whereof the token was an Elephant
Six-tusked, and white as milk of Kamadhuk—
Shot through the void; and, shining into her,
Entered her womb upon the right. Awaked,
Bliss beyond mortal mother's filled her breast,
And over half the earth a lovely light
Forewent the morn. The strong hills shook; the waves
Sank lulled; all flowers that blow by day came forth
As 'twere high noon; down to the farthest hells
Passed the Queen's joy, as when warm sunshine thrills
Wood-glooms to gold, and into all the deeps
A tender whisper pierced. "Oh ye," it said,
"The dead that are to live, the live who die,
Uprise, and hear, and hope! Buddha is come!"
Whereat in Limbos numberless much peace
Spread, and the world's heart throbbed, and a wind blew
With unknown freshness over lands and seas.
And when the morning dawned, and this was told,
The grey dream-readers said "The dream is good!
The Crab is in conjunction with the Sun;
The Queen shall bear a boy, a holy child
Of wondrous wisdom, profiting all flesh,
Who shall deliver men from ignorance,
Or rule the world, if he will deign to rule."

In this wise was the holy Buddha born.

Queen Maya stood at noon, her days fulfilled,
Under a Palsa in the Palace-grounds,
A stately trunk, straight as a temple-shaft,
With crown of glossy leaves and fragrant blooms;
And, knowing the time come—for all things knew—
The conscious tree bent down its bows to make
A bower about Queen Maya's majesty;
And Earth put forth a thousand sudden flowers

To spread a couch; while, ready for the bath,
The rock hard by gave out a limpid stream
Of crystal flow. So brought she forth her child
Pangless—he having on his perfect form
The marks, thirty and two, of blessed birth;
Of which the great news to the Palace came.
But when they brought the painted palanquin
To fetch him home, the bearers of the poles
Were the four Regents of the Earth, come down
From Mount Sumeru—they who write men's deeds
On brazen plates—the Angel of the East,
Whose hosts are clad in silver robes, and bear
Targets of pearl: the Angel of the South,
Whose horsemen, the Kumbhandas, ride blue steeds,
With sapphire shields: the Angel of the West,
By Nāgas followed, riding steeds blood-red,
With coral shields: the Angel of the North,
Environed by his Yakshas, all in gold,
On yellow horses, bearing shields of gold.
These, with their pomp invisible, came down
And took the poles, in cast and outward garb
Like bearers, yet most mighty gods; and gods
Walked free with men that day, though men knew not:
For Heaven was filled with gladness for Earth's sake,
Knowing Lord Buddha thus was come again.

But King Suddhōdana wist not of this;
The portents troubled, till his dream-readers
Augured a Prince of earthly dominance,
A Chakravartīn, such as rise to rule
Once in each thousand years; seven gifts he has—
The Chakra-ratna, disc divine; the gem;
The horse, the Aswa-ratna, that proud steed
Which tramps the clouds; a snow-white elephant,
The Hasti-ratna, born to bear his King;
The crafty Minister, the General
Unconquered, and the wife of peerless grace,
The Istrī-ratna, lovelier than the Dawn.
For which gifts looking with this wondrous boy,

The King gave order that his town should keep
High festival; therefore the ways were swept,
Rose-odours sprinkled in the street, the trees
Were hung with lamps and flags, while merry crowds
Gaped on the sword-players and posturers,
The jugglers, charmers, swingers, rope-walkers,
The nautch-girls in their spangled skirts, and bells
That chime light laughter round their restless feet;
The masquers wrapped in skins of bear and deer,
The tiger-tamers, wrestlers, quail-fighters,
Beaters of drum and twanglers of the wire,
Who made the people happy by command.
Moreover, from afar came merchant-men,
Bringing, on tidings of this birth, rich gifts
In golden trays; goat-shawls, and nard, and jade,
Turkises, "evening-sky" tint, woven webs—
So fine twelve folds hide not a modest face—
Waist-cloths sewn thick with pearls, and sandal-wood;
Homage from tribute cities; so they called
Their Prince Savārthasiddh, "All-Prospering,"
Briefer, Siddārtha.[1]

'Mongst the strangers came
A grey-haired saint, Asita, one whose ears,
Long closed to earthly things, caught heavenly sounds,
And heard at prayer beneath his peepul-tree
The Devas singing songs at Buddha's birth.
Wondrous in lore he was by age and fasts;
Him, drawing nigh, seeming so reverend,
The King saluted, and Queen Maya made
To lay her babe before such holy feet;
But when he saw the Prince the old man cried
"Ah, Queen, not so!" and thereupon he touched
Eight times the dust, laid his waste visage there,
Saying, "O Babe! I worship! Thou art He!
I see the rosy light, the foot-sole marks,
The soft curled tendril of the Swastika,[2]

[1] Buddha's proper name, meaning "He who has reached the goal."
[2] A Buddhist emblem, still in use today.

The sacred primal signs thirty and two,[1]
The eighty lesser tokens. Thou art Buddh,
And thou wilt preach the Law and save all flesh
Who learn the Law, though I shall never hear,
Dying too soon, who lately longed to die;
Howbeit I have seen Thee. Know, O King!
This is that Blossom on our human tree
Which opens once in many myriad years—
But opened, fills the world with Wisdom's scent
And Love's dropped honey; from thy royal root
A Heavenly Lotus springs: Ah, happy House!
Yet not all-happy, for a sword must pierce
Thy bowels for this boy—whilst thou, sweet Queen!
Dear to all gods and men for this great birth,
Henceforth art grown too sacred for more woe;
And life is woe, therefore in seven days
Painless thou shalt attain the close of pain."

Which fell: for on the seventh evening
Queen Maya smiling slept, and waked no more,
Passing content to Trāyastrinshas-Heaven,
Where countless Devas worship her, and wait
Attendant on that radiant Motherhead.
But for the Babe they found a foster-nurse,
Princess Mahāprajāpati—her breast
Nourished with noble milk the lips of Him
Whose lips comfort the Worlds.
When th' eighth year passed,
The careful King bethought to teach his son
All that a Prince should learn, for still he shunned
The too vast presage of those miracles,
The glories and the sufferings of a Buddh.
So, in full council of his Ministers,
"Who is the wisest man, great sirs," he asked,
"To teach my Prince that which a Prince should know?"
Whereto gave answer each with instant voice:
"King! Viswamitra is the wisest one,
The farthest-seen in Scriptures, and the best

[1] See list, *Bible of the World,* by R. O. Ballou, p. 242.

In learning, and the manual arts, and all."
Thus Viswamitra came and heard commands;
And, on a day found fortunate, the Prince
Took up his slate of ox-red sandal-wood
All-beautified by gems around the rim,
And sprinkled smooth with dust of emery,
These took he, and his writing-stick, and stood
With eyes bent down before the Sage, who said,
"Child, write this Scripture," speaking slow the verse
"Gāyatrī" named, which only High-born hear.
"Acharya, I write," meekly replied
The Prince, and quickly on the dust he drew—
Not in one script, but many characters—
The sacred verse; Nagri and Dakshin, Nī,
Mangal, Parusha, Yava, Tirthi, Uk,
Darad, Sikhyani, Mana, Madhyachar,
The pictured writings and the speech of signs
Tokens of cave men and the sea-peoples,
Of those who worship snakes beneath the earth
And those who flame adore and the sun's orb,
The Magians and the dwellers on the mounds;
Of all the nations all strange scripts he traced
One after other with his writing-stick,
Reading the master's verse in every tongue;
And Viswamitra said, "It is enough,
Let us to numbers.
After me repeat
Your numeration till we reach the Lakh,[1]
One, two, three, four, to ten, and then by tens
To hundreds, thousands." After him the child
Named digits, decads, centuries; nor paused,
The round lakh reached, but softly murmured on,
"Then comes the kōti, nahut, ninnahut,
Khamba, viskhamba, abab, attata,
To kumuds, gundhikas, and utpalas,
By pundarīkas unto padumas,
Which last is how you count the utmost grains
Of Hastagiri ground to finest dust;

[1] Ten thousand.

But beyond that a numeration is,
The Kātha, used to note the stars of night;
The Kōti-Kātha, for the ocean drops;
Ingga, the calculus of circulars;
Sarvanikchepa, by the which you deal
With all the sands of Gunga, till we come
To Antah-Kalpas, where the unit is
The sands of ten crore Gungas. If one seeks
More comprehensive scale, th' arithmic mounts
By the Asankya, which is the tale
Of all the drops that in ten thousand years
Would fall on all the worlds by daily rain;
Thence unto Maha-Kalpas, by the which
The Gods compute their future and their past."

" 'Tis good," the sage rejoined. "Most noble Prince,
If these thou know'st, needs it that I should teach
The mensuration of the lineal?"
Humbly the boy replied, "Acharya!
Be pleased to hear me. Paramānus ten
A parasukshma make; ten of those build
The trasarene, and seven trasarenes
One mote's-length floating in the beam, seven motes
The whisker-point of mouse, and ten of these
One likhya; likhyas ten a yuka, ten
Yukas a heart of barley, which is held
Seven times a wasp-waist; so unto the grain
Of mung and mustard and the barley-corn,
Whereof ten give the finger-joint, twelve joints
The span, wherefrom we reach the cubit, staff,
Bow-length, lance-length; while twenty lengths of lance
Mete what is named a 'breath,' which is to say
Such space as man may stride with lungs once filled,
Whereof a gow is forty, four times that
A yōjana; and, Master! if it please,
I shall recite how many sun-motes lie
From end to end within a yōjana."
Thereat, with instant skill, the little Prince
Pronounced the total of the atoms true.

But Viswamitra heard it on his face
Prostrate before the boy; "For thou," he cried,
"Art Teacher of thy teachers—thou, not I,
Art Gūrū. Oh, I worship thee, sweet Prince!
That comest to my school only to show
Thou knowest all without the books, and know'st
Fair reverence besides."
Which reverence
Lord Buddha kept to all his schoolmasters,
Albeit beyond their learning taught; in speech
Right gentle, yet so wise; princely of mien,
Yet softly-mannered; modest, deferent,
And tender-hearted, though of fearless blood;
No bolder horseman in the youthful band
E'er rode in gay chase of the shy gazelles;
No keener driver of the chariot
In mimic contest scoured the Palace-courts;
Yet in mid-play the boy would ofttimes pause,
Letting the deer pass free; would ofttimes yield
His half-won race because the labouring steeds
Fetched painful breath; or if his princely mates
Saddened to lose, or if some wistful dream
Swept o'er his thoughts. And ever with the years
Waxed this compassionateness of our Lord,
Even as a great tree grows from two soft leaves
To spread its shade afar; but hardly yet
Knew the young child of sorrow, pain, or tears,
Save as strange names for things not felt by kings,
Nor ever to be felt. Then it befell
In the Royal garden on a day of spring,
A flock of wild swans passed, voyaging north
To their nest-places on Himāla's breast.
Calling in love-notes down their snowy line
The bright birds flew, by fond love piloted;
And Devadatta, cousin of the Prince,
Pointed his bow, and loosed a wilful shaft
Which found the wide wing of the foremost swan
Broad-spread to glide upon the free blue road,
So that it fell, the bitter arrow fixed,

Bright scarlet blood-gouts staining the pure plumes.
Which seeing, Prince Siddārtha took the bird
Tenderly up, rested it in his lap—
Sitting with knees crossed, as Lord Buddha sits—
And, soothing with a touch the wild thing's fright,
Composed its ruffled vans, calmed its quick heart,
Caressed it into peace with light kind palms
As soft as plantain-leaves an hour unrolled;
And while the left hand held, the right hand drew
The cruel steel forth from the wound, and laid
Cool leaves and healing honey on the smart.
Yet all so little knew the boy of pain
That curiously into his wrist he pressed
The arrow's barb, and winced to feel it sting,
And turned with tears to soothe his bird again.

Then some one came who said, "My Prince hath shot
A swan, which fell among the roses here,
He bids me pray you send it. Will you send?"
"Nay," quoth Siddārtha, "if the bird were dead
To send it to the slayer might be well,
But the swan lives; my cousin hath but killed
The god-like speed which throbbed in this white wing."
And Devadatta answered, "The wild thing,
Living or dead, is his who fetched it down;
'Twas no man's in the clouds, but fall'n 'tis mine,
Give me my prize, fair Cousin." Then our Lord
Laid the swan's neck beside his own smooth cheek
And gravely spake, "Say no! the bird is mine,
The first of myriad things which shall be mine
By right of mercy and love's lordliness.
For now I know, by what within me stirs,
That I shall teach compassion unto men
And be a speechless world's interpreter,
Abating this accursed flood of woe,
Not man's alone; but, if the Prince disputes,
Let him submit his matter to the wise
And we will wait their word." So was it done;
In full divan the business had debate,

And many thought this thing and many that;
Till there arose an unknown priest who said,
"If life be aught, the saviour of a life
Owns more the living thing than he can own
Who sought to slay—the slayer spoils and wastes,
The cherisher sustains; give him the bird:"
Which judgment all found just; but when the King
Sought out the sage for honour, he was gone,
And some one saw a hooded snake glide forth,—
The gods come ofttimes thus! So our Lord Buddha
Began his works of mercy.

Yet not more
Knew he as yet of grief than that one bird's,
Which, being healed, went joyous to its kind.
But on another day the King said, "Come,
Sweet son! and see the pleasuance of the spring,
And how the fruitful earth is wooed to yield
Its riches to the reaper; how my realm—
Which shall be thine when the pile flames for me—
Feeds all its mouths and keeps the King's chest filled.
Fair is the season with new leaves, bright blooms,
Green grass, and cries of plough-time." So they rode
Into a land of wells and gardens, where,
All up and down the rich red loam, the steers
Strained their strong shoulders in the creaking yoke
Dragging the ploughs; the fat soil rose and rolled
In smooth long waves back from the plough; who drove
Planted both feet upon the leaping share
To make the furrow deep; among the palms
The tinkle of the rippling water rang,
And where it ran the glad earth 'broidered it
With balsams and the spears of lemon-grass.
Elsewhere were sowers who went forth to sow;
And all the jungle laughed with nesting-songs,
And all the thickets rustled with small life
Of lizard, bee, beetle, and creeping things
Pleased at the spring-time. In the mango-sprays
The sun-birds flashed; alone at his green forge
Toiled the loud coppersmith; bee-eaters hawked

Chasing the purple butterflies; beneath,
Striped squirrels raced, the mynas perked and picked,
The seven brown sisters chattered in the thorn,
The pied fish-tiger hung above the pool,
The egrets stalked among the buffaloes,
The kites sailed circles in the golden air;
About the painted temple peacocks flew,
The blue doves cooed from every well, far off
The village drums beat for some marriage-feast;
All things spoke peace and plenty, and the Prince
Saw and rejoiced. But, looking deep, he saw
The thorns which grow upon this rose of life:
How the swart peasant sweated for his wage,
Toiling for leave to live; and how he urged
The great-eyed oxen through the flaming hours,
Goading their velvet flanks: then marked he, too,
How lizard fed on ant, and snake on him,
And kite on both; and how the fish-hawk robbed
The fish-tiger of that which it had seized;
The shrike chasing the bulbul, which did hunt
The jewelled butterflies; till everywhere
Each slew a slayer and in turn was slain,
Life living upon death. So the fair show
Veiled one vast, savage, grim conspiracy
Of mutual murder, from the worm to man,
Who himself kills his fellow; seeing which—
The hungry ploughman and his labouring kine,
Their dewlaps blistered with the bitter yoke,
The rage to live which makes all living strife—
The Prince Siddārtha sighed. "Is this," he said,
"That happy earth they brought me forth to see?
How salt with sweat the peasant's bread! how hard
The oxen's service! in the brake how fierce
The war of weak and strong! i' th' air what plots!
No refuge e'en in water. Go aside
A space, and let me muse on what ye show."

So saying the good Lord Buddha seated him
Under a jambu-tree, with ankles crossed—

As holy statutes sit—and first began
To meditate this deep disease of life,
What its far source and whence its remedy.
So vast a pity filled him, such wide love
For living things, such passion to heal pain,
That by their stress his princely spirit passed
To ecstasy, and, purged from mortal taint
Of sense and self, the boy attained thereat
Dhyāna,[1] first step of "the path."
There flew
High overhead that hour five holy ones,
Whose free wings faltered as they passed the tree.
"What power superior draws us from our flight?"
They asked,—for spirits feel all force divine,
And know the sacred presence of the pure.
Then, looking downward, they beheld the Buddh
Crowned with a rose-hued aureole, intent
On thoughts to save; while from the grove a voice
Cried, "Rishis! [2] this is He shall help the world,
Descend and worship." So the Bright Ones came
And sang a song of praise, folding their wings;
Then journeyed on, taking good news to Gods.

But certain from the King seeking the Prince
Found him still musing, though the noon was past,
And the sun hastened to the western hills:
Yet, while all shadows moved, the jambu-tree's
Stayed in one quarter, overspreading him,
Lest the sloped rays should strike that sacred head;
And he who saw this sight heard a voice say,
Amid the blossoms of the rose-apple,
"Let be the King's son! till the shadow goes
Forth from his heart my shadow will not shift."

BOOK THE SECOND

Now, WHEN OUR LORD was come to eighteen years,
The King commanded that there should be built

[1] Meditation. [2] Seers.

Three stately houses, one of hewn square beams
With cedar lining, warm for winter days;
One of veined marbles, cool for summer heat;
And one of burned bricks, with blue tiles bedecked,
Pleasant at seed-time, when the champaks bud—
Subha, Suramma, Ramma, were their names.
Delicious gardens round about them bloomed,
Streams wandered wild, and musky thickets stretched,
With many a bright pavilion and fair lawn
In midst of which Siddārtha strayed at will,
Some new delight provided every hour;
And happy hours he knew, for life was rich,
With youthful blood at quickest; yet still came
The shadows of his meditation back,
As the lake's silver dulls with driving clouds.

Which the King marking, called his Ministers:
"Bethink ye, sirs! how the old Rishi spake,"
He said, "and what my dream-readers foretold.
This boy, more dear to me than mine heart's blood,
Shall be of universal dominance,
Trampling the neck of all his enemies,
A King of kings—and this is in my heart;—
Or he shall tread the sad and lowly path
Of self-denial and of pious pains,
Gaining who knows what good, when all is lost
Worth keeping; and to this his wistful eyes
Do still incline amid my palaces.
But ye are sage, and ye will counsel me;
How may his feet be turned to that proud road
Where they should walk, and all fair signs come true
Which gave him Earth to rule, if he would rule?"

The eldest answered, "Maharaja! [1] love
Will cure these thin distempers; weave the spell
Of woman's wiles about his idle heart.
What knows this noble boy of beauty yet,
Eyes that make heaven forgot, and lips of balm?

[1] Great king.

Find him soft wives and pretty playfellows;
The thoughts ye cannot stay with brazen chains
A girl's hair lightly binds."
And all thought good.
But the King answered, "If we seek him wives,
Love chooseth ofttimes with another eye;
And if we bid range Beauty's garden round,
To pluck what blossom pleases, he will smile
And sweetly shun the joy he knows not of."
Then said another, "Roams the barasingh[1]
Until the fated arrow flies; for him,
As for less lordly spirits, some one charms,
Some face will seem a Paradise, some form
Fairer than pale Dawn when she wakes the world.
This do, my King! Command a festival
Where the realm's maids shall be competitors
In youth and grace, and sports that Sākyas use.
Let the Prince give the prizes to the fair,
And, when the lovely victors pass his seat,
There shall be those who mark if one or two
Change the fixed sadness of his tender cheek;
So we may choose for Love with Love's own eyes,
And cheat his Highness into happiness."
This thing seemed good; wherefore, upon a day,
The criers bade the young and beautiful
Pass to the palace, for 'twas in command
To hold a court of pleasure, and the Prince
Would give the prizes, something rich for all,
The richest for the fairest judged. Thus flocked
Kapilavastu's maidens to the gate,
Each with her dark hair newly smoothed and bound,
Eyelashes lustred with the soorma-stick,
Fresh-bathed and scented; all in shawls and cloths
Of gayest; slender hands and feet new-stained
With crimson, and the tilka-spots[2] stamped bright.
Fair show it was of all those Indian girls
Slow-pacing past the throne with large black eyes
Fixed on the ground; for when they saw the Prince

[1] A stag.
[2] The beauty-spots between the eyebrows of Hindu women.

More than the awe of Majesty made beat
Their fluttering hearts, he sate so passionless,
Gentle, but so beyond them. Each maid took
With down-dropped lids her gift, afraid to gaze;
And if the people hailed some lovelier one
Beyond her rivals worthy royal smiles,
She stood like a scared antelope to touch
The gracious hand, then fled to join her mates
Trembling at favour, so divine he seemed,
So high and saint-like and above her world.
Thus filed they, one bright maid after another,
The city's flowers, and all this beauteous march
Was ending and the prizes spent, when last
Came young Yasōdhara, and they that stood
Nearest Siddārtha saw the princely boy
Start, as the radiant girl approached. A form
Of heavenly mould; a gait like Parvati's;
Eyes like a hind's in love-time; face so fair
Words cannot paint its spell; and she alone
Gazed full—folding her palms across her breasts—
On the boy's gaze, her stately neck unbent.
"Is there a gift for me?" she asked, and smiled.
"The gifts are gone," the Prince replied, "yet take
This for amends, dear sister, of whose grace
Our happy city boasts;" therewith he loosed
The emerald necklet from his throat, and clasped
Its green beads round her dark and silk-soft waist;
And their eyes mixed, and from the look sprang love.

Long after—when enlightenment was full—
Lord Buddha, being prayed why thus his heart
Took fire at first glance of the Sākya girl,
Answered, "We were not strangers, as to us
And all it seemed; in ages long gone by
A hunter's son, playing with forest girls
By Yamun's springs, where Nandadevi stands,
Sate umpire while they raced beneath the firs
Like hares at eve that run their playful rings;
One with flower-stars he crowned; one with long plumes

Plucked from eyed pheasant and the jungle-cock;
One with fir-apples; but who ran the last
Came first for him, and unto her the boy
Gave a tame fawn and his heart's love beside.
And in the wood they lived many glad years,
And in the wood they undivided died.
Lo! as hid seed shoots after rainless years,
So good and evil, pains and pleasures, hates
And loves, and all dead deeds, come forth again
Bearing bright leaves or dark, sweet fruit or sour.
Thus I was he and she Yasōdhara;
And while the wheel of birth and death turns round
That which hath been must be between us two."

But they who watched the Prince at prize-giving
Saw and heard all, and told the careful King
How sate Siddārtha heedless, till there passed
Great Suprabuddha's child, Yasōdhara;
And how—at sudden sight of her—he changed,
And how she gazed on him and he on her,
And of the jewel-gift, and what beside
Passed in their speaking glance.
The fond King smiled:
"Look! we have found a lure; take counsel now
To fetch therewith our falcon from the clouds.
Let messengers be sent to ask the maid
In marriage for my son." But it was law
With Sākyas, when any asked a maid
Of noble house, fair and desirable,
He must make good his skill in martial arts
Against all suitors who should challenge it;
Nor might this custom break itself for kings.
Therefore her father spake: "Say to the King,
The child is sought by princes far and near;
If thy most gentle son can bend the bow,
Sway sword, and back a horse better than they,
Best would he be in all and best to us:
But how shall this be, with his cloistered ways?"

Then the King's heart was sore, for now the Prince
Begged sweet Yasōdhara for wife—in vain,
With Devadatta foremost at the bow,
Ardjuna master of all fiery steeds,
And Nanda chief in sword-play; but the Prince
Laughed low and said, "These things, too, I have learned;
Make proclamation that they son will meet
All comers at their chosen games. I think
I shall not lose my love for such as these."
So 'twas given forth that on the seventh day
The Prince Siddārtha summoned whoso would
To match with him in feats of manliness,
The victor's crown to be Yasōdhara.

Therefore, upon the seventh day, there went
The Sākya lords, and town and country round,
Unto the maidān;[1] and the maid went too
Amid her kinsfolk, carried as a bride,
With music, and with litters gaily dight,
And gold-horned oxen, flower-caparisoned:
Whom Devadatta claimed, of royal line,
And Nanda and Ardjuna, noble both,
The flower of all youths there; till the Prince came
Riding his white horse Kantaka, which neighed,
Astonished at this great strange world without:
Also Siddārtha gazed with wondering eyes
On all those people born beneath the throne,
Otherwise housed than kings, otherwise fed,
And yet so like—perchance—in joys and griefs.
But when the Prince saw sweet Yasōdhara,
Brightly he smiled, and drew his silken rein,
Leaped to the earth from Kantaka's broad back,
And cried, "He is not worthy of this pearl
Who is not worthiest; let my rivals prove
If I have dared too much in seeking her."
Then Nanda challenged for the arrow-test
And set a brazen drum six gows away,
Ardjuna six and Devadatta eight;

[1] Anglo-Indian word, "parade ground."

But Prince Siddārtha bade them set his drum
Ten gows from off the line, until it seemed
A cowry-shell for target. Then they loosed,
And Nanda pierced his drum, Ardjuna his,
And Devadatta drove a well-aimed shaft
Through both sides of his mark, so that the crowd
Marvelled and cried; and sweet Yasōdhara
Dropped the gold sari[1] o'er her fearful eyes,
Lest she should see her Prince's arrow fail.
But he, taking their bow of lacquered cane,
With sinews bound, and strung with silver wire,
Which none but stalwart arms could draw a span,
Thrummed it—low laughing—drew the twisted string
Till the horns kissed, and the thick belly snapped:
"That is for play, not love," he said; "hath none
A bow more fit for Sākya lords to use?"
And one said, "There is Sinhahānu's bow,
Kept in the temple since we know not when,
Which none can string, nor draw if it be strung."
"Fetch me," he cried, "that weapon of a man!"
They brought the ancient bow, wrought of black steel,
Laid with gold tendrils on its branching curves
Like bison-horns; and twice Siddārtha tried
Its strength across his knee, then spake—"Shoot now
With this, my cousins!" but they could not bring
The stubborn arms a hand's-breadth nigher use;
Then the Prince, lightly leaning, bent the bow,
Slipped home the eye upon the notch, and twanged
Sharply the cord, which, like an eagle's wing
Thrilling the air, sang forth so clear and loud,
That feeble folk at home that day inquired
"What is this sound?" and people answered them,
"It is the sound of Sinhahānu's bow,
Which the King's son has strung and goes to shoot."
Then fitting fair a shaft, he drew and loosed,
And the keen arrow clove the sky, and drave

[1] Garment of Hindu women, wound round the body with one end thrown over the shoulder.

Right through that farthest drum, nor stayed its flight,
But skimmed the plain beyond, past reach of eye.

Next, Devadatta challenged with the sword,
And clove a Talas-tree six fingers thick;
Ardjuna seven; and Nanda cut through nine;
But two such stems together grew, and both
Siddārtha's blade shred at one flashing stroke,
Keen, but so smooth that the straight trunks upstood,
And Nanda cried, "His edge turned!" and the maid
Trembled anew seeing the trees erect;
Until the Devas of the air, who watched,
Blew light breaths from the south, and both green crowns
Crashed in the sand, clean-felled.

Then brought they steeds,
High-mettled, nobly-bred, and three times scoured
Around the maidān, but white Kantaka
Left even the fleetest far behind—so swift,
That ere the foam fell from his mouth to earth
Twenty spear-lengths he flew; but Nanda said,
"We too might win with such as Kantaka;
Fetch an unbroken horse, and let men see
Who best can back him." So the syces[1] brought
A stallion dark as night, led by three chains,
Fierce-eyed, with nostrils wide and tossing mane,
Unshod, unsaddled, for no rider yet
Had crossed him. Three times each young Sākya
Sprang to his mighty back, but the hot steed
Furiously reared, and flung them to the plain
In dust and shame; only Ardjuna held
His seat awhile, and, bidding loose the chains,
Lashed the black flank, and shook the bit, and held
The proud jaws fast with grasp of master-hand,
So that in storms of wrath and rage and fear
The savage stallion circled once the plain
Half-tamed; but sudden turned with naked teeth,
Gripped by the foot Ardjuna, tore him down,

[1] Groom (Anglo-Indian word).

And would have slain him, but the grooms ran in
Fettering the maddened beast. Then all men cried,
"Let not Siddārtha meddle with this Bhūt,
Whose liver is a tempest, and his blood
Red flame;" but the Prince said, "Let go the chains,
Give me his forelock only," which he held
With quiet grasp, and, speaking some low word,
Laid his right palm across the stallion's eyes,
And drew it gently down the angry face,
And all along the neck and panting flanks,
Till men astonished saw the night-black horse
Sink his fierce crest and stand subdued and meek,
As though he knew our Lord and worshipped him.
Nor stirred he while Siddārtha mounted; then
Went soberly to touch of knee and rein
Before all eyes, so that the people said,
"Strive no more, for Siddārtha is the best."

And all the suitors answered "He is best!"
And Suprabuddha, father of the maid,
Said, "It was in our hearts to find thee best,
Being dearest, yet what magic taught thee more
Of manhood 'mid thy rose-bowers and thy dreams
Than war and chase and world's work bring to these?
But wear, fair Prince, the treasure thou has won."
Then at a word the lovely Indian girl
Rose from her place above the throng, and took
A crown of mōgra-flowers, and lightly drew
The veil of black and gold across her brow,
Proud-pacing past the youths, until she came
To where Siddārtha stood in grace divine,
New lighted from the night-dark steed, which bent
Its strong neck meekly underneath his arm.
Before the Prince lowly she bowed, and bared
Her face celestial beaming with glad love;
Then on his neck she hung the fragrant wreath,
And on his breast she laid her perfect head,
And stooped to touch his feet with proud glad eyes,
Saying, "Dear Prince, behold me, who am thine!"

And all the throng rejoiced, seeing them pass
Hand fast in hand, and heart beating with heart,
The veil of black and gold drawn close again.

Long after—when enlightenment was come—
They prayed Lord Buddha touching all, and why
She wore this black and gold, and stepped so proud.
And the World-honoured answered, "Unto me
This was unknown, albeit it seemed half known;
For while the wheel of birth and death turns round,
Past things and thoughts, and buried lives come back.
I now remember, myriad rains ago,
What time I roamed Himāla's hanging woods,
A tiger, with my striped and hungry kind;
I, who am Buddh, couched in the kusa grass
Gazing with green blinked eyes upon the herds
Which pastured near and nearer to their death
Round my day-lair; or underneath the stars
I roamed for prey, savage, insatiable,
Sniffing the paths for track of man and deer.
Amid the beasts that were my fellows then,
Met in deep jungle or by reedy jheel,[1]
A tigress, comeliest of the forest, set
The males at war; her hide was lit with gold,
Black-broidered like the veil Yasōdhara
Wore for me; hot the strife waxed in that wood
With tooth and claw, while, underneath a neem
The fair beast watched us bleed, thus fiercely wooed.
And I remember, at the end she came,
Snarling, past this and that torn forest-lord
Whom I had conquered, and with fawning jaws
Licked my quick-heaving flank, and with me went
Into the wild with proud steps, amorously.
The wheel of birth and death turns low and high."

Therefore the maid was given unto the Prince
A willing spoil; and when the stars were good—
Mesha, the Red Ram, being Lord of heaven—

[1] A pool or lagoon in India after a flood.

The marriage feast was kept, as Sākyas use,
The golden gadi[1] set, the carpet spread,
The wedding garlands hung, the arm-threads tied,
The sweet cake broke, the rice and attar thrown,
The two straws floated on the reddened milk,
Which, coming close, betokened "love till death;"
The seven steps taken thrice around the fire,
The gifts bestowed on holy men, the alms
And temple-offerings made, the mantras[2] sung,
The garments of the bride and bridegroom tied.
Then the grey father spake: "Worshipful Prince,
She that was ours henceforth is only thine;
Be good to her, who hath her life in thee."
Wherewith they brought home sweet Yasōdhara,
With songs and trumpets, to the Prince's arms,
And love was all in all.
Yet not to love
Alone trusted the King; love's prison-house
Stately and beautiful he bade them build,
So that in all the earth no marvel was
Like Vishramvan, the Prince's pleasure-place.
Midway in those wide palace-grounds there rose
A verdant hill whose base Rohini bathed,
Murmuring adown from Himalay's broad feet,
To bear its tribute into Gunga's waves.
Southward a growth of tamarind trees and sāl,
Thick set with pale sky-coloured ganthi flowers,
Shut out the world, save if the city's hum
Came on the wind no harsher than when bees
Buzz out of sight in thickets. Northwards soared
The stainless ramps of huge Himāla's wall,
Ranged in white ranks against the blue—untrod,
Infinite, wonderful—whose uplands vast,
And lifted universe of crest and crag,
Shoulder and shelf, green slope and icy horn,
Riven ravine, and splintered precipice
Led climbing thought higher and higher, until
It seemed to stand in heaven and speak with gods.

[1] Seat cushion.
[2] Hymns, or metrical passages (prayers or formulas).

Beneath the snows dark forests spread, sharp-laced
With leaping cataracts and veiled with clouds:
Lower grew rose-oaks and the great fir groves
Where echoed pheasant's call and panther's cry,
Clatter of wild sheep on the stones, and scream
Of circling eagles: under these the plain
Gleamed like a praying-carpet at the foot
Of those divinest altars. Fronting this
The builders set the bright pavilion up,
Fair-planted on the terraced hill, with towers
On either flank and pillared cloisters round.
Its beams were carved with stories of old time—
Radha and Krishna and the sylvan girls—
Sita and Hanuman and Draupadi;
And on the middle porch God Ganesha,
With disc and hook—to bring wisdom and wealth—
Propitious sate, wreathing his sidelong trunk.
By winding ways of garden and of court
The inner gate was reached, of marble wrought,
White, with pink veins; the lintel lazuli,
The threshold alabaster, and the doors
Sandal-wood, cut in pictured panelling;
Whereby to lofty halls and shadowy bowers
Passed the delighted foot, on stately stairs,
Through latticed galleries, 'neath painted roofs
And clustering columns, where cool fountains—fringed
With lotus and nelumbo—danced; and fish
Gleamed through their crystal, scarlet, gold, and blue.
Great-eyed gazelles in sunny alcoves browsed
The blown red roses; birds of rainbow wing
Fluttered among the palms; doves, green and grey,
Built their safe nests on gilded cornices;
Over the shining pavements peacocks drew
The splendours of their trains, sedately watched
By milk-white herons and the small house-owls.
The plum-necked parrots swung from fruit to fruit;
The yellow sunbirds whirred from bloom to bloom,
The timid lizards on the lattice basked
Fearless, the squirrels ran to feed from hand;

For all was peace: the shy black snake, that gives
Fortune to households, sunned his sleepy coils
Under the moon-flowers, where the musk-deer played,
And brown-eyed monkeys chattered to the crows.
And all this House of love was peopled fair
With sweet attendance, so that in each part
With lovely sights were gentle faces found,
Soft speech and willing service; each one glad
To gladden, pleased at pleasure, proud to obey;
Till life glided beguiled, like a smooth stream
Banked by perpetual flow'rs, Yasōdhara
Queen of the enchanting Court.
But, innermost,
Beyond the richness of those hundred halls,
A secret chamber lurked, where skill had spent
All lovely fantasies to lull the mind.
The entrance of it was a cloistered square—
Roofed by the sky, and in the midst a tank—
Of milky marble built, and laid with slabs
Of milk-white marble; bordered round the tank
And on the steps, and all along the frieze
With tender inlaid work of agate-stones.
Cool as to tread in summer-time on snows
It was to loiter there; the sunbeams dropped
Their gold, and, passing into porch and niche,
Softened to shadows, silvery, pale, and dim,
As if the very Day paused and grew Eve
In love and silence at that bower's gate;
For there beyond the gate the chamber was,
Beautiful, sweet; a wonder of the world!
Soft light from perfumed lamps through windows fell,
Of nakre and stained stars of lucent film,
On golden cloths outspread, and silken beds,
And heavy splendour of the purdah's[1] fringe,
Lifted to take only the loveliest in.
Here, whether it was night or day none knew,
For always streamed that softened light, more bright
Than sunrise, but as tender as the eve's;

[1] Curtain with which Indian women are screened from strangers.

And always breathed sweet airs, more joy-giving
Than morning's, but as cool as midnight's breath;
And night and day lutes sighed, and night and day
Delicious foods were spread, and dewy fruits,
Sherbets new chilled with snows of Himalay,
And sweetmeats made of subtle daintiness,
With sweet tree-milk in its own ivory cup.
And night and day served there a chosen band
Of nautch girls,[1] cup-bearers, and cymballers,
Delicate, dark-browed ministers of love,
Who fanned the sleeping eyes of the happy Prince,
And when he waked, led back his thoughts to bliss
With music whispering through the blooms, and charm
Of amorous songs and dreamy dances, linked
By chime of ankle-bells and wave of arms
And silver vina-strings;[2] while essences
Of musk and champak, and the blue haze spread
From burning spices, soothed his soul again
To drowse by sweet Yasōdhara; and thus
Siddārtha lived forgetting.

Furthermore,
The King commanded that within those walls
No mention should be made of death or age,
Sorrow, or pain, or sickness. If one drooped
In the lovely Court—her dark glance dim, her feet
Faint in the dance—the guiltless criminal
Passed forth an exile from that Paradise,
Lest he should see and suffer at her woe.
Bright-eyed intendants watched to execute
Sentence on such as spake of the harsh world
Without, where aches and plagues were, tears and fears,
And wail of mourners, and grim fume of pyres.
'Twas treason if a thread of silver strayed
In tress of singing-girl or nautch-dancer;
And every dawn the dying rose was plucked,
The dead leaves hid, all evil sights removed:
For said the King, "If he shall pass his youth
Far from such things as move to wistfulness,

[1] Indian dancing girls. [2] Hindu musical instrument of the guitar kind.

And brooding on the empty eggs of thought,
The shadow of this fate, too vast for man,
May fade, belike, and I shall see him grow
To that great stature of fair sovereignty
When he shall rule all lands—if he will rule—
The King of kings and Glory of his time."

Wherefore, around that pleasant prison-house—
Where love was gaoler and delights its bars—
But far removed from sight, the King bade build
A massive wall, and in the wall a gate
With brazen folding-doors, which but to roll
Back on their hinges asked a hundred arms;
Also the noise of that prodigious gate
Opening, was heard full half a yōjana.[1]
And inside this another gate he made,
And yet within another—through the three
Must one pass if he quit that Pleasure-house.
Three mighty gates there were, bolted and barred,
And over each was set a faithful watch;
And the King's order said, "Suffer no man
To pass the gates, though he should be the Prince:
This on your lives—even though it be my son."

BOOK THE THIRD

In which calm home of happy life and love
Ligged our Lord Buddha, knowing not of woe,
Nor want, nor pain, nor plague, nor age, nor death,
Save as when sleepers roam dim seas in dreams,
And land awearied on the shores of day,
Bringing strange merchandise from that black voyage.
Thus ofttimes, when he lay with gentle head
Lulled on the dark breasts of Yasōdhara,
Her fond hands fanning slow his sleeping lids,
He would start up and cry, "My world! Oh, world!
I hear! I know! I come!" And she would ask,
"What ails my Lord?" with large eyes terror-struck;

[1] Yōjana, nine English miles.

For at such times the pity in his look
Was awful, and his visage like a god's.
Then would he smile again to stay her tears,
And bid the vinas sound; but once they set
A stringed gourd on the sill, there where the wind
Could linger o'er its notes and play at will—
Wild music makes the wind on silver strings—
And those who lay around heard only that;
But Prince Siddārtha heard the Devas play,
And to his ears they sang such words as these:—

We are the voices of the wandering wind,
Which moan for rest, and rest can never find;
Lo! as the wind is, so is mortal life,
A moan, a sigh, a sob, a storm, a strife.

Wherefore and whence we are ye cannot know,
Nor where life springs, nor whither life doth go;
We are as ye are, ghosts from the inane,
What pleasure have we of our changeful pain?

What pleasure hast thou of thy changeless bliss?
Nay, if love lasted, there were joy in this;
But life's way is the wind's way, all these things
Are but brief voices breathed on shifting strings.

O Maya's[1] *son! because we roam the earth*
Moan we upon these strings: we make no mirth,
So many woes we see in many lands,
So many streaming eyes and wringing hands.

Yet mock we while we wail, for, could they know,
This life they cling to is but empty show;
'Twere all as well to bid a cloud to stand,
Or hold a running river with the hand.

But thou that art to save, thine hour is nigh!
The sad world waiteth in its misery,

[1] Buddha's mother's name.

The blind world stumbleth on its round of pain;
Rise, Maya's child! wake! slumber not again!

We are the voices of the wandering wind:
Wander thou, too, O Prince, thy rest to find;
Leave love for love of lovers, for woe's sake
Quit state for sorrow, and deliverance make.

So sigh we, passing o'er the silver strings,
To thee who know'st not yet of earthly things;
So say we; mocking, as we pass away,
These lovely shadows wherewith thou dost play.

Thereafter it befell he sate at eve
Amid his beauteous Court, holding the hand
Of sweet Yasōdhara, and some maid told—
With breaks of music when her rich voice dropped—
An ancient tale to speed the hour of dusk,
Of love, and of a magic horse, and lands
Wonderful, distant, where pale peoples dwelled,
And where the sun at night sank into seas.
Then spake he, sighing, "Chitra brings me back
The wind's song in the strings with that fair tale:
Give her, Yasōdhara, thy pearl for thanks.
But thou, my pearl! is there so wide a world?
Is there a land which sees the great sun roll
Into the waves, and are there hearts like ours,
Countless, unknown, not happy—it may be—
Whom we might succour if we knew of them?
Ofttimes I marvel, as the Lord of day
Treads from the east his kingly road of gold,
Who first on the world's edge hath hailed his beam,
The children of the morning; oftentimes,
Even in thine arms and on thy breasts, bright wife,
Sore have I panted, at the sun's decline,
To pass with him into that crimson west
And see the peoples of the evening.
There must be many we should love—how else?
Now have I in this hour an ache, at last,

Thy soft lips cannot kiss away: oh, girl!
O Chitra! you that know of fairyland!
Where tether they that swift steed of thy tale?
My palace for one day upon his back,
To ride and ride and see the spread of the earth;
Nay, if I had yon callow vulture's plumes—
The carrion heir of wider realms than mine—
How would I stretch for topmost Himalay,
Light where the rose-gleam lingers on those snows,
And strain my gaze with searching what is round!
Why have I never seen and never sought?
Tell me what lies beyond our brazen gates."

Then one replied, "The city first, fair Prince!
The temples, and the gardens, and the groves,
And then the fields; and afterwards fresh fields,
With nullahs,[1] maidāns, jungle, koss[2] on koss;
And next King Bimbasāra's realm, and then
The vast flat world, with crores[3] on crores of folk."
"Good," said Siddārtha; "let the word be sent
That Channa yoke my chariot—at noon
To-morrow I shall ride and see beyond."

Whereof they told the King: "Our Lord, thy son,
Wills that his chariot be yoked at noon,
That he may ride abroad and see mankind."

"Yea!" spake the careful King, " 'tis time he sees;
But let the criers go about and bid
My city deck itself, so there be met
No noisome sight; and let none blind or maimed,
None that is sick, or stricken deep in years,
No leper, and no feeble folk come forth."
Therefore the stones were swept, and up and down
The water-carriers sprinkled all the streets
From spirting skins, the housewives scattered fresh
Red powder on their thresholds, strung new wreaths,
And trimmed the tulsi-bush before their doors.

[1] Ravines, river-beds. [2] A distance of over two English miles. [3] Millions (Hindu word).

The paintings on the walls were heightened up
With liberal brush, the trees set thick with flags,
The idols gilded; in the four-went ways
Suryadeva and the great gods shone
'Mid shrines of leaves; so that the city seemed
A capital of some enchanted land.
Also the criers passed, with drum and gong,
Proclaiming loudly, "Ho! all citizens,
The King commands that there be seen to-day
No evil sight: let no one blind or maimed,
None that is sick, or stricken deep in years,
No leper, and no feeble folk go forth.
Let none, too, burn his dead nor bring them out
'Till nightfall. Thus Suddhōdana commands."

So all was comely and the houses trim
Throughout Kapilavastu, while the Prince
Came forth in painted car, which two steers drew,
Snow-white, with swinging dewlaps, and huge humps
Wrinkled against the carved and lacquered yoke.
Goodly it was to mark the people's joy
Greeting their Prince; and glad Siddārtha waxed
At sight of all those liege and friendly folk
Bright-clad and laughing as if life were good.
"Fair is the world," he said, "it likes me well!
And light and kind these men that are not kings,
And sweet my sisters here, who toil and tend;
What have I done for these to make them thus?
Why, if I love them, should those children know?
I pray take up yon pretty Sākya boy
Who flung us flowers, and let him ride with me.
How good it is to reign in realms like this!
How simple pleasure is, if these be pleased
Because I come abroad! How many things
I need not if such little households hold
Enough to make our city full of smiles!
Drive, Channa! [1] through the gates, and let me see
More of this gracious world I have not known."

[1] Buddha's driver.

So passed they through the gates, a joyous crowd
Thronging about the wheels, whereof some ran
Before the oxen, throwing wreaths; some stroked
Their silken flanks; some brought them rice and cakes,
All crying, "*Jai! jai!* for our noble Prince!"
Thus all the path was kept with gladsome looks
And filled with fair sights—for the King's word was
That such should be—when midway in the road,
Slow tottering from the hovel where he hid,
Crept forth a wretch in rags, haggard and foul,
An old, old man, whose shrivelled skin, sun-tanned,
Clung like a beast's hide to its fleshless bones.
Bent was his back with load of many days,
His eyepits red with rust of ancient tears,
His dim orbs blear with rheum, his toothless jaws
Wagging with palsy and the fright to see
So many and such joy. One skinny hand
Clutched a worn staff to prop his quavering limbs,
And one was pressed upon the ridge of ribs
Whence came in gasps the heavy painful breath.
"Alms!" moaned he, "give, good people! for I die
To-morrow or the next day!" then the cough
Choked him, but still he stretched his palm, and stood
Blinking, and groaning 'mid his spasms, "Alms!"
Then those around had wrenched his feeble feet
Aside, and thrust him from the road again,
Saying, "The Prince! dost see? get to thy lair!"
But that Siddārtha cried, "Let be! let be!
Channa! what thing is this who seems a man,
Yet surely only seems, being so bowed,
So miserable, so horrible, so sad?
Are men born sometimes thus? What meaneth he
Moaning 'to-morrow or next day I die?'
Finds he no food that so his bones jut forth?
What woe hath happened to this piteous one?"
Then answer made the charioteer, "Sweet Prince!
This is no other than an aged man;
Some fourscore years ago his back was straight,
His eye bright, and his body goodly: now

The thievish years have sucked his sap away,
Pillaged his strength and filched his will and wit;
His lamp has lost its oil, the wick burns black;
What life he keeps is one poor lingering spark
Which flickers for the finish: such is age;
Why should your Highness heed?" Then spake the Prince:
"But shall this come to others, or to all,
Or is it rare that one should be as he?"
"Most noble," answered Channa, "even as he,
Will all these grow if they shall live so long."
"But," quoth the Prince, "if I shall live as long
Shall I be thus; and if Yasōdhara
Live fourscore years, is this old age for her,
Jālīni, little Hasta, Gautami,
And Gunga, and the others?" "Yea, great Sir!"
The charioteer replied. Then spake the Prince:
"Turn back, and drive me to my house again!
I have seen that I did not think to see."

Which pondering, to his beauteous Court returned
Wistful Siddārtha, sad of mien and mood;
Nor tasted he the white cakes nor the fruits
Spread for the evening feast, nor once looked up
While the best palace-dancers strove to charm:
Nor spake—save one sad thing—when wofully
Yasōdhara sank to his feet and wept,
Sighing, "Hath not my Lord comfort in me?"
"Ah, Sweet!" he said, "such comfort that my soul
Aches, thinking it must end, for it will end,
And we shall both grow old, Yasōdhara!
Loveless, unlovely, weak, and old, and bowed.
Nay, though we locked up love and life with lips
So close that night and day our breaths grew one,
Time would thrust in between to filch away
My passion and thy grace, as black Night steals
The rose-gleams from yon peak, which fade to grey
And are not seen to fade. This have I found,
And all my heart is darkened with its dread,
And all my heart is fixed to think how Love

Might save its sweetness from the slayer, Time,
Who makes men old." So through that night he sate
Sleepless, uncomforted.

And all that night
The King Suddhōdana dreamed troublous dreams.
The first fear of his vision was a flag
Broad, glorious, glistening with a golden sun,
The mark of Indra; but a strong wind blew,
Rending its folds divine, and dashing it
Into the dust; whereat a concourse came
Of shadowy Ones, who took the spoiled silk up
And bore it eastward from the city gates.
The second fear was ten huge elephants,
With silver tusks and feet that shook the earth,
Trampling the southern road in mighty march;
And he who sate upon the foremost beast
Was the King's son—the others followed him.
The third fear of the vision was a car,
Shining with blinding light, which four steeds drew,
Snorting white smoke and champing fiery foam;
And in the car the Prince Siddārtha sate.
The fourth fear was a wheel which turned and turned,
With nave of burning gold and jewelled spokes,
And strange things written on the binding tire,
Which seemed both fire and music as it whirled.
The fifth fear was a mighty drum, set down
Midway between the city and the hills,
On which the Prince beat with an iron mace,
So that the sound pealed like a thunderstorm,
Rolling around the sky and far away.
The sixth fear was a tower, which rose and rose
High o'er the city till its stately head
Shone crowned with clouds, and on the top the Prince
Stood, scattering from both hands, this way and that,
Gems of most lovely light, as if it rained
Jacynths and rubies; and the whole world came,
Striving to seize those treasures as they fell
Towards the four quarters. But the seventh fear was
A noise of wailing, and behold six men

Who wept and gnashed their teeth, and laid their palms
Upon their mouths, walking disconsolate.

These seven fears made the vision of his sleep,
But none of all his wisest dream-readers
Could tell their meaning. Then the King was wroth,
Saying, "There cometh evil to my house,
And none of ye have wit to help me know
What the great gods portend sending me this."
So in the city men went sorrowful
Because the King had dreamed seven signs of fear
Which none could read; but to the gate there came
An aged man, in robe of deer-skin clad,
By guise a hermit, known to none; he cried,
"Bring me before the King, for I can read
The vision of his sleep;" who, when he heard
The sevenfold mysteries of the midnight dream,
Bowed reverent and said, "O Mahārāj!
I hail this favoured House, whence shall arise
A wider-reaching splendour than the sun's!
Lo! all these seven fears are seven joys,
Whereof the first, where thou didst see a flag—
Broad, glorious, gilt with Indra's badge—cast down
And carried out, did signify the end
Of old faiths and beginning of the new;
For there is change with gods not less than men,
And as the days pass kalpas pass—at length.
The ten great elephants that shook the earth
The ten great gifts of wisdom signify,
In strength whereof the Prince shall quit his state
And shake the world with passage of the Truth.
The four flame-breathing horses of the car
Are those four fearless virtues which shall bring
Thy son from doubt and gloom to gladsome light;
The wheel that turned with nave of burning gold
Was that most precious Wheel of perfect Law
Which he shall turn in sight of all the world.
The mighty drum whereon the Prince did beat,
Till the sound filled all lands, doth signify

The thunder of the preaching of the Word
Which he shall preach; the tower that grew to heaven
The growing of the Gospel of this Buddh
Sets forth; and those rare jewels scattered thence
The untold treasures are of that good Law
To gods and men dear and desirable.
Such is the interpretation of the tower;
But for those six men weeping with shut mouths,
They are the six chief teachers whom thy son
Shall, with bright truth and speech unanswerable,
Convince of foolishness. O King! rejoice;
The fortune of my Lord the Prince is more
Than kingdoms, and his hermit-rags will be
Beyond fine cloths of gold. This was thy dream!
And in seven nights and days these things shall fall."
So spake the holy man, and lowly made
The eight prostrations, touching thrice the ground;
Then turned and passed; but when the King bade send
A rich gift after him, the messengers
Brought word, "We came to where he entered in
At Chandra's temple, but within was none
Save a grey owl which fluttered from the shrine."
The gods come sometimes thus.

But the sad King
Marvelled, and gave command that new delights
Be compassed to enthral Siddārtha's heart
Amid those dancers of his pleasure-house;
Also he set at all the brazen doors
A doubled guard.

Yet who shall shut out Fate?

For once again the spirit of the Prince
Was moved to see this world beyond his gates
This life of man, so pleasant, if its waves
Ran not to waste and woful finishing
In Time's dry sands. "I pray you let me view
Our city as it is," such was his prayer
To King Suddhōdana. "Your Majesty

In tender heed hath warned the folk before
To put away ill things and common sights,
And make their faces glad to gladden me,
And all the causeways gay; yet have I learned
This is not daily life, and if I stand
Nearest, my father, to the realm and thee,
Fain would I know the people and the streets,
Their simple usual ways, and workday deeds,
And lives which those men live who are not kings.
Give me good leave, dear Lord! to pass unknown
Beyond my happy gardens; I shall come
The more contented to their peace again,
Or wiser, father, if not well content.
Therefore, I pray thee, let me go at will
To-morrow, with my servants, through the streets."
And the King said, amidst his Ministers,
"Belike this second flight may mend the first.
Note how the falcon starts at every sight
New from his hood, but what a quiet eye
Cometh of freedom; let my son see all,
And bid them bring me tidings of his mind."

Thus on the morrow, when the noon was come,
The Prince and Channa passed beyond the gates,
Which opened to the signet of the King;
Yet knew not they who rolled the great doors back
It was the King's son in that merchant's robe,
And in the clerkly dress his charioteer.
Forth fared they by the common way afoot,
Mingling with all the Sākya citizens,
Seeing the glad and sad things of the town:
The painted streets alive with hum of noon,
The traders cross-legged 'mid their spice and grain,
The buyers with their money in the cloth,
The war of words to cheapen this or that,
The shout to clear the road, the huge stone wheels,
The strong slow oxen and their rustling loads,
The singing bearers with the palanquins,
The broad-necked hamals sweating in the sun,

The housewives bearing water from the well
With balanced chatties, and athwart their hips
The black-eyed babes; the fly-swarmed sweetmeat shops,
The weaver at his loom, the cotton-bow
Twanging, the millstones grinding meal, the dogs
Prowling for orts, the skilful armourer
With tong and hammer linking shirts of mail,
The blacksmith with a mattock and a spear
Reddening together in his coals, the school
Where round their Guru,[1] in a grave half-moon,
The Sākya children sang the mantras through,
And learned the greater and the lesser gods;
The dyers stretching waistcloths in the sun
Wet from the vats—orange, and rose, and green;
The soldiers clanking past with swords and shields,
The camel-drivers rocking on the humps,
The Brahman proud, the martial Kshatriya,[2]
The humble toiling Sudra; [3] here a throng
Gathered to watch some chattering snake-tamer
Wind round his wrist the living jewellery
Of asp and nāg, or charm the hooded death
To angry dance with drone of beaded gourd;
There a long line of drums and horns, which went,
With steeds gay painted and silk canopies,
To bring the young bride home; and here a wife
Stealing with cakes and garlands to the god
To pray her husband's safe return from trade,
Or beg a boy next birth; hard by the booths
Where the swart potters beat the noisy brass
For lamps and lotas; [4] thence, by temple walls
And gateways, to the river and the bridge
Under the city walls.

These had they passed
When from the roadside moaned a mournful voice,
"Help, masters! lift me to my feet; oh, help!
Or I shall die before I reach my house!"

[1] Hindu religious teacher.
[2] The second caste of warriors.
[3] The lowest, fourth caste, the servant class.
[4] Brass pots.

A stricken wretch it was, whose quivering fram
Caught by some deadly plague, lay in the dust
Writhing, with fiery purple blotches specked:
The chill sweat beaded on his brow, his mouth
Was dragged awry with twitchings of sore pai
The wild eyes swam with inward agony.
Gasping, he clutched the grass to rise, and rose
Half-way, then sank, with quaking feeble limbs
And scream of terror, crying, "Ah, the pain!
Good people, help!" whereon Siddārtha ran,
Lifted the woful man with tender hands,
With sweet looks laid the sick head on his knee,
And, while his soft touch comforted the wretch,
Asked, "Brother, what is ill with thee? what harm
Hath fallen? wherefore can'st thou not arise?
Why is it, Channa, that he pants and moans,
And gasps to speak, and sighs so pitiful?"
Then spake the charioteer: "Great Prince! this man
Is smitten with some pest; his elements
Are all confounded; in his veins the blood,
Which ran a wholesome river, leaps and boils
A fiery flood; his heart, which kept good time,
Beats like an ill-played drum-skin, quick and slow;
His sinews slacken like a bowstring slipped;
The strength is gone from ham, and loin, and neck,
And all the grace and joy of manhood fled:
This is a sick man with the fit upon him.
See how he plucks and plucks to seize his grief,
And rolls his bloodshot orbs, and grinds his teeth,
And draws his breath as if 'twere choking smoke!
Lo! now he would be dead; but shall not die
Until the plague hath had its work in him,
Killing the nerves which die before the life;
Then, when his strings have cracked with agony
And all his bones are empty of the sense
To ache, the plague will quit and light elsewhere.
Oh, sir! it is not good to hold him so!
The harm may pass, and strike thee, even thee."
But spake the Prince, still comforting the man,

"And are there others, are there many thus?
Or might it be to me as now with him?"
"Great Lord!" answered the charioteer, "this comes
In many forms to all men; griefs and wounds,
Sickness and tetters, palsies, leprosies,
Hot fevers, watery wastings, issues, blains
Befall all flesh and enter everywhere."
"Come such ills unobserved?" the Prince inquired.
And Channa said, "Like the sly snake they come
That stings unseen; like the striped murderer,
Who waits to spring from the Karunda bush,
Hiding beside the jungle path; or like
The lightning, striking these and sparing those,
As chance may send."

"Then all men live in fear?"

"So live they, Prince!"

"And none can say, 'I sleep
Happy and whole to-night, and so shall wake?' "

"None say it."

"And the end of many aches,
Which come unseen, and will come when they come,
Is this, a broken body and sad mind,
And so old age?"

"Yea, if men last as long."

"But if they cannot bear their agonies,
Or if they will not bear, and seek a term;
Or if they bear, and be, as this man is,
Too weak except for groans, and so still live,
And growing old, grow older, then—what end?"

"They die, Prince."

"Die?"

"Yea, at the last comes Death

In whatsoever way, whatever hour.
Some few grow old, most suffer and fall sick,
But all must die—behold, where comes the Dead!"

Then did Siddārtha raise his eyes, and see
Fast pacing towards the river-brink a band
Of wailing people; foremost one who swung
An earthen bowl with lighted coals; behind
The kinsmen, shorn, with mourning marks, ungirt,
Crying aloud, "O Rama,[1] Rama, hear!
Call upon Rama, brothers;" next the bier,
Knit of four poles with bamboos interlaced,
Whereon lay—stark and stiff, feet foremost, lean,
Chapfallen, sightless, hollow-flanked, a-grin,
Sprinkled with red and yellow dust—the Dead,
Whom at the four-went ways they turned head first,
And crying "Rama, Rama!" carried on
To where a pile was reared beside the stream:
Thereon they laid him, building fuel up—
Good sleep hath one that slumbers on that bed!
He shall not wake for cold, albeit he lies
Naked to all the airs—for soon they set
The red flame to the corners four, which crept,
And licked, and flickered, finding out his flesh
And feeding on it with swift hissing tongues,
And crackle of parched skin, and snap of joint;
Till the fat smoke thinned and the ashes sank
Scarlet and grey, with here and there a bone
White midst the grey—the total of the man.

Then spake the Prince: "Is this the end which comes
To all who live?"
"This is the end that comes
To all," quoth Channa; "he upon the pyre—
Whose remnants are so petty that the crows
Caw hungrily, then quit the fruitless feast—
Ate, drank, laughed, loved, and lived, and liked life well.
Then came—who knows?—some gust of jungle wind,

[1] Hindu god, seventh incarnation of Vishnu.

A stumble on the path, a taint in the tank,
A snake's nip, half a span of angry steel,
A chill, a fishbone, or a falling tile,
And life was over and the man is dead.
No appetites, no pleasures, and no pains
Hath such; the kiss upon his lips is nought,
The fire-scorch nought; he smelleth not his flesh
A-roast, nor yet the sandal and the spice
They burn; the taste is emptied from his mouth
The hearing of his ears is clogged, the sight
Is blinded in his eyes; those whom he loved
Wail desolate, for even that must go,
The body which was lamp unto the life,
Or worms will have a horrid feast of it.
Here is the common destiny of flesh:
The high and low, the good and bad, must die,
And then, 'tis taught, begin anew and live
Somewhere, somehow—who knows?—and so again
The pangs, the parting, and the lighted pile:—
Such is man's round."

But lo! Siddārtha turned
Eyes gleaming with divine tears to the sky,
Eyes lit with heavenly pity to the earth;
From sky to earth he looked, from earth to sky,
As if his spirit sought in lonely flight
Some far-off vision, linking this and that,
Lost—past—but searchable, but seen, but known.
Then cried he, while his lifted countenance
Glowed with the burning passion of a love
Unspeakable, the ardour of a hope
Boundless, insatiate: "Oh! suffering world;
Oh! known and unknown of my common flesh,
Caught in this common net of death and woe,
And life which binds to both! I see, I feel
The vastness of the agony of earth,
The vainness of its joys, the mockery
Of all its best, the anguish of its worst;
Since pleasures end in pain, and youth in age,

And love in loss, and life in hateful death,
And death in unknown lives, which will but yoke
Men to their wheel again to whirl the round
Of false delights and woes that are not false.
Me too this lure hath cheated, so it seemed
Lovely to live, and life a sunlit stream
For ever flowing in a changeless peace;
Whereas the foolish ripple of the flood
Dances so lightly down by bloom and lawn
Only to pour its crystal quicklier
Into the foul salt sea. The veil is rent
Which blinded me! I am as all these men
Who cry upon their gods and are not heard,
Or are not heeded—yet there must be aid!
For them and me and all there must be help!
Perchance the gods have need of help themselves,
Being so feeble that when sad lips cry
They cannot save! I would not let one cry
Whom I could save! How can it be that Brahm
Would make a world and keep it miserable,
Since, if, all-powerful, he leaves it so,
He is not good, and if not powerful,
He is not God?—Channa! lead home again!
It is enough! mine eyes have seen enough!"

Which when the King heard, at the gates he set
A triple guard; and bade no man should pass
By day or night, issuing or entering in,
Until the days were numbered of that dream.

BOOK THE FOURTH

But, when the days were numbered, then befell
The parting of our Lord—which was to be—
Whereby came wailing in the Golden Home,
Woe to the King and sorrow o'er the land,
But for all flesh deliverance, and that Law
Which whoso hears—the same shall make him free.

Softly the Indian night sinks on the plains
At full moon, in the month of Chaitra Shud,[1]
When mangoes redden and the asōka buds
Sweeten the breeze, and Rama's birthday comes,
And all the fields are glad and all the towns.
Softly that night fell over Vishramvan,
Fragrant with blooms and jewelled thick with stars,
And cool with mountain airs sighing adown
From snow-flats on Himāla high outspread;
For the moon swung above the eastern peaks,
Climbing the spangled vault, and lighting clear
Rohini's ripples, and the hills and vales,
And all the sleeping land; and near at hand
Silvering those roof-tops of the pleasure-house,
Where nothing stirred nor sign of watching was,
Save at the outer gates, whose warders cried
Mudra, the watchword, and the countersign
Angana, and the watch-drums beat a round;
Whereat the earth lay still, except for yelp
Of prowling jackals, and the ceaseless trill
Of crickets in the garden grounds.

Within—
Where the moon glittered through the lace-worked stone,
Lighting the walls of pearl-shell and the floors
Paved with veined marble—softly fell her beams
On such rare company of Indian girls,
It seemed some chamber sweet in Paradise
Where Devīs rested. All the chosen ones
Of Prince Siddārtha's pleasure-home were there,
The brightest and most faithful of the Court;
Each form so lovely in the peace of sleep,
That you had said "This is the pearl of all!"
Save that beside her or beyond her lay
Fairer and fairer, till the pleasured gaze
Roamed o'er that feast of beauty as it roams
From gem to gem in some great goldsmith-work,
Caught by each colour till the next is seen.

[1] March-April.

With careless grace they lay, their soft brown limbs
Part hidden, part revealed; their glossy hair
Bound back with gold or flowers, or flowing loose
In black waves down the shapely nape and neck.
Lulled into pleasant dreams by happy toils,
They slept, no wearier than jewelled birds
Which sing and love all day, then under wing
Fold head, till morn bids sing and love again.
Lamps of chased silver swinging from the roof
In silver chains, and fed with perfumed oils,
Made with the moonbeams tender lights and shades,
Whereby were seen the perfect lines of grace,
The bosom's placid heave, the soft stained palms
Drooping or clasped, the faces fair and dark,
The great arched brows, the parted lips, the teeth
Like pearls a merchant picks to make a string,
The satin-lidded eyes, with lashes dropped
Sweeping the delicate cheeks, the rounded wrists,
The smooth small feet with bells and bangles decked,
Tinkling low music where some sleeper moved,
Breaking her smiling dream of some new dance
Praised by the Prince, some magic ring to find,
Some fairy love-gift. Here one lay full-length,
Her vina by her cheek, and in its strings
The little fingers still all interlaced
As when the last notes of her light song played
Those radiant eyes to sleep, and sealed her own.
Another slumbered folding in her arms
A desert-antelope, its slender head
Buried with black-sloped horns between her breasts,
Soft nestling; it was eating—when both drowsed—
Red roses, and her loosening hand still held
A rose half-mumbled, while a rose-leaf curled
Between the deer's lips. Here two friends had dozed
Together, weaving mōgra-buds, which bound
Their sister-sweetness in a starry chain,
Linking them limb to limb and heart to heart,
One pillowed on the blossoms, one on her.
Another, ere she slept, was stringing stones

To make a necklet—agate, onyx, sard,
Coral, and moonstone—round her wrist it gleamed
A coil of splendid colour, while she held,
Unthreaded yet, the bead to close it up—
Green turkis, carved with golden gods and scripts.
Lulled by the cadence of the garden stream,
Thus lay they on the clustered carpets, each
A girlish rose with shut leaves, waiting dawn
To open and make daylight beautiful.
This was the ante-chamber of the Prince;
But at the purdah's fringe the sweetest slept—
Gunga and Gotami—chief ministers
In that still House of love.
The purdah hung,
Crimson and blue, with broidered threads of gold,
Across a portal carved in sandal-wood;
Whence by three steps the way was to the bower
Of inmost splendour, and the marriage-couch
Set on a dais soft with silver cloths,
Where the foot fell as though it trod on piles
Of neem-blooms. All the walls were plates of pearl,
Cut shapely from the shells of Lanka's wave;
And o'er the alabaster roof there ran
Rich inlayings of lotus and of bird,
Wrought in skilled work of lazulite and jade,
Jacynth and jasper; woven round the dome,
And down the sides, and all about the frames
Wherein were set the fretted lattices,
Through which there breathed, with moonlight and cool airs,
Scents from the shell-flowers and the jasmine sprays;
Not bringing thither grace or tenderness
Sweeter than shed from those fair presences
Within the place—the beauteous Sākya Prince,
And hers, the stately, bright Yasōdhara.

Half risen from her soft nest at his side,
The chuddar[1] fallen to her waist, her brow
Laid in both palms, the lovely Princess leaned

[1] A kind of fine plain-colored shawl.

With heaving bosom and fast-falling tears.
Thrice with her lips she touched Siddārtha's hand,
And at the third kiss moaned, "Awake, my Lord!
Give me the comfort of thy speech!" Then he:
"What is it with thee, O my life?" but still
She moaned anew before the words would come;
Then spake, "Alas, my Prince! I sank to sleep
Most happy, for the babe I bear of thee
Quickened this eve, and at my heart there beat
That double pulse of life and joy and love
Whose happy music lulled me, but—aho!—
In slumber I beheld three sights of dread,
With thought whereof my heart is throbbing yet.
I saw a white bull with wide-branching horns,
A lord of pastures, pacing through the streets,
Bearing upon his front a gem which shone
As if some star had dropped to glitter there,
Or like the kantha-stone the great Snake keeps
To make bright daylight underneath the earth.
Slow through the streets towards the gates he paced,
And none could stay him, though there came a voice
From Indra's temple, 'If ye stay him not,
The glory of the city goeth forth.'
Yet none could stay him. Then I wept aloud,
And locked my arms about his neck, and strove,
And bade them bar the gates; but that ox-king
Bellowed, and, lightly tossing free his crest,
Broke from my clasp, and bursting through the bars,
Trampled the warders down and passed away.
The next strange dream was this: Four Presences
Splendid, with shining eyes, so beautiful
They seemed the Regents of the Earth who dwell
On Mount Sumeru, lighting from the sky
With retinue of countless heavenly ones,
Swift swept unto our city, where I saw
The golden flag of Indra on the gate
Flutter and fall; and lo! there rose instead
A glorious banner, all the folds whereof
Rippled with flashing fire of rubies sewn

Thick on the silver threads, the rays wherefrom
Set forth new words and weighty sentences
Whose message made all living creatures glad;
And from the east the wind of sunrise blew
With tender waft, opening those jewelled scrolls
So that all flesh might read; and wondrous blooms—
Plucked in what clime I know not—fell in showers,
Coloured as none are coloured in our groves."

Then spake the Prince: "All this, my Lotus-flower!
Was good to see."

"Ay, Lord," the Princess said,
"Save that it ended with a voice of fear
Crying, 'The time is nigh! the time is nigh!'
Thereat the third dream came; for when I sought
Thy side, sweet Lord! ah, on our bed there lay
An unpressed pillow and an empty robe—
Nothing of thee but those!—nothing of thee,
Who art my life and light, my king, my world!
And, sleeping still, I rose, and sleeping saw
Thy belt of pearls, tied here below my breasts,
Change to a stinging snake; my ankle-rings
Fall off, my golden bangles part and fall;
The jasmines in my hair wither to dust;
While this our bridal-couch sank to the ground,
And something rent the crimson purdah down:
Then far away I heard the white bull low,
And far away the embroidered banner flap,
And once again that cry, 'The time is come!'
But with that cry—which shakes my spirit still—
I woke! O Prince! what may such visions mean
Except I die, or—worse than any death—
Thou shouldst forsake me, or be taken?"

Soft
As the last smile of sunset was the look
Siddārtha bent upon his weeping wife.
"Comfort thee, dear!" he said, "if comfort lives
In changeless love! for though thy dreams may be
Shadows of things to come, and though the gods

Are shaken in their seats, and though the world
Stands nigh, perchance, to know some way of help,
Yet, whatsoever fall to thee and me,
Be sure I loved and love Yasōdhara.
Thou knowest how I muse these many moons,
Seeking to save the sad earth I have seen;
And when the time comes, that which will be will.
But if my soul yearns sore for souls unknown,
And if I grieve for griefs which are not mine,
Judge how my high-winged thoughts must hover here
O'er all these lives that share and sweeten mine—
So dear! and thine the dearest, gentlest, best,
And nearest. Ah, thou mother of my babe!
Whose body mixed with mine for this fair hope,
When most my spirit wanders, ranging round
The lands and seas—as full of ruth for men
As the far-flying dove is full of ruth
For her twin nestlings—ever it has come
Home with glad wing and passionate plumes to thee,
Who art the sweetness of my kind best seen,
The utmost of their good, the tenderest
Of all their tenderness, mine most of all.
Therefore, whatever after this betide,
Bethink thee of that lordly bull which lowed,
That jewelled banner in thy dream which waved
Its folds departing, and of this be sure,
Always I loved and always love thee well,
And what I sought for all sought most for thee.
But thou, take comfort; and, if sorrow falls,
Take comfort still in deeming there may be
A way to peace on earth by woes of ours;
And have with this embrace what faithful love
Can think of thanks or frame for benison—
Too little, seeing love's strong self is weak—
Yet kiss me on the mouth, and drink these words
From heart to heart therewith, that thou mayst know—
What others will not—that I loved thee most
Because I loved so well all living souls.
Now, Princess! rest; for I will rise and watch."

Then in her tears she slept, but sleeping sighed—
As if that vision passed again—"The time!
The time is come!" Whereat Siddārtha turned,
And, lo! the moon shone by the Crab! the stars
In that same silver order long foretold
Stood ranged to say, "This is the night!—choose thou
The way of greatness or the way of good:
To reign a King of kings, or wander lone,
Crownless and homeless, that the world be helped."
Moreover, with the whispers of the gloom,
Came to his ears again that warning song,
As when the Devas spoke upon the wind:
And surely Gods were round about the place
Watching our Lord, who watched the shining stars.

"I will depart," he spake; "the hour is come!
Thy tender lips, dear Sleeper, summon me
To that which saves the earth but sunders us;
And in the silence of yon sky I read
My fated message flashing. Unto this
Came I, and unto this all nights and days
Have led me; for I will not have that crown
Which may be mine: I lay aside those realms
Which wait the gleaming of my naked sword:
My chariot shall not roll with bloody wheels
From victory to victory, till earth
Wears the red record of my name. I choose
To tread its paths with patient, stainless feet,
Making its dust my bed, its loneliest wastes
My dwelling, and its meanest things my mates;
Clad in no prouder garb than outcasts wear,
Fed with no meats save what the charitable
Give of their will, sheltered by no more pomp
Than the dim cave lends or the jungle-bush.
This will I do because the woful cry
Of life and all flesh living cometh up
Into my ears, and all my soul is full
Of pity for the sickness of this world;
Which I will heal, if healing may be found

By uttermost renouncing and strong strife.
For which of all the great and lesser Gods
Have power or pity? Who hath seen them—who?
What have they wrought to help their worshippers?
How hath it steaded man to pray, and pay
Tithes of the corn and oil, to chant the charms,
To slay the shrieking sacrifice, to rear
The stately fane, to feed the priests, and call
On Vishnu, Shiva, Surya,[1] who save
None—not the worthiest—from the griefs that teach
Those litanies of flattery and fear
Ascending day by day, like wasted smoke?
Hath any of my brothers 'scaped thereby
The aches of life, the stings of love and loss,
The fiery fever and the ague-shake,
The slow, dull, sinking into withered age,
The horrible dark death—and what beyond
Waits—till the whirling wheel comes up again,
And new lives bring new sorrows to be borne,
New generations for the new desires
Which have their end in the old mockeries?
Hath any of my tender sisters found
Fruit of the fast or harvest of the hymn,
Or bought one pang the less at bearing-time
For white curds offered and trim tulsi-leaves?
Nay; it may be some of the Gods are good
And evil some, but all in action weak;
Both pitiful and pitiless, and both—
As men are—bound upon this wheel of change,
Knowing the former and the after lives.
For so our scriptures truly seem to teach,
That—once, and wheresoe'er and whence begun—
Life runs its rounds of living, climbing up
From mote, and gnat, and worm, reptile, and fish,
Bird and shagged beast, man, demon, deva, God,

[1] Vishnu, the second of the Hindu Trinity, who takes care of the universe, and who incarnates as avataras to help mankind. Shiva, the third of the Trinity, the Destroyer; sometimes regarded as the One God. (Brahmā, as the creator Prajāpati, lord of all creatures, is the other member.) Surya is the Sun-God.

To clod and mote again; so are we kin
To all that is; and thus, if one might save
Man from his curse, the whole wide world should share
The lightened horror of this ignorance
Whose shadow is chill fear, and cruelty
Its bitter pastime. Yea, if one might save!
And means must be! There must be refuge! Men
Perished in winter-winds till one smote fire
From flint-stones coldly hiding what they held,
The red spark treasured from the kindling sun.
They gorged on flesh like wolves, till one sowed corn,
Which grew a weed, yet makes the life of man;
They mowed and babbled till some tongue struck speech,
And patient fingers framed the lettered sound.
What good gift have my brothers, but it came
From search and strife and loving sacrifice?
If one, then, being great and fortunate,
Rich, dowered with health and ease, from birth designed
To rule—if he would rule—a King of kings;
If one, not tired with life's long day but glad
I' the freshness of its morning, one not cloyed
With love's delicious feasts, but hungry still;
If one not worn and wrinkled, sadly sage,
But joyous in the glory and the grace
That mix with evils here, and free to choose
Earth's loveliest at his will: one even as I,
Who ache not, lack not, grieve not, save with griefs
Which are not mine, except as I am man;—
If such a one, having so much to give,
Gave all, laying it down for love of men,
And thenceforth spent himself to search for truth,
Wringing the secret of deliverance forth,
Whether it lurk in hells or hide in heavens,
Or hover, unrevealed, nigh unto all:
Surely at last, far off, sometime, somewhere,
The veil would lift for his deep-searching eyes,
The road would open for his painful feet,
That should be won for which he lost the world,
And Death might find him conqueror of death.

This will I do, who have a realm to lose,
Because I love my realm, because my heart
Beats with each throb of all the hearts that ache,
Known and unknown, these that are mine and those
Which shall be mine, a thousand million more
Saved by this sacrifice I offer now.
Oh, summoning stars! I come! Oh, mournful earth!
For thee and thine I lay aside my youth,
My throne, my joys, my golden days, my nights,
My happy palace—and thine arms, sweet Queen!
Harder to put aside than all the rest!
Yet thee, too, I shall save, saving this earth;
And that which stirs within thy tender womb,
My child, the hidden blossom of our loves,
Whom if I wait to bless my mind will fail.
Wife! child! father! and people! ye must share
A little while the anguish of this hour
That light may break and all flesh learn the Law.
Now am I fixed, and now I will depart,
Never to come again, till what I seek
Be found—if fervent search and strife avail."

So, with his brow he touched her feet, and bent
The farewell of fond eyes, unutterable,
Upon her sleeping face, still wet with tears;
And thrice around the bed in reverence,
As though it were an altar, softly stepped
With clasped hands laid upon his beating heart,
"For never," spake he, "lie I there again!"
And thrice he made to go, but thrice came back,
So strong her beauty was, so large his love:
Then, o'er his head drawing his cloth, he turned
And raised the purdah's edge:

There drooped, close-hushed,
In such sealed sleep as water-lilies know,
That lovely garden of his Indian girls;
The twin dark-petalled lotus-buds of all—
Gunga and Gotami—on either side,

And those, their silk-leaved sisterhood, beyond.
"Pleasant ye are to me, sweet friends!" he said,
"And dear to leave; yet, if I leave ye not,
What else will come to all of us save eld
Without assuage and death without avail?
Lo! as ye lie asleep so must ye lie
A-dead; and when the rose dies where are gone
Its scent and splendour? when the lamp is drained
Whither is fled the flame? Press heavy, Night!
Upon their down-dropped lids, and seal their lips,
That no tear stay me and no faithful voice.
For all the brighter that these made my life,
The bitterer it is that they and I,
And all, should live as trees do—so much spring,
Such and such rains and frosts, such winter-times,
And then dead leaves, with maybe spring again,
Or axe-stroke at the root. This will not I,
Whose life here was a God's!—this would not I,
Though all my days were godlike, while men moan
Under their darkness. Therefore farewell, friends!
While life is good to give, I give, and go
To seek deliverance and that unknown Light!"

Then, lightly treading where those sleepers lay,
Into the night Siddārtha passed: its eyes,
The watchful stars, looked love on him: its breath,
The wandering wind, kissed his robe's fluttered fringe;
The garden-blossoms, folded for the dawn,
Opened their velvet hearts to waft him scents
From pink and purple censers: o'er the land,
From Himalay unto the Indian Sea,
A tremor spread, as if earth's soul beneath
Stirred with an unknown hope; and holy books—
Which tell the story of our Lord—say, too,
That rich celestial musics thrilled the air
From hosts on hosts of shining ones, who thronged
Eastward and westward, making bright the night—
Northward and southward, making glad the ground.
Also those four dread Regents of the Earth,

Descending at the doorway, two by two,—
With their bright legions of Invisibles
In arms of sapphire, silver, gold, and pearl—
Watched with joined hands the Indian Prince, who stood,
His tearful eyes raised to the stars, and lips
Close-set with purpose of prodigious love.

Then strode he forth into the gloom, and cried:
"Channa, awake! and bring out Kantaka!"
"What would my Lord?" the charioteer replied—
Slow-rising from his place beside the gate—
"To ride at night when all the ways are dark?"

"Speak low," Siddārtha said: "and bring my horse,
For now the hour is come when I should quit
This golden prison, where my heart lives caged,
To find the truth; which henceforth I will seek,
For all men's sake, until the truth be found."

"Alas! dear Prince," answered the charioteer,
"Spake then for nought those wise and holy men
Who cast the stars, and bade us wait the time
When King Suddhōdana's great son should rule
Realms upon realms, and be a Lord of lords?
Wilt thou ride hence and let the rich world slip
Out of thy grasp, to hold a beggar's bowl?
Wilt thou go forth into the friendless waste
That hast this Paradise of pleasures here?"

The Prince made answer, "Unto this I came,
And not for thrones: the kingdom that I crave
Is more than many realms—and all things pass
To change and death. Bring me forth Kantaka!"

"Most honoured," spake again the charioteer,
"Bethink thee of my Lord thy father's grief!
Bethink thee of their woe whose bliss thou art—
How shalt thou help them, first undoing them?"
Siddārtha answered, "Friend, that love is false

Which clings to love for selfish sweets of love;
But I, who love these more than joys of mine—
Yea, more than joy of theirs—depart to save
Them and all flesh, if utmost love avail:
Go, bring me Kantaka!"

Then Channa said,
"Master, I go!" and forthwith, mournfully,
Unto the stall he passed, and from the rack
Took down the silver bit and bridle-chains,
Breast-cord and curb, and knitted fast the straps,
And linked the hooks, and led out Kantaka:
Whom, tethering to the ring, he combed and dressed,
Stroking the snowy coat to silken gloss;
Next on the steed he laid the numdah[1] square,
Fitted the saddle-cloth across, and set
The saddle fair, drew tight the jewelled girths,
Buckled the breech-bands and the martingale,
And made fall both the stirrups of worked gold.
Then over all he cast a golden net,
With tassels of seed-pearl and silken strings,
And led the great horse to the palace door,
Where stood the Prince; but when he saw his Lord,
Right glad he waxed and joyously he neighed,
Spreading his scarlet nostrils; and the books
Write, "Surely all had heard Kantaka's neigh,
And that strong trampling of his iron heels,
Save that the Devas laid soft unseen wings
Over their ears, and kept the sleepers deaf."

Fondly Siddārtha drew the proud head down,
Patted the shining neck, and said, "Be still,
White Kantaka! be still, and bear me now
The farthest journey ever rider rode;
For this night take I horse to find the truth,
And where my quest will end yet know I not,
Save that it shall not end until I find.
Therefore to-night, good steed, be fierce and bold!

[1] Coarse woolen cloth below the saddle.

Let nothing stay thee, though a thousand blades
Deny the road! let neither wall nor moat
Forbid our flight! Look! if I touch thy flank
And cry, 'On, Kantaka!' let whirlwinds lag
Behind thy course! Be fire and air, my horse!
To stead thy Lord; so shalt thou share with him
The greatness of this deed which helps the world;
For therefore ride I, not for men alone,
But for all things which, speechless, share our pain
And have no hope, nor wit to ask for hope.
Now, therefore, bear thy master valorously!"

Then to the saddle lightly leaping, he
Touched the arched crest, and Kantaka sprang forth
With armed hoofs sparkling on the stones, and ring
Of champing bit; but none did hear that sound,
For that the Suddha Devas, gathering near,
Plucked the red mohra-flowers and strewed them thick
Under his tread, while hands invisible
Muffled the ringing bit and bridle-chains.
Moreover, it is written when they came
Upon the pavement near the inner gates,
The Yakshas[1] of the air laid magic cloths
Under the stallion's feet, so that he went
Softly and still.
But when they reached the gate
Of tripled brass—which hardly fivescore men
Served to unbar and open—lo! the doors
Rolled back all silently, though one might hear
In daytime two koss off the thunderous roar
Of those grim hinges and unwieldy plates.

Also the middle and the outer gates
Unfolded each their monstrous portals thus
In silence, as Siddārtha and his steed
Drew near; while underneath their shadow lay,
Silent as dead men, all those chosen guards—
The lance and sword let fall, the shields unbraced,

[1] Goblins, spirits.

Captains and soldiers—for there came a wind,
Drowsier than blows o'er Malwa's fields of sleep,
Before the Prince's path, which, being breathed,
Lulled every sense aswoon: and so he passed
Free from the palace.

When the morning star
Stood half a spear's length from the eastern rim,
And o'er the earth the breath of morning sighed,
Rippling Anoma's wave, the border-stream,
Then drew he rein, and leaped to earth, and kissed
White Kantaka betwixt the ears, and spake
Full sweet to Channa: "This which thou hast done
Shall bring thee good, and bring all creatures good:
Be sure I love thee always for thy love.
Lead back my horse, and take my crest-pearl here,
My princely robes, which henceforth stead me not,
My jewelled sword-belt and my sword, and these
The long locks by its bright edge severed thus
From off my brows. Give the King all, and say
Siddārtha prays forget him till he come
Ten times a Prince, with royal wisdom won
From lonely searchings and the strife for light;
Where, if I conquer, lo! all earth is mine—
Mine by chief service!—tell him—mine by love!
Since there is hope for man only in man,
And none hath sought for this as I will seek,
Who cast away my world to save my world."

BOOK THE FIFTH

Round Rajagriha five fair hills arose,
Guarding King Bimbisāra's sylvan town:
Baibhāra, green with lemon-grass and palms;
Bipulla, at whose foot thin Sarsuti
Steals with warm ripple; shadowy Tapovan,
Whose steaming pools mirror black rocks, which ooze
Sovereign earth-butter from their rugged roofs;
South-east the vulture-peak Sailāgiri;
And eastward Ratnagiri, hill of gems.

A winding track, paven with footworn slabs,
Leads thee, by safflower fields and bamboo tufts,
Under dark mangoes and the jujube-trees,
Past milk-white veins of rock and jasper crags,
Low cliff and flats of jungle-flowers, to where
The shoulder of that mountain, sloping west,
O'erhangs a cave with wild figs canopied.
Lo! thou who comest thither, bare thy feet
And bow thy head! for all this spacious earth
Hath not a spot more dear and hallowed. Here
Lord Buddha sate the scorching summers through,
The driving rains, the chilly dawns and eves;
Wearing for all men's sakes the yellow robe,
Eating in beggar's guise the scanty meal
Chance-gathered from the charitable; at night
Couched on the grass, homeless, alone; while yelped
The sleepless jackals round his cave, or coughs
Of famished tiger from the thicket broke.
By day and night here dwelt the World-honoured,
Subduing that fair body born for bliss
With fast and frequent watch and search intense
Of silent meditation, so prolonged
That ofttimes while he mused—as motionless
As the fixed rock his seat—the squirrel leaped
Upon his knee, the timid quail led forth
Her brood between his feet, and blue doves pecked
The rice-grains from the bowl beside his hand.

Thus would he muse from noontide—when the land
Shimmered with heat, and walls and temples danced
In the reeking air—till sunset, noting not
The blazing globe roll down, nor evening glide,
Purple and swift, across the softened fields;
Nor the still coming of the stars, nor throb
Of drum-skins in the busy town, nor screech
Of owl and night-jar; wholly wrapt from self
In keen unravelling of the threads of thought
And steadfast pacing of life's labyrinths.
Thus would he sit till midnight hushed the world,

Save where the beasts of darkness in the brake
Crept and cried out, as fear and hatred cry,
As lust and avarice and anger creep
In the black jungles of man's ignorance.
Then slept he for what space the fleet moon asks
To swim a tenth part of her cloudy sea;
But rose ere the False-dawn, and stood again
Wistful on some dark platform of his hill,
Watching the sleeping earth with ardent eyes
And thoughts embracing all its living things;
While o'er the waving fields that murmur moved
Which is the kiss of Morn waking the lands,
And in the east that miracle of Day
Gathered and grew. At first a dusk so dim
Night seems still unaware of whispered dawn,
But soon—before the jungle-cock crows twice—
A white verge clear, a widening, brightening white,
High as the herald-star, which fades in floods
Of silver, warming into pale gold, caught
By topmost clouds, and flaming on their rims
To fervent golden glow, flushed from the brink
With saffron, scarlet, crimson, amethyst;
Whereat the sky burns splendid to the blue,
And, robed in raiment of glad light, the King
Of Life and Glory cometh!

Then our Lord,
After the manner of a Rishi, hailed
The rising orb, and went—ablutions made—
Down by the winding path unto the town;
And in the fashion of a Rishi passed
From street to street, with begging-bowl in hand,
Gathering the little pittance of his needs.
Soon was it filled, for all the townsmen cried,
"Take of our store, great sir!" and "Take of ours!"
Marking his godlike face and eyes enwrapt;
And mothers, when they saw our Lord go by,
Would bid their children fall to kiss his feet,
And lift his robe's hem to their brows, or run

To fill his jar, and fetch him milk and cakes.
And ofttimes as he paced, gentle and slow,
Radiant with heavenly pity, lost in care
For those he knew not, save as fellow-lives,
The dark surprised eyes of some Indian maid
Would dwell in sudden love and worship deep
On that majestic form, as if she saw
Her dreams of tenderest thought made true, and grace
Fairer than mortal fire her breast. But he
Passed onward with the bowl and yellow robe,
By mild speech paying all those gifts of hearts,
Wending his way back to the solitudes
To sit upon his hill with holy men,
And hear and ask of wisdom and its roads.

Midway on Ratnagiri's groves of calm,
Beyond the city, but below the caves,
Lodged such as hold the body foe to soul,
And flesh a beast which men must chain and tame
With bitter pains, till sense of pain is killed,
And tortured nerves vex torturer no more:
Yogis and Brahmacharis,[1] Bhikshus,[2] all
A gaunt and mournful band, dwelling apart.
Some day and night had stood with lifted arms,
Till—drained of blood and withered by disease—
Their slowly wasting joints and stiffened limbs
Jutted from sapless shoulders like dead forks
From forest trunks. Others had clenched their hands
So long and with so fierce a fortitude,
The claw-like nails grew through the festered palm.
Some walked on sandals spiked; some with sharp flints
Gashed breast and brow and thigh, scarred these with fire,
Threaded their flesh with jungle thorns and spits,
Besmeared with mud and ashes, crouching foul
In rags of dead men wrapped about their loins.
Certain there were inhabited the spots
Where death-pyres smouldered, cowering defiled

[1] Brahmana students. [2] Monks, devotees.

With corpses for their company, and kites
Screaming around them o'er the funeral-spoils:
Certain who cried five hundred times a day
The names of Shiva, knit with hissing snakes
About their sun-tanned necks and hollow flanks,
One palsied foot drawn up against the ham.
So gathered they, a grievous company;
Crowns blistered by the blazing heat, eyes bleared,
Sinews and muscles shrivelled, visages
Haggard and wan as slain men's, five days dead;
Here crouched one in the dust who noon by noon
Meted a thousand grains of millet out,
Ate it with famished patience, seed by seed,
And so starved on; there one who bruised his pulse
With bitter leaves lest palate should be pleased;
And next, a miserable saint self-maimed,
Eyeless and tongueless, sexless, crippled, deaf;
The body by the mind being thus stripped
For glory of much suffering, and the bliss
Which they shall win—say holy books—whose woe
Shames gods that send us woe, and makes men gods
Stronger to suffer than Hell is to harm.

Whom sadly eyeing spake our Lord to one,
Chief of the woe-begones: "Much-suffering sir!
These many moons I dwell upon the hill—
Who am a seeker of the Truth—and see
My brothers here, and thee, so piteously
Self-anguished; wherefore add ye ills to life
Which is so evil?"

Answer made the sage:
" 'Tis written if a man shall mortify
His flesh, till pain be grown the life he lives
And death voluptuous rest, such woes shall purge
Sin's dross away, and the soul, purified,
Soar from the furnace of its sorrow, winged
For glorious spheres and splendour past all thought."

"Yon cloud which floats in heaven," the Prince replied,
"Wreathed like gold cloth around your Indra's throne,
Rose thither from the tempest-driven sea;
But it must fall again in tearful drops,
Trickling through rough and painful water-ways
By cleft and nullah and the muddy flood,
To Gunga and the sea, wherefrom it sprang.
Know'st thou, my brother, if it be not thus,
After their many pains, with saints in bliss?
Since that which rises falls, and that which buys
Is spent; and if ye buy heav'n with your blood
In hell's hard market, when the bargain's through
The toil begins again!"

"It may begin,"
The hermit moaned. "Alas! we know not this,
Nor surely anything; yet after night
Day comes, and after turmoil peace, and we
Hate this accursed flesh which clogs the soul
That fain would rise; so, for the sake of soul,
We stake brief agonies in game with Gods
To gain the larger joys."

"Yet if they last
A myriad years," he said, "they fade at length,
Those joys; or if not, is there then some life
Below, above, beyond, so unlike life
It will not change? Speak! do your Gods endure
For ever, brothers?"

"Nay," the Yogis said,
"Only great Brahm endures: the Gods but live."

Then spake Lord Buddha: "Will ye, being wise,
As ye seem holy and strong-hearted ones,
Throw these sore dice, which are your groans and moans,
For gains which may be dreams, and must have end?
Will ye, for love of soul, so loathe your flesh,
So scourge and maim it, that it shall not serve
To bear the spirit on, searching for home,

But founder on the track before night-fall,
Like willing steed o'er-spurred? Will ye, sad sirs!
Dismantle and dismember this fair house,
Where we have come to dwell by painful pasts;
Whose windows give us light—the little light—
Whereby we gaze abroad to know if dawn
Will break, and whither winds the better road?"

Then cried they, "We have chosen this for road
And tread it, Rajaputra! [1] till the close—
Though all its stones were fire—in trust of death.
Speak, if thou know'st a way more excellent;
If not, peace go with thee!"

Onward he passed,
Exceeding sorrowful, seeing how men
Fear so to die they are afraid to fear,
Lust so to live they dare not love their life,
But plague it with fierce penances, belike
To please the Gods who grudge pleasure to man;
Belike to baulk hell by self-kindled hells;
Belike in holy madness, hoping soul
May break the better through their wasted flesh.
"Oh, flowerets of the field!" Siddārtha said,
"Who turn your tender faces to the sun—
Glad of the light, and grateful with sweet breath
Of fragrance and these robes of reverence donned
Silver and gold and purple—none of ye
Miss perfect living, none of ye despoil
Your happy beauty. Oh, ye palms! which rise
Eager to pierce the sky and drink the wind
Blown from Malaya and the cool blue seas,
What secret know ye that ye grow content,
From time of tender shoot to time of fruit,
Murmuring such sun-songs from your feathered crowns?
Ye, too, who dwell so merry in the trees—
Quick-darting parrots, bee-birds, bulbuls, doves—
None of ye hate your life, none of ye deem

[1] Son of a king, prince; "putra" means son.

To strain to better by foregoing needs!
But man, who slays ye—being lord—is wise,
And wisdom, nursed on blood, cometh thus forth
In self-tormentings!"

While the Master spake
Blew down the mount the dust of pattering feet,
White goats and black sheep winding slow their way,
With many a lingering nibble at the tufts,
And wanderings from the path, where water gleamed
Or wild figs hung. But always as they strayed
The herdsman cried, or slung his sling, and kept
The silly crowd still moving to the plain.
A ewe with couplets in the flock there was,
Some hurt had lamed one lamb, which toiled behind
Bleeding, while in the front its fellow skipped,
And the vexed dam hither and thither ran,
Fearful to lose this little one or that;
Which when our Lord did mark, full tenderly
He took the limping lamb upon his neck,
Saying, "Poor woolly mother, be at peace!
Whither thou goest I will bear thy care;
'Twere all as good to ease one beast of grief
As sit and watch the sorrows of the world
In yonder caverns with the priests who pray."

"But," spake he to the herdsmen, "wherefore, friends!
Drive ye the flocks adown under high noon,
Since 'tis at evening that men fold their sheep?"

And answer gave the peasants: "We are sent
To fetch a sacrifice of goats five-score,
And five-score sheep, the which our Lord the King
Slayeth this night in worship of his gods."
Then said the Master: "I will also go!"
So paced he patiently, bearing the lamb
Beside the herdsmen in the dust and sun,
The wistful ewe low bleating at his feet.

Whom, when they came unto the river-side
A woman—dove-eyed, young, with tearful face
And lifted hands—saluted, bending low:
"Lord! thou art he," she said, "who yesterday
Had pity on me in the fig-grove here,
Where I live lone and reared my child; but he
Straying amid the blossoms found a snake,
Which twined about his wrist, whilst he did laugh
And tease the quick-forked tongue and opened mouth
Of that cold playmate. But, alas! ere long
He turned so pale and still, I could not think
Why he should cease to play, and let my breast
Fall from his lips. And one said, 'He is sick
Of poison'; and another, 'He will die.'
But I, who could not lose my precious boy,
Prayed of them physic, which might bring the light
Back to his eyes; it was so very small
That kiss-mark of the serpent, and I think
It could not hate him, gracious as he was,
Nor hurt him in his sport. And some one said,
'There is a holy man upon the hill—
Lo! now he passeth in the yellow robe—
Ask of the Rishi if there be a cure
For that which ails thy son.' Whereon I came
Trembling to thee, whose brow is like a god's,
And wept and drew the face-cloth from my babe,
Praying thee tell what simples might be good.
And thou, great sir! didst spurn me not, but gaze
With gentle eyes and touch with patient hand;
Then draw the face-cloth back, saying to me,
'Yea! little sister, there is that might heal
Thee first, and him, if thou couldst fetch the thing;
For they who seek physicians bring to them
What is ordained. Therefore, I pray thee, find
Black mustard-seed, a tola; only mark
Thou take it not from any hand or house
Where father, mother, child, or slave hath died:
It shall be well if thou canst find such seed.'
Thus didst thou speak, my Lord!"

The Master smiled
Exceeding tenderly. "Yea! I spake thus,
Dear Kisagōtami![1] But didst thou find
The seed?"
"I went, Lord, clasping to my breast
The babe, grown colder, asking at each hut—
Here in the jungle and towards the town—
'I pray you, give me mustard, of your grace,
A tola—black'; and each who had it gave,
For all the poor are piteous to the poor;
But when I asked, 'In my friend's household here
Hath any peradventure ever died—
Husband, or wife, or child, or slave?' they said:
'O Sister! what is this you ask? the dead
Are very many, and the living few!'
So with sad thanks I gave the mustard back,
And prayed of others; but the others said,
'Here is the seed, but we have lost our slave!'
'Here is the seed, but our good man is dead!'
'Here is some seed, but he that sowed it died
Between the rain-time and the harvesting!'
Ah, sir! I could not find a single house
Where there was mustard-seed and none had died!
Therefore I left my child—who would not suck
Nor smile—beneath the wild-vines by the stream,
To seek thy face and kiss thy feet, and pray
Where I might find this seed and find no death,
If now, indeed, my baby be not dead,
As I do fear, and as they said to me."

"My sister! thou hast found," the Master said,
"Searching for what none finds—that bitter balm
I had to give thee. He thou lovedst slept
Dead on thy bosom yesterday: to-day
Thou know'st the whole wide world weeps with thy woe;
The grief which all hearts share grows less for one.
Lo! I would pour my blood if it could stay
Thy tears and win the secret of that curse

[1] See story of Kisā Gotamī, in the section, Some Buddhist Parables and Legends.

Which makes sweet love our anguish, and which drives—
O'er flowers and pastures to the sacrifice—
As these dumb beasts are driven—men their lords.
I seek that secret: bury thou thy child!"

So entered they the city side by side,
The herdsmen and the Prince, what time the sun
Gilded slow Sona's distant stream, and threw
Long shadows down the street and through the gate
Where the King's men kept watch. But when these saw
Our Lord bearing the lamb, the guards stood back,
The market-people drew their wains aside,
In the bazaar buyers and sellers stayed
The war of tongues to gaze on that mild face;
The smith, with lifted hammer in his hand,
Forgot to strike; the weaver left his web,
The scribe his scroll, the money-changer lost
His count of cowries; from the unwatched rice
Shiva's white bull fed free; the wasted milk
Ran o'er the lota while the milkers watched
The passage of our Lord moving so meek,
With yet so beautiful a majesty.
But most the women gathering in the doors
Asked, "Who is this that brings the sacrifice
So graceful and peace-giving as he goes?
What is his caste? whence hath he eyes so sweet?
Can he be Sākra[1] or the Devaraj[2]?"
And others said, "It is the holy man
Who dwelleth with the Rishis on the hill."
But the Lord paced, in meditation lost,
Thinking, "Alas! for all my sheep which have
No shepherd; wandering in the night with none
To guide them; bleating blindly towards the knife
Of Death, as these dumb beasts which are their kin."

Then some one told the King, "There cometh here
A holy hermit, bringing down the flock
Which thou didst bid to crown thy sacrifice."

[1] Another name for Indra. [2] Devaraj, ruler of the gods.

The King stood in his hall of offering,
On either hand the white-robed Brahmans ranged
Muttered their mantras, feeding still the fire
Which roared upon the midmost altar. There
From scented woods flickered bright tongues of flame,
Hissing and curling as they licked the gifts
Of ghee and spices and the Soma juice,
The joy of Indra. Round about the pile
A slow, thick, scarlet streamlet smoked and ran,
Sucked by the sand, but ever rolling down,
The blood of bleating victims. One such lay,
A spotted goat, long-horned, its head bound back
With munja grass; at its stretched throat the knife
Pressed by a priest, who murmured, "This, dread gods,
Of many yajnas[1] cometh as the crown
From Bimbisāra: take ye joy to see
The spirted blood, and pleasure in the scent
Of rich flesh roasting 'mid the fragrant flames;
Let the King's sins be laid upon this goat,
And let the fire consume them burning it,
For now I strike."
But Buddha softly said,
"Let him not strike, great King!" and therewith loosed
The victim's bonds, none staying him, so great
His presence was. Then, craving leave, he spake
Of life, which all can take but none can give,
Life, which all creatures love and strive to keep,
Wonderful, dear, and pleasant unto each,
Even to the meanest; yea, a boon to all
Where pity is, for pity makes the world
Soft to the weak and noble for the strong.
Unto the dumb lips of his flock he lent
Sad pleading words, showing how man, who prays
For mercy to the gods, is merciless,
Being as god to those; albeit all life
Is linked and kin, and what we slay have given
Meek tribute of the milk and wool, and set

[1] Sacrifices.

Fast trust upon the hands which murder them.
Also he spake of what the holy books
Do surely teach, how that at death some sink
To bird and beast, and these rise up to man
In wanderings of the spark which grows purged flame.
So were the sacrifice new sin, if so
The fated passage of a soul be stayed.
Nor, spake he, shall one wash his spirit clean
By blood; nor gladden gods, being good, with blood;
Nor bribe them, being evil; nay, nor lay
Upon the brow of innocent bound beasts
One hair's weight of that answer all must give
For all things done amiss or wrongfully,
Alone, each for himself, reckoning with that
The fixed arithmic of the universe,
Which meteth good for good and ill for ill,
Measure for measure, unto deeds, words, thoughts;
Watchful, aware, implacable, unmoved;
Making all futures fruits of all the pasts.
Thus spake he, breathing words so piteous,
With such high lordliness of ruth and right,
The priests drew down their garments o'er the hands
Crimsoned with slaughter, and the King came near,
Standing with clasped palms reverencing Buddh;
While still our Lord went on, teaching how fair
This earth were if all living things be linked
In friendliness and common use of foods,
Bloodless and pure; the golden grain, bright fruits,
Sweet herbs which grow for all, the waters wan,
Sufficient drinks and meats. Which when these heard,
The might of gentleness so conquered them,
The priests themselves scattered their altar-flames
And flung away the steel of sacrifice;
And through the land next day passed a decree
Proclaimed by criers, and in this wise graved
On rock and column: "Thus the King's will is:—
There hath been slaughter for the sacrifice
And slaying for the meat, but henceforth none
Shall spill the blood of life nor taste of flesh,

Seeing that knowledge grows, and life is one,
And mercy cometh to the merciful."
So ran the edict, and from those days forth
Sweet peace hath spread between all living kind,
Man and the beasts which serve him, and the birds,
On all those banks of Gunga where our Lord
Taught with his saintly pity and soft speech.

For aye so piteous was the Master's heart
To all that breathe this breath of fleeting life,
Yoked in one fellowship of joys and pains,
That it is written in the holy books
How, in an ancient age—when Buddha wore
A Brahman's form, dwelling upon the rock
Named Munda, by the village of Dālidd—
Drought withered all the land: the young rice died
Ere it could hide a quail; in forest glades
A fierce sun sucked the pools; grasses and herbs
Sickened, and all the woodland creatures fled
Scattering for sustenance. At such a time,
Between the hot walls of a nullah, stretched
On naked stones, our Lord spied, as he passed,
A starving tigress. Hunger in her orbs
Glared with green flame; her dry tongue lolled a span
Beyond the gasping jaws and shrivelled jowl:
Her painted hide hung wrinkled on her ribs,
As when between the rafters sinks a thatch
Rotten with rains; and at the poor lean dugs
Two cubs, whining with famine, tugged and sucked,
Mumbling those milkless teats which rendered nought;
While she, their gaunt dam, licked full motherly
The clamorous twins, and gave her flank to them
With moaning throat, and love stronger than want,
Softening the first of that wild cry wherewith
She laid her famished muzzle to the sand
And roared a savage thunder-peal of woe.
Seeing which bitter strait, and heeding nought
Save the immense compassion of a Buddh,
Our Lord bethought: "There is no other way

To help this murderess of the woods but one.
By sunset these will die, having no meat:
There is no living heart will pity her,
Bloody with ravin, lean for lack of blood.
Lo! if I feed her, who shall lose but I,
And how can love lose doing of its kind
Even to the uttermost?" So saying, Buddh
Silently laid aside sandals and staff,
His sacred thread, turban, and cloth, and came
Forth from behind the milk-bush on the sand,
Saying, "Ho! mother, here is meat for thee!"
Whereat the perishing beast yelped hoarse and shrill,
Sprang from her cubs, and, hurling to the earth
That willing victim, had her feast of him
With all the crooked daggers of her claws
Rending his flesh, and all her yellow fangs
Bathed in his blood: the great cat's burning breath
Mixed with the last sigh of such fearless love.

Thus large the Master's heart was long ago,
Not only now, when with his gracious ruth
He bade cease cruel worship of the Gods.
And much King Bimbisāra prayed our Lord—
Learning his royal birth and holy search—
To tarry in that city, saying oft,
"Thy princely state may not abide such fasts;
Thy hands were made for sceptres, not for alms.
Sojourn with me, who have no son to rule,
And teach my kingdom wisdom, till I die,
Lodged in my palace with a beauteous bride."
But ever spake Siddārtha, of set mind:
"These things I had, most noble King, and left,
Seeking the truth; which still I seek, and shall;
Not to be stayed though Sākra's palace ope'd
Its doors of pearl and Devīs [1] wooed me in.
I go to build the Kingdom of the Law,
Journeying to Gaya and the forest shades,
Where, as I think, the light will come to me;

[1] Feminine celestial spirits.

For nowise here among the Rishis comes
That light, nor from the Shasters,[1] nor from fasts
Borne till the body faints, starved by the soul.
Yet there is light to reach and truth to win;
And surely, O true Friend, if I attain
I will return and quit thy love."
Thereat
Thrice round the Prince King Bimbisāra paced,
Reverently bending to the Master's feet,
And bade him speed. So passed our Lord away
Towards Uravilva, not yet comforted,
And wan of face, and weak with six years' quest.
But they upon the hill and in the grove—
Alāra, Udra, and the ascetics five—
Had stayed him, saying all was written clear
In holy Shasters, and that none might win
Higher than *Sruti*[2] and than *Smriti*[3]—nay,
Not the chief saints!—for how should mortal man
Be wiser than the Jnana-Kānd,[4] which tells
That Brahm is bodiless and actionless,
Passionless, calm, unqualified, unchanged,
Pure life, pure thought, pure joy? Or how should man
Be better than the Karmma-Kānd,[5] which shows
How he may strip passion and action off,
Break from the bond of self, and so, unsphered,
Be God, and melt into the vast divine;
Flying from false to true, from wars of sense
To peace eternal, where the Silence lives?

But the Prince heard them, not yet comforted.

BOOK THE SIXTH

THOU, who wouldst see where dawned the light at last,
North-westwards from the "Thousand Gardens" go

[1] Also *shastra, sastra,* a Hindu sacred book, particularly a book of laws.
[2] The *Vedas,* orally handed down and considered as divine revelation.
[3] Name of a religious scripture.
[4] The knowledge portion of the *Vedas.*
[5] The ritualistic portion of the *Vedas.*

By Gunga's valley till thy steps be set
On the green hills where those twin streamlets spring,
Nilājan and Mohāna; follow them,
Winding beneath broad-leaved mahūa-trees,
'Mid thickets of the sansār and the bir,
Till on the plain the shining sisters meet
In Phalgu's bed, flowing by rocky banks
To Gāya and the red Barabar hills.
Hard by that river spreads a thorny waste,
Uruwelaya named in ancient days,
With sandhills broken; on its verge a wood
Waves sea-green plumes and tassels thwart the sky,
With undergrowth wherethrough a still flood steals,
Dappled with lotus-blossoms, blue and white,
And peopled with quick fish and tortoises.
Near it the village of Senāni reared
Its roofs of grass, nestled amid the palms,
Peaceful with simple folk and pastoral toils.

There in the sylvan solitudes once more
Lord Buddha lived, musing the woes of men,
The ways of fate, the doctrines of the books,
The lessons of the creatures of the brake,
The secrets of the silence whence all come,
The secrets of the gloom whereto all go,
The life which lies between, like that arch flung
From cloud to cloud across the sky, which hath
Mists for its masonry and vapoury piers,
Melting to void again which was so fair
With sapphire hues, garnet, and chrysoprase.
Moon after moon our Lord sate in the wood,
So meditating these that he forgot
Ofttimes the hour of food, rising from thoughts
Prolonged beyond the sunrise and the noon,
To see his bowl unfilled, and eat perforce
Of wild fruit fallen from the boughs o'erhead,
Shaken to earth by chattering ape or plucked
By purple parakeet. Therefore his grace
Faded; his body, worn by stress of soul,

Lost day by day the marks, thirty and two,
Which testify the Buddha. Scarce that leaf,
Fluttering so dry and withered to his feet
From off the sāl-branch, bore less likeliness
Of spring's soft greenery than he of him
Who was the princely flower of all his land.

And once, at such a time, the o'erwrought Prince
Fell to the earth in deadly swoon, all spent,
Even as one slain, who hath no longer breath
Nor any stir of blood; so wan he was,
So motionless. But there came by that way
A shepherd-boy, who saw Siddārtha lie
With lids fast-closed, and lines of nameless pain
Fixed on his lips—the fiery noonday sun
Beating upon his head—who, plucking boughs
From wild rose-apple trees, knitted them thick
Into a bower to shade the sacred face.
Also he poured upon the Master's lips
Drops of warm milk, pressed from his she-goat's bag,
Lest, being low caste, he, by touching, wrong one
So high and holy seeming. But the books
Tell how the jambu-branches, planted thus,
Shot with quick life, in wealth of leaf and flower,
And glowing fruitage interlaced and close,
So that the bower grew like a tent of silk
Pitched for a king at hunting, decked with studs
Of silver-work and bosses of red gold.
And the boy worshipped, deeming him some God;
But our Lord gaining breath, arose and asked
Milk in the shepherd's lota. "Ah, my Lord,
I cannot give thee," quoth the lad; "thou seest
I am a Sudra,[1] and my touch defiles!"
Then the World-honoured spake: "Pity and need
Make all flesh kin. There is no caste in blood,
Which runneth of one hue, nor caste in tears,
Which trickle salt with all; neither comes man
To birth with tilka-mark stamped on the brow,

[1] The lowest caste.

Nor sacred thread on neck. Who doth right deed
Is twice-born, and who doeth ill deeds vile.
Give me to drink, my brother; when I come
Unto my quest it shall be good for thee."
Thereat the peasant's heart was glad, and gave.

And on another day there passed that road
A band of tinselled girls, the nautch-dancers
Of Indra's temple in the town, with those
Who made their music—one that beat a drum
Set round with peacock-feathers, one that blew
The piping bansuli, and one that twitched
A three-string sitar. Lightly tripped they down
From ledge to ledge and through the chequered paths
To some gay festival, the silver bells
Chiming soft peals about the small brown feet,
Armlets and wrist-rings tattling answer shrill;
While he that bore the sitar thrummed and twanged
His threads of brass, and she beside him sang—

"Fair goes the dancing when the sitar's tuned;
Tune us the sitar neither low nor high,
And we will dance away the hearts of men.

The string o'er stretched breaks, and the music flies;
The string o'erslack is dumb, and music dies;
Tune us the sitar neither low nor high."

So sang the nautch-girl to the pipe and wires,
Fluttering like some vain, painted butterfly
From glade to glade along the forest path,
Nor dreamed her light words echoed on the ear
Of him, that holy man, who sate so rapt
Under the fig-tree by the path. But Buddh
Lifted his great brow as the wantons passed,
And spake: "The foolish ofttimes teach the wise;
I strain too much this string of life, belike,
Meaning to make such music as shall save.
Mine eyes are dim now that they see the truth,

My strength is waned now that my need is most;
Would that I had such help as man must have,
For I shall die, whose life was all men's hope."

Now, by that river dwelt a landholder
Pious and rich, master of many herds,
A goodly chief, the friend of all the poor;
And from his house the village drew its name—
"Senāni." Pleasant and in peace he lived,
Having for wife Sujāta, loveliest
Of all the dark-eyed daughters of the plain;
Gentle and true, simple and kind was she,
Noble of mien, with gracious speech to all
And gladsome looks—a pearl of womanhood—
Passing calm years of household happiness
Beside her lord in that still Indian home,
Save that no male child blessed their wedded love.
Wherefore, with many prayers she had besought
Lukshmi; and many nights at full-moon gone
Round the great Lingam, nine times nine, with gifts
Of rice and jasmine wreaths and sandal oil
Praying a boy; also Sujāta vowed—
If this should be—an offering of food
Unto the Wood-God, plenteous, delicate,
Set in a bowl of gold under his tree,
Such as the lips of Devs [1] may taste and take.
And this had been: for there was born to her
A beauteous boy, now three months old, who lay
Between Sujāta's breasts, while she did pace
With grateful footsteps to the Wood-God's shrine,
One arm clasping her crimson sari close
To wrap the babe, that jewel of her joys,
The other lifted high in comely curve
To steady on her head the bowl and dish
Which held the dainty victuals for the God.

But Radha, sent before to sweep the ground
And tie the scarlet threads around the tree,

[1] Devas (spirits).

Came eager, crying, "Ah, dear Mistress! look.
There is the Wood-God sitting in his place,
Revealed, with folded hands upon his knees.
See how the light shines round about his brow!
How mild and great he seems, with heavenly eyes!
Good fortune is it thus to meet the gods."

So,—thinking him divine,—Sujāta drew
Tremblingly nigh, and kissed the earth and said,
With sweet face bent, "Would that the Holy One
Inhabiting this grove, Giver of good,
Merciful unto me his handmaiden,
Vouchsafing now his presence, might accept
These our poor gifts of snowy curds, fresh made,
With milk as white as new-carved ivory!"

Therewith into the golden bowl she poured
The curds and milk, and on the hands of Buddh
Dropped attar from a crystal flask—distilled
Out of the hearts of roses: and he ate,
Speaking no word, while the glad mother stood
In reverence apart. But of that meal
So wondrous was the virtue that our Lord
Felt strength and life return as though the nights
Of watching and the days of fast had passed
In dream, as though the spirit with the flesh
Shared that fine meat and plumed its wings anew,
Like some delighted bird at sudden streams
Weary with flight o'er endless wastes of sand,
Which laves the desert dust from neck and crest.
And more Sujāta worshipped, seeing our Lord
Grow fairer and his countenance more bright:
"Art thou indeed the God?" she lowly asked,
"And hath my gift found favour?"

But Buddh said,
"What is it thou dost bring me?"

"Holy One!"
Answered Sujāta, "from our droves I took
Milk of a hundred mothers, newly-calved,

And with that milk I fed fifty white cows,
And with their milk twenty-and-five, and then
With theirs twelve more, and yet again with theirs
The six noblest and best of all our herds.
That yield I boiled with sandal and fine spice
In silver lotas, adding rice, well grown
From chosen seed, set in new-broken ground,
So picked that every grain was like a pearl.
This did I of true heart, because I vowed
Under thy tree, if I should bear a boy
I would make offering for my joy, and now
I have my son, and all my life is bliss!"

Softly our Lord drew down the crimson fold,
And, laying on the little head those hands
Which help the worlds, he said, "Long be thy bliss!
And lightly fall on him the load of life!
For thou hast holpen me who am no God,
But one, thy Brother; heretofore a Prince
And now a wanderer, seeking night and day
These six hard years that light which somewhere shines
To lighten all men's darkness, if they knew!
And I shall find the light; yea, now it dawned
Glorious and helpful, when my weak flesh failed
Which this pure food, fair Sister, hath restored,
Drawn manifold through lives to quicken life
As life itself passes by many births
To happier heights and purging off of sins.
Yet dost thou truly find it sweet enough
Only to live? Can life and love suffice?"

Answered Sujāta, "Worshipful! my heart
Is little, and a little rain will fill
The lily's cup which hardly moists the field.
It is enough for me to feel life's sun
Shine in my Lord's grace and my baby's smile,
Making the loving summer of our home.
Pleasant my days pass filled with household cares
From sunrise when I wake to praise the gods,

And give forth grain, and trim the tulsi-plant,
And set my handmaids to their tasks, till noon,
When my Lord lays his head upon my lap
Lulled by soft songs and wavings of the fan;
And so to supper-time at quiet eve,
When by his side I stand and serve the cakes.
Then the stars light their silver lamps for sleep,
After the temple and the talk with friends.
How should I not be happy, blest so much,
And bearing him this boy whose tiny hand
Shall lead his soul to Swarga,[1] if it need?
For holy books teach when a man shall plant
Trees for the travellers' shade, and dig a well
For the folks' comfort, and beget a son,
It shall be good for such after their death;
And what the books say that I humbly take,
Being not wiser than those great of old
Who spake with gods, and knew the hymns and charms,
And all the ways of virtue and of peace.
Also I think that good must come of good
And ill of evil—surely—unto all—
In every place and time—seeing sweet fruit
Groweth from wholesome roots, and bitter things
From poison stocks; yea, seeing, too, how spite
Breeds hate, and kindness friends, and patience peace
Even while we live; and when 'tis willed we die
Shall there not be as good a 'Then' as 'Now'?
Haply much better! since one grain of rice
Shoots a green feather gemmed with fifty pearls,
And all the starry champak's white and gold
Lurks in those little, naked, grey spring-buds.
Ah, Sir! I know there might be woes to bear
Would lay fond Patience with her face in dust.
If this my babe pass first I think my heart
Would break—almost I hope my heart would break;
That I might clasp him dead and wait my Lord—
In whatsoever world holds faithful wives—
Duteous, attending till his hour should come.

[1] Heaven.

But if Death called Senāni, I should mount
The pile and lay that dear head in my lap,
My daily way, rejoicing when the torch
Lit the quick flame and rolled the choking smoke.
For it is written if an Indian wife
Die so, her love shall give her husband's soul
For every hair upon her head a crore
Of years in Swarga. Therefore fear I not;
And therefore, Holy Sir! my life is glad,
Nowise forgetting yet those other lives
Painful and poor, wicked and miserable,
Whereon the gods grant pity! But for me,
What good I see humbly I seek to do,
And live obedient to the law, in trust
That what will come, and must come, shall come well."

Then spake our Lord, "Thou teachest them who teach,
Wiser than wisdom in thy simple lore.
Be thou content to know not, knowing thus
Thy way of right and duty: grow, thou flower!
With thy sweet kind in peaceful shade—the light
Of Truth's high noon is not for tender leaves
Which must spread broad in other suns, and lift
In later lives a crowned head to the sky.
Thou who hast worshipped me, I worship thee!
Excellent heart! learnéd unknowingly,
As the dove is which flieth home by love.
In thee is seen why there is hope for man
And where we hold the wheel of life at will.
Peace go with thee, and comfort all thy days!
As thou accomplishest, may I achieve!
He whom thou thoughtest God bids thee wish this."

"Mayest thou achieve!" she said, with earnest eyes
Bent on her babe; who reached its tender hands
To Buddh—knowing, belike, as children know,
More than we deem, and reverencing our Lord;
But he arose—made strong with that pure meat—
And bent his footsteps where a great Tree grew,

The Bōdhi-tree[1] (thenceforward in all years
Never to fade, and ever to be kept
In homage of the world), beneath whose leaves
It was ordained the Truth should come to Buddh:
Which now the Master knew; wherefore he went
With measured pace, steadfast, majestical,
Unto the Tree of Wisdom. Oh, ye Worlds!
Rejoice! our Lord wended unto the Tree!

Whom—as he passed into its ample shade,
Cloistered with columned dropping stems, and roofed
With vaults of glistering green—the conscious earth
Worshipped with waving grass and sudden flush
Of flowers about his feet. The forest-boughs
Bent down to shade him; from the river sighed
Cool wafts of wind laden with lotus-scents
Breathed by the water-gods. Large wondering eyes
Of woodland creatures—panther, boar, and deer—
At peace that eve, gazed on his face benign
From cave and thicket. From its cold cleft wound
The mottled deadly snake, dancing its hood
In honour of our Lord; bright butterflies
Fluttered their vans, azure and green and gold,
To be his fan-bearers; the fierce kite dropped
Its prey and screamed; the striped palm-squirrel raced
From stem to stem to see; the weaver bird
Chirped from her swinging nest; the lizard ran;
The koïl sang her hymn; the doves flocked round;
Even the creeping things were 'ware and glad.
Voices of earth and air joined in one song,
Which unto ears that hear said, "Lord and Friend!
Lover and Saviour! Thou who hast subdued
Angers and prides, desires and fears and doubts,
Thou that for each and all hast given thyself,
Pass to the Tree! The sad world blesseth thee
Who art the Buddh that shall assuage her woes.
Pass, Hailed and Honoured! strive thy last for us,
King and high Conqueror! thine hour is come;

[1] The Wisdom-Tree, famous in Buddhist scriptures; *bodhi,* wisdom.

This is the Night the ages waited for!"
Then fell the night, even as our Master sate
Under that Tree. But he who is the Prince
Of Darkness, Mara—knowing this was Buddh
Who should deliver men, and now the hour
When he should find the Truth and save the worlds—
Gave unto all his evil powers command.
Wherefore there trooped from every deepest pit
The fiends who war with Wisdom and the Light,
Arati, Trishna, Raga, and their crew
Of passions, horrors, ignorances, lusts,
The brood of gloom and dread; all hating Buddh,
Seeking to shake his mind; nor knoweth one,
Not even the wisest, how those fiends of Hell
Battled that night to keep the Truth from Buddh:
Sometimes with terrors of the tempest, blasts
Of demon-armies clouding all the wind
With thunder, and with blinding lightning flung
In jagged javelins of purple wrath
From splitting skies; sometimes with wiles and words
Fair-sounding, 'mid hushed leaves and softened airs
From shapes of witching beauty; wanton songs,
Whispers of love; sometimes with royal allures
Of proffered rule; sometimes with mocking doubts,
Making truth vain. But whether these befell
Without and visible, or whether Buddh
Strove with fell spirits in his inmost heart,
Judge ye:—I write what ancient books have writ.

The ten chief Sins came—Mara's mighty ones,
Angels of evil—Attavāda first,
The Sin of Self, who in the Universe
As in a mirror sees her fond face shown,
And, crying "I," would have the world say "I,"
And all things perish so if she endure.
"If thou be'st Buddh," she said, "let others grope
Lightless; it is enough that Thou art Thou
Changelessly; rise and take the bliss of gods
Who change not, heed not, strive not." But Buddh spake,

"The right in thee is base, the wrong a curse;
Cheat such as love themselves." Then came wan Doubt,
He that denies—the mocking Sin—and this
Hissed in the Master's ear, "All things are shows,
And vain the knowledge of their vanity;
Thou dost but chase the shadow of thyself;
Rise and go hence, there is no better way
Than patient scorn, nor any help for man,
Nor any staying of his whirling wheel."
But quoth our Lord, "Thou hast no part with me,
False Visikitcha! subtlest of man's foes."
And third came she who gives dark creeds their power
Sīlabbat-paramāsa, sorceress,
Draped fair in many lands as lowly Faith,
But ever juggling souls with rites and prayers;
The keeper of those keys which lock up Hells
And open Heavens. "Wilt thou dare," she said,
"Put by our sacred books, dethrone our gods,
Unpeople all the temples, shaking down
That law which feeds the priests and props the realms?"
But Buddha answered, "What thou bidd'st me keep
Is form which passes, but the free Truth stands;
Get thee unto thy darkness." Next there drew
Gallantly nigh a braver Tempter, he,
Kama, the King of passions, who hath sway
Over the gods themselves, Lord of all loves,
Ruler of Pleasure's realm. Laughing he came
Unto the tree, bearing his bow of gold
Wreathed with red blooms, and arrows of desire
Pointed with five-tongued delicate flame, which stings
The heart it smites sharper than poisoned barb:
And round him came into that lonely place
Bands of bright shapes with heavenly eyes and lips
Singing in lovely words the praise of Love
To music of invisible sweet chords,
So witching, that it seemed the night stood still
To hear them, and the listening stars and moon
Paused in their orbits while these hymned to Buddh
Of lost delights, and how a mortal man

Findeth nought dearer in the Three wide worlds
Than are the yielded loving fragrant breasts
Of Beauty and the rosy breast-blossoms,
Love's rubies; nay, and toucheth nought more high
Than is that dulcet harmony of form
Seen in the lines and charms of loveliness,
Unspeakable, yet speaking, soul to soul,
Owned by the bounding blood, worshipped by will
Which leaps to seize it, knowing this is best,
This the true heaven where mortals are like gods,
Makers and Masters, this the gift of gifts
Ever renewed and worth a thousand woes.
For who hath grieved when soft arms shut him safe,
And all life melted to a happy sigh,
And all the world was given in one warm kiss?
So sang they with soft float of beckoning hands,
Eyes lighted with love-flames, alluring smiles;
In wanton dance their supple sides and limbs
Revealing and concealing like burst buds
Which tell their colour, but hide yet their hearts.
Never so matchless grace delighted eye
As troop by troop these midnight-dancers swept
Nearer the Tree, each daintier than the last,
Murmuring "O great Siddārtha! I am thine,
Taste of my mouth and see if youth is sweet!"
Also, when nothing moved our Master's mind,
Lo! Kama waved his magic bow, and lo!
The band of dancers opened, and a shape,
Fairest and stateliest of the throng, came forth
Wearing the guise of sweet Yasōdhara.
Tender the passion of those dark eyes seemed
Brimming with tears; yearning those outspread arms
Opened towards him; musical that moan
Wherewith the beauteous shadow named his name,
Sighing, "My Prince! I die for lack of thee!
What heaven hast thou found like that we knew
By bright Rohini in the Pleasure-house,
Where all these weary years I weep for thee?
Return, Siddārtha! ah! return. But touch

My lips again, but let me to thy breast
Once, and these fruitless dreams will end! Oh, look!
Am I not she thou lovedst?" But Buddh said,
"For that sweet sake of her thou playest thus,
Fair and false Shadow! is thy playing vain;
I curse thee not who wear'st a form so dear,
Yet as thou art so are all earthly shows.
Melt to thy void again!" Thereat, a cry
Thrilled through the grove, and all that comely rout
Faded with flickering wafts of flame, and trail
Of vaporous robes.

Next, under darkening skies
And noise of rising storm, came fiercer Sins,
The rearmost of the Ten; Patigha—Hate—
With serpents coiled about her waist, which suck
Poisonous milk from both her hanging dugs,
And with her curses mix their angry hiss.
Little wrought she upon that Holy One
Who with his calm eyes dumbed her bitter lips
And made her black snakes writhe to hide their fangs.
Then followed Ruparaga—Lust of days—
That sensual Sin which out of greed for life
Forgets to live; and next him Lust of Fame,
Nobler Aruparaga, she whose spell
Beguiles the wise, mother of daring deeds,
Battles and toils. And haughty Mano came,
The Field of Pride; and smooth Self-Righteousness,
Uddhachcha; and—with many a hideous band
Of vile and formless things, which crept and flapped
Toad-like and bat-like—Ignorance, the Dam
Of Fear and Wrong, Avidya, hideous hag,
Whose footsteps left the midnight darker, while
The rooted mountains shook, the wild winds howled,
The broken clouds shed from their caverns streams
Of levin-lighted rain; stars shot from heaven,
The solid earth shuddered as if one laid
Flame to her gaping wounds; the torn black air
Was full of whistling wings, of screams and yells,
Of evil faces peering, of vast fronts

Terrible and majestic, Lords of Hell
Who from a thousand Limbos led their troops
To tempt the Master.
But Buddh heeded not,
Sitting serene, with perfect virtue walled
As is a stronghold by its gates and ramps;
Also the Sacred Tree—the Bōdhi-tree—
Amid that tumult stirred not, but each leaf
Glistened as still as when on moonlit eves
No zephyr spills the gathering gems of dew;
For all this clamour raged outside the shade
Spread by those cloistered stems:
In the third watch,—
The earth being still, the hellish legions fled,
A soft air breathing from the sinking moon—
Our Lord attained *Sammā-sambuddh;*[1] he saw,
By light which shines beyond our mortal ken,
The line of all his lives in all the worlds;
Far back, and farther back, and farthest yet,
Five hundred lives and fifty. Even as one,
At rest upon a mountain-summit, marks
His path wind up by precipice and crag,
Past thick-set woods shrunk to a patch; through bogs
Glittering false-green; down hollows where he toiled
Breathless; on dizzy ridges where his feet
Had well-nigh slipped; beyond the sunny lawns,
The cataract, and the cavern, and the pool,
Backward to those dim flats wherefrom he sprang
To reach the blue; thus Buddha did behold
Life's upward steps long-linked, from levels low
Where breath is base, to higher slopes and higher
Whereon the ten great Virtues wait to lead
The climber skyward. Also, Buddha saw
How new life reaps what the old life did sow;
How where its march breaks off its march begins;
Holding the gain and answering for the loss;
And how in each life good begets more good,

[1] Highest knowledge, perfect wisdom; the final liberation from the errors of mortal perceptions.

Evil fresh evil; Death but casting up
Debit or credit, whereupon th' account
In merits or demerits stamps itself
By sure arithmic—where no tittle drops—
Certain and just, on some new-springing life;
Wherein are packed and scored past thoughts and deeds,
Strivings and triumphs, memories and marks
Of lives foregone:

And in the middle watch
Our Lord attained *Abhidjna* [1]—insight vast
Ranging beyond this sphere to spheres unnamed,
System on system, countless worlds and suns
Moving in splendid measures, band by band
Linked in division, one, yet separate,
The silver islands of a sapphire sea
Shoreless, unfathomed, undiminished, stirred
With waves which roll in restless tides of change.
He saw those Lords of Light who hold their worlds
By bonds invisible, how they themselves
Circle obedient round mightier orbs
Which serve profounder splendours, star to star
Flashing the ceaseless radiance of life
From centres ever shifting unto cirques
Knowing no uttermost. These he beheld
With unsealed vision, and of all those worlds,
Cycle on epicycle, all their tale
Of Kalpas, Mahakalpas [2]—terms of time
Which no man grasps, yea, though he knew to count
The drops in Gunga from her springs to the sea,
Measureless unto speech—whereby these wax
And wane; whereby each of this heavenly host
Fulfils its shining life, and darkling dies.
Sakwal by Sakwal, depths and heights he passed
Transported through the blue infinitudes,
Marking—behind all modes, above all spheres,
Beyond the burning impulse of each orb—
That fixed decree at silent work which wills
Evolve the dark to light, the dead to life,

[1] Supernatural powers.

[2] World epochs and super-epochs.

To fulness void, to form the yet unformed,
Good unto better, better unto best,
By wordless edict; having none to bid,
None to forbid; for this is past all gods,
Immutable, unspeakable, supreme;
A Power which builds, unbuilds, and builds again,
Ruling all things accordant to the rule
Of virtue, which is beauty, truth, and use:
So that all things do well which serve the Power,
And ill which hinder; nay, the worm does well
Obedient to its kind; the hawk does well
Which carries bleeding quarries to its young;
The dewdrop and the star shine sisterly
Globing together in the common work;
And man who lives to die, dies to live well
So if he guide his ways by blamelessness
And earnest will to hinder not but help
All things both great and small which suffer life.
These did our Lord see in the middle watch.

But, when the fourth watch came, the secret came
Of Sorrow, which with evil mars the law,
As damp and dross hold back the goldsmith's fire.
Then was the Dukha-Satya [1] opened him
First of the "Noble Truths"; how Sorrow is
Shadow to life, moving where life doth move;
Not to be laid aside until one lays
Living aside, with all its changing states,
Birth, growth, decay, love, hatred, pleasure, pain,
Being and doing. How that none strips off
These sad delights and pleasant griefs who lacks
Knowledge to know them snares; but he who knows
Avidya—Delusion—sets those snares,
Loves life no longer, but ensues escape.
The eyes of such a one are wide, he sees
Delusion breeds Sankhāra, Tendency
Perverse; Tendency Energy—Vidnnān—
Whereby comes Namarūpa, local Form

[1] The truth regarding sorrows.

And Name and Bodiment, bringing the man
With senses naked to the sensible,
A helpless mirror of all shows which pass
Across his heart; and so Vedanā grows—
'Sense-life'—false in its gladness, fell in sadness,
But sad or glad, the Mother of Desire,
Trishna, that thirst which makes the living drink
Deeper and deeper of the false salt waves
Whereon they float, pleasures, ambitions, wealth,
Praise, fame, or domination, conquest, love;
Rich meats and robes, and fair abodes and pride
Of ancient lines, and lust of days, and strife
To live, and sins that flow from strife, some sweet,
Some bitter. Thus Life's thirst quenches itself
With draughts which double thirst, but who is wise
Tears from his soul this Trishna, feeds his sense
No longer on false shows, files his firm mind
To seek not, strive not, wrong not; bearing meek
All ills which flow from foregone wrongfulness,
And so constraining passions that they die
Famished; till all the sum of ended life—
The *Karma* [1]—all that total of a soul
Which is the things it did, the thoughts it had,
The 'Self' it wove—with woof of viewless time,
Crossed on the warp invisible of acts—
The outcome of him on the Universe,
Grows pure and sinless; either never more
Needing to find a body and a place,
Or so informing what fresh frame it takes
In new existence that the new toils prove
Lighter and lighter not to be at all,
Thus "finishing the Path"; free from Earth's cheats;
Released from all the Skandhas of the flesh;
Broken from ties—from Upādānas—saved
From whirling on the Wheel; aroused and sane
As is a man wakened from hateful dreams.
Until—greater than Kings, than Gods more glad!—
The aching craze to live ends, and life glides—

[1] Action or life, with its law of consequences in the present and future life.

Lifeless—to nameless quiet, nameless joy,
Blessed NIRVANA—sinless, stirless rest—
That change which never changes!
Lo! the Dawn
Sprang with Buddh's victory! lo! in the East
Flamed the first fires of beauteous day, poured forth
Through fleeting folds of Night's black drapery.
High in the widening blue the herald-star
Faded to paler silver as there shot
Brighter and brightest bars of rosy gleam
Across the grey. Far off the shadowy hills
Saw the great Sun, before the world was 'ware,
And donned their crowns of crimson; flower by flower
Felt the warm breath of Morn and 'gan unfold
Their tender lids. Over the spangled grass
Swept the swift footsteps of the lovely Light,
Turning the tears of Night to joyous gems,
Decking the earth with radiance, 'broidering
The sinking storm-clouds with a golden fringe,
Gilding the feathers of the palms, which waved
Glad salutation; darting beams of gold
Into the glades; touching with magic wand
The stream to rippled ruby; in the brake
Finding the mild eyes of the antelopes
And saying "It is day!" in nested sleep
Touching the small heads under many a wing
And whispering "Children, praise the light of day!"
Whereat there piped anthems of all the birds,
The Köil's fluted song, the Bulbul's hymn,
The "morning, morning" of the painted thrush,
The twitter of the sunbirds starting forth
To find the honey ere the bees be out,
The grey crow's caw, the parrot's scream, the strokes
Of the green hammersmith, the myna's chirp,
The never-finished love-talk of the doves:
Yea! and so holy was the influence
Of that high Dawn which came with victory
That, far and near, in homes of men there spread

An unknown peace. The slayer hid his knife;
The robber laid his plunder back; the shroff
Counted full tale of coins; all evil hearts
Grew gentle, kind hearts gentler, as the balm
Of that divinest Daybreak lightened Earth.
Kings at fierce war called truce; the sick men leaped
Laughing from beds of pain; the dying smiled
As though they knew that happy Morn was sprung
From fountains farther than the utmost East;
And o'er the heart of sad Yasōdhara,
Sitting forlorn at Prince Siddārtha's bed,
Came sudden bliss, as if love should not fail
Nor such vast sorrow miss to end in joy.
So glad the World was—though it wist not why—
That over desolate wastes went swooning songs
Of mirth, the voice of bodiless Prets and Bhūts
Foreseeing Buddh; and Devas in the air
Cried "It is finished, finished!" and the priests
Stood with the wondering people in the streets
Watching those golden splendours flood the sky,
And saying "There hath happed some mighty thing."
Also in Ran and Jungle grew that day
Friendship amongst the creatures; spotted deer
Browsed fearless where the tigress fed her cubs,
And cheetahs lapped the pool beside the bucks;
Under the eagle's rock the brown hares scoured
While his fierce beak but preened an idle wing;
The snake sunned all his jewels in the beam
With deadly fangs in sheath; the shrike let pass
The nestling-finch; the emerald halcyons
Sate dreaming while the fishes played beneath,
Nor hawked the merops, though the butterflies—
Crimson and blue and amber—flitted thick
Around his perch; the Spirit of our Lord
Lay potent upon man and bird and beast,
Even while he mused under that Bōdhi-tree,
Glorified with the Conquest gained for all,
And lightened by a Light greater than Day's.

Then he arose—radiant, rejoicing, strong—
Beneath the Tree, and lifting high his voice
Spake this, in hearing of all Times and Worlds:—

Many a House of life
Hath held me—seeking ever him who wrought
These prisons of the senses, sorrow-fraught;
Sore was my ceaseless strife!
But now,
Thou Builder of this Tabernacle—Thou!
I know Thee! Never shalt Thou build again
These walls of pain,
Nor raise the roof-tree of deceits, nor lay
Fresh rafters on the clay;
Broken Thy house is, and the ridge-pole split!
Delusion fashioned it!
Safe pass I thence—deliverance to obtain.

BOOK THE SEVENTH

Sorrowful dwelt the King Suddhōdana
All those long years among the Sākya Lords
Lacking the speech and presence of his Son;
Sorrowful sate the sweet Yasōdhara
All those long years, knowing no joy of life,
Widowed of him her living Liege and Prince.
And ever, on the news of some recluse
Seen far away by pasturing camel-men
Or traders threading devious paths for gain,
Messengers from the King had gone and come,
Bringing account of many a holy sage
Lonely and lost to home; but nought of him
The crown of white Kapilavustu's line,
The glory of her monarch and his hope,
The heart's content of sweet Yasōdhara,
Far-wandered now, forgetful, changed, or dead.

But on a day in the Wasanta-time,
When silver sprays swing on the mango-trees

And all the earth is clad with garb of spring,
The Princess sate by that bright garden-stream
Whose gliding glass, bordered with lotus-cups,
Mirrored so often in the bliss gone by
Their clinging hands and meeting lips. Her lids
Were wan with tears, her tender cheeks had thinned;
Her lips' delicious curves were drawn with grief;
The lustrous glory of her hair was hid—
Close-bound as widows use; no ornament
She wore, nor any jewel clasped the cloth—
Coarse, and of mourning-white—crossed on her breast.
Slow moved and painfully those small fine feet
Which had the roe's gait and the rose-leaf's fall
In old years at the loving voice of him.
Her eyes, those lamps of love,—which were as if
Sunlight should shine from out the deepest dark,
Illumining Night's peace with Daytime's glow—
Unlighted now, and roving aimlessly,
Scarce marked the clustering signs of coming Spring,
So the silk lashes drooped over their orbs.
In one hand was a girdle thick with pearls,
Siddārtha's—treasured since that night he fled—
(Ah, bitter Night! mother of weeping days!
When was fond Love so pitiless to love,
Save that this scorned to limit love by life?)
The other led her little son, a boy
Divinely fair, the pledge Siddārtha left—
Named Rahula—now seven years old, who tripped
Gladsome beside his mother, light of heart
To see the spring-bosoms burgeon o'er the world.

So, while they lingered by the lotus-pools,
And, lightly laughing, Rahula flung rice
To feed the blue and purple fish; and she
With sad eyes watched the swiftly-flying cranes,
Sighing, "Oh! creatures of the wandering wing,
If ye shall light where my dear Lord is hid,
Say that Yasōdhara lives nigh to death
For one word of his mouth, one touch of him!"—

Thus, as they played and sighed—mother and child—
Came some among the damsels of the Court
Saying, "Great Princess! there have entered in
At the south gate merchants of Hastinpūr,
Tripusha called and Bhalluk, men of worth,
Long travelled from the loud sea's edge, who bring
Marvellous lovely webs pictured with gold,
Waved blades of gilded steel, wrought bowls in brass,
Cut ivories, spice, simples, and unknown birds,
Treasures of far-off peoples; but they bring
That which doth beggar these, for He is seen!
Thy Lord,—our Lord,—the hope of all the land—
Siddārtha! they have seen him face to face,
Yea, and have worshipped him with knees and brows,
And offered offerings; for he is become
All which was shown, a Teacher of the wise,
World-honoured, holy, wonderful; a Buddh
Who doth deliver men and save all flesh
By sweetest speech and pity vast as Heaven:
And, lo! he journeyeth hither, these do say."

Then—while the glad blood bounded in her veins
As Gunga leaps when first the mountain snows
Melt at her springs—uprose Yasōdhara
And clapped her palms, and laughed, with brimming tears
Beading her lashes. "Oh! call quick," she cried,
"These merchants to my purdah, for mine ears
Thirst like parched throats to drink their blessed news.
Go bring them in,—but, if their tale be true,
Say I will fill their girdles with much gold,
With gems that Kings shall envy: come ye too,
My girls, for ye shall have guerdon of this
If there be gifts to speak my grateful heart."

So went those merchants to the Pleasure-House,
Full softly pacing through its golden ways
With naked feet, amid the peering maids,
Much wondering at the glories of the Court.
Whom, when they came without the purdah's folds,

A voice, tender and eager, filled and charmed
With trembling music, saying, "Ye are come
From far, fair Sirs! and ye have seen my Lord—
Yea, worshipped—for he is become a Buddh,
World-honoured, holy, and delivers men,
And journeyeth hither. Speak! for, if this be,
Friends are ye of my House, welcome and dear."

Then answer made Tripusha, "We have seen
That sacred Master, Princess! we have bowed
Before his feet; for who was lost a Prince
Is found a greater than the King of kings.
Under the Bōdhi-tree by Phalgū's bank
That which shall save the world hath late been wrought
By him,—the Friend of all, the Prince of all—
Thine most, High Lady! from whose tears men win
The comfort of this Word the Master speaks.
Lo! he is well, as one beyond all ills,
Uplifted as a god from earthly woes,
Shining with risen Truth, golden and clear.
Moreover as he entereth town by town,
Preaching those noble ways which lead to peace,
The hearts of men follow his path as leaves
Troop to the wind or sheep draw after one
Who knows the pastures. We ourselves have heard,
By Gaya in the green Tchīrnika grove,
Those wondrous lips and done them reverence:
He cometh hither ere the first rains fall."

Thus spake he, and Yasōdhara, for joy,
Scarce mastered breath to answer, "Be it well
Now and at all times with ye, worthy friends!
Who brings good tidings; but of this great thing
Wist ye how it befell?"

Then Bhalluk told
Such as the people of the valleys knew
Of that dread night of conflict, when the air
Darkened with fiendish shadows, and the earth
Quaked, and the waters swelled with Mara's wrath.

Also how gloriously that morning broke
Radiant with rising hopes for man, and how
The Lord was found rejoicing 'neath his Tree.
But many days the burden of release—
To be escaped beyond all storms of doubt,
Safe on Truth's shore—lay, spake he, on that heart
A golden load; for how shall men—Buddh mused—
Who love their sins and cleave to cheats of sense,
And drink of error from a thousand springs,
Having no mind to see, nor strength to break
The fleshly snare which binds them—how should such
Receive the Twelve Nidānas [1] and the Law
Redeeming all, yet strange to profit by,
As the caged bird oft shuns its opened door?
So had we missed the helpful victory
If, in this earth without a refuge, Buddh,
Winning the way, had deemed it all too hard
For mortal feet and passed, none following him.
Yet pondered the compassion of our Lord;
But in that hour there rang a voice as sharp
As cry of travail, so as if the earth
Moaned in birth-throe, *"Nasyami aham bhū*
Nasyati lóka!" SURELY I AM LOST,
I AND MY CREATURES: then a pause, and next
A pleading sigh borne on the western wind,
"Sruyatām dharma, Bhagwat!" OH, SUPREME!
LET THY GREAT LAW BE UTTERED! Whereupon
The Master cast his vision forth on flesh,
Saw who should hear and who must wait to hear,
As the keen Sun gilding the lotus-lakes
Seeth which buds will open to his beams
And which are not yet risen from their roots;
Then spake, divinely smiling, "Yea! I preach!
Whoso will listen let him learn the Law."

Afterwards passed he, said they, by the hills
Unto Benares, where he taught the Five,

[1] Causes. The twelve Nidānas form the chain of causation which carries on the misery of the world.

Showing how birth and death should be destroyed,
And how man hath no fate except past deeds,
No Hell but what he makes, no Heaven too high
For those to reach whose passions sleep subdued.
This was the fifteenth day of Vaishya
Mid-afternoon, and that night was full moon.

But, of the Rishis, first Kaundinya
Owned the Four Truths and entered on the Paths;
And after him Bhadraka, Asvajit,
Basava, Mahanāma; also there
Within the Deer-park, at the feet of Buddh,
Yasad the Prince with nobles fifty-four,
Hearing the blessed word our Master spake,
Worshipped and followed; for there sprang up peace
And knowledge of a new time come for men
In all who heard, as spring the flowers and grass
When water sparkles through a sandy plain.

These sixty—said they—did our Lord send forth,
Made perfect in restraint and passion-free,
To teach the Way; but the World-honoured turned
South from the Deer-park and Isipatan
To Yashti and King Bimbisāra's realm,
Where many days he taught; and after these
King Bimbisāra and his folk believed,
Learning the law of love and ordered life.
Also he gave the Master, of free gift,—
Pouring forth water on the hands of Buddh,—
The Bamboo-Garden, named Wéluvana,
Wherein are streams and caves and lovely glades;
And the King set a stone there, carved with this:—

"What life's course and cause sustain
These Tathāgato made plain;
What delivers from life's woe
That our Lord hath made us know."

And, in that Garden—said they—there was held
A high Assembly, where the Teacher spake

Wisdom and power, winning all souls which heard;
So that nine hundred took the yellow robe—
Such as the Master wears,—and spread his Law;
And this the gāthā [1] was wherewith he closed:—

"Evil swells the debts to pay,
Good delivers and acquits;
Shun evil, follow good; hold sway
Over thyself. This is the Way."

Whom, when they ended, speaking so of him,
With gifts, and thanks which made the jewels dull,
The Princess recompensed. "But by what road
Wendeth my Lord?" she asked: the merchants said,
"Yōjans [2] threescore stretch from the city-walls
To Rajagriha, whence the easy path
Passeth by Sona hither, and the hills.
Our oxen, treading eight slow koss a day,
Came in one moon."

Then the King, hearing word,
Sent nobles of the Court—well-mounted lords—
Nine separate messengers, each embassy
Bidden to say, "The King Suddhōdana—
Nearer the pyre by seven long years of lack,
Wherethrough he hath not ceased to seek for thee—
Prays of his son to come unto his own,
The Throne and people of this longing Realm,
Lest he shall die and see thy face no more."
Also nine horsemen sent Yasōdhara
Bidden to say, "The Princess of thy House—
Rahula's mother—craves to see thy face
As the night-blowing moon-flower's swelling heart
Pines for the moon, as pale asōka-buds
Wait for a woman's foot: if thou hast found
More than was lost, she prays her part in this,
Rahula's part, but most of all thyself."
So sped the Sākya Lords, but it befell

[1] A short religious poem, consisting of one verse.
[2] Short for *yōjanas,* each nine English miles.

That each one, with the message in his mouth,
Entered the Bamboo-Garden in that hour
When Buddha taught his Law; and—hearing—each
Forgot to speak, lost thought of King and quest,
Of the sad Princess even; only gazed
Eye-rapt upon the Master; only hung
Heart-caught upon the speech, compassionate,
Commanding, perfect, pure, enlightening all,
Poured from those sacred lips. Look! like a bee
Winged for the hive, who sees the mōgras spread
And scents their utter sweetness on the air,
If he be honey-filled, it matters not;
If night be nigh, or rain, he will not heed;
Needs must he light on those delicious blooms
And drain their nectar; so these messengers
One with another, hearing Buddha's words,
Let go the purpose of their speed, and mixed,
Heedless of all, amid the Master's train.
Wherefore the King bade that Udayi go—
Chiefest in all the Court, and faithfullest,
Siddārtha's playmate in the happier days—
Who, as he drew anear the garden, plucked
Blown tufts of tree-wool from the grove and sealed
The entrance of his hearing; thus he came
Safe through the lofty peril of the place,
And told the message of the King, and hers.

Then meekly bowed his head and spake our Lord
Before the people, "Surely I shall go!
It is my duty as it was my will;
Let no man miss to render reverence
To those who lend him life, whereby come means
To live and die no more, but safe attain
Blissful Nirvāna, if ye keep the Law,
Purging past wrongs and adding nought thereto,
Complete in love and lovely charities.
Let the King know and let the Princess hear
I take the way forewith." This told, the folk
Of white Kapilavastu and its fields

Made ready for the entrance of their Prince.
At the south gate a bright pavilion rose
With flower-wreathed pillars, and the walls of silk
Wrought on their red and green with woven gold.
Also the roads were laid with scented boughs
Of neem and mango, and full mussuks shed
Sandal and jasmine on the dust; and flags
Fluttered; and on the day when he should come
It was ordained how many elephants—
With silver howdahs [1] and their tusks gold-tipped—
Should wait beyond the ford, and where the drums
Should boom "Siddārtha cometh!" where the lords
Should light and worship, and the dancing girls
Where they should strew their flowers, with dance and song,
So that the steed he rode might tramp knee-deep
In rose and balsam, and the ways be fair;
While the town rang with music and high joy.
This was ordained, and all men's ears were pricked
Dawn after dawn to catch the first drum's beat
Announcing, "Now he cometh!"
But it fell—
Eager to be before—Yasōdhara
Rode in her litter to the city-walls
Where soared the bright pavilion. All around
A beauteous garden smiled—Nigrōdha named—
Shaded with bel-trees and the green-plumed dates,
New-trimmed and gay with winding walks and banks
Of fruits and flowers; for the southern road
Skirted its lawns, on this hand leaf and bloom,
On that the suburb-huts where base-borns dwelt
Outside the gates, a patient folk and poor,
Whose touch for Kshatriya and priest of Brahm
Were sort defilement. Yet those, too, were quick
With expectation, rising ere the dawn
To peer along the road, to climb the trees
At far-off trumpet of some elephant,
Or stir of temple-drum; and when none came,
Busied with lowly chores to please the Prince;

[1] A seat with a canopy and railing for the rider on elephant's back.

Sweeping their door-stones, setting forth their flags,
Stringing the fluted fig-leaves into chains,
New furbishing the Lingam, decking new
Yesterday's faded arch of boughs, but aye
Questioning wayfarers if any noise
Be on the road of great Siddārtha. These
The Princess marked with lovely languid eyes,
Watching, as they, the southward plain, and bent
Like them to listen if the passers gave
News of the path. So fell it she beheld
One slow approaching with his head close shorn,
A yellow cloth over his shoulder cast,
Girt as the hermits are, and in his hand
An earthen bowl, shaped melonwise, the which
Meekly at each hut-door he held a space,
Taking the granted dole with gentle thanks
And all as gently passing where none gave.
Two followed him wearing the yellow robe,
But he who bore the bowl so lordly seemed,
So reverend, and with such a passage moved,
With so commanding presence filled the air,
With such sweet eyes of holiness smote all,
That, as they reached him alms the givers gazed
Awestruck upon his face, and some bent down
In worship, and some ran to fetch fresh gifts
Grieved to be poor; till slowly, group by group,
Children and men and women drew behind
Into his steps, whispering with covered lips,
"Who is he? who? when looked a Rishi thus?"
But as he came with quiet footfall on
Nigh the pavilion, lo! the silken door
Lifted, and, all unveiled, Yasōdhara
Stood in his path crying, "Siddārtha! Lord!"
With wide eyes streaming and with close-clasped hands,
Then sobbing fell upon his feet, and lay.

Afterwards, when this weeping lady passed
Into the Noble Paths, and one had prayed
Answer from Buddha wherefore—being vowed

Quit of all mortal passion and the touch,
Flower-soft and conquering, of a woman's hands—
He suffered such embrace, the Master said:
"The greater beareth with the lesser love
So it may raise it unto easier heights.
Take heed that no man, being 'scaped from bonds,
Vexeth bound souls with boasts of liberty.
Free are ye rather that your freedom spread
By patient winning and sweet wisdom's skill.
Three eras of long toil bring Bodhisāts [1]—
Who will be guides and help this darkling world—
Unto deliverance, and the first is named
Of deep 'Resolve,' the second of 'Attempt,'
The third of 'Nomination.' Lo! I lived
In era of Resolve, desiring good,
Searching for wisdom, but mine eyes were sealed.
Count the grey seeds on yonder castor-clump,
So many rains it is since I was Ram,
A merchant of the coast which looketh south
To Lanka and the hiding-place of pearls.
Also in that far time Yasōdhara
Dwelt with me in our village by the sea,
Tender as now, and Lukshmi was her name.
And I remember how I journeyed thence
Seeking our gain, for poor the household was
And lowly. Not the less with wistful tears
She prayed me that I should not part, nor tempt
Perils by land and water. 'How could love
Leave what it loved?' she wailed; yet, venturing, I
Passed to the Straits, and after storm and toil
And deadly strife with creatures of the deep,
And woes beneath the midnight and the noon,
Searching the wave I won therefrom a pearl
Moonlike and glorious, such as Kings might buy
Emptying their treasury. Then came I glad
Unto mine hills, but over all that land
Famine spread sore; ill was I stead to live
In journey home, and hardly reached my door—

[1] Bodhisattvas.

Aching for food—with that white wealth of the sea
Tied in my girdle. Yet no food was there;
And on the threshold she for whom I toiled—
More than myself—lay with her speechless lips
Nigh unto death for one small gift of grain.
Then cried I, 'If there be who hath of grain,
Here is a kingdom's ransom for one life;
Give Lukshmi bread and take my moonlight pearl.'
Whereat one brought the last of all his hoard,
Millet—three seers—and clutched the beauteous thing.
But Lukshmi lived, and sighed with gathered life,
'Lo! thou didst love indeed!' I spent my pearl
Well in that life to comfort heart and mind
Else quite uncomforted; but these pure pearls,
My last great gain, won from a deeper wave—
The Twelve Nidānas and the Law of Good—
Cannot be spent, nor dimmed, and most fulfil
Their perfect beauty being freeliest given.
For like as is to Meru yonder hill
Heaped by the little ants, and like as dew
Dropped in the footmark of a bounding roe
Unto the shoreless seas, so was that gift
Unto my present giving; and so love—
Vaster in being free from toils of sense—
Was wisest stooping to the weaker heart;
And so the feet of sweet Yasōdhara
Passed into peace and bliss, being softly led."

But when the King heard how Siddārtha came
Shorn, with the mendicant's sad-coloured cloth,
And stretching out a bowl to gather orts
From base-borns' leavings, wrathful sorrow drave
Love from his heart. Thrice on the ground he spat,
Plucked at his silvered beard, and strode straight forth
Lackeyed by trembling lords. Frowning he clomb
Upon his war-horse, drove the spurs, and dashed,
Angered, through wondering streets and lanes of folk
Scarce finding breath to say, "The King! bow down!"
Ere the loud cavalcade had clattered by:

Which—at the turning by the Temple-wall,
Where the south gate was seen—encountered full
A mighty crowd; to every edge of it
Poured fast more people, till the roads were lost,
Blotted by that huge company which thronged
And grew, close following him whose look serene
Met the old King's. Nor lived the father's wrath
Longer than while the gentle eyes of Buddh
Lingered in worship on his troubled brows,
Then downcast sank, with his true knee, to earth
In proud humility. So dear it seemed
To see the Prince, to know him whole, to mark
That glory greater than of earthly state
Crowning his head, that majesty which brought
All men, so awed and silent, in his steps.
Nathless, the King broke forth, "Ends it in this
That great Siddārtha steals into his realm,
Wrapped in a clout, short, sandalled, craving food
Of low-borns, he whose life was as a God's?
My son! heir of this spacious power, and heir
Of Kings who did but clap their palms to have
What earth could give or eager service bring?
Thou should'st have come apparelled in thy rank,
With shining spears, and tramp of horse and foot.
Lo! all my soldiers camped upon the road,
And all my city waited at the gates;
Where hast thou sojourned through these evil years
Whilst thy crowned father mourned? and she, too, there
Lived as the widows use, foregoing joys;
Never once hearing sound of song or string,
Nor wearing once the festal robe, till now
When in her cloth of gold she welcomes home
A beggar-spouse in yellow remnants clad.
Son! why is this?"

"My Father!" came reply,
"It is the custom of my race."

"Thy race,"
Answered the King, "counteth a hundred thrones
From Maha Sammāt, but no deed like this."

"Not of a mortal line," the Master said,
"I spake, but of descent invisible,
The Buddhas who have been and who shall be
Of these am I, and what they did I do,
And this, which now befalls, so fell before,
That at his gate a King in warrior-mail
Should meet his son, a Prince in hermit-weeds;
And that, by love and self-control, being more
Than mightiest Kings in all their puissance,
The appointed helper of the Worlds should bow—
As now do I—and with all lowly love
Proffer, where it is owed for tender debts,
The first-fruits of the treasure he hath brought;
Which now I proffer."

Then the King amazed
Inquired "What treasure?" and the Teacher took
Meekly the royal palm, and while they paced
Through worshipping streets—the Princess and the King
On either side—he told the things which make
For peace and pureness, those Four noble Truths [1]
Which hold all wisdom as shores shut the seas,
Those eight right Rules whereby who will may walk—
Monarch or slave—upon the perfect Path
That hath its Stages Four and Precepts Eight,
Whereby whoso will live—mighty or mean,
Wise or unlearned, man, woman, young or old—
Shall, soon or late, break from the wheels of life,
Attaining blest Nirvāna. So they came
Into the Palace-porch, Suddhōdana
With brows unknit drinking the mighty words,
And in his own hand carrying Buddha's bowl,
Whilst a new light brightened the lovely eyes
Of sweet Yasōdhara and sunned her tears;
And that night entered they the Way of Peace.

[1] The Four Truths and Eightfold Path—see the summary of Buddha's teachings in the 'Sermon at Benares" (Section "Three Sermons by Buddha").

BOOK THE EIGHTH

A BROAD mead spreads by swift Kohāna's bank
At Nagara; five days shall bring a man
In ox-wain thither from Benares' shrines
Eastward and northward journeying. The horns
Of white Himāla look upon the place,
Which all the year is glad with blooms, and girt
By groves made green from that bright streamlet's wave.
Soft are its slopes and cool its fragrant shades,
And holy all the spirit of the spot
Unto this time: the breath of eve comes hushed
Over the tangled thickets, and high heaps
Of carved red stones cloven by root and stem
Of creeping fig, and clad with waving veil
Of leaf and grass. The still snake glistens forth
From crumbled work of lac and cedar-beams
To coil his folds there on deep-graven slabs;
The lizard dwells and darts o'er painted floors
Where Kings have paced; the grey fox litters safe
Under the broken thrones; only the peaks,
And stream, and sloping lawns, and gentle airs
Abide unchanged. All else, like all fair shows
Of life, are fled—for this is where it stood,
The city of Suddhōdana, the hill
Whereon, upon an eve of gold and blue,
At sinking sun Lord Buddha set himself
To teach the Law in hearing of his own.

Lo! ye shall read it in the Sacred Books
How, being met in that glad pleasaunce-place—
A garden in old days with hanging walks,
Fountains, and tanks, and rose-banked terraces
Girdled by gay pavilions and the sweep
Of stately palace-fronts—the Master sate
Eminent, worshipped, all the earnest throng
Watching the opening of his lips to learn
That wisdom which hath made our Asia mild;

Whereto four thousand lakhs of living souls
Witness this day. Upon the King's right hand
He sate, and round where ranged the Sākya Lords
Ananda, Devadatta—all the Court:
Behind stood Seriyut and Mugallan, chiefs
Of the calm brethren in the yellow garb,
A goodly company. Between his knees
Rahula smiled, with wondering childish eyes
Bent on the awful face, while at his feet
Sate sweet Yasōdhara, her heartaches gone,
Foreseeing that fair love which doth not feed
On fleeting sense, that life which knows no age,
That blessed last of deaths when Death is dead,
His victory and hers. Wherefore she laid
Her hand upon his hands, folding around
Her silver shoulder-cloth his yellow robe,
Nearest in all the world to him whose words
The Three Worlds waited for. I cannot tell
A small part of the splendid lore which broke
From Buddha's lips: I am a late-come scribe
Who love the Master and his love of men,
And tell this legend, knowing he was wise,
But have not wit to speak beyond the books;
And time hath blurred their script and ancient sense,
Which once was new and mighty, moving all.
A little of that large discourse I know
Which Buddha spake on the soft Indian eve;
So, too, I know it writ that they who heard
Were more—lakhs more—crores more—than could be seen,
For all the Devas and the Dead thronged there,
Till Heaven was emptied to the seventh zone
And uttermost dark Hells opened their bars;
Also the daylight lingered past its time
In rose-leaf radiance on the watching peaks,
So that it seemed Night listened in the glens
And Noon upon the mountains; yea! they write,
The Evening stood between them like some maid
Celestial, love-struck, rapt; the smooth-rolled clouds
Her braided hair; the studded stars the pearls

And diamonds of her coronal; the moon
Her forehead-jewel, and the deepening dark
Her woven garments. 'Twas her close-held breath
Which came in scented sighs across the lawns
While our Lord taught, and, while he taught, who heard—
Though he were stranger in the land, or slave,
High caste or low, come of the Aryan blood,
Or Mlech or Jungle-dweller—seemed to hear
What tongue his fellows talked. Nay, outside those
Who crowded by the river, great and small,
The birds and beasts creeping things—'tis writ—
Had sense of Buddha's vast embracing love
And took the promise of his piteous speech;
So that their lives—prisoned in shape of ape,
Tiger, or deer, shagged bear, jackal, or wolf,
Foul-feeding kite, pearled dove, or peacock gemmed,
Squat toad, or speckled serpent, lizard, bat;
Yea, or of fish fanning the river-waves—
Touched meekly at the skirts of brotherhood
With man who hath less innocence than these,
And in mute gladness knew their bondage broke
Whilst Buddha spake these things before the King:

[*The following presentation of Buddha's teachings is omitted. This material is better presented in the sections "Dhammapada," "Three Sermons by Buddha," "Some Buddhist Parables and Legends," and the "Surangama"—Ed.*]

These words the Master spake of duties due
To father, mother, children, fellows, friends;
Teaching how such as may not swiftly break
The clinging chains of sense—whose feet are weak
To tread the higher road—should order so
This life of flesh that all their hither days
Pass blameless in discharge of charities
And first true footfalls in the Eightfold Path;
Living pure, reverent, patient, pitiful;
Loving all things which live even as themselves;
Because what falls for ill is fruit of ill
Wrought in the past, and what falls well of good;

And that by howsomuch the householder
Purgeth himself of self and helps the world,
By so much happier comes he to next stage,
In so much bettered being. This he spake;
As also long before, when our Lord walked
By Rajagriha in the bamboo-grove:
For on a dawn he walked there and beheld
The householder Singāla, newly bathed,
Bowing himself with bare head to the earth,
To Heaven, and all four quarters; while he threw
Rice, red and white, from both hands. "Wherefore thus
Bowest thou, Brother?" said the Lord; and he,
"It is the way, Great Sir! our fathers taught
At every dawn, before the toil begins,
To hold off evil from the sky above
And earth beneath, and all the winds which blow."
Then the World-honoured spake: "Scatter not rice,
But offer loving thoughts and acts to all:
To parents as the East, where rises light;
To teachers as the South, whence rich gifts come;
To wife and children as the West, where gleam
Colours of love and calm, and all days end;
To friends and kinsmen and all men as North;
To humblest living things beneath, to Saints
And Angels and the blessed Dead above:
So shall all evil be shut off, and so
The six main quarters will be safely kept."

But to his Own, Them of the yellow robe—
Those who, as wakened eagles, soar with scorn
From life's low vale, and wing towards the Sun—
To these he taught the Ten Observances
The *Dasa-Sīl*, and how a mendicant
Must know the *Three Doors* and the *Triple Thoughts;*
The *Sixfold States of Mind;* the *Fivefold Powers;*
The *Eight High Gates of Purity;* the *Modes*
Of Understanding; Iddhi[1]*; Upekshā*[2];

[1] Dominion of spirit over matter, also certain major powers (Sanskrit: *riddhi*).
[2] The discipline of ignoring non-essentials.

The *Five Great Meditations,* which are food
Sweeter than Amrit[1] for the holy soul;
The *Jhānas*[2] and the *Three Chief Refuges.*[3]
Also he taught his Own how they should dwell;
How live, free from the snares of love and wealth;
What eat and drink and carry—three plain cloths,—
Yellow, of stitched stuff, worn with shoulder bare—
A girdle, almsbowl, strainer. Thus he laid
The great foundations of our Sangha well,
That noble Order of the Yellow Robe
Which to this day standeth to help the World.

So all that night he spake, teaching the Law;
And on no eyes fell sleep—for they who heard
Rejoiced with tireless joy. Also the King,
When this was finished, rose upon his throne
And with bared feet bowed low before his Son
Kissing his hem; and said, "Take me, O Son!
Lowest and least of all thy Company."
And sweet Yasōdhara, all happy now,—
Cried "Give to Rahula—thou Blessed One!
The Treasure of the Kingdom of thy Word
For his inheritance." Thus passed these Three
Into the Path.

Here endeth what I write
Who love the Master for his love of us.
A little knowing, little have I told
Touching the Teacher and the Ways of Peace.
Forty-five rains thereafter showed he those
In many lands and many tongues, and gave
Our Asia Light, that still is beautiful,
Conquering the world with spirit of strong grace:
All which is written in the holy Books,
And where he passed, and what proud Emperors
Carved his sweet words upon the rocks and caves:

[1] Nectar, or the immortal drink of the Vedic gods.
[2] Pali for Sanskrit *dyāna,* meditation, beatific vision.
[3] The Buddha, the Doctrine, and the Order (or Church).

And how—in fulness of the times—it fell
The Buddha died, the great Tathāgato,
Even as a man 'mongst men, fulfilling all:
And how a thousand thousand lakhs since then
Have trod the Path which leads whither he went
Unto Nirvāna, where the Silence lives.

Ah! Blessed Lord! Oh, High Deliverer!
Forgive this feeble script, which doth thee wrong,
Measuring with little wit thy lofty Love.
Ah! Lover! Brother! Guide! Lamp of the Law!
I take my refuge in thy name and thee!
I take my refuge in thy Law of Good!
I take my refuge in thy Order! OM!
The Dew is on the lotus!—Rise, Great Sun!
And lift my leaf and mix me with the wave.
Om mani padme hum, the Sunrise comes!
The Dewdrop slips into the shining Sea!

The Surangama Sutra

INTRODUCTION

In spite of the tremendous labors of Western scholars, I do not think there is a presentation which gives, in one short, consecutive discourse from original sources, the philosophic basis of Buddhist thought. There are able compilations by eminent scholars, notably *The Gospel of Buddha* (compiled from ancient records), by Dr. Paul Carus (Open Court, Chicago, 1894) and *Buddhism in Translations*, by Henry Clarke Warren (Harvard Oriental Series, Vol. 3, Harvard University Press, 1896, also available in the *Harvard Classics*). Dr. Carus's justly famous *Gospel of Buddha*, first published in 1894 and translated into seven or eight languages, seems to be the best compilation and the ideal book for the average reader. It is written in simple English and draws its sources from both Mahayana and Hinayana texts, while Warren's book confines itself to the latter sources (very largely from the *Visuddimagga*). What is difficult to find is one single, consecutive exposition of the Buddhist philosophy from the original sources which should give a fair idea of the Buddhist argument and its method and manner of approach and which can fit into the compass of the present volume.

The present selection from the *Surangama Sutra* gives, I believe, the best approach to the philosophic basis of Buddhist belief, for it must never be forgotten that Buddhism is a philosophy—it is a form of religious enlightenment built on a metaphysical basis. There is no other reason for the high prestige Buddhism has always enjoyed among the Chinese scholars. The present selection is a kind of *Essay on Human Understanding* and the *Gospel of St. John* combined, with the intellectual force of the one and the religious spirit of the other. We go through a process of intellectual inquiry that upsets all values, as we listen to the questions and answers between the Buddha and Ananda, his favorite young disciple; as the real meaning of the ultimate reality taught by Buddha, similar to the basis of Kantian idealism, seemed forever to be confused by our habitual notions of the physical world, the junior disciples were constantly thrown into perplexity and discouragement. Toward the end, before the final meaning was made plain, Ananda himself "broke into sobs" through utter bewilderment.

The style is familiar and challenges comparison with the *Gospel of St. John*. It shows Buddha's love for young Ananda (St. John), his compassion and pity for those slow of understanding, and his humor (in the remark to the King), and represents Buddha as several times chiding them all for their "easy forgetfulness" of the truth. In aptness and clarity of exposition, it has the marks of a philosophic masterpiece, which is the reason why I have chosen it rather than the *Lankāvatāra,* although the latter gives a more succinct outline of the Buddhist tenets with greater completeness. The translation is by Wei-tao and Dwight Goddard. The chief figures, besides Buddha, are Manjusri and Ananda, who in Chinese Buddhist temples are always worshipped on the right and left of Buddha.

Apart from its intrinsic merit, I have chosen the *Surangama* (Japanese for the Chinese name of the classic, *Shou ling yen*) rather than any of the texts from the Pali, because it represents Mahayana philosophy, a neglected branch of Western studies of Buddhism. Scholars have occupied themselves with the Buddhist *Tripitaka* ("Three Baskets") canons of the Hinayana School written in Pali.[1] The latter is called the "Lesser Vehicle" (*hsiao-ch'eng* in Chinese) of the so-called school of "Southern Buddhism," prevailing in Ceylon, Siam and Burma; while Mahayana is known as the "Greater Vehicle" (*ta-ch'eng* in Chinese) of "Northern Buddhism," prevailing in Thibet, China, Korea and Japan. The study of the Mahayana texts is making a proper beginning only in the last decade, and up to now only a few important Chinese Mahayana texts are available in English translations. The best known in the West, the *Lotus Sutra* (*Saddarma Pundarīka,* tr. by H. Kern, in the *Sacred Books of the East*, and *The Lotus of the Wonderful Law*, tr. by W. E. Soothill, Oxford, 1930) is only a popular text, and is not representative of the best in Mahayana literature.

[1] See list of these important Buddhist canons in *Buddhist Scriptures* by E. J. Thomas (Wisdom of the East Series) pp. 17-19, or for a more complete analytical list, see *History of Buddhist Thought,* by E. J. Thomas (Knopf), pp. 265-276.

Owing to the existence of the Pali Hinayana texts in better order and condition for the study of Western students, and owing to the influence of Mr. and Mrs. T. W. Rhys Davids, Mahayana Buddhism has not only been neglected, but has been even spoken of with contempt. Mr. and Mrs. Rhys Davids were not to blame when they spoke thus of Mahayana Buddhism, not only with a partisan, but also with what amounts to a sectarian hatred, regarding Mahayana Buddhism as "heterodox" and Hinayana as "orthodox"; this is entirely understandable for they devoted their lifetime to the study of the Pali texts. Perhaps I am speaking also with some bias as a Chinese, with Chinese associations. The word "bodhisattva," the most important doctrine of Mahayana religion, is such a common Chinese word that we use it in speaking of a sweet child (like the word "cherub") and of a clay doll. This is not the place to go into arguments. Suffice it to point out that the epithet "heretic" was not only hurled at each other by the Mahayana and Hinayana Buddhists, but also by the Hinayana Buddhists among themselves, of which there were eighteen divergent schools, that authenticity of material regarding Buddha's words can be as little claimed for the Pali texts as for the Sanskrit texts translated into Chinese, and that if the Mahayana texts were written down probably four or five centuries after the death of Buddha, so were the texts of Ceylon. Who can tell whether Xenophon or Plato gives us the real Socrates? Anyway, Mahayana philosophy stemmed out of Buddhism as naturally as Pauline theology stemmed out of Christ's teachings. The greatest of the Mahayana teachers was Asvaghosha, who was born in Oudh and lived toward the end of the first century. Like Paul, he was a haughty and learned scholar converted to Buddhism. Like Paul's stand on circumcision, he wrote the famous attack on the caste system, the *Vajrasūchū*. Unlike Paul, he wrote dramas, epics and lyrics. There is no question that here was truly a great mind. "There was no question he did not solve, no opponent he did not confound." Out of this great mind, the Mahayana religion grew. All questions of "heterodoxy" are inconsequential. Moreover, Mahayana religion rose when Brahmanism had come back to its own and the Hinayana Buddhists were losing their hold on the Hindu people.

What is far more important to point out here is that the Mahayana philosophy not only represents an important and natural development of Buddha's doctrines, but also shows a great advance, which accounts for its far greater prestige and popularity in China and Japan. First, it represents dissatisfaction with the doctrine of Nirvana as extinction.

Secondly, it represents dissatisfaction with the selfish salvation of the few Pratyekas and Arhats, and stands for the salvation of all, through the doctrine of the Bodhisattvas, beings who, having reached Nirvana, voluntarily abstain from that state by submitting to the cycle of re-births in order to save the world. Not until all mankind is delivered can the Buddhas be at peace. Thirdly, it represents the all-important principle of prayer and devotion (*bhakti*), and teaches salvation by faith rather than by works. And fourthly, it elevates the Buddha into a personal god. (Cf. the elevation of Krishna into a personal god by the Brahmans in the *Bhagavad-Gita.*) It is difficult to see how such developments could be prevented, or how they could be regarded as a "degeneration." Mere "historicity," which is an elusive hope, has, however, concerned the research scholars rather than the larger aspects of human wisdom.

The author of the *Sutra* is unknown. It was written in Sanskrit about the first century and known to the Chinese as *Shou-leng-yen Ching.* It was carried to China by a Hindu Master Paramartha who went by sea to South China, and was translated by him with the help of a Chinese scholar in A.D. 705 at Canton. It is a favorite work of Chinese scholar Buddhists, and the fact of its popularity may be attested by the fact that fifty-six commentaries and various elucidations have been known to exist in Chinese.

Students who are interested should read the Mahayana texts in *The Buddhist Bible,* by Dwight Goddard (published by Goddard, Thetford, Vt.). The works of Dr. D. T. Suzuki, dealing especially with one Mahayana school, the Zen in Japanese or Ch'an in Chinese: *Manual of Zen Buddhism, An Introduction to Zen Buddhism,* and his various *Essays,* are also extremely useful. The excellent works of Alan W. Watts, *The Spirit of Zen* (Wisdom of the East Series) and *The Legacy of Asia and Western Man* (University of Chicago) should be very useful in giving insight to the Oriental outlook.

Selections on Southern Buddhism are available. Besides the standard works of Carus and Warren mentioned above, there is an excellent small volume by E. J. Thomas, *Buddhist Scriptures* (Wisdom of the East Series, Murray). *The Bible of the World,* edited by Robert O. Ballou, also contains good material.

In particular, readers may be interested in the following Buddhist works. *Buddhist Legends* (Harvard Oriental Series, vols. 28, 29, 30), by E. W. Burlingame, is a complete translation, with good synopses, of the famous Commentary on the *Dhammapada,* giving a wealth of Buddhist parables to illustrate each of the 423 aphorisms of the *Dhammapada.* The *Dialogues of the Buddha* (*Dīgha-nikaya*) has been translated by Mr. and Mrs. Rhys Davids in 3 vols. (Oxford). The *Vissudhi Magga,* by Buddhaghosa, which is a very able piece of work, has been translated by P. M. Tin (*The Path of Purity,* Pali Text Society, Translation Series, 11, 17, 21).

I have supplied the section titles to make the development of thought easier to follow for the reader.

The Surangama Sutra

Translated by Wei-Tao and Dwight Goddard

INTRODUCTION

THUS HAVE I HEARD. Upon a memorable occasion, the Lord Buddha while staying at the Jetavana Meditation Hall in the city of Sravasti delivered a discourse to twelve hundred Great Disciples who were all great Arhats and free from all intoxicants, that is, they were all perfectly emancipated from sensual attachments and defilements. They were true heirs of their Lord Buddha and worthy to share their Lord's responsibility for the ever-continuing preaching of the Lord's Dharma. They had all transcended phenomenal existence and could manifest their gracious presence by a Buddhist influence wherever they sojourned. They were so highly advanced in their transcendental attainments that they were perfectly qualified to receive the Dharma from their Lord and Master and had so greatly profited from the Lord's teaching that they knew well how, with the Lord Buddha, to themselves turn the mysterious wheel of the true Dharma. They had kept the Precepts with such strict observance and perfect purity as to be qualified as perfect models for this triple world. They could assume innumerable appearance-bodies in response to the earnest prayer of any sentient being to rescue them and to perfect their emancipation. They were also willing to extend their helping hands into the future, so that all sentient beings in the future might become emancipated and free from all their fetters of earthly defilement.

Among the Great Bhikshus[1] present, acting as leaders, were the wise Sariputra, the Great Maudgalyayana, the Great Kaustila, Purna Meta-

[1] Monks.

luniputra, Subhuti, Upanishada, and many others equally well known and highly regarded. In addition there were present many Pratyaka-Buddhas,[1] who had mastered the teachings and perfected the practices, together with innumerable novice disciples. They all came to pay homage to Lord Buddha and also to associate themselves with all the great Bhikshus and their disciples in this great Dharma Assembly which had gathered for the "Summer Devotion" where they could make public confession and practice Dhyana together.

Besides the great company of Bhikshus and Disciples that had gathered from far and near, there were present Bodhisattva-Mahasattvas[2] from all the ten quarters of the Universe who had come to pay their highest respect to the Lord Shakyamuni Buddha as though it was an offering to a loving parent. Moreover, they came to entreat the Lord Buddha for some high teaching that would solve their mental puzzles and help them to get rid of the troublesome doubts which they occasionally experienced in their meditations.

Then the Lord Buddha ascended the Honorable Throne of Dharma and immediately became absorbed in profound contemplation with such noble solemnity and tranquillity that the whole company were spellbound by its profound silence and mystery. At the same time all the Bodhisattva-Mahasattvas, as numerous as the particles of sand in the river Ganges, with Manjusri the Great Bodhisattva at their head, gathered about the Lord Buddha and merged their deep meditation with the Lord Buddha's perfect Samadhi. Seldom, indeed, had any of them ever before experienced such serenity and quietness as then pervaded this Great Dharma Assembly. Wonderful music like the songs of the Kalavinka and Jiva-jiva birds seem to come from the Lord Buddha's perfect Samadhi and to fill the air with its heavenly music, and floating away to pervade the ten quarters of the Universe.

Upon this occasion, Prasenajit the King of Sravasti in celebration of the anniversary of his father's death, prepared a special feast of choice vegetables and dainties, and came personally to call upon the Lord Buddha and to invite him and all the Great Bodhisattvas-Mahasattvas to attend a reception at the royal palace. At the same time the elders

[1] Masters.

[2] Bodhisattvas, incarnations or rebirths of the Buddha, for the purpose of converting mankind—a peculiar doctrine of Mahayana Buddhism. Here, unlike the Pali texts of Hinayana Buddhism, saints and gods of all degrees were described as present at Buddha's discourse.

and wealthy laymen of the city added to the King's celebration by preparing jointly another feast and invited all the Disciples of the Lord Buddha to attend while the Lord and the Great Disciples were with the King. The Lord Buddha, knowing all about it, bade his Great Disciple Manjusri to first lead part of the Bodhisattvas-Mahasattva and Arhats[1] to attend the Laymen's homes and to receive their offerings.

Ananda was the only one of the Great Disciples who was noticeably absent. Owing to a previous engagement in a distant district, he had not yet returned. He was quite alone and when he reached the Meditation Hall upon his return, he found it deserted, not a single disciple about, nor were there any offerings from their patrons in sight. Then Ananda, thoughtful as ever, took his alms bowl and entered into the city begging food from house to house in regular order, his only thought being to receive the offerings from all alike even to the last *danapati*. It mattered nothing to Ananda whether the offering was small or generous, attractive or repulsive, whether the giver was of the Kshatriya[2] caste or the Candra[3] caste, to him the all important thing was to practice kindness and compassion on all alike with no discrimination whatever. He sought only to attain the inestimable merit of delivering all sentient beings, treating them all alike.

Ananda had heard that the Lord on one occasion had rebuked Subhuti and Mahakatyayana for showing discrimination towards Arahats in their practice of begging. He greatly admired the Lord's liberal mind and determined that he would not commit the same fault himself. He was proud of his good name and did not wish to give cause for people having suspicions or for slandering about himself, so he quietly crossed the dried moat that surrounded the city, entered the city-gate with solemn gravity. He was a noticeable figure in his neat attire and solemn manner as if he was on a special mission to receive some ceremonial offering.

While Ananda was begging in orderly succession, he came to the house of a prostitute named Maudenka who had a beautiful daughter named Pchiti. This young maiden was attracted by Ananda's youthful and attractive person and pleaded earnestly with her mother to conjure the young monk by the magic spell of "*bramanyika*." This the mother did and Ananda coming under the spell of its magic became fascinated by the charm of the young maiden and entered the house and her room.

[1] Saints. [2] Warrior (second) caste. [3] *Chandala,* an outcast.

As soon as the feast was ended, the Lord Tathagata[1] returned to the Meditation Hall in the Jeta Grove. King Prasenajit and his royal ministers and many of the prominent elders and wealthy laymen of the city returned with the Lord to listen further to his wonderful and precious teaching, the like of which they had never before heard. The Lord as usual first sitting quietly became absorbed in Samadhi,[2] radiating from the crown of his head rays of soft and tender brightness, like lotus petals surrounded by innumerable leaves. In the center of the Lotus petals there was a vision of the Nirmanakaya Buddha[3] sitting with feet crossed intuiting and radiating the intrinsic Dharani.

The Lord Buddha had known all along what was happening to Ananda and now called Manjusri and bade him repeat the Great Dharani at the place where Ananda was yielding to temptation. As soon as Manjusri reached the house, the magic spell lost its power and Ananda returned to self-control. Manjusri encouraged Ananda and Pchiti and they returned with him to meet the Lord Buddha.

CHAPTER ONE

THE MANY MANIFESTATIONS of the Wonderful Essence-Mind, and of the Perfect Principle of the Three Excellencies within the All-Inclusive Unity of the Womb of Tathagata.

1. THE CONUNDRUM OF THE PERCEIVING MIND AND ITS LOCATION: FALSENESS OF THE MECHANICAL APPROACH

When Ananda came into the presence of the Lord Buddha, he bowed down to the ground in great humanity, blaming himself that he had not yet fully developed the potentialities of Enlightenment, because from the beginning of his previous lives, he had too much devoted himself to study and learning. He earnestly pleaded with the Lord Buddha and with all the other Tathagatas from the ten quarters of the Universe,

[1] Title of the Buddha, "such-come" in Chinese, generally used to denote both the Buddha and the state of perfect godhead in wisdom ("Tathagataship") attainable by any man. It should be understood that there is no "God" in Buddhism, and that anybody can become a Buddha.

[2] A state of superconsciousness following meditation.

[3] "Transformation body," one of the three bodies of Buddha. The other two are "Dharmakaya" (body of the Law) and "Sambhogakaya" (the body of Bliss).

to support him in attaining perfect Enlightenment, that is, to support him in his practice of the Three Excellencies of Dhyana, Samadhi and Samapatti,[1] by some most fundamental and expedient means.

At the same time, all of the Bodhisattvas-Mahasattva, as numerous as the sands of the river Ganges, together with all the Arhats, Pratyaka-Buddhas, from all the ten quarters, with one accord and with gladness of heart, prepared to listen to the instruction to be given to Ananda by the Lord Buddha. With one accord they paid homage to the Lord and then resuming their seats, waited in perfect quietness and patience to receive the sacred teaching.

Then the Lord Buddha spoke to Ananda, saying:—Ananda, you and I are from the same ancestral blood and we have always cherished a fraternal affection for each other. Let me ask you a few questions and you answer me spontaneously and freely. When you first began to be interested in Buddhism what was it that impressed you in our Buddhist way of life and most influenced you to forsake all worldly pleasures and enabled you to cut asunder your youthful sexual cravings?

Ananda replied:—Oh, my Lord! The first thing that impressed me were the thirty-two marks of excellency in my Lord's personality.[2] They appeared to me so fine, as tender and brilliant, and transparent as a crystal.

From that time I have constantly thought about them and have been more and more convinced that these marks of excellence would be impossible for anyone who was not free from all sexual passion and desire. And why? Because when anyone becomes inflamed by sexual passion, his mind becomes disturbed and confused, he loses self-control and becomes reckless and crude. Besides, in sexual intercourse, the blood becomes inflamed and impure and adulterated with impure secretions. Naturally from such a source, there can never originate an aureole of such transcendently pure and golden brightness as I have seen emanating from the person of my Lord. It was because of this that I admired my Lord and it was this that influenced me to become one of thy true followers.

The Lord Buddha then said:—Very good, Ananda! All of you in this Great Dharma Assembly ought to know and appreciate that the reason why sentient beings by their previous lives since beginningless time

[1] *Dhyana,* meditation; *Samadhi,* a state of superconsciousness; *Samapatti,* a further state of heightened exaltation and spiritual powers.
[2] See *The Bible of the World,* by R. O. Ballou, p. 242.

have formed a succession of deaths and rebirths, life after life, is because they have never realized the true Essence of Mind and its self-purifying brightness. On the contrary they have been absorbed all the time busying themselves with their deluding and transient thoughts which are nothing but falsity and vanity. Hence they have prepared for themselves the conditions for this ever returning cycle of deaths and rebirths.

Ananda, if you are now desirous of more perfectly understanding Supreme Enlightenment and the enlightening nature of pure Mind-Essence, you must learn to answer questions spontaneously with no recourse to discriminating thinking. For the Tathagatas in the ten quarters of the universes have been delivered from the ever returning cycle of deaths and rebirths by this same single way, namely, by reliance upon their intuitive minds.

It is because of the straight-forwardness of their minds and the spontaneity of their mentations that the Tathagatas have ever remained, from beginningless time to endless time, of one pure Suchness, undisturbed by any complexity within their minds nor any rising thoughts of discrimination.

Then the Lord Buddha said:—Ananda, I want to question you; please listen carefully. You have just said that at the time your faith in me was awakened, that it was due to seeing the thirty-two marks of excellence. Let me ask you: What was it that gave you the sensation of seeing? What was it that experienced the sensation? And who was it that experienced the feeling of being pleased?

Ananda replied:—My Lord! At the time I experienced the sensation of being pleased, it was both through my eyes and my mind. When my eyes saw my Lord's excellencies, my mind immediately experienced a feeling of being pleased. It was then that I made up my mind to become thy disciple so that I might be delivered from the cycle of deaths and rebirths.

The Lord said:—From what you have just said, Ananda, your feeling of being pleased originated in your eyes and mind. But if you do not know where lies the perception of sight and where the activities of the mind originate, you will never be able to subjugate your worldly attachments and contaminations. It is like a king whose city was pestered by robbers and who tried to put an end to the thieving but was unsuccessful because he could not locate the secret hiding place of the robbers. So it is in the lives of human beings who are always being troubled by worldly attachments and contaminations, causing their perception of sight to become inverted and unreliable and seducing their thoughts and causing them to wander about ignorantly and uncontrolled. Ananda, let me ask you? Referring to your eyes and mind, do you know their secret hiding place?

Ananda replied:—Noble Lord! In all the ten different orders of life, the eyes are in the front of the face, as are my Lord's clear lotus eyes, and mine also. The same is true of the other sense organs, they are on the surface of the body, but the mind is hidden within the body.

The Lord Buddha interrupted:—Ananda, you are now sitting in the lecture hall, are you not? And when you are looking out to the Jetavana Grove, can you tell me where the hall and the grove are situated?

Certainly, my Lord. This quiet and splendid lecture hall and the Jetavana Grove are both situated in Anathapindika's beautiful park.

Now, Ananda, what do you see first, the people in this hall or the park outside?

I first see my Lord, then I see the noble audience, and other things in turn, and only afterward do I see the grove and the lovely park outside.

True, Ananda! Now tell me, while you are looking outside at the grove and park, what is it that enables you to distinguish the different views that your eyes see?

Noble Lord! It is because the windows and doors of the lecture hall are open wide. That is why I can see the distant views from inside the hall.

Then the Blessed Lord, in view of the great audience, reached out his golden hand and softly stroked Ananda's head, at the same time speaking to both him and the great assembly, saying:—

There is a particular Samadhi called, The Highest Samadhi, which was the Lord Buddha's Crowning Experience, and by it he attained a perfect realization of all manifestations and transformations. It was a wonderful door that opened to the mysterious Path that all the Tathagatas of all the ten quarters of all the universes have followed. It is of this Highest Samadhi that I am going to speak. Listen very carefully.

Then Ananda and the great audience bowed to the ground in deep adoration and then resumed their seats and waited humbly for the Master's solemn teaching.

The Lord Buddha then addressed Ananda and the great assembly, saying:—

Ananda, you have just said that from the inside of the lecture hall you can look out to the grove and the distant park because the windows and doors are open wide. It is possible that there are some within this very audience that only see these outside things and who are unable to see the Lord Tathagata within.[1]

Ananda interrupted:—But my Lord, how can it be that anyone in this hall who can see the grove and streams without can fail to see the Lord within?

It does seem absurd, Ananda, but it is just that way with you. You say that your mind exists within your body and that it is quite clear of all obstructions, but if this clear mind really exists within your body, then you ought to see the inside of your body first of all. But there are no sentient beings who can do this, that is, see both the inside and outside of their bodies. Though they may not see all the inside things—such as the heart, stomach, liver, kidneys, etc.—but at least they ought to see the growth of the finger-nails, the lengthening of the hair, the knotting of the sinews, the throbbing of the pulse. If the mind is within the body, why does it not see these things? But if the mind is within the body and can not see the things within, how can it see the things without the body? So you must see that what you have said about the perceiving mind, abiding within the body, is untrue.

With a respectful bow, Ananda said to the Lord:—Listening to the words of my Lord, I begin to realize that my mind, after all, may be outside my body. It may be like a lamp. If the lamp is within the room, it will certainly illumine the room first and then shining through the open door and windows will illumine the yard outside. If it was like that, why is it that one seeing only outside objects does not see the things within? It must be that the mind is like a lamp placed outside of a room, for then it would be dark within. If one can clearly understand what his mind is, he would no longer be puzzled, but would have the same intelligence and understanding that the Buddhas have. Would it not be so, my Lord?

The Lord replied:—Ananda, this morning all of the Bhikshus followed me to the city of Sravasti begging for food in regular order and afterwards all returned to this Grove. I was fasting at the time, but the others ate the food. What think you, Ananda? If only one of the Bhikshus ate the food, would the others be satisfied of their hunger?

[1] Here it is particularly clear that "Buddha" is not a particular god, but is that indefinable entity or state of perfect wisdom achieved by the godly.

Ananda replied:—No, my Lord, and why? Because, although all of these Bhikshus are Arahats, yet their physical bodies are individually separated. How could it be, that one Bhikshu eating, could satisfy the hunger of all?

The Lord Buddha replied:—Ananda if your perceiving, understanding mind is really outside your body, then what the mind perceives could not be felt by the body, and what the body feels could not be perceived by the mind. Look at my hand, Ananda. When your eyes are looking at it, does your mind make any discriminations about it?

Yes, my Lord, it makes discriminations.

The Lord continued:—But if your mind and body are in mutual correspondence, how can it possibly be said, that the mind exists outside the body? Therefore, Ananda, you ought to know that what you have just said about the mind existing outside the body is impossible.

Then Ananda said:—According to what my Lord says, the perceiving mind does not exist within the body because it does not see the things within, neither does it exist outside the body, because the mind and body are in mutual correspondence and therefore cannot be isolated from each other. Yet it seems to be that the perceiving mind must be in some locality.

Then the Lord Buddha questioned Ananda further:—But Ananda, where is its abiding place?

Ananda replied:—My Lord, since this perceiving mind cannot know the inside of its own body, but can see outside objects, it seems to me now, that it must be concealed in the sense organ itself. It may be like a man covering his eyes with a crystal bowl; though his eyes are covered yet there is no hindrance to his sight—the eye can still see clearly and make distinctions as usual. The reason that it does not see the inside of the body is because it is a part of the organ of the eye, and the reason it can see outside objects clearly is because it is hidden in the organ of the eye.

But, Ananda, you have just said that this perceiving mind concealed within the organ of the eye is like a crystal bowl covering the eyes. Now suppose a man has covered his eyes with a crystal bowl, but is still able to see outer objects such as mountains, rivers, etc., tell me, does he see the crystal bowl, also?

Yes, my Lord, while the man is covering his eyes with the crystal bowl, he sees the crystal bowl, also.

The Lord said:—Ananda, if your mind is just the same as the crystal bowl covering the eyes, why does your mind, while seeing the outside mountains and rivers, not see your own eyes, too? Or, supposing your mind does see your eyes, then your eyes will be regarded as any other objective thing and they will no longer regarded as a dependent organ. Or, if the mind cannot see everything, then how can it be said of the perceiving mind, that it is concealed within the organ of the eyes in the resemblance of a crystal bowl covering the eyes? Therefore, Ananda, what you have asserted, that this perceiving mind is concealed within the organ of the eyes like a crystal bowl covering the eyes, is impossible also.

Then Ananda said to the Lord Buddha:—Honored of the worlds! It may be like this:—As all sentient beings have their intestines inside the body and the opening outside the body, the intestines are hidden to their sight but the opening is visible. While I am standing before you and open my eyes, I see your brightness—this means to see the outside. When my eyes are closed, I see the hiddenness—this means to see the inside.

The Lord interrupted:—Ananda, when you close your eyes, you say you see the hiddenness, but this hidden condition, is it in an opposing direction to your eyes, or is it not? If it is directly opposed to your eyes, then the hiddenness must be in front of your eyes and then it cannot be thought of as a part of your inside. Or suppose it is meant as part of your inside, then when in any dark room, without the light of any such thing as sun, moon, or lamp, the whole dark space of the room might be regarded as your intestines or your heart. Or, if it is in a direction not opposite to your eyes, then how does it happen that the sight of your eyes is being affected at all?

Or, if you put aside this outside perception of sight and say that it is to be regarded as being in an inside opposite direction to your eyes, so that when you shut your eyes, you see darkness only, which would mean to see your inside body. But when you open your eyes and see the brightness, why do you not see your own face, also? If you do not see your own face, it would mean that the face is not in an inside opposite direction to your eyes. Or, supposing you can see your own face, then both this perceiving mind and the organ of sight must be in the open space, or they can no longer be thought of as being in an inside opposite direction.

If your perceptive mind is supposed to be in the open space, naturally it cannot belong to the body, and then, when the Lord Tathagata is in sight of your face which would mean that he is a part of your body, your eyes will, of course, get the perception, but the others parts of your body could not get into consciousness at the same time.

Or, if you persistently claim that the body and the eyes have each a separate consciousness, then there would be two perceiving minds, which would mean that your single personality would see two Buddhas. Therefore you should understand that it is utterly absurd for you to say that to see into the dimness of the eyes is the same as seeing into the inside of the body.

Then Ananda said to the Lord Buddha:—I have constantly learned from the instruction of my Lord and from the teaching of all four classes of Thy disciples that all the existences of phenomena are simply the manifestation of the mind itself and vice versa that all the existences of mind are the manifestation of phenomena. Now it seems to me that this thinking mind is really the essence of my mind, and that wherever it happens to meet outer objects, there is a manifestation of mind. That is, the perceiving mind is neither inside, nor outside, nor between the body.

The Lord interrupted, saying:—What you are just saying—that all the manifestations of thought are simply meant as all the existences of phenomena and that wherever the mind happens to meet outer objects, there is its manifestations. But if your mind has no substantiality of its own, how can it meet any outer objects? Or, if it should be that in spite of the mind having no substantiality of its own, it might happen to meet outer objects, then there would be another newly assumed datum of nineteen spheres of mentation, namely, the six objects, the six sense organs, the six perceptions, plus this newly assumed normality of thought considered as a "thing in itself." And then there must be assumed a new datum of seven objects,—the object of sight, the object of hearing, of smelling, of tasting, of touching, of the unified object of thought, plus this outer "thing of itself." No, your suggestion is by no means the right interpretation.

Ananda, your interpretation that the perceiving mind has a substantiality of its own at the point where the object and thought meet, would put fetters to your mind, like putting fetters to your hands and feet. Let me ask you in this way: does your mental consciousness arise within or without your body? If it arises within, you should be able to know the inside of your body; if it comes from outside your body, you should be able to first see your own face.

Ananda replied:—My Lord! I see with my eyes and I perceive with my mind. That does not mean that they are interchangeable.

The Lord Buddha continued:—Ananda, if your eyes can see by themselves, then supposing you are within a room, can the door share the perception of seeing? If the door shares with the eyes this perception of seeing, then all dead bodies that still have eye organs intact, should continue to see things. If they can still perceive, how can it be said that they are dead bodies.

Ananda, if we grant that your perceiving mind has some kind of substantially, is it one body or many bodies? Is it located in one place in your body or is it distributed all over the body? If it is one body, then if you bind one limb the others will feel bound. If they all feel bound, then there can be no sure knowledge of the exact place of the binding. Or, if the perception of being bound is located in one place, then the perceiving mind cannot be considered as one localized body. Or if the perceiving mind is considered to be many bodies or involved in many bodies, it would mean that there must be as many personalities, and the question would arise, which of these localized perceiving minds rightly belongs to you. Or if your mind is considered as being uniformally distributed over all parts of your body, then if your limb was tightly bound, then the whole body would feel the suffering. Or if not uniformally distributed, but only on some parts of the body, then if you touch your head and at the same touch your feet, one would know it and the other would not. We know that this is not so. Therefore, Ananda, you must see that your suggestion that wherever the mind happens to meet outer objects, there is localized a manifestation of mind is unreasonable.

Then Ananda said to the Lord Buddha:—Now I recall hearing my Lord Buddha say, at a time when he was teaching Brother Manjusri and other princes of the Dharma, that the mind neither abides inside nor outside the body. It seems to me, if it is inside and we cannot see the inside, and if it was outside we ought not to feel the outside. We know that we cannot see the inside of the body, so it must mean that the mind is not abiding inside the body; it must mean that in some way our mind and body are in mutural correspondence with each other through the faculty of perception, and that would mean that it is not abiding outside the body. Now, My Lord, I see that since our mind and body are in mutual correspondence and yet we cannot see the inside of our body, it must be that the perceiving understanding mind must be abiding between these things.

The Lord Buddha resumed:—Ananda, now you think that the mind must be abiding between somethings. Let us consider it. If it is abiding between somethings, there must be some particular place where it is abiding. We can not conceive of an indefinite abiding place. Now Ananda, supposing you guess between what things it is located. Is it located between outside things and our bodies? Then it would be on the surface of the body and could not mean any place within the body. If it is located between parts of our body, then it would be within the body. Or, if it is between external things, what is its standard of direction? Suppose we take the case of a man: if he is standing between things looking toward the east, he must be standing in the west; or if he is looking toward the west, he must be standing in the east; or if he is looking toward the south, he must be standing in the north. If the mind is between things but has no standard of direction, it is the same as saying that it has no existence; or even if it has some standard of direction, there can be no certainty about it (if by just turning he can be either in east or west or north or south). If the standard is uncertain, the mind will be confused naturally.

Ananda replied:—What I said of the mind being "between somethings," is not meant in that sense. On one occasion my Lord has said:—"As causal conditions, eyes and sights are mutually attracted," but there must be something that is manifested in the consciousness that is dependent upon the eyes. That is what I meant by the mind being "between somethings." The eyes note discriminations while objects and sights are insensible things. As consciousness develops between them, the conceiving mind must be localized between them.

The Lord Buddha interrupted, saying:—Ananda, if it is stated that the mind is existing between the sense organ and the object, then, let me ask, is the essence of mind separated into two parts or not? If it is, the object and essential mind will be confusingly mingled, and as the object can not be exactly the same as essential mind which possesses the consciousness, they must be opposite to each other. How then can you say, that the mind exists between them?

If the statement that the mind is separated into two parts has no ground, then the statement that the insensible object is imperceptive, means just the same as saying that it has no essence itself and must be, therefore, imperceptible. So the expression "between somethings," has no meaning.

Therefore, Ananda, you must admit that the statement that the mind exists between somethings, is an absurd statement that is incapable of interpretation.

Ananda then addressed the Lord Buddha, saying:—Noble Lord! Some time ago when my Lord was discussing the intrinsic Dharma with the four great Bodhisattva-Mahasattvas, Maudgalyayana, Subhuti, Purna, and Sariputra, I overheard my Lord to say, that the essence of the discerning, perceiving, conscious mind existed neither inside nor outside, nor between, in fact, that it had no location of existence. Since my Lord has interpreted this in his teachings just now, I have ceased to grasp any arbitrary conception as to the location of mind, but if this is true, and it is something intangible, in what sense can it be thought of as "my mind."

The Lord Buddha replied:—Ananda, as to what you have just said that the essence of the discerning, perceptive, conscious mind has no definite location anywhere, the meaning is clear; it is neither in this world, in the vast open spaces, neither in water, nor on land, neither flying with wings, nor walking, nor is it anywhere. But when you say that your mind no longer grasps any arbitrary conception of the existence of the phenomena of mind, what do you mean by it? Do you mean that the phenomena have no true existence, or that they have no tangible existence? If you mean that they have no true existence, that would mean that they are like hair on a tortoise, or like horns on a rabbit. But so long as you retain this notion of not grasping, you cannot mean perfect non-existence. But what do you mean? Of course if your mind is perfectly blank, it must mean, as far as you are concerned, absolute non-existence, but if you are still cherishing some arbitrary conception of phenomena, you must mean some kind of existence. How is it then, that so long as the notion of not-grasping of anything, as for instance, the notion of "my mind," that you mean its non-existence? Therefore, Ananda, you ought to see that what you have just said concerning the non-existence of anything just because you no longer cherish a conception of it within your mind, and that would mean the non-existence of a discerning, perceptive, conscious mind, would be quite absurd, would it not?

Thereupon, Ananda rose from his place in the midst of the assembly, adjusted his ceremonial scarf, knelt upon his right knee, placed the palms of his hands together, and respectfully addressed the Lord Buddha, saying:—

My Noble Lord! I have the honor of being thy youngest relative and thou hast always treated me with affectionate kindness. Although I am now only one of your many converts, thou dost still continue to show thy affection for me. But in spite of all I have gained mentally, I have not become liberated from contaminations and attachments and consequently I could not overcome the magic spell at the home of a harlot. My mind became confused and I was at the point of drowning in its defilement. I can see now that it was wholly due to my ignorance as to the right realization of what is true and essential Mind. I pray thee, Oh my Lord, to have pity and mercy upon me and show me the right Path to the spiritual graces of the Samapatti so that I may attain to self-mastery and become emancipated from the lure of evil myself, and be able to free all heretics from the bonds of their false ideas and craft.

2. THE TRUE NATURE OF MIND

When Ananda had finished his plea, he bowed humbly before the Lord Buddha, with hands and forehead touching the ground, and the whole audience, awed into intense excitement, waited with earnest and reverential hearts for the response of the Blessed One.

Suddenly in the Meditation Hall, filled with its awed and expectant throng, there appeared a most marvelous sight that transcended everything that had ever been seen before. The Hall was filled with a radiant splendor that emanated from the moon-life face of the Blessed One, like hundreds of thousands of sunbeams scintillating everywhere, and wherever the rays reached immediately there were seen celestial Buddha-lands. Moreover, the person of the Lord Buddha was vibrant with the six transcendental motions simultaneously manifesting and embracing all the Buddha-lands of the ten quarters of all the universes, as numerous as the finest particles of dust in the sunlight. And this all-embracing, blessed and transcendent glory united all these innumerable Buddha-lands into one single whole, and all the great Bodhisattvas of all these innumerable Buddha-lands were seen to be each in his own place with hands raised and pressed together expectantly waiting for the words of the Blessed One.

Then the Lord Buddha addressed the assembly, saying:—Ananda, from beginningless time, from life to life, all sentient beings have had their disturbing illusions that have been manifested in their natural development each under the conditioning power of his own individual karma, such as the seed-pod of the okra which when opening always drops three seeds in each group. The reason why all devoted disciples do not at once attain to supreme enlightenment is because they do not realize two primary principles and because of it some attain only to Arhatship, or to Pratyakaship, and some to even lower attainments, to the state of devas and heretics, and some to Mara kings and their dependents. The reason for these great differences is because, not knowing these two basic principles, they become confused in mind and fall into wrong practices. It is as if they were trying to cook fine delicacies by boiling stones or sand, which of course they could never do if they tried for countless kalpas.

What are these two fundamental principles, Ananda? The First Fundamental Principle is the primary cause of the succession of deaths and rebirths from beginningless time. [It is the Principle of Ignorance, the outgoing principle of individuation, manifestation, transformation, succession and discrimination.] From the working out of this Principle there has resulted the various differentiation of minds of all sentient beings, and all the time they have been taking these limited and perturbed and contaminated minds to be their true and natural Essence of Mind.

The Second Fundamental Principle is the primary cause of the pure unity of Enlightenment and Nirvana that has existed from beginningless time. [It is the Principle of integrating compassion, the in-drawing, unifying principle of purity, harmony, likeness, rhythm, permanency and peace.] By the in-drawing of this Principle within the brightness of your own nature, its unifying spirit can be discovered and developed and realized under all varieties of conditions. The reason why this unifying spirit is so quickly lost amongst the conditions is because you so quickly forget the brightness and purity of your own essential nature, and amid the activities of the day, you cease to realize its existence. That is why, Ananda, you and all sentient beings have fallen through ignorance into misfortune and into different realms of existence.

Now, Ananda, you wish to know the right road to Samapatti, so as to escape from the cycle of deaths and rebirths. Is it not so, Ananda? Then let me ask you some more questions. The Lord Tathagata raised one of his arms with hand and fingers clenched, saying:—Ananda, do you see this?

Yes, I see it, my Lord.

What do you see, Ananda?

I see my Lord raising one of his arms with hand clenched and its brightness blinds my eyes and warms my heart.

With what do you see it, Ananda?

I see it with my eyes, of course.

Then the Lord Buddha said:—Ananda, you have just answered me by saying that when the Tathagata by clenching his fingers made a shining fist, that its brightness shone into your eyes and warmed your heart. Very good. Now I will ask you:—While my fist is shining brightly and while you are looking at it closely, what is it that reveals the existence of your mind?

Ananda replied:—You are now asking me about the existence of my mind. To answer that question I must use my thinking and reasoning faculty to search and find an answer. Yes, now I understand. This thinking and reasoning being is what is meant as "my mind."

The Lord Buddha rebuked Ananda sharply and said:—Surely that is nonsense, to assert that your being is your mind.

Ananda stood up with hands pressed together and said with astonishment:—Why, my Lord, if my being is not my mind, what else can be my mind?

The Lord Buddha replied:—The notion that your being is your mind, is simply one of the false conceptions that arises from reflecting about the relations of yourself and outside objects, and which obscures your true and essential Mind. It is because, since from beginningless time down to the present life, you have been constantly misunderstanding your true and essential Mind. It is like treating a petty thief as your own son. By so doing you have lost consciousness of your original and permanant Mind and because of it have been forced to undergo the sufferings of successive deaths and rebirths.

Ananda, in dismay and confusion, said to the Lord:—I am your beloved cousin and owing to my appreciation of your marks of excellence, you have permitted me to become your disciple. So, in regard to my mind, it is not simply that my mind has offered adoration to my Lord Tathagata, but it has also offered praise to all the Buddhas and learned Masters of all the innumerable Buddha-lands. More than that, it is my mind that has been attempting all manner of difficult practices with great resolution and courage. These are all activities of my mind as well as of myself. How can they be separated? Even my evil acts of slandering the Dharma, neglecting good practices, these also are activities of my mind as well as of myself. Myself is my mind. If these acts can be shown to be not the activities of my mind, then I would be mindless, just like any other image made from a log or from earth. Oh, if I should give up my perceptions and consciousness, there would be nothing left that could be regarded as my self or as my mind. What do you mean, my Lord, when you say that my being is not my mind? As you can see, I am astonished and confused. And this audience, they are also in doubt. Pray have mercy upon us all and explain yourself clearly for we are only ignorant disciples.

Thereupon the Blessed Lord laid his hand affectionately upon the head of Ananda and proceeded to explain the true and Essence nature of Mind, desiring to awaken in them a consciousness of that which transcended phenomena. He explained to them how necessary it was to keep the mind free from all discriminating thoughts of self and not-self if they were to correctly understand it.

He continued:—Ananda and all my Disciples! I have always taught you that all phenomena and their developments are simply manifestations of mind. All causes and effects, from great universes to the fine dust only seen in the sunlight come into apparent existence only by means of the discriminating mind. If we examine the origin of anything in all the universe, we find that it is but a manifestation of some primal essence. Even the tiny leaves of herbs, knots of thread, everything, if we examine them carefully we find that there is some essence in its originality. Even open space is not nothingness. How can it be then that the wonderful, pure, tranquil and enlightened Mind, which is the source of all conceptions of manifested phenomena, should have no essence of itself.

If you must niggardly grasp this perceptive mind of discriminating consciousness that is dependent upon the different sense organs as being the same as Essential Mind, then the discriminative mind would have to forsake all those activities responding to any kind of form, sight, sound, odor, taste, touch, and seek for another and more perfect self-nature. You are now listening to my teaching and your minds are making discriminations by means of the sounds rising from my speaking, but when the sounds cease and all the perceptions arising from the sounds come to an end, still the mind goes on discriminating the memory of those sounds and you find it difficult to keep your mind in emptiness and tranquillity. This does not mean that I am instructing you not to grasp at these following activities, but I am instructing you to study their nature more closely. If your mind, after the object is removed from sight, still has its discriminating nature, does it necessarily mean that your discriminating mind has lost its substantiality? Does it not rather mean that you are now discriminating merely the shadows and reflections of unreal things which had their origin in objects in the presence of your sight? Objects certainly are not permanent; as they vanish, does your mind vanish, also, and become like hair on a tortoise, or a horn on a rabbit? If mind vanishes, then the Dharmakaya would be exterminated and who would be devoted to the practice of attaining perseverence in getting rid of the developments arising from the conceptions of phenomena? At this, Ananda and the great audience became more confused and speechless.

The Lord Buddha continued:—Ananda, if in this world disciples practiced meditation assiduously, though they attained all the nine stages of calmness in Dhyana, yet do not accomplish the attainment of Arhats free from the intoxicants arising from worldly contaminations and attachments, it is wholly due to their grasping this deceiving conception of discriminative thinking that is based on unrealities and mistaking the delusion as being a reality. Ananda, although you have learned a great deal, you are not yet ready for the maturity of Buddhahood.

3. THE MIND IS UNCHANGING; ONLY ITS REFLECTIONS CHANGE

WHEN ANANDA HEARD this solemn teaching, he became very sorrowful and with tears falling, with forehead, hands and feet touching the ground, he paid homage to the Lord. Then kneeling, he said:—

Noble Lord! Since I determined to follow thee and become thy disciple, I have always thought that I could rely upon thy supernormal strength and that it would not be difficult to put thy teachings into practice. I expected that the Lord would favor me with an experience of Samadhi in this body; I did not appreciate that the body and mind were different and could not be substituted for each other, so I have likely lost my own mind. Although I have become a disciple of Buddha, my heart is not yet absorbed in Enlightenment. I am like a prodigal son who has forsaken his father. I now see that in spite of my learning, if I am not able to put it into practice, I am no better than an unlearned man. It is like a man talking about food, but never eating and becoming satisfied. We are all entangled in these two hindrances: knowledge and learning, and vexation and suffering. I can now see that it is all due to our ignorance of the eternal and tranquil nature of true Mind. Pray, my Lord Tathagata, have mercy upon us all; show us clearly the mysterious, enlightening Mind, and open our true eye of Enlightenment.

Suddenly from the holy symbol on the breast of the Lord Tathagata, there shown forth a glorious, blazing brightness, which radiated forth brilliantly into hundreds and thousands of colored rays reaching to the ten quarters of the universes, which were instantly turned into innumerable Buddha-lands, and glorified all the holy shrines of the Tathagata, in all the ten quarters of the universes. And, finally, the scintillating splendor returned to rest on the crown of Ananda and upon the crown of each one in the assembly.

Then the Lord Buddha addressed Ananda, saying:—For the sake of all I will lift the luminous beacon of the Dharma so that by its light all sentient beings may realize the wonderful, mysterious nature of the pure enlightening Mind and acquire its true intrinsic Eye.

First, let me question you, Ananda. You saw my fist and it seemed bright to you. By what means did its brightness manifest itself? By what means was it seen, and by what means was the thought of brightness conceived?

Ananda replied:—My Lord, the brightness comes from the whole luminous body of my Lord which is as brightly shining as a valley filled with rubies. Your holy body, shining as it does, could not have originated except from Purity itself. Your hand being clenched was in the form of a fist. I saw it with my eyes, my mind conceived its brightness.

The Buddha said:—You say that it takes the movement of my fingers and the seeing of your eyes to give you the conception of a fist. Does that mean that the nature of the movement of the fingers and the seeing of the eyes and the thinking of the mind are all alike?

Ananda replied:—Yes, my Lord. If you had no hand, or I had no eyes, there could be no conception of a fist. There must be the meeting of the two conditions.

The Lord Buddha interrupted:—You state that the movement of the hand and the seeing of the eyes being in agreement, the mind conceives a fist. Is that wholly true? If a man loses his hand he loses it forever, but if a man loses his eyes, he does not wholly lose the sense of sight, nor does he lose the conception of a fist. Suppose you meet a blind man on the road and you ask him, "In your blindness, what do you see?" He will give you some such answer as this:—"I can only see darkness, nothing else." This means that the objects within the range of his former sight have become darkened; there is no loss of his conception of sight but the conception is of darkness.

Ananda asked:—My Lord, if the blind man can only perceive darkness, how can it mean that he still possesses the perception of sight?

The Buddha replied:—Ananda, this blind man of no eyes simply sees darkness just as any seeing man who is shut up in a dark room sees dark ness. Close your eyes, Ananda, what do you perceive but darkness?

Ananda had to admit that as far as perceiving darkness was concerned there was no difference between the blind man, the man in a dark room and himself with his eyes closed.

The Buddha resumed:—If the blind man seeing only darkness sud denly recovers his sight and again sees objects, we say that he sees them by means of his eyes. A lamp is suddenly brought into the dark room and we say that the man again sees objects by means of the lamp. That is not strictly true for while the lamp does reveal objects, it is the eyes that per ceive them. If it were otherwise and the seeing belonged to the lamp then it would no longer be a lamp and the seeing would have no relation to him. In a true sense, however, it is neither the lamp nor the eyes that perceives objects.

Although this was the second instruction that Ananda had had on this subject, he did not yet understand it and sat dazed hoping for a clearer interpretation of it in the kind and gentle tones of the Master and he waited with a pure and expectant heart for the Blessed One's further explanation.

The Lord Buddha, in great kindness, let his hand rest kindly on the head of Ananda and said to him:—Ananda, at the beginning of my perfect Enlightenment I went to the Deer Forest at Sarnath where Kaundinya and his four disciples were staying and gave them my first teaching. The teaching was this:—The reason why all sentient beings fail to attain enlightenment and Arhatship is because they have been led astray by false conceptions regarding phenomena and objects, which defiled their minds. Since that time they have understood the import of that teaching and have become enlightened.

Then Kaundinya rose from his seat and addressed the Lord, saying:—Blessed Lord! I am now the oldest in this assembly and am credited with having the best understanding of the Dharma. I attained Arhatship by realizing the significance of objective things. I was like a traveler seeking lodgings where I could satisfy my hunger and take my rest, but, like a traveler after he had satisfied his hunger and taken his rest, he could no longer stay there for a comfortable rest but must set out on another day's journey. If he was the inn-keeper he could do so, but the traveler is the symbol of impermanency. We may also draw a lesson from the sky. After a rain it is fresh and clear and the sun's rays penetrating the clouds light up the dust particles moving about in the air. We think of open space as a ymbol of motionlessness and permanency, while we think of dust par-icles as symbols of motion and impermanency.

The Lord Buddha was much pleased by the words of Kaundinya and aid:—So it is, it is, Kaundinya! Then raising his hand, he opened his ingers and then closed them, saying:—What do you see, Ananda?

Ananda replied:—I see my Lord standing before the assembly open-ng and closing his beautiful fingers.

The Lord resumed:—As you watch the fingers of my hand opening nd closing, does the perception of motion belong to my hand or to our eyes?

Ananda replied:—My Lord, while thy precious hand is opening and losing I recognize the motion as belonging to thy hand and not to ny eyes.

The Lord enquired:—Ananda, what is in motion and what is still?

Ananda replied:—My Lord, it is thy fingers that are in motion, but as o the perception of my eyes, while it can not be said that it possesses the nature of absolute stillness, it can hardly be said that it is in motion.

The Lord Buddha was pleased with this reply and said: So it is, Ananda. Then the Lord Buddha caused a bright beam of light to dart rom his hand and fall on Ananda's right side. Ananda quickly turned his head to look at it. Then the Lord caused another beam of light to fall on Ananda's left, and Ananda quickly turned his head to look at that. Then the Lord Buddha questioned Ananda, saying:—Ananda, what caused you to turn your heard about?

My Lord, it was because I saw a shining beam of light springing from my Lord's hand and darting first to my right and then to my left, and I turned my head to look at it.

Ananda, you say that when your eyes followed the light, you turned your head from right to left. Tell me was it your head or the perception of your sight that moved?

My Lord, it was my head that moved. As to the perception of sight, while it can not be said that it has the nature of motionlessness, neither can it be said that it has no motion.

The Lord was pleased with this reply and said:—So it is, Ananda. When I was looking at you as sentient beings do, it was your head that was moving about but my perception of sight did not move, and when you were looking at me, it was my hand opening and closing, not your "seeing" that moved. Ananda, can you not see the difference in nature in that which moves and changes, and that which is motionless and

unchanging? It is body which moves and changes, not Mind. Why d
you so persistently look upon motion as appertaining to both body an
mind? Why do you permit your thoughts to rise and fall, letting th
body rule the mind, instead of Mind ruling the body? Why do you le
your senses deceive you as to the true unchanging nature of Mind an
then to do things in a reversed order which leads to motion and cor
fusion and suffering? As one forgets the true nature of Mind, so he mis
takes the reflections of objects as being his own mind, thus binding hir
to the endless movements and changes and suffering of the recurrin
cycles of deaths and rebirths that are of his own causing. You shoul
regard all that changes as "dust-particles" and that which is unchangin
as being your own true Nature of Mind.

Then Ananda and all the assembly realized that from beginningles
time, they had forgotten and ignored their own true nature, had misin
terpreted conditional objects, and had confused their minds by false dis
criminations and illusive reflections. They felt like a little baby that ha
found its mother's breast, and became calm and peaceful in spirit. In thi
spirit they pressed their hands together and made devout obeisance t
the Blessed One. They besought the Lord Tathagata to teach them hov
to make distinctions between body and mind, between the real and th
unreal, between that which is true and that which is false, between th
manifested natures of deaths and rebirths on the one hand, and the in
trinsic nature of that which is un-born and never dies on the other hand
the one appearing and disappearing, the other forever abiding within th
essence of their own mind.

4. ASSURANCE OF IMMORTALITY OF THE MIND; THE BODY IS DESTRUCTIBLE, NOT THE MIND

His Highness King Prasenajit who was in the assembly, stood up anc
addressed the Lord Buddha, saying:—Honorable Lord, formerly befor
I had been under the instruction of my Lord, I visited Katyayana and
Vairotiputra (two heretic teachers). They both taught that after one's
death, the destruction of body and mind meant Nirvana. Afterwards, I
have been occasionally with thy Lord, I have had doubts within my
mind and even now the matter is not clear. How can I clearly understand
and realize this state of non-death and non-rebirth. I think that all the
disciples present who have not yet attained Arhatship, are equally desir-

us of more perfectly understanding this profound teaching from my ord Buddha.

The Lord addressed the King, saying:—Your Majesty! May I have e honor of asking you some questions about your present body. Is our Majesty's body as permanent and enduring as gold and steel, or is impermanent and destructible?

Oh, my Lord, my present body of flesh will soon come to destruction.

Your Majesty! While your body has not yet come to destruction, how o you know that it ever will?

My Lord, it is true that this body has not yet come to total destruction, ut as I have watched it and reflected about it, I have seen it constantly hanging and needing constant renewal. It seems as though it was slowly eing changed into ashes, gradually decreasing and fading away. From is I am convinced that it will ultimately come to destruction.

Yes, your Majesty, it is all too true. You are growing old and your ealth is becoming imperfect. Tell me a little about your present appearnce as compared with your boyhood.

Your Lordship! When I was a boy, my skin was tender and smooth, n young manhood my blood and energy were in full supply, now as I m getting old, my strength is failing, my appearance is languid and dull, ny brain is dull and uncertain, my hair has become grey and white, my ace wrinkled. All these changes certainly show that I can not live much onger. How can I compare my present with my youth?

The Lord Buddha replied kindly:—Your Majesty, do not be disouraged, your appearance will not become decrepit as quickly as all hat.

Your Lordship! It is true that these changes have been going on so ecretly that I have hardly felt them, but as winters and summers pass know that I have been gradually changing into my present condition. At twenty I was young for my age but my appearance was very different han at ten; at thirty I was older; at forty, still older; and now after twenty ears I am sixty and am what I am. I recollect that at fifty years of age I elt comparatively young and strong. Your Lordship! I am conscious hat these processes and changes are still going on secretly and that in a rief time, perhaps ten limited years, the end will come.

Moreover, your Lordship, as I think about these changes, I see that t is not a matter of changes in one or two decades, the process is going n yearly. And not only yearly, but month by month, yes, day by day. Now I think of it, the changes are going on faster than that even, breath by breath, changes incessantly going on faster than thoughts. In the end my body will be given over to destruction.

The Lord Buddha said:—Your Majesty from watching this process of change going on you have become convinced that ultimately your body will be given over to destruction. At the time of the destruction of your body, do you think there is anything within your body that is not destructible?

The King Prasenajit pressed his hands together and replied soberly:—Certainly, your Lordship, I do not know. I wish I did.

The Lord Buddha said: Your Majesty! I will now show you the nature of no-dying and no-rebirth. At the time you first saw the river Ganges your Majesty, how old were you?

The King replied:—I can remember when my mother brought me there to worship the Deva god. I was then just three years old. I can remember when we crossed the river; I can remember hearing it called the Ganges.

The Lord Buddha said:—Your Majesty! You were three years old at that time. As you have said, when ten years had passed, you were older and down to the age of sixty the processes of change have been going on year after year, month after month, day after day and thought after thought. Your Majesty, you said that when you first saw the river Ganges you were three years of age. Tell me, when you were thirteen years of age and saw the Ganges, how did it appear to you? Was the sight of it, your mind's perception of the sight, any different?

The King replied:—My sight of it was just the same as when I was three years of age. And now at my present age of sixty-two, while the sight of my eyes is not as good, my perception of the sight is just the same as ever.

The Lord Buddha continued:—Your Majesty! You have been saddened by the changes in your personal appearance since your youth—your greying hair and wrinkled face—but you say that your perception of sight compared with it when you were a youth, shows no change. Tell me, Your Majesty, is there any youth and old age in the perception of sight?

Not at all, your Lordship.

The Lord Buddha continued:—Your Majesty! Though your face has become wrinkled, in the perception of your eyes, there are no signs of age, no wrinkles. Then, wrinkles are the symbol of change, and the un-wrinkled is the symbol of the un-changing. That which is changing must suffer destruction, of course, but the un-changing is naturally free from deaths and re-births. How is it, Your Majesty, that the un-changing perception of Mind still suffers the illusion of deaths and rebirths and you are still clinging to the teaching of the heretic, who claimed that after the death of the body, everyone was completely destroyed?

After listening to this wonderful instruction that implied that after one's death something survived to reappear in a new body, the King and the whole assembly were much cheered and filled with joy. It was a most interesting occasion.

5. THE CONFUSING CONCEPTION OF THE PHENOMENAL WORLD

Then Ananda, after paying the usual reverence to the Lord Buddha, rose in his place and addressed the Lord, saying:—

Noble Lord! If the perception of the eyes and ears is free from death and re-birth, why did my Lord say that we had forgotten our true nature of mind and acted in a state of "reversed confusion"? Pray, my Lord, have pity on us all and purify our contaminated minds and clear away our attachments to them.

Immediately the Lord Buddha stretched out his arm with fingers pointing downward in some mystic *"mudra."* He said to Ananda:—As you are looking at my fingers, are they in an upright position or in a reversed position?

Ananda replied:—My Lord! Most people in this world would say that they were in a reversed position, but because the fingers are arranged in some mystic mudra, I do not know which is the upright position and which is the reverse.

The Lord replied:—Ananda, if human beings regard this as in a reversed position, what would they regard as an upright position?

Ananda replied:—My Lord, if you were to turn the hand so that the fingers were pointing up, that they would call an upright position.

The Lord Buddha suddenly turned his hand and said to Ananda:—If this interpretation of positions, reversed or upright, is simply made by turning the hand so that the fingers are pointing either up or down without any change in the location of the hand, that is, as viewed by beings in this world, then you should know that the essence of the Lord Tathagata's true body, the pure Dharmakaya, may be interpreted differently by viewing it from different viewpoints of attainment, as being either the Lord Tathagata's "True Omniscience" (upright position), or as the body of one's own mind, the "reversed position."

Now, Ananda, concentrate your mind on this and explain it to me:—When you say that your mind is in the reversed position, in what position is your body to be regarded? Is the body, also, in a reversed position?

At this question, Ananda and the whole assembly were confused and stared up at him with open mouths. What did he mean by a reversed position of both their body and mind?

In great compassion of heart, the Lord Buddha pitied Ananda and the great assembly. He spoke to them reassuringly, and his voice was like the subdued sound of the ocean's billows:—My good, faithful disciples! Have I not been constantly teaching you that all of the causes and conditions that characterize changing phenomena and the modes of the mind, and of the different attributes of the mind, and the independently developed conditions of the mind, are all simply manifestations of the mind; and all of your body and mind are but manifestations of the wonderful, enlightening, and true nature of the all-embracing and mysterious Essence of Mind.

My good, faithful disciples! Why do you so easily forget this natural, wonderful, and enlightening Mind of perfect Purity—this mysterious Mind of radiant Brightness? And why are you still bewildered in your realizing consciousness? Open space is nothing but invisible dimness; the invisible dimness of space is mingled with darkness to look like forms; sensations of form are mingled into illusive and arbitrary conceptions of phenomena; and from these false conceptions of phenomena, is developed the consciousness of body. So, within the mind, these jumblings of causes and conditions, segregating into groups and coming into contact with the world's external objects, there is awakened desire or fear which divide the mind and causes it to sink into either indulgence or anger. All of you have been accepting this confusing conception of phenomena as being your own nature of mind. As soon as you accepted it as your true mind, is it any wonder that you became bewildered and supposed it to be localized in your physical body, and that all the external things, mountains, rivers, the great open spaces, and the whole world, were outside the body. Is it any wonder that you failed to realize that everything you have so falsely conceived has its only existence within your own wonderful, enlightening Mind of True Essence.

In likeness you have abandoned all the great, pure, calm oceans of water, and clung to one bubble which you not only accept but which you regard as the whole body of water in all the hundreds of thousands of seas. In such bewilderment, you reveal yourselves as fools among fools. Though I move my fingers up or down, there is no change in the hand itself, but the world makes a distinction, and says that now it is upright, now it is reversed. Those who do this are greatly to be pitied.

6. THE PERCEIVING MIND AND THE "ESSENCE" OF MIND ARE ONE; PERMANENCE OF THE ENLIGHTENING MIND

ANANDA WAS profoundly moved by this teaching and through the kindness of the Lord Buddha was delivered from his foolish bewilderment. He sincerely repented and pressing his hands together reverenced the Lord Buddha, saying:—My Noble Lord! Though I have been listening to the Lord's wonderful teaching and have realized that this wonderful Enlightening Mind is by nature perfect in itself and is the permanent ground of my changing mind, but, as I have been listening to this Teaching of the Dharma, I think of my concentrating mind. I know that it is of a higher order than my conditional mind, but I dare not recognize it as being the pure, original ground of my mind. Pray, my Lord, have pity upon us all and kindly declare to us the complete teaching and remove this root of suspicion and doubt, so that we may attain to supreme Enlightenment.

The Lord Buddha replied to Ananda, saying:—Ananda, from what you have just said. I can see that you have been listening to my teaching with your conditional mind, and so my teachings have become conditional, also. It shows that you have not yet fully realized the pure Essence of your mind. It is like a man calling the attention of another man to the moon by pointing his finger toward it. The other man ought to look at the moon, but instead he looks at the finger and by so doing, not only misses the moon but misses the finger, also. And why? Because he has taken the finger to be the moon. Not only that, he has failed to notice the difference between darkness and brightness. And why? Because he takes the dark finger to be the moon's brightness. That is why he does not know the difference between darkness and brightness. Ananda, you are just as foolish as that man.

The Lord Buddha continued:—Ananda, if you take that which discriminates my teaching as your mind, then when it lays aside its conceptions of the discriminated teaching, the mind should still retain its own discriminating nature, which it does not. It is like a traveller seeking an inn where he may rest for a short time but not permanently. But the inn-keeper lives there permanently, he does not go away. It is the same with this difficulty. If the discriminating mind is your true Mind, it should never change. How can it be your true Mind when, as soon as the sound of my voice ceases, it has no discriminating nature?

Ananda, this is true not only as regards discriminations of sound, but also of sight and all other sensations, and if the mind is free from all conceptions of phenomena, inherently it must be free from discriminations in its own nature. And even if there is no discriminated object before it, the mind is neither vacuity nor phenomena. If it can be, that when you leave off all the conditions of phenomena, there shall remain no discriminating nature of mind, then both your mind and its Essence will have one individual and original nature, which would be their own and true reality.

Ananda said to the Lord Buddha:—Noble Lord, if both my mind and its Essence have one originality, why does the wonderful, enlightening original Mind, which has just been proclaimed by the Lord Buddha as being one with my discriminating mind, not return to its original state? Have pity upon us, my Lord, and explain it more clearly.

The Lord Buddha replied, saying:—Ananda, as you look at me with this enlightening Essence of sight, its perception of sight is the same thing and yet is not the same as the Enlightening Mind of the wonderful Essence. It is just like a reproduction of the true moon—that is, it is not merely a shadow of the moon. Now, Ananda, listen and I will show you the originality that has no need of returning at all.

Let us consider this great Lecture Hall which opens toward the east: when the crimson sun rises, it is filled with a glorious brightness; but when it is mid-night and no moonlight, and the sky overcast by clouds and mist, then there is dense darkness. Again, because it has doors and windows, the interior is visible, but if there were no doors or windows, the perception of sight would be hindered. Where there is only space, then there is only a common emptiness, but when discriminations are made, they straight away condition the sight. When the air is shut in by walls, it soon becomes close and gloomy and permeated with dust; when clear fresh air comes in, the dust soon disappears and the room becomes clear and refreshing to the eyes.

Ananda, during your life you have experienced many changes; I am now going to return these changes to their respective originalities. What do I mean by their respective originalities, Ananda? I will explain. In this Lecture Hall, first let us return the brightness to the crimson sun. Why? Because if there were no sun, there would be no brightness. That is, the origin of the brightness is in the sun, so let us return the brightness to the sun. Let us do the same with the other conditions; darkness returns to the dim moon, passage of light returns to the doors and windows, hindrance to light returns to the dense walls of the house, conditions return to discriminations, space returns to emptiness, closeness and gloominess return to dust and clearness and freshness return to the purifying air. Thus all the existencies in the world may be included in these eight kinds of phenomena.

Now, Ananda, let us consider the perceiving mind which distinguishes these eight kinds of phenomena and which we have already found has its ground in the enlightening nature of the Essence of Mind; to which one of these eight phenomena shall it be returned? If you return the faculty of perceiving to brightness, then when there is no brightness, there will be no perception of darkness. Though there may be all degrees of illumination between brightness and darkness, perception in its self-nature possesses no differentials. [Therefore, we can not return perceiving, which belongs to our Essence of Mind to the phenomena of brightness or any other of the eight classes of phenomena noted above.] Thus we see that those things which can be returned to their originalities do not belong to your own true nature; and that which we can not return to its originality, is the only thing which truly belongs to us. This shows that your mind has its own mysterious nature of brightness and purity, and when you try to refer your mind to the various classes of phenomena, you simply deceive and bewilder yourself, and, by so doing, you have lost your own true nature and have suffered endless mis-fortunes, like a vagrant adrift on the ocean of deaths and rebirths. That is why, I look upon you as being most pitiable.

7. THE PERCEPTION OF SIGHT IS INFINITE, UNIVERSAL AND IS ITSELF NOT AN OBJECT—THE BASIS OF BUDDHIST IDEALISM

Ananda was still in doubt as to the true nature of his mind, and begged the Lord Buddha for further elucidation, saying:—My Lord, though I now can see that the nature of the mind's perceiving is constant and does not need to be referred to any originality in phenomena, but how can I fully realize that it is my true and essential nature?

The Lord Buddha replied:—Ananda, you have not yet attained to the pure state of freedom from the intoxicants, but you have, with the aid of my Transcendental Power, advanced to the first attainment of Dhyana and thus acquired the state of Perfect Intelligence. In the state of Freedom from Intoxicants, Anuruddha looking upon the countries of this world, sees them as clearly as he sees an amala fruit lying in the palm of his hand. In that state the Bodhisattva-Mahasattvas, looking beyond this world, have seen with like clearness, all the worlds, even hundreds of thousands of worlds. It is the same with the Tathagatas of the ten quarters of all the universes. Their sight reaches everywhere; they see clearly all the Buddha-lands of Purity, greater in number than the fine particles of dust. But the perception of the eyes belonging to ordinary sentient beings cannot pierce through the thickness of a tenth of an inch.

Let us consider the palaces of the Four Heavenly Kings! How great the distances. How different the conditions of water and earth and air. In those Heavenly Realms there may be seen similarities to light and darkness, and all other phenomena of this world, but that is because of the lingering memory of objects seen in this world. Under those Heavenly conditions, you would still have to continue making distinctions between yourself and objects. But, Ananda, I challenge you, by the perception of your sight, to detect which is my True Essence and which manifestation.

Ananda, let us go to the extreme limit of our sight—to the palaces of the sun and moon—do you see anything there that belongs to our nature? Coming nearer to the Seven Golden Mountains that surround Mt. Sumaru, look carefully, what do you see? We see all sorts of brightness and glory, but nothing that belongs to our nature. Moving nearer, we come to the massing clouds, the flying birds, the hurrying winds, the rising of dust, the mountains, the familiar woods, trees, rivers, herbs, vegetables, animals, none of which belongs to our nature.

Ananda, regarding all these things, far or near, as perceived by the pure Essence of your perceiving eyes, they have different characteristics, but the perception of our eyes is always the same. Does this not mean, that this wonderful perception of sight is the true nature of our minds?

Ananda, if the perception of sight is not your own nature, but is to be regarded as an object, then since it is to be regarded as an object, my perception of sight is to be regarded as an object also, and you should be able to see my perception of sight. Moreover, if when you see the same thing that I do, you regard it as seeing my perception of sight, then since you have seen the sphere of my seeing, you should also see the sphere of my not seeing. Why can you not do so? Furthermore, if you falsely say that you see the sphere of my not seeing, it is then simply your own sphere of not seeing and it can not be the phenomena of my not seeing. And if not, how can it be that the phenomena of your not seeing is to be regarded as mine? Therefore, if you really do not see the sphere of my not seeing, then the selfness of this perception of sight can not be an object that can be seen with the eyes and touched with the hands. And if it is not an object, then why is it not your own true nature? If you still falsely regard your perception of sight as an object, the object should be able to see you, too. If you try to explain it in this way, the substantiality of an object and the selfness of the perception of sight of the object would be hopelessly jumbled together. No one would be able to tell which is subject and which object..

8. HOW THE PERCEPTION OF SIGHT, THOUGH BECOMING FINITE, STILL REMAINS UNCHANGEABLE AND TRANSCENDENTAL, WITHOUT ANALOGUE IN THE UNIVERSE

Ananda, as the nature of the perception of sight is universal, how can it be regarded as otherwise than your own true nature? What does it mean, Ananda, that you do not recognize the true nature that naturally belongs to you, and on the contrary, you are asking me to show you another reality?

Ananda said to the Blessed One:—Noble Lord! If the nature of the perception of my sight is my true nature and not any different, then when my Lord and I (in a Samapatti state) were visiting the transcendental, mystical, and magnificent palaces of the Four Heavenly Kings, and were sojourneying in the palaces of the sun and moon, the perception of our sight was then perfect and universal, reaching and including every part of the Saha world. But when we returned to this Jetavena Grove, we see only this Hall—a still, quiet place with doors and windows—and when we look out from within, we are able to see only the veranda and eaves. Now I learn from my Lord, that the essence of the perception of sight naturally permeates the whole universe. If that is so, why is it that now our perception of sight only embraces this little hall and nothing more? What does it mean, my Lord? Does it mean that the perception of sight is reduced from universality to the finiteness of mortal mind? Or is it that the perception of sight is partitioned off by walls and houses? I do not see where the point of your explanation lies. Please explain it more clearly, for we are very ignorant and stupid.

The Lord Buddha replied:—As all things in the universe, either great or small, external or internal, are objects in the presence of our sight, so it would not be right to say that our perception of sight has the potentiality of enlarging and reducing. For instance, take an empty square vessel. When you consider the space in the square vessel, is that square space fixed or changeable? If it is fixed, then if you put a round vessel inside of it, the square space would not permit the admission of the round vessel; or if it is changeable, then the space in the square vessel would no longer appear square. You said that you did not see where the point lies. Well here is the point: it is the nature of space to be neither fixed nor changeable [and the same is true of the mind's perception], as I have stated before, so it is absurd for you to repeat your question.

Or, Ananda [if you are still unconvinced], suppose you fill the square vessel with objects and then remove the vessel's squareness; are you still troubled as to the existence of shape in open space? Supposing that it is true that when we re-entered the Hall, the perception of our sight became limited, and when we look at the sun, it appears to lengthen to reach the surface of the sun. Or when we build a wall or a house, it appears to set apart or limit the perception of our sight, but when we make a hole in the wall, is the perception of our sight unable to look through and beyond? The point of my explanation is that changeableness is not an attribute of our perception of sight.

The Lord Buddha continued:—Ananda! Since beginningless time sentient beings have been led astray by mistaking the nature of their mind to be the same as the nature of any other object. As they thus lose their true and essential Mind their minds become bewildered by outer objects and the perception of their sight becomes changeable to conform to the dimensions of its visual field and to become limited strictly according to outer conditions. But if you can learn to see things by your true and essential Mind, right away you will become equal to all the Tathagatas—both your mind and your body will become perfectly enlightened and you will be in the same state of tranquillity and stillness as though you were sitting under the Bodhi tree. So perfectly univeralized will your mind have become that even at the point of a single hair all the kingdoms of the ten quarters of the universe will be seen.

9. WHAT BECOMES THEN OF THE BODY?

Ananda said:—Noble Lord, if the Essence of the perception of sight is my wonderful, enlightening Mind, then this wonderful Mind must be something which we can consider, and if the perception of sight is my true Essence, then what becomes of my present body and mind? I feel that both my body and mind have their separate existence, and yet this Essential perception of sight, even in its concentrated state of stillness, appears to make no discrimination of my body. If this Essential Nature of my perception of sight is truly my Mind then it should be able to show me in the presence of my sight, that it is my true self, but if it does, what becomes of my body, does it belong to me or not? This would seem to be contrary to what my Lord has previously said, that the object could not see the mind. We beg, my Lord to have pity upon us and enlighten our ignorant minds.

The Lord Buddha said:—Ananda, what you have just questioned, as to whether the perception of sight is something that can be considered as standing in your presence, is not true. If it was really present before your sight and you could really see it, then as the Essence of the perception of sight has a location, it will no longer be without a point of direction.

Suppose we were sitting in the Jetavana grove and our sight reached everywhere in the grove—to the streams, to the Royal Palace and its mansions, up to the sun and the moon and down to the River Ganges. All of these different phenomena, which we are supposing you are indicating with your hand as being within the purview of our sight, each has its distinctive characteristic; the grove is shady, the sun is bright, the wall is an obstacle to light, the opening in the wall is a passage for the light, and the same is true even of the smaller things, the trees, herbs, fine grasses, etc. Though in dimensions they all differ from one another, so long as it has appearance, there is nothing that is beyond the range of our sight or description. If the perception of sight is present before your sight, you should be able to point to me, which is your perception of sight and describe it to me.

If it is space that is the perception of sight, you ought to know, and if we were to remove perception of sight, what would you substitute for space? If one of the many objects is the perception of sight and has now become the perception of sight, what other object will you substitute for the first? Suppose you look closely, analyze all the phenomena before you, pick out the essential and enlightening, pure and wonderful nature of the perception of sight, and show it to me just as describable and tangible as the other things.

Ananda said to the Lord:—My Lord! Standing in the Lecture Hall of this imposing building and looking out into the far distances, to the vista of the Ganges, up to the sun and the moon, looking everywhere my hand can point and my sight can reach, there is nothing in sight but objects, and I see nothing that is analogous to my perception of sight. It is just as my Lord has taught us. I am simply a junior Arhat not yet free from the intoxicants, but it is the same with the Bodhisattva-Mahasattvas, we are all alike unable to detect the presence of anything to be called the perception of sight among all the appearances of phenomena, nor are we able to point out an analogous something that transcends all objects.

The Lord Buddha was greatly pleased with this reply and said:—So it is, Ananda, so it is! There is neither the Essence of the perception of sight, nor any other essential nature transcending all objects. There is no such "thing" as the perception of sight. Now let me ask you some more questions.

10. ALL PHENOMENA ARE ILLUSION; PHENOMENA AND SPACE "BELONG TO" THE PERCEPTION OF SIGHT

Suppose Ananda, that you and I are again sitting in the Jeta grove, looking over the gardens, even to the sun and moon, and seeing all the multitudinous objects, and no such thing as perception of sight can be pointed out to us. But, Ananda, among all these multitudinous phenomena, can you show me anything which does not belong to the perception of sight?

Ananda replied:—Noble Lord! True, I see every part of the Jeta grove, but see nothing which does not belong to perception of sight. And why? Because if the trees in the grove do not belong to the perception of sight, we could not call them trees. But if the trees belong to the perception of sight, why do we still call them trees? It is the same with space. If it does not belong to the perception of sight, we could not see space, and if it does belong to the perception of sight, why should we still call it space? I am convinced now that all objects whatsoever, be they little or big, wherever there are manifestations and appearances, all belong to the perception of sight.

Again, the Lord Buddha expressed agreement, saying:—So it is, Ananda, so it is!

Then all the junior disciples, except the older ones among them who had finished the practice of meditation, having listened to the discussion and not understanding the significance of the conclusion, became confused and frightened and lost control of themselves.

The Lord Tathagata, recognizing that the junior disciples were thrown into perplexity and discouragement by the teaching, took pity upon them and consoled them, saying to Ananda and to all of them:—

My good, pious disciples! Do not be disturbed by what has been taught. All that the supreme Teacher of the Dharma has taught are true and sincere words, they are neither extravagant nor chimerical. They are not to be compared with the puzzling paradoxes given by the famous heretic teachers. Do not be disturbed by what has been taught, but ponder upon its seriously and never give yourself up either to sadness or delight.

Thereupon the great disciple Manjusri, regarded by all as a Prince of the Lord's Dharma, took pity upon the confused ones among the Brothers, rose in his place and bowing with great reverence at the feet of the Lord Buddha, said to him:—Blessed Lord! There are some among the Brothers in this Assembly who have not yet fully realized the significance of these two seemingly ambiguous interpretations relating to whether phenomena and space belong to perception of sight, which have been presented by my Lord Tathagata.

Blessed Lord! If the conditioning causes in the presence of our sight, such as phenomenal objects, space etc., are meant as belonging to the perception of sight, they should have relations to be pointed out; or, if they are not meant as belonging to the perception of sight, they should not be seen by our sight. The Brothers do not see the point of the teaching and, therefore, have become confused and frightened. It does not mean that the roots of the Brothers' goodness in previous lives are too weak for such profound teaching, but for them the explanation needs to be very plain. I pray the Blessed Lord to be kind enough to bring out the Truth more simply as to what relations there are lying between the phenomenal objects and the Essence of the perception of sight. What are their origins, and how is the ambiguity as to whether they belong or do not belong, to be gotten rid of.

Then the Lord Buddha replied:—Manjusri and all my good pious Disciples! The Tathagatas in the ten quarters of the universe, together with all the great Bodhisattva-Mahasattvas, as they are intrinsically abiding in Samadhi, regard all of the perceptions of sight, their causes and conditions, and of all conceptions of phenomena, as being visionary flowers in the air, having no true nature of existence within themselves. But they regard the perceiving of sight as belonging to the Essence of the wonderful, pure, enlightening Mind (*Bodhi*). Why should there be any ambiguity as to belonging or not belonging, between the perception of sight and the perceiving of objects?

Manjusri, let me ask you, supposing there is another Manjusri, just such as you are. What do you think? Is there truly another Manjusri? Or is it an impossible supposition.

Blessed Lord, it is just as you say, it is impossible. I am the true Manjusri; it is impossible to have another of me. And why? Because if it was possible to have another in perfect likeness, there would be two Manjusris, but I would still be the one and true Manjusri. There is no ambiguity of one or two.

The Lord Buddha was pleased with this reply and continued:—It is just the same with this wonderful, enlightening perception of sight, the seeing of objects, as well as objects themselves, they all intrinsically belong to the pure, perfect, Essential Mind of the wonderful, enlightening, Supreme Bodhi. But they have been discriminated as phenomena of sight, space, the perception of seeing, hearing, etc. It is just like a man with defective eyes seeing two moons at the same time. Who can tell which is the true moon? Manjusri, there is only one true moon; there can be no ambiguity of one being true and the other untrue. Therefore, when one is looking upon these manifestations arising from the senses in contact with objects, he must remember that they are all illusion and then there will be no ambiguity. But if the feeling still persists that there is some ambiguity as to whether the essence of the perceiving mind is the wonderful, enlightening Mind of the True Essence or not, the wonderful enlightening Mind itself can free you from the ambiguity as to whether it is the True Mind or not.

11. "PERCEPTION" IS PURE REALITY AND IS NOT DEPENDENT ON CAUSES AND CONDITIONS

Ananda said:—Noble Lord! My Lord Dharma has said that the perceptions and their causes are universally permeating the ten quarters, that by nature they are tranquil and permanent, and that their nature is devoid of deaths and rebirths. If this is so, then what is the difference between it and the heretical teachings, such as the doctrine of "emptiness," the doctrine of "naturalism," and similar teaching, all of which teach that there is a "True Ego" universally permeating the ten quarters? My Lord has also given teachings to the wise Saraputra, our Brother, and to many others, on Mount Lankara, in which he explained to them that, while the heretics were always talking about "naturalism," my Lord taught the principle of "causes and conditions," which was fundamentally different from the teachings of the heretical philosophers. Now when I learn from my Lord's teaching that this nature of perception of sight is also natural in its origin, is devoid of death and rebirth, and is perfectly free from all sorts of illusive reversions, it does not seem to belong to your principle of "causes and conditions." How can it be distinguished from the "naturalism" taught by the heretics? Pray explain this to us, so that we do not fall into their heresy, and so that we may realize the wonderful, enlightening, and intelligent nature of our True Mind.

The Lord Buddha replied, saying:—Ananda, I have already explained it to you and shown you the Truth, but you have not realized it. On the contrary your mind is bewildered and you have mistaken my teaching of Mind-essence, as being "naturalism." Ananda, if your perception of sight belonged to "naturalism," then we should examine into the essence of its nature. Let us do so. In this wonderful, enlightening perception of sight, what would you take as belonging to itself? Does your perception of sight take its brightness from its own nature? Does it take its darkness from its own nature? Does it take its limitlessness from its own nature? Or its being limited by impenetrable objects as belonging to its own nature?

Amanda, if brightness belongs to it by nature, then it should not see darkness. If its ability to see everywhere in space belongs to it, then it should not be hindered by impenetrable objects. The opposite of this is true also. If darkness belongs to its nature, then there should be no brightness in the perception of sight. How then could it see the phenomena of brightness?

Then Ananda said to the Lord Buddha:—Noble Lord! If this wonderful perception of sight can not be explained as belonging to the principle of "naturalism," then how can it be explained as belonging to the principle of "cause and condition"? When I come to study the question of how the perception of sight can arise from causes and conditions, my mind is still confused. I beg my Lord to explain it for us once more.

The Lord Buddha replied:—Ananda, as to what you have just asked me about the nature of cause and condition, I would rather ask you a few questions first. Supposing the nature of your perception of sight was before us now for our examination. How could it be manifested to us? Would it be because of its brightness? Or its darkness? Or because of the clearness of space? Or because of the impenetrability of objects?

If the perception of sight is manifested by reason of its brightness, then we could not see darkness, or vice versa. And the same would be true if our perception of sight was manifested by the clearness of space, or the impenetrability of objects. Again, Ananda. Is the perception of sight manifested by the condition of brightness? Or the condition of darkness? Or the condition of the clearness of space? Or under the condition of impenetrable objects? If it is manifested under the condition of brightness, then it could not see darkness. And the same would be true of the opposite, or of open space and its opposite, impenetrable objects.

Ananda, you ought to realize that the nature of this essentially wonderful, intelligent, enlightening, perception of sight belongs to neither cause nor condition, to neither nature nor phenomena, to neither the ambiguities of being or not being, or of nothingness or not nothingness. Neither does the conception of sight belong to any conception of phenomena, and yet it embraces all phenomena.

Now, Ananda, after all these arguments, how can you discriminate within your mind, and how can you make distinctions and give them all those worldly fictitious names? You might as well try to take a pinch of space, or rub space with your hand. You would use up your strength and the air in the space would remain undisturbed. How would it be possible for you to catch and hold even a tiny bit of space? The same is true of your perception of sight.

Then Ananda said to the Lord Buddha:—Noble Lord! If this wonderful, enlightening nature of perception of sight, belongs neither to its own nature, nor to causes and conditions, then why did my Lord once explain to the Bhikshus that the nature of perception of sight is under four kinds of conditions, namely, space, brightness, mind and eyes? What did you mean by that explanation?

The Lord Buddha replied, saying:—Ananda! What I said about the causes and conditions in this phenomenal world, was not my supreme, intrinsic Teaching. Let me ask you again, Ananda:—When the people of this world say they can see this and that, what do they mean by it, Ananda?

My Lord, they mean that by the light of the sun or the moon or a lamp, they are able to see, and when devoid of the light of sun, moon or lamp, they are unable to see.

Suppose, Ananda, there is no light and they are unable to see things, does that mean that they cannot see the darkness? If it is possible to see darkness when it is too dark to see things, it simply means there is no light; it does not mean they can not see. Supposing, Ananda, they were in the light and could not see the darkness; does that mean, also, that they can not see? Here are two kinds of phenomena, light and darkness, and of both you say, 'he can not see.' If these two kinds of phenomena are mutually exclusive, then he can not see at all and that would mean, as far as the perception of sight is concerned, a temporary discontinuance of existence. But the fact is not so. Therefore, it is quite clear that you must mean that he can not see at all. I am puzzled to know just what you do mean, when you say, "he can not see in the darkness."

Listen, now Ananda, to what I am going to teach you. When you are seeing light, it does not mean that the perception of sight belongs to light, and when you are seeing darkness, it does not mean that the perception of sight belongs to darkness. It is just the same when you see through clear space, or cannot see through impenetrable objects. Ananda, you should understand the significance of those four things, for when you are speaking of the perception of sight you are not referring to the phenomena of seeing with the eyes, but to the intrinsic perception of sight that transcends the experiential sight of the eyes, and is beyond its reach. Then how can you interpret this transcendental perception of sight as being dependent upon causes and conditions, or nature, or a synthesis of all of them. Ananda, are you of all the Arahats so limited in understanding that you cannot comprehend that this Perception of Sight is pure Reality itself? This is a profound teaching and I want all of you to ponder upon it seriously. Do not become tired of it, nor indolent in realizing it. While it is the most profound of all teachings, it is the surest way to Enlightenment.

12. THE MYSTIC, INTUITIVE PERCEPTION OF REALITY; PARTICULARITIES DUE TO IMAGININGS OF THE SICK MIND

STILL ANANDA WAS NOT SATISFIED and said to the Lord Buddha:—Noble Lord! Although my Lord has explained to us the principles of causes and conditions, of naturalism, and all the phenomena of conformity and non-conformity, yet we do not fully realize any of them, and now as we listen to the teachings of our Lord about Perception of Sight, we become more puzzled than ever. We do not understand what you mean when you say that our mental perception of sight is not our intrinsic Perception of Sight. Pray, my Lord, have mercy upon us; give us the true eye of Transcendental Intelligence and reveal to us more clearly our Intuitive Mind of Brightest Purity. At this Ananda was so far overcome that he broke into sobs and bowed down to the ground waiting for the Lord's further instruction.

Thereupon the Blessed One had pity for Ananda and for all the younger members of the Assembly, and solemnly recited the Great Dharani which is the mystic way to the full attainment of Samadhi.

Then he said:—Ananda! Though you have an excellent memory, it seems to serve only to increase your knowledge. You are still a long way from the mysterious insight and reflection that accompany the attainment of Samapatti. Now, Ananda, listen carefully to me and I will teach you more particularly, not for your sake alone, but for the sake of all true disciples in the future, so that all alike may reap the fruit of Enlightenment.

The reason why all sentient beings in this world have ever been bound to the cycle of deaths and rebirths is because of two reverse, discriminative and false perceptions of the eyes which spring up everywhere to bind us to this present life and keep us turning about in the cycle of deaths and rebirths by every wind of karma. What are these two reverse perceptions of the eyes? One is the false perception of the eyes that is caused by individual and particular karma of any single sentient being. The other is the false perception of eyes that is caused by the general karma of many sentient beings.

Ananda, what is meant by the false perceptive karma that is caused by the individual and particular karma of single sentient beings? Supposing in this world there was someone who was suffering from inflammation of the eyes, so that when he looked at the light of a lamp in the night time, he would see a strange halo of different colors, surrounding the light. What do you think, Ananda? Is this strange bright halo caused by the lamp, or does it belong to the perception of the eyes? If it belongs to the lamp, then why do others with healthy eyes not perceive it? If it belongs to the perception of the eyes, then why does not every one see it? What is the strange sight only perceived by the single individual with the inflamed eyes?

Again, Ananda. If this halo that surrounds the light, exists independently of the lamp, then other objects near by should have like halos about them, screen, curtain, desk, table, etc. If it exists independently of the perception of the eyes, then it ought not to be seen by the eyes at all. How is it, that only the inflamed eyes see it?

Ananda, you should know that the sight really belongs to the lamp, but the halo is caused by the inflammation of the particular eyes, for the halo and the perception are both under the condition of the inflammation, but the nature that perceives the effect of the inflammation of the eyes is not sick itself. So, in conclusion, it should not be said that the halo belongs exclusively either to the lamp or to the perception of the eyes, nor should it be said that it belongs neither to the lamp nor to the perception of the eyes. It is just the same as the reflection of the moon in still water: it is neither the real moon nor its double. And why? Because the reproduction of any sight is always accounted for by causes and conditions, so that the learned and intelligent do not say that the origin of any sight that can be accounted for by causes and conditions, belongs to the object, nor does not belong to the object. It is the same with the sight caused by the inflamed eyes, which should not be said to be either independent of the perception of the eyes nor not independent of the perception of the eyes. Would it not be absurd to try and distinguish what part of the sight belongs to the eyes and what part belongs to the lamp? Would it not be more absurd to try and distinguish which part of the sight does not belong to the lamp and which part does not belong to the inflamed eyes?

Ananda! Now let us consider, what is meant by false perception of eyes that is caused by the general karma of many sentient beings. In this world there are many thousands of kingdoms, great and small. Supposing we think that in one of the smallest of these kingdoms, all of the people are under the influence of a common bad condition of mind, that is, they all see many sorts of unpropitious signs that are not seen by any other people—two suns, two moons, or different eclipses of the sun or moon, or halos about the sun or moon, or comets, with or without tails, or flying meteors seen only for an instant, or gloomy shadows like a great ear near the sun or moon, or sometimes rainbows seen early or late. Supposing that all these strange phenomena of evil omen are seen only by this small kingdom, and have never been seen or heard of by any other people. Now, Amanda, we will consider these two examples together. First let us refer to the individual and particular false perception of eyes as seen by a single individual in the strange halo about the night lamp. Though it appeared to belong to the conditions in the presence of sight yet, after all, it belonged to the perception of the inflamed eyes. The imaginary halo meant only the sickness of the perception of eyes; it had nothing whatever to do with sight in itself. That is, the nature of the perception of the eyes that sees an imaginary halo is not responsible for the viewing mistakes. For instance, Ananda, when you are viewing the whole appearance of a country, seeing its mountains, rivers, kingdoms, people etc., they seem to be discriminated particulars of fact, but in truth, they are all made up by the original, beginningless, sickness of perceiving eyes. To both the visual condition of the eyes and the perception of the eyes these particular sights seem manifested in our presence, but to our intuitive, enlightened nature it is seen to be, what it truly is, a morbid sight indicative of sick eyes. So any and all perceptions of enlightened nature, for instance, even the particular perception of eyes itself, are seen to be simply an obscuring mist. But our fundamental, intuitive, enlightening Mind that perceives this perception of eyes and its visual conditions can by no means be regarded as something imaginary and morbidly sick. Therefore, we must be careful not to plunge this intuitive nature that perceives this morbid mist that is discriminated by the perception of inflamed eyes into the same morbid mist. We must be careful to distinguish between the perception of our eyes and the intrinsic Perception of Sight by our enlightened Mind that is conscious of the fallible perception of the eyes.

Since this intrinsic Sight is not identical with the perception of the sight as perceived by the eyes, how can the perceptions of morbid sight, such as your common seeing, hearing, perceiving and discriminating, how can you continue to call it your True Mind, Ananda? Thus when you are regarding yourself, or me, or any of the ten species of sentient beings in this world, you are simply regarding the morbid mist of the perception of the eyes; it is not the true, unconditioned Sight. The nature of this intrinsic Sight naturally manifests no morbid mist in its transcendental Perceiving and, accordingly, your intrinsic Mind is not the same as your perceiving, experiential mind.

Ananda! Let us now regard those sentient beings with their general, common and false perception of eyes and compare them with this one person who is suffering under his individual and particular karma of false perception of eyes. This inflamed-eye individual who perceived an imaginary halo about the light, caused by the morbid mist in his perceiving mind, is perfectly typical of all the people in that little kingdom who saw the imaginary unpropitious signs in the heavens caused by the general and common karma of false perceptions of eyes. They are alike developments of a false perception of sight since beginningless time. For instance, in this great world with its continents and oceans, in the social world with all its races of people and kingdoms, all of these sentient beings and all the natural phenomena all have their origin in the intuitive, enlightening, non-intoxicating, mysterious, intrinsic Mind, but they are all manifestations of the false, morbid conditions that belong respectfully to the perceptions of the eyes, ears, nose, tongue, touch, discrimination, emotion, thinking. All these sentient beings are ever subject to the sufferings of an unceasing cycle of deaths and rebirths according to the general principle of causes and conditions.

Ananda! If you can remain perfectly independent of these false perceptions and of all conformity and non-conformity to them, then you will have exterminated all the causes leading to deaths and rebirths and, besides, you will have attained a perfectly matured enlightenment that is of the nature of non-death and non-rebirth. This is the pure Intrinsic Mind, the ever abiding Intuitive Essence.

[*This covers roughly half of the First Chapter. There follow discussions of the questions on the sole reality of the "Essence of Mind," with further developments on the falsity of the perception of the other senses of hearing, tasting and smelling, the twelve locations of contact between consciousness and objects, the eighteen spheres of mentation (sense-organs, sense-minds and sense perceptions) and their relations to the four elements (earth, fire, wind and water); these four elements with our perceptions and the notion of space constitute the "six elements" of the phenomenal world.*

[Chapter Two discusses the positive side of the intuitive perception, the untying of the "knots" of sense-perceptions and the acquiring of "transcendental sense-organs" corresponding to the six physical senses, with special emphasis on the transcendental sense of hearing as best suitable to the realization of the ultimate reality, which is easy to understand because a sound lingers in our ears after it ceases, being without shape and therefore "spiritual" in character.

[For a fair estimate of Buddhist thinking, however, it is always important to get back to the practical outcome of its religious spirit, or the Buddhist way of life. *The following selection from the Second Chapter is intended to supplement the above philosophical exposition.—Ed.]*

Thereupon the Blessed Lord, sitting upon his throne in the midst of the Tathagatas and highest Bodhisattva-Mahasattvas from all the Buddha-lands, manifested his Transcendent Glory surpassing them all. From his hands and feet and body radiated supernal beams of light that rested upon the crowns of each Tathagata, Bodhisattva-Mahasattva, and Prince of the Dharma, in all the ten quarters of all the universes, in number more numerous than the finest particles of dust. Moreover, from the hands and feet and bodies of all the Tathagatas, Bodhisattva-Mahasattvas and Princes of the Lord's Dharma, in all the ten quarters of the universes, went forth rays of glorious brightness that converged upon the crown of the Lord Buddha and upon the crowns of all the Tathagatas, Bodhisattva-Mahasattvas and Arhats present in the assembly. At the same time all the trees of the Jeta Park, and all the waves lapping on the shores of its lakes, were singing the music of the Dharma, and all the intersecting rays of brightness were like a net of splendor set with jewels and overarching them all. Such a marvelous sight had never been imagined and held them all in silence and awe. Unwittingly they passed into the blissful peace of the Diamond Samadhi and upon them all there fell like a gentle rain the soft petals of many different colored lotus blossoms—blue and crimson, yellow and white—all blending together and being reflected into the open space of heaven in all the tints of the spectrum. Moreover, all the differentiations of mountains and seas and rivers and forests of the Saha World blended into one another and faded away leaving only the flower-adorned unity of the Primal Cosmos, not dead and inert but alive with rhythmic life and light, vibrant with transcendental sounds of songs and rhymes, melodiously rising and falling and merging and then fading away into silence.

THE BUDDHIST WAY OF LIFE

"No teaching that is unkind can be the true teaching of Buddha."

Then Ananda and all the great assembly were purified in body and mind. They acquired a profound understanding and a clear insight into the nature of the Lord Buddha's Enlightenment and experience of highest Samadhi. They had confidence like a man who was about to set forth on a most important business to a far-off country, because they knew the route to go and to return. All the disciples in this great assembly realized their own Essence of Mind and purposed, henceforth, to live remote from all worldly entanglements and taints, and to live continuously in the pure brightness of the Eye of Dharma.

Then Ananda, rising in the midst of the assembly, straightened his robe, with the palms of his hands pressed together, knelt before the Lord Buddha. In the depths of his nature he was already enlightened and his heart was filled with happiness and compassion for all sentient beings and, especially, did he desire to benefit them by his newly acquired wisdom. He addressed the Lord Buddha, saying:—Oh my Lord of Great Mercy! I have now realized the True Door of Dharma for the attainment of Enlightenment, and have no more doubt about its being the only Door to Perfect Enlightenment. My Lord has taught us that those who are only starting the practice of Bodhisattvaship and have not yet delivered themselves, but who already wish to deliver others, that this is a sign of Bodhisattvaship. And when those who have attained Enlightenment have a deep purpose to enlighten others, that this is a sign of the Lord Tathagata's descent from the Pure Land for the deliverance of all the world. Although I have not yet delivered myself, I already wish to deliver all sentient beings of this present kalpa. Noble Lord! Sentient beings of this age and world are gradually becoming more and more alienated from my Lord's favor, and the propagation of heretical teachings, deceiving people and leading them astray, more and more flourishes. I want to persuade them to concentrate their minds in dhyana for the attainment of Samadhi. What can I do to help them arrange a True Altar to Enlightenment within their minds so that they may be kept far away from all deceiving temptations and in whose progress there shall be no retrogression or discouragement in the attainment of Enlightenment?

In response to this appeal, the Blessed One addressed the assembly:—

Ananda has just requested me to teach how to arrange a True Altar of Enlightenment to which sentient beings of this last kalpa may come for deliverance and protection. Listen carefully as I explain it to you.

Ananda and all in this assembly! In explaining to you the rules of the Vinaya,[1] I have frequently emphasized three good lessons, namely, (1) the only way to keep the Precepts is first to be able to concentrate the mind; (2) by keeping the Precepts you will be able to attain Samadhi; (3) by means of Samadhi one develops intelligence and wisdom. Having learned these three good lessons, one has gained freedom from the intoxicants and hindrances.

Ananda, why is concentration of mind necessary before one can keep the Precepts? And why is it necessary to keep the Precepts before one can rightly practice dhyana and attain Samadhi? And why is the attainment of Samadhi necessary before one may attain true intelligence and wisdom? Let me explain this to you. All sentient beings in all the six realms of existence are susceptible to temptations and allurements. As they yield to these temptations and allurements, they fall into and become fast bound to the recurring cycles of deaths and rebirths. Being prone to yield to these temptations and allurements, one must, in order to free himself from their bondage and their intoxication, concentrate his whole mind in a resolution to resist them to the uttermost. The most important of these allurements are the temptations to yield to sexual thoughts, desires and indulgence, with all their following waste and bondage and suffering. Unless one can free himself from this bondage and these contaminations and exterminate these sexual lusts, there will be no escape from the following suffering, nor hope of advancement to enlightenment and peacefulness. No matter how keen you may be mentally, no matter how much you may be able to practice dhyana, no matter to how high a degree of apparent Samadhi you may attain, unless you have wholly annihilated all sexual lusts, you will ultimately fall into the lower realms of existence. In these lower Mara realms of existence there are three ranks of evil ones:—the Mara king, evil demons, and female fiends, and all of them have each his and her own double who disguise themselves as "angels of light" who have attained supreme Enlightenment.

After my Parinirvana,[2] in the last kalpa[3] of this world, there will be plenty of all these kinds of evil spirits everywhere. Some of them will beset you openly with avarice and concupiscence and others of them will

[1] Religious discipline. [2] Near-Nirvāna. [3] Age, or Cycle.

pose as holy and learned masters. No one will escape their machinations to lure them into the swamps of defilement and thus to lose the Path to Enlightenment. Therefore, Ananda, and all of you, should persistently teach the people of this world to attain perfect concentration of mind, so that they may be enabled to keep the Precept of purity and thus be able to practice dhyana successfully and attain Samadhi. This is the clear teaching of all the Blessed Buddhas of the past, and it is my instruction at the present and it will be the instruction of all Tathagatas of the future.

Therefore, Ananda, a man who tries to practice dhyana without first attaining control of his mind is like a man trying to bake bread out of a dough made of sand; bake it as long as he will, it will only be sand made a little hot. It is the same with sentient beings, Ananda. They can not hope to attain Buddahood by means of an indecent body. How can they hope to attain the wonderful experience of Samadhi out of bawdiness? If the source is indecent, the outcome will be indecent; there will ever be a return to the never-ending recurrence of deaths and rebirths. Sexual lust leads to multiplicity; control of mind and Samadhi leads to enlightenment and the unitive life of Buddahood. Multiplicity leads to strife and suffering; control of mind and dhyana leads to the blissful peace of Samadhi and Buddahood.

Inhibition of sexual thoughts and annihilation of sexual lusts is the path to Samadhi, and even the conception of inhibiting and annihilating must be discarded and forgotten. When the mind is under perfect control and all indecent thoughts excluded, then there may be a reasonable expectation for the Enlightenment of the Buddhas. Any other teaching than this is but the teaching of the evil Maras. This is my first admonition as to keeping the Precepts.

The next important hindrance and allurement is the tendency of all sentient beings of all the six realms of existence to gratify their pride of egoism. To gain this one is prone to be unkind, to be unjust and cruel, to other sentient beings. This tendency lures them into the bondage of deaths and rebirth, but if this tendency can be controlled they will no longer be lured into this bondage for right control of mind will enable them to keep the Precept of kindness to all animate life. The reason for practicing dhyana and seeking to attain Samadhi is to escape from the suffering of life, but in seeking to escape from suffering ourselves, why should we inflict it upon others? Unless you can so control your minds that even the thought of brutal unkindness and killing is abhorrent, you will never be able to escape from the bondage of the world's life. No matter how keen you may be mentally, no matter how much you may be able to practice dhyana, no matter to how high a degree of Samadhi you may attain, unless you have wholly annihilated all tendency to unkindness toward others, you will ultimately fall into the realms of existence where the evil ghosts dwell.

There are three ranks of these ghosts:—the highest are the mighty ghosts, the next are the Yaksha ghosts who fly in the air, and the lowest are the Raksha ghosts that live under the earth. Each of these ghosts has his double that disguises itself as having attained enlightenment. After my Parinirvana in the last kalpa these different kinds of ghosts will be encountered everywhere deceiving people and teaching them that they can eat meat and still attain enlightenment. But how can any faithful follower of the Lord Tathagata kill sentient life and eat the flesh?

You of this great Assembly ought to appreciate that those human beings who might become enlightened and attain Samadhi, because of eating meat, can only hope to attain the rank of a great Raksha and until the end of their enjoyment of it must sink into the never ceasing round of deaths and rebirths. They are not true disciples of Buddha. If they kill sentient beings and eat the flesh, they will not be able to escape from this triple world. Therefore, Ananda, next to teaching the people of the last kalpa to put away all sexual lust, you must teach them to put an end to all killing and brutal cruelty.

If one is trying to practice dhyana and is still eating meat, he would be like a man closing his ears and shouting loudly and then asserting that he heard nothing. The more one conceals things, the more apparent they become. Pure and earnest bhikshus and Bodhisattva-Mahasattvas, when walking a narrow path, will never so much as tread on the growing grass beside the path. How can a bhikshu, who hopes to become a deliverer of others, himself be living on the flesh of other sentient beings?

Pure and earnest bhikshus, if they are true and sincere, will never wear clothing made of silk, nor wear boots made of leather because it involves the taking of life. Neither will they indulge in eating milk or cheese because thereby they are depriving the young animals of that which rightly belongs to them. It is only such true and sincere bhikshus who have repaid their karmic debts of previous lives, who will attain true emancipation, and who will no more be bound to wander to this triple world. To wear anything, or partake of anything for self-comfort, deceiving one's self as to the suffering it causes others or other sentient life, is to set up an affinity with that lower life which will draw them toward it. So all bhikshus must be very careful to live in all sincerity, refraining from even the appearance of unkindness to other life. It is such true hearted bhikshus who will attain a true emancipation. Even in one's speech and especially in one's teaching, one must practice kindness for no teaching that is unkind can be the true teaching of Buddha. Unkindness is the murderer of the life of Wisdom. This is the second admonition of the Lord Buddha as to the keeping of the Precepts.

Then there is the Precept of not taking anything that does not rightfully belong to one, not coveting it or even admiring it. One must learn to keep this Precept in all sincerity if he is to hope for escape from the chain of deaths and rebirths. The purpose of your practice of dhyana is to escape from the suffering of this mortal life. No matter how keen you may be mentally, no matter how much you may be able to practice dhyana, no matter to how high a degree of apparent Samadhi you may attain, unless you refrain from covetousness and stealing, you will fall into the realm of heretics.

There are three grades of these heretics:—the first grade are the spiritual heretics tempting one to rank and privilege and power and egoistic pride. The second grade are mental goblins tempting one to false ideas that will enhance one's knowledge and erudition. The third grade are the common heretics of this world who teach among human beings what is not true Dharma. You will be beset by these heretics on every hand, within and without. And each one of these heretic goblins will have his double who disguises himself as one who has attained supreme enlightenment and who sets himself up as a teacher of highest truth. After my Parinirvana, in the last kalpa of this world, there will be plenty of these goblin-heretics about, hiding themselves within the very personalities of the saints, the better to carry out their deceiving tricks. Sometimes they gain control of some great and good Master and teach under the prestige of his name. They often assert that they have received their Dharma from some notable Master, deceiving ignorant people, discouraging them and even causing them to go insane. In such deceptive ways do they spread their false and destructive heresies.

For all these various reasons, I teach my bhikshu-brothers not to covet comforts and privileges, but to beg their food, not here and there, or now and then, but to make it a regular habit so that they will be better able to overcome the greediness and covetousness that hinders their progress toward enlightenment. I teach them not to cook their own food even, but to be dependent upon others for even the poorest living so that they will realize their oneness with all sentient life and are but sojourners in this triple world. Under these conditions, how can bad men be tempted to put on our Buddhist garments and to offer the Dharma of all the Tathagatas as goods for sale? To do this is to accumulate all kinds of evil karma. Nevertheless, these heretics insist that their selfish and acquisitive acts are in conformity with Buddha's teaching and that Buddhism allows them to teach and act in these acquisitive ways. By so doing they defame the true Buddhist Bhikshus who have been tested and tried in some formal religious ceremony. On the contrary, they only reveal themselves as belonging to some heretical sect but, meanwhile, they have deluded and bewildered and turned astray or hindered many sentient beings so that they fall into the hells of suffering.

If after my Parinirvana there shall be bhikshus who undertake to practice dhyana and to attain Samadhi and who prove their sincerity and earnestness by some sacrifice before an image of the Tathagata, such as cutting off a part of their body, or burning a finger, or even burning one spot on their head with incense, such disciples immediately pay all their karmaic debts accumulated from beginningless time, and they will be immediately emancipated from the bondage of this triple world. Although such disciples will not at once attain Supreme Enlightenment, yet they reveal their right resolution and are on the right Path by the practice of dhyana.

But if they are not enough in earnest to sacrifice even the slightest comfort, even if they attain a measure of tranquillity, they will have to be reborn in a human body for the payment of the debts of previous lives. Thus I, myself, suffered for about three months to eat the rye in horse's fodder, so hungry was I, in recompense of the debt of an earlier life. Thus you must teach the people of this world who are practicing dhyana in the hope of attaining Samadhi, that they must abstain from stealing and covetousness.

Therefore, Ananda, if any of my disciples who are trying to practice dhyana, do not abstain from stealing and covetousness, their efforts will be like trying to fill a leaking pot with water; no matter how long they try, they will never succeed. So all of you, my bhikshu disciples, with the exception of your poor garments and your begging bowls should have nothing more in possession. Even the food that is left over from your begging after you have eaten should be given to hungry sentient beings and should not be kept for the next meal. Moreover, you should look upon your own body, its flesh, blood and bone, as not being your own but as being one with the bodies of all other sentient beings and so be ever ready to sacrifice it for the common need. Even when men beat you and scold you, you must accept it patiently and with hands pressed together bow to them humbly. Furthermore, you should not accept one teaching, or one principle, that is easy and agreeable, and reject the rest of the Dharma; you should accept all with equitable mind lest you misinterpret the Dharma to the new converts. Thus living, the Lord Buddha will confirm your attainment as one who has acquired the true Samadhi. As you teach the Dharma to others, be sure that your teaching is in agreement with the above so that it may be regarded as a true teaching of Buddha, otherwise it would be as heretical as the deceptive words of the goblin-heretics who are murderers of the life of Wisdom. This is the third admonition of the Lord Buddha as it relates to the Precepts.

Then there is the Precept of not deceiving nor telling lies. If the sentient beings of the six realms of existence should refrain from killing, stealing and adultery, and should refrain from even thinking about them, but should fail to keep the Precept of truthfulness and not be sincere in their practice of dhyana and their attainment of Samadhi, there would be no emancipation for them; they would fall into the ranks of the Maras who are satisfied with any slight attainment and who boast of it, or they would fall into the ranks of Maras who become prejudiced and egoistically assertive, and what is of more importance they would lose their seed of Buddhahood.

Such disciples presumptuously assume an attainment before they have attained it; they assume realization before they have realized it; they affect to be the most respected and competent masters, and speak to the people loftily, boasting:—"I have attained to the degree of Crotapanna, or to the degree of Sakradagamin, or to the degree of Anagamin, or to the degree of Arhat, or to the degree of Pratyaka-Buddha." They claim to have attained to the Ten Gradual Grounds of Tranquillity, or to the degree of those Bodhisattva-Mahasattvas who have attained to the stage of No Recension. Moreover, they covet the respect of people, they like to see them humble in their presence, they greedily watch for offerings from the people. Such disciples are to be regarded as no better than un-believers, no better than hardened Icchantikas. They not only lose their own seed of Buddahood, they destroy the seed of Buddahood in others. Such disciples progressively lose their nature of kindness and gradually lose the measure of understanding that they had attained and shall at last sink into the Sea of the Three Kinds of Suffering, namely, (1) the suffering of pain, (2) the loss of enjoyment, (3) the suffering of decay. They will not attain to Samadhi for a long, long time in after lives.

Nevertheless, Ananda, in the time after my Parinirvana, I urge all of you Bodhisattva-Mahasattvas and Arhats to choose to be reborn in the last kalpas wholly for the sake of delivering all sentient beings.[1] You should make use of all manner of transformations, such as disciples, laymen, kings, lords, ministers, virgins, boy-ennuchs, and even as harlots, widows, adulterers, thieves, butchers, pedlers, etc., so as to be able to mingle with all kinds of people and to make known the true emancipation of Buddhism and the following peace of Samadhi. You must never speak of your own true rank of Bodhisattva-Mahasattva and Arhat, you must never reveal the Lord Buddha's Secret Cause of Attainment, nor speak without discretion before those who are not practicing meditation. Except toward the end of your mortal life, you may disclose to your most worthy disciples the secret teachings and instruction, lest the evil heretics disturb and lure them away by their lies. To teach the world to observe the Precept of truthful sincerity, to practice dhyana with sincerity and to attain a true Samadhi, this is the clear and true instruction of the Lord Buddha.

Therefore, Ananda, if any disciple does not abstain from deceit, he is like a man moulding human dung instead of carving sweet-smelling sandalwood. I have always taught my bhikshu Brothers to keep their intuitive minds in straightforward sincerity as their true Altar of Enlightenment, and at all times, whether walking, standing, sitting or lying down, there should be no falsehood in your life. How disgraceful is it for heretics whose lives are filled with deceit to present themselves as having attained supreme enlightenment. They are like poverty stricken people who pretend to be kings or wealthy merchants, only to shame and destroy their own lives. For any such disciple who dares to represent himself as a Prince of the Dharma, there will be a terrible retribution.

It has always been a truism that any disease in a seed will reveal itself in diseased and abortive fruit. Such a disciple, seeking to attain the Lord Buddha's Enlightenment can be likened to a man trying to bite his own navel. How impossible for them to attain true Enlightenment. But bhikshus whose lives are as straight as the chord of a bow will certainly attain Samadhi. They need never fear the wiles of the Maras. They are

[1] The doctrine of "bodhisattvaship," voluntarily abstaining from Nirvana and continuing in the cycle of rebirths until the world is saved, is an essential tenet of Mahayana Buddhism. A "bodhisattva" therefore corresponds somewhat to the Christian idea of "Saviour."

the bhikshus who are certain to attain the Bodhisattva-Mahasattva's supreme understanding and insight. Any lesson or instruction that is in agreement with the foregoing can be relied upon as being a true teaching of the Lord Buddha. Differing from it, it is simply a false teaching of the heretics who have always been murderers of the Life of Wisdom. This is the fourth admonition of the Lord Buddha.

Ananda! As you have asked me as to the best method for concentrating the mind of those who have difficulty in following the common methods, I will now reveal to you the Lord Buddha's Secret Method for the attainment of Bodhisattva-Mahasattvahood. But you must remember that it is of first importance to fully observe the Four Precepts as explained above. To become a Bodhisattva-Mahasattva, one must have a nature as pure and clear and repellent as frost and ice, so that no false growths of leaves and branches shall sprout out from the true Mind, such as the three poisons of lust, hatred and infatuation; or the four wickednesses of the mouth: falsehood, slander, obscene words, and flattery.

Ananda! If any of the disciples in the last kalpa should be unable to overcome their old habits, you may teach them to recite this Dharani of mine. It is called, The Supreme Dharani of the Radiating Brightness of the Lord Buddha's Crowning Experience. It is the invisible transcendental power that rays out from the Tathagata's Wisdom Eye manifesting the unconditioned Essential Mind of the Lord Buddha. It is the transcendental radio-activity of Power and Glory that was revealed in me at the time of my Highest Samadhi, at the hour of my Perfect Enlightenment, as I sat amid the Lotus Blossoms under the Bodhi-tree.

Listen, Ananda! At the time you were helpless under the magic charm of the maiden Pchiti, what was it that released you and restored your control of mind? Your coming under her control was not a chance happening of this life, or of this kalpa alone: you had been in affinity with her for many a kalpa. Suddenly, when Manjusri repeated this Dharani, the bonds that bound you to her were destroyed, her passion for you was ended, and by once listening to my teaching she became enlightened. Although she was a prostitute and apparently had no interest in the Dharma, by the invisible power of my transcendental Dharani she immediately attained to the perfection of all dhyana practice. What this Dharani did for her and for you, it can do for all others. Rest assured all my Bhikshu Brothers in this great assembly, you who are earnestly seeking Supreme Attainment, rest assured that, by the power of this Great Dharani, you will attain Buddahood.

What Is Nirvana?

INTRODUCTION

Every student of Buddhism must be interested in a correct notion of Nirvana, the goal of this religious effort. Naturally this has puzzled many serious minds. Sir Edwin Arnold, in his Preface to "The Light of Asia" expresses the "firm conviction that a third of mankind would never have been brought to believe in blank abstractions, or in Nothingness as the issue and crown of Being." Yet what is it?

The foregoing philosophical exposition in the *Surangama Sutra* must have prepared the reader to expect a philosophic and at the same time mystic outcome of such speculations. The process of religious enlightenment is a process of divesting oneself of the illusions of the sensory world and constantly rising to a higher conception of an ideal world, such as arrived at by Kantian idealism. It is a steady process of dropping off of errors arising from the finite "discriminating mind," such as the habitual and ingrained notion of the ego and the individuality of things. From this, the reader can already deduce what the final outcome must be. It is the reaching of that unconditioned, infinite world. But then the mechanism of our thinking and language fails, because our words must fail to describe an unconditioned existence. To call it "destruction" is to assume that there is something to destroy, and to call it "emptiness" is to assume the contrast of a substantial world. When we read that Nirvana is "neither being, nor non-being," we realize that the words "being" and "non-being" are no longer adequate. If we could think of a world without our pet notions of space and time, that is, an unconditioned world, we would have a fair notion of what Nirvana means. The doggedly logical, finite mind can never rise to this conception, and therefore it is hard for western scholars to grasp its significance.

The following disquisition gives, in my opinion, the best description of the Mahayana conception of the Nirvana, found in the end of *Lankāvatāra Sutra*. The *Lankāvatāra Sutra* is very popular with the Chinese Buddhist students, there being four Chinese translations of it, in A.D. 420, 443, 513, and 700, of which the first one was lost. It gives a clear and well-reasoned outline of Buddhist metaphysics in a shorter, better-ordered and more complete scheme than the *Surangama*. Readers who are interested in such a clear summary are referred to "The Buddhist Bible," edited by Dwight Goddard (published by Goddard, Thetford, Vt.). But I have chosen the *Surangama,* rather than the *Lankāvatāra,* because the latter is like a well-written history of philosophy, while the former is like an original masterpiece in philosophy. Both employ the Buddhaesque method of dialogue, but anyone who examines both can have no doubt as to the superior aptness and freshness of Buddha's illustrations and the flesh-and-blood quality of the *Surangama*.

What Is Nirvana?

Then said Mahamati to the Blessed One[1]: Pray tell us about Nirvana?

The Blessed One replied: The term, Nirvana, is used with many different meanings, by different people, but these people may be divided into four groups: There are people who are suffering, or who are afraid of suffering, and who think of Nirvana; there are the philosophers who try to discriminate Nirvana; there are the class of disciples who think of Nirvana in relation to themselves; and, finally there is the Nirvana of the Buddhas.

Those who are suffering or who fear suffering, think of Nirvana as an escape and a recompense. They imagine that Nirvana consists in the future annihilation of the senses and the sense-minds; they are not aware that Universal Mind and Nirvana are One, and that this life-and-death world and Nirvana are not to be separated. These ignorant ones, instead of meditating on the imagelessness of Nirvana, talk of different ways of emancipation. Being ignorant of, or not understanding, the teachings of the Tathagatas, they cling to the notion of Nirvana that is outside what is seen of the mind and, thus, go on rolling themselves along with the wheel of life and death.

As to Nirvanas discriminated by the philosophers: there really are none. Some philosophers conceive Nirvana to be found where the mind-system no more operates owing to the cessation of the elements that make up personality and its world; or is found where there is utter indifference to the objective world and its impermanency. Some conceive Nirvana to be a state where there is no recollection of the past or present, just as when a lamp is extinguished, or when a seed is burnt, or when a fire goes out; because then there is the cessation of all the substrate,

[1] Buddha.

which is explained by the philosophers as the non-rising of discrimination. But this is not Nirvana, because Nirvana does not consist in simple annihilation and vacuity.

Again, some philosophers explain deliverance as though it was the mere stopping of discrimination, as when the wind stops blowing, or as when one by self-effort gets rid of the dualistic view of knower and known, or gets rid of the notions of permanency and impermanency; or gets rid of the notions of good and evil; or overcomes passion by means of knowledge;—to them Nirvana is deliverance. Some, seeing in "form" the bearer of pain, are alarmed by the notion of "form" and look for happiness in a world of "no-form." Some conceive that in consideration of individuality and generality recognizable in all things inner and outer, that there is no destruction and that all beings maintain their being for ever and, in this eternality, see Nirvana. Others see the eternality of things in the conception of Nirvana as the absorption of the finite-soul in Supreme Atman [1]; or who see all things as a manifestation of the vital-force of some Supreme Spirit to which all return; and some, who are especially silly, declare that there are two primary things, a primary substance and a primary soul, that react differently upon each other and thus produce all things from the transformations of qualities; some think that the world is born of action and interaction and that no other cause is necessary; others think that Ishvara is the free creator of all things; clinging to these foolish notions, there is no awakening, and they consider Nirvana to consist in the fact that there is no awakening.

Some imagine that Nirvana is where self-nature exists in its own right, unhampered by other self-natures, as the varigated feathers of a peacock, or various precious crystals, or the pointedness of a thorn. Some conceive being to be Nirvana, some non-being, while others conceive that all things and Nirvana are not to be distinguished from one another. Some, thinking that time is the creator and that as the rise of the world depends on time, they conceive that Nirvana consists in the recognition of time as Nirvana. Some think that there will be Nirvana when the "twenty-five" truths are generally accepted, or when the king observes the six virtues, and some religionists think that Nirvana is the attainment of paradise.

These views severally advanced by the philosophers with their various reasonings are not in accord with logic nor are they acceptable to the

[1] Here we see the Buddhistic rebellion against Brahmanism. In this section, we see the variety of schools of philosophy prevailing in the few centuries before Christ and the background against which developments of Buddhistic thought naturally arose.

wise. They all conceive Nirvana dualistically and in some causal connection; by these discriminations philosophers imagine Nirvana, but where there is no rising and no disappearing, how can there be discrimination? Each philosopher relying on his own textbook from which he draws his understanding, sins against the truth, because truth is not where he imagines it to be. The only result is that it sets his mind to wandering about and becoming more confused as Nirvana is not to be found by mental searching, and the more his mind becomes confused the more he confuses other people.

As to the notion of Nirvana as held by disciples and masters who still cling to the notion of an ego-self, and who try to find it by going off by themselves into solitude: their notion of Nirvana is an eternity of bliss like the bliss of the Samadhis—for themselves. They recognise that the world is only a manifestation of mind and that all discriminations are of the mind, and so they forsake social relations and practise various spiritual disciplines and in solitude seek self-realisation of Noble Wisdom by self-effort. They follow the stages to the sixth and attain the bliss of the Samadhis, but as they are still clinging to egoism they do not attain the "turning-about" at the deepest seat of consciousness and, therefore, they are not free from the thinking-mind and the accumulation of its habit-energy. Clinging to the bliss of the Samadhis, they pass to their Nirvana, but it is not the Nirvana of the Tathagatas. They are of those who have "entered the stream"; they must return to this world of life and death.

Then said Mahamati to the Blessed One: When the Bodhisattvas yield up their stock of merit for the emancipation of all beings, they become spiritually one with all animate life; they themselves may be purified, but in others there yet remain unexhausted evil and unmatured karma. Pray tell us, Blessed One, how the Bodhisattvas are given assurance of Nirvana? and what is the Nirvana of the Bodhisattvas?

The Blessed One replied: Mahamati, this assurance is not an assurance of numbers nor logic; it is not the mind that is to be assured but the heart. The Bodhisattva's assurance comes with the unfolding insight that follows passion hindrances cleared away, knowledge hindrance purified, and egolessness clearly perceived and patiently accepted. As the mortal-mind ceases to discriminate, there is no more thirst for life, no more sex-lust, no more thirst for learning, no more thirst for eternal life; with the disappearance of these fourfold thirsts, there is no more accumulation of habit-energy; with no more accumulation of habit-energy the defilements on the face of Universal Mind clear away, and the Bodhisattva attains self-realisation of Noble Wisdom that is the heart's assurance of Nirvana.

There are Bodhisattvas here and in other Buddha-lands, who are sincerely devoted to the Bodhisattva's mission and yet who cannot wholly forget the bliss of the Samadhis and the peace of Nirvana—for themselves. The teaching of Nirvana in which there is no substrate left behind, is revealed according to a hidden meaning for the sake of these disciples who still cling to thoughts of Nirvana for themselves, that they may be inspired to exert themselves in the Bodhisattva's mission of emancipation for all beings. The Transformation-Buddhas teach a doctrine of Nirvana to meet conditions as they find them, and to give encouragement to the timid and selfish. In order to turn their thoughts away from themselves and to encourage them to a deeper compassion and more earnest zeal for others, they are given assurance as to the future by the sustaining power of the Buddhas of Transformation, but not by the Dharmata-Buddha.

The Dharma which establishes the Truth of Noble Wisdom belongs to the realm of the Dharmata-Buddha. To the Bodhisattvas of the seventh and eighth stages, Transcendental Intelligence is revealed by the Dharmata-Buddha and the Path is pointed out to them which they are to follow. In the perfect self-realisation of Noble Wisdom that follows the inconceivable transformation death of the Bodhisattva's individualised will-control, he no longer lives unto himself, but the life that he lives thereafter is the Tathagata's universalised life as manifested in its transformations. In this perfect self-realisation of Noble Wisdom the Bodhisattva realises that for Buddhas there is no Nirvana.

The death of a Buddha, the great Parinirvana, is neither destruction nor death, else would it be birth and continuation. If it were destruction, it would be an effect-producing deed, which it is not. Neither is it a vanishing nor an abandonoment, neither is it attainment, nor is it of no attainment; neither is it of one significance nor of no significance, for there is no Nirvana for the Buddhas.

The Tathagata's Nirvana is where it is recognised that there is nothing but what is seen of the mind itself; is where, recognising the nature of the self-mind, one no longer cherishes the dualisms of discrimination; is where there is no more thirst nor grasping; is where there is no more attachment to external things. Nirvana is where the thinking-mind with all its discriminations, attachments, aversions and egoism is forever put away; is where logical measures, as they are seen to be inert, are no longer seized upon; is where even the notion of truth is treated with indifference because of its causing bewilderment; is where, getting rid of the four propositions, there is insight into the abode of Reality. Nirvana is where the twofold passions have subsided and the twofold hindrances are cleared away and the twofold egolessness is patiently accepted; is where, by the attainment of the "turning-about" in the deepest seat of consciousness, self-realisation of Noble Wisdom is fully entered into—that is the Nirvana of the Tathagatas.

Nirvana is where the Bodhisattva stages are passed one after another; is where the sustaining power of the Buddhas upholds the Bodhisattvas in the bliss of the Samadhis; is where compassion for others transcends all thoughts of self; is where the Tathagata stage is finally realised.

Nirvana is the realm of Dharmata-Buddha; it is where the manifestation of Noble Wisdom that is Buddhahood expresses itself in Perfect Love for all; it is where the manifestation of Perfect Love that is Tathagatahood expresses itself in Noble Wisdom for the enlightenment of all;—there, indeed, is Nirvana!

There are two classes of those who may not enter the Nirvana of the Tathagatas: there are those who have abandoned the Bodhisattva ideals, saying, they are not in conformity with the sutras, the codes of morality, nor with emancipation. Then there are the true Bodhisattvas who, on account of their original vows made for the sake of all beings, saying, "So long as they do not attain Nirvana, I will not attain it myself," voluntarily keep themselves out of Nirvana. But no beings are left outside by the will of the Tathagatas; some day each and every one will be influenced by the wisdom and love of the Tathagatas of Transformation to lay up a stock of merit and ascend the stages. But, if they only realised it, they are already in the Tathagata's Nirvana for, in Noble Wisdom, all things are in Nirvana fom the beginning.

Glossary of Hindu Words

PRONUNCIATION

The pronounciation of Sanskrit and Pali words in the transcription used in this book is simple. All vowels are pronounced as in Italian, except that the short *a,* has the sound of *u* in *but.* The consonant combinations, *dh, th, kh,* etc. are pronounced as aspirated stops, as in *"bird-house," "hothouse," "block house."* *G* is always hard, and *c* is always pronounced as *ch,* as in *church.* The difference between dental and lingual *d, t,* between lingual and palatal *sh,* and between the different *n*'s has been ignored for the convenience of the lay reader. Where the long marks are used over vowels, the long vowel is almost always accented.

VARIATIONS OF SPELLING AND NAMES

The editor has tried to achieve uniformity of spelling in the selections from different translators as far as possible. These selections use transcriptions with different degrees of exactness. Absolute uniformity is not possible without too much violence to the texts made by different translators. In the case of better-known Anglicized words, it is a question whether the retention of the accents is desirable. Moreover, in the general reading of books on Indian literature, such variations will be encountered again and again. It is well to know when such variations refer to the same word.

1. The palatal *sh* is variously rendered as *ç, s, ś* and *sh.* Thus the Hindu god may be spelled as *Çiva, Siva* or *Shiva,* and the word for "scripture" may be spelled as *çastra, sastra* or *shastra.*

2. English usage has established certain inconsistencies which are now

adopted. Thus the stem form is kept in *Nirvana* and *atman,* while *Brahma* and *karma* stand for *Brahman* and *karman*. Furthermore, the word *Brahmana* becomes *Brahman,* and is further Anglicized as *Brahmin*. Also the unaccented final *a* in Hindu words is almost silent in practice and we often find this letter abbreviated, especially in verse, as *Arjun* for *Arjuna*. There are also some minor variations in English and American spelling in the various texts.

3. There are differences between Sanskrit and Pali for the same words. The Sanskrit is the classic language of Hindu scriptures, the great epics and the Buddhist Mahayana texts translated into Chinese. Pali is a later form of the Sanskrit language, containing many simplifications, chiefly known as the language of the Buddhist *Tripitaka* (Hinayana "Pali Canons"). Thus the Sanskrit word *tripitaka* ("three baskets") becomes *tipitaka* in Pali. A few examples will show the simplification.

(SANSKRIT)	(PALI)
Nirvana	*Nibbana*
Sutra	*Sutta*
Bhikshu	*Bikkhu*
Dhyana	*Jhana*
Arahant	*Arahat*
Prajna	*Panna*

A great part of this glossary is based on that by Swami Vivekananda in "Raja Yoga" (Brentano).

Aditi. "The earliest name invented to express the infinite," Max Müller.

Adityas. The sons of Aditi, especially Varuna and the sun.

Agni. The god of fire and light, an important Vedic god.

Akasa. The all-pervading material of the universe.

Amitabha. Boundless light, later personified as Amitabha Buddha, or Amita, very popular in Chinese Buddhism.

Ananda. Bliss. Name of Buddha's cousin and favorite disciple.

Annutara Samyak Sambodhi. Most perfect knowledge, the highest state of Buddha knowledge.

Arahat (skt. *Arahant*). An enlightened one, a Buddhist saint (tr. into Chinese as *Lohan*).

Asana. Position of the body during meditation in *yoga* practice.

Asrama. Hermitage.

Asura. A high divine being in the Vedas; later a demon.
Atman. The eternal self, as distinguished from the false self; the universal principle in man.
Avidya. Ignorance; the active principle of ignorance which prevents us from seeing the truth.

Bhagavad. Blessed; also used as a title of Buddha.
Bhakti. Intense love of God; devotion or devotional practice of religion.
Bhikkhu (skt. *Bhikshu*). A monk, mendicant, friar, or religious devotee (tr. as *pich'iu* in Chinese).
Bhikkhuni (skt. *Bhikshuni*). A nun (tr. as *pich'iuni* in Chinese).
Bodhi. Wisdom. *Bodhi-tree,* or *Bo-tree,* the tree at Buddha-Gaya where Buddha attained enlightenment.
Bodhisatta (skt. *Bodhisattva*). "Essence of wisdom," one who is on his way to become a Buddha; in Mahayana Buddhism, one who has already attained Nirvana but voluntarily renounces it to save mankind.
Brahma. Anglicized form of skt. stem-form *Brahman* (nom. s. *Brahmā*). The world-soul personified, the chief god of Brahmanism.
Brahman. (1) Anglicized form of skt. *Brahmana.* A member of the Brahman caste, highest caste in India, from whom priests are chosen, but not necessarily a priest. A Brahmin. (2) Hindu word *Brahman,* (neuter) signifying the supreme essence, or world soul; when personified, it is *Brahmā* (masculine).
Brahmacharin. A Brahman student who has taken the religious vows.
Buddha. "The Enlightened." Name of Sakyamuni, the founder of Buddhism, but also may be anyone who has attained the state of godhead.

Chaitya. A shrine or temple.
Chandala. An outcast, son of a Sudra father and a Brahman mother.
Chandan. Sandal-tree; the fragrant sandal paste.
Channa. Name of Buddha's driver.
Chitta. The "mind-stuff" in the *yoga* doctrine.
Chowri. (Properly *Chamari*) the Indian yak, whose tail is used as a fan.

Devas. Gods, celestial beings.
Dhamma (skt. *Dharma*). An important Buddhist word with many meanings, the natural condition of things or beings, the law of their

existence, truth, religious truth, the Buddhist Doctrine, the law (Law), the ethical code of righteousness.

Dharana. Fixing the mind on one object in *yoga* practice.

Dharma (see *Dhamma*).

Dharmakaya. The body of the Law; one of the three bodies of Buddha (see *Nirmanakaya* and *Sambhogakaya*).

Dhyana (Pali *Jhana*). Meditation as a form of religious practice aiming at attaining a mystic vision. Tr. into Chinese as *Ch'an* and into Japanese as *Zen*. Name of an important Buddhist sect in China and Japan.

Gandhara. Name of a country famous for its horses.

Gandharva. A celestial musician.

Gatha. A short verse, with a religious meaning.

Gautama (see *Gotama*).

Gayatri. An especially sacred verse of the *Rigveda.*

Ghee. Clarified butter.

Gita. Song.

Gotami. A female member of the Gotama clan.

Gotama (skt. *Gautama*). Buddha's family name. (See also *Siddhartha* and *Sakyamuni*).

Guna. A quality or attribute, but more specifically the three *Gunas* refer to the three mystic elements or principles out of which all things and beings in this world are made: these are, *Sattva,* light or illumination principle, *Rajas,* activity or passion principle, and *Tamas,* dullness, heaviness or inertia principle.

Guru. A spiritual teacher or preceptor.

Hansa. Swan or goose.

Hari. The Lord, usually designating Vishnu.

Hinayana. "The Lesser Vehicle," name of the "Southern School" of Buddhism with its center in Ceylon, given by its opponents of the Mahayana School.

Iddhi (skt. *Riddhi*). Control of mind over matter, including powers of levitation and assuming any shape at will.

Indra. Important Vedic god of the firmament.

Isi. Pali word for skt. *Rishi,* which see.

Isvara (also *Iswara*). The Supreme Ruler, but always used to represent a personal and transcendent God.

Jain. Modernized form of skt. *Jaina;* an adherent of the Jain sect, or Jainism, emphasizing asceticism and self-mortification, criticized by Buddha.

Jataka. A Buddhist birth-story, i.e., a story telling about one of Buddha's previous lives as a human being or as an animal.

Jhana. Pali for skt. *Dhyana,* which see.

Kaivalya. The state of isolation or complete independence of the soul from the phenomenal world attained by *yoga* practice.

Kalpa. A world cycle.

Karma. Important Buddhist term, meaning work or deeds, with their necessary and natural consequences in this and future life.

Kisa Gotami (skt. *Krisha Gautami*), the slim or thin Gotami, name of the heroine in one of the Buddhist parables.

Krishna. The eighth incarnation of Vishnu; the personal god in *Bhagavad-Gita.*

Kriya-Yoga. Preliminary *yoga,* aiming at cleansing the mind.

Kshatriya. Member of the second, warrior, caste.

Magga (skt. *Marga*). The path; especially referring to the eightfold path of Buddhism, consisting of: right views, high aims, right speech, upright conduct, a harmless livelihood, perseverance in good, intellectual activity and earnest thought.

Mahayana. "The Greater Vehicle," name given themselves by followers of the "Northern School" of Buddhism now prevailing in Thibet, China, Korea and Japan. (See introduction to the selection, *Surangama Sutra*).

Manas. The deliberate faculty of the mind.

Mantra. Any prayer, holy verse, sacred or mystic word recited or contemplated during worship.

Mara. The Evil One, the tempter, the destroyer, the god of lust and sin.

Maya. Illusion; also name of Buddha's mother, with a curious similarity in sound to Maria.

Mrityu. Death; another name for the king of death, Yama.

Muni. A sage.

Nibbana. Pali word for *Nirvana,* which see.

Nirmanakaya. The body of the transformation (see *Dharmakaya*).

Nirvana. Freedom; extinction of "the illusions." Condition of emancipation from the finite world.

Om. The sacred mystic word said at the beginning of prayers, meaning the "Supreme Being," the "Bliss Absolute."

Paramita. Perfection or virtue.
Paulkasa. An outcast, son of a Sudra father and a Kshatriya mother.
Pitaka. "Basket." *Tripitaka* is the name of the "Three Baskets," or three bodies of Buddhist Canons.
Prajapati. The creator of the universe and lord of the creatures.
Prajna. Highest knowledge which leads to the realization of the Deity.
Prakriti. Nature.
Prana. Breath.
Pranayama. Control of breathing in *yoga* practice.
Pratyekabuddha. A Buddha who works out his individual salvation only.
Purusha. The soul behind the mind-consciousness, the Seer, the eternal in man.

Raja. "To shine"; royal.
Rajas. One of the three *Gunas*, which see.
Raja Yoga. "Royal Yoga," the science of conquering the inner nature.
Rakshas. A class of demons ranging at night and capable of assuming different forms.
Rasa. The mythical river in the firmament.
Rishi. A saint, an anchorite, a seer.

Sadhyas. Celestial beings.
Sakya. Name of Buddha's race, a royal race in the northern frontiers of Magadha.
Sakyamuni. "The Sage of the Sakyas," name of Buddha.
Samadhi. The state of spiritual ecstasy, achieved through meditation; the highest state attained through *yoga*.
Sambhogakaya. The body of Bliss (see *Dharmakaya*).
Samyama. "Control"; in *yoga* practice, the perfect control of the mind.
Sangha. The Buddhist church or brotherhood.
Sankhya. The name of the school of philosophy, founded by Kapila.
Sastra. Holy Scripture.
Sattva. See *Guna*.

Satyam. Truthfulness.
Siddhartha. Buddha's proper name.
Siddhas. *Yogas* who have attained supernatural powers.
Siddhis. The supernatural powers which come through *yoga.*
Siva. The destroyer of the Hindu Trinity. (See *Brahma* and *Vishnu*).
Sloka. The common verse form of sixteen-syllable lines, used in the Hindu epics.
Soma. Name of a plant and its juice, an intoxicating drink used in Vedic rituals; also personified as a god and identified with the moon.
Sudra. The fourth and lowest caste of servants and laborers. (See also *Brahman, Kshatriya* and *Vaisyas.*)
Surya. The Sun-god.
Sutra. "Thread," any essay or guide of a religious character.
Sutta. Pali for skt. *Sutra.*
Swami. A title meaning "master" or "spiritual teacher."
Swayamvara. A form of bridal, the bride selecting her husband from among suitors.

Tamas. See under *Guna.*
Tathagatha. A word denoting the highest religious enlightenment, used of Buddha and by Buddha of himself, generally explained as "the Perfect One"; translated into Chinese as "Thus Come," or *Julai.*

Udgitha. Ritual chant.
Urmya. An epithet of night.

Vaisyas. The third caste of merchants (see *Brahman, Kshatriya,* and *Sudra*).
Varuna. The old Vedic god of the sky.
Vayu. The wind.
Vedas. The Hindu Scriptures consisting of the *Rigveda,* the *Yajurveda,* the *Samaveda,* the *Arthavavedas;* also the *Brahmanas* and the *Upanishads.*
Vedanta. "The end of the Vedas," the final philosophy of the Vedas as expressed in the *Upanishads.*
Vishnu. The "Preserver" of the Hindu Trinity (see *Siva*), who takes care of the universe and incarnates from time to time to save mankind.
Visvakarman. The Creator of the universe.

Yakshas. A class of supernatural beings.
Yajna. Sacrifice.
Yama. Death; the King of Death.
Yasodhara. Wife of Buddha, who became one of the first Buddhist nuns.
Yoga. "Yoking," or joining the lower self to the higher self by means of mental control.
Yogi, or *Yogin.* One who practices *yoga.*
Yojana. The distance of about nine English miles.

THE
WISDOM
OF
CHINA

Introduction

Today the East and West must meet. It frightens one to read in the morning papers that Wendell Willkie was in Chungking one Friday and back in America the following Monday, over the week-end, as it were. It was almost like magic. No matter what will be the type of world cooperation after the war, we are sure that the East and the West will be living closely together, and dependent on each other. Somehow after the breaking-up of the nineteenth-century political world, a new world must be forged out of the elements of Anglo-Saxon, Russian and Oriental cultures. The "Wisdom of China" is an effort to unravel some of the mysteries of the Oriental, and specifically the Chinese point of view—some of the basic ways of looking at things as revealed in native Chinese literature and philosophy.

When we come to Chinese civilization, the general impression is that it is a human, rationalistic, and easily understandable type of culture. The Chinese temper is, on the whole, humanistic, non-religious and non-mystical. That is true only to a certain extent. I agree entirely on its being humanistic; I disagree on its being non-mystical, for any culture which has a broad and deep spiritual basis must be in a sense mystical. If by "non-mystical" is meant the modern servile and shallow worship of mechanistic and materialistic facts, accurately observed and well-tabulated, seemingly sufficient unto themselves, which is the prevalent type of thinking today, then I must repudiate that Chinese civilization ever fell so low. The fact is, any branch of knowledge, whether it be the study of rocks and minerals, or the study of cosmic rays, strikes mysticism as soon as it reaches any depth. Witness Dr. Alexis Carrel and A. S. Eddington. The nineteenth-century shallow rationalism naïvely believed that the question "What is a blade of grass?" could be answered adequately by considering the blade of grass as a purely mechanical phenomenon. The contemporary scientific attitude is that it cannot. Since Walt Whitman asked that question with his profound mysticism, no one has been able to answer it and no scientist will presume to answer it today. And let us remember, in that mysticism and distrust of the mechanistic view of the universe, Walt Whitman is Chinese. It is my conviction that the progress of contemporary science is forcing modern thought to develop in the direction of depth, and of a new synthesis of the mechanical and the spiritual, of matter and spirit.

In reviewing Chinese thought one is struck by the vast differences from the West both in style and method and in values and objectives. For what is the Chinese philosophy, and does China have a philosophy, say, like that of Descartes or Kant, a logically built and cogently reasoned philosophy of knowledge or of reality or of the universe? The answer is proudly "No." That is the whole point. So far as any systematic epistemology or metaphysics is concerned, China had to import it from India. The temperament for systematic philosophy simply wasn't there, and will not be there so long as the Chinese remain Chinese. They have too much sense for that. The sea of human life forever laps upon the shores of Chinese thought, and the arrogance and absurdities of the logician, the assumption that "I am exclusively right and you are exclusively wrong," are not Chinese faults, whatever other faults they may have. The very language of the Chinese philosophers is the market slang of the plebeians. China simply lacks the academic jargon which the American sociologists and psychologists love and which is so necessary for the construction of any air-tight academic theory. The fortress of academic aloofness from human life that Western scientists build around themselves by that jargon is one of the most amazing intellectual phenomena of the modern age. I notice that the scientists who popularize science and who write in the language that the common man can understand have a tendency to fall out of favor with the Royal Academies. In China, no college professor can call a "black-out" the "termination of illumination," and it is evident that we cannot build a systematic philosophy without this academic jargon. The Chinese scholar at once slips back into words like "black-out" and proverbs and analogies, like Emerson. The Chinese philosopher is like a swimmer who dives but must soon come up to the surface again; the Western philosopher is like a swimmer who dives into the water and is proud that he never comes up to the surface again and is happy in his profundity.

Generally, the reader will find reading Chinese philosophers like reading Emerson. Egon Friedell's characterization of Emerson's method and style may serve as a perfect description of all Chinese philosophers. "His propositions are there, unprepared, indisputable, like sailors' signals coming out of a misty deep." "He is an absolute Impressionist, in his style, his composition and his thought. He never propounds his ideas in a definite logical or artistic form, but always in a natural and often accidental order which they have in his head. He knows only provisional opinions, momentary truths. He never sacrifices even a single word, sentence, or idea to the architecture of the whole. Things like 'order of content,' 'introduction,' 'transitions' do not exist for him. He begins to develop this or that view, and we think he is going to weave it systematically, elucidate it from all sides and entrench it against all possible attack. But then, suddenly, some alien picture or simile, epigram or *aperçu* strikes him, full in the middle of his chain of thought, and the theme thenceforward revolves on a quite new axis. He calls his essays, 'Considerations by the Way,' but everything that he wrote might equally be so entitled."

China's peculiar contribution to philosophy is therefore the distrust of systematic philosophy. I confess this must distress many college sophomores who are so anxious to have systems that have no loopholes in them and are strongly entrenched against all possible attacks. They want to be able to say, either that criminals are born and not made, or else that criminals are made and not born, and they want to *prove* it. The Chinese reply is that there is no such air-tight system on earth, and has never been any. Such systems do not exist except in the minds of the deluded, logical dunderheads.

Furthermore, the Chinese can ask a counter-question, "Does the West have a philosophy?" The answer is also clearly "No." We need a philosophy of living and we clearly haven't got it. The Western man has tons of philosophy written by French, German, English, and American professors, but still he hasn't got a philosophy when he wants it. In fact, he seldom wants it. There are professors of philosophy, but there are no philosophers. When one asks about contemporary philosophy in America, one thinks of Professor Whitehead. But what has the philosophy of Professor Whitehead got to do with the common man? The fact is, the vast scientific knowledge of the modern age is disintegrating and falling by its own weight, so that philosophy itself has become a branch of physics or biology or mathematics. And when one reads the heavy volume of papers read before the Conference of Science,

Philosophy and Religion, trying to reunify modern knowledge, but comes upon such words as "objectives," "instrumentalities," and "procedures," and "determinant factors," and "processes," one has an instinctive distrust that science, philosophy and religion shall ever be reunited again.

Our international world is rapidly coming to the end of an era. So is our modern intellectual world. The world of ideas is definitely going to pieces, because our traditional values are gone. That brings us to the second difference between Oriental and Occidental philosophy; the difference in approach and values. It does look as if accurately observed and carefully tabulated facts are all that we have today; our moral values have disappeared, and they have disappeared in a curious manner that I shall try to explain. There is a definite difference in approach between Chinese and Western philosophy, the approach of values and the approach of facts. This difference is curiously brought out by the contact of the East and the West. It strikes the Western tourists as curious that the Chinese have no sense of accuracy, particularly of facts and figures. It is hopeless to get two Chinese to agree on the mileage between two neighboring towns or the population of either. And the Chinese equally cannot understand why a rough idea is not sufficient. On the other hand, it strikes the Chinese as equally curious that a Western writer cannot submit a magazine article and have it accepted without discoursing eloquently on the percentage of import of egg or butter into England, or the millimeters of Abyssinian cotton fibre, or a tabulation of so many million work-hours lost. A still more damning evidence is the popular assumption by politicians that a question like the second front could be settled by the "military" leaders who have "all the facts," and no sense of judgment whatsoever on moral, psychological and political issues. If the Chinese nation ever suffered from this statistical delusion, they would never have dared to take up arms against Japan's Army. As showing the Chinese ignorance of facts, there was a Chinese scholar who wrote in all seriousness that the human heart was on the right side of the chest; his technique was execrable—he could not possibly have felt his heart with his own hand. On the other hand, the Chinese can come back and reply, "What difference does it make whether the heart is on the right or on the left? If you cut it up, you are bound to see it anyway, and if you don't cut it up, you can't do anything with it. Generally you can't do anything with it, either, even if you do cut it up." The West will reply, "Ah yes, but we want to be scientific and exact and find out where the heart is." And the Chinese will reply again, "It doesn't matter where you find the heart is; it is much more important to place your heart in the right place." That represents briefly the difference between the approach of facts and the approach of values. H. G. Wells is suffering from the modern scientific Fact-Cult when he believes that we can reunify knowledge by his plan of a "world encyclopaedia." He seems to think that the gathering and systematic presentation of data confer upon the scientist a Godlike wisdom, that facts are like cold figures, and the human mind is like an adding machine, and that if you put all the facts into the machine, you automatically draw out the correct, infallible answer and the world will then be saved. The folly of this conception is beyond belief. We are suffering not from lack of facts, but rather from too many and from lack of judgment.

Chinese humanism, or Confucianism, concentrates on certain human values. Until we realize the vastness of the difference of approach, it will be found disappointing by Western readers. Confucianism excludes both physics and metaphysics, and concentrates on the values of human relationships. There are not so many things that we can discover about human relationships, and it seems so little. But Confucianism says there is the knowledge of essentials and the knowledge of externals; the knowledge of externals is the world of facts, and the knowledge of essentials is the world of human relationships and human behavior. Confucius says, Be a good son, a good brother and a good friend, and "if you have any energy left after attending to conduct, then study books." From the Confucian point of view, the little may be so much, and the much may be so little. For Chinese Humanism in its essence is the study of human relations (*jenlun*) through a correct appreciation of human values by the psychology of human motives to the end that we may behave as reasonable human beings (*tsuo jen*). That is all: but it may mean a great deal. The Confucian point of view is that politics must be subordinated to morals, that government is a makeshift of temporization, law a superficial instrument of order, and police force a foolish invention for morally immature individuals. "In presiding over law-suits, I am as good as anybody; the thing is so to aim that there shall be no lawsuits," says Confucius. And morally mature individuals behaving with dignity and self-respect can be brought about only by education and culture and by a sense of moral order through the cultivation of rituals and music. The conception of the means of achieving social and political order is poles apart from that of western economists and students of political science. "Guide the people with governmental measures and control or regulate them by the threat of punishment, and the people will try to keep out of gaol, but will have no sense of honor. Guide the people by morals and regulate them by *li* (the principle of social relationships), and the people will have a sense of honor and respect." At once an antipodal point is set up against the whole fabric of western social and political philosophy. The Confucian final test for any civilization is whether it produces good sons, good brothers, good husbands, good friends and good individuals who have a delicate sensibility and are most anxious to avoid hurting others' feelings. Perhaps that may be the final end of civilization; perhaps not—how can we know? Perhaps to the people of the twenty-fifth century, our social behavior as individuals and nations today may seem extremely uncouth. Perhaps some of the so-called world leaders today may seem to the man of the twenty-fifth century no more than barbarians with a tribalistic mind, as we today think of Hannibal. Meanwhile, the self-deception must continue.

But if we said to ourselves that the present disintegration of knowledge and collapse of values call for a restoration of certain human values, we would not know how to begin. The approach, the technique, the philosophical basis for the study of any kind of human values aren't there. So long as the mechanistic technique and materialistic method continue to dominate the thinking of our college professors, it is patent that such values cannot be rediscovered. And by "materialism" I do not mean the occupation with material progress, which is a popular charge against the Western world. I am all for material progress. I mean, rather, scientific materialism as a method and a technique and a point of view which has hopelessly paralyzed the European humanities and thrown it into utter rout and confusion.

It would be interesting to study how the professors of the humanities started the rout from their moral fortress and fled in fear of any distinction of good and evil or even moral emotions of any kind, how they came to live in mortal terror of taking sides and trained their minds to see all things objectively as mechanical phenomena, to be analyzed and explained and compared, how they ultimately came to be moral bats, disclaiming all judgments of morals and fearing moral platitudes like poison, and eventually had an abhorrence of the human free will and successfully eliminated conscience from their scholarship. The Dean of the Union Theological Seminary wrote an article in *Fortune,* telling of an incident which is typical and significant. He invited a scientific colleague to give a talk at the morning prayers to the students. The scientist declined on the ground that his realm was exact knowledge. Since questions of good and evil cannot in their nature be classified under exact knowledge and God himself shows very little possibility of being reduced to a mathematical formula, good and evil are out of bounds for the professor. What are we to do about a situation like this? Since God and Satan are eternal verities, in whatever sense you take it, but since there is no way of tackling the problems of good and evil by either percentages or statistical charts, the problem must remain unsolved and ignored.

It would be interesting to make a study of the invasion of the humanities by scientific materialism and of the betrayal of the humanities through the false instinct of their professors to ape the technique and paraphernalia of the natural sciences. There can be no conscience in the objective study of rocks and minerals or even of our animal friends, because the natural sciences call only for objectivity and an amoral academic attitude. When that scientific method is stolen and applied to the humanities, in the naïve belief that we are beginning to make the humanities true sciences, that amoral, objective method is carried over with it. It happens, however, that disinterestedness which is a virtue in the natural sciences is, and must be, a crime in the human sciences. Humanities built upon this basis must be both untrue and inadequate on account of the different nature of the object and data of study. All human sciences are false sciences, and can be called sciences only in a figurative sense. I understand there are not only intelligence tests, dealing with highly subjective matter like "social consciousness" and "personal charm" and "masculinity" and "femininity" and "force of character," but there is in a certain institution even a machine which gives you the correct percentage of a man's intelligence by just slipping the person's answers into the machine. The machine does everything. This is no more than a hoodlum trick practised by the professors on the well-meaning endowers of the institution.

Owing to the rapid rise of prestige of the natural sciences, about the middle of the nineteenth century, all branches of human studies were beginning to call themselves "sciences." The words "organism," "natural law," "origins" and "evolution" were applied to literary and historical studies. Auguste Comte had started the fashion by calling his new sociology "social physics" and society "an organism." What does he mean when he says, "Society is an organism" no one will be able to make out. There was a veritable orgy of "fundamental laws" even in literary and social studies. Taine applied them to literary history, Marx applied them to economics, Zola applied them to the novel, and even Sainte-Beuve called his literary and biographical studies "the science of souls."[1] But there is no need to go back to history; there are plenty of modern instances. Dr. J. B. Watson one day made the astounding discovery of the possibility of studying the human mind without reference to thinking and feeling, and thought he was on the point of making psychology a true science by eliminating such medieval terms as "consciousness," "will," "emotion," "memory" and "perception" and confining it to the measurements of mechanical impulses and response. His inspiration clearly came from his study of animal psychology. And as a result of the century of development, one need only think of Theodore Dreiser's view of man as a chemical compound, a trapped animal moving in the gigantic chaos of blind chance, blind urges and drives and moral irresponsibility. We have come to the end of the road.

It can be proved that the world has gone to pieces as a direct result of scientific materialism invading our literature and thought. The professors of the humanities are reduced to the position of finding mechanistic laws governing human activities, and the more rigorous the "natural laws" can be proved to be, and the more freedom of the will is proved to be a chimera, the greater is the professor's intellectual delight. Hence the economic interpretation of history, conceiving history as a determinist cage and man as a trapped biped animal moving in the direction of the supply for food. And Marx of course was proud of his "materialism" and his mechanistic view of history. For scientific materialism must spell determinism and determinism must spell despair. It is therefore not an accident that the most admired spirits of our times, not the greatest but the most in vogue, are pessimists. Our international chaos is founded upon our philosophic despair: the despair of Baudelaire, the despair of Huysmans, the despair of Hardy, the despair of Dreiser, the despair of T. S. Eliot, the eternal regret of Proust, the mild pessimism of Samuel Butler and Dean Inge and Aldous Huxley, and the violent despair of Picasso and the cubists and surrealists, Freudians, psychopaths and hyper-

[1] Taine said in his Preface to the *History of English Literature,* "Virtue and vice are products like vitriol and sugar." Zola derived his inspiration for "the experimental novel" from Claude Bernard's *Introduction to the Study of Experimental Medicine* and started the autopsy school of literature, practically regarding human society as a morgue.

esthetes. Only a robust mind like that of Walt Whitman who was not inflicted with the scientific spirit and who was in close touch with life itself and with the great humanity could retain that enormous love and enormous faith in the common man. It is interesting to point out that the flowers of New England culture were so close to the Chinese: Whitman in his mysticism and his love for this flesh-and-blood humanity, Thoreau in his pacifism and his rural ideal, and Emerson in his insight and epigrammatic wisdom. That flower can blossom no more because the spirit of industrialism has crushed it.

But such pseudo-scientific naturalism in the humanities must for ever remain inadequate and pathetic, because of the discrepancy between method and material. The tracing of mother love to ovary secretions must, in the nature of human life, be inadequate, and is in fact one of the wickedest lies of such pseudo-science. Old mother rats do recover a spell of mother love when they get an injection of ovary secretions; human mothers, apart from the comparatively short period of nursing, must depend upon something else—the daily associations and perhaps common struggles in poverty and stores of memories and habits of speech or some incorrigible foibles that endear the mother to the son and the son to the mother. The mother-and-son relationship of rats does not have that period. And what about the father who hasn't got ovary glands? How does he come to love his children? Science must for ever abjure the possibility of ever demonstrating that the father has any special secretions of any kind, when his wife conceives or has given birth to a baby. In the same way, our value of love between man and woman has been destroyed by this kind of science, which began by confusing love with sex and ended by interpreting love only in terms of sex. Love has been dethroned from its pedestal. For this we have the Freudians to thank:

No more privacy
Of mind and body; these students of mental history
Have stripped the fig-leaves, dispelled all mystery,
Have sent the naked, shivering soul to the scullery,
And turned the toilet into a public gallery;
They've dulled the glamor of love, soured the wine of romance,
Plucked the feathers of pride, exposed to naked glance
The Inner Sanctum of sovereign mind, dethroned from its dais,
And crowned the rank-smelling Libido in its place.

Our conception of the nature of man has been falsified, debased. The bottom has been knocked out of our human universe; the structure cannot hold; something must break. Out of the shattered fragments of modern knowledge a new world must be built, and the East and West must build it together.

Of the different selections in the China part, I shall speak in the separate Introductions. Both Taoism and Confucianism are well represented here. I will say here only that, for the immediate problems of this contentious modern world, it is more important to read Laotse than to read Confucius. I have been compelled to make many new translations of my own, including the translation of Laotse's *Book of Tao*. A knowledge of the *Book of History* and *Mencius* is necessary for the understanding of Chinese democratic ideas, of which so little is known to the West. But it may be equally enlightening to find the true spirit of Chinese culture in the family letters and proverbs, and particularly in the *Six Chapters of a Floating Life*. For the answer to the question "What is the spirit of Chinese civilization?" is to be found in the *Six Chapters,* in the picture of Chinese life, not as Chinese thinkers thought life ought to be lived but as the actual common people have lived it. The *Six Chapters,* as well as the *Family Letters of a Chinese Poet,* gives us some intimate glance into Chinese life, valuable because it was autobiography and not fiction, and was written by a Chinese for Chinese readers. The beauty and ugliness of Chinese family life are there, and there are both good and bad characters in it. But the fundamental temper of the Chinese spirit, its struggles, its longings, its resignations, and its casual glances along the wayside of life, are all there, written down sincerely by a common medium-educated Chinaman who made not too great a success either with his paintings or with his small trade as a commercial traveller.

CHINESE MYSTICISM

CONTENTS

Book One: The Principles of Tao

Book Two: The Application of Tao

Laotse, the Book of Tao

(*The Tao Teh Ching*)

INTRODUCTION

IF THERE IS ONE BOOK in the whole of Oriental literature which one should read above all the others, it is, in my opinion, Laotse's *Book of Tao*. If there is one book that can claim to interpret for us the spirit of the Orient, or that is necessary to the understanding of characteristic Chinese behavior, including literally "the ways that are dark," it is the *Book of Tao*. For Laotse's book contains the first enunciated philosophy of camouflage in the world; it teaches the wisdom of appearing foolish, the success of appearing to fail, the strength of weakness and the advantage of lying low, the benefit of yielding to your adversary and the futility of contention for power. It accounts in fact for any mellowness that may be seen in Chinese social and individual behavior. If one reads enough of this Book, one automatically acquires the habits and ways of the Chinese. I would go further and say that if I were asked what antidote could be found in Oriental literature and philosophy to cure this contentious modern world of its inveterate belief in force and struggle for power, I would name this book of "5,000 words" written some 2,400 years ago. For Laotse (born about B.C. 570) has the knack of making Hitler and other dreamers of world mastery appear foolish and ridiculous. The chaos of the modern world, I believe, is due to the total lack of a philosophy of the rhythm of life such as we find in Laotse and his brilliant disciple Chuangtse, or anything remotely resembling it. And furthermore, if there is one book advising against the multifarious activities and futile busy-ness of the modern man, I would again say it is Laotse's *Book of Tao*. It is one of the profoundest books in the world's philosophy.

The message of the book is simple and its dozen ideas are repeated in epigrammatic form again and again. Briefly the ideas are: the rhythm of life, the unity of all world and human phenomena, the importance of keeping the original simplicity of human nature, the danger of over-government and interference with the simple life of the people, the doctrine of *wu-wei* or "inaction," which is better interpreted as "non-interference" and is the exact equivalent of *laissez-faire,* the pervading influence of the spirit, the lessons of humility, quietude and calm, and the folly of force, of pride, and of self-assertion. All these will be understood if one understands the rhythm of life. It is profound and clear, mystic and practical.

Some of the greatest paradoxes in this book are: "Never be the first in the world (LXVII)." "The greatest cleverness appears like stupidity; the greatest eloquence seems like stuttering (XLV)." "The farther one pursues knowledge, the less one knows (XLVII)." "When two equally matched armies meet, it is the man of sorrow who wins (LXIX)." "Even in victory, there is no beauty, and he who calls it beautiful delights in slaughter (XXXI)." "A victory should be celebrated with the Funeral Rite (XXXI)." "For love is victorious in attack and invulnerable in defense. Heaven arms with love those it would not see destroyed (LXVII)." "He gives to other people, and has greater abundance (LXXXI)." "Requite hatred with virtue (LXIII)." "The honest ones I believe; the liars I also believe (XLVIII)." "He who knows does not speak, and he who speaks does not know (LVI)." (On *laissez-faire*): "Rule a big country as you would fry small fish (LX)." In fact, the whole book consists of such paradoxes.

The Book has been traditionally divided into two parts, since Hoshang Kung in the second century, B.C. Actually, the original collection consists of various epigrams, and if one reads the developments and connections between the different chapters, one sees even the chapter divisions were not original. (Some late editions of this Book have appeared without chapter divisions.) On the whole, one can make some rough divisions. Ch. I-X describe the general character of the doctrine. Ch. XI-XX develop the doctrine of inaction. Ch. XXI-XXVIII speak of the "models of Tao," and are more mystic. Ch. XXIX-XXXI contain forceful warnings against the use of force. Ch. XXXII-XXXVII speak of the rhythm of life. In Book Two, Ch. XXXVIII-XLIX again emphasize the use of gentleness, simplicity and quietude. Ch. L-LVI have to do with the preservation of life. From Ch. LVII on, the themes become more concrete. Ch. LVII-

LXVII give definite advice on government and management of human affairs. Ch. LXVIII-LXIX again touch upon war and camouflage. Ch. LXXII-LXXV contain Laotse's great sayings on crime and punishment. The last six chapters, LXXVI-LXXXI again give some general advice on the strength of weakness, with some very appropriate advice on peace settlements in Ch. LXXIX. In fact, if the chapters on war and peace could be made required reading for delegates to the Peace Conference, we would have a totally different world. "The virtuous man is for patching up, the vicious for fixing guilt, etc." The advice for big and small countries (Ch. LXI) also seems perfect.

Generally a chapter opens with some paradox and develops it with some parallel remarks, introduced with the word "Therefore." An explanation on the use of this word is important, for it will frequently be taken by the Western reader as misplaced and showing no real logical sequence. One should clearly understand, however, that Chinese logic is both indeterminate and synchronous, instead of determinate, exclusive and sequential as in Western logic. Hence cause may be an effect, and an effect may be part of the cause, which is often nearer the truth. Cause and effect in Chinese are not sequential, but are parallel aspects of the same truth. In Chinese, "therefore" is almost indistinguishable from "for." This is true of Laotse, Chuangtse and many Chinese writers. Isn't our distinction of cause and effect somewhat childish? Try to find out what is the cause of the present war, and one will discover many things about this logic of causality.

There have been many useful criticisms and emendations of the text of Laotse, especially the textual restorations of Yü Yüeh, Wang Niensun and others. On the other hand, there has been much useless contention over the shifting of phrases and passages and redivision of chapters by contemporary Chinese authors. These corrections and substitutions seem to derive from the schoolmaster's art of correcting pupils' compositions, cancelling a repetition here and shifting a sentence there where it seems to belong for better stylistic effect. It seems parallel construction must be put together in one paragraph and must never be allowed to appear in another place of the book. Any good writer can confirm the fact that a good essay never follows the schoolmaster's outline, and that where the essay has a fundamental unity of thought, any editor can transpose any sentence and fit it to another passage to the editor's own satisfaction. Corrections of this kind have no place in textual restorations of ancient authors. I am a "conservative" in this respect.

I have therefore followed the conservative division into eighty-one chapters, recognizing that the division was not original. Another interesting fault of these critics is to assume that the divisions were original and then complain that the chapters lack "unity of composition." The text of Laotse exists today in a fairly satisfactory form, making such transpositions and redivisions unnecessary. I have not unhesitatingly followed even the most famous restoration of Wang Niensun, because it does not improve upon the paradox, but rather takes away from it. Where the traditional text reads "Fine weapons are instruments of evil," Wang fairly well proved that the word "Fine" was a mistake for another word, like the English adverbial conjunction "now." But to ask how Laotse, the master of paradox, could say that "*fine* weapons are instruments of *evil,*" because what is "fine" is not "evil," is sheer stupidity.

Laotse is the most translated of all the Chinese books because of its small volume. I have seen nine translations in German, including the good one by Alexander Ular (Inselverlag). There are the twelve English translations by E. H. Parker, John Chalmers, M. E. Reynolds, Paul Carus, Dwight Goddard and Wei-Tao, Lionel Giles, Isabella Mears, Hu Tse-lin, "editors" of the Shrine of Wisdom, Walter Gorn Old, Ch'u Ta-Kao, John C. H. Wu and Arthur Waley, of which the last two mentioned are the best. I have profited most from the translations by Waley and Mears in my rendering into English. I have, however, found it necessary to make a new translation. Laotse's style is epigrammatic and his language is terse and vigorous, and I have tried to preserve its terse, epigrammatic quality and its sentence rhythm, but I have not tried to reproduce the rhyme in its many passages. Translation is an art of seeking the exact word, and when the exact word is found, circumlocutions can be avoided, and the style preserved. Translation also requires a certain stupidity, and the best translation is the stupid one which does not go out of its way for "brilliant" interpretations. Laotse's advice to "be aware of the Male, but keep to the Female" has been my principle. For only the stupid man has fidelity. Many translators betray that undue and incorrect stress on individual words in regard to their etymology as beginners in a foreign language place undue stress on individual syllables, the one arising from lack of familiarity, the other from lack of fluency. I have given footnotes for the sole purpose of making the meaning of the text more exact and clearer, and have avoided all comments of opinion. The chapter titles are not original, but are supplied by myself for the convenience of the readers.

Laotse, the Book of Tao

Translated by Lin Yutang

BOOK I: THE PRINCIPLES OF TAO

I. ON THE ABSOLUTE TAO

The Tao that can be told of
  Is not the Absolute Tao;
The Names that can be given
  Are not Absolute Names.

The Nameless is the origin of Heaven and Earth;
The Named is the Mother of All Things.

Therefore:
Oftentimes, one strips oneself of passion
  In order to see the Secret of Life;
Oftentimes, one regards life with passion,
  In order to see its manifest results.

These two (the Secret and its manifestations)
  Are (in their nature) the same;
They are given different names
  When they become manifest.

They may both be called the Cosmic Mystery: [1]
Reaching from the Mystery into the Deeper Mystery
Is the Gate to the Secret [2] of All Life.

[1] *Hsuän*—This word is the equivalent of "mystic" and "mysticism." Taoism is also known as the *Hsüanchiao,* or "Mystic Religion."
[2] *Miao* may also be translated as "Essence"; it means "the wonderful," the "ultimate," the "logically unknowable," the "quintessence," or "esoteric truth."

II. THE RISE OF RELATIVE OPPOSITES

When the people of the Earth all know beauty as beauty,
There arises (the recognition of) ugliness.
When the people of the Earth all know the good as good,
There arises (the recognition of) evil.

Therefore:
Being and non-being interdepend in growth;
Difficult and easy interdepend in completion;
Long and short interdepend in contrast;
High and low interdepend in position;
Tones and voice interdepend in harmony;
Front and behind interdepend in company.

Therefore the Sage:
Manages the affairs without action;
Preaches the doctrine without words;
All things take their rise, but he does not turn away from them;
He gives them life, but does not take possession of them;
He acts, but does not appropriate;
Accomplishes, but claims no credit.
It is because he lays claim to no credit
That the credit cannot be taken away from him.

III. ACTION WITHOUT DEEDS

Exalt not the wise,[3]
So that the people shall not scheme and contend;
Prize not rare objects,
So that the people shall not steal;
Shut out from sight the things of desire,
So that the people's hearts shall not be disturbed.

Therefore in the government of the Sage:
He keeps empty their hearts[4]
Makes full their bellies,

[3] Exalting the wise in government is a typically Confucianist idea.
[4] "Empty-heart" in the Chinese language means "open-mindedness," or "humility," a sign of the cultured gentleman. Throughout this book, "empty" and "full" are used as meaning "humility" and "pride" respectively.

Discourages their ambitions,
Strengthens their frames;
So that the people may be purified of their thoughts and desires.
And the cunning ones shall not presume to interfere.[5]
By action without deeds
May all live in peace.

IV. THE CHARACTER OF TAO

Tao is all-pervading,[6]
And its use is inexhaustible!
Fathomless!
Like the fountain head of all things.
Its sharp edges rounded off,
Its tangles untied,
Its light tempered,
Its turmoil submerged,
Yet crystal clear like still water it seems to remain.
I do not know whose Son it is,
An image of what existed before God.

V. NATURE

Nature is unkind:
It treats the creation like sacrificial straw-dogs.
The Sage is unkind:
He treats the people like sacrificial straw-dogs.[7]

How the universe is like a bellows!
Empty, yet it gives a supply that never fails;
The more it is worked, the more it brings forth.
By many words is wit exhausted.
Rather, therefore, hold to the core.[8]

[5] *Wei*, "to act," frequently used in this book to denote "interfere." *Wu-wei*, or "inaction" practically means non-interference, for it is the exact equivalent of *"laissez-faire."*
[6] *Ch'ung*, "empty," "mild," "formless," "filling all space." Another reading, *chung*, "Tao is an empty vessel."
[7] The doctrine of naturalism, the Sage reaching the impartiality and often the stolid indifference of Nature.
[8] Center, the original nature of man. "Hold to the core" is an important Taoist tenet.

VI. THE SPIRIT OF THE VALLEY

The Spirit of the Valley [9] never dies.
It is called the Mystic Female.[10]
The Door of the Mystic Female
Is the root of Heaven and Earth.

Continuously, continuously,
It seems to remain.
Draw upon it
And it serves you with ease.[11]

VII. LIVING FOR OTHERS

The universe is everlasting.
The reason the universe is everlasting
Is that it does not live for Self.[12]
Therefore it can long endure.

Therefore the Sage puts himself last,
And finds himself in the foremost place;
Regards his body as accidental,
And his body is thereby preserved.
Is it not because he does not live for Self
That his Self achieves perfection?

VIII. WATER

The best of men is like water;
Water benefits all things
And does not compete with them.
It dwells in (the lowly) places that all disdain,—
Wherein it comes near to the Tao.

In his dwelling, (the Sage) loves the (lowly) earth;
In his heart, he loves what is profound;

[9] The Valley, like the bellows, is a symbol of Taoistic "emptiness."
[10] The principle of *yin* the negative, the receptive, the quiescent.
[11] He who makes use of nature's laws accomplishes results "without labor."
[12] Gives life to others through its transformations.

In his relations with others, he loves kindness;
In his words, he loves sincerity;
In government, he loves peace;
In business affairs, he loves ability;
In his actions, he loves choosing the right time.
It is because he does not contend
That he is without reproach.

IX. THE DANGER OF OVERWEENING SUCCESS

Stretch (a bow) [13] to the very full,
And you will wish you had stopped in time.
Temper a (sword-edge) to its very sharpest,
And the edge will not last long.
When gold and jade fill your hall,
You will not be able to keep them safe.
To be proud with wealth and honor
Is to sow the seeds of one's own downfall.
Retire when your work is done,
Such is Heaven's way.[14]

X. EMBRACING THE ONE

In embracing the One [15] with your soul,
Can you never forsake the Tao?
In controlling your vital force to achieve gentleness,
Can you become like the new-born child?[16]
In cleansing and purifying your Mystic vision,
Can you strive after perfection?
In loving the people and governing the kingdom,
Can you rule without interference?

[13] Throughout Laotse, the idea of *ying*, "fullness" or "filled to the brim," associated with pride, is condemned as the opposite of "emptiness" or "humility," because success contains the seeds of downfall.
[14] The whole chapter is rhymed.
[15] Important phrase in Taoism.
[16] The babe as symbol of innocence, a common imagery found also in Chuangtse; sometimes the imagery of the "new-born calf" is used.

In opening and shutting the Gates of Heaven,
  Can you play the part of the Female?[17]
In comprehending all knowledge,
  Can you renounce the mind?[18]

To give birth, to nourish,
To give birth without taking possession,
To act without appropriation,
To be chief among men without managing them—
This is the Mystic Virtue.

XI. THE UTILITY OF NOT-BEING

Thirty spokes unite around the nave;
  From their not-being (losing of their individuality)
    Arises the utility of the wheel.
Mould clay into a vessel;
  From its not-being (in the vessel's hollow)
    Arises the utility of the vessel.
Cut out doors and windows in the house (-wall),
  From their not-being (empty space) arises the utility of the house.
Therefore by the existence of things we profit.
And by the non-existence of things we are served.

XII. THE SENSES

The five colors blind the eyes of man;
The five musical notes deafen the ears of man;
The five flavors dull the taste of man;
Horse-racing, hunting and chasing madden the minds of man;
Rare, valuable goods keep their owners awake at night.[19]

Therefore the Sage:
  Provides for the belly and not for the eye.[20]
  Hence, he rejects the one and accepts the other.

[17] The *Yin,* the receptive, the passive, the quiet.
[18] This section is rhymed throughout.
[19] Lit. "Keep one on one's guard."
[20] "Belly" here refers to the inner self, the unconscious, the instinctive; the "eye" refers to the external self or the sensuous world.

XIII. PRAISE AND BLAME

"Favor and disgrace cause one dismay;
What we value and what we fear are as if within our Self."

What does this mean:
"Favor and disgrace cause one dismay?"
Those who receive a favor from above
  Are dismayed when they receive it,
  And dismayed when they lose it.

What does this mean:
"What we value and what we fear [21] are as if within our Self?"
We have fears because we have a self.[22]
When we do not regard that self as self,
What have we to fear?

Therefore he who values the world as his self
  May then be entrusted with the government of the world;
And he who loves the world as his self—
  The world may then be entrusted to his care.

XIV. PREHISTORIC ORIGINS

Looked at, but cannot be seen—
  That is called the Invisible *(yi)*.
Listened to, but cannot be heard—
  That is called the Inaudible *(hsi)*.
Grasped at, but cannot be touched—
  That is called the Intangible *(wei)*.[23]
These three elude all our inquiries
And hence blend and become One.

Not by its rising, is there light,
Nor by its sinking, is there darkness.
  Unceasing, continuous,
  It cannot be defined,
And reverts again to the realm of nothingness.

[21] Interpreted as life and death. The text of Chuangtse confirms this interpretation.
[22] Lit. "body."
[23] Jesuit scholars consider these three words (in ancient Chinese pronounced nearly like *i-hi-vei*) an interesting coincidence with the Hebrew word, *"Jahve."*

That is why it is called the Form of the Formless,
The Image of Nothingness.
That is why it is called the Elusive:
Meet it and you do not see its face;
Follow it and you do not see its back.

He who holds fast to the Tao of old
In order to manage the affairs of Now
Is able to know the Primeval Beginnings
Which are the continuity[24] of Tao.

XV. THE WISE ONES OF OLD

The wise ones[25] of old had subtle wisdom and depth of understanding,
So profound that they could not be understood.
And because they could not be understood,
Perforce must they be so described:
Cautious, like crossing a wintry stream,
Irresolute, like one fearing danger all around,
Grave, like one acting as guest,
Self-effacing, like ice beginning to melt,
Genuine,[26] like a piece of undressed wood,[27]
Open-minded, like a valley,
And mixing freely,[28] like murky water.

Who can find repose in a muddy world?
By lying still, it becomes clear.
Who can maintain his calm for long?
By activity, it comes back to life.

He who embraces this Tao
Guards against being over-full.
Because he guards against being over-full,[29]
He is beyond wearing out and renewal.

[24] *Chi,* a word meaning "main body of tradition," "system" and also "discipline."
[25] Another ancient text, the "rulers."
[26] *Tun,* "thickness," like solid furniture, associated with the original simplicity of man, in opposition to "thinness," associated with cunning, over-refinement and sophistication.
[27] *P'u,* important Taoist idea, the uncarved, the unembellished, the natural goodness and honesty of man. Generally used to mean simplicity, plainness of heart and living.
[28] *Hun,* "muddled," "mixing freely," therefore "easygoing," "not particular." Taoist wisdom: a wise man should appear like a fool.
[29] Self-satisfaction, conceit.

XVI. KNOWING THE ETERNAL LAW

Attain the utmost in Humility; [30]
Hold firm to the basis of Quietude.

The myriad things take shape and rise to activity,
But I watch them fall back to their repose.
Like vegetation that luxuriantly grows
But returns to the root (soil) from which it springs.

To return to the root is Repose;
It is called going back to one's Destiny.
Going back to one's Destiny is to find the Eternal Law.[31]
To know the Eternal Law is Enlightenment.
And not to know the Eternal Law
Is to court disaster.

He who knows the Eternal Law is tolerant;
Being tolerant, he is impartial;
Being impartial, he is kingly; [32]
Being kingly, he is in accord with Nature; [33]
Being in accord with Nature, he is in accord with Tao;
Being in accord with Tao, he is eternal,
And his whole life is preserved from harm.

XVII. RULERS

Of the best rulers
The people (only) know [34] that they exist;
The next best they love and praise;
The next they fear;
And the next they revile.

[30] *Hsü:* emptiness, void. But in actual usage, this "emptiness" has no other meaning than "humility." Both "humility" and "quietude" are central Taoist ideas.

[31] *Ch'ang,* the "constant," the law of growth and decay, of necessary alternation of opposites, can be interpreted as the "universal law of nature," or the "inner law of man," the true self (*hsingming chih ch'ang*), the two being identical in their nature.

[32] *Wang;* a possible translation is "cosmopolitan," i.e. regarding the world as one.

[33] *T'ien,* heaven or nature. Both "t'ien" here and Tao in the next line are clearly used as adjectives; hence the translation "in accord with." *T'ien* very commonly means "nature," or "natural."

[34] Some texts read: "The people do *not* know."

When they do not command the people's faith,
Some will lose faith in them,
And then they resort to oaths!
But (of the best) when their task is accomplished, their work done,
The people all remark, "We have done it ourselves."

XVIII. THE DECLINE OF TAO

On the decline of the great Tao,
The doctrines of "love" and "justice"[35] arose.
When knowledge and cleverness appeared,
Great hypocrisy followed in its wake.

When the six relationships no longer lived at peace,
There was (praise of) "kind parents" and "filial sons."
When a country fell into chaos and misrule,
There was (praise of) "loyal ministers."

XIX. REALIZE THE SIMPLE SELF

Banish wisdom, discard knowledge,
And the people shall profit a hundredfold;
Banish "love," discard "justice,"
And the people shall recover love of their kin;
Banish cunning, discard "utility,"
And the thieves and brigands shall disappear.[36]
As these three touch the externals and are inadequate;
The people have need of what they can depend upon:
Reveal thy Simple Self,[37]
Embrace thy Original Nature,
Check thy selfishness,
Curtail thy desires.[38]

[35] Essential Confucian doctrines, usually translated (badly) as "benevolence" and "righ eousness."
[36] The ideas of Chapters 18 and 19 are fully developed by Chuangtse (Ch. X, "Openin Trunks").
[37] *Su,* the unadorned, uncultured, the innate quality, simple self; originally "plain si background" as opposed to superimposed colored drawings; hence the expression "reveal," "realize" *su.*
[38] The eight characters in these four lines sum up practical Taoist teachings.

XX. THE WORLD AND I

Banish learning, and vexations end.
  Between "Ah!" and "Ough!"[39]
  How much difference is there?
Between "good" and "evil"
  How much difference is there?
That which men fear
  Is indeed to be feared;
But, alas, distant yet is the dawn (of awakening)!

The people of the world are merry-making,
  As if eating of the sacrificial offerings,
  As if mounting the terrace in spring;
I alone am mild, like one unemployed,
  Like a new-born babe that cannot yet smile,
  Unattached, like one without a home.

The people of the world have enough and to spare,
But I am like one left out,
  My heart must be that of a fool,
  Being muddled, nebulous!

The vulgar are knowing, luminous;
  I alone am dull, confused.
The vulgar are clever, self-assured;
  I alone, depressed.
Patient as the sea,
  Adrift, seemingly aimless.

The people of the world all have a purpose;
  I alone appear stubborn and uncouth.
I alone differ from the other people,
  And value drawing sustenance from the Mother.[40]

[39] *Wei* and *o*. "*O*" an utterance of disapproval.
[40] Imagery of the sucking child, symbolizing drawing power from Mother Nature.

XXI. MANIFESTATIONS OF TAO

The marks of great Virtue[41]
Follow alone from the Tao.

The thing that is called Tao
  Is elusive, evasive.
Evasive, elusive,
  Yet latent in it are forms.
Elusive, evasive,
  Yet latent in it are objects.
Dark and dim,
  Yet latent in it is the life-force.
The life-force being very true,
  Latent in it are evidences.

From the days of old till now
Its Named (manifested forms) have never ceased,
By which we may view the Father of All Things.
How do I know the shape of Father of All Things?
  Through These![42]

XXII. FUTILITY OF CONTENTION

To yield is to be preserved whole.
To be bent is to become straight.
To be hollow is to be filled.
To be tattered is to be renewed.
To be in want is to possess.
To have plenty is to be confused.

Therefore the Sage embraces the One,[43]
And becomes the model of the world.

[41] *Teh* as manifestation of Tao, the active aspect of Tao, the moral principle, tr. by Waley as "power."
[42] Manifested forms.
[43] The Absolute, to which transient attributes revert.

He does not reveal himself,
  And is therefore luminous.[44]
He does not justify himself,
  And is therefore far-famed.
He does not boast of himself,
  And therefore people give him credit.
He does not pride himself,
  And is therefore the ruler among men.

It is because he does not contend
That no one in the world can contend against him.

Is it not indeed true, as the ancients say,
  "To yield is to be preserved whole?"[45]
Thus he is preserved and the world does him homage.

XXIII. IDENTIFICATION WITH TAO

Nature says few words:
Hence it is that a squall lasts not a whole morning.
A rainstorm continues not a whole day.
Where do they come from?
From Nature.
Even Nature does not last long (in its utterances),
  How much less should human beings?

Therefore it is that:
  He who follows the Tao is identified with the Tao.
  He who follows Virtue (*Teh*) is identified with Virtue.
  He who abandons (Tao) is identified with abandonment (of Tao).
He who is identified with Tao—
  Tao is also glad to welcome him.
He who is identified with Virtue—
  Virtue is also glad to welcome him.

[44] *Ming* with two meanings, "clear" (bright, sterling) and "clear-sighted" (wise, discerning).
[45] Another Chinese proverb: "Yield your land boundaries all your life and you never lose half; yield your way to fellow passengers all your life and you never lose a step."

He who is identified with abandonment—
  Abandonment is also glad to welcome him.
He who has not enough faith
  Will not be able to command faith from others.

XXIV. THE DREGS AND TUMORS OF VIRTUE

He who stands on tiptoe does not stand (firm);
He who strains his strides[46] does not walk (well);
He who reveals himself is not luminous;
He who justifies himself is not far-famed;
He who boasts of himself is not given credit;
He who prides himself is not chief among men.
  These in the eyes of Tao
  Are called "the dregs and tumors of Virtue,"
    Which are things of disgust.
Therefore the man of Tao spurns them.

XXV. THE FOUR ETERNAL MODELS

Before the Heaven and Earth existed
There was something nebulous:
  Silent, isolated,
  Standing alone, changing not,
  Eternally revolving without fail,
  Worthy to be the Mother of All Things.
I do not know its name
  And address it as Tao.
If forced to give it a name, I shall call it "Great."
Being great implies reaching out in space,
Reaching out in space implies far-reaching
Far-reaching implies reversion to the original point.

Therefore: Tao is Great,
    The Heaven is great,
    The Earth is great,
    The King is also great.

[46] Hurrying, striving, ambitious.

These are the Great Four in the universe,
And the King is one of them.

Man models himself after the Earth;
The Earth models itself after Heaven;
The Heaven models itself after Tao;
Tao models itself after Nature.[47]

XXVI. HEAVINESS AND LIGHTNESS

The Solid[48] is the root of the light;
The Quiescent is the master of the Hasty.

Therefore the Sage travels all day
  Yet never leaves his provision-cart.[49]
In the midst of honor and glory,
  He lives leisurely, undisturbed.
How can the ruler of a great country
Make light of his body in the empire?[50]
In light frivolity, the Center is lost;
In hasty action, self-mastery is lost.

XXVII. ON STEALING THE LIGHT

A good runner leaves no track.
A good speech leaves no flaws for attack.
A good reckoner makes use of no counters.
A well shut door makes use of no bolts,
  And yet cannot be opened.
A well-tied knot makes use of no rope,
  And yet cannot be untied.

[47] *Tse-jan,* lit. "self-so," "self-formed," "that which is so by itself."
[48] Literally "heavy," with the Earth as model. In Chinese, "heaviness" or "thickness" of character, meaning "honesty," "generosity," is associated with the idea of stable luck and endurance, whereas "thinness" or "lightness" of character, meaning "frivolity" or "sharpness," is associated with lack of stable luck.
[49] A pun on the phrase, containing the word "heavy."
[50] By rushing about.

Therefore the Sage is good at helping men;
For that reason there is no rejected (useless) person.
He is good at saving things;
For that reason there is nothing rejected.[51]
—This is called stealing[52] the Light.

Therefore the good man is the Teacher of the bad.
And the bad man is the lesson[53] of the good.

He who neither values his teacher
Nor loves the lesson
Is one gone far astray,
Though he be learned.
—Such is the subtle secret.

XXVIII. KEEPING TO THE FEMALE

He who is aware of the Male
But keeps to the Female
Becomes the ravine[54] of the world.
Being the ravine of the world,
He has the eternal power[55] which never fails,
And returns again to the (innocence of) the babe.

He who is conscious of the white (bright)
But keeps to the black (dark)
Becomes the model for the world.
Being the model for the world,
He has the eternal power which never errs,
And returns again to the Primordial Nothingness.

[51] The Sage uses each according to his talent.
[52] *Hsi,* to enter or secure by devious means such as invasion, attack at night, penetration, etc. The idea is cunningly to make use of knowledge of nature's law to obtain the best results. See full development by Chuangtse, especially in his parable of Prince Hui's cook. Ch. III.
[53] *Tse,* raw-material, resources, help, something to draw upon for profit, such as a lesson.
[54] See Ch. VI. The valley, or ravine is symbol of the Female Principle, the receptive, the passive.
[55] *Teh.*

He who is familiar with honor and glory
But keeps to obscurity
Becomes the valley of the world.
Being the valley of the world,
He has an eternal power which always suffices,
And returns again to pristine simplicity.

Break up this pristine simplicity[56]
And it is shaped into tools.
In the hands of the Sage,
They become the officials and magistrates.
Therefore the great ruler does not cut up.

XXIX. WARNING AGAINST INTERFERENCE

There are those who will conquer the world
And make of it (what they conceive or desire).
I see that they will not succeed.
(For) the world is God's own Vessel
It cannot be made (by human interference).
He who makes it spoils it.
He who holds it loses it.
For: Some things go forward,
Some things follow behind;
Some blow hot,
And some blow cold;[57]
Some are strong,
And some are weak;
Some may break,
And some may fall.
Hence the Sage eschews excess,
eschews extravagance,
eschews pride.

XXX. WARNING AGAINST THE USE OF FORCE

He who by Tao purposes to help the ruler of men
Will oppose all conquest by force of arms.[58]

[56] *P'u,* a piece of unhewn wood, symbol of unspoiled Nature.
[57] Lit. "blow out," "blow in." I follow Waley's rendering, which conveys the meaning perfectly.
[58] The Chinese character for "military" is composed of two parts: "stop" and "arms."

For such things are wont to rebound.
Where armies are, thorns and brambles grow.
The raising of a great host
Is followed by a year of dearth.[59]

Therefore a good general effects his purpose and stops.
He dares not rely upon the strength of arms;
Effects his purpose and does not glory in it;
Effects his purpose and does not boast of it;
Effects his purpose and does not take pride in it;
Effects his purpose as a regrettable necessity;
Effects his purpose but does not love violence.
(For) things age after reaching their prime.
That (violence) would be against the Tao.
And he who is against the Tao perishes young.

XXXI. WEAPONS OF EVIL

Of all things, soldiers[60] are instruments of evil,
Hated by men.
Therefore the religious man (possessed of Tao) avoids them.
The gentleman favors the left in civilian life,
But on military occasions favors the right.[61]

Soldiers are weapons of evil.
They are not the weapons of the gentleman.
When the use of soldiers cannot be helped,
The best policy is calm restraint.

Even in victory, there is no beauty,[62]
And who calls it beautiful
Is one who delights in slaughter.

Chinese pacifists interpret this as meaning disapproval of arms ("stop armament"), whereas it may just as well mean to stop the enemy by force. Etymologically, however, the word for "stop" is a picture of a footprint, so the whole is a picture of a "spear" over "footprints."

[59] These six lines are by Waley, for they cannot be improved upon.

[60] Another reading, "fine weapons." *Ping* can mean both "soldiers" and "weapons."

[61] These are ceremonial arrangements. The left is symbol of good omen, the creative; the right is symbol of bad omen, the destructive.

[62] Another equally good reading, "no boasting," "and who boasts of victory."

He who delights in slaughter
Will not succeed in his ambition to rule the world.

[The things of good omen favor the left.
The things of ill omen favor the right.
The lieutenant-general stands on the left,
The general stands on the right.
That is to say, it is celebrated as a Funeral Rite.]
The slaying of multitudes should be mourned with sorrow.
A victory should be celebrated with the Funeral Rite.[63]

XXXII. TAO IS LIKE THE SEA

Tao is absolute and has no name.
Though the uncarved wood is small,
It cannot be employed (used as vessel) by anyone.
If kings and barons can keep (this unspoiled nature),
The whole world shall yield them lordship of their own accord.

The Heaven and Earth join,
And the sweet rain falls,
Beyond the command of men,
Yet evenly upon all.

Then human civilization arose and there were names.[64]
Since names there were,
It were well one knew where to stop for repose.
He who knows where to stop for repose
May from danger be exempt.
Tao in the world
May be compared
To rivers that run into the sea.[65]

[63] One of the five Cardinal Rites of *Chou-li*. The last five lines but two read like a commentary, interpolated in the text by mistake. The evidence is conclusive: (1) The terms "lieutenant general" and "general" are the only ones in the whole text that are anachronisms, for these terms did not exist till Han times. (2) The commentary by Wang Pi is missing in this chapter, so it must have slipped into the text by a copyist's mistake. See also Ch. 69. Cf. Mencius, "The best fighter should receive the supreme punishment"; again "Only he who does not love slaughter can unify the empire."
[64] Names imply differentiation of things and loss of original state of Tao.
[65] Really to be compared to the sea, or to the rivers seeking repose in the sea.

XXXIII. KNOWING ONESELF

He who knows others is learned;
He who knows himself is wise.
He who conquers others has power of muscles;
He who conquers himself is strong.
He who is contented is rich.
He who is determined has strength of will.
He who does not lose his center endures,
He who dies yet (his power) remains has long life.

XXXIV. THE GREAT TAO FLOWS EVERYWHERE

The Great Tao flows everywhere,
(Like a flood) it may go left or right.
The myriad things derive their life from it,
And it does not deny them.
When its work is accomplished,
It does not take possession.
It clothes and feeds the myriad things,
Yet does not claim them as its own.
Often (regarded) without mind or passion,
It may be considered small.
Being the home [66] of all things, yet claiming not,
It may be considered great.
Because to the end it does not claim greatness,
Its greatness is achieved.

XXXV. THE PEACE OF TAO

Hold the Great Symbol [67]
And all the world follows,
Follows without meeting harm,
(And lives in) health, peace, commonwealth.

[66] Lit. "rendezvous."
[67] The symbol of Nature, Heaven or Earth. This chapter consists of rhymed three-word lines.

Offer good things to eat
And the wayfarer stays.
  But Tao is mild to the taste.
  Looked at, it cannot be seen;
  Listened to, it cannot be heard;
  Applied, its supply never fails.

XXXVI. THE RHYTHM OF LIFE

He who is to be made to dwindle (in power)
  Must first be caused to expand.
He who is to be weakened
  Must first be made strong,
He who is to be laid low
  Must first be exalted to power.
He who is to be taken away from
  Must first be given,
  —This is the Subtle Light.

Gentleness overcomes strength:
  Fish should be left in the deep pool,
  And sharp weapons of the state should be left
    Where none can see them.

XXXVII. WORLD PEACE

The Tao never does,
  Yet through it everything is done.
If kings and barons can keep the Tao,
  The world will of its own accord be reformed.
When reformed and rising to action,
  Let it be restrained by the Nameless pristine simplicity.
The Nameless pristine simplicity
  Is stripped of desire (for contention).
By stripping of desire quiescence is achieved,
And the world arrives at peace of its own accord.

BOOK II: THE APPLICATION OF TAO[68]

XXXVIII. DEGENERATION

The man of superior virtue is not (conscious of his) virtue,
  Hence he is virtuous.
The man of inferior virtue (is intent on) not losing virtue,
  Hence he is devoid of virtue.
The man of superior virtue never acts,
  Nor ever (does so) with an ulterior motive.
The man of inferior virtue acts,
  And (does so) with an ulterior motive.
The man of superior kindness acts,
  But (does so) without an ulterior motive.
The man of superior justice acts,
  And (does so) with an ulterior motive.
(But when) the man of superior *li*[69] acts and finds no response,
  He rolls up his sleeves to force it on others.

Therefore:
After Tao is lost, then (arises the doctrine of) kindness,
After kindness is lost, then (arises the doctrine of) justice.
After justice is lost, then (arises the doctrine of) *li*.
Now *li* is the thinning out of loyalty and honesty of heart.
  And the beginning of chaos.
The prophets are the flowering of Tao
  And the origin of folly.
Therefore the noble man dwells in the heavy (base),
  And not in the thinning (end).
He dwells in the fruit,
  And not in the flowering (expression).
Therefore he rejects the one and accepts the other.

[68] The name, the "Book of Teh" (virtue) was given to the Second Section by Hoshang Kung in the reign of Han Wenti (B.C. 179–157).
[69] *Li,* Confucian doctrine of social order and control, characterized by rituals; also courtesy, good manners.

XXXIX. UNITY THROUGH COMPLEMENTS

There were those in ancient times possessed of the One:
Through possession of the One, the Heaven was clarified,
Through possession of the One, the Earth was stabilized,
Through possession of the One, the gods were spiritualized,
Through possession of the One, the valleys were made full,
Through possession of the One, all things lived and grew,
Through possession of the One, the princes and dukes became the ennobled of the people.
—That was how each became so.

Without clarity, the Heavens might shake,
Without stability, the Earth might quake,
Without spiritual power, the gods might crumble,
Without being filling, the valleys might crack,
Without the life-giving power, all things might perish,
Without the ennobling power, the kings and barons might stumble and fall.

Therefore the nobility depend upon the common man for support,
And the exalted ones depend upon the lowly for their base.

That is why the princes and dukes call themselves "the orphaned," "the lonely one," "the unworthy."
Is it not true then that they depend upon the common man for support?
Truly, take down the parts of a chariot,
And there is no chariot (left).[70]
Rather than jingle like the jade,
Rumble like the rocks.

XL. THE PRINCIPLE OF REVERSION

Reversion is the action of Tao.
Gentleness is the function of Tao.
The things of this world come from Being,
And Being (comes) from Non-being.

[70] Another commonly accepted reading through word-substitution in the text: "Truly, the highest prestige requires no praise." Apart from the forced substitution of words, this reading makes no sense in the context.

XLI. QUALITIES OF THE TAOIST

When the highest type of men hear the Tao (truth),
They practice it diligently.
When the mediocre type hear the Tao,
They seem to be aware and yet unaware of it.
When the lowest type hear the Tao,
They break into loud laughter,—
If it were not laughed at, it would not be Tao.

Therefore there is the established saying:
"Who understands Tao seems dull of comprehension;
Who is advanced in Tao seems to slip backwards;
Who moves on the even Tao (Path) seems to go up and down."

Superior virtue appears like a hollow (valley);
Sheer white appears like tarnished;
Great character appears like insufficient;
Solid character appears like infirm;
Pure worth appears like contaminated.
Great space has no corners;
Great talent takes long to mature;
Great music is faintly heard;
Great Form has no contour;
And Tao is hidden without a name.
It is this Tao that is adept at lending (its power) and bringing fulfilment.

XLII. THE VIOLENT MAN

Out of Tao, One is born;
Out of One, Two;
Out of Two, Three;
Out of Three, the created universe.
The created universe carries the *yin* at its back and the *yang* in front;
Through the union of the pervading principles it reaches harmony.

To be "orphaned," "lonely" and "unworthy" is what men hate most.
Yet the kings and dukes call themselves by such names.
For sometimes things are benefited by being taken away from,
And suffer by being added to.

Others have taught this maxim,
Which I shall teach also:
"The violent man shall die a violent death."
This I shall regard as my spiritual teacher.

XLIII. THE SOFTEST SUBSTANCE

The softest substance of the world
Goes through the hardest.
That-which-is-without-form penetrates that-which-has-no-crevice;
Through this I know the benefit of taking no action.[71]
The teaching without words
And the benefit of taking no action
  Are without compare in the universe.

XLIV. BE CONTENT

Fame or one's own self, which does one love more?
One's own self or material goods, which has more worth?
Loss (of self) or possession (of goods), which is the greater evil?

Therefore: he who loves most spends most,
  He who hoards much loses much.
The contented man meets no disgrace;
Who knows when to stop runs into no danger—
He can long endure.

XLV. CALM QUIETUDE

The highest perfection is like imperfection,[72]
  And its use is never impaired.
The greatest abundance seems meagre,
  And its use will never fail.
What is most straight appears devious;

[71] Pervading influence of the spirit reaches everywhere, in contrast with superficial activities which create obstacles of their own. "That-which-is-without-form," etc. is further developed by Chuangtse (Ch. III).
[72] Because it assumes fluid form according to circumstances.

The greatest cleverness appears like stupidity;
The greatest eloquence seems like stuttering.
Movement overcomes cold,
(But) keeping still overcomes heat.
Who is calm and quiet becomes the guide for the universe.

XLVI. RACING HORSES

When the world lives in accord with Tao,
Racing horses are turned back to haul refuse carts.
When the world lives not in accord with Tao,
Cavalry abounds in the countryside.

There is no greater curse than the lack of contentment.
No greater sin than the desire for possession.
Therefore he who is contented with contentment shall be always content.

XLVII. PURSUIT OF KNOWLEDGE

Without stepping outside one's doors,
 One can know what is happening in the world,
Without looking out of one's windows,
 One can see the Tao of Heaven.

The farther one pursues knowledge,
 The less one knows.
Therefore the Sage knows without running about,
 Understands without seeing,
 Accomplishes without doing.

XLVIII. CONQUERING THE WORLD BY INACTION

The student of knowledge (aims at) learning day by day;
The student of Tao (aims at) losing day by day.
 By continual losing
 One reaches doing nothing (*laissez-faire*).
 By doing nothing everything is done.
He who conquers the world often does so by doing nothing.[73]
When one is compelled to do something,[74]
The world is already beyond his conquering.

[73] By moral influence.
[74] By ordering people about.

XLIX. THE PEOPLE'S HEARTS

The Sage has no decided opinions and feelings,[75]
But regards the people's opinions and feelings as his own.

The good ones I declare good;
The bad ones I also declare good.
  That is the goodness of Virtue.
The honest ones I believe;
The liars I also believe;
  That is the faith of Virtue.

The Sage dwells in the world peacefully, harmoniously.
The people of the world are brought into a community of heart,
And the Sage regards them all as his own children.

L. THE PRESERVING OF LIFE

Out of life, death enters.
The organs of life are thirteen;[76]
The organs of death are (also) thirteen.
What send man to death in this life are also (these) thirteen.
  How is it so?
Because of the intense activity of multiplying life.

It has been said that he who is a good preserver of his life
  Meets no tigers or wild buffaloes on land,
  Is not vulnerable to weapons in the field of battle.
The horns of the wild buffalo are powerless against him;
The paws of the tiger are useless against him;
The weapons of the soldier cannot avail against him.
  How is it so?
Because he is beyond death.[77]

[75] *Hsin,* Lit. "heart." Both thinking and feeling are denoted by this word. It is impossible to say a "decided heart."
[76] According to Han Fei, the four limbs and nine external cavities. Another orthodox reading is "three-tenths," but this makes less sense.
[77] Lit. "deathless."

LI. THE MYSTIC VIRTUE

Tao gives them birth,
Teh (virtue) fosters them.
The material world gives them form.
The circumstances of the moment complete them.
Therefore all things of the universe worship Tao and exalt Teh.
Tao is worshipped and Teh is exalted
Without anyone's order and is so of its own accord.

Therefore Tao gives them birth,
Teh fosters them,
Makes them grow, develops them,
Gives them a harbor, a place to dwell in peace,
Feeds them and shelters them.
It gives them birth and does not own them,
Acts (helps) and does not appropriate them,
Is superior, and does not control them.
—This is the Mystic Virtue.

LII. STEALING THE ABSOLUTE

There was a beginning of the universe
Which may be regarded as the Mother of Universe.
From the Mother, we may know her sons.
After knowing the sons, keep to the Mother.
Thus one's whole life may be preserved from harm.

Stop its apertures,
Close its doors,
And one's whole life is without toil.

Open its apertures,
Be busy about its affairs,
And one's whole life is beyond redemption.

He who can see the small is clear-sighted;
He who stays by gentility is strong.
Use the light,
And return to clear-sightedness—
Thus cause not yourself later distress.
—This is to steal the Absolute.

LIII. BRIGANDAGE

If I were possessed of Austere Knowledge,
Walking on the Main Path (Tao),
I would avoid the by-paths.
  The Main Path is easy to walk on,
  Yet people love the small by-paths.

The (official) courts are spic and span,
(While) the fields go untilled,
And the granaries are very low.
(Yet) clad in embroidered gowns,
And carrying fine swords,
Surfeit with good food and drinks,
(They are) splitting with wealth and possessions.
  —This is to lead the world toward brigandage.
  Is it not the corruption of Tao?

LIX. THE INDIVIDUAL AND THE STATE

Who is firmly established is not easily shaken.
Who has a firm grasp does not easily let go.
From generation to generation his ancestral sacrifices
  Shall be continued without fail.

Cultivated in the individual, Virtue will become genuine;
Cultivated in the family, Virtue will become abundant;
Cultivated in the village, Virtue will multiply;
Cultivated in the state, Virtue will prosper;
Cultivated in the world, Virtue will become universal.

Therefore:
  According to (the virtue of) the individual, judge the individual;
  According to (the virtue of) the family, judge the family;
  According to (the virtue of) the village, judge the village;
  According to (the virtue of) the state, judge the state;
  According to (the virtue of) the world, judge the world.
  How do I know the world is so.
  By this.[78]

[78] From within myself; or the meaning could be very well developed in the following chapter, since the chapter division is not original.

LV. THE VIRTUES OF THE CHILD

Who is rich[79] in virtue
Is like a child.
No poisonous insects sting him,
No wild beasts attack him,
And no birds of prey pounce upon him.
His bones are soft, his sinews tender, yet his grip is strong.
Not knowing the union of male and female, yet his organs are complete,
Which means his vigor is unspoiled.
Crying the whole day, yet his voice never runs hoarse,
Which means his (natural) harmony is perfect.
To know harmony is to be in accord with the eternal,
(And) to know eternity is called discerning.
(But) to improve upon life is called an ill-omen;
To let go the emotions through impulse[80] is called assertiveness.
(For) things age after reaching their prime;
That (assertiveness) would be against Tao.
And he who is against Tao perishes young.

LVI. BEYOND HONOR AND DISGRACE

He who knows does not speak;
He who speaks does not know.
Fill up its apertures,
Close its doors,
Dull its edges,
Untie its tangles,
Soften its light,
Submerge its turmoil,
—This is the Mystic Unity.[81]

Then love and hatred cannot touch him.
Profit and loss cannot reach him.
Honor and disgrace cannot affect him.
Therefore is he always the honored one of the world.

[79] Lit. "thick," "heavy."
[80] *Hsin,* lit. "mind," or "heart."
[81] All submerged in the One.

LVII. THE ART OF GOVERNMENT

Rule a kingdom by the Normal.
Fight a battle by (abnormal) tactics of surprise.[82]
Win the world by doing nothing.
How do I know it is so?

Through this:—
The more prohibitions there are, the poorer the people become.
The more sharp weapons there are,
The more prevailing chaos there is in the state.
The more skills of technique,
The more cunning [83] things are produced.
The greater the number of statutes,
The greater the number of thieves and brigands.

Therefore the Sage says:
I do nothing and the people are reformed [84] of themselves.
I love quietude and the people are righteous of themselves.
I deal in no business and the people grow rich by themselves.
I have no desires and the people are simple and honest by themselves.

LVIII. LAZY GOVERNMENT

When the government is lazy and dull,
Its people are unspoiled;
When the government is efficient and smart,
Its people are discontented.

Disaster is the avenue of fortune,
(And) fortune is the concealment for disaster.
Who would be able to know its ultimate results?
(As it is), there would never be the normal,

[82] *Cheng,* the normal, the straight, the righteous; *ch'i,* the abnormal, the deceitful, the surprising.
[83] *Ch'i,* same word as that used for "surprise tactics", with implied disapproval as being not proper for ruling a kingdom.
[84] *Hua,* touched, transformed, "civilized" by moral influence. The best explanation of "doing nothing."

But the normal would (immediately) revert to the deceitful,[85]
And the good revert to the sinister.
Thus long has mankind gone astray!

Therefore the Sage is square (has firm principles), but not cutting (sharp-cornered),
Has integrity but does not hurt (others),[86]
Is straight, but not high-handed,
Bright, but not dazzling.

LIX. BE SPARING

In managing human affairs, there is no better rule than to be sparing,[87]
To be sparing is to forestall;
To forestall is to be prepared and strengthened;
To be prepared and strengthened is to be ever-victorious;
To be ever-victorious is to have infinite capacity;
He who has infinite capacity is fit to rule a country,
And the Mother (principle) of a ruling country can long endure.
This is to be firmly rooted, to have deep strength,
The road to immortality and enduring vision.

LX. RULING A BIG COUNTRY

Rule a big country as you would fry small fish.[88]

Who rules the world in accord with Tao
Would find that the spirits lose their power.
It is not that the spirits lose their power,
But that they cease to do people harm.
It is not (only) that they cease to do people harm,
The Sage (himself) also does no harm to the people.
When both do not do each other harm,
Virtue (power) flows towards them.

[85] See Note 82.
[86] In removing corruption by artificial laws and statutes and punishments.
[87] Never do too much.
[88] Let alone, or the fish will become paste by constant turning about.

LXI. BIG AND SMALL COUNTRIES

A big country (must be like) the delta low-regions,
Being the concourse of the world,
(And) the Female of the world.
The Female overcomes the Male by quietude,
And achieves the lowly position by quietude.

Therefore if a big country places itself below a small country,
It absorbs[89] the small country;
(And) if a small country places itself below a big country,
It absorbs the big country.
Therefore some place themselves low to absorb (others),
Some are (naturally) low and absorb (others).
What a big country wants is but to shelter others,
And what a small country wants is but to be able to come in and be sheltered.
Thus (considering) that both may have what they want,
A big country ought to place itself low.

LXII. THE GOOD MAN'S TREASURE

Tao is the mysterious secret of the universe,
The good man's treasure,
And the bad man's refuge.
Beautiful sayings can be sold at the market,
Noble conduct can be presented as a gift.
Though there be bad people,
Why reject them?

Therefore on the crowning of an emperor,
On the appointment of the Three Ministers,
Rather than send tributes of jade and teams of four horses,
Send in the tribute of this Tao.
Wherein did the Ancients prize this Tao?
Did they not say, "to search for the guilty ones and pardon them?"
Therefore is (Tao) the treasure of the world.

[89] *Ch'ü*, takes, conquers, overcomes, wins over.

LXIII. DIFFICULT AND EASY

Accomplish do-nothing.
Attend to no-affairs.
Taste the flavorless.
Whether it is big or small, many or few,
Requite hatred with Virtue.
Deal with the difficult while yet it is easy;
Deal with the big while yet it is small.
The difficult (problems) of the world
Must be dealt with while they are yet easy;
The great (problems) of the world
Must be dealt with while they are yet small.
Therefore the Sage by never dealing with great (problems)
Accomplish greatness.

He who lightly makes a promise
Will find it often hard to keep his faith.
He who makes light of many things
Will encounter many difficulties.
Hence even the Sage regards things as difficult,
And for that reason never meets with difficulties.

LXIV. BEGINNING AND END

That which lies still is easy to hold;
That which is not yet manifest is easy to forestall;
That which is brittle (like ice) is easy to melt;
That which is minute is easy to scatter.
Deal with a thing before it is there;
Check disorder before it is rife.
A tree with a full span's girth begins from a tiny sprout;
A nine-storied terrace begins with a clod of earth.
A journey of a thousand *li* begins at one's feet.

He who acts, spoils;
He who grasps, lets slip.
Because the Sage does not act, he does not spoil,

Because he does not grasp, he does not let slip.
The affairs of men are often spoiled within an ace of completion,
By being careful at the end as at the beginning
Failure is averted.

Therefore the Sage desires to have no desire,
And values not objects difficult to obtain.
Learns that which is unlearned,
And restores what the multitude have lost.
That he may assist in the course of Nature
And not presume to interfere.

LXV. THE GRAND HARMONY

The Ancients who knew how to follow the Tao
Aimed not to enlighten the people,
But to keep them ignorant.
The reason it is difficult for the people to live in peace
Is because of too much knowledge.
Those who seek to rule a country by knowledge
Are the nation's curse.
Those who seek not to rule a country by knowledge
Are the nation's blessing.
Those who know these two (principles)
Also know the Ancient Standard,
And to know always the Ancient Standard
Is called the Mystic Virtue.
When the Mystic Virtue becomes clear, far-reaching,
And things revert back (to their source),
Then and then only emerges the Grand Harmony.

LXVI. THE LORDS OF THE RAVINES

How did the great rivers and seas become the Lords of the Ravines?
By being good at keeping low.
That was how they became the Lords of the Ravines.[90]

[90] See Chapter 6.

Therefore in order to be the chief among the people,
One must speak like their inferiors.
In order to be foremost among the people,
One must walk behind them.
Thus it is that the Sage stays above,
And the people do not feel his weight;
Walks in front,
And the people do not wish him harm.
Then the people of the world are glad to uphold him forever.
Because he does not contend,
No one in the world can contend against him.

LXVII. THE THREE TREASURES

All the world says: my teaching (Tao) greatly resembles folly.
Because it is great; therefore it resembles folly.
If it did not resemble folly,
It would have long ago become petty indeed!

I have Three Treasures;
Guard them and keep them safe:
The first is Love.[91]
The second is, Never too much.[92]
The third is, Never be the first in the world.
Through Love, one has no fear;
Through not doing too much, one has amplitude (of reserve power);
Through not presuming to be the first in the world,
One can develop one's talent and let it mature.

If one forsakes love and fearlessness,
forsakes restraint and reserve power,
forsakes following behind and rushes in front,
He is dead!

For love is victorious in attack,
And invulnerable in defense.[93]
Heaven arms with love
Those it would not see destroyed.

[91] *Ts'e,* tender love (associated with the mother).
[92] *Chien,* lit. "frugality," "be sparing;" see Chapter 59.
[93] See Chapters 31, 69.

LXVIII. THE VIRTUE OF NOT-CONTENDING

The brave soldier is not violent;
The good fighter does not lose his temper;
The great conqueror does not fight (on small issues);
The good user of men places himself below others.
—This is the Virtue of not contending,
Is called the capacity to use men,
Is reaching to the height of being
Mated to Heaven, to what was of old.

LXIX. CAMOUFLAGE

There is the maxim of military strategists;
I dare not be the first to invade, but rather be the invaded.[94]
Dare not press forward an inch, but rather retreat a foot.
That is, to march without formations,
To roll not up the sleeves,
To charge not in frontal attacks,
To arm without weapons.[95]
There is no greater catastrophe than to underestimate the enemy.
To underestimate the enemy might entail the loss of my treasures.[96]
Therefore when two equally matched armies meet,
It is the man of sorrow [97] who wins.

LXX. THEY KNOW ME NOT

My teachings are very easy to understand and very easy to practise,
But no one can understand them and no one can practise them.
In my words there is a principle.
In the affairs of men there is a system.

[94] *Invader* and *invaded,* lit. "host" and "guest." It is possible to read it differently by supplying the often dropped *when:* "When I dare not be the invader, then I will be the defender."

[95] Or to feel like being in this condition, i.e., the subjective condition of humility. This is entirely consistent with Laotse's philosophy of camouflage, the earliest in the world. Cf. "great eloquence is like stuttering" etc., Ch. 45.

[96] Possibly the "three Treasures" in Ch. 67.

[97] Who hates killing. See Ch. 31. The corrected text of Yü Yüeh would make this read, "The man who yields wins."

Because they know not these,
They also know me not.
Since there are few that know me,
Therefore I am distinguished.
Therefore the Sage wears a coarse cloth on top
And carries jade within his bosom.

LXXI. SICK-MINDEDNESS

Who knows that he does not know is the highest;
Who (pretends to) know what he does not know is sick-minded.
And who recognizes sick-mindedness as sick-mindedness is not sick-minded.
The Sage is not sick-minded.
Because he recognizes sick-mindedness as sick-mindedness,
Therefore he is not sick-minded.

LXXII. ON PUNISHMENT (1)[98]

When people have no fear of force,[99]
Then (as is the common practice) great force descends upon them.

Despise not their dwellings,
Dislike not their progeny.
Because you do not dislike them,
You will not be disliked yourself.
Therefore the Sage knows himself, but does not show himself,
Loves himself, but does not exalt himself.
Therefore he rejects the one (force) and accepts the other (gentility).

LXXIII. ON PUNISHMENT (2)

Who is brave in daring (you) kill,
Who is brave in not daring (you) let live.

[98] Chapters 72, 73, 74 and 75 are closely related in thought and similar in construction.
[99] *Wei,* military force or authority; sometimes also used in connection with "God's anger." Another interpretation, "when the people have no fear of God, then God's anger descends upon them." But this fits in not so well with the context. See next two chapters on the futility of punishment, especially the first two lines, Ch. 74.

In these two,
There is some advantage and some disadvantage.
(Even if) Heaven dislikes certain people,
Who would know (who are to be killed and) why?
Therefore even the Sage regards it as a difficult question.
Heaven's Way (Tao) is good at conquest without strife,
Rewarding (vice and virtue) without words,
Making its appearance without call,
Achieving results without obvious design.
The Heaven's Net is broad and wide,[100]
With big meshes, yet letting nothing slip through.

LXIV. ON PUNISHMENT (3)

The people are not afraid of death;
Why threaten them with death?
Supposing that the people *are* afraid of death,
And we can seize and kill the unruly,
Who would dare to do so? [101]
Often it happens that the executioner is killed.
And to take the place of the executioner
Is like handling the hatchet for the master carpenter.
He who handles the hatchet for the master carpenter
Seldom escapes injury to his hands.

LXXV. ON PUNISHMENT (4)

When people are hungry,
It is because their rulers eat too much tax-grain.
Therefore the unruliness of hungry people
Is due to the interference of their rulers.
That is why they are unruly.
The people are not afraid of death,
Because they are anxious to make a living.
That is why they are not afraid of death.
It is those who interfere not with their living
That are wise in exalting life.

[100] This has now become a Chinese proverb for "virtue always rewarded, vice always punished."

[101] Notice the similarity of construction with the first five lines of Chapter 73.

LXXVI. HARD AND SOFT

When man is born, he is tender and weak;
  At death, he is hard and stiff.
When the things and plants are alive, they are soft and supple;
When they are dead, they are brittle and dry.
  Therefore hardness and stiffness are the companions of death,
  And softness and gentleness are the companions of life.

Therefore when an army is headstrong,[102] it will lose in battle.
When a tree is hard, it will be cut down.
  The big and strong belong underneath.
  The gentle and weak belong at the top.[103]

LXXVII. BENDING THE BOW

The Tao (way) of Heaven,
Is it not like the bending of a bow?
  The top comes down and the bottom-end goes up,
  The extra (length) is shortened, the insufficient (width) is expanded.
It is the Way of Heaven to take away from those that have too much
And give to those that have not enough.
Not so with man's way:
  He takes away from those that have not
  And gives it as tribute to those that have too much.
Who can have enough and to spare to give to the entire world?
Only the man of Tao.
Therefore the Sage acts, but does not possess,
  Accomplishes but lays claim to no credit,
  Because he has no wish to seem superior.

LXXVIII. NOTHING WEAKER THAN WATER

There is nothing weaker than water
But none is superior to it in overcoming the hard,
For which there is no substitute.

[102] *Ch'iang* means "stiff," "strong," and "headstrong."
[103] As with twigs and trunks.

That weakness overcomes strength
And gentleness overcomes rigidity,
No one does not know;
No one can put into practice.

Therefore the Sage says:
"Who receives unto himself the calumny of the world
Is the preserver of the state.
Who bears himself the sins of the world
Is the king of the world."
Straight words seem crooked.

LXXIX. PEACE SETTLEMENTS

Patching up a great hatred is sure to leave some hatred behind.
How can this be regarded as satisfactory?
Therefore the Sage holds the left tally,[104]
And does not put the guilt on the other party.
The virtuous man is for patching up;
The vicious is for fixing guilt.[105]
But "the way of Heaven is impartial
It sides only with the good man."[106]

LXXX. THE SMALL UTOPIA

(Let there be) a small country with a small population,
Where the supply of goods are tenfold or hundredfold, more than they can use.
Let the people value their lives[107] and not migrate far.
Though there be boats and carriages,
None be there to ride them.
Though there be armor and weapons,
No occasion to display them.

[104] Sign of inferiority in an agreement.
[105] Wang Pi's commentary: "for pointing out faults."
[106] An ancient quotation appearing in many ancient texts.
[107] Lit. "death."

Let the people again tie ropes for reckoning,
  Let them enjoy their food,
  Beautify their clothing,
  Be satisfied with their homes,
  Delight in their customs.
The neighboring settlements overlook one another
So that they can hear the barking of dogs and crowing of cocks of their neighbors,
And the people till the end of their days shall never have been outside their country.

LXXI. THE WAY OF HEAVEN

True words are not fine-sounding;
  Fine-sounding words are not true.
A good man does not argue;
  He who argues is not a good man.
The wise one does not know many things;
  He who knows many things is not wise.
The Sage does not accumulate (for himself):
  He lives for other people,
  And grows richer himself;
  He gives to other people,
  And has greater abundance.
The Tao of Heaven
  Blesses, but does not harm.
The Way of the Sage
  Accomplishes, but does not contend.

Chuangtse, Mystic and Humorist

INTRODUCTION

JESUS WAS FOLLOWED BY ST. PAUL, Socrates by Plato, Confucius by Mencius, and Laotse by Chuangtse. In all four cases, the first was the real teacher and either wrote no books or wrote very little, and the second began to develop the doctrines and wrote long and profound discourses. Chuangtse, who died about B.C. 275, was separated from Laotse's death by not quite two hundred years, and was strictly a contemporary of Mencius. Yet the most curious thing is that although both these writers mentioned the other philosophers of the time, neither was mentioned by the other in his works.

On the whole, Chuangtse must be considered the greatest prose writer of the Chou Dynasty, as Ch'ü Yüan must be considered the greatest poet. His claim to this position rests both upon the brilliance of his style and the depth of his thought. That explains the fact that although he was probably the greatest slanderer of Confucius, and with Motse, the greatest antagonist of Confucian ideas, no Confucian scholar has not openly or secretly admired him. People who would not openly agree with his ideas would nevertheless read him as literature.

Nor can it be said truly that a pure-blooded Chinese could ever quite disagree with Chuangtse's ideas. Taoism is not a school of thought in China, it is a deep, fundamental trait of Chinese thinking, and of the Chinese attitude toward life and toward society. It has depth, while Confucianism has only a practical sense of proportions; it enriches Chinese poetry and imagination in an immeasurable manner, and it gives a philosophic sanction to whatever is in the idle, freedom-loving, poetic, vagabond Chinese soul. It provides the only safe, romantic release from the severe Confucian classic restraint, and humanizes the very humanists themselves. Therefore when a Chinese succeeds, he is always a Confucianist, and when he fails, he is always a Taoist. As more people fail than succeed in this world, and as all who succeed know that they succeed but in a lame and halting manner when they examine themselves in the dark hours of the night, I believe Taoist ideas are more often at work than Confucianism. Even a Confucianist succeeds only when he knows he never really succeeds, that is, by following Taoist wisdom. Tseng Kuofan, the great Confucian general who suppressed the Taiping Rebellion, had failed in his early campaign and began to succeed only one morning when he realized with true Taoist humility that he was "no good," and gave power to his assistant generals.

Chuangtse is therefore important as the first one who fully developed the Taoistic thesis of the rhythm of life, contained in the epigrams of Laotse. Unlike other Chinese philosophers principally occupied with practical questions of government and personal morality, he gives the only metaphysics existing in Chinese literature before the coming of Buddhism. I am sure his mysticism will charm some readers and repel others. Certain traits in it, like weeding out the idea of the ego and quiet contemplation and "seeing the Solitary" explain how these native Chinese ideas were back of the development of the Ch'an (Japanese *Zen*) Buddhism. Any branch of human knowledge, even the study of the rocks of the earth and the cosmic rays of heaven, strikes mysticism when it reaches any depth at all, and it seems Chinese Taoism skipped the scientific study of nature to reach the same intuitive conclusion by insight alone. Therefore it is not surprising that Albert Einstein and Chuangtse agree, as agree they must, on the relativity of all standards. The only difference is that Einstein takes on the more difficult and, to a Chinese, more stupid work of mathematical proof, while Chuangtse furnishes the philosophic import of this theory of relativity, which must be sooner or later developed by Western philosophers in the next decades.

A word must be added about Chuangtse's attitude toward Confucius. It will be evident to any reader that he was one of the greatest romanticizers of history, and that any of the anecdotes he tells about Confucius, or Laotse or the Yellow Emperor must be accepted on a par with those anecdotes he tells about the conversation of General Clouds and Great Nebulous, or between the Spirit of the River and the Spirit of the Ocean. It must be also plainly understood that he was a humorist with a wild and rather luxuriant fantasy, with an American love for exaggeration and for the big. One should therefore read him as one would a humorist writer, knowing that he is frivolous when he is profound and profound when he is frivolous.

The extant text of Chuangtse consists of thirty-three chapters, all of them a mixture of philosophic disquisition and anecdotes or parables. The chapters containing the most virulent attacks on Confucianism (not included here) have been considered forgery, and a few Chinese "textual critics" have even considered all of them forgery except the first seven chapters. This is easy to understand because it is the modern Chinese fashion to talk of forgery. One can rest assured that these "textual critics" are unscientific because very little of it is philological criticism, but consists of opinions as to style and whether Chuangtse had or had not enough culture to attack Confucius only in a mild and polished manner. (See samples of this type of "criticism" in my long introduction to *The Book of History*.) Only one or two anachronisms are pointed out, which could be due to later interpolations, and the rest is a subjective assertion of opinion. Even the evaluations of style are faulty, and at least a distinction should be made between interpolations and wholesale forgery. Some of the best pieces of Chuangtse are decidedly outside the first seven chapters, and it has not even occurred to the critics to provide an answer as to who else could have written them. There is no reason to be sure that even the most eloquent exposition of the thieves' philosophy, regarded by most as forgery, was not the work of Chuangtse, who had so little to do with the "gentlemen." On the other hand, I believe various anecdotes have been freely added by later generations into the extremely loose structure of the chapters.

I have chosen here eleven chapters, including all but one of the first best seven chapters. With one minor exception, these chapters are translated complete. The philosophically most important are the chapters on "Levelling All Things" and "Autumn Floods." The chapters, "Joined Toes," "Horses' Hoofs," "Opening Trunks" and "Tolerance" belong in one group with the main theme of protest against civilization. The most eloquent protest is contained in "Opening Trunks," while the most characteristically Taoistic is the chapter on "Tolerance." The most mystic and deeply religious piece is "The Great Supreme." The most beautifully written is "Autumn Floods." The queerest is the chapter on "Deformities" (a typically "romanticist" theme). The most delightful is probably "Horses' Hoofs" and the most fantastic is the first chapter, "A Happy

Excursion." Some of Chuangtse's parables in the other chapters will be found under "Parables of Ancient Philosophers" elsewhere in this volume.

I have based my translation on that of Herbert A. Giles. It soon became apparent in my work that Giles was free in his translation where exactness was easy and possible, and that he had a glib, colloquial style which might be considered a blemish. The result is that hardly a line has been left untouched, and I have had to make my own translation, taking advantage of whatever is good in his English rendering. But still I owe a great debt to my predecessor, and he has notably succeeded in this difficult task in many passages. Where his rendering is good, I have not chosen to be different. In this sense, the translation may be regarded as my own.

It should be noted that throughout the text, Giles translates "Heaven" as "God" where it means God. On the other hand, the term "Creator" is an exact rendering of *chao-wu,* or "he who creates things." I will not go into details of translation of other philosophic terms here.

Chuangtse

Translated by Lin Yutang

A HAPPY EXCURSION (CHAPTER I)

In the Northern Ocean there is a fish, called the *k'un,* I do not know how many thousand *li* in size. This *k'un* changes into a bird, called the *p'eng*. Its back is I do not know how many thousand *li* in breadth. When it is moved, it flies, its wings obscuring the sky like clouds.

When on a voyage, this bird prepares to start for the Southern Ocean, the Celestial Lake. And in the *Records of Marvels* we read that when the *p'eng* flies southwards, the water is smitten for a space of three thousand *li* around, while the bird itself mounts upon a great wind to a height of ninety thousand *li,* for a flight of six months' duration.

There mounting aloft, the bird saw the moving white mists of spring, the dust-clouds, and the living things blowing their breaths among them. It wondered whether the blue of the sky was its real colour, or only the result of distance without end, and saw that the things on earth appeared the same to it.

If there is not sufficient depth, water will not float large ships. Upset a cupful into a hole in the yard, and a mustard-seed will be your boat. Try to float the cup, and it will be grounded, due to the disproportion between water and vessel.

So with air. If there is not sufficient a depth, it cannot support large wings. And for this bird, a depth of ninety thousand *li* is necessary to bear it up. Then, gliding upon the wind, with nothing save the clear sky above, and no obstacles in the way, it starts upon its journey to the south.

A cicada and a young dove laughed, saying, "Now, when I fly with all my might, 'tis as much as I can do to get from tree to tree. And sometimes I do not reach, but fall to the ground midway. What then can be the use of going up ninety thousand *li* to start for the south?"

He who goes to the countryside taking three meals with him comes back with his stomach as full as when he started. But he who travels a hundred *li* must take ground rice enough for an overnight stay. And he who travels a thousand *li* must supply himself with provisions for three months. Those two little creatures, what should they know?

Small knowledge has not the compass of great knowledge any more than a short year has the length of a long year. How can we tell that this is so? The fungus plant of a morning knows not the alternation of day and night. The cicada knows not the alternation of spring and autumn. Theirs are short years. But in the south of Ch'u there is a *mingling* (tree) whose spring and autumn are each of five hundred years' duration. And in former days there was a large tree which had a spring and autumn each of eight thousand years. Yet, P'eng Tsu[1] is known for reaching a great age and is still, alas! an object of envy to all!

It was on this very subject that the Emperor T'ang[2] spoke to Chi, as follows:—"At the north of Ch'iungta, there is a Dark Sea, the Celestial Lake. In it there is a fish several thousand *li* in breadth, and I know not how many in length. It is called the *k'un*. There is also a bird, called the *p'eng*, with a back like Mount T'ai, and wings like clouds across the sky. It soars up upon a whirlwind to a height of ninety thousand *li*, far above the region of the clouds, with only the clear sky above it. And then it directs its flight towards the Southern Ocean.

"And a lake sparrow laughed, and said: Pray, what may that creature be going to do? I rise but a few yards in the air and settle down again, after flying around among the reeds. That is as much as any one would want to fly. Now, where ever can this creature be going to?"

Such, indeed, is the difference between small and great. Take, for instance, a man who creditably fills some small office, or whose influence spreads over a village, or whose character pleases a certain prince. His opinion of himself will be much the same as that lake sparrow's. The philosopher Yung of Sung would laugh at such a one. If the whole world flattered him, he would not be affected thereby, nor if the whole world blamed him would he be dissuaded from what he was doing. For Yung can distinguish between essence and superficialities, and understand what is true honor and shame. Such men are rare in their generation. But even he has not established himself.

[1] He is reputed to have lived 800 years. [2] B.C. 1783.

Now Liehtse[3] could ride upon the wind. Sailing happily in the cool breeze, he would go on for fifteen days before his return. Among mortals who attain happiness, such a man is rare. Yet although Liehtse could dispense with walking, he would still have to depend upon something.[4] As for one who is charioted upon the eternal fitness of Heaven and Earth, driving before him the changing elements as his team to roam through the realms of the Infinite, upon what, then, would such a one have need to depend?

Thus it is said, "The perfect man ignores self; the divine man ignores achievement; the true Sage ignores reputation."

The Emperor Yao[5] wished to abdicate in favor of Hsü Yu, saying, "If, when the sun and moon are shining, the torch is still lighted, would it be not difficult for the latter to shine? If, when the rain has fallen, one should still continue to water the fields, would this not be a waste of labor? Now if you would assume the reins of government, the empire would be well governed, and yet I am filling this office. I am conscious of my own deficiencies, and I beg to offer you the Empire."

"You are ruling the Empire, and the Empire is already well ruled," replied Hsü Yu. "Why should I take your place? Should I do this for the sake of a name? A name is but the shadow of reality, and should I trouble myself about the shadow? The tit, building its nest in the mighty forest, occupies but a single twig. The beaver slakes its thirst from the river, but drinks enough only to fill its belly. I would rather go back: I have no use for the empire! If the cook is unable to prepare the funeral sacrifices, the representative of the worshipped spirit and the officer of prayer may not step over the wines and meats and do it for him."

Chien Wu said to Lien Shu, "I heard Chieh Yü talk on high and fine subjects endlessly. I was greatly startled at what he said, for his words seemed interminable as the Milky Way, but they are quite detached from our common human experience."

"What was it?" asked Lien Shu.

"He declared," replied Chien Wu, "that on the Miao-ku-yi mountain there lives a divine one, whose skin is white like ice or snow, whose grace

[3] Philosopher about whose life nothing is known. The book *Liehtse* is considered a later compilation. See the section "Parables of Ancient Philosophers."

[4] The wind.

[5] B.C. 2357.

and elegance are like those of a virgin, who eats no grain, but lives on air and dew, and who, riding on clouds with flying dragons for his team, roams beyond the limits of the mortal regions. When his spirit gravitates, he can ward off corruption from all things, and bring good crops. That is why I call it nonsense, and do not believe it."

"Well," answered Lien Shu," "you don't ask a blind man's opinion of beautiful designs, nor do you invite a deaf man to a concert. And blindness and deafness are not physical only. There is blindness and deafness of the mind. His words are like the unspoiled virgin. The good influence of such a man with such a character fills all creation. Yet because a paltry generation cries for reform, you would have him busy himself about the details of an empire!

"Objective existences cannot harm him. In a flood which reached the sky, he would not be drowned. In a drought, though metals ran liquid and mountains were scorched up, he would not be hot. Out of his very dust and siftings you might fashion two such men as Yao and Shun.[6] And you would have him occupy himself with objectives!"

A man of the Sung State carried some ceremonial caps to the Yüeh tribes for sale. But the men of Yüeh used to cut off their hair and paint their bodies, so that they had no use for such things. The Emperor Yao ruled all under heaven and governed the affairs of the entire country. After he paid a visit to the four sages of the Miao-ku-yi Mountain, he felt on his return to his capital at Fenyang that the empire existed for him no more.

Hueitse[7] said to Chuangtse, "The Prince of Wei gave me a seed of a large-sized kind of gourd. I planted it, and it bore a fruit as big as a five-bushel measure. Now had I used this for holding liquids, it would have been too heavy to lift; and had I cut it in half for ladles, the ladles would have been too flat for such purpose. Certainly it was a huge thing, but I had no use for it and so broke it up."

"It was rather you who did not know how to use large things," replied Chuangtse. "There was a man of Sung who had a recipe for salve for chapped hands, his family having been silk-washers for generations. A stranger who had heard of it, came and offered him a hundred ounces of silver for this recipe; whereupon he called together his clansmen and said, 'We have never made much money by silk-washing. Now, we can

[6] Sage emperors.

[7] A sophist and friend of Chuangtse who often carried on debates with him.

sell the recipe for a hundred ounces in a single day. Let the stranger have it.'

"The stranger got the recipe, and went and had an interview with the Prince of Wu. The Yüeh State was in trouble, and the Prince of Wu sent a general to fight a naval battle with Yüeh at the beginning of winter. The latter was totally defeated, and the stranger was rewarded with a piece of the King's territory. Thus, while the efficacy of the salve to cure chapped hands was in both cases the same, its applications were different. Here, it secured a title; there, the people remained silk-washers.

"Now as to your five-bushel gourd, why did you not make a float of it, and float about over river and lake? And you complain of its being too flat for holding things! I fear your mind is stuffy inside."

Hueitse said to Chuangtse, "I have a large tree, called the ailanthus. Its trunk is so irregular and knotty that it cannot be measured out for planks; while its branches are so twisted that they cannot be cut out into discs or squares. It stands by the roadside, but no carpenter will look at it. Your words are like that tree—big and useless, of no concern to the world."

"Have you never seen a wild cat," rejoined Chuangtse, "crouching down in wait for its prey? Right and left and high and low, it springs about, until it gets caught in a trap or dies in a snare. On the other hand, there is the yak with its great huge body. It is big enough in all conscience, but it cannot catch mice. Now if you have a big tree and are at a loss what to do with it, why not plant it in the Village of Nowhere, in the great wilds, where you might loiter idly by its side, and lie down in blissful repose beneath its shade? There it would be safe from the axe and from all other injury. For being of no use to others, what could worry its mind?"

ON LEVELLING ALL THINGS

Tsech'i of Nankuo sat leaning on a low table. Gazing up to heaven, he sighed and looked as though he had lost his mind.

Yench'eng Tseyu, who was standing by him, exclaimed, "What are you thinking about that your body should become thus like dead wood, your mind like burnt-out cinders? Surely the man now leaning on the table is not he who was here just now."

"My friend," replied Tsech'i, "your question is apposite. Today I have lost my Self . . . Do you understand? . . . Perhaps you only know the music of man, and not that of Earth. Or even if you have heard the music of Earth, perhaps you have not heard the music of Heaven."

"Pray explain," said Tseyu.

"The breath of the universe," continued Tsech'i, "is called wind. At times, it is inactive. But when active, all crevices resound to its blast. Have you never listened to its deafening roar?

"Caves and dells of hill and forest, hollows in huge trees of many a span in girth—some are like nostrils, and some like mouths, and others like ears, beam-sockets, goblets, mortars, or like pools and poodles. And the wind goes rushing through them, like swirling torrents or singing arrows, bellowing, sousing, trilling, wailing, roaring, purling, whistling in front and echoing behind, now soft with the cool blow, now shrill with the whirlwind, until the tempest is past and silence reigns supreme. Have you never witnessed how the trees and objects shake and quake, and twist and twirl?"

"Well, then," enquired Tseyu, "since the music of Earth consists of hollows and apertures, and the music of man of pipes and flutes, of what consists the music of Heaven?"

"The effect of the wind upon these various apertures," replied Tsech'i, "is not uniform, but the sounds are produced according to their individual capacities. Who is it that agitates their breasts?

"Great wisdom is generous; petty wisdom is contentious. Great speech is impassioned, small speech cantankerous.

"For whether the soul is locked in sleep or whether in waking hours the body moves, we are striving and struggling with the immediate circumstances. Some are easy-going and leisurely, some are deep and cunning, and some are secretive. Now we are frightened over petty fears, now disheartened and dismayed over some great terror. Now the mind flies forth like an arrow from a cross-bow, to be the arbiter of right and wrong. Now it stays behind as if sworn to an oath, to hold on to what it has secured. Then, as under autumn and winter's blight, comes gradual decay, and submerged in its own occupations, it keeps on running its course, never to return. Finally, worn out and imprisoned, it is choked up like an old drain, and the failing mind shall not see light again.[8]

"Joy and anger, sorrow and happiness, worries and regrets, indecision and fears, come upon us by turns, with everchanging moods, like music from the hollows, or like mushrooms from damp. Day and night they

[8] Agitations of the soul (music of Heaven) compared to the agitations of the forest (music of Earth).

alternate within us, but we cannot tell whence they spring. Alas! Alas! Could we for a moment lay our finger upon their very Cause?

"But for these emotions I should not be. Yet but for me, there would be no one to feel them. So far we can go; but we do not know by whose order they come into play. It would seem there was a soul;[9] but the clue to its existence is wanting. That it functions is credible enough, though we cannot see its form. Perhaps it has inner reality without outward form.

"Take the human body with all its hundred bones, nine external cavities and six internal organs, all complete. Which part of it should I love best? Do you not cherish all equally, or have you a preference? Do these organs serve as servants of some one else? Since servants cannot govern themselves, do they serve as master and servants by turn? Surely there is some soul which controls them all.

"But whether or not we ascertain what is the true nature of this soul, it matters but little to the soul itself. For once coming into this material shape, it runs its course until it is exhausted. To be harassed by the wear and tear of life, and to be driven along without possibility of arresting one's course,—is not this pitiful indeed? To labor without ceasing all life, and then, without living to enjoy the fruit, worn out with labor, to depart, one knows not whither,—is not this a just cause for grief?"

"Men say there is no death—of what avail? The body decomposes, and the mind goes with it. Is this not a great cause for sorrow? Can the world be so dull as not to see this? Or is it I alone who am dull, and others not so?"

Now if we are to be guided by our prejudices, who shall be without a guide? What need to make comparisons of right and wrong with others? And if one is to follow one's own judgments according to his prejudices, even the fools have them! But to form judgments of right and wrong without first having a mind at all is like saying, "I left for Yüeh today, and got there yesterday." Or, it is like assuming something which does not exist to exist. The (illusions of) assuming something which does not exist to exist could not be fathomed even by the divine Yü; how much less could we?

For speech is not mere blowing of breath. It is intended to say something, only what it is intended to say cannot yet be determined. Is there speech indeed, or is there not? Can we, or can we not, distinguish it from the chirping of young birds?

[9] Lit. "true lord."

How can Tao be so obscured that there should be a distinction of true and false? How can speech be so obscured that there should be a distinction of right and wrong? [10] Where can you go and find Tao not to exist? Where can you go and find that words cannot be proved? Tao is obscured by our inadequate understanding, and words are obscured by flowery expressions. Hence the affirmations and denials of the Confucian and Motsean [11] schools, each denying what the other affirms and affirming what the other denies. Each denying what the other affirms and affirming what the other denies brings us only into confusion.

There is nothing which is not *this;* there is nothing which is not *that.* What cannot be seen by *that* (the other person) can be known by myself. Hence I say, *this* emanates from *that; that* also derives from *this.* This is the theory of the interdependence of *this* and *that* (relativity of standards).

Nevertheless, life arises from death, and *vice versa.* Possibility arises from impossibility, and *vice versa.* Affirmation is based upon denial, and *vice versa.* Which being the case, the true sage rejects all distinctions and takes his refuge in Heaven (Nature). For one may base it on *this,* yet *this* is also *that* and *that* is also *this. This* also has its 'right' and 'wrong', and *that* also has its 'right' and 'wrong.' Does then the distinction between *this* and *that* really exist or not? When *this* (subjective) and *that* (objective) are both without their correlates, that is the very 'Axis of Tao.' And when that Axis passes through the centre at which all Infinities converge, affirmations and denials alike blend into the infinite One. Hence it is said that there is nothing like using the Light.

To take a finger in illustration of a finger not being a finger is not so good as to take something which is not a finger to illustrate that a finger is not a finger. To take a horse in illustration of a horse not being a horse is not so good as to take something which is not a horse to illustrate that a horse is not a horse.[12] So with the universe which is but a finger, but a horse. The possible is possible: the impossible is impossible. Tao operates, and the given results follow; things receive names and are said to be what they are. Why are they so? They are said to be so! Why are they

[10] *Shih* and *fei* mean general moral judgments and mental distinctions: "right" and "wrong", "true" and "false", "is" and "is not," "affirmative" and "negative", also "to justify" and "condemn", to "affirm" and "deny."

[11] The followers of Motse were powerful rivals of the Confucianists in Chuangtse's days. See the selections from Motse.

[12] The meaning of these two sentences is made clear by a line below. "But if we put the different categories in one, then the differences of category cease to exist."

not so? They are said to be not so! Things are so by themselves and have possibilities by themselves. There is nothing which is not so and there is nothing which may not become so.

Therefore take, for instance, a twig and a pillar, or the ugly person and the great beauty, and all the strange and monstrous transformations. These are all levelled together by Tao. Division is the same as creation; creation is the same as destruction. There is no such thing as creation or destruction, for these conditions are again levelled together into One.

Only the truly intelligent understand this principle of the levelling of all things into One. They discard the distinctions and take refuge in the common and ordinary things. The common and ordinary things serve certain functions and therefore retain the wholeness of nature. From this wholeness, one comprehends, and from comprehension, one comes near to the Tao. There it stops. To stop without knowing how it stops—this is Tao.

But to wear out one's intellect in an obstinate adherence to the individuality of things, not recognizing the fact that all things are One,—this is called "Three in the Morning." What is "Three in the Morning?" A keeper of monkeys said with regard to their rations of nuts that each monkey was to have three in the morning and four at night. At this the monkeys were very angry. Then the keeper said they might have four in the morning and three at night, with which arrangement they were all well pleased. The actual number of nuts remained the same, but there was a difference owing to (subjective evaluations of) likes and dislikes. It also derives from this (principle of subjectivity). Wherefore the true Sage brings all the contraries together and rests in the natural Balance of Heaven. This is called (the principle of following) two courses (at once).

The knowledge of the men of old had a limit. What was the limit? It extended back to a period when matter did not exist. That was the extreme point to which their knowledge reached. The second period was that of matter, but of matter unconditioned (undefined). The third epoch saw matter conditioned (defined), but judgements of true and false were still unknown. When these appeared, Tao began to decline. And with the decline of Tao, individual bias (subjectivity) arose.

Besides, did Tao really rise and decline? [13] In the world of (apparent)

[13] *Ch'eng* and *k'uei,* lit.—"whole" and "deficient." "Wholeness" refers to unspoiled unity of Tao. In the following sentences, *ch'eng* is used in the sense of "success." It is explained by commentators that the "wholeness" of music exists only in silence, and that as soon

rise and decline, the famous musician Chao Wen did play the string instrument; but in respect to the world without rise and decline, Chao Wen did not play the string instrument. When Chao Wen stopped playing the string instrument, Shih K'uang, (the music master) laid down his drum-stick (for keeping time), and Hueitse (the sophist) stopped arguing, they all understood the approach of Tao. These people are the best in their arts, and therefore known to posterity. They each loved his art, and wanted to excel in his own line. And because they loved their arts, they wanted to make them known to others. But they were trying to teach what (in its nature) could not be known. Consequently (Hueitse) ended in the obscure discussions of the "hard" and "white"; and Chao Wen's son tried to learn to play the string instrument all his life and failed. If this may be called success, then I, too, have succeeded. But if neither of them could be said to have succeeded, then neither I nor others have succeeded. Therefore the true Sage discards the light that dazzles and takes refuge in the common and ordinary. Through this comes understanding.

Suppose here is a statement. We do not know whether it belongs to one category or another. But if we put the different categories in one, then the differences of category cease to exist. However, I must explain. If there was a beginning, then there was a time before that beginning, and a time before the time which was before the time of that beginning. If there is existence, there must have been non-existence. And if there was a time when nothing existed, then there must have been a time when even nothing did not exist. All of a sudden, nothing came into existence. Could one then really say whether it belongs to the category of existence or of non-existence? Even the very words I have just now uttered,—I cannot say whether they say something or not.

There is nothing under the canopy of heaven greater than the tip of a bird's down in autumn, while the T'ai Mountain is small. Neither is there any longer life than that of a child cut off in infancy, while P'eng Tsu himself died young. The universe and I came into being together; I and everything therein are One.

If then all things are One, what room is there for speech? On the other hand, since I can say the word 'one' how can speech not exist? If it does

---

as one note is struck, other notes are necessarily held in abeyance. The same thing is true of arguments: when we argue, we necessarily cut up truth by emphasizing certain aspects of it.

exist, we have One and speech—two; and two and one—three [14] from which point onwards even the best mathematicians will fail to reach (the ultimate); how much more then should ordinary people fail?

Hence, if from nothing you can proceed to something, and subsequently reach three, it follows that it would be still easier if you were to start from something. Since you cannot proceed, stop here.

Now Tao by its very nature can never be defined. Speech by its very nature cannot express the absolute. Hence arise the distinctions. Such distinctions are: "right" and "left," "relationship" and "duty," "division" and "discrimination," "emulation" and "contention." These are called the Eight Predicables.

Beyond the limits of the external world, the Sage knows that it exists, but does not talk about it. Within the limits of the external world, the Sage talks but does not make comments. With regard to the wisdom of the ancients, as embodied in the canon of *Spring and Autumn,* the Sage comments, but does not expound. And thus, among distinctions made, there are distinctions that cannot be made; among things expounded, there are things that cannot be expounded.

How can that be? it is asked. The true Sage keeps his knowledge within him, while men in general set forth theirs in argument, in order to convince each other. And therefore it is said that one who argues does so because he cannot see certain points.

Now perfect Tao cannot be given a name. A perfect argument does not employ words. Perfect kindness does not concern itself with (individual acts of) kindness.[15] Perfect integrity is not critical of others.[16] Perfect courage does not push itself forward.

For the Tao which is manifest is not Tao. Speech which argues falls short of its aim. Kindness which has fixed objects loses its scope. Integrity which is obvious is not believed in. Courage which pushes itself forward never accomplishes anything. These five are, as it were, round (mellow) with a strong bias towards squareness (sharpness). Therefore that knowledge which stops at what it does not know, is the highest knowledge.

Who knows the argument which can be argued without words, and the Tao which does not declare itself as Tao? He who knows this may be said to enter the realm of the spirit.[17] To be poured into without be-

[14] See Laotse, Ch. 42.

[15] See Laotse, Ch. 5.

[16] See Laotse, Ch. 58.

[17] Lit. in the "Palace of Heaven."

coming full, and pour out without becoming empty, without knowing how this is brought about,—this is the art of "Concealing the Light."

Of old, the Emperor Yao said to Shun, "I would smite the Tsungs, and the Kueis, and the Hsü-aos. Since I have been on the throne, this has ever been on my mind. What do you think?"

"These three States," replied Shun, "lie in wild undeveloped regions. Why can you not shake off this idea? Once upon a time, ten suns came out together, and all things were illuminated thereby. How much greater should be the power of virtue which excels the suns?"

Yeh Ch'üeh asked Wang Yi, saying, "Do you know for certain that all things are the same?"

"How can I know?" answered Wang Yi.

"Do you know what you do not know?"

"How can I know?" replied Yeh Ch'üeh.

"But then does nobody know?"

"How can I know?" said Wang Yi. "Nevertheless, I will try to tell you. How can it be known that what I call knowing is not really not knowing and that what I call not knowing is not really knowing? Now I would ask you this, If a man sleeps in a damp place, he gets lumbago and dies. But how about an eel? And living up in a tree is precarious and trying to the nerves. But how about monkeys? Of the man, the eel, and the monkey, whose habitat is the right one, absolutely? Human beings feed on flesh, deer on grass, centipedes on little snakes, owls and crows on mice. Of these four, whose is the right taste, absolutely? Monkey mates with the dog-headed female ape, the buck with the doe, eels consort with fishes, while men admire Mao Ch'iang and Li Chi, at the sight of whom fishes plunge deep down in the water, birds soar high in the air, and deer hurry away. Yet who shall say which is the correct standard of beauty? In my opinion, the doctrines of humanity and justice and the paths of right and wrong are so confused that it is impossible to know their contentions."

"If you then," asked Yeh Ch'üeh, "do not know what is good and bad, is the Perfect Man equally without this knowledge?"

"The Perfect Man," answered Wang Yi, "is a spiritual being. Were the ocean itself scorched up, he would not feel hot. Were the great rivers frozen hard, he would not feel cold. Were the mountains to be cleft by thunder, and the great deep to be thrown up by storm, he would not tremble with fear. Thus, he would mount upon the clouds of heaven, and driving the sun and the moon before him, pass beyond the limits of this mundane existence. Death and life have no more victory over him. How much less should he concern himself with the distinctions of profit and loss?"

Chü Ch'iao addressed Ch'ang Wutse as follows: "I heard Confucius say, 'The true Sage pays no heed to worldly affairs. He neither seeks gain nor avoids injury. He asks nothing at the hands of man and does not adhere to rigid rules of conduct. Sometimes he says something without speaking and sometimes he speaks without saying anything. And so he roams beyond the limits of this mundane world. These,' commented Confucius, 'are futile fantasies.' But to me they are the embodiment of the most wonderful Tao. What is your opinion?"

"These are things that perplexed even the Yellow Emperor," replied Ch'ang Wutse. "How should Confucius know? You are going too far ahead. When you see a hen's egg, you already expect to hear a cock crow. When you see a sling, you are already expecting to have broiled pigeon. I will say a few words to you at random, and do you listen at random.

"How does the Sage seat himself by the sun and moon, and hold the universe in his grasp? He blends everything into one harmonious whole, rejecting the confusion of this and that. Rank and precedence, which the vulgar sedulously cultivate, the Sage stolidly ignores, amalgamating the disparities of ten thousand years into one pure mould. The universe itself, too, conserves and blends all in the same manner.

"How do I know that love of life is not a delusion after all? How do I know but that he who dreads death is not as a child who has lost his way and does not know his way home?

"The lady Li Chi was the daughter of the frontier officer of Ai. When the Duke of Chin first got her, she wept until the bosom of her dress was drenched with tears. But when she came to the royal residence, shared with the Duke his luxurious couch, and ate rich food, she repented of having wept. How then do I know but that the dead may repent of having previously clung to life?

"Those who dream of the banquet, wake to lamentation and sorrow. Those who dream of lamentation and sorrow wake to join the hunt. While they dream, they do not know that they are dreaming. Some will even interpret the very dream they are dreaming; and only when they awake do they know it was a dream. By and by comes the great awakening, and then we find out that this life is really a great dream. Fools think they are awake now, and flatter themselves they know—this one is a prince, and that one is a shepherd. What narrowness of mind! Confucius and you are both dreams; and I who say you are dreams—I am but a dream myself. This is a paradox. Tomorrow a Sage may arise to explain it; but that tomorrow will not be until ten thousand generations have gone by. Yet you may meet him around the corner.

"Granting that you and I argue. If you get the better of me, and not I of you, are you necessarily right and I wrong? Or if I get the better of you and not you of me, am I necessarily right and you wrong? Or are we both partly right and partly wrong? Or are we both wholly right and wholly wrong? You and I cannot know this, and consequently we all live in darkness.

"Whom shall I ask as arbiter between us? If I ask some one who takes your view, he will side with you. How can such a one arbitrate between us? If I ask some one who takes my view, he will side with me. How can such a one arbitrate between us? If I ask some one who differs from both of us, he will be equally unable to decide between us, since he differs from both of us. And if I ask some one who agrees with both of us, he will be equally unable to decide between us, since he agrees with both of us. Since then you and I and other men cannot decide, how can we depend upon another? The words of arguments are all relative; if we wish to reach the absolute, we must harmonize them by means of the unity of God, and follow their natural evolution, so that we may complete our allotted span of life.

"But what is it to harmonize them by means of the unity of God? It is this. The right may not be really right. What appears so may not be really so. Even if what is right is really right, wherein it differs from wrong cannot be made plain by argument. Even if what appears so is really so, wherein it differs from what is not so also cannot be made plain by argument.

"Take no heed of time nor of right and wrong. Passing into the realm of the Infinite, take your final rest therein."

The Penumbra said to the Umbra. "At one moment you move: at another you are at rest. At one moment you sit down: at another you get up. Why this instability of purpose?" "Perhaps I depend," replied the Umbra, "upon something which causes me to do as I do; and perhaps that something depends in turn upon something else which causes it to do as it does. Or perhaps my dependence is like (the unconscious movements) of a snake's scales or of a cicada's wings. How can I tell why I do one thing, or why I do not do another?"

Once upon a time, I, Chuang Chou,[18] dreamt I was a butterfly, fluttering hither and thither, to all intents and purposes a butterfly. I was conscious only of my happiness as a butterfly, unaware that I was Chou. Soon I awaked, and there I was, veritably myself again. Now I do not know whether I was then a man dreaming I was a butterfly, or whether I am now a butterfly, dreaming I am a man. Between a man and a butterfly there is necessarily a distinction. The transition is called the transformation of material things.[19]

THE PRESERVATION OF LIFE

HUMAN LIFE is limited, but knowledge is limitless. To drive the limited in pursuit of the limitless is fatal; and to presume that one really knows is fatal indeed!

In doing good, avoid fame. In doing bad, avoid disgrace. Pursue a middle course as your principle. Thus you will guard your body from harm, preserve your life, fulfill your duties by your parents, and live your allotted span of life.

Prince Huei's cook was cutting up a bullock. Every blow of his hand, every heave of his shoulders, every tread of his foot, every thrust of his knee, every *whshh* of rent flesh, every *chhk* of the chopper, was in perfect rhythm,—like the dance of the *Mulberry Grove*, like the harmonious chords of *Ching Shou*.

"Well done!" cried the Prince. "Yours is skill indeed!"

"Sire," replied the cook laying down his chopper, "I have always devoted myself to Tao, which is higher than mere skill. When I first began to cut up bullocks, I saw before me whole bullocks. After three years' practice, I saw no more whole animals. And now I work with my mind and not with my eye. My mind works along without the control of the senses. Falling back upon eternal principles, I glide through such great joints or cavities as there may be, according to the natural

[18] Personal name of Chuangtse, "tse" being the equivalent of "Master."

[19] An important idea that recurs frequently in Chuangtse; all things are in constant flux and change, but are different aspects of the One.

constitution of the animal. I do not even touch the convolutions of muscle and tendon, still less attempt to cut through large bones.

"A good cook changes his chopper once a year,—because he cuts. An ordinary cook, one a month,—because he hacks. But I have had this chopper nineteen years, and although I have cut up many thousand bullocks, its edge is as if fresh from the whetstone. For at the joints there are always interstices, and the edge of a chopper being without thickness, it remains only to insert that which is without thickness into such an interstice. Indeed there is plenty of room for the blade to move about. It is thus that I have kept my chopper for nineteen years as though fresh from the whetstone.

"Nevertheless, when I come upon a knotty part which is difficult to tackle, I am all caution. Fixing my eye on it, I stay my hand, and gently apply my blade, until with a *hwah* the part yields like earth crumbling to the ground. Then I take out my chopper and stand up, and look around, and pause with an air of triumph. Then wiping my chopper, I put it carefully away."

"Bravo!" cried the Prince. "From the words of this cook I have learnt how to take care of my life."

When Hsien, of the Kungwen family, beheld a certain official, he was horrified, and said, "Who is that man? How came he to lose a leg? Is this the work of God, or of man?"

"Why, of course, it is the work of God, and not of man," was the reply. "God made this man one-legged. The appearance of men is always balanced. From this it is clear that God and not man made him what he is."

A pheasant of the marshes may have to go ten steps to get a peck, a hundred to get a drink. Yet pheasants do not want to be fed in a cage. For although they might have less worries, they would not like it.

When Laotse died, Ch'in Yi went to the funeral. He uttered three yells and departed.

A disciple asked him saying, "Were you not our Master's friend?"

"I was," replied Ch'in Yi.

"And if so, do you consider that a sufficient expression of grief at his death?" added the disciple.

"I do," said Ch'in Yi. "I had thought he was a (mortal) man, but now I know that he was not. When I went in to mourn, I found old persons weeping as if for their children, young ones wailing as if for their mothers. When these people meet, they must have said words on the occasion and shed tears without any intention. (To cry thus at one's death) is to evade the natural principles (of life and death) and increase human attachments, forgetting the source from which we receive this life. The ancients called this 'evading the retribution of Heaven.' The Master came, because it was his time to be born; he went, because it was his time to go away. Those who accept the natural course and sequence of things and live in obedience to it are beyond joy and sorrow. The ancients spoke of this as the emancipation from bondage. The fingers may not be able to supply all the fuel, but the fire is transmitted, and we know not when it will come to an end."

THIS HUMAN WORLD

YEN HUEI [20] went to take leave of Confucius. "Whither are you bound?" asked the Master.

"I am going to the State of Wei," was the reply.

"And what do you propose to do there?" continued Confucius.

"I hear," answered Yen Huei, "that the Prince of Wei is of mature age, but of an unmanageable disposition. He behaves as if the people were of no account, and will not see his own faults. He disregards human lives and the people perish; and their corpses lie about like so much undergrowth in a marsh. The people do not know where to turn for help. And I have heard you say that if a state be well governed, it may be passed over; but that if it be badly governed, then we should visit it. At the door of physicians there are many sick people. I would test my knowledge in this sense, that perchance I may do some good at that state."

"Alas!" cried Confucius, "you will be only going to your doom. For Tao must not bustle about. If it does it will have divergent aims. From divergent aims comes restlessness; from restlessness comes worry, and from worry one reaches the stage of being beyond hope. The Sages of old first strengthened their own character before they tried to strengthen that of others. Before you have strengthened your own character, what leisure have you to attend to the doings of wicked men? Besides, do you know into what virtue evaporates by motion and where knowledge ends? Virtue evaporates by motion into desire for fame and knowledge ends in contentions. In the struggle for fame men crush each other, while

[20] Best disciple of Confucius.

their wisdom but provokes rivalry. Both are instruments of evil, and are not proper principles of living.

"Besides, if before one's own solid character and integrity become an influence among men and before one's own disregard for fame reaches the hearts of men, one should go and force the preachings of charity and duty and the rules of conduct on wicked men, he would only make these men hate him for his very goodness. Such a person may be called a messenger of evil. A messenger of evil will be the victim of evil from others. That, alas! will be your end.

"On the other hand, if the Prince loves the good and hates evil, what object will you have in inviting him to change his ways? Before you have opened your mouth, the Prince himself will have seized the opportunity to wrest the victory from you. Your eyes will be dazzled, your expression fade, your words will hedge about, your face will show confusion, and your heart will yield within you. It will be as though you took fire to quell fire, water to quell water, which is known as aggravation. And if you begin with concessions, there will be no end to them. If you neglect this sound advice and talk too much, you will die at the hands of that violent man.

"Of old, Chieh murdered Kuanlung P'ang, and Chou slew Prince Pikan. Their victims were both men who cultivated themselves and cared for the good of the people, and thus offended their superiors. Therefore, their superiors got rid of them, because of their goodness. This was the result of their love for fame.

"Of old, Yao attacked the Ts'ung-chih and Hsü-ao countries, and Yü attacked the Yu-hus. The countries were laid waste, their inhabitants slaughtered, their rulers killed. Yet they fought without ceasing, and strove for material objects to the last. These are instances of striving for fame or for material objects. Have you not heard that even Sages cannot overcome this love of fame and this desire for material objects (in rulers)? Are you then likely to succeed? But of course you have a plan. Tell it to me."

"Gravity of demeanour and humility; persistence and singleness of purpose,—will this do?" replied Yen Huei.

"Alas no," said Confucius, "how can it? The Prince is a haughty person, filled with pride, and his moods are fickle. No one opposes him, and so he has come to take actual pleasure in trampling upon the feelings of others. And if he has thus failed in the practice of routine virtues, do you expect that he will take readily to higher ones? He will persist in his ways, and though outwardly he may agree with you, inwardly he will not repent. How then will you make him mend his ways?"

"Why, then," (replied Yen Huei) "I can be inwardly straight, and outwardly yielding, and I shall substantiate what I say by appeals to antiquity. He who is inwardly straight is a servant of God. And he who is a servant of God knows that the Son of Heaven and himself are equally the children of God.[21] Shall then such a one trouble whether his words are approved or disapproved by man? Such a person is commonly regarded as an (innocent) child. This is to be a servant of God. He who is outwardly yielding is a servant of man. He bows, he kneels, he folds his hands—such is the ceremonial of a minister. What all men do, shall I not do also? What all men do, none will blame me for doing. This is to be a servant of man. He who substantiates his words by appeals to antiquity is a servant of the Sages of old. Although I utter the words of warning and take him to task, it is the Sages of old who speak, and not I. Thus I shall not receive the blame for my uprightness. This is to be the servant of the Sages of old. Will this do?"

"No! How can it?" replied Confucius. "Your plans are too many. You are firm, but lacking in prudence. However, you are only narrow-minded, but you will not get into trouble; but that is all. You will still be far from influencing him because your own opinions are still too rigid."

"Then," said Yen Huei, "I can go no further. I venture to ask for a method."

Confucius said, "Keep fast, and I shall tell you. Will it be easy for you when you still have a narrow mind? He who treats things as easy will not be approved by the bright heaven."

"My family is poor," replied Yen Huei, "and for many months we have tasted neither wine nor flesh. Is that not fasting?"

"That is a fast according to the religious observances," answered Confucius, "but not the fasting of the heart."

"And may I ask," said Yen Huei, "in what consists the fasting of the heart?"

"Concentrate your will. Hear not with your ears, but with your mind; not with your mind, but with your spirit. Let your hearing stop with the ears, and let your mind stop with its images. Let your spirit, however, be like a blank, passively responsive to externals. In such open recep-

[21] Lit. "regarded as sons (i.e., fathered) by Heaven."

tivity only can Tao abide. And that open receptivity is the fasting of the heart."

"Then," said Yen Huei, "the reason I could not use this method was because of consciousness of a self. If I could apply this method, the assumption of a self would have gone. Is this what you mean by the receptive state?"

"Exactly so," replied the Master. "Let me tell you. Enter this man's service, but without idea of working for fame. Talk when he is in a mood to listen, and stop when he is not. Do without any sort of labels or self-advertisements. Keep to the One and let things take their natural course. Then you may have some chance of success. It is easy to stop walking: the trouble is to walk without touching the ground. As an agent of man, it is easy to use artificial devices; but not as an agent of God. You have heard of winged creatures flying. You have never heard of flying without wings. You have heard of men being wise with knowledge. You have never heard of men wise without knowledge.

"Look at that emptiness. There is brightness in an empty room. Good luck dwells in repose. If there is not (inner) repose, your mind will be galloping about though you are sitting still. Let your ears and eyes communicate within but shut out all knowledge from the mind. Then the spirits will come to dwell therein, not to mention man. This is the method for the transformation (influencing) of all Creation. It was the key to the influence of Yü and Shun, and the secret of the success of Fu Hsi and Chi Chü. How much more should the common man follow the same rule?"

(*Two sections are omitted here—Ed.*)

A certain carpenter Shih was travelling to the Ch'i State. On reaching Shady Circle, he saw a sacred *li* tree in the temple to the God of Earth. It was so large that its shade could cover a herd of several thousand cattle. It was a hundred spans in girth, towering up eighty feet over the hilltop, before it branched out. A dozen boats could be cut out of it. Crowds stood gazing at it, but the carpenter took no notice, and went on his way without even casting a look behind. His apprentice however took a good look at it, and when he caught up with his master, said, "Ever since I have handled an adze in your service, I have never seen such a splendid piece of timber. How was it that you, Master, did not care to stop and look at it?"

"Forget about it. It's not worth talking about," replied his master. "It's good for nothing. Made into a boat, it would sink; into a coffin, it would rot; into furniture, it would break easily; into a door, it would sweat; into a pillar, it would be worm-eaten. It is wood of no quality, and of no use. That is why it has attained its present age."

When the carpenter reached home, he dreamt that the spirit of the tree appeared to him in his sleep and spoke to him as follows: "What is it you intend to compare me with? Is it with fine-grained wood? Look at the cherry-apple, the pear, the orange, the pumelo, and other fruit-bearers? As soon as their fruit ripens they are stripped and treated with indignity. The great boughs are snapped off, the small ones scattered abroad. Thus do these trees by their own value injure their own lives. They cannot fulfill their alloted span of years, but perish prematurely because they destroy themselves for the (admiration of) the world. Thus it is with all things. Moreover, I tried for a long period to be useless. Many times I was in danger of being cut down, but at length I have succeeded, and so have become exceedingly useful to myself. Had I indeed been of use, I should not be able to grow to this height. Moreover, you and I are both created things. Have done then with this criticism of each other. Is a good-for-nothing fellow in imminent danger of death a fit person to talk of a good-for-nothing tree?"

When the carpenter Shih awaked and told his dream, his apprentice said, "If the tree aimed at uselessness, how was it that it became a sacred tree?"

"Hush!" replied his master. "Keep quiet. It merely took refuge in the temple to escape from the abuse of those who do not appreciate it. Had it not become sacred, how many would have wanted to cut it down! Moreover, the means it adopts for safety is different from that of others, and to criticize it by ordinary standards would be far wide of the mark."

Tsech'i of Nan-po was travelling on the hill of Shang when he saw a large tree which astonished him very much. A thousand chariot teams of four horses could find shelter under its shade.

"What tree is this?" cried Tsech'i. "Surely it must be unusually fine timber." Then looking up, he saw that its branches were too crooked for rafters; and looking down he saw that the trunk's twisting loose grain made it valueless for coffins. He tasted a leaf, but it took the skin off his lips; and its odour was so strong that it would make a man intoxicated for three days together.

"Ah!" said Tsech'i, "this tree is really good for nothing, and that is how it has attained this size. A spiritual man might well follow its example of uselessness."

In the State of Sung there is a land belonging to the Chings, where thrive the catalpa, the cedar, and the mulberry. Such as are of one span or so in girth are cut down for monkey cages. Those of two or three spans are cut down for the beams of fine houses. Those of seven or eight spans are cut down for the solid (unjointed) sides of rich men's coffins. Thus they do not fulfil their alloted span of years, but perish young beneath the axe. Such is the misfortune which overtakes worth.

For the sacrifices to the River God, neither bulls with white foreheads, nor pigs with high snouts, nor men suffering from piles, can be used. This is known to all the soothsayers, for these are regarded as inauspicious. The wise, however, would regard them as extremely auspicious (to themselves).

There was a hunchback named Su. His jaws touched his navel. His shoulders were higher than his head. His neck bone stuck out toward the sky. His viscera were turned upside down. His buttocks were where his ribs should have been. By tailoring, or washing, he was easily able to earn his living. By sifting rice he could make enough to support a family of ten. When orders came down for a conscription, the hunchback walked about unconcerned among the crowd. And similarly, in government conscription for public works, his deformity saved him from being called. On the other hand, when it came to government donations of grain for the disabled, the hunchback received as much as three *chung,* and of firewood, ten faggots. And if physical deformity was thus enough to preserve his body until the end of his days, how much more should moral and mental deformity avail!

When Confucius was in the Ch'u State, the eccentric Chieh Yü passed his door, saying, "O phœnix! O phœnix! How hast thy virtue fallen! Wait not for the coming years, nor hanker back to the past. When the right principles prevail on earth, prophets will fulfill their mission. When the right principles prevail not, they will but preserve themselves. At the present day, they are but trying to keep out of jail! The good fortunes of this world are light as feathers, yet none estimates them at their true value. The misfortunes of this life are weighty as the earth, yet none knows how to keep out of their reach. No more, no more, show off your virtue. Beware, beware, move cautiously on! O brambles, O brambles, wound not my steps! I pick my way about, hurt not my feet!"[22]

The mountain trees invite their own cutting down; lamp oil invites its own burning up. Cinnamon bark can be eaten; therefore the tree is cut down. Lacquer can be used, therefore the tree is scraped. All men know the utility of useful things; but they do not know the utility of futility.

DEFORMITIES, OR EVIDENCES OF A FULL CHARACTER[23]

IN THE STATE OF LU there was a man, named Wang T'ai, who had had one of his legs cut off. His disciples were as numerous as those of Confucius.

Ch'ang Chi asked Confucius, saying, "This Wang T'ai has been mutilated, yet he has as many followers in the Lu State as you. He neither stands up to preach nor sits down to give discourse; yet those who go to him empty, depart full. Is he the kind of person who can teach without words and influence people's minds without material means? What manner of man is this?"

"He is a sage," replied Confucius, "I wanted to go to him, but am merely behind the others. Even I will go and make him my teacher,—why not those who are lesser than I? And I will lead, not only the State of Lu, but the whole world to follow him."

"The man has been mutilated," said Ch'ang Chi, "and yet people call him 'Master.' He must be very different from the ordinary men. If so, how does he train his mind?"

"Life and Death are indeed changes of great moment," answered Confucius, "but they cannot affect his mind. Heaven and earth may collapse, but his mind will remain. Being indeed without flaw, it will not share the fate of all things. It can control the transformation of things, while preserving its source intact."

"How so?" asked Ch'ang Chi.

"From the point of view of differentiation of things," replied Confucius, "we distinguish between the liver and the gall, between the Ch'u State and the Yüeh State. From the point of view of their sameness, all things are One. He who regards things in this light does not even trouble about what reaches him through the senses of hearing and sight,

[22] The first part of this song is found in the *Analects*.

[23] This chapter deals entirely with deformities—a literary device for emphasizing the contrast of the inner and the outer man.

but lets his mind wander in the moral harmony of things. He beholds the unity in things, and does not notice the loss of particular objects. And thus the loss of his leg is to him as would be the loss of so much dirt."

"But he cultivates only himself," said Ch'ang Chi. "He uses his knowledge to perfect his mind, and develops his mind into the Absolute Mind. But how is it that people flock around him?"

"A man," replied Confucius, "does not seek to see himself in running water, but in still water. For only what is itself still can instil stillness into others. The grace of earth has reached only the pines and cedars; winter and summer alike, they are green. The grace of God has reached to Yao and to Shun, who alone attained rectitude. Happily he was able to rectify himself and thus become the means through which all were rectified. For the possession of one's original (nature) is evidenced in true courage. A man will, single-handed, brave a whole army. And if such a result can be achieved by one in search of fame through self-control, how much greater courage can be shown by one who extends his sway over heaven and earth and gives shelter to all things, who, lodging temporarily within the confines of a body with contempt for the superficialities of sight and sound, brings his knowledge to level all knowledge and whose mind never dies! Besides, he (Wang T'ai) is only awaiting his appointed hour to go up to Heaven. Men indeed flock to him of their own accord. How can he take seriously the affairs of this world?"

Shent'u Chia had only one leg. He studied under Pohun Wujen ("Muddle-Head No-Such-Person") together with Tsech'an[24] of the Cheng State. The latter said to him, "When I leave first, do you remain behind. When you leave first, I will remain behind."

Next day, when they were again together sitting on the same mat in the lecture-room, Tsech'an said, "When I leave first, do you remain behind. Or if you leave first, I will remain behind. I am now about to go. Will you remain or not? I notice you show no respect to a high personage. Perhaps you think yourself my equal?"

"In the house of the Master," replied Shent'u Chia, "there is already a high personage (the Master). Perhaps you think that you are the high personage and therefore should take precedence over the rest. Now I have heard that if a mirror is perfectly bright, dust will not collect on it, and that if it does, the mirror is no longer bright. He who associates for

[24] A well-known historical person, a model minister referred to in the *Analects*.

long with the wise should be without fault. Now you have been seeking the greater things at the feet of our Master, yet you can utter words like these. Don't you think you are making a mistake?"

"You are already mutilated like this," retorted Tsech'an, "yet you are still seeking to compete in virtue with Yao. To look at you, I should say you had enough to do to reflect on your past misdeeds!"

"Those who cover up their sins," said Shent'u Chia, "so as not to lose their legs, are many in number. Those who forget to cover up their misdemeanors and so lose their legs (through punishment) are few. But only the virtuous man can recognize the inevitable and remain unmoved. People who walked in front of the bull's-eye when Hou Yi (the famous archer) was shooting, would be hit. Some who were not hit were just lucky. There are many people with sound legs who laugh at me for not having them. This used to make me angry. But since I came to study under our Master, I have stopped worrying about it. Perhaps our Master has so far succeeded in washing (purifying) me with his goodness. At any rate, I have been with him nineteen years without being aware of my deformity. Now you and I are roaming in the realm of the spiritual, and you are judging me in the realm of the physical.[25] Are you not committing a mistake?"

At this Tsech'an began to fidget and his countenance changed, and he bade Shent'u Chia to speak no more.

There was a man of the Lu State who had been mutilated, by the name of Shushan No-toes. He came walking on his heels to see Confucius; but Confucius said, "You were careless, and so brought this misfortune upon yourself. What is the use of coming to me now?" "It was because I was inexperienced and careless with my body that I hurt my feet," replied No-toes. "Now I have come with something more precious than feet, and it is that which I am seeking to preserve. There is no man, but Heaven shelters him; and there is no man, but the Earth supports him. I thought that you, Master, would be like Heaven and Earth. I little expected to hear these words from you."

"Pardon my stupidity," said Confucius. "Why not come in? I shall discuss with you what I have learned." But No-toes left.

When No-toes had left, Confucius said to his disciples, "Take a good lesson. No-toes is one-legged, yet he is seeking to learn in order to make

[25] Lit. "The outside of frame and bones."

atonement for his previous misdeeds. How much more should those who have no misdeeds for which to atone?"

No-toes went off to see Lao Tan (Laotse) and said, "Is Confucius a Perfect One or is he not quite? How is it that he is so anxious to learn from you? He is seeking to earn a reputation by his abstruse and strange learning, which is regarded by the Perfect One as mere fetters."

"Why do you not make him regard life and death, and possibility and impossibility as alternations of one and the same principle," answered Lao Tan, "and so release him from these fetters?"

"It is God who has thus punished him," replied No-toes. "How could he be released?"

Duke Ai of the Lu State said to Confucius, "In the Wei State there is an ugly person, named Ait'ai (Ugly) T'o. The men who have lived with him cannot stop thinking about him. Women who have seen him, would say to their parents, 'Rather than be another man's wife, I would be this man's concubine.' There are scores of such women. He never tries to lead others, but only follows them. He wields no power of a ruler by which he may protect men's lives. He has no hoarded wealth by which to gratify their bellies, and is besides frightfully loathsome. He follows but does not lead, and his name is not known outside his own State. Yet men and women alike all seek his company. So there must be something in him that is different from other people. I sent for him, and saw that he was indeed frightfully ugly. Yet we had not been many months together before I began to see there was something in this man. A year had not passed before I began to trust him. As my State wanted a Prime Minister, I offered him the post. He looked sullenly before he replied and appeared as if he would much rather have declined. Perhaps he did not think me good enough for him! At any rate, I gave the post to him; but in a very short time he left me and went away. I grieved for him as for a lost friend, as though there were none left with whom I could enjoy having my kingdom. What manner of man is this?"

"When I was on a mission to the Ch'u State," replied Confucius, "I saw a litter of young pigs sucking their dead mother. After a while they looked at her, and then all left the body and went off. For their mother did not look at them any more, nor did she seem any more to have been of their kind. What they loved was their mother; not the body which contained her, but that which made the body what it was. When a man is killed in battle, his coffin is not covered with a square canopy. A man whose leg has been cut off does not value a present of shoes. In each case, the original purpose of such things is gone. The concubines of the Son of Heaven do not cut their nails or pierce their ears. Those (servants) who are married have to live outside (the palace) and cannot be employed again. Such is the importance attached to preserving the body whole. How much more valued is one who has preserved his virtue whole?

"Now Ugly T'o has said nothing and is already trusted. He has achieved nothing and is sought after, and is offered the government of a country with the only fear that he might decline. Indeed he must be the one whose talents are perfect and whose virtue is without outward form!"

"What do you mean by his talents being perfect?" asked the Duke.

"Life and Death," replied Confucius, "possession and loss, success and failure, poverty and wealth, virtue and vice, good and evil report, hunger and thirst, heat and cold—these are changes of things in the natural course of events. Day and night they follow upon one another, and no man can say where they spring from. Therefore they must not be allowed to disturb the natural harmony, nor enter into the soul's domain. One should live so that one is at ease and in harmony with the world, without loss of happiness, and by day and by night, share the (peace of) spring with the created things. Thus continuously one creates the seasons in one's own breast. Such a person may be said to have perfect talents."

"And what is virtue without outward form?"

"When standing still," said Confucius, "the water is in the most perfect state of repose. Let that be your model. It remains quietly within, and is not agitated without. It is from the cultivation of such harmony that virtue results. And if virtue takes no outward form, man will not be able to keep aloof from it."

Some days afterwards Duke Ai told Mintse saying, "When first I took over the reins of government, I thought that in guiding the people and caring for their lives, I had done all my duty as a ruler. But now that I have heard the words of a perfect man, I fear that I have not achieved it, but am foolishly squandering my bodily energy and bringing ruin to my country. Confucius and I are not prince and minister, but friends in spirit."

Hunchback-Deformed-No-Lips spoke with Duke Ling of Wei and the Duke took a fancy to him. As for the well-formed men, he thought their necks were too scraggy. Big-Jar-Goitre spoke with Duke Huan of Ch'i, and the Duke took a fancy to him. As for the well-formed men, he thought their necks were too scraggy.

Thus it is that when virtue excels, the outward form is forgotten. But mankind forgets not that which is to be forgotten, forgetting that which is not to be forgotten. This is forgetfulness indeed! And thus the Sage sets his spirit free, while knowledge is regarded as extraneous growths; agreements are for cementing relationships, goods are only for social dealings, and the handicrafts are only for serving commerce. For the Sage does not contrive, and therefore has no use for knowledge; he does not cut up the world, and therefore requires no cementing of relationships; he has no loss, and therefore has no need to acquire; he sells nothing, and therefore has no use for commerce. These four qualifications are bestowed upon him by God, that is to say, he is fed by God. And he who is thus fed by God has little need to be fed by man. He wears the human form without human passions. Because he wears the human form he associates with men. Because he has not human passions the questions of right and wrong do not touch him. Infinitesimal indeed is that which belongs to the human; infinitely great is that which is completed in God.

Hueitse said to Chuangtse, "Do men indeed originally have no passions?"

"Certainly," replied Chuangtse.

"But if a man has no passions," argued Hueitse, "what is it that makes him a man?"

"Tao," replied Chuangtse, "gives him his expressions, and God gives him his form. How should he not be a man?"

"If then he is a man," said Hueitse, "how can he be without passions?"

"Right and wrong (approval and disapproval)," answered Chuangtse, "are what I mean by passions. By a man without passions I mean one who does not permit likes and dislikes to disturb his internal economy, but rather falls in line with nature and does not try to improve upon (the materials of) living."

"But how is a man to live this bodily life," asked Hueitse, "if he does not try to improve upon (the materials of) his living?"

"Tao gives him his expression," said Chuangtse, "and God gives him his form. He should not permit likes and dislikes to disturb his internal economy. But now you are devoting your intelligence to externals, and wearing out your vital spirit. Lean against a tree and sing; or sit against a table and sleep! God has made you a shapely sight, yet your only thought is the *hard and white*." [26]

THE GREAT SUPREME

He who knows what is of God and who knows what is of Man has reached indeed the height (of wisdom). One who knows what is of God patterns his living after God. One who knows what is of Man may still use his knowledge of the known to develop his knowledge of the unknown, living till the end of his days and not perishing young. This is the fullness of knowledge.

Herein, however, there is a flaw. Correct knowledge is dependent on objects, but the objects of knowledge are relative and uncertain (changing). How can one know that the natural is not really of man, and what is of man is not really natural? We must, moreover, have true men before we can have true knowledge.

But what is a true man? The true men of old did not override the weak, did not attain their ends by brute strength, and did not gather around them counsellors. Thus, failing they had no cause for regret; succeeding, no cause for self-satisfaction. And thus they could scale heights without trembling, enter water without becoming wet, and go through fire without feeling hot. That is the kind of knowledge which reaches to the depths of Tao. The true men of old slept without dreams, and waked up without worries. They ate with indifference to flavor, and drew deep breaths. For true men draw breath from their heels; the vulgar only from their throats. Out of the crooked, words are retched up like vomit. When man's attachments are deep, their divine endowments are shallow.

The true men of old did not know what it was to love life or to hate death. They did not rejoice in birth, nor strive to put off dissolution. Unconcerned they came and unconcerned they went. That was all. They did not forget whence it was they had sprung, neither did they seek to inquire their return thither. Cheerfully they accepted life, waiting patiently for their restoration (the end). This is what is called not to

[26] Hueitse often discusses the nature of attributes, like the "hardness" and "whiteness" of objects.

lead the heart astray from Tao, and not to supplement the natural by human means. Such a one may be called a true man.

Such men are free in mind and calm in demeanour, with high foreheads. Sometimes disconsolate like autumn, and sometimes warm like spring, their joys and sorrows are in direct touch with the four seasons, in harmony with all creation, and none know the limit thereof. And so it is that when the Sage wages war, he can destroy a kingdom and yet not lose the affection of the people; he spreads blessing upon all things, but it is not due to his (conscious) love of fellowmen. Therefore he who delights in understanding the material world is not a Sage. He who has personal attachments is not humane. He who calculates the time of his actions is not wise. He who does not know the interaction of benefit and harm is not a superior man. He who pursues fame at the risk of losing his self is not a scholar. He who loses his life and is not true to himself can never be a master of man. Thus Hu Puhsieh, Wu Kuang, Po Yi, Shu Ch'i, Chi Tse, Hsü Yü, Chi T'o, and Shent'u Ti, were the servants of rulers, and did the behests of others, not their own.[27]

The true men of old appeared of towering stature and yet could not topple down. They behaved as though wanting in themselves, but without looking up to others. Naturally independent of mind, they were not severe. Living in unconstrained freedom, yet they did not try to show off. They appeared to smile as if pleased, and to move only in natural response to surroundings. Their serenity flowed from the store of goodness within. In social relationships, they kept to their inner character. Broad-minded, they appeared great; towering, they seemed beyond control. Continuously abiding, they seemed like doors kept shut; absent-minded, they seemed to forget speech. They saw in penal laws an outward form; in social ceremonies, certain means; in knowledge, tools of expediency; in morality, a guide. It was for this reason that for them penal laws meant a merciful administration; social ceremonies, a means to get along with the world; knowledge a help for doing what they could not avoid; and morality, a guide that they might walk along with others to reach a hill.[28] And all men really thought that they were at pains to make their lives correct.

For what they cared for was One and what they did not care for was

[27] All of these historical and semi-historical persons were good men who lost their lives, by drowning or starving themselves, or pretending insanity, in protest against a wicked world, or just to avoid being called into office.
[28] General attitude of fluidity towards life.

ONE also. That which they regarded as ONE was ONE, and that which they did not regard as ONE was ONE likewise. In that which was ONE, they were of God; in that which was not ONE, they were of man. And so between the human and the divine no conflict ensued. This was to be a true man.

Life and Death are a part of Destiny. Their sequence, like day and night, is of God, beyond the interference of man. These all lie in the inevitable nature of things. He simply looks upon God as his father; if he loves him with what is born of the body, shall he not love him also with that which is greater than the body? A man looks upon a ruler of men as one superior to himself; if he is willing to sacrifice his body (for his ruler), shall he not then offer his pure (spirit) also?

When the pond dries up and the fishes are left upon the dry ground, rather than leave them to moisten each other with their damp and spittle, it would be far better to let them forget themselves in their native rivers and lakes. And it would be better than praising Yao and blaming Chieh to forget both (the good and bad) and lose oneself in Tao.

The Great (universe) gives me this form, this toil in manhood, this repose in old age, this rest in death. And surely that which is such a kind arbiter of my life is the best arbiter of my death.

A boat may be hidden in a creek, or concealed in a bog, which is generally considered safe. But at midnight a strong man may come and carry it away on his back. Those dull of understanding do not perceive that however you conceal small things in larger ones, there will always be a chance of losing them. But if you entrust that which belongs to the universe to the whole universe, from it there will be no escape. For this is the great law of things.

To have been cast in this human form is to us already a source of joy. How much greater joy beyond our conception to know that that which is now in human form may undergo countless transitions, with only the infinite to look forward to? Therefore it is that the Sage rejoices in that which can never be lost, but endures always. For if we emulate those who can accept graciously long age or short life and the vicissitudes of events, how much more that which informs all creation on which all changing phenomena depend?

For Tao has its inner reality and its evidences. It is devoid of action and of form. It may be transmitted, but cannot be received. It may be obtained, but cannot be seen. It is based in itself, rooted in itself. Before heaven and earth were, Tao existed by itself from all time. It gave the spirits and rulers their spiritual powers, and gave Heaven and Earth their birth. To Tao, the zenith is not high, nor the nadir low; no point in time is long ago, nor by the lapse of ages has it grown old.

Hsi Wei obtained Tao, and so set the universe in order. Fu Hsi[29] obtained it, and was able to steal the secrets of eternal principles. The Great Bear obtained it, and has never erred from its course. The sun and moon obtained it, and have never ceased to revolve. K'an P'i[30] obtained it, and made his abode in the K'unlun mountains. P'ing I[31] obtained it, and rules over the streams. Chien Wu[32] obtained it, and dwells on Mount T'ai. The Yellow Emperor[33] obtained it, and soared upon the clouds to heaven. Chuan Hsü[34] obtained it, and dwells in the Dark Palace. Yü Ch'iang[35] obtained it, and established himself at the North Pole. The Western (Fairy) Queen Mother obtained it, and settled at Shao Kuang, since when and until when, no one knows. P'eng Tsu obtained it, and lived from the time of Shun until the time of the Five Princes. Fu Yüeh obtained it, and as the Minister of Wu Ting[36] extended his rule to the whole empire. And now, charioted upon the Tungwei (one constellation) and drawn by the Chiwei (another constellation), he has taken his station among the stars of heaven.

Nanpo Tsek'uei said to Nü Yü (or Female Yü), "You are of a high age, and yet you have a child's complexion. How is this?"

Nü Yü replied, "I have learnt Tao."

"Could I get Tao by studying it?" asked the other.

"No! How can you?" said Nü Yü. "You are not the type of person. There was Puliang I. He had all the mental talents of a sage, but not Tao of the sage. Now I had Tao, though not those talents. But do you think I was able to teach him to become indeed a sage? Had it been so, then to teach Tao to one who has a sage's talents would be an easy matter. It was not so, for I had to wait patiently to reveal it to him. In three days, he could transcend this mundane world. Again I waited for seven days

[29] Mythical emperor (B.C. 2852) said to have discovered the principles of mutations of *Yin* and *Yang*.

[30] With a man's head, but a beast's body.

[31] A river spirit.

[32] A mountain God.

[33] A semi-mythical ruler, who ruled in B.C. 2698-2597.

[34] A semi-mythical ruler, who ruled in B.C. 2514-2437, shortly before Emperor Yao.

[35] A water god with a human face and a bird's body.

[36] A monarch of the Shang Dynasty, B.C. 1324-1266.

more, then he could transcend all material existence. After he could transcend all material existence, I waited for another nine days, after which he could transcend all life. After he could transcend all life, then he had the clear vision of the morning, and after that, was able to see the Solitary (One). After seeing the Solitary, he could abolish the distinctions of past and present. After abolishing the past and present, he was able to enter there where life and death are no more, where killing does not take away life, nor does giving birth add to it. He was ever in accord with the exigencies of his environment, accepting all and welcoming all, regarding everything as destroyed and everything as in completion. This is to be 'secure amidst confusion,' reaching security through chaos."

"Where did you learn this from?" asked Nanpo Tsek'uei.

"I learned it from the Son of Ink," replied Nü Yü, "and the Son of Ink learned it from the Grandson of Learning, the Grandson of Learning from Understanding, and Understanding from Insight, Insight learned it from Practice, Practice from Folk Song, and Folk Song from Silence, Silence from the Void, and the Void learned it from the Seeming Beginning."

Four men: Tsesze, Tseyü, Tseli, and Tselai, were conversing together, saying, "Whoever can make Not-being the head, Life the backbone, and Death the tail, and whoever realizes that death and life and being and non-being are of one body, that man shall be admitted to friendship with us." The four looked at each other and smiled, and completely understanding one another, became friends accordingly.

By-and-by, Tseyü fell ill, and Tsesze went to see him. "Verily the Creator is great!" said the sick man. "See how He has doubled me up." His back was so hunched that his viscera were at the top of his body. His cheeks were level with his navel, and his shoulders were higher than his neck. His neck bone pointed up towards the sky. The whole economy of his organism was deranged, but his mind was calm as ever. He dragged himself to a well, and said, "Alas, that God should have doubled me up like this!"

"Do you dislike it?" asked Tsesze.

"No, why should I?" replied Tseyü. "If my left arm should become a cock, I should be able to herald the dawn with it. If my right arm should become a sling, I should be able to shoot down a bird to broil with it. If my buttocks should become wheels, and my spirit become a horse, I should be able to ride in it—what need would I have of a chariot? I obtained life because it was my time, and I am now parting with it in accordance with Tao. Content with the coming of things in their time and living in accord with Tao, joy and sorrow touch me not. This is, according to the ancients, to be freed from bondage. Those who cannot be freed from bondage are so because they are bound by the trammels of material existence. But man has ever given away before God; why, then, should I dislike it?"

By-and-by, Tselai fell ill, and lay gasping for breath, while his family stood weeping around. Tseli went to see him, and cried to the wife and children: "Go away! You are impeding his dissolution." Then, leaning against the door, he said, "Verily, God is great! I wonder what He will make of you now, and whither He will send you. Do you think he will make you into a rat's liver or into an insect leg?"

"A son," answered Tselai, "must go whithersoever his parents bid him, East, West, North, or South. *Yin* and *Yang* are no other than a man's parents. If *Yin* and *Yang* bid me die quickly, and I demur, then the fault is mine, not theirs. The Great (universe) gives me this form, this toil in manhood, this repose in old age, this rest in death. Surely that which is such a kind arbiter of my life is the best arbiter of my death.

"Suppose that the boiling metal in a smelting-pot were to bubble up and say, 'Make of me a Moyeh!' [37] I think the master caster would reject that metal as uncanny. And if simply because I am cast into a human form, I were to say, 'Only a man! only a man!' I think the Creator too would reject me as uncanny. If I regard the universe as the smelting pot, and the Creator as the Master Caster, how should I worry wherever I am sent?" Then he sunk into a peaceful sleep and waked up very much alive.

Tsesang Hu, Mengtse Fan, and Tsech'in Chang, were conversing together, saying, "Who can live together as if they did not live together? Who can help each other as if they did not help each other? Who can mount to heaven, and roaming through the clouds, leap about to the Ultimate Infinite, oblivious of existence, for ever and ever without end?" The three looked at each other and smiled with a perfect understanding and became friends accordingly.

Shortly afterwards, Tsesang Hu died, whereupon Confucius sent Tsekung to attend the mourning. But Tsekung found that one of his

[37] A famous sword.

friends was arranging the cocoon sheets and the other was playing string instruments and (both were) singing together as follows:

> "Oh! come back to us, Sang Hu,
> Oh! come back to us, Sang Hu,
> Thou hast already returned to thy true state,
> While we still remain here as men! Oh!"

Tsekung hurried in and said, "How can you sing in the presence of a corpse? Is this good manners?"

The two men looked at each other and laughed, saying, "What should this man know about the meaning of good manners indeed?" Tsekung went back and told Confucius, asking him, "What manner of men are these? Their object is to cultivate nothingness and that which lies beyond their corporeal frames. They can sit near a corpse and sing, unmoved. There is no name for such persons. What manner of men are they?"

"These men," replied Confucius, "play about beyond the material things; I play about within them. Consequently, our paths do not meet, and I was stupid to have sent you to mourn. They consider themselves as companions of the Creator, and play about within the One Spirit of the universe. They look upon life as a huge goiter or excrescence, and upon death as the breaking of a tumor. How could such people be concerned about the coming of life and death or their sequence? They borrow their forms from the different elements, and take temporary abode in the common forms, unconscious of their internal organs and oblivious of their senses of hearing and vision. They go through life backwards and forwards as in a circle without beginning or end, strolling forgetfully beyond the dust and dirt of mortality, and playing about with the affairs of inaction. How should such men bustle about the conventionalities of this world, for the people to look at?"

"But if such is the case," said Tsekung, "which world (the corporeal or the spiritual) would you follow?"

"I am one condemned by God," replied Confucius. "Nevertheless, I will share with you (what I know)."

"May I ask what is your method?" asked Tsekung.

"Fishes live their full life in water. Men live their full life in Tao," replied Confucius. "Those that live their full life in water thrive in ponds. Those that live their full life in Tao achieve realization of their nature in inaction. Hence the saying 'Fish lose themselves (are happy) in water; man loses himself (is happy) in Tao.' "

"May I ask," said Tsekung, "about (those) strange people?"

"(Those) strange people," replied Confucius, "are strange in the eyes of man, but normal in the eyes of God. Hence the saying that the meanest thing in heaven would be the best on earth; and the best on earth, the meanest in heaven."

Yen Huei said to Chungni[38] (Confucius), "When Mengsun Ts'ai's mother died, he wept, but without snivelling; his heart was not grieved; he wore mourning but without sorrow. Yet although wanting in these three points, he is considered the best mourner in the State of Lu. Can there be really people with a hollow reputation? I am astonished."

"Mr. Mengsun," said Chungni, "has really mastered (the Tao). He has gone beyond the wise ones. There are still certain things he cannot quite give up, but he has already given up some things. Mr. Mengsun knows not whence we come in life nor whither we go in death. He knows not which to put first and which to put last. He is ready to be transformed into other things without caring into what he may be transformed—that is all. How could that which is changing say that it will not change, and how could that which regards itself as permanent realize that it is changing already? Even you and I are perhaps dreamers who have not yet awakened. Moreover, he knows his form is subject to change, but his mind remains the same. He believes not in real death, but regards it as moving into a new house. He weeps only when he sees others weep, as it comes to him naturally.

"Besides, we all talk of 'me.' How do you know what is this 'me' that we speak of? You dream you are a bird, and soar to heaven, or dream you are a fish, and dive into the ocean's depths. And you cannot tell whether the man now speaking is awake or in a dream.

"A man feels a pleasurable sensation before he smiles, and smiles before he thinks how he ought to smile. Resign yourself to the sequence of things, forgetting the changes of life, and you shall enter into the pure, the divine, the One."

Yi-erh-tse went to see Hsü Yu. The latter asked him, saying, "What have you learned from Yao?"

"He bade me," replied the former, "practice charity and do my duty, and distinguish clearly between right and wrong."

[38] Personal name of Confucius.

"Then what do you want here?" said Hsü Yu. "If Yao has already branded you with charity of heart and duty, and cut off your nose with right and wrong, what are you doing here in this free-and-easy, unfettered, take-what-comes neighborhood?"

"Nevertheless," replied Yi-erh-tse. "I should like to loiter on its confines."

"If a man has lost his eyes," retorted Hsü Yu, "it is impossible for him to join in the appreciation of beauty of face and complexion or to tell a blue sacrificial robe from a yellow one."

"Wu Chuang's (No-Decorum's) disregard of her beauty," answered Yi-erh-tse, "Chü Liang's disregard of his strength, the Yellow Emperor's abandonment of his wisdom,—all these came from a process of purging and purification. And how do you know but that the Creator would rid me of my brandings, and give me a new nose, and make me fit to become a disciple of yourself?"

"Ah!" replied Hsü Yu, "that cannot be known. But I will give you an outline. Ah! my Master, my Master! He trims down all created things, and does not account it justice. He causes all created things to thrive and does not account it kindness. Dating back further than the remotest antiquity, He does not account himself old. Covering heaven, supporting earth, and fashioning the various forms of things, He does not account himself skilled. It is He whom you should seek."

Yen Huei spoke to Chungni (Confucius), "I am getting on."

"How so?" asked the latter.

"I have got rid of charity and duty," replied the former.

"Very good," replied Chungni, "but not quite perfect."

Another day, Yen Huei met Chungni and said, "I am getting on."

"How so?"

"I have got rid of ceremonies and music," answered Yen Huei.

"Very good," said Chungni, "but not quite perfect."

Another day, Yen Huei again met Chungni and said, "I am getting on."

"How so?"

"I can forget myself while sitting," replied Yen Huei.

"What do you mean by that?" said Chungni, changing his countenance.

"I have freed myself from my body," answered Yen Huei. "I have discarded my reasoning powers. And by thus getting rid of my body and mind, I have become One with the Infinite. This is what I mean by forgetting myself while sitting."

"If you have become One," said Chungni, "there can be no room for bias. If you have lost yourself, there can no more hindrance. Perhaps you are really a wise one. I trust to be allowed to follow in your steps."

Tseyü and Tsesang were friends. Once when it had rained for ten days, Tseyü said, "Tsesang is probably ill." So he packed up some food and went to see him. Arriving at the door, he heard something between singing and weeping, accompanied with the sound of a string instrument, as follows: "O Father! O mother! Is this due to God? Is this due to man?" It was as if his voice was broken and his words faltered.

Whereupon Tseyü went in and asked, "Why are you singing in such manner?" "I was trying to think who could have brought me to this extreme," replied Tsesang, "but I could not guess it. My father and mother would hardly wish me to be poor. Heaven covers all equally. Earth supports all equally. How can they make me in particular so poor? I was seeking to find out who was responsible for this, but without success. Surely then I am brought to this extreme by *Destiny*."

JOINED TOES

JOINED TOES AND EXTRA FINGERS seem to come from nature, yet, functionally speaking they are superfluous. Goiters and tumours seem to come from the body, yet in their nature, they are superfluous. And (similarly), to have many extraneous doctrines of charity and duty and regard them in practice as parts of a man's natural sentiments is not the true way of Tao. For just as joined toes are but useless lumps of flesh, and extra fingers but useless growths, so are the many artificial developments of the natural sentiments of men and the extravagances of charitable and dutiful conduct but so many superfluous uses of intelligence.

People with superfluous keenness of vision put into confusion the five colours, lose themselves in the forms and designs, and in the distinctions of greens and yellows for sacrificial robes. Is this not so? Of such was Li Chu (the clear-sighted). People with superfluous keenness of hearing put into confusion the five notes, exaggerate the tonic differences of the six pitch-pipes, and the various *timbres* of metal, stone, silk, and bamboo, of the *Huang-chung,* and the *Ta-lü.*[39] Is this not so? Of such was Shih K'uang (the music master). People who abnormally develop charity, exalt virtue and suppress nature in order to gain a reputation, make the world noisy with their discussions and cause it to follow impractical doctrines. Is this not so? Of such were Tseng and Shih.[40] People who commit excess in arguments, like piling up bricks and making knots, analyzing and inquiring into the distinctions of hard and white, identities and differences, wear themselves out over mere vain, useless terms. Is this not so? Of such were Yang and Mo.[41] All these are superfluous and devious growths of knowledge and are not the correct guide for the world.

He who would be the ultimate guide never loses sight of the inner nature of life. Therefore with him, the united is not like joined toes, the separated is not like extra fingers, what is long is not considered as excess, and what is short is not regarded as wanting. For duck's legs, though short, cannot be lengthened without dismay to the duck, and a crane's legs, though long, cannot be shortened without misery to the crane. That which is long in nature must not be cut off, and that which is short in nature must not be lengthened. Thus will all sorrow be avoided. I suppose charity and duty are surely not included in human nature. You see how many worries and dismays the charitable man has! Besides, divide your joined toes and you will howl: bite off your extra finger and you will scream. In the one case, there is too much, and in the other too little; but the worries and dismays are the same. Now the charitable men of the present age go about with a look of concern sorrowing over the ills of the age, while the non-charitable let loose the desires of their nature in their greed after position and wealth. Therefore I suppose charity and duty are not included in human nature. Yet from the time of the Three Dynasties downwards what a commotion has been raised about them!

Moreover, those who rely upon the arc, the line, compasses, and the square to make correct forms injure the natural constitution of things. Those who use cords to bind and glue to piece together interfere with the natural character of things. Those who seek to satisfy the mind of man by hampering it with ceremonies and music and affecting charity and devotion have lost their original nature. There is an original nature

[39] *Huang-chung* and *ta-lü* were the standard pitch-pipes.

[40] Tseng Ts'an and Shih Yü, disciples of Confucius.

[41] Yang chu and Motse (Mo Ti).

in things. Things in their original nature are curved without the help of arcs, straight without lines, round without compasses, and rectangular without squares; they are joined together without glue, and hold together without cords. In this manner all things live and grow from an inner urge and none can tell how they come to do so. They all have a place in the scheme of things and none can tell how they come to have their proper place. From time immemorial this has always been so, and it may not be tampered with. Why then should the doctrines of charity and duty continue to remain like so much glue or cords, in the domain of Tao and virtue, to give rise to confusion and doubt among mankind?

Now the lesser doubts change man's purpose, and the greater doubts change man's nature. How do we know this? Ever since the time when Shun made a bid for charity and duty and threw the world into confusion, men have run about and exhausted themselves in the pursuit thereof. Is it not then charity and duty which have changed the nature of man?

Therefore I have tried to show [42] that from the time of the Three Dynasties onwards, there is not one who has not changed his nature through certain external things. If a common man, he will die for gain. If a scholar, he will die for fame. If a ruler of a township, he will die for his ancestral honours. If a Sage, he will die for the world. The pursuits and ambitions of these men differ, but the injury to their nature resulting in the sacrifice of their lives is the same. Tsang and Ku were shepherds, and both lost their sheep. On inquiry it appeared that Tsang had been engaged in reading with a shepherd's stick under his arm, while Ku had gone to take part in some trials of strength. Their pursuits were different, but the result in each case was the loss of the sheep. Po Yi died for fame at the foot of Mount Shouyang.[43] Robber Cheh died for gain on the Mount Tungling. They died for different reasons, but the injury to their lives and nature was in each case the same. Why then must we applaud the former and blame the latter? All men die for something and yet if a man dies for charity and duty, the world calls him a gentleman; but if he dies for gain, the world calls him a low fellow. The dying being the same, one is nevertheless called a gentleman and the other called a low character. But in point of injury to their lives and nature, Robber Cheh was just another Po Yi. Of

[42] Beginning with this phrase, there is a marked change in style and vocabulary in this part of the chapter.
[43] Because he refused to serve a new dynasty.

what use then is the distinction of 'gentleman' and 'low fellow' between them?

Besides, were a man to apply himself to charity and duty until he were the equal of Tseng or Shih, I would not call it good. Or to flavours, until he were the equal of Shu Erh (famous cook), I would not call it good. Or to sound, until he were the equal of Shih K'uang, I would not call it good. Or to colours, until he were the equal of Li Chu, I would not call it good. What I call good is not what is meant by charity and duty, but taking good care of virtue. And what I call good is not the so-called charity and duty, but following the nature of life. What I call good at hearing is not hearing others but hearing oneself. What I call good at vision is not seeing others but seeing oneself. For a man who sees not himself but others, or takes possession not of himself but of others, possessing only what others possess and possessing not his own self, does what pleases others instead of pleasing his own nature. Now one who pleases others, instead of pleasing one's own nature, whether he be Robber Cheh or Po Yi, is just another one gone astray.

Conscious of my own deficiencies in regard to Tao, I do not venture to practice the principles of charity and duty on the one hand, nor to lead the life of extravagance on the other.

HORSES' HOOFS

Horses have hoofs to carry them over frost and snow, and hair to protect them from wind and cold. They eat grass and drink water, and fling up their tails and gallop. Such is the real nature of horses. Ceremonial halls and big dwellings are of no use to them.

One day Polo (famous horse-trainer),[44] appeared, saying, "I am good at managing horses." So he burned their hair and clipped them, and pared their hoofs and branded them. He put halters around their necks and shackles around their legs and numbered them according to their stables. The result was that two or three in every ten died. Then he kept them hungry and thirsty, trotting them and galloping them, and taught them to run in formations, with the misery of the tasselled bridle in front and the fear of the knotted whip behind, until more than half of them died.

The potter says, "I am good at managing clay. If I want it round, I

[44] Sun Yang, B.C. 658-619.

use compasses; if rectangular, a square." The carpenter says, "I am good at managing wood. If I want it curved, I use an arc; if straight, a line." But on what grounds can we think that the nature of clay and wood desires this application of compasses and square, and arc and line? Nevertheless, every age extols Polo for his skill in training horses, and potters and carpenters for their skill with clay and wood. Those who manage (govern) the affairs of the empire make the same mistake.

I think one who knows how to govern the empire should not do so. For the people have certain natural instincts—to weave and clothe themselves, to till the fields and feed themselves. This is their common character, in which all share. Such instincts may be called "Heaven-born." So in the days of perfect nature, men were quiet in their movements and serene in their looks. At that time, there were no paths over mountains, no boats or bridges over waters. All things were produced, each in its natural district. Birds and beasts multiplied; trees and shrubs thrived. Thus it was that birds and beasts could be led by the hand, and one could climb up and peep into the magpie's nest. For in the days of perfect nature, man lived together with birds and beasts, and there was no distinction of their kind. Who could know of the distinctions between gentlemen and common people? Being all equally without knowledge, their virtue could not go astray. Being all equally without desires, they were in a state of natural integrity. In this state of natural integrity, the people did not lose their (original) nature.

And then when Sages appeared, crawling for charity and limping with duty, doubt and confusion entered men's minds. They said they must make merry by means of music and enforce distinctions by means of ceremony, and the empire became divided against itself. Were the uncarved wood not cut up, who could make sacrificial vessels? Were white jade left uncut, who could make the regalia of courts? Were Tao and virtue not destroyed, what use would there be for charity and duty? Were men's natural instincts not lost, what need would there be for music and ceremonies? Were the five colours not confused, who would need decorations? Were the five notes not confused, who would adopt the six pitch-pipes? Destruction of the natural integrity of things for the production of articles of various kinds—this is the fault of the artisan. Destruction of Tao and virtue in order to introduce charity and duty—this is the error of the Sages. Horses live on dry land, eat grass and drink water. When pleased, they rub their necks together. When angry, they turn round and kick up their heels at each other. Thus far only do their natural instincts carry them. But bridled and bitted, with a moon-shaped metal plate on their foreheads, they learn to cast vicious looks, to turn their heads to bite, to nudge at the yoke, to cheat the bit out of their mouths or steal the bridle off their heads. Thus their minds and gestures become like those of thieves. This is the fault of Polo.

In the days of Ho Hsü,[45] the people did nothing in particular at their homes and went nowhere in particular in their walks. Having food, they rejoiced; tapping their bellies, they wandered about. Thus far the natural capacities of the people carried them. The Sages came then to make them bow and bend with ceremonies and music, in order to regulate the external forms of intercourse, and dangled charity and duty before them, in order to keep their minds in submission. Then the people began to labor and develop a taste for knowledge, and to struggle with one another in their desire for gain, to which there is no end. This is the error of the Sages.

OPENING TRUNKS, OR A PROTEST AGAINST CIVILIZATION

THE PRECAUTIONS taken against thieves who open trunks, search bags, or ransack tills, consist in securing with cords and fastening with bolts and locks. This is what the world calls wit. But a strong thief comes and carries off the till on his shoulders, with box and bag, and runs away with them. His only fear is that the cords and locks should not be strong enough! Therefore, does not what the world used to call wit simply amount to saving up for the strong thief? And I venture to state that nothing of that which the world calls wit is otherwise than saving up for strong thieves; and nothing of that which the world calls sage wisdom is other than hoarding up for strong thieves.

How can this be shown? In the State of Ch'i, the neighboring towns overlooked one another and one could hear the barking of dogs and crowing of cocks in the neighboring town. Fishermen cast their nets and ploughmen ploughed the land in a territory of over two thousand *li*. Within its four boundaries, was there a temple or shrine dedicated, a god worshipped, or a hamlet, county or a district governed, but in accordance with the rules laid down by the Sages? Yet one morning[46] T'ien Ch'engtse slew the ruler of Ch'i, and stole his kingdom. And not his kingdom only, but the wisdom-tricks which he had got from the Sages

[45] A mythical ruler.

[46] B.C. 481.

as well; so that although T'ien Ch'engtse acquired the reputation of a thief, he lived as securely and comfortably as ever did either Yao or Shun. The small States did not venture to blame, nor the great States to punish him, and for twelve generations his descendants ruled over Ch'i.[47] Was this not a stealing the State of Ch'i and its wisdom-tricks of the Sages in order to preserve their thieves' lives? I venture to ask, was there ever anything of what the world esteems as great wit otherwise than saving up for strong thieves, and was there ever anything of what the world calls sage wisdom other than hoarding up for strong thieves?

How can this be shown? Of old, Lungfeng was beheaded, Pikan was disembowelled, Changhung was sliced to death, Tsehsü was thrown to the waves. All these four were learned ones, but they could not preserve themselves from death by punishment.

An apprentice to Robber Cheh asked him saying, "is there then Tao (moral principles) among thieves?"

"Tell me if there is anything in which there is not Tao," Cheh replied. "There is the sage character of thieves by which booty is located, the courage to go in first, and the chivalry of coming out last. There is the wisdom of calculating success, and kindness in the equal division of the spoil. There has never yet been a great robber who was not possessed of these five qualities." It is seen therefore that without the teachings of the Sages, good men could not keep their position, and without the teachings of the Sages, Robber Cheh could not accomplish his ends. Since good men are scarce and bad men are the majority, the good the Sages do to the world is little and the evil great. Therefore it has been said, "If the lips are turned up, the teeth will be cold. It was the thinness of the wines of Lu which caused the siege of Hantan.[48]

When the Sages arose, gangsters appeared. Overthrow the Sages and set the gangsters free, and then will the empire be in order. When the stream ceases, the gully dries up, and when the hill is levelled the chasm is filled. When the Sages are dead, gangsters will not show up, but the empire will rest in peace. On the other hand, if the Sages do not pop off, neither will the gangsters drop off. Nor if you double the number of

[47] There is an anachronism here, for Chuangtse lived to see only the ninth generation of T'iens. At least the number "twelve" must have been slipped in by a later scribe. This evidence is not sufficient to vitiate the whole chapter, as some "textual critics" claim.

[48] Reference to a story. The states, Lu and Chao, both presented wine to the King of Ch'u. By the trickery of a servant, the flasks were exchanged, and Chao was blamed for presenting bad wine, and its city Hantan was besieged.

Sages wherewith to govern the empire will you do more than double the profits of Robber Cheh.

If pecks and bushels are used for measurement, the pecks and bushels themselves will also be stolen, along with the rice. If scales and steelyards are used for weighing, the scales and steelyards themselves will also be stolen along with the goods. If tallies and signets are used for good faith, the tallies and signets will also be stolen. If charity and duty are used for moral principles, charity and duty will also be stolen.

How is this so? Steal a hook and you hang as a crook; steal a kingdom and you are made a duke. (The teachings of) charity and duty remain in the duke's domain. Is it not true, then, that they are thieves of charity and duty and of the wisdom of the Sages?

So it is that those who follow the way of brigandage are promoted into princes and dukes. Those who are bent on stealing charity and duty together with the measures, scales, tallies, and signets can be dissuaded by no rewards of official regalia and uniform, nor deterred by fear of sharp instruments of punishment. This doubling the profits of robbers like Cheh, making it impossible to get rid of them, is the fault of the Sages.

Therefore it has been said, "Fishes must be left in the water; the sharp weapons of a state must be left where none can see them." [49] These Sages are the sharp weapons of the world; they must not be shown to the world.

Banish wisdom, discard knowledge,[50] and gangsters will stop! Fling away jade and destroy pearls, and petty thieves will cease. Burn tallies and break signets, and the people will revert to their uncouth integrity. Split measures and smash scales, and the people will not fight over quantities. Trample down all the institutions of Sages, and the people will begin to be fit for discussing (Tao). Confuse the six pitch-pipes, confine flutes and string instruments to the flames, stuff up the ears of Blind Shih K'uang, and each man will keep his own sense of hearing. Put an end to decorations, confuse the five colours, glue up the eyes of Li Chu, and each man will keep his own sense of sight. Destroy arcs and lines, fling away squares and compasses, snap off the fingers of Ch'ui the Artisan, and each man will use his own natural skill. Wherefore the saying, "Great skill appears like clumsiness." [51] Cut down the activities of Tseng

[49] See Laotse, Ch. 36.
[50] See Laotse, Ch. 19.
[51] See Laotse, Ch. 45.

and Shih,[52] pinch the mouths of Yang Chu and Motse, discard charity and duty, and the virtue of the people will arrive at Mystic Unity.[53]

If each man keeps his own sense of sight, the world will escape being burned up. If each man keeps his own sense of hearing, the world will escape entanglements. If each man keeps his intelligence, the world will escape confusion. If each man keeps his own virtue, the world will avoid deviation from the true path. Tseng, Shih, Yang, Mo, Shih K'uang, Ch'ui, and Li Chu were all persons who developed their external character and involved the world in the present confusion so that the laws and statutes are of no avail.

Have you never heard of the Age of Perfect Nature? In the days of Yungch'eng, Tat'ing, Pohuang, Chungyang, Lilu, Lihsü, Hsienyüan, Hohsü, Tsunlu, Chuyung, Fuhsi, and Shennung,[54] the people tied knots for reckoning. They enjoyed their food, beautified their clothing, were satisfied with their homes, and delighted in their customs. Neighboring settlements overlooked one another, so that they could hear the barking of dogs and crowing of cocks of their neighbors, and the people till the end of their days had never been outside their own country.[55] In those days, there was indeed perfect peace.

But nowadays any one can make the people strain their necks and stand on tiptoes by saying, "In such and such a place there is a Sage." Immediately they put together a few provisions and hurry off, neglecting their parents at home and their masters' business abroad, going on foot through the territories of the Princes, and riding to hundreds of miles away. Such is the evil effect of the rulers' desire for knowledge. When the rulers desire knowledge and neglect Tao, the empire is overwhelmed in confusion.

How can this be shown? When the knowledge of bows and crossbows and hand-nets and tailed arrows increases, then they carry confusion among the birds of the air. When the knowledge of hooks and bait and nets and traps increases, then they carry confusion among the fishes of the deep. When the knowledge of fences and nets and snares increases, then they carry confusion among the beasts of the field. When cunning and deceit and flippancy and the sophistries of the "hard" and "white" and identities and differences increase in number and variety, then they overwhelm the world with logic.

Therefore it is that there is often chaos in the world, and the love of

[52] See Note 40.

[53] *Hsüant'ung,* see Laotse, Ch. 1.

[54] All legendary ancient rulers.

[55] Cf. Laotse, Ch. 80.

knowledge is ever at the bottom of it. For all men strive to grasp what they do not know, while none strive to grasp what they already know; and all strive to discredit what they do not excel in, while none strive to discredit what they do excel in. That is why there is chaos. Thus, above, the splendor of the heavenly bodies is dimmed; below, the power of land and water is burned up, while in between the influence of the four seasons is upset. There is not one tiny worm that moves on earth or an insect that flies in the air but has lost its original nature. Such indeed is the world chaos caused by the desire for knowledge!

Ever since the time of the Three Dynasties downwards, it has been like this. The simple and the guileless have been set aside; the specious and the cunning have been exalted. Tranquil inaction has given place to love of disputation; and disputation alone is enough to bring chaos upon the world.

ON TOLERANCE

THERE HAS BEEN such a thing as letting mankind alone and tolerance; there has never been such a thing as governing mankind. Letting alone springs from the fear lest men's natural dispositions be perverted and tolerance springs from the fear lest their character be corrupted. But if their natural dispositions be not perverted, nor their character corrupted, what need is there left for government?

Of old, when Yao governed the empire, he made the people live happily; consequently the people struggled to be happy and became restless. When Chieh governed the empire he made the people live miserably; consequently the people regarded life as a burden and were discontented. Restlessness and discontent are subversive of virtue; and without virtue there has never been such a thing as stability.

When man rejoices greatly, he gravitates towards *yang* (the positive pole). When he is in great anger, he gravitates towards *yin* (the negative pole). If the equilibrium of positive and negative is disturbed, the four seasons are upset, and the balance of heat and cold is destroyed, man himself suffers physically thereby. It causes men to rejoice and sorrow inordinately, to live disorderly lives, be vexed in their thoughts, and lose their balance and form of conduct. When that happens, then the whole world seethes with revolt and discontent, and we have such men as Robber Cheh, Tseng, and Shih. Offer the entire world as rewards for the good or threaten the wicked with the dire punishments of the entire world, and it is still insufficient (to reform them). Consequently, with the entire world, one cannot furnish sufficient inducements or deterrents to action. From the Three Dynasties downwards, the world has lived in a helter-skelter of promotions and punishments. What chance have the people left for living the even tenor of their lives?

Besides, love (over-refinement) of vision leads to debauchery in colour; love of hearing leads to debauchery in sound; love of charity leads to confusion in virtue; love of duty leads to perversion of principles; love of ceremonies (*li*) leads to a common fashion for technical skill; love of music leads to common lewdness of thought; love of wisdom leads to a fashion for the arts; and love of knowledge leads to a fashion for criticism. If the people are allowed to live out the even tenor of their lives, the above eight may or may not be; it matters not. But if the people are not allowed to live out the even tenor of their lives, then these eight cause discontent and contention and strife, and throw the world into chaos.

Yet the world worships and cherishes them. Indeed deep-seated is the mental chaos of the world. Is it merely a passing mistake that can be simply removed? Yet they observe fasts before their discussion, bend down on their knees to practise them, and sing and beat the drum and dance to celebrate them. What can I do about it?

Therefore, when a gentleman is unavoidably compelled to take charge of the government of the empire, there is nothing better than inaction (letting alone). By means of inaction only can he allow the people to live out the even tenor of their lives. Therefore he who values the world as his own self may then be entrusted with the government of the world; and he who loves the world as his own self may then be entrusted with the care of the world.[56] Therefore if the gentleman can refrain from disturbing the internal economy of man, and from glorifying the powers of sight and hearing, he can sit still like a corpse or spring into action like a dragon, be silent as the deep or talk with the voice of thunder, the movements of his spirit calling forth the natural mechanism of Heaven. He can remain calm and leisurely doing nothing, while all things are brought to maturity and thrive. What need then would have I to set about governing the world?

Ts'ui Chü asked Lao Tan,[57] saying, "If the empire is not to be governed, how are men's hearts to be kept good?"

[56] See Laotse, Ch. 13.

[57] Laotse, Tan being one of the known personal names of Laotse (Li Tan, or Li Erh). "Lao" means "old," while "Li" is the family name.

"Be careful," replied Lao Tan, "not to interfere with the natural goodness of the heart of man. Man's heart may be forced down or stirred up. In each case the issue is fatal. By gentleness, the hardest heart may be softened. But try to cut and polish it, and it will glow like fire or freeze like ice. In the twinkling of an eye it will pass beyond the limits of the Four Seas. In repose, it is profoundly still; in motion, it flies up to the sky. Like an unruly horse, it cannot be held in check. Such is the human heart."

Of old, the Yellow Emperor first interfered with the natural goodness of the heart of man, by means of charity and duty. In consequence, Yao and Shun wore the hair off their legs and the flesh off their arms in endeavoring to feed their people's bodies. They tortured the people's internal economy in order to conform to charity and duty. They exhausted the people's energies to live in accordance with the laws and statutes. Even then they did not succeed. Thereupon, Yao (had to) confine Huantou on Mount Ts'ung, exile the chiefs of the Three Miaos and their people into the Three Weis, and banish the Minister of Works to Yutu, which shows he had not succeeded. When it came to the times of the Three Kings,[58] the empire was in a state of foment. Among the bad men were Chieh and Cheh; among the good were Tseng and Shih. By and by, the Confucianists and the Motseanists arose; and then came confusion between joy and anger, fraud between the simple and the cunning, recrimination between the virtuous and the evil-minded, slander between the honest and the liars, and the world order collapsed.

When the great virtue lost its unity, men's lives were frustrated. When there was a general rush for knowledge, the people's desires ever went beyond their possessions. The next thing was then to invent axes and saws, to kill by laws and statutes, to disfigure by chisels and awls. The empire seethed with discontent, the blame for which rests upon those who would interfere with the natural goodness of the heart of man.

In consequence, virtuous men sought refuge in mountain caves, while rulers of great states sat trembling in their ancestral halls. Then, when dead men lay about pillowed on each other's corpses, when cangued prisoners jostled each other in crowds and condemned criminals were seen everywhere, then the Confucianists and the Motseanists bustled about and rolled up their sleeves in the midst of gyves and fetters! Alas, they know not shame, nor what it is to blush!

[58] The founders of the Three Dynasties, Hsia, Shang and Chou (B.C. 2205-222).

Until I can say that the wisdom of Sages is not a fastener of cangues, and that charity of heart and duty to one's neighbor are not bolts for gyves, how should I know that Tseng and Shih were not the singing arrows[59] (forerunners) of (the gangsters) Chieh and Cheh? Therefore it is said, "Abandon wisdom and discard knowledge, and the empire will be at peace."

The Yellow Emperor sat on the throne for nineteen years, and his laws obtained all over the empire. Hearing that Kuangch'engtse was living on Mount K'ungt'ung, he went there to see him, and said, "I am told that you are in possession of perfect Tao. May I ask what is the essence of this perfect Tao? I desire to obtain the essence of the universe to secure good harvests and feed my people. I should like also to control the *yin* and *yang* principles to fulfil the life of all living things."

"What you are asking about," replied Kuangch'engtse, "is merely the dregs of things. What you wish to control are the disintegrated factors thereof. Ever since the empire was governed by you, the clouds have rained before thickening, the foliage of trees has fallen before turning yellow, and the brightness of the sun and moon has increasingly paled. You have the shallowness of mind of a glib talker. How then are you fit to speak of perfect Tao?"

The Yellow Emperor withdrew. He resigned the Throne. He built himself a solitary hut, and sat upon white straw. For three months he remained in seclusion, and then went again to see Kuangch'engtse.

The latter was lying with his head towards the south. The Yellow Emperor approached from below upon his knees. Kowtowing twice upon the ground, he said, "I am told that you are in possession of perfect Tao. May I ask how to order one's life so that one may have long life?"

Kuang Ch'engtse jumped up with a start. "A good question indeed!" cried he. "Come, and I will speak to you of perfect Tao. The essence of perfect Tao is profoundly mysterious; its extent is lost in obscurity.

"See nothing; hear nothing; guard your spirit in quietude and your body will go right of its own accord.

"Be quiet, be pure; toil not your body, perturb not your vital essence, and you will live forever.

"For if the eye sees nothing, and the ear hears nothing, and the mind

[59] Signal for attack.

thinks nothing, your spirit will stay in your body, and the body will thereby live forever.

"Cherish that which is within you, and shut off that which is without; for much knowledge is a curse.

"Then I will take you to that abode of Great Light to reach the Plateau of Absolute *Yang*. I will lead you through the Door of the Dark Unknown to the Plateau of the Absolute *Yin*.

"The Heaven and Earth have their separate functions. The *yin* and *yang* have their hidden root. Guard carefully your body, and material things will prosper by themselves.

"I guard the original One, and rest in harmony with externals. Therefore I have been able to live for twelve hundred years and my body has not grown old."

The Yellow Emperor kowtowed twice and said, "Kuangch'engtse is surely God . . ."[60]

"Come," said Kuangch'engtse, "I will tell you. That thing is eternal; yet all men think it mortal. That thing is infinite; yet all men think it finite. Those who possess my Tao are princes in this life and rulers in the hereafter. Those who do not possess my Tao behold the light of day in this life and become clods of earth in the hereafter.

"Nowadays, all living things spring from the dust and to the dust return. But I will lead you through the portals of Eternity to wander in the great wilds of Infinity. My light is the light of sun and moon. My life is the life of Heaven and Earth. Before me all is nebulous; behind me all is dark, unknown. Men may all die, but I endure forever."

When General Clouds was going eastwards, he passed through the branches of Fuyao (a magic tree) and happened to meet Great Nebulous. The latter was slapping his thighs and hopping about. When General Clouds saw him, he stopped like one lost and stood still, saying, "Who are you, old man, and what are you doing here?"

"Strolling!" replied Great Nebulous, still slapping his thighs and hopping about.

"I want to ask about something," said General Clouds.

"Ough!" uttered Great Nebulous.

"The spirits of Heaven are out of harmony," said General Clouds; "the spirits of the Earth are smothered; the six influences[61] of the weather

[60] Lit. "Heaven."

[61] *Yin, yang,* wind, rain, light and darkness.

do not work together, and the four seasons are no longer regular. I desire to blend the essence of the six influences and nourish all living beings. What am I to do?"

"I do not know! I do not know!" cried Great Nebulous, shaking his head, while still slapping his thighs and hopping about.

So General Clouds did not press his question. Three years later, when passing eastwards through the plains of the Sungs, he again fell in with Great Nebulous. The former was overjoyed, and hurrying up, said, "Has your Holiness[62] forgotten me? Has your Holiness forgotten me?"

He then kowtowed twice and desired to be allowed to interrogate Great Nebulous; but the latter said, "I wander on without knowing what I want. I rush about without knowing whither I am going. I simply stroll about, watching unexpected events. What should I know?"

"I too regard myself as rushing about," answered General Clouds; "but the people follow my movements. I cannot escape the people and what I do they follow. I would gladly receive some advice."

"That the scheme of empire is in confusion," said Great Nebulous, "that the conditions of life are violated, that the will of the Dark Heaven is not accomplished, that the beasts of the field are scattered, that the birds of the air cry at night, that blight strikes the trees and herbs, that destruction spreads among the creeping things,—this, alas! is the fault of those who would rule others."

"True," replied General Clouds, "but what am I to do?"

"Ah!" cried Great Nebulous, "keep quiet and go home in peace!"

"It is not often," urged General Clouds, "that I meet with your Holiness. I would gladly receive some advice."

"Ah," said Great Nebulous, "nourish your heart. Rest in inaction, and the world will be reformed of itself. Forget your body and spit forth intelligence. Ignore all differences and become one with the Infinite. Release your mind, and free your spirit. Be vacuous, be devoid of soul. Thus will things grow and prosper and return to their Root. Returning to their Root without their knowing it, the result will be a formless whole which will never be cut up. To know it is to cut it up. Ask not about its name, inquire not into its nature, and all things will flourish of themselves."

"Your Holiness," said General Clouds, "has informed me with power and taught me silence. What I had long sought, I have now found." Thereupon he kowtowed twice and took leave.

[62] Great Nebulous is here addressed as "Heaven." See Note 60.

The people of this world all rejoice in others being like themselves, and object to others being different from themselves. Those who make friends with their likes and do not make friends with their unlikes, are influenced by a desire to be above the others. But how can those who desire to be above the others ever be above the others? Rather than base one's judgement on the opinions of the many, let each look after his own affairs. But those who desire to govern kingdoms clutch at the advantages of (the systems of) the Three Kings[63] without seeing the troubles involved. In fact, they are trusting the fortunes of a country to luck, but what country would be lucky enough to escape destruction? Their chances of preserving it do not amount to one in ten thousand, while their chances of destroying it are ten thousand to nothing and even more. Such, alas! is the ignorance of rulers.

For to have a territory is to have something great. He who has something great must not regard the material things as material things. Only by not regarding material things as material things can one be the lord of things. The principle of looking at material things as not real things is not confined to mere government of the empire. Such a one may wander at will between the six limits of space or travel over the Nine Continents, unhampered and free. This is to be the Unique One. The Unique One is the highest among man.

The doctrine of the great man is (fluid) as shadow to form, as echo to sound. Ask and it responds, fulfilling its abilities as the help-mate of humanity. Noiseless in repose, objectless in motion, he brings you out of the confusion of your coming and going to wander in the Infinite. Formless in his movements, he is eternal with the sun. In respect of his bodily existence, he conforms to the universal standards. Through conformance to the universal standards, he forgets his own individuality. But if he forgets his individuality, how can he regard his possessions as possessions? Those who see possessions in possessions were the wise men of old. Those who regard not possessions as possessions are the friends of Heaven and Earth.

That which is low, but must be let alone, is matter. That which is humble, but still must be followed, is the people. That which is always there but still has to be attended to, is affairs. That which is inadequate, but still has to be set forth, is the law. That which is remote from Tao, but still claims our attention, is duty. That which is biased, but must be

[63] See Note 58.

broadened, is charity. Trivial, but requiring to be strengthened from within, that is ceremony. Contained within, but requiring to be uplifted, that is virtue. One, but not to be without modification, that is Tao. Spiritual, yet not to be devoid of action, that is God.

Therefore the Sage looks up to God, but does not offer to aid. He perfects his virtue, but does not involve himself. He guides himself by Tao, but makes no plans. He identifies himself with charity, but does not rely on it. He performs his duties towards his neighbors, but does not set store by them. He responds to ceremony, without avoiding it. He undertakes affairs without declining them, and metes out law without confusion. He relies on the people and does not make light of them. He accommodates himself to matter and does not ignore it. Things are not worth attending to, yet they have to be attended to. He who does not understand God will not be pure in character. He who has not clear apprehension of Tao will not know where to begin. And he who is not enlightened by Tao,—alas indeed for him!

What then is Tao? There is the Tao of God, and there is the Tao of man. Honor through inaction comes from the Tao of God: entanglement through action comes from the Tao of man. The Tao of God is fundamental: the Tao of man is accidental. The distance which separates them is great. Let us all take heed thereto!

AUTUMN FLOODS [64]

IN THE TIME OF AUTUMN FLOODS, a hundred streams poured into the river. It swelled in its turbid course, so that it was impossible to tell a cow from a horse on the opposite banks or on the islets.

Then the Spirit of the River laughed for joy that all the beauty of the earth was gathered to himself. Down the stream he journeyed east, until he reached the North Sea. There, looking eastwards and seeing no limit to its wide expanse, his countenance began to change. And as he gazed over the ocean, he sighed and said to North-Sea Jo, "A vulgar proverb says that he who has heard a great many truths thinks no one equal to himself. And such a one am I. Formerly when I heard people detracting from the learning of Confucius or underrating the heroism of Po Yi, I did not believe it. But now that I have looked upon your inexhaustibility

[64] This chapter further develops the ideas in Chapter "On Levelling All Things" and contains the important philosophical concept of relativity.

—alas for me! Had I not reached your abode, I should have been forever a laughing-stock to those of great enlightenment!"

To this North-Sea Jo (the Spirit of the Ocean) replied, "You cannot speak of ocean to a well-frog, which is limited by his abode. You cannot speak of ice to a summer insect, which is limited by his short life. You cannot speak of Tao to a pedagogue, who is limited in his knowledge. But now that you have emerged from your narrow sphere and have seen the great ocean, you know your own insignificance, and I can speak to you of great principles.

"There is no body of water beneath the canopy of heaven which is greater than the ocean. All streams pour into it without cease, yet it does not overflow. It is being continuously drained off at the Tail-Gate,[65] yet it is never empty. Spring and autumn bring no change; floods and droughts are equally unknown. And thus it is immeasurably superior to mere rivers and streams. Yet I have never ventured to boast on this account. For I count myself, among the things that take shape from the universe and receive life from the *yin* and *yang,* but as a pebble or a small tree on a vast mountain. Only too conscious of my own insignificance, how can I presume to boast of my greatness?

"Are not the Four Seas to the universe but like ant-holes in a marsh? Is not the Middle Kingdom to the surrounding ocean like a tare-seed in a granary? Of all the myriad created things, man is but one. And of all those who inhabit the Nine Continents, live on the fruit of the earth, and move about in cart and boat, an individual man is but one. Is not he, as compared with all creation, but as the tip of a hair upon a horse's body?

"The succession of the Five Rulers,[66] the contentions of the Three Kings, the concerns of the kind-hearted, the labors of the administrators, are but this and nothing more. Po Yi refused the throne for fame. Chungni (Confucius) discoursed to get a reputation for learning. This over-estimation of self on their part—was it not very much like your own previous self-estimation in reference to water?"

"Very well," replied the Spirit of the River, "am I then to regard the universe as great and the tip of a hair as small?"

"Not at all," said the Spirit of the Ocean. "Dimensions are limitless; time is endless. Conditions are not constant; terms are not final. Thus, the wise man looks into space, and does not regard the small as too little, nor the great as too much; for he knows that there is no limit to dimen-

[65] *Wei-lü,* a mythical hole in the bottom or end of the ocean.

[66] Mythical rulers before the Three Kings.

sions. He looks back into the past, and does not grieve over what is far off, nor rejoice over what is near; for he knows that time is without end. He investigates fullness and decay, and therefore does not rejoice if he succeeds, nor lament if he fails; for he knows that conditions are not constant. He who clearly apprehends the scheme of existence does not rejoice over life, nor repine at death; for he knows that terms are not final.

"What man knows is not to be compared with what he does not know. The span of his existence is not to be compared with the span of his non-existence. To strive to exhaust the infinite by means of the infinitesimal necessarily lands him in confusion and unhappiness. How then should one be able to say that the tip of a hair is the *ne plus ultra* of smallness, or that the universe is the *ne plus ultra* of greatness?"

"Dialecticians of the day," replied the Spirit of the River, "all say that the infinitesimal has no form, and that the infinite is beyond all measurement. Is that true?"

"If we look at the great from the standpoint of the small," said the Spirit of the Ocean, "we cannot reach its limit; and if we look at the small from the standpoint of the great, it eludes our sight. The infinitesimal is a subdivision of the small; the colossal is an extension of the great. In this sense the two fall into different categories. This lies in the nature of circumstances. Now smallness and greatness presuppose form. That which is without form cannot be divided by numbers, and that which is above measurement cannot be measured. The greatness of anything may be a topic of discussion, and the smallness of anything may be mentally imagined. But that which can be neither a topic of discussion nor imagined mentally cannot be said to have greatness or smallness.

"Therefore, the truly great man does not injure others and does not credit himself with charity and mercy. He seeks not gain, but does not despise the servants who do. He struggles not for wealth, but does not lay great value on his modesty. He asks for help from no man, but is not proud of his self-reliance, neither does he despise the greedy. He acts differently from the vulgar crowd, but does not place high value on being different or eccentric; nor because he acts with the majority does he despise those that flatter a few. The ranks and emoluments of the world are to him no cause for joy; its punishments and shame no cause for disgrace. He knows that right and wrong cannot be distinguished, that great and small cannot be defined.

"I have heard say, 'The man of Tao has no (concern for) reputation;

the truly virtuous has no (concern for) possessions; the truly great man ignores self.' This is the height of self-discipline."

"But how then," asked the Spirit of the River, "arise the distinctions of high and low, of great and small in the material and immaterial aspects of things?"

"From the point of view of Tao," replied the Spirit of the Ocean, "there are no such distinctions of high and low. From the point of view of individuals, each holds himself high and holds others low. From the vulgar point of view, high and low (honors and dishonor) are something conferred by others.

"In regard to distinctions, if we say that a thing is great or small by its own standard of great or small, then there is nothing in all creation which is not great, nothing which is not small. To know that the universe is but as a tare-seed, and the tip of a hair is (as big as) a mountain,—this is the expression of relativity.[67]

"In regard to function, if we say that something exists or does not exist, by its own standard of existence or non-existence, then there is nothing which does not exist, nothing which does not perish from existence. If we know that east and west are convertible and yet necessary terms, in relation to each other, then such (relative) functions may be determined.

"In regard to man's desires or interests, if we say that anything is good or bad because it is either good or bad according to our individual (subjection) standards, then there is nothing which is not good, nothing which is not bad. If we know that Yao and Chieh each regarded himself as good and the other as bad, then the (direction of) their interests becomes apparent.

"Of old Yao and Shun abdicated (in favor of worthy successors) and the rule was maintained, while Kuei (Prince of Yen) abdicated (in favor of Tsechih) and the latter failed. T'ang and Wu got the empire by fighting, while by fighting, Po Kung lost it. From this it may be seen that the value of abdicating or fighting, of acting like Yao or like Chieh, varies according to time, and may not be regarded as a constant principle.

"A battering-ram can knock down a wall, but it cannot repair a breach. Different things are differently applied. Ch'ichi and Hualiu (famous horses) could travel 1,000 *li* in one day, but for catching rats they were not equal to a wild cat. Different animals possess different

[67] Lit. "levelling of ranks or distinctions."

aptitudes. An owl can catch fleas at night, and see the tip of a hair, but if it comes out in the daytime it can open wide its eyes and yet fail to see a mountain. Different creatures are differently constituted.

"Thus, those who say that they would have right without its correlate, wrong; or good government without its correlate, misrule, do not apprehend the great principles of the universe, nor the nature of all creation. One might as well talk of the existence of Heaven without that of Earth, or of the negative principle without the positive, which is clearly impossible. Yet people keep on discussing it without stop; such people must be either fools or knaves.

"Rulers abdicated under different conditions, and the Three Dynasties succeeded each other under different conditions. Those who came at the wrong time and went against the tide are called usurpers. Those who came at the right time and fitted in with their age are called defenders of Right. Hold your peace, Uncle River. How can you know the distinctions of high and low and of the houses of the great and small?"

"In this case," replied the Spirit of the River, "what am I to do about declining and accepting, following and abandoning (courses of action)?"

"From the point of view of Tao," said the Spirit of the Ocean,[68] "how can we call this high and that low? For there is (the process of) reverse evolution (uniting opposites). To follow one absolute course would involve great departure from Tao. What is much? What is little? Be thankful for the gift. To follow a one-sided opinion is to diverge from Tao. Be exalted, as the ruler of a State whose administration is impartial. Be at ease, as the Deity of the Earth, whose dispensation is impartial. Be expansive, like the points of the compass, boundless without a limit. Embrace all creation, and none shall be more sheltered or helped than another. This is to be without bias. And all things being equal, how can one say which is long and which is short? Tao is without beginning, without end. The material things are born and die, and no credit is taken for their development. Emptiness and fullness alternate, and their relations are not fixed. Past years cannot be recalled; time cannot be arrested. The succession of growth and decay, of increase and diminution, goes in a cycle, each end becoming a new beginning. In this sense only may we discuss the ways of truth and the principles of the universe. The life of things

[68] From here on to the end of this paragraph, most of the passages are rhymed.

passes by like a rushing, galloping horse, changing at every turn, at every hour. What should one do, or what should one not do? Let the (cycle of) changes go on by themselves!"

"If this is the case," said the Spirit of the River, "what is the value of Tao?"

"Those who understand Tao," answered the Spirit of the Ocean, "must necessarily apprehend the eternal principles and those who apprehend the eternal principles must understand their application. Those who understand their application do not suffer material things to injure them.

"The man of perfect virtue cannot be burnt by fire, nor drowned by water, nor hurt by the cold of winter or the heat of summer, nor torn by bird or beast. Not that he makes light of these; but that he discriminates between safety and danger, is happy under prosperous and adverse circumstances alike, and cautious in his choice of action, so that none can harm him.

"Therefore it has been said that Heaven (the natural) abides within, man (the artificial) without. Virtue abides in the natural. Knowledge of the action of the natural and of the artificial has its basis in the natural, its destination in virtue. Thus, whether moving forward or backwards, whether yielding or asserting, there is always a reversion to the essential and to the ultimate."

"What do you mean," enquired the Spirit of the River, "by the natural and the artificial?"

"Horses and oxen," answered the Spirit of the Ocean, "have four feet. That is the natural. Put a halter on a horse's head, a string through a bullock's nose. That is the artificial.

"Therefore it has been said, do not let the artificial obliterate the natural; do not let will obliterate destiny; do not let virtue be sacrificed to fame. Diligently observe these precepts without fail, and thus you will revert to the True."

The walrus[69] envies the centipede; the centipede envies the snake; the snake envies the wind; the wind envies the eye; and the eye envies the mind. The walrus said to the centipede, "I hop about on one leg, but not very successfully. How do you manage all those legs you have?"

"I don't manage them," replied the centipede. "Have you never seen

[69] *K'uei,* a mythical, one-legged animal.

saliva? When it is ejected, the big drops are the size of pearls, the small ones like mist. At random they fall, in countless numbers. So, too, does my natural mechanism move, without my knowing how I do it."

The centipede said to the snake, "With all my legs I do not move as fast as you with none. How is that?"

"One's natural mechanism," replied the snake, "is not a thing to be changed. What need have I for legs?"

The snake said to the wind, "I wriggle about by moving my spine, as if I had legs. Now you seem to be without form, and yet you come blustering down from the North Sea to bluster away to the South Sea. How do you do it?"

"'Tis true," replied the wind, "that I bluster as you say. But any one who sticks his finger or his foot into me, excels me. On the other hand, I can tear away huge trees and destroy large buildings. This power is given only to me. Out of many minor defeats I win the big victory.[70] And to win a big victory is given only to the Sages."

When Confucius visited K'uang, the men of Sung surrounded him by several cordons. Yet he went on singing to his guitar without stop.

"How is it, Master," enquired Tselu, "that you are so cheerful?"

"Come here," replied Confucius, "and I will tell you. For a long time I have not been willing to admit failure, but in vain. Fate is against me. For a long time I have been seeking success, but in vain. The hour has not come. In the days of Yao and Shun, no man throughout the empire was a failure, though this was not due to their cleverness. In the days of Chieh and Chou, no man throughout the empire was a success, though this was not due to their stupidity. The circumstances happened that way.

"To travel by water without fear of sea-serpents and dragons,—this is the courage of the fisherman. To travel by land without fear of the wild buffaloes and tigers,—this is the courage of hunters. When bright blades cross, to look on death as on life,—this is the courage of the warrior. To know that failure is fate and that success is opportunity, and to remain fearless in times of great danger,—this is the courage of the Sage. Stop bustling, Yu! My destiny is controlled (by some one)."

Shortly afterwards, the captain of the troops came in and apologised, saying, "We thought you were Yang Hu; that was why we surrounded

[70] Now a slogan used in China in the war against Japan.

you. We find we have made a mistake." Whereupon he apologised and retired.

Kungsun Lung[71] said to Mou of Wei, "When young I studied the teachings of the elders. When I grew up, I understood the morals of charity and duty. I learned to level together similarities and differences, to confound arguments on "hardness" and "whiteness," to affirm what others deny, and justify what others dispute. I vanquished the wisdom of all the philosophers, and overcame the arguments of all people. I thought that I had indeed understood everything. But now that I have heard Chuangtse, I am lost in astonishment. I know not whether it is in arguing or in knowledge that I am not equal to him. I can no longer open my mouth. May I ask you to impart to me the secret?"

Prince Mou leaned over the table and sighed. Then he looked up to heaven and laughed, saying, "Have you never heard of the frog in the shallow well? The frog said to the turtle of the Eastern Sea, 'what a great time I am having! I hop to the rail around the well, and retire to rest in the hollow of some broken bricks. Swimming, I float on my armpits, resting my jaws just above the water. Plunging into the mud, I bury my feet up to the foot-arch, and not one of the cockles, crabs or tadpoles I see around me are my match. Besides, to occupy such a pool all alone and possess a shallow well is to be as happy as anyone can be. Why do you not come and pay me a visit?'

"Now before the turtle of the Eastern Sea had got its left leg down, its right knee had already stuck fast, and it shrank back and begged to be excused. It then told the frog about the sea, saying, 'A thousand *li* would not measure its breadth, nor a thousand fathoms its depth. In the days of the Great Yü, there were nine years of flood out of ten; but this did not add to its bulk. In the days of T'ang, there were seven years of drought out of eight; but this did not make its shores recede. Not to be affected by the passing of time, and not to be affected by increase or decrease of water,—such is the great happiness of the Eastern Sea.' At this the frog of the shallow well was considerably astonished, and felt very small, like one lost.

"For one whose knowledge does not yet appreciate the niceties of true and false to attempt to understand Chuangtse, is like a mosquito trying

[71] A Neo-Motseanist (of the Sophist school) who lived after Chuangtse. This section must have been added by the latter's disciples, as is easy to see from the three stories about Chuangtse which follow.

to carry a mountain, or an insect trying to swim a river. Of course he will fail. Moreover, one whose knowledge does not reach to the subtlest teachings, yet is satisfied with temporary success,—is not he like the frog in the well?

"Chuangtse is now climbing up from the realms below to reach high heaven. For him no north or south; lightly the four points are gone, engulfed in the unfathomable. For him no east or west; starting from the Mystic Unknown, he returns to the Great Unity. And yet you think you are going to find his truth by dogged inquiries and arguments! This is like looking at the sky through a tube, or pointing at the earth with an awl. Is not this being petty?

"Have you never heard how a youth of Shouling went to study the walking gait at Hantan? [72] Before he could learn the Hantan gait, he had forgotten his own way of walking, and crawled back home on all fours. If you do not go away now, you will forget what you have and lose your own professional knowledge."

Kungsun Lung's jaw hung open, his tongue clave to his palate, and he slunk away.

Chuangtse was fishing on the P'u River when the Prince of Ch'u sent two high officials to see him and said, "Our Prince desires to burden you with the administration of the Ch'u State."

Chuangtse went on fishing without turning his head and said, "I have heard that in Ch'u there is a sacred tortoise which died when it was three thousand (years) old. The prince keeps this tortoise carefully enclosed in a chest in his ancestral temple. Now would this tortoise rather be dead and have its remains venerated, or would it rather be alive and wagging its tail in the mud?"

"It would rather be alive," replied the two officials, "and wagging its tail in the mud."

"Begone!" cried Chuangtse. "I too will wag my tail in the mud."

Hueitse was Prime Minister in the Liang State, and Chuangtse was on his way to see him.

Some one remarked, "Chuangtse has come. He wants to be minister in your place."

[72] Capital of Chao.

Thereupon Hueitse was afraid, and searched all over the country for three days and three nights to find him.

Then Chuangtse went to see him, and said, "In the south there is a bird. It is a kind of phoenix. Do you know it? When it starts from the South Sea to fly to the North Sea, it would not alight except on the *wu-t'ung* tree. It eats nothing but the fruit of the bamboo, drinks nothing but the purest spring water. An owl which had got the rotten carcass of a rat, looked up as the phoenix flew by, and screeched. Are you not screeching at me over your kingdom of Liang?"

Chuangtse and Hueitse had strolled on to the bridge over the Hao, when the former observed, "See how the small fish are darting about! That is the happiness of the fish."

"You not being a fish yourself," said Hueitse, "how can you know the happiness of the fish?"

"And you not being I," retorted Chuangtse, "how can you know that I do not know?"

"If I, not being you, cannot know what you know," urged Hueitse, "it follows that you, not being a fish, cannot know the happiness of the fish."

"Let us go back to your original question," said Chuangtse. "You asked me how I knew the happiness of the fish. Your very question shows that you knew that I knew. I knew it (from my own feelings) on this bridge."

CHINESE DEMOCRACY

The Book of History

Documents of Chinese Democracy (*Shu Ching*)

INTRODUCTION

1. DOCUMENTS OF CHINESE DEMOCRACY

Much nonsense has been said about Chinese democracy or lack of it. This usually refers to the democratic machinery of government functioning in a typical modern republic like the United States of America, or with it as the standard of judgment (with electioneering, suffrage, Congressional control of the President, etc.). It does not refer to a true rule of the *demos*. On the other hand, when we speak of democracy as a way of life and talk of the spirit of democracy, it is so easy to take refuge under general terms like "freedom" and "dignity of the individual," which are all relative things either in modern America or in ancient China.

I still think that Abraham Lincoln's definition is the best. Taking that as the standard, I am forced to the conclusion that in ancient China, we have developed very definitely the idea of government for the people and by consent of the people, but not government by the people and of the people. On the other hand, considering democracy as a broad human ideal and not as a form of political machinery, I find these strange characteristics: that the Chinese temper is the democratic temper; that in fact the keeping of peace and order in the country depends not upon the government or the soldiers, but ninety per cent upon the self-government of the people; that the ideal, since the disastrous experiment of totalitarianism of the First Emperor of Ch'in in the end of the third century B.C., has always been to let the people alone; that *laissez faire* has been the key policy; that no other policy has been found to work; that the great Chinese empire was ruled without police always; that rule by force was long ago given up as impracticable and has not been attempted since the Ch'in Emperor's days; that the function of law has always been negative, and people regard it a shame to go to law courts; that there were no lawyers; that soldiers were despised, used by contending bandits struggling for the possession of the empire in times of chaos, but never relied upon in the normal running of government; that there was a sharp distinction between the "civil" (*wen*) and the "military" (*wu*), the former always taking precedence over the latter.

On the positive side, I find (1) since the Han Dynasty, the Chinese society has always been a truly classless society. The abolition of the feudal system of the Chou Dynasty and of the rights of primogeniture during the Han made the existence of aristocracy as a class impossible. (2) The selective service of the Imperial examinations in existence for about 1,500 years operated to form a constantly changing ruling class of scholars, insuring the rise of talent from the country. No one, not even the son of a beggar, was prevented from taking the examinations, if he had the talent, and no boy of talent, rich or poor, was ever overlooked by his village for training to rise to that ruling scholar class. Consequently, every one could become the Premier, or "There is no blood in premiers or generals," as the Chinese proverb says. (3) The theory of the right to revolt was perfected from the very earliest days, as will be seen from the following selections from the *Book of History* and *Mencius*. This is based on (4) the theory of the "mandate of Heaven," which is that the ruler ruled the people in trust from Heaven for the welfare of the people, and that when a ruler misruled, he automatically forfeited his right to rule. When Mencius was asked why, in contradiction to the theory of loyalty and obedience to the monarch, Emperor Wu rose in revolt against the tyrant Chou and overthrew the Shang Dynasty, his reply was that the King, by his misrule, was a common thief. In fact, the theory of the "mandate from Heaven" forms the outstanding feature of the entire *Book of History*. A corollary of that theory is that that mandate constantly changed, and that no king need think himself secure. "The favor of Heaven is not easily preserved; Heaven is difficult to depend on"; these statements abound in the *Book of History* and *Book of Poetry*. The threat of revolution was always there, and the word for "revolution" in Chinese (*kehming*) means "to change the mandate." Consequently, the divine right of kings became a very insecure and undependable thing. (5) The monarch was absolute in theory only; the system of imperial censors, appointed to censor, not the people, but the Emperor himself and the officials, was well defined and well developed. In the *History of the Press and Public Opinion in China* (University of Chicago), I have pointed out the instances when an Emperor could not even take a pleasure trip to the south at will, and when another could not appoint the son of his favorite concubine the Crown Prince, and the fight between the monarch and the censors and scholars dragged out for sixteen years.[1] (6) Connected with the censorship was the idea of the importance of public opinion. At the very dawn of Chinese civilization, in the reign of Shun (B.C. 2255–2198), his minister Kao-yao said, "Heaven hears and sees through (the ears and eyes of) our people. Heaven expresses its disapproval through the expressed disapproval of our people; such connection is there between the upper and lower (worlds)"—thus making the people's voice the voice of God. Also, in the Great Declaration (B.C. 1122), Emperor Wu declared to his hosts, "Heaven sees through the eyes of my people; Heaven hears through the ears of my people." These statements were later developed by Mencius, and became the philosophy of government of the court officials and historians, so that "to keep open the channels of speech" was always a cardinal tenet. (7) Back of it all was the concept that the people and ruler were complements in the structure of the state, found in several places in the *Book of History,* and further developed by Mencius. Mencius said regarding the different elements of a state, "The people are the most important, the spirits of the state the second, and the ruler the least important of all." As the book *Mencius* was prescribed reading in every school, every schoolboy learned this dictum from his childhood and had to commit it to memory. (8) Mencius further developed the theory of equality of all men. "The Sages are of the same species as ourselves." "All men can be Yao and Shun (ideal Sage emperors)." How did the Chinese find all these out? By common sense.

The peculiar developments of Chinese democracy can be understood only when we go back to the earliest sources of Chinese ideas. Why the Chinese never developed the parliamentary form of government, the election of rulers and the civil rights, will be apparent from any thoughtful study of Confucianism. The characteristics of Confucianism in the

[1] See *History of the Press,* etc., p. 65.

merging of morals and politics ("benevolent government" etc.), the emphasis on moral harmony as basis of political harmony, the total absence of any idea of "struggle" between ruler and subject or in any sphere will become apparent. It must be remembered that the philosophical basis of parliamentary government is distrust of the ruler. On the whole, Confucianism implies a naïve trust in the rulers, almost as naïve as the idea that a true government by the *demos* has ever become a reality. In fact, I would characterize the Confucian political ideal as strictly anarchism, in which moral culture of the people making government unnecessary becomes the ideal. If it is asked why the people of Chinatown in New York never have any use for the police, the answer is Confucianism. There never were any police in China for four thousand years. The people have got to learn to regulate their lives socially, and not rely upon the law. The law should be the resort of the scoundrel.

II. THE BOOK OF HISTORY

THE IMPORTANCE of the *Book of History* (*Shu King*) is basic. It is to Confucianism as the *Upanishads* are to Hinduism. Its basic importance comes not only from the fact that it contains the earliest historical documents and earliest Chinese writing, but also from the fact that it contains the deep moral wisdom which is the fountainhead of Confucian ideas. Confucius was strictly a historian, engaged in historical research, and spoke of himself as a transmitter rather than an innovator. He had a passion for history. After reading the *Book of History,* one can understand how Confucian ideas took their rise, including the Confucian gift for moralizing. An intensive study of Mencius will also show that he was extremely familiar with the *Book of History* and frequently quoted it to support his arguments. The whole idea of "benevolent government" (starting as a phrase with Mencius and not with Confucius) was developed from the *Book of History*. A casual reading of the Great Declaration will make this plain. Similarly, the ideas of "parental government," of the importance of moral example, of the "mandate of Heaven," and of the voice of the people as the voice of God, are all there.

The documents bearing most directly on democratic ideas and principles are: Common Possession of Pure Virtue, The Great Declaration, and Announcement of the Duke of Shao.

This work is a collection of important speeches and declarations given on historical or ceremonial occasions, like address to a host on the day of battle, or to a subjugated people after conquest, address to a people on the dedication of a new city, speech of a chief minister on his resignation from office, etc. In form it consists of "Declarations," "Announcements," "Counsels," "Charges" and recorded important conversations of wise rulers or counsellors of the state. These important speeches, like Lincoln's Gettysburg Address, were preserved in writing from the earliest times. There is an obscure tradition that there were one hundred pieces. Anyway, like the collection of *Liki,* it went through the hands of Confucius as the *Book of Poetry* was edited by him, and became one of the Confucian classics taught and studied by the Confucian scholars almost as their specialty. For it must be remembered that the Confucian School was principally an historical school, as distinguished from the others. How many such documents there were it is difficult to say, but it is certain that there were far more than the twenty-eight or twenty-nine pieces handed down in the Modern Script by Fu Sheng in the beginning of Han Dynasty. Quotations from it lay about in the works of the philosophers of the centuries after Confucius. The *Tsochüan* alone has sixty-eight quotations, of which only twenty-five are found in the Modern Script portion, the rest mostly in the Ancient Script portion.

As it now exists, in the standard text, there are fifty-eight pieces (counting the subdivisions), of which thirty-four are common to both Scripts, while twenty-four are based on the Ancient Script alone. It is this division that has called forth a great controversy about the authenticity of the Ancient Script portion.

III. ON THE AUTHENTICITY OF THE "ANCIENT SCRIPT"

THIS IS NOT THE PLACE to make a full and exhaustive discussion of the evidences for and against the Ancient Script of the *Book of History*. Inasmuch, however, as the present selection includes more documents of the Ancient Script than those common to the Modern Script and the Ancient Script, and inasmuch as some of the best passages occur in the Ancient Script portion, which is regarded by the majority of modern scholars as a forgery, a brief schematic outline of the reasons for including the Ancient Script portion must be given here for the lay reader.

A. What are Ancient and Modern Scripts?—When the first Ch'in Emperor burned the Confucian books in B.C. 213, most of them were destroyed. Four years later he died and his great empire began to crumble and in another three years, B.C. 206, it collapsed. There were many old scholars still living who had committed the texts to memory. A simplification of the Chinese script had taken place during the Ch'in reign by order of Li Sze, and the scholars began to write down what they remembered in the "Modern Script." Each particular version of the Confucian classics had a special tradition of interpretation which was handed down from teacher to student almost religiously. Then discoveries of ancient scripts kept coming to light. The most important one was the discovery of such texts in the walls of Confucius' house, evidently hidden there during the persecution, when Prince Kung of Lu began to tear it down to rebuild a better temple to Confucius. These were called the "Ancient Scripts." A separate tradition grew up, then, both with regard to text and interpretation. This division between the two traditions touches not only the *Book of History,* but also all the other Confucian classics. It must be remembered also that Ancient Scripts which modern scholars are trying to discredit include such standard texts as the *Tsochüan* and Mao's *Book of Poetry,* which are still our generally accepted sacred texts.

The attack on the Ancient Script tradition began with that on the *Book of History*. The first formidable attack on its authenticity was launched by Yen Jochü in the seventeenth century, followed soon by Hui Tung. In the eighteenth and nineteenth centuries, a fashion grew up to attack the Ancient Script of the different classics one after another, partly in regard to text, more chiefly in regard to interpretation of ancient institutions. These scholars of the Modern Script school went on with the crusade and devoted themselves to the barren studies of "bleary-eyed" *Kungyang* and "deformed" *Kuliang* in preference to the rich masterpiece, *Tsochüan,* and of Ch'i, Han and Lu versions of the *Book of Poetry,* in preference to the Mao. *Chouli* was regarded as a forgery. The results were extremely meager. The culprit of the forgery was usually traced to Wang Shu, or Liu Hsin. Finally, it culminated in the sweeping statement of K'ang Yuwei, the modern reformer associated with the reforms of 1898, who declared it was Confucius himself who forged all these books in order to lend an air of antiquity to his doctrines!

B. Chronology of the Survival of the Book of History.—The chronology of events concerning the survival of the two texts of the *Book of History* was as follows:

Third Century B.C.

In the time of Confucius (sixth century B.C.), about 100 or less pieces were known to have existed, according to a comparatively late tradition. In B.C. 213, during the burning of Confucian books, most copies were destroyed, but many were hidden away. Between Confucius and the burning of books, many scholars gave quotations from the *Book of History*. Some pieces may have been lost before then (witness the confusion regarding *Liki*).

Second Century B.C.

With the collapse of Ch'in and beginning of Han (B.C. 206), seven years after the burning, a scholar, Fu Sheng, who had hidden away his books in the wall, began to take them out, with many pieces missing, and to teach them to others. This was the *Modern Script,* of twenty-eight or twenty-nine pieces. During the reign of Han Wenti (B.C. 179–157), he was still living and over ninety years old. As he was too old to speak clearly, his daughter taught an official sent to his house by the Court. Owing to the difference in dialect, it was said that the official missed twenty or thirty per cent. From Han Wuti (B.C. 140–87), the preservation and teaching of this text were in the charge of a court official.

Between B.C. 140 and 128, Prince Kung of Lu tore down Confucius' house and discovered the Ancient Scripts of several classics. One of Confucius' descendants, K'ung Ankuo (who certainly lived between B.C. 156–74) took three months to read them by comparing them with the Modern Script and presented them to the Court; owing to some meddlers, these were not officially accepted for preservation and study by the Court. This is the *Ancient Script,* consisting of fifty-eight pieces. It is stated, and disputed, that K'ung also wrote a commentary (the *K'ung commentary*) and edited a preface. Szema Ch'ien, the great historian and author of *Shiki* (B.C. 145–before 86) saw both K'ung himself and his texts, and quoted them.

First Century B.C.

The titles and text of the Ancient Script were well-known to various Han scholars. Liu Hsiang (B.C. 79–6) in his bibliographical work was able to give titles of the fifty-eight pieces and count over seven hundred variations.

First and Second Centuries A.D.

Chia K'uei (A.D. 30–101), Ma Yung (A.D. 79–166) and Cheng K'ang-ch'eng (A.D. 127–200) wrote commentaries on the *Book of History,* but Ma Yung said there was "absolutely no teacher's tradition" in regard to the sixteen pieces (or twenty-four with subdivisions) of the Ancient Script. Cheng, however, quoted K'ung's explanations and gave a full list of the fifty-eight pieces, differing in some pieces from the present text. Between A.D. 25–56, one piece (*Wu-ch'eng*) was lost. These scholars also made use of one "volume" of Ancient Script in lacquer writing, discovered by Tu Lin who lived in the time of Kuangwuti (A.D. 25–57).

Third Century A.D.

Wang Shu (A.D. 159–256), the "forger" and a contemporary of Cheng, wrote a commentary on the *Book of History,* differing from Cheng's and agreeing with K'ung's. Huangfu Mi (A.D. 215–282) and Ho Yen (died 249) also made use of the K'ung commentaries in their works.

Fourth Century A.D.

In the reign of Yuanti (A.D. 317–322), Mei Tseh, a Recorder of the Interior, presented a copy of the K'ung text to the Emperor, which is our present official version, with fifty-eight pieces. Mei's tradition was traced back for five generations to Cheng Ch'ung in the time of Wang Shu. Mei was accused of forging the Ancient Script portion.

Fifth Century A.D.

Wang Shu's commentary and Cheng's commentary were accepted side by side, Wang's more in the south, Cheng's more in the north.

Sixth Century A.D.

In the T'ang Dynasty, K'ung Yingta (574–648) by imperial appointment wrote the commentary (*Chengyi*) on all fifty-eight pieces, incorporating the so-called K'ung commentaries. This became the standard text of the *Book of History* from then on to the present day.

C. The Question of Its Authenticity.—1. Intimidated by the vast display of erudition by the scholar critics, the majority of the modern scholars have accepted the Ancient Script as a forgery, in the sense that the present Ancient Script is not the genuine text of K'ung Ankuo, that certain subdivisions are unwarrantable, and that the so-called K'ung commentaries are not the genuine K'ung commentaries, though they believe generally in the Cheng commentaries. The last two points are less important than the first. Yen Jochü thought the Ancient Script had ceased to exist in Western Chin, and Mei Tseh was the forger, but Ting Yen thought it did exist in Western Chin and the forgery was by Wang Shu, and that because he was the grandfather-in-law of the first emperor of Western Chin, he was able to impose it on the scholars of the time. Ting Yen, however, concentrated on proving that the K'ung commentaries were not genuine, and that, furthermore, K'ung never wrote commentaries at all. Wei Yüan went further still in 1855 and attacked the Cheng and Ma commentaries, and even asserted that K'ung himself was of the Modern Script tradition, that in fact there was no distinction between Ancient and Modern Script schools in the Western Han at all. Such contradictory theses show how flimsy was the evidence from which each deduced his own conclusions.

2. In spite of the lengthy scholarly work of these "textual critics," I consider their methods as unscientific by the standards of modern textual criticism. These critics (including Yao Tsi-heng) combined enormous scholarly industry and erudition with loose reasoning, although Hui Tung was otherwise an extremely exact and conscientious scholar, being one of the best in the Manchu Dynasty. It must also be remembered that great scholars of the time, Mao Ch'iling and Tuan Yüts'ai, did not accept the theory, and later Sun Hsingyen adopted a conciliatory attitude. The case must be reopened.

3. Both Hui and Yen argued in a circle. The principal fact is that hundreds of quotations from the *Book of History* exist in ancient texts (*Analects, Mencius, Tsochüan, Shiki, Liki, Motse, Hsüntse,* etc.) which cannot be found in the twenty-eight pieces (or thirty-four with subdivisions) of the Modern Script, but most of them can be found in the Ancient Script portion. The argument was that the "forger" collected these quotations and with the help of other ancient ideas and phrases wove them into a patchwork, which was presented as the lost documents of the *Book of History*. Hui Tung went to the length of tracing these ideas and phrases and actual quotations to their "sources." He said there "was nothing wrong with their ideas." Yen said there is "not one important saying (in the forged texts) which did not have an ancient source." Even the casual use of words was proved to have been in consonance with the ancient usage. What does that prove?

4. The type of argument is as follows. I have examined Hui Tung's fifteen points and found that none of them holds, although on each point he merely drew a cautious, skeptical conclusion. If Mencius gave a quotation from the *Book of History* and it is found in the Ancient Script, they say, "You see there is the source of the forgery." If the words of the quotation do not quite agree, the Ancient Script is accused of "corrupting" them. If Mencius quoted directly from famous pieces like the "Speech of T'ang" or the "Great Declaration," and the Modern Script pieces do not contain those quotations, they argue that of course the present Modern Script is not complete in these pieces, while they dismiss the evidence that the quotations do exist in the "Announcement of T'ang" and the Ancient Script version of the "Great Declaration," as of no importance. The tracing of certain words of general use is still worse:

if *Tsochüan* used certain adjectives like "sincere" in connection with a certain person, that adjective may not be used of the same person by the Ancient Script without the charge of borrowing from *Tsochüan*. One of the chapters of *Liki* referred to the House of Yin as "Yi" in a certain sentence, and this Ancient Script has the same quotation; it is therefore argued that the Ancient Script should not have written it as Yi, whereas the right of the *Liki*'s text itself to do so is never questioned. This is arguing in a circle. But the type of loose reasoning mostly used is purely subjective and unscientific. According to the Ancient Script, Emperor Yü went to suppress the aborigines (Miao) after Shun had driven them out, and the critics exclaimed: Shun had driven them out, why should his successor fight them again? Moreover, as an emperor he should have sent his general instead! They wish to forget that repeated revolts of "pacified" aborigines are not so rare in history. According to the Ancient Script, a speech before the army was given by Emperor Shun, but these critics say, according to the Modern Script, the earliest speech before an army on the day of the battle is known to have been made by his immediate successor, Emperor Yü, and therefore this custom should not have begun with Shun, who was such a kind man. The assumption that the custom of addressing the hosts was suddenly invented by Yü is arbitrary and unwarranted. If in a Modern Script piece, Yao was described as offering the throne to Chi and Ch'i, then it was evidence of forgery for Yao to offer the same throne to Kao-yao also (in the Ancient Script piece). That is, Yao could have offered his throne to two persons successively, but not to three persons successively. As a matter of fact, Yao finally offered it to none of the three, but to Shun. If a certain piece of music (*Chiuko*), according to other ancient sources, is known only to have been played by Emperor Yü's son; then the mention of his father playing the same piece of music by the Ancient Script is adduced as evidence of contradiction to the ancient sources. There is no law forbidding a son from enjoying the same music as his father, and no evidence that that piece was composed by the son after the father died. In fact, many of the things mentioned by Mencius are just as "contradictory" to the tradition of the Modern Script, or just as much additions to the information in it, yet the authenticity of *Mencius* is not questioned. Such is the type of loose reasoning that leaves me unconvinced.

5. The only really "textual" criticism with regard to three words seems much better, but is connected with bad reasoning. The two words, *hsiang* for "premier" and *lun* for "discussion" are not known to have

occurred in the Five Classics. They abound, however, in the *Analects, Mencius* and *Tsochüan,* and the argument is not conclusive. It is really straining the point, however, to say that the word *yieh* (originally a "saw," then "fear," then "profession," "accomplishment") may be used in the latter senses in *Liki,* handed down by Confucius, but may not be used in the same senses in the *Book of History,* also handed down by Confucius. At the very worst, no word was used which was not current at the time of Confucius and Mencius.

6. The "motive" for the crime is insufficiently established. It is said that Wang Shu forged it to support his interpretations against Cheng's. Actually, Wang's commentaries dealt almost entirely with the Modern Script portion. Wang could have forged the K'ung commentaries, and not the text itself. Moreover, the critics, by their labors, proved that there was a continuity of tradition in the preservation of the Ancient Script, and that there was hardly a period when the Ancient Script was unknown or had disappeared.

7. There is no question but that several texts of all the Confucian classics existed side by side (e.g. four versions of the *Book of Poetry*), that none of them can claim to be an exact, complete, unspoiled version, that when texts were copied from generation to generation, corruption was inevitable, that all our texts, including the *Analects,* contain interpolations (usually at the end of chapters), and that the text of Mei Tseh is no exception. Mei was separated from the discovery of the Ancient Script in Confucius' walls by over four centuries. Even the assumption that there was only one correct, unspoiled, untouched text handed down by a kind of apostolic succession before the burning of books in B.C. 213 is incorrect. How did all the other books like *Motse, Mencius, Chuangtse, Ch'ü Yüan, Hsüntse, Kuoyü, Tsochüan* survive? Could even Confucius have the original text of the Canon of Yao 1,500 years old in his time? It is almost certain that variants were introduced, and that there were redivisions in at least two pieces. Redivisions and interpolations are part of the history of most ancient texts. But interpolations or redivisions are a different thing from forgery. It is also quite possible that the present K'ung commentaries may have been forged by Wang Shu, or some one else.

8. The fact remains that to cut out the Ancient Script portion from the *Book of History* would leave hundreds of quotations from it unaccounted for, especially when a quotation names the title of a particular piece, if we check it by the Modern Script. When Sun Hsingyen (A.D.

1753–1818) tried to do without the Ancient Script and restore the Great Declaration, the result was ridiculously meagre in content, with all the best quotations from this piece missing. The fact remains that the Ancient Script portion contains the richest parts of the work, and that irrespective of the argument whether our present copy is the original one found in Confucius' walls or any of the several found later, or just a later patchwork, most of its passages have, by the very labors of its critics, been proved to have existed as parts of the *Book of History* quoted in other works whose authenticity is not in question. Even as a patchwork of such quotations, it is an extremely useful piece of compilation. But more than that, the Ancient Script contains not only direct quotations, but also other material and ideas in the phraseology of the ancient times; the pieces have a good continuity and there are internal evidences of its authenticity; even the rhymes were ancient. It was such an able piece of work that it could deceive scholars for over 1,300 years, and it must have involved superhuman labors. I wish those critics would try such an undertaking of forgery themselves; even Confucius must shrink from the task. Finally, there is nothing regarding the condition of the text which we do not expect from one of that late date, and which we in fact find is true of both the *Analects* and the *Liki*.

9. The reader may therefore at least, pending the reopening of the case, regard those passages of the Ancient Script, which are supported by quotations found in other ancient sources like *Mencius,* as having certainly existed as parts of the *Book of History,* because Mencius said so. In the annotations I have tried to point out the supporting sources only for what I regard as the more important passages. Through these notes, the reader may gain some idea of the nature of the arguments for and against the Ancient Script. Incidentally, if the reader wishes to gather the most important "democratic" statements of this work, he need only check them through the footnotes.

I have used James Legge's translation, whose somewhat pretentious and quaint diction seems to suit these ancient documents well. I have made changes only in the spelling of proper names to conform with the current Wade romanization. Legge would spell, for instance, the name of the Chou Dynasty as "*K*âu". His curious spelling is due to the uniform spelling system of the Sacred Books of the East and to his Cantonese pronunciation.

The Book of History

Documents of Chinese Democracy (*Shu Ching*)

Translated by James Legge

THE CANON OF YAO [1]

(*Being the Book of T'ang. Modern and Ancient Scripts*) [2]

1. Examining into antiquity,[3] (we find that) the Ti Yao was styled Fang-hsün. He was reverential, intelligent, accomplished, and thoughtful,—naturally and without effort. He was sincerely courteous, and capable of (all) complaisance. The bright (influence of these qualities) was felt through the four quarters (of the land), and reached to (heaven) above and (earth) beneath.

He made the able and virtuous distinguished, and thence proceeded to the love of (all in) the nine classes of his kindred, who (thus) became harmonious. He (also) regulated and polished the people (of his domain), who all became brightly intelligent. (Finally), he united and

[1] Although having little to do with democracy, this document is interesting in itself as the oldest known piece of writing in Chinese. Emperor Yao reigned in B.C. 2357–2256. The Canon itself was written down probably centuries later.

[2] See Introduction.

[3] This shows that the Canon of Yao was not written at the time of Yao, but much later, which may be anywhere in the second millenium B.C. Chinese writing was supposed to have been invented by Ts'ang Chi, a minister of the Yellow Emperor, which is a tradition of legendary character. Recently excavated oracle bone inscriptions, dating back to about B.C. 2,000, show already advanced development.

harmonized the myriad states; and so the black-haired people were transformed. The result was (universal) concord.

2. He commanded the Hsis and Hos, in reverent accordance with (their observation of) the wide heavens, to calculate and delineate (the movements and appearances of) the sun, the moon, the stars, and the zodiacal spaces, and so to deliver respectfully the seasons to be observed by the people.

He separately commanded the second brother Hsi to reside at Yü-i, in what was called the Bright Valley, and (there) respectfully to receive as a guest the rising sun, and to adjust and arrange the labours of the spring. 'The day,' (said he), 'is of the medium length, and the star is in Niao;—you may thus exactly determine mid-spring. The people are dispersed (in the fields), and birds and beasts breed and copulate.'

He further commanded the third brother Hsi to reside at Nan-chiao, (in what was called the Brilliant Capital), to adjust and arrange the transformations of the summer, and respectfully to observe the exact limit (of the shadow). 'The day' (said he), 'is at its longest, and the star is in Huo;—you may thus exactly determine mid-summer. The people are more dispersed; and birds and beasts have their feathers and hair thin, and change their coats.'

He separately commanded the second brother Ho to reside at the west, in what was called the Dark Valley, and (there) respectfully to convoy the setting sun, and to adjust and arrange the completing labours of the autumn. 'The night' (said he), 'is of the medium length, and the star is in Hsü;—you may thus exactly determine mid-autumn. The people feel at ease, and birds and beasts have their coats in good condition.'

He further commanded the third brother Ho to reside in the northern region, in what was called the Sombre Capital, and (there) to adjust and examine the changes of the winter. 'The day' (said he), 'is at its shortest, and the star is in Mao;—you may thus exactly determine mid-winter. The people keep in their houses, and the coats of birds and beasts are downy and thick.'

The Ti [4] said, 'Ah! you, Hsis and Hos, a round year consists of three hundred and sixty-six days. Do you, by means of the intercalary month, fix the four seasons, and complete (the period of) the year. (Thereafter), the various officers being regulated in accordance with this, all the works (of the year) will be fully performed.'

[4] *Ti* means Emperor or Ruler.

3. The Ti said, 'Who will search out (for me) a man according to the times, whom I can raise and employ?' Fang-ch'i said, '(Your) heir-son Chu is highly intelligent.' The Ti said, 'Alas! he is insincere and quarrelsome:—can he do?'

The Ti said, 'Who will search out (for me) a man equal to the exigency of my affairs?' Huan-tao said, 'Oh! the merits of the Minister of Works have just been displayed on a wide scale.' The Ti said, 'Alas! when all is quiet, he talks; but when employed, his actions turn out differently. He is respectful (only) in appearance. See! the floods assail the heavens!'

The Ti said, 'Ho! (President of) the Four Mountains, destructive in their overflow are the waters of the inundation. In their vast extent they embrace the hills and overtop the great heights, threatening the heavens with their floods, so that the lower people groan and murmur! Is there a capable man to whom I can assign the correction (of this calamity)?' All (in the court) said, 'Ah! is there not Kun?' The Ti said, 'Alas! how perverse is he! He is disobedient to orders, and tries to injure his peers.' (The President of) the Mountains said 'Well but—. Try if he can (accomplish the work).' (Kun) was employed accordingly. The Ti said (to him), 'Go; and be reverent!' For nine years he laboured, but the work was unaccomplished.

The Ti said, 'Ho! (President of) the Four Mountains, I have been on the throne seventy years. You can carry out my commands;—I will resign my place to you.' The Chief said, 'I have not the virtue;—I should disgrace your place.' (The Ti) said, 'Show me some one among the illustrious, or set forth one from among the poor and mean.' All (then) said to the Ti, 'There is an unmarried man among the lower people, called Shun of Yü[5].' The Ti said, 'Yes, I have heard of him. What have you to say about him?' The Chief said, 'He is the son of a blind man. His father was obstinately unprincipled; his (step-) mother was insincere; his (half-) brother Hsiang was arrogant. He has been able, (however), by his filial piety to live in harmony with them, and to lead them gradually to self-government, so that they (no longer) proceed to great wickedness.' The Ti said, 'I will try him; I will wive him, and thereby see his behaviour with my two daughters.' (Accordingly) he arranged and sent down his two daughters to the north of the Kwei, to be wives in (the family of) Yü. The Ti said to them, 'Be reverent!'

[5] Emperor Shun who reigned in B.C. 2255–2206 as successor to Yao.

[*A division is made here in the Ancient Script, and what follows is given the name of the 'Canon of Shun,' while the Modern Script regards the whole as the Canon of Yao. A spurious paragraph of 28 words, added in A.D. 497, is omitted here.—Ed.*]

4. (Shun) carefully set forth the beauty of the five cardinal duties, and they came to be (universally) observed. Being appointed to be General Regulator, the affairs of every (official) department were arranged in their proper seasons. (Being charged) to receive (the princes) from the four quarters of the land, they were all docilely submissive. Being sent to the great plains at the foot of the mountains, notwithstanding the tempests of wind, thunder, and rain, he did not go astray.

The Ti said, 'Come, you Shun. I have consulted you on (all) affairs, and examined your words, and found that they can be carried into practice;—(now) for three years. Do you ascend the seat of the Ti.' Shun wished to decline in favour of some one more virtuous, and not to consent to be (Yao's) successor. On the first day of the first month, (however), he received (Yao's) retirement (from his duties) in the temple of the Accomplished Ancestor.

5. He examined the pearl-adorned turning sphere, with its transverse tube of jade, and reduced to a harmonious system (the movements of) the Seven Directors.

Thereafter, he sacrificed specially, but with the ordinary forms, to God; sacrificed with reverent purity to the Six Honoured Ones; offered their appropriate sacrifices to the hills and rivers; and extended his worship to the host of spirits.

He called in (all) the five jade-symbols of rank; and when the month was over, he gave daily audience to (the President of) the Four Mountains, and all the Pastors,[6] (finally) returning their symbols to the various princes.

In the second month of the year he made a tour of inspection eastwards, as far as Tai-chung, where he presented a burnt-offering to Heaven, and sacrificed in order to the hills and rivers. Thereafter he gave audience to the princes of the east. He set in accord their seasons and months, and regulated the days; he made uniform the standard-tubes, with the measures of length and of capacity, and the steel-yards; he regulated the five (classes of) ceremonies, with (the various) articles of introduction,—

[6] *Mu,* literally "shepherds (of the people)."

the five symbols of jade, the three kinds of silk, the two living (animals) and the one dead one. As to the five instruments of rank, when all was over, he returned them. In the fifth month he made a similar tour southwards, as far as the mountain of the south, where he observed the same ceremonies as at Tai. In the eighth month he made a tour westwards, as far as the mountain of the west, where he did as before. In the eleventh month he made a tour northwards, as far as the mountain of the north, where he observed the same ceremonies as in the west. He (then) returned (to the capital), went to (the temple of) the Cultivated Ancestor, and sacrificed a single bull.

In five years there was one tour of inspection, and there were four appearances of the princes at court. They gave a report (of their government) in words, which was clearly tested by their works. They received chariots and robes according to their merits.

He instituted the division (of the land) into twelve provinces, raising altars upon twelve hills in them. He (also) deepened the rivers.

He exhibited (to the people) the statutory punishments, enacting banishment as a mitigation of the five (great) inflictions; with the whip to be employed in the magistrates' courts, the stick to be employed in schools, and money to be received for redeemable offences. Inadvertent offences and those which could be ascribed to misfortune were to be pardoned, but those who transgressed presumptuously and repeatedly were to be punished with death. 'Let me be reverent! Let me be reverent!' (he said to himself.) 'Let compassion rule in punishment!'

He banished the Minister of Works to Yü island; confined Huan-tao on Mount Ch'ung; drove (the chief of) San-miao (and his people) into San-wei and kept them there; and held Kun a prisoner till death on Mount Yü. These four criminals being thus dealt with, all under Heaven acknowledged the justice (of Shun's administration).

6. After twenty-eight years the Ti deceased, when the people mourned for him as for a parent for three years. Within the four seas all the eight kinds of instruments of music were stopped and hushed. On the first day of the first month (of the) next year, Shun went to (the temple of) the Accomplished Ancestor.

7. He deliberated with (the President of) the Four Mountains how to throw open the doors (of communication between himself and the) four (quarters of the land), and how he could see with the eyes, and hear with the ears of all.

He consulted with the twelve Pastors, and said to them, 'The food!—it depends on observing the seasons. Be kind to the distant, and cultivate the ability of the near. Give honour to the virtuous, and your confidence to the good, while you discountenance the artful;—so shall the barbarous tribes lead on one another to make their submission.'

Shun said, 'Ho! (President of) the Four Mountains, is there any one who can with vigorous service attend to all the affairs of the Ti, whom I may appoint to be General Regulator, to assist me in (all) affairs, managing each department according to its nature? All (in the court) replied, 'There is Po-yü, the Minister of Works.' The Ti said, 'Yes. Ho! Yü, you have regulated the water and the land. In this (new office) exert yourself.' Yü did obeisance with his head to the ground, and wished to decline in favour of the Minister of Agriculture, or Hsieh, or Kao-yao. The Ti said, 'Yes, but do you go (and undertake the duties).'

The Ti said, 'Ch'i, the black-haired people are (still) suffering from famine. Do you, O prince, as Minister of Agriculture, (continue to) sow (for them) the various kinds of grain.'

The Ti said, 'Hsieh, the people are (still) wanting in affection for one another, and do not docilely observe the five orders of relationship. It is yours, as the Minister of Instruction, reverently to set forth the lessons of duty belonging to those five orders. Do so with gentleness.'

The Ti said, 'Kao-yao, the barbarous tribes trouble our great land. There are (also) robbers, murderers, insurgents, and traitors. It is yours, as the Minister of Crime, to use the five punishments to deal with their offences. For the infliction of these there are the three appointed places. There are the five cases in which banishment in the appropriate places is to be resorted to, to which places, though five, three localities are assigned. Perform your duties with intelligence, and you will secure a sincere (submission).'

The Ti said, 'Who can superintend my works, as they severally require?' All (in the court) replied, 'Is there not Shui?' The Ti said, 'Yes. Ho! Shui, you must be Minister of Works.' Shui did obeisance with his head to the ground, and wished to decline in favour of Shu, Ch'iang, or Po-yü. The Ti said, 'Yes, but do you go (and undertake the duties). Effect a harmony (in all the departments).'

The Ti said, 'Who can superintend, as the nature of the charge requires, the grass and trees, with the birds and beasts on my hills and in my marshes?' All (in the court) replied, 'Is there not Yi?' The Ti said, 'Yes. Ho! Yi, do you be my Forester.' did obeisance with his head to the ground, and wished to decline in favour of Chu, Hu, Hsiung, or Pi.[7] The Ti said, 'Yes, but do you go (and undertake the duties). You must manage them harmoniously.'

The Ti said, 'Ho! (President of the) Four Mountains, is there any one able to direct my three (religious) ceremonies?' All (in the court) answered, 'Is there not Po-i?' The Ti said, 'Yes. Ho! Po, you must be the Arranger in the Ancestral Temple. Morning and night be reverent. Be upright, be pure.' Po did obeisance with his head to the ground, and wished to decline in favour of K'uei[8] or Lung.[9] The Ti said, 'Yes, but do you go (and undertake the duties). Be reverential!'

The Ti said, 'K'uei, I appoint you to be Director of Music, and to teach our sons, so that the straightforward shall yet be mild; the gentle, dignified; the strong, not tyrannical; and the impetuous, not arrogant. Poetry is the expression of earnest thought; singing is the prolonged utterance of that expression; the notes accompany that utterance, and they are harmonized themselves by the standard-tubes. (In this way) the eight different kinds of musical instruments can be adjusted so that one shall not take from or interfere with another; and spirits and men are brought into harmony.' K'uei said, 'I smite the (sounding-) stone, I gently strike it, and the various animals lead on one another to dance.'

The Ti said, 'Lung, I abominate slanderous speakers and destroyers of the (right) ways, who agitate and alarm my people. I appoint you to be the Minister of Communication.[10] Early and late give forth my orders and report to me, seeing that everything is true.'

The Ti said, 'Ho! you, twenty and two men, be reverent; so shall you be helpful to the business (entrusted to me by) Heaven.'

Every three years there was an examination of merits, and after three examinations the undeserving were degraded, and the deserving advanced. (By this arrangement) the duties of all the departments were fully discharged; the (people of) San-miao (also) were discriminated and separated.

8. In the thirtieth year of his age, Shun was called to employment. Thirty years he was on the throne (with Yao). Fifty years afterwards he went on high and died.

[7] Four persons' names: Cedar (possibly Hog), Tiger, Bear and Grisly Bear.
[8] A horned animal.
[9] Dragon.
[10] *Na-yen,* strictly "to receive reports." The earliest reference to an office for communications between ruler and people that in later dynasties existed under various names.

THE COUNSELS OF THE GREAT YU

(*Book of Yü,*[11] *II. Ancient Script*)

1. Examining into antiquity, (we find that) the Great Yü[12] was styled Wen-ming. Having arranged and divided (the land), all to the four seas, in reverent response to the Ti, he said, 'If the sovereign can realize the difficulty of his sovereignship, and the minister the difficulty of his ministry, the government will be well ordered, and the black-haired people will sedulously seek to be virtuous.'

The Ti said, 'Yes; let this really be the case, and good words will nowhere lie hidden; no men of virtue and talents will be left neglected, away from court, and the myriad states will all enjoy repose. (But) to obtain the views of all; to give up one's opinion and follow that of others; to keep from oppressing the helpless, and not to neglect the straitened and poor;—it was only the (former) Ti who could attain to this.'

Yi said, 'Oh! your virtue, O Ti, is vast and incessant. It is sagely, spirit-like, awe-inspiring, and adorned with all accomplishments. Great Heaven regarded you with its favour, and bestowed on you its appointment. Suddenly you possessed all within the four seas, and became ruler of all under heaven.'

Yü said, 'Accordance with the right leads to good fortune; following what is opposed to it, to bad;—the shadow and the echo.' Yi said, 'Alas! be cautious! Admonish yourself to caution, when there seems to be no occasion for anxiety. Do not fail to observe the laws and ordinances. Do not find your enjoyment in idleness. Do not go to excess in pleasure. In your employment of men of worth, let none come between you and them. Put away evil without hesitation. Do not carry out plans, of (the wisdom of) which you have doubts. Study that all your purposes may be with the light of reason. Do not go against what is right, to get the praise of the people. Do not oppose the people's (wishes), to follow your own desires. (Attend to these things) without idleness or omission, and the barbarous tribes all around will come and acknowledge your sovereignty.'

Yü said, 'Oh! think (of these things), O Ti. The virtue (of the ruler) is seen in (his) good government, and that government in the nourish-

[11] Name of the rule of Shun. In this "Book," the *Ti,* or Ruler, refers to Shun.

[12] This "Yü" (different from that in Note 11) is the great Emperor Yü, founder of Hsia Dynasty and successor to Shun.

ing of the people.[13] There are water, fire, metal, wood, the earth, and grain,—these must be duly regulated; there are the rectification of (the people's) virtue, (the tools and other things) that supply the conveniences of life, and the securing abundant means of sustentation,—these must be harmoniously attended to. When the nine services (thus indicated) have been orderly accomplished, that accomplishment will be hailed by (the people's) songs. Caution them with gentle (words), correct them with the majesty (of law), stimulate them with the songs on those nine subjects,—in order that (your success) may not suffer diminution.' The Ti said, 'The earth has been reduced to order, and the (influences of) heaven produce their complete effect; those six magazines and three departments of (governmental) action are all truly regulated, and may be depended on for a myriad generations:—this is your merit.'

2. The Ti said, 'Come, you Yü. I have occupied my place for thirty and three years. I am between ninety and a hundred years old, and the laborious duties weary me. Do you, eschewing all indolence, take the leading of my people.'[14] Yü replied, 'My virtue is not equal (to the position), and the people will not repose in me. (But there is) Kao-yao with vigorous activity sowing abroad his virtue, which has descended on the black-haired people, till they cherish him in their hearts. O Ti, think of him! When I think of him, (my mind) rests on him (as the man fit for this place); when I would put him out of my thoughts, (my mind still) rests on him; when I name and speak of him, (my mind) rests on him (for this); the sincere outgoing of my thoughts about him is that he is the man. O Ti, think of his merits.'

The Ti said, 'Kao-yao, that of these my ministers and all (my people) hardly one is found to offend against the regulations of the government is owing to your being Minister of Crime, and intelligent in the use of the five punishments, thereby assisting (the inculcation of) the five cardinal duties, with a view to the perfection of my government, and that through punishment there may come to be no punishments,[15] but

[13] Yen Jo-chü who tried to prove that the whole Ancient Script was a forgery cites here a similar passage in *Tsochüan* to show the source of the forgery. The same evidence can be used to show that it was genuine, for *Tsochüan* expressly quotes from the *Book of History*. This is typical of Yen's method of reasoning and also of Hui Tung's. Almost all passages in this piece are traced to parallel passages in ancient texts (*Tsochüan, Book of Changes, Laotse, Motse, Hsüntse,* the *Analects,* etc.) most of which give them as quotations from the *Book of History*.

[14] Shun, like his predecessor Yao, did not give his throne to his son, but to the best man of proved ability in the kingdom. Hereditary succession began with Yü's son.

[15] Parallel passage in a quotation from Shang Yang's book.

the people accord with (the path of) the Mean. (Continue to) be strenu ous.' Kao-yao replied, 'Your virtue, O Ti, is faultless. You condescend tc your ministers with a kindly ease; you preside over the multitudes witl a generous forbearance. Punishments do not extend to (the criminal's) heirs, while rewards reach to (succeeding) generations. You pardon inad vertent faults, however great, and punish purposed crimes, howeve small.[16] In cases of doubtful crimes, you deal with them lightly; in case of doubtful merit, you prefer the high estimation. Rather than put a innocent person to death, you will run the risk of irregularity and error.[1] This life-loving virtue has penetrated the minds of the people, and this i why they do not render themselves liable to be punished by your officers. The Ti said, 'That I am able to follow and obtain what I desire in my government, the people responding everywhere as if moved by the wind —this is your excellence.'

The Ti said, 'Come, Yü. The inundating waters filled me with dread when you accomplished truly (all that you had represented), and com pleted your service;—thus showing your superiority to other men. Ful of toilsome earnestness in the service of the country, and sparing in you expenditure on your family, and this without being full of yourself an elated,—you (again) show your superiority to other men. You are with out any prideful assumption, but no one under heaven can contest witl you the palm of ability; you make no boasting, but no one under heave can contest with you the palm of merit.[18] I see how great is your virtue how admirable your vast achievements. The determinate appointmen of Heaven rests on your person; you must eventually ascend (the throne) of the great sovereign. The mind of man is restless, prone (to err); it affinity to what is right is small.[19] Be discriminating, be uniform (in th pursuit of what is right), that you may sincerely hold fast the Mean.[20] D not listen to unsubstantiated words; do not follow plans about which yo have not sought counsel. Of all who are to be loved, is not the ruler th chief? Of all who are to be feared, are not the people the chief? If th multitude were without their sovereign Head, whom should they sustai aloft? If the sovereign had not the multitude, there would be none t

[16] Parallel passage in Wang Ch'ung.
[17] Exact words of a quotation from the *Book of History (Book of Hsia)* given in *Tsochüa*
[18] See *Laotse,* Ch. 22, 24. The same idea is expressed in identical words in *Hsüntse,* and gen erally in *Book of Changes, Tsochüan* and *Yi Choushu,* so that it is hardly possible to poi even to Laotse as the ultimate source. Laotse himself quotes from ancient sayings.
[19] Parallel passage in Hsüntse.
[20] The *Analects* gives this quotation as from the *Book of History.*

guard the country for him. Be reverential! Carefully maintain the throne which you are to occupy, cultivating (the virtues) that are to be desired in you. If within the four seas there be distress and poverty, your Heaven-conferred revenues will come to a perpetual end. It is the mouth which sends forth what is good, and raises up war. I will not alter my words.'

Yü said, 'Submit the meritorious ministers one by one to the trial of divination, and let the favouring indication be followed.' The Ti replied, '(According to the rules for) the regulation of divination, one should first make up his mind, and afterwards refer (his judgment) to the great tortoise-shell.[21] My mind (in this matter) was determined in the first place; I consulted and deliberated with all (my ministers and people), and they were of one accord with me. The spirits signified their assent, and the tortoise-shell and divining stalks concurred. Divination, when fortunate, should not be repeated.' Yü did obeisance with his head to the ground, and firmly declined (the place). The Ti said, 'You must not do so. It is you who can suitably (occupy my place).' On the first morning of the first month, (Yü) received the appointment in the temple (dedicated by Shun) to the spirits of his ancestors, and took the leading of all the officers, as had been done by the Ti at the commencement (of his government).

3. The Ti said, 'Alas! O Yü, there is only the lord of Miao who refuses obedience; do you go and correct him.' Yü on this assembled all the princes, and made a speech to the host, saying, 'Ye multitudes here arrayed, listen all of you to my orders. Stupid is this lord of Miao, ignorant, erring, and disrespectful. Despiteful and insolent to others, he thinks that all ability and virtue are with himself. A rebel to the right, he destroys (all the obligations of) virtue. Superior men are kept by him in obscurity, and mean men fill (all) the offices. The people reject him and will not protect him. Heaven is sending down calamities upon him. I therefore, along with you, my multitude of gallant men, bear the instructions (of the Ti) to punish his crimes. Do you proceed with united heart and strength, so shall our enterprize be crowned with success.'

At the end of three decades,[22] the people of Miao continued rebellious against the commands (issued to them), when Yi came to the help of Yü, saying, 'It is virtue that moves Heaven; there is no distance to which it

[21] This very interesting and sensible idea is found also in The Great Plan elsewhere in the *Book of History* of the Modern Script collection.

[22] Another interpretation is thirty days.

does not reach. Pride brings loss, and humility receives increase;[23]—thi is the way of Heaven. In the early time of the Ti, when he was living by Mount Li, he went into the fields, and daily cried with tears to com passionate Heaven, and to his parents, taking to himself all guilt, and charging himself with (their) wickedness. (At the same time) with respectful service he appeared before Ku-sau,[24] looking grave and awe struck, till Kü also became transformed by his example. Entire sincerity moves spiritual beings,—how much more will it move this lord of Miao! Yü did homage to the excellent words, and said, 'Yes.' (Thereupon) he led back his army, having drawn off the troops. The Ti set about diffusing on a grand scale the virtuous influences of peace;—with shields and feathers they danced between the two staircases (in his courtyard). In seventy days, the lord of Miao came (and made his submission).[25]

THE COUNSELS OF KAO-YAO

(*Book of Yü, III. Modern and Ancient Scripts*)

1. Examining into antiquity, (we find that) Kao-yao[26] said, 'If (the sovereign) sincerely pursues the course of his virtue, the counsels (offered to him) will be intelligent, and the aids (of admonition that he receives) will be harmonious.' Yü said, 'Yes, but explain yourself.' Kao-yao said, 'Oh! let him be careful about his personal cultivation, with thoughts that are far-reaching, and thus he will produce a generous kindness and nice observance of distinctions among the nine branches of his kindred. All the intelligent (also) will exert themselves in his service; and in this way from what is near he will reach to what is distant.' Yü did homage to the excellent words, and said, 'Yes.' Kao-yao continued, 'Oh! it lies in knowing men, and giving repose to the people.' Yü said, 'Alas! to attain to both these things might well be a difficulty even to the Ti. When (the sovereign) knows men, he is wise, and can put every one into the office for which he is fit. When he gives repose to the people, his kindness is

[23] Parallel passage in *Book of Changes*.

[24] Shun's own wicked father. Parallel story with further details in *Mencius*.

[25] As an example of the bad reasoning used to prove the forgery of the Ancient Script, I may cite the case here where both Hui and Yen impatiently ask if the Miaos were "pacified" why there was another expedition later. Common sense should see that periodic and repeated revolts of pacified aborigines are by no means uncommon. Arguments of this type prove nothing.

[26] Minister of Justice under Emperor Shun.

elt, and the black-haired race cherish him in their hearts.[27] When he can
e (thus) wise and kind, what occasion will he have for anxiety about
Huan-tao? what to be removing a lord of Miao? what to fear any one
f fair words, insinuating appearance, and great artfulness?'

2. Kao-yao said, 'Oh! there are in all nine virtues to be discovered in
onduct, and when we say that a man possesses (any) virtue, that is as
nuch as to say he does such and such things.' Yü asked, 'What (are the
ine virtues)?' Kao-yao replied, 'Affability combined with dignity;
nildness combined with firmness; bluntness combined with respectful-
ess; aptness for government combined with reverent caution; docility
ombined with boldness; straightforwardness combined with gentleness;
n easy negligence combined with discrimination; boldness combined
vith sincerity; and valour combined with righteousness. (When these
ualities are) displayed, and that continuously, have we not the good
officer)? When there is a daily display of three (of these) virtues, their
ossessor could early and late regulate and brighten the clan (of which
e was made chief). When there is a daily severe and reverent cultiva-
ion of six of them, their possessor could brilliantly conduct the affairs of
he state (with which he was invested). When (such men) are all re-
eived and advanced, the possessors of those nine virtues will be em-
loyed in (the public) service. The men of a thousand and men of a
undred will be in their offices; the various ministers will emulate one
nother; all the officers will accomplish their duties at the proper times,
bservant of the five seasons (as the several elements predominate in
hem),—and thus their various duties will be fully accomplished. Let not
the Son of Heaven) set to the holders of states the example of indolence
r dissoluteness. Let him be wary and fearful, (remembering that) in
ne day or two days there may occur ten thousand springs of things. Let
im not have his various officers cumberers of their places. The work is
Heaven's; men must act for it!'

3. 'From Heaven are the (social) relationships with their several
luties; we are charged with (the enforcement of) those five duties;—
nd lo! we have the five courses of honourable conduct.[28] From Heaven

[27] Ideas like this, common in the *Book of History,* inspired Mencius in his theory of "benevo-
ent government." Mencius quoted the *Book of History* to the extent that we are justified
n saying that the *Book of History* was the fountainhead of his democratic ideas. The pas-
ages he quoted are often missing in the Modern Script and found in the Ancient Script.

[28] Legge's translation follows, as usual, the T'ang and Sung commentators. This Confucianist
nterpretation is not warranted by such Han commentators as Cheng K'ang-ch'eng, and not
y the text itself.

are the (social) distinctions with their several ceremonies; from us come the observances of those five ceremonies;—and lo! they appear in regular practice. When (sovereign and ministers show) a common reverence and united respect for these, lo! the moral nature (of the people) is made harmonious. Heaven graciously distinguishes the virtuous;—are there not the five habiliments, five decorations of them? Heaven punishes the guilty;—are there not the five punishments, to be severally used for that purpose? The business of government!—ought we not to be earnest in it? ought we not to be earnest in it?

'Heaven hears and sees as our people hear and see; Heaven brightly approves and displays its terrors as our people brightly approve and would awe;[29]—such connection is there between the upper and lower (worlds). How reverent ought the masters of territories to be!'

4. Kao-yao said, 'My words are in accordance with reason, and may be put in practice.' Yü said, 'Yes, your words may be put in practice, and crowned with success.' Kao-yao added, '(As to that) I do not know, but I wish daily to be helpful. May (the government) be perfected!'[30]

THE SONGS OF THE FIVE SONS

(Book of Hsia, III. Ancient Script.)

1. T'ai-K'ang[31] occupied the throne like a personator of the dead. By idleness and dissipation he extinguished his virtue, till the black-haired people all wavered in their allegiance. He, however, pursued his pleasure and wanderings without any self-restraint. He went out to hunt beyond the Lo, and a hundred days elapsed without his returning. (On this) Yi the prince of Ch'iung, taking advantage of the discontent of the people resisted (his return) on (the south of) the Ho.[32] The (king's) five brothers had attended their mother in following him, and were waiting for him on the north of the Lo; and (when they heard of Yi's movement)

[29] This translation is quite bad and inexact. It should read, "Heaven hears and sees through (the ears and eyes) of our people. Heaven expresses its disapproval through the expressed disapproval of our people." Compare almost similar expression in a quotation by Mencius from the Great Declaration (q.v.).

[30] According to the Ancient Script, the document ends here, while the Modern Script combines it with another document (Yi and Chi), not reproduced in this volume.

[31] Emperor T'ai-k'ang, who reigned B.C. 2188–2160, had five brothers who revolted against him. The "critics" do not approve of the idea of fratricide from a moral point of view and use it as an argument for the theory of "forgery" of this piece.

[32] The Yellow River.

all full of dissatisfaction, they related the Cautions of the great Yü [33] in the form of songs.

2. The first said,
'It was the lesson of our great ancestor:—
The people should be cherished,
And not looked down upon.[34]
The people are the root of a country;
The root firm, the country is tranquil.[35]
When I look at all under heaven,
Of the simple men and simple women,
Any one may surpass me.
If the One man err repeatedly,
Should dissatisfaction be waited for till it appears?
Before it is seen, it should be guarded against.[36]
In my dealing with the millions of the people,
I should feel as much anxiety as if I were driving six horses with rotten reins.
The ruler of men—
How should he be but reverent (of his duties)?'

The second said,
'It is in the Lessons:—
When the palace is a wild of lust,
And the country is a wild for hunting;
When spirits are liked, and music is the delight;
When there are lofty roofs and carved walls;—
The existence of any one of these things
Has never been but the prelude to ruin.' [37]

The third said,
'There was the lord of T'ao and T'ang,[38]
Who possessed this region of Chi.

[33] Their grandfather.
[34] Quotation given in a commentary on *Kuoyü* by Wei Chao (A.D. 204–273) as existing in the *Book of Hsia*, showing that Wei Chao knew this text, i.e., this text existed and was not unknown before Mei Cheh suddenly "forged" it in the following century.
[35] Huainantse (c. B.C. 178–122) says, "People are to the state as the foundations are to the city wall."
[36] Quotations exist in *Tsochüan* and *Kuoyü*.
[37] Story of Yü's sayings given in *Chankuots'eh*.
[38] "T'ao T'ang" is the name of Yao's rule.

Now we have fallen from his ways,
And thrown into confusion his rules and laws;—
The consequence is extinction and ruin.'

The fourth said,
'Brightly intelligent was our ancestor,
Sovereign of the myriad regions.
He had canons, he had patterns,
Which he transmitted to his posterity.
The standard stone and the equalizing quarter
Were in the royal treasury.
Wildly have we dropt the clue he gave us,
Overturning our temple, and extinguishing our sacrifices.'

The fifth said,
'Oh! whither shall we turn?
The thoughts in my breast make me sad.
All the people are hostile to us;
On whom can we rely?
Anxieties crowd together in our hearts;
Thick as are our faces, they are covered with blushes.
We have not been careful of our virtue;
And though we repent, we cannot overtake the past.' [39]

THE ANNOUNCEMENT OF T'ANG
(*Book of Shang, III. Ancient Script*)

1. When the king [40] returned from vanquishing Hsia and came to Po, he made a grand announcement to the myriad regions.

2. The king said, 'Ah! ye multitudes of the myriad regions, listen clearly to the announcement of me, the One man. The great God has conferred (even) on the inferior people a moral sense, compliance with which would show their nature invariably right.[41] To make them tran-

[39] Yen's accusation that "there is not enough rhyme" in these songs is entirely unfair.

[40] Emperor T'ang (reign B.C. 1783–1754), founder of the Shang Dynasty, had just overthrown Chieh, the last emperor of Hsia, and returned to the capital. In this announcement to bid for the support of the princes and the people is first found the famous theory of the "mandate of Heaven," which is that the ruler rules the people for the people's good in a mandate from Heaven. The right to revolt, in contradiction to the doctrine of loyalty to the monarch, early puzzled the Confucianists, and this theory was the answer. Mencius fully developed it.

[41] Quoted by Hanfeitse as a saying of Confucius.

quilly pursue the course which it would indicate is the work of the sovereign.

'The king of Hsia extinguished his virtue, and played the tyrant, extending his oppression over you, the people of the myriad regions. Suffering from his cruel injuries, and unable to endure the worm-wood and poison, you protested with one accord your innocence to the spirits of heaven and earth. The way of Heaven is to bless the good, and make the bad miserable.[42] It sent down calamities on (the House of) Hsia, to make manifest its guilt. Therefore I, the little child, charged with the decree of Heaven and its bright terrors, did not dare to forgive (the criminal). I presumed to use a dark-coloured victim-bull, and, making clear announcement to the Spiritual Sovereign in the high heavens, requested leave to deal with the ruler of Hsia as a criminal. Then I sought for the great Sage, with whom I might unite my strength, to request the favour (of Heaven) for you, my multitudes. High Heaven truly showed its favour to the inferior people, and the criminal [43] has been degraded and subjected. What Heaven appoints is without error;—brilliantly (now), like the blossoming of plants and trees, the millions of the people show a true reviving.'

3. 'It is given to me, the One man, to secure the harmony and tranquillity of your states and clans; and now I know not whether I may not offend against (the Powers) above and below. I am fearful and trembling, as if I were in danger of falling into a deep abyss. Throughout all the regions that enter on a new life under me, do not, (ye princes), follow lawless ways; make no approach to insolence and dissoluteness; let every one be careful to keep his statutes;—that so we may receive the favour of Heaven. The good in you I will not dare to keep concealed; and for the evil in me I will not dare to forgive myself. I will examine these things in harmony with the mind of God. When guilt is found anywhere in you who occupy the myriad regions, let it rest on me, the One man. When guilt is found in me, the One man, it shall not attach to you who occupy the myriad regions.[44]

[42] Parallel passages in *Tsochüan* and *Kuoyü.*

[43] Mencius says that when a ruler misrules, he is a common thief. Legge's translation of "inferior people" for "the people below" (i.e. on earth) is distinctly wrong.

[44] Quotation cited in the *Analects, Kuoyü, Motse* and *Shiki.* It is not found in the Speech of T'ang (Modern Script). In a case like this, Yen argues that T'ang did make this statement, but that it still must have been recorded in a lost Ancient Script, but not in the present spurious one!

'Oh! let us attain to be sincere in these things, and so we shall likewise have a (happy) consummation.

T'AI CHIA

(*Book of Shang, V. Ancient Script. Section 1 omitted here*)

Section 2

1. On the first day of the twelfth month of his third year, Yi Yin[45] escorted the young king in the royal cap and robes back to Po. (At the same time) he made the following writing:—

'Without the sovereign, the people cannot have that guidance which is necessary to (the comfort of) their lives; without the people, the sovereign would have no sway over the four quarters (of the kingdom).[46] Great Heaven has graciously favoured the House of Shang, and granted to you, O young king, at last to become virtuous. This is indeed a blessing that will extend without limit to ten thousand generations.'

2. The king did obeisance with his face to his hands and his head to the ground saying, 'I, the little child, was without understanding of what was virtuous, and was making myself one of the unworthy. By my desires I was setting at nought all rules of conduct, and violating by my self-indulgence all rules of propriety, and the result must have been speedy ruin to my person. Calamities sent by Heaven may be avoided, but from calamities brought on by one's self there is no escape.[47] Heretofore I turned my back on the instructions of you, my tutor and guardian;—my beginning has been marked by incompetency. Let me still rely on your correcting and preserving virtue, keeping this in view that my end may be good!'

3. Yi Yin did obeisance with his face to his hands and his head on the ground, and said, 'To cultivate his person, and by being sincerely virtuous, bring (all) below to harmonious concord with him;—this is the work of the intelligent sovereign. The former king was kind to the distressed and suffering, as if they were his children, and the people submitted to his commands,—all with sincere delight. Even in the states of the neighbouring princes, (the people) said, "We are waiting for our sovereign; when

[45] Yi Yin, exasperated at the conduct of the young king, had retired to the country in protest. Then the young king repented and went to see him.

[46] This sentence exists as a quotation from this document in *Shiki*.

[47] Exact words used by Mencius and in *Liki* as a quotation from this document.

our sovereign comes, we shall not suffer the punishments (that we now do)."

'O king, zealously cultivate your virtue. Regard (the example of) your meritorious grandfather. At no time allow yourself in pleasure and idleness. In worshipping your ancestors, think how you can prove your filial piety; in receiving your ministers, think how you can show yourself respectful; in looking to what is distant, try to get clear views; have your ears ever open to lessons of virtue;—then shall I acknowledge (and respond to) the excellence of your majesty with an untiring (devotion to your service).[48]

Section 3

1. Yi Yin again made an announcement to the king, saying, 'Oh! Heaven has no (partial) affection;[49]—only to those who are reverent does it show affection. The people are not constant to those whom they cherish;—they cherish (only) him who is benevolent. The spirits do not always accept the sacrifices that are offered to them;—they accept only the sacrifices of the sincere. A place of difficulty is the Heaven-(conferred) seat. When there are (those) virtues, good government is realized; when they are not, disorder comes. To maintain the same principles as those who secured good government will surely lead to prosperity; to pursue the courses of disorder will surely lead to ruin. He who at last, as at first, is careful as to whom and what he follows is a truly intelligent sovereign. The former king was always zealous in the reverent cultivation of his virtue, so that he was the fellow of God.[50] Now, O king, you have entered on the inheritance of his excellent line;—fix your inspection on him.'

2. '(Your course must be) as when in ascending high you begin from where it is low, and when in travelling far you begin from where it is near. Do not slight the occupations of the people;—think of their difficulties. Do not yield to a feeling of repose on your throne;—think of its perils. Be careful for the end at the beginning. When you hear words that are distasteful to your mind, you must enquire whether they be not right; when you hear words that accord with your own views, you must

[48] The whole spirit of Chinese history shows that emperors were restrained only by wise counsellors and public opinion from abusing their power. No Chinese ever thought of a *legal* restraint (constitution), as distinct from the moral restraint. Thus the development of the machinery of democracy was essentially different. The pattern of Chinese political ideas was already set in the *Book of History*.

[49] *Tsochüan* cites this as a quotation from the *Book of History*.

[50] The regular word for God, *Shangti*.

enquire whether they be not contrary to what is right. Oh! what attainment can be made without anxious thought? what achievement can be made without earnest effort? Let the One man be greatly good, and the myriad regions will be rectified by him.'[51]

3. 'When the sovereign does not with disputatious words throw the old rules of government into confusion, and the minister does not, for favour and gain, continue in an office whose work is done,—then the country will lastingly and surely enjoy happiness.'

THE COMMON POSSESSION OF PURE VIRTUE
(*Book of Shang, VI. Ancient Script*)

1. Yi Yin, having returned the government into the hands of his sovereign, and being about to announce his retirement, set forth admonitions on the subject of virtue.

2. He said, 'Oh! it is difficult to rely on Heaven;—its appointments are not constant.[52] (But if the sovereign see to it that) his virtue be constant, he will preserve his throne; if his virtue be not constant, the nine provinces will be lost by him. The king of Hsia could not maintain the virtue (of his ancestors) unchanged, but contemned the spirits and oppressed the people. Great Heaven no (longer) extended its protection to him. It looked out among the myriad regions to give its guidance to one who should receive its favouring appointment, fondly seeking (a possessor of) pure virtue, whom it might make lord of all the spirits. Then there were I, Yin, and T'ang, both possessed of pure virtue, and able to satisfy the mind of Heaven. He received (in consequence) the bright favour of Heaven,[53] so as to become possessor of the multitudes of the nine provinces, and proceeded to change Hsia's commencement of the year. It was not that Heaven had any private partiality for the lord of Shang;—it simply gave its favour to pure virtue. It was not that Shang sought (the allegiance of) the lower people;—the people simply turned to pure virtue. Where (the sovereign's) virtue is pure, his enterprizes are all fortunate; where his virtue is wavering and uncertain, his enterprizes are all unfortunate. Good and evil do not wrongly befall men, but Heaven sends down misery or happiness according to their conduct.'

[51] Parallel passage in *Liki*.

[52] This statement is repeated elsewhere in the *Book of History* (Prince Shih: Modern Script) and in the Great Odes of the *Book of Poetry*. For "appointments" read "mandate." The idea is that the ruler's right to rule may be easily forfeited by misconduct.

[53] Should read: "received the clear mandate of Heaven."

3. 'Now, O young king, you are newly entering on your (great) appointment,—you should be seeking to make new your virtue. At last, as at first, have this as your one object, so shall you make a daily renovation. Let the officers whom you employ be men of virtue and ability, and let the ministers about you be the right men. The minister, in relation to (his sovereign) above him, has to promote his virtue, and, in relation to the (people) beneath him, has to seek their good. How hard must it be (to find the proper man)! what careful attention must be required! (Thereafter) there must be harmony (cultivated with him), and a oneness (of confidence placed in him).

'There is no invariable model of virtue;[54]—a supreme regard to what is good gives the model of it. There is no invariable characteristic of what is good that is to be supremely regarded;—it is found where there is a conformity to the uniform consciousness (in regard to what is good). (Such virtue) will make the people with their myriad surnames all say, "How great are the words of the king!" and also, "How single and pure is the king's heart!" It will avail to maintain in tranquillity the rich possession of the former king, and to secure for ever the (happy) life of the multitudes of the people.'

4. 'Oh! (to retain a place) in the seven-shrined temple[55] of ancestors is a sufficient witness of virtue. To be acknowledged as chief by the myriad heads of families is a sufficient evidence of one's government. The sovereign without the people has none whom he can employ; and the people without the sovereign have none whom they can serve.[56] Do not think yourself so large as to deem others small. If ordinary men and women do not find the opportunity to give full development to their ability, the people's lord will be without the proper aids to complete his merit.'

THE CHARGE TO YÜEH

(*Book of Shang, VIII. Ancient Script*)

Section I

1. The king[57] passed the season of sorrow in the mourning shed for three years, and when the period of mourning was over, he (still) did not

[54] Parallel in the *Analects*.

[55] A point of great contention (five or seven shrines) between the students of the Ancient and the Modern Script, pointed out as evidence that Wang Shu forged this book.

[56] Quotation cited in *Kuoyü* as from the *Book of Hsia*.

[57] Wu-ting, the twentieth sovereign of Shang, B.C. 1324–1266.

speak (to give any commands). All the ministers remonstrated with him, saying, 'Oh! him who is (the first) to apprehend we pronounce intelligent, and the intelligent man is the model for others. The Son of Heaven rules over the myriad regions, and all the officers look up to and reverence him. They are the king's words which form the commands (for them). If he do not speak, the ministers have no way to receive their orders.' On this the king made a writing, for their information, to the following effect:—'As it is mine to serve as the director for the four quarters (of the kingdom), I have been afraid that my virtue is not equal to (that of my predecessors), and therefore have not spoken. (But) while I was reverently and silently thinking of the (right) way, I dreamt that God gave me a good assistant who should speak for me.' He then minutely recalled the appearance (of the person whom he had seen), and caused search to be made for him everywhere by means of a picture. Yüeh,[58] a builder in the wild country of Fu-yen, was found like to it.

2. On this the king raised and made (Yüeh) his prime minister, keeping him (also) at his side.

He charged him, saying, 'Morning and evening present your instructions to aid my virtue. Suppose me a weapon of steel;—I will use you for a whetstone. Suppose me crossing a great stream;—I will use you for a boat with its oars. Suppose me in a year of great drought;—I will use you as a copious rain. Open your mind, and enrich my mind. (Be you) like medicine, which must distress the patient, in order to cure his sickness.[59] (Think of me) as one walking barefoot, whose feet are sure to be wounded, if he do not see the ground.

'Do you and your companions all cherish the same mind to assist your sovereign, that I may follow my royal predecessors, and tread in the steps of my high ancestor, to give repose to the millions of the people. Oh! respect this charge of mine;—so shall you bring your work to a (good) end.'

3. Yüeh replied to the king, saying, 'Wood by the use of the line is made straight, and the sovereign who follows reproof is made sage. When the sovereign can (thus) make himself sage, his ministers, without being specially commanded, anticipate his orders;—who would dare not to act in respectful compliance with this excellent charge of your Majesty?'

[58] Fu Yüeh, who became one of the best ministers of the Dynasty, also credited with being a poet.

[59] Quoted by Mencius.

Section 2

1. Yüeh having received his charge, and taken the presidency of all the officers, he presented himself before the king, and said, 'Oh! intelligent kings act in reverence accordance with the ways of Heaven. The founding of states and the setting up of capitals, the appointing of sovereign kings, of dukes and other nobles, with their great officers and heads of departments, were not designed to minister to the idleness and pleasures (of one), but for the good government of the people.[60] It is Heaven which is all-intelligent and observing;—let the sage (king) take it as his pattern. Then his ministers will reverently accord with him, and the people consequently will be well governed.

'It is the mouth that gives occasion for shame; they are[61] the coat of mail and helmet that give occasion to war. The upper robes and lower garments (for reward should not be lightly taken from) their chests; before spear and shield are used, one should examine himself. If your Majesty will be cautious in regard to these things, and, believing this about them, attain to the intelligent use of them, (your government) will in everything be excellent. Good government and bad depend on the various officers. Officers should not be given to men because they are favourites, but only to men of ability. Dignities should not be conferred on men of evil practices, but only on men of worth.[62]

'Anxious thought about what will be best should precede your movements, which also should be taken at the time proper for them. Indulging the consciousness of being good is the way to lose that goodness; being vain of one's ability is the way to lose the merit it might produce.[63]

'For all affairs let there be adequate preparation;—with preparation there will be no calamitous issue. Do not open the door for favourites, from whom you will receive contempt. Do not be ashamed of mistakes, and (go on to) make them crimes. Let your mind rest in its proper objects, and the affairs of your government will be pure. Officiousness in sacrificing is called irreverence; and multiplying ceremonies leads to disorder. To serve the spirits acceptably (in this way) is difficult.'

2. The king said, 'Excellent! your words, O Yüeh, should indeed be put in practice (by me). If you were not so good in counsel, I should not

[60] Similar ideas, with different wording, were expressed by Motse.
[61] Should be rendered, "It is."
[62] Later this became a typical tenet of the Confucian school.
[63] Later became an important Taoist idea; see *Laotse*.

have heard these rules for my conduct.' Yüeh did obeisance with his head to the ground, and said, 'It is not the knowing that is difficult, but the doing.[64] (But) since your Majesty truly knows this, there will not be the difficulty, and you will become really equal in complete virtue to our first king. Wherein I, Yüeh, refrain from speaking (what I ought to speak), the blame will rest with me.'

Section 3

1. The king said, 'Come, O Yüeh. I, the little one, first learned with Kan P'an. Afterwards I lived concealed among the rude countrymen, and then I went to (the country) inside the Ho, and lived there. From the Ho I went to Po;—and the result has been that I am unenlightened. Do you teach me what should be my aims. Be to me as the yeast and the malt in making sweet spirits, as the salt and the prunes in making agreeable soup.[65] Use various methods to cultivate me; do not cast me away;—so shall I attain to practise your instructions.'

Yüeh said, 'O king, a ruler should seek to learn much (from his ministers), with a view to establish his affairs; but to learn the lessons of the ancients is the way to attain this. That the affairs of one, not making the ancients his masters, can be perpetuated for generations, is what I have not heard.

'In learning there should be a humble mind and the maintenance of a constant earnestness;—in such a case (the learner's) improvement will surely come. He who sincerely cherishes these things will find all truth accumulating in his person. Teaching is the half of learning;[66] when a man's thoughts from first to last are constantly fixed on learning, his virtuous cultivation comes unperceived.

'Survey the perfect pattern of our first king;—so shall you for ever be preserved from error. Then shall I be able reverently to meet your views, and on every side to look out for men of eminence to place in the various offices.

2. The king said, 'Oh! Yüeh, that all within the four seas look up to my virtue is owing to you. As his legs and arms form the man, so does a good minister form the sage (king). Formerly, there was the first premier of our dynasty, Pao-hang, who raised up and formed its royal

[64] Also found in *Tsochüan*. This became a proverb. Sun Yat-sen, preaching action, reverses it.
[65] See similar interesting analogy used by the king in Section 1. This, being not taken from quotations, seems to speak for its authenticity.
[66] Famous proverb on education, also found in the chapter on Education in *Liki*.

founder. He said, "If I cannot make my sovereign like Yao or Shun, I shall feel ashamed in my heart, as if I were beaten in the market-place."[67] If any common man did not get (all he should desire), he said, "It is my fault." (Thus) he assisted my meritorious ancestor, so that he became equal to great Heaven. Do you give your intelligent and preserving aid to me, and let not A-heng[68] engross all the good service to the House of Shang.

'The sovereign should share his government with none but worthy officers. The worthy officer should accept his support from none but the proper sovereign. May you now succeed in making your sovereign a (true) successor of the founder of his line, and in securing the lasting happiness of the people!'

Yüeh did obeisance with his head to the ground, and said, 'I will venture to respond to, and display abroad, your Majesty's excellent charge.'

THE GREAT DECLARATION
(*Book of Chou, I. Ancient Script*)[69]

Section 1

In the spring of the thirteenth year[70] there was a great assembly at Mengchin. The king said, 'Ah! ye hereditary rulers of my friendly states, and all ye my officers, managers of my affairs, hearken clearly to my declaration.

'Heaven and earth is the parent of all creatures;[71] and of all creatures

[67] Phrase used by Mencius in another connection, signifying public disgrace.
[68] Name of Yi Yin (see preceding document). For "engross" read "monopolize."
[69] This is one of the most important documents in the *Book of History*, and one of the most frequently quoted. Another Modern Script version exists, which is totally different. Different accounts, based on equally good sources, say that this document was originally in the Modern Script collection, or that it was found later in the time of Han Wuti (B.C. 140–87), or that a woman found it in the house of Laotse in the year B.C. 73. (Certainly many texts existed and the fantastic idea that the burning of books was effective must be discarded.) That Modern Script text has been restored by Sun Hsingyen (A.D. 1753–1818), but is still very meagre and inferior in quality, and leaves all the important quotations from this document unaccounted for. For this, if for no other reason, the Ancient Script version, containing the famous quotations, is adopted here.—*Ed.*
[70] B.C. 1122, the year of the founding of the great Chou Dynasty, the longest dynasty in China's history (B.C. 1122–B.C. 256). Eight hundred chiefs of states or tribes were gathered to overthrow the wicked Chou, last emperor of Shang.
[71] Compare Chuangtse's essay "The Great Supreme," where the same idea is expressed in the conversation of the four friends.

man is the most highly endowed. The sincerely intelligent (among men) becomes the great sovereign; and the great sovereign is the parent of the people.[72] But now, Shou,[73] the king of Shang, does not reverence Heaven above, and inflicts calamities on the people below. Abandoned to drunkenness and reckless in lust, he has dared to exercise cruel oppression. He has extended the punishment of offenders to all their relatives. He has put men into offices on the hereditary principle. He has made it his pursuit to have palaces, towers, pavilions, embankments, ponds, and all other extravagances, to the most painful injury of you, the myriads of the people. He has burned and roasted the loyal and good. He has ripped up pregnant women. Great Heaven was moved with indignation, and charged my deceased father Wen to display its terrors; but (he died) before the work was completed.

'On this account, I, Fa, the little child, have by means of you, the hereditary rulers of my friendly states, contemplated the government of Shang; but Shou has no repentant heart. He sits squatting on his heels, not serving God nor the spirits of heaven and earth, neglecting also the temple of his ancestors, and not sacrificing in it. The victims and the vessels of millet all become the prey of wicked robbers, and still he says, "The people are mine; the (heavenly) appointment is mine," never trying to correct his contemptuous mind.

'Heaven, for the help of the inferior people, made for them rulers, and made for them instructors, that they might be able to be aiding to God, and secure the tranquillity of the four quarters (of the kingdom). In regard to who are criminals and who are not, how dare I give any allowance to my own wishes?[74]

'"Where the strength is the same, measure the virtue of the parties; where the virtue is the same, measure their righteousness." Shou has hundreds of thousands and myriads of officers, but they have hundreds of thousands and myriads of minds; I have (but) three thousand officers, but they have one mind.[75] The iniquity of Shang is full. Heaven gives command to destroy it. If I did not obey Heaven, my iniquity would be as great.

'I, the little child, early and late am filled with apprehensions. I have received the command of my deceased father Wen; I have offered

[72] Origin of the theory of "parental government." Also expressed in the Great Plan, a chapter of the *Book of History* not reproduced in this volume.

[73] Another name for Chou, or its variant.

[74] Cited by Mencius in almost identical words.

[75] Cited by Kuantse.

special sacrifice to God; I have performed the due services to the great earth; and I lead the multitude of you to execute the punishment appointed by Heaven. Heaven compassionates the people. What the people desire, Heaven will be found to give effect to.[76] Do you aid me, the One man, to cleanse for ever (all within) the four seas. Now is the time!—It should not be lost.'

Section 2

On (the day) Wu-wu, the king halted on the north of the Ho. When all the princes with their hosts were assembled, the king reviewed the hosts, and made the following declaration:—'Oh! ye multitudes of the west, hearken all to my words.

'I have heard that the good man, doing good, finds the day insufficient; and that the evil man, doing evil, also finds the day insufficient.[77] Now Shou, the king of Shang, with strength pursues his lawless way. He has driven away the time-worn sires; and cultivates intimacies with wicked men. Dissolute, intemperate, reckless, oppressive, his ministers have become assimilated to him; and they form combinations and contract animosities, and depend on their power to exterminate one another. The innocent cry to Heaven. The odour of such a state is felt on high.

'Heaven loves the people, and the sovereign should reverently carry out (this mind of) Heaven. Chieh,[78] the sovereign of Hsia, would not follow the example of Heaven, but sent forth his poisonous injuries through the states of the kingdom:—Heaven therefore gave its aid to T'ang the Successful, and charged him to make an end of the appointment of Hsia. But the crimes of Shou exceed those of Chieh. He has degraded from office the greatly good man; he has behaved with cruel tyranny to his reprover and helper. He says that with him is the appointment of Heaven;[79] he says that a reverent care of his conduct is not worth observing; he says that sacrifice is of no use; he says that tyranny is no harm. The beacon for him to look to was not far off;—it was that king of Hsia. It would seem that Heaven is going by means of me to

[76] Twice quoted by *Kuoyü* and once by *Tsochüan*. This translation is not good enough. Literally: "What the people desire, Heaven will follow;" or "Heaven follows the people's will."

[77] Parallels in *Tsochüan* and the *Book of Poetry*.

[78] The last emperor of Hsia, who was similarly dissolute. This was a reminder to the Shang people that their first ruler also had revolted against a tyrant emperor.

[79] That is, the mandate of Heaven.

rule the people. My dreams coincide with my divinations; the auspicious omen is double. My attack on Shang must succeed.

'Shou has hundreds of thousands and millions of ordinary men, divided in heart and divided in practice;—I have of ministers, able to govern, ten men, one in heart and one in practice.[80] Though he has his nearest relatives with him, they are not like my virtuous men.[81] Heaven sees as my people see; Heaven hears as my people hear.[82] The people are blaming me, the One man, for my delay;—I must now go forward. My military prowess is displayed, and I enter his territories to take the wicked tyrant. My punishment (of evil) will be great, and more glorious than that executed by T'ang. Rouse ye, my heroes! Do not think that he is not to be feared;—better think that he cannot be withstood. (His) people stand in trembling awe of him, as if the horns were falling from their heads. Oh! unite your energies, unite your hearts;—so shall you forthwith surely accomplish the work, to last for all ages!'

Section 3

The time was on the morrow,[83] when the king went round his six hosts in state, and made a clear declaration to all his officers. He said, 'Oh! my valiant men of the west, from Heaven are the illustrious courses of duty, of which the (several) requirements are quite plain. And now Shou, the king of Shang, treats with contemptuous slight the five regular (virtues), and abandons himself to wild idleness and irreverence. He has cut himself off from Heaven, and brought enmity between himself and the people.

'He cut through the leg-bones of those who were wading in the morning; he cut out the heart of the worthy man. By the use of his power, killing and murdering, he has poisoned and sickened all within the four seas. His honours and confidence are given to the villainous and bad. He has driven from him his instructors and guardians. He has thrown to the winds the statutes and penal laws. He has imprisoned and enslaved the upright officer. He neglects the sacrifices to heaven and earth. He has discontinued the offerings in the ancestral temple. He makes con-

[80] Cited by *Tsochüan* and *Analects*.
[81] Cited by *Analects* and *Motse*.
[82] This most important statement is cited by Mencius. The people are the representatives of Heaven, or God, and the people's voice is God's voice. Hence the importance of public opinion as the basis of any true government. See my *History of the Press and Public Opinion in China* (Univ. of Chicago Press).
[83] Really, the next dawn.

trivances of wonderful device and extraordinary cunning to please his wife.—God will no longer indulge him, but with a curse is sending down on him this ruin. Do ye with untiring zeal support me, the One man, reverently to execute the punishment appointed by Heaven. The ancients have said, "He who soothes us is our sovereign; he who oppresses us is our enemy."[84] This solitary fellow Shou, having exercised great tyranny, is your perpetual enemy. (It is said again), "In planting (a man's) virtue, strive to make it great; in putting away (a man's) wickedness, strive to do it from the roots."[85] Here I, the little child, by the powerful help of you, all my officers, will utterly exterminate your enemy. Do you, all my officers, march forward with determined boldness to sustain your prince. Where there is much merit, there shall be large reward; where you do not so advance, there shall be conspicuous disgrace.

'Oh! (the virtue of) my deceased father Wen was like the shining of the sun and moon. His brightness extended over the four quarters of the land, and shone signally in the western region. Hence it is that our Chou has received (the allegiance of) many states. If I subdue Shou, it will not be from my prowess, but from the faultless (virtue of) my deceased father Wen. If Shou subdue me, it will not be from any fault of my deceased father Wen, but because I, the little child, am not good.'

THE METAL-BOUND COFFER

(Book of Chou, VI. Modern and Ancient Scripts)

1. Two years after the conquest of Shang[86] the king fell ill, and was quite disconsolate. The two (other great) dukes[87] said, 'Let us reverently consult the tortoise-shell about the king;' but the Duke of Chou[88] said, 'You must not so distress our former kings.' He then took the business on himself, and reared three altars of earth on the same cleared space; and having made another altar on the south of these, and facing the north, he took there his own position. Having put a round symbol of jade

[84] See *Mencius* (Bk. IV, Pt. 2, III, 1).

[85] Cited as a proverb by Wu Yüan in *Tsochüan*.

[86] B.C. 1121, or 1120.

[87] The Duke of Shao and T'ai-kung.

[88] The Duke of Chou, King Wu's brother, considered by Confucius to have laid down the governmental system and general pattern of rituals and music of the Chou Dynasty. Confucius said he often dreamed of him, which means it was Confucius' dream to restore the social order which had gone into decay in his time.

(on each of the three altars), and holding in his hands the lengthened symbol (of his own rank), he addressed the kings T'ai, Chi and Wen.[89]

The (grand) historiographer had written on tablets his prayer, which was to this effect[90]:—'A.B.,[91] your great descendant, is suffering from a severe and violent disease;—if you three kings have in heaven the charge of (watching over) him, (Heaven's) great son, let me Tan be a substitute for his person. I was lovingly obedient to my father; I am possessed of many abilities and arts, which fit me to serve spiritual beings. Your great descendant, on the other hand, has not so many abilities and arts as I, and is not so capable of serving spiritual beings. And moreover he was appointed in the hall of God to extend his aid all over the kingdom, so that he might establish your descendants in this lower earth. The people of the four quarters all stand in reverent awe of him. Oh! do not let that precious Heaven-conferred appointment fall to the ground, and (all the long line of) our former kings will also have one in whom they can ever rest at our sacrifices. I will now seek for your determination (in this matter) from the great tortoise-shell. If you grant me (my request), I will take these symbols and this mace, and return and wait for your orders. If you do not grant it, I will put them by.'

The duke then divined with the three tortoise-shells, and all were favourable. He opened with a key the place where the (oracular) responses were kept, and looked at them, and they also were favourable. He said, 'According to the form (of the prognostic) the king will take no injury. I, the little child, have got the renewal of his appointment from the three kings, by whom a long futurity has been consulted for. I have now to wait for the issue. They can provide for our One man.'

When the duke returned, he placed the tablets (of the prayer) in a metal-bound coffer, and next day the king got better.

2. (Afterwards), upon the death of King Wu, (the duke's) elder brother, he of Kuan, and his younger brothers, spread a baseless report through the kingdom, to the effect that the duke would do no good to the (king's) young son.[92] On this the duke said to the two (other great) dukes, 'If I do not take the law (to these men), I shall not be able to make my report to the former kings.'

[89] Ancestors of the king.

[90] The Duke of Chou offered to die in his brother's place.

[91] Literally, "So-and-So," standing for King Wu's name.

[92] King Ch'eng. The Duke, his uncle, was under suspicion of intending to rob him of his throne.

He resided (accordingly) in the east for two years, when the criminals were taken (and brought to justice). Afterwards he made a poem to present to the king, and called it 'the Owl.'[93] The king on his part did not dare to blame the duke.

In the autumn, when the grain was abundant and ripe, but before it was reaped, Heaven sent a great storm of thunder and lightning, along with wind, by which the grain was all broken down, and great trees torn up. The people were greatly terrified; and the king and great officers, all in their caps of state, proceeded to open the metal-bound coffer and examine the writings in it, where they found the words of the duke when he took on himself the business of being a substitute for King Wu. The two (great) dukes and the king asked the historiographer and all the other officers (acquainted with the transaction) about the thing, and they replied, 'It was really thus; but ah! the duke charged us that we should not presume to speak about it.' The king held the writing in his hand, and wept, saying, 'We need not (now) go on reverently to divine. Formerly the duke was thus earnest for the royal House, but I, being a child, did not know it. Now Heaven has moved its terrors to display his virtue. That I, the little child, (now) go with my new views and feelings to meet him, is what the rules of propriety of our kingdom require.'

The king then went out to the borders (to meet the duke), when Heaven sent down rain, and, by virtue of a contrary wind, the grain all rose up. The two (great) dukes gave orders to the people to take up the trees that had fallen and replace them. The year then turned out very fruitful.

THE ANNOUNCEMENT OF THE DUKE OF SHAO[94]

(Book of Chou, XII. Modern and Ancient Script)

1. In the second month, on the day Yi-wei, six days after full moon, the king[95] proceeded in the morning from Chou to Fang. (Thence) the Grand-Guardian[96] went before the Duke of Chou to survey the

[93] See the poem by the same name in the *Book of Poetry* (under "Some Great Ancient Poems" in this volume).

[94] This document contains the clearest exposition of the "mandate of Heaven" and how it changes from hand to hand. Those interested in pursuing the theory of the "mandate of Heaven," to which there are many references, may read Ch. 14, 16, 18 of the Book of Chou, in the *Shu King* (*Sacred Books of the East,* vol. III), in the same translation by James Legge.

[95] King Ch'eng, the second sovereign of Chou (B.C. 1115–1079), son of King Wu.

[96] Duke of Shao.

locality (of the new capital); and in the third month, on the day Wu-shan, the third day after the first appearance of the moon on Ping-wu, he came in the morning to Lo. He divined by the tortoise-shell about the (several) localities, and having obtained favourable indications, he set about laying out the plan (of the city). On Keng-hsü, the third day after, he led the people of Yin to prepare the various sites on the north of the Lo; and this work was completed on Chia-yin, the fifth day after.

On Yi-mao, the day following, the duke of Chou came in the morning to Lo, and thoroughly inspected the plan of the new city. On Ting-sze, the third day after, he offered two bulls as victims in the (northern and southern) suburbs; and on the morrow, Wu-wu, at the altar to the spirit of the land in the new city, he sacrificed a bull, a ram, and a boar. After seven days, on Chia-tse, in the morning, from his written (specifications) he gave their several orders to the people of Yin,[97] and to the presiding chiefs of the princes from the Hou, Tien, and Nan domains. When the people of Yin had thus received their orders, they arose and entered with vigour on their work.

(When the work was drawing to a completion), the Grand-Guardian went out with the hereditary princes of the various states to bring their offerings (for the king); and when he entered again, he gave them to the duke of Chou, saying, 'With my hands to my head and my head to the ground, I present these to his Majesty and your Grace. Announcements for the information of the multitudes of Yin must come from you, with whom is the management of affairs.'

2. 'Oh! God (dwelling in) the great heavens has changed his decree respecting his great son and the great dynasty of Yin.[98] Our king has received that decree. Unbounded is the happiness connected with it, and unbounded is the anxiety:—Oh! how can he be other than reverent?

'When Heaven rejected and made an end of the decree in favour of the great dynasty of Yin, there were many of its former wise kings in heaven. The king, however, who had succeeded to them, the last of his race, from the time of his entering into their appointment, proceeded in such a way as at last to keep the wise in obscurity and the vicious in office. The poor people in such a case, carrying their children and leading their wives, made their moan to Heaven. They even fled away, but were apprehended again. Oh! Heaven had compassion on the

[97] The new capital Lo (near modern Loyang) lay very near the territory of the conquered Yin (or Shang) people.

[98] Or Shang.

people of the four quarters; its favouring decree lighted on our earnest (founders). Let the king sedulously cultivate the virtue of reverence.

'Examining the men of antiquity, there was the (founder of the) Hsia dynasty. Heaven guided (his mind), allowed his descendants (to succeed him), and protected them. He acquainted himself with Heaven, and was obedient to it. But in process of time the decree in his favour fell to the ground.[99] So also is it now when we examine the case of Yin. There was the same guiding (of its founder), who corrected (the errors of Hsia), and (whose descendants) enjoyed the protection (of Heaven). He (also) acquainted himself with Heaven, and was obedient to it. But now the decree in favour of him has fallen to the ground. Our king has now come to the throne in his youth;—let him not slight the aged and experienced, for it may be said of them that they have studied the virtuous conduct of the ancients, and have matured their counsels in the sight of Heaven.

'Oh! although the king is young, yet he is the great son (of God). Let him effect a great harmony with the lower people, and that will be the blessing of the present time. Let not the king presume to be remiss in this, but continually regard and stand in awe of the perilous (uncertainty) of the people's (attachment).

'Let the king come here as the vice-regent of God, and undertake (the duties of government) in this centre of the land. Tan said, "Now that this great city has been built, from henceforth he may be the mate of great Heaven, and reverently sacrifice to (the spirits) above and beneath; from henceforth he may from this central spot administer successful government." Thus shall the king enjoy the favouring regard (of Heaven) all-complete, and the government of the people will now be prosperous.

'Let the king first subdue to himself those who were the managers of affairs under Yin, associating them with the managers of affairs for our Chou. This will regulate their (perverse) natures, and they will make daily advancement. Let the king make reverence the resting-place (of his mind);—he must maintain the virtue of reverence.

'We should by all means survey the dynasties of Hsia and Yin. I do not presume to know and say, "The dynasty of Hsia was to enjoy the favouring decree of Heaven just for (so many) years," nor do I pre-

[99] This changing of the mandate of Heaven became the established explanation or justification for the change of dynasties. In modern Chinese, the word for "revolution" means to "change mandate."

sume to know and say, "It could not continue longer." The fact simply was, that, for want of the virtue of reverence, the decree in its favour prematurely fell to the ground. (Similarly), I do not presume to know and say, "The dynasty of Yin was to enjoy the favouring decree of Heaven just for (so many) years," nor do I presume to know and say, "It could not continue longer." The fact simply was, that, for want of the virtue of reverence, the decree in its favour fell prematurely to the ground. The king has now inherited the decree,—the same decree, I consider, which belonged to those two dynasties. Let him seek to inherit (the virtues of) their meritorious (sovereigns);—(let him do this especially) at this commencement of his duties.

'Oh! it is as on the birth of a son, when all depends on (the training of) his early life, through which he may secure his wisdom in the future, as if it were decreed to him. Now Heaven may have decreed wisdom (to the king); it may have decreed good fortune or bad; it may have decreed a (long) course of years;—we only know that now is with him the commencement of his duties. Dwelling in this new city, let the king now sedulously cultivate the virtue of reverence. When he is all-devoted to this virtue, he may pray to Heaven for a long-abiding decree in his favour.

'In the position of king, let him not, because of the excesses of the people in violation of the laws, presume also to rule by the violent infliction of death;—when the people are regulated gently, the merit (of government) is seen. It is for him who is in the position of king to overtop all with his virtue. In this case the people will imitate him throughout the kingdom, and he will become still more illustrious.[100]

'Let the king and his ministers labour with a mutual sympathy, saying, "We have received the decree of Heaven, and it shall be great as the long-continued years of Hsia;—yea, it shall not fail of the long-continued years of Yin." I wish the king, through (the attachment of) the lower people, to receive the long-abiding decree of Heaven.'

3. (The duke of Shao) then did obeisance with his hands to his head and his head to the ground, and said, 'I, a small minister, presume, with the king's (heretofore) hostile people and all their officers, and with his (loyal) friendly people, to maintain and receive his majesty's dread command and brilliant virtue. That the king should finally obtain the decree all-complete, and that he should become illustrious,—

[100] Here we see the source of Confucius' ideas of government by moral example.

this I do not presume to labour for. I only bring respectfully these offerings to present to his majesty, to be used in his prayers to Heaven for its long-abiding decree.'[101]

THE SPEECH OF (THE MARQUIS OF) CH'IN[102]

(Book of Chou, XXX. Modern and Ancient Scripts)

Introduction by James Legge

THE state of Ch'in, at the time to which this speech belongs, was one of the most powerful in the kingdom, and already giving promise of what it would grow to. Ultimately, one of its princes overthrew the dynasty of Chou, and brought feudal China to an end.

Ch'in and Chin were engaged together in B.C. 631 in besieging the capital of Cheng, and threatened to extinguish that state. The marquis of Ch'in, however, was suddenly induced to withdraw his troops, leaving three of his officers in friendly relations with the court of Cheng, and under engagement to defend the state from aggression. These men played the part of spies in the interest of Ch'in, and in B.C. 629, one of them, called Chi-tse, sent word that he was in charge of one of the gates, and if an army were sent to surprise the capital, Cheng might be added to the territories of Ch'in. The marquis—known in history as duke Mu—laid the matter before his counsellors. The most experienced of them—Paili Hsi and Chien-shu—were against taking advantage of the proposed treachery; but the marquis listened rather to the promptings of ambition; and the next year he sent a large force, under his three ablest commanders, hoping to find Cheng unprepared for any resistance. The attempt, however, failed; and the army, on its way back to Ch'in, was attacked by the forces of Chin, and sustained a terrible defeat. It was nearly annihilated, and the three commanders were taken prisoners.

The marquis of Chin was intending to put these captives to death, but finally sent them to Ch'in, that duke Mu might himself sacrifice them to his anger for their want of success. Mu, however, did no such thing. He went from his capital to meet the disgraced generals, and comforted them, saying that the blame of their defeat was due to himself, who had refused to listen to the advice of his wise counsellors. Then also, it is said, he made the speech here preserved for the benefit of all his ministers, describing

[101] It is interesting to note the existence of the hostile conquered peoples, and to see how the Chou Dynasty ruled and united China for almost nine hundred years, and was thus able to stamp its own culture upon China as a whole.

[102] This is the last document of the *Book of History*, bringing it down to B.C. 628.

the good and bad minister, and the different issues of listening to them, and deploring how he had himself foolishly rejected the advice of his aged counsellors, and followed that of new men;—a thing which he would never do again.

The duke said, 'Ah! my officers, listen to me without noise. I solemnly announce to you the most important of all sayings. (It is this which) the ancients have said, "Thus it is with all people,—they mostly love their ease. In reproving others there is no difficulty, but to receive reproof, and allow it to have free course,—this is difficult." The sorrow of my heart is, that the days and months have passed away, and it is not likely they will come again (so that I might pursue a different course).

'There were my old counsellors.—I said, "They will not accommodate themselves to me," and I hated them. There were my new counsellors, and I would for the time give my confidence to them. So indeed it was with me; but hereafter I will take advice from the men of yellow hair, and then I shall be free from error. That good old officer!—his strength is exhausted, but I would rather have him (as my counsellor). That dashing brave officer!—his shooting and charioteering are faultless, but I would rather not wish to have him. As to men of quibbles, skilful at cunning words, and able to make the good man change his purposes, what have I to do to make much use of them?

'I have deeply thought and concluded.—Let me have but one resolute minister, plain and sincere, without other ability, but having a straightforward mind, and possessed of generosity, regarding the talents of others as if he himself possessed them; and when he finds accomplished and sage men, loving them in his heart more than his mouth expresses, really showing himself able to bear them:—such a minister would be able to preserve my descendants and people, and would indeed be a giver of benefits.

'But if (the minister), when he finds men of ability, be jealous and hates them; if, when he finds accomplished and sage men, he oppose them and does not allow their advancement, showing himself really not able to bear them:—such a man will not be able to protect my descendants and people; and will he not be a dangerous man?

'The decline and fall of a state may arise from one man. The glory and tranquillity of a state may also arise from the goodness of one man.'

Mencius

The Democratic Philosopher

INTRODUCTION

MENCIUS lived in B.C. 372–289, and was thus a contemporary of Plato who lived in B.C. 427–347 and of Aristotle who lived in B.C. 386–322. His birth was separated from the death of Confucius in B.C. 479 by 107 years, and he was about one generation older than Hsüntse who lived in B.C. 315–235, as Plato was that much older than Aristotle. His position in relation to Confucius was like that of Plato in relation to Socrates in developing the idealistic trends, while Hsüntse was in a sense similar to Aristotle in his philosophic realism. The analogy must not be forced; the chief difference between Mencius and Hsüntse was that Mencius believed in the innate goodness of human nature, while Hsüntse believed in its badness. Consequently Hsüntse believed in culture and restraint, while Mencius believed that culture consisted in seeking and retrieving the original goodness of man. "A great man is one who has not lost the child's heart." He tried to prove that the sense of mercy and the desire to do what is right are innate and instinctive, as when we instinctively rush forward to save a child crawling toward a well. Wickedness in human conduct is like the denuding of a hill by the woodsman's axe and grazing cattle, while it is the nature of a hill to be finely wooded. This original goodness could be developed or obstructed, but we all have it in ourselves to be like the Sages. "All men could be Yao and Shun." "The Sages are of the same species as ourselves." One of his best sayings is: "The sense of mercy is in all men; the sense of shame is in all men; the sense of courtesy and respect is in all men; the sense of right and wrong is in all men." He believed in the distinction between the human and the beastly in us, and that the distinctly human in us consists in the sense of mercy, the sense of right and wrong, etc. "He who has no sense of mercy is not a man, etc." He also admitted that the distinction between man and beast was "very small," but he urged that there is a greater self and a smaller self in us, and that "He who attends to his smaller self becomes a small man, and he who attends to his greater self becomes a great man."

Consequently there was a certain high idealism in Mencius, when he spoke of the *haojan chih ch'i,* the "expansive spirit" in us, which he beautifull pinned down in a phrase, "the air of the early dawn," which every early riser is familiar with. How to save and keep that air, or spirit, of the early dawn through the day, or how to guard the warm and good heart of the child through our life is the moral problem.

The definite contributions of Mencius' ideas to the democratic principle are as follows. First, that all men are equal. "The Sages are of the same species as ourselves." (Bk. VI, Pt. 1, VII, 3). Second, of the three elements of a state, "the people are the most important . . . and the ruler is the least important" (Bk. VII, Pt. 2, XIV, 1). Third, decisions of promotion and punishment are to be based not on what the government officials say, but on what all the people say (Bk. I, Pt. 2, VII, 4-5). Fourth, government must be for the welfare of the people, and the king must share his pleasures (parks and music) with the people (Bk. I, entire Part 1). Fifth, the relationships of the ruler and the people are reciprocal. "When a ruler regards his ministers as his hands and feet, they regard him as their belly and heart; when he regards them as dogs and horses, they regard him as a common citizen; when he regards them as dirt and grass, they regard him as a robber and enemy" (Bk. IV, Pt. 2, III, 1). Sixth, consequently, the right to revolt was vindicated. When T'ang's right to rebel against the tyrant emperor Chieh was questioned, he replied that the tyrant was a common thief (Bk. I, Pt. 2, VIII, 3). Finally, Mencius constantly elaborated the idea in the *Book of History* that the emperor ruled his country as a "mandate from Heaven" and forfeited it as soon as he misruled. Ultimately any one rules only because the people accept him (Bk. V, Pt. 1, V, 1-8).

From his general idealism, Mencius developed the theory of "benevolent government," which became the keystone of Chinese political philosophy. He also developed the sharp distinction between the "royal way" and the "dictator's way," or between government by winning the people's hearts and government by force; incidentally the "royal way" (*wangtao*) is what the Japanese say they are trying to set up in Manchuria. His idea of "parental government" was not original with him, but was already current in the Chinese tradition, as may be seen in the *Book of History*. The importance of Mencius arises from his extensive influence, holding a position in Chinese eyes next only to Confucius, his books being compulsory reading in elementary schools, committed to memory by all Chinese school children. Consequently, the theory of the "benevolent government" became an ideal held up by Chinese scholars, even as democracy is held up as an ideal by the Western democracies. That this ideal was not lived up to in times of a decaying dynasty is evident enough; over-taxation, wars, conscription and interference with the farmers' cultivation of the land were too evident in Mencius' own times and provided the very background against which he announced the benevolent government as a sure, unfailing remedy. Nevertheless, it was always held up as an ideal and profoundly influenced the whole character of Chinese government in times of peace. In fact, Chinese philosophy of history is firm on the fact that the very length of a dynasty's rule is in exact proportion to the kind of "kind and lenient government" that dynasty started out with.

I have used here the revised translation of 1874 by James Legge, and have not interfered with his text except in the correction of his Cantonese spelling of proper names. I regret, however, that Legge's translation is too literal to make easy reading; his methods amounted to translating every single word, even when two words formed a combination with a new meaning. This may be considered the general rule, that when we find a translation difficult to read, it is sure to be scholarly. Thus, to take a sentence much quoted by the Chinese in the present war, Legge rendered it thus, "Opportunities of time (vouchsafed by) Heaven are not equal to advantages of situation (afforded by) the Earth, and advantages of situation (afforded by) the Earth are not equal to (the union arising from) the accord of Men." This is literal enough, but what Mencius said was much briefer, in twelve Chinese words: "Weather is less important than terrain, and terrain is less important than the people's unity." This is no less literal, because "sky-times," or worse, "Heaven-opportunities-of-time," definitely and absolutely means in Chinese "weather" and nothing else. There is still no good translation of even such an important work as Mencius, and I have not had the opportunity to make a new translation. In all the important passages, however, I have indicated what an improved rendering might be. To translate "establishing a government of mercy with a heart of mercy" by "As when with a commiserating mind was practised a commiserating government" is almost to kill the original text. Something of the sonorous eloquence and fine idealism in Mencius which stirred the Chinese schoolboy's soul is gone. I say this not to disparage Legge; he did an inestimable service to China by translating single-handed all the important Chinese Classics, and it was a scholarly work conscientiously and in so many respects quite competently done. I say this to point out a more significant fact that the important work of translating Chinese classics and literature has only begun. Legge did this almost a century ago, and the Chinese scholars have not been too active in making their sacred texts known to the West. Legge's translation of the *Book of History,* undertaken twenty years after his first translation of Mencius, is much better. A complete new translation of the most important chapter of Mencius, Book VI, Part I, is available in my *Wisdom of Confucius,* Ch. XI.

I retain the chapter and verse numbers by Legge for convenience of reference. But it should be clearly understood that the following consists of selections from *Mencius* only.

Mencius

The Democratic Philosopher

Translated by James Legge

BOOK I, PART I

Chapter I

1 Mencius (went to) see King Huei of Liang.

2 The king said, "Venerable Sir, since you have not counted it far to come here, a distance of a thousand *li,* may I presume that you are likewise provided with (counsels) to profit my kingdom?"

3 Mencius replied, "Why must your Majesty use that word 'profit'? What I am likewise provided with are (counsels to) benevolence and righteousness,[1] and these are my only topics.

4 "If your Majesty say, 'What is to be done to profit my kingdom?' the great officers will say, 'What is to be done to profit our families?' and the (inferior) officers and the common people will say, 'What is to be done to profit our persons?' Superiors and inferiors will try to take the profit the one from the other, and the kingdom will be endangered. In the kingdom of ten thousand chariots, the murderer of his ruler will be (the chief of) a family of a thousand chariots. In the State of a thousand chariots, the murderer of his ruler will be (the chief of) a family of a hundred chariots. To have a thousand in ten thousand, and a hundred in a thousand, cannot be regarded as not a large allowance; but if

[1] "Love" and "justice" would be a better translation; the above is Legge's translation, while Giles translates them in Chuangtse as "charity" and "duty."

righteousness be put last and profit first, they will not be satisfied without snatching all.

5 "There never was a man trained to benevolence who neglected his parents. There never was a man trained to righteousness who made his ruler an after-consideration.

6 "Let your Majesty likewise make benevolence and righteousness your only themes;—why must you speak of profit?"

Chapter II

1 When Mencius (another day) was seeing king Huei of Liang, the king (went and) stood (with him) by a pond, and, looking round on the wild geese and deer, large and small, said, "Do wise and good (princes) also take pleasure in these things?"

2 Mencius replied, "Being wise and good, they then have pleasure in these things. If they are not wise and good, though they have these things, they do not find pleasure.

3 "It is said in the Book of Poetry:—

'When he planned the commencement of the Marvellous Tower,
He planned it, and defined it,
And the people in crowds undertook the work,
And in no time completed it.
When he planned the commencement, (he said), "Be not in a hurry;"
But the people came as if they were his children
The king was in the Marvellous Park,
Where the does were lying down,—
The does so sleek and fat;
With the white birds glistening.
The king was by the Marvellous Pond;—
How full was it of fishes leaping about!'

King Wen used the strength of the people to make his tower and pond, and the people rejoiced (to do the work), calling the tower 'the Marvellous Tower,' and the pond 'the Marvellous Pond,' and being glad that he had his deer, his fishes, and turtles. The ancients caused their people to have pleasure as well as themselves, and therefore they could enjoy it.

4 "In the Declaration of T'ang it is said, 'O sun, when wilt thou expire? We will die together with thee.' The people wished (for Chieh's death, though) they should die with him. Although he had his tower, his pond, birds and animals, how could he have pleasure alone?"

Chapter III

1 King Huei of Liang said, "Small as my virtue is, in (the government of) my kingdom, I do indeed exert my mind to the utmost. If the year be bad inside the Ho, I remove (as many of) the people (as) I can to the east of it, and convey grain to the country inside. If the year be bad on the east of the river, I act on the same plan. On examining the governmental methods of the neighbouring kingdoms, I do not find there is any (ruler) who exerts his mind as I do. And yet the people of the neighbouring kings do not decrease, nor do my people increase;—how is this?"

2 Mencius replied, "Your Majesty loves war; allow me to take an illustration from war. (The soldiers move forward at) the sound of the drum; and when the edges of their weapons have been crossed, (on one side) they throw away their buff-coats, trail their weapons behind them, and run. Some run a hundred paces and then stop; some run fifty paces and stop. What would you think if these, because (they had run but) fifty paces, should laugh at (those who ran) a hundred paces?" The king said, "They cannot do so. They only did not run a hundred paces; but they also ran." (Mencius) said, "Since your Majesty knows this, you have no ground to expect that your people will become more numerous than those of the neighbouring kingdoms.

3 "If the seasons of husbandry be not interfered with, the grain will be more than can be eaten. If close nets are not allowed to enter the pools and ponds, the fish and turtles will be more than can be consumed. If the axes and bills enter the hill-forests (only) at the proper times, the wood will be more than can be used. When the grain and fish and turtles are more than can be eaten, and there is more wood than can be used, this enables the people to nourish their living and do all offices for their dead, without any feeling against any. (But) this condition, in which (the people) nourish their living, and do all offices to their dead without having any feeling against any, is the first step in the Royal way.

4 "Let mulberry-trees be planted about the homesteads with their five acres, and persons of fifty years will be able to wear silk. In keeping fowls, pigs, dogs, and swine, let not their times of breeding be neglected, and persons of seventy years will be able to eat flesh.[2] Let there not be taken away the time that is proper for the cultivation of the field-allot-

[2] Should read "meat."

ment of a hundred acres, and the family of several mouths will not suffer from hunger. Let careful attention be paid to the teaching in the various schools, with repeated inculcation of the filial and fraternal duties, and gray-haired men will not be seen upon the roads, carrying burdens on their backs or on their heads. It has never been that (the ruler of a State) where these results were seen, persons of seventy wearing silk and eating flesh, and the black-haired people suffering neither from hunger nor cold, did not attain to the Royal dignity.

5 "Your dogs and swine eat the food of men, and you do not know to store up (of the abundance). There are people dying from famine on the roads, and you do not know to issue (your stores for their relief). When men die, you say, 'It is not owing to me; it is owing to the year.' In what does this differ from stabbing a man and killing him, and then saying, 'It was not I; it was the weapon'? Let your Majesty cease to lay the blame on the year,[3] and instantly the people, all under the sky, will come to you."

Chapter IV

1 King Huei of Liang said, "I wish quietly to receive your instructions."

2 Mencius replied, "Is there any difference between killing a man with a stick and with a sword?" "There is no difference," was the answer.

3 (Mencius continued) "Is there any difference between doing it with a sword and with governmental measures?" "There is not," was the answer (again).

4 (Mencius then) said, "In (your) stalls there are fat beasts; in (your) stables there are fat horses. (But) your people have the look of hunger, and in the fields there are those who have died of famine. This is leading on beasts to devour men.

5 "Beasts devour one another, and men hate them (for doing so). When he who is (called) the parent of the people conducts his government so as to be chargeable with leading on beasts to devour men, where is that parental relation to the people?

6 "Chung-ni[4] said, 'Was he not without posterity who first made wooden images (to bury with the dead)?' (So he said) because that man made the semblances of men and used them (for that purpose);—what shall be thought of him who causes his people to die of hunger?"

[3] Bad harvest.

[4] Personal name of Confucius.

Chapter V

1 King Huei of Liang said, "There was not in the kingdom a stronger State than Ch'in, as you, venerable Sir, know. But since it descended to me, on the east we were defeated by Ch'i, and then my eldest son perished; on the west we lost seven hundred *li* of territory to Ch'in; and on the south we have sustained disgrace at the hands of Ch'u. I have brought shame on my departed predecessors, and wish on their account to wipe it away once for all. What course is to be pursued to accomplish this?"

2 Mencius replied, "With a territory (only) a hundred *li* square it has been possible to obtain the Royal dignity.

3 "If your Majesty will (indeed) dispense a benevolent government to the people, being sparing in the use of punishments and fines, and making the taxes and levies of produce light, (so causing that) the fields shall be ploughed deep, and the weeding well attended to, and that the able-bodied, during their days of leisure, shall cultivate their filial piety, fraternal duty, faithfulness, and truth, serving thereby, at home, their fathers and elder brothers, and, abroad, their elders and superiors; you will then have a people who can be employed with sticks which they have prepared to oppose the strong buff-coats and sharp weapons of (the troops of) Ch'in and Ch'u.

4 "(The rulers of) those (States) rob their people of their time, so that they cannot plough and weed their fields in order to support their parents. Parents suffer from cold and hunger; elder and younger brothers, wives and children, are separated and scattered abroad.

5 "Those (rulers) drive their people into pitfalls or into the water; and your Majesty will go to punish them. In such a case, who will oppose your Majesty?

6 "In accordance with this is the saying, 'The benevolent has no enemy!' I beg your Majesty not to doubt (what I said)."

Chapter VI

1 Mencius had an interview with king Hsiang of Liang.

2 When he came out, he said to some persons, "When I looked at him from a distance, he did not appear like a ruler; when I drew near to him, I saw nothing venerable about him. Abruptly he asked me, 'How can the kingdom, all under the sky, be settled?'

2 "I replied, 'It will be settled by being united under one (sway).'

3 " 'Who can so unite it?' (he asked).

4 "I replied, 'He who has no pleasure in killing men can so unite it.

5 " 'Who can give it to them?' (he asked).

6 "I replied, "All under heaven will give it to him. Does your Majesty know the way of the growing grain? During the seventh and eighth months, when drought prevails, the plants become dry. Then the clouds collect densely in the heavens, and send down torrents of rain, so that the grain erects itself as if by a shoot. When it does so, who can keep it back? Now among those who are shepherds of men throughout the kingdom, there is not one who does not find pleasure in killing men. If there were one who did not find pleasure in killing men, all the people under the sky would be looking towards him with outstretched necks Such being indeed the case, the people would go to him as water flows downwards with a rush, which no one can repress."

Chapter VII

1 King Hsüan of Ch'i asked, saying, "May I be informed by you of the transactions of Huan of Ch'i and Wen of Chin?"

2 Mencius replied, "There were none of the disciples of Chung-n who spoke about the affairs of Huan and Wen, and therefore they have not been transmitted to (these) after-ages; your servant has not heard of them. If you will have me speak, let it be about (the principles of attain ing to) the Royal sway."

3 (The king) said, "Of what kind must his virtue be who can (attain to) the Royal sway?" (Mencius) said, "If he loves and protects the people, it is impossible to prevent him from attaining it."

4 (The king) said, "Is such a one as poor I competent to love and protect the people?" "Yes," was the reply. "From what do you know that I am competent to that?" "I have heard," said (Mencius), "from Hu Heh the following incident:—'The king,' said he, 'was sitting aloft in the hall, when some people appeared leading a bull past below it. The king saw it, and asked where the bull was going, and being answered that they were going to consecrate a bell with its blood, he said, "Let it go, I cannot bear its frightened appearance as if it were an innocent person going to the place of death." They asked in reply whether, if they did so they should omit the consecration of the bell; but (the king) said, "How can that be omitted? Change it for a sheep." ' I do not know whether this incident occurred."

5 "It did," said (the king), and (Mencius) replied, "The heart seem

in this is sufficient to carry you to the Royal sway. The people all supposed that your Majesty grudged (the animal), but your servant knows surely that it was your Majesty's not being able to bear (the sight of the creature's distress which made you do as you did)."

6 The king said, "You are right; and yet there really was (an appearance of) what the people imagined. (But) though Ch'i be narrow and small, how should I grudge a bull? Indeed it was because I could not bear its frightened appearance, as if it were an innocent person going to the place of death, that therefore I changed it for a sheep."

7 Mencius said, "Let not your Majesty deem it strange that the people should think you grudged the animal. When you changed a large one for a small, how should they know (the true reason)? If you felt pained by its (being led) without any guilt to the place of death, what was there to choose between a bull and a sheep?" The king laughed and said, "What really was my mind in the matter? I did not grudge the value of the bull, and yet I changed it for a sheep! There was reason in the people's saying that I grudged (the creature)."

8 (Mencius) said, "There is no harm (in their saying so). It was an artifice of benevolence. You saw the bull, and had not seen the sheep. So is the superior man affected towards animals, that, having seen them alive, he cannot bear to eat their flesh. On this account he keeps away from his stalls and kitchen."

9 The king was pleased and said, "The Ode [5] says,

'What other men have in their minds,
I can measure by reflection.'

This might be spoken of you, my Master. I indeed did the thing, but when I turned my thoughts inward and sought for it, I could not discover my own mind. When you, Master, spoke those words, the movements of compassion began to work in my mind. (But) how is it that this heart has in it what is equal to the attainment of the Royal sway?"

10 (Mencius) said, "Suppose a man were to make this statement to your Majesty, 'My strength is sufficient to lift three thousand catties, but it is not sufficient to lift one feather; my eyesight is sharp enough to examine the point of an autumn hair, but I do not see a waggon-load of faggots,' would your Majesty allow what he said?" "No," was the (king's) remark, (and Mencius proceeded), "Now here is kindness sufficient to reach to animals, and yet no benefits are extended from it to

[5] Book of Poetry.

the people;—how is this? is an exception to be made here? The truth is the feather's not being lifted is because the strength was not used; the waggon-load of firewood's not being seen is because the eyesight wa not used; and the people's not being loved and protected is because the kindness is not used. Therefore your Majesty's not attaining to the Roya sway is because you do not do it, and not because you are not able to do it."

11 (The king) asked, "How may the difference between him who does not do (a thing) and him who is not able to do it be graphicall set forth?" (Mencius) replied, "In such a thing as taking the T'ai moun tain under your arm, and leaping with it over the North sea, if you sa to people, 'I am not able to do it,' that is a real case of not being able. In such a matter as breaking off a branch from a tree at the order of a superior, if you say to people, 'I am not able to do it,' it is not a case o not being able to do it. And so your Majesty's not attaining to the Roya sway is not such a case as that of taking the T'ai mountain under you arm and leaping over the North sea with it; but it is a case like that o breaking off a branch from a tree.

12 "Treat with the reverence due to age the elders in your own family so that those in the families of others shall be similarly treated; trea with the kindness due to youth the young in your own family, so tha those in the families of others shall be similarly treated:—do this and the kingdom may be made to go round in your palm. It is said in the Book of Poetry,

> *'His example acted on his wife,*
> *Extended to his brethren,*
> *And was felt by all the clans and States;'*

telling us how (King Wen) simply took this (kindly) heart, and exer cised it towards those parties. Therefore the carrying out the (feeling of kindness (by a ruler) will suffice for the love and protection of all withi the four seas; and if he do not carry it out, he will not be able to protec his wife and children. The way in which the ancients came greatly to surpass other men was no other than this, that they carried out wel what they did, so as to affect others. Now your kindness is sufficient to reach to animals, and yet no benefits are extended from it to the people How is this? Is an exception to be made here?

13 "By weighing we know what things are light, and what heavy By measuring we know what things are long, and what short. All thing

are so dealt with, and the mind requires specially to be so. I beg your Majesty to measure it.

14 "Your Majesty collects your equipments of war, endangers your soldiers and officers, and excites the resentment of the various princes:—do these things cause you pleasure in your mind?"

15 The king said, "No. How should I derive pleasure from these things? My object in them is to seek for what I greatly desire."

16 (Mencius) said, "May I hear from you what it is that your Majesty greatly desires?" The king laughed, and did not speak. (Mencius) resumed, "(Are you led to desire it), because you have not enough of rich and sweet (food) for your mouth? or because you have not enough of light and warm (clothing) for your body? or because you have not enough of beautifully coloured objects to satisfy your eyes? or because you have not enough of attendants and favourites to stand before you and receive your orders? Your Majesty's various officers are sufficient to supply you with all these things. How can your Majesty have such a desire on account of them?" "No," said the king, "my desire is not on account of them." (Mencius) observed, "Then, what your Majesty greatly desires can be known. You desire to enlarge your territories, to have Ch'in and Ch'u coming to your court, to rule the Middle States, and to attract to you the barbarous tribes that surround them. But to do what you do in order to seek for what you desire is like climbing a tree to seek for fish."

17 "Is it so bad as that?" said (the king). "I apprehend it is worse," was the reply. "If you climb a tree to seek for fish, although you do not get the fish, you have no subsequent calamity. But if you do what you do in order to seek for what you desire, doing it even with all your heart, you will assuredly afterwards meet with calamities." The king said, "May I hear (what they will be)?" (Mencius) replied, "If the people of Tsou were fighting with the people of Ch'u, which of them does your Majesty think would conquer?" "The people of Ch'u would conquer," was the answer, and (Mencius) pursued, "So then, a small State cannot contend with a great, few cannot contend with many, nor can the weak contend with the strong. The territory within the seas would embrace nine divisions, each of a thousand *li* square. All Ch'i together is one of them. If with one part you try to subdue the other eight, what is the difference between that and Tsou's contending with Ch'u? (With the desire which you have), you must turn back to the proper course (for its attainment).

18 "Now if your Majesty will institute a government whose action shall all be benevolent, this will cause all the officers in the kingdom to

wish to stand in your Majesty's fields, the merchants, both travelling and stationary, all to wish to store their goods in your Majesty's market-places, travellers and visitors all to wish to travel on your Majesty's roads, and all under heaven who feel aggrieved by their rulers to wish to come and complain to your Majesty. When they are so bent, who will be able to keep them back?"

19 The king said, "I am stupid, and cannot advance to this. (But) I wish you, my Master, to assist my intentions. Teach me clearly, and although I am deficient in intelligence and vigour, I should like to try at least (to institute such a government)."

20 (Mencius) replied, "They are only men of education, who, without a certain livelihood,[6] are able to maintain a fixed heart. As to the people, if they have not a certain livelihood, they will be found not to have a fixed heart. And if they have not a fixed heart, there is nothing which they will not do in the way of self-abandonment, of moral deflection, of depravity, and of wild license. When they have thus been involved in crime, to follow them up and punish them, is to entrap the people. How can such a thing as entrapping the people be done under the rule of a benevolent man?

21 "Therefore an intelligent ruler will regulate the livelihood of the people, so as to make sure that, above, they shall have sufficient wherewith to serve their parents, and below, sufficient wherewith to support their wives and children; that in good years they shall always be abundantly satisfied, and that in bad years they shall not be in danger of perishing. After this he may urge them, and they will proceed to what is good, for in this case the people will follow after that with readiness.

22 "But now, the livelihood of the people is so regulated, that, above, they have not sufficient wherewith to serve their parents, and below, they have not sufficient wherewith to support their wives and children; (even) in good years their lives are always embittered, and in bad years they are in danger of perishing. In such circumstances their only object is to escape from death, and they are afraid they will not succeed in doing so; —what leisure have they to cultivate propriety and righteousness?

23 "If your Majesty wishes to carry out (a benevolent government), why not turn back to what is the essential step (to its attainment)?

24 "Let mulberry-trees be planted about the homesteads with their five acres,[6a] and persons of fifty years will be able to wear silk. In keeping

[6] Ts'an, property: same with the following paragraphs.

[6a] Really *mu*. The modern *mu* is one-sixth of an "acre."

fowls, pigs, dogs, and swine, let not their times of breeding be neglected, and persons of seventy years will be able to eat flesh. Let there not be taken away the time that is proper for the cultivation of the field-allotment of a hundred acres, and the family of eight mouths will not suffer from hunger. Let careful attention be paid to the teaching in the various schools, with repeated inculcation of the filial and fraternal duties, and gray-haired men will not be seen upon the roads, carrying burdens on their backs or on their heads. It has never been that (the ruler of a State) where these results were seen, the old wearing silk and eating flesh, and the black-haired people suffering neither from hunger nor cold, did not attain to the Royal dignity."

BOOK I, PART II

Chapter I

1 Chuang Pao, (having gone to) see Mencius, said to him, "I had an audience of the king. His Majesty told me about his loving music, and I was not prepared with anything to reply to him. What do you pronounce concerning (that) love of music?" Mencius said, "If the king's love of music were very great, the kingdom of Ch'i would be near to (being well governed)."

2 Another day, Mencius had an audience of the king, and said, "Your Majesty, (I have heard), told the officer Chuang about your love of music;—was it so?" The king changed colour, and said, "I am unable to love the music of the ancient kings; I only love the music that suits the manners of the (present) age."

3 (Mencius) said, "If your Majesty's love of music were very great Ch'i, I apprehend, would be near to (being well governed). The music of the present day is just like the music of antiquity (for effecting that)."

4 (The king) said, "May I hear (the proof of what you say)?" "Which is the more pleasant," was the reply,—"to enjoy music by yourself alone, or to enjoy it along with others?" "To enjoy it along with others," said (the king). "And which is the more pleasant," pursued (Mencius),—"to enjoy music along with a few, or to enjoy it along with many?" "To enjoy it along with many," replied (the king).

5 (Mencius went on), "Will you allow your servant to speak to your Majesty about music?

6 "Your Majesty is having music here.—The people hear the sound of your bells and drums, and the notes of your reeds and flutes, and they all, with aching heads, knit their brows, and say to one another, 'That's how our king loves music! But why does he reduce us to this extremity (of distress)? Fathers and sons do not see one another; elder brothers and younger brothers, wives and children, are separated and scattered abroad.' Again, your Majesty is hunting here. The people hear the noise of your carriages and horses, and see the beauty of your plumes and pennons, and they all, with aching heads, knit their brows, and say to one another, 'That's how our king loves hunting! But why does he reduce us to this extremity of distress? Fathers and sons do not see one another; elder brothers and younger brothers, wives and children, are separated and scattered abroad.' This is from no other cause, but that you do not give the people to have pleasure as well as yourself.

7 "Your Majesty is having music here.—The people hear the sound of your bells and drums, and the notes of your reeds and flutes, and they all, delighted and with joyful looks, say to one another, 'That sounds as if our king were free from all sickness! What fine music he is able to have!' Again, Your Majesty is hunting here.—The people hear the noise of your carriages and horses, and see the beauty of your plumes and pennons, and they all, delighted and with joyful looks, say to one another, 'That looks as if our king were free from all sickness! How he is able to hunt!' This is from no other reason but that you cause the people to have pleasure as well as yourself.

8 "If your Majesty now will make pleasure a thing common to the people and yourself, the Royal sway awaits you."

Chapter II

1 King Hsüan of Ch'i asked, "Was it so that the park of king Wen contained seventy square *li?"* Mencius replied, "It is so in the Records."

2. "Was it so large as that?" said (the king). "The people," said (Mencius), "still considered it small." "My park," responded (the king), "contains (only) forty square *li,* and the people still consider it large. How is this?" "The park of king Wen,"—said (Mencius), "contained seventy square *li,* but the grass-cutters and fuel-gatherers (had the privilege of) resorting to it, and so also had the catchers of pheasants and hares. He shared it with the people, and was it not with reason that they looked on it as small?

3 "When I first arrived at your frontiers, I enquired about the great prohibitory regulations before I would venture to enter (the country); and I heard that inside the border-gates there was a park of forty square *li,* and that he who killed a deer in it, whether large or small, was held guilty of the same crime as if he had killed a man. In this way those forty square *li* are a pitfall (trap) in the middle of the kingdom. Is it not with reason that the people look upon (your park) as large?"

Chapter VII

1 Mencius, having (gone to) see king Hsüan of Ch'i, said to him, "When men speak of 'an ancient kingdom,' it is not meant thereby that it has lofty trees in it, but that it has ministers (sprung from families that have been noted in it) for generations. Your Majesty has no ministers with whom you are personally intimate. Those whom you advanced yesterday are gone to-day, and you do not know it."

2 The king said, "How shall I know that they have no ability, and avoid employing them at all?"

3 The reply was, "A ruler advances to office (new) men of talents and virtue (only) as a matter of necessity. As he thereby causes the low to overstep the honourable and strangers to overstep his relatives, ought he to do so but with caution?

4 "When all those about you say (of a man), 'He is a man of talents and virtue,' do not immediately (believe them). When your great officers all say, 'He is a man of talents and virtue,' do not immediately (believe them). When your people all say, 'He is a man of talents and virtue,' then examine into his character; and, when you find that he is such indeed, then afterwards employ him. When all those about you say, 'He will not do,' do not listen to them. When your great officers all say, 'He will not do,' do not listen to them. When your people all say, 'He will not do,' then examine into his character; and when you find that he will not do, then afterwards send him away.

5 "When those about you all say (of a man), 'He deserves death,' do not listen to them. When your great officers all say, 'He deserves death,' do not listen to them. When your people all say, 'He deserves death,' then examine into his case; and when you find that he deserves death, then afterwards put him to death. In accordance with this we have the saying, 'The people put him to death.'

6 "Act in this way and you will be the parent of the people."

Chapter VIII

1 King Hsüan of Ch'i asked, saying, "Was it so that T'ang banished Chieh, and king Wu smote Chou?" Mencius replied, "It is so in the Records."

2 (The king) said, "May a subject put his ruler to death?"

3 The reply was, "He who outrages benevolence is called a ruffian,[7] he who outrages righteousness is called a villain. The ruffian and villain we call a mere fellow. I have heard of the cutting off of the fellow Chou[8]; I have not heard of the putting a ruler to death (in his case)."

Chapter X

1 The people of Ch'i attacked Yen, and conquered it.

2 King Hsüan asked, saying, "Some tell me not to take possession of it, and some tell me to take possession of it. For a kingdom of ten thousand chariots to attack another of the same strength, and to complete the conquest, of it in fifty days, is an achievement beyond (mere) human strength. If I do not take it, calamities from Heaven will surely come upon me:—what do you say to my taking possession of it?"

3 Mencius replied, "If the people of Yen will be pleased with your taking possession of it, do so.—Among the ancients there was (one) who acted in this way, namely king Woo. If the people of Yen will not be pleased with your taking possession of it, do not. Among the ancients there was one who acted in this way, namely king We.

4 "When with (the strength of) your kingdom of ten thousand chariots you attacked another of the same strength and they met your Majesty's army with baskets of rice and vessels of congee, was there any other reason for this but that they (hoped to) escape out of fire and water?[9]

If (you make) the water more deep and the fire more fierce, they will just in like manner make another revolution."

Chapter XI

1 The people of Ch'i having attacked Yen and taken possession of it, the (other) princes proposed to take measures to deliver Yen. King Hsüan said, "As the princes are many of them consulting to attack me, how shall I prepare myself for them?" Mencius replied, "I have heard

[7] *Tsei* should read "thief."

[8] The last tyrant emperor of Shang.

[9] "In deep water" or distress.

of one who with seventy *li* gave law to the whole kingdom, but I have not heard of (a ruler) who with a thousand *li* was afraid of others.

2 "The Book of History says, 'When T'ang began his work of punishment, he commenced with Ko. All under heaven had confidence in him. When the work went on in the east, the wild tribes of the west murmured. When it went on in the south, those of the north murmured. They said, "Why does he make us the last?" The looking of the people for him was like the looking in a time of great drought for clouds and rainbows. The frequenters of the markets stopped not; the husbandmen made no change (in their operations). While he took off their rulers, he consoled the people. (His progress) was like the falling of seasonable rain, and the people were delighted.' It is said (again) in the Book of History, 'We have waited for our prince (long); the prince's coming is our reviving.'

3 "Now (the ruler of) Yen was tyrannizing over his people, and your Majesty went and punished him. The people supposed that you were going to deliver them out of the water and the fire, and with baskets of rice and vessels of congee they met your Majesty's host. But you have slain their fathers and elder brothers, and put their sons and younger brothers in chains; you have pulled down the ancestral temple (of the rulers), and are carrying away its precious vessels:—how can such a course be admitted? (The other States of) the kingdom were afraid of the strength of Ch'i before; and now when with a doubled territory you do not exercise a benevolent government, this puts the arms of the kingdom in motion (against you).

4 "If your Majesty will make haste to issue an order, restoring (your captives) old and young, and stopping (the removal of) the precious vessels; (and if then) you will consult with the people of Yen, appoint (for them) a (new) ruler, and afterwards withdraw from the country:—in this way you may still be able to stop (the threatened attack)."

Chapter XII

1 There had been a skirmish between (some troops of) Tsou and Lu, (in reference to which,) duke Mu asked, saying, "Of my officers there were killed thirty-three men and none of the people would die in their defence. If I would put them to death, it is impossible to deal so with so many; if I do not put them to death, then there is (the crime unpunished of) their looking on with evil eyes at the death of their

officers, and not saving them:—how is the exigency of the case to be met?"

2 Mencius replied, "In calamitous years and years of famine the old and weak of your people who have been found lying in ditches and water-channels, and the able-bodied who have been scattered about to the four quarters, have mounted to thousands. All the while, your granaries, O prince, have been stored with rice and other grain, and your treasuries and arsenals have been full, and not one of your officers has told you (of the distress);—so negligent have the superiors (in your State) been, and cruel to their inferiors. The philosopher Tseng said, 'Beware, beware. What proceeds from you will return to you.' Now at last the people have had an opportunity to return (their conduct); do not you, O prince, blame them.

3 "If you will practice a benevolent government, then the people will love all above them, and will die for their officers."

BOOK II, PART I

Chapter VI

1 Mencius said, "All men have a mind which cannot bear (to see the sufferings of) others.[10]

2 "The ancient kings had this commiserating mind,[10] and they had likewise, as a matter of course, a commiserating government.[11] When with a commiserating mind there was practised a commiserating government, to bring all under heaven to order was (as easy) as to make (a small thing) go round in the palm.

3 "The ground on which I say that all men have a mind which cannot bear (to see suffering of) others is this:—Even now-a-days, when men suddenly see a child about to fall into a well, they will all experience a feeling of alarm and distress. They will feel so not that they may thereon gain the favour of the child's parents; nor that they may seek the praise of their neighbours and friends; nor from a dislike to the reputation of (being unmoved by) such a thing.[12]

4 "Looking at the matter from this case, (we may see that) to be without this feeling of distress is not human, and that it is not human

[10] Or simpler: "have a heart of mercy." Same with following sentences.
[11] Simpler: "a rule of mercy."
[12] Based on Mencian idea that human nature is innately good.

to be without the feeling of shame and dislike, or to be without the feeling of modesty and complaisance, or to be without the feeling of approving and disapproving.[13]

5 "That feeling of distress is the principle of benevolence; the feeling of shame and dislike is the principle of righteousness; the feeling of modesty and complaisance is the principle of propriety; and the feeling of approving and disapproving is the principle of knowledge.

6 "Men have these four principles just as they have their four limbs. When men, having these four principles, yet say of themselves that they cannot (manifest them), they play the thief with[14] themselves; and he who says of his ruler that he cannot (manifest them), plays the thief with his ruler.

7 "Since we all have the four principles in ourselves, let us know to give them all their development and completion, and the issue will be like that of a fire which has begun to burn, or of a spring which has begun to find bent. Let them have their full development, and they will suffice to love and protect all (within) the four seas; let them be denied that development, and they will not suffice for a man to serve his parents with."

BOOK II, PART II

Chapter I

1 Mencius said, "Opportunities of time (vouchsafed by) Heaven are not equal to advantages of situation (afforded by) the earth, and advantages of situation (afforded by) the earth are not equal to the strength (arising from the) accord of men.[15]

2 "(There is a city), with an inner wall of three *li* in circumference and an outer wall of seven. (The enemy) surround and attack it, but are not able to take it. Now, to surround and attack it, there must have been vouchsafed to them by Heaven the opportunity of time, and in such case

[13] Should read: "He who has not a heart of mercy is not a man; who has not a sense of shame is not a man; who has not a sense of courtesy and consideration for others is not a man; who is without a sense of right and wrong is not a man." Similar substitutions should be made for the following paragraph.

[14] Really "injure."

[15] Mencius is briefer: Weather is less important than terrain; terrain is less important than people's unity (morale). Same substitutions in the following two paragraphs will make them immediately clearer.

their not taking it is because opportunities of time (vouchsafed by) Heaven are not equal to advantages of situation (afforded by) the earth.

3 "(There is a city) whose walls are as high and moats as deep as could be desired, and where the arms and mail (of its defenders) are distinguished for their sharpness and strength, and the (stores of) rice and grain are abundant; yet it has to be given up and abandoned. This is because advantages of situation (afforded by) the earth are not equal to the (strength arising from the) accord of men.

4 "In accordance with these principles it is said, 'A people is bounded in not by the limits of dykes and borders; a State is secured not by the strengths of mountains and streams; the kingdom is overawed not by the sharpness of arms (and strength) of mail.' He who finds the proper course[16] has many to assist him, and he who loses it has few. When this—the being assisted by few—reaches the extreme point, (a ruler's) own relatives and connexions revolt from him. When the being assisted by many reaches its extreme point, all under heaven become obedient (to the ruler).

5 "When one to whom all under heaven are prepared to become obedient attacks one from whom his own relatives and connexions are ready to revolt, (what must the result be?) Therefore the true ruler will (prefer) not (to) fight, but if he do fight, he is sure to overcome."

BOOK III, PART I

Chapter III

13 (The Duke Wen of T'eng) sent Pi Chan to ask about the nine-squares system[17] of dividing the land. Mencius said to him, "Since your ruler, wishing to put in practice a benevolent government, has made choice of you, and put you into this employment, you must use all your efforts. Benevolent government must commence with the definition of the boundaries. If the boundaries be not defined correctly, the division of the land into squares will not be equal, and the produce (available for) salaries will not be evenly distributed. On this account, oppressive rulers and impure ministers are sure to neglect the defining of the boundaries. When the boundaries have been defined correctly, the divi-

[16] *Tao,* the true teaching.

[17] The ancient communal farm system, dividing a lot into nine equal squares, the middle one being the government farm.

sion of the fields and the regulation of the salaries may be determined (by you) sitting (at your ease).

14 "Although the territory of T'eng be narrow and small, there must be in it, I apprehend, men of a superior grade, and there must be in it countrymen. If there were not men of a superior grade, there would be none to rule the countrymen; if there were not countrymen, there would be none to support the men of superior grade.

15 "I would ask you, in the (purely) country districts, to observe the nine-square division, having one square cultivated on the system of mutual aid; and in the central parts of the State, to levy a tenth, to be paid by the cultivators themselves.[18]

16 "From the highest officers downwards, each one must have (his) holy field,[19] consisting of fifty acres.

17 "Let the supernumerary males have (their) twenty-five acres.

18 "On occasions of death, or of removing from one dwelling to another, there will be no quitting the district. In the fields of a district, those who belong to the same nine-squares render all friendly offices to one another in their going out and coming in, aid one another in keeping watch and ward, and sustain one another in sickness. Thus the people will be led to live in affection and harmony.

19 "A square *li* covers nine squares of land, which nine squares contain nine hundred acres. The central square contains the public fields; and eight families, each having its own hundred acres,[20] cultivate them together. And it is not till the public work is finished that they presume to attend to their private fields. (This is) the way by which the country-men are distinguished (from those of a superior grade).

20 "These are the great outlines (of the system). Happily to modify and adapt them depends on your ruler and you."

BOOK III, PART II

Chapter VIII

1 "Tai Ying-chih said (to Mencius), "I am not able at present and immediately to do with a tithe (only), and abolish (at the same time)

[18] Should read: "In the confines of the city (where land cannot be divided into nine-squares) to levy a tithe calculated by the tax-payers."
[19] For keeping up sacrifices.
[20] Really *mu,* one sixth of an acre.

the duties charged at the passes and in the markets. With your leave I will lighten all (the present extraordinary exactions) until next year, and then make an end of them. What do you think of such a course?"

2 Mencius said, "Here is a man who every day appropriates the fowls of his neighbours that stray to his premises. Some one says to him, 'Such is not the way of a good man,' and he replies, 'With your leave I will diminish my appropriations, and will take only one fowl a month, until next year, when I will make an end of the practice altogether.'

3 "If you know that the thing is unrighteous, then put an end to it with all despatch;—why wait till next year?"

Chapter X

1 K'uang Chang said (to Mencius), "Is not Mr. Ch'en Chung a man of true self-denying purity? He was living in Wu-ling, and for three days was without food, till he could neither hear nor see. Over a well there grew a plum tree, a fruit of which had been, more than half of it, eaten by worms. He crawled to it, and tried to eat (some of this fruit), when, after swallowing three mouthfuls, he recovered his sight and hearing."

2 Mencius replied, "Among the scholars of Ch'i I must regard Chung as the thumb (among the fingers). But still, how can he be regarded as having that self-denying purity? To carry out the principles which he holds, one must become an earth-worm, for so only can it be done.

3 "Now an earth-worm eats the dry mould above, and drinks the yellow spring below. Was the house in which Mr. Chung lives built by a Poyi? or was it built by a robber like Cheh? Was the grain which he eats planted by a Poyi? or was it planted by a robber like Cheh? These are things which cannot be known."

4 "But," said (Chang), "what does that matter? He himself weaves sandals of hemp, and his wife twists hempen threads, which they exchange (for other things)."

5 (Mencius) rejoined, "Mr. Chung belongs to an ancient and noble family of Ch'i. His elder brother Tai received from Kai a revenue of 10,000 *chung,* but he considered his brother's emolument to be unrighteous, and would not dwell in the place. Avoiding his brother, and leaving his mother, he went and dwelt in Wu-ling. One day afterwards, he returned (to their house), when it happened that some one sent his brother a present of a live goose. He, knitting his brows, said, 'What are you going to use that cackling thing for?' By-and-by, his mother killed the goose, and gave him some of it to eat. (Just then) his brother came

into the house and said, 'It's the flesh of that cackling thing,' on which he went out, and vomited it.

6 "Thus what his mother gave him he would not eat, but what his wife gives him he eats. He will not dwell in his brother's house, but he dwells in Wu-ling. How can he in such circumstances complete the style of life which he professes? With such principles as Mr. Chung holds, (a man must be) an earth-worm, and then he can carry them out."

BOOK IV, PART I

Chapter VII

1 Mencius said, "When right government prevails through the kingdom, (princes of) little virtue are submissive to those of great, and (those of) little worth to (those of) great. When bad government prevails, the small are submissive to the large, and the weak to the strong.[21] Both these cases are (the law of) Heaven. They who accord with Heaven are preserved; they who rebel against Heaven perish.

Chapter VIII

4 "A man must (first) despise himself, and then others will despise him. A family must (first) overthrow itself, and then others will overthrow it. A State must (first) smite itself, and then others will smite it.

5 "This is illustrated by the passage in the T'ai-chia, 'Calamities sent by Heaven may be avoided; but when we bring on the calamities ourselves, it is not possible to live.' "

Chapter IX

1 Mencius said, "Chieh and Chou's[22] losing the kingdom arose from their losing the people; and to lose the people means to lose their hearts. There is a way to get[23] the kingdom;—get the people, and the kingdom is got. There is a way to get the people;—get their hearts, and the people are got. There is a way to get their hearts;—it is simply to collect for them what they desire, and not to lay on them what they dislike.

[21] More exactly and clearly: "When the right teachings prevail, the moral inferior serve the moral superior, and the mental inferior serve the mental superior. When the right teachings do not prevail, the small serve the big and the weak serve the strong."

[22] The tyrant Chou, not the Chou Dynasty.

[23] Substitute "win" throughout, and it will immediately read better.

2 "The people turn to a benevolent (rule) as water flows downwards, and as wild beasts run to the wilds.

3 "Accordingly (as) the otter aids the deep waters, driving the fish to them, and (as) the hawk aids the thickets, driving the little birds to them, (so) did Chieh and Chou aid T'ang and Wu, driving the people to them.

4 "If among the present rulers throughout the kingdom there were one who loved benevolence, all the (other) princes would aid him by driving the people to him. Although he wished not to exercise the royal sway, he could not avoid doing so.

Chapter XIV

1 Mencius said, "Ch'iu acted as chief officer to the Head of the Chi family, whose (evil) ways he was unable to change, while he exacted from the people double the grain which they had formerly paid. Confucius said, 'He is no disciple of mine. Little children, beat the drum and assail him.'

2 "Looking at the subject from this case, (we perceive that) when a ruler who was not practising benevolent government, all (his ministers) who enriched him were disowned by Confucius;—how much more (would he have disowned) those who are vehement to fight (for their ruler)! Some contention about territory is the ground on which they fight, and they slaughter men till the fields are filled with them; or they fight for the possession of some fortified city, and slaughter men till the walls are covered with them. This is what is called 'leading land on to devour human flesh.'[24] Death is not enough for such a crime.

3 "Therefore those who are skillful to fight should suffer the highest punishment.[25] Next to them (should be punished) those who unite the princes in leagues; and next to them, those who take in grassy wastes, and impose the cultivation of the ground (upon the people)."

BOOK IV, PART II

Chapter III

1 Mencius addressed himself to king Hsüan of Ch'i, saying, "When a ruler regards his ministers as his hands and feet, they regard him as their

[24] Mencius is briefer; literally—"In a war for territory, the dead fill the countryside; in a war for cities, the dead fill the cities. This is to allow territories to devour human flesh."
[25] More simply: "The best fighters should receive the supreme punishment."

belly and heart; when he regards them as his dogs and horses, they regard him as they do any ordinary man;[26] when he regards them as the ground[27] or as grass, they regard him as a robber and an enemy."

Chapter VIII

Mencius said, "When men have what they will not do, they are prepared to act in what they do do (with effect)."[28]

Chapter XII

Mencius said, "The great man is he who does not lose his child's heart."[29]

Chapter XXXIII

1 "A man of Ch'i had a wife and a concubine, and lived together with them in his house. When their good-man went out, he was sure to get himself well filled with spirits and flesh and then return, and on his wife's asking him with whom he had been eating and drinking, they were sure to be all men of wealth and rank. The wife informed the concubine, saying, 'When the good-man goes out, he is sure to come back having partaken plentifully of spirits and flesh, and when I ask him with whom he has been eating and drinking, they are all men of wealth and rank. And yet no men of distinction ever come (here). I will spy out where our good-man goes.' (Accordingly) she got up early in the morning, and privately followed the good-man to where he was going. All through the city there was nobody who stood and talked with him. At last he came to those who were sacrificing among the tombs outside the outer wall on the east, and begged what they had left. Not being satisfied, he looked round him and went to another party;—and this was the way in which he got himself satiated. His wife went home, and informed the concubine, saying, 'It was to the good-man that we looked up in hopeful contemplation, and with whom our lot is cast for life;[30]—and these are his ways.' (On this) she and the concubine reviled their good-man, and wept together in the middle courtyard. (In the meantime) the good-man, knowing nothing of all this, came in with a jaunty air, carrying himself proudly to them.

[26] "A common citizen."
[27] "Dirt."
[28] "Men must refuse to do certain things before they can do (great) things."
[29] "The child's heart" (of innocence).
[30] "A husband is one whom one looks to for support for life."

2 "According to the view which a superior man takes of things, as to the ways by which men seek for riches, honours, gain, and advancement, there are few of their wives and concubines who might not be ashamed and weep together because of them."

BOOK V, PART I

Chapter V

1 Wan Chang said, "(It is said that) Yao gave the empire to Shun; was it so?" Mencius replied, "No; the emperor cannot give the empire to another."

2 "Yes; but Shun possessed the empire. Who gave it to him?" "Heaven gave it to him," was the reply.

3 " 'Heaven gave it to him'; did (Heaven) confer the appointment on him with specific injunctions?"

4 (Mencius) said, "No; Heaven does not speak. It simply showed its will by his (personal) conduct, and by (his conduct of) affairs."

5 " 'It showed its will by his (personal conduct of) affairs,' " returned the other;—"how was this?" (Mencius) said, "The emperor can present a man to Heaven, but he cannot make Heaven give that man the empire. A feudal prince can present a man to the emperor (to take his place), but he cannot make the emperor give the princedom to that man. A great officer can present a man to his prince, but he cannot cause the prince to make that man a great officer (in his own room). Anciently Yao presented Shun to Heaven, and Heaven accepted him; he displayed him to the people, and the people accepted him. Therefore I say, 'Heaven does not speak. It simply indicated its will by his (personal) conduct, and by (his conduct of) affairs.' "

6 (Chang) said, "I presume to ask how it was that (Yao) presented Shun to Heaven, and Heaven accepted him, and displayed him to the people, and the people accepted him." The reply was, "He caused him to preside over the sacrifices, and all the Spirits were well pleased with them; thus it was that Heaven accepted him. He caused him to preside over the conduct of affairs, and affairs were well administered, so that all the people reposed under him;—thus it was that the people accepted him. Heaven gave (the empire) to him, and the people gave it to him. Therefore I said, 'The emperor cannot give the empire to another.'

7 "Shun assisted Yao (in the government) for twenty and eight years;—this was more than man could have done, and was from Heaven. When the three years' mourning consequent on the death of Yao were accomplished, Shun withdrew from the son of Yao to the south of the southern Ho. The princes of the empire, however, repairing to court, went not to the son of Yao, but to Shun. Litigants went not to the son of Yao, but to Shun. Singers sang not about the son of Yao, but about Shun. Therefore I said that it was Heaven (that gave him the empire). It was after this that he went to the Middle State, and occupied the seat of the son of Heaven. If he had (before these things) taken up his residence in the palace of Yao, and applied pressure to his son, it would have been an act of usurpation, and not the gift of Heaven.

8 "This view (of Shun's obtaining the empire) is in accordance with what is said in The Great Declaration,—'Heaven sees as my people see, Heaven hears as my people hear.' "

BOOK VI, PART I[31]

Chapter I

1 Kaotse said, "(Man's) nature is like a willow tree, and righteousness is like a cup or a bowl.[32] The fashioning of benevolence and righteousness out of man's nature is like making cups and bowls from the willow tree."

2 Mencius replied, "Can you, in accordance with the nature of the willow tree, make cups and bowls from it? You will do violence and injury to the tree before you can make cups and bowls from it. If you will do violence and injury to the willow tree in order to make cups and bowls, will you also do violence and injury to a man, to fashion benevolence and righteousness (from him)? Your words, alas! would certainly with all men occasion calamity to benevolence and righteousness."[33]

[31] If the reader wishes to read a clearer translation of this most important portion of Mencius he should consult the new translation in *"Wisdom of Confucius"* (Modern Library), Chapter XI.
[32] Wicker basket.
[33] "Destroy the teachings of love and justice" by assuming that they are not in accord with our nature, but are external teachings forcing our nature into shape. Mencius believes goodness is in man's innate nature.

Chapter II

1 Kaotse said, "(Man's) nature is like water whirling round (in a corner). Open a passage for it on the east, and it will flow to the east; open a passage for it on the west, and it will flow to the west. Man's nature is indifferent to good and evil, just as water is indifferent to the east and west."

2 Mencius replied, "Water indeed will flow indifferently to the east or west, but will it flow indifferently up or down? The (tendency of) man's nature to goodness is like the (tendency of) water to flow downwards. There are none but have (this tendency to) goodness, (just as) water flows downwards.

3 "Now by striking water, and causing it to leap up, you may make it go over your forehead; and by damming and leading it, you may make it go up a hill; but are (such movements according to) the nature of water? It is the force applied which causes them. In the case of a man's being made to do what is not good, his nature is dealt with in this way."

Chapter III

1 Kaotse said, "(The phenomena of) life is what I call nature."

2 Mencius replied, "Do you say that life is nature just as you say that white is white?" "Yes," was the reply. (Mencius asked again), "Is the whiteness of a white feather like the whiteness of white snow, and the whiteness of white snow like that of white jade?" "Yes," returned (the other).

3 Mencius retorted, "Very well. Is the nature of a dog like the nature of an ox, and the nature of an ox like the nature of a man?"[34]

Chapter IV

1 Kaotse said, "(To delight in) food and in sexual pleasure is nature. Benevolence is from within, and not from without; righteousness is from without and not from within."[35]

2 Mencius said, "What is the ground of your saying that benevolence is from within, and righteousness from without?" (The other) replied, "There is a man older than I, and I give honour to his age;—it is not that there is in me a principle of reverence for age. It is just as when there is a

[34] Mencius was careful to insist that the human in us is different from the beastly.

[35] Justice, or duties to one's fellowmen, are created by social life, while love is innate. Mencius insists, however, that both are innate, including the love to do what is right (justice).

white man, and I consider him white;—according as he is so externally to me. It is on this account that I say (of righteousness) that it is from without."

3 (Mencius) said, "There is no difference to us between the whiteness of a white horse, and the whiteness of a white man, but I do not know that there is no difference between the regard with which we acknowledge the age of an old horse, and that with which we acknowledge the age of a man older (than ourselves)? And what is it which we call righteousness? The fact of a man's being older (than we)? or the fact of our giving honour to his age?"[36]

4 (Kao) said, "There is my younger brother; I love him. But the younger brother of a man of Ch'in I do not love; that is, it is (the relationship to) myself which occasions my complacency,[37] and therefore I say that benevolence is from within. I give the honour due to age to an old man of Ch'u, and to an old man of my own (kindred); that is, it is the age which occasions the complacency, and therefore I say that righteousness is from without."

5 (Mencius) answered him, "Our enjoyment of meat broiled by a man of Ch'in does not differ from our enjoyment of meat broiled by (one of) our (own kindred). Thus (what you insist on) takes place also in the case of (such) things; but is our enjoyment of broiled meat also from without?"

Chapter V

1 Mr. Meng Chi asked the disciple Kung-tu, saying, "On what ground is it said that righteousness is from within?"

2 (Kung-tu) replied, "It is the acting out of our feeling of respect, and therefore it is said to be from within."

3 (The other) said, "(In the case of) a villager one year older than your elder brother, to which of them will you show the (greater) respect?" "To my brother," was the reply. "But for which would you pour out spirits first?" (Kung-tu) said, "For the villager." (Meng Chi then argued), "Your feeling of respect rests on the one, but your reverence for age is rendered to the other; (righteousness) is certainly determined by what is without, and not by internal feeling."

4 The disciple Kung-tu was unable to reply, and reported (the conversation) to Mencius, who said, "(You should ask him), 'Which do you respect more, your uncle, or your younger brother?' He will reply, 'My

[36] Respect for age is subjective (and innate). [37] "I love (naturally) my own kind."

uncle.' (Ask him again), 'If your younger brother be personating a deceased ancestor, to whom will you show respect more,—(to him or to your uncle)?' He will say, 'To my younger brother.' (You can go on), 'But where is the (greater) respect due, as you said, to your uncle?' He will say, '(I show it to my younger brother), because he is in the position (of the deceased ancestor).' And then you must say, 'Because he is in that position;—and so ordinarily my respect is given to my elder brother, but a momentary respect is given to the villager.' "

5 When Meng Chi heard this, he observed, "When respect is due to my uncle, I give it to him; and when respect is due to my younger brother, I give it to him. The thing is certainly determined by what is without us, and does not come from within." Kung tu replied, "In winter we drink things warm, but in summer we drink things cold; but is then our eating and drinking determined by what is external to us?"

Chapter VI

1 The disciple Kung-tu said, "Kaotse says, '(Man's) nature is neither good nor bad.'

2 "Some say, '(Man's) nature may be made to do good, and it may be made to do evil; and accordingly, under Wen and Wu, the people loved what was good, and under Yu and Li they loved what was cruel.'

3 "Some say, 'The nature of some is good, and the nature of others is bad. Hence it was that under such a ruler as Yao, there appeared Hsiang; that with such a father as Kusau, there yet appeared Shun; and that, with Chou for their ruler and the son of their elder brother besides, there yet appeared Ch'i, the viscount of Wei, and prince Pikan.'

4 "And now you say, 'The nature is good.' Then are all those wrong?"

5 Mencius replied, "From the feelings proper to it, (we see) that it is constituted for the doing of what is good.[38] This is what I mean in saying that (the nature) is good.

6 "If (men) do what is not good, the guilt cannot be imputed to their natural powers.

7 "The feeling of compassionate distress belongs to all men; so does that of shame and dislike; and that of modesty and respect; and that of approving and disapproving.[39] The feeling of compassion and distress is the principle of benevolence; the feeling of shame and dislike is the

[38] "If allowed to follow their nature, they will do good."

[39] Read: "The heart of mercy is in all men; the sense of shame is in all men; the sense of courtesy and respect is in all men; the sense of right and wrong is in all men."

principle of righteousness; the feeling of modesty and respect is the principle of propriety; and the feeling of approving and disapproving is the principle of knowledge. Benevolence, righteousness, propriety, and knowledge are not fused into us from without; they naturally belong to us, and (a different view) is simply from want of reflection. Hence it is said, 'Seek, and you will find them; neglect, and you will lose them.' (Men differ from one another in regard to them); some as much again as others, some five times as much, and some to an incalculable amount; it is because they cannot fully carry out their (natural) endowments.

8 "It is said in the Book of Poetry,

> 'Heaven in giving birth to the multitudes of the people,
> To every faculty and relationship annexed its law:
> The people possess this normal nature,
> And they (consequently) love its normal virtue.'

Confucius said, 'The maker of this ode knew indeed the constitution (of our nature).' We may thus see that to every faculty and relationship there must belong its law, and that since the people possess this normal nature, they therefore love its normal virtue."

Chapter VII

1 Mencius said, "In good years the children of the people are most of them good, and in bad years they are most of them evil. It is not owing to their natural endowments conferred by Heaven, that they are thus different. It is owing to the circumstances in which they allow their minds to be ensnared and devoured that they appear so (as in the latter case).

2 "There now is barley.—Let the seed be sown and covered up; the ground being the same, and the time of sowing also the same, it grows luxuriantly, and when the full time is come, it is all found to be ripe. Although there may be inequalities (of produce), that is owing to (the difference of) the soil as rich or poor, to the (unequal) nourishment afforded by rain and dew, and to the different ways in which man has performed his business.

3 "Thus all things which are the same in kind are like to one another;—why should we doubt in regard to man, as if he were a solitary exception to this? The sage and we are the same in kind.[40]

4 "In accordance with this, Lungtse said, 'If a man make hempen

[40] Or, "are of the same species."

sandals, without knowing (the size of people's) feet, yet I know that he will not make them like baskets.' Sandals are like one another, because all men's feet are like one another.

5 "So with the mouth and flavours;—all mouths have the same relishes. Yiya (simply) appreciated before me what my mouth relishes. Suppose that his mouth, in its relish for flavours, were of a different nature from (the mouths of) other men, in the same way as dogs and horses are not of the same kind with us, how should all men be found following Yiya in their relishes? In the matter of tastes, the whole kingdom models itself after Yiya; that is, the mouths of all men are like one another.

6 "So it is with the ear also. In the matter of sounds, the whole kingdom models itself after the music-master K'uang; that is, the ears of all men are like one another.

7 "And so it is also with the eye. In the case of Tsetu, there is no one under heaven but would recognize that he was beautiful. Any one who did not recognize the beauty of Tsetu would (be said to) have no eyes.

8 "Therefore (I) say,—(Men's) mouths agree in having the same relishes; their ears agree in enjoying the same sounds; their eyes agree in recognizing the same beauty;—shall their minds alone be without that which they similarly approve? What is it then of which their minds similarly approve? It is the principles (of things), and the (consequent determinations of) righteousness. The sages only apprehended before me that which I and other men agree in approving.[41] Therefore the principles (of things) and (the determinations of) righteousness are agreeable to my mind just as (the flesh) of grass and grain-fed (animals) is agreeable to my mouth."

Chapter VIII

1 Mencius said, "The trees of Niu hill were once beautiful. Being situated, however, in the suburbs of (the capital of) a large State, they were hewn down with axes and bills; and could they retain their beauty? Still through the growth from the vegetative life day and night, and the nourishing influence of the rain and dew, they were not without buds and sprouts springing out. But then came the cattle and goats, and browsed upon them. To these things is owing the bare and stript appearance (of the hill); and when people see this, they think it was never finely wooded. But is this the nature of the hill?

[41] More exactly: "The sages are those who discover what is common to our hearts."

2 "And so even of what properly belongs to man; shall it be said that the mind (of any man) was without benevolence and righteousness?[42] The way in which a man loses the proper goodness of his mind is like the way in which (those) trees were denuded by axes and bills. Hewn down day after day, can it retain its excellence? But there is some growth of its life day and night, and in the (calm) air of the morning, just between night and day, the mind feels in a degree those desires and aversions which are proper to humanity; but the feeling is not strong; and then it is fettered and destroyed by what the man does during the day. This fettering takes place again and again; the restorative influence of the night is not sufficient to preserve (the proper goodness); and when this proves insufficient for that purpose, the (nature) becomes not much different from (that of) the irrational animals; and when people see this, they think that it never had those endowments (which I assert). But does this condition represent the feelings proper to humanity?

3 "Therefore if it receive its proper nourishment, there is nothing which will not grow; if it lose its proper nourishment, there is nothing which will not decay away.

4 "Confucius said, 'Hold it fast, and it remains with you; let it go, and you lose it. Its out-going and in-coming cannot be defined as to time and place.' It was the mental nature of which this was said."

Chapter IX

1 Mencius said, "It is not to be wondered at that the king is not wise!

2 "Suppose the case of the most easily growing thing in the world; —if you let it have one day's genial heat, and then expose it for ten days to cold, it will not be able to grow. It is but seldom that I have an audience (of the king), and when I retire, there come (all) those who act upon him like the cold. Though I succeed in bringing out some buds of goodness, of what avail is it?

3 "Now chess-playing is an art, though a small one; but without his whole mind being given, and his will bent to it, a man cannot succeed in it. Chess Ch'iu is the best chess-player in all the kingdom. Suppose that he is teaching two men to play;—the one gives all his mind to the game, and bends to it all his will, doing nothing but listen to Chess Ch'iu; the other, though he (seems to) be listening to him, has his whole mind running on a swan which he thinks is approaching, and wishes to bend his bow, adjust the arrow to the string, and shoot it. Though the latter is

[42] Better: "love and justice."

learning along with the former, his progress is not equal to his. Is it because his intelligence is not equal? Not so."

Chapter X

1 Mencius said, "I like fish, and I also like bears' paws. If I cannot get both together, I will let the fish go, and take the bears' paws. So I like life, and I also like righteousness. If I cannot keep the two together, I will let life go and choose righteousness.

2 "I like life indeed, but there is that which I like more than life; and therefore I will not seek to hold it by any improper ways. I dislike death indeed, but there is that which I dislike more than death, and therefore there are occasions when I will not avoid calamity (that may occasion death).

3 "If among the things which man likes there were nothing which he liked more than life, why should he not use all means by which he could preserve it? If among the things which man dislikes there were nothing which he disliked more than death, why should he not do everything by which he could avoid calamity (that might occasion it).

4 "(But as man is), there are cases when by a certain course men might preserve life, and yet they do not employ it; and when by certain things they might avoid calamity (that will occasion death), and yet they will not do them.

5 "Therefore men have that which they like more than life, and that which they dislike more than death. They are not men of talents and virtue only who have this mental nature. All men have it;—what belongs to such men is simply that they are able not to lose it.

6 "Here are a small basket of rice and a basin of soup;—and the case is one where the getting them will preserve life, and the want of them will be death. If they are offered to him in an insulting tone,[43] (even) a tramper on the road will not receive them, or if you first tread upon them, (even) a beggar will not stoop to take them.

7 "(And yet) a man will accept of ten thousand *chung*,[44] without any question as to the propriety and righteousness of his doing so. What can the ten thousand *chung* really add to him? (When he takes them), is it not that he may get beautiful mansions? or that he may secure the services of wives and concubines? or that the poor and needy of his acquaintance may be helped by him?

8 "In the former case, the (offered bounty) was not received, though

[43] Lit. "with a 'Tut!'"

[44] As official salary.

it would have saved from death, and now the man takes (the emolument) for the sake of beautiful mansions. (The bounty) that would have saved from death was not received, and (the emolument) is taken to get the services of wives and concubines. (The bounty) that would have saved from death was not received, and (the emolument) is taken that one's poor and needy acquaintances may be helped by him. Was it not possible then to decline (the emolument) in these instances? This is a case of what is called—losing the proper nature of one's mind."

Chapter XI

1 Mencius said, "Benevolence is (the proper quality of) man's mind, and righteousness is man's (proper) path.

2 "How lamentable is it to neglect this path and not pursue it, to lose this mind [45] and not know to seek it (again).

3 "When men's fowls and dogs are lost, they know to seek them (again); but they lose their mind, and do not know to seek it (again).

4 "The object of learning is nothing else but to seek for the lost mind." [46]

Chapter XII

1 Mencius said, "Here is a man whose fourth finger is bent, and cannot be stretched out straight. It is not painful, nor does it incommode his business; but if there were any one who could make it straight, he would not think it far to go all the way from Ch'iu to Ch'i (to find him);—because his finger is not like those of other people.

2 "When a man's finger is not like other people's, he knows to feel dissatisfied; but when his mind is not like other people's, he does not know to feel dissatisfied. This is what is called—ignorance of the relative (importance of things)."

Chapter XIII

Mencius said, "Anybody who wishes to cultivate a *t'ung* tree, or a *tse,* which may be grasped with the two hands, (perhaps) with one, knows by what means to nourish it; but in the case of their own persons men do not know by what means to nourish them. Is it to be supposed that

[45] The Chinese word *hsin* means both "heart" and "mind." Here the heart of original goodness is meant.

[46] "The lost heart of a child."

their regard for their own persons is inferior to their regard for a *t'ung* or a *tse*? Their want of reflection is extreme."

Chapter XIV

1 Mencius said, "Men love every part of their persons; and as they love every part, so they (should) nourish every part. There is not an inch of skin which they do not love, and so there is not an inch of skin which they will not nourish. For examining whether his (way of nourishing) be good or not, what other rule is there but simply this, that a man determine, (by reflecting) on himself, where it should be applied?

2 "Some parts of the body are noble, and some ignoble; some great, and some small. The great must not be injured for the small, nor the noble for the ignoble. He who nourishes the little belonging to him is a small man; he who nourishes the great is a great man.[47]

3 "Here is a plantation-keeper, who neglects his *wu* and *chia,* and nourishes his small jujube trees;—he is a poor plantation-keeper.

4 "He who nourishes one of his fingers, neglecting[48] his shoulders and back, without knowing that he is doing so, is a man (who resembles) a hurried wolf.[49]

5 "A man who (only) eats and drinks is counted mean by others; because he nourishes what is little to the neglect of what is great.

6 "If a man, (fond of) eating and drinking, do (yet) not fail (in nourishing what in him is great), how should his mouth and belly be accounted as no more than an inch of skin?"[50]

Chapter XV

1 The disciple Kung-tu asked, saying, "All are equally men, but some are great men, and others are little men; how is this?" Mencius replied, "Those who follow that part of themselves which is great are great men; those who follow that part which is little are little men."[51]

[47] This paragraph should read: "Now in our constitution there is a higher and a lower nature, and a smaller and a greater self. One should not develop the lower nature at the expense of the higher, or develop the smaller self at the expense of the greater self. He who attends to his smaller self becomes a small man, and he who attends to his greater self becomes a great man."

[48] "Losing."

[49] Should read: "deformed."

[50] "If a man eats and drinks, however, without forgetting about his greater self, then it may be said that the food taken into his mouth goes to nourish more than his external body."

[51] "Those who attend to their greater selves are great men; those who attend to their smaller selves are small men."

2 Kung-tu pursued, "All are equally men; but some follow that part of themselves which is great, and some that which is little; how is this?" Mencius said, "The ears and the eyes have it not in their office to think, and are (liable to be) obscured by things (affecting them); and when one thing comes into contact with another, it simply leads it away. But it is in the office of the mind to think. By thinking, it gets (the right view of things); when neglecting to think, it fails to do this.[52] These—(the senses and the mind)—are what Heaven has given to us. Let a man first stand in (the supremacy of) the greater (and nobler) part of his constitution, and the smaller part will not be able to take it from him.[53] It is simply this which makes the great man.[54]

Chapter XVI

1 Mencius said, "There is a nobility of Heaven, and there is a nobility of man. Benevolence, righteousness, self-consecration, and fidelity, with unwearied joy in the goodness (of these virtues),—these constitute the nobility of Heaven. To be a duke, a minister, or a great officer,—this constitutes the nobility of man.

2 "The men of antiquity cultivated their nobility of Heaven, and the nobility of man came in its train.

3 "The men of the present day cultivate their nobility of Heaven in order to seek for the nobility of man, and when they have obtained this, they throw away the other; their delusion is extreme. The issue is simply this, that they must lose (that nobility of man) as well."

Chapter XVII

1 Mencius said, "To desire to be what is considered honourable is the common mind of men. And all men have what is (truly) honourable in themselves; only they do not think of it.

2 "The honour which man confers is not the truly good honour. Those to whom Chao-meng gave honourable rank he could make mean again.[55]

[52] "The function of the mind is thinking; when you think, you keep your mind, and when you don't think, you lose your mind."
[53] "One who cultivates his higher self will find that his lower self follows of its own accord."
[54] The whole section is very important. See my translation *Wisdom of Confucius* (Modern Lib.) Chap. XI.
[55] "What people usually consider as an elevated rank or honor is not true honor, for he whom Chao Meng (a powerful ruling family of Chin) has honored, Chao Meng can also bring into dishonor."

3 "It is said in the Book of Poetry,

> 'You have made us to drink to the full of your spirits;
> You have satiated us with your kindness;'

meaning that (the guests) were filled with benevolence and righteousness, and therefore did not wish for the fat meat and fine millet of men. When a good reputation and far-reaching praise fall to (a man's) person, he does not desire the elegant embroidered garments of men."[56]

Chapter XVIII

1 Mencius said, "Benevolence subdues its opposite just as water subdues fire.[57] Those, however, who nowadays practise benevolence (do it) as if with a cup of water they could save a whole wagon-load of faggots which was on fire, and when the flames were not extinguished were to say that water cannot subdue fire. Such a course, moreover, is the greatest aid to what is not benevolent.[58]

2 "The final issue will simply be this, the loss (of that small amount of benevolence)."

Chapter XIX

Mencius said, "Of all seeds the best are the five kinds of grain, but if they are not ripe, they are not equal to the *ti* or the *pai*.[59] So the value of benevolence lies simply in its being brought to maturity."

Chapter XX

1 Mencius said, "Yi, in teaching men to shoot, made it a rule to draw the bow to the full, and his pupils were required to do the same.

2 "A master-workman, in teaching others, must use the compass and Shuns';—is it so?" Mencius said, "It is."

BOOK VI, PART II

Chapter II

1 Chiao of Ts'ao asked, saying, "(It is said,) 'All men may be Yaos and Shuns';—is it so?" Mencius said, "It is."

[56] "And when a man wears a mantle of fame, he does not care for the embroidered gown."
[57] "Kindness overcomes cruelty as water overcomes fire."
[58] "Those who practise kindness today are like those who take a cup of water to fight a carload of burning fuel, and when the fire is not put out exclaim, 'Water cannot overcome fire.' This is merely to help those who do not believe in kindness."
[59] Cockles.

2 (Ch'iao went on), "I have heard that king Wen was ten cubits high, and T'ang nine. Now I am nine cubits and four inches in height; but I can do nothing but eat my millet. What am I to do to realize that saying?"

3 The reply was, "What has the thing to do with this,—(the question of size)? It all lies simply in acting as such. Here is a man whose strength was not equal to that of a duckling or chicken,—he was (then) a man of no strength. (But) today he says, 'I can lift three thousand catties'; he is (now) a man of strength. And so, he who can lift the weight which Wu Huo lifted is just another Wu Huo. Why should a man make a want of ability the subject of his grief? It is only that he will not do the thing.

4 "To walk slowly, keeping behind his elders, is to perform the part of a younger. To walk rapidly, going before his elders, is to violate the duty of a younger. But is walking slowly what any man can not do? it is (only) what he does not do. The course of Yao and Shun was simply that of filial piety and fraternal duty.

5 "Do you wear the clothes of Yao, repeat the words of Yao, and do the actions of Yao, and you will just be a Yao. And if you wear the clothes of Chieh, repeat the words of Chieh, and do the actions of Chieh, you will just be a Chieh."

6 (Chiao) said, "When I have an audience of the ruler of Tsou, I can ask him to let me have a house to lodge in. I wish to remain here, and receive instruction at your gate."

7 (Mencius) replied, "The way (of truth) is like a great road; it is not difficult to know it. The evil is only that men will not seek for it. Do you go home, and seek it, and you will have abundance of teachers."

Chapter XV

1 Mencius said, "Shun rose (to the empire) from among the channeled fields. Fu Yüeh was called to office from the midst of his (building) frames and (earth-) beaters; Chiao Keh from his fish and and salt; Kuan Yiwu, from the hands of the officer in charge of him; Sun Shu-ao from (his hiding by) the sea-shore; and Poli Hsi from the market-place.

2 "Thus, when Heaven is about to confer a great office on any one, it first exercises his mind with suffering, and his sinews and bones with toil; it exposes his body to hunger, and subjects him to extreme poverty;

and it confounds his undertakings. In all these ways it stimulates his mind, hardens his nature, and supplies his incompetencies.[60]

3 "Men constantly err, but are afterwards able to reform. They are distressed in mind, and perplexed in thought, and then they arise to vigorous endeavour. When things have been evidenced in men's looks, and set forth in their words, then they understand them.

4 "If a ruler have not about his court families attached to the laws and able officers, and if abroad there are no hostile States or other external calamities, the State will generally come to ruin.[61]

5 "From such things we see how life springs from sorrow and calamity, and death from ease and pleasure."

BOOK VII, PART II

Chapter XIV

1 Mencius said, "The people are the most important element (in a country); the Spirits of the land and grain are the next; the ruler is the least important."

Chapter XXXVIII

4 "From Confucius to now there are (only) a hundred years and (somewhat) more;—so far from being remote is the distance from the sage in point of time, and so very near at hand is the sage's residence. In these circumstances, is there no one (to transmit his doctrines)? Yea, is there no one?"

[60] "Thus when Heaven is about to entrust a man with great work, it first causes distress to his mind, belabors his muscles and frame, starves his body, subjects him to want, and frustrates what he sets out to do. This is to stimulate his ambition, strengthen his character, and increase his capacity for doing what he could not do before."

[61] "If there be not old official families and wise counsellors within and enemies and foreign threats without, such a country often perishes."

Motse

The Religious Teacher

INTRODUCTION

MOTSE OR MO TI, is the only indigenous religious teacher China has produced. Both in method of thinking, and in his ideas, he seemed to stand on his own, although in his earlier chapters, there are some similarities with the Confucian point of view. For Motse seemed to have risen with his teachings in revolt against Confucianism. Among all Chinese philosophers, he comes closest to the Christian teachings, for he alone taught universal love as the basis of society and of peace, showed that Heaven loved the people equally, and insisted on the belief in the existence of the spirits. It is said that some missionaries are scared, instead of feeling encouraged, to find that the doctrines of the love of God and universal love were already known to the Chinese. It is almost as disheartening as reaching the South Pole to find that some one has already been there before. On the other hand, the broad-minded should be pleased that what is true can be independently discovered by the human mind. What should really discourage them is that the Chinese as a nation have rejected this doctrine after its reaching an enormous influence. They have rejected it so completely that the text of Motse, until our own generation, was among the most completely neglected of China's ancient texts, while all its early commentaries are lost.

Motse rose in revolt against Confucianism. He lived from B.C. 468 (or 441) to 401 (or 376), and was thus roughly one century behind Confucius. As Confucius died in 479, he might be said to have been born in the generation when his influence was spreading. Most probably born in Lu, Confucius' own country, he was fully familiar with the Confucian classics, like the *Book of Poetry* and *Book of History*. In temper he was more democratic than Confucius. Some of the most unflattering pictures of the Confucianists of his day come from his works. Huainantse tells us that "Motse studied the learning of the Confucianists and was taught the methods of Confucius. Deciding that their ceremonies were too complicated and difficult of practice, that the expensive funerals were a waste of money and impoverished the people, that their dresses interfered with proper attending to affairs, he renounced the teachings of the Chou Dynasty, and went back to (the simple and theocratic) Hsia system." Against Confucian love of music, he wrote or left three essays "Against Music." Against Confucian belief in fate, he left three essays "Against Fatalism." Against Confucian extravagance, he left several essays on "Thrift" and "Thrifty Funerals." Against Confucian agnosticism, he left three essays on "Recognizing the Spirits." Besides the two essays "Anti-Confucianism," such ideas are present in most of his essays.

On the positive side, he enunciated the clearest teachings "against offensive wars," and even developed in great detail the technique of defensive warfare. He also developed a system of logical method, and it was his followers who carried it further and became known as the Chinese "sophists," among whom Hueitse, constantly referred to by Chuangtse, was one. But what is more, Motse's teachings were a stern call to action, and unlike the other schools, showed an evangelistic zeal. Mencius referred to him as one who "would wear his head and his heels off to benefit the world." He taught and practised altruism, frugality and the hard life. Chuangtse said that his followers "wore coarse garments and walked in sandals, and day and night without cease lived the hard life as their goal." He sneered at the Confucianists, comparing them to bells which would sound only when struck, and not sound when not struck. Huainantse tells us that his "hundred eighty disciples would go through fire and walk on knives and face death without turning back."

His influence grew so great that for two centuries after Confucius, the Motseanists became the rivals of Confucianists. Mencius deplored the decay of Confucianism and said that the people of his time would be either followers of Motse or else followers of Yang Chu. In fact, it almost became an established religion. Chuantse says, his followers "regarded their Master as a Sage. They all wanted to be his priests, in the hope of succeeding to him."

Why its influence suddenly stopped completely remains a matter of speculation. Persecution could not do it, and there was no report of persecution. One explanation is the rise of Mencius, who powerfully combated its influence. Another explanation is that the Han Emperors made Confucianism into almost a state religion. A very possible explanation is that the warrior evangelists simply perished in the wars of the First Emperor of Ch'in. Which brings us to the truest explanation that Quixotic heroism and extreme altruism did not appeal to the native Chinese common sense.

Of all ancient texts, Motse can benefit most from editing. His essays, evidently written by his followers, contain many repetitions, so that three essays on the same subject may well be different versions of the same teachings, rather than a consecutive development of the same subject. I have made selections from the English translation of Y. P. Mei (*The Works of Motse,* Probsthain) which makes use of the best text of Sun Yi-jang. The baldness of the style is original, consonant with Motse's teachings on simplicity and frugality. His condemnation of offensive wars is direct to the point of naïveté, but some such plain speaking seems needed at the present time. That he has some wit is shown from the anecdotes about him I have collected from the last chapters of his works.

In contrast to Motse's teaching of universal love, I could produce a Chinese fascist, Shangtse, (fourth century B.C.) whose teachings are an exact replica of totalitarianism. Shangtse taught war and agriculture, but he taught agriculture because he believed peasants made the best soldiers. He exalted war and glorified the rule of force. As a result of the actual applications of his teachings, the dictatorial state of Ch'in came to power and vanquished all China. However, there is enough fascism in the West. The important thing is that both fascism and the doctrine of universal love collapsed in China and have never been tried again. Only in this light can we truly appreciate Confucianism.

Motse

The Religious Teacher

Translated by Y. P. Mei

ON THE NECESSITY OF STANDARDS

(Chapter 4)

Motse said: To accomplish anything whatsoever one must have standards. None has yet accomplished anything without them. The gentlemen fulfilling their duties as general and councillors have their standards. Even the artisans performing their tasks also have their standards. The artisans make square objects according to the square, circular objects according to the compasses; they draw straight lines with the carpenter's line and find the perpendicular by a pendulum. All artisans, whether skilled or unskilled, employ these five standards. Only, the skilled workers are accurate. Though the unskilled labourers have not attained accuracy, yet they do better by following these standards than otherwise. Thus all artisans follow the standards in their work.

Now, the government of the empire and that of the large states do not observe their standards. This shows the governors are even less intelligent that the artisans.

What, then, should be taken as the proper standard in government? How will it do for everybody to imitate his parents? There are numerous parents in the world but few are magnanimous. For everybody to imitate his parents is to imitate the unmagnanimous. Imitating the unmagnanimous cannot be said to be following the proper standard. How will it do for everybody to follow his teacher? There are numerous teachers in the world but few are magnanimous. For everybody to imitate his teacher is to imitate the unmagnanimous. Imitating the unmagnanimous cannot be taken as following the proper standard. How will it do for everybody to imitate his ruler? There are many rulers in the world but few are magnanimous. For everybody to imitate the ruler is to imitate the unmagnanimous. Imitating the unmagnanimous cannot be taken as following the right standard. So then neither the parents nor the teacher nor the ruler should be accepted as the standard in government.

What then should be taken as the standard in government? Nothing better than following Heaven. Heaven is all-inclusive and impartial in its activities, abundant and unceasing in its blessings, and lasting and untiring in its guidance. And, so, when the sage-kings had accepted Heaven as their standard, they measured every action and enterprise by Heaven. What Heaven desired they would carry out, what Heaven abominated they refrained from.

Now, what is it that Heaven desires, and what that it abominates? Certainly Heaven desires to have men benefit and love one another and abominates to have them hate and harm one another. How do we know that Heaven desires to have men love and benefit one another and abominates to have them hate and harm one another? Because it loves and benefits men universally. How do we know that it loves and benefits men universally? Because it claims all and accepts offerings from all. All states in the world, large or small, are cities of Heaven, and all people, young or old, honourable or humble, are its subjects; for they all graze oxen and sheep, feed dogs and pigs, and prepare clean wine and cakes to sacrifice to Heaven. Does this not mean that Heaven claims all and accepts offerings from all? Since Heaven does claim all and accepts offerings from all, what then can make us say that it does not desire men to love and benefit one another? Hence those who love and benefit others Heaven will bless. Those who hate and harm others Heaven will curse, for it is said that he who murders the innocent will be visited by misfortune. How else can we explain the fact that men, murdering each other, will be cursed by Heaven? Thus we are certain that Heaven desires to have men love and benefit one another and abominates to have them hate and harm one another.

The ancient sage-kings, Yü, T'ang, Wen, and Wu loved the people of the world universally, leading them to reverence Heaven and worship the spirits. Many were their benefits to the people. And, thereupon Heaven blessed them, establishing them emperors; and all the feudal lords of the empire showed them respect. (On the other hand) the wicked kings, Chieh, Chow, Yu, and Li, hated all the people in the world, seducing the people to curse Heaven and ridicule the spirits.

Great were their injuries to the people. Thereupon Heaven brought them calamity, depriving them of their empire and their lives; and posterity condemned them to this day. Chieh, Chow, Yu, and Li, then, are those that committed evil and were visited by calamities. And Yü, T'ang, Wen and Wu are those that loved and benefited the people and obtained blessings. Thus we have those who obtained blessings because they loved and benefited the people as well as those who were visited by calamities because they hated and harmed the people.

ON THE IMPORTANCE OF A COMMON STANDARD (III) [1]

(Chapter 13)

Motse said: The interest of the wise (ruler) lies in carrying out what makes for order among the people and avoiding what makes for confusion.

But what is it that makes for order among the people?

When the administration of the ruler answers to the desires of the people there will be order, otherwise there will be confusion.

How do we know it is so?

When the administration of the ruler answers to the desires of the subjects, it manifests an understanding of the approvals and disapprovals of the people. When there is such an understanding, the good will be discovered and rewarded and the bad will be discovered and punished, and the country will surely have order. When the administration of the ruler does not answer to the desires of the subjects, it shows a lack of understanding of the approvals and disapprovals of the subjects. When there is no such understanding then the good will not be discovered and rewarded and the bad will not be discovered and punished. With the good unrewarded and the evil unpunished, such a government will surely put the country into disorder. Therefore when rewards and punishments do not answer to the desires of the people, the matter has to be carefully looked into.

But how can the desires of the people (being so many and various) be met?

Therefore Motse said: It can be done only by adopting the principle of Identification with the Superior in government.[2]

[1] The title, *Shang T'ung,* is translated by Mr. Y. P. Mei as "Identification with the Superior" which I believe is unjustified. See Note 2.

[2] Should read: "It can be done only by exalting the common, unified standard of right in government."

How do we know the principle of Identification with the Superior can govern the empire?

Why not then examine the administration and the theory of government of the ancient times? In the beginning there was no ruler and everybody was independent. Since every one was independent, there would be one purpose when there was one man, ten purposes when there were ten men, a hundred purposes when there were a hundred men, a thousand purposes when there were a thousand men and so on until the number of men became innumerable and the number of different purposes became innumerable with it. And all of them approved their own ideas and disapproved those of others. And there was strife among the strong and struggle among the weak.

Thereupon Heaven wished to unify the standards in the world. The virtuous was selected and made emperor. Conscious of the insufficiency of his power alone to govern the empire, the emperor chose the next best (in virtue and wisdom) and honoured them to be the three ministers. Conscious of the insufficiency of their powers alone to assist the emperor, the three ministers in turn divided the empire into feudal states and assigned them to feudal lords. Conscious of the insufficiency of his power alone to govern all that were within his four borders, the feudal lord in turn selected his next best and commissioned them ministers and secretaries. Conscious of the insufficiency of their power alone to assist their feudal lord, the ministers and secretaries again selected their next best and appointed them district heads and clan patriarchs. Therefore in appointing the three ministers, the feudal lords, the ministers and secretaries, and the district heads and clan patriarchs, the emperor was not selecting them for wealth and honour, leisure and ease. It was to employ them to help in administration and jurisdiction. Hence, when Heaven established the empire and located the capital and commissioned the sovereign, kings, lords, and dukes, and appointed secretaries, scholars, professors, and elders,—it was not to give them ease, but only to divide up the task and let them help carry out the light of Heaven.

Why are the superiors now unable to govern their subordinates, and the subordinates unwilling to serve their superiors? It is because of a mutual disregard.

What is the reason for this? The reason is a difference in standards. Whenever standards differ there will be opposition. The ruler may think a man good and reward him. The man, though rewarded by the ruler, yet by the same act provokes the condemnation of the people. Therefore those who do good are not necessarily encouraged by rewards. The ruler may think a man evil and punish him. This man, though punished by the ruler, yet at the same time receives the approval of the people. Therefore those who do evil are not necessarily obstructed by punishments. Thus reward and honour from the ruler cannot encourage the good and his denunciation and punishment cannot prevent the evil. What is the reason for this? The reason is a difference in standards.

But how can the standards in the world be unified?

Motse said: Why not let each member of the clan organize his purposes and identify them with those of the patriarch? And let the patriarch give laws and proclaim to the clan: "Whoever discovers a benefactor to the clan shall report it; Whoever discovers a malefactor to the clan shall report it. Whoever reports the benefactor of the clan upon seeing one is equivalent to benefiting the clan himself. Knowing him the superior will reward him, hearing of him the group will praise him. Whoever fails to report a malefactor of the clan upon seeing one is equivalent to doing evil to the clan himself. Knowing him the superior will punish him, hearing of him the group will condemn him." Thereupon all the members of the clan wish to obtain reward and honour and avoid denunciation and punishment from their superior. Seeing the good they will report; seeing the evil they will report. And the patriarch can reward the good and punish the evil. With the good rewarded and the evil punished, the clan will surely have order. Now, why is it that the clan becomes orderly? Just because the administration is based on the principle of Identification with the Superior.[3]

Now that the clan is in order, is that all there is of the way of governing the feudal state?

By no means. The state is composed of many clans. They all like their own clan and dislike other clans. And there is strife among the strong and struggle among the weak. Therefore the clan patriarchs should again organize the purposes in the clan and identify them with those of the feudal lord. The feudal lord also should give laws and should proclaim to the state: "Whoever discovers a benefactor of the state shall report it; whoever discovers a malefactor of the state shall report it. Whoever reports a benefactor of the state upon seeing one is equivalent to benefiting the state himself. Knowing him the superior will reward

[3] Should read: "is based on unification of the standard of right."

him, hearing of him the people will praise him. Whoever fails to report a malefactor of the state upon seeing one is equivalent to doing evil to the state himself. Knowing him the superior will punish him, hearing of him the people will condemn him." Thereupon all people in the state wish to obtain reward and honour and avoid denunciation and punishment from their superior. Seeing the good they will report, seeing the evil they will report. And the feudal lord can reward the good and punish the evil. With the good rewarded and the evil punished, the feudal state will surely have order. Now, why is it that the state becomes orderly? Just because the administration is based on the principle of Identification with the Superior.[4]

Now that the feudal state is in order, is that all there is to the way of governing the empire?

By no means. The empire is composed of many states. They all like their own state and dislike other states. And there is strife among the strong and struggle among the weak. Therefore the feudal lord should again organize the purposes in the state and identify them with those of the emperor. The emperor also should give laws and should proclaim to the empire: "Whoever discovers a benefactor of the empire shall report it; whoever discovers a malefactor of the empire shall report it. Whoever reports a benefactor of the empire upon seeing one is equivalent to benefiting the state himself. Knowing him the superior will reward him, hearing of him the people will praise him. Whoever fails to report a malefactor upon seeing one is equivalent to doing evil to the empire himself. Knowing him the superior will punish him, hearing of him the people will condemn him." Thereupon all the people in the empire will wish to obtain reward and honour and avoid denunciation and punishment from their emperor. Seeing the good and the evil they will report. And the emperor can reward the good and punish the evil. With the good rewarded and the evil punished, the empire will surely have order. Now why is it that the empire becomes orderly? Just because the administration is based on the principle of Identification with the Superior.[5]

Now that the empire becomes orderly, the emperor will further organize the purposes in the empire and identify them with the Will of Heaven.[6]

[4] See Note 3.
[5] See Note 3.
[6] Should read: "The emperor will again gather all the standards of right of the world and unify them with (the will of) Heaven. See "Will of Heaven" I.

UNIVERSAL LOVE (II)
(*Chapter 15*)

Motse said: The purpose of the magnanimous[7] is to be found in procuring benefits for the world and eliminating its calamities.

But what are the benefits of the world and what its calamities?

Motse said: Mutual attacks among states, mutual usurpation among houses, mutual injuries among individuals; the lack of grace and loyalty between ruler and ruled, the lack of affection and filial piety between father and son, the lack of harmony between elder and younger brothers—these are the major calamities in the world.

But whence did these calamities arise, out of mutual love?

Motse said: They arise out of want of mutual love. At present feudal lords have learned only to love their own states and not those of others. Therefore they do not scruple about attacking other states. The heads of houses have learned only to love their own houses and not those of others. Therefore they do not scruple about usurping other houses. And individuals have learned only to love themselves and not others. Therefore they do not scruple about injuring others. When feudal lords do not love one another there will be war on the fields. When heads of houses do not love one another they will usurp one another's power. When individuals do not love one another they will injure one another. When ruler and ruled do not love one another they will not be gracious and loyal. "When father and son do not love each other they will not be affectionate and filial. When elder and younger brothers do not love each other they will not be harmonious. When nobody in the world loves any other, naturally the strong will overpower the weak, the many will oppress the few, the wealthy will mock the poor, the honoured will disdain the humble, the cunning will deceive the simple. Therefore all the calamities, strifes, complaints, and hatred in the world have arisen out of want of mutual love. Therefore the benevolent disapproved of this want.

Now that there is disapproval, how can we have the condition altered?

Motse said: It is to be altered by the way of universal love and mutual aid.

[7] *Jen,* variously translated as "benevolence," "charity," "love," "kindness." *Jenjen* philosophically means the "true man" in Confucianism, and in general usage the "good, kind man." Throughout this translation the word "magnanimous" refers to *jen.*

But what is the way of universal love and mutual aid?

Motse said: It is to regard the state of others as one's own, the houses of others as one's own, the persons of others as one's self. When feudal lords love one another there will be no more war; when heads of houses love one another there will be no more mutual usurpation; when individuals love one another there will be no more mutual injury. When ruler and ruled love each other they will be gracious and loyal; when father and son love each other they will be affectionate and filial; when elder and younger brothers love each other they will be harmonious. When all the people in the world love one another, then the strong will not overpower the weak, the many will not oppress the few, the wealthy will not mock the poor, the honoured will not disdain the humble, and the cunning will not deceive the simple. And it is all due to mutual love that calamities, strifes, complaints, and hatred are prevented from arising. Therefore the benevolent exalt it.

But the gentlemen of the world would say: "So far so good. It is of course very excellent when love becomes universal. But it is only a difficult and distant ideal."

Motse said: This is simply because the gentlemen of the world do not recognize what is to the benefit of the world, or understand what is its calamity. Now, to besiege a city, to fight in the fields, or to achieve a name at the cost of death—these are what men find difficult. Yet when the superior encourages them, the multitude can do them. Besides, universal love and mutual aid is quite different from these. Whoever loves others is loved by others; whoever benefits others is benefited by others; whoever hates others is hated by others; whoever injures others is injured by others. Then, what difficulty is there with it (universal love)? Only, the ruler fails to embody it in his government and the ordinary man in his conduct.[8]

UNIVERSAL LOVE (III)
(*Chapter* 16)

. . . . .

Yet the objection is not all exhausted. It is asked: "It may be a good thing, but can it be of any use?"

[8] This is half of the second essay in "Universal Love," of which there are three, with repetitions. Motse further proves his point by illustrations from ancient history and answers criticisms of Universal Love as "impracticable," etc. The idea of Universal Love is closely connected with "the will of Heaven" and is further developed all through Motse's works.

Motse replied: If it were not useful then even I would disapprove of it. But how can there be anything that is good but not useful? Let us consider the matter from both sides. Suppose there are two men. Let one of them hold to partiality and the other to universality. Then the advocate of partiality would say to himself, how can I take care of my friend as I do of myself, how can I take care of his parents as my own? Therefore when he finds his friend hungry he would not feed him, and when he finds him cold he would not clothe him. In his illness he would not minister to him, and when he is dead he would not bury him. Such is the word and such is the deed of the advocate of partiality. The advocate of universality is quite unlike this both in word and in deed. He would say to himself, I have heard that to be a superior man one should take care of his friend as he does of himself, and take care of his friend's parents as his own. Therefore when he finds his friend hungry he would feed him, and when he finds him cold he would clothe him. In his sickness he would serve him, and when he is dead he would bury him. Such is the word and such is the deed of the advocate of universality.

These two persons then are opposed to each other in word and also in deed. Suppose they are sincere in word and decisive in deed so that their word and deed are made to agree like the two parts of a tally, and that there is no word but what is realized in deed, then let us consider further: Suppose a war is on, and one is in armour and helmet ready to join the force, life and death are not predictable. Or suppose one is commissioned a deputy by the ruler to such far countries like Pa, Yüeh, Ch'i and Ching, and the arrival and return are quite uncertain. Now (under such circumstances) let us inquire upon whom would one lay the trust of one's family and parents. Would it be upon the universal friend or upon the partial friend? It seems to me, on occasions like these, there are no fools in the world. Even if he is a person who objects to universal love, he will lay the trust upon the universal friend all the same. This is verbal objection to the principle but actual selection by it—this is self-contradiction between one's word and deed. It is incomprehensible, then, why people should object to universal love when they hear it.

Yet the objection is still not exhausted. It raises the question, when one does not think in terms of benefits and harm to one's parents would it be filial piety?

Motse replied: Now let us inquire about the plans of the filial sons for their parents. I may ask, when they plan for their parents, whether they desire to have others love or hate them? Judging from the whole doctrine (of filial piety), it is certain that they desire to have others love their parents. Now, what should I do first in order to attain this? Should I first love others' parents in order that they would love my parents in return, or should I first hate others' parents in order that they would love my parents in return? Of course I should first love others' parents in order that they would love my parents in return. Hence those who desire to be filial to one another's parents, if they have to choose (between whether they should love or hate others' parents), had best first love and benefit others' parents. Would any one suspect that all the filial sons are stupid and incorrigible (in loving their own parents)? We may again inquire about it. It is said in the "Ta Ya" among the books of the ancient kings: "No idea is not given its due value; no virtue is not rewarded. When a peach is thrown to us, we would return with a prune." This is to say whoever loves others will be loved and whoever hates others will be hated. It is then quite incomprehensible why people should object to universal love when they hear it.

CONDEMNATION OF OFFENSIVE WAR (I)
(*Chapter 17*)

Suppose a man enters the orchard of another and steals the other's peaches and plums. Hearing of it the public will condemn it; laying hold of him the authorities will punish him. Why? Because he injures others to profit himself. As to seizing dogs, pigs, chickens, and young pigs from another, it is even more unrighteous than to steal peaches and plums from his orchard. Why? Because it causes others to suffer more,[9] and it is more inhumane and criminal. When it comes to entering another's stable and appropriating the other's horses and oxen, it is more inhumane than to seize the dogs, pigs, chickens, and young pigs of another. Why? Because others are caused to suffer more; when others are caused to suffer more, then the act is more inhumane and criminal. Finally, as to murdering the innocent, stripping him of his clothing, dispossessing him of his spear and sword, it is even more unrighteous then to enter another's stable and appropriate his horses and oxen. Why?

[9] A clause seems to have been lost here, when we compare this sentence with the following sentences expressing the same meaning. The correct text here seems also to be, "Because others are caused to suffer more; when others are caused to suffer more, it is more inhumane and criminal."

Because it causes others to suffer more; when others are caused to suffer more, then the act is more inhumane and criminal.

All the gentlemen of the world know that they should condemn these things, calling them unrighteous. But when it comes to the great attack of states, they do not know that they should condemn it. On the contrary, they applaud it, calling it righteous. Can this be said to be knowing the difference between righteousness and unrighteousness?

The murder of one person is called unrighteous and incurs one death penalty. Following this argument, the murder of ten persons will be ten times as unrighteous and there should be ten death penalties; the murder of a hundred persons will be a hundred times as unrighteous and there should be a hundred death penalties. All the gentlemen of the world know that they should condemn these things, calling them unrighteous. But when it comes to the great unrighteousness of attacking states, they do not know that they should condemn it. On the contrary, they applaud it, calling it righteous. And they are really ignorant of its being unrighteous. Hence they have recorded their judgment to bequeath to their posterity. If they did know that it is unrighteous, then why would they record their false judgment to bequeath to posterity?

Now, if there were a man who, upon seeing a little blackness, should say it is black, but, upon seeing much, should say it is white; then we should think he could not tell the difference between black and white. If, upon tasting a little bitterness one should say it is bitter, but, upon tasting much, should say it is sweet; then we should think he could not tell the difference between bitter and sweet. Now, when a little wrong is committed people know that they should condemn it, but when such a great wrong as attacking a state is committed, people do not know that they should condemn it. On the contrary, it is applauded, called righteous. Can this be said to be knowing the difference between the righteous and unrighteous? Hence we know the gentlemen of the world are confused about the difference between righteousness and unrighteousness.

CONDEMNATION OF OFFENSIVE WAR (II)
(*Chapter 18*)

Now, about a country going to war. If it is in winter it will be too cold; if it is summer it will be too hot. So it should be neither in winter nor in summer. If it is in spring it will take people away from sowing and planting; if it is in autumn it will take people away from reaping and harvesting. Should they be taken away in either of these seasons, innumerable people would die of hunger and cold. And, when the army sets out, the bamboo arrows, the feather flags, the house tents, the armour, the shields, the sword hilts—innumerable quantities of these will break and rot and never come back. The spears, the lances, the swords, the poniards, the chariots, the carts—innumerable quantities of these will break and rot and never come back. Then innumerable horses and oxen will start out fat and come back lean or will not return at all. And innumerable people will die because their food will be cut off and cannot be supplied on account of the great distances of the roads. And innumerable people will be sick and die of the constant danger and the irregularity of eating and drinking and the extremes of hunger and over-eating. Then, the army will be lost in large numbers or entirely; in either case the number will be innumerable. And this means the spirits will lose their worshippers, and the number of these will also be innumerable.

Why then does the government deprive the people of their opportunities and benefits to such a great extent? It has been answered: "I covet the fame of the victor and the possessions obtainable through the conquest. So I do it."

Motse said: But when we consider the victory as such, there is nothing useful about it. When we consider the possessions obtained through it, it does not even make up for the loss. Now about the siege of a city of three *li* or a *kuo*[10] of seven *li*—if these could be obtained without the use of weapons or the killing of lives, it would be all right. But (as a matter of fact) those killed must be counted by the ten thousand, those widowed or left solitary must be counted by the thousand, before a city of three *li* or a *kuo* of seven *li* could be captured. Moreover the states of ten thousand chariots now have empty towns to be counted by the thousand, which can be entered without conquest; and their extensive lands to be counted by the ten thousand (of *mu*),[11] which can be cultivated without conquest. So, land is abundant but people are few. Now to pursue the people to death and aggravate the danger feared by both superiors and subordinates in order to obtain an empty city—this is to give up what is needed and to treasure what is already in abundance. Such an undertaking is not in accordance with the interest of the country.

Those who endeavour to gloss over offensive wars would say: "These states perished because they could not gather and employ their multi-

[10] Outer city.

[11] A *mu* is one-sixth of an acre.

tudes. I can gather and employ my multitudes and wage war with them; who, then, dare to be unsubmissive?"

Motse said: You might be able to gather and employ your multitudes, but can you compare yourself with the ancient Ho Lü of Wu? Ho Lü of Wu (about 510 B.C.) in the ancient days drilled his soldiers seven years. With armour on and weapons in hand they could cover three hundred *li* (in a day) before encamping (for the night). Passing Chu Lin, they emerged at the narrow Pass of Min. They engaged in battle (with the state of Ch'u) at Po Chü. Subduing Ch'u, (Ho Lü) gave audience to Sung and Lu. By the time of Fu Ch'ai,[12] he attacked Ch'i in the north, encamped on the Wen River, fought at Ai Ling and greatly defeated Ch'i and compelled surety at Kuei Chi. None of the nine tribes dared to show disrespect. Reaching home, however, he would not reward the orphaned or give to the numerous rustics. He depended on his own might, gloated over his success, praised his own cleverness, and neglected instructing and training his people. He built the Monument of Ku Su [13] which was not completed even in seven years. By this time (the people of Wu) felt tired and disheartened. Seeing the friction between the superior and the subordinates in Wu, Kou Chien of Yüeh gathered his multitudes to take revenge. He broke into its *kuo* on the north, moved away its royal boat, and surrounded its palace. And thus Wu perished. . . .

XIX. CONDEMNATION OF OFFENSIVE WAR (III)
(*Chapter 19*)

Motse said: What does the world now praise to be good? Is not an act praised because it is useful to Heaven on high, to the spirits in the middle sphere, and to the people below? Certainly no other reason is needed for praise than to be useful to Heaven on high, to the spirits in the middle, and to the people below. Even the stupid would say it is praiseworthy when it is helpful to Heaven on high, to the spirits in the middle, and to the people below. And what the world agrees on is just the way of the sage-kings.

Now to capture a state and to destroy an army, to disturb and torture the people, and to set at naught the aspirations of the sages by confusion—is this intended to bless Heaven? But the people of Heaven are gathered

[12] Ho Lü's son (about 490 B.C.)
[13] Capital of the state of Wu, now Soochow.

ogether to besiege the towns belonging to Heaven. This is to murder nen of Heaven and dispossess the spirits of their altars and to ruin the state and to kill the sacrificial animals. It is then not a blessing to Heaven on high. Is it intended to bless the spirits? But men of Heaven are murdered, spirits are deprived of their sacrifices, the earlier kings[14] are neglected, the multitude are tortured and the people are scattered; it is hen not a blessing to the spirits in the middle. Is it intended to bless the people? But the blessing of the people by killing them off must be very meagre. And when we calculate the expense, which is the root of the calamities of living, we find the property of innumerable people is exhausted. It is, then, not a blessing to the people below either.

Have we not heard it said that, when a warring state goes on an expedition, of the officers there must be several hundred, of the common people there must be several thousand, and of the soldiers and prisoners there must be ten thousand, before the army can set out? It may last for several years, or at the shortest, several months. So, the superior will have no time to attend to their offices, the farmers will have no time to sow or reap, the women will have no time to weave or spin: that is, the state will lose its men and the people will neglect their vocations. Besides, the chariots will break and horses will be exhausted. As to tents, army supplies, and soldiers' equipment—if one-fifth of these can remain (after the war) it would already be beyond expectation. Moreover, innumerable men will be missing and lost on the way, and will become sick from the long distances, meagre rations, hunger and cold, and die in the ditches. Now the calamity to the people and the world is tremendous. Yet the rulers enjoy doing it. This means they enjoy injuring and exterminating the people; is this not perversity?

THE WILL OF HEAVEN (I)
(*Chapter 26*)

Now, what does Heaven desire and what does it abominate? Heaven desires righteousness and abominates unrighteousness. . . . But how do we know Heaven desires righteousness and abominates unrighteousness? For, with righteousness the world lives and without it the world dies; with it the world becomes rich and without it the world becomes poor; with it the world becomes orderly and without it the world

[14] Meaning the ancestral spirits of the state.

becomes chaotic. And Heaven likes to have the world live and dislikes to have it die, likes to have it rich and dislikes to have it poor, and likes to have it orderly and dislikes to have is disorderly. Therefore we know Heaven desires righteousness and abominates unrighteousness.

How do we know Heaven loves the people? Because it teaches them all. How do we know it teaches them all? Because it claims them all. How do we know it claims them all? Because it accepts sacrifices from them all. How do we know it accepts sacrifices from all? Because within the four seas all who live on grains feed oxen and sheep with grass, and dogs and pigs with grains, and prepare clean cakes and wine to do sacrifice to God on High and the spirits. Claiming all the people, why will Heaven not love them? Moreover, as I have said, for the murder of one innocent individual there will be one calamity. Who is it that murders the innocent? It is man. Who is it that sends down the calamity? It is Heaven. If Heaven should be thought of as not loving the people, why should it send down calamities for the murder of man by man? So, I know Heaven loves the people.

To obey the will of Heaven is to accept righteousness as the standard. To oppose the will of Heaven is to accept force as the standard. Now what will the standard of righteousness do?

Motse said: He who rules a large state does not attack small states: he who rules a large house does not molest small houses. The strong does not plunder the weak. The honoured does not disdain the humble. The clever does not deceive the stupid. This is beneficial to Heaven above, beneficial to the spirits in the middle sphere, and beneficial to the people below. Being beneficial to these three it is beneficial to all. So the most excellent name is attributed to such a man and he is called sage-king.

The standard of force is different from this. It is contradictory to this in word and opposed to this in deed like galloping with back to back. Leading a large state, he whose standard is force, attacks small states; leading a large house he molests small houses. The strong plunders the weak, the honoured disdains the humble. The clever deceives the stupid. This is not beneficial to Heaven above, or to the spirits in the middle sphere, or to the people below. Not being beneficial to these three, it is beneficial to none. So, the most evil name in the world is attributed to him and he is called the wicked king.

Motse said: The will of Heaven to me is like the compasses to the wheelwright and the square to the carpenter. The wheelwright and the carpenter measure all the square and circular objects with their square and compasses and accept those that fit as correct and reject those that do not fit as incorrect. The writings of the gentlemen of the world of the present day cannot be all loaded (in a cart), and their doctrines cannot be exhaustively enumerated. They endeavour to convince the feudal lords on the one hand and the scholars on the other. But from magnanimity and righteousness they are far off. How do we know? Because I have the most competent standard in the world to measure them with.

THE WILL OF HEAVEN (II)
(*Chapter 27*)

And hence Motse said: If the gentlemen of the world really desire to follow the way and benefit the people, they must not disobey the will of Heaven, the origin of magnanimity and righteousness.

Now that we must obey the will of Heaven, what does the will of Heaven desire and what does it abominate? Motse said: The will of Heaven abominates the large state which attacks small states, the large house which molests small houses, the strong who plunder the weak, the clever who deceive the stupid, and the honoured who disdain the humble—these are what the will of Heaven abominates. On the other hand, it desires people having energy to work for each other, those knowing the way to teach each other, and those possessing wealth to share with each other. And it desires the superior diligently to attend to government and the subordinates diligently to attend to their work....

The rule of Heaven over the world is not unlike the rule of the feudal lord over the state. In ruling the state does the feudal lord desire his ministers and people to work for mutual disadvantage? If leading a large state one attacks small states, if leading a large house one molests small houses—if by doing this one seeks reward and commendation (from the feudal lord) he cannot obtain it. On the contrary, punishment will visit him. Now, the rule of Heaven over the world is not unlike this. If leading a large state one attacks small states, if leading a large house one molests small houses—if by doing this one seeks reward and commendation (from Heaven) he cannot obtain it. On the contrary, punishment will visit him. When (man) does not do what Heaven desires, but does what Heaven abominates, Heaven will also not do what man desires but do what he abominates. What man abominates are disease and calamities. Therefore not to do what Heaven desires but do what it abominates is to lead the multitudes in the world to calamity. . . .

Now Heaven loves the whole world universally. Everything is prepared [15] for the good of man. Even the tip of a hair is the work of Heaven. Substantial may be said of the benefits that are enjoyed by man. Yet there is no service in return. And they do not even know this to be unmagnanimous and unfortunate. This is why I say the gentlemen understand only trifles and not things of importance.

Moreover I know Heaven loves men dearly not without reason. Heaven ordered the sun, the moon, and the stars to enlighten and guide them. Heaven ordained the four seasons, Spring, Autumn, Winter and Summer, to regulate them. Heaven sent down snow, frost, rain, and dew to grow the five grains and flax and silk so that the people could use and enjoy them. Heaven established the hills and rivers, ravines and valleys, and arranged many things to minister to man's good or bring him evil. He appointed the dukes and lords to reward the virtuous and punish the wicked, and to gather metal and wood, birds and beasts, and to engage in cultivating the five grains and flax and silk to provide for the people's food and clothing. This has been taking place from antiquity to the present. Suppose there is a man who is deeply fond of his son and has used his energy to the limit to work for his benefit. But when the son grows up he returns no love to the father. The gentlemen of the world will all call him unmagnanimous and miserable. Now Heaven loves the whole world universally. Everything is prepared for the good of man. The work of Heaven extends to even the smallest things that are enjoyed by man. Such benefits may indeed be said to be substantial, yet there is no service in return. And they do not even know this to be unmagnanimous. This is why I say the gentlemen of the world understand only trifles but not things of importance.

THE WILL OF HEAVEN (III)
(*Chapter 28*)

How do we know the gentlemen of the world are far from righteousness? For, the lords in the large states compete in saying: "Being a big

[15] The term here used in the text is "chiao sui." Its exact meaning is not ascertainable.—*Original note.*

state, if I do not attack the small states, in what way am I big?" Therefore they mustered their warriors and soldiers, and arranged their boat and chariot forces to attack some innocent state. They broke into its borders, cut down its fields, felled its trees, tore down its inner and outer city walls, and filled up its moats and ditches, burned its ancestral temples and seized and killed its sacrificial victims. Of the people the strong were killed, the weak were brought back in chains and ropes. The men were turned into servants and grooms and prisoners. The women were made to be waitresses (to pour wine). Yet, the warring lord did not even know that this is unmagnanimous and unrighteous. He announced to the neighbouring lords: "I have attacked a state, defeated an army, and killed so many generals." And the neighbouring lords did not know that this is unmagnanimous and unrighteous either, but with furs and silk sent envoys to offer congratulations. And the warring lords were even doubly ignorant of its being unmagnanimous and unrighteous. They recorded it on the bamboos and silk and kept them in the archives so that the descendants would imitate their royal ancestors, saying: "Why not let us open up the archives and let us learn of the achievements of our ancestors?" Then they would surely not learn: "Such and such is the regime of Wu," but would learn: "I have attacked states, reversed armies, and killed so many of their generals." Now that the warring lords do not understand this to be unmagnanimous and unrighteous and neighbouring lords do not understand this to be unmagnanimous and unrighteous, therefore attacks and assaults go on generation after generation without end.

What do I mean when I say people do not understand things of importance but understand trifles? Supposing some one entered the orchard and garden of another and took the other's peaches and prunes, melon and ginger, he will be punished by the superior when caught and condemned by the public when heard of. Why? Because he did not share the toil but takes the fruit and appropriates what is not his. How much more is this true with him who jumps over another's fence and maltreats the children of the other; of him who digs into another's storehouse and carries away the other's gold, jade, silk and cloth; of him who breaks into another's fold and steals the other's oxen and horses; and of him who kills an innocent person? In the government of the lords of to-day all—from the one who kills an innocent person to the one who jumps over another's fence and maltreats the other's children, who digs into another's warehouse and carries away his gold, jade, silk and cloth, who breaks into another's fold and steals his oxen and horses, and who enters another's orchard and garden and takes his peaches and prunes, melons and ginger, all these are punished quite the same as they would be even in the government of Yao, Shun, Yu, T'ang, Wen and Wu. Now the lords and chiefs in the world all attack and absorb others. This is a thousand and ten thousand times worse than killing one innocent individual, a thousand and ten thousand times worse that jumping over another's fence and maltreating his children or digging into another's storehouse and carrying away his gold, jade, silk and cloth, a thousand and ten thousand times worse than breaking into another's fold and stealing his oxen and horses, or entering another's orchard and garden and taking his peaches and prunes, melons and ginger. Yet, they claim it to be righteous....

ANTI-CONFUCIANISM (II)
(*Chapter 39*)

Once, Confucius was in straits between Ts'ai and Ch'en having only vegetable soup without even rice to eat. After ten days of this, Tse Lu cooked a pig for him. Confucius did not inquire whence the meat came, and ate. Tse Lu robbed some one of his garment and exchanged it for wine. Confucius did not inquire whence the wine came, and drank. But when Lord Ai received Confucius, Confucius would not sit on a mat that was not placed straight and would not eat meat that was not cut properly. Tse Lu went to him and asked: "Why the reverse to what you did on the borders of Ch'en and Ts'ai?" Confucius answered: "Come, let me tell you. Then, our goal was to keep alive. Now our goal is to behave righteously." Now when hunger-stricken he was not scrupulous about the means of keeping alive, and when satiated he acted hypocritically to appear refined. What foolery, perversion, villainy, and pretension can be greater than this! . . . .

KENG CHU[16]
(*Chapter 46*)

Wu Matse said to Motse: "Though you love universally the world cannot be said to be benefited; though I do not love (universally) the world cannot be said to be injured. Since neither of us has accomplished any-

[16] Name of one of the many disciples of Motse.

thing, what makes you then praise yourself and blame me?" Motse answered: Suppose a conflagration is on. One person is fetching water to extinguish it, and another is holding some fuel to reinforce it. Neither of them has yet accomplished anything, but which one do you value? Wu Matse answered that he approved of the intention of the person who fetches water and disapproved of the intention of the person who holds fuel. Motse said: (In the same manner) do I approve of my intention and disapprove of yours.

Wu Matse said to Motse: "For all the righteousness that you do, men do not help you and ghosts do not bless you. Yet you keep on doing it. You must be demented." Motse said: Suppose you have here two employees. One of them works when he sees you but will not work when he does not see you. The other one works whether he sees you or not. Which of the two would you value? Wu Matse said that he would value him that worked whether he saw him or not. Motse then said: Then you are valuing him who is demented.

A pupil of Tse Hsia asked Motse whether there could be any struggle among the superior men. Motse said: The superior men do not struggle. The pupil of Tse Hsia said: "There is struggle even among the dogs and hogs, how can there be no struggle among men?" Motse said: What a shame! T'ang and Wu are praised with words; but dogs and hogs are brought into comparison in conduct. What a shame!"

THE MIDDLE WAY

The Aphorisms of Confucius

INTRODUCTION

ONE OF THE MOST CURIOUS FACTS of world history is that three of the world's greatest and most influential thinkers were born within two decades of each other. Laotse was probably born in B.C. 570, Buddha in 563, and Confucius in 551. The dates of Laotse's life are highly uncertain, but many records of the immediately following centuries, including the *Shiki,* contain various stories of Confucius going to Laotse as an older man for advice. Anyway, it is certain that Buddha was older than Confucius only by twelve years.

It seems destined that Confucius will be known to the West chiefly through his aphorisms, running very close to platitudes. What must not be forgotten is that Confucianism was primarily an historical school, that as Chang Hsüeh-ch'eng says, all the Confucian Classics are history, and that that body of historical learning which provides the ideal and the background for his social teachings can hardly interest the West today. It had a very definite and well-defined system of moral and social philosophy, and I have tried elsewhere [1] to indicate what that system is. To the Chinese, that system of moral and social order, based on history, is contained in the one word *li,* which has such a broad meaning that it is untranslatable. In the narrowest sense, it means "rituals," "propriety," and just "good manners"; in an historical sense, it means the rationalized system of feudal order; in a philosophic sense, it means an ideal social order with "everything in its place"; and in a personal sense, it means a pious, religious state of mind, very near to the word "faith," which means to me a valid, unified body of beliefs implicitly accepted, concerning God

[1] See my long introduction to *The Wisdom of Confucius* (Modern Library).

and nature and man's place in the universe, as distinguished from the knowledge of externals or accidentals. It is this valid, unified body of beliefs implicitly accepted, concerning God and nature and man's place in the universe which the modern world lacks, and it is this lack which cuts the modern world adrift. Among the Chinese scholars, Confucianism is known as the "religion of *li*," the nearest translation for which would be "religion of moral order." It subjects the political order to the moral social order, making the latter the basis of the former, to the extent that it disbelieves in a merely political solution and can be identified with ideal anarchism. (See the selections on "Government.") Any full exposition of the Confucian system of ideas is out of the question here, and readers are referred to *The Wisdom of Confucius,* where both a *Life* of Confucius and his longer discourses are available.

Anyway, Confucius said of himself, "I transmit, and do not create." The fact that some modern Chinese scholars have charged Confucius with forging all the Chinese classics may be cited to show how closely tied up with historical learning the whole Confucian tradition is. From Motse, we learn that a half century after Confucius died, the Confucian scholars wore a special cap and "talked an ancient language." Chuangtse constantly maligned the Confucianists and Confucius himself for talking about Yao and Shun, the sage emperors who were 1,700 years old in Confucius' days. Confucius had a passion for historical research and was the greatest editor of ancient books of his days. But from this body of historical learning, he discerned and established a clear and definite system of social and moral philosophy, and with a hard, common sense, pronounced certain Johnsonian dicta on questions of moral conduct.

It is these moral aphorisms and pronouncements, gathered together in the *Analects,* like Bartlett's *Familiar Quotations* without rhyme or order, which the Chinese regard as the essence of Confucian teachings. There they stand, so deep in wisdom and so mellow in tone, a tribute to the nation which worships them. Like mellow old masters, and unlike magazine covers, these sayings of the *Analects* are for the connoisseurs, i.e., for the moral connoisseurs. The gentleness of touch, the softness of tone, the skill coming from mastery are best appreciated by those who have thought deeply about human problems. And like looking at an old master, one person will admire certain details and aspects, and another will admire others. For 2,500 years, they have always exasperated the young inquiring mind, looking for exciting truths and brilliant intellectual sorties, and always won over that mind when it grows older and natures. This accounts for its classic, immortal influence on generations of men.

This idea is further developed in the introduction to "The Golden Mean." This is the same as the Aristotelean Golden Mean, a rather sad discovery for ardent students of moral conduct. It is the discovery that the gentleman can do nothing exciting or out of the way to distinguish himself except by his indistinguishability from other gentlemen. If courage is but the mean between foolhardiness and cowardice, courage is somewhat nondescript and can hardly be sensational. If the good management of money is but the mean between extravagance and being a miser, neither can that staid, sensible keeping of family accounts have anything heroic about it, or reach psychopathic proportions to provide delightful material for the "realist" writers. If therefore we must be gentlemen, we'll have to be contented with just being gentlemen. But in this plebeianism, there is great content. Plebeianism satisfies.

In these selections translated by myself, I have classified them and given headings of my own, and made an arrangement differing from that in the *Analects*. I have also added some selections from the *Liki* to make certain points clearer. A few minor revisions have been made from the text in "*Wisdom of Confucius*." For further comments on the nature of the *Analects* and the method of studying it, see also the Introduction to these *Aphorisms* in that text.

The Aphorisms of Confucius

Translated by Lin Yutang

I. DESCRIPTION OF CONFUCIUS BY HIMSELF AND OTHERS

DUKE YEH (OF CH'U) asked Tselu about Confucius, and Tselu did not make a reply. Confucius said, "Why didn't you tell him that I am a person who forgets to eat when he is enthusiastic about something, forgets all his worries when he is happy, and is not aware that old age is coming on?"

Tselu was stopping for the night at the Stone Gate and the gate-keeper asked him, "Where are you from?" "I'm from Confucius," replied Tselu. "Oh, is he the fellow who knows that a thing can't be done and still wants to do it?"

Weisheng Mou said to Confucius, "Why are you so self-important and constantly rushing about? Don't you talk a little bit too much?" "It isn't that I want to talk. It's because I hate (the present moral chaos)."

Confucius said, "At fifteen I began to be seriously interested in study. At thirty I had formed my character. At forty I had no more perplexities. At fifty I knew the will of heaven. At sixty nothing that I heard disturbed me.[1] At seventy I could let my thought wander without trespassing the moral law."

Yen Huei and Tselu were sitting together with Confucius, and Confucius said, "Why don't you each tell me your ambitions in life?" Tselu replied, "It is my ambition in life to go about with a horse and carriage and a light fur coat and share them with my good friends until they are all worn out without any regret." Yen Huei said, "It is my ambition

[1] Here is an example of the great responsibility and room for conjecture on the part of a translator of ancient texts. The original text merely consists of two works "Ears accord."

never to show off and never to brag about myself." Then Tselu said, "May I hear what is your ambition?" And Confucius replied, "It is my ambition that the old people should be able to live in peace, all friends should be loyal and all young people should love their elders."

There were the famous recluses, Poyi, Schuch'i, Yuchung, Yiyi, Chuchang, Liuhsia Huei and Shaolien. Confucius said, "Not to compromise with their own ideals and not to be disgraced—these were Poyi and Shuch'i." He said of Liuhsia Huei and Shaolien that they compromised with their ideals and were disgraced, but that they managed to maintain a standard in their words and their conduct. He said of Yuchung and Yiyi that they escaped from society and were unconventional or untrammeled in their speech, and that they were able to live a clean private life and to adjust themselves according to the principle of expediency in times of chaos. "I am different from these people; I decide according to the circumstances of the time, and act accordingly." [2]

A great official asked Tsekung, "Is the Master a Sage? Why is it that he is so many-sided?" Tsekung replied, "Heaven has sent him to become a Sage, and he is many-sided, to boot." When Confucius heard this he said, "Perhaps this great official knows me well. I was a poor man's son and can therefore do many things that belong to a common man. Does a gentleman know all these things? No, he doesn't." Tsechang said, "Confucius said, 'I did not enter the government, that was how I had time for learning the arts.' "

Confucius said, "There is pleasure in lying pillowed against a bent arm after a meal of simple vegetables with a drink of water. On the other hand, to enjoy wealth and power without coming by it through the right means is to me like so many floating clouds."

Confucius said, "There are three things about the superior man that I have not been able to attain. The true man has no worries; the wise man has no perplexities; and the brave man has no fear." Tsekung said, "But, Master, you are exactly describing yourself."

Confucius said, "In the study of literature, I am probably as good as anyone, but personally to live the life of the superior man, I don't think I have succeeded."

Confucius said, "As to being a Sage and a true man, I am not so pre-

[2] Literally, in five words, "No *may*, no *may not*." Later Mencius fully commented upon this, saying that Confucius was a great flexible character, acting according to the requirements of the occasion. He could be an official if necessary, and he could refuse to be an official if necessary. In contrast with the other recluses mentioned, there was a positive urge in his character, as well as a philosophic resignation.

sumptuous. I will admit, however, that I have unceasingly tried to d
my best and to teach other people."

Confucius said, "Do you think I know a great deal? I don't. Ther
was an uneducated man who asked me about something, and I couldn'
say a word in reply. I merely discussed the two sides of the questio
and was at my wit's end."

Confucius said, "In every hamlet of ten families, there are alway
some people as honest and straight as myself, but none who is so de
voted to study."

Confucius said, "I may perhaps compare myself to my old frien
Laop'eng. I merely try to describe (or carry on) the ancient tradition
but not to create something new. I only want to get at the truth an
am in love with ancient studies."

Confucius said, "To silently appreciate a truth, to learn continuall
and to teach other people unceasingly—that is just natural with me."

"The things that trouble or concern me are the following: lest
should neglect to improve my character, lest I should neglect my studie
and lest I should fail to move forward when I see the right course, o
fail to correct myself when I see my mistake."

Confucius said, "I'm not born a wise man. I'm merely one in lov
with ancient studies and work very hard to learn them."

Confucius said, "Ah Sze, do you suppose that I merely learned a grea
deal and tried to remember it all?" "Yes, isn't that what you do?
"No," said Confucius, "I have a system or a central thread that run
through it all."

Confucius said, "There are some people who do not understand
subject, but go ahead and invent things out of their own head. I an
not like those people. One can come to be a wise man by hearing a grea
deal and following the good, and by seeing a great deal and remem
bering it."

Confucius said, "Sometimes I have gone the whole day without foo
and a whole night without sleep, occupied in thinking and unable t
arrive at any results. So I decided to study again."

Confucius said, "Whenever walking in a company of three, I ca
always find my teacher among them (or one who has something t
teach me). I select a good person and follow his example, or I see a ba
person and avoid being like him myself."

Confucius said, "I won't teach a man who is not anxious to lear
and will not explain to one who is not trying to make things clear t

himself. And if I explain one-fourth and the man doesn't go back and reflect and think out the implications in the remaining three-fourths for himself, I won't bother to teach him again."

Confucius said, "There was never yet a person who came to me with the present of dried meat (equivalent of tuition) that I have refused to teach something."

The young men of a certain village, Hu, were given to mischief, and one day some young people from that village came to see Confucius, and the disciples were surprised that Confucius saw them. Confucius said, "Don't be too hard on people. What concerns me is how they come, and not what they do when they go away. When a man approaches me with pure intentions, I respect his pure intentions, although I cannot guarantee what he does afterwards."

Confucius was in difficulties at K'uang and he said, "Since King Wen died, is not the tradition of King Wen in my keeping or possession? If it be the will of Heaven that this moral tradition should be lost, posterity shall never again share in the knowledge of this tradition. But if it be the will of Heaven that this tradition shall not be lost, what can the people of K'uang do to me?"

Confucius said, "Heaven has endowed me with a moral destiny (or mission). What can Huan T'uei (a military officer who was driving him away) do to me?"[3]

Confucius said, "Give me a few more years to take up the study of the *Book of Changes* at the age of fifty, then I hope I shall be able to be free from making serious mistakes (or errors of judgment)."

These were the things Confucius often talked about: Poetry, history, and the performance of ceremonies—all these were what he often talked about.

Confucius seldom talked about profit or destiny or true manhood.[4]

Confucius did not talk about monsters, physical exploits, unruly conduct and the heavenly spirits.

Confucius taught four things: Literature, personal conduct, being one's true self and honesty in social relationships.

[3] See Chapter II, Section 4, in *The Wisdom of Confucius* for fuller details.

[4] There is no other topic which Confucius and his disciples more constantly talked about than "true manhood." See below Section VI. This is therefore a palpable falsehood, unless it means that Confucius refused to admit that many persons whom his disciples admired could be called "true men."

Confucius fished with a fishing rod, but would not use a net. While shooting he would not shoot a bird at rest.[5]

Confucius denounced or tried to avoid completely four things: arbitrariness of opinion, dogmatism, narrowmindedness and egotism.

Confucius was gentle but dignified, austere yet not harsh, polite and completely at ease.

Yen Huei heaved a sigh and said, "You look up to it and it seems so high. You try to drill through it and it seems so hard. You seem to see it in front of you, and all of a sudden it appears behind you. The Master is very good at gently leading a man along and teaching him. He taught me to broaden myself by the reading of literature and then to control myself by the observance of proper conduct. I just felt being carried along, but after I have done my very best, or developed what was in me, there still remains something austerely standing apart, uncatchable. Do what I could to reach his position, I can't find the way."

Shusun Wushu said to the officials at court, "Tsekung is a better man than Confucius." Tsefu Chingpo told this to Tsekung, and Tsekung said, "It is like the matter of housewalls. My housewall comes up only to the shoulder, and the people outside are therefore able to see my beautiful house, whereas the wall of Confucius is twenty or thirty feet high, and unless you go right inside, you do not see the beauty of its halls and the grandeur of its furniture. But there are very few people who can penetrate inside that household. What Shusun says is therefore perfectly easy to understand."

Again Shusun Wushu tried to belittle the greatness of Confucius, and Tsekung said, "There's no use trying. Confucius cannot be belittled. Other great men are like mounds or hillocks which you can climb up, but Confucius is like the moon and the sun, which you can never reach. A man can shut his eyes to the sun and the moon, but what harm can it do to the sun and the moon? You are just trying to do the impossible."

II. THE EMOTIONAL AND ARTISTIC LIFE OF CONFUCIUS

When Yen Huei died, Confucius wept bitterly and his followers said, "You are all shaken up." Confucius said, "Am I all shaken up? But if I don't feel all shaken up at the death of this person, for whom else shall I ever feel shaken up?"

[5] Both being unfair.

Confucius never ate his fill in the company of people in mourning. If he wept on that day, then he did not sing.

What Confucius took very seriously were: The ceremonial bath before religious worship, war, and sickness.

Someone asked Confucius about the meaning of the Grand Sacrifice to the Imperial Ancestors, and Confucius said, "I don't know. One who knows the meaning of the Grand Sacrifice would be able to rule the world as easily as pointing a finger at the palm."

When Confucius offered sacrifice to his ancestors, he felt as if his ancestors were present bodily, and when he offered sacrifice to the other gods, he felt as if the gods were present bodily. Confucius said, "If I don't offer sacrifice by being personally present, it is as if I didn't sacrifice at all."

Wangsun Chia asked, "Why do people say that it is better to get on good terms with the kitchen god than with the god of the southwestern corner of the house?" Confucius replied, "Nonsense, if you have committed sins against Heaven, you haven't got a god to pray to."[6]

Tsekung wanted to do away with the ceremony of sacrificing the lamb in winter. Confucius said, "Ah Sze, you love the lamb, but I love the institution."

Confucius said, "Respect the heavenly and earthly spirits and keep them at a distance."

Confucius said, "My, how old I have grown! For a long time I have not dreamed of Duke Chou again."[7]

Confucius heard the music of Hsiao in Ch'i, and for three months he forgot the taste of meat, saying, "I never thought that music could be so beautiful." When Confucius was singing with some other men and liked the song, he always asked for an *encore* and then would join in the chorus.

Confucius said, "Wake yourself up with poetry, establish your character in *li* and complete your education in music."

Confucius said, "Since my return to Lu from Wei, I have been able to classify the different kinds of music, and the *ya* and the *sung* are restored to their proper place."

[6] These gods in modern China are supposed to intercede for human beings before Heaven.

[7] Duke Chou was the symbol of the moral ruler and founder of the governmental system of the Chou Dynasty which Confucius was trying to restore.

Yen Huei asked about running a government. Confucius replied, "Use the calendar of Hsia Dynasty (the Hsia year begins with "January," or about February in the solar calendar, while the Chou year begins with "November"), adopt the (heavy and strong and comparatively unadorned wooden) carriages of the Shang Dynasty, and use the imperial crown of the Chou Dynasty. For music, adopt the dance of *Hsiao*. Suppress the music of Cheng and keep away the petty flatterers. The music of Cheng is lascivious, and the petty flatterers are dangerous."

(Tselu was playing the *seh*, and) Confucius said, "How dare Ah Yu play such atrocious music in my house!" The disciples then began to look down upon Tselu and Confucius said, "Ah Yu has entered the hall, but he has not entered the inner room."[8]

Confucius would not use navy blue or scarlet for the binding and collar of his dress. He would not have red or purple pajamas. In summer he would wear underclothes beneath the thin (transparent) coarse or fine linen gown. He would match a lamb coat with a black material; match a coat of white fawn with white material, and match a fox coat with brown (or yellow) material. He always wore a nightgown longer than his body by half. At home he wore a long-haired fox coat. Except during mourning, he wore all sorts of pendants (on his girdle).

For him rice could never be white enough and mince meat could never be chopped fine enough. When the fool was mushy or the flavor had deteriorated, or when the fish had become bad or the meat was tainted, he would not eat. When its color had changed, he would not eat. When the smell was bad, he would not eat. When it was not cooked right, he would not eat. When food was not in season, he would not eat. When the meat was not cut properly, he would not eat. When a food was not served with its proper sauce, he would not eat. Although there was a lot of meat on the table, he would not take it out of proportion with his rice; as for wine, he drank without any set limit, but would stop before getting drunk. Wine or shredded meat bought from the shops he would not eat. A meal without ginger on the table, he would not eat. He did not overeat.

During thunderstorms, his face always changed color.

[8] The orthodox interpretation is that Tselu had made some progress in learning the teachings of Confucius, but had not mastered them yet. I am inclined to think that Confucius meant that Tselu was playing only in the outside hall and not in the inner chamber, and that therefore it was not so unforgivable after all.

III. THE CONVERSATIONAL STYLE

Tselu, Tseng Hsi, Jan Ch'iu and Kunghsi Hua were sitting together one day and Confucius said, "Do not think that I am a little bit older than you and therefore am assuming airs. You often say among yourselves that people don't know you. Suppose someone should know you, I should like to know how you would appear to that person." Tselu immediately replied, "I should like to rule over a country with a thousand carriages, situated between two powerful neighbors, involved in war and suffering from famine. I should like to take charge of such a country and in three years, the nation will become strong and orderly." Confucius smiled at this remark and said, "How about you, Ah Ch'iu?" Jan Ch'iu replied, "Let me have a country sixty or seventy *li* square or perhaps only fifty or sixty *li* square. Put it in my charge, and in three years, the people will have enough to eat, but as for teaching them moral order and music, I shall leave it to the superior man." (Turning to Kunghsi Hua) Confucius said, "How about you, Ah Ch'ih?" Kunghsi Hua replied, "Not that I say I can do it, but I'm willing to learn this. At the ceremonies of religious worship and at the conference of the princes, I should like to wear the ceremonial cap and gown and be a minor official assisting at the ceremony." "How about you, Ah Tien?" The latter (Tseng Hsi) was just playing on the *seh*, and with a bang he left the instrument and arose to speak. "My ambition is different from theirs." "It doesn't matter," said Confucius, "we are just trying to find out what each would like to do." Then he replied, "In late spring, when the new spring dress is made, I would like to go with five or six grown-ups and six or seven children to bathe in the River Yi, and after the bath go to enjoy the breeze in the Wuyu woods, and then sing on our way home." Confucius heaved a deep sigh and said, "You are the man after my own heart."

Confucius said, "Do you think that I have hidden anything from the two or three of you? No, I have hidden nothing from you. There is nothing that I do that I don't share with the two or three of you. That is I."

Confucius went to the city of Wu (where his disciple Tseyu had been made the magistrate), and heard the people singing to the accompaniment of string instruments. Confucius grinned and said to Tseyu, "You are trying to kill a chicken with a big cleaver for killing a cow." "But

I heard from you," replied Tseyu, "that when the superior man had learned culture, he became kind to people, and when the common people learned culture, they would become well-disciplined." Confucius (turned to the other disciples and) said, "You fellows, what he says is right. I was only pulling his leg."

Some people of Tahsiang said, "Great indeed is Confucius! He knows about everything and is an expert at nothing." When Confucius heard this, he said, "Now what am I going to specialize in? Shall I specialize in archery, or in driving a carriage?"

The Secretary of Justice of Ch'en asked Confucius if Duke Chao of Lu understood propriety (or *li*) and Confucius replied that he did. After Confucius had left, the Secretary asked Wuma Ch'i to come in and said to him, "Is a superior man partial to his own country? I heard that a superior man should not be partial. Duke Chao married a princess of Wu, who was of the same family name, and called her Mengtse of Wu. Now if that man understands propriety, who doesn't?" Later on Wuma Ch'i told this to Confucius, and Confucius said, "How lucky I am! Whenever I make a mistake, people are sure to discover it."

Tsekung said, "Here is a beautiful piece of jade. Shall it be kept in a casket? Shall it be offered for a sale at a good price?" Confucius remarked, "Sell it! Sell it! I'm the one waiting for a good price for sale!"

Someone asked about Tsech'an (a good minister of Cheng) and Confucius said, "He is a kind man." The man then asked about Prince Tseshi (of Ch'u), and Confucius said, "Oh, that fellow! oh, that fellow!"

Confucius asked Kungming Chia about Kungshu Wentse, "Is it true that your Master doesn't talk, doesn't laugh and doesn't take goods from the people?" Kungming Chia replied, "That is an exaggerated story. My Master talks only when he should talk and people are not bored with his talk. He laughs only when he is happy, and people are not bored with his laughter. And he takes goods from the people only when it is right to do so, and people do not mind his taking their goods." Confucius said, "Really! Is that so?"

Tsekung loved to criticize people, and Confucius said, "Ah Sze, you're clever, aren't you? I have no time for such things."

Confucius said, "I greatly admire a fellow who goes about the whole day with a well-fed stomach and a vacuous mind. How can one ever do it? I would rather that he play chess, which would seem to me to be better.

"I have seen people who gather together the whole day and never talk of anything serious among themselves, and who love to play little clever tricks. Marvellous, how can they ever do it!"

Confucius said, "I am going to remain quiet!" Tsekung remarked, "If you remain quiet, how can we ever learn anything to teach to the others?" And Confucius said, "Does Heaven talk? The four seasons go their way in succession and the different things are produced. Does Heaven talk?"

Confucius said, "I have sometimes talked with Huei for a whole day, and he just sits still there like a fool. But then he goes into his own room and thinks about what I have said and is able to think out some ideas of his own. He is not a fool."

IV. THE JOHNSONIAN TOUCH

Confucius said, "By looking at a man's faults, you know the man's character."[9]

Tsekung asked Confucius, "What kind of a person do you think can be properly called a scholar?" Confucius replied, "A person who shows a sense of honor in his personal conduct and who can be relied upon to carry out a diplomatic mission in a foreign country with competence and dignity can be properly called a scholar." "What kind of a person would come next?" "One who is known to be a good son in his family and has a reputation for humility and respect in a village." "What kind of a person would come next after that?" "A person who is extremely careful of his conduct and speech and always keeps his word. That is a priggish, inferior type of person, but still he can rank below the above two types." "What do you think of the officials today?" "Oh!" said Confucius, "those rice-bags! They don't count at all."

Confucius was once seriously ill, and Tselu asked his disciples to serve as stewards (for his funeral to emulate the style of official families).

[9] *Liki,* Chapter XXXII, gives a fuller quotation, as follows: "Confucius said, 'There are three kinds of true manhood. There are some who show the same behavior as the true man but proceed from different motives. So those who show the same behavior as the true man are not necessarily true men. Some have the same faults as the true men, and these you can be sure are the true men. The true men are happy and natural in their true manhood; the wise men choose the behavior of true manhood because it pays; and those who are afraid to get in jail take the course of true manhood much against their will. . . ." This is also an example of the way in which certain excellent sayings of Confucius are incorporated in the *Analects* without their contexts. The above saying itself, so much like Sainte-Beuve's, seems to point the way to a truer conception of Confucius' character by examining Confucius' foibles.

When Confucius got a little better, he remarked, "The scoundrel! He has gone on preparing to do these things behind my back. I have no stewards in my house and he wanted to pretend that I had. Whom can I deceive? Can I deceive God?"

Confucius saw Queen Nancia and Tselu was displeased. Confucius swore an oath, "If I had said or done anything wrong during the interview, may Heaven strike me! May Heaven strike me!"

Tsai Yu slept in the daytime and Confucius remarked, "There is no use trying to carve on a piece of rotten wood, or to whitewash a wall made of earth from a dunghill. Why should I bother to scold him?" Confucius said, "At first when I heard a man talk, I expected his conduct to come up to what he said. But now when I hear a man talk, I reserve my judgment until I see how he acts. I have learned this lesson from Tsai Yu."

(*Confucius hates a bad pun.*) Duke Ai asked about the customs of the worship of the Earth, and Tsai Yu replied, "The Hsias planted pine trees on the altar, the Shangs used cypresses, and the Chous used chestnuts, in order to make the people nuts." (Literally "give the people the creeps," a pun on the Chinese word *li.*) When Confucius heard this, he said, "Oh, better forget your history! Let what has come, come! Don't try to remedy the past!"

Ju Pei wanted to see Confucius and Confucius declined by saying that he was sick. When the man was just outside the door, Confucius took a string instrument, the *seh,* and sang, in order to let him hear it (and know that he was not sick after all).

Yang Ho wanted to see Confucius, and Confucius would not see him. Yang then presented Confucius with a leg of pork, and Confucius took care to find out when he would not be at home and then went to pay his return call, but met him on the way. Yang Ho said to Confucius, "Come, I want to talk to you!" And he said, "Can you call a man kind who possesses the knowledge to put the country in order, but allows it to go to the dogs?" "Of course not," said Confucius. "Can you call a man wise who loves to get into power and yet lets an opportunity pass by when it comes?" "Of course not," said Confucius. "But the time is passing swiftly by," said Yang Ho. Confucius replied (sarcastically), "Yes, sir, I'm going to be an official." (Yang Ho was a powerful but corrupt official in Lu, and Confucius refused to serve under him.)

Baron Ch'eng Ch'en assassinated Duke Chien (in Ch'i), and Confucius took a ceremonial bath and went to see the Duke of Lu and said,

"Ch'en Heng has assassinated the Duke, his superior. We must send a punitive expedition." "You speak to the three Barons (of Lu)." Confucius replied, "You know in my capacity as an official, I have to inform you formally of this matter." "You speak to the three Barons," said the Duke again. Confucius then went to speak to the three Barons who disapproved, and Confucius said to them, "You know in the capacity of an official I have to inform you formally of this matter."

Yuan Jang (who was reputed to sing at his mother's death) squatted in Confucius' presence and Confucius said, "As a child, you were impudent; after you are grown up, you have absolutely done nothing; and now in your old age you refuse to die! You blackguard!" And Confucius struck him in the shin with a cane.

Baron K'ang Chi was worried about thieves and burglars in the country and consulted Confucius about it. Confucius replied, "If you yourself don't love money the people will not steal, even though you reward the thieves."

Baron K'ang Chi was richer than Duke Chou and Jan Ch'iu (Confucius' disciple who was his secretary) continued to tax the people in order to enrich the Baron. Confucius said (to his disciples), "He is not my disciple. You fellows may beat the drum and denounce him. You have my permission."

Baron K'ang Chi was going to attack Ch'uanyu and Jan Ch'iu and Tselu came to see Confucius and said, "The Baron is going to send an expedition against Ch'uanyu." Confucius said, "Ah Ch'iu, isn't this your fault? The town of Ch'uanyu was originally designated by the ancient emperors as a fief to maintain the worship of the Tungmeng Hill, and besides it is situated within the boundaries of Lu, and the ruler was directly appointed by the founder of the Dynasty. How can you ever think of sending an expedition to take it over (to enlarge the territory of the Baron)?" "The Baron wants it. We don't," replied Jan Ch'iu. "Ah Ch'iu," said Confucius, "the ancient historian Chou Jen said, 'Do your best according to your official capacity, and if you can't stop it, then you quit.' If a person is approaching danger and you do not assist him, or if a person is falling down and you do not support him, then what is the use of being an assistant or guide? What you have just said is wrong. When a tiger or a buffalo escapes from the fenced enclosure or when a piece of sacred jade is found broken in its casket, whose fault is it (but that of the keeper)?" "But this Ch'uanyu lies right next to Pi (city of the Baron)," said Jan Ch'iu, "and if we don't take it now, it will remain a constant threat to our defense in the future." Confucius replied, "Ah Ch'iu, a gentleman hates the person who is embarked upon a course for selfish gains and then tries to create all sorts of pretexts. I have heard that a man in charge of a state or a family doesn't worry about there being too few people in it, but about the unequal distribution of wealth, nor does he worry about poverty, but about general dissatisfaction. For when wealth is equally distributed, there is no poverty; when the people are united, you cannot call it a small nation, and when there is no dissatisfaction (or when people have a sense of security), the country is secure. Accordingly, if people in the neighboring cities do not pay homage to you, you attend to the civil development in your own country to attract them, and when they come, you make it so that they would like to settle down and live in peace. Now you two as secretaries assisting your chief, have not been able to induce people in the neighboring cities to pay homage and come to you. You see the country of Lu divided against itself without being able to do anything about it, and then you set about thinking of starting wars right inside the country. I'm afraid that what the Baron will have to worry about will not be the city of Ch'uanyu, but trouble right within your doors."

V. WIT AND WISDOM

Confucius said, "To know what you know and know what you don't know is the characteristic of one who knows."

Confucius said, "A man who does not say to himself, 'What to do? What to do?'—indeed I do not know what to do with such a person!"

Confucius said, "A man who has committed a mistake and doesn't correct it is committing another mistake."

Confucius said, "A melon-cup that no longer resembles a melon-cup and people still say, 'A melon-cup! A melon-cup!' "

Confucius said, "It is said, 'It is difficult to be a king, but it is not easy to be a minister, either.' "

Baron Wen Chi said that he always thought three times before he acted. When Confucius heard this, he remarked, "To think twice is quite enough."

Confucius said, "I do not expect to find a saint today. But if I find a gentleman, I shall be quite satisfied."

Confucius said, "A man who has a beautiful soul always has some beautiful things to say, but a man who says beautiful things does not necessarily have a beautiful soul. A true man (or truly great man) will always be found to have courage, but a courageous man will not always be found to have true manhood."

Confucius said, "A man who brags without shame will find great difficulty in living up to his bragging."

Confucius said, "The man who loves truth (or learning) is better than the man who knows it, and the man who finds happiness in it is better than the man who loves it." [10]

Confucius said, "In speaking to a sovereign, one must look out for three things: To talk before you are asked is called 'impulsiveness.' To fail to talk when you are asked is called 'lack of candor.' And to talk without noticing the sovereign's mood is called 'blindness.' "

Confucius said, "When you find a person worthy to talk to and fail to talk to him, you have missed your man. When you find a man unworthy to talk to and you talk to him, you have missed (i.e., wasted) your words. A wise man neither misses his man, nor misses his words."

Confucius said, "A gentleman does not praise a man (or put him in office) on the basis of what he says, nor does he deny the truth of what one says because he dislikes the person who says it (if it is good)."

Tsekung asked Confucius, "What would you say if all the people of the village like a person?" "That is not enough," replied Confucius. "What would you say if all the people of a village dislike a person?" "That is not enough," said Confucius. "It is better when the good people of the village like him, and the bad people of the village dislike him."

Confucius said, "The common man often gets in trouble because of his love for the water (literally "gets drowned" in it); the gentleman often gets into trouble because of his love for talking; and the great man often gets into trouble because of his love for the people. All of them get submerged in what they come close to or are familiar with. Water seems so familiar to the people, but easily drowns them because it is a thing that seems so easy to approach and yet is dangerous to get too near to. Talking easily leads one into trouble because when you talk, you use so many words, and it is easy to let them out of your mouth, but difficult to take them back. The people often get one into trouble because they are mean and not open-minded; you can respect them, but you must not insult or offend them. Therefore the gentleman must be very careful."

[10] There is no indication in the text as to whether the reference is to loving truth or loving learning. It uses only the word "it."

Confucius said, "The people who live extravagantly are apt to be snobbish (or conceited), and the people who live simply are apt to be vulgar. I prefer the vulgar people to the snobs."

Confucius said, "It is easy to be rich and not haughty; it is difficult to be poor and not grumble."

Confucius said, "When a country is in order, it is a shame to be a poor and common man. When a country is in chaos, it is a shame to be rich and an official."

Confucius said, "Can you ever imagine a petty soul serving as a minister of the state? Before he gets his post, he is anxious to get it, and after he has got it, he is anxious about losing it, and if he begins to be anxious about losing it, then there is nothing that he will not do."

Confucius said, "Do not worry about people not knowing you, but strive so that you may be worth knowing."

Confucius said, "A gentleman blames himself, while a common man blames others."

Confucius said, "If a man would be severe toward himself and generous toward others, he would never arouse resentment."

Confucius said, "A man who does not think and plan long ahead will find trouble right by his door."

Confucius said, "Polished speech often confuses our notion of who is good and who is bad. A man who cannot put up with small losses or disadvantages will often spoil a big plan."

Confucius said, "In talking about a thoroughbred, you do not admire his strength, but admire his temper."

Someone said, "What do you think of repaying evil with kindness?" Confucius replied, "Then what are you going to repay kindness with?" "Repay kindness with kindness, but repay evil with justice (or severity)."

Confucius said, "When you repay kindness with kindness, then the people are encouraged to do good. When you repay evil with evil, then people are warned from doing bad."

Confucius said, "To repay evil with kindness is the sign of a generous character. To repay kindness with evil is the sign of a criminal." (*Liki,* Chapter XXXII.)

Confucius said, "Men are born pretty much alike, but through their habits they gradually grow further and further apart from each other."

Confucius said, "Only the highest and the lowest characters don't change."

Confucius said, "I have seen rice plants that sprout, but do not blossom, and I have seen rice plants that blossom, but don't bear grains."

Confucius said, "Even though a man had the beautiful talent of Duke Chou, but if he were proud and egoistic, he would not be worth looking at."

Confucius said, "If the superior man is not deliberate in his appearance (or conduct), then he is not dignified. Learning prevents one from being narrow-minded. Try to be loyal and faithful as your main principle. Have no friends who are not as good as yourself. When you have mistakes, don't be afraid to correct them."

Confucius said, "When you see a good man, try to emulate his example, and when you see a bad man, search yourself for his faults."

Confucius said, "Well, well! I have never yet seen a person who knows his own faults and accuses himself before himself!"

Confucius said, "Don't criticize other people's faults, criticize your own."

Tsekung said, "What do you think of a person who is not snobbish (or subservient to the great) when he is poor, and not conceited when he is rich?" Confucius replied, "That's fairly good. It would be better if he were happy when he was poor, and had self-discipline when he was rich."

Confucius said, "You can kill the general of an army, but you cannot kill the ambition in a common man."

VI. HUMANISM AND TRUE MANHOOD

HUMANISM

Confucius said, "It is man that makes truth great, and not truth that makes man great."

Confucius said, "Truth may not depart from human nature. If what is regarded as truth departs from human nature, it may not be regarded as truth."

Tselu asked about the worship of the celestial and earthly spirits. Confucius said, "We don't know yet how to serve men, how can we know about serving the spirits?" "What about death?" was the next question, and Confucius said, "We don't know yet about life, how can we know about death?"

A certain stable was burned down. On returning from the court, Confucius asked, "Was any man hurt?" And he did not ask about the horses.

THE MEASURE OF MAN IS MAN

Confucius said, "To one who loves to live according to the principles of true manhood without external inducements and who hates all that is contrary to the principles of true manhood without external threats of punishments, all mankind seems but like one man only. Therefore the superior man discusses all questions of conduct on the basis of himself as the standard, and then sets rules for the common people to follow." (*Liki,* Chapter XXXII.)

Confucius said, "True manhood requires a great capacity and the road thereto is difficult to reach. You cannot lift it by your hands and you cannot reach it by walking on foot. He who approaches it to a greater degree than others may already be called 'a true man.' Now is it not a difficult thing for a man to try to reach this standard by sheer effort? Therefore, if the gentleman measures men by the standard of the absolute standard of righteousness, then it is difficult to be a real man. But if he measures men by the standard of man, then the better people will have some standard to go by." (*Liki,* Chapter XXXII.)

Confucius said, "To a man who feels down in his heart that he is happy and natural while acting according to the principles of true manhood, all mankind seems like but one man." (What is true of the feelings of one person will serve as the standard of feelings for all people.) (*Liki,* Chapter XXXII.)

Tsekung asked, "If there is a man here who is a benefactor of mankind and can help the masses, would you call him a true man?" "Why, such a person is not only a true man," said Confucius, "he is a Sage. Even the Emperors Yao and Hsun would fall short of such a standard. Now a true man, wishing to establish his own character, also tries to establish the character of others, and wishing to succeed himself, tries also to help others to succeed. To know how to make the approach from one's neighbors (or from the facts of common, everyday life) is the method or formula for achieving true manhood."

Confucius said, "Is the standard of true manhood so far away, after all? When I want true manhood, there it is right by me."

THE GOLDEN RULE

Chung Kung asked about true manhood, and Confucius replied, "When the true man appears abroad, he feels as if he were receiving distinguished people, and when ruling over the people, he feels as if he were worshipping God. What he does not want done unto himself, he does not do unto others. And so both in the state and in the home, people are satisfied."

Tsekung said, "What I do not want others to do unto me, I do not want to do unto them." Confucius said, "Ah Sze, you cannot do it."

Confucius said, "Ah Ts'an, there is a central principle that runs through all my teachings." "Yes," said Tsengtse. When Confucius left, the disciples asked Tsengtse what he meant, and Tsengtse replied, "It is just the principle of reciprocity (or *shu*)."

Tsekung asked, "Is there one single word that can serve as a principle of conduct for life?" Confucius replied, "Perhaps the word 'reciprocity' (*shu*) will do. Do not do unto others what you do not want others to do unto you."

TRUE MANHOOD

Confucius said, "For a long time it has been difficult to see examples of true men. Everybody errs a little on the side of his weakness. Therefore it is easy to point out the shortcomings of the true man." (*Liki*, Chapter XXXII.)

Confucius said, "For a long time it has been difficult to find examples of true men. Only the superior man can reach that state. Therefore the superior man does not try to criticize people for what he himself fails in, and he does not put people to shame for what they fail in. . . ." (*Liki*, Chapter XXXII.)

Confucius said, "To find the central clue to our moral being which unites us to the universal order (or to attain central harmony), that indeed is the highest human attainment. For a long time people have seldom been capable of it."

Yen Huei asked about true manhood, and Confucius said, "True manhood consists in realizing your true self and restoring the moral order or discipline (or *li*). If a man can just for one day realize his true self, and restore complete moral discipline, the world will follow him. To be a true man depends on oneself. What has it got to do with others?"

Confucius said, "Humility is near to moral discipline (or *li*); simplicity of character is near to true manhood; and loyalty is near to sincerity of heart. If a man will carefully cultivate these things in his conduct, he may still err a little, but he won't be far from the standard of true manhood. For with humility or a pious attitude, a man seldom commits errors; with sincerity of heart, a man is generally reliable; and with simplicity of character, he is usually generous. You seldom make a mistake when you start off from these points." (*Liki*, Chapter XXXII.)

Confucius said, "Yen Huei's heart does not leave the condition of true manhood for as long as three months. The others are able to reach that level only for a month or for a few days."

Someone said, "Would you call a man who has succeeded in avoiding aggressiveness, pride, resentment and greed a true man?" Confucius said, "I would say that he is a very rare person, but I do not know whether he can be called a true man."

Tsechang asked Confucius: "Secretary Tsewen (of Ch'u) was three times made a secretary and didn't seem to show particular satisfaction at his appointment, and three times he was relieved of his office and did not seem to show any disappointment. And when he was handing over the affairs of his office to his successors, he explained everything to the latter. Now what would you say about such a person?" Confucius said, "I would call him a sincere, faithful person." "Would you say that he is a true man?" "I do not know," said Confucius. "How should I call him a true man?"[11]

Someone said that Chung Kung (a disciple of Confucius) was a true man and that he was not a glib talker. Confucius said, "What is the use of being a glib talker? The more you talk to defend yourself, the more the people hate you. I do not know about his being a true man. What is the use of being a glib talker?"

Count Wu Meng asked if Tselu was a true man, and Confucius said, "I do not know." On being asked again, Confucius said, "You can put Yu in charge of a country with a thousand carriages and let him take care of its finance. But I do not know about his being a true man." "How about Ch'iu?" Confucius said, "You can put Ch'iu in charge of a township of a thousand families or make him the steward of a household with a hundred carriages (that is, of a minister), but I do not know about his being a true man." "How about Ch'ih (Kunghsi Hua)?" Confucius said, "You can let Ch'ih stand at court, dressed in his official gown and girdle and let him entertain the guests, but I do not know about his being a true man."

[11] An actual example like this shows how inadequate it is to translate the Chinese word *jen* as "kindness," "benevolence" or "a kind person," or "a benevolent person."

FURTHER DESCRIPTIONS OF THE TRUE MAN

Confucius said, "One who is not a true man cannot long stand poverty, nor can he stand prosperity for long. A true man is happy and natural in living according to the principles of true manhood, but a wise man thinks it is advantageous to do so."

Confucius said, "Only a true man knows how to love people and how to hate people."

Confucius said, "How can the superior man keep up his reputation when he departs from the level of the true man? The superior man never departs from the level of true manhood for the time of a single meal. In his most casual moments, he lives in it, and in the most compromising circumstances, he still lives in it."

Confucius said, "If a man is not a true man, what is the use of rituals? If a man is not a true man, what is the use of music?"

Confucius said, "The wise man has no perplexities, the true man has no sorrow, and the brave man has no fear."

Confucius said, "A true man is very slow to talk." Someone asked, "Can a man who is slow to talk then be called a true man?" Confucius said, "Because it is so difficult for a man to do what he says, of course he would be very slow to talk."

VII. THE SUPERIOR MAN AND THE INFERIOR MAN

Confucius said, "The superior man understands what is right; the inferior man understands what will sell."

Confucius said, "The superior man loves his soul; the inferior man loves his property. The superior man always remembers how he was punished for his mistakes; the inferior man always remembers what presents he got."

Confucius said, "The superior man is liberal towards others' opinions, but does not completely agree with them; the inferior man completely agrees with others' opinions, but is not liberal toward them."

Confucius said, "The superior man is firm, but does not fight; he mixes easily with others, but does not form cliques."

Confucius said, "The superior man blames himself; the inferior man blames others."

Confucius said, "The superior man is easy to serve, but difficult to please, for he can be pleased by what is right, and he uses men according to their individual abilities. The inferior man is difficult to serve, but easy to please, for you can please him (by catering to his weaknesses) without necessarily being right, and when he comes to using men, he demands perfection."

Confucius said, "You can put a superior man in an important position with large discretionary powers, but you cannot give him a nice little job; you can give an inferior man a nice little job, but you cannot put him in an important position with great discretionary powers."

Confucius said, "The superior man is not one who is good for only one particular kind of position."

Confucius said, "The superior man is broad-minded toward all men and not a partisan; the inferior man is a partisan, but not broad-minded toward all."

Confucius and his followers had to go for days without food in Ch'en, and some of his followers felt ill and were confined to bed. Tselu came to see Confucius in low spirits and asked, "Does the superior man also land in difficulties?" Confucius said, "Yes, the superior man also sometimes finds himself in difficulties, but when an inferior man finds himself in difficulties, he is likely to do anything."

Confucius said, "The superior man attends to the spiritual things and not to his livelihood. You let him cultivate a farm, and he will be starved, but if you let him attend to his studies, he will find riches in it. The superior man does not worry about his poverty, but worries about the spiritual things."

Confucius said, "The superior man is always candid and at ease (with himself or others); the inferior man is always worried about something."

Confucius said, "The superior man develops upwards; the inferior man develops downwards."

Confucius said, "The superior man is dignified and at ease, but not proud; the inferior man is proud, but not dignified."

Confucius said, "The superior man keeps to the standard of right, but does not (necessarily) keep his promise."

Szema Niu asked Confucius about being a gentleman, and Confucius replied, "A gentleman has no worry and no fear." "Does having no worry and no fear then constitute a gentleman?" Confucius said, "If he looks within himself and is sure that he has done right, what does he have to fear or worry about?"

Confucius said, "The superior man goes through his life without any one preconceived course of action or any taboo. He merely decides for the moment what is the right thing to do."

Confucius said, "The superior man doesn't insist on good food and good lodging. He is attentive to his duties and careful in his speech, and he finds a great man and follows him as his guide. Such a person may be called a lover of learning."

Confucius said, "A scholar who intends to follow the truth and is ashamed of his poor dress and poor food is not worth talking to."

Confucius said, "A scholar who is in love with living comforts is not worthy to be called a scholar."

Confucius said, "A man who serves his king and three times finds his advice rejected and still does not leave the country, is hanging on to his post for the sake of the salary. Even though he says that it is not the salary that attracts him, I won't believe him." (*Liki*, Chapter XXXII.)

Confucius said, "A gentleman is ashamed that his words are better than his deeds."

Confucius said, "A gentleman is careful about three things: In his youth, when his blood is strong, he is careful about sex. When he is grown up, and his blood is full, he is careful about getting into a fight (or struggle in general). When he is old and his blood is getting thinner, he is careful about money." (A young man loves women; a middle-aged man loves struggle; and an old man loves money.)

VIII. THE MEAN AS THE IDEAL CHARACTER AND TYPES OF PERSONS THAT CONFUCIUS HATED

THE PEOPLE OF THE MEAN

Confucius said, "Since I cannot find people who follow the Mean (or Golden Mean) to teach, I suppose I will have to work with those who are brilliant or erratic (*k'uang*) and those who are a little dull but careful (*chuan*). The brilliant but erratic persons are always ready to go forward (or are too active), and the dull but careful persons always hold themselves back (or are not active enough)."

Confucius said, "The goody-goodies are the thieves of virtue."[12]

[12] In the Confucian teachings, there are, therefore, four classes of persons, which were clearly recognized and more fully commented upon by Mencius. According to Mencius, the people who followed the Mean are the ideal human material. Secondly, according to Mencius, since this ideal material cannot be obtained, Confucius preferred to work with the brilliant but erratic; this is the class that Mencius described as "being of an idealistic and expansive nature, always saying, 'The ancient people! The ancient people!' and

Confucius said (when he was wandering in Ch'en and decided to return to his country to devote himself to editing books and teaching), "Let us go home! The scholars of our country are brilliant but erratic, but they are anxious to go forward, and have not lost their original simplicity of character."

Tsekung asked whether Shih (Tsechang) or Shang (Tsehsia) was the better man. Confucius said, "Ah Shih goes a little too far (or is above the normal) and Ah Shang doesn't go far enough (or is a little below the normal)." "Then is Ah Shih a better person?" Confucius said, "To go a little too far is as bad as not going far enough." [13]

Confucius said to Tsehsia, "You must be a gentleman-scholar and not a petty scholar."

---

being free and easy in their ways without trying to conceal their fault." As examples of this class, Mencius quoted a few people who violated Confucian canons of conduct. (According to Chuangtse, they were reputed to sing at their friends' funerals.) Mencius then went on to say that "since Confucius could not get brilliant but erratic people, he would be content to work with those who were anxious to be correct, the *chuan,* who came after the *k'uang* as a class." In describing the last or fourth class, the thieves of virtue, Mencius said that Confucius said, "The kind of people whom I don't mind failing to come into my house or visiting me when passing my door, are the *hsiangyuan* (or goody-goodies). The *hsiangyuan* are the thieves of virtue." Then in answer to a question about this class of people, Mencius described them as follows: "They say, 'Why be idealistic like those people? When their words do not tally with their conduct and their conduct does not tally with their words, they say, "The ancient people! The ancient people!" Why are they so supercilious toward the world and so cool and detached in their conduct? When a man lives in the present world and acts according to the standard of the present world, and succeeds, it is quite enough!' They are the class of people who are quite contented to secure the approval of society. These are the *hsiangyuan." Hsiangyuan* literally means what the country folk call "good men," or "goody-goodies." The questioner then asked Mencius, "Since all the country folk call them 'good men,' and everywhere they go they are called 'good men' (or 'nice people' or 'respectable people'), why did Confucius call them 'thieves of virtue'?" Mencius then said, "You want to criticize them and they seem so perfect; you want to lampoon them, and they seem so correct; they fall in with the current conventions and thoroughly identify themselves with the ways of the times. In their living, they seem to be so honest and faithful, and in their conduct they seem to be so moral. Everybody likes them and they are quite pleased with themselves. But it is impossible to lead them into the ways of Emperors Yao and Hsun. Therefore Confucius said, 'The goody-goodies (or *hsiangyuan,* or the so-called "respectable people") are the thieves of virtue.' " Directly after this description, Mencius quoted what Confucius had said about the things that resemble the real things but are not the real things, and the types of persons that he hated. See below toward the end of this section.

[13] Evidences seem to show that Tsechang was the more brilliant one and more interested in philosophic principles, while Tsehsia, who later became a great teacher specializing in the teaching of the *Book of Songs* after Confucius' death, was the type of a humdrum, conscientious professor.

Confucius said, "When a man has more solid worth than polish, he appears uncouth, and when a man has more polish than solid worth, he appears urbane. The proper combination of solid worth and polish alone makes a gentleman."

Confucius said, "The earlier generations were primitive or uncouth people in the matter of ritual and music; the later generations are refined (literally "gentlemen") in the matter of ritual and music. But if I were to choose between the two, I would follow the people of the earlier generations."[14]

TYPES OF PERSONS THAT CONFUCIUS HATED

Confucius said, "The ancient people had three kinds of faults, and nowadays we haven't even got them. The ancient people who were impulsive were just unconventional in their ways, but today the impulsive people indulge themselves. The ancient people who were correct and smug were the lease austere and careful in their conduct, but today the smug people are always condemning other people and are bad-tempered. The ancient lower class were simple and honest souls, but today the lower class are a deceitful lot."

Tsekung asked, "Does the superior man also have certain things that he hates?" "Yes, there are things that the superior man hates," said Confucius. "He hates those who like to criticize people or reveal their weaknesses. He hates those who, in the position of inferiors, like to malign or spread rumors about those in authority. He hates those who are chivalrous and headstrong but are not restrained by propriety. He hates those who are sure of themselves and are narrow-minded." "But what do you hate, Ah Sze?" "I hate those who like to spy on others and think they are very clever. I hate those who think they are brave when they are merely unruly. And I hate the wily persons who pretend to be honest gentlemen."

Confucius said, "A man who is impulsive and headstrong without having the virtue of simple honesty, who doesn't know a thing and has not enough wit to speak or behave cautiously, or who has no particular ability and withal has not the virtue of honesty or faithfulness—why, there is nothing to be done about such a person."

[14] A choice between uncouth simplicity and decadent elaborateness and formalism—a very important point, considering the common charge of formalism against Confucianism. This common criticism was certainly justifiable when it was directed against the Confucianists in the centuries after him.

Confucius said, "I hate things that resemble the real things but ar not the real things. I hate cockles because they get mixed up with th corn. I hate the ingratiating fellows, because they get mixed up wit the good men. I hate the glib talkers because they confuse us with hones people. I hate the music of Cheng, because it brings confusion int classical music. I hate the purple color, because it confuses us with th red color. I hate the goody-goodies because they confuse us with th virtuous people." (Mencius.)

Confucius said, "A man who appears dignified and austere but is al hollow and weak inside seems to me to be like a little petty burgla who slips into the house through a hole at night."

Confucius said, "Women and the inferior people are most difficult t deal with. When you are familiar with them, they become cheeky, an when you ignore them, they resent it."

Confucius said, "I hate the garrulous people."

Confucius said, "A glib talker with an ingratiating appearance i seldom a gentleman."

Confucius said, "The gentleman does not judge a person entirely by his words. Therefore in a cultured world, we have flowery conduct, and in an uncultured world, we have flowery speeches." (*Liki*, Chapter XXXII.)

IX. GOVERNMENT

THE MORAL IDEAL OF GOVERNMENT

Confucius said, "Guide the people with governmental measures and control or regulate them by the threat of punishment, and the people will try to keep out of jail, but will have no sense of honor or shame. Guide the people by virtue and control or regulate them by *li*, and the people will have a sense of honor and respect."

Confucius said, "When the kingdom of Ch'i moves a step forward, it will have reached the culture of the kingdom of Lu, and when the kingdom of Lu moves a step forward, it will have reached the stage of true civilization."

Confucius said, "In presiding over lawsuits, I'm as good as any man. The thing is to aim so that there should be no lawsuits."

Someone asked Confucius, "Why don't you go into the government?" Confucius replied, "Doesn't the *Book of History* speak about the good son? When the sovereign is a good son, and a good brother, and applies he same principles to the government of the nation, that is also what ve call government. Why should I go into the government?"

Yutse said, "We seldom find a man who is a good son and a good rother that is disrespectful to authority, and we never find a man who s not disrespectful to authority wanting to start a rebellion."

OVERNMENT BY MORAL EXAMPLE

Confucius said, "A sovereign who governs a nation by virtue is like the North Polar Star, which remains in its place and the other stars revolve round it."

Baron K'ang Ch'i asked Confucius concerning government, and Confucius replied, "Government is merely setting things right. When you ourself lead them by the right example, who dares to go astray?"

Baron K'ang Ch'i asked Confucius concerning government, saying, 'If I kill off the bad citizens, and associate with the good citizens, what lo you think?" Confucius replied, "What's the need of killing off people on the part of a ruler of a country? If you desire what is good, the people vill become good also. The character of the ruler is like wind, and the haracter of the common people is like grass, and the grass bends in he direction of the wind."

Confucius said, "When the ruler himself does what is right, he will ave influence over the people without giving commands, and when the uler himself does not do what is right, all his commands will be of no vail."

Confucius said, "If a ruler rectifies his own conduct, government is n easy matter, and if he does not rectify his own conduct, how can e rectify others?"

ACTORS OF GOVERNMENT

Tsekung asked about government, and Confucius replied: "People must have sufficient to eat; there must be a sufficient army; and there must be confidence of the people in the ruler." "If you are forced to give up one of these three objectives, what would you go without first?" asked Tsekung. Confucius said, "I would go without the army first." 'And if you were forced to go without one of the two remaining factors, what would you rather go without?" asked Tsekung again. "I would ather go without sufficient food for the people. There have always been leaths in every generation since man lived, but a nation cannot exist without confidence in its ruler."

X. ON EDUCATION, RITUAL AND POETRY

Confucius said, "Education begins with poetry, is strengthened throug proper conduct (self-discipline) and consummated through music."

Confucius said, "The gentleman broadens himself by scholarship o learning, and then regulates himself by *li* (proper conduct or moral dis cipline). Then he will not fall away from the proper principles."

Yutse said, "Among the functions of *li*, the most valuable is that i establishes a sense of harmony. This is the most beautiful heritage o the ancient kings. It is a guiding principle for all things, big and smal If things do not go right, and you are bent only on having social har mony (or peace) without regulating the society by the pattern of *l* (or the principle of social order),[15] still things won't go right."

Confucius said, "We are saying all the time, *'Li! Li!'* Does *li* mear merely a collection of jades and silks (in ceremonial use)? We are say ing all the time 'Music! Music!' Does music merely mean playing abou with drums and bells?"

Tseshia asked (concerning a passage in the *Book of Songs*), "Wha is the meaning of the passage, 'She has a winning smile, and her eye are so clear and bright. Her dress is of a colored design on a plain back ground'?" Confucius said, "In painting, we must have a plain back ground." "Does that mean that the ceremonial forms of *li* must be basec on a background of simplicity of character?"[16] Confucius said, "Now you have contributed a fresh thought, Ah Shang! You are worthy tc discuss the *Book of Songs*."

Lin Fang asked concerning the foundation of *li*, and Confucius re plied, "You are asking an important question! In this matter of rituals or ceremony, rather than be extravagant, be simple. In funeral ceremonies, rather than be expertly familiar, it is more important to have the rea sentiment of sorrow."

Confucius said, "If you have the wisdom to perceive a truth, but have not the manhood to keep to it, you will lose it again, though you have discovered it. If you have the wisdom to perceive a truth, and the true manhood to keep to it, and fail to preserve decorum in your public appearance, you will not gain the people's respect for authority. If you

[15] See Chapters VI, VII, VIII, "Discourses on the Social Order," in *Wisdom of Confucius.*

[16] This is the orthodox interpretation, and probably correct. This sentence consists of merely three words in the original: "*Li*—behind—is-that-so?"

have the wisdom to perceive a truth, the manhood to keep to it, and have decorum of appearance, but fail to be imbued with the spirit of *li* (or social discipline) in your actions or conduct, it is also not satisfactory."

Confucius said, "Ah Sze is worthy to discuss the *Book of Songs* with me. I tell him something, and he comes up with a fresh suggestion."

Confucius said, "One phrase will characterize all the three hundred poems (actually three hundred and five), and that is: Keep the heart right."

Ch'en K'ang asked Poyu (or Li, the name of Confucius' only son, meaning "a carp"), "Is there anything special that you were taught by your father?" Poyu replied, "No. One day he was standing alone and I ran past the court, and he asked me, 'Have you learned poetry?' And I said, 'Not yet.' He said, 'If you don't study poetry, your language will not be polished.' So I went back and studied poetry. Another day he was standing alone, and I went past the court, and he said to me, 'Have you studied the ceremonies?' And I said, 'Not yet.' And he said, 'If you don't study the ceremonies, you have no guide for your conduct.' And I went back and studied the ceremonies. I was taught to study these two things." Ch'en K'ang came away quite pleased and said, "I asked him one question and learned three things. I learned what Confucius said about poetry. I learned what he said about ceremonies. And I learned that the Master taught his own son in exactly the same way as he taught his disciples (was not partial to his son)."

Confucius said, "Reading without thinking gives one a disorderly mind, and thinking without reading makes one flighty (or unbalanced)."

Confucius said, "Isn't it a great pleasure to learn and relearn again?"

Confucius said, "A man who goes over what he has already learned and gains some new understanding from it is worthy to be a teacher."

Confucius said, "That type of scholarship which is bent on remembering things in order to answer people's questions does not qualify one to be a teacher."

Confucius said, "The ancient scholars studied for their own sake; today the scholars study for the sake of others (out of obligations to their teachers, their parents, etc.)."

Confucius said, "Ah Yu, have you heard of the six sayings about the six shortcomings?" "No," said Tselu. "Sit down, then, and I will tell you. If a man loves kindness, but doesn't love study, his shortcoming will be ignorance. If a man loves wisdom but does not love study, his shortcoming will be having fanciful or unsound ideas. If a man loves honesty and does not love study, his shortcoming will be a tendency to spoil or upset things. If a man loves simplicity but does not love study, his shortcoming will be sheer following of routine. If a man loves courage and does not love study, his shortcoming will be unruliness or violence. If a man loves decision of character and does not love study, his shortcoming will be self-will or headstrong belief in himself."

Confucius said, "Those who are born wise are the highest type of people; those who become wise through learning come next; those who learn by sheer diligence and industry, but with difficulty, come after that. Those who are slow to learn, but still won't learn, are the lowest type of people."

Confucius said, "The young people should be good sons at home, polite and respectful in society; they should be careful in their conduct and faithful, love the people, and associate themselves with the kind people. If after learning all this, they still have energy left, let them read books."

The Golden Mean of Tsesze

INTRODUCTION

I THINK it was the late Professor Herbert A. Giles who described the character of Confucius as that of a typical English schoolmaster. Nothing would have pleased Confucius better than this description. Actually, the Chinese gentleman, like the English gentleman, or at least the perfect one, is an indescribable and indefinable nonentity whom you will not recognize if you pass him on the street, just as the perfect English pronunciation is one which betrays no accent of any particular locality. The essence of the English gentleman is the ability to pass into unrecognizability from one's fellowmen, and the essence of Confucian culture is the moral effort to aspire to achieve the commonplace. It is by holding to the doctrine of the Golden Mean, or the Middle Way, that commonplaceness can be achieved. Confucius confessed, "There are those who seek for the abstruse and strange and live a singular life in order to leave their names to posterity. This I would never do." He also once drew a sharp distinction between the famous man and the truly great man, and described the "famous" man as one who was "bound to be talked about at home when he was at home, and bound to be talked about abroad when he was abroad." It is this doctrine of the Golden Mean which Confucian scholars hold to be the fundamental philosophy of all human conduct, and is intended to transform the Chinese people into a nation of village schoolmasters.

The Golden Mean represents probably the best philosophical approach to Confucian moral philosophy. In this book are contained such great sayings as the following: "What is God-given is what we call human nature. To fulfil the law of human nature is what we call the moral law. The cultivation of the moral law is what we call culture." "Being true to oneself is the law of God. To learn to be true to oneself is the law of man." There is in it the great humanistic dictum, "Truth does not depart from human nature. If what is regarded as truth departs from human nature, it may not be regarded as truth." There is the important Confucian teaching that the measure of man is man, and that the standard of human goodness is not to be sought in Heaven, but in one's fellowman. There is the further somewhat mystic recognition of the identity of the moral law within and the law of the universe without.

The Golden Mean forms one of the *Four Books* formerly prescribed for study in all elementary schools. It formed originally Chapter XXXI of *Liki,* and like certain chapters of the *Liki,* its authorship is ascribed to Tsesze, the grandson of Confucius and allegedly teacher of Mencius. An examination of the style of the book reveals that probably it consisted originally of two separate parts, one distinguished by its beauty of style and a highly philosophical mind in the author, while the other consists of sundry quotations from Confucius on the Golden Mean, put together without much correlation or order. I have rearranged the text and given sectional headings, the reasons for which are given fully in the Introduction to this piece in *The Wisdom of Confucius* (Modern Library).

For the convenience of serious students who wish to compare the original text, I have inserted in parentheses at the beginnings of sections the original numbers of the "chapters." The translation is by the late brilliant Ku Hungming, with certain revisions of my own, to correspond more nearly with the original text.

The Golden Mean of Tsesze

Translated by Ku Hungming

I. THE CENTRAL HARMONY

(I) WHAT IS GOD-GIVEN is what we call human nature. To fulfil the law of our human nature is what we call the moral law. The cultivation of the moral law is what we call culture.

The moral law is a law from whose operation we cannot for one instant in our existence escape. A law from which we may escape is not the moral law. Wherefore it is that the moral man (or the superior man) watches diligently over what his eyes cannot see and is in fear and awe of what his ears cannot hear.

There is nothing more evident than that which cannot be seen by the eyes and nothing more palpable than that which cannot be perceived by the senses. Wherefore the moral man watches diligently over his secret thoughts.

When the passions, such as joy, anger, grief, and pleasure have not awakened, that is our *central* self, or moral being (*chung*). When these passions awaken and each and all attain due measure and degree, that is *harmony,* or the moral order (*ho*). Our central self or moral being is the great basis of existence, and *harmony* or moral order is the universal law in the world.

When our true central self and harmony are realised, the universe then becomes a cosmos and all things attain their full growth and development.

II. THE GOLDEN MEAN

(II) Confucius remarked: "The life of the moral man is an exemplif cation of the universal moral order (*chung-yung,* usually translated a "the Mean").[1] The life of the vulgar person, on the other hand, is contradiction of the universal moral order.

"The moral man's life is an exemplification of the universal orde because he is a moral person who unceasingly cultivates his true self o moral being. The vulgar person's life is a contradiction of the universa order, because he is a vulgar person who in his heart has no regard for, o fear of, the moral law."

(III) Confucius remarked: "To find the central clue to our mora being which unites us to the universal order, that indeed is the highes human attainment. For a long time, people have seldom been capabl of it."

(IV) Confucius remarked: "I know now why the moral life is no practiced. The wise mistake moral law for something higher than wha it really is; and the foolish do not know enough what moral law really is I know now why the moral law is not understood. The noble nature want to live too high, high above their moral ordinary self; and ignobl natures do not live high enough, i.e., not up to their moral ordinary tru self. There is no one who does not eat and drink. But few there are wh really know flavor."

(V) Confucius remarked: "There is in the world now really no mor social order at all."

(VII) Confucius remarked: "Men all say 'I am wise'; but when driven forward and taken in a net, a trap, or a pitfall, there is not one who knows how to find a way of escape. Men all say, 'I am wise'; but in finding the true central clue and balance in their moral being (i.e., their normal, ordinary, true self), they are not able to keep it for a round month."

(VIII) Confucius remarked of his favorite disciple, Yen Huei: "Huei was a man who all his life sought the central clue in his moral being, and when he got hold of one thing that was good, he embraced it with all his might and never lost it again."

[1] *Chung* means "central," and *yung* means "constant." The whole idea expresses the conception of a norm. It is possible that Sections 2, 3, 4, 5, 6 originally formed a separate book, later amalgamated with the other Sections (1, 7, 8, 9, 10). The styles of the two parts are quite different. This accounts for the abrupt change from *chungho* (central harmony) in the first section to *chungyung* (Golden Mean) in the second section.

(IX) Confucius remarked: "A man may be able to put a country in
rder, be able to spurn the honors and emoluments of office, be able to
rample upon bare, naked weapons; with all that he is still not able to
ind the central clue in his moral being."

(X) Tselu asked what constituted strength of character.

Confucius said: "Do you mean strength of character of the people of
he southern countries or force of character of the people of the northern
ountries; or do you mean strength of character of your type? To be
atient and gentle, ready to teach, returning not evil for evil; that is
he strength of character of the people of the southern countries. It is the
deal place for the moral man. To lie under arms and meet death without
egret; that is the strength of character of the people of the northern
ountries. It is the ideal of brave men of your type. Wherefore the man
vith the true strength of moral character is one who is gentle, yet firm.
Iow unflinching is his strength! When there is moral social order in the
ountry, if he enters public life he does not change from what he was
vhen in retirement. When there is no moral social order in the country,
ie is content unto death. How unflinching is his strength!"

(XI) Confucius remarked: "There are men who seek for the abstruse
nd strange and live a singular life in order that they may leave a name
o posterity. This is what I never would do. There are again good men
vho try to live in conformity with the moral law, but who, when they
ave gone half way, throw it up. I never could give it up. Lastly, there
re truly moral men who unconsciously live a life in entire harmony with
he universal moral order and who live unknown to the world and un-
oticed of men without any concern. It is only men of holy, divine
atures who are capable of this."

III. MORAL LAW EVERYWHERE

(XII) The moral law is to be found everywhere, and yet it is a secret.

The simple intelligence of ordinary men and women of the people
may understand something of the moral law; but in its utmost reaches
there is something which even the wisest and holiest of men cannot
understand. The ignoble natures of ordinary men and women of the
people may be able to carry out the moral law; but in its utmost reaches
even the wisest and holiest of men cannot live up to it.

Great as the Universe is, man is yet not always satisfied with it. For
there is nothing so great but the mind of the moral men can conceive

of something still greater which nothing in the world can hold. There is nothing so small but the mind of the moral man can conceive of something still smaller which nothing in the world can split.

The *Book of Songs* says: "The hawk soars to the heavens above and fishes dive to the depths below." That is to say, there is no place in the highest heavens above nor in the deepest waters below where the moral law is not to be found. The moral man finds the moral law beginning in the relation between man and woman; but ending in the vast reaches of the universe.

(XVI) Confucius remarked: "The power of spiritual forces in the Universe—how active it is everywhere! Invisible to the eyes, and impalpable to the senses, it is inherent in all things, and nothing can escape its operation."

It is the fact that there are these forces which makes men in all countries fast and purify themselves, and with solemnity of dress institute services of sacrifice and religious worship. Like the rush of mighty waters, the presence of unseen Powers is felt; sometimes above us, sometimes around us.

In the *Book of Songs* it is said:

"The presence of the Spirit:
It cannot be surmised,
How may it be ignored!

Such is the evidence of things invisible that it is impossible to doubt the spiritual nature of man.

IV. THE HUMANISTIC STANDARD

(XIII) Confucius said: "Truth does not depart from human nature. If what is regarded as truth departs from human nature, it may not be regarded as truth. The *Book of Songs* says: 'In hewing an axe handle, the pattern is not far off.' Thus, when we take an axe handle in our hand to hew another axe handle and glance from one to the other, some still think the pattern is far off. Wherefore the moral man in dealing with men appeals to the common human nature and changes the manner of their lives and nothing more.

"When a man carries out the principles of conscientiousness and reciprocity he is not far from the moral law. What you do not wish others should do unto you, do not do unto them.

"There are four things in the moral life of a man, not one of which I have been able to carry out in my life. To serve my father as I would expect my son to serve me: that I have not been able to do. To serve my sovereign as I would expect a minister under me to serve me: that I have not been able to do. To act towards my elder brothers as I would expect my younger brother to act towards me: that I have not been able to do. To be the first to behave towards friends as I would expect them to behave towards me: that I have not been able to do.

"In the discharge of the ordinary duties of life and in the exercise of care in ordinary conversation, whenever there is shortcoming, never fail to strive for improvement, and when there is much to be said, always say less than what is necessary; words having respect to actions and actions having respect to words. Is it not just this thorough genuineness and absence of pretense which characterizes the moral man?"

(XV) The moral life of man may be likened to traveling to a distant place: one must start from the nearest stage. It may also be likened to ascending a height: one must begin from the lowest step. The *Book of Songs* says:

> "When wives and children and their sires are one,
> 'Tis like the harp and lute in unison.
> When brothers live in concord and at peace
> The strain of harmony shall never cease.
> The lamp of happy union lights the home,
> And bright days follow when the children come."

Confucius, commenting on the above, remarked: "In such a state of things what more satisfaction can parents have?"

(XIV) The moral man conforms himself to his life circumstances; he does not desire anything outside of his position. Finding himself in a position of wealth and honor, he lives as becomes one living in a position of wealth and honor. Finding himself in a position of poverty and humble circumstances, he lives as becomes one living in a position of poverty and humble circumstances. Finding himself in uncivilized countries, he lives as becomes one living in uncivilized countries. Finding himself in circumstances of danger and difficulty, he acts according to what is required of a man under such circumstances. In one word, the moral man can find himself in no situation in life in which he is not master of himself.

In a high position he does not domineer over his subordinates. In a subordinate position he does not court the favors of his superiors. He puts in order his own personal conduct and seeks nothing from others; hence he has no complaint to make. He complains not against God, nor rails against men.

Thus it is that the moral man lives out the even tenor of his life calmly waiting for the appointment of God, whereas the vulgar person takes to dangerous courses, expecting the uncertain chances of luck.

Confucius remarked: "In the practice of archery we have something resembling the principle in a moral man's life. When the archer misses the center of the target, he turns round and seeks for the cause of his failure within himself."

V. CERTAIN MODELS

(VI) Confucius remarked: "There was the Emperor Shun. He was perhaps what may be considered a truly great intellect. Shun had a natural curiosity of mind and he loved to inquire into ordinary conversation. He ignored the bad (words?) and broadcast the good. Taking two extreme counsels, he took the mean between them and applied them in dealings with his people. This was the characteristic of Shun's great intellect."

(XVII) Confucius remarked: "The Emperor Shun might perhaps be considered in the highest sense of the word a pious man. In moral qualities he was a saint. In dignity of office he was the ruler of the empire. In wealth all that the wide world contained belonged to him. After his death his spirit was sacrificed to in the ancestral temple, and his children and grandchildren preserved the sacrifice for long generations.

"Thus it is that he who possesses great moral qualities will certainly attain to corresponding high position, to corresponding great prosperity, to corresponding great name, to corresponding great age.

"For God in giving life to all created things is surely bountiful to them according to their qualities. Hence the tree that is full of life. He fosters and sustains, while that which is ready to fall He cuts off and destroys.

The *Book of Songs* says:

> That great and noble Prince displayed
> The sense of right in all he wrought;
> The spirit of his wisdom swayed
> Peasant and peer; the crowd, the court.

So Heav'n, that crowned his sires, restored
The countless honors they had known;
For Heav'n aye keepeth watch and ward,
The Mandate gave to mount the throne.

It is therefore true that he who possesses exceedingly great moral qualities will certainly receive the divine mandate to the Imperial throne."

(XVIII) Confucius remarked: "The man perhaps who enjoyed the most perfect happiness was the Emperor Wen. For father he had a remarkable man, the Emperor Chi, and for son also a remarkable man, the Emperor Wu. His father laid the foundation of his House and his son carried it on. The Emperor Wu, continuing the great work begun by his ancestor, the great Emperor, his grandfather Chi and his father the Emperor Wen, had only to buckle on his armor and the Empire at once came to his possession. In dignity of office he was the ruler of the Empire; in wealth all that the wide world contained belonged to him. After his death his spirit was sacrificed to in the ancestral temple, and his children and grandchildren preserved the sacrifice for long generations.

"The Emperor Wu received Heaven's mandate to rule in his old age. His brother, Duke Chou, ascribed the achievement of founding the Imperial House equally to the moral qualities of the Emperors Wen and Wu. He carried the Imperial title up to the Great Emperor (Wen's grandfather) and the Emperor Chi (Wen's father). He sacrificed to all the past reigning Dukes of the House with Imperial honors.

("This rule is now universally observed from the reigning princes and nobles to the gentlemen and common people. In the case where the father is a noble and the son is a simple gentleman, the father, when he dies, is buried with the honors of a noble, but sacrificed to as a simple gentleman. In the case where the father is a simple gentleman and the son a noble, the father, when he dies, is buried as a simple gentleman, but sacrificed to with the honors of a nobleman. The rule for one year of mourning for relatives is binding up to the rank of a noble, but the rule for three years of mourning for parents is blinding for all up to the Emperor. In mourning for parents there is only one rule, and no distinction is made between noble and plebeian.") [2]

(XIX) Confucius remarked: "The Emperor Wu and his brother, Duke Chou, were indeed eminently pious men. Now, true filial piety

[2] The foregoing paragraph is part of the original Confucian text. In content, however, it resembles a commentary.

consists in successfully carrying out the unfinished work of our forefathers and transmitting their achievements to posterity.

"In spring and autumn they repaired and put in order the ancestral temple, arranged the sacrificial vessels, exhibited the regalia and heirlooms of the family, and presented the appropriate offerings of the season.

"The principle in the order of precedence in the ceremonies of worship in the ancestral temple is, in the first place, to arrange the members of the family according to descent. Ranks are next considered, in order to give recognition to the principle of social distinction. Services rendered are next considered as a recognition of distinction in moral worth. In the general banquet those below take precedence of those above in pledging the company, in order to show that consideration is shown to the meanest. In conclusion, a separate feast is given to the elders, in order to recognize the principle of seniority according to age.

"To gather in the same places where our fathers before us have gathered; to perform the same ceremonies which they before us have performed; to play the same music which they before us have played; to pay respect to those whom they honored; to love those who were dear to them—in fact, to serve those now dead as if they were living, and now departed as if they were still with us: this is the highest achievement of true filial piety.

"The performance of sacrifices to Heaven and Earth is meant for the service of God. The performance of ceremonies in the ancestral temple is meant for the worship of ancestors. If one only understood the meaning of the sacrifices to Heaven and Earth, and the significance of the services in ancestral worship in summer and autumn, it would be as easy to govern a nation as to point a finger at the palm."

VI. ETHICS AND POLITICS[3]

(XX) Duke Ai (ruler of Lu, Confucius' native state) asked what constituted good government.

Confucius replied: "The principles of good government of the Emperors Wen and Wu are abundantly illustrated in the records preserved. When the men are there, good government will flourish, but when the men are gone, good government decays and becomes extinct. With the right men, the growth of good government is as rapid as the growth of

[3] This section must have been placed here from other "ancient records." Confucius had a number of interviews with Duke Ai, some in the "Great Tai" collection.

vegetation is in the right soil. Indeed, good government is like a fast-growing plant. The conduct of government, therefore, depends upon the men. The right men are obtained by the ruler's personal character. To cultivate his personal character, the ruler must use the moral law (*tao*). To cultivate the moral law, the ruler must use the moral sense (*jen,* or principles of true manhood).

"The moral sense is the characteristic attribute of man. To feel natural affection for those nearly related to us is the highest expression of the moral sense. The sense of justice (*yi* or propriety) is the recognition of what is right and proper. To honor those who are worthier than ourselves is the highest expression of the sense of justice. The relative degrees of natural affection we ought to feel for those who are nearly related to us and the relative grades of honor we ought to show to those worthier than ourselves: these give rise to the forms and distinctions in social life (*li,* or principles of social order). For unless social inequalities have a true and moral basis (or unless those being ruled feel their proper place with respect to their rulers), government of the people is an impossibility.

"Therefore it is necessary for a man of the governing class to set about regulating his personal conduct and character. In considering how to regulate his personal conduct and character, it is necessary for him to do his duties toward those nearly related to him. In considering how to do his duties toward those nearly related to him, it is necessary for him to understand the nature and organization of human society. In considering the nature and organization of human society it is necessary for him to understand the laws of God.

"The duties of universal obligation are five, and the moral qualities by which they are carried out are three. The duties are those between ruler and subject, between father and son, between husband and wife, between elder brother and younger, and those in the intercourse between friends. These are the five duties of universal obligation. Wisdom, compassion and courage[4]—these are the three universally recognized moral qualities of man. It matters not in what way men come to the exercise of these moral qualities, the result is one and the same.

"Some men are born with the knowledge of these moral qualities; some acquire it as the result of education; some acquire it as the result of hard experience. But when the knowledge is acquired, it comes to one and the same thing. Some exercise these moral qualities naturally and easily; some because they find it advantageous to do so; some with effort and

[4] Ku translates them as "intelligence, moral character and courage."

difficulty. But when the achievement is made it comes to one and the same thing."

Confucius went on to say: "Love of knowledge is akin to wisdom. Strenuous attention to conduct is akin to compassion. Sensitiveness to shame is akin to courage.

"When a man understands the nature and use of these three moral qualities, he will then understand how to put in order his personal conduct and character. When a man understands how to put in order his personal conduct and character, he will understand how to govern men. When a man understands how to govern men, he will then understand how to govern nations and empires.

"For every one called to the government of nations and empires there are nine cardinal directions to be attended to:

1. Cultivating his personal conduct.
2. Honoring worthy men.
3. Cherishing affection for, and doing his duty toward, his kindred.
4. Showing respect to the high ministers of state.
5. Identifying himself with the interests and welfare of the whole body of public officers.
6. Showing himself as a father to the common people.
7. Encouraging the introduction of all useful arts.
8. Showing tenderness to strangers from far countries.
9. Taking interest in the welfare of the princes of the Empire.

"When the ruler pays attention to the cultivation of his personal conduct, there will be respect for the moral law. When the ruler honors worthy men, he will not be deceived (by the crafty officials). When the ruler cherishes affection for his kindred, there will be no disaffection among the members of his family. When the ruler shows respect to the high ministers of state, he will not make mistakes. When the ruler identifies himself with the interests and welfare of the body of public officers, there will be a strong spirit of loyalty among the gentlemen of the country. When the ruler becomes a father to the common people, the mass of the people will exert themselves for the good of the state. When the ruler encourages the introduction of all useful arts, there will be sufficiency of wealth and revenue in the country. When the ruler shows kindness to the strangers from far countries, people from all quarters of the world will flock to the country. When the ruler takes interest in the condition and welfare of the princes of the Empire, he will inspire awe and respect for his authority throughout the whole world.

"By attending to the cleanliness and purity of his person and to the propriety and dignity of his dress, and in every word and act permitting nothing which is contrary to good taste and decency; that is how the ruler cultivates his personal conduct. By banishing all flatterers and keeping away from the society of women, holding in low estimation possession of worldly goods, but valuing moral qualities in men—that is how the ruler gives encouragement to worthy men. By raising them to high places of honor and bestowing ample emoluments for their maintenance; sharing and sympathizing with their tastes and opinions—that is how the ruler inspires love for his person among the members of his family. By extending the powers of their function and allowing them discretion in the employment of their subordinates—that is how the ruler gives encouragement to the high ministers of state. By dealing loyally and punctually with them in all engagements which he makes with them and allowing a liberal scale of pay—that is how the ruler gives encouragement to men in the public service. By strictly limiting the time of their service and making all imposts as light as possible—that is how the ruler gives encouragement to the mass of the people. By ordering daily inspection and monthly examination and rewarding each according to the degree of his workmanship—that is how the ruler gives encouragement to the mass of the people. By ordering daily inspection and monthly examination and rewarding each according to the degree of his workmanship—that is how the ruler encourages the artisan class. By welcoming them when they come and giving them protection when they go, commending what is good in them and making allowance for their ignorance—that is how the ruler shows kindness to strangers from far countries. By restoring lines of broken succession and reviving subjugated states, putting down anarchy and disorder wherever they are found, and giving support to the weak against the strong, fixing stated times for their attendance and the attendance of their envoys at court, loading them with presents when they leave, while exacting little from them in the way of contribution when they come—that is how the ruler takes interest in the welfare of the princes of the empire.

"For every one who is called to the government of nations and empire, these are the nine cardinal directions to be attended to; and there is only one way by which they can be carried out.

"In all matters success depends on preparation; without preparation there will always be failure. When what is to be said is previously determined, there will be no difficulty in carrying it out. When a line of conduct is previously determined, there will be no occasion for vexation. When general principles are previously determined, there will be no perplexity to know what to do."

VII. BEING ONE'S TRUE SELF

"If the people in inferior positions do not have confidence in those above them, government of the people is an impossibility. There is only one way to gain confidence for one's authority: if a man is not trusted by his friends, he will not have confidence in those above him. There is only one way to be trusted by one's friends: if a man is not affectionate toward his parents, he will not be trusted by his friends. There is only one way to be affectionate toward one's parents: if a man, looking into his own heart, is not true to himself, he will not be affectionate toward his parents. There is only one way for a man to be true to himself. If he does not know what is good, a man cannot be true to himself.

"Being true to oneself is the law of God. Try to be true to oneself is the law of man.[5]

"He who is naturally true to himself is one who, without effort, hits upon what is right, and without thinking understands what he wants to know, whose life is easily and naturally in harmony with the moral law. Such a one is what we call a saint or a man of divine nature. He who learns to be his true self is one who finds out what is good and holds fast to it.

"In order to learn to be one's true self, it is necessary to obtain a wide and extensive knowledge of what has been said and done in the world; critically to inquire into it; carefully to ponder over it; clearly to sift it; and earnestly to carry it out.

"It matters not what you learn; but when you once learn a thing, you must never give it up until you have mastered it. It matters not what you inquire into, but when you inquire into a thing, you must never give it up until you have thoroughly understood it. It matters not what you try to think out, but when you once try to think out a thing you must never give it up until you have got what you want. It matters not what you try to sift out, but when you once try to sift out a thing, you must never give it up until you have sifted it out clearly and distinctly. It matters not

[5] This part from the beginning of the section is found in the *Book of Mencius,* Book IV, Part I. The complete interview is found also in "Confucius' Family Records" (*K'ungtse Chiayu*), without the section that follows immediately.

what you try to carry out, but when you once try to carry out a thing you must never give it up until you have done it thoroughly and well. If another man succeed by one effort, you will use a hundred efforts. If another man succeed by ten efforts, you will use a thousand efforts.

"Let a man really proceed in this manner, and, though dull, he will surely become intelligent; though weak, he will surely become strong."

(XXI) To arrive at understanding from being one's true self is called nature, and to arrive at being one's true self from understanding is called culture. He who is his true self has thereby understanding, and he who has understanding finds thereby his true self.[6]

VIII. THOSE WHO ARE ABSOLUTE TRUE SELVES

(XXII) Only those who are their absolute true selves in the world can fulfil their own nature; only those who fulfil their own nature can fulfil the nature of others; only those who fulfil the nature of others can fulfil the nature of things; those who fulfil the nature of things are worthy to help Mother Nature in growing and sustaining life; and those who are worthy to help Mother Nature in growing and sustaining life are the equals of Heaven and Earth.

(XXIII) The next in order are those who are able to attain to the apprehension of a particular branch of study. By such studies, they are also able to apprehend the truth. Realization of the true self compels expression; expression becomes evidence; evidence becomes clarity or luminosity of knowledge; clarity or luminosity of knowledge activates; active knowledge becomes power and power becomes a pervading influence. Only those who are absolutely their true selves in this world can have pervading influence.

(XXIV) It is an attribute of the possession of the absolute true self to be able to foreknow. When a nation or family is about to flourish, there are sure to be lucky omens. When a nation or family is about to perish, there are sure to be signs and prodigies. These things manifest themselves in the instruments of divination and in the agitation of the human body. When happiness or calamity is about to come, it can be known beforehand. When it is good, it can be known beforehand. When it is evil, it can also be known beforehand. Therefore he who has realized his true self is like a celestial spirit.

[6] This paragraph constitutes a "chapter" by itself in the Chinese text. The translation of this paragraph and the following two paragraphs is entirely mine, differing from Ku's.

(XXV) Truth means the fulfilment of our self; and moral law means following the law of our being. Truth is the beginning and end (the substance) of material existence. Without truth there is no material existence. It is for this reason that the moral man values truth.

Truth is not only the fulfilment of our own being; it is that by which things outside of us have an existence. The fulfilment of our being is moral sense. The fulfilment of the nature of things outside of us is intellect. These, moral sense and intellect, are the powers or faculties of our being. They combine the inner or subjective and outer or objective use of the power of the mind. Therefore, with truth, everything done is right.

(XXVI) Thus absolute truth is indestructible. Being indestructible, it is eternal. Being eternal, it is self-existent. Being self-existent, it is infinite. Being infinite, it is vast and deep. Being vast and deep, it is transcendental and intelligent. It is because it is vast and deep that it contains all existence. It is because it is transcendental and intelligent that it embraces all existence. It is because it is infinite and eternal that it fulfils or perfects all existence. In vastness and depth it is like the Earth. In transcendental intelligence it is like Heaven. Infinite and eternal, it is the Infinite itself.

Such being the nature of absolute truth, it manifests itself without being seen; it produces effects without motion; it accomplishes its ends without action.

The principle in the course and operation of nature may be summed up in one word: because it obeys only its own immutable law, the way in which it produces the variety of things is unfathomable.

Nature is vast, deep, high, intelligent, infinite and eternal. The heaven appearing before us is only this bright, shining mass; but in its immeasurable extent, the sun, the moon, stars and constellations are suspended in it, and all things are embraced under it. The Earth, appearing before us, is but a handful of soil; but in all its breadth and depth, it sustains mighty mountains without feeling their weight; rivers and seas dash against it without causing it to leak. The mountain appearing before us is only a mass of rock; but in all the vastness of its size, grass and vegetation grow upon it, birds and beasts dwell on it, and treasures of precious minerals are found in it. The water appearing before us is but a ladleful of liquid; but in all its unfathomable depths, the largest crustaceans, dragons, fishes, and turtles are produced in them, and all useful products abound in them.

In the *Book of Songs* it is said:

"The ordinance of God,
How inscrutable it is and goes on for ever."

That is to say, this is the essence of God. It is again said:

"How excellent it is,
The moral perfection of King Wen."

That is to say, this is the essence of the noble character of the Emperor Wen. Moral perfection also never dies.

IX. EULOGY ON CONFUCIUS

(XXVII) Oh, how great is the divine moral law of the Sage. Overflowing and illimitable, it gives birth and life to all created things and towers high up to the very heavens. How magnificent it is! How imposing the three hundred principles and three thousand rules of conduct! They await the man who can put the system into practice. Hence it is said: Unless there be the highest moral character, the highest moral law cannot be realized.

Wherefore the moral man, while honoring the greatness and power of his moral nature, yet does not neglect inquiry and pursuit of knowledge. While broadening the scope of his knowledge, he yet seeks to exhaust the mystery of the small things. While seeking to attain the highest understanding he yet orders his conduct according to the middle course (literally "*chungyung*."). Going over what he has already learned, he gains some new knowledge. Earnest and simple, he respects and obeys the laws and usages of social life (*li*).

Therefore, when in a position of authority, he is not proud; in a subordinate position, he is not insubordinate. When there is moral social order in the country, what he speaks will bring prosperity to the nation; and when there is no moral social order in the country, his silence will ensure forbearance for himself.[7]

In the *Book of Songs* it is said:

"With wisdom and good sense,
He guards his life from harm."

That is the description of the moral man.

[7] Here we see the connection between the realization of the true self and harmony with the outside world, between "sincerity" and "harmony."

(XXIX) To attain to the sovereignty of the world, there are three important things necessary, which would make it perfect.

(XXVIII)[8] Although a man may occupy a position of authority, yet, unless he possesses the moral character fitting him for his task, he may not take upon himself to make changes in the established religious and artistic institutions (literally "ritual and music"). Although one may possess the moral character fitting him for his task, yet, unless he occupies the position of authority, he may not take upon himself to make changes in the established religious and artistic institutions.

Confucius remarked: "I have tried to understand the moral and religious institutions (*li*) of the Hsia Dynasty, but what remains of those institutions in the present state of Ch'i does not furnish sufficient evidence. I have studied the moral and religious institutions of the Shang (Yin) Dynasty; the remains of them are still preserved in the present state of Sung. I have studied the moral and religious institutions of the present Chou Dynasty, which being now in use, I follow in practice."

(XXIX) Coming from those in power, a system may be lacking in historical authority ("historic evidences"), however excellent it may be; what is lacking in historical authority cannot command credence; and what cannot command credence the people will never obey. Coming from those not in authority, a system may not command respect, however excellent it may be; what does not command respect cannot command credence; and what cannot command credence the people will never obey.

Therefore every system of moral laws must be based upon the man's own consciousness, verified by the common experience of mankind, tested by due sanction of historical experience and found without error, applied to the operations and processes of nature in the physical universe and found to be without contradiction, laid before the gods without question or fear, and able to wait a hundred generations and have it confirmed without a doubt by a Sage of posterity. The fact that he is able to confront the spiritual powers of the universe without any fear shows that he understands the laws of God. The fact that he is prepared to wait a hundred generations for confirmation from the Sage of posterity without any misgiving shows that he understands the laws of man.

Wherefore it is that it is true of the really great moral man that

[8] The following two paragraphs are incorporated here from "Chapter 28." The "three important things" (position, character and appeal to history) become otherwise unintelligible.

every move he makes becomes an example for generations; every act he does becomes a model for generations and every word he utters becomes a guide for generations. Those who are far away look up to him, while those who are near do not decrease their respect for him. In the *Book of Songs* it is said:

> "There they found no fault of him,
> Here they never tire of him;
> Thus from day to day and night to night
> They will perpetuate his praise!"

There never was a moral man who did not answer this description and who yet could obtain timely recognition throughout the world.

(XXX) Confucius taught the truth originally handed down by the ancient Emperors Yao and Shun, and he adopted and perfected the system of social and religious laws established by the Emperors Wen and Wu. He shows that they harmonize with the divine order which governs the revolutions of the seasons in the Heaven above and that they fit in with the moral design which is to be seen in physical nature upon the Earth below.

These moral laws form one system with the laws by which Heaven and Earth support and contain, overshadow and canopy all things. These moral laws form the same system with the laws by which the seasons succeed each other and the sun and moon appear with the alternations of day and night. It is this same system of laws by which all created things are produced and develop themselves each in its order and system without injuring one another, and by which the operations of Nature take their course without conflict or confusion; the lesser forces flowing everywhere like river currents, while the great forces of Creation go silently and steadily on. It is this (one system running through all) that makes the Universe so impressively great.

(XXXI) It is only the man with the most perfect divine moral nature who is able to combine in himself quickness of apprehension, intelligence, insight and understanding—qualities necessary for the exercise of command, magnanimity, generosity, benignity and gentleness—qualities necessary for the exercise of patience; originality, energy, strength of character and determination—qualities necessary for the exercise of endurance, piety, noble seriousness, order and regularity—qualities necessary for the exercise of dignity, grace, method, subtlety and penetration—qualities necessary for the exercise of critical judgment.

Thus all-embracing and vast is the nature of such a man. Profound it is and inexhaustible, like a living spring of water, ever running out with life and vitality. All-embracing and vast, it is like Heaven. Profound and inexhaustible, it is like the abyss.

As soon as such a man shall make his appearance in the world, all people will reverence him. Whatever he says, all people will believe it. Whatever he does, all people will be pleased with it. Thus his fame and name will spread and fill all the civilized world (literally "China"), extending even to savage countries, wherever ships and carriages reach, wherever the labor and enterprise of man penetrate, wherever the heavens overshadow and the earth sustain, wherever the sun and moon shine, wherever frost and dew fall. All who have life and breath will honor and love him. Therefore we may say: "He is the equal of God."

(XXXII) It is only he in this world who has realized his absolute self that can order and adjust the great relations of human society, fix the fundamental principles of morality, and understand the laws of growth and reproduction of the Universe.

Now, where does such a man derive his power and knowledge, except from himself? How simple and self-contained his true manhood! How unfathomable the depth of his mind! How infinitely grand and vast the moral height of his nature! Who can understand such a nature except he who is gifted with the most perfect intelligence and endowed with the highest divine qualities of character, and who has reached in his moral development the level of the gods?

X. EPILOGUE

In the *Book of Songs* it is said:

> "Over her brocaded robe,
> She wore a plain and simple dress,"

in that way showing her dislike of the loudness of its color and magnificence. Thus the ways of the moral man are unobtrusive and yet they grow more and more in power and evidence; whereas the ways of the vulgar person are ostentatious, but lose more and more in influence until they perish and disappear.

The life of the moral man is plain, and yet not unattractive; it is simple, and yet full of grace; it is easy, and yet methodical. He knows that accomplishment of great things consists in doing little things well.

He knows that great effects are produced by small causes. He knows the evidence and reality of what cannot be perceived by the senses. Thus he is enabled to enter into the world of ideas and morals.

In the *Book of Songs* it is said:

> "How deep the fish may dive below,
> And yet it is quite clearly seen."

Therefore the moral man must examine into his own heart and see that he has no cause for self-reproach, that he has no evil thought in his mind. Wherein the moral man is superior to other men consists even in those things that people do not notice.

In the *Book of Songs* it is said:

> "In your secret chamber even you are judged;
> See you do nothing to blush for,
> Though but the ceiling looks down upon you."

Therefore the moral man, even when he is not doing anything, is serious; and, even when he does not speak, is truthful.

In the *Book of Songs* it is said:

> "All through the solemn rite not a word was spoken,
> And yet all strife was banished from their hearts."

Hence the moral man, without the inducement of rewards, is able to make the people good; and without the show of anger, to awe them into fear more than if he had used the most dreadful instruments of punishment.

In the *Book of Songs,* it is said:

> "He makes no show of his moral worth,
> Yet all the princes follow in his steps."

Hence the moral man, by living a life of simple truth and earnestness, alone can help to bring peace and order in the world.

In the *Book of Songs,* it is said:

> "I keep in mind the fine moral qualities
> Which make no great noise or show."

Confucius remarked: "Among the means for the regeneration of mankind, those made with noise and show are of the least importance."

In another place in the *Book of Songs,* it is said:

> "His virtue is light as hair."

Still a hair is something material. "The workings of Almighty God have neither sound nor smell." That is the highest development of our moral nature.

CHINESE POETRY

Chinese Poetry

INTRODUCTION

Poetry is the most difficult form of literature to translate, particularly Chinese poetry. Nevertheless, through the labors of many talented scholars, it has been possible for the West to appreciate something of the spirit of the Chinese poetic genius. Chinese poetic development is important, and almost all good Chinese scholars leave behind a volume of poems as well as prose. Only T'ang poetry is comparatively well known, and of this not one ten-thousandth part has been translated. Not even one-twentieth part of Li Po's works has been translated, so enormous was his output. "T'ang poetry" is a name for one kind of verse with a conventional and strictly prescribed pattern, later used in official examinations for imperial service, and therefore learned by every ambitious scholar. It is therefore not confined to poetry written in the T'ang Dynasty, although Li Po and Tu Fu represented its peak of development. Again, T'ang poetry is only one corner of Chinese poetry, and the T'ang poets, including Li Po and Tu Fu wrote some of their best things in the so-called "ancient poetry," i.e., freer style. The whole field of Sung *Ts'e,* poems written to music, with complicated meters, and Yüan dramas, and other dramatic poetry is practically unknown to the West.

The following selections give some samples of Ancient Poems, T'ang Poems, and folk poetry.

Some Great Ancient Poems

These selections are from the classic *Book of Poetry,* edited by Confucius. History records that there were 3,000 ancient poems, and from these, Confucius made a selection of 305 poems, and moreover arranged them according to their music. A great majority of them were folk songs, or "Songs of the States," while some were sacred odes used at royal sacrifices. There are five of these odes belonging to the Shang Dynasty (B.C. 1783–1122). The background for this collection is, according to *Feng Shu T'ung,* the ancient custom of annual collecting of folk songs by officers for the purpose of finding out the state of public opinion. As will be seen, many of these were satires of the government, for the Chinese people from the earliest days showed an unusual propensity to criticize their government.

The difference between T'ang poetry and the *Book of Poetry* is the difference between a carefully arranged flower twig in a vase, where every angle and curve is carefully studied, and the luxuriant growth of a wild garden. These poems represent to us the voice of the ancient people, fresh and direct and unaffected, and sometimes unashamed. A flirt spoke the voice of a flirt, which is impossible in the poems of the T'ang scholars. We hear also an amazing variety of themes, of elopements, the maiden's longings, the forsaken wife, the divorced woman, the luxury of the rich, the hunt, wars, soldiers on service, and satires against the wealthy class.

I have tried here to give a few representative samples, by two translators who know Chinese thoroughly and one who does not. Of all translations of Chinese poetry, I think Helen Waddell's is the best, (*Lyrics from the Chinese,* Holt). She based her translations on James Legge's translation and his notes, and her translations are far from literal. Her method is to catch the essence or spirit of a poem and weave it into an exquisite creation with whatever material from the poem she needs for that particular purpose. And she is completely successful. One cannot help being impressed by the fact that the fleeting thought, the sudden heart cry of a second of some peasant woman some three thousand years ago in China can be recaptured for us in the English language by one who does not know her language. Herbert A. Giles' two poems are quite charming. Dr. Legge's translations in regard to diction, rhythm and general effect, often fall short of the true poetic level, but he did not mistranslate, and his work gives us the means of getting a glimpse of the scope and variety of the *Book of Poetry*. He has translated the *Book* complete, and some of his verses are certainly successful. Really the *Book of Poetry* is easier to translate than the T'ang poems, because there is not the problem of rendering the sophisticated subtleties of the poet's choice of words. The ancient poems can be very tender, but that tenderness is always fresh and whole and unaffected.

Ch'ü Yüan

Ch'ü Yüan (B.C. 343–c. 290) ranks undoubtedly as one of the three or four greatest poets of China characterized by his intensity of feeling, his rich mythological details, and his somber imagination. The Songs of Ch'u belong in an entirely different category from either the poems of Confucian China, or from the later T'ang poems. His poems are at the same time among those most difficult to read in Chinese.

Li Po

Li Po (A.D. 701–762) is selected here as representing the T'ang poets. He is the Prince of Chinese Poets, and is known among the Chinese as the "Poet Fairy" while Tu Fu is known as the "Poet Sage," which sufficiently characterizes the two friends. His poetry is chiefly distinguished by *élan* and romantic abandon, and a magic fairylike quality which transforms the world before him by the very use of his language. It can hardly be hoped that readers will understand his charm and melody, for Li Po has veritably the soul of music. His poems sing by themselves with an inevitableness and freedom from effort. Every syllable, every tone and every imagery co-operates to hypnotize the Chinese reader. The language he used could be simple or most ornate as he wished, but when he struck an inevitable phrase, we felt as if we had been ignorant of the Chinese language or dumb, or else we might have said it. A reliable account of Li Po's life, as well as translations of biographical notes on the poet by Chinese authors, may be found in the Introduction to Obata's *Li-Po, the Chinese Poet* (Dutton). A clear account of the general field of Chinese poetry, with some details on technique, may be found in Kiang Kang-hu's essay on "Chinese Poetry" in the introduction to Witter Bynner's *Jade Mountain* (Knopf). I regard Witter Bynner's translation of *Li Po* as on the whole the best. I have supplied a few necessary footnotes.

The Tale of Meng Chiang

The tale is one of the best known to all Chinese children. The present selection is a translation by Genevieve Wymsatt (*The Lady of the Long*

Wall, Columbia University Press) from what is known as a Chinese "drum story." The "drum story" is still one of the most popular forms of story-telling in China, and this material may be regarded as representative of Chinese folk poetry. The authors of such drum stories are generally unknown, but there is a stock of literary phrases, born of the drama, which is ever available at the hand of the professional singers who improve upon them to suit their purposes as they hand them down from generation to generation. Their language is not entirely un-literary, but it has the great virtue of being always intelligible to the common people. This is the story of the bride who went in search of her husband, conscripted to build the Great Wall, in the third century B.C., and who, upon discovering her husband's bones, wept so profusely that a section of the Great Wall melted down. It was a real story, with later alterations, that gained immediate popularity even in Han days and has never lost its hold on the people for 2,000 years.

The "drum story" can best be explained as a monologue, told with all the modulation and gestures of a monologue reciter's art, to the rhythm of a hand-drum beaten by the story-teller himself. At times, it breaks out into song. Miss Wimsatt's admirable verse rendering gives the reader a sense of the varied rhythm and dramatic intensity of the original.

Mortal Thoughts of a Nun

This is an extract from a popular Chinese drama, very much enjoyed by the Chinese audience. It is the only bit of dramatic poetry included in this anthology. Incidentally it shows the typically humorous, common-sense and irreligious attitude of the Chinese people.

Some Great Ancient Lyrics

I. POEMS TRANSLATED BY HELEN WADDELL

I

Written in B.C. 718. It is the Chinese rendering of 'the world well lost.' Possibly, as one Yen Ts'an of the thirteenth century insists, 'intended to show the error of licentious connections.'

THE gourd has still its bitter leaves,
And deep the crossing at the ford.
I wait my lord.

The ford is brimming to its banks;
The pheasant cries upon her mate.
My lord is late.

The boatman still keeps beckoning,
And others reach their journey's end.
I wait my friend.

II

Written in B.C. 826. It is inconsistent with the finest ideal of chastity that a Chinese woman should break her perpetual widowhood.

AH, let it drift, that boat of cypress wood,
There in the middle of the Ho.
He was my mate,

And until death I will go desolate.
Ah Mother! God!
How is it that ye will not understand?

Ah, let it drift, that boat of cypress wood,
  There in the middle of the Ho.
  He was my King.
I swear I will not do this evil thing.
Ah Mother! God!
How is it that ye will not understand?

III

Written in the twelfth century before Christ. It is possibly the oldest drinking-song in the world.

THE dew is heavy on the grass,
  At last the sun is set.
Fill up, fill up the cups of jade,
  The night's before us yet!

All night the dew will heavy lie
  Upon the grass and clover.
Too soon, too soon, the dew will dry,
  Too soon the night be over!

IV

Written in the twelfth century before Christ, *c.* 1121.

THE morning glory climbs above my head,
Pale flowers of white and purple, blue and red.
  I am disquieted.

Down in the withered grasses something stirred;
I thought it was his footfall that I heard.
  Then a grasshopper chirred.

I climbed the hill just as the new moon showed,
I saw him coming on the southern road.
  My heart lays down its load.

V

Written B.C. 680. The 'Little Preface': 'A man's praise of his Poor Wife.'

I WENT out at the Eastern Gate,
I saw the girls in clouds,
Like clouds they were, and soft and bright,
But in the crowds
I thought on the maid who is my light,
Down-drooping, soft as the grey twilight;
She is my mate.

I went out by the Tower on the Wall,
I saw the girls in flower,
Like flowering rushes they swayed and bent,
But in that hour
I thought on the maid who is my saint,
In her thin white robe and her colouring faint;
She is my all.

VI

Written 718 B.C. from the harem of the Palace of Wei.

THE wind blows from the North.
He looks and his eyes are cold.
He looks and smiles and then goes forth,
My grief grows old.

The wind blows and the dust.
To-morrow he swears he will come.
His words are kind, but he breaks his trust,
My heart is numb.

All day the wind blew strong,
The sun was buried deep.
I have thought of him so long, so long,
I cannot sleep.

The clouds are black with night,
The thunder brings no rain.
I wake and there is no light,
I bear my pain.

VII

Written B.C. 769 by a divorced woman.

YELLOW's the robe for honour,
And green is for disgrace.
I wear the green and not the gold,
And turn away my face.

I wear the green of scorning,
Who wore the gold so long.
I think upon the Sages,
Lest I should do them wrong.

It is for her he shames me.
I sit and think apart.
I wonder if the Sages knew
A woman's heart.

VIII

Written B.C. 826. He complains of a broken assignation.

THE willows by the Eastern Gate
Are deep in sheltering leaves.
You said 'Before the night grows late,'
—There's twittering in the eaves.

The willows by the Eastern Gate
All night in shadow are.
You said 'Before the night grows late,'
—There shines the morning star.

IX

Written B.C. 718.

I CANNOT come to you. I am afraid.
I will not come to you. There, I have said.
Though all the night I lie awake and know
That you are lying, waking, even so.
Though day by day you take the lonely road,
And come at nightfall to a dark abode.

Yet if so be you are indeed my friend,
Then in the end,
There is one road, a road I've never gone,
And down that road you shall not pass alone.
And there's one night you'll find me by your side.
The night that they shall tell me you have died.

X

Written *c.* 605 B.C.

THE rushes on the marsh are green
  And in the wind they bend.
I saw a woman walking there,
  Near daylight's end.

On the black water of the marsh,
  The lotus buds swim white.
I saw her standing by the verge
  At fall of night.

All the long night I lie awake,
  And sleep I cannot find.
I see her slim as any rush
  Sway in the wind.

I shut my eyes and see again
  The whiteness of her throat,
On the black water of the night
  Like lotus float.

XI

Written B.C. 718.

THE K'e still ripples to its banks,
  The moorfowl cry.
My hair was gathered in a knot,
  And you came by.

Selling of silk you were, a lad
  Not of our kin;
You passed at sunset on the road
  From far-off Ts'in.

The frogs were croaking in the dusk;
  The grass was wet.
We talked together, and I laughed;
  I hear it yet.

I thought that I would be your wife;
  I had your word.
And so I took the road with you,
  And crossed the ford.

I do not know when first it was
  Your eyes looked cold.
But all this was three years ago,
  And I am old.

XII

Written 769 B.C.

MY lord is gone away to serve the King.
The pigeons homing at the set of sun
Are side by side upon the courtyard wall,
And far away I hear the herdsmen call
The goats upon the hill when day is done.
But I, I know not when he will come home.
    I live the days alone.

My lord is gone away to serve the King.
I hear a pigeon stirring in the nest,
And in the field a pheasant crying late.
—She has not far to go to find her mate.
There is a hunger will not let me rest.
The days have grown to months and months to years,
And I have no more tears.

XIII

Written 675 B.C. "Is there anything whereof it may be said, 'See, this is new? it hath been already of old time, which was before us.'"

I WOULD have gone to my lord in his need,
Have galloped there all the way,
But this is a matter concerns the State,
And I, being a woman, must stay.

I watched them leaving the palace yard,
In carriage and robe of state.
I would have gone by the hills and the fords;
I know they will come too late.

I may walk in the garden and gather
Lilies of mother-of-pearl.
I had a plan would have saved the State.
—But mine are the thoughts of a girl.

The Elder Statesmen sit on the mats,
And wrangle through half the day;
A hundred plans they have drafted and dropped,
And mine was the only way.

XIV

780 B.C. Jacques Bonhomme complains of the useless stars.

I SEE on high the Milky Way,
But here's a rougher road.
The Sacred Oxen shining stand;
They do not draw our load.

The Sieve is sparkling in the South,
But good and ill come through.
The Ladle opens wide its mouth,
And pours out naught for you.

At dawn the Weaving Sisters sleep,
At dusk they rise again;
But though their Shining Shuttle flies,
They weave no robe for men.

XV

Written in the seventh century before Christ.

On the moor is the creeping grass,
Parched, thirsting for the dew,
And over it the swallows dip and pass,
The live-long summer through.
I came at sunset, fevered with the heat,
Seeking I knew not what with listless feet.

On the moor is the creeping grass,
Deep-drenchèd with the dew,
And over it the swallows dip and pass,
The live-long summer through.
You came at sunrise, ere the dew was dried.
And I am satisfied.

II. TWO POEMS TRANSLATED BY HERBERT A. GILES [1]

To a Young Gentleman

Don't come in, sir, please!
Don't break my willow-trees!
Not that *that* would very much grieve me;
But alack-a-day! what would my parents say?
And love you as I may,
I cannot bear to think what that would be.

[1] From *Chinese Poetry in English Verse,* Bernard Quaritch, London, 1898.

Don't cross my wall, sir, please!
Don't spoil my mulberry-trees!
Not that *that* would very much grieve me;
But alack-a-day! what would my brothers say?
And love you as I may,
I cannot bear to think what that would be.

Keep outside, sir, please!
Don't spoil my sandal-trees!
Not that *that* would very much grieve me;
But alack-a-day! what would the world say?
And love you as I may,
I cannot bear to think what that would be.

To a Man

You seemed a guileless youth enough,
Offering for silk your woven stuff;
But silk was not required by you:
I was the silk you had in view.
With you I crossed the ford, and while
We wandered on for many a mile
I said, "I do not wish delay,
But friends must fix our wedding-day. . . .
Oh, do not let my words give pain,
But with the autumn come again."

And then I used to watch and wait
To see you passing through the gate;
And sometimes when I watched in vain,
My tears would flow like falling rain;
But when I saw my darling boy,
I laughed and cried aloud for joy.
The fortune-tellers, you declared,
Had all pronounced us duly paired;
"Then bring a carriage," I replied,
"And I'll away to be your bride."

The mulberry-leaf, not yet undone
By autumn chill, shines in the sun.
O tender dove, I would advise,
Beware the fruit that tempts thy eyes!
O maiden fair, not yet a spouse,
List lightly not to lovers' vows!
A man may do this wrong, and time
Will fling its shadow o'er his crime;
A woman who has lost her name
Is doomed to everlasting shame.

The mulberry-tree upon the ground
Now sheds its yellow leaves around.
Three years have slipped away from me,
Since first I shared your poverty;
And now again, alas the day!
Back through the ford I take my way.
My heart is still unchanged, but you
Have uttered words now proved untrue;
And you have left me to deplore
A love that can be mine no more.

For three long years I was your wife,
And led in truth a toilsome life;
Early to rise and late to bed,
Each day alike passed o'er my head.
I honestly fulfilled my part;
And you—well, you have broke my heart.
The truth my brothers will [1] not know,
So all the more their gibes will flow.
I grieve in silence and repine
That such a wretched fate is mine.

Ah, hand in hand to face old age!—
Instead, I turn a bitter page.
Oh for the river-banks of yore;
Oh for the much-loved marshy shore;
The hours of girlhood, with my hair
Ungathered, as we lingered there.

[1] "shall" might be an improvement.

The words we spoke, that seemed so true,
I little thought that I should rue;
I little thought the vows we swore
Would some day bind us two no more.[2]

III. POEMS TRANSLATED BY JAMES LEGGE

The New Tower

(Satirizing the marriage of Duke Hsüan and his queen, who had been contracted to marry his son.)

The New tower, fresh and bright, they show,
Where its vast volume rolls the Ho;—
    For bride a palace rare.
To Wei she came, a mate to find;
She sought a husband young and kind,
    But found this mis-shaped bear.

There stands the New tower grand and high,
Where with still stream the Ho flows by;—
    For bride a palace rare.
To Wei she came, a mate to find;
She sought a husband young and kind,
    But found this mis-shaped bear.

As when the net for fish they set,
And lo! a goose ensnared they get,
    They stamp with sudden ire;
So might *she* stamp who came to wed
The genial son, and in his stead
    Got but the hump-backed sire.

The Gudeman's Awa

The gudeman's awa, for to fecht wi' the stranger,
  An' when he'll be back, oh! my hert canna tell.
The hens gae to reist, an' the beests to their manger,
  As hameward they wend frae their park on the hill.
    But hoo can I, thus left alane,
    Help thinking o' my man that's gane?

[2] Original last line reads: "Why talk about it any more?"

The gudeman's awa, for to fecht wi' the stranger,
An' lang will it be ere he see his fireside.
The hens gae to reist, an' the beests to their manger,
As the slantin' sunbeams throu the forest trees glide.
Heaven kens the lanesome things I think.
Heaven sen' my man his meat an' drink!

The Gudeman's Come Hame

The gudeman's come hame, an' his face weers a bloom,
His organ o' reeds he hads in his left han';
An' his richt han' ca's me to come till his room:—
It's siccan a joy; it's mair nor I can stan'.

The gudeman's come hame, an' he's pleesed I'll engage,
His gran' fether screen he hads in his left han';
An' his richt han' ca's me to come till the stage:—
It's siccan a joy; it's mair nor I can stan'.

The Cock is Crawin'

(*Translated into Scotch by Dr. Legge's nephew.*)

Says oor gudewife, "The cock is crawin'."
Quoth oor gudeman, "The day is dawin'."
"Get up, gudeman, an' tak a spy;
See gin the mornin'-star be high,
Syne tak a saunter roon' aboot;
There's rowth o' dyukes and geese to shoot.

"Lat flee, and bring them hame to me,
An' sic a dish as ye sall pree.
In comin' times as ower the strings
Your noddin' heed in rapture hings,
Supreme ower care, nor fasht wi' fears,
We'll baith grow auld in worth and years.

"An' when we meet the friends ye like,
I'll gie to each some little fyke;—
The lasses beads, trocks to their brithers,
An' auld-warld fairlies to their mithers.
Some nick-nack lovin' hands will fin',
To show the love that dwalls within."

The Artful Boy

O dear! that artful boy
Refuses me a word!
But, Sir, I shall enjoy
My food, though you're absurd!

O dear! that artful boy
My table will not share!
But, Sir, I shall enjoy
My rest, though you're not there!

By the Eastern Gate

By th' eastern gate, flat lies the ground,
And madder there grows on the slope.
Hard by my lover's house is found;—
He keeps away, and mocks my hope.

Where chestnuts grow, near th' eastern gate,
There stands a row, where is your home.
My heart turns aye to you, its mate,
But ah! to me you never come!

The Student With Blue Collar

You student, with the collar blue,
Long pines my heart with anxious pain.
Although I do not go to you,
Why from all word do you refrain?

O you, with girdle strings of blue,
My thoughts to you for ever roam!
Although I do not go to you,
Yet why to me should you not come?

How reckless you, how light and wild,
There by the tower upon the wall!
One day, from sight of you exiled,
As long as three long months I call.

On the Moor

On the moor, where thickly grew
Creeping grass, bent down with dew,
There a handsome man drew nigh,
'Neath whose forehead, broad and high,
Gleamed his clear and piercing eye.
'Twas by accident we met;
Glad was I my wish to get.

Where the grass creeps o'er the moor,
With the dew all covered o'er,
There the finest man found I,
'Bove whose clear and piercing eye,
Rose his forehead, broad and high.
Chance gave us a meeting rare,
And we both were happy there.

On Comes Her Chariot

(Satirizing the open shamelessness of a queen.)

On comes her chariot, fast and loud,
With screen of bamboos finely wove,
And leather bright, vermilion-hued;—
Ts'e's daughter hastes to lawless love.
To this from Loo the road is smooth and plain;
'Twas but last night she started with her train.

Her four black steeds are beautiful;
Soft are the reins the driver holds.
The road from Loo is smooth and plain;—
Ts'e's daughter's heart its joy unfolds.
Full of complacency is she; nor shame
Abashes her, nor fear of evil name.

Broad flow the waters of the Wan,
And crowds of travellers go by.
The road from Loo is smooth and plain;—
She looks around with careless eye.
That many see her gives her no concern;
Her thoughts to her licentious fancy turn.

On sweep the waters of the Wan;
More numerous are the travellers now.
The road from Loo is smooth and plain;—
Ts'e's daughter shows her brazen brow.
At ease and proud, she holds her onward way,
Careless of what all think of her display.

A Soldier's Thought of Home

To the top of that tree-clad hill I go,
And towards my father I gaze,
Till with my mind's eye his form I espy,
And my mind's ear hears how he says:—
"Alas for my son on service abroad!
He rests not from morning till eve.
May he careful be, and come back to me!
While he is away, how I grieve!"

To the top of that barren hill I climb,
And towards my mother I gaze,
Till with my mind's eye her form I espy,
And my mind's ear hears how she says:—
"Alas for my child on service abroad!
He never in sleep shuts an eye.
May he careful be, and come back to me!
In the wild may his body not lie!"

Up the lofty ridge I, toiling, ascend,
And towards my brother I gaze,
Till with my mind's eye his form I espy,
And my mind's ear hears how he says:—
"Alas! my young brother, serving abroad,
All day with his comrades must roam.
May he careful be, and come back to me,
And die not away from his home!"

The Woodman's Song

(One of the finest and most direct satires. I have taken the liberty of substituting an exact translation of the two lines at the end of each verse, where Dr. Legge versifies on his own.—Ed.)

K'an-k'an upon the sandal trees
The woodman's strokes resound.
Then on the bank he lays the trunks
His axe brings to the ground;
The while the stream goes rippling by,
Its waters cool and clear.
You sow no seed; no harvest tasks
Your soft hands take in charge;
And yet each boasts three hundred farms,
And stores the produce large.
You never join the hunt's halloo,
Nor dare to share its toils;
Yet lo! your wide courtyards are seen
Hung round with badgers' spoils.
That gentleman!
He does not eat the bread of idleness indeed!

K'an-k'an upon the sandal wood
The woodman's strokes resound,
Then by the river's side he lays
What fit for spokes is found;
The while the river onward flows,
Its waters clear and smooth.
You sow no seed; no harvest tasks
Your dainty fingers stain;
And yet each boasts three million sheaves;—
Whence gets he all that grain?
You never join the hunt's halloo,
Nor brave its ventures bold;
Yet lo! your wide courtyards display
Those boars of three years old.
That gentleman!
He does not eat the bread of idleness indeed!

K'an-k'an resound the woodman's strokes
 Upon the sandal wood;
Then on the river's lip he lays
 What for his wheels is good;
The while the river onward flows,
 Soft rippled by the wind.
You sow no seed; no harvest tasks
 Your soft hands undertake;
Yet grain each boasts, three hundred binns;—
 Who his that grain did make?
You never join the hunt's halloo;
 Your feeble courage fails;
Yet lo! your wide courtyards display
 Large strings of slaughtered quails.
That gentleman!
 He does not eat the bread of idleness indeed!

Large Rats

(The poet proposes to leave his country Wei.)

Large rats, large rats, let us entreat
That you our millet will not eat.
But the large rats we mean are you,
With whom three years we've had to do,
And all that time have never known
One look of kindness on us thrown.
We take our leave of Wei and you;
That happier land we long to view.
O happy land! O happy land!
There in our proper place we'll stand.

Large rats, large rats, let us entreat
You'll not devour our crops of wheat.
But the large rats we mean are you,
With whom three years we've had to do;
And all that time you never wrought
One kindly act to cheer our lot.

To you and Wei we bid farewell,
Soon in that happier State to dwell.
O happy State! O happy State!
There shall we learn to bless our fate.

Large rats, large rats, let us entreat
Our springing grain you will not eat.
But the large rats we mean are you,
With whom three years we've had to do.
From you there came not all that while
One word of comfort 'mid our toil.
We take our leave of you and Wei;
And to those happier coasts we flee.
O happy coasts, to you we wend!
There shall our groans and sorrows end.

Owl, O Owl!

(Written in B.C. 1113, by the great Duke of Chou, brother of King Wu. King Wu was dead and his young son was on the throne. Two of the young king's brothers had rebelled, and the Duke, who was assisting the young king, was compelled to fight the rebellion for three years. The Duke wrote this, comparing the rebels trying to destroy the Imperial house to the owls.—Ed.)

Owl, O owl, hear my request,
And do not, owl, destroy my nest.
You have taken my young,
Though I over them hung,
With the nursing of love and of care.
Pity me, pity me! Hear my prayer.

Ere the clouds the sky had obscured,
The mulberry roots I secured.
Door and window around,
Them so firmly I bound,
That I said, casting downward my eyes,
"Dare any of you my house despise?"

I tugged with my claws and I tore,
And my mouth and my claws were sore.
So the rushes I sought,
And all other things brought;
For to perfect the house I was bent,
And I grudged no toil with this intent.

My wings are deplorably torn,
And my tail is much injured and worn.
Tossed about by the wind,
While the rain beats unkind,
Oh! my house is in peril of harm,
And this note I scream out in alarm.

IV. ODES TRANSLATED BY JAMES LEGGE

Two Sacrificial Odes

I. THE TSAI SHU

(The 'Preface' says that this ode was used in spring, when the king in person turned up some furrows in the field set apart for that purpose, and prayed at the altars of the spirits of the land and the grain, for an abundant year.)

They clear away the grass and the bushes; and the ground is laid open by their ploughs. In thousands of pairs they remove the roots, some in the low wet land, some along the dykes.

There are the master and his eldest son; his younger sons, and all their children; their strong helpers and their hired servants. How the noise of their eating the viands brought to them resounds! (The husbands) think lovingly of their wives; (the wives) keep close to their husbands. (Then) with their sharp ploughshares they set to work on the south-lying acres.

They sow their various kinds of grain, each seed containing in it a germ of life. In unbroken lines rises the blade, and, well nourished, the stalks grow long. Luxuriant looks the young grain, and the weeders go among it in multitudes.

Then come the reapers in crowds. And the grain is piled up in the fields, myriads, and hundreds of thousands, and millions (of stacks); for the spirits and for sweet spirits, to offer our ancestors, male and female, and to provide for all ceremonies.

Fragrant is their aroma, enchancing the glory of the state. Like pepper is their smell, to give comfort to the aged.

It is not here only that there is this (abundance); it is not now only that there is such a time:—from of old it has been thus.

II. THE CH'U TS'E

(A poetic description of sacrificial and festive services in the ancestral temple, and their connection with husbandry.)

Thick grew the tribulus (on the ground), but they cleared away its thorny bushes. Why did they this of old? That we might plant our millet and sacrifice millet; that our millet might be abundant, and our sacrificial millet luxuriant. When our barns are full, and our stocks can be counted by tens of myriads, we proceed to make spirits and prepared grain, for offerings and sacrifice. We seat the representatives of the dead, and urge them to eat:—thus seeking to increase our bright happiness.

With correct and reverent deportment, the bulls and rams all pure, we proceed to the winter and autumnal sacrifices. Some flay (the victims); some cook (their flesh); some arrange (the meat); some adjust (the pieces of it). The officer of prayer sacrifices inside the temple gate. And all the sacrificial service is complete and brilliant. Grandly come our progenitors; their spirits happily enjoy the offerings; their filial descendant receives blessing:—they will reward him with great happiness, with myriads of years, life without end.

They attend to the furnaces with reverence; they prepare the trays, which are very large;—some for the roast meat, some for the broiled. Wives presiding are still reverent, preparing the numerous (smaller) dishes. The guests and visitors present the cup all round. Every form is according to rule; every smile and word are as they should be. The spirits quietly come, and respond with great blessings,—myriads of years as the (fitting) reward.

We are very much exhausted, and have performed every ceremony without error. The able officer of prayer announces (the will of the spirits), and goes to the filial descendant to convey it:—'Fragrant has been your filial sacrifice, and the spirits have enjoyed your spirits and viands. They confer on you a hundred blessings; each as it is desired, each as sure as law. You have been exact and expeditious; you have been correct and careful; they will ever confer on you the choicest favours, in myriads and tens of myriads.'

The ceremonies having thus been completed and the bells and drums having given their warning, the filial descendant goes to his place, and the able officer of prayer makes his announcement, 'The spirits have drunk to the full.' The great representatives of the dead then rise, and the bells and drums escort their withdrawal, (on which) the spirits tranquilly return (to whence they came). All the servants, and the presiding wives, remove (the trays and dishes) without delay. The (sacrificer's) uncles and cousins all repair to the private feast.

The musicians all go to perform, and give their soothing aid at the second blessing. Your viands are set forth; there is no dissatisfaction, but all feel happy. They drink to the full, and eat to the full; great and small, they bow their heads, (saying), 'The spirits enjoyed your spirits and viands, and will cause you to live long. Your sacrifices, all their seasons, are completely discharged by you. May your sons and your grandsons never fail to perpetuate these services!'

Ch'ü Yüan

Translated by Arthur Waley

THE GREAT SUMMONS

When Ch'ü Yüan had been exiled from the Court for nine years, he became so despondent that he feared his soul would part from his body and he would die. It was then that he made the poem called "The Great Summons," calling upon his soul not to leave him.

GREEN Spring receiveth
The vacant earth;
The white sun shineth;
Spring wind provoketh
To burst and burgeon
Each sprout and flower.
In those dark caves where Winter lurketh
Hide not, my Soul!
O Soul come back again! O, do not stray!

O Soul come back again and go not east or west, or north or south!
For to the East a mighty water drowneth Earth's other shore;
Tossed on its waves and heaving with its tides
The hornless Dragon of the Ocean rideth:
Clouds gather low and fogs enfold the sea
And gleaming ice drifts past.
O Soul go not to the East,
To the silent Valley of Sunrise!

O Soul go not to the South
Where mile on mile the earth is burnt away
And poisonous serpents slither through the flames;

Where on precipitous paths or in deep woods
Tigers and leopards prowl,
And water-scorpions wait;
Where the king-python rears his giant head.
O Soul, go not to the South
Where the three-footed tortoise spits disease!

O Soul go not to the West
Where level wastes of sand stretch on and on;
And demons rage, swine-headed, hairy-skinned,
With bulging eyes;
Who in wild laughter gnash projecting fangs.
O Soul go not to the West
Where many perils wait!

O Soul go not to the North,
To the Lame Dragon's frozen peaks;
Where trees and grasses dare not grow;
Where a river runs too wide to cross
And too deep to plumb,
And the sky is white with snow
And the cold cuts and kills.
O Soul seek not to fill
The treacherous voids of the north!

O Soul come back to idleness and peace.
In quietude enjoy
The lands of Ching and Ch'u.
There work your will and follow your desire
Till sorrow is forgot,
And carelessness shall bring you length of days.
O Soul come back to joys beyond all telling!

Where thirty cubits high at harvest-time
The corn is stacked;
Where pies are cooked of millet and bearded-maize.
Guests watch the steaming bowls
And sniff the pungency of peppered herbs.
The cunning cook adds slices of bird-flesh,

Pigeon and yellow-heron and black-crane.
They taste the badger-stew.
O Soul come back to feed on foods you love!

Next are brought
Fresh turtle, and sweet chicken cooked in cheese
Pressed by the men of Ch'u.
And pickled sucking-pig
And flesh of whelps floating in liver-sauce
With salad of minced radishes in brine;
All served with that hot spice of southernwood
The land of Wu supplies.
O Soul come back to choose the meats you love!

Roasted daw, steamed widgeon and grilled quail—
On every fowl they fare.
Boiled perch and sparrow broth,—in each preserved
The separate flavour that is most its own.
O Soul come back to where such dainties wait!

The four strong liquors are warming at the fire
So that they grate not on the drinker's throat.
How fragrant rise their fumes, how cool their taste!
Such drink is not for louts or serving-men!
And wise distillers from the land of Wu
Blend unfermented spirit with white yeast
And brew the *li* of Ch'u.
O Soul come back and let your yearnings cease!

Reed-organs from the lands of T'ai and Ch'in
And Wei and Cheng
Gladden the feasters, and old songs are sung:
The "Rider's Song" that once
Fu-hsi, the ancient monarch, made;
And the harp-songs of Ch'u.
Then after prelude from the flutes of Chao
The ballad-singer's voice rises alone.
O Soul come back to the hollow mulberry-tree! [1]

[1] The harp.

Eight and eight the dancers sway,
Weaving their steps to the poet's voice
Who speaks his odes and rhapsodies;
They tap their bells and beat their chimes
Rigidly, lest harp and flute
Should mar the measure.
Then rival singers of the Four Domains
Compete in melody, till not a tune
Is left unsung that human voice could sing.
O Soul come back and listen to their songs!

Then women enter whose red lips and dazzling teeth
Seduce the eye;
But meek and virtuous, trained in every art;
Fit sharers of play-time,
So soft their flesh and delicate their bones.
O Soul come back and let them ease your woe!

Then enter other ladies with laughing lips
And sidelong glances under moth-eyebrows;
Whose cheeks are fresh and red;
Ladies both great of heart and long of limb,
Whose beauty by sobriety is matched.
Well-padded cheeks and ears with curving rim,
High-arching eyebrows, as with compass drawn,
Great hearts and loving gestures—all are there;
Small waist and necks as slender as the clasp
Of courtiers' brooches.
O Soul come back to those whose tenderness
Drives angry thoughts away!

Last enter those
Whose every action is contrived to please;
Black-painted eyebrows and white-powdered cheeks.
They reek with scent; with their long sleeves they brush
The faces of the feasters whom they pass,
Or pluck the coats of those who will not stay.
O Soul come back to pleasures of the night!

A summer-house with spacious rooms
And a high hall with beams stained red;
A little closet in the southern wing
Reached by a private stair.
And round the house a covered way should run
Where horses might be trained.
And sometimes riding, sometimes going afoot
You shall explore, O Soul, the parks of spring;
Your jewelled axles gleaming in the sun
And yoke inlaid with gold;
Or amid orchises and sandal-trees
Shall walk in the dark woods.
O Soul come back and live for these delights!

Peacocks shall fill your gardens; you shall rear
The roc and phœnix, and red jungle-fowl,
Whose cry at dawn assembles river storks
To join the play of cranes and ibises;
Where the wild-swan all day
Pursues the glint of idle king-fishers.
O Soul come back to watch the birds in flight!

He who has found such manifold delights
Shall feel his cheeks aglow
And the blood-spirit dancing through his limbs.
Stay with me, Soul, and share
The span of days that happiness will bring;
See sons and grandsons serving at the Court
Ennobled and enriched.
O Soul come back and bring prosperity
To house and stock!

The roads that lead to Ch'u
Shall teem with travellers as thick as clouds,
A thousand miles away.
For the Five Orders of Nobility
Shall summon sages to assist the King
And with godlike discrimination choose
The wise in council; by their aid to probe

The hidden discontents of humble men
And help the lonely poor.
O Soul come back and end what we began!

Fields, villages and lanes
Shall throng with happy men;
Good rule protect the people and make known
The King's benevolence to all the land;
Stern discipline prepare
Their natures for the soft caress of Art.
O Soul come back to where the good are praised!

Like the sun shining over the four seas
Shall be the reputation of our King;
His deeds, matched only in Heaven, shall repair
The wrongs endured by every tribe of men,—
Northward to Yu and southward to Annam,
To the Sheep's Gut Mountain and the Eastern Seas.
O Soul come back to where the wise are sought!

Behold the glorious virtues of our King
Triumphant, terrible;
Behold with solemn faces in the Hall
The Three Grand Ministers walk up and down,—
None chosen for the post save landed-lords
Or, in default, Knights of the Nine Degrees.
At the first ray of dawn already is hung
The shooting-target, where with bow in hand
And arrows under arm,
Each archer does obeisance to each,
Willing to yield his rights of precedence.
O Soul come back to where honour still
The name of the Three Kings.[2]

[2] Yü, T'ang and Wen, the three just rulers of antiquity.

Li Po

Translated by Witter Bynner from the texts of Kiang Kang-hu

IN THE QUIET NIGHT

So bright a gleam on the foot of my bed—
Could there have been a frost already?
Lifting myself to look, I found that it was moonlight.
Sinking back again, I thought suddenly of home.

A BITTER LOVE

How beautiful she looks, opening the pearly casement,
And how quiet she leans, and how troubled her brow is!
You may see the tears now, bright on her cheek,
But not the man she so bitterly loves.

A SIGH FROM A STAIRCASE OF JADE

(Written to Music)

Her jade-white staircase is cold with dew;
Her silk soles are wet, she lingered there so long . . .
Behind her closed casement, why is she still waiting,
Watching through its crystal pane the glow of the autumn moon?

A FAREWELL TO MÊNG HAO-JAN ON HIS WAY TO YANG-CHOU

You have left me behind, old friend, at the Yellow Crane Terrace,
On your way to visit Yang-chou in the misty month of flowers;
Your sail, a single shadow, becomes one with the blue sky,
Till now I see only the river, on its way to heaven.

THROUGH THE YANG-TSZE GORGES

From the walls of Po-ti high in the coloured dawn
To Kiang-ling by night-fall is three hundred miles,[1]
Yet monkeys are still calling on both banks behind me
To my boat these ten thousand mountains away.

A SONG OF PURE HAPPINESS

(Written to Music for Lady Yang)

I

Her robe is a cloud, her face a flower;
Her balcony, glimmering with the bright spring dew,
Is either the tip of earth's Jade Mountain
Or a moon-edged roof of paradise.

II

There's a perfume stealing moist from a shaft of red blossom,
And a mist, through the heart, from the magical Hill of Wu—
The palaces of China have never known such beauty—
Not even Flying Swallow with all her glittering garments.

III

Lovely now together, his lady and his flowers
Lighten for ever the Emperor's eye,
As he listens to the sighing of the far spring wind
Where she leans on a railing in the Aloe Pavilion.

[1] Suggesting the speed of the current and the boat.

A MESSAGE TO MÊNG HAO-JAN

Master, I hail you from my heart,
And your fame arisen to the skies. . . .
Renouncing in ruddy youth the importance of hat and chariot,
You chose pine-trees and clouds; and now, white-haired,
Drunk with the moon, a sage of dreams,
Flower-bewitched, you are deaf to the Emperor . . .
High mountain, how I long to reach you,
Breathing your sweetness even here!

A FAREWELL TO A FRIEND

With a blue line of mountains north of the wall,
And east of the city a white curve of water,
Here you must leave me and drift away
Like a loosened water-plant hundreds of miles. . . .
I shall think of you in a floating cloud;
So in the sunset think of me.[2]
. . . We wave our hands to say good-bye,
And my horse is neighing again and again.

ON HEARING CHÜN THE BUDDHIST MONK FROM SHU PLAY HIS LUTE

The monk from Shu with his green silk lute-case,
Walking west down O-mêi Mountain,
Has brought me by one touch of the strings
The breath of pines in a thousand valleys.
I hear him in the cleansing brook,
I hear him in the icy bells;
And I feel no change[3] though the mountain darkens
And cloudy autumn heaps the sky.

[2] More literally: The sailing clouds understand the traveller's thoughts. The setting sun must go away like parting friends.
[3] Before I know it.

ON CLIMBING IN NAN-KING TO THE TERRACE OF PHŒNIXES

Phœnixes that played here once, so that the place was named for them,
Have abandoned it now to this desolate river;
The paths of Wu Palace are crooked with weeds;
The garments[4] of Chin are ancient dust.
. . . Like this green horizon halving the Three Peaks,
Like this island of White Egrets dividing the river,
A cloud has arisen between the Light of Heaven and me,
To hide his city from my melancholy heart.

DOWN CHUNG-NAN MOUNTAIN TO THE KIND PILLOW AND BOWL OF HU SSÜ

Down the blue mountain in the evening,
Moonlight was my homeward escort.
Looking back, I saw my path
Lie in levels of deep shadow . . .
I was passing the farm-house of a friend,
When his children called from a gate of thorn
And led me twining through jade bamboos
Where green vines caught and held my clothes.
And I was glad of a chance to rest
And glad of a chance to drink with my friend. . . .
We sang to the tune of the wind in the pines;
And we finished our songs as the stars went down,
When, I being drunk and my friend more than happy,
Between us we forgot the world.[5]

DRINKING ALONE WITH THE MOON

From a pot of wine among the flowers
I drank alone. There was no one with me—
Till, raising my cup, I asked the bright moon
To bring me my shadow and make us three.

[4] The scholar class.
[5] A Taoistic word is used here, hardly translatable: "forgetting the cycle or wheel of life."

Alas, the moon was unable to drink
And my shadow tagged me vacantly;
But still for a while I had these friends
To cheer me through the end of spring. . . .
I sang. The moon encouraged[6] me.
I danced. My shadow tumbled after.
As long as I knew, we were boon companions.
And then I was drunk, and we lost one another.
. . . . Shall goodwill ever be secure?
I watch the long road of the River of Stars.

IN SPRING

Your grasses up north are as blue as jade,
Our mulberries here curve green-threaded branches;
And at last you think of returning home,
Now when my heart is almost broken. . . .
O breeze of the spring, since I dare not know you,
Why part the silk curtains by my bed?

THE MOON AT THE FORTIFIED PASS

(Written to Music)

The bright moon lifts from the Mountain of Heaven
In an infinite haze of cloud and sea,
And the wind, that has come a thousand miles,
Beats at the Jade Pass battlements. . . .
China marches its men down Po-têng Road
While Tartar troops peer across blue waters of the bay . . .[7]
And since not one battle famous in history
Sent all its fighters back again,
The soldiers turn round, looking toward the border,
And think of home, with wistful eyes,
And of those tonight in the upper chambers
Who toss and sigh and cannot rest.

[6] Paced back and forth.

[7] Really the Chinghai (Blue Waters) Bay.

A SONG OF AN AUTUMN MIDNIGHT

(Written to a Su-chou Melody)

A slip of the moon hangs over the capital;
Ten thousand washing-mallets are pounding;
And the autumn wind is blowing my heart
For ever and ever toward the Jade Pass. . . .
Oh, when will the Tartar troops be conquered,
And my husband come back from the long campaign!

A SONG OF CH'ANG-KAN

(Written to Music)

My hair had hardly covered my forehead.
I[8] was picking flowers, playing by my door,
When you, my lover, on a bamboo horse,
Came trotting in circles and throwing green plums.
We lived near together on a lane in Ch'ang-kan,
Both of us young and happy-hearted.
. . . At fourteen I became your wife,
So bashful that I dared not smile,
And I lowered my head toward a dark corner
And would not turn to your thousand calls;
But at fifteen I straightened my brows and laughed,
Learning that no dust could ever seal our love,
That even unto death I would await you by my post
And would never lose heart in the tower of silent watching.[9]
. . . Then when I was sixteen, you left on a long journey
Through the Gorges of Ch'ü-t'ang, of rock and whirling water.
And then came the Fifth-month, more than I could bear,
And I tried to hear the monkeys in your lofty far-off sky.
Your footprints by our door, where I had watched you go,
Were hidden, every one of them, under green moss,
Hidden under moss too deep to sweep away.

[8] A female person is speaking.

[9] Allusion to a lover who kept a tryst with his sweetheart under a bridge. He refused to leave his rendezvous when the flood came and his girl still had not appeared. He was drowned. A second allusion to a woman who watched for her husband's return at a particular spot until she turned into stone.

And the first autumn wind added fallen leaves.
And now, in the Eighth-month, yellowing butterflies
Hover, two by two, in our west-garden grasses. . . .
And, because of all this, my heart is breaking
And I fear for my bright cheeks, lest they fade.
. . . Oh, at last, when you return through the three Pa districts,
Send me a message home ahead!
And I will come and meet you and will never mind the distance,
All the way to Chang-fêng Sha.

T'IEN-MU MOUNTAIN ASCENDED IN A DREAM

A seafaring visitor will talk about Japan,
Which waters and mists conceal beyond approach;
But Yüeh people talk about Heavenly Mother Mountain,
Still seen through its varying deepnesses of cloud.
In a straight line to heaven, its summit enters heaven,
Tops the five Holy Peaks, and casts a shadow through China
With the hundred-mile length of the Heavenly Terrace Range,
Which, just at this point, begins turning southeast.
. . . My heart and my dreams are in Wu and Yüeh
And they cross Mirror Lake all night in the moon.
And the moon lights my shadow
And me to Yien River—
With the hermitage of Hsieh still there
And the monkeys calling clearly over ripples of green water.
I wear his pegged boots
Up a ladder of blue cloud,
Sunny ocean half-way,
Holy cock-crow in space,
Myriad peaks and more valleys and nowhere a road.
Flowers lure me, rocks ease me. Day suddenly ends.
Bears, dragons, tempestuous on mountain and river,
Startle the forest and make the heights tremble.
Clouds darken with darkness of rain,
Streams pale with pallor of mist.
The Gods of Thunder and Lightning
Shatter the whole range.
The stone gate breaks asunder

Venting in the pit of heaven,
An impenetrable shadow.
. . . But now the sun and moon illumine a gold and silver terrace,
And, clad in rainbow garments, riding on the wind,
Come the queens of all the clouds, descending one by one,
With tigers for their lute-players and phœnixes for dancers.
Row upon row, like fields of hemp, range the fairy figures. . . .
I move, my soul goes flying,
I wake with a long sigh,
My pillow and my matting
Are the lost clouds I was in.
. . . And this is the way it always is with human joy:
Ten thousand things run for ever like water toward the east.
And so I take my leave of you, not knowing for how long.
. . . But let me, on my green slope, raise a white deer
And ride to you, great mountain, when I have need of you.
Oh, how can I gravely bow and scrape to men of high rank and men of
high office
Who never will suffer being shown an honest-hearted face!

PARTING AT A WINE-SHOP IN NAN-KING

A wind, bringing willow-cotton, sweetens the shop,
And a girl from Wu, pouring wine, urges me to share it
With my comrades of the city who are here to see me off;
And as each of them drains his cup, I say to him in parting,
Oh, go and ask this river running to the east
If it can travel farther than a friend's love!

HARD ROADS IN SHU

(Written to Music)

O, but it is high and very dangerous!
Such travelling is harder than scaling the blue sky.
. . . Until two rulers of this region
Pushed their way through in the misty ages,
Forty-eight thousand years had passed
With nobody arriving across the Ch'in border.

And the Great White Mountain, westward, still has only a bird's path [10]
Up to the summit of O-mei Peak—
Which was broken once by an earthquake and there were brave men lost,
Just finishing the stone rungs of their ladder toward heaven.[11]
. . . High, as on a tall flag, six dragons drive the sun,
While the river, far below, lashes its twisted course.
Such height would be hard going for even a yellow crane,
So pity the poor monkeys who have only paws to use.
The Mountain of Green Clay is formed of many circles—
Each hundred steps, we have to turn nine turns among its mounds.
Panting, we brush Orion and pass the Well Star,
Then, holding our chests with our hands and sinking to the ground with a groan,
We wonder if this westward trail will never have an end.
The formidable path ahead grows darker, darker still,
With nothing heard but the call of birds hemmed in by the ancient forest,
Male birds smoothly wheeling, following the females;
And there come to us the melancholy voices of the cuckoos
Out on the empty mountain, under the lonely moon . . .
Such travelling is harder than scaling the blue sky.
Even to hear of it turns the cheek pale,
With the highest crag barely a foot below heaven.
Dry pines hang, head down, from the face of the cliffs,
And a thousand plunging cataracts outroar one another
And send through ten thousand valleys a thunder of spinning stones.
With all this danger upon danger,
Why do people come here who live at a safe distance?
. . . Though Dagger-Tower Pass be firm and grim,
And while one man guards it
Ten thousand cannot force it,
What if he be not loyal,
But a wolf toward his fellows?
. . . There are ravenous tigers to fear in the day
And venomous reptiles in the night

[10] Mountain trail.
[11] "Only after able-bodied men perished from landslides was the suspended plank-road completed." (A road of planks was laid out on the side of the high cliffs of the Yangtse Gorges, providing entrance to Szechuen. The scene suggests the Burma Road.)

With their teeth and their fangs ready
To cut people down like hemp.
. . . Though the City of Silk be delectable, I would rather turn home quickly.
Such travelling is harder than scaling the blue sky . . .
But I still face westward with a dreary moan.

ENDLESS YEARNING

(Written to Music)

"I am endlessly yearning
To be in Ch'ang-an.
. . . Insects hum of autumn by the gold brim of the well;
A thin frost glistens like little mirrors on my cold mat;
The high lantern flickers; and deeper grows my longing.
I lift the shade and, with many a sigh, gaze upon the moon,
Single as a flower, centred from the clouds.
Above, I see the blueness and deepness of sky.
Below, I see the greenness and the restlessness of water . . .
Heaven is high, earth wide; bitter between them flies my sorrow.
Can I dream through the gateway, over the mountain?
Endless longing
Breaks my heart."

BRINGING IN THE WINE

(Written to Music)

See how the Yellow River's waters move out of heaven.
Entering the ocean, never to return.
See how lovely locks in bright mirrors in high chambers,
Though silken-black at morning, have changed by night to snow.
. . . Oh, let a man of spirit venture where he pleases
And never tip his golden cup empty toward the moon! [12]
Since heaven gave the talent, let it be employed!
Spin a thousand pieces of silver, all of them come back!
Cook a sheep, kill a cow, whet the appetite,
And make me, of three hundred bowls, one long drink!
. . . To the old master, Ts'ên,

[12] Never let the golden cup wait idly upon the moon.

And the young scholar, Tan-ch'iu,
Bring in the wine!
Let your cups never rest!
Let me sing you a song!
Let your ears attend!
What are bell and drum, rare dishes and treasure?
Let me be forever drunk and never come to reason!
Sober men of olden days and sages are forgotten,
And only the great drinkers are famous for all time.
. . . Prince Ch'ên paid at a banquet in the Palace of Perfection
Ten thousand coins for a cask of wine, with many a laugh and quip.
Why say, my host, that your money is gone?
Go and buy wine and we'll drink it together!
My flower-dappled horse,
My furs worth a thousand,
Hand them to the boy to exchange for good wine,
And we'll drown away the woes of ten thousand generations!

The Tale of Meng Chiang

A "drum story," in five cantos, translated by
Genevieve Wimsatt

PROLOGUE

(To the beat of the drum)

Shrewd the trader, Lü Pu-wei! [1]
Knowing Time must well repay
Cost and care, he dares devise
Schemes to market merchandise
Rare and strange—beguileful eyes!

Though the greedy hand essay
"Spring and Autumn's" brush again—
Daring competition—when
Discords and confusions rise
Loathed their records pass away
Never graved on hearts of men.
Crime, bequeathed from age to age,
Carries as its appanage
Wrongs born of an elder day;
Cursed through the historic page
Runs the name that all despise.
Lü takes on the regal guise
Rightful to the Line of Ying; [2]
Kingdoms six devouring,
Ch'in is battened great in size.

[1] Real father of Ch'in the First Emperor, the builder of the Great Wall.
[2] Ying is the clan name of the Ch'in rulers.

"To make the kingdom firm," Mêng Tzu[3] has said,
"Place no dependence upon streams and hills."
But Ch'in Shih Huang, first to be heralded
As Emperor of one great nation, wills
To build the Wall. The white bones of the dead
Lie near in heaps, the living flee in dread;

World-wide have tyranny and terror spread;
To the Four Seas go streaming such rank ills
That even genii weep and demons wail;
When books are burned, and lettered men are thrust
Alive into the grave, then to the dust
Is learning leveled, law and order fail
When States are riven and no Rites prevail.

CANTO I: LEAVING THE VILLAGE

She is a crystal holding Heaven's light
And glints of sunny Earth, this Mêng Chiang,
The faithful lady of Fan Ch'i Liang.
Most steadfast of all those that love the right,
Alone she stands; for since her lord was reaved
To labor at the Great Long Wall a blight
Has lain upon her beauty; she has grieved
Until her waist is like the willow wand;
 On her rouge-rejecting cheek
 Sorrow fades the colors faint;
 Left unsleek, her eyebrows speak
 All of heart-ache, naught of paint.
The East Room dream, too fleet, too fond,
Fades with the night;
The bamboo screen has been hooked up; beyond
The Northern Bourn her tranced thought wings its flight
To where the wintered sun shows dull and slight.

Wistful, she muses, "Where
Is my lord forced to bear
The heavy bricks? The scholar is but slim
And frail—and who will pity him?

[3] Same as Mengtse.

His strength is slight—and who will spare
The student? Is there none to care
How we may fare?
    Ruthless overseers dare
    Roar their biddings, crack their thongs;
    Blows and cursings are his share—
    Hapless, must he bear these wrongs?

"My lord, why bid your wife's heart follow you
Across the myriad miles? I sit alone
And watch the shadows of the lamp imbrue
The empty room with gloom. My thoughts pursue
The moon-wheel's downward track. I scan the zone
Edging the far sky where white clouds are rifting;
The shifting wind has autumn in its tone,
And down the ancient highway, drifting, drifting,
Red leaves are blown.

"To wait and wait
Breaks heart and hope—when will this vigil end?
I sigh for him, my lord of bitter fate;
When will that sun ascend
Shining on his return? Disconsolate,
I pledge my life to seek him, though there be
Outstretched to sunder us ten thousand *li!*
Though downward to the Yellow Springs I fare,[4]
Yet, even there,
My wish fulfilled may follow me."
Despite her little bow-shaped shoes,[5] despite
Her tiny hose, her small teeth gleaming white,
Her shapely brows, this lady's soul is bright
As gold and chrysolite,
Like iron is her heart.
A gown of cotton for her wear,
A paltry pin thrust in her hair,
Her charmfulness and graces furled,

[4] To the grave.
[5] Evidently an anachronism for those days, accepted by the average Chinese audience.

She goes through blowing wind and dripping rain,
And under moonbeams falling on the world
Slantwise and sinister. Alone to dare
The road affrights her heart; yet not in vain
Has she been urgent to prepare
Warm clothing for Fan Ch'i Liang to wear
In winter. Neither loyalty nor gain
Will tempt a runner to the drear campaign
Where stands the wall; but she herself will bear
The bundle on her back!
Ahead she sees
The falling, withered leaves, the frosted trees—
Suddenly cold and cutting veers the breeze!
Maples by the river's edge . . .
From the hut of fisher folk
Lonely curls the evening smoke . . .
Flocking wild geese in a wedge
Sink obliquely toward the sedge . . .
Broad, broad the sky—where is he now forlorn?
Wide, wide the earth, and one alone must mourn.

With willow waist and downcast almond eyes,
Delicate, diffident, she treads the way
With lily steps, on aching feet; her gay
Kingfisher [6] sleeves are useless when she tries.
To screen her powdered face from dust and grit;
Too sorrowful to lift her bright attire,
She lets her girdle drag through mud and mire,
Locking her brows in pain; her bundles weigh
Heavy and heavier as bit by bit
Her strength is spent.
Ah, Lady, thus to rain
Tears to the wind but wounds the heart in vain!

She sighs, "Hs-s-s-s-si, High Heaven, on what day
Shall he again behold his native land?
Departing for the Wall he cautioned me,
" 'The time of my returning needs must be
Uncertain. The Imperial Decree,

[6] Embroidered with kingfisher feather.

The Royal Messenger's command,
Who dares resist? Ai! Ai! Once I am dead,
And my white bones cast out upon the sand,
Never again may we rest head by head
On the same pillow, like the mated birds
Flying in pairs! O True Wife, heed my words;
Never oppose what you can not withstand;
Credit no dream that once again may shine
The shattered mirror! [7] Do not be misled
To think this petty property of mine
Could keep you. Do not bring to naught
The bright hopes of your spring! Your own forethought
Will tell you I perhaps shall find it hard
To come again.'

"My Lord, your words were fraught
With pity; yet recall what kind of wife
Was yours in quiet days of wedded life.
Have you forgot our heart-to-heartedness,
Matching like fish and water? [8] Why regard
Your mate as dust and ashes? Tireless
The hot blood surges in my breast; unmarred
My clear heart is a scepter of pure jade.
Knowing my purpose good I dare rely
Upon my strength. With constancy to aid
Even the heart of Heaven may be swayed.

I, when I was small and young,
From my honored father heard
Precepts, and still heed the word
Of the parent-mentor's tongue;
Ever has my heart preferred
Principles correct and straight;
Furthermore, my lord conferred
Precious counsels on his mate.

How should I venture now to turn my back
On admonitions of a learned sire,
Forget a husband's exhortations, slack
The duty that both need and right require?

[7] Symbol of separation of husband and wife.

[8] Symbol of marital happiness.

"Therefore, not by ten thousand *li* deterred,
Seeking my lord I take the track
That leads to distant boundaries."

CANTO II: IN THE DREAM

"Even the crackle of a falling leaf
Affrights the heart made timorous by grief!"

"Soon the autumn wind will send
Sun-rays slanting toward the west—
In the shelter of what home
Shall this way-worn body rest?
In the marshes where I roam,
In this alien Land-of-others,
Are there fathers? Are there mothers?
Far and wide the dried grass smothers
All the landscape; 'neath a sky
Darkly frigid, here am I!
Back to the village copse the ravens fly,
Dotting the dusk and chattering on high;
How should this timid one be undismayed
Facing the road where twilight shadows lie?
Hark! Again, again the knell
Sounding from a distant bell!
Ahead, perhaps, some hamlet site is near;
I hasten onward toward the peal I hear,
And glimpse a spot of lamplight in the glade!"
In haste the lady wipes away a tear,
And walks into the forest where the shade
Is darkest. In the gloomy depths appear
A rustic temple and a tiny shrine
Built to Lung Wang, the Dragon King.[9]
She asks herself, "What if I laid
Myself beneath the Lung Wang's sheltering
Table of sacrifice to pass the night . . .
Only a flake of body now is mine,

[9] The King of the Sea.

Wasted so thin and slight
That none would note it there . . .
Often before
I have drunk water from the forest spring
To quench my thirst; but now no store
Of food in earthen vessels could I bring
Along with me, and how shall I be fed?"

Without surcease the lady's tears are shed;
Before the holy place of worshipping
She makes her k'o t'ous,[10] while her prayers implore:

"O Dragon King, look down with grace
On Mêng Chiang, and pardon her
That she profanes your holy place,
Misfortune-driven traveller,
Hiding from the wind and frost!"

She drops her bundle to accost
The god; then from the stones embossed
With mould of ages sweeps a space,
And in the altar's cold embrace
Clenching her teeth, shutting her almond eyes,
Herself as cold as ice, she lies.

The autumn night winds penetrate her dress
In waves; lifting her head the lady spies
The hooked moon hanging slantwise in the skies;
The bright rays fall upon her dress like rime.
Toward the Cold Mansion of the Moon Goddess
Mêng Chiang Nü sighs her distress:
"Ai, Ch'ang-O, fair Lunar Queen,
Why are you thus pitiless
Toward your humble votaress?
Spacious Heaven knows your light,
On the Myriad Things your sheen
Falls in glory, silver white;
Clean and cold your beams make bright

[10] Kowtow, or kotow.

Earth's ten corners; distant are
Both celestial and terrene
Frontiers, yet these feet are less
Than three inches; long and far
Winds the road, yet must this slight
Body trail its endlessness.
I plead the holy plea, bestow a dream
On my Beloved to bring him cheer
(Clothes, too, to keep him warm in those extreme
North wilds where frost falls most severe),
Compassionate the last branch of the tree
Left sere and drear!
And pity me,
Mêng Chiang Nü, toiling ten thousand *li!*
Though this small wife not twice ten years has faced
The dusty, windy world, yet see
The shades that nest within her breast,
And on her cheeks the tracks the tears have traced!"

No sooner does the lady drowse
Than down a stretch of darkness she is led
Into the Land of Dreams.
Here is a man with knitted brows,
Holding his grief in check—tears in his eyes—
His body covered with a rotting shred
Of cloth—racked with despair he seems.

Sadly he bows his head
Before the lady as he sighs,
"Ah, Wife, do you not know Fan Ch'i Liang?
Searching for me you have not winced to tread
Ten thousand *li*. Now only in this wise,
With shattered bones, with body broke and dead
Your lord indemnifies
The toils and hardships of his Mêng Chiang!"

The dreamer in the dream replies,
"Ah, Husband, you have come!" She laughs and cries
And calls, "My Lord! My Lord . . ." She springs to press
Closer her greeting—"Lord, all happiness!"

"Already from the plum blossoms the sounds of autumn call;
Already on the lattice silk athwart the moon-beams fall. . . ."

Startled, the lady wakes. All overhead
Cluster the stars, upon the earth is spread
The hoarfrost. She recalls the dream departed
And muses, "This can not but make me dread
Some great misfortune! In the dream he said
The fragments of his bones, his body's dust
Should be my compensation, so I must
Ponder this vision all but broken-hearted . . .

"Perhaps, over wide waters and high hills
This dream has traveled joltingly, and thus
Its contents were inverted, goods and ills . . .
A dream is only what the dreamer wills,"
She solaces herself. "My vagrant thought
Was masterless . . . Ah, is it fate
That I should seek my mate
Beneath the earth? If destiny has wrought
This condemnation, how can I do aught
But meet the doom? Yet let one hope abide—
At last to rest me by my husband's side!
Now am I fearful lest without avail
I perish half way on the road and fail
To meet my lord. Hsi! Hsi! that I am frail
And soft as water! At the midnight hour
Empty and shaking in the dark I cower
Beneath the altar stone."

The sky is pale
Before the rising sun, the frost-touched vale
Is damp, the ravens from the tree tops flit,
And orioles begin to dart and twit
Along the ancient way.

The lady rises with the dawn to say
Adieu to each and every little Kuei[11]

[11] Earthly spirit.

Guarding the shrine. Before the Dragon King
She lifts her eyes and kneels to pray.
Her jade-fine fingers fix the covering
About the bundle; in her heart is strife
Of hope and sorrow; bowed beneath her load
She sighs.
"Of all the ills that here are rife
To journey with no goal is first and worst—
Yet, even this, the utmost ill of life,
Attests the unity of man and wife."

CANTO III: OVERNIGHT AT THE INN

"Rustling sounds of early fall . . .
Down the ancient highway brawl
Whirling leaf and dusty squall . . ."

From her locked brows the paint is blown,
The rouge is rifled from her face,
Her tender breast at night has known
The soaking dews; with swaying grace
She wavers in the wind's embrace.

"Where are you now, my lord, alive, or dead?
Not knowing this I can not rightly know
Toward what end I should strive.
I dream that on my brows I still can feel
The paint strokes that you sketched there long ago[12] . . .
We two have played the harp amid the flowers
In the serenity of moon-lit hours
Heralding autumn's coming. . . . Now I go
Toward the Long Wall . . . and will the end reveal
My Lord? Stark desolation lowers
Along the road I tread, wishing in vain
That you might come to share the evening meal . . .
Perhaps, never again
Shall we two steal
Together up the stairs. . . .

[12] Allusion to a scholar who painted her eyebrows for his bride.

Hsi, hsi! What crime,
My lord, did you commit in that dim time
Before your birth that we must bear this woe?
I sigh, and rub my bruised soles where the pain
Is sharpest. Now am I
Like the small floweret, yellow, dry. . . .

"When, suddenly, the gusts of autumn blow,
Against my shoulders, red, red leaves are whirled:
The saddest spot, perhaps, in all the world
Is but the pathway where few footprints show.
Deep in these woods, from maple tree and oak
Thick falling leaves darken the air like smoke;
Sometimes I pass a newly rifled tomb;
Sometimes, dark footprints on the frosted bridge
Spanning the freshet's spume;
Sometimes I see the cock perched on the ridge
A-top the rush-thatched inn and hear him crow,
While in the moonlight of the court below
The watch dogs bark before the wattled door;
Sometimes the blackbirds to the tree tops soar . . .
Over these scenes of solitude I pore,
And one by one they fill my heart with gloom."

The sun has reached its high meridian,
And still the lady has not broken fast;
Early or late, she knows, the traveler can
Get porridge at the village inn. At last
She finds a hostel where the holder's clan
Is dwelling. Here the Good Dame of the inn
Notes that although the lady's traveling gear
Is scant and poor, yet is her air
Gentle and elegant.
She asks, "What fare,
A meal or less, would you be served with here?"

The guest replies, "Only what you prepare
For every day, rice gruel from the pot,
That is enough."

She eats a frugal share
Of congee, then, revived, she starts to blot
And pat the moisture from her peach bloom cheeks
And willow brows with every winsome phase
Of charm, and myriad shy, engaging ways.

Watching her lovely guest the hostess speaks,
"What a fine lady! There's nobility
About her, though there's trouble in her gaze."

She questions, "Gentle Lady, tell me where
You come from, tell me where you think to go."

Mêng Chiang Nü sighs as the tear drops flow,
"The Long Wall is our endless enemy!
To labor at its building did they tear
My husband from his home. My heart has striven
Toward him in vain across ten thousand *li,*
To barren hill tops have my tears been given!
Boundary wind and winter snow
Chill the world; the thin smoke driven
By the tempest to and fro
Saps the sun's enfeebled glow;
Laden, toward my lord I go—
Bearing bundles dulls the woe—
Plodding onward fagged and slow
Numbs the heart by sorrow riven.
As, when the stream runs dry the rocks appear,
So, at the journey's end, when I draw near
The Great Long Wall my heart shall be at rest.
Yet, even this, the uncompleted quest,
Is better than the aching, breaking heart,
The shedding of the futile, bloody tear!"

"Nonsense!" the Good Dame says. "Let be! Let be!
How tramp a thousand—nay, ten thousand *li!*
The eighth and ninth months shift the seasons cold.
One body small, one pair of tiny feet,
While in the mountains lurk the bandits bold,

And everywhere there's crime and knavery!
The wind blows straight south-west. Lady, behold,
You face north-east. Your journey was begun
When summer smiled, but now the autumn's done.
These facts have force to wake the sympathy
Of mere on-lookers, Lady, have they none
To wake your fears? Wherever there may be
A comely woman, who will guarantee
There'll spring no brigand armed with club and knife?"

The pilgrim answers, "Sages all agree
That of the Five Relations of this life
Foremost is that between the Man and Wife.
This is, for womankind, the only one
To hold, the other four are not our care.
I have received with glad humility
Your kind instructions, and I am aware
Of all these perils. Yet, caught in the snare
Of this hard enterprise, my foolish heart
Can rest no more in quiet. I depart
Determined that there shall be no returning
(Although our meeting be beneath the ground!)
Until the silken strand of love shall wind
To rest upon the paired Teals'[13] burial mound,
Or on the high crests of the Fir Trees yearning
Together with their branches intertwined."[14]

The hostess, shaken by the lady's pain
Lets her lips quiver and her tear drops rain
To see such piteous courage.
"Ai!" she sobs,
"For you and your mishaps my old heart throbs!
To change the past, whatever can we do?
You must not go! You can not well remain!
I'd like to venture this old frame of mine,

[13] Usually translated as "mandarin ducks" who swim in pairs and are the symbol of marital happiness.
[14] The two trees with intertwined branches, also a symbol of union between lovers.

Could it avail, to come along with you!
For though it, also, is but weak, yet two
Are better than one lady all alone."

Mêng Chiang draws a long and trembling breath,
And answers, "Should I dare to be the death
Of one so venerable who has shown
Me kindness? Such an act would ill accord
With the Proprieties! My heart shall hoard
Your mother-fondness. On some other day
When I return from searching for my lord,
All this shall I repay."

The Good Dame, seeing nothing can be done
To change the lady's purpose, goes to spread
Mats for the resting place;
Then these two light the lamp, and face to face
Sit talking on and on.
Ah, from the shed
The rooster crows in protest at delay!
The night-watch drums with dawn are quieted;
Taking her bundle, making no more stay
For rest, the lady hastens on her way.

CANTO IV: SIGHS ON THE ROAD

Gustily the night winds sigh,
Dawn is near,
Fresh and magical and clear;
Fallen leaves
Frolic over hill and mere;
Dense dew cleaves
Glistening to the grasses dry;
Stars appear
Lusterless against the sky;
Through the high
Boughs of trees the sun-beams strike;
Wanders here

Mêng Chiang, the pilgrim fair,
    Treading where
Prints of human feet are rare.
    From the West
Blows the wind her shadow-like
    Form must breast;
Tinged with blood her tears are shed
    Jewel-red;
Up the rocky road must tread
    Feet that wear
Shoes embroidered and compressed—
    Where to rest?
In her bones aching is bred;
    Hsi! Hsi! Hsi!
Like the faded yellow bloom
    Presently
She must meet the autumn doom.
    How to bear
Killing cold, and not despair?
    How to dare
Cutting blasts of winter blown
    To the bone?

Her tiny feet traverse the icy zone,
Daunted by winter's wrath she is alone
Like the thin rush left shaking in the breeze.
    Heavy-hearted, in a daze,
    Staring down that road of sighs,
    There she sees before her eyes
    Myriad mountain peaks arise
    Purple in the distant haze.
"Oh, Highest Heaven," Mêng Chiang makes moan,
"My heart is breaking, and who hears my pleas?
Who listens to my prayer when I complain
At this embitterment of heart and brain?
Where is the Great Long Wall?"
                                        At length,
Her eyes still stinging from the squall,
She girds her strength

And mounts the lifting *li* that crawl
Over the mountains, asking all
She meets for tidings of her lord.

Just now at Shan Hai Kuan,[15] peasants advise,
The Long Wall builders push the work abhorred.

Glad hope and newborn cheer suffuse
The lady's heart at this good news.
"Then, right ahead my high-road lies!
If once again I see his face
The hardships of this enterprise
Will vanish from my mind without a trace!"

Now turn to this, mark how Ch'in Shih Huang Ti
To guard the nation builds the Great Long Wall,
And orders Mêng T'ien to oversee
The work for speediest accomplishment.
The people's wealth is drained and spent,
Their strength is taxed, their energy
Is sapped, the marrow of their bones
Is sucked; ground down by heavy toil they die.

Over high mountain peaks the masses haul
Water, and up the steep ascent
Panting, they drag the heavy stones.
They clamber over cliff and crag—
Even by star-and-moonlight who dares lag?
The corpses of the laborers that fall
Are flung into the Wall, the bones of men
Dead from hard work are piled up mountain-tall
Along the way.
Up to the Jasper River[16]
Rises the breath of bitter discontent;
A shiver shakes the earth, the Heavens quiver
Hearing the loud lament.

[15] The eastern end of the Great Wall, northeast of Tientsin, where the Great Wall runs into the sea.
[16] The Milky Way.

Fan Ch'i Liang, torn from his native land,
Conscripted in the Wall-ward driven band
Of laborers, what hope is there for him?
How can the man of letters long withstand
This unremitting toil? The ending grim
Must be his death before the term is past.

Ai! Ai! That hence the scholar's soul is torn
To track the sinking moon and trail the whim
Of veering winds!
Some fellow workmen mourn
Their friend, and pitying his fate forlorn
Bury his body in the rubble massed
Between the bricks.
This is a day of rest
To celebrate the bright Mid-Autumn Feast;
From work the driven masons are released
By the Imperial Officer's command.
And just today Mêng Chiang ends her quest,
Reaching the bourn by farthest frontiers spanned.

Here the scene is different;
Here the Long Wall girds each bleak
Mountain peak to mountain peak
Where the Pass bellipotent
Rears into the firmament.

Sighing, the lady gazes on the view—
"Truly," she muses, "can a fixed resolve
Upturn the seas and make the hills revolve!
But for firm heart and constant mind
Who could have found strength to pursue
This road, leaving ten thousand *li* behind,
Ascending step by step?
But where so few
Families dwell it may be hard to find
Someone to lead me to my husband's side!"

She stands perplexed, not knowing what to do,
When, suddenly, she sees some workers stride

Straight toward the Portal. One, with countenance
Weathered and sad, with clothing torn and frayed,
Holds spirit money.[17]
"Surely, there's a chance
They know him! Why should I not ask their aid?"
Mêng Chiang Nü hastens her shy advance
Meeting the group, and crying, "Sirs, please wait
A moment!"
Now the workers check their gait,
Hailing the stranger with sedate
Greetings. They see that though her glance
Is modest, yet her spirit is depressed;
That though her cotton skirt is torn,
Her clothing dusty, and rude pins of thorn
Fasten her hair, yet here is manifest
The stamp of one well bred and nobly born—
She is a crystal holding Heaven's light,
With beauty graced, with gentle virtues blessed.
The lady asks, "Among the men impressed
To labor here where hill and sea unite,
Sirs, does Fan Ch'i Liang toil with the rest?
He is my husband."
Moved, the masons say,
"It is for him that we have come today!
Because our brother Fan was young and slight,
And unaccustomed to the fag and moil
Of heavy labor he has died from toil.
And since we fellow workers could not bear
To leave his corpse exposed to sun and air,
In the Long Wall we buried him by night.

"Now, at Mid-Autumn when the builders share
A feast, we come with simple rite
To burn our paper money, and attest
Our friendship."
While the laborers recite
Their tale, they see the lady's form recoil
And drop, her almond eyes close in despair.

[17] Paper money burnt for the use of the deceased in the underworld.

CANTO V: RECOGNIZING THE BONES

"Parting from loved ones most embitters life . . .
Close is the bond uniting man and wife."

Once Mêng Chiang hears that her lord is dead,
To the Nine Heavens ranged beyond the skies
Torn from her breast her ravaged spirit flies.

"Like the frail flower that the marchers tread,
Like the pale moon by clouds discomfited . . ."

From choking throat break forth her stifled cries;
She screams, "Ah, Husband!" careless of the eyes
Regarding her, benumbed and stupefied
She crumbles to the ground; senseless she lies
Her eyes wide open fixed against the light,
Staring, her peach-like mouth drooping and wryed,
Her red lips silver white.

She stirs, she moans, "Hsi, I am slain!
Why should High Heaven thus requite
The good? My lord was careful to observe
All the Proprieties; there was no Rite
Ignored by him; learned, he could explain
The Classics; dutiful, he did not swerve
From Righteousness; he studied to attain
To moral excellence, and was resigned
To follow all that Heaven should ordain.
He knew the Sacred Books and could define
Their teachings. Many are the hearts that yearn
To see Fan Ch'i Liang return
To glorify his name. Who knows that he
Is vanished like a stone tossed in the sea,
Not to be seen, not to be heard again?

"The rest house on the long road where we parted,
His earnest words, his last farewell to me
That might have moved the stony-hearted,

Can I forget? My lord, did you not say,
'Husband and wife, like wood birds flying free,
Are paired; yet when the day
Of doom has come they, too, must separate.
Do I not wish that man might be
Ever triumphant, woman dear?
That bonds of married unity
Might never warp or terminate?
Ai! Ai! In what forgotten sphere
Were sinned those sins which antedate
And mold the punishments which here
We blindly bear to expiate
Old crimes? What man can conquer Fate?
From the Long Wall there is no track
By which the builder may come back.
We two, I think, shall meet no more,
Except as in the fortunate
Dream of the Duke of Chou of yore.'

"Now are fulfilled the words you spoke afore!
You have met misadventures strange and sore!
To what horizons desolate
Have you called for me to commiserate
Your lonely soul?
I only know that wide and great
Stretches an empty universe; I dare
Not turn to look behind; before me where
Is there a home? No path leads on ahead;
There is no roadway back, only one gate
Opens to me . . .
Hs-s-s-si! when I am dead
There is no fear but that the pallid dust
Of my blanched bones, unburied, will be whirled
By aimless winds across the world!"
The workmen, hearing Mêng Chiang lament,
Seeing her cry as though her heart would break,
Press forward, urging, "Lady, only take
A little rest, and cease your bitter weeping!"

Quickly the lady stills the turbulent
Outburst of grief, and thanks the builders, keeping
Her tears in check.
"The grace that you have shown
In burying my husband shall be scored
Upon my heart as though engraved on bone.
My words are weak, my woman's strength is spent . . .
Sirs, tell me where my husband lies alone
That I may seek his grave."
With one accord
The workers weep, and say, "Lady, we, too,
Will go along and at the grave bemoan
Our brother's spirit and condole with you."

Mêng Chiang Nü fastens the rain cloth straight
About the pack, shoulders the heavy weight,
And follows. As late autumn floods break through
Wrecking their channels, so her tears are poured,
Breaking her heart.
Soon there beyond the Pass
Along the coast she sees the rolling mass
Of waters swirl itself against the blue
Clouds to the very roof of Heaven soared.
Wall and Eastern Sea unite
At the shore; a thousand times
On the grisly ramp that climbs
Unresisted to the height,
Parapet repeats the threat
Caught from farther parapet.
Here bricks are piled, and ashes strew the ground,
Over the dreary scene the rude winds fling
Deep dust, sweeping the acrid smoke to sting
The eyes; bleak winter's glacial blasts confound
The soul.
Mêng Chiang Nü cries, shuddering,
"This deadly cold! What mortal could endure
The rigors of this plain? On the bleak moor
My husband's body lies beneath a mound
Of yellow earth amid the autumn wood!"

Then to the group her eyes in question cling—
"But here, in this abandoned, barren space,"
She puzzles, "Sirs, there is no sign or trace
Of any grave . . ."
They answer, as sighs wring
Their hearts, "Lady, let it be understood
This is Imperial Ground, a seizin place
Held by the Reigning House; who would—who could—
Dare raise a burial mound? Here at the base
Of the Long Wall our brother's body lies.
Moved by our sense of common brotherhood,
We have devoted to his memory
A three-foot stone, white, bearing on its face
Your husband's now-immortal name to be
His tomb-tablet."
The workers point, "Here, see,
Just at this stone!"
The lady bends above
The slab sunk at the Wall, whereon a name
That neither sun nor wind can quite erase,
Nor grinding dust, shows mistily.

Mêng Chiang's heart burns with her baffled love
Like straw devoured by flame;
Against the Wall she beats her wasted frame,
Crying,
"Ah, Husband, whither strays
Your orphaned spirit? Now for whom
Has your small wife embraced the doom
Of homelessness, and all these days
Traveled the myriad-*li*-long ways?
Despite the distance and the gloom,
This foolish-hearted one has clung
To the fond hope that through the maze
She still might find her lord among
The living. Now the wild grass plume
Flickers its shadow on your tomb—
Like sunken pearl, like shattered jade,
You perish, leaving me to gaze

Upon a moon that mists consume,
Swift-sinking stars that dull and fade,
Clouds that the winds have rent and frayed!
My world forever and forever
Is but a lotus-pod adrift—
Though Fate itself had willed this gift
Of meeting, now it could be—never!"

Mêng Chiang's love and fervent purpose rise
Straight from the earth and pierce the very skies!
Ai, of a truth, such constancy can sway
The Heavens, and move even Shên and Kuei.[18]
This lady, searching for her husband's bones,
Cries, and the Wall is riven, earth and stones!

Startled, the Wall Official makes report
Of this event to the Imperial Court.
The Son of Heaven, Shih Huang Ti, elects
The lady for his palace!
She rejects
The summons! Clasping to her faithful breast
Her husband's bones, she stands upon the crest
Of the Long Wall—a leap, a flash, and she
Is lost forever in the Eastern Sea!

Now Shih Huang Ti approves her constancy,
And issues an Imperial Decree
For rites and ceremonies in her name,
Ordering that a temple to her fame
Be built close by the wall beyond the Portal—
The lady, Mêng Chiang, is an Immortal!

[18] *Shen,* the celestial spirits; *Kuei,* the earthly spirits.

The Mortal Thoughts of a Nun

Translated from a popular drama by Lin Yutang

A young nun am I, sixteen years of age;
My head was shaven in my young maidenhood.

For my father, he loves the Buddhist sutras,
And my mother, she loves the Buddhist priests.

Morning and night, morning and night,
I burn incense and I pray, for I
Was born a sickly child, full of ills.
So they sent me here into this monastery.

Amitabha! Amitabha!
Unceasingly I pray.
Oh, tired am I of the humming of the drums and the tinkling of the bells;
Tired am I of the droning of the prayers and the crooning of the priors;
The chatter and the clatter of unintelligible charms,
The clamor and the clangor of interminable chants,
The mumbling and the murmuring of monotonous psalms.
Prajnaparamita, Mayura-sutra,
Saddharmapundarika—
Oh, how I hate them all!

While I say Mitabha,
I sigh for my beau.
While I chant saparah,
My heart cries, "Oh!"
While I sing tarata,
My heart palpitates so!

Ah, let me take a stroll,
Let me take a stroll!

(She comes to the Hall of the Five Hundred Lohans, or Arahats, Buddhist saints, who are known for their distinctive facial expressions.)

Ah, here are the Lohan,
What a bunch of silly, amorous souls!
Every one a bearded man!
How each his eyes at me rolls!

Look at the one hugging his knees!
His lips are mumbling my name so!
And the one with his cheek in his hand,
As though thinking of me so!
That one has a pair of dreamy eyes,
Dreaming dreams of me so!

But the Lohan in sackcloth!
What is he after,
With his hellish, heathenish laughter?
With his roaring, rollicking laughter,
Laughing at me so!
—Laughing at me, for
When beauty is past and youth is lost,
Who will marry an old crone?
When beauty is faded and youth is jaded,
Who will marry an old, shrivelled cocoon?

The one holding a dragon,
He is cynical;
The one riding a tiger,
He is quizzical;
And that long-browed handsome giant,
He seems pitiful,
For what will become of me when my beauty is gone?

These candles of the altar,
They are not for my bridal chamber.

These long incense-containers,
    They are not for my bridal parlor.
And the straw prayer-cushions,
    They cannot serve as quilt or cover.

  Oh, God!
Whence comes this burning, suffocating ardor?
    Whence comes this strange, infernal, unearthly ardor?
I'll tear these monkish robes!
    I'll bury all the Buddhist sutras;
I'll drown the wooden fish,
    And leave all the monastic putras!

I'll leave the drums,
    I'll leave the bells,
        And the chants,
            And the yells,
And all the interminable, exasperating, religious chatter!
I'll go downhill, and find me a young and handsome lover—
Let him scold me, beat me!
    Kick or ill-treat me!
I will *not* become a Buddha!
I will *not* mumble mita, prajna, para!

SKETCHES OF CHINESE LIFE

Chinese Tales

INTRODUCTION

THE DIFFERENCE between China and the modern world that we call Western is that in the West children believe in fairies while in China the adults do so. The capacity for belief is what the modern world has lost on the whole, to our advantage or disadvantage no one can say. Shakespeare believed in a lot of things that we wise prophets of the latter days do not. But we terribly misjudge when we project our idea of verifiable truth and confuse it with poetic truth or the truth of imagination. Our whole attitude toward truth has been vitiated by our scientific training and we can no longer be interested in a truth that cannot pull a locomotive or work a steam shovel. What we have lost is fancy, or that pleasurable borderland between truth and fiction where the two merge and it becomes unimportant which is which. That is why we can no longer produce the great myths that were associated with religion; the self-conscious mind of the modern man has lost its simple naïveté. But this difference is no longer between Eastern and Western; it is a difference between this scientific age and all previous ages of all countries. Man did delight in fairies before the nineteenth century, except for a few staid, rationalist souls like Voltaire and Wang Ch'ung.

Consequently, Chinese literature abounds in tales of ghosts, goblins, fox spirits, genii and double personalities. Such stories may be read in Herbert A. Giles' *Strange Stories from a Chinese Studio* (Boni and Liveright). The best collection of Chinese short stories is *Chinku Ch'ikuan,* eleven of which have been excellently translated by E. Butts Howell (*Inconstancy of Madame Chuang* and *The Restitution of the Bride,* Brentano). These are longer stories and show a higher development of the story-teller's art. It is needless to say that the vast fund of Chinese stories has scarcely been touched.

In the present selection, I have chosen a few shorter ones that are either typical or have some special significance. The first two stories of judgments are interesting as showing resemblance to a biblical story. "The Chinese Cinderella" should be interesting to students of folk-lore. "The Tale of Ch'ienniang" is typical of those weird tales wherein a man's spirit can depart from its body. The next two are early tales of the fourth century with a peculiar droll humor, typical of the period. "The Brothers' Search for Their Father" and "The Private History of Queen Feiyen" are strictly true stories and belong to history rather than fiction. I have chosen them because they are "curious" from the Western point of view, but are strictly authentic. Like the "Six Chapters of a Floating Life," they may be regarded as documents affording real glimpses into Chinese life. All these stories have never been translated into English before, except "The Tale of Ch'ienniang" which was included in *My Country and My People*. Of course, I have not included Chinese jokes and humorous stories which form something of a dessert by themselves.

Chinese Tales

Translated by Lin Yutang

THE JUDGMENT BETWEEN TWO MOTHERS

(From Fengshut'ung, Second Century)

(This and the following story with the same motive are told in *Fengshut'ung,* written by Ying Shao who lived certainly in the years A.D. 178–197. The resemblance with the biblical story of Solomon's judgment in *Kings* is striking. A story of the same theme is found in the Commentary to the *Jātakas,* or Buddhist "birth stories," probably written by Buddhaghosha in the fifth century, A.D. in India.[1] The two stories, however, are not found in the present copy of *Fengshut'ung,* but in Ma Tsung's *Yilin* of the T'ang Dynasty, which is a book of selections from the ancient philosophers, very much prized because many of its selections vary from present texts, of Laotse, Chuangtse, Mencius, etc., or preserve passages from ancient books known to have existed but are now lost. Ying Shao's work was well known and the official bibliography of the History of Shui around A.D. 600, recorded the book as consisting of thirty-one volumes, while the present copy consists only of ten volumes. The *Yilin* itself is known to have been a book of selections based on an earlier work by Yu Chungyung of the Liang Dynasty (A.D. 546–556). Chinese translations of Buddhist works began in the first century, A.D. The resemblance with Solomon's story could well have been a coincidence.—*Ed.*)

In Yingch'uan,[2] there were two brothers living in the same house, and both sisters-in-law were expecting. The elder woman had a miscarriage, but did not let any one know about it. When both women were in confinement and the younger sister-in-law was delivered of a boy, the

[1] Rhys Davids, *Buddhist Birth-Stories.* I, xiii, xliv.

[2] Ying Shao's own native district, in present Honan.

elder one stole her child at night and, for three years, the dispute could not be settled. When the case was brought before the Chief Minister Huang Pa,[3] he ordered the baby to be placed ten steps away from the two mothers. At a signal, the two women rushed for the child and it seemed the baby was being torn to pieces and neither would give it up. The baby was crying desperately, and the mother was afraid he might be hurt and let him go. The elder woman was very pleased, while the younger woman looked very sorrowful. Then Huang Pa declared, "It is the younger one's child." He indicted the elder woman and she was indeed found guilty.

THE JUDGMENT ON A DISPUTE

(*From Fengshut'ung, Second Century*)

At Linhuai, a silk merchant was carrying a piece of waterproof silk to the city for sale. There came a rain and he spread it over his head for shelter, and soon another man came to stand under it. When the rain had stopped, both of them claimed that the silk was his own. The Chief Minister Hsüeh Hsüan said, "This piece of waterproof silk is only worth several hundred cash. Why fight over it?" Thereupon he cut it in two and gave each one half. As he continued to watch them, he saw the owner was protesting that he had been wronged, while the other man seemed well satisfied. And so he knew to which one the silk rightfully belonged, and the other man was found guilty and punished.

THE CHINESE CINDERELLA

(*From Yuyang Tsatsu, Ninth Century*)

(This is the earliest-known Cinderella story in writing in the world. The Cinderella story is one of most widespread folk tales in the world, and hundreds of versions have been collected and studied and compared by scholars.[4] However, according to Professor R. D. Jameson, an authority on this topic in the Far East, who has kindly corresponded with me on the subject, "It [the version here] antedates the earliest Western version by Des Perriers in his *Nouvelles Récréations et Iojeux Devis,* Lyon, 1558, by some 700 years." The Chinese version is from *Yuyang Tsatsu,* a book of weird, supernatural tales as well as historical learning, written by Tuan Ch'eng-shih, who died in

[3] Well-known character in the time of the Three Kingdoms.

[4] Marion Rolfe Cox, *Cinderella, Three Hundred and Forty-five Variants* (London, Folklore Society, 1893).

63 A.D. The story was told him by an old servant of his family who was rom Yungchow [modern Nanning] in Kwangsi, and who came from the ave people [aborigines] of that district. Tuan was a premier's son and a cholar, and in *Yuyang Tsatsu,* in several instances, he traced certain Chinese olk tales to Buddhist classics, for in the ninth century, Buddhist supernatural tories were well known and popular in China. However, this story was stated o have come first hand from an oral tradition. There are well-known Siamese ersions of the Cinderella story, and Nanning is very close to Indo-China. n response to my inquiry whether this version could have come from India, rofessor Jameson said, "So far as my evidence goes, at least, the oldest version n print is Chinese. We know far too little of the process of the human magination and far too many spots on the folkloristic map of Asia are entirely unexplored to justify, it seems to me, too much speculation." The striking thing about this Chinese version is that it contains the elements of both he Slavonic tradition, where an animal friend is an important feature, and the Germanic tradition, where the loss of the slipper at a ball is the important eature. The cruel stepmother and stepsisters are common to both.—*Ed.*)

Once, before the time of Ch'in[5] and Han there was a chief of a mountain cave whom the natives called Cave Chief Wu. He married two women, one of whom died leaving him a baby girl named Yeh Hsien. She was very intelligent and clever at working on gold and her father loved her dearly, but when he died she was maltreated by her stepmother who often forced her to cut wood and sent her to dangerous places to draw water from deep wells.

One day, Yeh Hsien caught a fish more than two inches long with red fins and golden eyes and she brought it home and placed it in a basin of water. Every day it grew larger and larger until finally the bowl wouldn't hold it at all and she placed it in the pond back of her home. Yeh Hsien used to feed it with what she had saved from her own food. When she came to the pond, the fish would rise to the surface and pillow its head on the bank, but if anyone else came to the water's edge it would never appear.

This curious behavior was noticed by the stepmother and she waited for the fish but the latter would never come up. One day she resorted to a ruse and said to the girl, "Aren't you tired from work? I will give you a new jacket." Then she made Yeh Hsien take off her old clothing, and sent her off to a distance of several hundred *li* to draw water from

[5] B.C. 222–206.

another well. The mother then put on Yeh Hsien's dress, and hiding sharp knife in her sleeve, went towards the pond and called to the fish. When the fish put its head out of the water, she killed it. The fish was by that time already over ten feet long, and when it was cooked, it tasted so many times better than other fish. And the mother buried its bones in a dunghill.

Next day, Yeh Hsien came back and when she approached the pond she found the fish had vanished. Thereupon she wept in the wilds when a man with disheveled hair and in a ragged garment descended from the sky and comforted her, saying, "Do not cry. Your mother has killed the fish, and its bones are buried under a dunghill. Go home and carry the bones to your room and hide them. Whatever you shall want pray to it and your wish will be granted." Yeh Hsien followed his advice, and it was not long before she had gold and jewelry and finery of such costly texture that they would have delighted the heart of any young maiden.

The night of the cave festival Yeh Hsien was told to stay at home and watch the fruit orchard. When the lonely girl saw that her mother had gone a long distance, she arrayed herself in a green silk jacket and followed to the cave. Her sister who had recognized her turned to the mother, saying, "Is that girl not strangely like my elder sister?" The mother also seemed to recognize her. When Yeh Hsien became aware of their glances she ran away, but in such haste that she dropped one of her slippers which fell into the hands of the cave people.

When the mother came back home, she found her daughter sleeping with her arms around a tree; so she put aside any thoughts she may have had (about the identity of the finely dressed lady).

Now near the caves, there was an island kingdom called T'o Huan. Through its strong army, it ruled over a couple of dozen islands, and its territorial waters covered several thousand *li*. The cave people therefore sold the slipper to the T'o Huan Kingdom, where it found its way to the King. The King made (the women of) his household try it on, but the slipper was an inch too short for those who had small feet. Then he had all of the women of the Kingdom try it, and none could fit.

The King then suspected the cave man of getting the slipper from dubious sources and imprisoned and tortured him. But that unfortunate soul could not tell where the shoe came from. Finally it was placed by the roadside and couriers were sent from house to house to arrest anyone who had the slipper. The King was greatly puzzled.

The house was searched and Yeh Hsien was found. She was made to ut the slippers on, and they fitted her perfectly. She then appeared in er slippers and her green silk dress, looking like a goddess. Then a eport was made to the King, and the King brought Yeh Hsien to his land home, together with her fish bones.

After Yeh Hsien had left the cave, the mother and sister were killed y flying stones. The cave people pitied them and buried them in a it and erected a tomb which they called "The Tomb of Regretful Vomen." The cave people worshipped them as the goddesses of match-nakers and whenever anyone asked them a favor regarding marriage, ney were sure to have their prayer granted.

The King returned to his island and made Yeh Hsien his first wife. ut during the first year of their marriage he asked the fish bones for o many jades and precious things that they refused any longer to rant his wishes. He then took the bones and buried them close by the ea, with a hundred bushels of pearls, lined with a border of gold. When is soldiers rebelled against him, he went to the spot, but the tide had ashed them away and they have never been found to this day. This ory was told me by an old servant of my family, Li Shih-yüan. He omes from the cave people of Yungchow, and remembers many strange ories of the South.

THE TALE OF CH'IENNIANG

(*A Tale of the T'ang Dynasty*)

h'ienniang was the daughter of Mr. Chang Yi, an official in Hunan. ne had a cousin by the name of Wang Chou, who was a brilliant and andsome young man. They had grown up together from childhood, nd as her father was very fond of the young boy, he had said that he ould take Wang Chou as his son-in-law. This promise they had both eard, and as she was the only child, and they were very close together, eir love grew from day to day. They were now grown-up young peo-e, and even had intimate relationships with each other. Unfortunately, er father was the only man who failed to perceive this. One day a young ficial came to beg for her hand from her father, and, ignoring or for-etting his early promise, he consented. Ch'ienniang, torn between love nd filial piety, was ready to die with grief, while the young man was so sgusted that he decided he would go abroad rather than stay and see s sweetheart become the bride of another person. So he made up a pretext and informed his uncle that he had to go away to the capital. A the uncle could not persuade him to stay, he gave him money and presen and prepared a farewell feast for him. Wang Chou, sad to take leave c his lover, was thinking it all over at the feast and he told himself that was best to go, rather than remain to carry on a hopeless romance.

So Wang Chou set out on a boat of an afternoon, and before he ha gone a few miles, it was already dark. He told the boatman to tie up th boat along shore and rest for the night. That night he could not slee and toward midnight he heard the sound of quick footsteps approachin In a few minutes the sound had drawn near the boat. He got up an inquired, "Who is there at this hour of the night?" "It is I, eve Ch'ienniang," was the reply. Surprised and delighted beyond measur he led her down the boat, and there she told him that she had hoped t be his wife, that her father had been unfair to him, and that she coul not bear parting from him. She was afraid, too, that he, lonely and trave ing in strange parts, might be driven to take his own life. So she ha braved the censure of society and the anger of her parents and come t follow him wherever he should go. Thus they were happy together an continued their journey to Szechuen.

Five years passed happily and she bore him two sons. But they had n news from the family, and she was daily thinking of her parents. It wa the only thing that marred their happiness. She did not know wheth her parents were living and well or not, and one night she began tellin Wang Chou how unhappy she was, and that since she was the only chil she felt guilty of great filial impiety to leave the old parents in this ma ner. "You have a good daughter's heart, and I am with you," said h husband. "Five years have passed; surely they are not still angry wit us. Let's go home." Ch'ienniang was overjoyed to hear this, and so the made preparations to go home with their two children.

When the boat had reached her home town, Wang Chou said Ch'ienniang, "I do not know what state of mind your parents are i So let me go alone first to find out." His heart was palpitating as h drew near his father-in-law's house. On seeing his father-in-law, Wan Chou knelt down and kowtowed, and begged for forgiveness. On hea ing this, Chang Yi was greatly surprised, and said, "What are you talkin about? Ch'ienniang has been lying unconscious in bed for these last fi years since you left. She has never even left her bed." "I am not lying said Wang Chou. "She is well and waiting in the boat."

Chang Yi did not know what to think, so he sent two maid-servan to see Ch'ienniang. They saw her sitting, well dressed and happy in the boat, and she even told the servants to convey her love to her parents. Bewildered, the two maid-servants ran home to make their report, and Chang Yi was still more greatly puzzled. Meanwhile, she who was lying in bed in her chamber had heard of the news, and it seemed her illness was gone, and there was light in her eyes. She rose up from her bed and dressed herself before her mirror. Smiling and without saying a word, she came straight to the boat. She who was in the boat was starting for home, and they met on the river bank. When the two came close together, their bodies melted into one shape, and their dresses were double, and there appeared the old Ch'ienniang, as young and as lovely as ever.

Both her parents were overjoyed, but they bade their servants keep the secret and not tell their neighbors about it, in order to avoid gossip. So no one, except the close relatives of the Chang family, ever knew of this strange happening.

Wang Chou and Ch'ienniang lived on as husband and wife for over forty years before they died.[6]

THE MAN WHO SOLD GHOSTS

(*From Soushenchi, Fourth Century*)

When Sung Tingpo of Nanyang was a young man, he was walking one night when he met a ghost. He asked the ghost who he was and the ghost said he was a ghost. "Who are you?" asked the ghost in return, and Tingpo lied to him and answered, "I am a ghost, too." The ghost then asked him where he was going, and Tingpo replied, "I am going to Wanshih town." "I am going there, too," said the ghost. So they went along together. After a mile or so, the ghost said it was stupid for both of them to walk, when they could carry one another by turn. "That is a good idea," said Tingpo. The ghost carried Tingpo first, and after a mile he said, "You are too heavy for a ghost. Are you one really?" Tingpo explained that he was a new ghost and was therefore somewhat heavier. Tingpo then began to carry the ghost, but it was very light as if he were carrying no weight at all. They thus carried one another by turns and Tingpo began to ask the ghost what ghosts were afraid of. "What ghosts are most afraid of is human saliva," the ghost replied. They then went along until they came to a stream. Tingpo let the ghost go ahead and observed that the ghost made no noise in the

[6] The story is supposed to have happened around the year A.D. 690.

water at all, but when he went in, the ghost heard the swish-swash in the water and asked him for an explanation. Tingpo again explained, "Don't be surprised, for I am a new ghost and am not quite used to getting across the water yet." When they were approaching the town, Tingpo began to carry the ghost on his back and gripped him very tight. The ghost began to shout and cry and struggled to get down, but Tingpo gripped him still more tightly. When he reached the streets, he let the ghost down, when it changed itself into a goat. Tingpo spat on the goat so that it could not change itself again, and sold it for fifteen hundred cash and went home. That was why there was a saying by Shih Ts'ung, "Tingpo sold a ghost for fifteen hundred cash."

IT'S WONDERFUL TO BE DRUNK

(*From Soushenchi, Fourth Century*)

Ti Hsi was a native of Chungshan and he could make "thousand-day wine" which would make a man drunk for a thousand days. There was a man of the district by the name of Hsüan Shih who wanted to taste this wine at his home. The next day, he went to see Ti Hsi and asked for a drink, and the latter said, "My wine is not quite thoroughly fermented, and I dare not offer it to you." "Even so, let me have a sip," said Hsüan. Ti Hsi could not say "no" and he gave him a cup. "That's wonderful," said Hsüan, "give me another cup." "You should go home now," replied Ti Hsi. "Come back another day. This cup alone will enable you to get drunk for a thousand days." Hsüan left, looking a little foolish, and when he went home, he died under the influence of the wine. His family never suspected it and wept and buried him.

After three years had passed, Ti Hsi said to himself, "Hsüan must be awake by this time. I must go to see him." When he reached Hsüan's home, he inquired if Hsüan was at home. His family was greatly surprised and said, "He has been dead for a long time. We have already taken off the mourning." Ti Hsi was frightened and said, "Why, it's my wonderful wine which can make one drunk for a thousand days. He ought to be ready to wake up just about now." He then ordered Hsüan's family to dig up the grave and open the coffin to see what was happening. There was a mist of vapor shooting up from the grave high into the sky, and accordingly he ordered the work to be begun. When the coffin top was taken off, the man was seen to be opening his eyes and yawning and said, "Oh, it's wonderful to be drunk!" Then he asked Ti Hsi, "What kind of wine is it that you make? Just one cup has such an effect. I have just waked up. What time of the day is it?" The people standing on top of the grave laughed at him, but a strong smell from the grave assailed their nostrils, and all of them fell drunk for three months.

IT'S GOOD TO BE HEADLESS

(*From Luyichi, Ninth Century*)

In the time of Han Wuti (B.C. 140–87), Chia Yung of Ts'angwu was serving as magistrate of Yüchang. One day he went out to fight bandits. He was wounded and lost his head. Yung mounted his horse and returned to the camp. The soldiers and people of the camp all came to look at him, and Yung spoke from his chest, "I was defeated by the bandits and they cut off my head. Tell me, in your opinion, does it look better to have a head or be without a head?" The officers wept and said, "It's better to have a head." And Yung replied, "I don't think so. It's just as good to be without a head."

THE BROTHERS' SEARCH FOR THEIR FATHER

(*Eighteenth Century*)

(The "Search of Two Filial Sons of Yüyao for Their Father across a Thousand Miles," is a true story written by Weng Kwangp'ing of Wukiang, and is attached to a book of genealogy of the Clan of Weng of Yüyao, in Chekiang. The style is that of the usual biography of ancestors, with which Chinese literature abounds, though few searches for relatives are quite so dramatic as this one. It is included here as showing the part which the family plays in Chinese society. It may make some thinking Christian missionaries hesitate to destroy Chinese ancestral worship and break up both the cornerstone of the Chinese social system and their living, concrete sense of continuity with the past. According to Confucian teachings, filial piety is the basis of moral character, and as will be seen in this sketch, good moral habits are first formed in the family during childhood.—*Ed.*)

This record of two sons' search for their father across a thousand miles is written concerning the efforts of granduncles of our clan Chishan and Luyeh to search for their father. Chishan's posthumous name[7] was Yünhuai, and his literary name was Chihshan. Luyeh's

[7] Name of a deceased ancestor.

posthumous name was Yünpiao and his literary name was Chinkung. Their family had lived for generations in Yüyao Hsien in eastern Chekiang. Their father was Ancestor Tahuan, whose posthumous name was Ying. He was one of the Confucian scholars of the town, deep in his scholarship and quiet in temperament. He used to sit silently the whole day, and whenever he passed a beautiful mountain landscape, his mind dwelled on poetic, unearthly thoughts. All his writings were devoted to expounding the (Sung) Confucian philosophy of reason, free of Buddhist or Taoist ideas. Thus he was much admired as a pure Confucianist in his village.

Ancestor Tahuan's wife had a brother, surnamed Wu, who was appointed magistrate of Kungch'eng in Kwangsi. When he was going to his office, he mortgaged his land to the clan relatives of Ancestor Tahuan. The mortgagee, however, considered it poor land and insisted on having Ancestor Tahuan's land instead, and Ancestor Tahuan generously changed the deed and gave him his own land in exchange. The interest he had to pay on this mortgage was fifteen hundred bushels a year. In the years 1690 and 1691, there was a drought, and the clan relatives pressed for payment of capital and interest very hard. Ancestor did not know what to do but was urged by the man to go to Kwangsi If he did not go, he would give the impression of being not willing to do his best. At last he was compelled to take the journey, but he sang on the way while tapping on the side of the boat. On the fifth day of the eleventh month, 1692, when his boat was stopping at Hsint'angchan, in Ch'iyang Hsien of Yungchow, Hunan, he suddenly disappeared at night. The son of the magistrate of Kungch'eng (his brother-in-law) who was with him on the same boat, reported it to the magistrate, and a great search was instituted for him for five days in vain. A messenger was then sent home to report the news, when Madame Wu[8] heard the news, she bit her finger until it bled and fell unconscious. When she came to again, she looked up and sighed, "Alas! My husband is calling me. He didn't want to go at first, and when he was about to start, he called for a lamp and lifted the bed curtain to look at his two sons. The brothers were fast asleep, but he turned round to look again and with sighs and tears in his eyes he left the room. I saw him to the door, and he said to me, 'Don't think about me. It will be your responsibility to

[8] That is, Madame Weng, wife of the missing person. In literary Chinese, the wife is designated by her own family name.

bring them up.' As I think of them now, these were inauspicious words."

She then sent an old servant to Kwangsi. In 1693, the magistrate of Kungch'eng (her brother) died in his office, and his son was bringing his coffin home together with the old servant. On their way, they passed Hsint'angchan, where their boat stopped, and a public notice was posted, describing Ancestor Tahuang's appearance and giving details of his native place, his names and the date of his disappearance. They searched for several days without results. When the old servant returned with the report to Madame Wu, she again wept until she became unconscious. When she came to, she said, "Now there is no more hope." And she took the cap and gown of her husband and placed them on the altar and the relatives put on the regular dress of mourning and wept and poured the wine of sacrifice morning and night. A divination was made at the Temple to Kuankung with the following verse as the oracle:

A small boat stops at the river bank in rain and wind.
The brothers look at one another in their dreams.
Already torn apart by death at the ends of the earth,
Yet there comes the unexpected news of returning alive.

The divination was taken three times and each time the oracle came out the same, which very much surprised the family. At the time of the disappearance, Chishan was eight years old, and Luyeh was only three. Since they had this divination corroborated three times, their mother used to carry Luyeh on her breast and wept in the courtyard, saying, "Son, can you grow up to search for your father?" and was satisfied only when the child nodded.

After three years, the mother died with that regret in her breast. While she was still alive, she called to her two daughters, and pointing to her two sons, said, "The reason why I did not die after I heard the news in the year *jenshen* (1692) was the hope that when they grew up I might be able to bring them along and personally search for him in the districts of Yungchow and Hengchow. Even if I could not see him alive again, I might be buried in the same grave with him. But now there is no more hope." The four children wept by her side and received her last instructions. Afterwards the two sons often embraced each other and wept, as if they didn't want to live. Again they inquired from people who had gone with their father to Kwangsi, but none could give any clue. Their cousin-sister still remembered the verse which Ancestor Tahuan wrote when his boat was stopping at Hsint'angchan, the last two lines of which ran:

From where could be seen in cold frost the ancient temple bell
A speck of translucent light shone from the Buddhist lamp.

The family accordingly conjectured together, believing that since he was writing verse in the boat at night, he could not have been lost on shore. When they inquired further from people who had again visited Kungch'eng, these people had forgotten even the name of the location of the mishap. The two sons were greatly distressed, and said to one another, "Are we brothers to lose by comparison with Miss Ts'ao O?"[9]

In the year, 1697, Chishan was already thirteen, and he went to Kwangsi, bringing along an old servant with him. At Liuchow, both young master and servant fell ill, and the servant soon died. The boy carried his own bedding and crossed the Hsiang River to Hunan, and nearly died in the waves. Alone and sick at heart, he used to cry in the journey, and it happened that a merchant of his district met him and brought him home. His cousin-sister welcomed him home and said with tears in her eyes, "I know you are taking this trip in accordance with your mother's wish. However, is that all your mother expected of you brothers? Have you forgotten what your mother said your father had said at his departure? Have you forgotten what she said when she was living? Your parents wanted you to grow up and be independent. Now are you already independent? You have undertaken a journey of a thousand miles at your age, without thinking of the true wish of your father and mother. Should you deprive them of their ancestral sacrifices without accomplishing anything, would you not grieve them in their graves?" Thereupon the two brothers wept and took her advice to heart, giving up the idea of going abroad again.

At this time, Ancestor Tahuan's family fortune was all used up and they could not support themselves. Chishan therefore worked as an apprentice in a pharmacist shop, while Luyeh was adopted as son by a certain uncle; but when the said uncle had two sons of his own later, Luyeh became superfluous and his brother took him home. Chishan

[9] Ts'ao O was a girl who went in search of her father who had been drowned and finally drowned herself. It was said that after five days her corpse was found holding her father's corpse. The story is well preserved in a famous stone inscription now very much prized as a model for calligraphy.

asked his younger brother what he wanted to do, and Luyeh replied that he would like to be a scholar. "Good," said the brother. "Your sister-in-law and I will take care of your board and tuition and expenses." Luyeh began then to work hard at his studies and train his character under a teacher, and the people of the village began to say, "Tahuan has a worthy son. The orphans are coming up, and his progeny will prosper." When Luyeh was nineteen (in 1711), he was studying at his village and was going to attend the district examinations. There was a flood, and Chishan made a raft and rowed him home himself. When the results were published, his name came out first, and thus he became a "student of the district."

Three years thereafter, Luyeh brought a servant and went to Hunan to search for his missing father, but without finding any trace. On his way to Kwangsi, he passed rivers and climbed over high peaks. The servant's expression suddenly changed and he rushed towards Luyeh with a knife. The latter dodged and the servant rolled down the precipice and died. He then carried his own baggage on his shoulder and begged his way about. After going through many hardships, he came home without finding anything. At this time, his elder brother had by thrift and hard work saved up enough to buy a land of a hundred *mu* (sixteen acres), so that he could continue to pay for his brother's tuition and expenses.

In the year 1723, Luyeh was successful at the national examinations and became a *chinshih*,[10] and returned home. Chishan already had a son, and the brothers were both happy and sad when they met, and discussed together how they might find traces of their missing father. They then pricked their arms with a needle and wrote in blood a prayer of several hundred words, with which they asked again for divination at the Temple to Kuankung. The oracle again spoke of "returning alive," and they said to each other, "Can the god lie to us?" They swore to find their father, and would not return until they had found him. It was therefore planned that they should leave their families in the care of the two sisters. But there was high water in the sea, and the fields were flooded, and thinking it impossible to burden their sisters with the extra expense at such a time, they gave up the idea.

In the winter of the following year, the two brothers secretly made up a traveling luggage and, behind closed doors, practised carrying it on

[10] Scholar of the third rank, who had passed successively the district, the provincial and the national examinations.

their shoulders for a long journey without letting even their families know about it. In the second month of 1725, Luyeh also had a son born to him, and on the third day of the baby's birth, the two brothers left their homes without letting any one know. For two years, they wandered in Hunan and Kwangsi and even went up the Lushan and the ghost valleys of Nanchang district, roaming in the thick forests amidst roaring tigers and wolves. Disregarding all danger, they went all over the mountains and whenever there was a Buddhist temple, they would stop and pray to the Buddhas. The people of Nanchang were greatly touched by the conduct of these filial sons and felt sorry for them.

Their two sisters thought of the long absence of the brothers, and sent a servant to Yungchow to look for them. Luyeh's friend, Shao Hungchieh, was also sojourning at Yungchow at this time and met their servant. He inquired about the situation and the servant replied that he knew nothing, but that he had heard a monk of Feiyüntu say that Mr. Weng's two filial sons had gone one to the Tungting Lake, and the other to Hengshan. In the eleventh month of 1726, the two brothers met at the Hsiangshan Temple in Chuanchow, Kwangsi, by previous agreement. Hungchieh went at once to see them, and saw that the brothers' faces were tanned and their bones stuck out. They were wearing straw sandals and carrying dry food, as if intending to start for some other place. Hungchieh tried to dissuade them and said to them, "Now you two are making a mistake. I have read your father's writings; they are strictly Confucianist without any taint of Buddhist or Taoist thoughts. On account of the verse he left referring to the Buddhist lamp, you are searching for him among the Buddhist and Taoist priests. I am afraid you are misjudging your father. Moreover, he merely happened to write his last lines at Hsint'angchan. You must trace the matter back to where it took place, instead of going all over the country to look for him. You are wearing yourselves out to no good purpose. Why not have a boat made to order, to be used as your home? Go up and down the districts of Yungchow and Hengchow, and stop at whatever islet, rocky shore, or branch stream, or hamlet or valley or town or highroads. After acquainting yourselves with the general topography of the place and the nature of the roads and rivers, then make inquiries among the farmers and fishermen and woodcutters. Then again in the quiet hours of the early dawn or when the moon is setting and the ravens are crying, sing the last verse your father wrote before he disappeared. I know that the celestial and earthly spirits will listen to your prayer and show you the way."

The brothers thought it good advice, and accordingly had a carpenter get ready the timber for making a boat. In the first month of 1727, the boat was completed, and on its mast hung a flag with the words, "The boat of certain Weng brothers of Yüyao in search of their father." Thus they went up and down between Yungchow and Hengchow for over a half year.

Toward the end of the eighth month, their boat was stopping at White Sand Islet in Kiangkan. The brothers were weeping with their faces toward the river. An old man carrying a cane came to Kiangkan. His name was Cheng Haihuan (Sea-Returned), and he came up to the two brothers and said to them, "If you are searching for a living father, then I dare not say a word. If the contrary, he is buried there in this islet." The brothers were greatly surprised and asked for details, and Haihuan said, "My home is at Niaowotang, about seven miles from Kiangkan. My brother was called Haisheng (Sea-Born, or Sea-Alive). My brother's wife gave birth to a son on the seventh of the eleventh month in 1692. Haisheng was going to inform his wife's family and was drowned on the way while crossing the river. He was prevented from sinking by decaying reeds in the water, and was thus saved. Among the reeds, he saw a corpse and told me about it on his return. I went with him to see the corpse and pulled it ashore. The body was clothed in silk and was thin and white. We chose a spot and buried it, thinking it was a fellow sufferer like my brother. When the family of the magistrate of Kung-ch'eng was returning home and searching for your father, I read the notice and thought the details agreed, and was going to report when an old man of the village stopped me, saying, 'The notice does not speak of drowning. They are looking for a living person and you come with a report of a dead man. How are you going to ask the corpse to rise from its grave and identify himself? I am afraid it will be difficult for you brothers to answer their questions satisfactorily.' I therefore gave up, and when Haisheng heard about it, he ran after the official messenger, but the latter had already gone far away. For over thirty years now since that time, no one has mentioned this affair again. Now Haisheng, my brother, is dead, and I am old. I heard that you filial sons are looking for your father abroad and the wayfarers who heard of it all shed tears. How can I bear not to tell you what I know? When I pulled your father's body from the water, it was only two days after he was drowned at Hsint'ang. Haisheng's son, who was born then, is called Jusheng, and still living. Otherwise, I should not be able to remember the exact date."

The two brothers then followed the old man to his home and asked how it all happened. Haisheng's wife was still living and they said that at the time of the burial, they had picked up several articles found on the body, and that now only a key and a key-case still remained. The two brothers at once asked for the key and key-case and sent a good walker to take them home to their cousin-sister. When the latter saw it, she was greatly touched and said, "This case was my present to uncle, embroidered by my own hand. When his trunk was sent home, there was a lock without the key to it. We opened it somehow and it was thus that we found the verse he wrote at Hsint'ang."

After three months, the good runner came back with the lock for the trunk, and the key was found to fit perfectly. The two brothers were then certain [11] it was indeed their father who had been drowned at Hsint'angchan and buried at the White Sand Islet. If it had not been for the information furnished by Haihuan, they would not have been able to clear up this eternal regret of their lives. And the oracle spoke of "returning alive," which fitted in with the names of brothers Haisheng and Haihuan (Sea-Returned and Sea-Alive). The god's oracle really fits in marvelously.

The brothers then requested from the magistrate permission for removing the remains of their father for burial in their native place in Chekiang. The magistrate showed great consideration for their feelings and gave the permission, but the inhabitants of the islet all came to the magistrate and said that the islet was formerly deserted but had now grown into quite a hamlet, all because of the protecting power of this grave. They asked therefore that the remains should not be removed. The magistrate respected their opinion and said to the brothers, "Your father's spirit has been enjoying peace in this soil. I think you had better not disturb his bones. Besides, the hamlet has grown up because of the grave, and every spring and autumn, it will receive sacrifices like a god. I think your father should be well satisfied with it."

The brothers then built a hut by the grave and stayed in it for three months, after which they invoked the spirit and brought a small model coffin home. Several years afterwards, Chishan died, and Luyeh was appointed magistrate of Tungpo (in Honan), where he sent for his

[11] Without absolute certainty, the brothers could not, according to custom, pay due ceremony to the grave as that of their father.

brother's family and looked after them in his official residence like his own. Soon he was transferred to Wuning, which was only about thirty miles from Ch'iyang Hsien (in which lay Hsint'angchan), and he therefore erected a Memorial Temple at Hoput'ang near the site of his father's grave. He purchased some land, whose produce was to be used for keeping up the sacrifices, and appointed some inhabitants and the descendants of Cheng Haihuan to look after the Temple generation after generation.

The magistrate of Ch'iyang, Chüehlo Cho-erh-pu,[12] set up a stone inscription telling the story. Luyeh ended up as district magistrate of Taochow (Yungchow) and left a good name for his administration, which is recorded in the Chapter on Famous Officials in the Provincial Records (*Fuchih*) of Hunan. There are the following records of the life of the two brothers: "The Story of a Search for Father" by Shao Hungchieh and Wu Hsiwen,[13] "History of the White Sand Islet" by Ch'iu Yinyü, "Story of Seeking for Father" by Chang Ts'anchih (which is a mere outline of events), the record of Shih Yühuei, the biographical sketches by Li Tsuhuei and Chang Kengchih. They vary in some details and in omissions, and I, Kuangp'ing, have therefore made use of all this material to write this sketch, in order to show that the filial conduct of the two men was enough to touch the gods' heart and make the spirits weep. For this reason, they went through the dangers of the waves and the wild beasts and yet were preserved and able to find the location of their father's grave. Therefore I have taken the liberty to edit it and put it at the back of the genealogy book of the clan, in order not only to let him serve as a model for our whole clan, but also to tell the story to all who are yet to be born as sons of men in the world.

THE PRIVATE HISTORY OF QUEEN FEIYEN

(*First Century, B.C.*)

(The "Private History of Queen Feiyen" is written by one Ling Yüan, Commander of Hotung in Han Dynasty, a contemporary of Yang Hsiung (first decades of the Christian era). It belongs to that vast storehouse of private notes on current or historical events in Chinese literature, of the nature of Pepys' Diaries, that are not found in official histories. It is apparently a story told by some old woman in the palace, possibly Fanyi in the story, and has all the faults and virtues of old-womanish gossip, which belongs to

[12] A Manchu, as indicated by the Manchu name.
[13] Friend and relative mentioned above.

the school of unconscious realism. The style is that of a half-educated clerk, with what might be called "misspellings" and "ungrammatical" passages, and there is utterly no sense of composition. But it gives us a very intimate glimpse into the licentious court life of China, which probably has not varied in the last two thousand years. The unconscious realists beat the conscious realists in realism, and I have had to delete passages that would be considered downright obscene by Western literary standards. It is a pity, because if sex were not so much hedged about, there might be less psychosis. On the other hand, I do not want the book to be banned in Boston. Apart from the light it throws incidentally on court life and ancient beauty aids, the interest of the story lies in the jealousy of two sisters, and there is no question but that the real heroine of the story is not Feiyen, but her younger sister.—*Ed.*)

Queen Chao Feiyen's[14] father Feng Wanchin and grandfather Feng Tali were makers of musical instruments and musicians in the employ of the Prince of Kiangtu. Wanchin was not content to carry on the musical lore handed down in his family, but composed a type of music without the regular verse form, with many embellishments and sad airs. This he called poignant or mad melodies, and it was very touching to hear. The granddaughter of the Prince, Princess of Kusu, who was married to Commander Chao Manman of Kiangtu, fell in love with Wanchin. She was not happy at dinner unless she was sharing the same bowl with Wanchin, and they had relations with one another. Chao Manman was a jealous man, and besides had been suffering from a secret disease and so had abstained from sleeping with his wife. So when the Princess conceived, she was very much frightened and retired to her palace on pretext of illness. She gave birth to two daughters, the elder one called Yichu and the second one called Hoteh, whom she sent to Wanchin's home, but they took the family name of Chao (The Princess's husband).

Yichu was a very intelligent child, and she studied a copy of Peng Tsu's "Treatise on Circulation Systems" and mastered the art of regulating circulations. When she grew up, she was very pretty with a slender, lithesome figure, and people called her Feiyen ("Flying Swallow"). Hoteh's skin was so smooth that water would not stay on it when she came out of the bath. She was good at singing and had a soft, low voice. Both sisters were distinguished beauties.

When Wanchin died, their family had lost its fortune, and the sisters moved on to the capital Ch'angan, where they were known as the daugh-

[14] Empress Chao of Han Ch'engti, who ruled in B.C. 32–17.

ters of Chao, or as some say, the "other children" of Manman. They were then staying in the same alley with Chao Lin, who was an officer in the household of Princess of Yang-o. Thus coming under his protection, they often presented Lin with their own embroidery work, and soon they were staying in Lin's home and were accepted as his daughters. Lin's eldest daughter was serving in the palace, and she returned home on account of sickness and later died. In this way, Feiyen and her sister often went to serve in the home of the Princess of Yang-o, taking the opportunity to learn song and dance. Sometimes they would be so occupied with it that they forgot their meals. They got very little pay for their service and were often short of money, but they would spend on powder and cream and beauty aids without regard of cost, for which they were laughed at.

Feiyen had relations with a neighbor who was an archer of the Imperial Park. She was poor and shared the same bed with Hoteh. On a snowy night, she would stand by her house, waiting in the open for the archer. By regulating her breath, she could keep her body warm and remain without shiver, so that the archer thought she was a fairy. Through the influence of her mistress's family, she was sent up to the palace. Her cousin, Fanyi, who was a keeper of curtains at the palace, knew of Feiyen's affair with the archer, and was afraid for her. When she received the Emperor's favor, Feiyen denied him; she closed her eyes and wept till her tears wetted her cheeks and kept her legs shivering. For three nights, the Emperor was thus denied, but he did not feel offended. Some of the palace favorites asked the Emperor, and the latter replied, "She is full and soft as if without bones, and is very modest and shy, unlike you wenches. She is a virtuous girl." . . . From then on, she stayed in the inner palace and was made Empress Chao.

The Emperor was in his private room in the Wanyang Hall, looking over the list, and Fanyi, who was close by, took the opportunity to tell him that Feiyen had a sister by the name of Hoteh, who was both beautiful and had a much gentler temper than her sister. The Emperor sent a servant, Lü Yenfu, with a jewelled hand-cart to welcome her. Hoteh declined, saying, "Unless my sister calls me, I dare not go. You can return to the palace with my head." Upon Yenfu's report, Fanyi took the Empress's silk-covered order book and sent for Hoteh. The Emperor prepared to receive her in his bedroom in the Yünkuang Hall. Hoteh had come with a fresh ointment of aloes wood perfume; her hair was done up in the "new coiffure" and her eyebrows were painted in the "distant hill-line" style, with a small red beauty spot painted on her face. She was wearing the "lazy suit," with a short embroidered skirt, narrow sleeves and plum-patterned socks. When she was presented through Fanyi, she said, "My sister is terribly jealous, and she can easily ruin and disgrace me. I am not afraid of death, but unless it is with my sister's consent, I would rather die than suffer disgrace." Without looking up, she retired. Her voice was soft and clear, and those present sighed in admiration. The Emperor therefore sent her back to her home.

Now there was one Lady Chao, who used to serve Emperor Hsüan as a keeper of incense but who was now a white-haired woman serving as a teacher of the palace maids. She spat when she spoke of the Empress, "She is a flood which is going to overwhelm us." [15] The Emperor therefore followed Fanyi's advice and opened up the Yüant'iao Hall for the Empress's residence, presenting her with a cloud-pattern curtain, marble tables and a gold nine-paneled collapsible screen. And Fanyi said to the Empress, "The Emperor is without an heir, and Your Majesty should be thinking of the Imperial line. Why not speak to the Emperor and ask him to take one who can give him a son?" The Empress approved and that night, Hoteh was presented to the Emperor, who was greatly pleased with her. He felt all over her body and called her the Land of Voluptuousness, and said to Fanyi, "I am going to live and die in this Land, rather than imitate Emperor Wuti who sought the Land of Immortality." Fanyi cried "Ten Thousand Years!" and congratulated him, saying, "Your Majesty now has met a fairy." The Emperor immediately gave her twenty-four pieces of fish-scale, gold-spotted brocade. Hoteh thus received the special favor of the Emperor, and she was given the official title of Lady (*Chiehyü*) Chao.

Hoteh used to go to see her sister, greeting her with the ceremony of a child to its parent. One day, the sisters were sitting together, and apparently by mistake, the Empress spat on the sleeve of Hoteh's dress. "See, Sister," the latter said, "you have made marks on my purple sleeve, looking just like mosses on rocks. The Imperial Tailors [16] would not be able to make a sleeve with such a design." The Empress in her own court had relations with palace attendants and servants who had many children, and Hoteh tried her best to protect her by often saying

[15] The Han Imperial House was supposed to have risen to power on the strength of the fire element.

[16] Strictly, officers in charge of the furniture, upholstery and dresses of the Imperial Household.

to the Emperor with tears in her eyes, "My sister has a bad temper. If enemies should ever frame her up, we sisters should be dead." For that reason, those who informed the Emperor of the Empress's conduct were killed. And the attendants and servants wore fancy-colored trousers and did what they pleased at Yüant'iao Hall with complete freedom. But the Empress still failed to produce an heir to the throne.

The Empress used to bathe herself with a bath of five ingredients and seven perfumes, sit in the seat of perfumed *aquilaria agallocha* wood, and drench herself with the etherean hundred-ingredient perfume water. Her sister bathed herself simply with nutmeg and used the powder of flower essence, but the Emperor once told Fanyi, "Although the Empress breathes an exotic perfume, it cannot be compared with the natural fragrance of the Lady Chao's flesh." There was one Li Yanghua, who used to serve in Prince Yi of Kiangtu's court, and who was the niece of the sisters' grandfather. In her old age, she came to live with the sisters' family as their aunt. Yanghua was an expert in beauty aids, and she used to advise the Empress to use the nine-curved aloes wood ointment and take a medicine from the navel of the male muskdeer for relaxing the muscles. This latter was also taken by Hoteh, but when often taken by women, the monthly flow would become thin. One day, the Empress spoke about this to the Court Pharmacist, Shangkuan Wu, and Wu said, "If this is the case, how can you have children?" She taught her to douche herself with a kind of fern,[17] but still it did not work.

The tribes of Cambodia sent a tribute of a giant mother-of-pearl and a Nightless Pearl, which shone like moonlight. Their soft glow made anyone look beautiful in it. The Emperor gave the mother-of-pearl to the Empress and the pearl to Hoteh. The Empress fixed the shell in a curtain of golden threads, which gave a light like the full moon. Some time afterwards, the Emperor remarked to Lady Chao, "The Empress does not look so beautiful in daytime as she does at night. One feels like being transported into a different world." When she heard this, she decided to give the Nightless Pearl to the Empress as a birthday present, but did not tell her about it. When Lady Chao heard from the Emperor that a new title was going to be conferred upon the Empress, she sent in her presents to the Empress with the following memorandum: "On this auspicious day when the spirits of Heaven and Earth blend in harmony and when my sister ascends the Empress's throne, our ancestors are greatly honored and I am extremely delighted, and beg to present

[17] *Yanghua*, not known in present Chinese *Materia Medica;* possibly *aspidium filix-mas.*

the following twenty-seven articles in congratulation: 1 gold-sprinkled stitched mattress, 1 *aquilaria agallocha* lotus bowl, 1 five-colored concentric knot, 1 piece of mandarin-duck designed gold-thread brocade, 1 crystal screen, 1 Nightless Pearl, 1 perfumed wild-cat-skin cushion, 1 perfumed tiger-skin with sandalwood statue, 2 carved ambergris fish, 1 single stalk precious lotus, 1 seven-paneled water-calthrop-shaped mirror, 4 pure gold finger rings, 1 vanishing gauze dress, 3 perfumed *wenlo* silk hand rests, 1 jar glamor hair ointment, 3 bed incense cases, 2 pairs ivory antiseptic chopsticks,[18] 1 case white jade cream. I am asking my maid Kuo Yüchiung to bring them to you." The Empress gave her in return a colored bed curtain of cloud brocade, a jade pot and aloes wood incense. Lady Chao said she would not think of taking these things if they were not given her by her sister, and the Emperor showed his appreciation.

It was then ordered that the Emperor was to go and stay at Yichow for three years, and a special brocade curtain and bed decorated with *aquilaria agallocha* wood was ordered for the Lady Chao. The latter received His Majesty at the Taiyi Lake, and a great boat was made, supposed to contain the whole palace household. A tower was erected in the middle of the lake forty feet high. The Emperor was wearing a flowing-line seamless gown, and the Empress was wearing a purple skirt sent as tribute from Annam and a light-green gauze dress. She was singing the song, "Oh, Waft the Wind" in the high towers, and the Emperor was beating time by striking a jade bowl with an ivory hair brooch, while the Empress's favorite attendant, Feng Wufang, was asked to play the hand-pipes (*sheng*) in accompaniment. When the Empress was singing the song, "Down the Stream" dreamily, a sudden gust of wind arose, and her voice rose with the wind, while Wufang whistled gently along with it. The wind blew up her skirt, and she cried, "Look at me, look at me!" and she raised her flowing sleeves and said, "Oh, fairy, oh, fairy! You have forsaken the old for the new. Have you forgotten me?" And the Emperor (seeing that the wind was blowing her off), said to Wufang, "Hold her!" Wufang stopped playing and caught the Empress by her shoe. After a while, the wind stopped and the Empress wept and said, "Your Majesty was kind to me and saved me from becoming a fairy." And she felt very sad, and tears came down her cheeks, and the Emperor loved her the more. He gave Wufang thousands of pieces of silver and granted him permission to enter the Empress's bedroom.

[18] That changed color after contact with poison.

Some days afterwards, some court favorites split their skirts and called it "the skirt for holding the fairy."

Lady Chao was growing in the favor of the Emperor, and received the title of Chaoyi. She wished to live near her sister, and the Emperor built for her the Shaopin Studio, the Luhua Hall, the Hanfeng Hall, the P'och'ang Hall, the Ch'iu-an Hall, all with front and back courts. He also built for her a heated room, a room of ice jars, an orchid bath room, with many inner chambers and connecting corridors, decorated with gold and jade, with the wall covered with white jade in a multitude of designs. Her quarters were connected with those of her sister's, through a gate called the "Approach to the Fairies."

Now the Empress, being secure in the Emperor's favor, grew more licentious every day, and she asked magicians to secure for her drugs for staying old age. An emissary from the P'oyi tribes of the Southwest had come with tributes to the Emperor, and he was a man who after a wine feast could go without sleep for twenty-four hours. He was staying in the office for foreign emissaries and there was a singular glamor about his appearance. The Empress heard about it and asked him what special magic he had. And the foreigner replied, "My magic consists in regarding heaven and earth and life and death all alike and leveling the differences between existence and non-existence, so that through all transformations I remain unchanged." The Empress asked Fanyi's follower Puchou to give him a thousand pieces of silver, but the foreigner said, "Who wishes to learn my teachings must refrain from licentious living and telling lies." Accordingly, the Empress was discouraged. One day, Fanyi was serving the Empress at bath, and they were chatting happily together. The Empress told her what the foreigner had said, and Fanyi slapped her hands and said with a laugh, "I remember that when I was in Kiangtu, Aunt Li Yanghua used to keep some fighting ducks in a pond, but was worried on account of the beavers that came to prey upon them. A woman, Nuei, of Chuli, got a wildcat that preyed upon the beavers and gave it to our aunt, but said that the wildcat itself had to be fed with ducks. Aunt was angry and strangled the wildcat. This is just like what the foreigner says." The Empress broke into a loud laughter and said, "The dirty foreigner! He is not worth my strangling."

There was one attendant who had intimate relations with the Empress, by the name of Yen Red-Phoenix, who could scale walls and houses. He also had relations with the younger sister, now called Chaoyi.

He was just leaving Chaoyi's house, when the Empress happened to come in. Now it was the custom that on the fifth of October, the Emperor was to go to the Lingan Temple for worship. On this day, people played the clay pipe and beat the drum, and danced and sang with their arms joined together while their feet tapped the ground. When Red Phoenix came to assist in the music, the Empress said to Chaoyi, "Who does Red Phoenix come for?" And Chaoyi replied, "He comes for you. Can it be for anybody else?" The Empress was angry and pushed her cup at Chaoyi's face and replied, "Can a mouse bite a human being?" And Chaoyi replied, "He wears your clothes and has seen your underwear. That is quite enough. He does not have to bite anybody." Now Chaoyi had always been humble toward her sister and the Empress was completely surprised by her insolent tone, and she stared for a long time without reply. Fanyi took off her hair brooch and kowtowed on the ground until she bled, and pulled Chaoyi to apologize to her sister. Chaoyi performed the bow and said, weeping, "Sister, have you forgotten how we used to share the bed together and how we could not sleep for the cold and you asked me to snuggle close to your back? Now we have been lucky and are honored far above all the others. Besides, there is no rival from the outside. Can we bear to quarrel between ourselves?" Then the Empress also shed tears and held Chaoyi's hand and she took a brooch of purple jade with nine young birds and put it in her sister's hair. Thus the sisters were reconciled. The Emperor came to hear about the affair, but he was afraid of the Empress's temper and dared not ask her, but asked Chaoyi. The latter replied, "She was merely jealous of me. The Han Imperial House rose by the power of the fire element; that was why she referred to Your Majesty as Red Dragon and Phoenix." The Emperor believed her and was greatly pleased.

Once the Emperor went out to hunt on an early snowy morning and caught an illness. He became impotent, and nothing availed except by holding Chaoyi's legs . . . but Chaoyi would not keep still, but turned about, which prevented His Majesty from holding her leg for long. Fanyi said to Chaoyi, "His Majesty has tried all medicines brought by the magicians without avail, but Your Majesty's leg alone has worked. God has given you a great blessing. Why do you turn about to defy the Emperor?" And Chaoyi replied, "Fortunately I do turn about, and that is how I can still hold his affection. If I do as my sister does and ask him to hold my leg, he would be tired of me soon. How then shall I be able to excite him?" She was spoiled by the Emperor and, when she was ill, would not take food or drink unless the Emperor fed her with a spoon or chopsticks, and when she had to take bitter medicine, she would take it only from the Emperor's own mouth.

When Chaoyi took a bath at night in the Orchid Bathroom, her body shone in the candle light. The Emperor used to take a peep at her, and a maid told Chaoyi about it, and Chaoyi wrapped herself in a towel and had the candles removed. Another day, the Emperor promised the maids gold[19] if they would keep quiet. Some maid coming out through the curtain chanced upon the Emperor and went in and informed Chaoyi, and Chaoyi hid herself. From then on, His Majesty used to peep at her from behind the curtains of the Orchid Bath, and he carried about him a lot of gold so that whenever he saw a maid passing by, he would stop her and give her some gold. The maids were greedy for gold and passed out and in one after another without stop. He gave the night attendants as much as over a hundred pieces of gold in one night.

The Emperor then became deprived of his sexual powers, and the Chief Physician could not do anything about it. He searched for rare medicines and obtained *shensüchiao* ("Carefully Use Gum"), which was given to Chaoyi. Chaoyi used to give the Emperor one pill for one occasion. One night Chaoyi was drunk and gave him seven pills. His Majesty embraced her all night . . . and laughed hysterically. The next morning . . . His Majesty fell unconscious . . . and soon he died.[20] The attendants reported this to the Empress, and the Empress wanted to have Chaoyi tried. Chaoyi said, "I have handled His Majesty as a mother handles a child. And of all women in the world, he has loved and honored me. How can I stand with my hands at my back like a prisoner in court to explain intimate details?" She then beat her chest and cried, "Your Majesty! Where have you gone?" Then she threw up blood and died.

[19] *Chin* can also refer to silver.

[20] The details of Ch'engti's death agree with the Biographies of the Empresses in Han History.

Six Chapters of a Floating Life

INTRODUCTION

Yün, I think, is one of the loveliest women in Chinese literature. She is not the most beautiful, for the author, her husband, does not make that claim, and yet who can deny that she is the loveliest? She is just one of those charming women one sometimes sees in the homes of one's friends, so happy with their husbands that one cannot fall in love with them. One is glad merely to know that such a woman exists in the world and to know her as a friend's wife, to be accepted in her household, to be able to come uninvited to her home for lunch, or to have her put a blanket around one's legs when one falls asleep while she is discussing painting and literature and cucumbers in her womanish manner with her husband. I daresay there are a number of such women in every generation, except that in Yün I seem to feel the qualities of a cultivated and gentle wife combined to a greater degree of perfection than falls within our common experience. For who would not like to go out secretly with her against her parents' wish to Taihu Lake and see her elated at the sight of the wide expanse of water, or watch the moon with her by the Bridge of Ten Thousand Years? And who would not like to go with her, if she were living in England, and visit the British Museum, where she would see the mediaeval illuminated manuscripts with tears of delight? Therefore, when I say that she is one of the loveliest women in Chinese literature and Chinese history—for she was a real person—I do not think I have exaggerated.

Her life, in the words of Su Tungp'o, "was like a spring dream which vanished without a trace." Had it not been for a literary accident, we might not have known that such a woman lived, loved and suffered. I am translating her story just because it is a story that should be told the world; on the one hand, to propagate her name, and on the other, because in this simple story of two guileless creatures in their search for beauty, living a life of poverty and privations, decidedly outwitted by life and their cleverer fellowmen, yet determined to snatch every moment of happiness and always fearful of the jealousy of the gods, I seem to see the essence of a Chinese way of life as really lived by two persons who happened to be husband and wife. Two ordinary artistic persons who did not accomplish anything particularly noteworthy in the world, but merely loved the beautiful things in life, lived their quiet life with some good friends after their own heart—ostensibly failures, and happy in their failure. They were too good to be successful, for they were retiring, cultivated souls, and the fact that they were disowned by their elders could not be counted against them, but was all to their credit. The cause of the tragedy lay simply in the fact that she knew how to read and write and that she loved beauty too much to know that loving beauty was wrong. As a daughter-in-law who could read and write, she had the unpleasant task of writing letters for her mother-in-law to her father-in-law abroad who wanted to marry a concubine, and she got so excited over a sing-song girl that she secretly arranged to have her husband take her as his concubine, and fell seriously ill because a more powerful young man snatched her away. There we see an elementary, though entirely innocent, conflict between her artistic temperament and the world of reality, a conflict further seen in her disguising herself as a man in order to see the "illuminated flowers" on a god's birthday. Was it morally wrong for a woman to disguise herself as a man or to take a passionate interest in a beautiful sing-song girl? If so, she could not have been conscious of it. She merely yearned to see and know the beautiful things in life, beautiful things which lay not within the reach of moral women in ancient China to see. It was the same artistically innocent, but morally indecorous, urge that made her wish to visit like a man all the famous mountains in China which, since she could not do as a moral young woman, she was willing to look forward to in her old age. But she did not see the mountains, for she had already seen a beautiful sing-song girl, and that was indecorous enough for her parents to disown her as a sentimental young fool, and the rest of her life had to be spent in a struggle with poverty, with too little leisure and money for such delights as climbing famous mountains.

Did Shen Fu, her husband, perhaps idealize her? I hardly think so. The reader will be convinced of this when he reads the story itself. He made no effort to whitewash her or himself. In him, too, lived the spirit of truth and beauty and the genius for resignation and contentment so characteristic of Chinese culture. I cannot help wondering what this commonplace scholar must have been like to inspire such a pure and loyal love in his wife, and to be able to appreciate it so much as to write for us one of the tenderest accounts of wedded love we have ever come across in literature. Peace be to his soul! His ancestral tomb is somewhere in the neighbourhood of Soochow, and if we are lucky, we may still be able to find it. I do not think it would be wrong to prepare some incense and fruits and say some prayers on our knees to these two sweet souls. If I were there, I would whistle the melodies of Maurice Ravel's "Pavane," sad as death, yet smiling, or perhaps Massenet's "Melodie," tender and resigned and beautiful and purged of all exciting passions. For in the presence of these souls, one's spirit also becomes humble, not before the great, but before the small things of life, for I truly believe that a humble life happily lived is the most beautiful thing in the universe. Inevitably, while reading and re-reading and going over this little booklet, my thoughts are led to the question of happiness. For those who do not know it, happiness is a problem, and for those who do know it, happiness is a mystery. The reading of Shen Fu's story gives one this sense of the mystery of happiness, which transcends all bodily sorrows and actual hardships—similar, I think, to the happiness of an innocent man condemned to a life-long sentence with the consciousness of having done no wrong, the same happiness that is so subtly depicted for us in Tolstoy's "Resurrection," in which the spirit conquers the body. For this reason, I think the life of this couple is one of the saddest and yet at the same time "gayest" lives, the type of gaiety that bears sorrow so well.

The Chinese title for this book is "Fousheng Liu Chi" or "Six Chapters of a Floating Life," of which only four remain. (The reference is to a passage in Li Po's poem, "Our floating life is like a dream; how many times can one enjoy oneself?") In form, it is unique, an autobiographical story mixed with observations and comments on the art of living, the little pleasures of life, some vivid sketches of scenery and literary and art criticism. The extant version was first published in 1877 by Yang Yinch'üan, who picked it up from a secondhand bookstore, with the two last chapters missing. According to the author's own testimony, he was born in 1763, and the fourth chapter could not have been written before 1808. A brother-in-law of Yang's and a well-known scholar, by the name of Wang T'ao,[1] had seen the book in his childhood, so that it is likely that the book was known in the neighbourhood of Soochow in the second or third decade of the nineteenth century. From Kuan Yi-ngo's poems and from the known headings of the last chapters, we know that the Fifth Chapter recorded his experiences in Formosa, while the Sixth Chapter contained the author's reflections on the Way of Life. I have the fond hope that some complete copy of the book is still lying somewhere in some private collections or secondhand shops of Soochow, and if we are lucky, it is not altogether impossible that we may discover it still.

[1] Wang T'ao was the Chinese scholar who assisted James Legge in his translation of Chinese Classics at Hong Kong.

Six Chapters of a Floating Life

by Shen Fu

Translated by Lin Yutang

CHAPTER I: WEDDED BLISS

I WAS BORN in 1763, under the reign of Ch'ienlung, on the twenty-second day of November. The country was then in the heydey of peace and moreover, I was born in a scholars' family, living by the side of Ts'ang lang Pavilion in Soochow. So altogether I may say the gods have been unusually kind to me. Su Tungp'o said: "Life is like a spring dream which vanishes without a trace." I should be ungrateful to the gods if I did not try to put my life down on record.

Since the *Book of Poems* begins with a poem on wedded love, I thought I would begin this book by speaking of my marital relations and then let other matters follow. My only regret is that I was not properly educated in childhood; all I know is a simple language and I shall try only to record the real facts and real sentiments. I hope the reader will be kind enough not to scrutinize my grammar, which would be like looking for brilliance in a tarnished mirror.

I was engaged in my childhood to one Miss Yü, of Chinsha, who died in her eighth year, and eventually I married a girl of the Ch'en clan. Her name was Yün and her literary name Suchen. She was my cousin, being the daughter of my maternal uncle, Hsinyü. Even in her childhood, she was a very clever girl, for while she was learning to speak, she was taught Po Chüyi's poem, *The P'i P'a Player,* and could at once repeat it. Her father died when she was four years old, and in the family there were only her mother (of the Chin clan) and her younger brother K'ech'ang and herself, being then practically destitute. When Yün grew up and had learnt needle-work, she was providing for the family of three, and contrived always to pay K'ech'ang's tuition fees punctually. One day, she picked up a copy of the poem *The P'i P'a Player* from a paper basket, and from that, with the help of her memory of the lines, she learnt to read. Between her needlework, she gradually learnt to write poetry. One of her poems contained the two lines:

"Soaked in autumn, one's figure becomes thin,
Touched by frost, the chrysanthemum grows fat."

When I was thirteen years old, I went with my mother to her maiden home and there we met. As we were two young innocent children, she allowed me to read her poems. I was quite struck by her talent, but feared she was too clever to be happy. Still I could not help thinking of her all the time, and once I told my mother, "If you choose a girl for me, I won't marry any one except cousin Su." My mother also liked her for being so gentle, and gave her her gold ring as a token for the betrothal.

This was on July 16 in the year 1775. In the winter of this year one of my girl cousins was going to get married and I again accompanied my mother to her maiden home. Yün was of the same age as myself, but ten months older, and as we had been accustomed to calling each other 'elder sister' and 'younger brother' from childhood, I continued to call her 'Sister Su.'

At this time the guests in the house all wore bright dresses, but Yün alone was clad in a dress of quiet colour, and had on a new pair of shoes. I noticed that the embroidery on her shoes was very fine, and learnt that it was her own work, so that I began to realize that she was gifted at other things, too, besides reading and writing.

Of a slender figure, she had drooping shoulders, and a rather long neck, slim but not to the point of being skinny. Her eye-brows were arched and in her eyes there was a look of quick intelligence and soft refinement. The only defect was that her two front teeth were slightly inclined forward, which was not a mark of good omen. There was an air of tenderness about her which completely fascinated me.

I asked for the manuscripts of her poems and found that they consisted mainly of couplets and three or four lines, being unfinished poems, and I asked her the reason. She smiled and said: "I have had no teacher in poetry, and wish to have a good teacher-friend who could help me to finish these poems." I wrote playfully on the label of this book of poems the words: "Beautiful Lines in an Embroidered Case," and did not realize that in this case lay the cause of her short life.

That night, when I came home from my relatives' place in the country, whither I had accompanied my female cousin the bride, it was already midnight, and I felt very hungry and asked for something to eat. A maid-servant gave me some dried dates, which were too sweet for me. Yün secretly pulled me by the sleeve into her room, and I saw that she had hidden away a bowl of warm congee and some dishes to go with it. I was beginning to take up the chopsticks and eat it with great gusto when Yün's cousin Yüheng called out: "Sister Su, come quickly!" Yün quickly shut the door and said: "I am very tired and going to bed." Yüheng forced the door open and seeing the situation, said with a malicious smile at Yün, "So, that's it! A while ago I asked for congee and you said there was no more, but you really meant to keep it for your future husband." Yün was greatly embarrassed and everybody laughed at her, including the servants. On my part, I rushed away home with an old servant in a state of excitement.

Since the affair of the congee happened, she always avoided me when I went to her home afterwards, and I knew that she was only trying to avoid being made a subject of ridicule.

On the twenty-second of January in 1780, I saw her on our wedding night, and found that she had the same slender figure as before. When her bridal veil was lifted, we looked at each other and smiled. After the drinking of the customary twin cups between groom and bride, we sat down together at dinner and I secretly held her hand under the table, which was warm and small, and my heart was palpitating. I asked her to eat and learnt that she had been keeping fast for several years already. I found that the time when she began her fast coincided with my small-pox illness, and said to her laughingly: "Now that my face is clean and smooth without pock-marks, my dear sister, will you break your fast?" Yün looked at me with a smile and nodded her head.

This was on the twenty-second, my wedding night. On the twenty-fourth, my own sister was going to get married, and as there was to be a national mourning and no music was to be allowed on the twenty-third, we gave my sister a send-off dinner on the night of the twenty-second, and Yün was present at table. I was playing the finger-guessing game with the bridesmaids in the bridal chamber and being a loser all the time, fell asleep drunk like a fish. When I woke up the next morning, Yün had not quite finished her morning toilet.

That day, we were kept busy entertaining guests and towards evening, music was played. After midnight, on the morning of the twenty-fourth, I, as the bride's brother, sent my sister away and came back towards three o'clock. The room was then pervaded with quietness, bathed in the silent glow of the candle-lights. I went in and saw Yün's woman servant taking a nap behind the bed, while Yün had taken off her bridal costume, but had not yet gone to bed. Her beautiful white neck was bent before the bright candles, and she was absorbed reading a book. I patted her on the shoulder and said: "Sister, why are you still working so hard? You must be quite tired with the full day we've had."

Quickly Yün turned her head and stood up saying: "I was going to bed when I opened the book-case and saw this book and have not been able to leave it since. Now my sleepiness is all gone. I have heard of the name of *Western Chamber* for a long time, but to-day I see it for the first time. It is really the work of a genius, only I feel that its style is a little bit too biting."

"Only geniuses can write a biting style," I smiled and said.

The woman servant asked us to go to bed and left us and shut the door. I began to sit down by her side and we joked together like old friends after a long separation. I touched her breast in fun and felt that her heart was palpitating too. "Why is Sister's heart palpitating like that?" I bent down and whispered in her ear. Yün looked back at me with a smile and our souls were carried away in a mist of passion. Then we went to bed, when all too soon the dawn came.

As a bride, Yün was very quiet at first. She was never sullen or displeased, and when people spoke to her, she merely smiled. She was respectful towards her superiors and kindly towards those under her. Whatever she did was done well, and it was difficult to find fault with her. When she saw the grey dawn shining through the window, she would get up and dress herself as if she had been commanded to do so. "Why?" I asked. "You don't have to be afraid of gossip, like the days when you gave me that warm congee." "I was made a laughing-stock on account of that bowl of congee," she replied, "but now I am not afraid of people's talk; I only fear that our parents might think their daughter-in-law lazy."

Although I wanted her to lie in bed longer, I could not help admiring her virtue, and so got up myself, too, at the same time with her. And so every day we rubbed shoulders together and clung to each other like an object and its shadow, and the love between us was something that surpassed the language of words.

So the time passed happily and the honeymoon was too soon over. At this time, my father Chiafu was in the service of the Kueich'i district government, and he sent a special messenger to bring me there, for, it should be noted that, during this time, I was under the tutorship of Chao Shengtsai of Wulin. Chao was a very kindly teacher and to-day the fact that I can write at all is due entirely to his credit.

Now, when I came home for the wedding, it had been agreed that I could go back any time. So when I got this news, I did not know what to do. I was afraid Yün might break into tears, but on the other hand she tried to look cheerful and comforted me and urged me to go, and packed up things for me. Only that night I noticed that she did not look quite her usual self. At the time of parting, she whispered to me: "Take good care of yourself, for there will be no one to look after you."

When I went up on board the boat, the peach and pear trees on the banks were in full bloom, but I felt like a lonely bird that had lost its companions and as if the world was going to collapse around me. As soon as I arrived, my father left the place and crossed the river for an eastward destination.

Thus three months passed, which seemed to me like ten insufferable long years. Although Yün wrote to me regularly, still for two letters that I sent her, I received only one in reply, and these letters contained only words of exhortation and the rest was filled with airy, conventional nothings, and I felt very unhappy. Whenever the breeze blew past my bamboo courtyard, or the moon shone upon my window behind the green banana leaves, I thought of her and was carried away into a region of dreams.

My teacher noticed this, and sent word to my father, saying that he would give me ten subjects for composition and let me go home. I felt like an exiled prisoner receiving his pardon.

Strange to say, when I got on to the boat and was on my way home, I felt that a quarter of an hour was like a long year. When I arrived home, I went to pay my respects to my mother and then entered my room. Yün stood up to welcome me, and we held each other's hands in

ilence, and it seemed then that our souls had melted away or evapo-
ated like a mist. My ears tingled and I did not know where I was.

It was June, then, and the rooms were very hot. Luckily, we were
ext door to the Lotus Lover's Lodge of the Ts'anglang Pavilion on the
ast. Over the bridge, there was an open hall overlooking the water,
alled "After My Heart"—the reference was to an old poem: "When
he water is clear, I will wash the tassels of my hat, and when the water is
nuddy, I will wash my feet." By the side of the eaves, there was an old
ree which spread its green shade over the window, and made the
eople's faces look green with it; and across the creek, you could see
eople passing to and fro. This was where my father used to entertain
is guests. I asked for permission from my mother to bring Yün and
tay there for the summer. She stopped embroidery during the summer
nonths because of the heat, and the whole day long, we were either
eading together, or discussing the ancient things, or else enjoying the
noon and passing judgments on the flowers. Yün could not drink, but
ould take at most three cups when compelled to, and I taught her
iterary games in which the loser had to drink. We thought there could
not be a more happy life on earth than this.

One day Yün asked me: "Of all the ancient authors, which one should
we regard as the master?" And I replied: "*Chankuots'eh* and Chuangtse
are noted for their agility of thought and expressiveness of style,
K'uang Heng and Liu Hsiang are known for their classic severity,
Szema Ch'ien and Pan Ku are known for their breadth of knowledge,
Han Yü is known for his mellow qualities, Liu Tsungyüan for his
rugged beauty, Ouyang Hsiu for his romantic abandon, and the Su's,
father and sons, are known for their sustained eloquence. There are,
besides, writings like the political essays of Chia Yi and Tung Chung-
shu, the euphuistic prose of Hsü Ling and Yü Hsin, the memorandums
of Lu Chih, and others more than one can enumerate. True appreciation, however, must come from the reader himself."

"The ancient literature," Yün said, "depends for its appeal on depth
of thought and greatness of spirit, which I am afraid it is difficult for a
woman to attain. I believe, however, that I do understand something of
poetry."

"Poetry was used," I said, "as a literary test in the imperial examinations of the T'ang Dynasty, and people acknowledge Li Po and Tu Fu
as the master poets. Which of the two do you like better?"

"Tu's poems," she said, "are known for their workmanship and artistic refinement, while Li's poems are known for their freedom an naturalness of expression. I prefer the vivacity of Li Po to the severit of Tu Fu."

"Tu Fu is the acknowledged king of poets," said I, "and he is take by most people as their model. Why do you prefer Li Po?"

"Of course," said she, "as for perfection of form and maturity o thought, Tu is the undisputed master, but Li Po's poems have the way ward charm of a nymph. His lines come naturally like falling flower and flowing water, and are so much lovelier for their spontaneity. I an not saying that Tu is second to Li; only personally I feel, not that love Tu less, but that I love Li more."

"I say, I didn't know that you are a bosom friend of Li Po!"

"I have still in my heart another poet, Po Chüyi, who is my first tutor as it were, and I have not been able to forget him."

"What do you mean?" I asked.

"Isn't he the one who wrote the poem on *The P'i P'a Player*?"

"This is very strange," I laughed and said. "So Li *Po* is your bosom friend, *Po* Chüyi is your first tutor and your husband's literary name is San*po*. It seems that your life is always bound up with the *Po's*"

"It is all right," Yün smiled and replied, "to have one's life bound up with the *Po's,* only I am afraid I shall be writing *Po* characters all my life." (For in Soochow we call misspelt words *"po* characters.") And we both laughed.

"Now that you know poetry," I said, "I should like also to know your taste for *fu* poems."

"The *Ch'uts'e* is, of course, the fountainhead of *fu* poetry, but I find it difficult to understand. It seems to me that among the Han and Chin *fu* poets, Ssuma Hsiangju is most sublime in point of style and diction."

"Perhaps," I said, "Wenchün was tempted to elope with Hsiangju not because of his *ch'in* music, but rather because of his *fu* poetry," and we laughed again.

I am by nature unconventional and straightforward, but Yün was a stickler for forms, like the Confucian schoolmasters. Whenever I put on a dress for her or tidied up her sleeves, she would say "So much obliged" again and again, and when I passed her a towel or a fan, she must receive it standing up. At first I disliked this and said to her: "Do you mean to tie me down with all this ceremony? There is a proverb which says, 'One who is overcourteous is crafty.'" Yün blushed all over and said: "I am merely trying to be polite and respectful; why do you charge me with craftiness?" "True respect is in the heart, and does not require such empty forms," said I, but Yün said, "There is no more intimate relationship than that between children and their parents. Do you mean to say that children should behave freely towards their parents and keep their respect only in their heart?" "Oh! I was only joking," I said. "The trouble is," said Yün, "most marital troubles begin with joking. Don't you accuse me of disrespect later, for then I shall die of grief without being able to defend myself." Then I held her close to my breast and caressed her and then she smiled. From then on our conversations were full of 'I'm sorry's' and 'I beg your pardon's.' And so we remained courteous to each other for twenty-three years of our married life like Liang Hung and Meng Kuang of old, and the longer we stayed together, the more passionately attached we became to each other. Whenever we met each other in the house, whether it be in a dark room or in a narrow corridor, we used to hold each other's hands and ask: 'Where are you going?' and we did this on the sly as if afraid that people might see us. As a matter of fact, we tried at first to avoid being seen sitting or walking together, but after a while, we did not mind it any more. When Yün was sitting and talking with somebody and saw me come, she would rise and move sideways for me to sit down together with her. All this was done naturally almost without any consciousness, and although at first we felt uneasy about it, later on it became a matter of habit. I cannot understand why all old couples must hate each other like enemies. Some people say 'if they weren't enemies, they would not be able to live together until old age.' Well, I wonder!

On the seventh night of the seventh moon of that year [1780], Yün prepared incense, candles and some melons and fruits, so that we might together worship the Grandson of Heaven [1] in the Hall called "After My Heart." I had carved two seals with the inscription "That we might remain husband and wife from incarnation to incarnation." I kept the seal with positive characters, while she kept the one with negative characters, to be used in our correspondence. That night, the moon was shining beautifully and when I looked down at the creek, the ripples shone like golden chains. We were wearing light silk dresses and sitting together with a small fan in our hands, before the window overlooking the creek. Looking up at the sky, we saw the clouds sailing through the

[1] The seventh day of the seventh moon is the only day in the year when the pair of heavenly lovers, the Cowherd ("grandson of heaven") and the Spinning Maid are allowed to meet each other across the Milky Way.

heavens, changing at every moment into a myriad forms, and Yün said "This moon is common to the whole universe. I wonder if there is an other pair of lovers quite as passionate as ourselves looking at the sam moon to-night?" And I said: "Oh! there are plenty of people who wil be sitting in the cool evening and looking at the moon, and perhap also many women criticising or enjoying the clouds in their chambers but when a husband and wife are looking at the moon together, hardly think that the clouds will form the subject of their conversation." By and by, the candle-lights went out, the moon sank in the sky, and we removed the fruits and went to bed.

The fifteenth of the seventh moon was All Souls' Day. Yün prepared a little dinner, so that we could drink together with the moon as ou company, but when night came, the sky was suddenly overcast with dark clouds. Yün knitted her brow and said: "If it be the wish of God that we two should live together until there are silver threads in ou hair, then the moon must come out again to-night." On my part I fel disheartened also. As we looked across the creek, we saw will-o'-the wisps flitting in crowds hither and thither like ten thousand candle lights, threading their way through the willows and smartweeds. And then we began to compose a poem together, each saying two lines at a time, the first completing the couplet which the other had begun, and the second beginning another couplet for the other to finish, and after a few rhymes, the longer we kept on, the more nonsensical it became until it was a jumble of slapdash doggerel. By this time, Yün was buried amidst tears and laughter and choking on my breast, while I felt the fragrance of the jasmine in her hair assail my nostrils. I patted her on the shoulder and said jokingly, "I thought that the jasmine was used for decoration in women's hair because it was round like a pearl; I did not know that it is because its fragrance is so much finer when it is mixed with the smell of women's hair and powder. When it smells like that even the citron cannot remotely compare with it." Then Yün stopped laughing and said: "The citron is the gentleman among the different fragrant plants because its fragrance is so slight that you can hardly detect it; on the other hand, the jasmine is a common fellow because it borrows its fragrance partly from others. Therefore, the fragrance of the jasmine is like that of a smiling sycophant." "Why, then," I said "do you keep away from the gentleman and associate with the common fellow?" And Yün replied, "I am amused at the gentleman that loves the common fellow." While we were thus bandying words about, i was already midnight, and we saw the wind had blown away the clouds in the sky and there appeared the full moon, round like a chariot wheel, and we were greatly delighted. And so we began to drink by the side of the window, but before we had tasted three cups, we heard suddenly the noise of a splash under the bridge, as if some one had fallen into the water. We looked out through the window and saw there was not a thing, for the water was as smooth as a mirror, except that we heard the noise of a duck scampering in the marshes. I knew that there was a ghost of some one who had been drowned by the side of the Ts'anglang Pavilion, but knowing that Yün was very timid, dared not mention it to her. And Yün sighed and said: "Alas! Whence cometh this noise?" and we shuddered all over. Quickly we shut the window and carried the wine pot back into the room. A lamp light was then burning as small as a pea, and the curtains moved in the dark, and we were shaking all over. We then put out the light and went inside the bed curtain, and Yün already ran up a high fever. Soon I had a high temperature myself, and our illness dragged on for about twenty days. True it is that when the cup of happiness overflows, disaster follows, as the saying goes, and this was also an omen that we should not be able to live together until old age.

On the fifteenth of the eighth moon, or the Mid-Autumn Festival, I had just recovered from my illness. Yün had now been a bride in my home for over a year, but still had never been to the Ts'anglang Pavilion itself next door. So I first ordered an old servant to tell the watchman not to let any visitors enter the place. Toward evening, I went with Yün and my younger sister, supported by an amah and a maid-servant and led by an old attendant. We passed a bridge, entered a gate, turned eastwards and followed a zigzag path into the place, where we saw huge grottoes and abundant green trees. The Pavilion was situated on the top of a hill. Going up by the steps to the top, one could look around for miles, where in the distance chimney smoke arose from the cottages against the background of clouds of rainbow hues. Over the bank, there was a grove called the "Forest by the Hill" where the great officials used to entertain their guests. Later on, the Chengyi College was erected on this spot, but it wasn't there yet. We brought a blanket which we spread on the Pavilion floor, and then sat round together, while the watchman served us tea. After a while, the moon had already arisen from behind the forest, and the breeze was playing about my sleeves, while the moon's image sparkled in the rippling water, and all worldly cares were banished from our breasts. "This is the end of a perfect day," said Yün. "Wouldn't it be fine if we could get a boat and row around the Pavilion!" At this time, the lights were already shining from people's homes, and thinking of the incident of the fifteenth night of the seventh moon, we left the Pavilion and hurried home. According to the custom at Soochow, the women of all families, big and small, came out in groups on the Mid-Autumn night, a custom which was called "pacing the moonlight." Strange to say, no one came to such a beautiful neighbourhood as the Ts'anglang Pavilion.

My father Chiafu was very fond of adopting children; hence I had twenty-six adopted brothers. My mother, too, had nine adopted daughters, of whom Miss Wang, the second, and Miss Yü, the sixth, were Yün's best friends. Wang was a kind of a tom-boy and a great drinker while Yü was straightforward and very fond of talking. When they came together, they used to chase me out, so that the three of them could sleep in the same bed. I knew Miss Yü was responsible for this, and once I said to her in fun: "When you get married, I am going to invite your husband to come and keep him for ten days." "I'll come here, too, then," said Miss Yü, "and sleep in the same bed with Yün. Won't that be fun?" At this Yün and Wang merely smiled.

At this time, my younger brother Ch'it'ang was going to get married, and we moved to Ts'angmi Alley by the Bridge of Drinking Horses. The house was quite big, but not so well furnished as the one by the Ts'anglang Pavilion. On the birthday of my mother, we had theatrical performances at home, and Yün at first thought them quite wonderful. Scorning all taboos, my father asked for the performance of a scene called "Sad Parting," and the actors played so realistically that the audience were quite touched. I noticed across the screen that Yün suddenly got up and disappeared inside for a long time. I went in to see her and the Misses Yü and Wang also followed suit. There I saw Yün sitting alone before her dressing table, resting her head on an arm. "Why are you so sad?" I asked. "One sees a play for diversion," Yün said, "but to-day's play only breaks my heart." Both Wang and Yü were laughing at her, but I defended her. "She is touched because hers is a profoundly emotional soul." "Are you going to sit here all day long?" asked Miss Yü. "I'll stay here until some better selection is being played," Yün replied. Hearing this, Miss Wang left first and asked my mother to select more cheerful plays like *Ch'ihliang* and *Househ*. Then Yün was persuaded to come out and watch the play, which made her happy again.

My uncle Such'un died early without an heir, and my father made me succeed his line. His tomb was situated on Longevity Hill in Hsi-k'uatang by the side of our ancestral tombs, and it was our custom to go and visit the grave every spring. As there was a beautiful garden called Koyüan in its neighbourhood, Miss Wang begged to come with us. Yün saw that the pebbles on this hill had beautiful grains of different colours, and said to me: "If we were to collect these pebbles and make them into a grotto, it would be even more artistic than one made of Hsüanchow stones." I expressed the fear that there might not be enough of this kind. "If Yün really likes them, I'll pick them for you," said Miss Wang. So we borrowed a bag from the watchman, and went along collecting them. Whenever she saw one, she would ask for my opinion. If I said 'good,' she would pick it; and if I said 'no,' she would discard it. Very soon we had a fairly full bag and Miss Wang was perspiring all over. "If we get any more, we shan't be able to carry them home," she said. "I have been told," said Yün, as we were going along, "that mountain fruits must be gathered by monkeys, which seems quite true." Miss Wang was furious and stretched both hands as if to scratch her. I stopped her and said to Yün by way of reproof: "You cannot blame her for being angry, because she is doing all the work and you stand by and say such unkind things." Then on our way back, we visited the Koyüan Garden, in which we saw a profusion of flowers of all colours. Wang was very childish; she would break a flower branch for no reason, and Yün scolded her, saying: "You are not going to put it in a vase or in your hair. Why destroy flowers like that?" "Oh! what's the harm? These flowers don't feel anything." "All right," I said, "you will be punished for this one day by marrying a pock-marked bearded fellow for your husband to avenge the flowers." Wang looked at me in anger, threw the flowers to the ground, and kicked them into the pond. "Why do you all bully me?" she said. However, Yün made it up with her, and she was finally pacified.

Yün was at first very quiet and loved to hear me talk, but I gradually taught her the art of conversation as one leads a cricket with a blade of grass. She then gradually learnt the art of conversation. For instance, at meals, she always mixed her rice with tea, and loved to eat stale pickled bean-curd, called 'stinking bean-curd' in Soochow. Another thing she liked to eat was a kind of small pickled cucumber. I hated both of these things, and said to her in fun one day: "The dog, which has no stomach, eats human refuse because it doesn't know that refuse stinks, while the beetle rolls in dunghills and is changed into a cicada because it wants to fly up to heaven. Now are you a dog or a beetle?" To this Yün replied: "One eats bean-curd because it is so cheap and it goes with dry rice as well as with congee. I am used to this from childhood. Now I am married into your home, like a beetle that has been transformed into a cicada, but I am still eating it because one should not forget old friends. As for pickled cucumber, I tasted it for the first time in your home." "Oh, then, my home is a dog's kennel, isn't it?" Yün was embarrassed and tried to explain it away by saying: "Of course there is refuse in every home; the only difference is whether one eats it or not. You yourself eat garlic, for instance, and I have tried to eat it with you. I won't compel you to eat stinking bean-curd, but cucumber is really very nice, if you hold your breath while eating. You will see when you have tasted it yourself. It is like Wuyien, an ugly but virtuous woman." "Are you going to make me a dog?" I asked. "Well, I have been a dog for a long time, why don't you try to be one?" So she picked one with her chopsticks and pushed it into my mouth. I held my breath and ate it and found it indeed delicious. Then I ate it in the usual way and found it to have a marvellous flavour. And from that time on, I loved the cucumber also. Yün also prepared pickled bean-curd mixed with sesame seed oil and sugar, which I found also to be a delicacy. We then mixed pickled cucumber with pickled bean-curd and called the mixture 'the double-flavoured gravy.' I said I could not understand why I disliked it at first and began to love it so now. "If you are in love with a thing, you will forget its ugliness," said Yün.

My younger brother Ch'it'ang married the daughter of Wang Hsüchou. It happened that on the wedding day, she wanted some pearls. Yün took her own pearls, which she had received as her bridal gift, and gave them to my mother. The maid-servant thought it a pity, but Yün said: "A woman is an incarnation of the female principle, and so are pearls. For a woman to wear pearls would be to leave no room for the male principle. For that reason I don't prize them." She had, however, a peculiar fondness for old books and broken slips of painting. Whenever she saw odd volumes of books, she would try to sort them out, arrange them in order, and have them rebound properly. These were collected and labelled "Ancient Relics." When she saw scrolls of calligraphy or painting that were partly spoilt, she would find some old paper and paste them up nicely, and ask me to fill up the broken spaces.[2] These were kept rolled up properly and called "Beautiful Gleanings." This was what she was busy about the whole day when she was not attending to the kitchen or needle-work. When she found in old trunks or piles of musty volumes any writing or painting that pleased her, she felt as if she had discovered some precious relic, and an old woman neighbour of ours, by the name of Feng, used to buy up old scraps and sell them to her. She had the same tastes and habits as myself, and besides had the talent of anticipating my wishes, doing things without being told and doing them to my perfect satisfaction.

Once I said to her: "It is a pity that you were born a woman. If you were a man, we could travel together and visit all the famous places of the world."

"Oh! this is not so very difficult," said Yün. "Wait till I am middle-aged. Even if I cannot accompany you to the five sacred mountains then, we can travel to the nearer places, like Huch'iu and Lingyen, as far south as the West Lake and as far north as P'ingshan [in Yangchow]."

"Of course this is all right, except that I am afraid when you are middle-aged, you will be too old to travel."

"If I can't do it in this life, then I shall do it in the next."

"In the next life, you must be born a man and I will be your wife."

"It will be quite beautiful if we can then still remember what has happened in this life."

"That's all very well, but even a bowl of congee has provided material for so much conversation. We shan't be able to sleep a wink the whole wedding night, but shall be discussing what we have done in the previous existence, if we can still remember what's happened in this life then."

"It is said that the Old Man under the Moon is in charge of matrimony," said Yün. "He was good enough to make us husband and wife in this life, and we shall still depend on his favour in the affair of marriage in the next incarnation. Why don't we make a painting of him and worship him in our home?"

So we asked a Mr. Ch'i Liut'i, who specialised in portraiture, to make a painting of the Old Man under the Moon, which he did. It was a picture of the Old Man holding a red silk thread in one hand and a walking-stick with the Book of Matrimony suspended from it in the other.

[2] The author was a painter, and for a time painted for his living. Some of his paintings still remain.

He had white hair and a ruddy complexion, apparently bustling about in a cloudy region. Altogether it was a very excellent painting of Ch'i's. My friend Shih Chot'ang wrote some words on it and we hung the picture in our chamber. On the first and fifteenth of every month, we burnt incense and prayed together before him. I do not know where this picture is now, after all the changes and upsets in our family life. "Ended is the present life and uncertain the next," as the poet says. I wonder if God will listen to the prayer of us two silly lovers.

After we had moved to Ts'angmi Alley, I called our bedroom the "Tower of Guests' Fragrance," with a reference to Yün's name,[3] and to the story of Liang Hung and Meng Kuang who as husband and wife were always courteous to each other "like guests." We rather disliked the house because the walls were too high and the courtyard was too small. At the back, there was another house, leading to the library. Looking out of the window at the back, one could see the old garden of Mr. Lu, then in a dilapidated condition. Yün's thoughts still hovered about the beautiful scenery of the Ts'anglang Pavilion.

At this time, there was an old peasant woman living on the east of Mother Gold's Bridge and the north of Kenghsiang. Her little cottage was surrounded on all sides by vegetable fields and had a wicker gate. Outside the gate, there was a pond about thirty yards across, surrounded by a wilderness of trees on all sides. This was the old site of the home of Chang Shihch'eng of the Yüan Dynasty. A few paces to the west of the cottage, there was a mound filled with broken bricks, from the top of which one could command a view of the surrounding territory, which was an open country with a stretch of wild vegetation. Once the old woman happened to mention the place, and Yün kept on thinking about it. So she said to me one day: "Since leaving the Ts'anglang Pavilion, I have been dreaming about it all the time. As we cannot live there, we must put up with the second best. I have a great idea to go and live in the old woman's cottage." "I have been thinking, too," I said, "of a place to go to and spend the long summer days. If you think you'll like the place, I'll go ahead and take a look. If it is satisfactory, we can carry our beddings along and go and stay there for a month. How about it?" "I'm afraid mother won't allow us." "Oh! I'll see to that," I told her. So the next day, I went there and found that the cottage consisted only of two rooms, which could be partitioned into four. With paper windows and bamboo beds, the house would be quite a delight-

[3] "Yün" in Chinese means a fragrant weed.

fully cool place to stay in. The old woman knew what I wanted and gladly rented me her bedroom, which then looked quite new, when I had repapered the walls. I then informed my mother of it and went to stay there with Yün.

Our only neighbours were an old couple who raised vegetables for the market. They knew that we were going to stay there for the summer, and came and called on us, bringing us some fish from the pond and vegetables from their own fields. We offered to pay for them, but as they wouldn't take any money, Yün made a pair of shoes for them, which they were finally persuaded to accept. This was in July when the trees cast a green shade over the place. The summer breeze blew over the water of the pond, and cicadas filled the air with their singing the whole day. Our old neighbour also made a fishing line for us, and we used to angle together under the shade. Late in the afternoons, we would go up on the mound to look at the evening glow and compose lines of poetry, when we felt so inclined. Two of the lines were:

> "Beast-clouds swallow the sinking sun,
> And the bow-moon shoots the falling stars."

After a while, the moon cut her image in the water, insects began to cry all round, and we placed a bamboo bed near the hedgerow to sit or lie upon. The old woman then would inform us that wine had been warmed up and dinner prepared, and we would sit down to have a little drink under the moon. After we had a bath, we would put on our slippers and carry a fan, and lie or sit there, listening to old tales of retribution told by our neighbour. When we came in to sleep about midnight, we felt our whole body nice and cool, almost forgetting that we were living in a city.

There along the hedgerow, we asked the gardener to plant chrysanthemums. The flowers bloomed in the ninth moon, and we continued to stay there for another ten days. My mother was also quite delighted and came to see us there. So we ate crabs in the midst of chrysanthemums and whiled away the whole day. Yün was quite enchanted with all this and said: "Some day we must build a cottage here. We'll buy ten *mu* of ground, and around it we'll plant vegetables and melons for our food. You will paint and I will do embroidery, from which we could make enough money to buy wine and compose poems over dinners. Thus, clad in simple gowns and eating simple meals, we could live a very happy life together without going anywhere." I fully agreed with her.

Now the place is still there, while the one who knows my heart is dead. Alas! such is life!

About half a *li* from my home, there was a temple to the God of Tungt'ing Lake, popularly known as the Narcissus Temple, situated in the Ch'uk'u Alley. It had many winding corridors and a small garden with pavilions. On the birthday of the God, every clan would be assigned a corner in the Temple, where they would hang beautiful glass lamps of a kind, with a table in the centre, on which were placed vases on wooden stands. These vases were decorated with flowers for competition. In the day time, there would be theatrical performances, while at night the flower-vases were brilliantly illuminated with candlelights, a custom which was called "Illuminated Flowers." With the flowers and the lanterns and the smell of incense, the whole place resembled a night feast in the Palace of the Dragon King. The people there would sing or play music, or gossip over their tea-cups. The audience stood around in crowds to look at the show and there was a railing at the curb to keep them within a certain limit.

I was asked by my friend to help in the decorations and so had the pleasure of taking part in it. When Yün heard me speaking about it at home, she remarked: "It is a pity that I am not a man and cannot go to see it." "Why, you could put on my cap and gown and disguise yourself as a man," I suggested. Accordingly she changed her coiffure into a queue, painted her eyebrows, and put on my cap. Although her hair showed slightly round the temples, it passed off tolerably well. As my gown was found to be an inch and a half too long, she tucked it round the waist and put on a *makua* on top. "What am I going to do about my feet?" she asked. I told her there was a kind of shoes called "butterfly shoes," which could fit any size of feet and were very easy to obtain at the shops, and suggested buying a pair for her, which she could also use as slippers later on at home. Yün was delighted with the idea, and after supper, when she had finished her make-up, she paced about the room, imitating the gestures and gait of a man for a long time, when all of a sudden she changed her mind and said: "I am not going! It would be so embarrassing if somebody should discover me, and besides, our parents would object." Still I urged her to go. "Who doesn't know me at the Temple?" I said. "Even if they should find it out, they would laugh it off as a joke. Mother is at present in the home of the ninth sister. We could steal away and back without letting anyone know about it."

Yün then had such fun looking at herself in the mirror. I dragged her along and we stole away together to the Temple. For a long time nobody in the Temple could detect it. When people asked, I simply said she was my boy cousin, and people would merely curtsy with their hands together and pass on. Finally, we came to a place where there were some young women and girls sitting behind the flower show. They were the family of the owner of that show, by the name of Yang. Yün suddenly went over to talk with them, and while talking, she casually leant over and touched the shoulder of a young woman. The maid-servants near by shouted angrily: "How dare the rascal!" I attempted to explain and smooth the matter over, but the servants still scowled ominously on us, and seeing that the situation was desperate, Yün took off her cap and showed her feet, saying "Look here, I am a woman, too!" They all stared at each other in surprise, and then, instead of being angry, began to laugh. We were then asked to sit down and have some tea. Soon afterwards we got sedan chairs and came home.

When Mr. Ch'ien Shihcho of Wukiang died of an illness, my father wrote a letter to me, asking me to go and attend the funeral. Yün secretly expressed her desire to come along, since on our way to Wukiang, we would pass the Taihu Lake, which she wished very much to see. I told her that I was just thinking it would be too lonely for me to go alone, and that it would be excellent, indeed, if she could come along, except that I could not think of a pretext for her going. "Oh! I could say that I am going to see my mother," Yün said. "You can go ahead, and I shall come along to meet you." "If so," I said, "we can tie up our boat beneath the Bridge of Ten Thousand Years on our way home, where we shall be able to look at the moon again as we did at the Ts'anglang Pavilion."

This was on the eighteenth day of the sixth moon. That day, I brought a servant and arrived first at Hsükiang Ferry, where I waited for her in the boat. By and by, Yün arrived in a sedan chair, and we started off, passing by the Tiger's Roar Bridge, where the view opened up and I saw sailing boats and birds on the sand-banks. The water was a white stretch, joining the sky at the horizon. "So this is Taihu!" Yün exclaimed. "I know now how big the universe is, and I have not lived in vain! I think a good many ladies never see such a view in their whole life-time." As we were occupied in conversation, it wasn't very long before we saw swaying willows on the banks, and we knew we had arrived at Wukiang.

I went up to attend the funeral ceremony, but when I came back, Yün was not in the boat. I asked the boatman and he said: "Don't you see some one under the willow trees by the bridge, watching the cormorants catching fish?" Yün, then, had gone up with the boatman's daughter. I followed her there, and saw that she was perspiring all over, still leaning on the boatman's daughter and standing there absorbed looking at the cormorants. I patted her shoulder and said, "You are wet through." Yün turned her head and said, "I was afraid that your friend Ch'ien might come to the boat, so I left to avoid him. Why did you come back so early?" "In order to catch the renegade!" I replied.

We then came back hand-in-hand to the boat, and when we stopped at the Bridge of Ten Thousand Years, the sun had not yet gone down. And we let down all the windows to allow the river breeze to come in, and there, dressed in light silk and holding a fan, we sliced a melon to cool ourselves. Soon the evening glow was casting a red hue over the bridge, and the distant haze enveloped the willow trees in darkness. The moon then came up, and all along the river we saw a stretch of lights coming from the fishing boats. I asked my servant to go astern and have a drink with the boatman.

The boatman's daughter was called Suyün. She was quite a likeable girl, and I had known her before. I beckoned her to come and sit together with Yün on the bow of the boat. We did not put on any light, so that we could the better enjoy the moon, and there we sat drinking and playing literary games with wine as forfeit. Suyün just stared at us, listening for a long time before she said: "Now I am quite familiar with all sorts of wine-games, but have never heard of this one. Will you explain it to me?" Yün tried to explain it by all sorts of analogies to her, but still she failed to understand. Then I laughed and said: "Will the lady teacher please stop a moment? I have a parable for explaining it, and she will understand at once." "You try it, then!" "The stork," I said, "can dance, but cannot plow, while the buffalo can plow, but cannot dance. That lies in the nature of things. You are making a fool of yourself by trying to teach the impossible to her." Suyün pummelled my shoulder playfully, and Yün said: "Hereafter let's make a rule: let's have it out with our mouths, but no hands! One who breaks the rule will have to drink a big cup." As Suyün was a great drinker, she filled a cup full and drank it up at a draught. "I suggest that one may be allowed to use one's hands for caressing, but not for striking," I said. Yün then playfully pushed Suyün into my lap, saying, "Now you can caress her to your full." "How stupid of you!" I laughed in reply. "The beauty of caressing lies in doing it naturally and half unconsciously. Only a country bumpkin will hug and caress a woman roughly." I noticed that the jasmine in her hair gave out a strange fragrance, mixed with the flavour of wine, powder and hair lotion, and remarked to her: "The 'mean little fellow' stinks all over the place. It makes me sick." Hearing this, Suyün struck me with her fist in a rage, saying:

"Who told you to smell it?"

"She breaks the rule! Two cups!" Yün shouted.

"He called me 'mean little fellow.' Why shouldn't I strike him?" explained Suyün.

"He really means by the 'mean little fellow' something which you don't understand. You finish these two cups first and I'll tell you."

When Suyün had finished the two cups, Yün told her of our discussion about the jasmine at the Ts'anglang Pavilion.

"Then the mistake is mine. I must be penalised again," said Suyün. And she drank a third cup.

Yün said then that she had long heard of her reputation as a singer and would like to hear her sing. This Suyün did beautifully, beating time with her ivory chop-sticks on a little plate. Yün drank merrily until she was quite drunk, when she took a sedan-chair and went home first, while I remained chatting with Suyün for a moment, and then walked home under the moonlight.

At this time, we were staying in the home of our friend Lu Panfang, in a house called Hsiaoshuanglou. A few days afterwards, Mrs. Lu heard of the story from someone, and secretly told Yün: "Do you know that your husband was drinking a few days ago at the Bridge of Ten Thousand Years with two sing-song girls?" "Yes, I do," replied Yün, "and one of the sing-song girls was myself." Then she told her the whole story and Mrs. Lu had a good laugh at herself.

When I came back from eastern Kwangtung in July, 1794, there was a cousin of mine, by the name of Hsü Hsiufeng, who had brought home with him a concubine. He was crazy about her beauty and asked Yün to go and see her. After seeing her, Yün remarked to Hsiufeng one day, "She has beauty, but no charm." "Do you mean to say that when your husband takes a concubine, she must have both beauty and charm?" answered Hsiufeng. Yün replied in the affirmative. So from that time on, she was quite bent on finding a concubine for me, but was short of cash.

At this time there was a Chekiang sing-song girl by the name of Wen

Lenghsiang, who was staying at Soochow. She had composed four poems on the Willow Catkins which were talked about all over the city, and many scholars wrote poems in reply, using the same rhyme-words as her originals, as was the custom. There was a friend of mine, Hsienhan of Wukiang, who was a good friend of Lenghsiang and brought her poems to me, asking me to write some in reply. Yün wasn't interested because she did not think much of her, but I was intrigued and composed one on the flying willow catkins which filled the air in May. Two lines which Yün liked very much were:

> "They softly touch the spring sorrow in my bosom,
> And gently stir the longings in her heart."

On the fifth day of the eighth moon in the following year, my mother was going to see Huch'iu with Yün, when Hsienhan suddenly appeared and said: "I am going to Huch'iu, too. Will you come along with me and see a beautiful sing-song girl?" I told my mother to go ahead and agreed to meet her at Pant'ang near Huch'iu. My friend then dragged me to Lenghsiang's place. I saw that Lenghsiang was already in her middle-age, but she had a girl by the name of Hanyüan, who was a very sweet young maiden, still in her 'teens. Her eyes looked like an autumn lake that cooled one by its cold splendour. After talking with her for a while, I learnt that she knew how to read and write. There was also a younger sister of hers, by the name of Wenyüan, who was still a mere child. I had then no thought of going with a sing-song girl, fully realizing that, as a poor scholar, I could not afford to give a feast in return. But since I was there already, I tried to get along as best I could.

"Are you trying to seduce me?" I said to Hsienhan secretly.

"No," he replied, "someone had invited me to-day to a dinner in Hanyüan's place in return for a previous dinner. It happened that the host himself was invited by an important person, and I am acting in his place. Don't you worry!"

I felt then quite relieved. Arriving at Pant'ang, we met my mother's boat, and I asked Hanyüan to go over to her boat and meet Yün. When Yün and Han met each other, they instinctively took to each other like old friends, and later they went hand-in-hand to see the famous hill. Yün was especially fond of a place called "A Thousand Acres of Clouds," and she remained there for a long time, lost in admiration of the scenery. We returned to the Bank of Rural Fragrance where we tied up the boats and had a jolly drinking party together.

When we started on our way home, Yün said: "Will you please go over to the other boat with your friend, while I share this one with Han?" We did as she suggested, and I did not return to my boat until we had passed the Tut'ing Bridge, where we parted from my friend and Hanyüan. It was midnight by the time we returned home.

"Now I have found a girl who has both beauty and charm," Yün said to me. "I have already asked Hanyüan to come and see us to-morrow, and I'll arrange it for you." I was taken by surprise.

"You know we are not a wealthy family. We can't afford to keep a girl like that, and we are so happily married. Why do you want to find somebody else?"

"But I love her," said Yün smilingly. "You just leave it to me."

The following afternoon, Hanyüan actually came. Yün was very cordial to her and prepared a feast, and we played the finger-guessing game and drank, but during the whole dinner, not a word was mentioned about securing her for me. When Hanyüan had gone, Yün said, "I have secretly made another appointment with her to come on the eighteenth, when we will pledge ourselves as sisters. You must prepare a sacrificial offering for the occasion"; and pointing to the bracelet on her arm, she continued, "if you see this bracelet appear on Hanyüan's arm, you'll understand that she has consented. I have already hinted at it to her, but we haven't got to know each other as thoroughly as I should like to yet." I had to let her have her own way.

On the eighteenth, Hanyüan turned up in spite of a pouring rain. She disappeared in the bedroom for a long time before she came out hand-in-hand with Yün. When she saw me, she felt a little shy, for the bracelet was already on her arm. After we had burnt incense and pledged an oath, we continued to drink again. It happened that Hanyüan had an engagement to go and visit Shih-hu Lake, and soon she left.

Yün came to me all smiles and said, "Now that I have found a beauty for you, how are you going to reward the go-between?" I asked her for the details.

"I had to broach the topic delicately to her," she said, "because I was afraid that she might have someone else in mind. Now I have learnt that there isn't anyone, and I asked her, 'Do you understand why we have this dinner today?' 'I should feel greatly honoured if I could come to your home, but my mother is expecting a lot of me and I can't decide by myself. We will watch and see,' she replied. As I was putting on the bracelet, I told her again, 'The jade is chosen for its hardness as a token of fidelity and the bracelet's roundness is a symbol of everlasting faithfulness. Meanwhile, please put it on as a token of our pledge.' She replied that everything depended on her mother. So it seems that she is willing herself. The only difficulty is her mother, Lenghsiang. We will wait and see how it turns out."

"Are you going to enact the comedy *Linhsiangpan* of Li Liweng right in our home?"

"Yes!" Yün replied.

From that time on, not a day passed without her mentioning Hanyüan's name. Eventually Hanyüan was married by force to some influential person, and our arrangements did not come off. And Yün actually died of grief on this account.

CHAPTER II: THE LITTLE PLEASURES OF LIFE

I REMEMBER that when I was a child, I could stare at the sun with wide, open eyes. I could see the tiniest objects, and loved to observe the fine grains and patterns of small things, from which I derived a romantic, unworldly pleasure. When mosquitoes were humming round in summer, I transformed them in my imagination into a company of storks dancing in the air. And when I regarded them that way, they were real storks to me, flying by the hundreds and thousands, and I would look up at them until my neck was stiff. Again, I kept a few mosquitoes inside a white curtain and blew a puff of smoke round them, so that to me they became a company of white storks flying among the clouds, and their humming was to me the song of storks singing in high heaven, which delighted me intensely. Sometimes I would squat by a broken, earthen wall, or by a little bush on a raised flower-bed, with my eyes on the same level as the flower-bed itself, and there I would look and look, transforming in my mind the little plot of grass into a forest and the ants and insects into wild animals. The little elevations on the ground became my hills, and the depressed areas became my valleys, and my spirit wandered in that world at leisure. One day, I saw two little insects fighting among the grass, and while I was all absorbed watching the fight, there suddenly appeared a big monster, overturning my hills and tearing up my forest—it was a little frog. With one lick of his tongue, he swallowed up the two little insects. I was so lost in my young imaginary world that I was taken unawares and quite frightened. When I had recovered myself, I caught the frog, struck it several dozen times and chased it out of the courtyard. Thinking of this incident afterwards when I was grown up, I understood that these two little insects were committing adultery by rape. "The wages of sin is death," so says an ancient proverb, and I wondered whether it was true of the insects also. I was a naughty boy, and once my ball (for we call the genital organ a 'ball' in Soochow) was bitten by an earthworm and became swollen. [Believing that the duck's saliva would act as an antidote for insect bites,] they held a duck over it, but the maid-servant, who was holding the duck, accidentally let her hand go, and the duck was going to swallow it. I got frightened and screamed. People used to tell this story to make fun of me. These were the little incidents of my childhood days.

When I was grown up, I loved flowers very much and was very fond of training pot flowers and flower trees. When I knew Chang Lanp'o, I learnt from him the secrets of trimming branches and protecting joints, and later the art of grafting trees and making rockeries. The orchid was prized most among all the flowers because of its subdued fragrance and graceful charm, but it was difficult to obtain really good classic varieties. When Lanp'o died, he presented me with a pot of spring orchids, whose flowers had lotus-shaped petals; the centre of the flowers was broad and white, the petals were very neat and even at the "shoulders," and the stems were very slender. This type was classical, and I prized it like a piece of old jade. When I was working away from home, Yün used to take care of it personally and it grew beautifully. After two years, it died suddenly one day. I dug up its roots and found that they were white like marble, while nothing was wrong with the sprouts, either. At first, I could not understand this, but ascribed it with a sigh merely to my own bad luck, which might be unworthy to keep such flowers. Later on, I found out that some one had asked for some of the flowers from the same pot, had been refused, and had therefore killed it by pouring boiling water over it. Thenceforth I swore I would never grow orchids again.

Next in preference came the azalea. Although it had no smell, its flowers lasted a long time and were very beautiful to look at, in addition to its being easy to train up. Because Yün loved these flowers so much, she would not stand for too much cutting and trimming, and that was the reason why it was difficult to make them grow into trees. The same thing was true of the other pot flowers.

The chrysanthemum, however, was my passion in the autumn of every year. I loved to arrange these flowers in vases, but not to raise them in pots, not because I did not want to have them that way, but because I had no garden in my home and could not take care of them myself. What I bought at the market were not properly trained and not to my liking. When arranging chrysanthemum flowers in vases, one should take an odd, not an even, number, and each vase should have flowers of only one colour. The mouth of the vase should be broad, so that the flowers can lie easily together. Whether there be half a dozen flowers or even thirty or forty of them in a vase, they should be so arranged as to come up together straight from the mouth of the vase, neither overcrowded, nor too much spread out, nor leaning against the mouth of the vase. This is called "keeping the handle firm." Sometimes they can stand gracefully erect, and sometimes spread out in different directions. In order to avoid a bare monotonous effect, they should be mixed with some flower buds and arranged in a kind of studied disorderliness. The leaves should not be too thick and the stems should not be too stiff. In using pins to hold the stems up, one should break the long pins off, rather than expose them. This is called "keeping the mouth of the vase clear." Place from three to seven vases on a table, depending on the size of the latter, for if there were too many of them, they would be overcrowded, looking like chrysanthemum screens at the market. The stands for the vases should be of different height, from three or four inches to two and a half feet, so that the different vases at different heights would balance one another and belong intimately to one another as in a picture with unity of composition. To put one vase low in the centre with two high at the sides, or to put a low one in front and a tall one behind, or to arrange them in symmetrical pairs, would be to create what is vulgarly called "a heap of gorgeous refuse." Proper spacing and arrangement must depend on the individual who has an understanding of pictorial composition.

In the case of flower bowls or open dishes, the method of making a support for the flowers is to mix refined resin with elm bark, flour and oil, and heat up the mixture with hot hay ashes until it becomes a kind of glue, and with it glue some nails upside down on to a piece of copper. This copper plate can then be heated up and glued on to the bottom of the bowl or dish. When it is cold, tie the flowers in groups by means of wire and stick them on those nails. The flowers should be allowed to incline sideways and not shoot up from the centre; it is also important that the stems and leaves should not come to closely together. After this is done, put some water in the bowl and cover up the copper support with some clean sand, so that the flowers will seem to grow directly from the bottom of the bowl.

When picking branches from flower trees for decoration in vases, it is important to know how to trim them before putting them in the vase, for one cannot always go and pick them oneself, and those picked by others are often unsatisfactory. Hold the branch in your hand and turn it back and forth in different ways in order to see how it lies most expressively. After one has made up one's mind about it, lop off the superfluous branches, with the idea of making the twig look thin and sparse and quaintly beautiful. Next think how the stem is going to lie in the vase and with what kind of bend, so that when it is put there, the leaves and flowers can be shown to the best advantage. If one just takes any old branch in hand, chooses a straight section and puts it in the vase, the consequence will be that the stem will be too stiff, the branches will be too close together and the flowers and leaves will be turned in the wrong direction, devoid of all charm and expression. To make a straight twig crooked, cut a mark half way across the stem and insert a little piece of broken brick or stone at the joint; the straight branch will then become a bent one. In case the stem is too weak, put one or two pins to strengthen it. By means of this method, even maple leaves and bamboo twigs or even ordinary grass and thistles will look very well for decoration. Put a twig of green bamboo side by side with a few berries of Chinese matrimony vines, or arrange some fine blades of grass together with some branches of thistle. They will look quite poetic, if the arrangement is correct.

In planting new trees, it does not matter if the trunk comes up from the ground at an angle, for if let alone for a year, it will grow upwards by itself. On the other hand, if one lets the stem come up in a perpendicular line, it will be difficult later on for it to have a dynamic posture. As to the training of pot flowers, one should choose those with claw-like roots coming above the surface of the ground. Lop off the first three branches from the ground before allowing the next one to grow up, making a bend at every point where a new branch starts off. There should be seven such bends, or perhaps nine, from the lower end of a tree to its top. It is against good taste to have swollen joints at these bends, or to have two branches growing directly opposite each other at the same point. These must branch off in all directions from different points, for if one only allows those on the right and left to grow up, the effect will be very bare, or "the chest and back will be exposed," as we say. Nor, for instance, should they grow straight from the front or behind. There are "double-trunked" and "treble-trunked" trees which all spring from the same root above the ground. If the root were not claw-shaped, they would look like planted sticks and would on that account be disqualified.

The proper training of a tree, however, takes at least thirty to forty years. In my whole life, I have seen only one person, old Wan Ts'aichang of my district, who succeeded in training several trees in his life. Once I also saw at the home of a merchant at Yangchow two pots, one of boxwood and one of cypress, presented to him by a friend from Yüshan, but this was like casting pearls before swine. Outside these cases, I have not seen any really good ones. Trees whose branches are trained in different horizontal circles going up like a pagoda or whose branches turn round and round like earthworms are incurably vulgar.

When arranging miniature sceneries with flowers and stones in a pot, design so that a small one could suggest a painting, and a big one the infinite. One should make it so that, with a pot of tea, one could lose oneself in a world of imagination; and only this kind should be kept in one's private studio for enjoyment. Once I planted some narcissus and could not find any pebbles from Lingpi for use in the pot, and I substituted them with pieces of coal that looked like rocks. One can also take five or seven pea sprouts of different size, and plant them in sand in an oblong earthen basin, decorated with charcoal instead of pebbles. The black of the charcoal will then contrast vividly with the white of the pea sprouts, quite interesting to look at. It is impossible to enumerate all the possible variations, but if one exercises one's ingenuity, it will be found to be an endless source of pleasure. For instance, one can take some calamus seeds in the mouth, chew them together with cold rice soup, and blow them on to pieces of charcoal. Keep them in a dark damp place and fine little calamus will grow from them. These pieces of charcoal can then be placed in any flower basin, looking like moss-covered rocks. Or one can take some old lotus seeds, grind off slightly both ends, and put them in an egg-shell, making a hen sit on it together with other eggs. When the little chickens are hatched, take the egg out also and plant the old lotus seeds in old clay from swallows' nests, prepared with twenty per cent of ground asparagus. Keep these then in a small vessel filled with river water, and expose them to the morning sun. When the flowers bloom, they will be only the size of a wine cup, while the leaves will be about the size of a bowl, very cute and beautiful to look at.

As to the planning of garden pavilions, towers, winding corridors and out-houses, the designing of rockery and the training of flower-trees, one should try to show the small in the big, and the big in the small, and provide for the real in the unreal and for the unreal in the real. One reveals and conceals alternately, making it sometimes apparent and sometimes hidden. This is not just rhythmic irregularity, nor does it depend on having a wide space and great expenditure of labour and material. Pile up a mound with earth dug from the ground, and decorate it with rocks, mingled with flowers; use live plum-branches for your fence, and plant creepers over the walls. Thus one can create the effect of a hill out of a flat piece of ground. In the big, open spaces, plant bamboos that grow quickly and train plum-trees with thick branches to screen them off. This is to show the small in the big. When a courtyard is small, the wall should run in convex and concave lines, decorated with green, covered with ivy and inlaid with big slabs of stone with inscriptions on them. Thus when you open your window, you seem to face a rocky hillside, alive with rugged beauty. This is to show the big in the small. Contrive so that an apparently blind alley leads suddenly into an open space and a kitchen leads through a backdoor into an unexpected courtyard. This is to provide for the real in the unreal. Let a door lead into a blind courtyard and conceal the view by placing a few bamboo trees and a few rocks before it. Thus you suggest something which is not there. Place low balustrades along the top of a wall so as to suggest a roof garden. This is to provide for the unreal in the real.

Poor scholars who live in crowded houses should follow the method of the boatmen in our native district who make clever arrangements with their limited space on the bows of their boats by devising certain modifications, such as making a series of successive elevations one after another, and using them as beds, of which there may be three in a little room, and separating them with papered wooden partitions. The effect will be compact and wonderful to look at, like surveying a long stretch of road, and one will not feel the cramping of space. When my wife and I were staying at Yangchow, we lived in a house of only two beams, but the two bedrooms, the kitchen and the parlour were all arranged in this method, with an exquisite effect and great saving of space. Yün once said to me laughingly, "The arrangements are exquisite enough, but after all, they lack the luxurious atmosphere of a rich man's house." It was so indeed.

Once I visited my ancestral tombs on the hill and found some pebbles of great beauty, with faint tracings on them. On coming back, I talked it over with Yün, and said: "People mix putty with Hsüanchow stones in white stone basins, because the colours of the two elements blend. These yellow pebbles of this hill, however, are different, and although they are rugged and simple, they will not blend in colour with putty. What can we do?" "Take some of the worse quality," she said, "pound them into small pieces and mix them in the putty before it is dry, and perhaps when it is dry, the colour will be uniform." So we did as she suggested, and took a rectangular Yihsing earthen basin, on which we piled up a mountain peak on the left coming down in undulations to the right. On its back, we made rugged square lines in the style of rock paintings of Ni Yünlin, so that the whole looked like a rocky precipice overhanging a river. At one corner we made a hollow place, which we filled with mud and planted with multi-leaf white duckweed, while the rocks were planted with dodder. This took us quite a few days to finish. In late autumn, the dodder grew all over the hill, like wistarias hanging down from a rock. The red dodder flowers made a striking contrast to the white duckweed, which had grown luxuriantly, too, from the pond underneath. Looking at it, one could imagine oneself transported to some fairy region. We put this under the eaves, and discussed between ourselves where we should build a pavilion by the water, where we should put a farmer's hut, and where we should put a stone inscription: "Where petals fall and waters flow." And Yün further discussed with me where we could build our home, where we could fish, and where we could go up for a better view of the distance, all so absorbed in it as if we were moving to live in that little imaginary universe. One night, two cats were fighting for food and the whole thing fell down from the eaves, broken into pieces, basin and all. I sighed and said, "The gods seem to be jealous of even such a little effort of ours." And we both shed tears.

To burn incense in a quiet room is one of the cultivated pleasures of a leisurely life. Yün used to burn aloes-wood and *shuhsiang* [a kind of fragrant wood from Cambodia]. She used to steam the wood first in a cauldron thoroughly, and then place it on a copper wire net over a stove, about half an inch from the fire. Under the action of the slow fire, the wood would give out a kind of subtle fragrance without any visible noke. Another thing, the "buddha's fingers" [a variety of citrus] ould not be smelt by a drunken man, or it would easily rot. It is also ad for the quince to perspire [as under atmospheric changes], and hen it does so, one should wash it with water. The citrus alone is easy take care of, because it is not afraid of being handled. There are different ways of taking care of "buddha's fingers" and the quince which annot be expressed in so many words. I have seen people who take one f these things, which have been properly kept, and handle or smell it arelessly and put it down again roughly, which shows that they do not now the art of preserving these things.

In my home I always had pot flowers on my desk. "You know very ell about arranging flowers in vases for all kinds of weather," said ün to me one day. "I think you have really understood the art, but ere is a way of sticking insects on to a painting which you haven't ied yet. Why don't you try?"

"I'm afraid," I replied, "that I cannot hold the insect's legs still. What an I do?"

"I know a way, except that I am afraid it would be too cruel," said ün.

"Tell me about it," I asked.

"You know that an insect does not change its colour after death. You an find a mantis or cicada or a butterfly; kill it with a pin and use a ne wire to tie its neck to the flowers, arranging its legs so that they ither hold on to the stem or rest on the leaves. It would then look like live one. Don't you think it is very good?"

I was quite delighted and did as she suggested, and many of our iends thought it very wonderful. I am afraid it is difficult to find ladies owadays who show such an understanding of things.

When I was staying with my friend Mr. Hua at Hsishan with Yün, Irs. Hua used to ask Yün to teach her two daughters reading. In that ountry house, the yard was wide open and the glare of the summer un was very oppressive. Yün taught them a method of making movable creens of growing flowers. Every screen consisted of a single piece. She ook two little pieces of wood about four or five inches long, and laid hem parallel like a low stool, with the hollow top filled by four horiontal bars over a foot long. At the four corners, she made little round oles on which she stuck a trellis-work made of bamboo. The trellis vas six or seven feet high and on its bottom was placed a pot of peas vhich would then grow up and entwine round the bamboo trellis. This

could be easily moved by two persons. One can make several of thes
things and place them wherever one pleases, before windows or door
and they will look like living plants, casting their green shade into th
house, warding off the sun and yet allowing the wind to come through
They can be placed in any irregular formation, adjustable accordin
to time and circumstances, and are, therefore, called "movable flowe
screens." With this method, one can use any kind of fragrant weeds c
the creeper family, instead of peas. It is an excellent arrangement fc
people staying in the country.

My friend Lu Panfang's name was Chang and his literary nam
Ch'unshan. He was very good at painting pine trees, plum blossom
and chrysanthemums, as well as writing the *lishu* style of calligraphy
besides specialising in carving seals. I stayed in his home called Hsiac
shuanglou for a year and a half. The house faced east and consisted o
five beams, of which I occupied three. From it one could get a beautifu
view of the distance in rain or shine. In the middle of the court, ther
was a tree, the *osmanthus fragrans,* which filled the air with a kind c
delicate fragrance. There were corridors and living rooms, and the plac
was quite secluded. When I went there, I brought along a man-servan
and an old woman, who also brought with them a young daughter. Th
man-servant could make dresses and the old woman could spin; there
fore Yün did embroidery, the old woman spun and the man-servan
made dresses to provide for our daily expenses. I was by nature ver
fond of guests and whenever we had a little drinking party, I insiste
on having wine games. Yün was very clever at preparing inexpensiv
dishes; ordinary foodstuffs like melon, vegetables, fish and shrimps ha
a special flavour when prepared by her. My friends knew that I wa
poor, and often helped pay the expenses in order that we might ge
together and talk for the whole day. I was very keen on keeping th
place spotlessly clean, and was, besides, fond of free and easy ways wit
my friends.

At this time, there were a group of friends, like Yang Pufan, als
called Ch'anghsü, who specialised in portrait sketches; Yüan Shaoyü
also called P'ai, who specialised in painting landscape; and Wan
Hsinglan, also called Yen, good at painting flowers and birds. They al
liked the Hsiaoshuanglou because of its seclusion, so they would brin
their painting utensils to the place and I learnt painting from them
They would then either write "grass-script" or "*chüan*-script" or carv
seals, from which we made some money which we turned over to Yün

defray expenses for teas and dinners. The whole day long, we were cupied in discussing poetry or painting only. There were, moreover, iends like the brothers Hsia Tanan and Hsia Yishan, the brothers iao Shanyin and Miao Chihpo, Chiang Yünhsiang, Lu Chühsiang, hou Hsiaohsia, Kuo Hsiaoyü, Hua Hsingfan, and Chang Hsienhan. hese friends came and went as they pleased, like the swallows by the ves. Yün would take off her hair-pin and sell it for wine without a cond's thought, for she would not let a beautiful day pass without mpany. To-day these friends are scattered to the four corners of the rth like clouds dispersed by a storm, and the woman I loved is dead, ke broken jade and buried incense. How sad indeed to look back upon ese things!

Among the friends at Hsiaoshuanglou, four things were tabooed: rstly, talking about people's official promotions; secondly, gossiping bout law-suits and current affairs; thirdly, discussing the conventional ght-legged essays for the imperial examinations; and fourthly, playg cards and dice. Whoever broke any of these rules was penalized to rovide five catties of wine. On the other hand, there were four things hich we all approved: generosity, romantic charm, free and easy ways, nd quietness. In the long summer days when we had nothing to do, e used to hold examinations among ourselves. At those parties, there ould be eight persons, each bringing two hundred cash along. We egan by drawing lots, and the one who got the first would be the fficial examiner, seated on top by himself, while the second one would e the official recorder, also seated in his place. The others would then e the candidates, each taking a slip of paper, properly stamped with seal, from the official recorder. The examiner then gave out a line f seven words and one of five words, with which each of us was to make he best couplet. The time limit was the burning of a joss-stick and we vere to tease our brains standing or walking about, but were not allowed o exchange words with each other. When a candidate had made the ouplets, he placed them in a special box and then returned to his seat. After all the papers had been handed in, the official recorder then opened he box and copied them together in a book, which he submitted to the xaminer, thus safeguarding against any partiality on the latter's part. Of these couplets submitted, three of the seven-word lines and three of he five-word lines were to be chosen as the best. The one who turned in he best of these six chosen couplets would then be the official examiner for the next round, and the second best would be the official recorder.

One who had two couplets failing to be chosen would be fined twent cash, one failing in one couplet fined ten cash, and failures handed i beyond the time limit would be fined twice the amount. The offici examiner would get one hundred cash "incense money." Thus we coul have ten examinations in a day and provide a thousand cash with whic to buy wine and have a grand drinking party. Yün alone was allowe the privilege of thinking out her lines on her seat.

Once Yang Pufan made a sketch of Yün and myself working at garden with wonderful likeness. One night, the moon was very brigh and was casting a wonderfully picturesque shadow of an orchid flowe on the wall. Inspired by some hard drinking, Hsinglan said to m "Pufan can paint your portrait sketch, but I can paint the shadows c flowers."

"Will the sketch of flowers be as good as that of a man?" I asked.

Then Hsinglan took a piece of paper and placed it against the wal on which he traced the shadow of the orchid flower with ink. Whe we looked at it in the day time, there was a kind of haziness about th lines of leaves and flowers, suggestive of the moonlight, although i could not be called a real painting. Yün liked it very much and m friends wrote inscriptions on it.

There are two places in Soochow called the South Garden and th North Garden. We would go there when the rape flowers were i bloom, but there was no wine shop near by where we could have a drink. If we brought eatables along in a basket, there was little fu drinking cold wine in the company of the flowers. Some proposed tha we should look for something to drink in the neighbourhood, an others suggested that we should look at the flowers first and then com back for a drink, but this was never quite the ideal thing, which shoul be to drink warm wine in the presence of flowers. While no one coul make any satisfactory suggestion, Yün smiled and said, "Tomorrow you people provide the money and I'll carry a stove to the place my self." "Very well," they all said. When my friends had left, I asked Yün how she was going to do it. "I am not going to carry it myself," sh said. "I have seen *wonton* sellers in the streets who carry along a stov and a pan and everything we need. We could just ask one of thes fellows to go along with us. I'll prepare the dishes first, and when w arrive, all we need is just to heat them up, and we will have everythin ready including tea and wine."

"But what about the kettle for boiling tea?"

"We could carry along an earthen pot," she said, "remove the *wonton* eller's pan and suspend the pot over the fire by a spike. This will then erve us as a kettle for boiling water, won't it?"

I clapped my hands in applause. There was a *wonton* seller by the name of Pao, whom we asked to go along with us the following afternoon, agreeing to pay him a hundred cash, to which Pao agreed. The following day my friends, who were going to see the flowers, arrived. I told them about the arrangements, and they were all amazed at Yün's ngenious idea. We started off after lunch, bringing along with us some straw mats and cushions. When we had arrived at the South Garden, we chose a place under the shade of willow trees, and sat together on the ground. First we boiled some tea, and after drinking it, we warmed up the wine and prepared the dishes. The sun was beautiful and the breeze was gentle, while the yellow rape flowers in the field looked like a stretch of gold, with people in blue gowns and red sleeves passing by the rice fields and butterflies flitting to and fro—a sight which could make one drunk without any liquor. Very soon the wine and dishes were ready and we sat together on the ground drinking and eating. The *wonton* seller was quite a likable person and we asked him to join us. People who saw us thus enjoying ourselves thought it quite a novel idea. Then the cups, bowls and dishes lay about in great disorder on the ground, while we were already slightly drunk, some sitting and some lying down, and some singing or shouting. When the sun was going down, I wanted to eat congee, and the *wonton* seller bought some rice and cooked it for us. We then came back with a full belly.

"Did you enjoy it to-day?" asked Yün.

"We would not have enjoyed it so much, had it not been for Madame!" all of us exclaimed. Then merrily we parted.

A poor scholar should try to be economical in the matter of food, clothing, house and furniture, but at the same time be clean and artistic. In order to be economical, one should "manage according to the needs of the occasion," as the saying goes. I was very fond of having nice little suppers with a little liquor, but did not care for many dishes. Yün used to make a tray with a plum-blossom design. It consisted of six deep dishes of white porcelain, two inches in diameter, one in the centre and the other five grouped round it, painted gray and looking like a plum flower. Both its bottom and its top were bevelled and there was a handle on the top resembling the stem of a plum flower, so that, when placed on the table, it looked like a regular plum blossom dropped on the table, and on opening, the different vegetables were found to be contained i the petals of the flower. A case like this with six different dishes woul be quite enough to serve a dinner for two or three close friends. I second helping was needed, more could be added. Besides this, we mad another round tray with a low border for holding chop-sticks, cups an the wine pot. These were easily moved about and one could have th dinner served at any place one wished. This is an example of econom in the matter of food. Yün also made all my collars, socks and my littl cap. When clothes were torn, she would cut out one piece to men another, making it always look very neat and tidy. I used to choos quiet colours for my clothes, for the reason that dirty spots would no show easily, and one could wear them both at home and abroad. Thi is an instance of economy in the matter of dress. When I first took u my residence at the Hsiaoshuanglou, I found the rooms too dark, bu after papering the walls with white paper, they were quite bright again During the summer months, the ground floor was quite open, becaus the windows had all been taken down, and we felt that the place lacke privacy. "There is an old bamboo screen," suggested Yün, "why don' we use it and let it serve in place of a railing?"

"But how?" I asked.

"Take a few pieces of bamboo of black colour," she replied, "and mak them into a square, leaving room for people to pass out and in. Cut of half of the bamboo screen and fasten it on the horizontal bamboo, abou the height of a table, letting the screen come down to the ground. The put four vertical pieces of short bamboo in the centre, fasten these i place by means of a string, and then find some old strips of black clot and wrap them up together with the horizontal bar with needle an thread. It would give a little privacy and would look quite well, beside being inexpensive." This is an instance of "managing according to th needs of the occasion." This goes to prove the truth of the ancient sayin that "slips of bamboo and chips of wood all have their uses."

When the lotus flowers bloom in summer, they close at night an open in the morning. Yün used to put some tea leaves in a little sil bag and place it in the centre of the flower at night. We would take i out the next morning, and make tea with spring water, which woul then have a very delicate flavour.

CHAPTER III: SORROW

WHY IS IT that there are sorrows and hardships in this life? Usually they are due to one's own fault, but this was not the case with me. I was fond of friendship, proud of keeping my word, and by nature frank and straightforward, for which I eventually suffered. My father Chiafu, too, was a very generous man; he used to help people in trouble, bring up other people's sons and marry off other people's daughters in innumerable instances, spending money like dirt, all for the sake of other people. My wife and I often had to pawn things when we were in need of money, and while at first we managed to make both ends meet, gradually our purse became thinner and thinner. As the proverb says, "To run a family and mix socially, money is the first essential." At first we incurred the criticism of the busybodies, and then even people of our own family began to make sarcastic remarks. Indeed "absence of talent in a woman is synonymous with virtue," as the ancient proverb says.

I was born the third son of my family, although the eldest; hence they used to call Yün *"san niang"* at home, but this was later suddenly changed into *"san t'ait'ai."* This began at first in fun, but later became a general practice, and even relatives of all ranks, high and low, addressed her as *"san t'ait'ai."* I wonder if this was a sign of the beginning of family dissension.[4]

When I was staying with my father at the Haining yamen in 1785, Yün used to enclose personal letters of hers along with the regular family correspondence. Seeing this, my father said that, since Yün could write letters, she should be entrusted with the duty of writing letters for my mother. It happened that there was a little family gossip and my mother suspected that it had leaked out through Yün's letters, and stopped her writing. When my father saw that it was not Yün's handwriting, he asked me, "Is your wife sick?" I then wrote to enquire from her, but got no reply. After some time had elapsed, my father was angry with her and spoke to me, "Your wife seems to think it beneath her to write letters for your mother!" Afterwards when I came home, I found out the reason and proposed to explain the matter, but Yün stopped me, saying, "I would rather be blamed by father than incur the displeasure of mother." And the matter was not cleared up at all.

[4] *"San"* means "number three." The meaning of *"niang"* and *"t'ait'ai"* varies with local usage, but generally *"niang"* refers to a young married woman in a big household, while *"t'ait'ai"* suggests the mistress of an independent home.

In the spring of 1790, I again accompanied my father to the magistrate's office at Hankiang [Yangchow]. There was a colleague by the name of Yü Fout'ing, who was staying with his family there. One day, my father said to Fout'ing, "I have been living all my life away from home, and have found it very difficult to find some one to look after my personal comforts. If my son would sympathize with me, he should try to look for one from my home district, so that there will be no dialect difficulty." Fout'ing passed on the word to me, and I secretly wrote to Yün, asking her to look round for a girl. She did, and found one of the Yao clan. As Yün was not quite sure whether my father would take her or not, she did not tell mother about it. When the girl was leaving, she merely referred to her as a girl in the neighbourhood who was going for a pleasure trip. After learning, however, that my father had instructed me to bring the girl to his quarters for good, she listened to some one's advice and invented the story that this was the girl my father had had in mind for a long time. "But you said she was going for a pleasure trip! Now why does he marry her?" remarked my mother. And so Yün incurred my mother's displeasure, too.

I was staying at Chenchow in 1792. My father happened to be ill at Yangchow, and I went there to see him, accompanied by my younger brother Ch'it'ang. In her letter to me, Yün mentioned that Ch'it'ang had borrowed some money from a woman neighbour, for which she was the guarantor, and that now the creditor was pressing for repayment. I asked Ch'it'ang about it, and he was rather displeased, thinking that Yün was meddling with his affairs. So I merely wrote a postscript at the end of a letter with the words: "Both father and son are sick and we have no money to pay the loan. Wait till younger brother comes home, and let him take care of it himself." Soon my father got well and I left for Chenchow again. Yün's reply came when I was away and was opened by my father. The letter spoke of Ch'it'ang's loan from the neighbouring woman, and besides contained the words, "Your mother thinks that old man's illness is all due to that Yao girl. When he is improving, you should secretly suggest to Yao to say that she is homesick, and I'll ask her parents to come to Yangchow to take her home. In this way we could wash our hands of the matter." When my father saw this, he was furious. He asked Ch'it'ang about the loan and Ch'it'ang declared that he knew nothing about it. So my father wrote a note to me, "Your wife borrowed a loan behind your back and spread scandals about your brother. Moreover, she called her mother-in-law 'your mother' and called her father-in-law 'old man.' This is the height of impudence. I have already sent a letter home by a special messenger, ordering her dismissal from home. If you have any conscience at all, you should realize your own fault!" I received this letter like a bolt from the blue, and immediately wrote a letter of apology to him, hired a horse and hurried home, afraid that Yün might commit suicide. I was explaining the whole matter at home, when the family servant arrived with my father's letter, which detailed her various points of misconduct in a most drastic tone. Yün wept and said, "Of course I was wrong to write like that, but father-in-law ought to forgive a woman's ignorance." After a few days, we received another letter from father: "I won't be too harsh on you. You bring Yün along and stay away from home, and do not let me see your face again."

It was proposed then that Yün might stay at her maiden home, but her mother was dead and her younger brother had run away from home, and she was not willing to go and be a dependent on her kinsfolk. Fortunately, my friend Lu Panfang heard of the matter and took pity on us, and asked us to go and stay in his home at Hsiaoshuanglou. After two years had passed, my father began to know the whole truth. It happened that shortly after I returned from Lingnan [in Kwangtung], my father personally came to the Hsiaoshuanglou and said to Yün, "Now I understand everything. Why not come home?" Accordingly we returned happily to the old home and the family was reunited. Who would suspect that the affair of Hanyüan was still brewing ahead!

Yün used to have woman's troubles, with discharges of blood. The ailment developed as a consequence of her brother K'ehch'ang running away from home and her mother dying of grief over it which affected Yün's health very much. Since coming to know Hanyüan, however, the trouble had left her for over a year and I was congratulating myself that this friendship proved better than all medicine. Then Han was married to an influential person, who had offered a thousand dollars for her and, furthermore, undertook to support her mother. "The beauty had therefore fallen into the hands of a barbarian." I had known of this for some time, but dared not mention it to Yün. However, she went to see her one day and learnt the news for herself. On coming back, she told me amidst sobs, "I did not think that Han could be so heartless!"

"You yourself are crazy," I said. "What do you expect of a sing-song girl? Besides, one who is used to beautiful dresses and nice food like her would hardly be satisfied with the lot of a poor housewife. It were better like this than to marry her and find it to one's cost afterwards.

I tried my best to comfort her, but Yün could never quite recove from the shock of being betrayed and her troubles came again. She wa confined to bed and no medicine was of any avail. The illness then be came chronic and she grew greatly emaciated. After a few years, ou debts piled up higher and higher, and people began to make unpleasan remarks. My father also began to dislike her more and more on accoun of the fact that she had been a sworn sister to a sing-song girl. I wa placed in an embarrassing position between father and wife, and fron that time on, I did not know what human happiness was.

Yün had given birth to a daughter, named Ch'ingchün, who was ther fourteen years old. She knew how to read, and being a very under standing child, quietly went through the hardships with us, often under taking the pawning of jewelleries and clothing. We had also a son namec Fengsen, who was then twelve and was studying with a private tutor I was out of job for many years, and had set up a shop for selling books and paintings in my own home. The income of the shop for three days was hardly sufficient to meet one day's expenses, and I was hard pressec for money and worried all the time. I went through the severe winte without a padded gown and Ch'ingchün too was often shivering in he thin dress, but insisted on saying that she did not feel cold at all. Fo this reason, Yün swore that she would never see any doctor or take any medicine.

It happened once that she could get up from bed, when my frienc Chou Ch'unhsü, who had just returned from the yamen of Prince Fu wanted to pay for some one to embroider a buddhist book, the *Prajna-paramita Sutra*. Yün undertook to do it, being attracted by the handsome remuneration and besides believing that embroidering the text of a buddhist sutra might help to bring good luck and ward off calamities My friend, however, was in a hurry to depart and could not wait, and Yün finished it in ten days. Such work was naturally too much of a strain for a person in her condition, and she began to complain of dizzi-ness and back-ache. How did I know that even Buddha would not show mercy to a person born under an evil star! Her illness then became very much aggravated after embroidering the buddhist sutra. She needec more attention and wanted now tea and now medicine, and the people in the family began to feel weary of her.

There was a Shansi man who had rented a house on the left of my ar shop, and used to lend money at high interest for his living. He often asked me to do some painting for him, and in this way came to know me. There was a friend of mine who wanted to borrow fifty dollars from him and asked me to guarantee the loan. I could not refuse him and consented, but my friend eventually ran away with the money. The creditor, of course, came to me as the guarantor for the money, and made a lot of fuss about it. At first, I tried to pay back a part of the loan with my painting, but finally I just had nothing left to offer him in place of cash. At the end of the year, my father came home, and one day the creditor was creating a lot of noise in the house, demanding repayment of the loan. He called me to him and scolded me saying, "We belong to a scholars' family; how could we fail to repay a loan from such common people?" While I was trying to explain the matter, there appeared a messenger from Mrs. Hua, a childhood friend of Yün's, who had heard about her illness and had sent him to inquire after her health. My father thought that this messenger was from the sing-song girl Han, and became still more infuriated. "Your wife does not cultivate the feminine virtues, but has become sworn sister to a sing-song girl. You yourself do not associate with good friends, but go about with low-class people. I cannot bear to put you to death, but will allow you three days. Make up your own mind what you are going to do in the meantime, or else I will prosecute you at court for filial impiety!" When Yün heard of this, she wept and said, "It is all my fault that we have displeased our parents. I know that if I die, you will not be able to bear my death, and if we separate, you will not be able to bear the parting. Let's ask Mrs. Hua's servant to come in, and I will try to get up from bed and have a talk with him."

I then asked Ch'ingchün to assist her mother to get up and escort her outside her bedroom, where we asked the messenger from Mrs. Hua whether his mistress had sent him specially to enquire after her illness, or he was merely taking a message on his way. "My mistress has long heard of your illness," replied the servant, "and was thinking of coming personally to see you, but refrained because she thought she had never been here before. When I was leaving, she told me to say that if Madame didn't mind living in a poor country home, she would like her to come to her place for a rest, in order to fulfil a pledge of their childhood days." The messenger was referring to a girlhood pledge between Yün and Mrs. Hua, when they were doing embroidery work together under the same lamplight, that they should assist each other in sickness or trouble.

"You go back quickly then, and tell your mistress to send a boat secretly for us within two days," she instructed the servant.

When the man had retired from the interview with her, he said to me, "You know that Mrs. Hua is as good to your wife as to her own sister and she won't at all mind your coming along too. As for the children, I am afraid that it will be inconvenient for you either to bring them along or to leave them here to trouble your parents. I should suggest that you make some arrangements for them within these two days."

There was a cousin of mine by the name of Wang Chinch'en who had a son called Yünshih, for whom he wished to secure the hand of my daughter. "I hear," said Yün, "that this son of Wang's is rather weak and useless. At best, he would be good only for carrying on, but not for building up a family fortune, but there is no fortune in the family for him to carry on. However, they are a scholars' family and he is the only son. I don't mind giving Ch'ingchün to him." So I said to Chinch'en, "We are cousins and, of course, I should be glad to give Ch'ingchün to your son, but I am afraid it is difficult under the circumstances for us to keep her until she should grow up. I propose, therefore, that you bring the matter up to my parents after we have gone to Hsishan, and take her over as your 'child daughter-in-law.' I wonder what you think of it?" Chinch'en was very pleased and agreed to my suggestion. As for my son Fengsen, I also asked a friend of mine by the name of Hsia Yishan to place him in a shop as an apprentice.

As soon as these arrangements had been made, Mrs. Hua's boat arrived. This was on the twenty-fifth of December, 1800. "If we should leave like this," said Yün, "I am afraid the neighbours will laugh at us, and besides, we haven't repaid the loan due to the Shansi man. I don't think he will let us off. We must leave quietly before dawn to-morrow."

"But can you stand the early damp of the morning in your present state of health?" I asked.

"Oh! I wouldn't worry about that," she said. "It's all a matter of fate how long one is going to live!"

I secretly informed my father about this arrangement, which he also thought best. That night, I first brought a little bag down to the boat and asked Fengsen to go to bed first. Ch'ingchün was weeping by her mother's side, and this was Yün's parting instruction to her: "Mamma was born under an evil star and is, besides, sentimentally passionate. That is why we've come to this. However, your father is very kind to me and you have nothing to worry on my account. I am sure that, in two or three years, we shall be able to manage so that we can be reunited. When you go to your new home, you must try to be a better daughter-in-law than your mother. I know that your parents-in-law will be very kind to you because they are very proud of this match. Whatever we have left behind in the trunks and bags are yours, and you can bring them along. Your younger brother is still young, and therefore we have not let him know. At the time of parting, we are going to say that mamma is going away to see a doctor and will return in a few days. You can explain the whole thing to him when we have gone a long distance, and just let grandfather take care of him."

There was with us at this time an old woman who was the one that had let us her country house, as mentioned in the first chapter. She was going to accompany us to the country, and was now sitting in the room, silently and continually wiping her tears. In the small hours of the morning, we warmed up some congee and ate it together. Yün forced herself to smile and joke, saying, "We first met round a bowl of congee and now we are parting also round a bowl of congee. If some one were to write a play about it, it should be entitled, 'The Romance of the Congee.' " Fengsen heard these words in his sleep, woke up and asked, while yawning:

"What is mamma doing?"

"Mamma is going to see a doctor," Yün replied.

"But why so early?"

"Because the place is so far away. You stay at home with sister and be a good boy and don't annoy grandmother. I am going away with papa and shall be home within a few days."

When the cock had crowed three times, Yün, buried in tears and supported by the old woman, was going out by the back door, when Fengsen suddenly wept aloud and cried: "I know mamma is not coming back!"

Ch'ingchün hushed him up, afraid that the noise might wake up other people, and patted him. All this time, I felt as if my bowels were torn to shreds and I could not say a single word except asking him to stop crying. After Ch'ingchün had closed the door on us, Yün walked along for just about a dozen paces and found she could no more, and I carried her on my back, while the old woman carried the lantern before us. We were almost arrested by a night sentinel when coming near the river, but luckily through the old woman's ruse, Yün passed off as her sick daughter, and I her son-in-law. The boatmen, who were all servants of the Hua family, came to the rescue and helped us down to the boat. When the boat was untied and we were moving, Yün broke down completely and wept bitterly aloud. Actually, mother and son never saw each other again.

Mr. Hua, whose name was Tach'eng, was living on the Tungkao Hill at Wusih, in a house facing the hillside. He tilled the field himself and was a very simple, honest soul. Mrs. Hua, whose family name was Hsia, was, as I have mentioned, Yün's sworn sister. We arrived that day at their home about one o'clock. Mrs. Hua came with her two little daughters to the boat to meet us, and we were all very happy to see each other. She supported Yün up the river bank to her home and gave us a most cordial welcome. The neighbouring women and children all came crowding into the house to look at Yün, some enquiring for news and some expressing their sympathy with her, so that the whole house was full of their twitter.

"Now I really feel like the fisherman who went up to the Peach-Blossom Spring,"[5] said Yün to Mrs. Hua.

"I hope sister won't mind these people. The country folk are merely curious."

And so we lived at the place very happily and passed the New Year there. Hardly twenty days had passed since our arrival when the festival of the fifteenth day of the first moon came and Yün was already able to leave her bed. That night we watched a dragon lantern show in a big yard for threshing wheat, and I noticed that Yün was gradually becoming her normal self again. I felt very happy and secretly discussed our future plans with her.

"I don't think we ought to be staying here for ever, but, on the other hand, we have no money to go elsewhere. What shall we do?" I said.

"Your wife has thought about it too," said Yün. "I have an idea. You know the husband of your sister, Mr. Fan Hueilai, is now serving as treasurer in the Salt Bureau of Chingkiang. Do you remember that, ten years ago, we lent him ten dollars, and it happened that we did not have sufficient money and I sold my hairbrooch to make up the amount?"

"Why, I'd forgotten all about it!" I replied.

"Why don't you go and see him? I hear Chingkiang is only a short way from here," said Yün.

I took her advice and started off on the sixteenth of the first moon, in 1801. The weather was quite mild, and one felt too warm even in a

[5] Reference to an idyllic retreat mentioned in an essay by T'ao Yüanming.

elvet gown and a serge *makua*. That night I stayed at an inn at Hsishan, nd rented some bedding for my bed. Next morning I took a sailing oat for Kiangyin. The wind was against us and there was a slight rain. t night, we arrived at the mouth of the river by Kiangyin. I felt chilled o the bones and bought some wine to warm myself up, in that way pending the last cash I had with me. I lay there the whole night thinking vhat I should do, rotating in my mind the idea of perhaps pawning my nside jacket in order to get money for the ferry.[6]

On the nineteenth, the north wind became still severer and snow lay bout the fields and I shed tears. I calculated the expenses for the room nd the ferry boat and dared not buy another drink. While I was shiver- ng both in my body and my heart, suddenly I saw an old man in sandals nd a felt hat enter the shop, carrying a yellow bag on his back. He ooked at me and seemed to know me.

"Aren't you Mr. Ts'ao of Taichow?" I asked.

"Yes," replied the old man. "Were it not for you, I should have died ong ago in the gutter. Now my little daughter is still living and well, nd she remembers you with gratitude all the time. What a pleasant urprise for us to meet here! What has brought you to this place?"

It should be explained that when I was working in the yamen of aichow some years ago, there was a Mr. Ts'ao of a humble family vho had a beautiful daughter already betrothed to some one, and n influential person had lent him money with the object of obtaining is daughter. In this way he was involved in a lawsuit. I helped him in he affair and managed to return his daughter to the family of the be- rothed. Old Ts'ao came to offer his services at the yamen as a token of is gratitude and kowtowed to thank me. That was how I came to know im. I told him how I was on my way to see my brother-in-law and how had run into the snow.

"If it clears up to-morrow," said Ts'ao, "I shall accompany you, for am passing that way myself." And he took out some money to buy vine, showing the greatest cordiality toward me.

On the twentieth, as soon as the morning temple bell had struck, I lready heard the ferry-man crying at the bank for passengers to come board. I got up in a hurry and asked Ts'ao to go together. "No hurry. Ve must eat something before going down to the boat," said Ts'ao. hen he paid the room and board for me and asked me to come out or a drink. As I had been delayed so long on my way and was anxious

Kiangyin is on the south bank of the Yangtse.

to start off, I was in no mood for eating, but merely chewed two piece of sesame-seed cake. When I got to the boat, there was a piercing win blowing over the river, and I was shivering all over.

"I am told there is a native of Kiangyin who hanged himself a Chingkiang, and his wife has engaged this boat to go there," said Ts'ao "We have to wait till she comes, before we can cross the river."

So I waited there, hungry and cold, till noon before we started of When we arrived at Chingkiang, there was already an evening haz lying over the countryside.

"There are two yamen at Chingkiang, one inside the city and the othe outside. Which one is your relative working in?"

"I really don't know," I said, walking dismally behind him.

"In that case we might just as well stop here and call on him tomo row," said Ts'ao.

When I entered the inn, my shoes and socks were already drenche through and covered with mud, and I had them dried before the fir I was all in, hurried through my meal and dropped into a sound slee Next morning when I got up, my socks were half burnt by fire. Ts'a again paid for my room and board. When I arrived at Hueilai's home i the city, he had not got up yet, but hurriedly put on his gown and cam out to see me. When he saw the state I was in, he was quite astonishe and said, "Why, what's the matter with brother-in-law? You look s shabby!"

"Don't ask me questions. Lend me two dollars first, if you have an with you. I want to pay back a friend who came along with me."

Hueilai gave me two Mexican dollars which I gave to Ts'ao, bu Ts'ao would not take them; only after my insistence did he receive on dollar before going away. I then told Hueilai about all that had hap pened, as well as the purpose of my visit.

"You know we are brothers-in-law," said Hueilai, "I should help yo even if I did not owe you the debt. The trouble is, our salt boats on th sea were recently captured by pirates, and we are still trying to straighte up the accounts, and I am afraid I shan't be able to help you muc Would it be all right if I tried to provide twenty dollars in repayment o the old debt?" As I was not expecting much anyway, I consented. Aft staying there for two days, the sky had cleared up and the weath became milder and I came home, arriving at Mrs. Hua's house on th twenty-fifth.

"Did you run into the snow on the way?" inquired Yün. I told h what had happened on the way and she remarked sadly, "When it snowed, I thought you had already arrived at Chingkiang, but you were then still on the river! It was very lucky of you to have met old Ts'ao. Really Heaven always provides for good people."

After a few days, we received a letter from Ch'ingchün informing us that her younger brother had already found a job as apprentice through the good offices of my friend Yishan. Ch'ingchün herself was also brought to Chinch'en's home on the twenty-fourth of January, with the permission of my father. Thus my children's affairs were all settled, but it was hard for parents and children to part like this.

The weather was clear and mild in the beginning of February. With the money I had obtained from my brother-in-law, I made arrangements for a trip to Yangchow, where my old friend Hu K'engt'ang was working at the Salt Bureau. I obtained a post there as secretary at the imperial tax bureau and felt more settled. In the eighth moon of the following year, 1802, I received a letter from Yün which said: "I have completely recovered now. I don't think it is right for us to be staying at a friend's place for ever, and wish very much to come to Yangchow, and see the famous P'ingshan." I then rented a two-roomed house on a river outside the First-in-Spring Gate of Yangchow city, and went personally to bring Yün to our new home. Mrs. Hua presented us with a little boy servant, called Ah Shuang, who was to help us in cooking and general housework. She also made an agreement with us that some day we should live together as neighbours. As it was already in the tenth moon and it was too cold at P'ingshan, I asked her to come next spring for a visit.

I was fully hoping, then, that we were going to have a quiet life and Yün's health would steadily recover and that eventually we might be reunited with our family. In less than a month, however, the yamen was reducing its staff and cut off fifteen persons. As I was only indirectly recommended by a friend, naturally I was among those sent away. Yün at first thought of different plans for me; she tried to be cheerful and comforted me, and never said a word of complaint. Thus we dragged on till the second moon of 1803, when she had a severe relapse, with profuse discharges of blood. I wanted to go again to Chingkiang for help, but Yün said:

"It is better to go to a friend than to a relative for help."

"You are quite right," I said, "but all my friends are themselves in trouble and won't be able to help us, however kind they are."

"All right, then," she said. "The weather is quite mild now and I don't think there will be any snow. Go quickly and come back quickly, but don't worry on my account. Take good care of yourself and increase not the burden of my sins."

At this time, we were already unable to meet our daily expenses, but in order to ease her mind, I pretended to her that I was going to hire a donkey. As a matter of fact, I took the journey on foot, merely eating some wheat cakes in my pocket whenever I felt hungry. I went in a south-easterly direction and crossed two creeks. After going for eighty or ninety *li,* I found a deserted country without any houses around. As night came, I saw only a stretch of yellow sands under the starry sky. There I found a little shrine of the God of Earth, about five feet high, enclosed by a low wall, with two little cypress trees in front. Then I kowtowed to the God and prayed: "I am Mr. Shen of Soochow on my way to a relative's. I've lost my bearings and intend to borrow thy temple to pass a night here. Protect me, I pray!" I then put away the little stone incense tripod and tried to crawl in. The shrine, however, was too small for my body by half and I managed to sit on the ground, leaving my legs outside. I turned my travelling cap round, using the back to cover my face, and thus sat there listening with my eyes closed, but all I could hear was the whistling of winds blowing by. My feet were sore and my spirit was tired and soon I dozed off.

When I woke up, it was already broad daylight and suddenly I heard people's footsteps and sounds of talking outside the low enclosure. Immediately I peeped out and saw that it was the peasants, who were going to a fair, passing by. I asked them for directions and they told me that I was to go straight south for ten *li* until I should reach Taihsing City, and after going through the city, to go southeast for ten *li* until I should come across an earthen mound; after passing eight such mounds, I would then arrive at Chingkiang. All I had to do was to follow the main road. I turned back then, put the incense tripod back in its original place, thanked the God for the night's rest and started off. After passing Taihsing, I took a wheelbarrow and arrived at Chingkiang about four o'clock in the afternoon.

I sent in my card and waited for a long time before the watchman came out and said, "Mr. Fan is away on official business to Ch'angchow." From the way he talked, I thought this was merely a pretext for not seeing me. I asked him when his master was coming home.

"I don't know," replied the servant.

"Then I am going to stay here until he returns, even if I have to wait a year."

The watchman guessed the purpose of my visit and secretly asked me, "Is Mrs. Fan really your own sister by the same mother?"

"If she weren't my own sister, I wouldn't have decided to wait until Mr. Fan's return."

The watchman then asked me to stay. After three days, I was told that Mr. Fan had returned and was given twenty-five dollars, with which I hurriedly hired a donkey and returned home.

I found Yün very sad and sobbing at home. When she saw me, she said rather abruptly, "Do you know that Ah Shuang ran away yesterday with our things? I have asked people to go about looking for him, but so far with no results. I don't mind losing the things, but the boy was given to me by his own mother, who told me repeatedly on parting to take good care of him. If he is running home, he will have to cross the Yangtse River, and I don't know what may happen to him. Or if his parents should hide him away and ask me for their son, what are we to do? And how am I going to face my sworn sister?"

"Please calm yourself," I said. "I think there is no ground for such anxiety. One who hides away his own son must do it for blackmail, but they know perfectly well that we haven't got any money. Besides, since the boy's coming here half a year ago, we have given him food and clothing, and have never struck him or been harsh to him, as everybody round here knows. I think the real fact is that the boy was a rascal and, seeing that we were in a bad way, stole our things and ran away. As for Mrs. Hua, it is she, rather than you, that should feel uneasy—for sending you such a scamp. The thing to do is for us to report the matter immediately to the magsitrate, and prevent any future complications."

Yün felt a little easier after hearing my view of the situation, but from then on she often cried out in her sleep "Ah Shuang has run away!" or "How could Han be so heartless!" and her illness became worse and worse every day. I wanted to send for a doctor, but Yün stopped me saying:

"You know my illness started in consequence of deep grief over my mother's death following upon K'ehch'ang's running away, then it was aggravated through my passion for Han and finally made worse by my chagrin at this recent affair. Besides, I was often too cautious and afraid of making mistakes. I have tried my best to be a good daughter-in-law, and have failed, and have consequently developed dizziness and palpitation of the heart. The illness is now deep in my system and no doctor will be of any avail, and you may just as well spare yourself the expense. As I look back upon the twenty-three years of our married life I know that you have loved me and been most considerate to me, in spite of all my faults. I am happy to die with a husband and understanding friend like you and I have no regrets. Yes, I have been as happy as a fairy at times, with my warm cotton clothing and frugal but full meals and the happy home we had. Do you remember how we used to enjoy ourselves amongst springs and rocks, as at the Ts'anglang Pavilion and the Hsiaoshuanglou? But who are we to enjoy the good luck of a fairy, for which only those are worthy who have lived a virtuous life from incarnation to incarnation? We had, therefore, offended God by trying to snatch a happiness that was above our lot; hence our various earthly troubles. It all comes of your too great love, bestowed upon one who is ill-fated and unworthy of this happiness."

After a while she spoke again amidst sobs, "Every one has to die once. My only regret is, we have to part half-way from each other for ever, and I am not able to be your wife until the end of your days and see with my own eyes the wedding of Fengsen." After saying this, tears rolled down her eyes as big as peas. I tried to comfort her by saying, "You have been ill for eight years, and this is not the first time that you are in a critical condition. Why do you suddenly say such heart-breaking words?"

"I have been dreaming lately," she said, "of my parents who have sent a boat to welcome me home. Whenever I close my eyes, I feel my body is so light, so light, like one walking among the clouds. It seems that my spirit has already departed and only my body remains."

"This is the effect of your extreme weakness," I said. "If you will take some tonic and rest yourself properly, I am sure you will get well."

Then Yün sighed again and said, "If there were the slightest ray of hope, I would not have told you all these things. But now death is approaching and it is high time I spoke my mind. I know you have displeased your parents all on my account; therefore when I die, your parents' attitude will change round, and you yourself will feel more at ease toward your parents. You know they are already very old, and when I die, you should return to them as soon as possible. If you cannot bring my remains back to the native district for burial, you can temporarily keep my coffin here and then see to its removal afterwards. I hope you will find another one who is both beautiful and good to take my place and serve our parents and bring up my children, and then I shall die content." At this point, I broke down completely and fell to weeping as if my bowels had been cut through.

"Even if you should leave me half-way like this," I said, "I shall never marry again. Besides, 'it is difficult to be water for one who has seen the great seas, and difficult to be clouds for one who has seen the Yangtse Gorges.'" Then Yün held my hand and was going to say something again, but she could only mumble the words "Next incarnation!" half audibly again and again. Suddenly she began to feel short of breath, her chin was set, her eyes stared wide open, and however I called her name, she could not utter a single word. Two lines of tears began to roll down her face. After a while, her breath became weaker, her tears gradually dried up and her spirit departed from this life for ever. This was on the thirtieth of the third moon, 1803. A solitary lamp was shining then in the room, and a sense of utter forlornness overcame me. In my heart opened a wound that shall be healed nevermore!

My friend Hu K'engt'ang kindly helped me with ten dollars, and together with this and what I could obtain by selling what I had in the house, I saw to her proper burial.

Alas! Yün was a woman with the heart and talent of a man. From the time she was married into my home, I had been forced to run about abroad for a living, while she was left without sufficient money, and she never said a word of complaint. When I could stay at home, our sole occupation was the discussion of books and literature. She died in poverty and sickness without being able to see her own children, and who was to blame but myself? How could I ever express the debt I owe to a good chamber companion? I should like to urge upon all married couples in the world neither to hate nor to be too passionately attached to each other. As the proverb says, "a loving couple can never reach grand old age together." Mine is a case in point.

According to custom, the spirit of the deceased is supposed to return to the house on a certain day after his death, and people used to arrange the room exactly as the deceased had left it, putting his old clothes on the bed and his old shoes by the bedside for the returning spirit to take a farewell look. We called this in Soochow "closing the spirit's eyes." People also used to invite Taoist monks to recite incantations, calling to the spirit to visit the deathbed and then sending it away. This was called "welcoming the spirit." At Yangchow the custom was to prepare wine and dishes and leave them in the dead man's chamber, while

the whole family would run away, in order to "avoid the spirit." I
often happened that things were stolen while the house was thus de
serted. On this day, my landlord, who was staying with me, left th
house, and my neighbours urged me to leave the offerings at home an
get away also. To this I gave a cold, indifferent reply, for I was hopin
to see the spirit of Yün again. There was a certain Chang Yümen o
the same district who warned me saying, "One may be very well pos
sessed by the evil spirit, when one's mind dwells on the uncanny.
should not advise you to try it, for I rather believe in the existence o
ghosts."

"This is the very reason I am going to stay—because I believe tha
ghosts do exist," I replied.

"To encounter the spirit of the deceased on its return home has an
evil influence on living men," Chang replied. "Even if your wife's spirit
should return, she is living in a world different from ours. I am afraid
you won't be able to see her form, but will, on the other hand, be affected by her evil influence."

I was so madly in love with her that I did not care. "I don't care a bit
about it," I said to him. "If you are so concerned about me, why not
stay on and keep me company?"

"I'll stay outside the door. If you should see anything strange, just call
for me."

I then went in with a lamp in my hand and saw the room was exactly as she had left it, only my beloved was not there, and tears welled up in my eyes in spite of myself. I was afraid then that with my wet eyes, I should not be able to see her form clearly, and I held back my tears and sat on the bed, waiting for her appearance with wide open eyes. Softly I touched her old dress and smelt the odour of her body which still remained, and was so affected by it that I fainted off. Then I thought to myself, how could I let myself doze off since I was waiting for the return of her spirit? I opened my eyes and looked round and saw the two candle-lights burning low on the table as small as little peas. It gave me a goose-flesh and I shuddered all over. Then I rubbed my hands and my forehead and looked carefully and saw the pair of candle-lights leapt higher and higher till they were over a foot long and the papered wooden frame of the ceiling was going to catch fire. The sudden glow of the lights illuminated the whole room and enabled me to look round clearly, when suddenly they grew small and dark as before. At this time I was in a state of excitement and wanted to call in my companion, when I thought that her gentle female spirit might be scared away by the presence of another living man. Secretly and in a quiet tone, I called her name and prayed to her, but the whole room was buried in silence and I could not see a thing. Then the candle-lights grew bright again, but did not shoot high up as before. I went out and told Yümen about it, and he thought me very brave, but did not know that I was merely in love.

After Yün's death, I thought of the poet Lin Hoching who "took the plum-trees for his wives and a stork for his son," and I called myself "Meiyi," meaning "one bereaved of the plum-tree." I provisionally buried Yün on the Golden Cassia Hill outside the West Gate of Yangchow, at the place which was commonly known as "The Precious Pagoda of the Ho Family." I bought a lot and buried her there, according to her dying wish, bringing home with me the wooden tablet for worship. My mother was also deeply touched by the news of her death. Ch'ingchün and Fengsen came home, wept bitterly and went into mourning.

"You know father is still angry with you," said my brother Ch'it'ang. "You'd better stay away at Yangchow for some time and wait till father returns home, when I shall speak for you and then write for you to come home."

I then kowtowed to my mother and parted from my daughter and son and wept aloud for a while, before I departed again for Yangchow, where I painted for my living. Thus I was often enabled to loiter round and weep over Yün's grave, forlorn soul that I was! And whenever I passed our old house, the sight was too much for me to bear. On the festival of the ninth day of the ninth moon, while all the other graves were yellow, hers was still green. The graveyard keeper said to me, "This is a propitious place for burial, that is why the spirit of the earth is so strong." And I secretly prayed to her, "O Yün! The autumn wind is blowing high, and my gowns are still thin. If you have any influence, protect me and arrange that I may have a job to pass the old year, while waiting abroad for news from home."

Soon afterwards one Mr. Chang Yü-an, who had a post as secretary at the Kiangtu yamen, was going to bury his parents at home in Chekiang, and asked me to take his place for three months. And thus I was provided against the winter. After I left that place, Chang Yümen asked me to stay at his home. He was out of a job too, and told me that he was finding it hard to meet the expenses at the end of the year. I gave him all the twenty dollars I had in my pocket, and told him that this was the money I had reserved for bringing Yün's coffin home and that he could pay me back when I heard word from my family.

So that year I passed the New Year at Chang's home. I was waiting for mail from home morning and night, but no news came at all. In March of 1804, I received a letter from my daughter Ch'ingchün, informing me of my father's illness. I wanted very much to go home to Soochow, but was afraid of father's anger. While I was still hesitating, I received a second letter from her, telling me that father had died. Sorrow went into my heart and pierced my bones and I cried to heaven in vain, for I knew it was too late. Brushing aside all considerations, I dashed home under the starry sky. I knocked my head against the coffin until I bled and wailed bitterly. Alas! my father had a hard time all his life working away from home, and he begot such an unfilial son as I, who was neither able to minister to his pleasure while he was alive, nor able to serve him at his deathbed. Great, indeed, is my sin!

"Why didn't you come home earlier then?" said my mother, seeing me weeping so bitterly.

"Had it not been for Ch'ingchün's letter," I said, "I would not even have heard of it at all." My mother cast a look at my brother's wife and kept silent.

I then kept watch over the coffin in the hall, but for seven days and seven nights not one in the whole family spoke to me about family affairs or discussed the funeral arrangements with me. I was ashamed of myself for not fulfilling a son's duties and would not ask them questions, either.

One day some men suddenly appeared at our house to ask for repayment of a loan, and made a lot of noise in the hall. I came out and said to them, "I don't blame you for pressing for repayment of the debt. But isn't it rather mean of you to create such a turmoil, while my father's remains are scarcely cold yet?" One among them then secretly explained to me, "Please understand we have been sent here by somebody. You just get away for a moment, and we will ask for repayment directly from the man who called us here."

"I'll return myself what I owe! You had better all go away!"

My wish was immediately obeyed, and the people having left, I called Ch'it'ang to my presence and remonstrated with him, "Although elder brother is stupid, I have never committed any great wrongs. If you are thinking of my being made heir to uncle, remember that I did not receive a single cent of the family fortune. Do you suppose I came home to divide property with you instead of for the funeral? A man ought to stand on his own feet; I have come empty-handed, and empty-handed I will go!" After saying this, I left him and went behind the curtain again and cried bitterly before the coffin.

I then said good-bye to my mother and went to tell Ch'ingchün that I was going to a mountain to become a Taoist monk. While Ch'ingchün was just trying to persuade me not to do so, some friends of mine arrived. They were the brothers Hsia Nanhsün, literary name Tan-an, and Hsia Fengt'ai, literary name Yishan. They remonstrated with me in a very severe tone, and thus began:

"We don't blame you for being angry with this kind of a family, but although your father is dead, your mother is still living, and although your wife has died, your son is not independent yet. Have you really the heart to become a monk?"

"What am I going to do then?" I replied.

"For the time being," said Tan-an, "you could put up at our home. I hear that his honour Shih Chot'ang is coming home on leave from his office. Why don't you wait till he comes and see him about it? I am sure he will be able to give you a position."

"This is hardly proper," I said. "I am still in the hundred days of my mourning, and your parents are still living."

"Don't worry on that account," said Yishan, "for our father, too, joins us in the invitation. If you think it's not quite proper to do so, then there is a temple on the west of our home where the abbot is a good friend of mine. How about putting up there?" To this I agreed.

Then Ch'ingchün said to me, "Grandfather has left us a family property certainly not less than three or four thousand dollars. If you will not have a share of the property, will you not even take along your travelling bag? I'll fetch it myself and bring it to the temple for you." In this way not only did I get my travelling bag, but also found ingeniously stuck in it some books, paintings, ink slabs and pots for holding writing brushes. The monk put me up at the Tower of Great Mercy. The tower faced south and on its east was a buddha. I occupied the western room which had a moon window exactly opposite the buddha, this being the room where pilgrims used to have their meals. At the door, there was a most imposing standing figure, representing the God of War holding a huge knife in his hand. A big maiden hair tree stood in the yard, three fathoms in circumference, and cast a heavy shade over the whole tower. At night the wind would blow past the tree, making a roaring noise. Yishan often brought some wine and fruit to the place to have a drink between ourselves.

"Are you not afraid of staying here alone on a dark night?" he asked.

"No," I replied. "I have lived a straight life and have a free conscience, why should I be afraid?"

It happened that shortly after I moved in, there was a pouring rain which continued day and night for over a month. I was always afraid that some branch of the maiden hair tree might break off and crash on to the roof, but, thanks to the protection of the gods, nothing happened. In the country around us, however, a great number of houses had fallen down and all the rice fields were flooded. I spent the days painting with the monk as if nothing had happened.

In the beginning of July, the sky cleared up and I went to the Ts'ungming Island as a personal secretary of Yishan's father, whose name was Shunhsiang and who was going there on business. For this I received twenty dollars as remuneration. When I returned, they were making my father's grave and Ch'it'ang asked Fengsen to tell me that he was in need of money for the burial expenses and would I lend him ten or twenty dollars? I was going to turn over the money I had to him, but Yishan would not allow it and insisted on contributing half of the amount. I then went ahead to my father's grave, accompanied by Ch'ingchün.

After the burial, I returned to the Tower of Great Mercy. At the end of September, Yishan had some rent to collect from his crops at Yungt'ai Beach in Tunghai and I accompanied him there, where I stayed for two months. When I returned, it was already late winter and I moved to his home at the Snow-and-Wild-Goose Hut to pass the New Year. He was better to me than my own kin.

In July, 1805, Chot'ang returned home from the capital. This was his "fancy name," while his real name was Yünyü and his literary name Chihju. He was a childhood chum of mine, took the first place in the imperial examinations in 1790 during the reign of Ch'ienlung, and then became magistrate of Chungking in Szechuen. During the rebellion of the White Lily Secret Society, he won great merit for himself fighting the rebels for three years. When he returned, we were very glad to see each other. On the ninth day of the ninth moon, he was going again to his office at Chungking with his family and asked me to accompany him. I then said good-bye to my mother at the home of Lu

Shangwu, the husband of my ninth sister, for by this time my father's home had already been sold. My mother gave me parting instructions as follows: "You should try your best to glorify the name of the family, for your younger brother will never amount to anything. Remember I depend entirely on you." Fengsen was seeing me off, but on the way he suddenly began to cry pitifully, and I bade him go home.

When our boat arrived at Kingk'ou [Chinkiang], Chot'ang said he wanted to see an old friend of his, Wang T'ifu, who was a *chüjen* and was working at the Salt Bureau in Yangchow. He was going out of his way to call on him and I accompanied him there, and thus had another chance to look at Yün's grave. Then we turned back and went up the Yangtse River and enjoyed all the scenery on the way. When we arrived at Kingchow we learned that my friend had been promoted a *taotai* at Tungkuan [in Honan]. He, therefore, asked me to stay at Kingchow with his son Tunfu and family, while he went to pass the New Year at Chungking with just a small entourage and went directly to his new office via Chengtu. In February of the following year, his family at Szechuen then followed him there by boat up the river as far as Fanch'eng. From that point on, we had to travel by land. The way was very long and the expenses very heavy; with the heavy load of men and luggage, horses died and cartwheels were often broken on the road and it was altogether a tortuous journey. It was March when we arrived at Tungkuan, when Chot'ang was again transferred to Shantung as inspector. As he was out of money and his family could not follow him there, we remained temporarily at the T'ungch'uan College. Only at the end of October did he receive his salary from his Shantung office, which enabled him to send for his family. In his letter he enclosed a note from Ch'ingchün, which informed me that Fengsen had died in April. Then I began to understand that the tears he shed when sending me off from home were tears of farewell. Alas! Yün had only one son and must even he be taken away and not allowed to continue her line! Chot'ang was also greatly touched at the news, and presented me with a concubine. From that time on, I was again thrown into life's mad turmoil, a floating dream from which I do not know when I shall wake up!

CHAPTER IV: THE JOYS OF TRAVEL

For thirty years I worked as a government clerk in different yamens and practically visited every province except Szechuen, Kweichow and

Yunnan. Unfortunately, I was not free to wander where I liked, inasmuch as I was always attached to some office, and could therefore only hastily enjoy such natural scenery as came my way, getting at most a general impression of things without the opportunity to explore the more unfrequented and out-of-the-way spots. I am by nature fond of forming my own opinions without regard to what others say. For instance, in the criticism of painting and poetry, I would value highly certain things that others look down upon, and think nothing of what others prize very highly. So it is also with natural scenery, whose true appreciation must come from one's own heart or not at all. There are famous scenic spots that do not at all appeal to me, and, on the other hand, certain places that are not at all famous but delighted me intensely. I will merely record here the places that I have visited.

When I was fifteen, my father Chiafu was working at the yamen at Shanyin with one official Chao, who employed a certain old scholar of Hangchow by the name of Chao Ch'üan, literary name Shengtsai, as private tutor for his son, and I was made by my father to study under him. Once I had the opportunity of visiting Hushan Hill, which was over ten *li* from the city and could be reached only by a waterway. On approaching the hill, I saw there was a stone cave with a rock jutting out horizontally as if it was going to fall down. My boat passed under this and went inside the cave, commonly known as "Shuiyüan" (Water Park), which was very spacious within and surrounded on all sides by perpendicular rocks. There was a stone open tower overlooking the water, consisting of five beams, and a stone inscription on the opposite rock bearing the words, "Looking at Jumping Fish." The water was very deep at this spot and people said that there were some gigantic fish in it. I threw some crumbs down, but saw only small ones hardly a foot long come up to nibble them. A road led from the back of the open tower to "Hanyüan" (Land Park), where there was a jumble of rockery, standing in irregular profusion, some of them only as broad as the palm of a hand, and others being stone pillars with their tops ground even, and capped with huge rocks. The whole thing was artificial, the workman's marks being too apparent, and nothing good could be said for them. After going round the place, I had a picnic in the Water Park at the open tower by the waterside. I asked an attendant to fire some crackers, which made a noise like thunder, reverberating throughout the whole valley. This was my first taste of the joys of travel in my young days. Unfortunately I was not able to visit Lant'ing[7] and Emperor Yün's Tomb, a sin of omission which I very much regret to this day.

. . . .

In the eighth moon of 1781, my father returned home, laid up with a cold. He would ask for fire when in a cold fit, and ask for ice when in high fever, despite my repeated advice to the contrary, and in this way, it turned into typhoid, which grew from bad to worse every day. I attended on him day and night and never slept a wink for almost a month. My wife, Yün-niang, also fell seriously ill at this time and was confined to bed; everything was in a muddle and I felt very miserable. "I am afraid I shall never get well," said my father to me one day, calling me to his bedside for final instructions. "I don't think you can make a living with the knowledge derived from a few books, and I am going to place you in charge of a sworn brother of mine, Chiang Ssutsai, who will bring you up to follow my profession." Ssutsai turned up next day and I kowtowed to him as pupil to tutor by my father's bedside. Soon afterwards, however, my father was attended to by a famous doctor, Mr. Hsü Kuanlien, and gradually got well; Yün, too, was cured by the same doctor and was able to leave her bed. Thus I began my training as a yamen clerk. I mention this unpleasant episode here in my record of the joys of travel, because through this change of profession, I was enabled to leave my studies and travel a great deal.

My teacher's name was Hsiang. I followed him in the winter of that year to the yamen of Fenghsien. There was a colleague of mine, also learning the same profession at the place; his name was Ku Chinchien, literary name Hungkan and "fancy name" Purple Haze. Ku was also a native of Soochow and was by nature a bighearted, frank and straightforward fellow. As he was a year older, I called him 'elder brother,' and he called me 'younger brother' and we became fast friends. Hungkan was in fact the best friend I had in this world. Unfortunately he died at twenty-two, and now in my forty-sixth year I doubt if I could find another friend like him in this wide, wide world. I remember that when we began our friendship, our minds were full of noble thoughts and we often thought of living a quiet life in the mountains.

. . . .

In the spring of 1783, I accompanied my teacher to Yangchow and in this way got a glimpse of the Chinshan and Chiaoshan Hills [at

[7] Made famous by Wang Hsichih's essay.

Chinkiang]. The former should be looked at from a distance, and the latter at close range; unfortunately I failed to visit these hills, although I passed them many times. On crossing the Yangtse River to the north, I saw before my very eyes the "walls of green willows" of Yangchow, as the poet Wang Yüyang described it. The P'ingshan Hall was about two or three *li* from the city, but was reached by a winding route of eight or nine *li*. Although this entire landscape was built by human labour it was so ingeniously planned that it looked like a bit of nature, suggesting to me the "marble halls" and "emerald pools" and phantom gardens of Fairyland itself. The beauty of the place consisted in the fact that over a dozen private villas and home gardens combined to form a huge park, stretching all the way from the city to the hill, with a unity all its own. From the point of view of landscape designing, the most difficult part to lay out satisfactorily was a space of over a *li* that lay close by the city wall. A city should, in order to be picturesque, be built against a background of a vast countryside with ranges of hills in the distance; it was, therefore, a most difficult problem to have pavilions and parks around it without achieving a stupid, closed-in effect. But the whole thing was so contrived, with a pavilion here and a terrace there, and glimpses of walls and rocks and trees and bamboo groves so cleverly designed that there was not the slightest bit of obtrusiveness to the tourist's eye. Only a master architect of the mind could have conceived and executed this.

The stretch began with the Rainbow Garden immediately adjoining the city wall, and after a turn to the north, came the Rainbow Bridge: I do not know whether the garden took its name from the bridge or the bridge from the garden. Rowing past these places, one came to the scene called "Spring Willows on a Long Embankment." It was a striking proof of the ingenuity of the designer, that this scene was placed at this spot and not immediately close to the city wall. With another turn to the west, there was an artificial mound with a temple on it, called "The Little Chinshan."[8] This was also a master stroke, for with this hill blocking the view, the picture became tightened and wonderfully compact. I was told that owing to the fact that the soil here consisted mainly of sand, they had tried several times to build the mound without success, until wooden piles had to be sunk into the ground at successive heights

[8] Or Little Gold Hill, after the Chinshan of Chinkiang.

and then earth piled on to them, the whole work thus costing several tens of thousands of dollars. No one except the rich merchants [of Yangchow] could have carried through a project like this.

After this we came to the Tower of Triumphal Delight, where the waterway became broader and people used to hold annual boat races on the Dragon Boat Festival. This was spanned over by the Lotus Bridge running north and south. The Bridge was situated on a central point, and on its top were five pavilions, with four at the corners and one at the centre, called by the natives of Yangchow "Four Dishes and One Soup." I did not like it because the design was too laborious or suggested too much mental effort. On the south of the Bridge there was the Lotus-Seed Temple, with a Thibetan dagoba rising straight up from its midst and its golden dome rising into the clouds; with the terra-cotta walls and temple roofs nestling under the kind shade of pine-trees and cypresses and the sounds of temple bells and *ch'ing* [musical stone] coming to the traveller's ears intermittently—all combining to achieve a unique effect that could not be duplicated in any other pleasure garden of the world.

After passing by the bridge I saw a high three-storeyed tower with projecting eaves and painted girders in rainbow hues, decorated with rocks from the Taihu Lake and surrounded by white marble balustrades. This place was called "Where the Five Clouds Are Abundant," its position in this picture suggesting the main turning-point of a literary composition. After this we came to a place known as "Morning Sun on the Szechuen Hill"—rather commonplace and uninteresting to me, besides being artificial. As we were approaching the hill the waterway narrowed down and lost itself in four or five bends formed by blocking the water's path with earth piled on the banks and planting them with bamboos.

It was then as if the spirit of the place had spent itself when, all of a sudden, a beautiful view opened up before my eyes with the "Forest of Ten Thousand Pines" of the P'ingshan Hall before me. The three characters "P'ingshant'ang" were written by Ouyang Hsiu himself.[9] The genuine spring, called the "Fifth Best Spring East of Huai River" was situated in a grotto, being nothing but a well whose water tasted like that of natural mountain springs, this being usually confused with the

[9] This was where the Sung scholar stayed and has now been made a temple to his honour.

other well at the Lotus Pavilion with an iron cover on top bearing six holes, whose water was flat and tasteless. The Garden of Nine Peaks was situated in another secluded spot outside the South Gate; it had a natural charm of its own and in my opinion should be regarded as the best of all the gardens round the place. I did not go to K'angshan and have no idea what it is like.

The above is merely a rough sketch of the place, with no attempt to go into its artistic beauties and details of workmanship. In general, I would say, the place looked more like a beautiful woman in a gorgeous costume than a pretty country maid washing on a river bank. It happened that I visited the place shortly after it had been done up expressly for the visit of Emperor Ch'ienlung, and thus saw it at its best—an opportunity which rarely comes to a person in a life-time.

In the spring of 1784, I accompanied my father to the yamen of Wukiang under the magistrate Mr. Ho, where I had colleagues like Chang Pinchiang of Shanyin, Chang Yingmu of Wulin, [Hangchow] and Ku Aich'üan of T'iaoch'i. There we had the privilege of preparing a provisional palace for the Emperor at Nantouyü, and thus had the honour of seeing His Majesty a second time. One day [during this occasion], I suddenly thought of returning home when it was already approaching sundown. I got a small "fast boat," which was the kind used for fast official errands with two oars at the sides and two *yaolu* at the stern. This kind was called in Kiangsu "Horse's Head on the Surf" because it went so fast on the Taihu water. Quick as riding upon a stork in the air, I reached the Wumen Bridge in a second, and reached home before supper was ready.

The people of my district were usually given to luxuries, and on this day they were still more extravagant. I saw dazzling lanterns and heard music of the flute and song all over the place, suggesting to me the "painted beams and carved girders," "beaded curtains and embroidered screens," "jade railings," and "screens of [women in] embroidered shoes" mentioned in ancient literature. I was dragged about by my friends to help them in arranging flowers and hanging silk sashes. In our spare time, we would get together and indulge ourselves in wine and song or go about the place. Like all young people, we went through all this din and commotion without feeling tired. I would not have seen all this, if I had been living in an out-of-the-way village, even though it was a time of national peace and order.

That year Ho, the magistrate, was dismissed for some reason or other, and my father went to work with another magistrate Wang at Haining [in Chekiang]. There was a Mr. Liu Hueichieh at Kashing, a devoted buddhist, who came to call on my father. His home was situated by the side of the Tower of Mist and Rain [at Kashing], and had an open tower called Moon-in-the-Water Lodge overlooking the river. This was where he used to recite buddhist books and was arranged spick and span like a monk's studio. The Tower of Mist and Rain was in the middle of the Mirror Lake, and had an open terrace looking out on green willows on the banks all around; had there been more bamboos, the view would have been perfect. Fishing boats lay about on the stretch of calm water—a scene which seemed to be best looked at under the moonlight. The monks there could prepare very excellent vegetarian food.

At Haining I was working with Shih Hsinyüeh of Nanking and Yü Wuch'iao of Shanyin as my colleagues. Hsinyüeh had a son called Choheng, who was gentle and quiet of disposition, being the second best friend I had in life. Unfortunately, we met only for a short time and then parted like duckweed on the water. I also visited the "Garden of Peaceful Eddies" of Mr. Ch'en, which occupied over a hundred *mu* and had any number of towers, buildings, terraces and winding corridors. There was a wide pond with a zigzag bridge of six bends across it; the rocks were covered with ivy and creepers which helped to make them look so much more natural; a thousand old trees reared their heads to the sky, and in the midst of singing birds and falling flowers, I felt like transported into a deep mountain forest. Of all the gardens I had seen built with artificial rockeries and pavilions on a flat ground, this was the one which approached nature most. One day we had a dinner at the Cassia Tower and the flavours of the food were simply lost in the fragrance of the flowers around—with the exception of pickled ginger, which remained sharp and pungent. The ginger is by its nature the more biting the older it becomes, and it seems to me extremely appropriate therefore for it to be compared to old dour, veteran ministers of state, who often have more guts than the young ones.

Going out of the South Gate, one came upon the great sea, its white-crested bores rushing by twice daily with the ebb and tide like miles-long silvery embankments. There were surf-riding boats lying in wait with the bow facing the on-coming bore. At the bow of the boat was placed a wooden board shaped like a big knife for cutting the water when the bore came. With a movement of the cutter, the tide was divided and the boat took a dive into the water. After a while it came up again, and turning round, it followed the surf up the bay for miles with a tremendous speed.

On the embankment, there was a pagoda in an enclosure where I once viewed the bore on a mid-autumn night with my father. About thirty *li* eastwards further down the embankment, there was the Needle Hill, which rose up abruptly and ended up in the sea. A tower on its top bore the signboard: "The Sea is Wide and the Sky Empty," from which place one could gain an unlimited view of the universe, with nothing except angry sea waves rising to meet the sky.

I received an invitation to go to Chich'i in Huichow [in Anhui] from the magistrate Mr. K'eh there, when I was twenty-five years of age. I took a river junk from Hangchow, sailed up the Fuch'un River and visited the Fishing Terrace of Yen Tzuling. This so-called "Fishing Terrace" was located half-way up the hill in the form of an overhanging cliff over a hundred feet above the water level. Could it be that it was on the same level with the river in the Han Dynasty? On a moon-lit night, our boat anchored at Chiehk'ou, where there was an inspector's office. The moon seemed so small on the top of the high mountain and rocks stood up above the surface of the water, making a most enchanting picture. I also got a glimpse of the foot of Huangshan, or the Yellow Mountains, but unfortunately could not go up and explore the whole place.

The town of Chich'i is a very small one, being situated in a mountainous region and inhabited by a people of very simple ways. . . . There was a village, called the Benevolence Village, thirty *li* from the city, where they had a festival of flowers and fruit-trees every twelve years, during which a flower show was held. I was lucky enough to be there at the time and gladly undertook the journey to the place. There being no sedan-chairs or horses for hire, I taught the people to make some bamboos into carrying poles, and tie a chair on them, which served as a makeshift. There was only another colleague going along with me, one Hsü Ch'eht'ing, and all the people who saw us carried on the conveyance were greatly amused. When we reached the place, we saw there was a temple, but did not know what god they worshipped. There was a wide open space in front of the temple where they had erected a provisional theatrical stage, with painted beams and square pillars, which looked very imposing at a distance, but at close range were found to consist of painted paper wrapped around the poles and varnished over with paint. Suddenly gongs were struck and there were four men carrying a pair of candles as big as broken pillars, and eight persons carrying a pig the size of a young calf. This pig, it was pointed out to me, had been raised and kept by the village in common for twelve years expressly for this occasion to be used as an offering to the god. Ch'eht'ing laughed and said, "This pig's life is long, isn't it? but the god's teeth are also sharp, aren't they? I don't think I could enjoy such a huge pig, if I were a god." "However, it shows the religious devotion of the villagers," said I.

We entered the temple and saw the court and corridors were filled up with potted flowers and trees. These had not been artificially trained, but were chosen for their rugged and strange lines in their natural state, being mostly pine-trees from the Yellow Mountains, I believe. Then the theatrical performances began and the place was crowded full with people and we went away to avoid the noise and commotion. In less than two years, however, I left the place owing to differences of opinion with my colleagues, and returned home.

During my stay at Chich'i, I saw how unspeakably dirty politics was and how low men could stoop in official life, which made me decide to change my profession from scholar to business man. I had a paternal uncle by marriage by the name of Yüan Wanchiu, who was a wine brewer by profession, living at the Fairy Pond of P'anch'i. I then went into this business with Shih Hsinching as partner. Yüan's wines were sold chiefly overseas, and after a year there came the rebellion of Lin Shuangwen in Formosa, traffic on the sea was interrupted, and we lost money. I was then compelled to return to my profession as a salaried man, in which capacity I stayed four years in Kiangpei [northern Kiangsu], during which period I did not enjoy any travel worth recording.

Afterwards we were staying at the Hsiaoshuanglou, living like fairies on earth. The husband of my female cousin, Hsü Hsiufeng, then happened to return from Eastern Kwangtung. Seeing that I was out of a job, he said to me, "I don't see how you can get along forever living by your pen and making your breakfast out of morning dew. Why don't you come along with me to Lingnan? I am sure you can make a lot of money there." Yün also approved and said to me, "I think you should go while our parents are still strong and you are still in your prime. It is better to make some money once for all than to live from hand to mouth like this."

I then got together some capital with the help of my friends for this venture, and Yün also personally attended to the purchase of embroidered goods, Soochow wine and wine-treated crabs, things that were not produced in Kwangtung. With the permission of my parents, I started on the tenth of October with Hsiufeng, going by way of Tungpa and coming upon the Yangtse at Wuhu. This being my first trip up the Yangtse, it gave me quite a thrill. Every night when the boat lay at anchor, I would have a little drink on the bow of the boat. Once I saw a fisherman carrying a little net hardly three feet wide; the meshes were about four inches wide and its four corners were tied with strips of iron, which were apparently used as sinkers. "Although Mencius told us that a fishing net should not be too fine," I said, chuckling, "I don't see how they are going to catch any fish with such big meshes and a tiny net." Hsiufeng explained that this kind was made specially for catching *pien* fish. I noticed the net was tied to a long rope and let down into the water every now and then, as if trying to see if there was any fish around. After a while, the fisherman gave a sudden pull and there was a big *pien* fish right enough caught in it. "It is true that one is never too old to learn!" I remarked with a sigh.

One day I saw a solitary hilly island rising abruptly from the middle of the river, and learned from Hsiufeng that this was the famous "Little Orphan." There were temples and towers hidden among the frost-covered wood, but unfortunately we were prevented from visiting the place, as our boat was passing by very fast with the wind. When arriving at the famous Tower of Prince T'en, I realized that the geographical reference to this Tower contained in the sketch by Wang Tzu-an was entirely erroneous, just as the location of Chunching Tower of Soochow was changed to the Main Wharf of Hsümen Gate.

We then embarked at the Tower on a "sampan." with upturned bow and stern, and sailed up past Kungkuan as far as Nanan, where we left the boat. The day of my arrival there happened to be my thirtieth birthday and Hsiufeng prepared a dinner of noodles in my honour. Next day we passed the Tayü Pass. On the top of the Pass there was a pavilion with a signboard reading: "I look up and the sun seems near," referring to the height of the place. The peak here was split in twain by a perpendicular cleavage in the cliffs which rose up like walls, leaving a path in the centre like a stone alleyway.[10] There were two stone inscriptions at the entrance to the Pass, one bearing the words, "Retreat heroically before a rushing torrent" and the other containing the wise counsel: "Be satisfied with your luck this time." There was a temple on top in honour of a certain General Mei, I do not know of what dynasty.[11] I do not know what people mean by speaking of "plum flowers on the Pass," because I did not see a single plum-tree there; perhaps it was called the "*Mei* (plum) Peak" after General Mei. December was there and the pots of plum flowers which I had brought along as gifts to friends had already blossomed and the flowers had fallen off and the leaves turned yellow.

Coming out on the other side of the Pass, I saw an entirely different type of scenery. On the left, there was a hill with beautiful rocks, whose name I have forgotten, and I was informed by my sedan-chair bearers that there was a "Fairy's Bed" on it, which I had to forego the pleasure of visiting, as I was in a hurry to proceed on my way.

On reaching Nanhsiung, we engaged an old "dragon boat." At the Buddhist Hill Hamlet, I saw that over the walls of people's homes were placed many potted flowers, whose leaves were like *ilex pedunculosa* and whose flowers were like peony, in three different colours of red, pink and white. These were camelias.

We reached Canton on the fifteenth of December and stayed inside the Chinghai Gate, where we rented a three-roomed flat on the street from one Mr. Wang. Hsiufeng's customers were all local officials, and I accompanied him on his rounds of official calls. There were then many people who came to buy our goods for weddings and other ceremonial occasions, and in less than ten days all my stocks were sold. On the New Year's Eve, there were still plenty of mosquitoes humming like thunder. People wore padded gowns with crape gowns on top during the New Year calls, and I noticed that not only was the climate here so different, but that even the native inhabitants, who had assuredly the same anatomy as ours, had such a different facial expression.

On the sixteenth of January, I was asked by three friends of my native district working in the yamen to go and see the sing-song girls on the river—a custom which was called "making rounds on the river." The

[10] This is the pass on the frontier between Kiangsi and Kwangtung.

[11] This was General Mei Chüan who was one of the first Chinese colonizers of Kwangtung at the beginning of Han Dynasty.

prostitutes were called "laochü." Coming out by the Chinghai Gate, we went down little boats which looked like egg-shells cut in two, covered with a roof-matting. First we came to Shamen where the sing-song boats, called "flower boats," were anchored in two parallel rows with a clear space in the centre for small boats to pass up and down. There were about twenty boats in one group, which were all tied up to horizontal logs to secure them against high wind. Between the boats, there were wooden piles sunk into the bottom of the river, with moveable rattan rings on top allowing the boats to rise and fall with the tide. The women keepers of these sing-song girls were called "shut'oup'o," whose hair was done up in a high coiffure by being wound round a hollow rack of silver wires over four inches high. Their temples were decorated with flowers held there by means of long "ear picks," and they wore black jackets and long black trousers coming down to the instep of the foot, set in contrast by sashes of green or red tied round their waists. They wore slippers without stockings like actresses on the stage, and when people came down to the boats, they would personally welcome them with a smile and lift the curtain for them to enter the cabin. There were chairs and tea tables on the sides and a big divan in the centre, with a door leading into the stern of the boat. As soon as the woman shouted "Welcome guests!" we heard a confusion of footsteps of girls coming out. Some had regular coiffures, and some had their queues done up on top of their heads, all powdered like white-washed walls and rouged like the pomegranate flowers; some in red jackets and green trousers and others in green jackets and red trousers; some bare-footed and wearing silver bracelets on their ankles and others in short socks and embroidered "butterfly shoes"; again some squatting on the divan and some leaning against the door, and all looking attentively but silently at us. I turned to Hsiufeng and said, "What is all this for?" "They are for you to choose," said Hsiufeng. "Call any one of them that you like and she will come up to you." I then beckoned to one, and she came forward with a smiling face and offered me a betel-nut. I took a bite and finding it to be most harsh and unpalatable, spat it out. While attempting to clean my lips with a piece of paper, I saw it was besmeared with red like blood, and this conduct of mine aroused a great laughter from the whole company.

We then passed on to the Arsenal, and found the girls at the latter place to be dressed in the same costume, except that all of them, old and young, could play the *p'ip'a.* When I spoke to them, they would answer "Mi-eh?" which means "What is it?"

"People say that one should not come to Kwangtung in one's youth, only for fear of being enticed by sing-song girls," I said. "But when I look at these with their uncouth dresses and their barbarian dialect, I don't see where's the danger."

"The Swatow girls," said a friend of mine, "are dressed exquisitely. You might have a look there."

When we went there, we found the boats to be tied up in rows as at Shamen. There was a well-known brothel keeper called Suniang, who was dressed like a woman in a Chinese circus. The girls' dresses had high collars, with silver locks hanging from their necks; their hair came down as far as the eyebrows in front and reached the shoulders at the back, with a coiffure on top looking like a maid-servant's coils; those with bound feet wore petticoats and the others wore short socks and also "butterfly shoes" beneath their long slim pants. Their dialect was barely intelligible to me, but I disliked the strange costume and was not interested.

"You know there are Yangchow sing-song girls across the river from Chinghai Gate," said Hsiufeng, "and they are all in Soochow dress. I am sure if you go, you will find some one to your liking."

"This so-called Yangchow group," explained a friend, "consists only of a brothel keeper called 'Widow Shao' and her daughter-in-law called Big Missie, who really come from Yangchow; the rest all come from Kiangsi, Hunan, Hupeh and Kwangtung."

We then went to see these Yangchow girls, and saw that there were only about a dozen boats tied up in two rows opposite each other. The women here had all puffy coiffures, broad sleeves and long petticoats, were slightly powdered and rouged and spoke an intelligible dialect to me. This so-called 'Widow Shao' was very cordial to us. One of my friends then called a "wine boat," of which the bigger kind were called "henglou" and the smaller kind "shakut'ing." He wanted to be the host and asked me to choose my girl. I chose a very young one, called Hsi-erh, who had a pair of very small feet and whose figure and expression resembled Yün, while Hsiufeng called a girl by the name of Ts'uiku, and the rest of the company asked for their old acquaintances. We then let the boat anchor in the middle of the river and had a wine feast lasting until about nine o'clock. I was afraid that I might not be able to control myself and insisted on going home, but the city gate had been locked up at sundown, in accordance with the custom on the coast cities, of which I was informed for the first time.

At the end of the dinner, some were lying on the couch smoking opium, and some were fooling round with the girls. Amahs began to bring in bedding and were going to make the beds for us to put up there for the night—all in the same cabin. I secretly asked Hsi-erh if she could put up there for the night. She suggested a "loft"—which was a cabin on the top of a boat—but did not know whether it was occupied. I proposed then that we go and take a look, and got a sampan to row us over to Widow Shao's boat, where I saw the boat lights shining in two parallel rows like a long corridor. The loft was unoccupied then and the woman welcomed me saying, "I knew that our honourable guest was coming to-night and have purposely reserved it for you." "You are indeed the 'Fairy under the Lotus Leaves'," I said, complimenting her with a smile. An amah then led the way with a candle in her hand up the ladder at the stern and came to the cabin, which was very small like a garret and was provided with a long couch and tables and chairs. Going through another curtained door, I entered what was the inner room, this being directly above the main cabin below. There was a bed at the side, and a square glass window in the centre admitted light from the neighbouring boats, so that the room was quite bright without a lamp of its own. The bedding, curtains and the dressing-table were all of a fine quality.

"We can get a beautiful view of the moon from the terrace," Hsi-erh suggested to me. I then crawled out through a window over the hatchway and reached what was the top of the stern. The deck was bounded on three sides with low railings. A full moon was shining from a clear sky on the wide expanse of water, wine boats were lying here and there like floating leaves, and their lights dotted the water surface like stars in the firmament. Through this picture, small sampans were threading their way and the music of string instruments and song was mixed with the distant rumble of the waves. I felt quite moved and said, "This is the reason why 'one shouldn't visit Kwangtung in one's youth!' " Unfortunately my wife Yün was not able to accompany me here.[12] I turned round and looked at Hsi-erh and saw that her face resembled Yün's under the hazy moonlight, and I escorted her back to the cabin, put out the light and went to bed.

[12] Yün was living then, for the story is not told in chronological order from chapter to chapter, as the reader might suppose.

Next morning Hsiufeng and the other friends appeared at the cabin early at dawn. I hastily put on my gown and got up to meet them, but was scolded by everyone for deserting them last night. "I was afraid of you people teasing me at night and was only trying to get a little privacy," I explained. Then we went home together.

A few days after this, I went with Hsiufeng to visit the Sea Pearl Temple. This was situated in the middle of the river and surrounded like a city by walls with gun-holes about five feet from the water in which were placed cannon for defence against pirates. As the tide rose and fell the gun-holes seemed to shift up and down above the water level—an optical illusion which was truly amazing. The "Thirteen Foreign Firms" were situated on the west of the Yulanmen or Secluded Orchid Gate, the building structures looking just like those in a foreign painting. Across the water was a place called the "Garden Patch," being full of flower trees, for it was the flower market of Canton. I had always prided myself on knowing every variety of flower, but here I found that thirty or forty per cent of the flowers were unknown to me. I asked for their names and found that some of them were never recorded in the *Ch'ünfangp'u* ("Dictionary of Flowers"), perhaps accountable through the difference of dialects.

The Sea Screen Temple was built on a gigantic scale. Inside the temple gate, there was a banyan tree over ten fathoms in circumference, whose thick evergreen foliage looked like a green umbrella. The railings and pillars of this temple were all made of "iron-pearwood." There was a linden tree whose leaves resembled those of the persimmon. One could scrape off the outer surface of these leaves after immersing them in water for some time, when the network of the fibre could be seen as fine as the wings of a cicada, and have them bound up into little volumes for the purpose of copying Buddhist texts.

We looked for Hsi-erh among the flower boats on our way home, and it happened that both Ts'uiku and Hsi-erh were free. After having a cup of tea, we were going to leave but were begged again and again to stay. I had a mind to go to the loft again, but it was occupied at the time by a guest of Big Missie's, the widow's daughter-in-law. So I suggested to the widow that if the girls could come along to our house, I would be glad to spend an evening with them. The widow agreed, and Hsiufeng returned home first to order a dinner, while I followed later with the girls. While we were chatting and joking together, our landlord Wang

Moulao unexpectedly turned up and was therefore asked to join us. We were just raising the wine-cups to our lips, when we heard a great noise of people downstairs, as if some men were attempting to come up. What really happened was that our landlord had a ne'er-do-well nephew who had learnt that we had invited sing-song girls to the house and was trying to blackmail us. Hsiufeng said regretfully, "This all comes of Sanpo's[13] sudden desire for some fun. I shouldn't have followed his example." "This is no time for argument," I said. "We must think of some ways and means to get out of the situation." Moulao offered to go down and speak to the people while I instructed the servants to order two sedan-chairs for the girls to slip away first, and then see how we could manage to get out of the city. We learnt that the people could not be persuaded to leave the house, nor were they coming up. Meanwhile, the two sedan-chairs were ready, and I ordered my servant, who was a strong, agile fellow, to lead the way; Hsiufeng followed him with Ts'uiku, while I and Hsi-erh brought up the rear; thus we rushed downstairs, intending to break through. With the help of the servant, Hsiufeng and Ts'uiku disappeared outside the door, but Hsi-erh was caught by someone. I raised my leg and kicked the fellow's arm. Released from the hold, Hsi-erh dashed out and I escaped after her. My servant was standing guard at the door to prevent the rascals from pursuing us.

"Have you seen Hsi-erh?" I asked my servant.

"Ts'uiku has gone ahead in a sedan-chair," replied the servant, "and I have seen Hsi-erh come out also, but haven't seen her going into a sedan-chair."

I then lighted a torch and saw that the empty sedan-chair was still standing there. Hurriedly I rushed to the Chinghai Gate and saw Hsiufeng standing there by the side of Ts'uiku's sedan-chair. In answer to my enquiry about Hsi-erh, he said that she might have gone off in an opposite direction by mistake. Quickly I turned back and passed a dozen houses before I heard somebody calling to me from a dark corner. I held up the light and saw it was indeed herself. I then put her in a sedan-chair and was starting, when Hsiufeng rushed to the place and informed me that there was a water-gate at the Yulanmen, and that he had asked somebody to bribe the gate-keeper.

"Ts'uiku has gone ahead, and Hsi-erh should follow immediately," he said.

[13] Author's name.

"You leave the girls in my care, while you go home and try to talk the rascals down," I told Hsiufeng.

When we arrived at the water-gate, it had indeed been opened for us, and Ts'uiku had been waiting there. Holding Hsi-erh with my left arm and Ts'uiku with my right, I crawled out of the water-gate with them like fugitives. There was a light shower and the roads were slippery, and when we reached Shamen, the place was still full of music and song. Someone in a sampan knew Ts'uiku and called out to her to come aboard.

Only after going down the boat did I discover that Hsi-erh's hair was all dishevelled and all her hairpins and bangles had disappeared.

"Why, have you been robbed?" I asked.

"No," she smiled. "I was told that they are all solid gold and they belong to my adopted mother. I secretly put them away in my pocket as we were coming downstairs. It would be awful if I were robbed and you had to pay for the loss."

I heard what she said and felt very grateful to her. I then asked her to dress up again and not to tell her adopted mother about the whole incident, but merely to say that there were too many people in our house and that she preferred to come back to the boat. Ts'uiku told this to her mother accordingly, adding that they had had a full dinner and wanted only some congee.

By this time the guest at the loft had already left and the widow asked Ts'uiku also to accompany me to the room. I noticed that Ts'uiku's and Hsi-erh's embroidered shoes were already wet through and covered with mud. We three then sat down to have some congee together, in default of a proper evening meal. During the conversation under the candle-light, I learned that Ts'uiku came from Hunan and Hsi-erh from Honan, and that Hsi-erh's real family name was Ouyang, but that after the death of her father and the remarriage of her mother, she had been sold by a wicked uncle of hers. Ts'uiku told me how hard the sing-song girls' life was: they had to smile when not happy, had to drink when they couldn't stand the wine, had to keep company when they weren't feeling well, and had to sing when their throats were tired; besides, there were people of a rough sort who would, at the slightest dissatisfaction, throw wine-pots, overturn tables and indulge in loud abuse and on top of that, the girls might receive all the blame, as far as the woman keeper was concerned. There were also ill-bred customers who must continue their horse-play throughout the night until it was quite unbearable. She said that Hsi-erh was young and had just arrived, and the woman was very kind to her on that account. While recounting all her troubles, some tears had unconsciously rolled down Ts'uiku's cheeks, and Hsi-erh was also weeping silently. I then took Hsi-erh in my lap and comforted her, while I asked Ts'uiku to sleep in the outer room because she was a friend of Hsiufeng's.

From this time on, they would send for us every five or ten days, and sometimes Hsi-erh would come personally in a sampan to the river bank to welcome me. Every time I went, I had Hsiufeng for company, without asking any other guests or hiring another boat, and this cost us only four dollars a night. Hsiufeng used to go from one girl to another, or "jump the trough," in the sing-song slang, and sometimes even had two girls at the same time, while I stuck only to Hsi-erh. Sometimes I went alone and either had a little drink on the deck or a quiet talk at the loft. I did not ask her to sing, or compel her to drink, being most considerate to her, and we felt very happy together. The other girls all envied her, and some of them, while unoccupied and learning that I was at the loft, would come and visit me. Thus I came to know every single one of them there, and when I went up the boat, I was greeted with a chorus of welcome. I had enough to do to give each a courteous reply, and this was a welcome that could not be bought with tens of thousands of dollars.

For four months I stayed there, spending altogether over a hundred dollars. I always regarded the experience of eating fresh *lichi* there as one of the greatest joys in my life. Later on, the woman wanted me to marry Hsi-erh for the sum of five hundred dollars. Her insistence rather annoyed me and I planned to return home. Hsiufeng, on the other hand, was very far gone with the girls, and I persuaded him to buy a concubine and returned to Soochow by the original route. Hsiufeng went back the following year, but my father forbade me to accompany him. After that I accepted an invitation to work under magistrate Yang of Ch'ingp'u. On coming home, Hsiufeng recounted to me how Hsi-erh had several times attempted suicide because I didn't go back. Alas!

> Awaking from a half year's Yang-group dream,
> I acquired a fickle name among the girls.[14]

During the two years at Ch'ingp'u, after my return from Kwangtung, I did not visit any place worthy of mention. It was soon after this

[14] This is an adaptation from two famous lines by Tu Mu.

that Yün and Han met each other and caused a great sensation among our relatives and friends, and Yün's health broke down on account of disappointment in Han. I had set up, with one Mr. Ch'eng Mo-an, a shop for selling books and paintings next door to our house, which helped somewhat to pay for the expenses of the doctor and medicine.

Two days after the Mid-Autumn Festival, I was invited by Wu Yünk'eh together with Mao Yihsiang and Wang Hsinglan to go and visit the Little Quiet Lodge at the Western Hill. It happened that I had an order to execute and asked them to go ahead first. "If you will come along," said Wu, "we shall wait for you to-morrow noon at the Come Ye Storks Temple by the Shuita Bridge at the foot of the hill." To this proposition I agreed, and on the following day, I asked Ch'eng to stay behind and keep shop for me, while I went on foot alone. Passing through the Ch'angmen Gate, I reached the foot of the hill, went over the Shuita Bridge and followed the country path westwards until I saw a temple facing south, girdled by a clear stream outside its walls. Someone answered the door and asked me where I had come from. On being told the purpose of my visit, he informed me with an amused smile that this was the Tehyün Temple, as I might see from the characters above the gate, and that I had already passed the Come Ye Storks. I said that I had not seen any temple this side of the bridge, and then he pointed out to me a mud wall enclosing a bamboo thicket. I then retraced my steps to the foot of the wall, where I saw a small closed door. Peeping through a hole in the door, I saw some winding paths, a low fence and some delightfully green bamboo trees in the yard, but not a soul in the place. I knocked and there was no reply. Someone passed by and said to me, "There is a stone in a hole in the wall which is used for knocking." I followed his instruction and after repeated knocking, indeed an acolyte appeared.

I then went in along the path, passed a little stone bridge, and after turning west, saw a monastery door with a black-varnished signboard bearing characters in white "Come Ye Storks," with a long postscript which I did not stop to read. Entering it and passing through the first hall, I was struck by the extreme neatness and cleanliness of the place, and realized that its owner must be a person who loved quiet and solitude. Suddenly I saw another acolyte appear down the corridor on the left with a wine-pot in his hand. I shouted to him in a loud voice and demanded to know where my friends were. Then I heard Hsinglan's voice chuckling in the room: "How about it now? I knew that Sanpo would keep his word!" Then Yünk'eh came out to welcome me and said "We have been waiting for you to have breakfast with us. Why do you come so late?" Behind him stood a monk who nodded to me, and I learned his monastic name was Chuyi.

I entered the room, which consisted merely of three beams, with a signboard reading "The Cassia Studio." Two cassia trees were standing in full bloom in the courtyard. Both Hsinglan and Yihsiang got up and shouted to me, "You must be penalized three cups for coming late!" On the table, there were very nice, pretty vegetarian and non-vegetarian dishes, with both yellow and white wine. I inquired how many places they had visited, and Yünk'eh told me that it was already late when they arrived the night before, and that they had visited only the two places Tehyün and Hot'ing that morning. We then had a very enjoyable drinking party for a long time, and after dinner we went again in the direction of Tehyün and Hot'ing and visited eight or nine places as far as the Huashan Hill, all beautiful in their own ways, but impossible to go into with full details here.

There was a Lotus Peak on top of the Huashan Hill, but as it was already getting late, we promised ourselves we would visit it another time. At this spot, the cassia flowers reached the greatest profusion. We had a nice cup of tea under the flowers and then took mountain sedan-chairs back to the Come Ye Storks Temple. A table was already laid in a little open hall on the east of the Cassia Studio. Monk Chuyi was by nature reticent, but a great drinker and very fond of company. At first we played a game with a twig of cassia,[15] and later each one was required to drink one round, and we did not break up till the second watch in the night.

"The moon is so beautiful to-night," I said. "It would be a pity to sleep in here. Can't we find a nice and high place, where we could enjoy the moon and spend the time in a way worthy of a night like this?"

"Let's go up to the Flying Stork Pavilion," suggested Chuyi.

"Hsinglan has brought a *ch'in* along," said Yünk'eh, "but we haven't heard him play on it yet. How about going there and playing it for us?"

We then started together and saw on our way a stretch of trees enveloped in the silvery shadows of the night and buried in the fragrance of *osmanthus fragrans*. All was peace and quiet under the moon-

[15] This is a game similar to "Going to Jerusalem." A twig of cassia blossoms was passed round from hand to hand as long as the beat of the drum continued. The one found with the twig in his hand when the drum stopped beating was required to drink.

light and the universe seemed a stretch of long silence. Hsinglan played for us the "Three Stanzas of Plum-Blossoms" with ethereal lightness. Caught by the gaiety of the moment, Yihsiang also took out his iron flute and played a low, plaintive melody. "I am sure," remarked Yünk'eh, "of all the people who are enjoying the moon to-night at Shih-hu Lake, none can be quite as happy as we." This was true enough because it was the custom at Soochow for people to gather together under the Pacing Spring Bridge at the Shih-hu Lake on the eighteenth of the eighth moon and look at the golden chain of the moon's image in the water; the place was packed full with people in pleasure boats, and music and song were kept up throughout the night, but although they were supposed to be enjoying the moon, actually they were only having a night of carousal in the company of prostitutes. Soon the moon went down and the night was cold, and we retired to sleep after having thoroughly enjoyed ourselves.

The next morning, Yünk'eh said to all of us, "There is a Temple of Candour round about here in a very secluded spot. Have any of you been there?" We all replied that we had not even heard of the name, not to speak of having been to the place.

"This Temple of Candour is surrounded by hills on all sides," explained Chuyi, "and it is so entirely out-of-the-way that even monks cannot stay there for a long time. The last time I was there several years ago, the place was in ruins. I hear it has been rebuilt by the scholar P'eng Ch'ihmu, but have not seen it since. I suppose I could still locate the place, and if you all agree, I'll be your guide."

"Are we going there on an empty stomach?" asked Yihsiang.

"I have already prepared some vegetarian noodle," said Chuyi laughingly, "and we can ask the Taoist monk to follow us with a case of wine."

After eating the noodle, we started off on foot. As we passed the Garden of High Virtue, Yünk'eh wanted to go into the White Cloud Villa. We entered the place and had seated ourselves, when a monk came out gracefully and curtsied to Yünk'eh saying, "Haven't seen you for two months! And what's the news from the city? And is the Governor still in his yamen?"

"The baldhead snob!" said Yihsiang, and got up abruptly and swept out of the room. Hsinglan and I followed him out, barely able to conceal our laughter. Yünk'eh and Chuyi remained behind to exchange a few words with the monk out of mere politeness and then also took leave. . . .

In the spring of 1804 during the reign of Chiach'ing, I was about to leave home and become a recluse consequent upon the death of my father, when my friend Hsia Yishan kindly invited me to stay at his home. In the eighth moon of that year he asked me to accompany him to Tunghai, where he was going to collect crops from his farms at the Yungt'ai Beach. This sandy beach belonged to Ts'ungming *hsien* and was reached by the sea over a hundred *li* from Liuho. The beach had newly arisen from the bottom of the Yangtse River and been only recently cultivated; there were no streets yet and very little human habitation, and the place was covered with reeds for miles round. There was, besides Mr. Hsia, only one Mr. Ting who owned property there and had a grainage with over a score of rooms, which was surrounded on all sides by a moat and outside this, by an embankment grown over with willows.

Ting's personal name was Shihch'u; he came from Ts'ungming and was the head of the whole beach settlement. He had a shroff by the name of Wang and these two were frank, jolly souls, being very fond of company, and treated us like old friends soon after our arrival. He used to kill a pig and provide a whole jar of wine to entertain us at dinner; at such drinking parties, he always played the finger guessing game, being ignorant of any games of poetry, and being equally innocent of any musical knowledge, used to crow when he felt like singing. After treating himself to a generous drink, he would call the farm-hands together and make them hold wrestling or boxing matches for a pastime. He kept over a hundred head of cattle which stayed unsheltered on the embankments at night, and also a pack of geese for the purpose of raising an alarm against pirates. In the day-time, he would go hunting with his eagle and his dogs among the reeds and marshes, and return with a good bag of game. I used to accompany him in these hunts and lie down anywhere to sleep when tired.

Once he took me to the farms where the grains were ripe; these were all serially numbered and around each farm was built a high embankment for protection against the tides. This was provided with a lock for regulating the water level, being opened during high tide to let in the water when the field was too dry, and at low tide to let the water out when it was overflooded. The farm-hands' cottages were scattered all over the place, but the men could gather together at instant notice.

These men addressed their employer as "master of the property," and were very obedient and charmingly simple and honest. Roused by any act of injustice, they could be fiercer than wild beasts, but if you said a word that appealed to their fair play, they could be just as quickly pacified. It was a life of simple struggle with the elements of nature, dreary and powerful and wild, like that of primæval times.

There one could see the sea from one's bed, and listen to the roaring waves that sounded like war-drums from one's pillow. One night I suddenly saw miles and miles away a red light, about the size of a big basket, bobbing up and down upon the high sea, and the horizon reddened as if illuminated by a great fire. "There is a 'spirit fire,'" said Shihch'u to me. "Its appearance is an omen that very soon more land will rise up from the bottom of the river." Yishan was usually of a romantic turn of mind, and he became all the more abandoned and carefree in his ways here. In the absence of all conventional restraints, I would yell and sing on the back of a buffalo or, inspired by alcohol, dance and cavort on the beach and do anything my fancy dictated. This was the pleasantest and most romantic bit of travel that I ever enjoyed in my life. Business done, we left the place and came home in October.

Of all the scenic beauties of Soochow I like best "A Thousand Acres of Clouds," and next the Sword Pond. With the exception of these two places, they are all too much belaboured by human effort and contaminated by the atmosphere of social luxury, thereby losing all the quiet native charm of nature. Even the newly erected Pagoda Shadows Bridge and the Temple of Pokung are only interesting as preserving an historical interest. The Yehfangpin, which I playfully wrote with another three characters meaning the "Bank of Rural Fragrance" is only a place for sing-song girls to flirt with passers-by in their promenades. Inside the city, there is the famous Shihtsulin ("Lion's Forest"), supposed to be in the style of the famous painter Ni Yünlin, which, despite its many old trees and elegant rocks, resembles on the whole more a refuse heap of coal ashes bedecked with moss and ant-holes, without any suggestion of the natural rhythm of sweeping hills and towering forests. For an uncultivated person like myself, I just fail to see where its beauty lies.

The Lingyenshan [16] is associated with the famous beauty of old,

[16] This and the following hills are all within a short distance of Soochow.

Hsishih, who lived here as the court favourite of the King of Wu. There are places of interest on top like Hsishih's Cave, the Corridor of Musical Shoes and the Canal for Picking Fragrance. However, it is a straggling type of landscape, in need of some tightening, and is therefore not to be compared with the T'ienp'ing and Chihhsing hills in charm and beauty.

The Tengweishan is also known as 'Yüan Tomb'; it faces the Chinfeng Peak on the east and the Taihu Lake on the west, and with its red cliffs and green towers, the whole hill looks like a painting. The inhabitants here plant plums for their living, and when these flowers are in bloom, there is a stretch of white blossoms for miles and miles looking like snow, which is the reason why the place is called "The Sea of Fragrant Snow." There are four old cypress trees on the left of the hill which have been given the four respective names, "Pure," "Rare," "Antique" and "Quaint." "Pure" goes up by a long straight trunk, spreading out a foliage on top resembling a parasol; "Rare" couches on the ground and rolls itself into three zigzag bends resembling the character *chih* (Z); "Antique" is baldheaded at the top and broad and stumpy, with its straggling limbs half dried-up and resembling a man's fingers; and "Quaint's" trunk twists round spirally all the way up to its highest branches. According to tradition, these trees are older than the Han Dynasty. In January of 1805, Yishan's father Shuhsiang, his uncle Chiehshih and four of the younger generation went to P'ushan for the spring sacrifice at their ancestral temple as well as to visit their ancestral tombs, and I was invited to accompany them. We first visited Lingyenshan on our way, came out by the Hushan Bridge and arrived at the Sea of Fragrant Snow by way of Feichia River to look at the plum blossoms there. Their ancestral temple at P'ushan was buried in this "Sea of Fragrant Snow" and in the all-pervading glory of the plum-flowers, even our coughs and spittings seemed perfumed. I painted twelve pictures of the trees of P'ushan and presented them to Chiehshih as a souvenir.

In September of the same year, I accompanied His Honour Shih Chot'ang on the voyage to his office at Chungking in Szechuen. Following the Yangtse up, we came to Yüanshan Hill, where was Yü's Tomb, belonging to a loyal Chinese minister at the end of the Mongol Dynasty. By the side of his tomb, there was a hall called the Majestic View Pavilion, a three-roomed affair, facing the South Lake in front and looking out on the Ch'ienshan Hill at its back. The Pavilion was situated on a knoll and therefore commanded an open view of the distance. It was open on the north side, and by its side was a long covered corridor. The tree leaves were just turning red, resplendent like peach and pear blossoms.

At this time Chiang Shoupeng and Ts'ai Tsech'in were travelling with me. Outside the South Gate there was Wang's Garden, which consisted of a long narrow strip of land running east and west, being limited on the south by the lake and on the north by the city wall, presenting a most difficult problem for the architect. The problem was ingeniously solved, however, by having serried terraces and storeyed towers. By 'serried terraces' is meant building of courtyards on the roof gardens, provided with rockeries and flower trees in such a manner that visitors would hardly suspect a house underneath; the rockeries standing on what was solid ground below and the courtyards on tops of buildings, so that the flowers actually grew upon the soil. And by 'storeyed towers' is meant crowning an upper storey with an open tower on top, and again crowning the latter with an open terrace, so that the whole consisted of four storeys going from one to another in an artfully irregular manner; there were also small pools actually holding water at different levels so that one could hardly tell whether one was standing on solid ground or on a top floor. The basic structures consisted entirely of bricks and stone, with the supports made in the western style. It was fortunately situated on the lake, so that one actually gained a better unobstructed view of the surrounding country than from an ordinary garden on a piece of flat ground. This garden seemed to me to show a marvellous human ingenuity.

The Tower of Yellow Stork at Wuchang is situated on the Yellow Stork Cliff, being connected with the Yellow Stork Hill at the back, popularly known as the Snake Hill. The three-storeyed Tower with its beautifully painted eaves and girders, stood on top of the city overlooking the Han River in a way that counterbalanced the Ch'ingch'üan Tower at Hanyang on the opposite shore. I went up the Tower one snowy day with Chot'ang; the beautiful snow flakes dancing in the sky above and silver-clad hills and jade-bedraggled trees below gave one the impression of a fairy world. Little boats passed up and down the river, tossed about by the waves like falling leaves in a storm. Looking at a view like this somehow made one feel the vanity of life and the futility of its struggles. There were a lot of poems written on the walls of the Tower, which I have all forgotten with the exception of a couplet running as follows:[17]

"When the yellow stork comes again,
let's together empty the golden goblet,
pouring wine-offering
over the thousand-year green meadow
on the isle.

"Just look at the white clouds sailing off,
and who will play the jade flute,
sending its melodies
down the fifth-moon plum-blossoms
in the city?"

That year in November we reached Kingchow. Chot'ang had then received the news of his promotion to *taot'ai* at Tungkuan, and I was asked to stay behind at Kingchow, thus forfeiting an opportunity to see the beautiful hills and waters of Szechuen, to my great regret. Chot'ang went there alone, leaving me with Ts'ai Tzuch'in and Hsi Chiht'ang and his son Tunfu and family. . . .

Towards New Year's Eve it snowed, and the weather was very severe. During the New Year festival we were free from the red-tape of New Year calls, but spent the days firing fire-crackers, flying kites and making paper lanterns to amuse ourselves. Soon the warm wind of spring awakened all the flowers and the spring showers moistened the earth, and Chot'ang's concubines arrived from up-river with his young daughter and baby boy. Tunfu then began to pack up and we started on the voyage north together, going on land from Fanch-eng, and went straight to Tungkuan.

Passing from the west of Wenhsiang *hsien* of Honan, we came to the Hankukuan Pass, which Laotzu passed through on the back of a black cow when he was retiring from the world. There was an inscription which bore the words, "The Purple Air Comes from the East." The Pass consisted of a narrow foot-path between two high mountains, barely allowing two horses to go together. About ten *li* from Han-

[17] In a Chinese couplet, which one sees everywhere in halls and parlours and temples, every word in one member must have a word of the same class and reversed tone in the corresponding position in the other member. With the exception of "the's," this can be seen in the translation given herewith.

kukuan was the Tungkuan Pass, with a perpendicular cliff on one side and the Yellow River on the other. A fortress was erected at this strategic spot with a series of most imposing towers and ramparts, but there were few inhabitants around the place and hardly any traffic. The line which Han Yü wrote, "The sun is shining upon Tungkuan with its doors all open" seems also to refer to the desolate appearance of the place. . . .

I stayed in the southern part of the garden in a boat-shaped house, where there was a courtyard with a pavilion on top of a mound, from which one could obtain a general view of the whole garden. The house was protected by the green shade of trees on all sides so that one did not feel the heat in summer. Chot'ang kindly named the studio for me: "An Unanchored Boat." This was the best house I ever lived in during the period I served as a yamen secretary. There were scores of varieties of cultivated chrysanthemums around the mound, but unfortunately Chot'ang was promoted to an inspectorship in Shantung before the season for chrysanthemums came.

It was then that this family moved to the T'ungch'uan College where I accompanied them, while Chot'ang went to his office first. Tsech'in, Chiht'ang and myself were left without anything to do then and we often went for an outing. One day we went on horseback to the Huayin Temple, passing through the Huafeng village, the place where old Emperor Yao prayed three times for his people. There were at the Temple many locust trees dating back to the Ch'in Dynasty and cypress trees of the Han Dynasty, mostly three or four fathoms in circumference, some locust trees growing inside a cypress, and some cypresses growing inside a locust tree. There were any number of old stone inscriptions in the different courtyards, with one in particular consisting of the characters for "Good Luck" and "Longevity" written by Ch'en Hsiyi. There was a Jade Fountain Court at the foot of the Huashan where Ch'en had departed from this earth as a Taoist fairy. His image, in a couching position, lay on a stone bed in a very small cave. At this place, the water was very clear and the sands nice and clean; most of the vegetation was of a deep red colour and there was a very rapid mountain stream flowing through a thick bamboo grove. A square pavilion stood outside the cave with the signboard: "Carefree Pavilion." By its side were three old trees, whose barks were cracked like broken coal and whose leaves resembled those of the locust tree, but were of a deeper colour. I did not know their name, but the natives aptly and conveniently called them "carefree trees."

I have no idea how many thousand feet high the Huashan mountains are and regret very much not having been able to pack up some dry provisions and go exploring them for a few days. On my way back I saw some wild persimmons, which were of a ripe colour. I picked one from the tree while on horseback, and was going to eat it then and there. The native people tried to stop me, but I wouldn't listen to them. Only after taking a bite did I find it to have a very harsh flavour. So much so that I quickly spat it out and had to come down from horseback and rinse my mouth at a spring before I could speak, to the great merriment of my native advisers. For persimmons should be boiled in order to take away their harsh flavour, but I learned this a little too late.

In the beginning of October, Chot'ang sent a special messenger to bring his family to Shantung, and we left Tungkuan and came to Shantung by way of Honan. The Taming Lake is in the western part of Tsinan city in Shantung, with places of interest like the Lihsia and Shuihsiang Pavilions. It was most enjoyable to go boating around the lake with a few bottles of wine, and enjoy the fragrance of lotus flowers under the cool shade of willow trees in summer. I went there, however, on a winter day and saw only a stretch of cold water against some sparse willow trees and a frosty sky. The Paotu Spring ranks first among the seventy-two springs of Tsinan. The spring consists of three holes with water gushing forth from underneath and bubbling up like a boiling cauldron, in strange contrast to other springs whose water usually flows downwards. There is a storeyed building on the pond, with an altar to Lüchu inside, where the tourists used to stop and taste tea made from the spring water.

In the second month of the following year, I went to my office at Laiyang (Shantung). In 1807, Chot'ang was demoted to be *Hanlin,* and I followed him to the capital (Peking). I never saw the reputed mirage on the coast of Tengchow.

CHINESE WIT AND WISDOM

Parables of Ancient Philosophers

INTRODUCTION

ALL ANCIENT CHINESE PHILOSOPHERS spoke parables and drew stories from actual life or invented them to illustrate their points. It will be seen from the parables contained in the selections from Chuangtse that this was a typical and habitual mode of expression with the early philosophers of the fourth and third centuries, B.C., and that the narrator could invent conversations by Confucius, Laotse, Ts'angwutse and the Yellow Emperor with absolute freedom. I have included here some of the best and most popular ones from the ancient texts. The first two are by Chuangtse which are not included in the preceding selections from that philosopher. The great majority come from the book of Liehtse; very little is known about this person, who was alleged to have lived at the time of or before Chuangtse (who died about B.C. 275), and the books under his name are generally considered to be of a much earlier date, but contain the same Taoist point of view. Han Fei, or Hanfeitse, who died in B.C. 234, was one of the great philosophers of the Legalist School, with traces of Taoist influence. Liu Hsiang was a famous and important author and editor of Han Dynasty and lived in B.C. 77–6. The *Chankuots'eh* is a well-known book containing the clever speeches and strategies of scholars of the Warring Kingdoms (fourth and third centuries, B.C.). It is a book full of witticisms and profound or clever speeches used by scholars who traveled about to counsel the kings during that period of wars and alliances and counter-alliances. Finally I have included one parable ("The Blind Man's Idea of the Sun") by the great genial poet of Sung Dynasty, Su Tungp'o. This parable has been used by Albert Einstein to illustrate the average man's idea of his theory of relativity.

Parables of Ancient Philosophers

Translated by Lin Yutang

THE MAN WHO SPURNED THE MACHINE

When Tsekung, the disciple of Confucius, came south to the state of Ch'u on his way to Chin, he passed through Hanyin. There he saw an old man engaged in making a ditch to connect his vegetable garden with a well. He carried a pitcher in his hand, with which he was bringing up water and pouring it into the ditch, with very great labor and little results.

"If you had a machine here," said Tsekung, "in a day you could irrigate a hundred times your present area. The labor required is trifling compared with the work done. Would you not like to have one?"

"What is it?" asked the gardener, looking up at him.

"It is a contrivance made of wood, heavy behind and light in front. It draws water up smoothly in a continuous flow, which bubbles forth like boiling soup. It is called a well-sweep."

Thereupon the gardener flushed up and said with a laugh, "I have heard from my teacher that those who have cunning implements are cunning in their dealings, and those who are cunning in their dealings have cunning in their hearts, and those who have cunning in their hearts cannot be pure and incorrupt, and those who are not pure and incorrupt in their hearts are restless in spirit. Those who are restless in spirit are not fit vehicles for Tao. It is not that I do not know of these things. I should be ashamed to use them."

Tsekung's countenance fell, humiliated, and he felt discomfited and abashed. It was not till they had gone thirty *li* that he recovered his composure.

"Who was that man?" asked his disciples. "Why did your face change color after seeing him and why did you seem lost for a whole day?"

"I thought," replied Tsekung, "there was only one man (Confucius) in this world. But I did not know there was this man. I have heard from the Master that the test of a scheme is its practicability and the goal of effort is success, and that we should achieve the greatest results with the least labor. Not so this manner of man. Coming into life, he lives among the people, not knowing whither he is bound, infinitely complete in himself. Success, utility and the knowledge of skills would certainly make man lose the human heart. But this man goes nowhere against his will and does nothing contrary to his heart, master of himself, above the praise and blame of the world. He is a perfect man."

—CHUANGTSE

DO-NOTHING SAY-NOTHING

When Knowledge traveled north, across the Black Water and over the Dark Steep Mountain, he met Do-nothing Say-nothing and asked him about Tao, and Do-nothing Say-nothing did not reply.

He turned back and went to the south of the White Water, up the Fox Hill and asked All-in-extremes about Tao. "Ha! I know. I will tell you . . ." But just as he was about to speak, he seemed to forget what he was going to say and Knowledge also received no reply.

Then he came back to the royal palace and asked the Yellow Emperor concerning Tao. And the latter said, "Man becomes alive from the collection of the vital spirit. When the vital spirit collects, he is alive, and when it scatters, he dies. If life and death are steady companions, why should I care?

"Therefore all things are one. What we love is the mystery of life. What we hate is corruption in death. But the corruptible in turn becomes mysterious life, and mysterious life once more becomes corruptible. The world is permeated by one spirit. Therefore the Sage places value upon Unity."

"Then you and I know Tao, and they don't," said Knowledge.

"Do-nothing Say-nothing was right," replied the Yellow Emperor. "All-in-extremes was quite near it. But you and I are still far from Tao. He who knows does not speak, and he who speaks does not know."

"I asked Do-nothing Say-nothing about Tao," said Knowledge, "but he did not answer me. Not that he would not, but he could not. So I asked All-in-extremes. He was just going to tell me, but he did not tell me. Not that he would not, but just as he was going to do so, he forgot what he wanted to say. Now I ask you and you are able to tell me. Why do you say, therefore, that you are far from Tao?"

"Of the two," replied the Yellow Emperor, "the former was genuinely right, because he really did not know. The latter was quite near it, because he had forgotten. You and I are still far from Tao, because we know."

When All-in-extremes heard this remark, he praised the Yellow Emperor for knowing what he was talking about.

—CHUANGTSE

THE CONCEALED DEER

There was a woodcutter in Cheng who came across a frightened deer in the country and shot and killed it. Afraid that other people might see it, he hid it in a grove and covered it with chopped wood and branches, and was greatly delighted. Soon afterwards, however, he forgot where he had hid the deer, and believed it must have all happened in a dream. As a dream, he told it to everybody in the streets. Now among the listeners there was one who heard the story of his dream and went to search for the concealed deer and found it. He brought the deer home and told his wife, "There is a woodcutter who dreamed he had killed a deer and forgot where he hid it, and here I have found it. He is really a dreamer."

"You must have dreamed yourself that you saw a woodcutter who had killed a deer. Do you really believe that there was a real woodcutter? But now you have really got a deer, so your dream must have been a true one," said his wife.

"Even if I've found the deer by a dream," answered the husband, "what's the use of worrying whether it is he who was dreaming, or I?"

That night, the woodcutter went home, still thinking of his deer, and he really had a dream, and in that dream, he dreamed back the place of hiding of the deer and also its finder. Early at dawn, he went to the finder's house and found the deer. The two then had a dispute and they went to a judge to settle it. And the judge said to the woodcutter:

"You really killed a deer and thought it was a dream. Then you really had a dream and thought it was reality. He really found the deer and is now disputing with you about it, but his wife thinks that he had dreamt that he had found a deer shot by someone else. Hence no one really shot the deer. Since we have the deer before our eyes, you may divide it between you two."

The story was brought to the ears of the King of Cheng, and the King of Cheng said, "Ah, ah! Isn't the judge dreaming again that he is dividing the deer for people?"

—LIEHTSE

THE MAN WHO FORGOT

There was a man in Sung by the name of Huatse, who developed in his middle age a peculiar malady of forgetting everything. He would take a thing in the morning and forget about it at night, and receive a thing at night and forget about it in the morning. While in the streets he forgot to walk, and while standing in the house, he forgot to sit down. He could not remember the past in the present, and could not remember the present in the future. And the whole family were greatly annoyed by it. They consulted the soothsayer and they could not divine it, and they consulted the witch and prayers could not cure it, and they consulted the physician and the physician was helpless. But there was a Confucian scholar in the country of Lu who said he could cure him. So the family of Huatse offered him the half of their property if he should cure him of this strange malady. And the Confucian scholar said:

"His malady is not something which can be cured by soothsaying or prayer or medicine. I shall try to cure his mind and change the objects of his thought, and maybe he'll be cured."

So he exposed Huatse to cold and Huatse asked for clothing, exposed Huatse to hunger, and Huatse asked for food, and shut Huatse up in a dark room, and Huatse asked for light. He kept him in a room all by himself for seven days and cared not what he was doing all this time. And the illness of years was cured in a day.

When Huatse was cured and learned about it, he was furious. He scolded his wife and punished his children and drove away the Confucian scholar from his house with a spear. The people of the country asked Huatse why he did so, and Huatse replied:

"When I was submerged in the sea of forgetfulness, I did not know whether the heaven and earth existed or not. Now they have waked me up, and all the successes and disappointments and joys and sorrows and loves and hatreds of the past decades have come back to disturb my breast. I am afraid that in the future, the successes and disappointments and joys and sorrows and loves and hatreds will continue to oppress my mind as they are oppressing me now. Can I ever recover even a moment of forgetfulness?"

—LIEHTSE

CHI LIANG'S PHYSICIANS

Yang Chu had a friend by the name of Chi Liang. One day Chi Liang fell ill, and after seven days, he became very serious. His sons wept by his bedside and asked for a doctor.

"I have such unworthy sons," said Chi Liang to Yang Chu. "Will you not sing a song to make them understand?"

So Yang Chu sang:

Heaven does not know
Why it is so,
How can we men
Divine it then?
Misfortune comes
In heaven's ways,
Fare well or ill,
It's man who pays.
Neither you nor I
Know what is gout,
Can then the witch
Or the doctor
Know what it's all about?

Chi Liang's sons still failed to understand, and asked for three doctors. One's name was Chiao, the second was called Yu and the third was called Lu. And the physician Chiao said to Chi Liang:

"You do not live properly. Your sickness comes from hunger and overeating and sexual indulgence. Your spirit is distracted. This is not due to heaven or to the evil spirits. Although the case is serious, it can be cured." Chi Liang said, "He is a common doctor," and sent him away.

The doctor Yu said, "You are suffering from a weak constitution and you were not properly nursed at infancy. It's not a matter of days, but of years. It cannot be cured." And Chi Liang said, "He is a good doctor. Feed him."

The doctor Lu said, "Your sickness comes neither from heaven, nor from men, nor from the evil spirits. There was one who controlled it, when you were first conceived in your mother's womb, and there was one knew about it. What's the use of medicine?" Chi Liang said, "He is a divine doctor," and sent him away with costly presents.

And Chi Liang soon got well by himself.

—LIEHTSE

HONEST SHANGCH'IU KAI

Mr. Fan[1] had a son by the name of Tsehua, who succeeded very well in establishing his personal influence, and was very much admired by the whole kingdom. He was a good friend of the King of Chin, and although he refused office, his power was higher than that of the Three Chief Ministers. When the light of his eyes lighted upon a person, the government at once honored him, and when he spoke ill of a person, the government at once degraded him. The scholars who congregated in his house equalled those at the court. He made his warriors fight duels of wit or of strength, even to the point of hurting each other, which he did not try to stop. Thus day and night they amused themselves so that such customs grew up in the country.

Among the "guests" of the house of the Fan family were Hosheng and Tsepo. One day the two men were walking in the countryside and stopped at the hut of a farmer by the name of Shangch'iu K'ai. During the night, Hosheng and Tsepo talked about the great power of Tsehua, and said that he could make or ruin a man and make a rich man poor and a poor man rich at his will. The farmer, Shangch'iu K'ai, had known starvation and cold and he overheard the conversation against

[1] A very powerful family of the Chin State. In the time of the Warring Kingdoms, a wealthy class had grown up, and it was the custom for many wealthy families to keep a great many scholars, swordsmen and warriors in their homes. Some had as many as three thousand such "guests" and they acquired a tremendous political influence, being sometimes able to influence the fortunes of war and the fate of kingdoms.

the north wall. Therefore he borrowed some food and putting it in a basket across his shoulder, started out for the home of Tsehua.

Now the followers of Tsehua were all from well-known families. They wore white jackets and rode in carriages, walked with a leisurely pace and held their heads high. When they saw the farmer was shabby and old, a feeble fellow with a dark face, they thought him a fool, and soon began to tease and cheat him and make fun of him. They would strike and pummel him and push and pull him about and do anything they liked with him, but Shangch'iu K'ai did not show any feeling of offense. When the followers were tired of this teasing, they went up with him to a high tower and said among themselves, "Whoever can jump down from the tower shall be rewarded with a hundred pieces of silver." Many people offered to try, and Shangch'iu, innocently believing in their words, jumped down first. He flew down like a bird and alighted on the ground, without hurting himself. The followers thought it was just a stroke of luck, and were not surprised by it. Again they pointed to a deep bend of the river and said, "There is a precious pearl in the water. You can dive in and get it." Shangch'iu K'ai indeed took their word for it and dived into the water and soon emerged with a real pearl. Only then did they begin to suspect there was something in the farmer, and Tsehua ordered that he be placed among those entitled to eat meat and wear silk. Soon a fire broke out, and Tsehua said, "If you can go through the fire and rescue some of the brocades, whatever you can bring out shall be yours." Shangch'iu K'ai placidly walked toward the fire and went back and forth through the flames. He came out without being scorched by the flames or blackened by the ashes.

The followers of the Fan family then believed he was a man of God and apologized to him, saying, "We did not know that you were a man of God, and have cheated you. We did not know that you were a divine saint and have abused you. Do you regard us as fools, or do you consider us blind or deaf? Please explain to us your secret doctrine."

"I have no secret doctrine," replied the farmer. "Even my mind does not know how I have done it. However, there is a point which I will tell you. When you two were stopping at my house, I heard you talking about the power of the Fan family, saying that they could make or ruin a man and make a rich man poor and a poor man rich. And I had no doubts in mind, but sincerely believed you. That was why I was willing to come such a long distance. And I thought all that you people said was sincere. I was only worried that I might not have enough faith in me and might not do all that was in my power. I was not conscious where my body was and what was good and what was bad for me. I had only this sincere mind, and matter could not go against it. Now that I know you people are cheating me, my mind is full of suspicions and I have to be constantly on the look out. When I think of how I escaped being burned or drowned in the water, I am still trembling and excited. How dare I go near the fire or water now?"

From that time on, the followers of Fan dared not abuse beggars or horse doctors they met on the way, but always came down from their carriage and bowed to them. When Tsai Wo heard the story, he told Confucius about it, and Confucius said, "Don't you know? The absolutely sincere man can influence matter, his power can move heaven and earth and influence the spirits, and he can go through the universe without meeting any obstruction, not to speak of going through fire and water and such common dangers. Shangch'iu K'ai was able to overcome matter even when he was being cheated; how much more when you and I are both sincere? Remember it, young man."

—LIEHTSE

THE MAN WHO WORRIED ABOUT HEAVEN

There was a man of the country of Ch'i who was worrying that the sky might one day fall down, and he would not know where to hide himself. This so much troubled him that he could not eat or sleep. There was another who was worried about this man's worry, and he went to explain it to him, saying, "The sky is only formed of accumulated air. There is no place where there is no air. Whenever you move or breathe, you are living right in this sky. Why do you need ever to worry that the sky will fall down?" The other man said, "If the sky were really nothing but air, would not the sun and moon and the stars fall down?" And the man who was explaining said, "But the sun, the moon and the stars are also nothing but accumulated air (gases) [1] which has become bright. Even if they should fall down, they would not hurt anybody." "But what if the earth should be destroyed?" And the other replied,

[1] *Ch'i* in Chinese means ether, air, breath, gas and any invisible spiritual force. "Gas" would make better reading here, but the Taoist conception is that all the universe is formed of a certain spiritual force. It is an extremely useful word, bridging the difficulty between material and immaterial concepts, such as we find in the theories of light.

"The earth is also only formed of accumulated solids, which fill all space. There is no place where there are no solids. As you walk and stamp on the ground, you are moving the whole day on this earth. Why do you ever need to worry that it may be destroyed?" Then that man seemed to understand and was greatly pleased, and the one who was explaining it to him also felt he understood and was greatly pleased.

When Ch'anglutse heard about it, he laughed and said, "The rainbow, the clouds and mists, the winds and rains and the four seasons—are all these not formed of accumulated air in the sky? The mountains and high peaks, the rivers and seas, metal and stone, water and fire—are these not formed of accumulated solids on the earth? Since we know they are formed of accumulated air and accumulated solids, how can we say then that they are indestructible? The infinitely great and the infinitesimally small cannot be exhaustively known or explored, or conjectured about—that is a matter taken for granted. Those who worry about the destruction of the universe are of course thinking too far ahead, but those who say they cannot be destroyed are also mistaken. Since the heaven and earth must be destroyed, they will end finally in destruction. And when they are destroyed, why shouldn't one worry about it?"

Liehtse heard about what Ch'anglutse had said, and laughed and said, "Those who say that heaven and earth are destructible are wrong, and those who say they are indestructible are also wrong. Destruction and indestructibility are not things we know anything about. However, they are both the same. Therefore one lives and does not know about death; one dies and does not know about life; one comes and does not know about going away; and one goes away and does not know about coming. Why should the question of destruction or non-destruction ever bother our minds?"

—LIEHTSE

THE OLD MAN WHO WOULD MOVE MOUNTAINS

The two mountains Taihang (in Shansi) and Wangwu cover a territory of seven hundred square *li,* and are ten thousand cubits high. They were formerly situated in the south of Chichou and north of Hoyang. Old Man Fool of the North Mountain was about ninety years old and he lived in a house facing the mountain. He did not like to go up and down the mountain when he left home, and asked his family o come together and said to them, "You and I shall set to work with all ur strength and level this mountain so that we may have a level path eading straight to Yünan (Honan), and reaching clear to the northern bank of the Han River (in Hupeh). What do you say?" The family greed, but his wife said, "With your strength, you can't even do anyhing with the K'ueifu Hill. How can you do anything with the Taiiang and Wangwu? Besides, where are you going to put away all the ocks and soil?" The various people said, "We can throw them into the nd of the Puhai (Gulf of Peichili, south of Manchuria) and north of Yintu (Siberia)."

He then led three of his children and grandchildren who could carry oads, and began to chip the rocks and shovel the soil, and carried them n baskets to the end of Puhai. An orphan boy of the neighbor's widow by the name of Chingch'eng, who had just shed his milk teeth, jumped along and came to help them, and returned home only once a season.

The wise man of Hoch'ü laughed at the old man and tried to stop him, saying, "What a fool you are! With all the strength and years left to you, you can't even scratch the surface of this mountain. What can you do about the rocks and soil?" Old Man Fool of North Mountain drew a deep sigh and said, "It's only your mind that is not made up; when it is made up, nothing can stop it. You are of less use than the widow's son. When I die, there will be my children (to carry on the work), and the children will have grandchildren, and the grandchildren will again have children, and the children will again have children, and the children will again have grandchildren. So my children and grandchildren are endless, while the mountain cannot grow bigger in size. Why shouldn't it be leveled some day?"

The wise man could not make any reply. Now the Snake Spirit heard about it and was worried about his own safety, and he went to speak to God. God had pity on the old man's sincerity of heart and ordered the two sons of K'uafu to carry the two mountains and placed one in Sutung and one in Yungnan. From then on, the south of Chichow and north of Han River became level ground.

—LIEHTSE

CONFUCIUS AND THE CHILDREN

Confucius was traveling east and met two children arguing with one another. He asked them what they were arguing about, and one child said, "I say the sun is nearer to us in the morning and farther away from us at noon, and he says the sun is farther away from us in the morning and nearer to us at noon." One child said, "When the sun begins to come up, it is big like a carriage cover, and at noon it is like a dinner plate. So it must be farther away when it looks smaller, and nearer us when it looks bigger." The other child said, "When the sun comes up, the air is very cool, and at noon it burns like hot soup. So it must be nearer when it is hot and farther away when it is cool." Confucius could not decide who was right, and the children laughed at him and said, "Whoever said that you were a wise guy?"

—LIEHTSE

THE MAN WHO SAW ONLY GOLD

There was a man of Ch'i who desired to have gold. He dressed up properly and went out in early morning to the market. He went straight to the gold dealer's shop and snatched the gold away and walked off. The officers arrested him and questioned him: "Why, the people were all there. Why did you rob them of gold (in broad daylight)?" And the man replied, "I only saw the gold. I didn't see any people."

—LIEHTSE

LOOKS LIKE A THIEF

There was a man who had lost money, and thought that his neighbor's son had stolen it. He looked at him and it seemed his gait was that of a thief, his expression was that of a thief, and all his gestures and movements were like those of a thief. Soon afterwards he found the money in a bamboo drain-pipe. Again he looked at the neighbor's son and neither his movements nor his gestures were those of a thief.

—LIEHTSE

MEASUREMENTS FOR SHOES

A certain man of Cheng was going to buy himself a new pair of shoes. First he took measurements of his feet, and left them in his seat. These he forgot to bring along when he went to the streets, and after entering a shoe shop, he said to himself, "Oh, I have forgotten to bring along the measurements, and must go back to bring them." So he did. But when he returned, the shop was closed already and he failed to buy any shoes. Someone said to him, "Why didn't you let them try the shoes on your feet?" And the man replied, "I would rather trust the measurements than trust myself."

—HANFEITSE

KING HUAN LOST HIS HAT

King Huan of Ch'i was drunk one day and lost his hat. For three days he shut himself up for shame, without giving audience. Kuan Chung said to the King, "This is disgrace for a ruler. Why don't you make amends by some generous act?" Accordingly, the King opened the granary and distributed grains to the poor for three days. The people praised the King for his generosity, and said, "Why does not he lose his hat again?"

—HANFEITSE

HOW THE TONGUE SURVIVED THE TEETH

Ch'ang Ch'uang was sick and Laotse went to see him. The latter said to Ch'ang Ch'uang, "You are very ill. Have you not something to say to your disciple?" "Even if you did not ask me, I was going to tell you," replied Ch'ang Ch'uang. "Do you know why one has to get down from one's carriage when coming to one's old village?" And Laotse replied, "Doesn't this custom mean that one should not forget one's origins?" "Ah, yes," said Ch'ang Ch'uang.

Then the sick man asked again, "Do you know why one should run when passing under a tall tree?" "Doesn't this custom mean we should respect what is old?" "Ah, yes," said Ch'ang Ch'uang.

Then Ch'ang Ch'uang opened his mouth wide and asked Laotse to look into it, and said, "Is my tongue still there?" "It is," replied Laotse. "Are my teeth still there?" asked the old man. "No," replied Laotse.

"And do you know why?" asked Ch'ang Ch'uang. "Does not the tongue last longer because it is soft? And is it not because the teeth are hard that they fall off earlier?" replied Laotse.[1] "Ah, yes," said Ch'ang Ch'uang. "There you have learned all the principles concerning the world. I have nothing else to teach you."

—LIU HSIANG

THE OWL AND THE QUAIL

An owl met a quail, and the quail asked, "Where are you going?" "I am going east," was the owl's reply. "May I ask why?" then asked the quail. "The people of the village hate my screeching noise," replied the owl. "That is why I am going east." Then said the quail, "What you should do is to change that screeching noise. If you can't, you will be hated for it even if you go east."

—LIU HSIANG

THE TIGER AND THE FOX

King Hsüan of Ch'u asked his ministers, "I hear that the people in the north are afraid of Chao Hsisü. Is this true?" The ministers did not make any reply, but Chiang Yi said to the King, "There was a tiger that was looking for animals for food and got hold of a fox. And the fox said, 'How dare you eat me? God of Heaven has made me the chief of the animal kingdom. If you eat me, you will be sinning against God. If you do not believe what I say, come along. I shall walk in front, and you follow behind.' The tiger went along with the fox accordingly, and the animals fled at their approach. The tiger was not aware that the animals were not afraid of the fox, but of himself. Now Your Royal Highness has a territory of five thousand square *li* and an army of a million soldiers, and you gave the entire power to Chao Hsisü. Therefore the people of the north are afraid of his power while they are really afraid of the King's army, as the animals were afraid of the tiger."

—CHANKUOTS'EH

[1] Gentleness overcomes strength, typically Taoist idea.

THE CRANE AND THE CLAM

hao was going to invade Yen. Su Tai went to speak to King Huei of
hao on Yen's behalf. "This morning," said Su Tai, "when I was
oming on my way, I was passing the Yi River. There I saw a clam
unning itself in the sun, and a crane came along to peck at its flesh, and
e clam shut its shell on the crane's beak tightly. The crane said, "If
doesn't rain today and doesn't rain tomorrow, there will be a dead
lam." And the clam also said, "If you can't get out today and can't
et out tomorrow, there will be a dead crane." Neither of the two was
illing to let go, when a fisherman came up and caught them both.
ow if you go and attack Yen, the two countries will be locked in battle
or a long time until the people of both countries are exhausted. I am
fraid the strong Ch'in will be the fisherman. You might think this over
arefully." "Good," said the King, and he gave up the idea.

—CHANKUOTS'EH

THE BLIND MAN'S IDEA OF THE SUN

here was a man born blind. He had never seen the sun and asked about
of people who could see. Someone told him, "The sun's shape is like
brass tray." The blind man struck the brass tray and heard its sound.
ater when he heard the sound of a bell, he thought it was the sun.
gain someone told him, "The sunlight is like that of a candle, and the
lind man felt the candle, and thought that was the sun's shape. Later
e felt a (big) key and thought it was a sun. The sun is quite different
rom a bell or a key, but the blind man cannot tell their difference be-
ause he has never seen the sun. The truth (Tao) is harder to see than
he sun, and when people do not know it they are exactly like the blind
nan. Even if you do your best to explain by analogies and examples, it
till appears like the analogy of the brass tray and the candle. From
vhat is said of the brass tray, one imagines a bell, and from what is
aid about a candle, one imagines a key. In this way, one gets ever
urther and further away from the truth. Those who speak about Tao
ometimes give it a name according to what they happen to see, or
magine what it is like without seeing it. These are mistakes in the
ffort to understand Tao.

—SU TUNGP'O

Family Letters of a Chinese Poet

INTRODUCTION

THE FAMILY LETTERS of Cheng Panch'iao (A.D. 1693–1765) and the "Si
Chapters of a Floating Life" serve, I think, better than anything else t
show the kindly temper of the Chinese people and the typical spirit o
Chinese culture at its best, though not idealized, but as it was actuall
lived in China. An ancient proverb, quoted in *Tienlun,* says "Do no
brag about yourself; see how you write family letters." For it is in suc
family letters that one's true character comes out. The "Six Chapters o
a Floating Life" shows how a Chinese couple took failure; these famil
letters show how one scholar took success. Beside the essential kindlines
and spirit of democratic living, all talks of the political machinery an
party machines for democratic government pale into insignificance
There has been a curious emphasis on politics when we speak of de
mocracy, as if Congressmen made a republic, an assumption which i
totally unwarranted. This political emphasis was repudiated by Con
fucius and the Chinese nation as a whole, long ago. I have chosen Chen
Panch'iao's family letters rather than Tseng Kuofan's, because these ar
fewer in number. But the spirit revealed is the same in both. Tsen
Kuofan's family letters could fill two thousand-page volumes, and it i
interesting to note that Tseng Kuofan, the greatest general and mos
honored man of his time, whose letters deeply influence Chiang Kai-shek
constantly wrote home to find out if his daughter already had learne

) make shoes and advise his "mandarin" family to raise vegetables and ogs and poultry.

Cheng Panch'iao was a man distinguished equally in poetry, painting nd calligraphy, which is a rare attainment. In all three he achieved n inimitable style. He was sniffed at by the Confucian scholars, which neans he was great. His ideas were strictly Confucian, but he was "un- sual." As an evidence of his "unusualness," the story is recorded of how e arranged the marriage of his elder daughter. His daughter was of mar- iageable age and not yet engaged. He had a friend whom he greatly espected as a scholar, and the friend had a son. One day, after supper, e said to his daughter, "Come along with me. I will take you to a good lace." His daughter followed him to the friend's place, when he said o her, "Now you stay here and be a good daughter-in-law." He turned ound and left. He was also unusual in the sense that he was different rom the Confucian Pecksniffs and could not stand over-taxation of he people. When he was magistrate in Weihsien, Shantung, there was year of bad harvest, and he petitioned the Governor for relief of the oor, which greatly angered the official. Thereupon he asked for sick eave and returned home. His poetry is distinguished by great feeling for he poor and distressed, couched in the most homely terms, and if well ranslated, would give even a more vivid feeling of his great heart than hese family letters. His paintings of bamboo and orchids were espe- ially distinguished.

In his preface to his poems, he said that the book contained all he vanted published. "If after my death, someone should republish it in ny name and include in it the nonsense I have written as obligations to riends or on social occasions, I shall be a ghost and strike the fellow's kull."

There are only sixteen letters altogether. I have omitted Letters III, V, IX, XI, XII, the second postscript to XIII, and the first part of XVI, s being too difficult for the average reader to follow in his critical pinions of Chinese authors and historical personalities. The best things n the letters are those concerning treatment of servants' and poor neigh- ors' children. They are the last word on charity of spirit (see especially Letters XIII, XIV).

Family Letters of a Chinese Poet

by Cheng Panch'iao

Translated by Lin Yutang

I. TO BROTHER MO FROM T'AOKUANG TEMPLE, HANGCHOW, WRITTEN IN 1732

THERE IS NO ONE IN THE WORLD who is not a descendant of the Yellow Emperor, and Yao and Shun. But today some have unfortunately be come slaves, slave girls, concubines and poor laborers, living in povert and distress and unable to help themselves; it would be wrong to assum that their ancestors were slaves, slave girls, concubines and poor laborer in generations ago. Once they make up their minds and are willing t work hard, some of them become rich and honored in their own lif time, and others become so in the next generation. Is there such a thin as blood among kings, dukes, premiers and generals? [1] Some scions o former noble or well-known families taunt others on their birth an brag about their previous generations, saying, "Who is he, and yet he i high up? I am such and such a person, and yet I am down and out There is no justice in heaven or in the affairs of man." Alas! they d not know that this is exactly the justice of heaven and of human affairs Heaven rewards the good and punishes the licentious; it is in accord ance with reason that he is good and therefore rewarded, and you ar licentious and therefore poor. What is wrong with that? For the wa

[1] Current proverb: "There is no blood in premiers and generals."

Heaven goes in a cycle. His ancestors were poor, and now it is his
rn to be rich and honored; your ancestors were rich and honored, and
ɔw it is your turn to be poor. Again, what is wrong about that? This
the way of heaven and also of human affairs.

After I, your foolish brother, became a government graduate
siuts'ai), whenever I found in the old trunks at our home some deed
a slave sold into our family in the former generation, I at once
ırned it over the oil lamp. I did not even return it to the person con-
rned, for I felt if I did, it would be an obvious act and increase the
an's embarrassment. Since I began to employ people, I have never
quired contracts. If we can get along with the servant, we keep him;
d if not, we send him away. Why keep such a piece of paper to pro-
de a pretext for our next generations to use it as a claim or a means
extortion? To act with such a heart is to have consideration for others,
hich is to have consideration for ourselves. If we try always to obtain
legal hold, once we get into the meshes of legality, we shall never be
le to get out again. We shall only become poor more quickly and
saster will follow immediately. The posterity of such people will soon
involved in scandals and meet with unexpected disasters. You just
ok at the people of the world who are shrewd at calculations; do they
er succeed in overcoming others by their shrewd calculations? They
e only calculating toward their own ruin. What a pity! Remember
is, my younger brother.

II. TO FOURTH BROTHER MO, WRITTEN WHILE READING AT CHIAOSHAN

he world is filled with monks. But they are not sent here from Thibet,
ıt are fathers and brothers of China who have no home to go to or
ho have entered the faith. When we shave, we become monks, and
hen they let their hair grow again, they become ourselves. It would
a mistake to look at them with anger, call them heretics and treat
em with hatred and disgust. From the time Buddha was born in the
ign of Emperor Chao of Chou[2] until he passed away, he never set
ot on Chinese soil. Eight hundred years later, Emperor Han Mingti[3]
ought on all this trouble through his wild fancies and dreams. Buddha
mself had nothing to do with it. Now instead of blaming Emperor

.c. 1052–1002. The chronology is bad.
.D. 58–75, when the first Buddhist monks reached China.

Han Mingti, we are all blaming Buddha, who is perfectly innoce Besides, since Ts'angli (Han Yü) exposed the Buddhist doctrines, Co fucianism has come back into its own, and the Buddhist religion gradually on the wane. The rulers have followed the Six Classics a Four Books as the means of regulating family life and governing t empire. To denounce Buddhism at this late hour would be as meanin less as chewing candle-wax. The monks are sinners against Buddh They rob and kill and seek after women and are greedy and snobbis for they have not followed the doctrines of purifying their hearts a seeking their original nature. The government graduates are also si ners against Confucius, for they are neither kind nor wise, and devc of courtesy or justice. They are no longer concerned with the keeping the ancient tradition and of Confucian teachings. The governme graduates love to abuse the monks and the monks love to abuse t government graduates. The proverb says, "Let each one sweep off t snow at his door-step, and not interfere with the frost on the neig bors' roof." What do you think of this? The idea has just occurred to n and I am putting it down and sending it for you to read. I have a shown this to Monk Wufang and it gave him a good laugh.

V. TO BROTHER MO, WRITTEN AT SHUANGFENGKO CHIAOSHAN

There is a cemetery lot at Hochiachuang, which costs twelve ounces silver. Father once wanted to buy it, but on account of a grave witho an owner there, which had to be removed, he said, "Alas! How c one dig up another person's grave to make room for one's own?" Fath therefore never did buy the lot. But if we don't buy it, someone e will, and that ownerless grave will be dug up. I am thinking of writi to cousin Ho to find out what has happened to it. If it's not yet sold shall send him twelve ounces of silver and buy it for burial ground myself and my wife. We shall leave that grave untouched as a place buffaloes to lie down, and set up an inscription in stone asking c posterity never to disturb that grave. Would this not be in accordar with our deceased father's kindly thought and an improvement up it? We shouldn't believe in geomancers. If we always try to ret generosity and eschew meanness of heart, even an unlucky grave w turn into good ground. There can be no doubt about this point. Wh our posterity visit our graves on the annual *ch'ingming* festival, th ıall also offer sacrifices to that grave, with one chicken, a cup of wine, bowl of rice and a hundred packs (of hundred) of paper money. Let .is be an established rule. June, 10, 1734.

I. TO BROTHER MO, WRITTEN ON A BOAT AT HUAIAN

one loves other people, he himself becomes worthy of love; if one ıtes other people, he himself deserves hatred. The best point about (Su) ungp'o is that he felt all his life that there was no bad man in this world. your foolish elder brother, have all my life criticized people without incing words, but whenever someone has one good point or special ›ility, or said one good word or done one good deed, I have never iled to praise it with all my heart. It is because I love people that henever I have several thousand dollars, I must use it all. And when am in need of help, other people have often helped me. I always love iticizing people, particularly the government graduates. But, come think about it, the trouble with the graduates is that they are so ›und up with themselves. On the other hand, if they were not so bound › with themselves, they wouldn't be graduates. But I think it is unfair criticize the graduates alone—who nowadays are not bound up with emselves? I am an old man now and living alone. I must watch out r this habit of mine. It is good to love people, and a bad habit to crit-ize people. Su Tungp'o suffered on account of this habit.[4] And cer-inly a person like myself should be more careful than he. You must so often remind me of this point, old brother.

VII. TO BROTHER MO, FROM THE MAGISTRATE'S RESIDENCE AT FANHSIEN

he family cemetery at Ch'ayüansze belongs in common to the East ate branch of our clan. Because there was no other place, I buried our .rents there, and thanks to its power, I have become a *chinshih*.[5] For veral years now I have occupied an official post without any mishap, hich means that I have robbed the clan of its luck and monopolized it myself. Can my heart feel at ease? It is pitiful to see our relatives at

Ie was exiled to a southern district because he could not help making fun of Wang ıshih who was in power.

›ne who passed successfully the national examinations, equivalent to a doctor's degree, t much more highly honored.

East Gate catch fish and shrimps, working on their boats and repairir nets, living in huts and eating chaffs and wheat gruel. They pick floatir heart, radish and water-bamboo and boil them and if they have buc wheat cakes to go along with them, they consider them delicacies ar the young children fight for them. Whenever I think of them, tears fi my eyes. When you bring money from my salary home, you should di tribute it from house to house. Although the six families at the Sou Gate, the eighteen families at Chuhuengchiang and the lone family Hsiat'ien are more distant relatives, they are of the same blood, ar should be given something also. Where is young granduncle Ch'ilir Such an orphan without parents to depend upon is often bullied by tl people of the village. You should find out where he is and comfort hir All relatives in the four generations counting from our great-grandfath should be given each two dollars, and it will be easier later for us get along with them. Hsü Tsungyü and Lu Poyi are my college frienc and we used to go about daily together. I still remember discussir ancient literatures with them in an old temple deep into the night wi the falling leaves flying about. Sometimes we sat on the stone lions ar discussed ancient warfare and all topics in the universe. They have bee unfortunate, and must also be given a share of my money for old frien ship's sake. People usually think a great deal of their own writings ar scholarship and believe that getting degrees is an easy matter for ther but do not realize it is all due to luck. Suppose I should happen to l still unsuccessful in the examinations, to whom could I complain? Th is therefore not something to make one conceited toward friends. Tl principal thing is to cement good-will among relatives and membe of the clan and remember old friends; for the rest, you can do wh you think fit in the way of helping the neighbors and people of t village. Spend it all; I shall spare the details.

VIII. SECOND LETTER TO BROTHER MO, FROM THE MAGISTRATE'S RESIDENCE AT FANHSIEN

The house you bought is well enclosed and indeed suitable for residen except that I feel the courtyard is too small, and when you look at t sky, it is not big enough. With my unfettered nature, I do not like Only a hundred steps north from this house, there is the Parrot Brid and another thirty steps from the Bridge is the Plum Tower, with vaca spaces all around. When I was drinking in this tower in my young da

I used to look out and see the willow banks and the little wooden bridge with decrepit huts and wild flowers against a background of old city walls, and was quite fascinated by it. If you could get fifty thousand cash, you could buy a big lot for me to build a cottage there for my old days. My plan is to build an earthern house with courtyard, and plant bamboos and flowers and trees around. There will be a pebble walk leading from the gate to the house door. There will be two rooms, one for the parlor, and the other for study, where I can keep books, paintings, brushes, ink-slabs, wine-kettle and tea service, and where I can discuss literature and write poetry with some good friends and the younger generation. Behind this will be the family living rooms, with three main rooms, two kitchens and one room for servants. Altogether there will be eight rooms, all covered with a hay-thatch, and I shall be quite content. Early in the morning before sunrise, I shall be able to see the red glow of morning clouds over the Eastern Sea,[6] and at sunset, the sun will shine from behind the trees. When one stands upon a high place in the courtyard, one can already see the haze and water and the bridge in the distance, and when giving a party at night, people outside will be able to see our lights across the wall. It will be only thirty steps to your house on the south, and will be separated from the little garden only by a small creek. So it is quite ideal.

Some may say, "It will be indeed comfortable, but there may be thieves." They do not know that thieves are but poor people. I would open the door and invite them to come in, and discuss with them what they would like to share with me. They can take away whatever they like, and if really nothing will suit them, they can take away the great Wang Hsienchih's antique carpet and pawn it for a hundred cash to meet their immediate needs. Please, my younger brother, bear this in mind, for this is your stupid brother's provision for spending a happy old age. I wonder whether I can have what I so desire.

X. FOURTH LETTER TO BROTHER MO, FROM THE MAGISTRATE'S RESIDENCE AT FANHSIEN

I received a letter from home on the twenty-sixth of the tenth month, and was delighted to learn that we got twenty-five hundred bushels from the new fields at the autumn harvest. From now on I can afford

[6] Cheng's native place is Hinhua, in Eastern Fukien, near the coast.

to be a farmer during the remainder of my days. We must have all sorts of things made—mortars, grinding-stones, sieves, bamboo pans, big and small brooms and rice measures of all kinds. The women of the family shall lead the maids in housework and all learn to pound rice, shake grains and work with their hands and feet. It will give an atmosphere of living on land and bringing up children there. On a cold, icy day, when poor relatives come to our door, first give them a big bowl of (boiled) toasted rice, which, helped out with a small dish of pickled ginger, is the best means of warming up the aged and the poor. In our leisure days, we can eat cakes of broken rice and cook "muddle congee," and eat it sinking our head into the bowl held between the hands. On a frosty or snowy morning, this makes the whole body warm. Alas! I hope to be a farmer until the end of my days!

I think the best class of people in the world are the farmers. Scholars should be considered the last of the four classes.[7] The most well-to-do farmers have a hundred *mu* (about sixteen acres), the second seventy or eighty *mu,* and the next fifty or sixty *mu.* They all toil and labor to feed the rest of the world. Were it not for the farmers, we should all starve. We scholars are considered one class higher than the farmers because we are supposed to be good sons at home and courteous abroad, and maintain the ancient tradition of culture; in case of success, we can serve and benefit the people, and in case of failure, we can cultivate our personal lives as an example to the world. But this is no longer true. As soon as a person takes a book in hand, he is thinking of how to pass the examinations and become a *chüjen* or *chinshih,* how to become an official and get rich and build fine houses and buy large property. It is all wrong from the very start, and the further one goes, the more wicked one becomes. It will all come to a bad end. Those who are not successful at the examinations are still worse; they prey upon the people of the village, with a small head and thievish eyes. True, there are many who hold firm to their principles, and there are everywhere some who set the highest standards for themselves. But the good suffer on account of the bad, with the result that we have to shut up. The moment we open our mouths, people will say, "All you scholars know how to talk. As soon as you become officials, you will not be saying the same things." That is why we have to keep quiet and accept the insults.

[7] Cheng here reverses the traditional Chinese classification which is in the following order: scholars, farmers, artisans and business men.

The artisans make tools and turn them to good use, while the business men make possible the exchange of goods. They are all of some use to the people, while the scholars alone are a great nuisance to them. One should not be surprised to find them considered the lowest of the four classes of people, and I doubt that they are entitled to even that.

I have always thought the most of the farmers. The new tenants should be treated with courtesy. They should call us "hosts" and we should call them "guests." The host-and-guest relationship is reciprocal. What reason is there to suppose that we are higher than they? We must be courteous to them and love them. If they ask for help, help them, and if they cannot repay, make it easy for them. It has seemed ludicrous to me that all the T'ang poets who wrote poems about the Cowherd and the Spinning Maid described only the parting of the lovers and lost sight of the original meaning of their names. For the Spinning Maid reminds us where our dress comes from, and the Cowherd reminds us where our food comes from; therefore they are the most honored among the stars of Heaven. If Heaven thinks a great deal of them, shall man look down upon them? The hard-working farmers who toil to give us the essentials of living may be said to have followed the example of these stars.

The women of our town cannot weave coarse silk or cotton, but they can still cook and sew and do their part nobly. Recently many listen to the drum-stories or play at cards. The manners are becoming loose and should be corrected.

Although we have three hundred *mu* of land, they are mortgaged property and cannot be depended upon. Hereafter we should buy two hundred *mu,* so that we brothers shall have each one hundred *mu,* which is in accordance with the ancient teaching that each farmer was to receive a hundred *mu*. More than that will be robbery of other people's property and a crime. There are many people in this world who have no land, and who are we that we should be so greedy? Where shall the poor ones be forced to go? It may be argued that there are plenty of people whose lands stretch for miles in thousands of *mu,* and what can we do about it? The reply is, "Let others attend to their affairs, while we attend to ours. When good customs prevail, unite around the King in harmony. When the customs degenerate, abstain from walking in evil company." Let this be the family tradition of Panch'iao.

XIII. SECOND LETTER TO BROTHER MO FROM THE MAGISTRATE'S RESIDENCE AT WEIHSIEN

My only son was born to me in my fifty-second year. Of course, I love him, but there is a correct way of loving one's children. Even in games, he should be taught to show the heart of mercy and generosity, and avoid cruelty. What I hate most is to have caged birds; we enjoy them while they are shut up in prison. What justification is there that we are entitled to thwart the instincts of animals to please our own nature? As for tying up a dragon-fly by the hair or tying a crab with a piece of string, it affords the children some fun only for a little while, and soon the little thing is dead. Now nature creates all things and nourishes them all. Even an ant or an insect comes from the combination of forces of the *yin* and *yang* and the five elements. God also loves them dearly in his heart, and we who are supposed to be the crown of all creation cannot even sympathize with God's heart. How then is the animal world going to have a place of refuge? Snakes and centipedes, tigers, leopards and wolves are most dangerous animals. But since Heaven has given birth to them, what right have we to take their lives? If they were all meant to be killed, then why in the first place did Heaven give them life? All we can do is to drive them far away so that they shall not harm us. What wrong has the spider committed by spinning its web? Some kill them without mercy on the fairy-tale that they curse the moon or that they may make the walls crumble down. On what authority is such a statement based, by which we kill animals' lives? Will this do? Will this do? As I am away from home, you should watch over my son. Develop his heart of kindness and stop his cruelties. Don't spare him because he is your nephew, and not your son. The children of our servants are also a part of humankind. We should be equally kind to them and should not permit our children to bully them. When there are fish or eatables, we must also share them with their children and see them happy and jump about. If our own children are eating and let the servants' children stand far away looking on, their parents will see it and, while pitying them and being unable to help them, will shout to them to go away. Is this not heart-rending for the parents? Now to be a scholar and be a college graduate or a doctor is a small thing; the important thing is to be reasonable and be a good man. Read this to sister-in-law Kuo and sister-in-law Jao, and let them know that there is a proper and an improper way of loving their children.

Postscript. Regarding what I have just said about not keeping birds in cages, I must say that I always love birds, but that there is a proper way of doing it. One who loves birds should plant trees, so that the house shall be surrounded with hundreds of shady branches and be a country and a home for birds. Thus, at dawn, when we wake up from sleep and are still tossing about in bed, we hear a chorus of chirping voices like a celestial harmony. And when we get up and are putting on our gowns or washing our faces or gargling our mouths or sipping the morning tea, we see their gorgeous plumes flitting about. Before we have time to look at one, we are attracted by another. This is a pleasure that far exceeds that of keeping one bird in a cage. Generally the enjoyment of life should come from a view regarding the universe as a park, and the rivers and streams as a pond, so that all beings can live in accordance with their nature. Great indeed is such happiness! How shall the keeping of a bird in a cage or a fish in a jar be compared with it in generosity of spirit and in kindness?

XIV. THIRD LETTER TO BROTHER MO FROM WEIHSIEN

The wealthy families usually do their best to secure the best teachers for their children, but the successful scholars usually come from the poor children who are invited to study at their schools, and not from their own children. In a few years, the wealthy families go down; some depend upon others for a living; some become beggars, and some are barely able to carry on without fear of want, but are illiterate. Sometimes one out of a hundred such rich children will become a successful scholar, but his writings will lack depth and true feelings, the title to immortality. Is it not true therefore that wealth can make a man stupid and poverty can strengthen a man's ambition and enlighten his mind?

Although I am a humble official, my son may be already considered heir of an official family. I do not know whether he will make good or fail, but if the children who are studying with him in our home can become successful, I shall be quite happy and contented. We should be most careful in regard to his relationships with his teacher and schoolmates. My son is only six and is the youngest at school. The eldest among his schoolmates should be addressed as *hsiensheng,* and the next eldest should be addressed as "elder brothers." He should not be permitted to call them directly by their names. We have plenty of writing brush and ink and paper at our home and should distribute them to the school children. I have often observed how a son of a poor widow tried for ten days to get money for buying writing paper to make a writing pad and failed. We should keep an eye on such a boy and give it to him unintentionally. And when it rains, and a poor boy is not able to go home, we should ask him to stay for supper, and at dusk send him home with an old pair of shoes. His parents love him, and though they may not be able to make good clothes for him, they generally provide a good pair of shoes and socks for him to come to school. Once that pair gets wet with mud, it will be difficult for them to get another pair.

It is difficult to get a good teacher, but it is more important to respect him. One should be careful in selecting a teacher for the school, but once he is chosen, he must be treated with due respect and not found fault with. Once in officialdom, it is impossible for us to stay at home to coach the children. The teacher one invites is usually just a better scholar of the village, but by no means a famous writer. It is easy to laugh secretly at his mistakes or openly point out his errors. The teacher will become ill at ease and will not be able to devote his mind to teaching, while the pupils will lose respect for him and not work hard at their lessons. This would be a matter of regret. It would be far better to make use of what the teacher excels in and make the pupils profit by it. If he is really not qualified, we should wait till the next year and employ another teacher, but meanwhile there should be no decrease in our courtesy toward him.

XV. FOURTH LETTER TO BROTHER MO FROM WEIHSIEN

When a man goes to school, he cannot be certain that he will become an official. But whether he becomes an official or not, he should not forget the true object of study. If one fails in the examinations, the knowledge gained still remains his own and it should not be regarded as a losing investment. I, for instance, have become successful and am reputed to have a good knowledge of books. But when I ask myself, I cannot say how many books I have really absorbed into my heart. All we do usually is to borrow from one book and adapt from others, thus gaining a reputation by cheating. The scholars owe a debt to the books, while the books owe nothing to them.

Formerly someone asked Shen Chinsze what to do to avoid poverty, and his reply was to read books. The man thought Shen's advice was impractical, but it is practical. A man loses his character by rushing about and attending to worthless affairs and in the end gains nothing. It would be better for him to wander about in the land of books and history, without any object of seeking benefit, but suddenly coming upon some truth before his very eyes. Who believes in this advice will become successful and who does not will remain poor. It all depends on whether one has the wit to realize it and whether he has persistence.

XVI. FIFTH LETTER TO BROTHER MO FROM THE MAGISTRATE'S RESIDENCE AT WEIHSIEN

Calligraphy and painting are considered fine arts, but are also vulgar occupations. Is it not a vulgar thing for a man who cannot do some service to the country and improve the life of the people to occupy himself with pen and ink for the amusement of other people? It was harmless for Su Tungp'o who took the entire universe into his heart to paint a tree or a rock with a dry brush. But Wang Mochieh (Wang Wei) and Chao Tse-ang (Mengfu) were merely two painters in the times of T'ang and Sung. If you examine their poetry and prose, you will not find a single line that has to do with the welfare of the people. Place these two persons among Fang (Hsüanling), Tu (Juhwei), Yao (Ts'ung) and Sung (Ching), and among Han (Ch'i), Fan (Chungyen), Fu (Pi) and Ouyang (Hsiu),[8] and where will they be? The talents of *protégés* of officials' homes and the skills of friends of leisure are good only for trimming flowers, building pavilions and terraces, and examining curios and tasting tea. They are worthy to give orders to the doormen and butlers, but what are they? Your stupid brother had no profession in youth, achieved nothing in middle age and lives in poverty in old age. I have therefore been forced to earn a living by my writing brush, but in reality it may be regarded a shame and a disgrace. I hope you will have some higher ambition and not fall into my footsteps. The ancient people said of Chuko Liang that he was "indeed a famous scholar,"

[8] The first four are famous, good ministers of T'ang and the last four are famous ministers of Sung.

which means that the term "famous scholar" could be applied worthily only to him. Now the city is full of painters and writers of calligraphy who are called "famous scholars." Would this not make Cho Liang's cheeks burn and turn the high-minded ones' teeth cold (make them sneer)?

The Epigrams of Lusin

INTRODUCTION

It is difficult to discuss or evaluate a contemporary writer who died only in 1936. But it is still more difficult to talk of God, and Lusin is God to the leftist writers of China today. Whether he will be pleased with that position or not, if his spirit is conscious, is not such a simple question to one who is acquainted with the highly complicated involutions of Lusin's ideas. Anyway, in one of his epigrams he says, "By the time a great man becomes fossilized and is worshipped as great, he is already a puppet." I suppose it is quite harmless to discuss a Chinese god in the English language which he does not understand. The reason for including a short selection from Lusin in this anthology of the wisdom of China is obvious: he is one of the most biting satirists of Chinese culture, and even such a short selection will show the mood and temper of modern China, especially that of young China in regard to its ancient culture. Behind some of his short epigrams one gets a glimpse of the gigantic spiritual and mental turmoil of a China in revolt against the past. Lusin represents the Literature of Revolt. But this is in itself a sign of life.

In the following selection, I have drawn less from his direct views on proletarian literature and class warfare, which are quite familiar to Western students of the ideas of Soviet Russia, and have concentrated more upon his epigrams on life as epigrams. It must not be forgotten also that the charm he has cast upon his readers is due to his style and his bitter sarcasm and occasional wit, while as a leader of the theory of proletarian literature, his views of ancient Chinese culture, his continual cry of revolt and his strictly Marxian view of the function of literature are eagerly and uncritically accepted as the Bible. That his views of

China's culture seem shallow and unsound, especially after the five years of war which have opened the eyes of the leftists themselves to the inner strength of China's ancient ideals, and that a radical young China is willing to take Lusin's word for it when he discourages them from touching ancient books by calling them poison, must be taken as necessary phases of the age of revolt. Behind it one sees a heartrending spirit of repentance and, best of all, an unquestionable zeal for reform. After all, China was a little too placid and lethargic in accepting the modern world. For that reason he directed his full venom at those who would preserve China's national heritage, because, as seen in actual circumstances, it is these people who stand in the way of reform. But the war and the migration inland are teaching young China about ancient China in a way that "critics" and "satirists" cannot. For the strength of China's sound peasantry is indisputably the strength of Confucian morals.

Lusin is a warrior more than a "literary man." It always seems to me that he was happiest when he saw or imagined his face bruised and groggy. And it is his uncompromising, challenging, fighting spirit that so charms his readers, for the public always loves a good fighter. When teaching in the Amoy University, he once saw a pig rubbing its back against a tree associated with love and romance, and he could not help stooping down to fight the pig. A friend asked him why he did so, and he would not explain. The following is both characteristic of his style and his spirit:

"I am sometimes aware that I am wicked. For instance, I stop drinking and take cod-liver oil to lengthen my life, not entirely for the sake of those who love me, but principally because of those who are my enemies —so that some regret may remain in their too perfect world. . . . I still mean to live in this society, for a reason that I have often announced, and that is, purposely to make the so-called gentlemen uncomfortable for a few more days. So I still purposely leave a few pieces of armor on my body and stand erect to give them some regret in their world, until I am wearied and tired, and then I will go away."

This is typical of his style:

"There are two kinds of difficult crises in a man's life. One is when you come to a cross-road. According to Motse, one ought to weep and turn back. But I would neither weep nor turn back, but would first sit down at the cross-road for a little rest or a little nap, and then choose a relatively better road to travel. If I come across a fool, perhaps I will rob him of his food to stop my hunger, but will not ask him for the way, because I know he cannot tell me. If I should meet a tiger, I would climb up a tree, and come down only after he could not stand his hunger and had gone away. If he didn't go away, I would rather die of hunger on the top of the tree, and moreover tie myself to a bough so that he shall not have the pleasure of eating even my dead body. But if there is no tree, what then? I will offer myself to him and invite him to eat me, but must bite a morsel off him first. The second kind of crisis is when you come to an extremity. It is said that Yüan Tsi also wept and turned back on his way, as Motse advised on coming to a cross-road. One must still go on and make one's way by cutting through the brambles and undergrowths. But I have never yet come to a place where there is no road, but all brambles. I do not know whether there is such a thing as an extremity, or merely that I have not come across one."

"Lusin" is his pen name, his real name being Chou Shujen. It is because he is more a warrior than a "literary man" that in reading his writings, one continually smells blood, gunpowder, and sweat and tears. As was said of Heinrich Heine, his coffin should be laid, not with a pen, but with a sword. The structure of his ideas is fairly simple: all that belongs to China's ancient culture is putrid and poisonous, and all that Lunacharsky says about literature is perfect. He advises China's young men to "read few, or absolutely no, Chinese books, but read foreign books"; he compares Chinese ancient books to "poison" or "arsenic" and says the reading of them makes him sleepy; he says "although there is a strain of teaching in ancient books for taking up responsibility toward society, but mostly it is the optimism of corpses; while although there is a strain of cynicism and decadence in foreign books, it is the cynicism and decadence of living men." He advocates the abolition of Chinese writing, believes in the "Europeanization of Chinese syntax" and is for imitation of foreign grammar. He urges the young men to worship Darwin and Ibsen rather than Confucius and Kuan Yü, and sacrifice to Apollo rather than to the God of Pestilence. These ideas are incredibly naïve and hardly show a sense of discernment either of the East or of the West. They are taken very seriously, and it is a true fact that "leftist professors" advise China's young men not to read Chinese ancient works, though they themselves read them on the sly to improve their style, like pharmacists who are qualified to handle arsenic. This self-deception is going on today. But China needed a man like Lusin to wake the millions up from the self-complacency and lethargy and accumulated inertia of four thousand years. Perhaps China needs still more Lusins. But the young China that listens to Lusin and accepts his ideas is a China no longer self-complacent, but humble and anxious to learn from the West, and humility is the beginning of wisdom.

The Epigrams of Lusin

Translated by Lin Yutang

1 Those who were officials in former regimes wish to restore the ancient culture; those who are officials now wish to maintain the *status quo*; and those who are not yet officials cry for reform.

2 When you talk with famous scholars, the best thing is to pretend that occasionally you do not quite understand them. If you understand too little, you will be despised; if you understand too much, you will be disliked; if you just fail occasionally to understand them, you will suit each other very well.

3 Do not guard yourself against those who call themselves thieves, for when you find out the opposite, they turn out to be gentlemen. Guard yourself against those who call themselves gentlemen, for when you discover the opposite, they turn out to be thieves.

4 The man who is hated by the man you hate is a good person.

5 Jesus said that it is easier for a camel to go through the needle's eye than for a rich man to enter into the kingdom of God, and he had to go through Gethsemane. Now the rich men of the West are worshipping Jesus, and it is the poor who are going through Gethsemane.

6 The bourgeosie love to hear scandals, particularly scandals about persons they know.

7 In the war between the so-called celestial spirits and the devils, both are fighting not for the control of heaven, but for the control of hell. Therefore irrespective of who wins, hell still remains hell.

8 I think it is difficult to say whether there is such a thing as hope or not. Hope is like a road in the country; there was never a road, but when many people walk on it, the road comes into existence.

9 The so-called "peace" is an interval between wars.

10 One who knows many subjects is liable to be shallow; one who knows only one subject is apt to be perverse.

11 A woman has a maternal instinct and a childish instinct, but not the instinct of a wife. Her wife-instinct is a combination of her maternal and childish instincts.

12 A bee gives a sting and loses its life; a satirist gives a sting and preserves his.

13 I used to think that a man was sentenced to death or imprisonment because he was guilty; now I know that he is found guilty because he is disliked.

14 I have hated too many things in this society and ought to be hated by others myself. This gives me a feeling of living in a human world.

15 There was a ruffian in Tientsin during the Boxer trouble who always demanded two dollars for carrying a person's luggage. Even if the luggage was very light, he said he wanted two dollars. Even if the distance was very small, he still wanted two dollars. Even if the person didn't want him to carry the luggage at all, he still wanted two dollars. The ruffian's conduct was execrable, but his insistent spirit was admirable. The same may be applied to demanding women's rights. If one says to you, "This is outmoded," your answer is "I want women's rights." If one says to you, "This is unworthy of you," your answer still is, "I want women's rights." If one says to you, "Don't be so anxious. Everything will be well when the economic system is changed," your answer still should be, "I want women's rights."

16 Chinese people love compromise. If you say to them, "This room is too dark, we must have a window made," they will all oppose you. But if you say, "Let's take off the roof," they will compromise with you and say "Let's have a window."

17 The Chinese people worship the malign spirits, like the God of Pestilence and the God of Fire, and bully the honest gods, like the God of the Earth and the God of the Kitchen. They do the same with their emperors.

18 China is like a room with invisible walls. You are liable to knock your head against something. The man who is willing to fight these walls and bump his head without minding pain wins.

19 I often think that we ought to apply the new law to the new and the old law to the old. When old officials of the Manchu Dynasty commit a crime, we ought to flog their bottoms.

20 The Chinese culture is the culture of serving one's masters, achieved at the cost of the misery of multitudes. Those who praise Chinese culture, whether they be Chinese or foreigners, assume that they belong to the ruling class.

21 People hate Buddhist monks and nuns, Mohammedans and Christians, but no one hates a Taoist. To understand the reason for this is to understand half of China.

22 There is a favorite way with those who know old literature. When a new idea is introduced, they call it "heresy" and must bend all their efforts to destroy it. When that new idea, after hard struggle, has won a place for itself, they then discover that "it's same thing as what was taught by Confucius." They object to all imported things, saying that this is "to convert Chinese into barbarians," but when the barbarians become rulers of China, they discover these "barbarians" are also descendants of the Yellow Emperor.

23 The Chinese have only two names for foreign races: one is "foreign races," the other is "Your Majesty."

24 When the Chinese are in power, and see that others cannot do anything to them . . . they are autocrats and have no use for moderation; when they begin to talk of "moderation," they know they have to be moderate; and when they are out of luck, then they begin to speak of "fate." They would be contented even with being slaves and find themselves in perfect harmony with the universe.

25 Who says that the Chinese do not change? When new things are introduced, they want to reject them, but when they begin to see that there is something in them, they begin to change. But they do not change by adapting themselves to the new things, but by adapting the new things to themselves.

26 Buddhism was once fought against in China. But when the (Sung) philosophers of reason began to talk of contemplation and monks learned to write poetry, then the time was ripe for the discovery that "the three religions come from the same source."

27 A friend of mine has said, "The question is not whether we can preserve our national heritage, but whether the national heritage can preserve us." To preserve ourselves is the first thing. The question is whether it has or has not the power to preserve us, and not whether it is "national heritage."

28 I think our immediate needs at present are the three things: first, self-preservation, second, food and clothing, and third, development.

Anything which stands in the way of these three things ought to be ruthlessly trampled down—be it man or ghost, or the Three Scripts and Five Canons, or the "Hundred Sung" or "Thousand Yüan" editions,[1] be it the astrolabe or the Divination Chart,[2] the golden statue or jade Buddha, or family secrets for medicines or pills made by secret processes.

29 Rather than worship Confucius and Kuan Kung, one should worship Darwin and Ibsen. Rather than Sacrifice to the God of Pestilence and the Five Classes of Spirits, one should worship Apollo.[3]

30 The greatest and most enduring art of China is that of men acting the role of women on the stage. . . . The best part about men acting as women is that the men in the audience see the men are acting as women, and the women in the audience see that the women are being acted by men.

31 Both talking and writing are the signs of those who have failed. Those who are engaged in fighting the evil forces have no time for these, and those who are successful keep quiet.

32 We have hereafter only two roads to choose: one is to embrace the ancient literature and die, the other is to forsake the ancient literature and live.

33 Immaturity need not be ashamed before maturity just as a child need not be ashamed before an old man. This is true of writing; a young writer need not be ashamed of his immaturity, for if his personality is not thwarted, he will grow and mature in time, while there is no hope for senility and decay.

34 The great judge of man's soul is at the same time its defendant. The judge on his bench enumerates the crimes the soul has committed while the defendant tries his best to paint a picture of its good points. The judge exposes the dirt in his soul, while the defendant reveals the beauty among its dirt. In this way, the depths of the human soul can be revealed.

35 The literature of former days is like watching a fire from across the water; in present-day literature, the author himself is being scorched by the fire and he is bound to feel it deeply, and when he begins to feel it deeply, he is bound to take part in the social struggle.

[1] Names of two famous collections of rare editions.

[2] Both mentioned in the *Book of History*.

[3] This has justified the witticism that the American bug is better than the Chinese bug and the American moon is better than the Chinese moon. Lusin knew principally Japanese and some German, besides Chinese.

One Hundred Proverbs

INTRODUCTION

THE FOLLOWING COLLECTION OF PROVERBS is taken from a cheap edition of a "popular" book of games, riddles, jokes, verse oddities and anecdotes, by an anonymous author so undistinguished that its signatures are at once disarming. It is called "A Night's Talk," written by "Mr. Tut-Tut!" and revised by "Mr. Pfui-Pfui!" From internal evidence, it appears to have been written in the seventeenth century.

A word about the moral elevation of this Mr. Tut-Tut is therefore necessary. Mr. Tut-Tut merely inherited a tradition of folk and literary wisdom and, like Benjamin Franklin, wrote some extremely good proverbs himself. Back of these proverbs are all the subtlety and depth of Laotse, the common sense of Confucius, the practical shrewdness of Han Fei, the hard cynicism of Yang Chu, the super-mundane breadth of a Buddhist monk and the tender sensualism of a Chinese poet, blended together in spirit so that they represent China's wisdom of the ages. They seem to let us look at life through the window of a Chinese scholar's hut. For the Chinese literature of the earliest times started out with an amazing fondness for moralizations (witness *Tsochüan* and *Chankouts'eh*), and through the centuries, every scholar was content to note down a moral truth, or give it a new expression, no matter how often that truth had been observed before. In one sense, Chinese literature is strewn with proverbs and moral maxims. Then, especially beginning with the Sung Dynasty, quite a few writers began consciously to write books of maxims and observations on human nature and human life. Deepened by the Buddhist outlook and refined by T'ang poetry, these maxims soon assumed a special form and delicacy of expression, with all the subtleties of poetic diction. In the sixteenth and seventeenth centuries, when the so-called *hsiaop'in,* or casual essays, reached special perfection, we see a sudden growth of such books of maxims, by Ch'en Chiju, T'u Lung, Chang Ch'ao, etc. I have already translated "The Epigrams of Chang Ch'ao" (about half of the original book) in *The Importance of Living,* while the present ones are more in the nature of proverbs.

These hundred proverbs I have selected are distinctly of a popular type and many are culled from sources which I can recognize. But they are popular also in another special sense. They represent the average content of couplet scrolls that are invariably seen in Chinese households, similar to the custom half a century ago when American homes used to hang biblical maxims in the parlor or bedroom. In other words, they are sayings which the Chinese call good, and to which their hearts give an instinctive assent. Some of these are seen in couplet scrolls and almost all of them can be used for such purposes. Almost all of them are put in the form of literary couplets, a form developed to the last degree of nicety in the "T'ang poems," where in a verse of eight lines, the middle four lines must perforce be in the form of two couplets. And good lines of poetry should be popular because every perfect line should have a melody and inevitableness of expression besides the thought, like a proverb.

It is therefore singular, but not unintelligible that proverbs of such moral elevation should be found in a cheap book of games, riddles and jokes. One should be surprised nowadays to find such proverbs in the *New York World-Telegram's* "Year Book," but one need not be surprised at all to find them in "Poor Richard's Almanac." That is the difference between the past world and the present one, between the world of simple wisdom and the world of well-verified, well-tabulated and well-indexed Infallible Sacred Facts. These facts are our god today. They are almost all we have.

There is often a touch of cynicism in these maxims, but that can hardly be a fault. An idealist who has outgrown his idealism is a danger to society, but a cynic who has outgrown his cynicism is one of the kindest persons on earth. After reading these, one can enjoy the games and jokes and riddles better.

One Hundred Proverbs

by Mr. Tut-Tut

Translated by Lin Yutang

1 Men and women who know each other easily are cheap lovers; persons who easily make friends are not lifelong friends.

2 To have a peace of mind not quite perfect is to deepen the awareness of peace; to enjoy pleasure not quite to the limit is to prolong the flavor of those pleasures.

3 The silkworm weaves its cocoon and stays inside, therefore it is imprisoned; the spider weaves its web and stays outside, therefore it is free.

4 An intelligent person often talks with his eyes; a shallow man often swallows with his ears.

5 Endure a small insult and be safe from a big insult; suffer some small loss and be safe from a big loss. Where you miss an advantage in a deal, you gain an advantage.

6 There are heroes with hearts of steel and beards of frost, and beauties with faces like a flower, breathing fragrance with their smiles—the same human skull, yet what different acts of farce!

7 Personal talent coupled with a slow temper becomes great talent; wisdom coupled with a pacifist mind becomes true wisdom.

8 It would be indeed an ideal world if warriors did not have the air of the army, scholars did not have the air of bookish dogmatism, mountain recluses did not have the smell of mists and clouds and monks did not smell of incense and the altar.

9 Do not open your heart to the grim silent one; guard your tongue before the garrulous fool.

10 Talk not of your personal success to one who has failed; forge not your failures in your moment of success.

11 Avoid the mean person, but do not make him your persona enemy; get close to the gentleman, but do not always say "Yes" to him

12 Who cannot be of use to society and therefore wears the mask of cynics is afraid to meet the true hero; who is not fit to sit on top bu insists on sitting on top is safe among his futile friends.

13 Who makes his mind the slave of his body is like a plodding horse or cattle; who sacrifices his body to fame is like a caged pheasan or wild goose.

14 The true hero hardens his nature and controls his mind; the mock variety makes a show of his talent and flies off his temper.

15 Who likes to insult people through his writings is like a sorceress; who likes to flatter people through his writings is like a fortune-teller.

16 The ancients blamed Heaven for their mishaps; the moderns blame the earth—that is why they change the sites of their ancestors' graves.

17 A private garden should have a section of rustic wildness; if it merely dazzles by its sumptuousness, the vulgarity of it suffocates one's breath.

18 No one is safe from flattery, therefore the art of flattery is infinitely various; the crowd of blackmailers is legion, therefore the flow of rumors is difficult to stop.

19 All the universe is an inn; search not specially for a retreat of peace: all the people are your relatives; expect therefore troubles from them.

20 It is most difficult for love to last long, therefore who loves passionately is in the end cured of love; human nature is eternal, therefore who follows his nature in the end retains his orignial nature.

21 The blessing of health is realized on the sickbed; the blessing of a peaceful home is realized when that peace is upset.

22 All people are in financial troubles sometimes. The failure to realize the meaning of poverty must be also considered a fault of the wealthy and successful. Moreover, there are heroes among the poor: the right thing is to open your eyes and broaden your chest.

23 Thrift is an aid to integrity; loyalty guides one toward a steady character. (Who lives within his means is not tempted.—*Ed.*)

24 To suffer an insult from those one fears is not true patience; to suffer an insult from those one does not fear is true patience.

25 Who does not enjoy his happy moments cannot after all be called lucky; who feels happy in extremities is the real cultivated scholar.

26 To see through fame and wealth is to gain a little rest; to see through life and death is to gain a big rest.

27 Swim not in the tides of the world, and storms will not beat upon your breast.

28 To be elated at success and disappointed at failure is to be the child of circumstances; how can such a one be called master of himself?

29 Stupidity prevents one from committing mistakes; leisure confers upon one many privileges. (A folk proverb, especially as a guide to officialdom: Do much, err much; do little, err little; do nothing, err nothing. This, however, differs in sense from the maxim which warns against the man with flighty ideas and unsteady purpose.—*Ed.*)

30 Disasters arise from hatred; good luck comes from goodness of heart.

31 Accumulate learning as you would accumulate wealth; seek moral goodness as you would seek official rank and honor; love your parents as you would love your wife and children; look after the country well as you would look after your own official post.

32 Who is narrow of vision cannot be big-hearted; who is narrow of spirit cannot take long, easy strides.

33 Who gives me goods hurts my spirit; who gives me fame injures my life.

34 Do not be cool toward a close relative on account of some small quarrel; do not forget an old act of kindness because of a recent dispute.

35 In moments of satisfied conceit, one speaks words of untruth; in moments of heated anger, one speaks words offending courtesy.

36 Be firm in your acts, but easy in your heart; be strict with yourself, but gentle with your fellowmen.

37 God gives me bad luck, I meet it with a generous heart. God gives me labor and toil, I meet it with an easy-going mind. God gives me trials and adversities, I understand them by means of Tao (comprehension of the rhythm of life).

38 Some who do not save in times of plenty regret it in times of need; some who do not study in youth regret it on occasions when knowledge is of use; some who talk freely when drunk regret it when they are sober; some who do not give themselves a little rest in the days of their health regret it when they are confined to bed.

39 Who likes to spread secrets should not be told a secret; who loves to criticize affairs cannot be entrusted with affairs.

40 Keep your mind busy to accomplish things; keep your mind open to understand things.

41 If a scholar, being poor, cannot help people with money but will on occasions wake up a man from his folly or save a man from trouble with a word of advice, that is also a form of (religious) merit.

42 The man of real ability shows his ability in his face; the happy man conceals his talents.

43 Humility is a good thing, but over-humility is near to crookedness; silence is a virtue, but undue silence bespeaks a deceitful mind.

44 Who does evil and is afraid of letting it be known has still a seed of good in his evil; who does good and is anxious to have it known has still a root of evil in his good.

45 Who does not have self-respect invites disgrace; who is not on the look-out against himself courts disaster; who is not satisfied with himself will grow; who is not sure of his own correctness will learn many things.

46 One should not miss the flavor of being sick, nor miss the experience of being destitute.

47 Who is indignant at false gossip invites rumor; who is pleased with words of praise attracts the flatterers.

48 By sometimes thinking of the period of illness, one's worldly ambitions become milder; by sometimes thinking of death, one's religious thoughts grow.

49 On occasions of a great or difficult crisis, you see a man's stature; on occasions of good luck or mishap, you see a man's great or small mind; in moments of satisfaction or anger, you see a man's degree of moral culture (*hanyang*); in a man's refusal or acceptance of a course of action with or against the crowd, you see a man's sense of judgment.

50 When God wishes to send disaster upon a person, He first sends him a little luck to elate him and see whether he can receive it in a worthy manner; when God wishes to send blessing upon a person, He first sends him a little mishap and sees how well he can take it.

51 Talent grows strong through personal force; character becomes firm through the will.

52 The noisy person cannot have calm judgment; the timid soul cannot have superior sense; the man of inordinate desires cannot do

generous deeds; the man of many words cannot have a steady mind; the man of physical prowess cannot have refinement.

53 He who is a good judge of men corrects what he hears by what he sees; he who is not a good judge of men corrupts what he sees by what he hears.

54 The clever man often worries; the loyal person is often overworked.

55 The great hypocrite weeps to make people believe him; women and cowards weep to make people pity them.

56 A girl who flirts with her looks is not chaste; a scholar who flirts with his knowledge is not honest.

57 When a mean person plans to injure a gentleman, his heart is cruel, his plans are well laid out and his action is firm; therefore the gentleman can seldom escape. When a gentleman intends to punish a mean person, his heart is kind, his plans are incomplete, and he cannot quite go to the limit; therefore more often he himself is victimized by it.

58 The amasser of wealth is rich materially and poor in his mind; the contented man is materially poor and rich in his mind.

59 Virtue in a rich person is the ability to give, in a poor man it is the refusal to beg, in a man of high position it is a humble attitude toward fellowmen, and in a man of low position it is the ability to see through life.

60 There is never a quarrel that cannot be settled when both parties repent, never a friendship that does not succeed when both parties are attracted toward one another, never a stroke of bad luck that can be avoided when both parties have lost their temper.

61 The braggart is seldom loyal; the glib talker is seldom honest.

62 The proud spirit, the chivalric spirit and the beautiful spirit suffuse fragrance even when their bones are dead; words of cool detachment, witty words and words of charm carry weight though their volume be small.

63 Such is the power of literature: it speaks of joy and makes one dance; it speaks of sorrow and makes one weep; it speaks of retirement and makes one detached; it speaks of love and makes one tender; it speaks of danger and makes one shiver; it speaks of pent-up anger and makes one cautious; it speaks of indignation and makes one lay one's hand on the sword; it speaks of incitement to action and makes one throw down the pen; it speaks of the high and makes one soar up to the clouds; it speaks of the low and makes one roll down the rocks. It

shakes our heart and dazzles our eyes, but this has nothing to do with stylistic embellishments.

64 Of the things that are good, only study is good without accompanying evil; the love of mountains and rivers is good without accompanying evil; taking pleasure in the moon, the breeze, flowers and bamboos is good without accompanying evil; sitting in upright posture in silence is good without accompanying evil.

65 Wine dispels sorrow, and the best part is when one is slightly drunk; carefree fancies go into poems, and the best lines are obtained without effort.

66 There are four rules for living in the mountains: let there be no formation in trees, no arrangement of rocks, no sumptuousness in the living house, and no contrivance in the human heart.

67 One should see the flowers' shadow in the water, the bamboos' shadow under the moon, and the beauty's shadow behind a door screen.

68 There must be no straining after effect in the arts of leisure: to go after the fanciful in dress, the exotic in food, and quality in daily utensils is uncleanliness in the pursuit of leisure, and the worm of corruption in the pursuit of leisure.

69 To stay up in the mountains is a fine thing, but the slightest attachment turns it into a market; the appreciation of old paintings is a refined hobby, but the slightest greed of possession turns one into a merchant; wine and poetry provide occasions of pleasure, but the slightest loss of freedom turns them into hell; generous hospitality is a magnanimous habit, but when one is surrounded by common fellows, it is again like entering a sea of distress.

70 If a man can keep ten thousand volumes of rare books, have them bound in precious brocade, and perfumed with rare incense, while he himself lives in a mud house with a screen of reed, paper windows and mud walls, and lives all his life in simple cotton dress, that one might be called an extraordinary person on this earth.

71 Hide your expression of personal dislike in the wine cup; conceal your pity for mankind in your poems.

72 The sun and moon shoot past like a bullet in our floating life; only sleep affords a little extension of our span of life. Business affairs fly about like thick dust to belabor our lives; only sleep affords a little reprieve. Gorging oneself with fish and meat morning and night besmirches our taste; only sleep gives opportunity for a short fast. Contention and strife disturb our peace; only sleep restores for us a short Golden

Age. As for seeing novel things in our sleep—travelling abroad and being able to walk without legs and fly without wings—it provides us also with a little fairyland.

73 Pass famous mountains as you read rare books, a few steps at a time if you are tired, or going a hundred miles when you are feeling fit. One does not go by a schedule, but only stops at what pleases the eye and delights the mind.

74 To go to see the prune flowers after snow, pay a visit to the chrysanthemums during frost, tend the orchid during rain, or listen to the swaying bamboos before the breeze—such are the joys of leisure of a rustic fellow, but they are also moments of the greatest meaning to the scholar.

75 When the tea is well-brewed and the incense has a pure fragrance, it's a delight if friends drop in; when birds twitter and flowers drop their petals, even solitude is contentment for the soul.

76 You are reading when incense is burning and all your human obligations are fulfilled, while outside the screen the flower petals are dropping and the moon has come up to the top of the pine trees, and you suddenly hear the temple bell and push open the window and see the Milky Way—such a moment is superior to daytime.

77 If a man's house is not secluded, his mind does not wander far; if a man's face does not show a little sadness, his thoughts are not deep.

78 With the door shut and living in idleness, I associate with the musty volumes the year round; meeting an old friend and falling into conversation, we carry on the discussion deep into the night.

79 They say there is a devil in the drunkard and a ghost in the poet; I think these people have perfect mastery of themselves, so that when the spirits move, they give the spirits a free hand.

80 Floating down the stream in spring in a small boat, even the most conventional spirit feels emancipated; listening to the rain at night over a lone wine cup, even the most stout-hearted will feel touched.

81 Whither shall we dispose of the pure breeze and shining moon of the universe? Into the wine cup and bag of poetry. How shall we take leave of the changing elements of human passion? By closing the door and lying on a high pillow.

82 Sometimes plant bamboos while there is a drizzling rain; close the gate and tend the flowers in idleness; take up a pen and leisurely check up mistakes in old editions; draw spring water and try several pots of the season's tea.

83 During a drizzling rain, open a volume leisurely; against the breeze, play the string instrument alone.

84 Only watch how the flowers bloom, how the flowers fade; say not this man is right, that man is wrong.

85 Let the red dust of the road and the white foams of the river circle round the southern city; lose not to the bright moon among flowers and the pure breeze among pines a good nap in my northern room.

86 Living in the mountains has eight advantages over living in the city: no strict conventions, no strange visitors, no mulling over wine and meat, no fights over property, no concerns over the treacherous human heart, no quarrels over right and wrong, no pressing for literary articles, no gossip about officials.

87 When the rain is over and the air is cool, when your affairs are few and your mind is at ease, you listen to the lingering notes of some neighbor's flute chasing after the clear clouds and the receding rain, and every note seems to drop and sink into your soul.

88 When wild geese cry in the sky, the mountain clouds touch your tower, and a thousand peaks bid the rain proceed, you approach a couch for an afternoon nap, and even your dreams will partake of poetry.

89 Rather be laughed at by the world, be not fooled by the Creator; rather be disturbed by the gentleman, be not familiar with the petty people.

90 If indeed we can confer wealth and poverty upon ourselves, then God has no control; if our happiness and disappointments depend on what others say of us, then the gossip-makers have their way.

91 Poverty is not a disgrace; disgrace lies in poverty without ambition. A mean position is not a cause for contempt; contempt belongs to one in a mean position without ability. Old age is no cause for regret; regret that one is old, having lived in vain. Death is no cause for sorrow; sorrow that one dies without benefit to the world.

92 So long as I have legs, so long as I have eyes, wherever I go I am the lord of the mountains and rivers and the winds and the breeze.

93 Whenever you do a thing, act so that it will give your friends no occasion for regret and your foes no cause for joy.

94 Some one skill enables one to make a living; too many abilities make one a slave.

95 Poetry is for pleasing the spirit, and wine is for pleasing the soul. If with poetry one becomes jealous of fame, and with wine one falls into a drunken brawl, wherefore does either please the spirit or the soul?

96 Talk not of arbitrary opinions in your mouth, hang not sorrow n the tip of your eyebrow—this is to be a human fairy. Plant flowers nd bamboos where they belong, keep fish and poultry to suit your own leasure—this is economics of living in the mountains.

97 Look at a beauty as you look at beautiful clouds, and your mortal assions will be milder; listen to the song of flutes as you listen to the owing water, what harm is there?

98 Money sometimes prevents trouble; too much money breeds it.

99 Stupid sons don't ruin a family; it is the clever ones who do.

100 A hero may be willing to lose the world, but he will not be willing to lose his concubine and his horse.

The Pronunciation of Chinese Names

1 Every vowel in the Romanized spelling of Chinese is pronounced.
2 The vowels have as their basis the usual Latin values:

a as in *father*
e as in *eight*
eh as in *burr*
erh as in a Scotch *burr*
i as in *machine* and *in*
o as in *old*
u as in *goose*
ü as in German *lügen*

3 The vowel sound in combinations like *tse, sze* does not exist in English. It is made with difficulty by Westerners, but is actually the vowel sound produced when the sound of *z* is prolonged and definitely vocalized ("buzzing" sound). In this instance, I depart from the Wade system, which renders it as *tzŭ,* because of its cumbersomeness. It frequently appears in names like *Laotse, Chuangtse, Tsengtse, Tsesze.*

4 The vowel sound indicated by the combination *ih* does not exist in English. It is made when the tongue and lip positions of the English *sh* are held unchanged and vocalized. For practical purposes, read the *ih* as *ee* (or if possible as a sound in between *she* and *shir*); there's no use trying to reproduce the sound exactly.

5 The important diphthongs are: *ia, ai, ou, uo, ei, ieh, ua*—all pro-

ounced with their individual approximate Latin values (*h* in *ieh* is not ronounced). *ao* may be pronounced nearly as *ow* in *owl*.

6 Combinations like *in, ing, an, ang* are pronounced with the usual atin values for the sounds (*in, ing, ahn, ahng*). But *en, eng* are proounced as *ern, erng,* or for practical purposes as *un, ung* (*sun, sung*) in nglish, whereas Chinese *un, ung* must be pronounced as *oon, oong*.

7 The distinction between *sh* and *hs* is a nuisance for English readers: ead both as *sh* for practical purposes. Technically, the sound *hs* is differnt and comes invariably before *i* and *ü*. Since the two groups are learly separated by the occurrence or absence of a following *i* or *ü*, that istinction in spelling between *sh* and *hs* is totally unnecessary for Chinese eaders, and meaningless for Westerners.

8 The Chinese language distinctly differentiates between aspirated nd unaspirated *p, t, k, ch, ts*. For practical purposes read *p, t, k, ch, ts* as , *d, g, j, dz,* and read *p', t', k', ch', ts'* like the regular English *p, t, k, ch, ts*.

9 Remember therefore to follow the Latin values for the vowels as general principle, and for practical purposes read:

hs as *sh*	*eh* as *er*
ih as *ee* (or *ir*)	*en* as *un*
ieh as *y-ay*	*eng* as *ung*

10 In particular, the closest pronunciation for the following words s as indicated below:

Tao [*tow*] as in *towel*
Laotse [loutsi] *lou* as in *loud*
Chuangtse [jwahng-tsi]
Liehtse [lee-ay-tsi]

TABLE OF CHINESE DYNASTIES

NAME	DATES	CENTURIES (*approximate*)	REMARKS
(Mythical)	2697-2206 B.C.	XXVII-XXIII	Legendary
Hsia	2205-1784 B.C.	XXII-XIX	Together with Chou, calle "Santai" or "Three Dynasties
Shang (Yin)	1783-1123 B.C.	XVIII-XII	
Chou	1122-222 B.C.	XI-III	Classic period; Ch'unch'i period 722-481; Chanku period 403-221
Ch'in	221-207 B.C.	end of III	Reunified China
Han	206 B.C.-A.D. 219	II B.C.-A.D. II	"Eastern Han" from A.D. 2
Wei	220-264	middle III	Wei, Wu and Shu forming th "Three Kingdoms" from abou A.D. 200
Chin	265-419	mid. III-IV	"Eastern Chin" from 317. Bar-barians' kingdoms in Nort China 304-439
"North and South"			
Sung	420-478	V-VI	These are called "North an South" Dynasties for distinc-tion. Together with precedin Wu and Eastern Chin, calle "Six Dynasties," a term re-ferring to southern culture
Ch'i	479-501		
Liang	502-556		
Ch'en	557-588		
Sui	589-617	round A.D. 600	Reunified China
T'ang	618-906	VII-IX	
"Wutai"			
Liang	907-922	first half X	These are called "Wutai," o "Five Dynasties" for distinction from other dynasties of the same name
T'ang	923-935		
Chin	936-946		
Han	947-950		
Chou	951-959		
Sung	960-1276	latter half X-XIII	"Southern Sung" from 1127 onward, with Northern China under Manchus and Mongols
Yüan (Mongol)	1277-1367	end of XIII-mid. XIV	Foreign rule
Ming	1368-1643	mid. XIV-mid. XVII	Restored to Chinese rule
Ch'ing (Manchu)	1644-1911	mid. XVII-XIX	Foreign rule
Republic	1911-	XX	